Theatre in Europe: a documentary history

This volume explores the professional English uments collected here, many published for the first time, chronicle the exciting and flourishing world of the theatre through the reigns of Henry VIII to Charles I and the Commonwealth. These exciting primary sources offer first-hand accounts, including the daily life and work of the actor, and the most complete coverage yet of all the playhouses, both public and private, including the Rose, the Globe, the Red Lion and the Swan. The volume documents the various theatre companies of children, costumes and stage property matters, audience reception and behaviour and ecclesiastical and governmental legislation. A full linking narrative and extensive bibliography detailing the location of the primary sources provide an important reference work and valuable research tool.

Theatre in Europe: a documentary history

General Editors

Glynne Wickham
John Northam
W. D. Howarth

This series presents a comprehensive collection of primary source materials for teachers and students, and serves as a major reference work for studies in theatrical and dramatic literature. The volumes focus individually on specific periods and geographical areas, encompassing English and European theatrical history. Each volume will present primary source material in English, or in English translation, relating to actors and acting, dramatic theory and criticism, theatre architecture, stage censorship, settings, costumes, and audiences. These sources include such documents as statutes, proclamations, inscriptions, contracts, and playbills. Additional documentation from contemporary sources is provided through correspondence, reports and eyewitness accounts. The volumes also provide not only the exact source and location of the original documents, but also complementary lists of similar documents. Each volume contains an Introduction, narrative linking passages, notes on the documents, a substantial bibliography and an index offering detailed access to the primary material.

Published

Restoration and Georgian England, 1669–1788, compiled and introduced by David Thomas and Arnold Hare, edited by David Thomas

National Theatre in Northern and Eastern Europe, 1746–1900, edited by Laurence Senelick

German and Dutch Theatre, 1600–1848, compiled by George W. Brandt and Wiebe Hogendoorn, edited by George W. Brandt

Naturalism and Symbolism in European Theatre, 1850–1918, edited by Claude Schumacher

French Theatre in the Neo-classical Era, 1550–1789, edited by William D. Howarth

The Medieval European Stage, 500–1500, edited by william Tydeman

Romantic and Revolutionary theatre, 1789–1860, edited by Donald Roy

Theatre in Europe: a documentary history

English Professional Theatre, 1530–1660

Edited by

GLYNNE WICKHAM
Emeritus Professor of Drama, University of Bristol

HERBERT BERRY
Emeritus Professor of English, University of Saskatchewan

WILLIAM INGRAM
Emeritus Professor of English, University of Michigan

CAMBRIDGE UNIVERSITY PRESS

CAMBRIDGE UNIVERSITY PRESS
Cambridge, New York, Melbourne, Madrid, Cape Town, Singapore, São Paulo, Delhi

Cambridge University Press
The Edinburgh Building, Cambridge CB2 8RU, UK

Published in the United States of America by Cambridge University Press, New York

www.cambridge.org
Information on this title: www.cambridge.org/9780521230124

© Cambridge University Press 2000

This publication is in copyright. Subject to statutory exception
and to the provisions of relevant collective licensing agreements,
no reproduction of any part may take place without the written
permission of Cambridge University Press.

First published 2000
This digitally printed version 2008

A catalogue record for this publication is available from the British Library

Library of Congress Cataloguing in Publication data

English professional theatre, 1530–1660 / edited by Glynne Wickham,
  Herbert Berry and William Ingram.
      p. cm. (Theatre in Europe)
  Includes bibliographical references and index.
  ISBN 0 521 23012 8 (hardback)
  1. Theatre – England – History – sixteenth-century sources. 2. Theatre –
England – History – seventeenth-century sources. I. Wickham, Glynne
William Gladstone. II. Berry, Herbert. III. Ingram, William.
IV. Series.
PN2589.E55 2000   792'.0942'09031 – dc21   99-16741 CIP

ISBN 978-0-521-23012-4 hardback
ISBN 978-0-521-10082-3 paperback

Contents

List of illustrations | *page* vii
List of documents | viii
General editor's preface | xli
Preface | xliii
Abbreviations | xlv

Introduction | 1

Part one: documents of control, 1530–1660
Edited by Glynne Wickham

I Henry VIII, 1530–1547 | 17
II Edward VI, 1547–1553 | 33
III Mary I, 1553–1558 | 39
IV Elizabeth I, 1558–1603 | 48
V James I and Charles I, 1603–1625 and 1625–1647 | 120

Part two: players and playing
Edited by William Ingram

VI Introduction | 153
VII The popular image of the stage player | 157
VIII A representative life: Augustine Phillips | 191
IX Patrons and playing companies | 204
X Players and their playing places | 211
XI Costumes, properties and playbooks | 229
XII Players travelling in the provinces | 243
XIII Companies of children | 260
XIV Some illustrative instances of professional theatrical life and practice | 275

Part three: playhouses, 1530–1660
Edited by Herbert Berry

XV Introduction | 287
XVI The Red Lion | 290

XVII–XX	The Four Inns	295
XXI	St Paul's	306
XXII	Newington Butts	320
XXIII	The Theatre	330
XXIV	The first Blackfriars	388
XXV	The Curtain	404
XXVI	The Rose	419
XXVII	The Swan	437
XXVIII	The Boar's Head	452
	Appendix: the buildings and the theatrical enterprise in them	488
XXIX	The first Globe	493
XXX	The second Blackfriars	501
XXXI	The first Fortune	531
XXXII	Whitefriars	547
XXXIII	The Red Bull	564
	Appendix: Woodford's lawsuit against Holland	592
XXXIV	The Hope	595
XXXV	The second Globe	607
XXXVI	The Phoenix	623
XXXVII	The second Fortune	638
XXXVIII	Salisbury Court	649

Bibliography 675
Index 685

List of illustrations

1 The Curtain playhouse (?), from *The View of the Cittye of London from the North towards the Sowth*, c. 1600–10 or later (courtesy of Clive and Philip Burden, Rickmansworth, Herts.) *page* 404

2 The remains of the Rose playhouse, (a) as built in 1587, and (b) as rebuilt in 1592, from the provisional plans of the excavation in 1989 (courtesy of the Museum of London). The five large blank spaces, three down the middle and two on the right, have to do with a building erected on the site in the 1950s and since removed 420 and 421

3 The interior of the Swan playhouse, from Arend van Buchell's copy in the Library of the University of Utrecht of a lost letter of Johannes de Witt, c. 1596 437

4 The Whitefriars playhouse (?), from A. W. Clapham, 'The Topography of the Carmelite Priory of London', p. 26, a reproduction of a plan at the British Museum, now lost. The playhouse must have been in the 'Hale', i.e., hall. The Thames is beyond the top of the drawing and Fleet Street beyond the bottom 548

5 The Red Bull playhouse during a performance of drolls in the 1650s (?), from Francis Kirkman, *The Wits, or Sport upon Sport*, frontispiece 565

6 (a) The Hope playhouse and Baiting House, and (b) the second Globe playhouse, from Wenceslas Hollar, Long Bird's-Eye View (1647). Hollar reversed the labels for the buildings 608

7 A Phoenix playhouse (?), from Wenceslas Hollar, The Great Map, as reproduced in *A Collection of Early Maps of London, 1553–1667*, sheet 19. The playhouse is probably the larger of the two buildings in the middle that have three pitched roofs. The street in the lower left corner is Drury Lane, and that across the top is Wild Street 624

8 Unidentified playhouses of Caroline times, (a) from the title page of William Alabaster, *Roxana*, a Latin play, and (b) from the title page of Nathaniel Richards, *Messallina*. The second drawing is probably derived from the first 650

List of documents

Asterisks before titles indicate illustrated documents

PART ONE: DOCUMENTS OF CONTROL

I *Henry VIII, 1530–1547*

1. William Newhall, town clerk of Chester, censors references to the Pope's jurisdiction over performances of the Whitsun plays in the city, 1532 — page 18
2. Sir Richard Morrison urges king Henry VIII to use the theatre to destroy respect for the Pope in England, c. 1535 — 20
3. Payments to John Bale and his fellow-actors — 21
4. Henry VIII orders the justices in York to arrest and imprison papists who write and perform religious plays, 1536/1537 — 21
5. The Duke of Suffolk writes to Thomas Cromwell about an allegedly satirical and subversive play at Huxton, 1537 — 22
6. Three actors convicted of heresy and burned at Salisbury, 1541 — 22
7. The bishops in Convocation petition the King to censor public performances of plays in London, 1542 — 23
8. An Act of Parliament for the Advancement of True Religion and for the Abolition of the Contrary, 1543 — 23
9. (a–f) Excerpts from letters between the Chancellor of Cambridge University, the Vice-Chancellor and the Privy Council relating to a performance of Thomas Kirchmayer's play *Pammachius* at Christ's College, 1545 — 25
10. A Proclamation banning public performances of all plays in London without the prior consent of the Lord Mayor and Aldermen, 1545 — 30
11. London's Court of Aldermen prohibit the posting of playbills and all unauthorised performances of plays in their wards, 1545 — 31
12. The Court of Aldermen orders its officers to destroy all playbills posted on Sunday mornings and to arrest the actors, 1547 — 32

II *Edward VI, 1547–1553*

13. Hereford City Council abolishes its Corpus Christi guild plays, 1548 — 33
14. An Act of Parliament for the Uniformity of Service and Administration of the Sacraments, 1549 — 34
15. A Royal Proclamation of 6 August 1549, forbidding all dramatic performances between 9 August and the feast of All Saints next coming (1 November) — 34
16. Another Proclamation forbidding both the printing of plays and public

List of documents ix

	performances without prior approval and written licence from the King or his Privy Council, 1551	35
17	The Marquis of Dorset's players are licensed to play only in their patron's presence, 1551	37
18	Martin Bucer, as Regius Professor Divinity at Cambridge, advises the King of the need to appoint a committee to censor plays prior to performance	37
	*(a) A brass plate in the chancel floor of Great St Mary's Church, Cambridge commemorating the burial, exhumation, burning and reburial of Martin Bucer in 1551, 1557 and 1560 respectively	38

III Mary I, 1553–1558

19	A Proclamation reimposing and reinforcing Edward VI's restrictions on the printing and performance of all plays without prior written permission from the Queen or her Council, 1553	39
20	A sequence of government orders for the arrest, interrogation and prosecution of offending play-makers and players, 1555–1558	41
	(a.1–2) At Hatfield Bradock, Essex, 1555	41
	(b) An Order directed at all travelling companies of players, 1556	42
	(c) The Court of Aldermen in London forbids performances of plays on Sundays and other Holy Days, 1557	42
	(d) A letter 'of the utmost urgency' from the Privy Council to the Lord President of the North (the Earl of Shrewsbury), ordering the arrest and interrogation of Sir Francis Leek's players, 1557, newly located and freshly transcribed for the first time since 1822	42
	(e) The Privy Council orders the Lord Mayor of London to arrest a company of players for examination by the Commissioners for Religion, 1557	44
	(f) The Privy Council orders the Mayor of Canterbury to imprison a company of actors pending examination of their playbook, 1557	44
	(g) Letters from the Lord Chancellor instructing the Lord Lieutenant of Essex (Lord Rich) to punish the players who fought with the Watch, and to all justices in that county to prohibit the performance of all plays throughout the summer months, 1557	44
	(h) The Privy Council returns the playbook and examinations of the players arrested in Canterbury (20f) to the mayor and instructs him to proceed against them in accordance with the law, 1557	45
	(i) Two letters from the Privy Council to the Lord Mayor of London respecting the conduct of players at the Boar's Head inn, 1557	45
21	A sequence of documents relating to an abortive performance of an heretical play in Islington, North London, 1557	46–7
	(a) Henry Machyn records the arrest of the players in his diary on Sunday, 12 December 1557	46

x   List of documents

    (b) The Privy Council orders the Bishop of London to proceed against one of these players (now in prison) 15 December 1557 — 46
    (c) The presumed leader of these players, Sir John Rough, is condemned to be burned for heresy, 20 December 1557 — 46
    (d) Sir John Rough burned at Smithfield, 22 December 1557 — 47

IV   Elizabeth I, 1558–1603

(a) From 1558 to 1570

22   An Act of Parliament for the Uniformity of Common Prayer and Divine Service in the Church and the use of the Sacraments, 1559 — 50
23   An order of the Court of Aldermen relating to the Queen's first Proclamation of 7 April, and its application in London, 1559 — 51
24   The Queen's second Proclamation relating to the licensing of players, May 1559 — 51
25   (a) Excerpts from Injunctions from the Queen governing the printing of books and plays under licence, June 1559 — 52
    (b) A warrant from the Queen authorising the individuals named in the previous Injunction to license the printing of books and plays, July 1559 — 53
26   Documents relating to visitations of plague in London, 1564–9 — 54–6
    (a) A Precept from the Lord Mayor and aldermen forbidding performances of plays, February 1564 — 54
    (b) A letter from the Archbishop of Canterbury to Sir William Cecil asking him to arrange for performances of plays to be forbidden for a year or more, 1564 — 55
    (c) A Precept from the Lord Mayor to the aldermen of London ordering them to forbid performances of plays within their wards until further notice, 1569 — 56
27   Documents relating to the regulation of performance of plays in inns and taverns within the City of London, 1565–1569 — 56–7
    (a) An Order of the Court of Aldermen forbidding performances of plays in inns, taverns and victualling houses where admission is charged for them, 1565 — 56
    (b) A precept from the Lord Mayor particular to the aldermen for the ward of Cheapside reinforcing the above Order (**27a**), 1565 — 56
    (c) A Precept from the city council prohibiting all horse- or cart-drawn transportation, and all performances of plays, after 5.00 p.m. on Sundays to allow time for the cleansing of the City streets, 1569 — 57
28   Documents regulating performances of plays on Sundays, in Lent and on other occasions — 57–61
    (a) Robert Fryer, a London goldsmith, is bound over in recognisance of £10.00 to refuse to allow plays to be performed in his 'mansion' before 4.00 p.m. on any Sunday or other festival Holy Day and to refuse admission to audiences before 3.00 p.m. between April and the end of August 1566 — 57
    (b) Bonds in the sum of £40.00 each are to be taken from all large householders within the City of London where plays are regularly

List of documents xi

		presented, restricting performances to daylight hours, 'and that between the hours of 3 & 4 of the clock', 3 February 1569	58
	(c)	This Order is reinforced by a Precept from the Lord Mayor to the aldermen of each ward in the City to the same effect, 3 February 1569	59
	(d)	A Proclamation from Guildhall banning all performances of plays from 12 May to 1 September to prevent outbreaks of plague in London, 1569	59
	(e)	This ban is extended until the end of October with an additional obligation imposed on at least one member of every household to attend Common Prayer in their parish church on Mondays, Tuesdays, Wednesdays and Saturdays, 1569	59
	(f)	The Court of Aldermen order John Rose of Bridewell to desist from holding puppet shows in that ward of the City, November 1568	60

(b) *From 1570 to 1580*

29		Extracts from an Act of Parliament for the punishment of vagabonds and for the relief of the poor, 1572	62
30–33		Documents relating to the suppression of annual performances of religious Guild plays in York, Chester and Wakefield, 1568–1576	
30	(a)	The Dean of York advises the Lord Mayor not to proceed with the proposed production of the York Creed Play, 1568	64
	(b)	York City Council agrees to submit the text of their Pater Noster Play to the Archbishop for his examination, 1572	65
	(c)	York City Council asks to recover the prompt-copies of the Creed Play, Pater Noster Play and Corpus Christi plays from the Archbishop, 1575	65
31	(a)	The Mayor of Chester, John Hankey, decides to sanction performance of the Whitsun plays, notwithstanding advice from the Archbishops of Canterbury and York to the contrary, 1572	65
	(b)	The Whitsun (or Chester) plays proceed despite substantial public disapproval, 1572	65
	(c)	The Whitsun plays proceed, despite an Inhibition from the Archbishop of York forbidding performances since this arrived too late to cancel them, 1572	66
	(d)	The Whitsun plays are again performed despite public opposition to this decision, 1572	66
32	(a)	The city council, after a year's interval without performances, debate whether or not to resume them, 1574	66
	(b)	The city council votes, by a majority of 21, to proceed with reformed versions of the traditional texts, 1575	66
	(c)	These performances took place despite orders received from the Archbishop of York and the Lord President of the North to reverse this decision, 1575	66
	(d)	Following these performances, the Mayor of Chester is arrested and conveyed to London for examination by the Privy Council, 1575	67

xii   List of documents

(e) The mayor, Sir John Savage, writes to his successor asking the city council to supply the Privy Council with a Certificate testifying the decision to proceed with production of the plays was taken by majority vote of the whole council and was not his alone, 1575 — 67

(f) An extract from the Certificate requested, exculpating both Sir John Savage and his predecessor as mayor, Mr. Hankey, from any blame, and despatched on the same day as Sir John's letter was received, 1575 — 68

33 An Order from the Diocesan Court of High Commission in the North to the town council in Wakefield insisting that any proposal to perform their cycle of Corpus Christi plays may only be permitted to proceed in appropriately revised texts, 1576 — 69

34 A Patent appointing Edmund Tilney to the Mastership of the Revels Office within the Royal Household, 1581 — 70

*(a) Edmund Tilney's monument in St Leonard's Parish Church, Streatham, London, SW 16 — 72

35 An Edict from the Court of Common Council for the regulation of all theatrical performances in London responding to the issue of Edmund Tilney's Patent, 1582 — 73–7

36 (a) The Privy Council forbids public performances of plays throughout Lent, 1579 — 77

(b) The Lord Mayor orders all aldermen in London to stop performances of plays advertised within their wards at night before they begin, 1579 — 77

(c) From 1581 to 1603

37 The Privy Council rebukes the Justices of the Peace in Surrey and Middlesex for failing to implement its Order to close all playhouses as a precautionary measure against plague between May and September 1580 — 81

38 (a) The Lord Mayor instructs the sheriffs and aldermen to prohibit the posting of playbills throughout the City of London, and anywhere else in adjoining suburbs, November 1581 — 81

(b) The Privy Council asks the Lord Mayor to rescind its Order earlier in the year to close all playhouses, since the recent outbreak of plague is now over and unlikely to return, November 1581 — 82

(c) The Privy Council records its receipt of a petition from the players to reopen London's playhouses and its own request to the Lord Mayor to do so, but on weekdays only, December 1581 — 82

39 The Privy Council forbids 'all manner of public concourse ... preaching and Divine Service at Churches excepted', 1593 — 83

40 An Order from the Lord Mayor to the officers of the Ironmongers Company instructing them to charge all their freemen to prohibit their 'servants, apprentices, journeymen and children' from attending plays both within the City and in the suburbs, 1582 — 85

List of documents xiii

41	The Lord Mayor informs the Privy Council that its ban on performances of plays on Sundays until after divine services have ended will fail in its purpose while audiences continue to absent themselves from City churches in order to secure places in the playhouses before performances begin, 1582	86
42	The Lord Mayor seeks help from Sir Francis Walsingham in persuading the Privy Council to enforce stricter controls over actors and playhouse owners in the suburbs, 1588	86
43	The Lord Mayor uses the recent collapse of seating scaffolds with fatal consequences at Beargardens to urge the Privy Council to make the justices in Surrey and Middlesex enforce government regulations respecting plays, players and playhouses more rigorously in future, 1583	87
44	(a–c) Letters from the Privy Council to the justices in Surrey and Middlesex rebuking them for their laxity in permitting performances of plays to proceed on Sundays, 1587	88–9
45	'Two letters of one tenor' from the Privy Council to the justices in Surrey and Middlesex, rebuking them severely for their repeated failure to enforce government regulations respecting the suburban playhouses, 1601	89
46	An army officer writes to the Queen's secretary suggesting that playhouse receipts should be taxed to provide relief for the poor, 1587	90
47	(a) The Vestry of St Saviour's, Southwark, instructs its churchwardens to discuss tithes with the actors and playhouse managers on Bankside towards relief for the poor in the parish as suggested by the Archbishop of Canterbury, the Bishop of London and the Master of the Revels, 1600	91
	(b) Twenty seven inhabitants in the parish of Finsbury, North London, petition the Privy Council to license the building of the Fortune playhouse to help in raising funds for poor relief, 1600	91
48	The Lord Mayor informs Lord Burghley of the action he has taken against the Lord Admiral's and Lord Strange's players, 1589	93
49	Letters from the Privy Council to the Archbishop of Canterbury, the Lord Mayor of London and the Master of the Revels about the licensing of plays prior to performance, 1589	94–6
50	The Lord Mayor solicits help from the Archbishop of Canterbury to persuade Edmund Tilney to relinquish his powers of jurisdiction over plays, players and playhouses in London, 1592	96
51	The Lord Mayor thanks the Archbishop for his promise of support, 1592	97
52	(a) The Court of the Mercers' Company debate the Lord Mayor's request to consider funding an annuity for Edmund Tilney to persuade him to relinquish his licensing powers, but decide to defer an answer until the attitude of other London livery companies is known, 1592	98
	(b) The Court of the Merchant Taylors' Company debate this issue and arrive at a similar decision, 1592	98

xiv List of documents

53	An exasperated Court of Common Council at Guildhall ask the Privy Council to forbid all performances of plays in and around London, 'instantly and forever', 1597	99
54	The Privy Council instructs magistrates in Surrey and Middlesex to forbid performances of plays between August and November and to give orders for the demolition of the Theatre, the Curtain and the playhouses on Bankside, July 1597	100
55	The Privy Council orders the arrest of Thomas Nashe, co-author of *The Isle of Dogs*, and those members of the Earl of Pembroke's players not yet imprisoned, August 1597	102
56	The Privy Council instructs the Master of the Revels to deny a licence to an intrusive and unwanted company of players said to be presenting plays in London without the Council's consent, 1598	104
57	The Countess of Derby pleads with her uncle, Lord Burghley, to secure a licence for her husband's company to continue to present his own and other plays in London, 1599	105
58	Extracts from Orders of the Privy Council governing performances of plays in London's public playhouses, 1600	106
59	The Privy Council informs the Lord Mayor of its decision to license a third company of players to present plays at the Boar's Head inn, 1602	109
60	The Privy Council instructs the High Sheriff of Suffolk to forbid performance of a Whitsun play at Hadley, 1597	110
61	A memorandum submitted to the Privy Council by the bishop of Chester relating to complaints received from the clergy in Lancashire about plays and players, 1590	111
62	A letter from the Privy Council ordering the Earl of Derby to forbid all recreational entertainments in northern counties at times of divine service, and to send persistent offenders to London for interrogation, 1592	112
63	A Warrant and two letters from the Vice-Chancellor of Cambridge University relating to travelling companies of players, 1592	113–17
64	(a) Rules for the better regulation of acting companies seeking to perform plays in Canterbury, 1595	117–18
	(b) Bristol City Council bans the use of its guildhall to visiting companies of professional players, 1595/6	118–19

V *James I and Charles I, 1603–1647*

(a) *From 1603 to 1625: London*

65	A Royal Proclamation forbidding all forms of entertainment on Sundays, 1603	122
66	James I's Patent enrolling the former Lord Chamberlain's company of players into his own household as the King's Men, 1603	123
67	The Duke of Lennox writes to all magistrates and constables asking them to respect his licence as sufficient authority for his players to perform in public playhouses, 1604	124
68	Ben Jonson's preface to the printed text of *The Masque of Queens*, 1609	125

List of documents xv

69 Sir Thomas Lake informs Lord Salisbury of the King's decision to withdraw the licence granted to the Children of the Queen's Revels at Blackfriars, 1608 ... 126

70 A letter from the Privy Council to the King's secretary informing him about the action taken to suppress performances of Thomas Middleton's *A Game at Chess* and to interrogate the King's players, 1624 ... 127

    (b) From 1625 to 1647

71 (a) Charles I distinguishes between asseverations and oaths which must be deleted from play-texts before they may be performed, 1633/1634 ... 128
    (b) Charles I authorises the Master of the Revels to license Philip Massinger's *The King and the Subject* for performance with the title changed and one speech deleted, 1638 ... 129

72 Extracts from the Patent awarded to William Davenant by Charles I to build a theatre near Fleet Street in London, 1639 ... 130

73 (a) Parliament revises the Statutes governing the Punishment of Rogues, Vagabonds and Sturdy Beggars, 1604 ... 131
    (b) Parliament legislates against the use by players of the Holy Names of God, Christ Jesus, the Holy Ghost and the Trinity in any play by making any actor who so offends liable to a fine of £10.00 for each offence, 1606 ... 131

74 (a) Parliament passes an Ordinance forbidding all performances of stage plays indefinitely, September 1642 ... 132
    (b) Parliament orders the Lord Mayor of London and the Justices of the Peace in Westminster, Surrey and Middlesex to suppress stage plays and commit all players found acting in them to prison, 1647 ... 132
    (c) Parliament bans all further performances of stage plays; decrees that all actors are from henceforth to be regarded as Rogues and Vagabonds punishable under the Statutes, and orders all playhouses in and around London to be defaced or demolished, 1647/1648 ... 133
    *(d) The title page of this Ordinance as printed for publication 11 February 1647/1648 ... 134

    (c) From 1603 to 1647: the provinces

75 Notice of receipt of four royal Proclamations delivered to the city council in Leicester, 1603; one of them forbids all forms of public entertainment on Sundays ... 136

76 (a) The Diocesan Court sentences Edward Bartholomew and other actors for performing a play at Alvechurch, Worcestershire on a Sunday, 1611 ... 136
    (b) John Browning is convicted of having attended a performance of a play on Sunday and absented himself from church to do so, 1611 ... 137

77 Sir Edward Coke orders the mayor and justices in Coventry to prohibit all performances of plays on the forthcoming Sunday, 28 March 1615 ... 137

xvi List of documents

78   The Privy Council thanks the Mayor of Canterbury for the action he has taken against players performing in the city in Lent in defiance of Injunctions forbidding them, 1636   137
79   Proceedings taken against an ale-house keeper in Warrington, Lancashire, and a group of amateur actors who rehearsed or performed a play in his loft on a Sunday during Morning Prayer, 1632   138
80   Judgement is given by the magistrates at Ormskirk in Lancashire at the Quarter Sessions respecting these actors, 1632   139
81   Leicester City Council revises its regulations governing payments to visiting companies of actors and attendance by councillors at their performances, 1607   140
82   Costs for repairs to the city hall in Leicester following visits of travelling companies of players, 1605 and 1608   141
83   Extract from the deposition of two members of the Queen's players arrested for performing in the town hall at Cambridge without having obtained permission to do so, 1606   142
84   York City Council licenses the Princess Elizabeth's players to perform in the city, 1612   142
85   Conditions governing use of the town hall in Worcester for the performance of plays, 1622   143
86   The Lord Chamberlain writes to all mayors and county magistrates instructing them to arrest all actors suspected of travelling under dubious licences and to send them to London for examination by the Privy Council, 1617   143
87   The Privy Council acknowledges safe receipt of a Patent sent by the Mayor of Banbury that he suspected to be a forgery, and instructs him to send the actors who presented it to London for interrogation   145
88   Francis Wambus, leader of the Princess Elizabeth's players, challenges the Mayor of Norwich to test the strength of a Royal Patent against that of merely local powers of restraint, 1624   146
89   The Lord Chamberlain instructs provincial mayors and magistrates on how to handle travelling companies of actors presenting licences purporting to have been issued under the Privy Seal, 1622   148

PART TWO: PLAYERS AND PLAYING

VII   *The popular image of the stage player*

90   Contention over the funeral obsequies for Henry VIII, 1547   157
91   Players and play-watchers equally corrupt (William Bavande, 1559)   158
92   Playing a dishonest and wicked occupation (Henry Cornelius Agrippa, 1569)   159
93   Players offend the majesty of God (Geoffrey Fenton, 1574)   159
94   A dialogue between Youth and Age (John Northbrooke, 1577)   160
95   Players a mixture of good and bad (Stephen Gosson, 1579)   161
96   Players incline their audience to wickedness (?Anthony Munday, 1580)   162
97   Players are to be loathed (Stephen Gosson, 1582)   164

98	Players as painted sepulchres and double-dealing ambidexters (Phillip Stubbes, 1583)	166
99	Players as unwholesome weeds (William Rankins, 1587)	167
100	Players as immoral profiteers (Samuel Cox, 1590)	168
101	The adventures of Roberto (Robert Greene, 1592)	169
102	The opinions of Pierce Penniless (Thomas Nashe, 1592)	171
103	Accusations of sexual perversion and stage-playing, 1600	172
104	Cambridge students, aspiring to be stage-players, talk with Burbage and Kemp (*The Return from Parnassus*, c.1601)	173
	*(a) Woodcut of Will Kemp, 1600	174
105	Christopher Beeston accused of fornication, 1602	175
106	Players work in an ancient and honourable tradition (Thomas Heywood, 1612)	175
107	The proper name for a player is Hypocrite (I. G., 1615)	178
108	Description of a common player (John Cocke, 1615)	179
109	The character of an excellent player (Sir Thomas Overbury, 1615)	180
110	Anonymous funeral elegy for Richard Burbage, 1619	181
	(a) Portrait of Richard Burbage	184
111	Players as exemplars of womanishness (Robert Burton, 1621)	185
112	Players as unfit subjects for legal redress, 1625	185
113	Players not to be confused with their roles (Philip Massinger, 1626)	185
114	Character of a virtuous player (John Earle, 1628)	186
115	Players as the very dregs of men (William Prynne, 1632)	187
116	Thomas Barnes, carpenter, pretends to be a player, 1632	189
117	Players as speaking pictures (Richard Baker, 1662)	189

VIII   A representative life: Augustine Phillips

118	Augustine Phillips as Sardanapalus, 1590	191
119	Phillips and his colleagues licensed to travel, 1593	191
120	Phillips assessed by the subsidy commissioners, 1593	192
121	Phillips resident in Horseshoe Court, 1593–1594	192
122	Phillips's first daughter baptised, 1594	192
123	Phillips's jig of the slippers, 1595	192
124	Phillips still resident in Horseshoe Court, 1595–1596	193
125	Another daughter baptised, 1596	193
126	Phillips no longer resident in Horseshoe Alley, 1596–1597	193
127	A stillborn child buried, 1597	193
128	Churching of Anne Phillips after the delivery of her stillborn child, 1597	194
129	Phillips a player in Jonson's *Every Man in His Humour*, 1598	194
130	Phillips living near the Swan playhouse in 1598–159?	194
131	Phillips a player in Jonson's *Every Man Out of His Humour*, 1599	194
132	The Phillips family perhaps in a new dwelling, 1599	194
133	Phillips examined about the Essex Rebellion, 1601	195
134	Phillips resettled in St Saviour's parish in Southwark, 1601	195
135	Possible marriage of Elizabeth Phillips, 1603	195

xviii List of documents

136	Phillips resident again in Horseshoe Alley, 1602–1603	196
137	Phillips still in Horseshoe Alley in 1603–04	196
138	Phillips among those named to be the King's players, 1603	196
139	Phillips a player in Jonson's *Sejanus*, 1603	196
140	Phillips takes part in the royal coronation, 1604	196
141	Phillips's only son buried, 1604	197
142	Augustine Phillips as a moneylender, 1604	197
143	Vacating the premises in Horseshoe Alley, 1604–1605	197
144	Augustine Phillips makes his will, 1605	198
145	Death and burial of Augustine Phillips, 1605	199
146	Probate of the will; widow Anne Phillips named as executrix	199
147	Second probate of the will	199
148	Phillips's acting remembered and commended by Thomas Heywood, 1612	200
149	Burial of Anne Phillips Witter, 1618	200
150	John Witter's lawsuit, 1619; 1, 2, 3 and 4	200–3

IX Patrons and playing companies

(a) The Earl of Leicester

151	Lord Robert Dudley intercedes for his company of stage-players, 1559	205
152	Leicester's players petition to be his household servants, c. 1572	205
153	Royal Patent for the Earl of Leicester's players, 1574	206
*(a)	Portrait of the Earl of Leicester, 1575	207

(b) The Queen

154	Formation of the Queen's players, 1583	208
155	Comment on the Queen's players	208
*(a)	Drawing of Richard Tarlton	209

(c) The King

| 156 | Warrant to expand the King's company, 1633 | 210 |

X Players and their playing places

157	The Swan playhouse and the Earl of Pembroke's players, 1597; 1, 2, 3 and 4	211–16
158	Lease of one thirty-second part of the income of the Fortune playhouse, 1608	216
159	Agreement between a company of players and a playhouse owner, 1613	217
160	Players draft articles of grievance against Phillip Henslowe, 1615	218
161	Edward Alleyn leases out the Fortune playhouse, 1618	220
162	The so-called 'Sharers' Papers', 1635; 1 to 7	221–8

XI Costumes, properties and playbooks

163	*Rastell* v *Walton*, a lawsuit about playing costumes, ?1530; 1 to 11	229–33
164	Getting costumes for a play before the King, 1552	233
165	A lawsuit about playscripts, 1572	234
166	Richard Jones and James Tunstall, players, buy gowns from Phillip Henslowe, 1594	235

List of documents xix

167	Inventory lists belonging to Phillip Henslowe, 1598	236
168	Samuel Rowley asks Phillip Henslowe to pay for playscripts, 1601	238
169	A dispute over ownership of costumes, properties and playbooks, ?1619	239
170	Cast-off garments as costumes for players, 1629	241

XII Players travelling in the provinces

171	What happened when players came to a town	243
172	A town's reasons for not wishing to welcome players, 1580	243
173	The Earl of Worcester's players told not to perform at Leicester, 1584	244
174	The Queen's players in an affray at Norwich, 1583	246
175	Various players discouraged from playing, twelve instances, 1580 to 1635	250
176	The Lord Chamberlain (the Earl of Pembroke) directs the Mayor of Norwich to confiscate exemplifications, June 1617	254
177	The Privy Council authorises the Mayor of Norwich to prohibit playing in his city, 1623	255
178	Francis Wambus, stage-player, contends with the Mayor of Norwich for the right to play, 1624; i–v	255–8

(a) Permissions to travel and protections from arrest

179	Request for a passport for players travelling through Holland, 1592	258
180	Sir Henry Herbert's Protection from Arrest, 1624	258
181	Permission for players to travel and play, 1636	259

XIII Companies of children

182	William Hunnis seeks help in taking over the theatre at Blackfriars, 1580	260
183	William Hunnis appeals for more money, 1583	261
184	Thomas Giles' commission to impress children, 1585	262
185	Nathaniel Giles' commission to impress children, 1597	263
186	Henry Clifton's son Thomas forced to be a stage-player, 1601	264
187	Ben Jonson's elegy for Salomon Pavy, a boy-player, ?1604	267
188	Abel Cooke's apprenticeship and reinstatement, 1607	268
189	Articles of Agreement for a children's company, 1608	269
190	The Queen sees to it that a company of children is allowed at Bristol, 1615–1618	
	(a) Letter from the Master of the Revels concerning a forthcoming Patent for the children of the Queen's chamber of Bristol, 10 July 1615	271
	(b) Patent for the children of the Queen's chamber of Bristol, 17 July 1615	272
	(c) The Mayor of Exeter's letter to Sir Thomas Lake, June 1618?	273
	(d) Letter confirming John Daniel's Patent, undated	273

XIV Some illustrative instances of professional theatrical life and practice

| 191 | George Maller, glazier, and his apprentice Thomas Arthur, 1529 | 275 |
| 192 | A woman and child reportedly killed at a play, 1587 | 277 |

xx   List of documents

193	Edward Alleyn, on tour, writes to his wife, 1593	277
	*(a) Portrait of Edward Alleyn	279
	*(b) Portrait of Joan Woodward Alleyn	280
194	Ben Jonson kills Gabriel Spencer in a duel, 1598	281
195	Indictment of Ben Jonson for the killing of Gabriel Spencer, 1598	281
196	Edward Alleyn as moneylender, 1607	282
197	Robert Dawes contracts to play for Phillip Henslowe, 1614	282

PART THREE: PLAYHOUSES, 1560–1660

XVI   *The Red Lion*

198	Players perform at Mile End, 6 August 1501	291
199	Brayne complains about the carpenter's work on the scaffolds, 15 July 1567	291
200	Brayne complains about the carpenter's work on the stage, autumn 1568	291

XVII–XX   *The Four Inns*

201	Fencers use the Bel Savage and Bull for their prizes, 1568, 1575	296
	(a) The Bel Savage, 13 June 1568	296
	(b) The Bull, 7 June 1575	296
202	The Bel Savage is in business as a playhouse, 1575	297
203	How spectators paid to see plays at the Bel Savage, 1576	297
204	The Bell is in business as a playhouse, 12–21 February (Shrovetide) 1577	297
205	All four inns are probably in business as playhouses, 24 August 1578	298
206	Italian tourists are to take note of playing at the Bull, 1578	298
207	James Burbage attends a play at the Cross Keys, 23 June 1579	298
	(a) Burbage's question for a witness, John Hynd, 1592	298
	(b) Hynd's reply, 24 July 1592	298
208	A despiser of plays approves of two at the Bel Savage and two at the Bull, 22 July 1579	299
209	A fencer wants to play a prize at the Bull, 1–24 July 1582	
	(a) The Earl of Warwick to the Lord Mayor of London, 1 July 1582	299
	(b) The Lord Mayor replies to the Earl of Warwick, 24 July 1582	299
210	The Queen's men are allowed to play at the Bull and Bell, 28 November 1583	
	(a) The Queen's men may play at the Bull and the Bell, 28 November 1583	300
	(b) The City notes the result, *c.* November 1584	301
211	Richard Tarlton plays at the Bull and the Bell and jests at the Cross Keys, 1583–1588	301
	(a) At the Bull	301
	(b) At the Bell and Cross Keys	301
212	Tarlton sings his last 'theme' at the Bel Savage, *c.* 1588	302
213	The Lord Mayor stops playing in the City, but Strange's men defy him at the Cross Keys, 6 November 1589	302
214	The Bel Savage has a perilously high stage, *c.* 1590	302

List of documents   xxi

215	Diabolical events take place on the stage at the Bel Savage, c. 1590	303
216	The Bull is noted as a place where actors speak fustian, 1592	303
217	Francis and Anthony Bacon's mother warns Anthony of the dangers of living near the Bull, c. 1 May 1594	303
218	The Lord Chamberlain's men want to continue playing at the Cross Keys, 8 October 1594	304
219	City authorities suppress the playhouses in the four inns, c. 1596	
	(a) The City did suppress the four inns	304
	(b) Three of them were out of business by 1596	305
220	The privy council administers a *coup de grâce*, 22 June 1600	305
221	The playhouses in the four inns are remembered, and vestiges survive, 1664	305

XXI St Paul's

222	Sebastian Westcott and John Heywood take boys to the court of Princess Elizabeth, 13 February 1552	308
223	Westcott and Heywood lead the boys of St Paul's in a performance before Queen Elizabeth, 7 August 1559	308
224	Westcott has the right to draft boys into his choir from anywhere, 30 June 1560	309
225	One of Westcott's boys is 'stolen', and the privy council tries seriously to find him, 3 December 1575	309
226	The London authorities find that the boys play for great gain at St Paul's, 8 December 1575	309
227	The privy council includes St Paul's boys among companies of professional players, 24 December 1578	
228	The playhouse at St Paul's and the Marprelate Controversy, October–November 1589	
	(a) Nashe? 20 October 1589?	310
	(b) Lyly? end of October 1589?	310
	(c) Harvey, 5 November 1589	311
	(d) The Lord Mayor to Lord Burghley, 6 November 1589	311
	(e) The Privy Council order, 12 November 1589	311
229	Plays are no longer being performed publicly at St Paul's, 1591, 1596	
	(a) Lyly, 4 October 1591	312
	(b) Nashe, 1596	312
230	But the boys may perform for a private occasion in a private house, autumn 1592	312
231	John Howe, a verger in the cathedral, testifes about where the playhouse was, 1599	313
232	The children of St Paul's have begun playing again, thanks to the Earl of Derby, 13 November 1599	313
233	The children of St Paul's are playing old-fashioned plays, 8 September 1600	314
234	People do not sit on the stage at St Paul's because it is very little, c. 1601	314
235	The boys of St Paul's act a play about a vexed local matter, January and February 1603	

xxii   List of documents

		(a) The Attorney General's bill, 6 May 1603	315
		(b) Chapman's reply, 19 May 1603	315
		(c) Chapman's testimony, 30 May 1603	315
		(d) Woodford's reply, 23 May 1603	316
		(e) Woodford's testimony, 3 June 1603	316
		(f) Peers' reply, 7 June 1603	316
236	William Percy may offer five of his plays to the children of St Paul's, 1603–ff.		317
237	Peers and Woodford quarrel, and Edward Kirkham becomes a master of the boys of St Paul's, 1604–1606		
		(a) Peers assaults Woodford, 2 December 1604	317
		(b) Kirkham is a master, spring 1606	317
238	The boys of St Paul's perform before two kings at Greenwich, 30 July 1606		318
239	Rival companies of players bribe the people at St Paul's to keep the playhouse closed, 1608–1610		
		(a) Keysar's assertion, 2 May 1610	318
		(b) The King's men's answer, 19 June 1610	318

XXII   Newington Butts

240	The officers of Canterbury Cathedral describe the playhouse plot, 30 November 1590; 5 and 6 April 1595		
		(a) The playhouse	321
		(b) The plot	322
		(c) The plot revised	322
241	An actor, Jerome Savage, has the part of Hicks' land including the playhouse, 1576–1578		322
242	Hicks and his son-in-law try to remove Savage from the playhouse property, and Savage sues them, May 1577		
		(a) Savage's bill of complaint, undated	323
		(b) The reply of Honingborne, 10 May 1577	324
		(c) Hicks' reply, 14 May 1577	326
243	The playhouse is to stop alluring people to plays, 10 November 1578		326
244	The playhouse has been defying an order to stop playing, 13 May 1580		326
245	The playhouse is closed, like its competitors nearer to the City of London, 11 May 1586		327
246	Peter Honingborne has the playhouse and Richard Cuckow the rest of Hicks' property 1590, 1591		
		(a) 30 November 1590	327
		(b) 26 February 1591	327
247	The playhouse is disused, but Lord Strange's men play there briefly, before 25 September 1593		327
248	The Lord Admiral's and Lord Chamberlain's men play jointly at Newington Butts, 3–13 June 1594		328
249	Paul Buck, perhaps a player, acquires the playhouse on condition that he ends playing there, 6 July 1594		329
250	The playhouse has been replaced by houses, 5 October 1599		329
251	The playhouse is remembered, 1631		329

XXIII   The Theatre

252	James Burbage leases property in Holywell from Giles Allen in which to build a playhouse, 13 April 1576	333
253	The playhouse has been in business for some time, 1 August 1577	336
254	Burbage is to share the lease with John Brayne but cannot because it has been pawned, 9 August 1577	336
255	A 'brabble' over a matter at the Theatre, 5 October 1577	337
256	Clergymen find the Theatre a sumptuous school for wickedness and vice, 3 November and 2 December 1577	
	(a) T. W., 3 November 1577	337
	(b) Northbrooke, 2 December 1577	337
257	Burbage bonds himself to give Brayne half the Theatre, but they argue and violence ensues, 22 May 1578	337
258	Burbage and Brayne seek arbitration of their disagreements, 12 July 1578	
	(a) Robert Miles, 30 July 1592	338
	(b) Ralph Miles, 26 April 1592	339
	(c) Nicoll, 31 July 1592	339
259	The gorgeous Theatre, 24 August 1578	339
260	Swordsmen in the Theatre, 25 August 1578	340
261	Burbage and Brayne mortgage the lease on the property for £125, 26 September 1579	340
262	Wholesome plays at the Theatre, 1579	340
263	Unwholesome plays at the Theatre, 1579	341
264	Burbage and Brayne are indicted for malefactions at plays at the Theatre, 21 February 1580	341
265	An earthquake shakes the Theatre, 6 April 1580	341
266	Another riot at the Theatre, 10 April 1580	342
267	The mortgage on the Theatre property is forfeit, 27 September 1581	
	(a) Hyde deposes, 8 December 1590	342
	(b) Burbage deposes, 16 February 1591	342
	(c) Hyde deposes, 12 February 1592	342
	(d) Hyde deposes, 21 February 1592	343
268	A scurvy play at the Theatre set out by a virgin, 22 February 1582	343
269	James Burbage hires men to prevent Edmund Peckham from seizing the Theatre, spring 1582	
	(a) Cuthbert Burbage's bill, 26 January 1600	343
	(b) Deposition of Randolph May, a painter, 15 May 1600	343
	(c) Deposition of Oliver Tilte, a yeoman, 15 May 1600	344
270	Hyde attempts to collect money owing for the mortgage on the Theatre, June 1582	344
271	Richard Tarlton and the Queen's men are at the Theatre, 1583–ff.	345
272	One Browne causes a brawl at the door of the Theatre, 10 June 1584	345
273	James Burbage resists an attempt by the city of London to suppress the Theatre, 14 June 1584	345
274	Allen denies that Burbage has observed the terms of the lease and refuses to extend it, 1 November 1585	

xxiv List of documents

	(a) Cuthbert Burbage's bill, 26 January 1600	346
	(b) Allen's answer, 4 February 1600	347
	(c) Deposition of Philip Baker, 26 April 1600	347
	(d) Deposition of Henry Johnson, 26 April 1600	347
	(e) Deposition of William Smyth, 15 May 1600	347
275	James Burbage shows that he has indeed spent £200 on buildings other than the Theatre, 20 November 1585	348
276	The Theatre is tied commercially to its neighbour, the Curtain, for seven years from Michaelmas 1585	
	(a) James Burbage, 16 February 1591	348
	(b) John Allein, an actor, 6 May 1592	348
	(c) Henry Lanman, owner of the Curtain, 30 July 1592	349
277	John Brayne dies, apparently childless; his widow accuses Robert Miles of murder, July–August 1586	
	(a) James Burbage's bill, 1588	349
	(b) Deposition of Henry Bett, 30 September 1591	349
278	Margaret Brayne collects her husband's share of profits at the Theatre and Curtain, autumn 1586–1587?	
	(a) Deposition of Henry Bett, 30 September 1591	350
	(b) Deposition of Ralph Miles, 10 February 1592	350
	(c) Deposition of Robert Miles, 30 July 1592	350
279	Margaret Brayne and Robert Miles sue one another, then combine against the Burbages, 1586–1588	351
280	John Hyde, the mortgagee, tries to collect the money owing on the mortgage, 1587–1588	
	(a) Hyde, 8 December 1590	351
	(b) George Clough, 8 December 1590	352
281	James Burbage countersues Margaret Brayne in Chancery, autumn 1588	352
282	Margaret Brayne and Robert Miles respond in Chancery, autumn 1588	355
283	Cuthbert Burbage pays off the mortgage and takes possession of the lease, 7 June 1589	
	(a) Ralph Miles, 10 February 1592	355
	(b) John Hyde, 12 February 1592	356
	(c) Giles Allen, January 1601	356
284	A play against Martin Marprelate is played at the Theatre, 1589	357
285	Chancery orders that the arbitrament of 1578 be observed, 13 November 1590	357
286	The Burbages suspect Miles and Margaret Brayne of murdering John Brayne and of adultery, November 1590	357
287	Margaret Brayne tries to claim half the Theatre, and the Burbages defy her, 14 November 1590–spring 1591	
	(a) Cuthbert Burbage, 16 February 1591	358
	(b) James Burbage, 16 February 1591	359
	(c) Nicholas Byshop, 29 January and 6 April 1592	360
	(d) John Allein, an actor, 6 February and 6 May 1592	361
	(e) Ralph Miles, 10 February and 26 April 1592	362
288	The Burbages have the work done on buildings other than the Theatre valued again, July 1591	363

289	The Burbages spend £30 to £40 on 'further building and repairing' the Theatre, winter 1591–1592	
	(a) Bryan Ellam, carpenter, 25 February, 1592	364
	(b) Richard Hudson, 25 February 1592	364
290	Margaret Brayne dies leaving her child and lawsuits to Robert Miles, 8–13 April 1593	364
291	Robert Miles takes up Margaret Brayne's lawsuit against James Burbage in Chancery, 11 February 1594	365
292	Chancery combines the two lawsuits about the Theatre, 14 March 1595	365
293	Robert Miles effectually loses his case against James Burbage, 28 May 1595	366
294	*Hamlet* is being acted at the Theatre, 1595–1596	367
295	The Burbages negotiate with Giles Allen to renew the lease on the Theatre property, 1596–1598	
	(a) Cuthbert Burbage's bill, 26 January 1600	367
	(b) Allen's answer, 4 February 1600	367
	(c) Two of Allen's interrogatories, 5 June 1600	369
	(d) Robert Vigerous, lawyer, replies, 14 August 1600	369
	(e) Thomas Nevill, gentleman, replies, 10 October 1600	370
	(f) Henry Johnson answers other questions, 26 April 1600	370
	(g) John Goburne answers, 23 May 1600	371
296	Robert Miles sues Cuthbert Burbage and Giles Allen, April–May 1597	372
297	Requests hesitates to accept Miles' lawsuit, 9 May 1597	375
298	Requests accepts Miles' lawsuit, 27 May 1597, but Miles evidently drops it	375
299	The Theatre is abandoned, before 8 September 1598	375
300	Cuthbert Burbage has the Theatre dismantled so that parts can be used in a new playhouse, Christmas 1598	
	(a) Allen in King's Bench, January 1599?	376
	(b) Allen's reply in Requests, 4 February 1600	376
	(c) Allen in the Star Chamber, 23 November 1601	376
	(d) Cuthbert Burbage in Requests, 26 January 1600	377
	(e) Allen's tenant, Henry Johnson, in Requests, 26 April 1600	377
	(f) Allen's tenant, John Goburne, in Requests, 26 April 1600	378
	(g) The Burbages' friend, William Smyth, in Requests, 15 May 1600	378
301	Giles Allen sues Burbages for trespass, 20 January 1599?	378
302	Cuthbert Burbage countersues Giles Allen in Requests, 26 January 1600	378
	(a) Cuthbert Burbage's bill of complaint, 26 January 1600	378
	(b) Giles Allen's answer, 4 February 1600	379
	(c) Cuthbert Burbage's replication, 27 April 1600	382
303	Requests stops Allen's lawsuit in King's Bench, 10–22 April 1600	
	(a) A court order, 10 April 1600	383
	(b) A court order, 22 April 1600	384
304	Cuthbert Burbage accuses Allen of pressing the lawsuit in King's Bench despite a court order, 11 June 1600	384

xxvi   List of documents

305	Requests orders Giles Allen arrested for contempt as a result of Cuthbert Burbage's accusation, 11 June 1600	
	(a) A court order, 11 June 1600	384
	(b) Allen's recollection of being arrested	384
306	Requests decides for Cuthbert Burbage in his lawsuit against Giles Allen, 18 October 1600	385
307	Giles Allen files two more lawsuits against Cuthbert Burbage, 1601–1602	
	(a) Early 1601	386
	(b) 23 November 1601	386

XXIV   The first Blackfriars

308	Richard Farrant asks Sir William More for a lease on a 'house' in Blackfriars, 27 August 1576	390
309	More leases the playhouse property to Farrant for twenty-one years, 29 September and 20 December 1576	390
310	Farrant makes his will, leaving the playhouse property to his wife, 30 November 1580	393
311	Farrant's widow pleads with More for permission to sublet the playhouse property, 25 December 1580	393
312	Anne Farrant sublets the playhouse to William Hunnis and John Newman, just before 19 September 1581	394
313	A great many comedies have been played in the first Blackfriars playhouse, 6 April 1582	394
314	Hunnis pleads impoverishment because of the expenses of the children of the Chapel Royal, November 1583	395
315	Anne Farrant sues William Hunnis and John Newman in Common Pleas for not paying their rent, autumn 1583	395
316	Hunnis and Newman countersue Anne Farrant in Requests, 20 January 1584	
	(a) Newman and Hunnis' bill of complaint, 20 January 1584	396
	(b) Anne Farrant's answer, 27 January 1584	397
	(c) Newman and Hunnis' replication, 27 May 1584	399
	(d) Court orders, January–June 1584	399
317	Anne Farrant appeals to Sir Francis Walsingham about More's seizure of the playhouse property, autumn? 1584	400
318	More explains how and why he seized the playhouse property, c. summer–autumn 1584	401
319	Anne Farrant appeals to the privy council about More's seizure of the playhouse property, 13 January 1587	403

XXV   The Curtain

320	The Curtain estate is described in 1567, 1572 and 1581	
	(a) 20 February 1567	407
	(b) 23 August 1572	407
	(c) 18 March 1581	407
321	The Curtain playhouse and its neighbour, the Theatre, are in business, 2 December 1577	408

		List of documents	xxvii
322	The Curtain and the Theatre represent London playhouses in general, 1577–1592		
	(a) 1579		408
	(b) 1 March 1583		408
	(c) 3 May 1583		409
	(d) 1587		409
	(e) August 1589		409
	(f) 23 June 1592		409
323	Fencers play their 'prizes' at the Curtain, 1579–1583		
	(a) 25 August 1579		409
	(b) 30 April 1583		410
324	The City of London tries to suppress the Curtain, 14 June 1584		410
325	Contemporaries describe the Curtain, 1585–1611		
	(a) Samuel Kiechel, 1585		410
	(b) Johannes de Witt, 1596		410
	(c) John Day, William Rowley, George Wilkins, 1607		411
	(d) The owners, 1611		411
326	The owners of the Curtain and Theatre agree to share the profits of the two playhouses, 1585–1592		411
327	The privy council orders the Theatre and Curtain to be speedily pulled down, 28 July 1597		411
328	The Lord Chamberlain's men move from the Theatre to the Curtain, autumn 1598		
	(a) Marston, 8 September 1598		412
	(b) Guilpin, 15 September 1598		412
	(c) Armin, 1600, 1605		412
329	A Swiss sees a play at the Curtain, September or October 1599		412
330	A barber is charged with stealing a purse at a play at the Curtain, March 1600		413
331	The privy council allows the Fortune to open provided that the Curtain is closed, 22 June 1600		413
332	But playing continues at the Curtain: the privy council suppresses a play there, 10 May 1601		414
333	The privy council allows Queen Anne's men to play at the Curtain after the plague of 1603–1604, 9 April 1604		414
334	Entertainments continue at the Curtain after the departure of the Queen's men, 1605–1615		
	(a) The Venetian ambassador in London, 1611–1615		415
	(b) Wentworth Smith, 1615		416
	(c) 1615		416
335	The Curtain is decayed and, as the freeholders think, is no longer a playhouse, 1 July 1611		416
336	Prince Charles' (I) men are at the Curtain, early 1620–1623		
	(a) February 1620		417
	(b) 1622		417
	(c) 1623		417
337	Prince Charles' (I) men leave the Curtain to lesser companies, 1623–1625		417

xxviii   List of documents

338   The Curtain ceases to be a playhouse but continues to house other entertainments and then people, 1625–1698
    (a)   Fencers at the Curtian, 1625–ff.   418
    (b)   The Curtain is still standing, 1660   418
    (c)   The playhouse is a garden and houses, 1698   418

XXVI   The Rose

339   Philip Heslowe acquires the lease on the property where he will build the Rose, 24 March 1585   423
340   Henslowe provides for food and drink at the Rose and takes a partner, 10 January 1587   423
341   The Rose is open, and the government takes an interest, 29 October 1587 and 12 April 1588
    (a)   The privy council writes to the Surrey justices, 29 October 1587   426
    (b)   The sewer commission alludes to the Rose, 12 April 1588   426
342   Henslowe rebuilds the Rose, February – April 1592 and Lent 1595
    (a)   1592   427
    (b)   1595   430
343   Henslowe takes Lord Strange's men into the Rose and begins his 'Diary', 19 February 1592   431
344   After the plague of 1592–1594, Henslowe takes the Lord Admiral's men into the Rose, 14 May, 15 June 1594   431
345   The parish tries, and apparently fails, to raise money from its playhouses, 1 May, 19 July 1598
    (a)   On 20 April 1598 and again on 1 May   432
    (b)   On 19 July 1598   432
346   The Rose is busy, August–September 1598   432
347   The first Globe is built across the street from the Rose, May 1599, and Henslowe's receipts diminish   433
348   Henslowe builds the Fortune, moves the Admiral's men into it, and finds new players for the Rose, 1600–1603
    (a)   28–29 October 1600   433
    (b)   August 1602 to 12 March 1603   434
349   Henslowe inquires about renewing his lease of the property where the Rose stood, 25 June 1603   434
350   Henslowe does not renew his lease, and the Rose comes to an end, 1604–1622
    (a)   25 January 1604–25 April 1606   434
    (b)   After 1620   435
    (c)   June 1622   436

XXVII   The Swan

351   The playhouse is being built, and the City objects, 3 November 1594   440
352   A German prince includes the Swan among the active playhouses in London, 26 June 1596   440
353   A Dutchman describes the playhouses in London, especially the Swan, c. 1596   441

List of documents xxix

354	A play at the Swan, *The Isle of Dogs*, has disastrous results there, 28 July 1597	441
355	Francis Langley sues players who have abandoned the Swan for the Rose, November 1597–1598	
	(a) The bill, 1–16 November 1597	442
	(b) Langley's answer, 24 November 1597	443
	(c) The replication of the five players, 6 February 1598	444
	(d) An order of the court, 29 May 1598	446
356	The churchwardens of St Saviour's assume that the Swan is still in business, 20 April–19 July 1598	446
357	A challenge in extemporaneous versifying takes place at the Swan, before 7 September 1598	446
358	Peter Bromvill, a French acrobat, performs at the Swan, 15 May 1600	446
359	Richard Vennar uses the Swan for a celebrated fraud, 6 November 1602	447
360	A display of fencing at the Swan has a tragic result, 7 February 1603	448
361	Alexander Walshe, a fruiterer, occupies the Swan, *c*. March 1606	448
362	Players use the Swan from perhaps May 1610 to the summer of 1614	
	(a) Accounts of the overseers of the poor, April 1610–April 1615	449
	(b) An allusion to a new play at the Swan, 1610	449
	(c) A play perhaps acted at the Swan by Lady Elizabeth's men, *c*. 1611	449
363	The players have forsaken the Swan to play in Middlesex, spring–summer 1614	449
364	A Swan song at the Swan: players perform there again, 1620–spring 1621	450
365	The Swan is used occasionally, but for fencing, not playing, after 1620	450
366	The Swan is decayed in 1632, but used by the Court of Requests, 1 October 1634	
	(a) 1632	450
	(b) 1 October 1634	450

XXVIII The Boar's Head

367	The privy council prevents a lewd play from being performed at the Boar's Head, 5 and 6 September 1557	
	(a) 5 September 1557	455
	(b) 6 September 1557	456
368	Oliver Woodliffe leases most of the Boar's Head so that he can build a playhouse in it, 28 November 1594	456
369	Woodliffe subleases most of the Boar's Head to Richard Samwell for eighteen years, 13 April 1598	
	(a) Woodliffe, 20 May 1603	457
	(b) Browne, 30 May 1603	458
	(c) The elder Samwell, 11 April 1600	458
	(d) Moxlay, 22 October 1600	458
370	Samwell and Woodliffe build a primitive playhouse in the Boar's Head, summer 1598	
	(a) The date of building	458
	(b) The cost of building	459

xxx List of documents

371 Woodliffe and Samwell build a new and much more expensive playhouse, July 1599
    (a) The date of building   459
    (b) Sequence of events   460
    (c) The cost of building   461
372 Samwell sells his part of the Boar's Head to Robert Browne, mid-October, 1599
    (a) The transaction   461
    (b) The date   462
373 Woodliffe sells his part of the Boar's Head to Francis Langley for £400, 7 November 1599
    (a) Francis Langley, 17 April 1600   463
    (b) Richard Langley, January 1601   463
    (c) An order of Chancery, 6 May 1601   464
    (d) Woodliffe, 20 May 1603   464
374 Langley tries to seize Samwell's galleries, autumn 1599 – April 1600
    (a) The argument   464
    (b) Events, September–November 1599   465
    (c) Langley invades the playhouse, 13 December 1599   466
    (d) Langley invades the playhouse, 16 December 1599   466
    (e) Langley invades the playhouse, 24 December 1599   467
    (f) Langley invades the playhouse, 26 December 1599   469
    (g) Arrests   470
375 Bishop accuses Browne and Mago of damaging posts and fixed seats at the Boar's Head, 20 May 1600
    (a) Autumn 1600   475
    (b) Spring 1601   475
376 Francis Langley forfeits his first bond, and Woodliffe sues Richard Langley, 19 January–12 February 1601   476
377 Francis and Richard Langley seek a way to escape Woodliffe and the Boar's Head, late April–May 1601
    (a) 6 May 1601   476
    (b) 20 May 1601   477
    (c) 22 May 1601   477
378 Brown argues in Chancery that the galleries belong to him by a verbal lease, late April–June 1601
    (a) The court order, 9 May 1601   478
    (b) One of Browne's questions   478
    (c) The younger Samwell's answer, 11 June 1601   478
379 Browne ceases to pay the half profits of the western gallery to Woodliffe or Langley, 22 August 1601
    (a) A court order, 15 January 1602   479
    (b) A court order, 15 October 1602   479
    (c) Woodliffe's bill, 20 May 1603   479
    (d) Browne's reply, 30 May 1603   479
380 Browne leases the Boar's Head to Worcester's men for shares in their plays, late summer 1601   480

381	Langley raids the playhouse and Worcester's men agree to pay him £3 a week for twenty weeks, autumn 1601		
	(a) Browne replies to Woodliffe's lawsuit, 30 April 1603		480
	(b) Browne questions Mago and Marsh, carpenters, July 1603		480
	(c) Marsh replies, 25 July 1603		480
	(d) Mago replies on the same day		481
382	Worcester's men legalise themselves and make the Boar's Head their permanent home, 31 March 1602		481
383	Worcester's men quarrel with Browne, he sues them, and they move to the Rose, autumn 1601–17 August 1602		
	(a) 13 May 1602		481
	(b) 29 May 1602		482
	(c) 8 June 1602		482
	(d) 28 June 1602		482
384	The Langleys escape from the Boar's Head, July–15 October 1602		482
385	A bailiff effectively closes down the Boar's Head, Christmas 1602		483
386	Woodliffe regains the stage, tiring-house and western gallery from Richard Langley, before 28 January 1603		484
387	Browne has regained the use of the stage, tiring-house and western gallery, 20 May 1603		
	(a) Woodliffe's bill, 20 May 1603		484
	(b) Browne's reply, 30 May 1603		485
388	The Boar's Head takes leave of the law courts, July, October 1603		485
389	Worcester's men plan to return to the Boar's Head, winter–spring 1603–1604		485
390	The Queen's men are at the Boar's Head, 1604–1607, and Prince Charles' (I) men are there, 1609		
	(a) 12 April, 1607		486
	(b) 16 June 1607		486
	(c) 1609		487
391	The leases fall in, Christmas 1615 and Lady Day 1616, and the playhouse ends, before 23 June 1618		
	(a) 23 June, 1618		487
	(b) 27 December 1621		487
392	The Boar's Head is remembered, c. 1660		487

XXIX The first Globe

393	A consortium leases two plots of ground in Southwark for the site of the Globe, Christmas 1598		
	(a) The lawsuit of 1616		495
	(b) The lawsuit of 1632–1637		496
394	The Theatre is pulled down so that much of it can be used in building the Globe, 28–ff. December 1598–1599		496
395	The consortium builds the Globe for £700 and opens it, spring 1599		
	(a) The consortium raises money		497
	(b) The consortium spends about £700		497
	(c) The playhouse is newly built, 16 May 1599		497
396	A Swiss sees *Julius Caesar* at the Globe, 21 September 1599		497

List of documents

397	The privy council licenses the Lord Chamberlain's men to play at the Globe, 22 June 1600	498
398	The Globe has its share of critical spectators, 1610	498
399	Foreign tourists visit the Globe, 30 April 1610; 1611	
	(a) Prince Lewis Frederick of Württemberg	498
	(b) Prince Otto of Hesse-Cassel, 1611	499
400	The Globe burns to the ground during a performance of *Henry VIII*, 29 June 1613	
	(a) Letter, Thomas Lorkin to Sir Thomas Puckering, 30 June 1613	499
	(b) Letter, Sir Henry Wotton to Edmund Bacon, 2 July 1613	499
	(c) Letter, Henry Bluett to Richard Weeks, 4 July 1613	500
	(d) Ben Jonson, 'Execration upon Vulcan', after 1621	500

XXX The second Blackfriars

401	James Burbage buys the parliament chamber and allied properties, 4 February 1596	506
402	Neighbours petition the privy council to prevent the playhouse from opening, November 1596	507
403	Richard Burbage leases the playhouse to Henry Evans for twenty-one years, 2 September 1600	
	(a) May 1612	508
	(b) 5 November 1612	509
404	Evans stumbles a second time at a Blackfriars playhouse, December 1600–January 1602	
	(a) Giles seizes a child to make an actor of him, 13 December 1600	510
	(b) The decision about Evans, 23–30 January 1602	511
	(c) The decision about Giles and the children, 23–30 January 1602	511
405	Evans distances himself from the playhouse and his other possessions, 21 October 1601, 20 April 1602	
	(a) Evans and Hawkins' bond for £200, 20 April 1602	512
	(b) Kirkham, Rastall and Kendall's bond for £50, 20 April 1602	513
	(c) The Children of the Queen's Revels, 4 February 1604	513
406	Spectators who sit on the stage are a souce of revenue at the playhouse, 1603–1604	514
407	The King ends the career of the child-actors in the Blackfriars playhouse, shortly after 11 March 1608	514
408	Richard Burbage regains the playhouse and moves the King's men into it, 9–10 August 1608	
	(a) Richard Burbage leases the playhouse to a consortium, 9 August 1608	516
	(b) Evans surrenders the old lease, 10 August 1608	516
409	People concerned with the playhouse in the time of the child-actors sue one another, spring 1608–1612	
	(a) Evans sues Kirkham, Rastall, and Kendall in King's Bench, spring 1608	517
	(b) Kirkham and Rastall sue Hawkins in King's Bench, autumn 1608	517
	(c) Kirkham sues Evans in Chancery, spring 1609	518
	(d) Kirkham and Kendall's widows sue Samuel Daniel in Chancery, 9 May 1609	518

List of documents   xxxiii

	(e)	Keysar sues the Blackfriars consortium in Requests, 8 February 1610	519
	(f)	Kirkham sues Evans in King's Bench twice, summer 1611	519
	(g)	Evans sues Kirkham in Chancery, 5 May 1612	520
	(h)	Kirkham sues Edward Painton in Chancery, 1 July 1612	521
410	Neighbours repeatedly try to have the playhouse closed, 1618–1641		
	(a)	December 1618–March 1619	522
	(b)	October–December 1633	523
411	The consortium renews the leases, 24 June 1629	525
412	Actresses appear at Blackfriars with a French troupe, autumn 1629	526
413	Fashionable people quarrel at plays at Blackfriars, 1632–1636		
	(a)	Lord Thurles and Captain Essex, late January 1632	527
	(b)	Sir John Suckling and John Digby, 18 November 1634	527
	(c)	Lord Digby and Will Crofts, spring 1635	528
	(d)	The Duke of Lennox and the Lord Chamberlain, January 1636	528
414	The Queen joins the audience at Blackfriars, 1634–1638	528
415	The Blackfriars playhouse comes to an end, 1642–1655?		
	(a)	The Burbages sell the playhouse, 1651	529
	(b)	The playhouse in 1652	529
	(c)	The playhouse pulled down, 1655?	530

XXXI The first Fortune

416	Edward Alleyn acquires the property on which he builds the playhouse, 22 December 1599		
	(a)	Alleyn buys Brewe's lease, 22 December 1599	533
	(b)	Alleyn buys the freehold, 30 May 1610	533
417	Henslowe and Alleyn contract with a carpenter, Peter Street, to build the first Fortune, 8 January 1600	534
418	Neighbours object to the building of the playhouse, 12 January–8 April 1600		
	(a)	The Lord Admiral writes to the Middlesex justices, 12 January 1600	537
	(b)	The privy council writes to the Middlesex justices, 9 March 1600	538
	(c)	Parishioners petition the privy council, c. 1 April 1600	538
	(d)	The privy council writes to the Middlesex justices, 8 April 1600	539
419	Alleyn and the Lord Admiral's men are performing in the first Forune playhouse, autumn 1600	539
420	Henslowe and Alleyn formalise their partnership in the playhouse, 4 April 1601	540
421	Alleyn lays out about £120 a year on the first Fortune, 1602–1608	541
422	Alleyn and Henslowe contemplate sharing profits with leading members of the company at the Fortune, 1608	541
423	A character in a play describes the first Fortune and its audience, c. 1610	542
424	Criminal acts are perpetrated at the Fortune, 1611–1613		
	(a)	Two butchers abuse gentlemen, c. 26 February 1611	543
	(b)	Jigs attract ill-disposed persons, 1 October 1612	543
	(c)	A justice's son is stabbed, 5 June 1613	543
425	Alleyn inherits Henslowe's part of the Fortune then leases the playhouse to the players, 1616–1618	544

xxxiv   List of documents

426	The players feast the Spanish ambassador at the Fortune, 16 July 1621	545
427	The first Fortune is destroyed by fire, 9 December 1621	546

XXXII Whitefriars

428	The playhouse exists, 29 September 1607	550
429	The investors in the playhouse experience difficulties, autumn 1607	
	(a) Cooke's reply, January 1615	551
	(b) Cooke's deposition, 5 February 1616	552
430	The investors in the playhouse try to run it in a businesslike way, spring 1608	
	(a) Androwes' bill of complaint, 9 February 1609	553
	(b) Slatier answers, 17 February 1609	557
431	The children of the King's Revels lose their lease on the playhouse, c. late March–early April 1608	559
432	The children of Blackfriars succeed those of the King's Revels at Whitefriars, 1609	560
433	The constables of St Dunstan in the West file a complaint about the playhouse, 21 December 1609	561
434	The Blackfriars children become the Children of the Queen's Revels at Whitefriars, 4 January 1610	561
435	Sheriffs stop a play being performed by apprentices at the Whitefriars playhouse, 21 February 1613	562
436	The lease runs out at Whitefriars, the players leave, the playhouse dies, 1613–1615	562

XXXIII The Red Bull

437	Martin Slatier asks the privy council to let the work on the playhouse continue, before 31 May 1605	568
438	The Red Bull is first mentioned as open when the Queen's men are there, autumn 1607	568
439	Notable outrages are committed at the Red Bull, May 1610–c. 1623	
	(a) 29 May 1610	569
	(b) 3 March 1613	569
	(c) c. 1623	569
440	Fools learn a fool's eloquence at the Red Bull, 1613, 1615	
	(a) 1613	570
	(b) 1615	570
441	Thomas Woodford sues Aaron Holland over the profits of the galleries and stage at the Red Bull, 1613–1624	
	(a) Woodford's bill of complaint, 25 October 1623	570
	(b) Holland's answer, 6 November 1623	571
	(c) The court's decision, 3 May 1624	579
442	The Queen's men get into difficulties at the Red Bull because of negligent management, 1615	579
443	The Queen's men leave the Red Bull, and Prince Charles' (I) men arrive, spring 1617	580

List of documents   xxxv

444	Prince Charles' (I) men and the Queen's men, now the company of the Revels, swap playhouses, 1619	580
445	A felt maker's apprentice sitting on the stage is injured by an actor's sword, 10 March 1623	581
446	The Red Bull is used for a fencing prize, 21 March 1623	581
447	The Revels Company disappears, and Prince Charles' (I) men return to the Red Bull, before 30 July 1623	582
448	A play at the Red Bull combines two current sensational events, 3–15 September 1624	
	(a) The ballad concludes	582
	(b) Dekker answers, 3 February 1625	583
	(c) Dekker deposes, 24 March 1626	583
449	The Red Bull is re-edified and perhaps enlarged, 1622–1630	583
450	Prince Charles' (I) men disband, and the Red Bull company moves into the Red Bull, 1625	584
451	A French company with women plays at the Red Bull, 22 November 1629	584
452	A notable company, Prince Charles' (II) men, have taken up residence at the Red Bull, 18 July 1634	584
453	Great disorders occur at the Red Bull, January–August 1638	
	(a) 16 January 1638	585
	(b) 23 August 1638	585
454	Players at the Red Bull get into trouble for acting a play that mocks officials, 29 September 1639	
	(a) The complaint	585
	(b) The specific charges	585
	(c) The action taken	586
455	Sophisticates mock the plays and playing at the Red Bull, 1638–1641	
	(a) 1638	586
	(b) 1638	586
	(c) 1641	587
456	The players at the Red Bull and the second Fortune swap playhouses, Easter 1640	
	(a) The swap	587
	(b) The new company asks the Red Bull audience to be civil	587
457	After the closing of the playhouses in 1642, the Red Bull is often used for illegal performances	
	(a) 3 February 1648	588
	(b) 9 February 1648	588
	(c) 2 January 1649	588
	(d) 20 December 1649	588
	(e) 22 January 1650	588
	(f) 22 September 1652	589
	(g) 9 June 1653	589
	(h) 15–22 November 1654	589
	(i) 29 December 1654	590
	(j) 16–23 May 1655	590
	(k) 14 September 1655	590

xxxvi List of documents

458 The regular playing of plays is illegal again, and the Red Bull resumes, then ends as a playhouse, 1660–1664
    (a) Pepys, 23 March 1661   590
    (b) Pepys, 26 May 1662   591
    (c) Davenant, summer 1663   591
    (d) Pepys, 25 April 1664   591

XXXIV The Hope

459 Henslowe and Jacob Meade engage a carpenter to build the Hope, 29 August 1613, and work gets under way
    (a) The contract   598
    (b) The work gets under way   600
460 Henslowe and Meade raise a company of actors for the Hope and arrange for animal baiting, March–April 1614   600
461 A projected 'trial of wit' at the Hope becomes a fiasco, 7 October 1614   600
462 Ben Jonson comments on the Hope in the induction to *Bartholomew Fair*, 31 October 1614   602
463 Players quarrel with the management partly about baiting and then leave, 1615–1617
    (a) Lady Elizabeth's men quarrel with Henslowe, 1615   603
    (b) Prince Charles' men leave, winter of 1616–1617   603
464 The Hope is a place mainly for baiting bears and bulls, 1621–1622
    (a) Henry Farley, before 20 May 1621   604
    (b) Edward Alleyn, 5 February 1622   604
465 The Spanish ambassador takes delight in animal baiting at the Hope, *c.* 5 July 1623   604
466 The Hope is used for entertainments other than plays and baiting, 1631–1632
    (a) Edward Howes, 1631   605
    (b) Nicholas Goodman, 1632   605
    (c) Sir Henry Herbert, June 1632   605
467 The Hope is said to have been pulled down, 25 March 1656   605

XXXV The second Globe

468 The sharers add six years to their lease, 26 October 1613, and are promised nine more, 15 February 1614
    (a) Bodley adds six years to the lease, 26 October 1613   611
    (b) Brend promises to add nine years, 15 February 1614   611
469 To raise money for rebuilding the Globe, the sharers tax themselves £120 for each share, 1613–1614   611
470 Hemmings directs the building of the second Globe; it costs £1,400 and a house adjoining £200: spring 1614
    (a) Atkins, 1 October 1634   612
    (b) A statement of fact for both sides, 5 February 1634   613
471 Plays are being performed at the second Globe, the fairest playhouse that ever was in England, 30 June 1614

List of documents   xxxvii

	(a) John Chamberlain writes to Alice Carleton, 30 June 1614	613
	(b) The water poet's tribute, 1614	613
472	The King's men use the second Globe only during the summer, and its audiences prefer crude plays, c. 1616–ff.	
	(a) Goodman, 1632	614
	(b) Crosfield, 18 July 1634	614
	(c) Davenant, August 1635	614
	(d) Shirley, 1640	614
473	An ambassador objects to a play at the second Globe and says the place could hold 3,000 people, 6–17 August 1624	
	(a) John Chamberlain to Sir Dudley Carleton, 21 August 1624	615
	(b) A Spanish accout of the ambassador's protest, 10 August 1624	615
	(c) Another Spanish account of the ambassador's protest, 10 August 1624	616
474	The second Globe is used for things other than plays, February 1631 and March 1635	
	(a) February 1631	616
	(b) March 1635	616
475	The sharers sue Sir Matthew Brend for an extension of their lease, 28 January–10 May 1632	
	(a) The sharers' bill of complaint, 28 January 1632	616
	(b) Brend's reply, 6 February 1632	618
	(c) The sharers' replication, 10 May 1632	619
476	A play about witchcraft is a great success at the Globe, 11–15 August 1634	619
477	The sharers and Brend reach a compromise in their lawsuit, 18 November 1634	620
478	Financial arrangements between sharers and players are explained, summer 1635	621
479	Brend returns to court, and the sharers' lawsuit against him ends, 28 November 1637	621
480	The second Globe is closed, 2 September 1642, and comes to an end, 1644–1655	
	(a) 15 April 1644	622
	(b) 17 October 1655	622

XXXVI The Phoenix

481	Christopher Beeston subleases property for the playhouse, 9 August 1616 and 4 May 1633	
	(a) Buildings erected 1609–ff.	626
	(b) The property in 1616	626
482	Beeston is converting the cockpit into a playhouse, 15 October 1616	627
483	The Queen's men are still at the Red Bull, 23 February 1617	627
484	Apprentices wreck the Phoenix on Shrove Tuesday during a performance by the Queen's men, 4 March 1617	
	(a) By the privy council, 5 March 1617	628
	(b) By John Chamberlain, 8 March 1617	628
	(c) By Edward Sherburne, 8 March 1617	629

xxxviii   List of documents

485   The Queen's men return to the Red Bull, then reopen the Phoenix on or about 3 June 1617 — 629
486   Contemporary playwrights allude to the nature of the building, 1619–1640
    (a)   The Phoenix is made of bricks, and the Queen's men do not prosper there — 630
    (b)   The auditorium is compared to a sphere — 630
    (c)   The stage may have had three doors and a balcony — 630
487   When the Queen dies, Beeston removes the Queen's men to put Prince Charles' (I) men into the Phoenix, 1619
    (a)   The answer of three Queen's men, 18 November 1619 — 630
    (b)   Beeston's answer, 23 November 1619 — 631
488   Beeston removes Prince Charles' (I) men and installs Lady Elizabeth's, 1622 — 631
489   Beeston removes Lady Elizabeth's men and installs Henrietta Maria's during the plague of 1625
    (a)   Henrietta Maria's men are first recorded, 5 July 1627 — 631
    (b)   They are at the Phoenix, 1629 — 632
490   A French company, including actresses, plays at the Phoenix wihout apparent objections, Lent 1635 — 632
491   Beeston removes Henrietta Maria's men and installs the King's and Queen's boys, 1636–1637
    (a)   Beeston expels Henrietta Maria's men, after 10 May 1636 — 632
    (b)   Beeston leads a new company at court, 7, 14 February 1637 — 633
    (c)   Beeston is made governor of the boys, 21 February 1637 — 633
    (d)   Beeston tries the boys out in public, *c.* 12 May 1637 — 633
492   Beeston dies, leaving the Phoenix to his widow and son, William, late 1638 — 633
493   William Beeston is confirmed as director of the company at the Phoenix, 5 April 1639 — 634
494   William Beeston gets into trouble and is replaced at the Phoenix by William Davenant, early May–June 1640
    (a)   Beeston is threatened but is a success, spring 1640 — 634
    (b)   Beeston mounts a play critcising the King, 1–2 May 1640 — 635
    (c)   Beeston is imprisoned and the playhouse closed, 4–6 May 1640 — 635
    (d)   Davenant is director at the Phoenix, 27 June 1640 — 635
495   Davenant flees London because of the Army Plot, and William Beeston resumes at the Phoenix, May 1641 — 636
496   The Phoenix is closed with all the other playhouses, 2 September 1642, then is sometimes used illegally
    (a)   Illegal performances, 1647–1648 — 636
    (b)   The Phoenix is said to have been pulled down, 1649 — 637
    (c)   Beeston tries to buy the Phoenix, October–March 1650–1651 — 637

XXXVII   *The second Fortune*

497   Alleyn forms a consortium to own the second Fortune playhouse for fifty-one years, 20 May 1622 — 640

498	The playhouse may open in March, and the Palsgrave's men are there c. 23 May 1623		
	(a) The almanac		641
	(b) The affidavit		641
499	Contemporaries describe the second Fortune playhouse, 1627–1699		
	(a) The playhouse sign, c. 1627		642
	(b) The second Fortune is far fairer than the first, 1631		642
	(c) The playhouse has two gates, 1643		642
	(d) The playhouse has, among other things, brick walls, 1656		642
	(e) The playhouse was round, 1699		642
500	Naval seamen riot at the Fortune, mid-May 1626; and apprentices catch Dr Lambe there, 13 June 1628		
	(a) Men of the Royal Navy		643
	(b) Apprentices and Dr Lambe		643
501	The Fortune is compared unfavourably with the Blackfriars, 1632		644
502	Memorable players perform at the Fortune during the last two years of legal playing there, 1640–1642		
	(a) Cane, 1650		644
	(b) Fowler and Cane, 1654		644
	(c) Smith, Worth and Fowler, 1664		645
	(d) Cane, 1673		645
503	The playhouse is closed with all the others in 1642 but is used for illegal performances, 1643–1649		
	(a) Fencing, 19–26 April 1645		645
	(b) Plays, 2 August 1647		645
	(c) A play, 20 January 1648		646
	(d) Plays, 12–19 September 1648		646
	(e) Rope-dancing, 2–9 January 1649		646
504	The second Fortune playhouse comes to an end, 1649–1739		
	(a) The Fortune is said to have been pulled down on the inside, 1649		647
	(b) A prediction that the place would reopen, 1653		647
	(c) The building is ruinous, 18 July 1656		647
	(d) But a man says it is being refurbished, 15 October 1658		647
	(e) The site is to be redeveloped, 1660–1661		648
	(f) The Fortune is no more, 1661–1662		648
	(g) But the ruins of the playhouse are said still to exist, 1739		648

XXXVIII Salisbury Court

505	Richard Gunnell and William Blagrave lease land and buildings for the playhouse, 6 July 1629	652
506	The Earl of Dorset leases the playhouse property to John Herne, 15 July 1629	652
507	The playhouse is to be built, 24 October 1629	653
508	Gunnell and Blagrave spend about £1,000 converting the barn into a playhouse, 1629–1630	
	(a) Beeston, 25 June 1658	654
	(b) The successors (in a petition to the Earl of Dorset), c. 1658	654

List of documents

509	Contemporaries describe the playhouse		
	(a) The playhouse was small		654
	(b) Size, shape, seats, boxes and viewing rooms		655
510	The playhouse opens, c. 25 November 1630		
	(a) Prynne's book		655
	(b) Randolph's play		656
	(c) Edmond Malone quoting the Master of the Revels		656
511	Awkward events at the playhouse, 1634–1635		
	(a) Violence, 27 March 1634		657
	(b) Blasphemy on stage, 16 February 1635		657
512	Richard Brome is contracted to write plays for Salisbury Court, 20 July 1635 – spring 1639		
	(a) The owners' and players' bill, 12 February 1640		657
	(b) Brome's answer, 6 March 1640		660
513	Richard Heton becomes manager at Salisbury Court, 1636–1637, and establishes a new regime there, 1639		
	(a) 'Instructions' for the patent, early 1639		664
	(b) Draft of the first part of the patent, 1639		665
	(c) 'My intention for the rest' of the patent, 1639		666
	(d) 'Instructions', dated 14 September 1639		666
	(e) A note		667
514	An elaborate production mounted on the stage at Salisbury Court, 1637		667
515	The stage at Salisbury Court is itself on stage there, c. 1638		668
516	The playhouse is closed with all the others in 1642 but is used for illegal performances, 1647–1649		
	(a) 5 or 6 October 1647		669
	(b) 2 January 1649		669
517	William Beeston buys the playhouse to save it from becoming a brewery, 1649–1652		
	(a) Beeston agrees to buy the lease on the playhouse, winter 1648–1649		670
	(b) Soldiers are said to have pulled down the playhouse, 24 March 1649		670
	(c) Beeston completes purchase, 25 March, 1652		670
	(d) Beeston explains his purchase, 25 June 1658		671

General editor's preface

In appointing appropriately qualified editors for all the volumes in this documentary history it has been our aim to provide a comprehensive collection of primary source materials for teachers and students on which their own critical appraisal of theatrical history and dramatic literature may safely be grounded.

Each volume presents primary source documents in English, or in English translation, relating to actors and acting, dramatic theory and criticism, theatre architecture, stage censorship, settings, costumes and audiences. Editors have, in general, confined their selection to documentary material in the strict sense (statutes, proclamations, inscriptions, contracts, working drawings, playbills, prints, account books, etc.), but exceptions have been made in instances where prologues, epilogues, excerpts from play-texts and private correspondence provide additional contemporary documentation based on an author's authority or that of eye-witnesses to particular peformances and significant theatrical events.

Unfamiliar documents have been preferred to familiar ones, short ones to long ones; and among long ones recourse has been taken to excerpting for inclusion all passages which either oblige quotation by right of their own intrinsic importance or lead directly to a clearer understanding of other documents. In every instance, however, we have aimed to provide readers not only with the exact source and location of the original document, but with complementary lists of similar documents and of secondary sources offering previously printed transcripts.

Each volume is equipped with an introductory essay, and in some cases introductory sections to each chapter, designed to provide readers with the appropriate social background – religious, political, economic and aesthetic – as context for the documents selected; it also contains briefer linking commentaries on particular groups of documents and concludes with an extensive bibliography.

Within this general presentational framework, individual volumes will vary considerably in their format – greater emphasis having to be placed, for example, on documents of control in one volume than in another, or with dramatic theory and criticism figuring less prominently in some volumes than in others – if each volume is to be an accurate reflection of the widely divergent interests and concerns of different European countries at different stages of their historical development, and the equally sharp differences in the nature and quality of the surviving documents volume by volume.

William D. Howarth
Bristol University, 1999

Preface

This volume differs from its predecessors in this series in two principal respects. Firstly, its editors have been obliged because of limited space to exclude all forms of amateur and occasional dramatic entertainments other than those documented as charting the slow but inexorable suppression of overtly religious plays whether organised and financed under ecclesiastical or civic auspices, or presented by small groups of players licensed to travel and present short plays to public audiences for their private gain, between 1530 and the 1580s.

The vacuum created by the disappearance of these highly popular, recreational and festive celebrations invited ever-increasing numbers of professionally organised players, licensed to travel, to extend the numbers of people willing to pay to see them perform a small repertoire of more secularly orientated plays, and thus to establish themselves and their families on a firmer financial footing in their own chosen profession.

Secondly, in the light of this editorial decision, we then chose to divide all those documents relating directly to the rise and fall of a wholly professional theatre in England during the reigns of Elizabeth I, James I and Charles I into three self-contained sections, with each assigned to its own editor.

The first of these sections seeks to cover all those documents relating to the efforts of successive Tudor and early Stuart governments to acquire control over play-makers, players and playing places, with responsibility for doing this assigned to me.

The second, compiled by Professor Ingram, concerns actors, and their struggle to obtain recognition as members of a legitimate profession within the limitations imposed upon them by (1) increasingly restrictive government regulations, (2) their own entrepreneurial abilities to acquire performance spaces where the pricing and collection of admission charges could be brought within their own control, and (3) a rising tide of outspoken hostility in some ecclesiastical and commercial sectors of their own society to their unconventional, nomadic and supposedly hypocritical and parasitical lifestyle.

The third section, compiled by Professor Berry, covers all those 'private' and 'public' playhouses, acquired or purpose-built, in London between the accession of Elizabeth I in 1558 and the outbreak of the Civil War. This section also traces the many lawsuits which arose out of disputes relating to profits accruing to ground landlords, owners, investors and shareholders. These provide much of the information we still possess about these playhouses, their audiences, their dimensions and arrangements made for financing their upkeep.

It is to my co-editors, therefore, that my thanks must go in the first instance, for their patience, forbearance and diligence over many years in supplying readers with both the documents and the narratives which introduce and link them in the second and third sections of this volume. Further thanks are also due to them for their willingness to assemble the bibliography and index which conclude the volume as single entities embracing all three sections of the book.

All three of us wish to thank the archivists and librarians in many cities both in this country and in North America for their generous assistance in making documents in their care available to us – often at times chosen to fit in with our travel arrangements rather than their convenience. Such thanks must go, in particular, to staff at the Public Record Office, the British Library, the Corporation of London Records Office and at the Folger and the Huntington Libraries in Washington, DC, and at Passadena, California, respectively.

Grateful acknowledgement is also due on my part for the help received from Mr Timothy Duke, Chester Herald at the College of Arms in London, in deciphering the coats-of-arms surrounding Edmund Tilney's tomb in St. Leonard's Church, Streatham, and to Mr David Partner for his photographs of that monument and the more modest one commemorating Martin Bucer in Great St Mary's Church, Cambridge.

Thanks are likewise due to the Trustees of Dulwich Art Gallery and the photographic department of the British Library for permissions to reproduce the portraits of Robert Dudley, the Earl of Leicester, and those of the six Elizabethan and Jacobean actors which appear as illustrative documents in this book.

Lastly, I must record my special thanks to the librarian at Lambeth Palace and to the city archivists at Chester, Leicester and Canterbury for their invaluable help in locating some particularly elusive documents and in deciphering others now in their care which have been badly damaged at some time during the past 400 years.

Glynne Wickham
Emeritus Professor of Drama
and Hon. Fellow, Bristol
University 1999

Abbreviations

Add.Charter	Additional Charters, British Library
Add.MS	Additional Manuscripts, British Library
APC	*Acts of the Privy Council of England*
BL	British Library, St Pancras, London
CLRO	Corporation of London Records Office, Guildhall, London
CRS	Hotson, *The Commonwealth and Restoration Stage*
CSP, Dom.	*Calendar of State Papers, Domestic*
CSP, Ven.	*Calendar of State Papers, Venetian*
Dulwich	Library of the College of God's Gift (Dulwich College), Dulwich, London
ED and S	Hazlitt, *The English Drama and Stage under the Tudor and Stuart Princes, 1543–1664* (1869)
EDC	J. T. Murray, *English Dramatic Companies, 1558–1642*, 2 vols. (London 1910)
EES	Wickham, *Early English Stages*
ES	Chambers, *The Elizabethan Stage*
Folger	Folger Shakespeare Library, Washington, DC
GL	Guildhall Library, Guildhall, London
Government Regulation	Gildersleeve, *Government Regulation of the Elizabethan Drama*
Henslowe's Diary	Edited by Foakes and Rickert
HMC	Historical Manuscripts Commission
HMSO	Her Majesty's Stationery Office
Huntingdon	Huntingdon Library, San Marino, California
J and CS	Bentley, *The Jacobean and Caroline Stage*
LMA	London Metropolitan Archives (formerly Greater London Record Office), Clerkenwell, London
LP	*Calendar of Letters and Papers, Foreign and Domestic, Henry VIII*
MSC	Malone Society *Collections*

List of documents

OED	*Oxford English Dictionary*
Office of the Revels, Eliz. I	Feuillerat, *Documents Relating to the Office of the Revels in the Time of Queen Elizabeth*
PRO	Public Record Office, Kew, London
REED	Records of Early English Drama
Revels at Court, Ed. VI and Mary	Feuillerat, *Documents Relating to the Revels at Court in the Time of King Edward VI and Queen Mary*
SHC	Surrey History Centre, Woking
SR	Stationers' Register, as compiled in *The Transcript of the Registers of the Stationers Company, 1553–1640*
STC	*A Short-Title Catalogue of English Books, 1475–1640*
Statutes	*Statutes of the Realm*

Introduction

The period of English theatrical history covered in this volume begins and ends with revolutions affecting every aspect of religious, political, social, economic and artistic life in unprecedented ways.

The first of these revolutions was brought about by King Henry VIII's decision in 1531 to abrogate the Supremacy of the Pope in the government of ecclesiastical affairs in England and to vest it in his own person. The second took place a century later when the outbreak of civil war in 1642 brought with it a ban on all professional acting as a legitimate occupation in Britain that continued until the restoration of the monarchy in 1660.

Until the first of these revolutions, plays and play-acting had been universally recognised and welcomed as occasional (if as essentially amateur) adornments of a recreational and educative kind to the celebration of the principal feast days in the Roman Catholic calendar – Christmas, Epiphany, Easter, Whitsun (and, from the start of the fourteenth century onwards, Corpus Christi), together with most of those festivals dedicated to the apostles, saints and martyrs. All of these feasts were recognised as public holidays, distinguishing Holy Days of national or local significance from the hard grind of daily working life. Thus, by the start of the sixteenth century, plays (scripted by priests, clerks, schoolmasters or university dons) along with fairs, mummings (mimes and dances grounded in more ancient agricultural festivals of pre-Christian origin) and a wide range of athletic games had been absorbed into English social life for long enough to be regarded as licensed customs hallowed by tradition, and welcomed within the palaces, castles and manor-houses of the aristocracy (ecclesiastical and courtly), the livery halls of the wealthy merchant guilds and on village greens alike. A way was thus already open for spirited and enterprising young men to contemplate escaping from the drudgery of near-serfdom as agricultural labourers, household servants or apprenticed tradesmen into a lifestyle offering both greater personal freedom of action and hope of larger material rewards, by turning exceptional, but already recognised, mimetic talent into a professional career. This process had advanced far enough for King Henry VII to equip himself with a small company of six players, led by John English, within his own household.

These men became recognisable by the Royal Livery that they were entitled to wear; the retaining fee and rewards for Court performances accorded to them; and by a Patent to travel in order to seek out other audiences willing to pay to hear and see them. By royal decree, these same privileges were extended throughout his reign to favoured members of the nobility, both temporal and spiritual. Henry VIII adopted this practice on his accession in 1509 and extended the number of players in his own company from six to eight shortly afterwards. At least one of these players was a choirboy apprenticed to the leader of the company to play female roles.

By 1530 it had become customary to commission talented poets of the standing of Henry Medwall, John Skelton and John Heywood to write (or 'make') plays for these companies of professional actors.

This natural, evolutionary progression from an amateur towards a professionally orientated dramatic and theatrical mode of development, however, was destined to be rudely fractured in 1531 by the King's decision to challenge the hitherto acknowledged right of the Pope in Rome to regulate the Church in England. It did so by introducing a political dimension, hitherto largely absent, into all aspects of theatrical life.

THE FIRST REVOLUTION

Following the first attempts, however, to reform the government of ecclesiastical affairs in England after 1531, this view of theatrical activity became inescapably intertwined with national politics if only because a drama born from within the Roman Catholic Church could not hope to escape accusations from ardent reformers (led by Thomas Cranmer as Archbishop of Canterbury and Thomas Cromwell as Lord Chancellor) of being a product and continuing manifestation of Roman Catholic superstition, idolatry and other propagandist snares set for the unwary by Antichrist himself – alias the Pope.

As these views gained credence among the ecclesiastical hierarchy and senior civil servants, upon whom both the King and the central government in London relied to establish the legitimacy of their views, so the continuance of both plays and play-acting came to be placed under close scrutiny, along with all other visual interpretations of Roman Catholic doctrine as represented by stained glass and statuary in English churches and by the preaching and practices of all monks and friars.

Given the uncertainties, however, which persisted among the population at large throughout the rest of Henry VIII's reign about whether ultimate authority over expressions of religious belief in England rested with the Church or the State, it was virtually inevitable that future efforts to regulate public performances of plays re-enacting biblical history or the legendary lives of Catholic Saints and Martyrs by the imposition of censorship and statutory controls would become both more oppressive in intention and more varied in their results. This was because the further north and west of London decisions had to be taken at local level, the more frequently opportunities arose for ambiguities of interpretation to colour the judgements of the many individual civic and ecclesiastical officials charged with their enforcement: and some of these personal loyalties in matters of religious belief and political persuasions spilled over into the decisions made.

This was a situation that, following the death of King Henry VIII in 1547, could only be aggravated by those changes in the religious allegiances adopted by successive sovereigns which persisted to a greater or lesser degree throughout the rest of the Tudor era. The young King Edward VI, guided by the Regent – Lord Protector Somerset – and his Lutheran-minded Archbishop of Canterbury – Thomas Cranmer – made determined efforts between 1548 and 1553 to impose more explicitly Protestant controls over the content of plays and the conduct of all players (whether amateur or professional) through Proclamations, Orders of his Privy Council and statutory regulation. Following the accession of Queen Mary I, while his controls were stiffened, they were switched by her principal advisers – Cardinal Pole and her consort, King Philip II of Spain – to support the return of Papal Supremacy over the Church in England for the next five years. These efforts culminated in the creation of theatrical martyrs, burned at the stake for heresy, playmakers and actors alike (see docs 6 and 21a and b). This, however, was a situation that would not be repeated following the accession of Queen Elizabeth I.

Students, therefore, who seek factual information or enlightenment from the documents transcribed and presented in this volume about the erratic development of dramatic art and theatrical representation in England between 1530 and 1558 and beyond, must constantly bear in mind the abiding presence of two factors common to both the objectives of the policy makers in London on the one hand and to the degree of acceptance or resistance to them on the other hand that was encountered in different geographical areas of this country, taken as a whole.

First, the stage, along with the pulpit and the lecterns of schools, universities and the law schools (the Inns of Court in London) was not only among the primary sources of moral education, but potentially the most subversive. This explains why it should have taken another century for Tudor and Stuart governments to find effective means to control it by Proclamations, Decrees and other legislative and judicial means.

Secondly, the social status, lifestyle and economy of actors, and that of the playmakers whom they commissioned to supply them with performable scripts, were governed throughout this long period by three imperatives: their constant need to find audiences in the provinces, as well as in London and at Court, willing to pay to hear and see them perform; next, a continuing sequence of writers who could supply them with new plays that would attract popular audiences without landing them in prison for alleged expressions of heretical, libellous or seditious intentions; and, thirdly, an aristocratic patron willing to employ, maintain and protect a private company of players.

These three imperatives led in turn to the creation of a fourth: performance spaces, or playhouses, where admission could be controlled, prices of admission advertised in advance, and seating or standing room within the auditorium arranged to accord with the prices charged for admission, and which could be regarded by the company as their home base for all professional purposes.

Since the last of these imperatives obliged all professional companies to seek financial support from people with money to invest who regarded playhouses as offering, at least potentially, a profitable capital investment, they often teamed up with ground landlords and business speculators (whose interest in dramatic art was always questionable) in order to acquire the funding needed to purchase property and either build on that land or adapt the buildings already on it to meet their own requirements. These awkward partnerships frequently led to quarrels about contracts and shares of the profits earned from the resultant playhouses: and these, in their turn, frequently led to lengthy and costly lawsuits to which we owe much of the surviving evidence relating to these playhouses.

Thus every aspect of dramatic art and theatrical representation, ranging from the subject matter of all plays through the performance of them to public audiences, including the performance spaces in which they were given, come under ever-increasing government legislative control between 1530 and the end of the Tudor era in 1603. Just as in the latter half of the twentieth century successive governments in this country and the whole population alike have had to come to terms with the advent of radio, television and computer technology (as has been the case worldwide), so all Tudor and early Stuart governments had to come to terms with the invention of printing and with the arguments that surrounded acknowledgement of acting as a legitimate, professional occupation in England.

Both of these questions became the more acute and inflammatory as divisions in religious belief began to govern political, moral and educational ideology from the 1530s onwards. Thus, as play-making and acting began to shift from amateur and occasional activities towards professional and regular entertainment, pursued as much for monetary gain as for recreational and didactic purposes, Tudor governments found themselves under increasing pressure to impose censorship through national and local legislation upon all actors, play-makers and owners of performance spaces alike. This they achieved on a largely experimental basis involving frequent conflicts between representatives of the Church, the State and the Judiciary, with each fighting jealously to preserve its own special privileges and interests.

These conflicts reached their climax during the latter half of the reign of Queen Elizabeth I within the City of London, following the establishment of purpose-built playhouses in the capital and its suburbs. By then such residual claims as the Church had formerly exercised over the theatre, both in London and in the provinces, had been largely subsumed into the controlling hands of the Privy Council assisted by its Ecclesiastical Commissions. What still remained to be decided was whether the Court of Common Council at Guildhall within the City of London, and city and town councils elsewhere in the kingdom, would or would not yield up to the Queen and her Privy Councillors such prerogatives as they had formerly exercised over where, when and on what conditions plays could be performed in public places situated on land they regarded as subject to their own jurisdiction.

If the Court appeared to have won this struggle by the end of the sixteenth century, that can be attributed principally to the increased powers accorded to an officer within the Royal Household itself – the Master of the Revels. Created by King Henry VIII in 1545, this office consisted of a master, a comptroller and a yeoman: it was initially only intended to assist the Lord Chamberlain in the discharging of his responsibilities for the provision of recreational entertainments within the royal palaces. After 1581, however, the Master's responsibilities were extended to cover the issue of licences governing all play-texts, whether in manuscript only or in print, together with all acting companies and their playhouses; but it would take Edmund Tilney, the Master then in post, a full twenty years to complete this process, by which time Queen Elizabeth I was herself a dying woman and her godson, King James VI of Scotland, was eagerly awaiting a summons from her Privy Council to travel south to London as her designated successor.

If this success story respecting the long-drawn-out struggle for the right to control the advance of the professional theatre in England may be regarded as a by-product of Tudor absolutism in the government of all aspects of both Church and State, it also opened a route forward to the second revolution that would overtake it within the next forty years.

Claiming to have succeeded to the English throne by Divine Right, King James chose, within months of his accession, to silence all future controversy stirred up by Puritan preachers, some masters and wardens of affluent livery companies and like-minded members of provincial town and city councils, by taking control over the major acting companies, their managers and their playhouses into his own hands and those of other leading members of his family – initially the Queen and the heir apparent, Henry, Prince of Scotland and Duke of Cornwall. Had he confined himself to this compromise, the likelihood is that it would have been accepted, however grudgingly, by all his opponents; but instead he chose to extend these privileges to other members of his family and to a Scottish cousin, the Duke of Lennox. This provided excuses for the opening of more playhouses in London and an extension of the number of acting companies touring in the provinces, some of them under more dubious credentials. When his example was followed by his successor, King Charles I in 1625, these autocratic actions served to divorce English actors and their play-makers from the popular franchise they had previously enjoyed, and on which their right to earn their livings by performing plays before public audiences had been built. Once all actors could be branded by their opponents as 'royal slaves' and found themselves more frequently rewarded outside London for agreeing 'not to play' than for any performance actually given, that right can be said to have been forfeited.

In this emasculated state from 1625 onwards, acting as a legitimate profession in England again became open to question, as did the future of an aristocratic Court in an increasingly mercantile-orientated and libertarian-minded society.

THE SECOND REVOLUTION

The Puritan revolution, simmering and threatening to break out since the opening of the Long Parliament on 3 November 1640, finally erupted into civil war when the King raised the royal standard at Nottingham on 22 August 1642.

In one sense this revolution was short-lived when compared with its predecessor, since it was seemingly reversed by the restoration of the Monarchy and the reopening of playhouses in London licensed from 1662 onwards to serve the needs of acting companies retained by King Charles II and his brother, James, Duke of York. Yet in another sense it was far more radical in its longer-term effects: for not only did it bring about major changes in the style of theatrical architecture, playwriting and scenic representation on London's stages, but it succeeded in ensuring that theatre-going, as a licensed and reputable pastime, would fail to re-establish itself on any regular, popular basis anywhere in the British Isles other than in London.

The outbreak of civil war in August 1642, however, confronted all professional actors immediately with agonising choices and decisions to be made for themselves and their families.

Denied survival in their former profession by the enforced closure of all playhouses and the cessation of all regular performances in London, they had to choose immediately between continuing to offer their services to those heads of the royal households who had previously supported them in their chosen way of life, or to desert and seek salvation by offering them to the Parliamentary cause.

Either way, the likelihood was that the most probable means of earning an alternative living would be through enlistment in one or other of the respective armies. In the event, only one of the actors previously engaged in the royal households – Eyllaerdt Swanston of the King's Men – chose to desert to the other side. This in itself provides evidence that most actors assumed that if they were ever to return to their preferred way of life it could only be guaranteed by a short war concluding in a royal victory. In that hope they were to be disappointed, but they could well have been buoyed up in the belief that a majority of their audiences would remain as loyal to them as they themselves had proved to be to their royal patrons.

In this belief they were not altogether mistaken, for not only were there many humble men and women servicing London's playhouses as gatherers of admission monies, as scriveners who copied out actors' lines and cues, as printers of plays and playbills and as purveyors of refreshments whose livelihoods were suddenly cut off, but many more who cared little for their new masters in Whitehall and still less for the bigoted and self-righteous preachers who had dispossessed them of their favourite recreational pastime.

Between them these malcontents sufficed numerically for as long as playhouses in London remained standing and vacant to encourage the bravest spirits among the erstwhile professional actors to band together and take the risks of staging occasional performances, the times and places of which were advertised locally by word of mouth, to earn some money. Others stayed in London and took other forms of employment.

These risks included betrayal, forcible suppression by platoons of armed soldiers and the subsequent despoliation of scripts, stage costumes and the playhouses themselves. Supporting documentary evidence for several such incidents, together with some instances of more positive assistance, is offered in part three of this book, 'Playhouses'.

In the provinces, these risks proved to be too great to take, for not only were there no longer any licensed companies of professional actors to take plays on tour, but no hope either of persuading city or town councils to lease their guildhalls to serve as playhouses. If dramatic entertainments were thus to be attempted they could only be offered in private houses, gardens, fairgrounds or other unlicensed premises and on a largely amateur basis; and in the provinces that was a situation destined to last far beyond the resumption of professional theatrical activity in London following the Restoration of the Monarchy in 1660.

This is a theatrical world, however, that lies outside the confines of this volume; but it is one that has already been fully discussed and documented within this series in *Restoration and Georgian England, 1660–1788*, assembled by David Thomas and Arnold Hare, and published by Cambridge University Press in 1989.

THE DOCUMENTS

Three principal groups of documents follow: those covering the efforts of successive Tudor and early Stuart governments to bring control over the theatre into their own hands; those depicting the fortunes of professional actors and the widely varying degrees of esteem in which they were held by the populace at large; and those relating to the twenty-three playhouses which were built or rented in London during this period, the so-called Shakespearean era. This part of the book treats the documents of the time that explain the ownership of the buildings and the buildings themselves, and, less extensively, those that explain the history of each playhouse from beginning to end.

Collectively, these three groups of documents – despite the many gaps in our knowledge of their dimensions, interior appearance, maintenance costs and daily usage, which time, fires, wars, carelessness and other hazards have combined to create among them during the past 400 years – recall with surprising vividness and authenticity the rise and fall of the professional stage in England between 1530 and 1642.

What will not be found here is any comprehensive account of the many dramatic entertainments organised and executed by amateurs on an occasional basis. Nor should readers expect to find any systematic coverage of the careers of the many outstanding play-makers or their plays during this period.

These are serious omissions, but the reason for enforcing both of them is the same. So many documents relating to the professional stage in England have survived that the contributors to this volume were faced at the outset with having to decide whether the space allotted to them by the publishers would or would not permit them to include any other aspects of theatrical life, as represented by occasional academic, courtly and civic dramatic entertainments, within the limits of a single volume. As we strove to ration the number of printed pages and illustrations allowed to us between the professional stage, amateur theatricals and biographies restricted to only the most dynamic, innovative and productive of play-makers, it soon became obvious that any attempt to do this would result in failure to do justice to any of them. Thus, given the worldwide renown of the English professional theatre during the period assigned to this volume, we decided, very reluctantly, to confine our endeavours to that topic alone. Even so, we recognised that our approach would still have to be selective and illustrative rather than exhaustive.

In reaching this decision we drew some comfort, however, from the fact that the careers and plays of all the major play-makers, together with most of the surviving expressions of continuing (and often innovative) amateur activities, had already been printed in many highly reputable, scholarly editions. With nothing of any importance to add to these published records, we concluded that if sacrifices had to be accepted, these were the two areas which would have to be omitted from this volume. Outweighing all arguments to the contrary was the fact that to do justice to the sum total of the surviving documents relating to the play-makers – the most notable of the amateur entertainments devised for Queen Elizabeth I on her summer progresses through the provinces; the Lord Mayor of London's annual civic pageants (often scripted by professional play-makers) and the scenic and choreographic splendours of early Stuart Court Masques (scripted by Samuel Daniel, Ben Jonson, Thomas Campion and others) and staged with the aid of all the latest Italian, neoclassical precepts governing theatrical representation (a proscenium arch concealing changeable scenery constructed and painted in receding perspective, borrowed and implemented with striking success in England by Inigo Jones and aided by equally creative musicians and dancing masters) – would require another volume, possibly two. This, however, was a course of action which our publishers felt unable to contemplate, given the financial restraints governing their own activities at the present time.

All the documents which are to be found in this volume, therefore, are confined exclusively to the rise and fall of a popular professional theatre in England between 1530 and 1660. For the convenience of readers, these have been divided into three principal sections: 'Documents of Control', 'Players and Playing', and 'Playhouses'.

Each of these sections is accompanied by its own general introduction. Thereafter, brief editorial commentaries introduce each different aspect of the subject matter illustrated by the documents included in that section of the book.

In all three sections, the documents selected for inclusion have been transcribed from the original manuscripts or, occasionally, from the first printed edition where this is the primary source, as cited under each numbered heading. References are also given in these headings to the principal secondary sources whenever the manuscript in question has already been reputably transcribed, edited and printed. Spellings and punctuation, however, have been altered (with only a few exceptions retained to preserve the authenticity of some original documents – most notably the word Enterlude and Interlude – between 1530 and 1570) to conform with modern usage. Some exceptions will also be found after 1570 respecting references to the major Elizabethan and early Stuart acting companies. Here we have agreed to retain the words 'actors', 'players', 'servants' and 'companies' as given in the documents with or without the use of capitalization rather than seek to impose uniformity upon them for no other reason than to try to make them conform to some common style of nineteenth-century or more modern invention.

In many instances, the compilers of all three sections, in order to conserve space, have only quoted that part (or parts) of particular documents which serve to confirm or advance knowledge of the topic under discussion with reliable, supportive evidence. This course of action seemed to be especially desirable where protracted lawsuits, bureaucratically worded parliamentary Statutes, and Decrees issued (and frequently reissued as occasion demanded) by provincial town clerks were concerned.

In other cases where the addition of glossarial or other explanatory footnotes appeared to be helpful, these have been uniformly placed immediately below each document throughout the book. All references to published material are given in condensed form, the full form being supplied in the bibliography.

The abbreviations used throughout this book are explained in a list of abbreviations, which, together with the index and bibliography, are not subdivided section by section but are all presented as entities complete in themselves and applicable to the whole book. The list of abbreviations is placed after the editor's preface and before the general introduction. The bibliography and index follow the text.

In cases where documents in one section must self-evidently recur in another, a choice has been made – again to conserve space – to assign lengthy quotations from them to the section in which readers are most likely to expect to find them, but all such overlaps have been signalled by cross reference. The most notable example of this occurs in respect of the Privy Council's reaction to a performance of *The Isle of Dogs*, a play attributed to Ben Jonson and Thomas Nashe and presented by the Earl of Pembroke's company of players at the Swan Playhouse in July 1597. As this response was as immediate as it was extreme, it has to figure in 'Documents of Control': but as its consequences resulted in the arrest and imprisonment of both Ben Jonson and the actors concerned, and in premature termination of the London season brought about by the instant closure of all its playhouses, coupled with an unprecedented order for their demolition, the case for placing the relevant documents under 'Players and Playing' or 'Playhouses' is at least as compelling as that for confining them to 'Documents of Control' simply because these happen to precede the other two sections in this book. In this instance, it quickly becomes clear that only by a combination of cross referencing with some measure of common sense in the apportionment of a long sequence of documents between all three sections of the book can all the surviving evidence be offered to readers without recourse to lengthy and tedious repetition.

Notwithstanding these occasional awkward editorial requirements, it remains abundantly clear from the documents themselves that Tudor and early Stuart professional actors owed both their initial survival, and the remarkable success story which they subsequently imposed upon it, to their own ability to recognise that the restraints imposed upon them by their licences to earn their livings from play-acting were no more restricting or inhibiting than those applying to other men and boy-apprentices seeking to earn their keep in troubled times.

Spelt out, this meant that provided they could retain the active support of their noble patrons (to whom they owed their licences) and provided they could avoid giving grave offence to those government officials who claimed the right to issue or withdraw these licences, they could continue to exploit every new opportunity that appeared to be open to them to acquire larger audiences willing to pay to hear and see them perform their plays. Of these, outstandingly the most important was to secure and retain the favour and support of the many illiterate citizens who at that time still formed the majority of the population.

Their evident success in achieving this, however, served to impose a further restraint upon their remaining freedom of action – an obligation to preserve a conservative approach to the dramatic structure and content of the plays they commissioned for inclusion in their repertoire. Thus medieval Moral Interludes and familiar Saint Plays remained the preferred models throughout the sixteenth century and at least the first decade of the seventeenth. In these respects provision for romance, sensational horrors and heroics spiced with comic incident derived from Italian Renaissance sources together with an abiding respect for folklore and the supernatural, figured as priorities in most commissions issued to prospective play-makers by actors regardless of whether they were work-a-day journalists or university graduates aspiring to be recognised as men of letters. The actor-managers then reinforced their own control over prospective play-makers by requiring the submission of a 'Plott' or scenario, outlining the intended storyline and the actions required of the principal characters to advance it, scene by scene to its conclusion. It was then left to the company to discuss it and either to accept it or reject it. Companies retained their control over the completed scripts (after payment of an agreed fee) by acquiring the copyright in the manuscript which would then be used as the prompter's copy for all rehearsals and performances. Actors were only given copies of their own lines and cues, to prevent scripts falling into unscrupulous hands.

While the pragmatism that informed this approach to plays and their authors undoubtedly succeeded in securing the survival of some professional companies through the reigns of Edward VI and Mary I, it could only inhibit adoption of any of those avant-garde, neoclassical alternatives which were by then being promoted by amateur enthusiasts at Oxford and Cambridge universities, at the London law schools and in many schools and choir schools. While controversy still raged in Protestant ecclesiastical circles about the propriety of reviving plays by pagan authors, the risks of inviting a response from both Church and Government officials carrying punitive penalties with it were too great to be contemplated. So too were those satirical situation comedies of a Graeco-Roman kind intended to pillory the vices and follies of self-important members of bourgeois society in all walks of professional life. Not until late in the reign of Elizabeth I were gestures made by the company managers towards Ben Jonson, and such young play-makers among university graduates as George Peele, Thomas Nashe, Thomas Lodge, Christopher Marlowe, Robert Greene, George Chapman and John Marston, allowing them to provide their audiences with some degree of novelty and surprise. These gestures generated substantial financial returns to actor-managers and play-makers alike, but they continued also to carry risks of a punitive response. At least five of the plays so commissioned from these authors landed both them and the actors in serious trouble with the licensing authorities that led on to court cases, fines and even imprisonment. It is thus hardly surprising that Sir Philip Sidney's eloquent and forcefully argued plea for a more rational approach to dramatic genre, play construction, avoidance of subplots and theatrical representation as argued in his *Defence of Poesie* (first printed in 1595) went virtually unheeded by all English professional acting companies in Elizabethan England.

Only after the accession of James I in 1603, were play-makers allowed to usurp responsibility for both the style and content of an entire play and then only on the rarest of occasions. Ben Jonson's two essays in Graeco-Roman tragedy (both commissioned by the King's Men), *Sejanus* and *Catiline, his Conspiracy*, offer us examples, but both proved to be box-office disasters; so much so, however, that Jonson himself vowed never to repeat this experiment. A similar fate awaited his neoclassically structured comedy, *Epicoene* (anglicised as *The Silent Woman* and then nicknamed *The Silent Audience* because so few of its members remained in the auditorium by the end of the performance to applaud it).

A similar disregard or disrespect for neoclassical ideas concerning theatre architecture and scenic representation characterises all documents relating to Elizabethan and Jacobean public and private playhouses erected in London, with the notable exception of Johannes de Witt's famous sketch of the interior of the Swan (made during his visit to London, probably in 1596) with its Latin annotations to label particular areas within the auditorium (see fig. 3). So here again the surviving documents bear witness to an ingrained desire to preserve the dimensions, shapes and internal arrangements of the familiar and well-tested near-circular bull- and bear-baiting arenas and the spacious rectangular yards of coaching-inns, and eclipse all evidence of any desire (prior to the 1630s) to copy, or even experiment with, Italianate attempts to reconstruct the theatres of classical antiquity. References to a proscenium arch designed to conceal changeable scenery systematically arranged and painted in receding perspective of the kind offered to the Stuart Court by Inigo Jones to embellish Masques from 1604 onwards and erected on temporary stages at vast expense figure nowhere in our documents. The reason for this can only be that such spectacular, occasional and costly entertainments were virtually irrelevant to the daily concerns of professional actors. In the first place Masques, although commissioned by the royal patrons of the licensed acting companies, were nearly always staged to please small but exclusively aristocratic audiences and privately paid for out of the Exchequer. Secondly, all Masques, although presented as dramatic entertainments, were specifically constructed to flatter their royal sponsors and to provide the largely amateur participants with elaborate poetic and musical opportunities to select dancing partners from among their élite audiences. They were *not* plays: no money changed hands between audiences and players, and many more workmen had to be recruited and paid to paint the scenery and operate the machinery needed to change it than any professional actor-manager could afford to employ within his own company. The same reasoning applied to the staging of those academic plays and entertainments occasionally mounted by Oxford and Cambridge Colleges to honour royal visitors.

Once, therefore, all this negative evidence derived from exceptionally wealthy and largely amateur-organised sources has been collated with the evidence that survives from the documents recording the activities habitually undertaken by professional companies of actors on a year-in, year-out basis in order to protect, sustain and, if possible, improve the income earned from them in their own interest, and that of their families whom they had to support even when absent from home on provincial tours, it becomes easier to understand their abiding distrust of all aspects of neoclassical dramatic theory. But if readers can accept this reasoning, it at once places a question mark over the ultimate failure of the professional companies from 1620 onwards to maintain their earlier hold over the respect and affection accorded to them by popular audiences outside of London; for that is an established fact amply testified to by the documents themselves.

Is this then to be attributed to an ingrained distrust of innovations presumptuously offered to professionals by amateurs? Or did it arise out of the players' enforced acquiescence in their own incorporation into the service of the Stuart Royal Household in 1603? Or was it a steadily rising tide of militantly Protestant opposition to the supposedly hypocritical, parasitical and effeminate lifestyle of all actors that accounts for the downfall of professional acting in 1642 and its prohibition through the ensuing eighteen years? Or did all of these factors contribute in some measure to this débâcle?

Here, alas, the documents alone fail to supply any definitive answer. It must thus be left to each individual reader of this book to supply his or her own speculative solution to an as yet unresolved conundrum.

THE ILLUSTRATIONS

Such limited pictorial evidence as has survived from English and continental European sources concerning Tudor and early Stuart playhouses, actors and theatrical representation has been repeatedly used to illustrate books, monographs and shorter articles throughout this century. All of them are thus already familiar and obtainable in libraries.

Virtually all of them, moreover, were conveniently collected and reprinted by R.A. Foakes in *Illustrations of the English Stage, 1580–1642* (London: Scolar Press, 1985). They are there grouped under classified headings: A. Maps and panoramas; B. Drawings, plans and vignettes; C. Illustrations in printed texts; D. Miscellaneous illustrations; E. Other illustrations. Each picture is supplemented by a detailed analysis of its provenance, its reliability and an accompanying bibliography.

It thus seemed pointless, when pressed to conserve space, to repeat this process within little more than a decade. Instead, therefore, we have chosen only to reproduce those pictures which can be regarded both as documents in their own right because they supplement those printed within the text with additional, visual information or because they add evidence not previously published.

Examples of the former include the portraits of the actor Edward Alleyn and his wife, Joan (née Woodward). Since her stepfather, Philip Henslowe, was the builder and manager of the Rose and Fortune playhouses, compiler of the invaluable 'Diary' that bears his name and, later – together with his son-in-law – joint Master of the King's Bears and Beasts, first at Bear Gardens and then at the Hope Playhouse, these portraits serve in themselves to explain how it became possible for the creator of Marlowe's Tamburlaine and Dr Faustus and Kyd's Hieronimo, a despised 'common player', to acquire the wealth needed to build and endow a prestigious grammar school – the College of God's Gift at Dulwich.

Among those illustrations that are less familiar, or have not been previously published, is that of the tomb of Edmund Tilney, Master of the Revels in the Households of both Queen Elizabeth I and James I, who managed during his 25-year tenure of that office to acquire virtually dictatorial powers of control over all aspects of the English professional stage. The photograph of his tomb in St Leonard's Church, Streatham (here published for the first time) provides readers with a vivid sense not only of his wealth and standing in the eyes of his contemporaries, but of his own high opinion of himself, his office and his achievements.

All illustrations, therefore, are numbered throughout parts I and II of this book as documents, supplemented by an (a) as a suffix with an asterisk attached to relate each of them to the corresponding verbal document in the text to which it offers additional, factual information: those in part III, since each refers in a more general sense to a particular playhouse, are numbered, listed and referred to as figures in the text.

Part one: documents of control, 1530–1660

Edited by GLYNNE WICKHAM

I Henry VIII, 1530–1547

There is no evidence of any serious desire in government circles before 1530 to interfere with an author's liberty to write plays or with an actor's to perform them. Books, admittedly, could not be printed without the sovereign's consent, *cum privilegio regis*; but evidence of books being suppressed for giving offence is slender.[1] Plays, being the work of 'makers', were not regarded as literature and, accordingly, only found their way into print in exceptional circumstances. The content of religious plays had always been regulated in manuscript by appropriate officials of the Roman Catholic Church acting on the ultimate authority of the Pope: secular entertainments at Court (and in all noble households) were similarly regulated by the standard procedures set out in House Order Books under the control of the Lord Chamberlain.[2]

Henry VIII's decision, however, to open divorce proceedings against Queen Katherine of Aragon in 1529, culminating in his abolition of papal authority in England and his marriage to Ann Boleyn in 1533, served not only to fan the flames of a rising tide of populist anticlericalism, but also to politicise religious drama.

It was within this twin context that writers and actors discovered that religious plays – especially Moralities, Moral Interludes and Saint Plays – could easily be adapted for polemical use as weapons with which to advance or to oppose the reformation of the Anglican Church along lines already pioneered in Luther's Germany and in Switzerland.

That Henry VIII and his Council were unprepared for this turn of events may be discerned from the largely localised and often contradictory actions taken to control it between 1530 and the King's death in 1547. These include, on the one hand, threateningly suppressive actions in Ipswich, Chester, Cambridge, York, Suffolk, Salisbury and London; and on the other hand, supportive gestures backed by the Lord Chancellor,[3] the Archbishop of Canterbury[4] and other senior representatives of the Lords temporal and the Lords spiritual in the provinces. Nevertheless, the start of formal, legislative action directed against the stage during this period indicates just as clearly that the government was becoming increasingly aware of the danger the theatre was coming to represent as an instrument for stirring up opposition to government policy in the first instance, and calls for rebellion against it in the second. This, of course, was an inevitable consequence of integrating matters of heretical opinion in religious affairs with government policies in secular matters.

Thus what started as legitimately outspoken attacks on papal interference in the government of the English Church advanced steadily to include far more controversial and sensitive claims relating to the primacy of Latin or English as the allowed language of the Anglican liturgy; celebration of the sacraments, saints, saints' days, images, and church vestments; and the alleged abuses of the whole Roman Catholic hierarchy from monks and parish priests to abbots and bishops. Thus what Henry VIII and his Privy Council sought to control was expressions of religious opinion, contrary to those laid down by the government, presented in emotive rhetoric and inflammatory spectacle on stages in public places and likely to lead to breaches of the King's Peace. No evidence survives to suggest any desire in government circles to control, let alone to suppress, any other aspect of dramatic art.

[1] See *EES*, I, 60 and 125–6; also fig.1.
[2] See *EES*, I, 275ff: S. Westfall, *Patrons and Performance*, 122–34.
[3] Thomas Cromwell joined the Privy Council in 1531 and became First Secretary in 1534.
[4] Thomas Cranmer became Archbishop of Canterbury in January 1533.

The first intimation of the trouble ahead appears in the removal of all references to papal control over performances of the Chester cycle in 1532.[1] It occurs in the form of deletion in ink of the offending phrases in the standard document issued annually by the town clerk announcing the forthcoming production, during the first three days of Whitsunweek. The original manuscript in the city archives has been badly damaged by fire; but a sixteenth century copy survives in the British Library from which most of the words now missing from the original can be supplied.

[1] A year earlier, in Ipswich, Suffolk, the Corpus Christi Guild decreed that their play should be 'laid aside for ever'; but there is no proof that this draconian action was a product of religious reform. Rather it was a consequence of Cardinal Wolsey's dismissal as chancellor in 1529 and the suppression of his college in Ipswich in 1530.

I William Newhall, town clerk of Chester, censors references to the Pope's jurisdiction in the city from the Proclamation announcing arrangements for the performance of the Chester Cycle, 1532

City of Chester, Assembly Files, CCA: A/F/1, fo. 12. Reproduced in *EES*, I, 340–3. Words and phrases in the above missing through damage are here supplied from collation with BL, MS Harl. 2013, fo. 1. See also REED, *Chester*, 27–8. It is for this reason that this document, unlike any other in this book, is reproduced here on a line-by-line basis in the original spelling and punctuation, instead of in modern English as is generally the case throughout.

The pro*c*lamac*ion* for the plaies newly made by William Newhall
(...) pentice the first yere of his entre   2

fforasm (...) as of old tyme not only for the Augmentacion &
incres (...) faith of o (...) auyo*ur* iesu Crist & to exort the mynd*es*
of the co*m*mon people (...) doctryne th(...)f but also for the
co*m*menwelth & pr*os*peritie of this Citie a play (...) & diu*er*se   6
stor(...) of the bible begynnyng with the creac*i*on & fall of
Lucifer & endy (...) iugement of th(.) world to be declared &
plaied in the Witsonweke was devised & m (...) henry ffraun*ses*
o 'sometyme' o monk of this o 'dissolued' o monesty who obteyned
& gate of Clement then beyng (...) daiez of p*ar* (...) & of the
Busshop of Chest*er* at that tyme beyng xl^ti daiez of p*ar*don   12
g (...) thensforth (..) eu*er*y p*er*son resortyng in pecible man*ner*
with gode devoc*i*on to here & se the s (...) frome tyme to tyme
asoft as they shalbe plaied within this Citie o [And that euery

Henry VIII, 1530–1547   19

~~person (. . .) disturbyng the same plaiez in eny manner wise to be
accursed by thauctoritie of the s(. . .) pope cleme(. . .) bulles vnto
suche tyme as he or they be absolued therof~~ ○] / Whiche plaiez   17
were d (. . .) to the honour of god by Iohn arneway then mair of
this Citie of chester & his brethern & holl cominal(..) therof to
be bro (. . .) forthe declared & plaid at the Costes & chargez of
the craftes men & occupacons of (. . .) said Citi(.) whiche hitherunto   22
haue from tyme to tyme vsed & performed the same accordin (. . .)
   Wherefore Maister mair in the kyngez name straitly chargeth
& commaundeth that euery person & (. . .) of what esta(..) degre
or condicion so euer he (..) they be resortyng to the said plaiez
do vse th(. . .) pecible witho (. . .) akyng eny assault affrey or   27
other disturbans wherby the same (. . .) shalbe disturbed & that no
manner person or persons who so euer he or they be do vse or
we (. . .) Vnlaufull wepons within the precynct of the said Citie
duryng the tyme of the said p (. . .) ○ [~~not only opon payn of
cursyng by thauctoritie of the said Pope Clement bulles but also~~] ○   32
opon payn of enprisonment of their bodiez & makyng fyne
to the kyng at maister mairis pleasure (. . .) god saue the kyng
& maister mair &c.
         per me W newhall factum tempore
         Willelmo Sneyde draper secundo tempore   37
         sui maioralitatis

   [By me, W. Newhall, made during the time of William Sneyde, draper, in
   his second year as mayor]

A/F/1, fo. 12 missing readings supplied from BL, Harley 2013, fo. 1
line 2 / (. . .): clarke of the   line 3 / fforasm(. . .): for as much
line 4 / (. . .): of the holy & Catholick   line 4 / o (. . .) auyour: our Sauiour
line 5 / (. . .): to good deuotion & holsome line 5 / th(. . .)f: therof
line 6 / (. . .): & declaration   line 7 / stor(. . .): storyes
line 8 / endy (. . .): ending with the generall line 8 / th(.): the
line 9 / m (. . .): made by one Sir   line 11 / (. . .): bushop of rome a 1000
line 11 / par(. . .): pardon   line 13 / g (. . .): grauntted from
line 13 / (..): to   line 14 / s (. . .): sayd playes
line 16 / (. . .): or persons   line 17 / s(. . .): sayd
line 17 / cleme(. . .): clemants   line 19 / d(. . .): deuised
line 20 / cominal(..): cominalty   line 21 / bro(. . .): brought
line 22 / (. . .)y: the   line 23 / accordin(. . .): accordingly
line 25 / (. . .): persons   line 25 / esta(..): estate
line 26 / (..): or   line 27 / th(. . .): themselves
line 27 / witho (. . .) akyng: without making line 28 / (. . .): playes
line 30 / we (. . .): weare any   line 31 / p(. . .): play

The first indication of a realisation in London that the Court could play an influential role in control of the theatre survives in a memorandum prepared by the Lord Chancellor's secretary, Richard Morrison, c. 1535, and addressed to the King entitled 'A Discourse touching the Reformation of the Laws of England'. In it he advocated the elimination of papal power in England; but he goes beyond such action as had been taken in Chester to suggest that since plays have been used by the Papacy for generations to indoctrinate illiterate citizens with superstition and idolatry, steps should now be taken to employ similar methods to re-educate the King's subjects in the new ideologies of religious reform.

2   Sir Richard Morrison urges King Henry VIII to use the theatre to destroy respect for the Pope in England, c. 1535

BL, Cotton MS Faustina. C.ii, fos. 15b–18b. Reproduced by Sydney Anglo, *Journal of the Warburg and Courtauld Institute*, 20 (1957), 177–9

Expedient and very necessary it is, that unto the time he [*i.e.* the Pope] be destroyed of all princes, banished out of all Christendom, the ungodliness, hurts and evils that have come and may come through him to every Christian realm were daily by all means opened, incul[ca]ted and driven into peoples' heads, taught in schools to children, played in plays before the ignorant people, sung in minstrels' songs, and books in English purposely to be devised to declare the same at large ...

The priests yearly with procession make a perambulation round about the limits and extremes of their benefices, for the safeguard of their rights and tithes; likewise have the bishops general processions for the maintenance of their dioceses: how much more ought there be a yearly time appointed, partly to teach and preach the usurped power of the Bishop of Rome; how he usurped upon Kings and princes; how and whereby he and his adherents went about to destroy this Realm, that the people may abhor him and his doings and not hereafter be distrained with him: and chiefly for the maintenance and safety of your Grace's right to your most godly authority of Supreme Head of the Church of England and other your dominions to set forth and declare the same that your subjects may know and do their due obedience unto your most royal Majesty according to their duty.

In summer, commonly upon the Holy Days in most places of your Realm, there be plays of Robin Hood, Maid Marion, Friar Tuck wherein beside the lewdness and ribaldry that there is opened to the people, disobedience also to your officers is taught, whilst these good bloods go about to take from the Sheriff of Nottingham one that for offending the laws should have suffered execution. How much better is it that those plays should be forbidden and deleted, and others devised to set forth and declare lively before the people's eyes the abomination and wickedness of the Bishop of Rome, monks, friars, nuns and such like, and to declare and open to them the obedience that your subjects, by God's and man's laws, owe unto your Majesty. Into the common people things sooner enter by the eyes than by the ears; remembering more better that they see than that they hear ...

That Thomas Cromwell and Thomas Cranmer acted almost instantly upon this advice, with or without the King's permission, cannot be doubted after reading any of the surviving plays of John Bale, written between 1536 and 1540, who both of them patronised and may even have commissioned. In *Kyng Johan*,[1] *Three Lawes, God's Promises* and *The Temptations of our Lord*, Bale attacks the Pope, monks, friars, pardoners and all aspects of Roman Catholic dogma (including the sacraments) regarded by the reformers as superstitious and idolatrous. Formerly a Carmelite friar, Bale had renounced his vows and married, and was recruited by Cromwell when a parish priest at Thorndon, Suffolk, not only to write these plays but to lead a company of players willing to perform them.[2] His own roles, declared in the cast lists prefacing the plays, were those of Prologue, Expositor (Chorus) and Epilogue: in *Three Lawes* he doubled as the Vice, Infidelity, its most demanding role.

[1] A performance of 'an interlude concerning King John at my Lord of Canterbury's at Christmas time', 1538, became the subject of a subsequent interrogation as reported in a letter from Cranmer to Cromwell dated 11 January. PRO, SPI/142, pp. 33–6; XIV. 1. no. 47(2).
[2] Evidence that Cromwell maintained a company of players himself survives from Cambridge, where they were paid for performances at King's College (1536–7); and before the mayor (1537–8 and 1539–40). See REED, *Cambridge*, I, 112, 114 and 119.

3 Payments to John Bale and his fellow actors
CSP, Dom. XIV(2), Henry VIII (Thomas Cromwell's Accounts) 1537–9, fos. 337, 339

September 1538   Bale and his fellows at St Stephen's beside Canterbury for playing before my Lord, 40s.

January 1539   Bale and his fellows for playing before my Lord, 30s.

While Bale was striving to advance his career in the service of the government by writing and producing Protestant polemical plays in southern counties, repressive action was being taken in northern ones against plays promoting Roman Catholic doctrines.

4 Henry VIII writes to the justices in York ordering them c. 1536–7 to arrest and imprison papists who write and perform religious interludes
James O. Halliwell, *Letters of the Kings of England* (London, 1848), I, 354. Transcribed in *EES*, II(1), 62–3 and REED, *York*, II, app. 4, 649–50[1]

Trusty and well-beloved, we greet you well. And whereas we understand by certain report the late evil and seditious rising in our ancient city of York, at the acting of a religious interlude of St Thomas the Apostle, made in the said city on the 23rd of August now past;[2] and whereas we have been credibly informed that the said rising was owing to the seditious conduct of certain papists who took part in preparing for the said interlude, we will and require you that from henceforward ye do your utmost to prevent and hinder any such commotion in future, and for this ye have my warrant for apprehending and putting in prison any papists who shall, in performing interludes which are founded on any portions of the Old or New Testament, say or make use of any language which may tend to excite those who are beholding the same to any breach of the peace.

Given, etc.

[1] Halliwell, when translating and publishing this letter, claimed to have found the Latin original among the Rawlinson manuscripts in the Bodleian Library. No trace of it has been found since; but its contents place it in the immediate context of 'The Pilgrimage of Grace' – an uprising in protest against the dissolution of monastic houses – which had begun in York and spread as far west as Cumberland. The King, having won a temporary breathing space by promising to meet the protestors to listen to their complaints, then reneged on his word and ordered his officers to punish all concerned.

[2] On 19 April 1536, York City Council decreed that 'Corpus Christi Play shall be spared for this year and not played for so much as Pater Noster Play ought by Course (*rotation*) to be played this year. Therefore it is agreed that the said Pater Noster Play shall be played upon Lammas Day [1 Aug] next.' On June 19th a decision was taken to postpone the performance until 'Sunday next after Lammas Day'. See REED, *York*, I, 262–3.

Further cause for alarm was provided in Suffolk in 1537 arising out of a May Day play which was alleged to be both satirical and subversive in its aims and content.

5 Letters from the Duke of Suffolk to Thomas Cromwell, 16 and 26 May 1537

PRO, SPI/120, pp.100–5: PRO, SPI/120, pp. 202–3, LP, Henry VIII, xii.i.557 and 585

Wharton [*the Duke of Norfolk's comptroller*] also told him of a May game played last May day, 'which play was of a King how he should rule his realm'; in which one played husbandry and said many things against gentlemen more than was in the book of the play. He has been sent for but cannot yet be found. He [*the Duke*] has ordered the justices of this shire to have regard to light persons especially at games and plays. Would like the King's letters to the same effect.

Signed, Hoxston, May 16th

Wharton has not yet brought me the book of prophecy, nor the man who keeps it, nor him that played the part of Husbandry. At Huxton, Suffolk.

Signed, May 26th

Shortly after Cromwell's disgrace and execution, accompanied by the King's own reversion to more orthodox Anglo-Catholic beliefs in 1540, evidence accumulated of sterner efforts to bring plays, players and audiences under firmer government control. These start with the prosecution of a citizen of London, and the execution of three ex-priests turned actor in Salisbury, in 1541.

6 John Foxe, *Actes and Monuments of these latter and perillous dayes touching matters of the Church*

2 vols. (London, 1570), ed. S.R. Catley, v.446 and 448

1541. Shoreditch, London   Shermons, Keeper of the Carpenter's Hall in Christ's parish, was presented for procuring an interlude to be openly played, wherein priests were railed on and called knaves.

1541. Salisbury, Wiltshire   Richard Spencer, Ramsay and Hewet, Martyrs who suffered at Salisbury. About the same time also a certain priest was burned at

Salisbury who, leaving his papistry, had married a wife, and became a player in interludes, with one Ramsay and Hewet, which three men were all condemned and burned; against whom, and especially against Spencer, was laid matter concerning the sacrament of the altar. He suffered in Salisbury.

A year later, when the English bishops were gathered in Convocation at Canterbury, the situation appeared serious enough, especially in and near London, for them to ask the King to take action.

7 Minute of the 7th session of Convocation, 14 February 1542
PRO, LPFD, Henry VIII, 17.79

The bishops advised a petition to the King, to correct the public plays and comedies which are acted in London, to the contempt of God's Word.

Within a year they had their answer in an Act of Parliament which set out to define what religious subject matter could and could not be discussed in stage plays.

8 An Act for the Advancement of True Religion, and for the Abolition of the Contrary, 34/35 Henry VIII, 1543, c 1
Statutes, III, 894, para.7

After explaining the need for this Act of Parliament on account of

the ignorance, fond opinions, errors and blindness of divers and sundry his subjects of this his realm in abusing, and not observing, nor following the commandments, precepts and laws of Almighty God, nor the very true and perfect religion of Christ, notwithstanding such wholesome doctrines and documents as His Majesty hath heretofore caused to be set forth for that purpose . . .

and specifying as principal offenders those

pretending to be learned, and to have the perfect and true knowledge, understanding and judgement of the sacred and holy scriptures, and some others of their perverse, froward and malicious minds, wills and intents, intending to subvert the very true and perfect exposition, doctrine and declaration of the said scripture, after their perverse fantasies . . .

it explains that these same offenders

have taken upon them, not only to preach, teach, declare and set forth the same by words, sermons, disputations, and arguments, but also by printed books, printed ballads, plays, rhymes, songs and other fantasies, subtly and craftily instructing His Highness's people, and specially the youth of his realm untruely, and otherwise than the scripture ought or should be taught, declared or expounded, and contrary to the very sincere and godly meaning of the same.

Finally, it reveals its principal objective:

For reformation wherof, His Majesty most virtuously, and prudently considereth, and thinketh that it is and shall be most requisite, expedient and necessary, not only by laws dreadful and penal, to take away, purge and cleanse this His Highness's Realm, territories, confines, dominions and countries, of all such books writings, sermons, disputations, arguments, ballads, plays, rhymes, songs, teachings and instructions as be pestiferous and noisome, with all the causes, instruments and means of the same . . . And therefore be it enacted, ordained and established, by our said sovereign lord the King, the lords spiritual and temporal, and the commons in this present Parliament assembled, and by authority of the same, that all manner of books of the Old and New Testament in English, being of the crafty, false and untrue translation of Tyndale, and all other books and writings in the English tongue, teaching or comprising any matters of Christian religion, articles of the faith, or Holy Scripture, or any part of them, contrary to that doctrine which, since the year of Our Lord MDXI is, or any time during the King's Majesty's life, our said sovereign lord that now is, King Henry the VIII, which Our Lord long preserve, shall be set forth by His Highness, with such superscription and subscription, as hereafter shall be declared, shall be by authority of this present Act clearly and utterly abolished, extinguished and forbidden to be kept or used in this Realm, or elsewhere in any of the King's dominions.

Then follows a qualifying clause which proves beyond all doubt that, as yet, the government sought only to prohibit the writing and acting of unorthodox religious plays which could be classified as heretical, seditious, or both.

[para. 9] Provided always, and be it enacted by the authority aforesaid, that it shall be lawful to all and every person and persons to set forth songs, plays and enterludes, to be used and exercised within this Realm and other the King's dominions, for the rebuking and reproaching of vices, and the setting forth of virtue: so always the said songs, plays or enterludes meddle not with interpretations of scripture, contrary to the doctrine set forth, or to be set forth, by the King's Majesty, our said sovereign lord that now is, King Henry the Eight in form aforesaid. Anything contained in this Act to the contrary notwithstanding.

> To legislate is one thing; to enforce quite another. A glaring, and exceptionally well documented example of this occurred a year later in respect of a performance of Thomas Kirchmayer's *Pammachius* (presumably in John Bale's translation) at Cambridge University.

On 16 January 1545 the Fellows of Christ's College decided to perform this violently anti-Catholic play on the following Shrove Tuesday (Carnival), and in doing so precipitated a crisis that came to involve not only the Heads of all the Cambridge Colleges, but the Vice-Chancellor, the Chancellor, and finally the Privy Council.

Shortly after the performance, an outraged junior fellow – Master Cuthbert Scott – informed his chancellor – Stephen Gardiner, Bishop of Winchester and a Privy councillor – of what had happened: news of it also appears to have reached him from someone resident in the town. This confronted Gardiner with an embarrassing dilemma since his duty as chancellor obliged him to protect the freedom of the university while his office as a Privy Councillor required him to uphold the Statute for the Advancement of True Religion of 1543. This conflict of loyalties is apparent throughout the lengthy correspondence between himself and the Vice-Chancellor, Matthew Parker,[1] which began as a discreet enquiry on 27 March and ended both threateningly and abusively two months later on 18 May.

Since this correspondence survives in the Library of Corpus Christi College and has been printed several times between 1838 and 1981,[2] only excerpts which illustrate the course it took and the conclusions eventually reached are included here.

[1] Matthew Parker, Master of Corpus Christi College, was elected Vice-Chancellor in succession to Thomas Smith on 25 January 1545, nine days after the decision had been taken at Christ's College to perform *Pammachius*. Parker was appointed Archbishop of Canterbury by Elizabeth I on 18 July 1559.
[2] Lamb, *A Collection of Letters, and other Documents, Statutes* 1838; Cooper, *Annals of Cambridge*, 1842; Parker, *Correspondence*, Parker Society 49, 1853; REED, *Cambridge*, 1990.

9 Excerpts from letters between the Chancellor of Cambridge University, the Vice-Chancellor and the Privy Council relating to a performance of Thomas Kirchmayer's play *Pammachius* at Christ's College, 1545

(a) CCL: 106. fos. 223–3v, transcribed in REED, *Cambridge*, I, 133; (b) CCL: 106. fos. 224–5, reproduced in full in REED, *Cambridge*, I, 134–6; (c) CCL: 106. fos. 227–8, reproduced in REED, *Cambridge*, I, 137–8; (d) CCL: 106. fos. 229–30, reproduced in REED, *Cambridge*, I, 138–40; (e) CCL: 106. fo. 231, reproduced in REED, *Cambridge*, I, 140; (f) CCL: 119. fos. 30–1.

(a) Stephen Gardiner to Matthew Parker and Thomas Smith,[1] 27 March

Master Vice-Chancellor; I have been informed that the youth in Christ's College, contrary to the mind of the Master and President,[2] has of late played a tragedy called *Pammachius*, a part of which tragedy is so pestiferous as were intolerable.[3] I will give no credit to this information but as I shall hear from you, wherein I pray you that I may shortly by you know the truth. If it be not so, I will be glad; and if it be so I intend further to travail, as my duty is, for the reformation of it. I know mine office there, and mind to do in it as much as I may; requiring you therefore that in such matters of innovation and disorder I may be diligently advertised from you from time to time . . .

The Vice-Chancellor, in his reply dated 3 April,[4] claims to have done what was asked of him in making 'a more exact enquiry of the tragedy late played in Christ's College'. He further claims that the decision to perform it had been taken by the Fellows and that 'it cost the College wellnigh 20 nobles allowed by the Master and the Company [i.e. the Fellows]'. He admits that the complete text did include 'slanderous, cavillatious and suspicious sentence', but claims that the Master and Senior Fellows had wisely agreed 'to omit all such matter whereby offence might justly have risen'.

[1] Parker's immediate predecessor.
[2] Henry Lockwood.
[3] This phrase directly parallels that used to justify the introduction of the Act for the Advancement of True Religion of 1543. See 8 p. 23 above.
[4] See REED, *Cambridge*, I, 134.

The Chancellor, however, was not to be fobbed off with this ingenuous disclaimer. Instead, he sent one of his own chaplains in person to Cambridge bearing a much stiffer call for action.

(b) Stephen Gardiner to Matthew Parker, 23 April 1545

And to the intent it may appear that howsoever youth [i.e. undergraduates] either of frailty, lightness or malice would abuse their gifts, we that be Heads and rulers over them should not be seen either by suffrance or negligence to be blameworthy of their fault, I will and require you that upon receipt of these my letters you assemble the Masters and Presidents of the Colleges, with the Doctors of the University, declaring unto them this matter: to require them to assist you in the trial of truth concerning the said tragedy, and that by due examination of such as were there, it may be truly known what was uttered, and so by their judgement approved as good . . .

He then proceeds to specify that it is the reported breaches of the Act for the Advancement of True Religion of 1543 that concern him (see 8). Here it is the Privy Councillor, rather than the Chancellor, who is addressing himself to the Vice-Chancellor:

which by the Order established by the King's Majesty in this Church is reproved, or by them [i.e. the actors] reproved which by the King's Majesty is allowed. I have heard specialities [i.e. more especially] that they reproved Lent fastings, all ceremonies and, albeit the words of the Sacrament and Mass were not named, yet the rest of the matter written in that tragedy in the reproof of them was expressed. And if, as you wrote to me, they left out somewhat unspoken, it should appear that the rest, being spoken, was upon a judgement by consideration and deliberation allowed; which, if it be true, is a lamentable case, and such as has not chanced that such as [have] by the King's Majesty's privileges and supportation be there preserved in quiet to learn all virtue, should presumptuously mock and scorn the direction of their Prince in matter of religion: I touch only herein the truth of obedience, for I esteem such offenders for unlearned and ignorant, unmeet to discern what is truth in the matter: but if the King's Majesty's directions be not obeyed there, and by us dissembled, how shall we charge the rudeness abroad that may allege their example for pretence of their fault. This matter is greater than were expedient to be true, and is more certaintly reported unto me than of lightly wode [*sic?* likelihood] can be totally false . . .

He ends this long letter by reverting to the duties incumbent on him as Chancellor, and on Parker as Vice-Chancellor, to protect the reputation of the University lest it lose its privileges and, above all else, its lucrative endowments:

Many have of late repined at the King's Majesty's munificence in our privileges and otherwise;[1] and let not us give cause that they should [worthily so] justly so do. Our obedience should be example to all other, in public directions, without occasion of all slander. If learning should now be an instrument to stir up dissension, and trouble the common quietness, their opinion should be confirmed which, not many years past, have laboured to prove in books printed in English that the Universities be the corruption of the Realm. Oxford liveth quietly with fewer privileges than we have: there be those that would we had as few as they.

On receipt of this double-barrelled salvo from the Chancellor, the Vice-Chancellor did as he was bidden; but the meeting of Heads of Colleges and senior members of the University proved inconclusive since so many of them 'whether of purpose or of chance were absent'. Of those who were present, he could only find two who had taken offence, one of whom was Cuthbert Scott, who had supplied the Chancellor with the original complaint.

[1] He is referring here to the fact that the Universities had thus far escaped the fate of the monasteries.

Nevertheless, such was the trouble that they had stirred up, both in the University and in the town, that he felt obliged to undertake a second enquiry among the actors who had performed the play, to ask them to surrender the prompt-copy. This Parker sent to Gardiner, together with the depositions of two of the actors.

(c) Sworn statements of John Crane and Nicholas Greenwall, actors in *Pammachius* at Christ's College, 8 May 1545

In the presence of Matthew Parker, Master Doctor Wigon, Doctor Lockwood, Doctor Wendeye, these words, spoken under oath, written by the parties following:

> I, John Crane, do say that Mr Scott did affirm the tragedy of *Pammachius* to be throughout poison, – about the 16th day of January.   John Crane.

> Witnesseth that I, Nicholas Greenwell heard him say that the tragedy was all, throughout, poison: 16th day of January.   Nicholas Greenwall

And whereas we said that our intent was to pluck down the Pope's usurped power, he answered that under that pretence we would speak against all goodness.
John Crane.

[*signed*] Matthew Parker: Edward Wigan: Henry Lockwood: Thomas Wendeye.

After reading the prompt-book of *Pammachius* in the light of these enquiries, Gardiner told Parker that 'where all other proof faileth, there the book maketh an abundant proof of their lewdness to me here'. On that account he is only the more deeply shocked that no one in authority in the University has taken any punitive action against the players. He ends this reply as follows:

(d) Stephen Gardiner to Matthew Parker, 12 May 1545

Requiring you Master Vice-Chancellor to communicate these my letters with the Masters, Presidents and Doctors and, on my behalf to desire them gravely to consider of what moment the good order of youth is, and to withstand the lewd conduct of such as have neither shame nor fear of punishment and correction. The lesson of obedience would be well taught and practised, and I will be more diligent to know how men profit in it than I have been. I have showed the whole Council [*i.e.* the Privy Council] the words spoken by Master Scott from whom you shall shortly receive answer in that matter. And as touching those that were chief players in the tragedy, I hear very evil matter; and I pray you call them unto you and know whether they will acknowledge and confess their fault or no, and to signify the same to me. And so fare you well.

The Privy Council met at St James' on 16 May 1545, and included in its business for that day the drafting of a letter to the Vice-Chancellor of Cambridge University, 'touching a certain tragedy lately played there, and certain words spoken by one Scott touching the same, saying the said tragedy was poison' (*APC*; I (1542–7), 162).

(e) A letter from the Privy Council to Matthew Parker, 16 May 1545

We have considered such words as you signified to your Chancellor, our very good Lord the Bishop of Winchester, to have been spoken by one, Master Scott, touching a certain tragedy played at Christ's College, and think it right expedient that calling the parties before you, you should admonish them to endeavour themselves so to employ their wits and studies in knowledge of that is good, true and wholesome as all that is indeed poison, either in learning or manners, be expelled and put out; and no such matter, either in play or earnest, to be moved or meddled with as should offend the laws and quiet of this Realm, so as you that be there assembled and under the King's Majesty's special protection be maintained to live quietly for the increase of virtue and learning do also in your manner and behaviour practice rest and quietness, and exclude all occasions that might impeach the same. Whereas you that be Heads and Governors must have such special cure and care as if any misorder be among the youth you reform it from time to time, and do that may be for your discharge in that behalf. And thus discharging the said Master Scott noted to have spoken the said words, to do for reformation of those that have misused themself in playing of the said tragedy as to your wisdoms shall be thought requisite.

It is to be presumed that since this affair had receded into the past and had not resulted in any breach of the peace, the Council decided to take a lenient view of it at Gardiner's behest, and to conclude the matter with a stern warning against any repetition. This message was then rammed home two days later in a final letter (this time in official Latin and of undisguised severity) from the Chancellor to the Vice-Chancellor.

(f) Stephen Gardiner to Matthew Parker, 18 May 1545

The text given here is that of Alan Nelson's translation for REED, *Cambridge*, I, 141. The Latin text is printed by Lamb (*Collection of Letters*) and Cooper (*Annals of Cambridge*) and is in REED, *Cambridge*.

The event itself shows that all proper defence has died among you. Your own men deride your own affairs in your own precincts. Indeed they guaranteed the truth of this with ostentation in the tragedy *Pammachius* when, while [*possibly* because] you were looking on and dithering, after they deservedly hissed the bishop of Rome from the stage, they forced off all the doctors with the same authority by jeering.

I do not think it right to expect that things which take place publicly within your bounds, and take place for the purpose of being public, would remain within your walls and not become known among others. Many understand the state of your affairs and are clearly aware of your disputes and disagreements. They notice many things which you do not imagine, and this first of all, that there is virtually no college in which one does not find partisanship among various factions, while the head at one time promotes his own interests [and] at another allows the helm to be blown about by the winds [of factionalism], and taken counsel for himself rather than for those entrusted to him. And [further they notice that] just as Sophocles wrote that life is sweetest when we are conscious of nothing, so some of your own think that life is safest when they are doing nothing. But they are also wrong, and even though they may be undisturbed for a time, those who fail to carry out a duty entrusted to them, sometimes offering a reason contrary to expectation, are surely not safe.

Nothing of this kind happens among the Oxonians, and someone has said to me that there would be a more suitable administration at your university if the vice-chancellor were chosen by the decision of the chancellor alone, according to their [*i.e.* Oxford's] example. But I have always shrunk from such changes except when the situation clearly demands them. And now I have undertaken in the matter of the tragedy that everything be left in your jurisdiction. Therefore, take care that you may be held worthy of so great a responsibility, and I in turn will arrive with all my resources and judgment to preserve all your rights whole and undiminished for you . . .

Evidence that the Fellows of Christ's College, Cambridge had reason to suppose that in their privileged position they could ignore at least the strict letter of the Statute of 1543 and proceed with their production of *Pammachius* in a deftly cut version survives from London in the form of a Proclamation, dated 6 February 1545, aimed directly at stopping all performances of contentious plays which continued to be performed, 'in divers and many suspicions, dark and inconvenient places of this our most dread and most benign sovereign Lord the King's City and Chamber of London wherein no such plays ought to be played'.

10   A Proclamation is issued from Guildhall for the Abolishment of Interludes, London, 6 February 1545

CLRO, City Letter Books, Q, fo. 169 and Journals of the Court of Common Council xv, fos. 241b and 242. Transcribed in MSC, II.3.291–2; also in *EES*, II(1), app. B, 327–8

Forasmuch as by reason and occasion of the manifold and sundry Enterludes and Common Plays that now of late days have been by divers and sundry persons more commonly and busily set forth and played [than] heretofore has been accustomed in divers and many suspicions, dark and inconvenient places of this our most dread and most benign sovereign Lord the King's City and Chamber of London wherein no such plays ought to be played. And that namely and chiefly upon the Sunday and other Holy Days in the time of Evensong and other Divine Service celebrate [*d*] and said in the said City, to which places a great part of the youth of the same City and many other light, idle and evil disposed persons daily and continually frequenting, haunting and following the same plays have not only been the rather moved and provoked thereby to all provity [*sic*? proclivity] and readiness of divers and sundry kinds of vice and sin. And the said youth, by that occasion not only provoked to the unjust wasting and consuming of their masters' goods, the neglecting and omission of their faithful service and due obedience to their said masters, but also to the no little loss and hinderance of God's honour and the Divine Service aforesaid and to the augmenting of many other inconveniences more which daily spring and ensue thereof to the high displeasure of Almighty God, the great nourishment and increase of much vice, sin and idleness, and to the great decay and hurt of the commonwealth of the said City; as of Archery and other lawful and laudable exercises as our said most gracious sovereign Lord is credibly informed.

His Highness therefore straightly charges and commandes that no manner of person or persons from henceforth, of whatsoever estate, degree or condition he or they be of, presume or take upon him or them at any time hereafter to play or set forth, or cause to be played, any manner of Enterlude or common play within any manner of place or places of this His Grace's said City, unless it be in the houses of noblemen, or of the Lord Mayor, Sheriffs or Aldermen of the same his Highness's City for the time being; or else in the houses of gentlemen, or of the substantial and said commoners or head parishioners of the same City; or in the open streets of the said City as in time past it hath been used and accustomed; or in the Common Halls of the Companies, Fellowships or Brotherhoods of the same City. And that at the request and desire of the same Companies, Fellowships and Brotherhoods and in their Common Assemblies and presence at times meet and convenient for the same and in none otherwise.

And further, that no manner of person or persons of what estate, degree or condition soever he or they be of, presume at any time hereafter, or take upon him or them to set up, affix . . .

Both manuscript texts break off here and are clearly incomplete. The word following 'affix' was probably 'bills', and the sense of the sentence that no plays were to be publicly advertised whether by bill posting or by any other means within the city. Two years earlier, the Court of Aldermen had issued an Order specifically directed at bill posters and unauthorised performances.

11   Order of the Court of Aldermen: Common Plays or Interludes, 2 April 1545

CLRO, Repertory, x, fos. 322b–3. Transcribed in MSC, II. 3.289–90

Item: it is agreed that every of my Masters the Aldermen shall cause diligent search and watch to be made in their several wards for such persons as commonly use to set up bills for plays or interludes within this City; and to cause the same bills to be pulled down and the setters-up to be attached and committed to Ward, and as much inquisition to be made as by any convenient means can be devised to try out the maker and setter-up the bills of my Lord Mayor's gate against Dr Wilson and Dr Weston.

And that none of all my said Masters the Aldermen permit from henceforth any interludes or plays to be had or used within any of their several Wards, but that they likewise attach and commit unto Ward all and every such person and persons as will take upon them to play and make interludes in their said Wards, there to remain until they shall find good sureties that they shall no more so use themselves.

This Order was evidently often defied or ignored since it became necessary to repeat it within two months of the death of Henry VIII. In this case, it is specifically directed against performances on Sundays. This marks the start of a running battle that was to last for nearly a hundred years (see 65, 77 and 78, 81 and 84). The reason for this was that Sunday was the only day of the week allowed as a public holiday on which labourers, tradesmen and apprentices were free to engage in recreational activities: and of these, play-going was rapidly becoming the most popular.

12 The Court of Aldermen impose a ban on the advertising of plays and Interludes on Sundays, 17 March 1547

CLRO, Repertory xi, fo. 315b (339b); Letter Book Q, fo. 198. Transcribed in MSC ii.3.293

Item: It is agreed that every one of my Master[s] the Aldermen shall from henceforth cause their Bedells[1] of their Wards to pull down upon Sundays in the morning all such bills of interludes as the common players of the same interludes shall cause to be affixed or set up upon any post or other place within their several Wards, and to bring them to my Lord Mayor.

A month after the Court of Common Council at Guildhall had issued its Proclamation of 6 February 1545 (10, above), laying claim to regulate all dramatic activity in the City of London, the King took steps to achieve the same objective within the Court's domain by reorganising the Office of the Revels within the Royal Household to create a new post of 'Master of Games, Revels and Masks'. The first holder of it was Sir Thomas Cawarden, who was appointed to it by Royal Patent on 11 March 1545.[2]

This pair of assertively definitive documents, read in conjunction, mark the start of the battle for control over all aspects of the theatre in England that was to be fought out between the Church, the City of London and the Crown throughout the Tudor era. For its ultimate resolution in favour of the Crown see **65, 66, 73a** and **b**, and **74a–c**.

[1] Beadles.
[2] PRO, LPXX/1, 465(28), Patent Rolls, 36. Henry VIII, C66/753, m. 23.

II Edward VI, 1547–1553

Since the Prince of Wales was only nine at his accession, responsibility for the government of the country was deputed to a Council of Regency headed by Edward Hertford, Duke of Somerset. Somerset, having taken the young King into his own custody, then persuaded the Privy Council to accord him the title of Lord Protector.

Somerset was a Protestant whose radical beliefs inclined closer to those of John Calvin than to those which Henry VIII had tried to reimpose on the country since 1540. In consequence, many of the more extreme reformers who, like John Bale (see 3) had served Cromwell and then fled abroad after his execution, returned to England, encouraged by the torrent of Reformist religious legislation that was rushed through the first parliament of the new reign. This included the repeal of Henry VIII's Act for the Advancement of True Religion (see 8); the Chantries Act, which assigned all chantries, free chapels, colleges, hospitals and guilds to the Crown; the abolition of the Feast of Corpus Christi and public observance of many Saints' Days; and the introduction of a new liturgy in English – Cranmer's Book of Common Prayer – use of which became mandatory on 9 June 1549.

All measures taken to acquire firmer control over plays, play-makers and players during Edward's brief reign must therefore be considered within this wider context of religious reform which sought to move much further and faster than conservative opinion (especially in northern and western districts) was then ready to go. Thus the Chantries Act (1. Ed. VI c. 14), by dissolving religious guilds, served also to destroy the *raison d'être* for the performance of the many religious plays that had been for so long entrusted to their care,[1] threatening their continuance and provoking local unrest in consequence.

[1] The Corpus Christi Play at Chester, the York Creed Play and the Croxton Play of the Sacrament provide examples.

13 Hereford City Council decides to abolish its Corpus Christi Guild plays, 18 December 1548

Great Black Book, Hereford Record Office, fos. 27–8. Transcribed in full in REED, *Herefordshire and Worcestershire*, 119, and in part in *EES*, II(1), 69

Forasmuch as there was before this time divers Corporations of Artificers, crafts and occupations in the said City who were bound by their grants of their Corporations yearly to bring forth and set forward divers pageants of ancient histories in the procession in the said City upon the Day and Feast of Corpus Christi which now is and are omitted and surceased. Wherefore it is agreed . . .

This entry proceeds to set out in great detail how each craft guild concerned is henceforth to divert its former production funds to the upkeep and maintenance of the city.

The importance of this change in Hereford and in most other areas of southern England lies in the obvious difficulties which would confront anyone trying in future to link plays, thus officially disestablished, to some other festival.

Elsewhere the effects of the Reformist legislation were serving to aggravate existing animosities between extremist wings of radical and conservative opinion where all forms of oratorical propaganda were concerned, especially in London.

An immediate storm warning of what lay ahead surfaced there in the Borough of Southwark in 1547 while the Bishop of Winchester, Stephen Gardiner, was arranging a Requiem Mass for Henry VIII. Writing on 5 February to a fellow member of the Privy Council, Sir William Paget, he warns him that a company of players is proposing to perform a play simultaneously, 'to try who shall have most resort; they in game or I in earnest', and begs him to ask the Lord Protector to ban the performance.[1] The outcome of this plea has gone unrecorded; but the Privy Council wasted no time in preparing action to deal with such incidents in a wider context.

[2] PRO, SP10/1, fos. 8–9ᵛ; *CSP, Dom.*, Ed. VI (1547–53), 5.

Efforts were made in the first instance to establish a form of liturgical observance in English instead of in Latin, and then to impose it legally by Act of Parliament throughout the Kingdom. A section of this Act was drafted to apply specifically to the stage, and became mandatory on 9 June 1549.

14 An Act for the Uniformity of Service and Administration of the Sacraments throughout the Realm, 1549

Section III, Statutes, IV.i.37–8. Reproduced in *EES*, II(1), 67

And it is ordained and enacted by the authority above said, that if any person or persons whatsoever after the said Feast of Pentecost next coming,[1] shall in any enterludes, plays, songs, rhymes, or by other open words, declare or speak anything in the derogation, depraving or despising of the same book [*i.e.* The Book of Common Prayer] or of anything therein contained, or any part thereof . . . that then . . .

A list of penalties follows, all of which are severe.[2]

This Act was succeeded two months later with a Proclamation issued in the King's name forbidding all theatrical performances for at least three months.

[1] i.e. 9 June 1549.
[2] For the first offence a fine of £10; for the second, a fine of £20; for the third, forfeiture of goods and life imprisonment.

15 Edward VI's Proclamation forbidding all dramatic performances, 6 August 1549

The original, which appears to have been lost, was transcribed by J. P. Collier in *Annals of the Stage* (1831), I, 144–5, then collated with *Such Proclamations as have been set forth by the King's Majesty* (London, 1550), 8v, by W.C. Hazlitt for the Roxburghe Library in 1869 and then reprinted in *ED and S*, 8–9; *EES*, II(1), 67; also in *Government Regulation*, 6–7.

Forasmuch as a great number of those that be Common Players of Enterludes and Plays, as well within the City of London, as elsewhere within the realm, do for the most part play such Enterludes as contain matter tending to sedition and condemning of sundry good orders and laws, where upon are grown, and daily are like to grow and ensue, much disquiet, division, tumults and uproars in this realm: the King's Majesty . . . straightly chargeth and commandeth all and every His Majesty's subjects . . . that from the 9th day of this present month of August until the Feast of All Saints next coming (*Nov. 1st*) they, nor any of them, openly or secretly, play in the English tongue any kind of Interlude, Play, Dialogue or other matter set forth in form of Play in any place public or private within this realm, upon pain that whosoever shall play in English any such Play, Enterlude or other matter, shall suffer imprisonment, and further punishment at the pleasure of His Majesty . . .

A final paragraph charges all,

mayors, sheriffs, bailiffs, constables, headboroughs, tithing men [and] justices of the peace . . . in all the partes throughout the realm . . .

to ensure that the provisions of this Proclamation are everywhere strictly enforced.

That these measures failed in their intentions is evident from the government's decision to issue a second Proclamation within eighteen months of the first. That of April 1551 is far longer than its predecessor; and three-quarters of it is taken up with general, moral exhortations to live peaceably with one's neighbours, and to avoid heretical and seditious rumour-mongering, both verbally and in writing. It concludes, however, with two very tough paragraphs directed against plays and players. What is new about them is evidence of a dawning consciousness in Court circles that a form of censorship will have to be imposed on the subject matter of all stage plays *in advance* of their performance.

This Proclamation also reveals that the Court, having successfully reduced the powers previously exercised by the Church in such affairs to those of an Agent of the Crown, recognised that it still had to recover from the Common Council of the City of London the authority which the latter had annexed to itself in its own Proclamation of 6 February 1545 (see 9) where control over plays performed in the capital were concerned.

16 Second Proclamation of Edward VI relating (among other things) to dramatic performances throughout the Kingdom, 28 April 1551, 'for the reformation of vagabonds, tellers of news, sowers of seditious rumours, *players*, and printers without licence and divers other disordered persons'

Broadsheet, Society of Antiquaries. Transcribed in full in *ED and S*, 9–14; and in part (as here) in *EES*, II(1), 67–9

And furthermore, His Majesty straightly chargeth and commandeth, that no man be so hardy either to devise any tale, rumour or talk, touching His Majesty, his

Council, Magistrates, Justices, Officers, or Ministers; nor, hearing any such tale, rumour or talk, to tell, report, or speak the same again to any other person or persons, than to either one of His Council, or a Justice of the Peace; and then withal to show also of whom he had the same, to the intent that the same person from whom the tale or rumour cometh may be punished for the devising of it, if he devised it, or for the telling of it to any other person, than by this Proclamation is appointed.

And for because divers Printers, Booksellers and Players of Enterludes, without consideration or regard to the quiet of the realm, do print, sell and play whatsoever any light and fantastical head listeth to invent and devise, whereby many inconveniences hath, and daily doth arise and follow among the King's Majesty's loving and faithful subjects: His Highness therefore straightly chargeth and commandeth that from henceforth no printer, or other person, do print nor sell within the Realm or any other His Majesty's dominions any matter in the English tongue; nor they nor any other person do sell or otherwise dispose abroad any matter, printed in any foreign dominion in the English tongue unless the same be first allowed by His Majesty, or His Privy Council in writing signed with His Majesty's most gracious hand or the hands of six of his said Privy Council, upon pain of imprisonment without bail or main price, and further fine at His Majesty's pleasure.

Nor that any common players or other persons, upon like pains, to play in the English tongue, any manner Enterlude, play or matter, without they have special licence to show for the same in writing under His Majesty's sign, or signed by 6 of His Highness's Privy Council: willing and straightly charging and commanding all Justices, Mayors, Sheriffs, Bailiffs, Constables and other officers and Ministers, diligently to enquire for and search out all manner offenders within the limits and compass of their commissions; and specially all such as shall offend against any the points or branches expressly set forth in this Proclamation, and to punish the same without remission.

Willing likewise, and also straightly charging and commanding all his good, true, loving and faithful subjects to be aiding, helping, and assisting to all and every officer in the execution of their charges as they tender the favour of His Majesty, and the preservation of the Commonwealth, as they will answer to His Majesty for the contrary at their utmost peril.

God Save the King.

This broadsheet is signed by the King's typographer, Richard Grafton, and dated 1551.

Two months later, efforts appear also to have been made to prevent players, maintained in the private households of the nobility, from travelling.

17 The Privy Council wrote to the Marquis of Dorset about his company of actors, 21 June 1551

PRO, PC 2/4, p. 332: *APC*, Ed. VI, III (1550–2), 21 June 1551, 307

Another [letter] to the said Lord Marquis signifying license to be granted for to have his players, to play only in his Lordship's presence.

As yet, the government had still to decide how to administer the censorship of play-texts, which it had just introduced in its Proclamation of April 1551. Advice on this question reached the King in the form of a New Year present from the newly appointed Regius Professor of Divinity at Cambridge, Martin Bucer.

As one of John Calvin's most ardent and able disciples, Bucer had established his headquarters in Strasbourg; but in 1549 threats of arrest forced him to leave France. Seeking refuge in England, he was befriended by Archbishop Cranmer, who obtained the vacant Chair of Divinity for him at Cambridge. There he wrote his *De Regno Christi* (*Christ's Kingdom*), which included a chapter entitled 'De Honestis Ludis' ('Concerning Legitimate Recreations').[1] Bucer's views are liberal insofar as he does not seek to suppress plays or acting; but the grounds on which he justifies both are primarily those of advancing instruction in the articles of the Christian faith as interpreted by Calvin and Lord Protector Somerset. How is this to be achieved? His answer is uncompromising: by recourse to censorship.

[1] lit.: 'honest', 'virtuous', 'appropriate', i.e. acceptable, allowable, tolerable.

18 Martin Bucer advises Edward VI to appoint censors to control play-texts, 1 January 1552

De Regno Christi was first printed in 1557, and then again in *Scripta Anglicana*, 1577, ii.54ff. The Latin text of 'De Honestis Ludis' is reproduced in *ES*, IV, 188–90: the extract in translation given here is from *EES* II(1), 111 and 329–31.

In order that Christ's people may profit from religious comedies and tragedies, men will have to be appointed to the task of preventing any comedy or tragedy which they have not seen beforehand and decided should be acted: they must be men both outstanding in their knowledge of this kind of literature and also of established and constant zeal for Christ's Kingdom.

Neither the King nor Bucer had time to put this advice into practice. Bucer died later that year and Edward VI followed him eighteen months later. It was thus left to his successor, Queen Mary I, to give these proposals the force of law. When she did so, being a convinced Roman Catholic, it was in a direction quite contrary to that envisaged by Bucer.[1]

[1] The volatile state of religious and theatrical opinion at that time may be judged by the fact that when Bucer died he was buried in Great St Mary's; then exhumed under Mary I and publicly burned in the marketplace as a heretic; and finally restored to the Church following Elizabeth I's accession.

(a) A Victorian brass plate, replacing the original tomb and monument, in memory of Martin Bucer, sometime Regius Professor of Holy Theology, whose body was interred in this chancel AD 1551. It was exhumed AD 1557 and burned in the market place. This second burial AD 1560 now honours his memory

Photo: David Partner

III Mary I, 1553–1558

Within twelve days of the death of King Edward VI on 6 July 1553, the *coup d'état* devised and headed by the Duke of Northumberland to replace him with his own, Protestant daughter-in-law, Lady Jane Grey, had failed: and on 19 July the rightful heir, Princess Mary Tudor – the daughter of Henry VIII and Katherine of Aragon – was welcomed into London.

Having bravely persisted in maintaining her right to practise the Roman Catholic faith ever since her father divorced her mother, she immediately declared her intention to remain true to it as queen; and in this she was supported by her Privy Council, who were agreeable to the repeal of most of her half-brother's ecclesiastical legislation, but who had no intention of enabling papal authority to be restored in England or to re-establish the monasteries and return the lands and other property that had been stripped from them.

A Proclamation was issued within a month of her arrival in the capital aimed at preventing breaches of the peace resulting from 'false and untrue reports and rumours spread by some light and evil disposed persons', included among whom are preachers and players of interludes.[1] This opens with a paragraph that sets out the Queen's personal position in matters of religion side by side with that which is to be allowed to her subjects. The prospects, however, of a return to a more tolerant religious regime which this preamble to the Proclamation may have engendered were short-lived: and when, a year later, the Queen chose King Philip II of Spain to become her consort, fear mixed with anger among Protestants of all persuasions led inexorably to a major confrontation between government and people, and to ever more restrictive and punitive action against the theatre.

[1] This was approved by the Privy Council at its meeting on 16 August 1553, where it is described in the minutes taken at Richmond as 'A Proclamation for reformation of busy meddlers in matters of religion, and for redress of preachers, printers and players.' Transcribed in *APC*, IV (1552–4), 426.

19   Proclamation of Queen Mary I, August 18th 1553. By the Queen

Broadsheet in the Library of the Society of Antiquaries. Transcribed in full in *ED and S*, 15–18: in part in *EES*, II(1), 71–2, and *Government Regulation*, 10–11

First; Her Majesty being presently by the only goodness of God settled in her just possession of the imperial crown of this realm and other dominions thereunto belonging, can not now hide that religion (which God and the world knoweth she hath ever professed from her infancy hitherto) which as Her Majesty is minded to observe and maintain for herself by God's Grace during her time, and would be glad the same were of all her subjects quietly and charitably embraced. And yet she doth signify unto all Her Majesty's said loving subjects, that of her most gracious disposition and clemency, Her Highness mindeth not to compel any her said subjects thereunto, unto such time as further Order by common assent may be taken therein.

Given a Privy Council as large and riven by as many factions as Mary's was, it was never likely that this compromise would hold for long: and even if it did, the subsequent provisions within this Proclamation respecting plays and players are just as uncompromising and even more severe than those issued by Edward VI (see **15** and **16**).

And furthermore, forasmuch also as it is well known, that sedition and false rumours have been nourished and maintained in this realm by the subtlety and malice of some evil disposed persons, which take upon them without sufficient authority to preach, and to interpret the Word of God after their own brain in churches and other places both public and private. *And also by playing of Interludes* and printing false fond books, ballads, rhymes and other lewd treatises in the English tongue, concerning doctrine in matters now in question and controversy, touching the high points and mysteries of the Christian religion; which books, ballads, rhymes and treatises are chiefly by the Printers and Stationers set out to sale to Her Grace's subjects, of an evil zeal for lucre and covetous of vile gain.

Her Highness therefore straightly chargeth and commandeth all and every her said subjects, of whatsoever state, condition, or degree they be, that none of them presume from henceforth to preach, or by way of reading in churches, or other public or private places (except in the schools and universities) to interpret or teach any scriptures, or any manner points of doctrine concerning religion. Neither also to print any books, matter, ballad, rhyme, *interlude*, process or treatise, *nor to play any interlude*, except they have Her Grace's special licence in writing for the same upon pain to incur Her Highness's indignation and displeasure.

A final paragraph instructs 'all Mayors, Sheriffs, Justices of Peace, Bailiffs, Constables and all other public officers and ministers' to ensure that these provisions are strictly observed, just as Edward VI had done two years earlier (**15** and **16**); but the net is here drawn tighter than ever before by the extension of the injunctions to cover the Printers and Stationers Company. Thenceforward the Crown could claim the right to censor all plays prior to publication as well as all manuscript playscripts intended only as prompt-copies prior to public performance.

Scholarly opinion today is still divided on who was responsible for the collapse of this invitation to arrive at a tolerant compromise in matters of religious belief – the Queen herself, or divisions between radical Protestants and conservative Anglo-Catholics within the Privy Council. What is certain is that while Parliament was prepared to repeal Edward VI's Act of Uniformity (see **13**) in 1553, it steadfastly refused to repeal the Act of Royal Supremacy; it is just as certain that the Queen took it upon herself (as much in loyalty to her Spanish mother as for any other reason) to propose a marriage with Philip II of Spain. This wedding was arranged in December 1553 and effected on 25 July 1554, despite the popular agitation against it which arose in Kent, Devon, Essex, Wales and the Midlands in the months prior to the event.

There is no documentary evidence that any of these serious disturbances was precipitated by dramatic performances.[1] It thus seems that only in the years after the wedding did the stage again become regarded by the government as a major *agent provocateur* that must be more securely muzzled. Evidence of this survives both from northern counties, and from Essex, Kent and London. There can, however, be no doubt that these risings derived from hatred of Spanish tyranny in the Netherlands and from fear that Mary's Spanish consort might seize the English throne for himself, rather than from the formal reunion with Rome that followed the arrival of Cardinal Pole as papal legate in London in November 1554.[2] Nevertheless within three months of this event arrests for heresy began with burning at the stake as the penalty for conviction. Thenceforward, no writer of Protestant polemical Interludes could hope to escape notice from the host of spies and informers employed as Crown agents and ready to accuse them and the actors of heresy, sedition or both.

[1] The only play to have survived which sets out to match anti-Catholic polemic with sharply anti-Protestant satire is *Respublica*, sometimes attributed to Nicholas Udall; this was performed at Court 'as a Christmas device' in 1553/4 by a company of six boys. Edited for Early English Text Society by W. W. Greg, 1952. On the boy companies see below pages 260–73.
[2] Formalised by the 'Act repealing all Statutes, Articles and Provisions made against the Apostolic See of Rome . . .', Statutes, IV.i.c. 3, 246. One effect of this was to restore the old liturgical calendar and with it the Feast of Corpus Christi. Associated plays were revived at York and Chester in 1553; at Lincoln in 1554, as also at Coventry and Wakefield; and finally in London in 1557. See REED, *York*, 1.307; REED, *Chester*, 54; *Records of Plays and Players in Lincolnshire, 1300–1585*, ed. Stanley Kahrl for MSC, VIII, 65. York Arch. Soc., Record Series, LXXIV, 20–1; Machyn, *Diary*, 138.

It is within this broad political context, rather than in one of narrow, religious sectarianism, that the prosecutions of play-makers and players which began in 1555 and continued through the rest of Mary's reign must be viewed. Quoted below there follows an illustrative sequence of Orders for the arrest, interrogation and prosecution of play-makers and players issued between 1555 and 1558.

20 (a.1) The Privy Council orders the Lord Lieutenant of Essex to ban a play at Hatfield Bradock, Essex, 14 February 1555

PRO, PC2/7, p. 39: *APC*, Mary I (1554–6), V, 234

A letter to the Lord Rich that where there is a stage play appointed to be played this Shrovetide at Hatfield Bradock in Essex, his Lordship is willed to stay the same and to examine who should be the players; what the effect of the play is; with such other circumstances as he shall think meet; and to signify the same hither.

(a.2) An Order for a second letter to be sent to Lord Rich, 19 February 1555

PRO, PC2/7, p. 373: *APC*, Mary I (1554–6), V, 237–8

A letter of thanks to the Lord Rich for his trouble in staying the stage-play which was appointed to be played this Shrovetide at Hatfield in Essex, requiring him, for that he noteth the players to be honest householders and quiet persons, to set them again at liberty; and to have an eye and special care to stop the like occasions of assembling the people together hereafter.

(b) A General Order controlling acting companies, 7 May 1556
PRO, SP11/8, no. 50: CSP, Dom. (1547–80), 82

Orders against players and pipers strolling through the Kingdom, disseminating seditions and heresies.

(c) The Court of Aldermen forbids the performance of all plays on Sundays and other Holy Days in London, 9 March 1557
CLRO, Repertory XIII(2), fo. 484b. Transcribed in MSC, II.3.297

Entreludes. Item: for certain good and necessary causes and considerations especially moving the Court, it was this day ordered and agreed by the same that there shall be precepts made out forthwith by my Lord Mayor to every of my Masters the Aldermen that none of them from henceforth do in any wise permit or suffer any interludes or stage plays to be played within any place of their several wards upon the Sundays or other Holy Days as they will answer to the contrary at their peril.[1]

[1] The Lord Mayor, William Blakewell, issued his Precept that same day carrying the Order itself into immediate effect. CLRO, Journal XVII, fo. 26; Letter Book S, fos. 118–19b. Transcribed in MSC, II.3.298.

A month later, trouble broke out in Yorkshire, where a company of players maintained by Sir Francis Leke, or Leek, was alleged to have been touring a seditious play (probably about the Spanish marriage) which casts some light on **20b** above. When news of this reached the Privy Council in London, it responded by writing to the Lord President of the North (the Earl of Shrewsbury), instructing him to arrest the players and to question both them and their patron immediately.

(d) A letter 'of the utmost urgency' from the Privy Council to the Lord President of the North, ordering the arrest and interrogation of Sir Francis Leek's players, 1557

This letter, written in the hand of the clerk to the Privy Council, was in the possession of Sir Edmund Lodge, a Pursuivant at Arms and Fellow of the Society of Antiquaries, in 1791 when he transcribed and printed it in his *Illustrations of British History* (3 vols., I, 212–13): from him the manuscript passed into the possession of the College of Arms. Unknown to Sir

Edmund Chambers, it was there when he was preparing *The Elizabethan Stage* for publication in 1924; but it had been found there by John Strype when he transcribed and printed it again in *Ecclesiastical Memorials relating chiefly to Religion and the Reformation of it* in 1822 (vol. III(2), 413–14). He described it there as *Ex Epist. comit. Salop. in offic. Armor* [From the Letters of the Earl of Shrewsbury in the College of Arms].

It was still there when the Historical Manuscripts Commission published its *Calendar of the Shrewsbury and Talbot Papers* in 1971, but it has since been reassigned to the Library of Lambeth Palace, where it now resides and is catalogued as MS 3194, fo. 229. The transcription given below has been newly made for this book from that source. An exceptionally rare and interesting feature of it is the address provided for the bearer who was to carry it north. This reads as follows:

[fo.229b] To our very good Lord, the Earl of Shrewsbury, President of the King and Queen's Majesties' Council in the North. Haste, haste post haste, haste, haste with all diligence possible.
    Delivered at St James the 30th of April at four of the clock
    at after noon.

[fo.229] After our right hearty commendations to your good Lordship, whereas we have been lately informed that certain lewd persons, to the number of 6 or 7 in a company, naming themselves to be servants unto Sir Francis Leke, and wearing his livery, and badge, on their sleeves, have wandered about those North parts, and represented certain plays and enterludes, containing very naughty and seditious matter touching the King and Queen's Majesties, and the state of this Realm, and to the slander of Christ's true and Catholic religion contrary to all good order and to the manifest contempt of Almighty God, and dangerous example to others: we have thought meet to pray your Lordship to give order forthwith unto all the Justices of the Peace within your rule, that from henceforth they do in no wise suffer any plays, enterludes, songs, or any such like pastimes whereby the people may any ways be stirred to disorder, to be used by any manner persons, or under any colour or pretence within the limits of your charge.

Praying you also, not only to write unto Sir Francis Leke willing him to cause the said players that name themselves his servants to be sought for, and sent forthwith unto you, to be further examined, and ordered according to their deserts, but also to give him straight charge and commandment in their Majesties' names, that he suffer not any of his servants hereafter to go about the Country, and use any plays, songs or enterludes, as he will answer to the contrary.

And in case any person shall attempt to set forth these sort of games or pastimes at any time hereafter, contrary to this Order; and do wander for that purpose, abroad in the Country; your Lordship shall do well to give the Justices of Peace in charge to see them apprehended out of hand, and punished as vagabonds by virtue of the Statute made against loitering and idle persons. And thus we bid your good Lordship most heartily well to fare.
    From St James, the 30th of April 1556.[1]

No document could illustrate better than does this one the degree of fear, bordering on panic, engendered in government circles by the power of the stage over largely illiterate audiences to unleash civil disorder in troubled times which could quickly turn into outright rebellion. In that year alone (1557) the Privy Council sent Orders of a similar kind to local authorities in London, Kent and Essex.

[1] I have to thank the Librarians of both the College of Arms and Lambeth Palace for their assistance in tracking down this manuscript to its present location.

(e) An Order to the Lord Mayor of London to arrest a company of players and hand them over for interrogation, Westminster, 14 June 1557
PRO, PC2/7, p. 631: *APC*, Mary I (1556–8), VI, 102

A letter to the Lord Mayor of London that where there were yesterday certain naughty plays played in London (as the Lords are here informed), he is willed both to make search for the said players, and having found them to send them to the Commissioners for Religion to be by them further ordered, and also to take order that no play be made henceforth within the City except the same be first seen and allowed, and the players authorised.

(f) An Order to the Mayor of Canterbury, Kent, to hold a company of actors in prison pending examination of their playbook, Westminster, 27 June 1557
PRO, PC2/7, p. 640: *APC*, Mary I (1556–8) VI, 110 (see also **20h**)

A letter to John Fuller, Mayor of Canterbury, of thanks for his diligence in the apprehending and committing of the players to Ward, whom they are willed to keep so until they shall receive further order from hence; and in the mean [time] their lewd playbook is committed to the consideration of the King and Queen's Majesties' Learned Council, who are willed to declare what the same weigheth unto in the law, whereupon they shall receive further order from hence touching the said players.

During the course of this troublesome month, an Order was issued in Star Chamber to all Justices of the Peace banning performances of all plays throughout the summer as becomes clear from a letter to the Lord Lieutenant of Essex about a riot which had arisen at a play.

(g) At the Lord Chancellor's House, London, 11 July 1557
PRO, PC2/7, p. 648: *APC*, Mary (1556–8), VI, 118–19

A letter to the Lord Rich of thanks for his committing them that fought with the Watch to Ward, praying him to cause them at the next Sessions to be further punished according to the Order of the laws and his Lordship's discretion: and, touching the players, it is signified to his Lordship that order was given in the Star Chamber openly to the Justices of the Peace of every Shire this last Term that they should suffer no players, whatsoever the matter was, to play, especially this summer, which Order his Lordship is willed to observe, and to cause them that shall enterprise the contrary to be punished.

Eodem die [The same day]

A letter to the Justices of the Peace of the County of Essex to suffer no players to play any enterlude within that County, but to see them punished that shall attempt the same; wherein they were admonished this last Term in the Star Chamber, and therefore it is thought strange that they have not accordingly accomplished the same.

(h) A second Order to the Mayor of Canterbury relating to the play and players that formed the subject of the Council's earlier letter of 27 June (20f). Richmond, 11 August 1557

PRO, PC2/7, p. 674: APC, Mary I (1556–8), VI, 148–9

A letter to the mayor and Aldermen of Canterbury with the lewd playbook sent hither by them and the examinations also of the players thereof, which they are willed to consider, and to follow the order hereof signified unto them, which was that, upon understanding what the law was touching the said lewd play, they should thereupon proceed against the players forthwith according to the same and the qualities of their offences, which Order they are willed to follow without delay.

If this letter is read in the context of 21a–d below, the prospects for these actors and their play-maker can only be regarded as ominous.

(i) Two letters from the Privy Council to the Lord Mayor of London respecting the conduct of players at the Boar's Head Inn, 1557

Two more Orders were sent by the Privy Council to the Lord Mayor of London, respecting a company of actors at the Boar's Head inn: the first for their arrest in September 1557 and the second for their release, both of which are given in full by Berry, 367a and 367b.

Documents 20a to 20h, covering the years 1555 to 1557, illustrate how ineffectual the government's attempts to censor plays before they were performed, as had been provided for in Mary's Proclamation of 18 August 1553 (18), actually were. Indeed, by 1557–8, the theatre was manifestly presenting a more serious threat to the stability of the Court's authority in London, despite all the measures taken against plays and players since 1531, than it had ever done before.

The last four documents of Mary I's reign relating to control of the theatre occur within a period of a mere two weeks – 12 to 22 December 1557. They survive from two sources: a Londoner's diary and the minutes of the Privy Council. Taken in sequence, these documents offer a clear picture of how the law operated when at its most efficient, even if they fail to identify the roles played by author, actors and audience with a similar degree of clarity.

21   (a) A Londoner records a clandestine performance of a satirical play about the mass in the northern suburb of Islington that was stopped by the police

BL, MS Cotton, Vitellius Fv: *The Diary of Henry Machyn, Citizen and Merchant Taylor of London, AD 1550 to AD 1563*, edited for Camden Society by John Gough Nichols, 1st series, 42 (1848), 160

The 12th day of December, being Sunday, there met certain persons that were Gospellers and some pretended players at Islington, taking [*i.e.* mistaking] certain men and one Ruff, a Scott and a friar, for the reading of a lecture and other matters: and the Communion was played, – and [*i.e.* or] should have been, but the guard came too soon, or ever the chief matter was begun.[1]

[1] Machyn's shaky grammar suggests a second-hand rather than an eye-witness report. It may thus be presumed that (a) Ruff was a Scottish Presbyterian disguised as a friar; (b) that the performance was arranged and advertised as a celebration of mass; (c) that news of this intended subterfuge had been leaked by an informer to the watch or to higher authority; (d) that the dramatic satire substituted for the mass was abruptly stopped with the arrest of the players.

(b) The Privy Council orders the Bishop of London to proceed against the leader of this company of 'pretended' players in the Ecclesiastical Court. St James', 15 December 1557

PRO, PC2/7, p. 742: *APC*, Mary I (1556–8), VI, 216

A letter to the Bishop of London,[1] with the examination enclosed of a Scottish man named John Roughe, presently sent to Newgate [*prison*], against whom he is required to proceed by order of the laws.

[1] i.e. the bishop of the diocese sitting, together with two Justices of the Peace, in the Ecclesiastical Court: in this case the Bishop of London.

(c) Henry Machyn learns of the verdict of the Ecclesiastical Court against John Ruff and records it in his diary

Machyn's *Diary*, 20 December 1557, p. 161

The 20th day of December was condemned for heresy Sir John Ruff, priest, a Scott,[1] and a woman for to be burned at Smithfield . . . [*entry left unfinished*]

[1] The fact that Ruff (or Rough) was both a Gospeller (see 20a) and a Knight had presumably become known to the Privy Council at his 'examination' (see 20b).

(d) The leader of this group of actors (and presumably the author of the play) is burned at the stake

Machyn's *Diary*, 22 December 1557, p. 161

The 22nd day of December were burned in Smithfield 2; one Sir John Ruff the friar[1] and a Scott, and a woman, for heresy.

Such then were the penalties attaching to use of the stage for the advancement of religious and political ideologies in England in the middle of the sixteenth century.

[1] i.e. the gospeller who acted the part of the friar in the heretical play.

IV Elizabeth I, 1558–1603

When the Protestant Princess Elizabeth, daughter of Henry VIII and Ann Boleyn, succeeded her childless Roman Catholic half-sister in 1558, the ground rules for control of the theatre had at least been firmly laid, even if much still had to be learnt about how to implement them effectively.

Firstly, authority over the subject matter of stage plays (which the Roman Catholic Church had exercised up to 1530) had been subsumed by Henry VIII's Act of Supremacy into that of the Crown: this Act had never been repealed by Parliament despite Mary I's efforts to abolish it. Thus, while Lord Mayors, Mayors, Sheriffs, Lord Lieutenants, and Justices of the Peace could still claim the right to read a play before licensing it for public performances, they did so as the local representatives of the Crown itself, and could in turn be held to blame for any failure to discharge their duties in this respect.[1]

Secondly, the Crown had successfully established the right to exercise control over actors and acting, in part through Henry VIII's Act Concerning Punishment of Beggars and Vagabonds, and in part through Henry VII's earlier Acts governing the maintenance of liveried household servants among the nobility and gentry.[2] Thus, in theory, any company of actors that took plays on tour without the written authority of the master of the household whose livery it wore could be arrested under the vagrancy laws of 1531 as revised and strengthened by Edward VI between 1547 and 1552,[3] and then tried for heresy, sedition or any breach of the King's Peace; but, as events of the past thirty years had forecast, Elizabeth I and her Council still had to find ways of dealing with this problem *before* rather than *after* the performance had taken place. Much of the Elizabethan legislation concerned with the theatre is thus motivated by a growing awareness of the need to resolve it quickly.

The government's difficulties in this respect were compounded by the rapid growth in the number of organised professional companies and the corresponding increase in the popularity and frequency of their performances, especially in London. Revisions of the vagrancy laws in 1563, 1572, 1576 and 1584–5 represent attempts to deal with these issues.[4] Even here, however, Elizabeth I was already equipped with a weapon which had lain dormant in the government's hands ever since Henry VIII had reorganised the Revels Office within his own household, providing it with a master, directly responsible to the Lord Chamberlain, in 1545 (see 34, below). Further revisions of the powers and functions of this office in 1573, and again in 1589, chart the route forward to an ultimate solution to these problems.

What still lay ahead were the vexed questions of (i) the revivals of Corpus Christi community dramas in northern counties, which neither the ecclesiastical nor the civil authorities had made any serious efforts to stop; and (ii) the as yet wholly unregulated situation governing use of and control over performance spaces.

It took the threats to national security arising from the abortive Northern Rebellion in 1569 followed by the excommunication of the Queen by Papal Bull in 1570 to stir the government into taking steps to suppress all surviving Corpus Christi and Whitsun plays between 1574 and 1581.

Control over performance spaces, however, proved to be far more difficult to secure, and had finally to be left to James I to resolve on his accession in 1603. The principal reason for this was that, prior to 1558, players of interludes did not expect to be able to use any buildings resembling what we would describe as a playhouse or theatre on a regular basis either in London or in the provinces.

Theirs was still a medieval, makeshift world of fit-ups in market squares, town halls, livery halls, chapels, inns, gardens and large rooms in noblemen's private houses. The rapidly increasing profitability of professional performances after Elizabeth I's accession, however, made it inevitable that companies would seek to obtain some security of tenure over performance spaces, and that in doing so they would provoke disputes between local and central government relating to ownership of and jurisdiction over such places. These conflicts were aggravated by two other phenomena, both of which lacked any precedent which could be invoked to settle them.

The first of these was a question of hygiene, provoked by the advent of epidemics of plague thought to be spread by large crowds assembled in confined places of the kind chosen by players for their performances. The second was the discovery that young people, when free of the need to earn a living on Sundays and other public holidays, preferred to devote their leisure and their savings to patronising plays and playhouses rather than to attending church services and listening to sermons. On these two accounts Elizabeth I's Privy Council found itself besieged throughout her reign both by the bishops and by the civic authorities in and outside London, to ban acting and to close playhouses.[5] Yet as all of the most prestigious acting companies were, at least titularly, in the service of the Queen and members of the Privy Council or their friends, capitulation to this clamour could only result in a serious sacrifice of prerogatives hitherto unchallenged. Not surprisingly, that was resisted.

The changes of stance towards control over the stage outlined above fall into three distinct chronological phases. The first of these, covering the decade between the Queen's accession and the 1570s, was characterised by a tolerant, *laissez-faire* approach to existing legislation designed to prevent the stage being used to advance heretical or seditious opinions.

This state of affairs ended with the flight of Mary, Queen of Scots, from her own country into England in 1568, followed in 1569 by a Catholic insurrection in the north and by an intemperately worded Papal Bull issued in February 1570, excommunicating Elizabeth I, placing the whole kingdom under interdict and urging her subjects to rise up and depose her. These events roused the government, in the interest of national security, into trying to tighten its control over both the subject matter of plays and the movements of itinerant acting companies. Measures were thus taken during the next fifteen years to suppress all remaining Corpus Christi plays, to reorganise the Revels Office and extend its powers from regulating entertainments at Court to include more general responsibilities for the control of plays and players both in London and in the provinces; and thirdly to extend censorship of all subject matter likely to offend against public decency and morality.[6]

The third and last phase from the early 1580s to the Queen's death in 1603 was again marked by serious threats from abroad to national security, to the Queen's life and to Protestantism itself which obliged the government to tighten its own hold on control over the theatre still further. This was achieved through the establishment of a Licensing

Commission in 1589; an extension of the powers of the Revels Office to include the licensing of the newly built playhouses in and around London; and restriction of the number of companies authorised to perform in them after 1597.

The documents illustrating these changes are accordingly presented in three sections which correspond to these phases, and – to assist readers – are further subdivided to reflect major differences of approach to control of the theatre in and outside London.

[1] See **24**, below. The Crown retained a vestigial interest in play texts whenever the Crown or its Agents chose to refer an incident to the Ordinary. See **25a**, **25b** and notes below.
[2] See Statutes, ii.240 and 522.
[3] See Statutes, iv.5, 115, 131 and 173.
[4] Statutes, iv.411, 590, 610 and 718.
[5] See **26a–c** and **28a–c**, below.
[6] See **30a–33**.

GENERAL LEGISLATION, 1558–1569

To exorcise the ghosts of a five-year reversion to Roman Catholicism, Elizabeth I immediately restored the Book of Common Prayer, making its use obligatory by bringing back a revised version of Edward VI's Act of Uniformity on to the statute book in April 1559 (see **13**).

22   An Act for the Uniformity of Common Prayer and Divine Service in the Church, and the use of the Sacraments

Statutes, 1. Eliz. c. 2.356, para. 3

And it is ordained and enacted by the authority aforesaid, that if any person or persons whatsoever, after the said Feast of the Nativity of St John Baptist [24 June] next coming, shall in any Enterludes, Plays, Songs, Rhymes, or by other open words, declare or speak anything in derogation, depraving or despising of the same Book [of Common Prayer] or of anything therein contained . . . then every such person, being thereof lawfully convicted in form aforesaid, shall forfeit to the Queen . . . [etc.]

The list of penalties copies those imposed by Edward VI (see **14**, note 2); for the first offence, a fine of 100 marks; for the second, a fine of 400 marks; and for the third, forfeiture of all personal goods and life imprisonment. Failure to pay the first fine would result in a six-month prison sentence, and failure to pay the second a full year. Nevertheless, no one is to be executed for these offences, and the Act is clearly restricted in its intentions, as far as the theatre is concerned, to preventing riots arising out of expressions of heretical opinions. The Proclamations, however, which accompanied the placing of this Act on the statute book were more far-reaching and ambitious. There were two of them, the first being issued on 7 April and the second on 16 May 1559. No copy of the former is extant, but evidence of its existence survives from a passage in Holinshed's *Chronicle*,[1] and from reference to it by the Court of Aldermen in London.

[1] London, 1577, III, 1184; reproduced in *ES*, IV, 262–3.

23   18 April 1559. An Order of the Court of Aldermen relating to the Queen's Proclamation

CLRO, Repertory XIV, fo. 153. Transcribed in MSC, II.3.298–9

At this Court it was ordered that the Queen's Majesty's Proclamation, lately set forth and made within this City for the staying of Interludes within the said City should forthwith be entered in the Journal of Record and then be conveyed to Mr Recorder to be delivered on again unto Mr Secretary Cecil forasmuch as he hath sent to my Lord Mayor for it.

The wording of this Order – especially the repetition of 'within the said City'[1] – suggests that this first Proclamation was intended as a stopgap measure applying to London only, pending the drafting and printing of the second one covering the whole country that was to be issued a month later.

[1] cf. the words 'within any city or town corporate' used in the second Proclamation (see 24).

24   The Queen's second Proclamation against plays, 16 May 1559

Two copies survive of which one is in the British Library and the other in the Bodleian Library at Oxford. Reproduced in full in *ED and S*, 19–20, and in *ES*, IV, 263–4; also, in part, in *EES*, II, 1, 75.

Forasmuch as the time wherein common Interludes in the English tongue are wont usually to be played is now past until All Hallowtide [1 November], and that also some that have been of late used are not convenient in any ordered Christian Common weal to be suffered; the Queen's Majesty doth straightly forbid all manner Interludes to be played, either openly or privately, except the same be notified beforehand and licensed within any city or town corporate by the Mayor or other chief officers of the same; and within any shire by such as shall be Lieutenants for the Queen's Majesty in the same shire, or by two Justices of the Peace inhabiting within that part of the shire where they shall be played.

And for instruction to every of the said officers, Her Majesty doth likewise charge every of them as they will answer: that they permit none to be played, wherein either matters of religion or of the governance of the estate of the Commonwealth shall be handled, or treated: being no meet matters to be written or treated upon but by men of authority, learning and wisdom, nor to be handled before any audience but of grave and discreet persons.[1] All which parts of this Proclamation Her Majesty chargeth to be inviolately kept. And if any shall attempt to the contrary, Her Majesty giveth all manner of officers that have authority to see common peace kept, in commandment to arrest and imprison the parties so offending for space of fourteen days or more, as cause shall need. And further also, until good assurance may be found and given, and no more to offend in the like.

And further Her Majesty giveth special charge to her nobility and gentlemen, as they profess to obey and regard Her Majesty, to take good order in this behalf with their servants being players, that this Her Majesty's commandment may be duly kept and obeyed.

Given at our Palace of Westminster, the 16th day of May, the first year of our reign.

Imprinted at London in Paul's Churchyard by Richard Jugge and John Cawood, Printers to the Queen's Majesty. *Cum privilegis Regiae Majestatis.*

The provisions made to regulate performances of stage plays within the Act of Uniformity and this Proclamation were supplemented within the next two months by a government Injunction covering the printing of plays, and the issue of a Patent establishing a High Commission for ecclesiastical causes to enforce the Injunction.

[1] It is this clause which allows so overtly political a play as Thomas Sackville's and Thomas Norton's *Gorboduc* to be presented privately at the Inns of Court in the presence of the Queen in 1561, revived at Court in 1562 and printed in 1566.

25 (a) Excerpts from *Injunctions given by the Queen's Majesty concerning both the clergy and laity of this realm* (governing the printing of books and plays under licence), c.13 June 1559

Transcribed in full by E. Cardwell in *Documentary Annals of the Reformed Church of England* (1844), I, 229–30 from Bodl. 4to I.2.Th. Seldon

Item: Because there is a great abuse in the printers of books, which for covetousness chiefly, regard not what they print, so they may have gain . . . the Queen's Majesty straightly chargeth and commandeth, that no manner of person shall print any manner of book or paper, of what sort, nature or in what language soever it be, except the same be first licensed by Her Majesty, by express words in writing, or by six [members] of her Privy Council: or be perused and licensed by the Archbishops of Canterbury and York, the Bishop of London, the Chancellors of both Universities, the Bishop being Ordinary and the Archdeacon also of the place, where any such shall be printed; or by two of them, whereof the Ordinary of the place to be always one. And that the names of such as shall allow the same to be added in the end of every such work, for a testimony of the allowance thereof. And because many pamphlets, plays and ballads be often times printed, wherein regard would be had that nothing therein should be either heretical, seditious, or unseemly for Christian ears: Her Majesty likewise commandeth, that no manner of person shall enterprise to print any such, except the same be to him licensed by such Her Majesty's Commissioners, or three of them, as be appointed in the City of London, to hear and determine divers causes Ecclesiastical, tending to the execution of certain Statutes, made [by] the last Parliament for uniformity of order in religion.

The rest of this Injunction is addressed directly to the wardens of the Stationers Company, warning them 'to be obedient' to all provisions set out in it.

(b) Excerpts from the Queen's Warrant authorising the individuals nominated in the previous Injunction to license the printing of books (including printed plays), 19 July 1559

PRO, Patent Rolls, 1. Eliz. I, p. 9, m. 23–dorso. Transcribed in part in *ES*, IV, 265–6: also in Cardwell, *Documentary Annals*, I, 255–9

Elizabeth, by the grace of God, &c., to the Reverend Father in God Matthew Parker nominated Bishop of Canterbury, and Edmond Grindall nominated Bishop of London [and others] greeting. Where at our Parliament . . . there were two Acts and Statutes made and established, the one entitled An Act for the Uniformity of Common Prayer . . . and the other entitled An Act restoring to the Crown the Ancient Jurisdiction of the State Ecclesiastical and Spiritual . . . and whereas divers seditious and slanderous persons do not cease daily to invent and set forth false rumours, tales, and seditious slanders . . . but also have set forth divers seditious books within this our realm of England, meaning thereby to move and procure strife, division, and dissension amongst our loving and obedient subjects . . .

Wherefore we . . . have authorised, assigned, and appointed you to be our Commissioners, and by these presents do give our full power and authority to you or six of you . . . to inquire for all offences, misdoers, and misdemeanours . . . contrary to the tenor and effect of the said several Acts and Statutes, and either of them . . . and to hear, and determine all the premises . . . and to visit, reform, redress, order, correct, and amend . . . errors, heresies, crimes, abuses, offences, contempts, and enormities spiritual and ecclesiastical . . .

This Patent concludes with a dangerously vague clause inviting the Commissioners to extend their brief far beyond the licensing of printed books and plays by instructing them

to inquire of and search out all ruleless men, quarrellers, vagrant and suspect persons within our city of London and ten miles compass about the same city, and of all assaults and affrays done and committed within the same city and the compass aforesaid.

It was this clause that equipped the Anglican church, as Puritan sentiment advanced within its own ranks, to attack plays, players and playhouses in London during the 1580s and 1590s. Despite this, however, the legislative action taken by the government during the first year of Elizabeth I's reign sufficed to allow dramatic art to develop in its own way without any serious trouble throughout the whole of the next decade.

LOCAL LEGISLATION, 1560–1570

London

The measures adopted by the Lord Mayor and the Court of Aldermen to regulate theatrical performances in the capital were all addressed to the resolving of local problems. These can be grouped under three headings:

(i) Attempts to control the spread of infectious diseases, especially epidemics of plague.
(ii) Efforts to secure jurisdiction over performance places in the City, especially inns, taverns, and large private houses and gardens.
(iii) Endeavours, starting in 1569, to prevent the depletion of Church congregations from the competition supplied by performances of stage plays on Sundays, Saints' Days and at other times prescribed for divine services.

PLAGUE

The first great plague of the reign struck London in June 1563 and raged until the early months of 1564, with deaths over the whole period totalling more than 20,000.

26 (a) 12 February 1564. A Precept from the Lord Mayor and Aldermen forbidding performances of plays

CLRO, Journal xviii, fo. 184: Letter Book T, fo. 189. Transcribed in MSC, ii.3.299–300 (incorrectly noted as dated 30 September 1563 in ES, iv, 266)

My Lord Mayor and his right worshipful Brethren the Aldermen of this gracious Sovereign Lady the Queen's Majesty's City of London earnestly and continually pondering and considering the danger and peril of the great and contagious sickness of the plague which of a great season hath grievously reigned and continued within the said City, and is not yet utterly extinct or ceased; and foreseeing therewithal the foments [lit.: heatings; i.e. summer's warmth] and occasions of the maintenance and increase thereof, and studiously and carefully seeking and minding to the uttermost of their powers (as much as in in [sic] them may lie), utterly revoke and avoid all and every such cause and matter as by man's conjecture might in any wise occasion or increase the same sickness have, among other things, esteemed, perceived and adjudged the great and frequent confluences, congregations and assemblies of great numbers and multitude of people pressed together in small rooms to be very dangerous in that behalf: and do therefore straightly charge and command on our Sovereign Lady the Queen's Majesty's behalf that no manner of person or persons do from henceforth take upon him or them to set forth, or openly or privately play, or to permit or suffer to be set forth or played, within his or their mansion house, yard, garden, orchard or other whatsoever place or places within the said City or the Liberties thereof, any manner of enterlude or stage play at any time hereafter without the special licence of the said Lord Mayor first had and obtained for the same upon pain of imprisonment of their bodies at the discretion of the said Lord M. and Aldermen. Given at the Guildhall of the said City, the 12th day of February in 6th year of the reign of our said Sovereign Lady Elizabeth by the grace &c.,

Blackwell

God save the Queen.

The Bishop of London wrote to the Queen's secretary eleven days later to the same effect, but in a more moralistic tone.

(b) 23 February 1564. A letter from Edmund Grindal to Sir William Cecil asking for a Proclamation to be issued to forbid performances of plays for a year or more

BL, MS Lansdowne 7, fo. 141. Transcribed in MSC, I.148 and ES, IV, 266–7: also in EES, II, i, 77

Mr Calfhill this morning showed me your letter to him, wherein ye wish some politic orders to be devised against Infection. I think it very necessary, and will do mine endeavour both by exhortation, and otherwise. I was ready to crave your help for that purpose afore, as one not unmindful of the parish.

By search I do perceive that there is no one thing of late is more like to have renewed this contagion than the practice of an idle sort of people which have been infamous in all good commonweals: I mean these Histriones, common players, who now daily, but specially on holy days, set up bills, whereunto the youth resorteth excessively & there taketh infection: besides that God's word by their impure mouths is profaned, and turned into scoffs: for remedy wherof in my judgement ye should do very well to be a mean, that a Proclamation were set forth to inhibit all plays for one whole year (and if it were for ever, it were not amiss) within the City, or 3 miles compass, upon pains as well to the players, as to the owners of the houses where they play their lewd enterludes.[1]

[1] No reply to this letter is extant: nor does it seem that one was needed given the action already taken by the Court of Common Council at Guildhall. Rather does it appear that Grindal is at once seeking to excuse his own inaction and to link visitations of plague with divine vengeance for the tolerance accorded to plays and players by the government.

For the next five years deaths from plague in London declined to under thirty a year; but in March 1569 it again assumed serious enough proportions for performances of plays to be forbidden from the end of May to the end of September (see 28d). A further injunction against them was prepared by the Court of Common Council at the start of the autumn season.

(c) 11 November 1569. A Precept by the Lord Mayor

CLRO, Journal XIX, fo. 197b; Letter Book, v, fo. 265b. Transcribed in MSC, II.3.306–7

By the Mayor,

Where of late you had in Commandment by precept for the avoiding of Infection this time of God's visitation with the plague that all great resort, assembly, and concourse of people assembled and drawn together by reason of any plays, interludes or other shows should by you within your said ward not only be forbidden but also not suffered to be frequented and used for that thereby the said infection did spread itself abroad in the City.

These are therefore to will and require you, that you in no wise permit or suffer any manner of enterludes, plays, or shows, to be played or set forth within any part of your said ward until further order be taken on that behalf.

Given at the Guildhall of the City of London, the 11th day of November, 1569. Backwell.[1]

[1] The summary of this Precept, inset in the margin, also instructs all Aldermen to ensure that 'the householders & servants [in their wards] shall come to common service there to pray &c.'

INNS AND TAVERNS

By the mid-1560s hotels, taverns and restaurants in London were being used by itinerant acting companies so often that the city council started taking steps to regulate them. Their first target was all such places within the immediate vicinity of Guildhall, in Cheapside.

27 (a) 29 November 1565. An Order of the Court of Aldermen forbidding performances of plays in inns

CLRO, Repertory xv, fo. 500b. Transcribed in MSC, II.3.300

Item: It was ordered that precepts shall immediately be made out to every of my masters the Aldermen [*not*] to permit and suffer from henceforth any plays or enterludes in any Tavern, Inn, Victualling house or other place within any of their said wards where any money shall be demanded or paid for the sight or hearing of the same plays.

(b) 29 November 1565. Precept by the Lord Mayor to the Aldermen of the Ward of Cheape

CLRO, Journal xviii, fo. 362. Transcribed in MSC, II.3.300–1

By the Mayor.

On the Queen our Sovereign Lady's behalf we straightly charge and command you that ye immediately upon the receipt hereof, calling before you all the Constables and such other the common officers of your said ward as ye shall think meet and necessary, do take and appoint such order to be immediately taken within your said ward that no manner of common play or enterlude be from henceforth permitted or suffered by any manner vintner or tavern keeper, innholder or victaller, or by any other person or persons to be made holden or kept in any their taverns, inns, victualling houses or in any other place or places where any manner of sum or sums of money shall be demanded, collected or gathered of any manner of person or persons for the hearing or seeing of any such play or enterlude, but that ye do utterly stay and abolish the same, advertising us of the names of all such as ye shall find disobedient and contrariant in this behalf. Fail ye not hereof as ye will answer for the contrary at your peril.

Given at the Guildhall of the said City the 29th day of November, 1565.
        Blackwell.

A further Precept issued four years later helps to explain the Council's concern about this matter.

(c) 3 January 1569. A Precept that no carriage either on horseback, by cart or car shall be carried out of any inn or house of this City on the Sabbath day, and that there shall no plays be played after 5 of ye clock, and for the cleansing and avoiding of filth and ordure in the streets

CLRO, Journal XIX, fo. 138b; Letter Book v, fo. 209b. Transcribed in MSC, II.3.302–3

By the mayor,

On the Queen our most dread sovereign Lady's behalf we straightly charge and command you that ye immediately upon the sight hereof take ... like order with the said Constables and other inhabitants of your said ward that they or any of them shall not permit or suffer any enterlude or other kind of play to be had or played within your said ward in any house, Inn or Brewhouse before this time used or hereafter to be used as a place of common resort of people thereto for that purpose after the hour of 5 of the clock in the afternoon at any time between this and Shrovetide next upon pain of like imprisonment of the offenders therein.

Given ... etc. Blackwell.

SUNDAYS, SAINTS' DAYS AND OTHER RELIGIOUS SERVICES

The Elizabethan debate about the propriety of allowing plays to be performed at times prescribed for religious services was not wholly new since Bishop Gardiner had drawn the Privy Council's attention to it as early as 1547 (see p. 32 above). When it re-emerged in 1563, it did so in a more hostile and moralistic vein as manifested in the Bishop of London's letter to Secretary Cecil already quoted (see **25b**). Not until 1566, however, did the city council start to concern itself seriously with this issue.

28 (a) 30 April 1566. Robert Fryer, Goldsmith, is bound over in recognisance of £10.00 not to allow plays to be performed in his house before 4.00 p.m. on Sundays

CLRO, Repertory XVI, fo. 42b; Letter Book v, fo. 21b. Transcribed in MSC, II.3.301

The Condition etc., that if the said Recognizancer do not at any time hereafter before the last day of August now next coming permit or suffer any manner of Stage Play or Interlude to be played within any part of his mansion before the hour of 4 of the clock in the afternoon upon any Sunday or other festival or Holy Day, or permit or suffer any manner of people to enter or come into his said house upon any of the said days before the hour of 3 of the clock in the afternoon of every of the said days to that intent to see or hear any such play or interlude before the said last day of the said month of August, that then &c. [*i.e.* shall be null and void].

This idea of regulating days and times of performances by obliging the owner of a popular performance space to surrender a very large deposit to observe local bye-laws was extended to cover the whole city by a Lord Mayor's Precept on 3 January 1569 (see **26c**) and an Order of the Court of Aldermen, dated 3 February 1569.[1] This was a plague year, but infection did not assume alarming proportions until the autumn.

[1] Provided there was no breach in the terms of such bonds before the date of their expiry, they were rendered null and void.

(b) Court Order of 3 February 1569, relating to plays and interludes

CLRO, Repertory XVI, fo. 442b, misdated Thursday 1 February; Letter Book v, fo. 222. Transcribed in MSC, II.3.303–4.

Item: It was this day ordered by the Court here that precepts shall be made forth with expedition to every of my Masters the Aldermen to take order without delay that no manner of Interlude be from henceforth had or played in any of their Wards but in the daytime, and that between the hours of 3 & 4 of the clock, & that they do take bonds of all those in whose houses or other rooms any such plays or interludes shall be made or kept in the sum of £40.00 that they shall not suffer any person or persons repairing or coming to their said houses under the pretence or colour of hearing or seeing of any such interlude or play to enter into any chamber or other close or secret place within their said houses during the time of the said play.

This Order was simultaneously reinforced by a further Precept from the Lord Mayor.

(c) 3 February 1569. A Precept that no person resorting to any play shall be suffered to stand in any house, chamber or other close place

CLRO, Journal XIX, fo. 143b; Letter Book v, fo. 125. Transcribed in MSC, II.3.304.

By the Mayor,
   On the Queen our Sovereign Lady's behalf we straightly charge and command you that ye immediately upon the receipt hereof, calling before you all the householders of your said ward in whose houses, yards, courts or gardens, or other place or places whatsoever any enterludes or plays have heretofore been accustomed or used to be had played or kept, to take such order & direction with every of them that none of them or any other householder within your said Ward do from henceforth permit or suffer any such enterlude or play to be had, made or played within any of their said houses, yards, courts or gardens, or other place or places, within your said Ward, but only in the daytime; and that only between the hours of 3 and 5 of the clock in the afternoon. And that ye do take bond of every such person in whose house, yard, court or garden, or other place whatsoever any such enterludes or plays shall hereafter be had, played or made, of & in the sum of £40, that they or any of them shall not permit or suffer any manner of persons resorting or coming to any of their said houses under the colour & pretence to hear or see any

such enterlude or play to have [*sic?* leave] or enter into any chamber or other secret or close place or places within any of their said houses during the time of any such enterlude or play, but that they do cause all the said persons resorting as aforesaid to their said houses for the intent and purpose afore expressed still to remain and stand in the open [market] place & places where the same enterludes or plays shall be had, played or made during all the time of the same plays; And then honestly to depart. Fail ye not thus to do as ye tender the honour of this City of London & will answer for the contrary at your peril.

Given . . . etc. Blackwell.

(d) A Proclamation from Guildhall banning all performances of plays from 12 May to 1 September to prevent outbreaks of plague in London, 1569

CLRO, Journal XIX, fo. 167b. Transcribed in *ES*, IV, 267

In the Proclamation the Lord Mayor sought to ban all performances of plays both within 'this City and the liberties and suburbs of the same'. To plays and interludes he adds 'disguisings', and to innkeepers and taverners he adds 'tablekeepers, hall-keepers and brewers'. While the ban on performances is total until 'the lst day of September', the reason for the issue of this Proclamation specifically links the risk of plague to 'great resort, access and assemblies of great multitudes of people . . . to the intent to hear & see certain stage plays . . . on the Sabbath days and other solemn feasts commanded by the Church to be kept holy'. No financial penalties are attached to this Proclamation, but it is to be presumed that those enacted three months earlier still applied.

In September, despite these precautions, the plague returned. This provoked a further Precept from the Lord Mayor.

(e) 26 September 1569. A Precept forbidding the resumption of performances until the end of October and requiring at least one representative of every household to attend their respective parish churches on Mondays, Tuesdays, Wednesdays and Saturdays during the time of Common Prayer

CLRO, Journal XIX, fo. 188; Letter Book v, fo. 251b.

By the Mayor,

Whereas of late I did ordain and set forth by Proclamation [*i.e.* 12 May, see above] within this City for the avoiding of infection of sickness which, by reason of great resort, assembly, and concourse of people might be occasion to the increase, that there should not be any plays, enterludes or other shows (whereby the people might be gathered together into great companies) suffered to be played, set forth or showed within this City, liberties or suburbs of the same until the last day of this September now ensuing; and for that it hath pleased Almighty God at this point to visit this City with sickness of the plague, these shall be therefore to will and require you that you in no wise permit or suffer any manner of Enterludes, plays or shows to be played or set forth within any part of your Ward afore the last day of October now next ensuing.

 Given ... etc. Blackwell

As October ended, deaths from plague were still increasing. On 8 November, a further Order was issued by the Court of Aldermen 'for the staying & utter denying of all manner of enterludes & plays ... upon Sundays or any other time whatsoever' until further notice.[1] This was followed up on 11 November by a Precept from the Lord Mayor to the same effect.[2]

[1] CLRO, Repertory XVI, fo. 513; Letter Book V, fo. 264b. Transcribed in MSC, II.3.306.
[2] CLRO, Journal XIX, fo. 197b; Letter Book V, fo. 265b. Transcribed in MSC, II.3.306–7.

 Four important points emerge clearly from the documents particular to London reproduced here. The first is that professionally organised companies of actors were visiting the capital often enough throughout each year to provoke the city council into trying to control their activities. The second is that the actors' favourite (and most profitable) performance spaces were located in the largest hotels, taverns and restaurants, and in the most spacious private houses of wealthy merchants in central London. The third is that large influxes of citizens flocking to attend these performances into narrow and already crowded streets created traffic and policing problems which forced the council to intervene to protect the interests of businessmen and local residents. Lastly, sporadic epidemics of plague, induced as much by primitive and unhygienic sanitary conditions as by anything else, supplied rapidly growing numbers of Puritan propagandists with a heaven-sent chance to equate these visitations with their own hostility to plays and players.

 It is thus easy to understand why Guildhall should have seized the initiative from Whitehall during this decade for licensing all performance spaces in and around London, and why it should have taken another three decades for the court to recover this aspect of control over theatrical performances back into its own hands.

 One isolated document remains to be listed. This speaks for itself.

(f) 16 November 1568. An Order of the Court of Aldermen concerning puppets

CLRO, Repertory XVI, fo. 414; Letter Book V, fo. 200b. Transcribed in MSC, II.3.302

Item: John Rose of Bridewell was this day straightly charged and commanded by the Court here utterly to desist and leave of that kind of pastime that he there useth to make with puppets and such other like things whereby great numbers of people do thither resort in such wise as is not there to be suffered at his peril.[1]

[1] This Order leaves him free to give his shows elsewhere.

The provinces

Outside of London, the measures taken to regulate performance and printing of plays during the first year of Elizabeth I's reign appear to have been far more successful than those of her three predecessors between 1530 and 1558. At the least, there are no extant records of breaches of the peace or of any other need for punitive action to be taken against particular authors or actors of the kind illustrated in 4, 5, 6, 9, 11, 12, 20a-i and 21.

In northern counties ample evidence survives to prove that revivals of Corpus Christi plays and other religious community dramas were allowed to continue without serious let or hindrance.[1] In southern counties there is evidence that enthusiasm for them steadily waned in Kent, Essex, Suffolk and Norfolk as well as in London itself without any record of external pressure from the Privy Council. Even in Norwich, where a new version of the Grocer's play of the Fall was written in 1565, the pageant itself had encountered such hard times by 1570 that it was broken up and sold off to settle debts.[2]

Where records of adult itinerant, professional companies of actors in the service of the nobility and gentry are concerned, only one document thus far appears to have survived. This is a letter from Robert Dudley, Earl of Leicester, to the Lord President of the North, seeking his permission for his own players to travel and present their plays in Yorkshire (see 151). Dated June 1559, this simply fulfils the obligation imposed on all noblemen maintaining a private, liveried company of actors by the Queen's Proclamation of May 1559 (24, above) requiring all plays to be licensed before being presented to public audiences.

[1] In York, the only pageants to be dropped from the Corpus Christi cycle were those of the Death, Assumption and Coronation of the Virgin.
[2] See REED, Norwich, pp. lxvi–lxvii.

GENERAL LEGISLATION, 1570–1585: FROM THE NORTHERN REBELLION TO EDMUND TILNEY'S APPOINTMENT AS MASTER OF THE REVELS

Mary, Queen of Scots, had arrived in England as an uninvited guest in May 1568. With her army routed, and branded by her Scottish subjects as a murderess, an adulteress and an unscrupulous papist, she came to England as a refugee. She was accorded asylum in honourable custody, at first in Carlisle and then in Yorkshire. Yet within a year she had let herself become involved in a rebellion spearheaded by Catholic peers in the north. This was swiftly suppressed in December 1569; but by February 1570, Elizabeth I had been excommunicated and her subjects had again been urged to rise up and depose her.

In one sense, the Pope's decision served only to expose his impotence to achieve his own ends. Firstly it ignored the high degree of respect and affection that Elizabeth had earned from most of her subjects – Protestant and Catholic alike – since her accession; secondly it warned the Queen and her Council that the Bull of Excommunication would be supplemented by exhortations to the Catholic Kings of Europe to mount an invasion of England to depose the Queen and place Mary on the throne instead.

Nearly two years passed in fruitless discussions about what to do with Mary before her involvement in a second conspiracy was unmasked in November 1571.[1] By the time Parliament next met in May 1572, Elizabeth had asked for the Spanish Ambassador to be withdrawn for his part in it; and the House of Lords, having tried the Duke of Norfolk for high treason, pronounced him guilty and sentenced him to death. Presented with the death warrant, Elizabeth refused to sign it.

Parliament had thus to decide how to deal both with that situation and with the public fury aroused by Mary's flagrant abuse of the refuge and hospitality accorded to her in England. Under intense pressure from her bishops, nobles and commons to sign death warrants for Norfolk and Mary, Elizabeth finally signed Norfolk's (who was executed on 2 June) but vetoed Mary's. Instead, Mary was to remain a prisoner and a continuing source of anxiety to the Queen, her Council and her subjects for the next fifteen years.

This was a situation that made wholesale reappraisal of security precautions obligatory. Forty years of legislative action aimed at restricting the power of plays and players to use the stage as an instrument for arousing emotional responses to heretical and seditious claims and counter-claims in public places ensured that the theatre must be placed within this review. It was; but the measures actually taken between 1572 and 1584 were governed, as before, as much by internal pressures as by those from abroad.

[1] This became known as the Ridolfi Plot. Roberto Ridolfi was a Florentine banker, resident in London, and employed there as an agent by the Pope. The objective was to persuade the Duke of Norfolk to marry Mary and, with the help of Spanish troops, restore both Scotland and England to Catholicism.

Actors and acting

The first targets were the nomadic professional acting companies. Within a month of Norfolk's execution, Parliament revised Henry VIII's Statute for the 'Punishment of Beggars and Vagabonds', originally promulgated in 1531 and already amended on several occasions,[1] to include all actors and entertainers claiming to earn their living from touring plays and shows outside their own county boundaries.

[1] The most recent was that of 1563, 5. Eliz. I, Statutes IV. 1, c. 3. 411.

29 Extracts from An Act for the Punishment of Vagabonds and for the Relief of the Poor and Impotent, 29 June 1572

Statutes IV.i.590–8. Transcribed in *ED and S*, 21–3 and, in part, in *ES*, IV, 269–71

[Clause 5] And for the full expressing what person and persons shall be intended within this branch to be Rogues, Vagabonds and Sturdy Beggars, to have and receive the punishment aforesaid for the said lewd manner of life. It is now published, declared and set forth by the Authority of this present Parliament, that all and every such person & persons . . . using subtle, crafty or unlawful Games or Plays . . . – being whole and mighty in body and able to labour, having not Land or Master, nor using any lawful Merchandise, Craft or Mystery whereby he or she might get his or her living and can give no reckoning how he or she doth lawfully get his or her living; and all Fencers, Bearwards, Common Players in Enterludes, & Minstrels, not belonging to any Baron of this Realm or towards any other honourable Personage of greater Degree; all Jugglers, Pedlars, Tinkers, and petty Chapmen; which said Fencers, Bearwards, Common Players in Enterludes, Minstrels, Jugglers, Pedlars, Tinkers and petty Chapmen shall wander abroad, and have not licence of two Justices of the Peace at the least, whereof one to be of the Quorum, when and in what Shire they shall happen to wander . . . shall be taken, adjudged and deemed Rogues, Vagabonds and Sturdy Beggars.

Although this Act claims to be explanatory, it is also highly restrictive; for not only does it bring actors and other entertainers into its embrace for the first time, but it withdraws from the whole squirearchy and gentry up to and including the rank of Baron, their former right to maintain a company of travelling players if they so wished and could afford to do so.[1] A later clause of this Act, however, is so worded as to allow the Crown to override its own law in this respect, should it wish to do so.

[Clause 12] Provided always, that it shall be lawful to the Lord Chancellor, or Lord Keeper of the Great Seal of England for the time being to make Licence under the said Great Seal, as heretofore hath been accustomed, and that the said Licence and Licences shall as largely extend as the contents of them will bear; anything to the contrary notwithstanding.

This clause was put to the test on 14 July 1573, when the Privy Council wrote to the Lord Mayor of London asking him

to permit liberty to certain Italian players to make show of an instrument of strange motions [? puppets? *Commedia dell 'arte*] within the City.[2]

And again, in a second letter, five days later,

marvelling that he did it not at their first request.[3]

A year later, on 7 May 1574, the Council acted more firmly when deciding to issue a Royal Patent authorising the Earl of Leicester's company, led by James Burbage, to perform their repertoire of 'comedies, tragedies, enterludes and stage plays . . . as well within the city of London and liberties of the same, as also within the liberties and freedoms of any [of] our cities, towns, boroughs &c. whatsoever as without the same, throughout our realm of England'.[4] This unique privilege was granted on the explicit provisos that all plays in this repertoire would first have been 'seen and allowed' by the Master of the Revels and that none of them would be either published, or performed 'in the time of great and common plague in our City of London'.[5]

A further clause in the Statute of 1572 (no. 34, vi.1.597–8) stipulated that 'Justices of the Peace for Counties shall not interfere with Justices for Cities' – i.e. in administering the provisions set out in it. Likewise justices in cities or boroughs corporate were restrained from attempting to extend their powers of jurisdiction outwards into surrounding counties. The effect of this clause in London was to prohibit the city council from legislating against plays, players and playhouses in the suburban areas of the adjoining counties of Surrey and Middlesex.[6]

---

[1] It is to be noted that this Act does not forbid such companies to perform within their own shire or county, or for their master's private entertainment.
[2] PRO, PC2/10, p. 150. Transcribed in *APC*, VIII (1571–5), 131. Also in *ES*, IV, 271.
[3] PRO, PC2/10, p. 151. Transcribed in *APC*, VIII (1571–5), 132. Also in *ES*, IV, 271.
[4] For the full text of this Patent, see Ingram, 153.
[5] For the City's response to this Patent, see 35.
[6] This Statute was renewed in 1576 to run for a further seven years (IV.i.610); it was renewed again in 1584/5 until the end of the ensuing parliament (IV.i.718).

Play-texts: religious drama in York, Chester and Wakefield

The next aspect of theatrical affairs to receive attention from the government was the continuance of overtly religious community drama in northern counties. With the Queen of Scots still resident there (although in protective custody and at a safe distance both from the border and from London), Corpus Christi cycles and other religious plays of Roman Catholic provenance, even when presented in expurgated and reformed texts, were thought to be too provocative and dangerous to permit. Steps were accordingly taken by the Privy Council, working through its agent – the Ecclesiastical Commission for the North – to suppress them. The first sacrificial victim was the city of York.

In February 1568, York City Council had ordered that the Creed Play be presented in place of the Corpus Christi plays which had been performed the previous year; the prompt-copy was sent to the Dean of York to peruse and amend if necessary. The Dean was a newly appointed member of the Ecclesiastical Commission for the North.[1]

[1] PRO, C66/1042, m. xx.

30 (a) Dean Hutton's reply to the Lord Mayor respecting the Creed Play, 24 March 1568

York City Library, York House Books, B24 (106a). Transcribed in REED, *York*, I, 353, and in part in Gardner, *Mysteries' End*, 73, and in *EES*, I, 115.

... as I find so many things that I much like because of the antiquitie, so I see many things that I cannot allow because they be disagreeing from the sincerity of the Gospel, the which things, if they should either be altogether cancelled or altered into other matter, the whole drift of the play should be altered; and therefore I dare not put my pen unto it because I want [lack] both skill and leisure to amend it; though, in goodwill, I assure you if I were worthy to give your Lordship and your right worshipful brethren councel, surely mine advice should be that it should not be played; for, though it was plausible 40 years ago, and would now also of the ignorant sort be well liked, yet now, in the happy time of the Gospel, I know the learned will mislike it, and how the State will bear with it I know not ...

In the light of this letter, the city council rescinded its earlier Order, and on 30 March agreed 'to have no play this year'. The text of the Creed Play has never been seen again.[1] However, the Corpus Christi plays were performed the following year, seemingly without interference (June 1569); but that was to be the last time, for the Northern Rebellion broke out five months later. Its suppression in December was followed by more than 500 executions.[2] In the ensuing climate of fear and suspicion, no amount of further study and revision could save the plays.

The corporation still possessed its copy of the Pater Noster Play, and at council meetings on 14 April and 14 May 1572, it was agreed that this should be performed on Corpus Christi after it had been 'perused, amended and corrected'.[3] Following the performance on 5 June, Edmund Grindal, the newly appointed Archbishop of York, asked to see the prompt-copy.

[1] See 30c.
[2] See *Cambridge Modern History*, III, 282.
[3] York City Library, House Books Y: B25, fo. 6 and fos. 12v–13, transcribed in REED, *York*, I, 365.

(b) 30 July 1572. The city council agrees to send the text of the Pater Noster Play to the Archbishop

York City Library, House Books Y: B25, fo. 19. Transcribed in REED, *York*, I, 368

And now my said Lord Mayor declared to this said worshipful assembly that my Lord Archbishop of York requested to have a copy of the Books of the Pater Noster Play: whereupon it is now agreed by these presents that his Grace shall have a true copy of all the said books even as they were played this year.

Like the Creed Play and Corpus Christi plays before it, the Pater Noster Play was not returned as becomes evident from the minute of a council meeting three years later.

(c) The city council attempts to recover the prompt-copies of all of its plays, 8 July 1575

York City Library, House Books Y: B26, fo. 27. Transcribed in REED, *York*, I, 378

Also, it was now agreed that, before Michaelmas next, Mr. Allyn, Mr. Maskewe, Alderman Mr Robert Brooke and Mr. Andrew Trewe shall go and require of my Lord Archbishop his Grace all such the play books as pertain to this City now in his Grace's custody, and that his Grace will appoint two or three sufficiently learned to correct the same wherein by the law of this Realm they are to be reformed . . .

A final attempt to revive the Corpus Christi plays was made in 1579, but it failed.[1]

[1] See York City Library, York House Books Y: B27, fo. 151. The Council minute of 8 April is reproduced in REED, *York*, I, 390. Although these plays, and their like in other northern cities, were predominantly organised, presented and performed under amateur auspices, their disappearance from the annual calendar of recreational activities encouraged professional companies to fill the vacuum created by their suppression.

In 1572, while York was performing its Pater Noster Play for the last time, Chester was to learn that it could no longer present its religious plays without interference from the government or its agents. The first indication of this survives in a sequence of entries in those records known as the Mayors' Lists for 1571/2.

31 (a) Mayor's List 1

BL, MS Harl. 1046, fo. 163v (Whitsun) Mayor, John Hankey. Transcribed in REED, *Chester*, 96–7

This year the Mayor would needs have the plays (commonly called Chester plays) to go forward, against the wills of the Bishops of Canterbury, York and Chester.

(b) Mayor's List 5

BL, MS Harl. 2125, fo. 39v. Mayor, John Hankey. Transcribed in REED, *Chester*, 97

The Whitsun plays were played this year to the dislike of many.

(c) Mayor's List 8

BL, MS Harl. 2133, fo. 43. Mayor, John Hankey. Transcribed in REED, *Chester*, 97

This year Whitsun plays were played; and an Inhibition was sent from the Archbishop [*i.e.* York] to stay them, but it came too late.

(d) Mayor's List 10

BL, Add. MS 2977, item 246. Mayor, John Hankey. Transcribed in REED, *Chester*, 97

In this year the whole plays were played, though many of the City were sore against the setting forth thereof.

In 1572/3 and 1573/4 wiser counsels prevailed and performances were neither authorised nor given; but, on 30 May 1574/5, when Sir John Savage was mayor, the City Council debated

32 (a)

City of Chester Archives, Assembly Files, CCA: A/F/3, fo. 25. Transcribed in REED, *Chester*, 103–4. Following the Reformation, Whitsun replaced Corpus Christi as the city's principal ecclesiastical midsummer festival.

whether the accustomed plays, called the Whitsun plays, shall be set forth and played at Midsummer next or not.

A decision was taken by 33 votes to 12

(b)

City of Chester Archives, Assembly files, CCA: A/F/3, fo. 25. Transcribed in REED, *Chester*, 104

that they be set forth in the best fashion with such reformation as Mr Mayor with his advice shall think convenient.

In 1575, the plays were again authorised to proceed. No record of any Injunction to the contrary is extant, but an item in the Mayor's List dated 'Midsummer' suggests that one had been received but ignored. This states that the performances took place

(c)

BL, MS Harl. 1046, fo. 164v: Mayor's List 1. Transcribed in REED, *Chester*, 109. The author of this document describes the cycle as 'the popish plays of Chester'.

in contempt of an Inhibition and the Primate's letters from York and from the Earl of Huntingdon [*i.e.* the Lord President of the North].

Confronted with this 'contempt', the Lord President, perhaps fearing that to arrest Savage while still in office might make matters worse, bided his time for four months. Then, on the day that Savage surrendered his chain of office to his successor, the commission pounced.

(d) Sir John Savage arrested and conveyed to London, 4 October 1575

BL, MS Harl. 1046, fo. 104b. Mayor's List 1. Transcribed in REED, *Chester*, 109–10

... he was served by a Pursuivant from York the same day that the new Mayor was elected as they came out of the Common Hall. Notwithstanding, the said John Savage took his way towards London; but how his matter sped is not known. Also, Mr Hankey was served by the same Pursuivant for the like contempt when he was Mayor.[1] Divers others of the citizens and players were troubled for the same matter.

[1] See 31a–d.

It was left to the Privy Council to make an example of these two mayors. Having questioned Savage and listened to his defence, the Council ordered him to produce a Certificate from the city council proving the order to proceed with the performances was not of his making, but approved and endorsed by the entire Council for the financial good of the whole city.

(e) A letter from Sir John Savage to the Mayor of Chester sent from London, 10 November 1575

City of Chester Archives, Corporation Lease Book, CCA: CHB/3, fo. 28. Transcribed in REED, *Chester*, 112

After my right hearty commendations, where it hath been informed to the Privy Council that I caused the plays last at Chester to be set forward only of myself, which yourselves do know the contrary. And that they were by common assembly appointed as remaineth in Record.[1] For the easing and qualifying all controversies grown about the same, I am most heartily to desire you to send me a Certificate under your hands and seal of your City to testify that the same plays were set forward as well by the Council of the City as for the common wealth of the same, whereby their honours may be better satisfied thereof. And hoping thereby to reduce all such matters quiet as are risen now against me and Mr Hankey,[2] whom you must make mention of in the Certificate as well as of myself, which I pray you may be sent me with as much convenient speed as is possible ...

[1] See 32a and b.
[2] See 31c.

This letter was received by Savage's successor, Henry Hardware, and brought to the attention of the city council on 21 November and duly minuted.[1] The Certificate requested was drafted and despatched that same day. It starts by setting out the charges levelled against Savage and Hankey, and then dismisses them as 'surmises' which the Mayor and his brethren know 'to be untrue'. It goes on to declare that this claim is supported by the records in the council's minute books for the years in question, and concludes by exonerating them of the charges laid against them.

[1] City of Chester Archives, Assembly Books, CCA: AB/1, fos. 162v–3. Transcribed in REED, *Chester*, 113–14.

(f) An extract from the Certificate exculpating Sir John Savage and, before him, Mr Hankey, from having acted illegally during their respective tenures of the Office of Lord Mayor, when authorising performances of the Whitsun plays in Chester in 1573 and 1575, 21 November 1575

City of Chester Archives, Assembly Books, CCA: AB/1, fos. 162v–3. Transcribed in REED, *Chester*, 113–14.

And that the said plays, set forth in their several mayoralities, was severally done by th'assent, consent, goodwill and agreement of the Aldermen, Sheriffs, Sheriff's peers and Common Council of the said City . . . whereunto and for the performance whereof the whole Citizens of the City are bound and tied by oath as they are to other their orders.[1] And that they, the said Sir John Savage and John Hankey, nor either of them, did nothing in their several times of mayoralities touching the said plays but by the assent, consent and agreement of the Aldermen, Sheriffs and Common Council of the said City in the self safe same manner and form as the same now is penned and read to this Assembly. And it is further ordered that, as well the said several letters of the said Sir John Savage touching his said request, as also the said such Certificate, shall be entered verbatim in the said book called the Table Book of the said City for the enrolments of all the indentures, leases and deeds concerning the lands of the said City. All which was and is so done accordingly.

As if this were not enough to satisfy the Privy Council, to protect Savage and Hankey and all other individuals directly concerned, and to cover Henry Hardware (the new mayor) and his fellow-councillors, the council issued a proclamation,

To all true Christian people to whom this present writing shall come to be heard or read[2]

covering, in great detail, the whole affair from the council's decision to proceed with the performance of the Whitsun plays in the spring of 1572 to the despatch of the Certificate exempting Mr Hankey and Sir John Savage from any blame on 21 November 1575.

The Privy Council, on receiving the Certificate, appears to have released Savage and dropped all charges brought against Hankey and others, having successfully ensured that no one in Chester would dare to revive these 'popish plays'.

[1] This sentence clears the 'Divers others of the citizens and players' who in 32d are said to have been 'troubled for the same matter'.
[2] City of Chester, Corporation Lease Book, CCA: CHB/3, fo. 28v, 21 November 1575. A seventeenth-century copy is in BL, MS Harl. 2173, fos. 107v–8. Transcribed in REED, *Chester*, 114–17.

Nevertheless, the Ecclesiastical Commission for the North was on the warpath again in the spring of 1576, with its eyes now trained on the town of Wakefield.

33   A Order from the Diocesan Court of High Commission in the North for a letter to be sent to the civic authorities in Wakefield relating to their Corpus Christi play, 27 May 1576: The Deanery, York

York City Library, Court Book, 1575–80, fo. 19. Transcribed by Gardner in *Mysteries' End*, 78, and in part in *EES*, I, 115–16

This day, upon intelligence given to the said Commission that it is meant and purposed that in the town of Wakefield shall be played in Whitsun week next or thereabouts a play, commonly called Corpus Christi play, which hath been heretofore used there, wherein they are done [given] to understand that there be many things used which tend to the derogation of the Majesty and glory of God, the profanation of the sacraments and the maintenance of superstition and idolatry, the said Commissioners decreed a letter to be written and sent to the Bailiffs, Burgesses and other the inhabitants of the said town of Wakefield that in the said play no pageant be used or set forth wherein the Majesty of God the Father, God the Son, or God the Holy Ghost, or the administration of the sacraments of Baptism or of the Lord's Supper be counterfeited or represented, or anything played which tend to the maintenance of superstition and idolatry, or which be contrary to the laws of God and [*deleted*] or of the Realm.[1]

Surviving records from Coventry, and from such northern towns as Kendal and Carlisle, unfortunately fail to supply exact dates for the suppression of their locally organised religious plays; but government action against their continuance in York, Chester and Wakefield between 1572 and 1576 (as illustrated in **31a–33**) makes it virtually certain that serious efforts to revive them after 1580, if they had not altogether ceased, became ever more infrequent, and that a great era of amateur, community drama had been snuffed out. Thereafter, the provision of leisure time theatrical entertainment rested almost exclusively in the hands of touring professional companies, many of them from London, and the goodwill of local mayors, sheriffs and Justices of the Peace in according them the right to use suitable local buildings for their performances.[2]

[1] On the relevance of this document to the deletions and corrections in the MS text of the Townley Cycle, see Gardner, *Mysteries' End*, 78–9.
[2] See Ingram, **193**, below.

The Revels Office

A third area of theatrical activity to attract attention from the Privy Council following the Northern Rebellion of 1569 was the Revels Office within the Royal Household. Its first master, Sir Thomas Carwarden, had been appointed by Henry VIII under Royal Patent on 11 March 1545, to take responsibility for the provision of all entertainments at Court.[1] He held this office through four reigns, supported by a staff of three – his clerk, clerk-comptroller and yeoman – until he died on 29 August 1559.

Carwarden was succeeded by Sir Thomas Benger who, like his predecessor, was appointed for life at an annual fee of £10 under Royal Patent by Elizabeth I, dated 18 January 1560, as master of all forms of dramatic entertainment required at Court.[2] By 1572, however, Benger had ceased to exercise his duties, delegating all of them, including the annual audit of the accounts, to his clerk, Thomas Blagrave. Besieged by creditors, many of whom had waited in vain for up to five years or more for the settlement of their bills, Blagrave appealed to Lord Burghley (formerly Sir William Cecil), the Lord Treasurer, for help.[3] Faced with this situation, caused largely by bureaucratic lethargy but exacerbated by Benger's inefficiency, Burghley initiated a wholesale review of the organisation and administration of the office in the summer of 1573, by calling for a report on its workings from each member of its staff of three.[4]

Blagrave's powers as acting master were greatly extended a year later by the Patent awarded to the Earl of Leicester's players on 7 May 1574 (see p. xx above and 193 below), since this authorised him to license all that company's plays for performance, not only at Court, but anywhere in England including the City of London. This represents the Privy Council's first move towards placing direct control over the theatre in the hands of a single agent responsible only to one of its own members, the Lord Chamberlain.

When Benger died in 1577, Blagrave expected to succeed him; but Burghley thought otherwise, preferring Edmund Tilney, who was accorded a Patent as master on 24 July 1579, backdated to March 1578.[5] This was a stop-gap measure pending completion of his review. A second Patent was thus issued to Tilney two years later incorporating all those reforms to the organisation and administration of the Revels Office suggested in the reports which Burghley himself, backed by the Privy Council, thought to be desirable.

[1] PRO, C66/753, m. 23. Transcribed in *Office of the Revels, Eliz. I*, 53.
[2] PRO, C66/952, m. 10. Transcribed in *Office of the Revels, Eliz. I*, 54. This is also in Latin and its wording virtually the same as Cawarden's.
[3] See E.K. Chambers, *Notes on the History of the Revels Office Under the Tudors*, 26.
[4] All three reports are in BL, MS Lansdowne 83, and are reproduced in *ibid.*, 31–49.
[5] PRO, C66/1181, m. 8. Transcribed in the original Latin in *Office of the Revels, Eliz. I*, 55.

34 Elizabeth I's Patent appointing Edmund Tilney as Master of the Revels, 24 December 1581

PRO, C66/1606, m. 34, no. 46. Reproduced in full in *Office of the Revels, Eliz. I*, 51–2, and in *ES*, IV, 285–6

Elizabeth, by the grace of God &c. To all manner our Justices, Mayors, Sheriffs, Bailiffs, Constables and all other our Officers, Ministers, true liege men and subjects; and to every of them greeting. We let you wit [know] that we have authorised, licensed and commanded, and by these presents do authorise, license and command our well-beloved Edmund Tilney, Master of our Revels ...

The Patent then proceeds to list the powers invested in his office.

(1) To purchase 'at reasonable prices' all raw materials needed for the construction of costumes, properties and settings.
(2) To hire 'all carriages for the same both by land and water'.
(3) To punish anyone who will 'obstinately disobey or refuse ... to accomplish and obey our commandment and pleasure in that behalf or withdraw them-

selves from our said works [i.e. the Queen's]'. with imprisonment for as long as the Master himself regards as appropriate to the offence.[1]

(4) To protect anyone working for the office from arrest (or to secure the immediate release of anyone who has been so arrested), should those workmen have a clause in their contract for other work specifying a deadline. In short, these men are not to be sued for failing to meet the deadline for their other work, provided they return promptly to that work when Tilney has discharged them.[2]

Then follows the most radical of the reforms which extend Tilney's powers to embrace the licensing of *all* plays, players and playing places.

And, furthermore, also we have and do by these presents authorise and command our said servant Edmund Tilney, Master of our said Revels, by himself or his sufficient deputy or deputies to warn, command and appoint in all places within this our Realm of England, as well within franchises and liberties as without, all and every player or players with their play-makers either belonging to any nobleman or otherwise bearing the name or names of using the faculty of play-makers or players of Comedies, Tragedies, Enterludes, or what other shows soever from time to time and at all times to appear before him with all such plays, Tragedies, Comedies or shows as they shall have in readiness, or mean to set forth and then to present and recite before our said Servant or his sufficient deputy whom we ordain and appoint and authorise by these presents of all such shows, plays, players and playmakers, together with their playing places, to order and reform, authorise and put down, as shall be thought meet or unmeet unto himself or his said deputy in that behalf . . .

The final clause provides the master with the same powers to punish any offending players or play-makers at his own discretion, and requires all officers to whom the Patent is addressed to be aiding, supporting and assisting from time to time as the case shall require.

[1] This clause is aimed perhaps as much at creditors who refuse to co-operate until outstanding bills have been paid, as at anyone else.
[2] This clause is aimed at cutting the costs of unnecessary piece-work and overtime as well as at securing greater technical efficiency and reliability.

LOCAL LEGISLATION: LONDON, 1570–1581

Inclusion within the Queen's Patent to the Earl of Leicester's company in May 1574 of the words, 'as well within our City of London and Liberties of the same, as also within the liberties and freedoms of any [of] our Cities, towns, Boroughs, &c.' was taken by the Common Council in London to represent an unprecedented and unwarrantable attempt by the Privy Council to usurp its own powers of jurisdiction within London itself.[1]

[1] See pp. 57–60 above and 35.

(a) Edmund Tilney's monument, erected above his tomb in the Parish Church of St Leonard, Streatham, London, SW16[1]

Photo: David Partner

The monument is placed in the narthex and is said to have been designed by Tilney himself. Surrounded by nine coats of arms, it carries the following inscription:

Here lieth interred, Edmund Tilney of Leatherhead in the County of Surrey, Esquire, Master of the Revels unto Queen Elizabeth deceased and to King James, in an(n)o [ ][2] who was the only son of Philip Tilney, Gentleman Usher of the Privy Chamber unto King Henry VIIIth, and of Malin, his wife, both of the Purlieu here;[3] and who was a younger son of Sir Philip Tilney, Knight Banneret, and Treasurer of the Scottish wars under Thomas, Duke of Norfolk, whose sister the said Duke had then married for his second wife; and who was son unto Hugh Tilney of Boston in the County of Lincoln, Esquire, that was a younger brother unto Sir Frederick Tilney, Knight, who married the daughter and heir of Sir Simon Thorpe of Ashfeldthorpe in the County of Norfolk; by whom he had Elizabeth, first married to the Lord Barnes and afterwards unto the foresaid Thomas, Duke of Norfolk to his first wife; by whom and by Agnes Tilney, his second wife, he had all his succession and from whom all are descended – the Marquis of Winchester and the Earls of Arundel, Derby, Sussex, Essex, Nottingham, Suffolk, Northampton, Dorset and the Viscount Binden, and the Barons Berkeley, Stafford, Scroop, Morley, Sheffield, Hunsdon, Knollys and Arundel.

[1] This Church was badly damaged by fire in May 1975 but has subsequently been restored.
[2] Although he died in 1608/9, this space has been left empty by the 'stone cutter near unto Charing Cross' as if the monument had been commissioned by Tilney some years before his death, and suggesting that this omission went unnoticed by engraver and relatives alike when it came to be erected.
[3] Presumably an area either within or adjacent to the parish of Streatham.

Guildhall responded accordingly by issuing a lengthy Edict of its own some six months later in an attempt to recover control over all aspects of theatrical activity within the City. This was closely modelled on its earlier Edict of 1545 (see 10), but was far more moralistic and censorious in its actual wording. Fear of plague and breaches of the peace provided excuse enough for issuing it.

35 An Act of Common Council for the regulation of all theatrical performances in London, 6 December 1574

BL MS Lansdowne 20. Transcribed in MSC, 1.2.175–8 and in ES, IV, 273–6: also in ED and S, 27–31

Whereas heretofore sundry great disorders and inconveniences have been found to ensue to this City by the inordinate haunting of great multitudes of people, specially youth, to plays, enterludes, and shows, namely occasion of frays and quarrels, evil practices of incontinency in great Inns, having chambers and secret places adjoining to their open stages and galleries, inveighing and alluring of maids, specially orphans and good citizens' children under age, to privy and unmeet contracts, the publishing of unchaste, uncomely and unshamefast speeches and doings, withdrawing of the Queen's Majesty's subjects from divine service on Sundays and Holydays – at which times such plays were chiefly used, – unthrifty waste of the money of the poor and fond persons;[1] sundry robberies by picking and cutting of purses; uttering of popular, busy and seditious matters; and many other corruptions of youth, and other enormities besides that also sundry slaughters and mayhemmings of the Queen's subjects have happened by ruins of scaffolds, frames and stages, and by engines, weapons and powder used in plays.

Having thus branded plays and playing places as a prime source of sexual promiscuity and general corruption of young minds, the city fathers next proceed to smear them as the Almighty's prime instrument for punishing Londoners with visitations of plague.

And where[as] in time of God's visitation by the plague such assemblies of the people in throng and press have been very dangerous for spreading of Infection; and for the same and other great causes by the authority of the honourable Lords, Mayors of this City, and the Aldermen and their brethren, and specially upon the severe and earnest admonition of the Lords of the most honourable Council, with signifying of Her Majesty's express pleasure and commandment in that behalf, such use of plays, Interludes and shows hath been during this time of sickness forbidden and restrained:[2] And for that the Lord Mayor and his Brethren the Aldermen, together with the grave and discreet Citizens in the Common Council assembled, do doubt and fear least upon God's merciful withdrawing of his hand of sickness from us (which God grant!) the people, specially the meaner and most unruly sort, should with sudden forgetting of His visitation, without fear of God's wrath, and without due respect of this good and politic means that he hath ordained for the preservation of Commonweals and peoples in health and good order, return to the undue use of such enormities to the great offence of God, the Queen's Majesty's commandments and good governance.

It never seems to have occurred to these legislators that large assemblies of people crowded into small City churches to listen to sermons might be just as responsible for the spread of plague as actors and play-goers in the yards and gardens of 'great Inns'. However, with this lengthy, justificatory preamble concluded, the Common Council proceeds to list the actions it now proposes to take to prevent any recurrence of these evils. The first measure is aimed at the actors.

Now, therefore, to the intent that such perils may be avoided and the lawful, honest and comely use of plays, pastimes and recreations in good sort only permitted, and good provision had for the safety and well ordering of the people there assembled, be it enacted by the Authority of this Common Council, that from henceforth no play, comedy, tragedy, enterlude nor public show shall be openly played or showed within the liberties of the City, wherein shall be uttered any words, examples or doings of any unchastity, sedition, nor suchlike unfit and uncomely matter, upon pain of imprisonment by the space of fourteen days of all persons offending in any such open playing or showings, and £5 for every such offence.

The second measure is aimed at the owners and managers of the performance spaces, and is clearly intended to override any attempt by the Master of the Revels to dictate to the City in such matters.

Elizabeth I, 1558–1603   75

And that no Innkeeper, Tavern Keeper nor other person whatsoever within the liberties of this City shall openly show or play, nor cause or suffer to be openly showed or played, within the house, yard, or any other place within the liberties of this City any play, enterlude, comedy, tragedy, matter, or show, which shall not be first perused and allowed in such order and form, and by such persons as by the Lord Mayor and Court of Aldermen for the time being shall be appointed, nor shall suffer to be interlaced, added, mingled or uttered in any such play, enterlude, comedy, tragedy, or show any other matter than such as shall be first perused and allowed as is above said. And that no person shall suffer any plays, enterludes, comedies, tragedies or shows to be played or showed in his house, yard, or other place whereof he then shall have rule or power, but only such persons and in such places as upon good and reasonable considerations showed shall be thereunto permitted and allowed by the Lord Mayor and Aldermen for the time being: neither shall take or use any benefit or advantage of such permission or allowances before or until such person be bound to the Chamberlain of London for the time being with such sureties and in such sum and such form for the keeping of good order and avoiding of the discords and inconveniences abovesaid, as by the Lord Mayor and Court of Aldermen for the time being shall seem convenient: neither shall use or exercise any such Licence, or permission, at or in any times in which the same for any reasonable consideration of sickness [*i.e.* plague] or otherwise shall be by the Lord Mayor and Aldermen by public Proclamation, or by Precept, to such persons restrained or commanded to stay and cease, nor in any usual time of divine service in the Sunday or Holyday, nor receive any to that purpose in time of service to see the same, upon pain to forfeit for every offence £5.

That the City's determination to retain control over the owners and managers of public playing places was not as wholly altruistic, as the wording of the Edict suggests, becomes evident in the next clause: this relates to the taxation of all admission receipts in order to subsidise some of the City's costs for the relief of the sick, the aged and the unemployed.

And be it enacted that every person so to be licensed or permitted shall, during the time of such continuance of such license or permission, pay or cause to be paid to the use of the poor in hospitals of the City, or of the poor of the City visited with sickness, by the discretion of the said Lord Mayor and Aldermen, such sums and payments and in such form as between the Lord Mayor and Aldermen for the time being on the one party and such person so to be licensed or permitted on the other party shall be agreed, upon pain that in want of every such payment, or if such person shall not first be bound with good sureties to the Chamberlain of London for the time being for the true payment of such sums to the poor, that then every such licence or permission shall be utterly void, and every doing by force or colour of such licence or permission shall be adjudged an offence against this Act in such manner as if no such licence or permission had been had, nor made, any such licence or permission to the contrary notwithstanding.

76 Documents of control, 1530–1660

And be it likewise enacted that all sums and forfeitures to be incurred for any offence against this Act, and all forfeitures of Bonds to be taken by force, mean or occasion of this Act shall be employed to the relief of the poor in hospitals of this City, or the poor infected or diseased in this City of London, as the Lord Mayor and Court of Aldermen for the time being shall adjudge meet to be distributed; and that the Chamberlain of London shall have and recover the same to the purposes aforesaid by Bill, Plaint, Action of Debt, or information to be commenced and pursued in his own name in the Court of the Outer Chamber of the Guildhall of London called the Mayor's Court, in which suit no Essoine nor Wager of Law for the defendants shall be admitted or allowed.[3]

Having thus defined the parameters of its own vested interests where regulation of theatrical performances in London was concerned, the Council tactfully concluded this Act by exempting from it all privately organised performances in the London houses of the nobility, and all such wealthy citizens as the Lord Mayor and aldermen, commissioned to celebrate special occasions.

Provided alway that this Act (otherwise than touching the publishing of unchaste, seditious, and unmeet matters) shall not extend to any plays, en[terludes], comedies, tragedies, or shows to be played or showed in the private house, dwelling, or lodging of any nobleman, citizen, or gentleman, which shall or will then have the same there so played or showed in his presence for the festivity of any marriage, assembly of friends, or other like cause without public or common collection of money of the Auditory or beholders thereof, reserving always to the Lord Mayor and Aldermen for the time being the judgement and construction according to equity what shall be counted such a playing or showing in a private place, anything in this Act to the contrary notwithstanding.

[1] i.e. simple, naïve.
[2] This refers to an Order of the Privy Council of 15 November 1574 (PRO, PC2/10, p. 285), restraining all performances within a ten-mile radius of London until Easter 1575. Printed in *APC*, VIII (1571–5), 313, and in *ES*, IV, 272–3.
[3] i.e. excuses, special pleading or testimony to a defendant's plea under oath.

With this Act of Common Council from Guildhall and the Patent awarded from Whitehall to the Earl of Leicester's company of actors excepted, most of the legislation respecting control of plays and playhouses in London between 1570 and 1581, as during the 1560s, related to efforts to prevent the spread of plague in summer and autumn months and to stamp out performances on Sundays and at other times prescribed for church services. The frequent directives affecting inn- and tavern-keepers, however, came slowly to be replaced after 1576 by efforts to stop fights and vandalism in or near the new, custom-built playhouses,[1] and to persuade the Surrey and Middlesex magistrates responsible for them to comply with Guildhall's own wishes respecting days and times allowed for performances and the banning of them in times of plague.

Plague reached epidemic proportions in 1570, 1574, 1577, 1578 and 1581. Proclamations were issued in each of these years advertising special measures including a ban on all performances for several months, 1574 alone excepted.[2] Fear of it sufficed to precipitate Orders from Guildhall, Whitehall and sometimes both, covering relatively short periods in the summer and autumn of 1572, 1573, 1575, 1576 and 1580.

All of these Injunctions, however, affected the movements and economy of all adult acting companies licensed to perform in London during the months in question, obliging them to seek an income by touring in the provinces: the losses incurred by the owners of the playhouses were just as serious.[3]

Other familiar irritants provoking action from the Council include the illicit posting of playbills,[4] avoidance of taxes for relief of the poor,[5] and breaches of the ban on performances on Sundays.[6]

[1] Feb./April 1580; July 1581; April/July 1583.
[2] Proclamation nos. 1570 (658), 1577 (719 and 722), 1578 (724, 725 and 729), 1581 (760).
[3] See 38b and 38c; also p. 84.
[4] Order of the Court of Aldermen, 29 April 1574. CLRO, Repertory XVIII, fo. 198. Transcribed in MSC, II.3.308–9.
[5] Order of the Court of Aldermen, 8 December 1575. CLRO, Repertory XIX, fos. 18a, 18b. Transcribed in MSC, II.3.309–10.
[6] Order of the Court of Aldermen, 7 December 1581. CLRO, Repertory XX, fo. 267b. Transcribed in MSC, II.3.312. For the corresponding Minute of the Privy Council on 3 December 1581, see PRO, PC2/13/569–70: transcribed in *APC*, XIII (1581–2), 269–70, and in *ES*, IV, 284.

Notable exceptions are two Injunctions issued in March 1579 and January 1580, forbidding respectively performances during Lent and at night.

36 (a) Minute of the Privy Council forbidding performances in Lent, 13 March 1579

PRO, PC2/12/427: transcribed in *APC*, XI (1579), 73–4, and in *ES*, IV, 278

To the Lord Mayor of London to take order within the City and in all other places within his jurisdiction that there be no players suffered to play during this time of Lent, until it be after the Easter week: and also to advertise their Lordships whose players they be, and in what places they have played since the beginning of this Lent, and that this order may be observed hereafter yearly in the Lent time, etc.

To the Justices of the Peace in Middlesex to forbid all manner of players in the Suburbs of London and other places near adjoining to the same, that they do not in any wise exercise the same during this time of Lent, and that this order may be observed hereafter yearly during the time of Lent, etc.

(b) The Lord Mayor instructs all aldermen to watch out for and to stop any theatrical performance at night within their respective wards before they begin

CLRO, Journal XXI, fo. 7: Letter Book Z, fo. 15b. Transcribed in MSC, II.3.310–11

Where I am credibly informed that there hath been now of late within this City some disorder by reason of certain plays or enterludes used and played by night in diverse suspect places within this City, the same beginning about 7 or 8 of the clock in the evening and continuing until 11 or 12 of the clock whereunto suspicious, lewd & idle persons commonly resort so that if speedy care and reformation be not had great inconveniences are like to ensue. These therefore are in the Queen's Majesty's name straightly to charge and command you that from henceforth from time to time you cause diligent search and enquiry to be made throughout your said Ward; and when you shall understand of such plays or enterludes you cause as well the players as the owners of the houses where any such shall be to be apprehended and committed to Ward, there to remain until further order shall be by me taken for their deliverance. And of your doing herein to certify me from time to time as occasion shall require. Fail ye not hereof as you will answer the contrary at your peril.

Given this 11th of January, 1579.   Sebright.[1]

[1] William Sebright was the town clerk. The evidence provided by this Precept of the acting companies' ability to tailor their play-scripts to fit satisfactorily into a variety of performance spaces in private houses by artificial light in central London should warn historians of Elizabeth and Jacobean playhouses against making dogmatic pronouncements about plays being written after 1576 to fit special architectural features of particular playhouses.

REGULATION OF PLAYS, PLAYERS AND PLAYHOUSES, 1581–1603

While threats from abroad to the security of both the Realm and the Anglican Church steadily increased through the 1580s, the surviving documents relating to government control of the theatre fail to reveal any direct connection with such notorious historical events as the formation of the Catholic League in 1585, the execution of Mary Queen of Scots in 1587, or the defeat of the Spanish Armada in 1588. Rather do they strongly suggest that the enhanced powers given to the Master of the Revels under Edmund Tilney's revised Patent of 1581[1] had finally provided Elizabeth I's Privy Council with sufficient authority to control the stage in London (with only a few notable exceptions to existing regulations) until the end of her reign.

Outside London, the responsibilities delegated to the Lord President of the North, the Ecclesiastical Commissioners and the Lords Lieutenant, sheriffs and justices in each county were by then both well enough defined and well enough known to have reduced complaints against the subject matter of plays and the conduct of the actors who performed them to negligible proportions.

Within London itself, however – at least during the 1580s – the Court of Common Council viewed Tilney's Patent with the same degree of suspicion and hostility as it had the Patent awarded to the Earl of Leicester's company in 1574.[2] Both were regarded as attempts by the Privy Council to interfere with and, if necessary, to override its own jealously guarded powers of jurisdiction within the City precincts. As a result, relationships between Guildhall and Whitehall became increasingly strained and acrimonious. Yet there is no documentary evidence to warrant attaching any blame for this to Tilney's use of his new powers; rather does it appear that the principal cause of friction derived from the decision of the theatre managers and actors to transfer their principal activities to London's suburban districts situated within the jurisdiction of the Justices of the Peace in Middlesex and Surrey, or in the few remaining areas that could still be described as Liberties within the City itself because the land in question, and the buildings on it, was by then in private hands.[3] What infuriated Guildhall about this situation was that it allowed all residents of the City to attend performances less than a mile outside the limits of its own judicial powers, thus constantly frustrating local legislation governing outbreaks of plague and attendance at parish churches on Sundays within the City itself;[4] nor could the relatively relaxed attitude of the county justices towards both of these problems have done anything but exacerbate this frustration.[5]

Whether this situation had arisen inadvertently or with the connivance of the Privy Council it is impossible to determine from the surviving documents. Either way, however, it was one which served its own interests well since most of the adult acting companies still allowed to rehearse and perform in public in London were in the liveried service of its members. What is certain is that the Crown did nothing to change that situation until 1598. In that year Parliament revised the Statute governing the Punishment of Rogues and Vagabonds to reduce the number of authorised acting companies to those belonging to barons and noblemen of greater degree,[6] and the Council reinforced it with specific instructions to the county justices in Middlesex and Surrey.[7]

Thus, from 1581 onwards, while Guildhall might still entertain hopes that the Court might be persuaded to abandon its stubbornly protectionist attitude towards plays and players, it had to come to terms with the facts of theatrical life as ordered in London by the Privy Council in the cause of providing the Queen with entertainment of the highest obtainable quality between Michaelmas and Shrovetide annually.

On the credit side of the balance sheet, Guildhall could claim by then to have been victorious in forcing the adult acting companies to quit many of their former, habitual performance spaces within the City of London itself. (For exceptions see pp. 299–305, below.) They could also take comfort from knowledge that the government had yielded to pressure to reduce the number of itinerant adult companies permitted to perform in the new suburban playhouses to less than ten. Beyond that, the Lord Mayor and Aldermen could also continue to exploit fear of plague with a view to forcing even these privileged companies to reduce the time they spent in or near London and thus to damage their economy. Further pressure to this end could be applied by banning performances throughout the forty days of Lent and by consistently refusing to license performances on Sundays and saints' days, provided the bishops could be persuaded to add their voices to those of the city magistrates when addressing the Privy Council to this effect.[8]

On the debit side, however, the justices in Surrey and Middlesex – thanks to the City's own earlier actions – had by then become the principal beneficiaries of the taxes levied on all admissions to playhouses from which to finance poor-relief in the parishes – notably those in Shoreditch, Moorfields and Southwark – under their control.[9] It is thus not surprising that they should have continued to adopt a more relaxed and pragmatic attitude to actors and performances than did the preachers and merchants in London itself where threats of plague, breaches of the peace, absenteeism from the workplace and performances on Sundays, in Lent and on other Holy Days were concerned.

Despite inevitable overlaps between these three causes of friction between 1581 and 1603, it becomes easier to distinguish what they actually were if, as here, they are presented to readers as separate groups distinguishing the documents particular to each of them rather than sequentially in their original chronological order. Within each of these three groups, only those examples which illustrate new aspects of these same issues will be cited verbatim among the documents which follow.

If the surviving documents of control relating to outbreaks of plague (or to precautionary measures taken to prevent them) outnumber all others during these two decades, those relating to the increasingly sensitive issue of the priorities to be attached to attendance at church services on Sundays and at sermons (both at parish churches and at other advertised locations) and to the strict observance of Lent and other Holy Days come a close second. The third group concerns serious breaches of the peace in or near named inns and playhouses, or to particular issues pertaining to named companies of actors. Since these appear in the subsequent sections of this book relating respectively to theatres and to actors and acting, again only a few illustrative examples will be quoted here and appropriately cross-referenced.

Occasionally the generally accepted ground rules were so seriously ignored or breached as to warrant exceptional punitive and corrective measures designed to prevent any recurrence. A sequence of documents relating to the establishment of a Licensing Commission in 1589 offers one such example; another relating to a performance of Thomas Nashe and Ben Jonson's *The Isle of Dogs* at the Swan Theatre in 1597 provides a second; those documents concerned with Philip Henslowe and Edward Alleyn's efforts to replace the decayed Rose Theatre on Bankside with a new one in Middlesex (the Fortune in Clerkenwell) in 1600–2 provide a third. All of these incidents will be treated in full and cross-referenced, where necessary, to other sections of this book.

The final pages of this section provide a brief survey of such actions as were thought to be needed locally in the provinces to control itinerant groups of actors and other entertainers.

[1] See 34.
[2] See pp. 73–6, above.
[3] See Berry, pp. 309–3; 506–9, and 550–9, below.
[4] See 104; also 43.
[5] See 37, 44a and b and 45.
[6] See p. 103 below.
[7] See 56.
[8] By 1601, if not earlier, they had won over the Privy Council's support. See 45.
[9] See 35.

Injunctions against theatrical performances in times of plague, on Sundays and through Lent

PLAGUE

London was free of any serious outbreak of plague throughout the 1580s; but deaths attributed to it reached totals high enough for precautionary restraints to be issued from Guildhall banning performances for short periods in the summer of every year except 1585 and again from 1588 to 1591.

These were reinforced by Orders from the Privy Council directed to the justices in Middlesex and Surrey as well as to the Lord Mayor covering the periods 17 April to Michaelmas (29 September) 1580, 10 July to Michaelmas 1581, and 7 May until after Bartholomewtide (24 August) 1586. Of these, the first (17 April 1580: transcribed in *APC*, XI (1578–80), 449) provides evidence that the patrons of London's major acting companies then and later – the Earl of Leicester, the Lord Admiral and Lord Hunsden – were all present at the meeting on 17 April 1580, at which it was agreed that 'the great resort of people to plays is thought to be very dangerous, &c.' and concluded, 'and further to have a good regard to the execution of the statute against rogues and vagabonds'. This letter was addressed only to the Justices of Middlesex (which by then included both the Theatre and the Curtain): but finding (possibly on being prompted by the Lord Mayor of London) that it appeared to have been ignored by the justices in Surrey for at least six weeks, it was then followed up by a stern warning to them.

37 Minute of the Privy Council, 13 May 1580, rebuking the Justices of the Peace in Surrey for failing to implement its Order of 17 April

PRO, PC2/13.10. Transcribed in *APC*, xii (1580–1), 15, and in *ES*, iv, 280

... whereas their Lordships do understand that notwithstanding their late Order given to the Lord Mayor to forbid all plays within and about the City until Michaelmas next for avoiding of infection, nevertheless certain players do play sundry days each week at Newington Butts on that part of Surrey without the jurisdiction of the said Lord Mayor contrary to their Lordships' Order. Their Lordships require the Justices not only to enquire who they be that disobey their commandment in that behalf, and not only to forbid them expressly for playing in any of these remote places near unto the City until Michaelmas, but to have regard that within the precinct of Surrey none be permitted to play. If any do, to commit them and to advertise, etc[1]

In 1581 the Order running from 10 July to September was renewed until November because of a sharp increase in the number of deaths reported.[2] When the Lord Mayor issued a further, unilateral injunction on 14 November, the Privy Council again intervened, but this time to ask for it to be withdrawn. This request, however, appears to have failed to elicit the desired response from Guildhall, obliging the Council to follow it up with a fuller and more sternly worded letter on 3 December. All three Orders are given here in sequence.

[1] See 244.
[2] CLRO, Remembrancia, I, 221. Transcribed in *ES*, iv, 281–2.

38 (a) The Lord Mayor of London's Precept to the sheriffs and aldermen against football play and stage plays, 14 November 1581

CLRO, Journal xxx, fo. 151v. Transcribed in *ES*, iv, 283

These shall be straightly to charge and command you that you take present order ... And also that you give straight charge and commandment to all the inhabitants within the same [*i.e.* your own] ward, that they do not at any time hereafter, suffer any person or persons whatsoever, to set up or fix any papers or briefs upon any posts, houses, or other places within your Ward for the show or setting out of any plays, enterludes, or prizes within this City,[1] or the liberties and suburbs of the same, or to be played or showed in any other place or places within two miles of this City; and that if any such be set up, the same presently to be pulled down and defaced. Fail you not hereof, as you will, etc.

[1] For earlier Injunctions against posters and advertisements see 10 and 11 above.

(b) The Privy Council asks the Lord Mayor to rescind this Order, 18 November 1581

CLRO, Remembrancia, I, 295. Transcribed in *ES*, IV, 283–4

Whereas for avoiding the increase of infection within your City this last summer you received Order from us for the restraint of plays until Michaelmas last. For that (thanks be to God) the sickness is very well ceased and not likely in this time of the year to increase: Tendering the relief of these poor men the players and their readiness with convenient matters for Her Highness's solace this next Christmas, which cannot be without their usual exercise therein; we have therefore thought good to require you forthwith to suffer them to use such plays in such sort and usual places as hath been heretofore accustomed, having careful regard for continuance of such quiet orders in the playing places as [here]tofore you have had.

When Guildhall failed to respond to this request, the players petitioned the Privy Council to intervene formally on their behalf a fortnight later.

(c) The Privy Council records its receipt of this petition and its decision to order the Lord Mayor to lift his restraint on public performances, 3 December 1581

PRO, PC2/13, p. 10. Transcribed in *APC*, XIII (1581–2), 269–70 and in *ES*, IV, 284–5

Item 1: Whereas certain companies of players heretofore using their common exercise of playing within and about the City of London have of late in respect of the general infection within the City been restrained by their Lordships commandment from playing, the said players this day exhibited a petition unto their Lordships, humbly desiring that as well in respect of their poor estates, having no other means to sustain them, their wives and children but their exercise of playing, and were only brought up from their youth in the practice of music and playing, as for that the sickness within the City was well slaked [*i.e.* cured] so as no danger of infection could follow by the assemblies of people at their plays, it would please their Lordships therefore to grant them licence to use their said exercise of playing as [here]tofore they had done.

Item 2: Their Lordships, thereupon, for the considerations aforesaid, as also for that they [*i.e.* the players] are to present certain plays before the Queen's Majesty for her solace in the Christmas time now following, were contented to yield unto their said humble petition, and ordered that the Lord Mayor of the City of London should suffer and permit them the use and exercise of their trade of playing in and about the City as they have heretofore accustomed upon the weekdays only (being Holy Days or other days) so as they do forbear wholly to play on the Sabbath day, either in the forenoon or afternoon, which to do they are by this their Lordships' Order expressly denied and forbidden.

This directive was followed up three months later by the issue of the second, revised Patent to Edmund Tilney greatly extending the powers of the Master of the Revels on the Council's behalf both in and outside the City of London.[1]

In May 1586 the Privy Council again issued its own orders restraining plays in public places 'in respect of the heat of the year now drawing on, and for the avoiding of infection like to grow and increase by the ordinary assemblies of people to those places'. On this occasion, however, it not only addressed separate letters to the Surrey justices and the Lord Mayor, but took the opportunity to inform the Lord Mayor that

their Lordships have taken the like order for the prohibiting of the use of plays at the theatre and the other places about Newington out of his charge.[2]

Between 1588 and 1592 London's acting companies seem to have escaped harassment on account of plague even from Guildhall. In August 1592, however, this disease again assumed epidemic proportions obliging both Guildhall and Whitehall to ban performances. The precautionary measures taken in June thus came to be extended on a virtually continuous basis through the rest of that year and throughout 1593, the only exception being the Christmas to Shrovetide period from 29 December 1592 to 1 February 1593.[3] This situation repeated itself through 1593/4 with performances allowed only between 26 December 1593 and February 1594. It was not until the early summer months of 1594 that anything approaching a normal theatrical season in or near London could resume.

[1] See 34.
[2] PRO, PC2/14.84.. Transcribed in *APC*, xiv (1586–7), 99, and in *ES*, iv, 302. See **244** and **245**.
[2] See *ES*, iv, 347–9.

The gravity with which this state of affairs was viewed at the time is vividly illustrated in Orders issued both to Guildhall and to the Surrey and Middlesex magistrates by the Privy Council in January 1593.

39 The Privy Council forbids 'all manner of public concourse', 28 January 1593

PRO, PC2/10, p. 285. Transcribed in *APC*, xxiv (1592–3), 31, and in *ES*, iv, 313–14

A letter to the Lord Mayor and Aldermen of the City of London. Forasmuch as by the Certificate of the last week it appeareth the infection doth increase, which by the favour of God and with your diligent observance of Her Majesty's commandments and the means and orders prescribed to be put in execution within the City of London may speedily cease. Yet, for the better furtherance thereof we think it fit that all manner of concourse and public meetings of the people at plays, bear-baitings, bowlings and other like assemblies for sports be forbidden. And therefore [we] do hereby require you, and in Her Majesty's name straightly charge and command you, forthwith to inhibit within your jurisdiction all plays, baiting of bears, bulls, bowling and any other like occasions to assemble any numbers of people together (preaching and Divine Service at Churches excepted) whereby no occasions be offered to increase the infection within the City, which you shall do both by Proclamation to be published to that end, and by special watch and observation to be had at the places where the plays, bear-baitings, bowlings and like pastimes are usually frequented.[1] And if you shall upon the publication find any so undutiful and disobedient as they will, notwithstanding this prohibition, offer to play, bait bears or bulls, bowl, &c., you shall presently cause them to be apprehended and committed to prison, there to remain until by their [Lordships'] Order they shall be dismissed. And to the end the like assemblies within the out-liberties adjoining to the City [may be prohibited], we have given direction to the Justices of the Peace and other public officers of the Counties of Middlesex and Surrey to hold the like course, not only within the said liberties but also within the distance of seven miles about the City, which we doubt not they will carefully see to be executed, as you for your parts within the City will do the like, in regard of Her Majesty's commandment, the benefit of the City and for the respects already signified unto you.

[1] The exceptionally detailed wording of this Order raises an important question: where, if anywhere and other than the old inn-yards, within the City itself in 1593 did any of the activities listed take place? These questions are only the more pertinent in the context of the concluding sentences of this Order. Did large private houses remain exempted? See 35.

The plight of the adult acting companies resulting from these virtually continuous Injunctions against performances in London covering nearly two whole years, if not disastrous, was desperate enough to provoke several of them into asking for remedial assistance.

Philip Henslowe who, between 1591 and 1592, had laid out a substantial capital sum to enlarge the audience capacity and to improve the stage facilities at the Rose, was even persuaded to forward a petition received from the Thames ferrymen to his patron, the Lord High Admiral, pleading for the ban on performances there to be lifted as an act of Christian charity for the relief of their wives and children; it was signed by the Queen's barge-master and fifteen royal watermen.[1]

Lord Strange's company of actors likewise petitioned the Privy Council to relieve their distress on account of the high costs of touring the provinces which will be 'a mean to bring us to division and separation'.[2]

With the lifting of all restraints on performances in London and its suburbs in May/June 1594, however, the acting companies returned to the capital to enjoy a clear run of seven consecutive years free of the anxieties that had accompanied outbreaks of plague. A single exception was a brief precautionary restraint operative only between July and September 1596.

Performances were again forbidden during the Queen's last illness on March 19th, 1603; but almost immediately after her death and the accession of James VI and I, plague returned causing 33,000 deaths and enforcing the closure of all playhouses throughout that year.

[1] Dulwich, MS i, Articles 16–18. Transcribed in *Henslowe's Diary*, 284–5; also in *ES*, IV, 312. See also W.W. Greg, *Henslowe's Papers* (London, 1904–8).
[2] See **193** and note 1 above.

SUNDAYS, HOLY DAYS AND LENT

With Calvinist and other Puritan-minded ecclesiastical and mercantile opinion in London insisting that recurrent epidemics of plague must be interpreted as an unmistakable sign of God's vengeance for the moral depravity of a population addicted to plays and players – especially on Sundays and in Lent – the Court of Common Council found itself under ever-increasing pressure to suppress the new purpose-built playhouses in the suburbs. Denied the judicial powers needed to do this by the Privy Council, yet faced with county magistrates both in Surrey and Middlesex who took a less austere view of the theatre than they did, they were nevertheless acutely aware that the majority of the audiences who flocked to the suburban playhouses were residents of the City itself and thus, theoretically, subject to their jurisdiction. Yet in the early 1580s the only means of redress open to the Lord Mayor and his brethren at Guildhall was to persuade the Privy Council to support their cause. Strenuous efforts were made accordingly to achieve this objective between the spring of 1582 and the summer of 1583.

Guildhall started this campaign in April 1582, by enlisting the support of the livery companies in the City.

40   Lord Mayor's Precept to the officers of the Ironmongers Company, 3 April 1582

Company Court Books xxx. Transcribed in J. Nicholl, *Some Account of the Worshipful Company of Ironmongers* (2nd edn, 1866), 128; and in *ES*, IV, 287

These shall be straightly to charge and command you, that forthwith upon the receipt hereof you call before you all the freemen of your said Company, and give to everyone of them straightly charge and commandment that they or any of them do at any time hereafter suffer any of their servants, apprentices, journeymen or children to repair or go to any plays, pieces, or enterludes, either within the City or suburbs thereof, or to any place without the same, upon pain of every servant so offending, or master so suffering, to be punished at the discretion of me and my brethren. Fail you not hereof as you will answer the contrary at your peril. Given at Guildhall, the 3rd day of April, 1582.

Sebright [Town Clerk]

A week later, Guildhall could gain some satisfaction on receipt of a letter from the Privy Council stating that while it had decided to license 'certain companies of players to exercise their playing in London', it had refused them this right on ordinary public holidays until 'after evening prayer', and had forbidden them to perform on Sundays.[1] The Lord Mayor replied by return explaining to 'the honourable the Lords and other of the Queen's Majesty's most honourable Council' that this licence failed fully to meet his own and the aldermen's objections (41).

[1] PRO, PC2/13, pp. 691–2, 11 April 1582. Transcribed in *APC*, XIII (1580–1), 404. See also CLRO, Remembrancia, 1.317; transcribed in *MSC*, I.i.52–3, and in *ES*, IV, 287–8.

41 A letter from the Lord Mayor to the Privy Council, 13 April 1582

CLRO, Remembrancia, 1, 319. Transcribed in MSC, I.i.34, and in *ES*, IV, 288–9

I have received signification of your Lordships' pleasure by your letters for enlarging the restraint of players on holydays in the afternoon, being not the Sabbath day, so as the same may be done after service and without disturbance of common prayer and service of God which, as the experience is among us, peradventure not made known to your Lordships, can very hardly be done. For though they begin not their plays till after evening prayer, yet all the time of the afternoon before they take in hearers and fill the place with such as be thereby absent from serving God at Church, and attending to serve God's enemy in an Inn. If, for remedy hereof, I should also restrain the letting in of the people till after service in Church, it would drive the action of their plays into very inconvenient time of night, especially for servants and children to be absent from their parents' and masters' attendance and presence.

The Lord Mayor concludes this letter by invoking fear of a recurrence of plague in the months ahead, and requesting a formal restraint against all performances on that account; but the Privy Council appears to have taken no action.

In May of the following year the Lord Mayor turned his attention to the problem of the playhouses in the suburbs and appealed directly to the Queen's secretary, Sir Francis Walsingham, for help. Having issued a precautionary restraint on the performance of plays in the City earlier that year, he explains why this will prove to be ineffective unless pressure is brought to bear upon the Middlesex and Surrey magistrates to reinforce his own order.

42 A private letter from the Lord Mayor of London to Sir Francis Walsingham, 3 May 1583

CLRO, Remembrancia, 1, 538. Transcribed in MSC, I.i.63 and in *ES*, IV, 294

According to our duty, I and my brethren have had care for stay of infection of the plague, and published orders in that behalf which we intend, God willing, to execute with diligence. Among other, we find one very great and dangerous inconvenience – the assembly of people to plays, bear-baiting, fencers, and profane spectacles at the Theatre and Curtain and other like places, to which do resort great multitudes of the basest sort of people; and many infected with sores running on them, being out of our jurisdiction, and some whom we cannot discern by any diligence; and which be otherwise perilous for contagion, beside the withdrawing from God's service, the peril of ruins of so weak buildings, and the advancement of incontinency and most ungodly confederacies, the terrible occasion of God's wrath and heavy striking with plagues. It availeth not to restrain them in London unless the like Orders be in those places adjoining to the liberties, for amendment whereof I beseech your honour to be mean[1] to the most honourable Council; and the rather I am to make that humble suit, for that I would be loathe to sustain Her Majesty's heavy displeasure when such foreign and extraordinary occasions shall be above all our abilities by any diligence or foresight to redress it.

[1] i.e. to enlist the support of the Privy Council.

As no action appears to have followed from this indirect and private approach to the Council, the Lord Mayor decided to appeal directly to it two months later. Using as his excuse the need to reply to a letter from the Council relating to provisions for the maintenance of archery, he lays the blame for its neglect among the citizens and consequent decay on 'assemblers to unlawful spectacles, as bear-baiting, unchaste enterludes and other like'.

43   Extract from a letter from the Lord Mayor to the Privy Council, 3 July 1583

CLRO, Remembrancia, I, 520. Transcribed in MSC, I.i.64, and in ES, IV, 294–5

... [which have provoked the] drawing of God's wrath and plagues upon us, whereof God hath in His judgement shewed a late terrible example at Paris Garden, in which place in great contempt of God the scaffolds are new builded, and the multitudes on the Sabbath day called together in most excessive number.[1] These things are objected to us, both in open sermons at Paul's Cross and elsewhere in the hearing of such as repair from all parts of to [sic? delete of] our shame and grief when we cannot remedy it. The reproach also to us as the sufferers and maintainers of such disorders is published to the whole world in books. We have herewith moved [i.e. resolved], as becometh us in conscience and in regard of our honesty and credits, not to be accounted senseless of the fear of God and of our duties to Her Majesty and the preservation of her subjects in our charge, have endeavoured – and your good favours concurring will more endeavour – ourselves for redress of such enormities within our jurisdiction, specially on the Sabbath and days appointed for common prayer. Which our travails shall yet be vain and to no effect without your honourable help and assistance. It may therefore please your good Lordships both to give your allowance of our proceeding in such reformation within our liberties, and to send your Lordships' letters of request and commandment to the Justices of the Counties and Governors of precincts adjoining to this City to execute like Orders as we shall do for the honour of God and service of Her Majesty.

[1] Some of the seating at Beargardens collapsed on Sunday 13 January 1583, killing some spectators and maiming many more. The Lord Mayor wrote to Lord Burghley the next day alleging that the Surrey magistrates were claiming that they lacked any authority to forbid such performances. See BL, MS Lansdowne 37, fo. 8. Transcribed in ES, IV, 92. Clearly, however, this was not the first time that scaffolds and stages had collapsed (see 35).

By 1584, even if Guildhall had failed in its efforts to persuade the Privy Council to extend the frontiers of its own jurisdiction to embrace the suburban playhouses, it could at least claim to have reached agreement with the Privy Council that *all* performances on Sundays should be forbidden. On the other hand, no one knew better than the theatre owners and the acting companies that larger audiences (and thus higher receipts) could be secured on public holidays than on any day in the working week. It is scarcely surprising therefore that they should have continued to defy it, notwithstanding the Orders already cited to the contrary. Thus further measures had to be taken in 1587, 1591, and even as late as 1601, to stop it.

44 Letters from the Privy Council to the justices in Surrey and Middlesex rebuking them for their laxity in permitting performances to be given on Sundays, 29 October 1587

(a) PRO, PC2/14, p. 477. Transcribed in *APC*, xv (1587–8), 271–2, and in *ES*, iv, 304–5; (b) PRO, PC2/14, p. 478. Transcribed in *APC*, xv (1587–8) 272

(a) To the Justices of Surrey

Whereas the inhabitants of Southwark had complained unto their Lordships declaring that the Order by their Lordships set down for the restraining of plays and enterludes within that County on the Sabbath days is not observed, and especially within the Liberty of the Clink and in the Parish of St Saviours in Southwark, which disorder is to be ascribed to the negligence of some of the Justices of Peace in that County; They are required to take such strict Order for the staying of the said disorder as is already taken by the Lord Mayor within the Liberties of the City, so as the same be not hereafter suffered at the times forbidden in any place of that County.

(b) To the Justices of Middlesex

Foreasmuch as Order is taken by the Lord Mayor within the precincts of the City for the restraining of plays and interludes on the Sabbath day, according to such direction as hath been heretofore given by their Lordships in that behalf, they are required to see the like observed and kept within that County, as well in any places privileged as otherwise.

Despite the unequivocal nature of these Orders, these abuses continued. On 25 July 1591, the Privy Council was moved to write again to the Lord Mayor and to the Middlesex and Surrey magistrates complaining that their Orders forbidding 'the playing of enterludes and plays on the Sabbath day' are still being neglected 'to the profanation of this day'. These Orders also reveal that by that time Orders of some sort had been issued to restrain performances of plays on Thursdays to remove any competition from the rival entertainment of bear-baiting, and that these were being flouted as brazenly as the ban on Sunday performances. This is made explicit in the concluding sentences.

(c) The Privy Council to the Justices of Middlesex and Surrey, 25 July 1591

PRO, PC2/18, p. 440. Transcribed in *APC*, XXI (1591), 395, and in *ES*, VI, 307

These shall be therefore to require you not only to take Order hereafter that there may no plays, enterludes or comedies be used or publicly made and showed either on the Sunday or on the Thursdays, because on the Thursdays those other games usually have been always accustomed and practised. Whereof see you fail not hereafter to see this our Order duly observed for the avoiding of the inconveniences aforesaid.

The veiled threat of the concluding sentence to this sternly worded reproof, coupled with the onslaughts of plague between 1592 and 1594, may have succeeded in achieving the Council's immediate objectives; but by 1601 its Orders were again being so flagrantly breached as to provoke it into rebuking the Surrey and Middlesex magistrates in unprecedentedly hostile terms.

45 Extracts from 'two letters of one tenor' from the Privy Council to the Justices of Middlesex and Surrey, 31 December 1601

PRO, PC2/26, p. 514. Transcribed in *APC*, XXXII (1601–4), 466 and *ES*, IV, 332–3

It is in vain for us to take knowledge of great abuses and disorders complained of and to give Order for redress if our directions find no better execution and observation than it seemeth they do; and we must needs impute the fault and blame thereof to you, or some of you, the Justices of the Peace that are put in trust to see them executed and performed . . .

Referring specifically to earlier orders issued on 22 June 1600,[1] to restrain the excessive number of playhouses and the immoderate use of stage plays in and about the City the Council claim that

instead of restraint and redress of the former disorders, the multitude of playhouses is much increased, and that no day passeth over without many stage plays in one place or other within and about the City publicly made . . .

Calling for instant reform, the Council again lays the blame for these present abuses on the magistrates and concludes both letters with specific instructions about the action to be taken.

. . . yet we have neither understood of any redress made by you, nor received any Certificate at all of your proceedings therein, which default or omission we do now pray and require you forthwith to amend, and to cause our said former Order to be put duly in execution; and especially to call before you the owners of all the other playhouses (excepting the two houses in Middlesex and Surrey afore-mentioned [*i.e.* the Fortune and the Globe]), and to take good and sufficient bonds of them not to exercise, use or practise, nor to suffer from henceforth to be exercised, used or practised any stage playing in their houses; and if they shall refuse to enter into such bonds, then to commit them to prison until they shall conform themselves.

[1] CLRO, Remembrancia, II, 188, transcribed in *APC*, xx (1599–1600), 395 and in MSC, I.i.80–3.

The bonds, or financial sureties, to be taken from the playhouse owners and managers thus continued to be as useful to the Privy Council as a disciplinary measure as it had been to Guildhall when attempting to control the inn and tavern keepers within the City during the 1560s and 1570s.[1]

[1] See 35, especially pp. 75–6.

A second financial weapon often used for disciplinary purposes was the attempt to tax admission receipts to assist with the raising of funds in particular parishes and wards towards the cost of hospitals, alms-houses and other supplementary measures for the relief of the poor and indigent.

46 A highly literate, but anonymous, army officer writes to Sir Francis Walsingham, the Queen's secretary, suggesting that the taxing of playhouse receipts should become part of government fiscal policy, 25 January 1587
BL, MS Harl. 286, fo. 102

The daily abuse of Stage Plays is such an offence to the godly, and so great a hindrance to the gospel, as the papists do exceedingly rejoice at the blemish thereof, and not without cause. For every day in the week the players' bills are set up in sundry places of the City, some in the name of Her Majesty's men, some the Earl of Leicester's, some the Earl of Oxford's, the Lord Admiral's and divers others: so that when the bells toll to the Lectorer [*i.e.* for the public reading of the Scriptures] the trumpets sound to the Stages whereat the wicked faction of Rome laugheth for joy, while the godly weep for sorrow. Woe is me! The playhouses are pestered when churches are naked: at the one it is not possible to get a place; at the other void seats are plenty.

The profaning of the Sabbath is redressed; but as bad a custom entertained, and yet still our long-suffering God forbeareth to punish. It is a woeful sight to see two hundred proud players get in their silks, where five hundred poor people starve in the streets. But if needs this mischief must be tolerated, whereat (no doubt) the highest frowneth, yet for God's sake (Sir), let every Stage in London pay a weekly pension to the poor ... Now, me thinks, I see your honour smile, and say to yourself, these things are fitter for the pulpit than a soldier's pen: but God (who searches the heart and reins [kidneys] knoweth that I write not hypocritically, but from the very sorrow of my soul.

There is no record that any legislation was ever laid before Parliament to impose such a tax on playhouse owners or acting companies; but by 1600 general acceptance of some such form of taxation at local authority level had become generally accepted.[1] Evidence of further attempts at enforcement is forthcoming from two surviving documents: the first relates to the Rose and the Globe, and the second to the Fortune.

[1] Doc. 35 however, supplies evidence that Guildhall had been attempting to do this since 1574.

47 (a) St Saviour's Parish Church, Southwark, 28 March 1600
LMA, P92/Sav/450 (1581/2–1628), Vestry Minute Book, fo. 339

It is ordered that the churchwardens shall talk with the players for tithes for their playhouses and for the rest of the[ir] new town houses there about within the Liberty of the Clink, and for money for the poor, according to the Order taken before my Lords of Canterbury, London and the Master of the Revels.

(b) Certificate sent to the Privy Council by twenty seven inhabitants of Finsbury supporting the issue of a licence to build a new playhouse, the Fortune, within their parish, undated but *c*. January 1600
Dulwich, MS i, Article 28. Transcribed in Henslowe's *Diary*, 289–90, and in *ES*, IV, 327–8

In all humbleness, we the Inhabitants of the Lordship of Finsbury, within the Parish of St Giles without Cripplegate, London, do certify unto your honours: That where the Servants of the right honourable Earl of Nottingham have lately gone about to erect and set up a new Playhouse within the said Lordship, we could be contented that the same might proceed and be tolerated (so it stand with your honour's pleasure) for the reasons and causes following:

First, because the place appointed out for that purpose standeth very tolerable, near unto the Fields, and so far distant and remote from any person or place of account as that none can be annoyed thereby:

Secondly, because the Erectors of the said house are contented to give a very liberal portion of the money weekly towards the relief of our Poor, the number and necessity whereof is so great that the same will redound to the continual comfort of the said Poor:

Thirdly and lastly we are the rather contented to accept this means of relief of our Poor, because our Parish is not able to relieve them: neither have the Justices of the Shire taken any Order for any supply out of the County, as is enjoined by the late Act of Parliament.[1]

[1] See pp. 537–9 below.

BRAWLS AND OTHER PUBLIC DISORDERS INVOLVING ACTORS AND PLAYHOUSES

So great was the appetite for plays among men and women of all trades and classes in late-Elizabethan London (as **46** reveals) – ranging from the Queen herself to 'the basest sort of people' – it is not surprising that the largest number of documents of control (after those governing performances in times of plague and on Sundays and other religious holidays) should be those relating to the conduct of the playhouses and the acting companies who used them. Most of these relate to serious breaches of the Queen's Peace and are treated fully in subsequent sections of this book.[1] They are thus only mentioned here to amplify such blanket-phrases as 'frequent and great disorders and abuses' which occur so often in the letters and Orders issued from Guildhall and by the Privy Council already cited.

Starting in 1580 with the indictment of John Brayne and James Burbage concerning an affray at the Theatre, they include fighting between the Earl of Oxford's players and members of the Inns of Court that same year, and between members of the Inns and the Earl of Berkeley's players in 1581.[2] A third dispute arose between the Lord Mayor and the Earl of Warwick's fencer over a prize fight in 1582.[3]

The deaths and injuries resulting from the collapse of rotten seating at Beargardens in 1583 have already been cited.[4] A second dispute about a fencing prize fight, this time at the Theatre, occurred later that year, as did another arising from the Master of the Revels' decision to ask Guildhall to provide a performance space in the City for the new company of actors whom he had assembled to serve the Queen under her name.[5]

In 1584 a riot took place at the Curtain Playhouse,[6] and in 1589 the Lord Mayor found it necessary to write to Lord Burghley about the conduct of the Lord Admiral's Men and Lord Strange's Men (see **48**).

Between 1592 and 1595 further disputes arose relating to the Rose and the Swan playhouses in Southwark, and to the Theatre in Shoreditch. This pattern repeated itself between 1596 and the end of Elizabeth I's reign respecting the conduct of actors and their audience at the Blackfriars, the Swan, the Rose, the Fortune, the Curtain and the Boar's Head.

Of these many incidents, those of 1589 (associated with the Martin Marprelate controversy) at the Theatre and at the Curtain or the Rose, and those of 1597 at the Swan (following performances of Thomas Nashe and Ben Jonson's *The Isle of Dogs*) assumed serious enough proportions in the opinion of the Privy Council to warrant draconian action. Critical discussion of the government of the Church of England on the stage in the Marprelate plays led directly to the creation of a Licensing Commission: *The Isle of Dogs*, in which certain noblemen and foreign dignitaries saw themselves as having been scurrilously lampooned, resulted in an order to close and demolish all playhouses in and around London, and another to arrest and imprison the authors and actors concerned. Since the consequences of both of these incidents were unprecedented, the documents relating to them are quoted here.

[1] See especially **194** and **195**.
[2] See **264** and **266** below: CLRO, Remembrancia, I, 224; see *ES*, ii, 100.
[3] See **209a** and **b** below: CLRO, Remembrancia, I, 359; reproduced in *MSC*, I.i.55, and in *ES*, IV, 289.
[4] See **43**; also BL, MS Lansdowne 37, fo. 8.
[5] See **272** below: CLRO, Remembrancia, I, 498; and CLRO, Remembrancia, I, 553 and 554.
[6] BL, MS Lansdowne 41, fo. 31: transcribed in *MSC*, I.2.163–4, and in *ES*, IV, 297.

Alleged breaches of statutory legislation by play-makers, actors and playhouse owners

The Licensing Commission, 1589

During the first week of November 1589 both the Lord Admiral's and Lord Strange's Men rashly decided to add their voices to those of the London pamphleteers who were then engaged in a series of satirical attacks on the government of the Church of England. They did this as opponents to these satirists; but in choosing to accept plays or to interpolate characters and dialogue into existing plays, or to add Bergomasks (short farces) tacked on to performances of plays as afterpieces, they laid themselves open to accusations of engaging in inflammatory conduct on public stages.[1]

The only known play-makers whose names surface in the pamphlets are those of Thomas Nashe and John Lyly, who may thus have provided the texts which caused the Master of the Revels to intervene by trying to prohibit further performances. As the language of the pamphlets makes mention of Apes, Maid Marian and a May Game, satirical Bergomasks would seem to have offered the most likely source of offence. The playhouses named in this context in the pamphlets include the Theatre, the Curtain, St Paul's and 'St Thomas à Waterings', but as that was the place of public execution for Surrey (two miles south of London Bridge) this is generally assumed to have been intended as a joke.[2] The Lord Mayor names only the Cross Keys inn.[3]

[1] On the Marprelate Controversy, see *ES*, IV, 229–33.
[2] See 228 and 284.
[3] See 48. The Lord Mayor does not specify in this letter that 'the great offence' given was occasioned by the content of the performance. It could thus have been occasioned by performing there without a licence; but the reference to Tilney's objections makes this seem unlikely.

Proceedings against the offending companies began on 3 and 4 November 1589, and were translated into action on 6 November.

48 The Lord Mayor writes to Lord Burghley acknowledging receipt of his letter directed to Mr Young and passed on to him (not extant) and describes the action that he has taken against offending actors, 6 November 1589

BL, MS Lansdowne 60, fo. 47. Transcribed in MSC, 1.2.180, and in *ES*, IV, 305–6; also in *ED and S*, 34–5

Where, by a letter of your Lordship's directed to Mr Young, it appeared unto me that it was your honour's pleasure I should give order for the stay of all plays within the City, in that Mr Tilney did utterly mislike the same. According to which your Lordship's good pleasure, I presently sent for such players as I could hear of: so as there appeared yesterday [5 November] before me the Lord Admiral's and the Lord Strange's players, to whom I specially gave in Charge and required them in her Majesty's name to forbear playing until further Order might be given for their allowance in that respect. Whereupon, the Lord Admiral's players very dutifully obeyed; but the others, in very contemptuous manner, departing from me, went to the Cross Keys and played that afternoon to the great offense of the better sort that knew they were prohibited by Order from your Lordship. Which, as I might not suffer, so I sent for the said contemptuous persons, who having no reason to alledge for their contempt, I could do no less but this evening commit some of them to one of the Compters [prisons], and do mean, according to your Lordship's direction, to prohibit all playing until your Lordship's pleasure therein be further known.

Six days later the matter had reached the Privy Council, where it was decided to act with unprecedented firmness. Orders were thus issued to establish a Licensing Commission of three people who in future would be required to read, purge and finally license all plays prior to their performance in London. The Court, the City and the Church were to be equally represented on this commission. The Court was to be represented by the Master of the Revels, deputising for the Lord Chamberlain; the City by an individual nominated by the Lord Mayor; and the Church 'by some fit person well learned in Divinity' to be appointed by the Archbishop of Canterbury.

49 Letters from the Privy Council to the Archbishop of Canterbury, the Lord Mayor of London and the Master of the Revels concerning the licensing of stage plays before performance, 12 November 1589

The letters to the Lord Mayor and Master of the Revels are known only from the minute in which the Privy Council directed a clerk to prepare the letter. The letter to the Archbishop has been similarly known, but the original letter has come to light and was sold at Sotheby's in 1996 to an anonymous buyer. Sotheby's reproduced the letter in their catalogue for the sale, 'English Literature and History, London, 16 and 17 December 1996', p. 34. The minutes about the letters to the Lord Mayor and Master of the Revels are at the PRO, PC2/16, pp. 388–9, and are transcribed in *APC*, xviii (1589–90), 214–16

(i) (The letter to the Archbishop)
Whereas there hath grown some inconvenience by the common plays and interludes played and exercised in and about the City of London, in that the players do take upon them to handle in their plays certain matters of Divinity and of State unfit to be suffered, for redress whereof we have thought good to appoint some persons of judgement and understanding to view and examine their plays before they be permitted to present them publicly. And because it is most proper to your lordship and those that are of the Commission Ecclesiastical to have the censuring of such matters as are of Divinity, we think it meet, and so desire your lordship, that some fit person well learned in Divinity be appointed by you to join with the Master of the Revels and one other to be nominated by the Lord Mayor, and they jointly and with some speed to view and consider of such comedies or tragedies as are and shall be publicly played by the companies of players in and about the City of London, and they to give their allowance of such as they shall think

Elizabeth I, 1558–1603

meet to be played and to forbid the rest, which we desire to be done with some speed, and so bid your lordship right heartily farewell. From the court at Richmond, the 12th of November 1589.[1]

(ii) A letter to the Lord Mayor of London that whereas their Lordships have already signified unto him to appoint a sufficient person learned and of judgement for the City of London to join with the Master of the Revels and with a divine to be nominated by the Lord Archbishop of Canterbury for the reforming of the plays daily exercised and presented publicly in and about the City of London wherein the players take upon them, without judgement or decorum, to handle matters of Divinity and State; he is required, if he have not as yet made choice of such a person, that he will do so forthwith, and thereof give knowledge to the Lord Archbishop and the Master of the Revels that they may all meet accordingly.

(iii) A letter to the Master of the Revels requiring him [to join] with two others, the one to be appointed by the Lord Archbishop of Canterbury and the other by the Lord Mayor of London, to be men of learning and judgement, and to call before them the several companies of players (whose servants soever they be) and to require them by the authority hereof to deliver unto them their books that they may consider of the matters of their comedies and tragedies, and thereupon to strike out or reform such parts and matters as they shall find unfit and undecent to be handled in plays, both for Divinity and State, commanding the said companies of players, in Her Majesty's name, that they forbear to present and play publicly any comedy or tragedy other than such as they three shall have seen and allowed: which, if they shall not observe, they shall then know from their Lordships that they shall be not only severely punished, but made [in]capable of the exercise of their profession forever hereafter.

The wording of this final sentence is so threatening and explicit that, once recorded in the minutes for future reference, it was likely to be carried into effect if ever any play or plays resembling in their subject matter those which had brought the Licensing Commission into existence were to be presented in a London playhouse. This goes far towards explaining the action taken by the Council eight years later following performances of *The Isle of Dogs* at the Swan (see 55 and 56).

[1] I owe the transcription of this letter to Professor Berry, who also drew my attention to the notice of its retrieval as first given in the Sotheby sale catalogue cited on p. 94 above.

However, through the next two years the Commission appears to have operated satisfactorily; but by the spring of 1592 differences of opinion among its members had become so acute that Guildhall decided to approach the Archbishop of Canterbury and seek his support in an attempt to buy out the Master of the Revels. The method proposed was to try to raise a levy from the twelve great livery companies in the City from which to purchase an annuity for Tilney large enough to persuade him to drop out from the triumvirate.

After a lengthy preamble embracing the usual complaints about (a) the corruption of youth, (b) absenteeism in working hours, and (c) the profanation of religion, the Lord Mayor invites Archbishop Whitgift's assistance.

50 The Lord Mayor of London to John Whitgift, Archbishop of Canterbury, 25 February 1592

CLRO, Remembrancia, I, 635. Transcribed in MSC, I.i.68, and in *ES*, IV, 307–8

In consideration whereof we most humbly beseech your Grace for your godly care for the reforming of so great abuses tending to the offence of Almighty God, the profanation and slander of his true religion, & the corrupting of our youth, which are the seed of the Church of God and the commonwealth among us, to vouchsafe us your good favour and help for the reforming and banishing of so great evil out of this City, which ourselves of long time – though to small purpose – have so earnestly desired and endeavoured by all means that possibly we could . . .

He then reaches the heart of the matter which is that so long as Tilney, claiming the authority of his Patent of 1581, is allowed to safeguard the Court's protectionist policy towards public performances of plays in and around London in its own autocratic interests, nothing can or will be done to change this situation.

And because we understand that the Queen's Majesty is and must be served at certain times by this sort of people, for which purpose she hath granted her Letters Patent to Mr Tilney, Master of her Revels, by virtue whereof he being authorised to reform, exercise or suppress all manner of players, plays and playing houses whatsoever, did first license the said playing houses within this City for Her Majesty's said service, which before that time lay open to all the Statutes for the punishing of these and such like disorders.[1] We are most humbly and earnestly to beseech your Grace to call unto you the said Master of Her Majesty's Revels, with whom also we have conferred of late to that purpose, and to treat with him, if by any means it may be devised,[2] that Her Majesty may be served with these recreations as hath been accustomed (which in our opinions may easily be done by the private exercise of Her Majesty's own players in convenient place),[3] and the City freed from these continual disorders which thereby do grow and increase daily among us . . .

The letter concludes in the same pietistic vein as it began and ends with a special plea in the name of

the preachers and ministers of the Word of God about this City, who have long time and yet do make their earnest, continual complaint unto us for the redress hereof.

The plan was approved by Whitgift, almost by return of post, as is evident from a second letter sent to him by the Lord Mayor,[4] telling him that practical steps are being taken by

Guildhall to secure and expedite 'the consideration to be made to Mr Tilney' to abandon his claims to license plays and players in and around London.

[1] By 'lay open to all the Statutes', he means leaving Guildhall and the clergy free to interpret their application in London as they wished. The inference is that they could do so again if Tilney's hated Patent could be short-circuited.
[2] That 'any means' includes financial remuneration is clear from the subsequent correspondence (see 51 and 52a and b). The reason for this was to compensate him for any loss of fees from licences issued under his Patent of 1581.
[3] i.e. in the Revels Office itself, or in noblemen's private houses, or in rooms in one of the royal palaces: anywhere, in other words, other than in public playhouses in London. He also seems to be suggesting that the number of companies called to Court could thus be reduced to one.
[4] Whitgift's reply is no longer extant.

51 The Lord Mayor writes to the Archbishop of Canterbury thanking him for his support and suggested plan of action, 6 March 1592

CLRO, Remembrancia, I, 646. Transcribed in MSC, I.i.70, and in ES, IV, 308–9

I received your Grace's letter, wherein I understood the contents of the same, and imparted the same presently to my Brethren the Aldermen in our Common Assembly: who, together with myself yield unto your Grace our most humble thanks for your good favour and godly care over us in vouchsafing us your help for the removing of this great inconvenience which groweth to this City by plays and players.

As touching the consideration to be made to Mr Tilney and other capitulations that are to pass betwixt us for the better effecting and continuance of this restraint of the said plays in and about this City, we have appointed certain of our Brethren the Aldermen to confer with him forthwith, purposing to acquaint your Grace with our Agreement and whole proceeding herein as occasion shall require.[1]

On 18 March the Lord Mayor himself and the Master of the Grocer's Company, William Horne, were commissioned to negotiate with Tilney.[2] No record survives of this meeting or of Tilney's response to it; but by 22 March the whole scheme had already collapsed in the light of the reply given to the Lord Mayor by the Master of the Merchant Taylor's Company (the wealthiest in the City) to his request to raise money towards the provision of an annuity for the Master of the Revels to compensate him for the loss of the fee income, under his Patent, that he had been receiving from the issue of licences to acting companies and playhouse owners for the past eight years.

[1] I have capitalised the word 'Agreement' since here it can only mean a negotiated settlement, drawn up on the lines suggested by the Court of Common Council as a discussion document to be presented to Tilney.
[2] CLRO, Repertory XX, fo. 345. Transcribed in ES, IV, 309.

Prior to the meeting between Tilney and the City's representatives, the Lord Mayor had written to the masters of the livery companies about the proposed annuity. Evidence of receipt survives from two companies' records: the Mercers' and the Merchant Taylors.

52 (a) Minute from the Acts of the Mercers Company of London dated 17 March 1592

Mercer's Co., Acts (of the Court of Assistants) III, 470b. Transcribed in MSC, III.166

At this Court the Precept directed to this Company for their contribution to Mr Tilney, Master of the Revels, for the putting down of plays was read; and for divers good causes and forcible reasons there alleged, it is not thought good to allow anything yearly unto him. Nevertheless, this matter is further referred till the Company may see what other Companies will do herein; and then this Company to conclude as they shall see cause.

The Guild Court Book of the Merchant Taylors Company provides a similar answer.

(b) Extract from the minutes of the Merchant Taylors

Court Books, III, fo. 244b. Transcribed in full in C.M. Clode, *Early History of the Guild of Merchant Taylors* (London, 1888), 236–7, and in MSC, III.166–7. Also cited from Clode in *ES*, I, 296 and IV, 309

Upon consideration of which Precept, albeit the Company think it a very good service to be performed, yet weighing the damage of the precedent and innovation of raising Annuities upon the Companies of London – what further occasions it may be drawn unto, together with their great charge otherwise which this troublesome time hath brought, and is likely to bring – they think this no fit course to remedy this mischief, but wish some other way were taken in hand to expel out of our City so general a contagion of manners and other inconveniences; wherein, if any endeavour or travail of this Company might further the matter, they would be ready to use their service therein. And this to be certified as the complete answer if it shall appear by conference with other Companies that the process requireth necessarily a return of the complete Certificate and answer in this behalf.

Since nothing more is heard of the matter either from the companies or the Lord Mayor or the Archbishop, it has to be presumed that the scheme foundered and that Tilney came out of the affair with his powers over the theatre in London greatly enhanced. By 1597, however, Guildhall had become so exasperated that the Lord Mayor again took it upon himself to challenge Tilney's authority. By then, moreover, the conduct of playwrights, actors and theatre managers (or owners) was causing sufficient alarm for both the Privy Council and Parliament to intervene by imposing punitive measures on all three between July 1597 and March 1598, and by introducing new, regulatory controls which changed the status quo and greatly strengthened the Court's authority over the stage in London and the provinces during the last five years of Elizabeth I's reign.

Punitive action against plays, players and playhouse owners, July 1597 to March 1598

On 28 July 1597 the Lord Mayor sent a long letter to the Privy Council recapitulating Guildhall's exasperation with the recurrent disorders and abuses attributed to players and playhouses: this concluded with a useful, tabulated summary of its principal grievances. On the same day, the Council issued its own orders banning all performances for the next three months and, more surprisingly, demanding that all purpose-built playhouses be demolished forthwith.

We possess no clue to help us decide in which order these two letters were written: it is thus impossible for us to determine whether the Privy Council's orders to the justices of Middlesex and Surrey represent a direct response to the Lord Mayor's appeal, or whether they were issued independently on the strength of information received earlier from private informants (see p. 101 below).

53 The Court of Common Council at Guildhall writes to the Privy Council asking that plays in and about London be forbidden both instantly and for ever, 28 July 1597

CLRO, Remembrancia, II, 171. Transcribed in MSC, I.i.78, and in ES, IV, 321–2

We have signified to your Honours many times heretofore the great inconvenience which we find to grow by the common exercise of Stage Plays . . .

For avoiding whereof we are now again most humble and earnest suitors to your Honours to direct your letters as well to ourselves as to the Justices of Peace of Surrey and Middlesex for the present stay, and final suppressing, of the said Stage Plays, as well at the Theatre, Curtain and Bankside as in all other places in and about the City. Whereby we doubt not but, the opportunity and the very cause of many disorders being taken away, we shall be more able to keep the worse sort of such evil and disordered people in better order than heretofore we have been.

Then follows the tabulated list of 'The inconveniences that grow by Stage Plays about the City of London'. Heading the list is the perennial charge of immorality.

(1) They are a special cause of corrupting their youth, containing nothing but unchaste matters, lascivious devices, shifts of cozenage [*i.e.* deceit and trickery], and other lewd and ungodly practices; being so as that they impress the very quality and corruption of manners which they represent, contrary to the rules and art prescribed for the making of Comedies, even among the Heathen, who used them seldom and at certain set times, and not all the year long as our manner is. Whereby, such as frequent them, being of the base and refuse sort of people, or such young gentlemen as have small regard of credit or conscience, draw the same into imitation, and not to the avoiding the like vices which they represent.

Next come crime and immorality.

(2) They [*i.e.* playhouses] are the ordinary places for vagrant persons, masterless men, thieves, horse stealers, whoremongers, cozeners, coney-catchers, contrivers of treason, and other idle and dangerous persons to meet together and to make their matches, to the great displeasure of Almighty God and the

hurt and annoyance of Her Majesty's people, which cannot be prevented nor discovered by the Governors of the City for that they are out of the City's jurisdiction.

Thirdly, absenteeism from work and worship:

(3) They maintain idleness in such persons as have no vocation, and draw apprentices and other servants from their ordinary works and all sorts of people from the resort unto sermons and other Christian exercises, to the great hindrance of trades and prophanation of religion established by Her Highness within this Realm.

The last complaint, as might be expected, relates to the spread of plague:

(4) In the time of sickness it is found by experience that many, having sores, and yet not heart-sick, take occasion hereby to walk abroad and to recreate themselves by hearing a play; whereby others are infected, and themselves also many things miscarry.

54 The Privy Council orders the magistrates in Middlesex and Surrey to forbid performances for the next three months and, in the meantime, to effect the demolition of the playhouses within their jurisdiction, 28 July 1597

PRO, PC2/22/327. Transcribed in *APC*, xxvii (1597), 313–14, and in *ES*, iv, 322–3

(i) A letter to Robert Wrothe, William Fleetwood, John Barne, Thomas Fowler and Richard Skevington, Esquires, and the rest of the Justices of Middlesex nearest to London.

Her Majesty being informed that there are very great disorders committed in the common playhouses, both by lewd matters that are handled on the stages and by resort and confluence of bad people, hath given direction that not only no plays shall be used within London or about the City, or in any public place during this time of summer, but that also those playhouses that are erected and built only for such purposes shall be plucked down – namely the Curtain and the Theatre near to Shoreditch, or any other within that County.

These are therefore in Her Majesty's name to charge and command you that you take present order there be no more plays used in any public place within three miles of the City until All Hallowtide next; and likewise that you do send for the owners of the Curtain, Theatre or any other common playhouse and enjoin them by virtue hereof forthwith to pluck down quite the stages, galleries and rooms that are made for people to stand in, and so to deface the same as they may not be employed again to such use; which, if they shall not speedily perform, you shall

advertize us, that Order may be taken to see the same done according to Her Majesty's pleasure and commandment. And hereof praying you not to fail, we, etc
...

(ii) The like to Mr Bowier, William Gardiner, and Bartholomew Scott, Esquires, and the rest of the Justices of Surrey, requiring them to take the like Order for the playhouses in the Bankside, in Southwark or elsewhere in the said County within three miles of London.

Here it must be noted that while all three of the preceding orders *may* have been issued in the routine course of concluding City and government business before the start of the August vacation, they can as easily, in the light of document 55 and the entries in *Henslowe's Diary* cited below, be construed as retaliatory responses to an offensive play then being performed by the Earl of Pembroke's Men at the Swan Theatre: *The Isle of Dogs*.

On 6 August Philip Henslowe recorded in his diary that he had bound Richard Jones, a member of the Earl of Pembroke's Men, to join the Lord Admiral's company at the Rose; and that he had also paid Jones a similar sum (2d in each case) to secure the services of another of Pembroke's men, Robert Shaa.[1] On 10 August he made a similar entry respecting William Borne: to this he adds two highly significant phrases. Firstly that he 'came and offered himself to come and play with my Lord Admiral's Men at my house called by the name of the Rose'; and secondly, 'beginning immediately after this Restraint is recalled by the Lords of the Council, which Restraint is by the means of playing *The Isle of Dogs*'.[2] That it was, indeed, performances of this play that had provoked the Privy Council into issuing its orders to the magistrates of Middlesex and Surrey on 28 July (24b) is confirmed by the survival of two further documents. The first is a letter from the Privy Council's chief spy-catcher and inquisitor, Richard Topcliffe, to its secretary, Sir Robert Cecil: the second is a letter from the Council itself to the magistrates in Surrey.

Topcliffe's letter is dated 10 August and concludes by recommending to Sir Robert an unnamed person (probably the bearer of the letter) as, 'the first man that discovered to me that seditious play called *The Isle of Dogs*'.[3] From this letter we can thus be sure that action against the offending actors and play-makers had already been taken before 10 August: and Henslowe's memoranda cited above narrow down the actual date still further to within the week of 29 July at earliest to 5 August at latest.[4] That this action, however, had miscarried in its intentions is revealed in the Privy Council's second letter to the Surrey magistrates (including Richard Topcliffe) sent on 15 August, which indicates that Ben Jonson, a co-author of the play, and several of Pembroke's Men were already in prison.

[1] Dulwich, MS i, fo. 232b; reproduced in *Henslowe's Diary*, 239–40. See also 55.
[2] *Henslowe's Diary*, 240.
[3] Hatfield House, Cecil Papers, MS vii, 343. Reproduced in *ES*, iii, 455. See also *EES* ii(2), 11f., and Ingram 'The Isle of Dogs', *A London Life in the Brazen Age*, 167–86, 313–14.
[4] The Rose was still open for a performance of *The Witch of Islington* on 28 July (*Henslowe's Diary*, 58 (fo. 27v)): Richard Jones was seeking employment there by 6 August.

55 The Privy Council orders the arrest of the other members of the company and the other co-author, Thomas Nashe, for interrogation, 15 August 1597

PRO, PC2/22, p. 346. Transcribed in *APC*, xxvii (1597), 338, and in *ES*, iv, 323; *EES*,ii(2), 10; and *Government Regulation*, 97

Upon information given us of a lewd play that was played in one of the playhouses on the Bankside, containing very seditious and slanderous matter, we caused some of the players to be apprehended and committed to prison, whereof one of them was not only an actor but a maker of part of the said play. [*That was Ben Jonson.*]

For as much as it is thought meet that the rest of the players or actors in that matter shall be apprehended to receive such punishment as their lewd and mutinous behaviour doth deserve, these shall be therefore to require you to examine those of the players that are committed, whose names are known to you, Mr Topcliffe, what is become of the rest of their fellows that either had their parts in the devising of that seditious matter, or that were actors or players in the same; what copies they have given forth of the said play and to whom; and such other points as you shall think meet to be demanded of them, wherein you shall require them to deal truly as they will look to receive any favour.[1]

We pray you also to peruse such papers as were found in Nashe his lodgings which Ferrys, a Messenger of the Chamber, shall deliver unto you, and to certify us the examinations you take . . .

[1] The phrases 'to receive such punishment as their lewd and mutinous behaviour doth deserve' and 'as they will look to receive any favour' point directly back to the Council's minute of 12 November 1589, which spells out what form that punishment will take. (See **49**)

Despite the terminal date of 1 November placed on the Council's original restraint of 28 July, it was relaxed nearly a month earlier: on 8 October the Council ordered the release of Ben Jonson, Robert Shaa (or Shaw) and Gabriel Spencer from prison, and Henslowe recorded in his diary that on 'The 11th of October began my Lord Admiral's and my Lord of Pembroke's men to play at my house, 1597'. He so describes the company until the end of November, when he reverts to describing it simply as the Lord Admiral's.[1] And there the matter seems to have ended as far as the Privy Council was concerned. That, however, was not to be the case for the actors since Henslowe had only offered contracts to the leading members of the company. These fortunate few then found themselves sued by the owner of the Swan playhouse, Francis Langley, for breaking the contracts they had signed with him.[2] What Langley appears to have overlooked on reopening the Swan in November and taking this action is that where the Rose was relicensed to open in October, the Swan was not: moreover, while the rest of Pembroke's company, on being released from prison were able to reform in the Earl's name as a touring company in the provinces, they were never licensed again to perform in London.[3]

While, therefore, we possess sufficient documentary evidence to reconstruct with a fair claim to accuracy the sequence of events that followed directly from the performances of

The Isle of Dogs at the Swan in July 1597, no such certainty can be attached to the cause and purposes of the Privy Council's orders issued at that time to the magistrates of Middlesex and Surrey to demolish all purpose-built playhouses standing on land within their jurisdiction.

[1] *Henslowe's Diary*, 71–3 (fos. 35v–36v).
[2] See ch. **157** and **355**, below: also *ES*, II, 132–3.
[3] See *ES*, II, 133–4.

Efforts to reach an acceptable compromise, 1599 to 1603

What is certain is that work had begun on the demolition of the Theatre by 28 December 1598, and had been completed by 20 January 1599; but this was because the Lord Chamberlain's company had by then despaired of securing a renewal of their lease. No attempt was made to pluck down or deface any of the other playhouses, even the Swan. What is surprising is the confidence displayed by Philip Henslowe within a matter of days of the issue of the Privy Council's orders that the Rose would reopen in the autumn, and which allowed him to engage the leading members of Pembroke's disgraced company to appear there as members of the Lord Admiral's company.

By February, 1598, however, it becomes a little clearer that the rash behaviour of Pembroke's men at the Swan in July 1597 may have rudely interrupted a series of very delicate negotiations already in progress between the Queen, her Council and the principal, licensed acting companies relating to the future of the theatre in London; and that this caused the Council to reveal its hand much earlier than it had planned to do. Here the ground shifts from documented fact to hypothesis derived from documents.

The first of these is the wholesale revision of the existing Statute governing the Punishment of Rogues and Vagabonds which received the Royal Assent on 9 February 1598, and which must thus have been ready to lay before Parliament by November 1597 at latest. This abolished all earlier versions and imposed much harsher penalties on anyone found guilty of disobeying the new one.[1] Acting companies must in future, if they sought to travel as professional players, produce their master's warrant to do so under his hand and seal: and the right previously accorded to mayors and county magistrates to license them to travel was withdrawn.

The second such document is an order from the Privy Council addressed directly to the Master of the Revels which was issued a day after the new Act governing Punishment of Rogues and Vagabonds had reached the Statute Book (**56**). This reveals that agreement had been reached at some earlier date – certainly prior to the Christmas festivities of 1597/8 – for two adult companies only to provide the Court with plays: the Lord Chamberlain's and the Lord Admiral's. Tilney is reminded of this in the context of information recently received that a third company is reported to be claiming the same official authorisation to prepare productions for the forthcoming Shrovetide festivities. He is then instructed to suppress this impertinent company forthwith.

[1] Statutes, iv.973, 43 Eliz. c. 9. Reproduced in *ES*, IV, 324–5. For the Statute of 1572 to which these revisions were made, see **29**.

56 The Privy Council to the Master of the Revels, 19 February 1598, with copies to the magistrates in Middlesex and Surrey

PRO, PC2/23, p. 181. Transcribed in *APC*, xxviii (1597–8), 327, and in *ES*, iv, 325

Whereas licence hath been granted unto two companies of stage players retained unto us, the Lord Admiral and Lord Chamberlain, to use and practise stage plays, whereby they might be the better enabled and prepared to show such plays before Her Majesty as they shall be required at times meet and accustomed, to which end they have been chiefly licensed and tolerated as aforesaid; and whereas there is also a third company who of late (as we are informed) have by way of intrusion used likewise to play, having neither prepared any play for Her Majesty nor are bound to you, the Master of the Revels, for performing such orders as have been prescribed and are enjoined to be observed by the other two companies before mentioned. We have therefore thought good to require you upon receipt hereof to take order that the aforesaid third company may be suppressed, and none suffered hereafter to play but those two formerly named belonging to us, the Lord Admiral and Lord Chamberlain, unless you shall receive other direction from us.

Given the entire sequence of events as documented above between July 1597 and February 1598 – a mere six months – it becomes difficult to suppose that the Privy Council was not already in the process of negotiating such a settlement with the Lord Chamberlain and the Lord Admiral (with the probable agreement of the Archbishop of Canterbury, and apparently that of the Lord Mayor) in the early summer of 1597 and thus shortly before the arrival in London of ambassadors from the Emperor of Russia and the King of Poland. The lampooning of one or more of these distinguished guests of the Court on the stage of a public playhouse in *The Isle of Dogs* would demand instant punitive action.[1] If this, or some equally grave offence occurred while these private and confidential negotiations towards a final resolution to London's theatrical problems were in progress, that alone would explain why this punitive action was as draconian as the wording of the Privy Council's instructions of 28 July 1597 unquestionably was in requiring the immediate demolition and defacement of all playhouses in and about London together with the arrest and imprisonment of the offending play-makers and players. With this threat to deny all actors the right to earn a living by performing plays in London hanging over their heads for the next three months at least, a breathing space could be gained before discussions were resumed after the departure of the offended foreign dignitaries and after the playhouse owners and acting companies had learned that, in future, they must either accept the Court as their master or forfeit the right to work in their chosen profession. With an example already made of Francis Langley and the Earl of Pembroke's men at the Swan, theatrical life then resumed its normal pattern at the start of the autumn season with one playhouse closed (if not yet demolished) and one company disbanded and banished. Against that background, discussions resumed with the results already cited and spelt out clearly in the Council's instructions to the Master of the Revels of 10 February 1598 (56).

With Lent approaching, the Council thus had good reason to suppose that it had recovered full control over plays and players in London. Yet two days before it ended two businessmen in the City thought it worth their while to enter into a contract to refurbish the Boar's Head inn without Aldgate to serve as a playhouse on an experimental basis. Thus when Oliver Woodliffe and Richard Samwell signed this agreement on 13 April, it may well have been on the assumption that the homeless 'third company' would need it if these actors wished to renew their abortive bid to establish themselves as a licensed company in time for the start of the autumn of 1599.[2] By then the Theatre had been demolished; the Swan lay empty and unlicensed as, seemingly, did the Curtain. This gamble paid off; for between October 1598 and February 1599 an unnamed company of actors played at the Boars Head without any recorded interference from either Whitehall or Guildhall. This proved to have been profitable enough for Woodliffe and Samwell to invest much larger sums of money in the building of a more elaborate playhouse to eclipse the antiquated Curtain. To assist them in this enterprise, they enlisted the support of an experienced actor-manager, Robert Browne. Browne had gained this experience both with the Earl of Worcester's and the Lord Admiral's men, and had toured extensively in Germany. By the autumn of 1599 he was the leader of the Earl of Derby's company and was aspiring, on his master's behalf, to bring that company to Court. To this end, the earl's wife was prevailed upon to write to her uncle, Lord Burghley, asking him to use his influence to bring this dream to fruition. The earl, like the Earl of Oxford, was himself a play-maker.

[1] See *ES*, III, 454–5.
[2] See 369 below.

57 Elizabeth, Countess of Derby, writes to Robert Cecil, Lord Burghley, asking him to add Robert Browne and his fellow-actors to the two companies presently allowed to perform in London, (?) summer 1599[1]

Hatfield House, Cecil Papers, 186/24. Transcribed in HMC, Salisbury, MS XIII, 609, and in Berry, *The Boar's Head Playhouse*, 34: see also *ES*, II, 127, and *MSC*, II.2.147–8

Good uncle: Being importuned by my Lord to entreat your favour that his man Browne, with his company, may not be barred from their accustomed playing, in maintenance whereof they have consumed the better part of their substance. If so vain a matter shall not seem troublesome to you, I could desire that your furtherance might be a mean to uphold them, for that my Lord, taking delight in them, it will keep him from more prodigal courses.

[1] The earl was not a member of the Privy Council: Lord Burghley was. The company was called to Court in February 1600, and would have to have prepared itself in London before then. The letter is undated, but is thus likely to have been written in the late summer of 1599.

Nepotism and collusion within the Privy Council thus secured both the presence of Browne's company in London through the autumn season with impunity, and Woodliffe and Samwell in their joint investment in the Boar's Head playhouse. This collaborative enterprise culminated in an invitation to perform at Court during the following Shrovetide festivities on 3 and 5 February 1600. These performances were well enough received to warrant recalling the company to Court the following Christmas (1 and 6 January 1601).[1]

For that to happen, the Master of the Revels must have licensed both the company and the playhouse throughout that year.

Naturally enough this success fuelled expectations among City entrepreneurs that they could safely copy this example. It was within this climate of opinion that Philip Henslowe and Edward Alleyn decided to quit the Rose on Bankside (where they were meeting fierce competition from the recently established Lord Chamberlain's men at the Globe) and erect a new playhouse in Middlesex to replace it. Having taken good care to keep the Privy Council informed of their intentions and to secure the goodwill of the churchwardens in Finsbury,[2] they succeeded in this objective; but even with the active help of their patron, the Earl of Nottingham, it took a full year of patient negotiation before they could make their move to the new Fortune playhouse in the autumn of 1600.[3]

Other City speculators with similar ambitions were, however, to be disappointed. One such was John Wolf, a stationer who in April 1600 found himself required by the Middlesex magistrates to hand over a bond of £40 for starting to

build a Playhouse in Nightingale Lane near East Smithfield ... contrary to Her Majesty's Proclamation and Orders set down in Her Highness's Court of Star Chamber.[4]

Since nothing more is heard of this project, it is to be presumed that he abandoned it and that his bond was treated as null and void.

That Wolf was not the only one to be copying Woodliffe's and Samwell's example, however, becomes evident three months later when the Privy Council felt sufficiently provoked or alarmed to issue further Orders to clarify the situation and to 'restrain the excessive number of Playhouses and the immoderate use of stage plays in and about the City'.

[1] PRO (Pipe Office), 1599/1600, fo. 57a, and 1600/1, fo. 69b. In MSC, VI.31 and 32; also *ES*, IV, 112 and 113.
[2] See **418**; also *ES*, IV, 327–8.
[3] See **419**; also *ES*, II, 435–43.
[4] J.C. Jeaffreson, *Middlesex County Records*, I, 260, citing an abstract entry in Roll of the General Sessions of the Peace for Middlesex. Transcribed in *ES*, IV, 327.

58 Extracts from Orders of the Privy Council to regulate performances of plays in public playhouses in London, 22 June 1600

PRO, PC2/25, pp. 233–4. Transcribed in *APC*, xxx (1599–1600), 395; CLRO, Remembrancia, II, 188; MSC, I.i.80–3. See also *ES*, IV, 329–31

These orders start by restating the position arrived at in the Council's instructions to the Master of the Revels and the county magistrates of 19 February 1598 (see **56**), authorising the existence of two playhouses, but then proceed to amplify them in several important respects.

First, that there shall be about the City two houses and no more allowed to serve for the use of the common stage plays, of the which houses one shall be in Surrey in that place which is commonly called the Bankside or thereabouts, and the other in Middlesex.

The latter is then expressly specified as being

the house now in hand to be built by the said Edward Alleyn. [*i.e.* The Fortune]

    This is not to be regarded as an additional playhouse: it is to be allowed on the strict understanding that it will replace the Curtain, which is 'either to be ruined and plucked down, or to be put to some other good use'.
    Strangely, neither the Rose nor the Boar's Head is named in this context since the Lord Admiral's company was still at the Rose in June, and the Boar's Head extensions were finished by then, and the Fortune was about to open.
    The Lord Chamberlain's company is to have a house on Bankside. Having been given the freedom

to make their own choice which they will have of [divers houses that are there], choosing one of them and no more . . .[1]

Having opted for the Globe,

it is ordered that the said house and none other shall be there allowed.

While again neither the Rose nor the Swan is named, the clear inference of the Order is that, like the Curtain in Middlesex, both will be 'ruined and plucked down, or put to some other good use'. The Council then stipulates that these licences are to be conditional upon strict observance of three specific restraints. Firstly, permission to use the Globe excludes all others:

And especially it is forbidden that any stage plays shall be played (as some times they have been) in any Common Inn for public assembly in or near about the City.[2]

    Secondly, forasmuch as these stage plays, by the multitude of houses and company of players have been too frequent, not serving for recreation, but inviting and calling the people daily from their trade and work to mis-spend their time, it is likewise ordered that the two several companies of players assigned unto the two houses allowed [*i.e.* the Fortune and the Globe] may play each of them in their several [*i.e.* respective] house twice a week and no oftener.

The third condition is that,

they shall refrain to play on the Sabbath day, upon pain of imprisonment and further penalty, and that they shall forbear altogether in the time of Lent, and likewise at such time and times as any extraordinary sickness or infection of disease shall appear to be in and about the City.

Copies of these Orders were sent, together with a covering letter, to the county magistrates and the Lord Mayor. This letter concludes with a blunt warning that they will be held no less responsible for the successful implementation of this 'new deal' than the playhouse managers and actors: the time for complaints has passed.

But as we have done our parts in prescribing the Orders, so, unless you perform yours in looking to the due execution of them, we shall lose our labour; and the want of redress must be imputed unto you and others unto whom it appertaineth: and therefore we do hereby authorise and require you to see the said Orders to be put in execution and to be continued, as you do wish the amendment of the aforesaid abuses and will remove the blame for thereof from yourselves.[3]

[1] The Council met twice to consider these regulations and revised the original draft with interpolations incorporating the results of the choices made by these two companies. See *ES*, IV, 329, and 397 below.
[2] There are no records of any London inn still being used for this purpose at this late date. This clause may have been included as a warning to inn- and tavern-keepers as well as to players, or it may have been obliquely aimed at the owners of the Boar's Head. See Berry, *Boar's Head*, 373a; but, by then, it may no longer have been regarded as a 'Common Inn'.
[3] PRO, PC2/22, p. 230. Transcribed in *APC*, XXX (1599–1600), 411, and in *ES*, IV, 331–2.

In the light of this letter and the Orders which accompanied it, it is difficult to understand how Lord Burghley and Edmund Tilney found it possible to admit the presence of the Earl of Derby's company that same autumn at the Boar's Head without any protest from either the Lord Mayor or the Middlesex magistrates. The simplest explanation would be that sufficient sums of money changed hands to secure tolerance for an exception made to humour the Queen: but as we lack any evidence, no firm answer can be given. Suffice it to say that a year later the Lord Mayor and the City magistrates had become incensed enough by this and other 'exceptions' to risk renewing their complaints to the Council. They were rewarded for their pains by tersely worded replies referring them back to the Council's Orders and covering letter of 22 June 1600, and laying the blame for all subsequent infringements of those regulations squarely on their own failure to enforce them efficiently. See 58.

Despite these indignant disclaimers, the Council must have known that the breaches of their regulations complained of were not confined to the presence of the Earl of Derby's men at the Boar's Head. Indeed, on 10 May 1601 the Council had itself written to the Middlesex magistrates to that effect (PRO, PC E351/541–91, transcribed in *APC*, XXXI (1601–2), p. 346, and in *ES* IV, 332).

We do understand that certain players that use to recite their plays at the Curtain in Moorfields do represent upon the stage in their interludes the persons of some gentlemen of good desert and quality that are yet alive under obscure manner, but yet in such sort as all the hearers may take notice both of the matter and the persons that are meant thereby.

Like Pembroke's men and their play-makers at the Swan in 1597, these offending authors and actors are to be arrested, examined and, if found guilty,

to answer their rash and indiscreet dealing before us.

The culprits have never been identified; but if, as has generally been supposed, the Earl of Worcester's company had moved, without licence, into the vacant Rose playhouse with Henslowe's consent,[1] the most likely company to have been occupying the vacant Curtain at this time was that of the Earl of Oxford who, like Derby, was himself a play-maker. This supposition receives some support from the documented facts: by the opening of the autumn season in October 1601, these two companies had merged to join Browne at the Boar's Head, his own company having moved into the provinces; the merged company then appeared at Court under Worcester's name on 3 January 1602.[2]

[1] See *ES*, II, 225 and 409; and **348**, below.
[2] PRO (Pipe Office), 1601/2, m. 83a; CLRO, Remembrancia, II, 189. Transcribed in MSC, I.i.85 and *ES*, IV, 114. See also **382** below.

Thus, by the start of 1602 it was clear that however these earlier breaches of the Council's Orders were viewed and whoever was held to blame for them, the long-running issue of an obstructive third company could no longer be fudged. In the two years since the Privy Council had ordered the Master of the Revels to suppress it in February 1598 (see **56**), the Court had come round to wanting to legitimise a third company to employ at Christmas and Shrovetide. To achieve this, it must select a reliable company and allocate a suburban playhouse for its use. After further correspondence between Whitehall and Guildhall, the Court expressed its wish to do this by authorising the Privy Council to write a conciliatory letter to the Lord Mayor communicating its decision. This letter, dated 31 March 1602, is signed by Lord Burghley, the Earl of Nottingham and the Earl of Worcester and by five others.

59 The Privy Council informs the Lord Mayor of London of its decision to authorise the licensing of a third company of adult actors and to assign the playhouse at the Boar's Head for their use, 31 March 1602

CLRO, Remembrancia, II, 189. Transcribed in MSC, I.i.85–6, and in *ES*, IV, 334–5; also Berry, *Boar's Head*, 56–7

We received your letter signifying some amendment of the abuses or disorders by the immoderate exercise of stage plays in and about the City by means of our late Order renewed for the restraint of them; and withal showing a special inconvenience yet remaining by reason that the servants of our very good Lord, the Earl of Oxford, and of me the Earl of Worcester, being joined by agreement together in one Company (to whom, upon notice of Her Majesty's pleasure, at the suit of the Earl of Oxford, toleration hath been thought meet to be granted, notwithstanding the restraint of our said former Orders), do not tie themselves to one certain place and house, but do change their place at their own disposition, which is as disorderly and offensive as the former offence of many houses.[1]

And as the other Companies that are allowed, namely of me, the Lord Admiral, and the Lord Chamberlain, be appointed their certain houses; and one and no more to each Company; so we do straightly require that this third Company be likewise [appointed] to one place. And because we are informed the house called the Boar's Head is the place they have especially used and do best like of, we do pray and require you that the said house, namely the Boar's Head, may be assigned unto them, and that they be very straightly charged to use and exercise their plays in no other but that house as they will look to have that toleration continued and avoid farther [*sic?* further] displeasure.

This carefully worded concordat brought the long struggle between the City and the Court for control over the stage in and around London to an end. While the Crown had emerged as the victor, the City could at least claim to have succeeded in banishing adult actors and stage plays (if not those presented by children) from central London, and in reducing the number of companies licensed to exercise their skills in the suburbs to three, with each of these restricted to performing in a single licensed playhouse on two afternoons (other than on Sundays and throughout Lent) in any one week. A year later the Queen died.

[1] This phrase vividly illuminates the sort of cat and mouse games being played with the magistrates by companies of touring actors passing through London while at least three vacant and unlicensed playhouses remained standing and inviting use; especially so when a company, to escape the clutches of the Middlesex magistrates, had only to cross the river and begin again in Surrey.

PROVINCIAL LEGISLATION, 1580–1603

Following the suppression of virtually all surviving religious community drama associated with saints' days and the former feast of Corpus Christi during the 1570s (see pp. 64–9 above), and Edmund Tilney's appointment as Master of the Revels under his revised Patent of 1581 (34), Elizabeth I's Privy Council seems rarely to have been troubled by serious breaches of existing legislation governing the conduct of players and their performances in the provinces.

How was this achieved? The answer lies partly in clearer understanding and stricter enforcement by the Lords Lieutenant and Justices of the Peace of what was allowed and what was not under Elizabethan Statutes and Proclamations relating to plays and players, and partly in the annual visitations carried out, if not by themselves then by their chosen representatives, by the archbishops and bishops in every parish in their respective dioceses when enquiries were made whether the church or churchyard had been abused by any entertainers and, if so, by whom. Mayors and town councillors likewise began to adopt a more restrictive stance towards requests from acting companies for the use of guildhalls and other civic buildings under their control.

Only on one occasion have we any evidence that the Privy Council felt obliged to intervene directly on its own initiative.

60 The Privy Council, acting on information received from the High Sheriff of Suffolk, instructs him to forbid the proposed performance of local Whitsun plays at Hadley, 6 May 1597

PRO, PC2/22, p. 228. Transcribed in *APC*, xxvii (1597), 97, and in *ES*, iv, 321

We do understand by your letter of the third of this instant of a purpose in the town of Hadley to make certain stage plays at this time of the Whitsun Holydays next ensuing, and thither to draw a concourse of people out of the country thereabouts, pretending herein the benefit of the town, which purpose we do utterly mislike, doubting what inconveniences may follow thereon, especially at this time of scarcity, when disordered people of the common sort will be apt to misdemean themselves. We do therefore require you straightly to prohibit the officers and all others in the town of Hadley not [sic] to go forward with the said plays, and to cause the stage prepared for them to be plucked down, letting them know that they are to obey this our Order as they will answer it at their peril. We thank you for the care you take to keep the country in good order.

Records also survive of two appeals from provincial dignitaries for help from the Privy Council to deal with local problems created by actors which, under existing legislation, they felt unable to handle themselves. The first of these was received from the Bishop of Chester in 1590.

In Cheshire and Lancashire an influential group of Puritan preachers and local residents who were all strict Sabbatarians had campaigned tirelessly throughout most of the previous decade to prohibit all forms of entertainment at any time and anywhere on Sundays, ranging from performances of plays to the simplest provision of music in ale-houses. They attributed the failure of this campaign principally to the landed gentry in those two counties, from among whose ranks most of the local magistrates and justices were recruited and appointed, and to their laxity or indifference on the Bench when offenders were brought before them. Their cause thus resembles that of the Lord Mayor of London when complaining to the Privy Council about the repeated failure of magistrates in Surrey and Middlesex to arrest and punish playhouse owners and actors for flouting restraints and injunctions against performances on Sundays, in Lent, and in time of plague in suburban areas adjacent to the city.

61 Memorandum submitted to the Privy Council by the Bishop of Chester summarising the report received by him from the Lancashire Preachers, *c.* October/November 1590

PRO, SP 12/235, fo. 146. Reproduced in REED, *Lancashire*, 227[1]

The Lord's Day is generally profaned, with unlawful trades and markets; with heathenish and popish pastimes; some tending to the nourishing of idolatrous superstition; other some to the increase of whoredom and drunkenness. All purposely maintained and countenanced by the Gentry and better sort, for the hindrance and defacing of the religious and holy exercises of the Sabbath.

[1] For earlier documents leading up to this report, including a letter from Edward Fleetwood, Rector of Wigan, to Lord Burghley of approximately the same date, see REED, *Lancashire*, 6–10, 214 and 219–26.

After a delay of eighteen months the Privy Council finally responded to this report by issuing instructions to the Earl of Derby in his capacity as Lord Lieutenant of the Counties and Chancellor of the Duchy of Lancaster.

62 A letter from the Privy Council to the Earl of Derby asking him to instruct all local magistrates to forbid entertainments and sports of all kinds during times of Divine Service and to send all persistent offenders to London to answer the charges against them in the Council's presence, Greenwich, 23 June 1592

PRO, PC 2/19, p. 14. Transcribed in REED, *Lancashire*, 228, and in *ES*, IV, 311

Whereas we are informed that there are certain May Games, Morris Dances, Plays, Bear-baitings, Ales and other like pastimes used ordinarily in those Counties under your Lordship's lieutenancy on the Sundays and Holydays at the time of Divine Service, and other godly exercises, to the disturbance of the service and bad example that those kind of pastimes should be used in such sort and at such time when men do assemble together for the hearing of God's Word and to join in Common Prayers, which sports are most ordinarily used at those undue seasons by such as are evil affected in religion purposely by those means to draw the people from the service of God and to disturb the same.

These shall be therefore to pray your Lordship, by virtue hereof, to give knowledge not only to the Bishop of that diocese of this common and unsufferable disorder, but to give special direction to all the Justices in their several divisions by all means to forbid and not to suffer these or the like pastimes to be in any place whatsoever on the Sunday or Holyday at the time of Divine Service.

And if, notwithstanding this straight prohibition and special Order taken, any shall presume to use the said sports or pastimes in the time [of] service, sermons, or other Godly exercises, you shall cause the favourers, maintainers, or chief offenders to be sent up hither to answer this their contentions [*sic?* contentious] and lewd behaviour before us.

Thus, while the Council carefully refrains from prohibiting all games and pastimes on Sundays outside of periods set aside for services and sermons, it does authorise the Earl and his officers to arrest 'favourers, maintainers or chief offenders' and send them to London 'to answer this their contentions and lewd behaviour' before the Council – a phrase which can readily be stretched to embrace Catholic recusants, presumptuous squires and other sympathisers who collude with the culprits by protecting them.

The next occasion on which the Council was approached for assistance followed a year later, this time from Cambridge, as an immediate sequel to the grim epidemic of plague which struck London in August 1592, and was to last until April 1594 (see pp. 83–5 above). Banned by official restraints from performing in London, the actors had no option but to tour the provinces. Some of them set up their flags in small towns in the immediate vicinity of Cambridge and advertised forthcoming performances in the city to attract students in the colleges to come and see them. Heads of colleges, on finding themselves no more able to prevent their students from quitting their lecture rooms to flock to these performances than were the Puritan preachers in London and elsewhere from preferring plays to sermons, prevailed upon the Vice-Chancellor to support efforts to restore discipline. He responded by writing first to the constables of the village of Chesterton, where the players were in residence, and then to both the Chancellor, Lord Burghley, and the Privy Council.

This correspondence spans some ten months between Michaelmas 1592 and the end of July 1593, and consists of some five letters, all of them long ones. It starts with a Warrant (grounded on orders issued by the Privy Council, c. 1575–6)[1] instructing the constables of Chesterton to stop both the players from performing their plays and local residents from aiding and abetting them. The Vice-Chancellor at that time was Robert Some. This Warrant, together with the subsequent letters that passed between the Vice-Chancellor, the Chancellor and the Privy Council illustrate in remarkable detail the sort of difficulties that must have confronted local authorities throughout the country when attempting to enforce government legislation respecting touring companies of actors.

In Cambridge, the first such difficulty arose from the fact that one of the two constables at Chesterton to whom the Vice-Chancellor had addressed his Warrant was sick: the next was that his deputy proved to be incompetent. The third was that the Vice Chancellor, when drafting his Warrant, had failed to notice that the Privy Council's Orders restraining performances of plays from being given within a five-mile radius of Cambridge (on the authority of which the Warrant was based) were about to expire.[2] This, however, was noticed by the licensing magistrate for Chesterton, Lord North, who proclaimed the Warrant to be invalid, and allowed the players to perform. To make matters worse, he said so in front of the actors and assured them that the Vice Chancellor dare not arrest them.[3]

All of this is revealed in a letter from the Vice-Chancellor to the Chancellor, Lord Burghley, asking him to secure a renewal of the original restraint from the Privy Council. That same day (18 September) he and the heads of colleges sent a supplementary letter addressed directly to the Council. In this they explain the action they have taken and ask for the constables, actors and everyone else who had ignored the Vice-Chancellor's Warrant to be summoned before the Council to answer for their contempt. They do not, however, admit the Council's restraint on which the Warrant was based to have been out of date, nor do they ask for it to be renewed.

[1] A document answering this description is preserved in Cambridge University Archives (Lett. 9A4), dated 30 October 1576: it is printed in REED, *Cambridge*, 1, 276–7.
[2] The most probable expiry date was Michaelmas Day (29 September) 1592. It could thus be argued that the Warrant was already invalid by the time Constable Oliver Reed delivered it to the licensing magistrate, Lord North. See note 1, above.
[3] The leader of the offending troupe of actors was either John or Lawrence Dutton, both of whom were members of the Queen's Company. This may explain why Lord North saw fit to let them perform and to tell them they could do so without risk of being arrested for doing so.

63 Excerpts from a Warrant and two letters from the Vice-Chancellor of Cambridge University, September 1592

(a) The Warrant addressed to Richard Cobb and Oliver Reeve, constables of Chesterton, near Cambridge, Michaelmas Day, 1592

BL, MS Lansdowne 71, Art. 82, fo. 201. Reproduced in MSC, 1.2.197–8, and in REED, *Cambridge*, 1, 339–40

Whereas there be certain persons lately repaired unto the University and Town of Cambridge, having in purpose either there or in some other place near unto, by the showing of certain Interludes, Plays or Tragedies, to procure the assembly of Her Majesty's subjects and people otherwise than in diverse good respects, and especially at this time by reason of danger by infection of sickness is thought convenient, and otherwise than is agreeable with Order therein given by the Lords of Her Majesty's most Honourable Privy Council . . .

These shall be to will and require you, and by virtue of the said Letters, in Her Majesty's name straightly to charge and command you, and either of you, that if at this present, either they, the said persons, be repaired, or any hereafter of like condition (during the time of your being in office) do make their repair unto that Her Majesty's Town to the foresaid end and purpose, with endeavour there to put such their exercises in practice, that immediately thereupon you fail not, by virtue hereof, straightly to inhibit all and every the inhabitants of the said town from the furthering and aiding of them or any of them in that their endeavour. As namely from the suffering of them, or any of them, to take the use of any of their rooms, houses or yards in that town to that end and intent. As also that by virtue hereof you require the said parties so endeavouring not to proceed in the execution of that their purpose there as they will answer the same at their peril . . .

The Warrant concludes with an order to arrest anyone disobeying it in any respect and to bring them to the Vice-Chancellor for questioning. A postscript is appended, noting that

by reason Richard Cobb the Constable was sick, the execution of this business was commited to Oliver Reeve who dealt therein in such sort as appeareth by the supplication unto the Lords of Her Majesty's Honourable Privy Council.

(b) A letter from the Vice-Chancellor and Heads of Colleges to the Chancellor of Cambridge University, Lord Burghley, 18 September 1592

BL, MS Lansdowne 75, Art. 8, fo. 16. Transcribed in full in MSC, 1.2.190–2, and in REED, *Cambridge*, 1, 340–1

We sent a Warrant (grounded upon the Letters of the Lords of Her Majesty's most Honourable Privy Council) to inhibit certain players who were purposed (as we heard) to play at Chesterton. How slightly that Warrant was regarded, as well by the Constables and the inhabitants of Chesterton as by the players themselves (whereof one Dutton is a principal) appeared by their bills set up upon our College gates, and by their playing in Chesterton, notwithstanding our said Warrant to the contrary.

One of the Constables told us that he heard the players say that they were licensed by the Lord North to play in Chesterton. We cannot charge his Lordship otherwise with that particular: but we are able to justify that the Lord North upon like occasion heretofore, being made acquainted with the said Letters of the Lords of the Council, returned answer in writing that those Letters were no perpetuity.[1]

And likewise also in this very action [? occasion], when the players came to him for his Lordship's allowance for their playing in Chesterton, and some of us did tell his Lordship that we had the Lords of the Council's Letters to the contrary, he openly uttered, in the hearing as well of the players as of diverse Knights and Gentlemen of the Shire then present, that the date of those Letters was almost expired. And he said then further to the players that although they should play at Chesterton, yet the Vice-Chancellor durst not commit them therefore.[2]

How well such speeches sound, and what they may work in the heads of the rude multitudes, we leave to your Honour's wisdom to consider: but duty would not suffer us to conceal the same from your Lordship's Knowledge.

With that said, the writers of this letter list the documents supporting their case that they are enclosing with it, and then conclude as follows:

That which we chiefly desire, and very humbly crave (the correction of the contempt reserved to your good Lordship's own honourable wisdom) is, that for the better defence of our ancient Charters, your Lordship would be pleased to procure that those your former honourable Letters by your good Lordship and the rest of the Lords of Her Majesty's most honourable Privy Council may be renewed; whereby the rather the great disorders of Chesterton (which Town hath and doth continually annoy our University) may be met withall, and many occasions of stirs and dangers may be prevented.

This comes as near to an admission that the Vice-Chancellor and his colleagues had allowed the validity of the Council's earlier restraint to expire on or before the date on which they issued their Warrant as they were willing to make.

[1] This probably refers to an incident in September 1580, the correspondence about which is preserved in Cambridge University Archives, Lett. 9 (E.7.6) and reproduced in REED, *Cambridge*, 1, 291–2.
[2] These accusations have the same frustrated ring of righteous indignation about them as the complaints of the Lancashire Preachers levelled at the landed gentry and especially the local Magistrates among them during the 1580s and early 1590s. See 61 and 62.

In the letter they sent to the Privy Council that same day, they approached this question more obliquely.

(c) A letter from the Vice-Chancellor and Heads of Colleges at Cambridge University to the Privy Council, 18 September 1592

BL, MS Lansdowne 71, Art. 83, fos. 202v–3. Transcribed in full in MSC, 1.2.192–5, and in REED, *Cambridge*, 1, 341–3.

That whereas, about seventeen years since, information was given unto your Lordships touching the misdemeanour of divers bad persons which, wandering about the Country under the colour of licences for the making of shows, and playing of Enterludes, and setting forth of other vain games and pastimes, did thereby allure very many of our Scholars from the good course of their studies and usual exercises for the increase of learning; upon which information it pleased your good Lordships to address unto the Vice-Chancellor and Heads of the said University your Honourable Letters, thereby fully authorising and strictly charging them and other Justices of Peace within five miles of Cambridge to repress such disorders . . . Yet so it is . . . that now of late some evil-disposed persons, encouraged (as it may seem) by such as carry no great good affection to the increase of learning, or the peaceable government of this society [*i.e.* Lord North and 'divers Knights and gentlemen of the shire'] notwithstanding they have been made acquainted with the aforesaid Order by your Lordships taken in that behalf, have nevertheless presumed – some slily and by stealth, some boldly and openly – to cross the true meaning of that your honourable commandment.

They end this very long and self-justificatory letter with a plea to the Council to summon everyone guilty of defying their Warrant at Chesterton before the Council,

that by due examination of all persons your Lordships may know the manner of their offence, and so to correct the same as to your honourable wisdoms shall seem convenient.

There is no evidence to support the idea that the Privy Council took any action to follow up this suggestion: indeed, the council only renewed the restraint on performances in and around Cambridge at the end of July 1593, when the same orders were simultaneously issued to the Vice-Chancellor of Oxford University.[1]

[1] PRO, PC2/20, pp. 516–17. Reproduced in REED, *Cambridge*, I, 348–9.

Elsewhere in the kingdom, actors and local magistrates appear to have arrived at a satisfactory *modus vivendi* within the bounds of existing legislation; but some evidence does survive that foreshadows troubles that were to become acute by the end of the Queen's reign.

The first of these was occasioned by the increasing frequency of outbreaks of plague in London and the accompanying restraints on performances in the capital which forced the major acting companies to embark on provincial tours more often, and for longer periods of time, than in earlier years. This in its turn branded actors as likely carriers of infectious disease, thus making them less welcome as guests in large towns, more especially those within a hundred miles of London, where sporadic outbreaks of plague were not uncommon. The governing body of Cambridge University had become convinced by the 1590s that plague would spread through the colleges if public performances of plays by London companies were permitted to take place in or near the town (see 63a).

Further afield, the frequency of requests from touring companies for permission to use civic buildings as playhouses began to interfere so seriously with the normal uses of these buildings for civic and judicial purposes as to suggest a need to ration such requests. No less serious from a civic viewpoint was the rising costs of repairing the damage done to the flooring and fittings of these buildings by actors and audiences alike. As early as 1571–2,

Liverpool had decided to withdraw the use of its town hall from all actors other than those described as 'not deniable' – i.e. liveried companies carrying Letters Patent from a powerful nobleman: and even these companies were only to be licensed to perform in it on paying 5 shillings in advance into a fund to be set up to meet the cost of repairs after the actors' departure.[1]

Actors who presumed upon the status they claimed to be due to them under their Letters Patent to the extent of ignoring local regulations aroused resentment, even among their most loyal admirers and promoters. Such was the case in Coventry where, in November 1600, an entry was placed in the chamberlains' and wardens' account books to the following effect:

Be it had in mind that the Lord Chandos' players were committed to prison for their contempt against Master Mayor, and there remained until they made their submission under their hands as appeareth in the file of Record under their hands to be seen.[2]

[1] See REED, *Lancashire*, 39, citing Town Book 2, LIRO: 352 MIN/COUI 1/2, 17/18 October. A week later, order was taken at another Port Moot to ban the introduction of 'monstrous and strange beasts' into the hall. Others were to follow (see pp. 39–41)
[2] See REED, *Coventry*, 355, citing Wardens' Account Book II, CRO A7(b), p. 329.

In other areas actors had earned an equally unfortunate reputation for being persistent Sabbath breakers and overstaying their welcome, especially in Cheshire and Lancashire as already remarked (see **61** and **62** above). This was taken into account in Canterbury in 1595 when the Burgmote met to discuss restrictions to be imposed on touring companies seeking permission to perform in the town.

64 (a) Rules for the better regulation of acting companies seeking permission to perform in Canterbury, 15 April 1595

Canterbury Cathedral Archives, Burgmote Books, CC.A3, fos. 261b and 262. Transcribed, with some inaccuracies, in *English Dramatic Companies*, II, 233

Also for that to suffer players to play on the Sabbath day is a profanage of the Sabbath and a matter highly displeasing to God; and the continuance of them so long time as commonly hath been used is deemed very inconvenient and hurtful to the state and good quiet of this City and impoverishing thereof, especially the same being so late as usually they have been in the night time; it is, therefore, at this Burgmote, holden here on Tuesday this fifteenth of April in the xxxviith year of the Queen's Highness' reign, by full consent (as a matter for the good of the same City) decreed and agreed from henceforth for ever to be observed and kept.

On the basis of this primary objection to the behaviour of touring companies of professional players, councillors then took this opportunity to introduce and impose far more restrictive regulations upon these same visiting companies when seeking to perform their plays in Canterbury on weekdays in summer months.

That there shall not any plays, enterludes, tragedies or comedies be played, or players suffered to play within this City or Liberties of the same, on any Sabbath days nor above two days together at any time. And no players so to be suffered for any such two days, to be suffered to play again within the said City or Liberties thereof within twenty and eight days next after such time as they shall have last played within the same two days. And whensoever any such players shall fortune to play in any two days as before, they shall not exceed the hour of nine of the clock in the night of any of those days.

If they do, then these players to be noted what they are, and not to be suffered at any time after to play within this City. And for better the performance hereof Mr Mayor of this City for the time being shall so often and whensoever any players do come unto this City disclose unto them the tenor of this Decree, and give to them commandment that they do in every respect accomplish the same upon pain to them not to be suffered to play again at any other time. And that the same Mayor do send for the host of the house where any such players shall have their abode, or be playing, and to let him also understand the tenor hereof which, if he shall suffer to be in his house broken and not observed, he shall forfeit and lose 40 shillings to the uses of the poor of this City, and that of him to be bestowed by 'Distress',[1] to be taken for every such contempt and offence by the Town Sergeant.

This document, taken together with those that immediately precede it, can leave no doubt that by the end of Elizabeth I's reign the mayors and town councillors of cities in the provinces, backed by most bishops and preachers, were learning to adopt as tough a regulatory stance against visiting groups of professional actors as that which, by then, the Privy Council had taken in its dealings with the resident companies and playhouse owners in London, where performances after nightfall in public playhouses had already been banned for many years.

[1] A legal process, authorising creditors to confiscate goods or monies to redeem fines or other debts owing, but not paid.

Less than a year later, Bristol City Council took similar, if even more restrictive action against use of its guildhall by players. There, however, interference with its use for judicial purposes is supplied as the primary reason for the council's decision, rather than the Sabbatarian objections offered in Canterbury.

(b) An Ordinance of Bristol City Council banning use of Guildhall to visiting companies of professional players, 3 February 1595/6

Bristol City Record Office, Ordinances of the Common Council, 04272, fo. 64. Transcribed in REED, *Bristol*, 148

It is ordered that there shall not be any players in Interludes suffered at any time hereafter to play in the Guild Hall, being the place of Justice. And that if any Mayor of this City shall, at any time hereafter, license or permit any such players to play in the said Guild Hall, then every such Mayor, breaking this Ordinance, shall forfeit and pay to the Chamberlain to the use of the Mayor and Commonality five pounds of current English money to be deducted out of his fee of £40 due to be unto him by the Chamberlain. And that no such players be suffered to play in this City, or within the liberties thereof, at any time after sunset.

Notwithstanding the penalty incurred under this Ordinance, from 1596 onwards successive mayors chose to welcome travelling companies of professional players on an occasional rather than a regular basis, and to pay them sums ranging between 10 shillings and £2 out of their own pockets.

Confronted, however, by this loss of the regularly licensed playhouse provided by the Guild Hall, Bristol rapidly filled this gap by providing one of its own from 1604/5 onwards.[1]

Nine years later, moreover, when Queen Anne was ceremonially received into the city on a state visit, a Patent was secured in her name from James I authorising the establishment of a company of boy-actors to be known 'under the name and title of Her Majesty's Royal Chamber of Bristol'.[2] By 1633, however, the city's account books declared unequivocally that Bristol had finally decided to join other provincial towns and cities in only making payments to players 'to rid them out of Town'.[3]

---

[1] Following the withdrawal of the Guildhall from regular use by players, increasing pressure came to be placed upon both acting companies and wealthy citizens to follow London's example in establishing a reliable, alternative performance space. Here Bristol, as England's second largest and most prosperous city, succeeded where others failed; for within a decade, a rich merchant, Nicholas Woolfe (a cutler by trade) had decided to transform a large room or rooms in his private residence in Wine Street in the centre of the city into a playhouse.

In his will (executed some ten years later in June 1614) he specifies that after his death a portion of the rents received from lettings of this playhouse are to be donated to the city to support a vareity of local charities. Records of such payments then appear in the city's Account Books for the next fifteen years. These are then followed in the early 1630s by those pertaining to a second playhouse built and managed by Richard Barker on Redcliffe Hill in the surburban Parish of St Mary Redcliffe. See *REED, Bristol*, pp. xxxvii, xl, lix and 195–233.

[2] This company was led by John Daniel, brother of the poet Samuel Daniel, and was authorised to tour its repertoire of plays throughout the Kingdom. For the Patents, see **190a** to **190d**.

[3] Bristol Record Office, Mayor's Audits, 04026(20), p. 238, 23 June 1633.

V James I and Charles I, 1603–1625 and 1625–1649

REGULATION OF PLAYS, PLAYERS AND PLAYHOUSES, 1603–1642

London

For at least a year following the accession of James the Sixth and First, it must have seemed as if the new king had not only confirmed but reinforced the settlement reached in 1602 between the Privy Council on the one hand and the city and county magistrates on the other. This had authorised three companies of actors, three licensed public playhouses, with the managers of all three made directly responsible to the Lord Chamberlain and Master of the Revels respecting days and times of performances and the payment of licence fees and local taxes.

At first, such optimism was further strengthened by the issue of a Royal Proclamation on 17 May 1603, forbidding entertainments of all descriptions on Sundays (see **65**), and then by the issue of Royal Patents two weeks later formally transferring the three companies of actors previously maintained by the Lord Chamberlain, the Lord Admiral and the Earl of Worcester respectively into the service of the Royal Household in the King's, Prince Henry's and the Queen's names (see **66**). These changes were reinforced a year later by an Act of Parliament revising yet again the Statute for the Punishment of Rogues and Vagabonds and Sturdy Beggars by finally withdrawing the privilege of maintaining a travelling company of actors even from noblemen of the highest degree (see **73a**).

Where, however, this situation might in theory have held throughout the reign, in practice it contained within itself the seeds of its own undoing. In the first place, property speculators in London cannot have failed to notice that while Prince Henry (the inheritor of the Lord Admiral's company) was still only nine years old, his younger brother, Prince Charles, and his sister, the Princess Elizabeth, could soon be expected to reach an age when each might claim the right to maintain a company of their own and require a theatre in which to house it (see *ES*, iv, 241–3 and 246–7). Not only that: members of the Scottish peerage who had accompanied James to London might also claim the right to retain the privileges accorded to them in Scotland. One such appeared as early as October 1604 in the person of the Duke of Lennox, a cousin of the King, who insisted that his company be allowed to perform in London (see **67**).

No less problematic were the two companies of boy-actors based during the last years of Queen Elizabeth I's reign at Blackfriars and St Pauls. Those at St Pauls belonged, as choristers, to the cathedral, and so could be left, as before, under the continuing care and control of the Dean and Chapter. The boys at Blackfriars, however, could not. The simplest answer to that problem was to treat them and their manager, Edward Kirkham, like the adult companies and to transfer them into one or other of the Royal Households. Of these, the Queen's was chosen; and in 1604 the company was renamed the 'Children of the Queen's Revels' and licensed to present performances at Blackfriars.

Where, however, the playhouse in Blackfriars as refurbished by the Burbage family in 1596/7 could compete with any public playhouse, that at St Pauls could not. Thus, under circumstances that are virtually undocumented, this company of boys appears to have been handed over to a syndicate headed by Martin Slater at some time between 1604 and 1606/7 and renamed as the 'Children of the King's Revels'; they were licensed from 1608 onwards to perform in a new playhouse within Whitefriars.[1]

It was also foreseeable that if many noblemen who had previously maintained players were in future to be denied the right to create and maintain a company of actors travelling under the protection of their hands and seals, groups of dissident actors within the licensed royal companies might be expected to risk amplifying their own patents with duplicates under cover of which to travel on provincial circuits as subsections of the legitimate London companies. By 1616 this had become a common enough occurrence for the Privy Council to feel obliged to intervene (see **86**).

Then, as now, there are always lawyers, accountants and entrepreneurs who earn or supplement their living by finding ways and means by which it becomes possible to stretch or circumvent new laws: it should thus occasion no surprise that when James I died in 1625 there were seven public playhouses still standing in London and inviting use instead of the three originally prescribed in 1603, together with two private houses. Likewise, there were five licensed acting companies instead of the three originally allowed.

Nevertheless, from the standpoint of the Lord Mayor and his fellow aldermen in London, as also from that of the bishops and preachers, the Surrey and Middlesex magistrates, and their Puritan-minded friends in Parliament, even this situation could be regarded as acceptable since they had only to deal with the monarch's personal representative – the Lord Chamberlain, or his deputy, the Master of the Revels – instead of with a plethora of innkeepers, playhouse owners, actor-managers and actors (maintained by an unknown quantity of dukes, earls and lesser lords) as they had had to do in Tudor times.

Yet Jacobean legislation did nothing to inhibit the output of plays licensed for performance and certainly increased the number which subsequently appeared in print, a fact which greatly enhanced the standing of their authors by advancing them from the despised status of common play-makers to that of dramatic poets and men of letters in contemporary society. Confirmation of this change was forthcoming both in the conferment of a poet-laureate's crown upon Ben Jonson in 1617 (at least in respect of its stipendiary benefits) and upon William Davenant as his successor twenty years later, as also in the interest displayed by Charles I in reading stage plays before they were licensed for performance (see **71a** and **b**).

Actors, however, fared less well. Ever stricter enforcement of Lent together with serious, if less frequent, outbreaks of plague combined to cause playhouses to be closed for substantial periods of time forcing actors to seek their living from provincial tours. Yet, local licensing authorities were beginning to find good reasons to refuse them the use of their habitual performance spaces – especially town and livery halls – or to reduce the number of days of use of them which they were willing to allow (see **64** and **83–85**); and even if companies licensed to travel under Royal Patents could not be denied permission to perform, it was soon discovered that they could be graciously received but paid 'not to play'. Any company that chose to ignore this compromise could then be arrested and prosecuted for contempt (see **85**). By the 1630s, provincial records illustrate with great clarity that this method of dealing with unwanted visiting companies had reduced the number of towns in which they had found audiences eager to pay to see their plays so severely as to force both the King's and the Queen's men in 1636–7 to petition their patrons for funds to stave off bankruptcy. Nothing can explain more clearly why, when Parliament finally decided to challenge Royal Patents by closing the London playhouses in 1642, these long-standing and legally protective instruments proved to be such broken reeds. The plain fact was that the theatre in England had already lost the popular franchise on which it had been grounded during the Middle Ages, and which had enabled it to survive an ever-swelling tide of religious and commercial hostility throughout the reign of Elizabeth I. Partly by reducing the appeal of their repertoire to conform more closely to the fashionable, restrictive and largely imported tastes of the early Stuart courts and partly by stretching the legitimate limits of their licences wider and more often than many councils in provincial cities were prepared to allow, travelling companies of actors came to be viewed with such suspicion and distrust as to find themselves more often asked to move on than to perform.

[1] The first house to be found for them was in the former Carmelite friary at Whitefriars, but its lease expired in 1613, obliging the company to find another (see **431**, **432** and **434** below).

Royal Proclamations, Patents and direct interventions in theatrical affairs

The most striking change in the methods adopted to control the stage to manifest itself during the first four decades of the Stuart era was the determination both James I and Charles I displayed in bringing the licensing of acting companies, playhouses and plays under their personal authority.

James I, shortly after his arrival in London, used the existing Restraint on all theatrical performances to introduce two new measures. The first, on 7 May 1603, was to make it a punishable offence to present or perform any game or play on Sundays throughout the realm: the second was to remove the three companies allowed to perform in London out of the service of members of the Privy Council into that of his own household and those of the Queen and the heir apparent.

65 Extract from Proclamation 944 forbidding all forms of entertainment on Sundays, 7 May 1603

Transcribed in *ES*, IV, 335, citing John Strype's *Annals*, IV, 528. See *Stuart Royal Proclamations*, I, 14, ed. James F. Larkin and Paul F. Hughes (Oxford, 1973).

And for that we are informed that there hath been heretofore great neglect in this Kingdom of keeping the Sabbath day: For better observing of the same, and avoiding of all impious profanation of it, we do straightly charge and command that no bear-baiting, bull-baiting, enterludes, common plays, or other like disordered or unlawful exercises, or pastimes, be frequented, kept or used at any time hereafter upon the Sabbath day.

This Proclamation gave even the strictest Sabbatarians everything that they had clamoured for but failed to obtain during the 1580s and 1590s (see **53** above).

66 James I issues a Royal Patent enrolling the company of actors formerly known as the Lord Chamberlain's Men as Grooms of the Chamber within his personal household and to be known henceforth as the King's Men, 17 May 1603[1]

PRO, C66/1608/m. 4. Transcribed in *ES*, II, 208–9; also in *ED and S*, 38–40 and *Government Regulation*, 36–7

Know ye that We of our special grace, certain knowledge and mere motion have licensed and authorised, and by these presents do license and authorise these Our Servants, Lawrence Fletcher, William Shakespeare, Richard Burbage, Augustine Philips, John Heminges, Henry Condell, William Sly, Robert Armyn, Richard Cowley, and the rest of their Associates freely to use and exercise the art and faculty of playing comedies, tragedies, histories, enterludes, morals, pastorals, stage plays and such others like as they have already studied, or hereafter shall use or study, as well for the recreation of our loving subjects as for our solace and pleasure when we shall think good to see them during our pleasure.

And the said comedies ... and such like to show and exercise publicly to their best commodity, when the infection of the plague shall decrease,[2] as well within their now usual house called the Globe within our County of Surrey, as also within any Town Halls or Moothalls or other convenient places within the liberties and freedom of any other city, university, town, or borough whatsoever within our said realms and dominions.

Willing and commanding you, and every of you, as you tender our pleasure, not only to permit and suffer them herein without any your lets, hindrances or molestations during our said pleasure, but also to be aiding and assisting to them, if any wrong be to them offered. And to allow them such former courtesies as hath been given to men of their place and quality; and also what further favour you shall show to these Our Servants for Our sake We shall take kindly at your hands.

[1] Signed under the Privy Seal, 17 May and issued on 19 May. It is addressed to all Magistrates and subjects alike.
[2] Precautionary measures were taken against plague on 19 April 1603.

This Patent was followed shortly afterwards by two more transferring the Earl of Worcester's company into the Queen's Household and the Lord Admiral's into that of Henry Stuart, Prince of Scotland and Duke of Cornwall. (See *ES* iv, 229–30 and 186 n.1.). The same method was adopted a year later to deal with the company of boy-actors using the playhouse in Blackfriars (see **189** below). This seemingly stable situation, however, was challenged in October 1604 by a member of the Scottish peerage who had accompanied the King to London, Ludovic Stuart, Duke of Lennox.[1]

[1] The duke was a cousin of the King, and all restraints on performances because of plague had been lifted when he wrote this letter.

67 The Duke of Lennox equips his company of actors with a letter to all magistrates and constables asking them to respect his licence as sufficient authority to perform their plays in public, 13 October 1604

Dulwich, MS i, Article 40. Transcribed in Greg, *Henslowe Papers*, 62, and in *ES*, IV, 337

Sir, I am given to understand that you have forbidden the company of players (that call themselves mine) the exercise of their plays. I pray you to forbear any such course against them; and seeing they have my licence, to suffer them to continue the use of their plays: and until you receive other signification from me of them, to afford them your favours and assistance.

This request seems to have been ignored in London, and this company was not called to Court.

Between 1610 and 1611, however, the King himself drove a coach and horses through his earlier restrictive provisions by issuing two more Patents authorising his younger son, Prince Charles, and his daughter, the Princess Elizabeth, to recruit companies of their own and to select playhouses of their own choice. Since no record of any consultation with Guildhall or the Middlesex and Surrey magistrates about these decisions has survived, it must be assumed that the Lord Chamberlain and his deputy, the Master of the Revels, possessed sufficient authority under the King's Seal to license both companies to play 'in such usual houses as themselves shall provide'.[1]

That the Court was above its own laws also became apparent in the mysterious circumstances that surround allowance for the construction of a new playhouse – the Red Bull in Clerkenwell – in 1604/5.[2] By 1609, when yet another Royal Patent authorised the Queen's men to move there from the Boar's Head,[3] its existence had become a *fait accompli*.

This move had the immediate effect of leaving both the Boar's Head and the antiquated, but vacant, Curtain free to accommodate the two new royal companies about to be licensed in 1610/11 to perform in London. Thus by that year the three public playhouses originally accepted by the city and county magistrates as allowable in London in 1603 had already swollen to five on no firmer basis than by royal decree. When the Hope came to be added to this list in 1613, five became six; but its owners, Philip Henslowe and Edward Alleyn, as Masters of the King's Bears, could plead that it was a replacement for the decaying Beargardens. This line of argument was a thin one since the Hope was expressly designed to allow bear-baiting to alternate with stage plays and was closely modelled on the Swan: yet, given the Privy Council's pressing need to accommodate Princess Elizabeth's company, this clearly offered a convenient compromise. The building contract is dated 29 August 1613: the company began playing there in 1614 (see **460**).

When James I again used the issue of a Royal Patent to rehouse the Children of the Revels in a second playhouse within the liberty of Blackfriars in 1615, it resulted in a fiasco. Local residents, already angry about the traffic and parking problems caused by the influx of coaches, horses and grooms to the existing Blackfriars playhouse, petitioned the Privy Council to stop the building of another and found themselves supported by the Lord Mayor. Under this degree of pressure the King relented. The whole matter was referred to the Lord Chief Justice; and on receipt from him of assurances that the wording of the Patent had been exploited by the leader of the company, Philip Rosseter, to suit his own advantage, it was annulled four months after it had been issued (see **410**).

The precedent of replacing an old playhouse with a new one was followed more successfully a year later by Christopher Beeston at the Cockpit (or Phoenix) in Drury Lane to enable the Queen's men to move out of the reputedly dingy and uncomfortable Red Bull.[4] Its opening, however, was greeted with riots and serious damage to its fabric at the hands of gangs of unruly apprentices (see **484a–c** below). Permission was likewise obtained from Charles I for the building of a new private playhouse at Salisbury Court south of Fleet Street which supposedly replaced that formerly in the Whitefriars: this opened in November 1630 (see **510**).

No less important than the frequent use of Royal Patents, however, was the increasingly intimate relationship that developed in Court circles under the early Stuarts between dramatic poets and actors on the one hand, and the royal family itself on the other. One reason for this is attributable to Queen Anne's decision to upgrade the status and artistic quality of masques in the calendar of Court entertainments. No sooner had she arrived in London than she decided to appear on the stage in person and to commission Samuel Daniel and Ben Jonson to prepare librettos: she also secured the return of Inigo Jones from her father's court in Denmark to provide changeable landscape scenery as background to her own and her friends' appearances in exotic roles as masquers. She appeared as Pallas Athenae in Daniel's vision of *Twelve Goddesses* on Twelfth Night, 1604, and as Euphoris, daughter of Oceanus and Niger, in Jonson's *Masque of Blackness* on Twelfth Night, 1605. By 1610/11 these same poets were providing roles for her children in *Tethys Festival* and *Oberon* respectively.[5]

---

[1] See **485** below: also *EES*, II(2), 64–5 and 106–7.
[2] See **436** below.
[3] See **437** below.
[4] John Webster in 'To the Reader', prefaced to the printed text of *The White Devil* (1612), blamed the play's failure on its staging in 'so dull a time of winter', and 'in so open and black a theatre'. He then adds that he has since noticed that 'most of the people who come to that playhouse resemble ignorant asses'.
[5] Both masques were commissioned to celebrate Prince Henry's investiture as Prince of Wales.

Ben Jonson, in a prefatory note to the printed text of *The Masque of Queens* (1609), went so far as to attribute credit for the invention of antimasques to her.

68 Preface to the printed text of *The Masque of Queens*, 1609

It increasing now to the third time of my being used in these services to Her Majesty's personal presentations, with the bodies whom she pleaseth to honour; it was my first and special regard to see that the nobility of the invention should be answerable to the dignity of the persons. For which reason I chose the argument to be, *A celebration of honourable and true Fame, bred out of Virtue*: observing that rule of the best artist,[1] to suffer no object of delight to pass without mixture of profit and example. And because Her Majesty (best knowing that a principal part of life, in these spectacles, lay in their variety) had commanded me to think on some dance, or show, that might precede hers, and have the place of a foil, or false masque: I was careful to decline, not only from others, but mine own steps in that kind, since the last year, I had an antimasque of boys;[2] and therefore now devised that twelve women, in the habit of hags, or witches sustaining the persons of Ignorance, Suspicion, Credulity, etc., the opposites to good Fame, should fill that part; not as a masque, but a spectacle of strangeness, producing multiplicity of gesture, and not unaptly sorting with the current, and whole fall of the device.

While it can be argued that all Court Masques remained essentially amateur and occasional entertainments, the steady growth in the complexity and popularity of antimasques made increasing demands on dramatic expertise which only professional actors could supply.

By then the King, himself a poet of high repute in France and Germany as well as in Scotland, had already made it plain to several English dramatic poets and actors that he would not tolerate abuse of the privileges accorded to them as sworn-in servants of the royal households by ordering their arrest following performances of *Eastward Ho!* (1605), *The Isle of Gulls* (1606), *The Conspiracy and Tragedy of Charles, Duke of Biron* (1608) and a lost play about an ill-fated silver mining enterprise in Scotland (1608).[3]

George Chapman and Ben Jonson were threatened with loss of their ears and split noses after *Eastward Ho!*, but were reprieved – perhaps after successfully pinning the blame for the offending jokes about the Scots on its co-author, John Marston, who escaped into hiding. John Day seems likewise to have escaped after *The Isle of Gulls*, but the disgrace of the Children of the Queen's Revels became public knowledge when they were stripped of their privilege of performing in the Queen's name. It was the French ambassador rather than James I who protested about Chapman's history in two parts of Charles, Duke of Biron; but the result was the same. The play was called in and savagely cut before being licensed for printing, and Chapman appears to have stopped writing for the stage for at least the next five years. James I, however, left no one in any doubt about his own response to John Marston's play about the Scottish silver mines.

[1] He is here citing Horace's *Art of Poetry*.
[2] This reference is to his masque for Lord Haddington's wedding.
[3] The mines in question had been discovered at Hilderston near Linlithgow; they were operated on the King's behalf to little or no profit.

69 Sir Thomas Lake informs Lord Salisbury of the King's response to the action taken respecting the Children of the Revels' plays at Blackfriars, 11 March 1608

Transcribed in *CSP Dom.*, 1603–10, 73–4, and in *ES*, II, 53–4.

His Majesty was well pleased with that which your Lordship advertiseth concerning the committing of the players that have offended in the matters of France; and commanded me to signify to your Lordship that for the others who have offended in the matter of the mines and other lewd words, which is the Children of the Blackfriars, that though he had signified his mind to your Lordship by my Lord of Montgomery yet I should repeat it again: that his Grace had vowed they should never play more, but should first beg their bread, and he would have his vow performed. And therefore my Lord Chamberlain, by himself, or your Lordship at the table, should take Order to dissolve them, and to punish the maker besides.[1]

Marston was certainly committed to Newgate prison in June but vanished shortly afterwards.[2] The boys likewise were dismissed from the Blackfriars, and their lease of it reverted to the Burbages and the King's men as a house for their own use in winter.[3]

[1] On the future of the King's and the Queen's Revels companies, see **189**.
[2] He seems thereafter to have severed all former connections with the theatre; entered into holy orders, and accepted appointment to a living at Christchurch, Hampshire, in 1616, which he resigned shortly before his death in 1634.
[3] See **408** below.

That these harsh lessons were well learned seems clear from the fact that there is no record of any repetition of such offences until 1624, when the King's men were arrested and examined for performing Thomas Middleton's *A Game at Chess* at the Globe. This play had been duly licensed and had run for nine consecutive performances when it was visited by the Spanish ambassador who reported it to James I as a transparent attack on his predecessor, Count Gondomar, and directed at the proposed marriage of the Prince of Wales to the Spanish Infanta. On 12 August the King instructed the Privy Council to suppress further performances and question everyone responsible. Warrants to this effect were duly issued and the leaders of the King's men appeared before the Council.

70   **A letter from the Privy Council to the King's secretary reporting on the performances of *A Game at Chess*, 21 August 1624**

PRO, PC/2/32, pp. 424–5. Transcribed in *APC*, James I (1623–5), VI, 305, and in MSC, I, 4 and 5, 380–1; see also *J and CS*, I, 10–12

After etc. According to His Majesty's pleasure signified to this Board by your letter of the 12th of August touching the suppressing of a scandalous comedy, acted by the King's Players, we have called before us some of the principal actors and demanded of them by what licence and authority they have presumed to act the same: in answer whereunto they produced a book, being an original and perfect copy thereof (as they affirmed) seen and allowed by Sir Henry Herbert, Knight, Master of the Revels, under his own hand, and subscribed in the last page of the said book. We, demanding further whether there were no other parts or passages represented on the stage than those expressly contained in the book, they confidently protested they added or varied from the same nothing at all.

The poet, they tell us, is one Middleton who, shifting out of the way, and not attending the Board with the rest as we expected, we have given Warrant to a messenger for the apprehending of him.

To those that were before us we gave sound and sharp reproof, making them sensible of His Majesty's high displeasure therein, giving them straight charge and command that they presume not to act the said comedy any more, nor that they suffer any play or enterlude whatsoever to be acted by them, or any of their company, until His Majesty's pleasure be further known.

This matter, however, was not to end there. The letter continues:

We have caused them likewise to enter into Bond for their attendance upon the Board whensoever they shall be called.

As for our certifying to His Majesty (as was intimated by your letter) what passages in the said comedy we should find to be offensive and scandalous, we have thought it our duties for His Majesty's clearer information to send herewithal the book itself, subscribed as aforesaid by the Master of the Revels, that so, either yourself, or some other whom His Majesty shall appoint to peruse the same, may see the passages themselves out of the original, and call Sir Henry Herbert before you to know a reason of his licensing thereof who (as we are given to understand) is now attending at Court.

So, having done as much as we conceived agreeable with our duties in conformity with His Majesty's royal commandments, and that which we hope shall give him full satisfaction, we shall continue our humble prayers to Almighty God for his health and safety.[1]

A week later, when Middleton could not be found, a Warrant was issued to arrest his son Edward, who was required on 30 August to surrender an Indemnity to be held until such time as he was discharged from it by the Privy Council. Within a year the King had died: Thomas Middleton returned to London to resume his work as chronologer to the City but, like John Marston before him, never wrote for the stage again.[2]

[1] Herbert had succeeded Sir John Astley as Master as recently as 20 July 1623. On the play itself and the licence for its performance, see *J and CS*, I, 10–15.
[2] His appointment as chronologer, or historian, to the City began in 1620. The Orders relating to his son, Edward, are transcribed in MSC, 1.4 and 5, 381, from PRO, PC2/32, pp. 428–9, and in *APC* James I (1623–5), VI, 307–8.

Charles I, perhaps alerted by his father's angry response to this affair, took a keen interest in reading manuscript copies of stage plays before they were licensed, and it may be due as much to this as for any other reason that no similar scandals erupted again in London playhouses until 1639/40.[1] Two instances follow, both of them taken from the record book kept by his Master of the Revels, which reveal the attention he gave to such matters.

[1] These were troubled times. In September 1639, Prince Charles' company at the Red Bull was thus inviting trouble when its members were arrested and examined for alleged libel of lawyers and subject matter that 'reflected upon the present Government'. PRO, PC2/50, p. 653. Transcribed in PC Reg., Charles I, xvi.653; and in MSC, 1.4 and 5.394–5 and *J and CS*, VI, 228–9. In May 1640 the manager of the Phoenix was likewise arrested for presenting a subversive play. The actors were imprisoned for three days: Beeston lost his licence and was replaced by Davenant. See *J and CS*, VI, 74.

71 (a) Charles I offers his opinion on oaths used by characters in William Davenant's comedy *The Witts*, 9 January 1633/4

Sir Henry Herbert's Record Book, ed. J.Q. Adams, 22[1]

This morning, being the 9th of January, 1633, the King was pleased to call me into his withdrawing chamber to the window, where he went over all that I had crossed

[out] in Davenant's playbook; and allowing of *faith* and *slight* to be asseverations only, and no oaths, marked them to stand, and some other few things; but in the greater part allowed of my reformations. This was done upon a complaint of Mr Endymion Porter's in December.

He then added, for future reference:

The King is pleased to take *faith, death, slight*, for asseverations, and no oaths, to which I do humbly submit as my master's judgement: but, under favour, conceive them to be oaths, and enter them here, to declare my opinion and submission.

The 10th of January, 1633, I returned unto Mr Davenant his playbook of *The Witts*, corrected by the King.

[1] On 'oaths', see 73b.

(b) Charles I authorises the Master of the Revels to license Philip Massinger's play, *The King and the Subject*, for the King's men provided the title is changed and one speech is deleted, 5 June 1638

Adams, ed., *Record Book*, 22–3

The name of *The King and the Subject* is altered,[1] and I allowed the play to be acted, the reformations most strictly observed, and not otherwise, the 5th of June, 1638.

At Greenwich the 4th of June Mr W. Murray gave me power from the King to allow of the play, and told me that he would warrant it.

At least one of these reformations had been made by the King. The speech in question is then copied out verbatim in the record book.

> Monies? We'll raise supplies what ways we please,
> And force you to subscribe to blanks, in which
> We'll mulct you as wee [*sic*] shall think fit. The Caesars
> In Rome were wise, acknowledging no laws
> But what their swords did ratify, the wives
> And daughters of the senators bowing to
> Their wills as deities, etc.

This is a piece taken out of Phillip Massinger's play called *The King and the Subject*, and entered here forever to be remembered by my son and those that cast their eyes on it, in honour of King Charles, my master, who reading over the play at Newmarket, set his mark upon the place with his own hand, and in these words:

This is too insolent, and to be changed.

Note that the poet makes it the speech of a King, Don Pedro, King of Spain, and spoken to his subjects.

[1] This play was never printed: its new title may have been *The Tyrant* which was registered with the Stationers' Company in 1660 and attributed to Massinger.

By 1639, Davenant was on good enough terms with the King to be awarded a Patent to build himself a new playhouse that would accommodate stage scenery near Fleet Street in either the parish of St Dunstan or that of St Bride: but this was withdrawn six months later when it was recognised that the designated site had been found to be 'inconvenient and unfit'.[1]

Two passages within this Patent merit quotation here; the one because the description it provides of the proposed new theatre suggests one resembling the Teatro San Cassiano in Venice which had opened for opera in 1637; the other because it provides the justification for Davenant's claim, following the Restoration, that his Patent was still valid.

[1] Both the Patent and Davenant's Indenture are printed in *J and CS*, VI, 305–8.

72 Extracts from the Patent awarded by Charles I to William Davenant to build a theatre in or near Fleet Street, 26 March 1639

PRO, PC66/1608, m. 4. Transcribed in *J and CS*, VI, 305–6, citing Rymer's *Foedera*, XX, 377–8

Know ye, that We . . . upon the humble Petition of our Servant, William Davenant, Gentleman . . . do give and grant . . . full Power Licence and Authority that he . . . may lawfully, quietly and peaceably frame, erect, new-build and set up, upon a parcel of ground . . . already allotted to him for that use, or in any other place that is or hereafter shall be assigned and allotted out to the said William Davenant . . . a theatre or playhouse, with necessary tiring and retiring rooms and other places convenient, containing in the whole forty yards square at the most, wherein plays, musical entertainments, scenes or other like presentments, may be presented . . .

The Indenture which Davenant subsequently signed on 2 October 1639 surrendered only the right accorded to him in the original Patent to build his playhouse or opera house in the immediate vicinity of Fleet Street. He could thus claim, as he did in 1660, that he was still legally possessed of his right to build a playhouse.

Statutory legislation

Parliament was only called upon to legislate in theatrical matters four times between 1603 and the outbreak of the Civil War.

The first occasion was in 1604, when its authority was called upon to withdraw from barons and all noblemen of higher degree their former right to license a company of players under their own hand and seal to perform plays in counties other than their own. This object was achieved by equating any member or members of their companies who did so in future with all other vagrants and by exposing them to punishment by branding, banishment or, on conviction for a second offence, to summary execution without benefit of clergy (see Clause 3).

The second occurred two years later when an Act was passed to reinforce James I's Proclamation banning all entertainments on Sundays by forbidding the use of the name (let alone representation) of God, Christ, or Holy Ghost in any stage play.

73 (a) **Parliament revises the Elizabethan Statutes governing the Punishment of Rogues, Vagabonds and Sturdy Beggars, 7 July 1604**

1 Jac. 1, c. 7, Statutes, iv.1024–5. Transcribed in *ES*, iv, 336–7. Further revisions made in 1610 are set out in Statutes, 7 Jac. 1, iv.1159–61.

Clause 1: after referring back in detail to the Elizabethan Statute of 1598 (see p. 103 above), that of 1604 proceeds:

Sithence the making of which Act divers Doubts and Questions have been moved and grown by diversity of opinions taken in and upon the letter of the said Act: for a plain declaration whereof be it declared and enacted, that from henceforth no Authority to be given or made by any Baron of this Realm or any other honourable Personage of greater Degree, unto any other person or persons, shall be available to free and discharge the said persons, or any of them, from the pains and punishments in the said Statute mentioned, but that they shall be taken within the offence and punishment of the same Statute.

The punishments in question were then amended and stiffened in Clause 3 of this Statute.

(b) **An Act to restrain abuses of players, 27 May 1606**

Statutes, iv.1097. Transcribed in *ED and S*, 42, and in *ES*, iv, 338–9

For the preventing and avoiding of the great abuse of the Holy Name of God in stage plays, interludes, May games, shows and such like: Be it enacted by our Sovereign Lord the King's Majesty, and by the Lords spiritual and temporal, and Commons in this present Parliament assembled, and by the authority of the same, that if at any time or times, after the end of this present session of Parliament, any person or persons do or shall in any stage play, interlude, show, May game or pageant jestingly or profanely speak or use the Holy Name of God, or of Christ Jesus, or of the Holy Ghost, or of the Trinity, which are not to be spoken but with fear and reverence [? such person or persons] shall forfeit for every such offence by him or them committed Ten Pounds; the one moiety thereof to the King's Majesty, his heirs and successors, the other moiety thereof to him or them that will sue for the same in any Court of Record at Westminster, wherein no Essoin [Excusal], Protection or Wager of Law [statements on oath] shall be allowed.

When James I died in 1625, his Proclamation banning all entertainments on Sundays expired with him. Charles I, on his accession, instead of renewing it, chose to leave it to his first Parliament to translate it into a Statute. This resulted in the 'Act for punishing of divers abuses committed on the Lord's Day called Sunday', of 8 June 1625.[1] When Parliament next interested itself in the theatre, it was to challenge the King's autocratic behaviour in seeking to make himself the sole licenser of plays, players and playhouses throughout the realm. It did so in three distinct phases, the first of which was to issue a temporary injunction on 2 September 1642, so worded as to correspond with the distracted estate of England, threatened with a cloud of blood by a civil war

and to

avert the wrath of God.[2]

[1] Statutes, 1 Charles I c. 1, 1625, V.1. Transcribed in *ED and S*, 59–60.
[2] See 74a.

Statutory legislation following the outbreak of civil war

During the course of the Civil War, what has since come to be known as the Long Parliament intervened in theatrical affairs hesitantly in 1642; more forcefully in 1647; and definitively in 1648.

74 (a) An Ordinance of the Lords and Commons concerning stage plays, 2 September 1642

BL, MS E115.15. Transcribed in *ED and S*, 63, and in part in Hotson, *CRS*, 5–6

And whereas public sports do not well agree with public calamities, nor public stage plays with the seasons of humiliation, this being an exercise of sad and pious solemnity, and the other being spectacles of pleasure, too commonly expressing lascivious mirth and levity: it is therefore thought fit and ordained by the Lords and Commons in this Parliament assembled, that while these sad causes and set-times of humiliation do continue, public stage plays shall cease and be foreborne.

This Ordinance, together with the exigencies of the war itself, appear to have sufficed for the next five years. In 1647, however, Parliament passed a second Ordinance intended this time to seize control over the theatre in London.

(b) An Ordinance for the Lord Mayor of the City of London, and the Justices of the Peace, to suppress stage plays, interludes etc., 22 October 1647

BL, MS E518.48. Transcribed in *ED and S*, 64, and in Hotson, *CRS*, 27

For the better suppression of stage plays, interludes and common players.

It is this day ordered, by the Lords and Commons in Parliament assembled, that the Lord Mayor, Justices of the Peace, and Sheriffs of the City of London and Westminster, the Counties of Middlesex and Surrey . . . are hereby authorised and required to enter into all houses [*i.e.* playhouses] . . . where stage plays, interludes, or other common plays are or shall be acted or played: and all such common players or actors, as they upon view of them . . . shall be proved . . . to have acted or played in such playhouses or places above said . . . to commit to any common gaol or prison . . .

There they are to remain to await sentence under the Statute governing the punishment of Rogues and Vagabonds (see **73a**).

The following February, as the Civil War was drawing to its close, Parliament finally plucked up its courage to suppress all plays, players and playhouses without exception and for ever. In its wording, this third Ordinance (effectively the Long Parliament's first Act) releases all the venom of Puritan hostility to play acting that had accumulated during the past hundred years: and it is aimed unequivocally at substituting Parliament's own authority for that of the King over all aspects of theatrical legislation in England.

(c) An Ordinance for suppression of all stage plays and interludes, 9 February 1647 (old calendar); 1648 (our calendar)

Reproduced in full in *ED and S*, 67–70, from the copy of the original printed Quarto in the Bodleian Library. See **74d**

Whereas the Acts of stage plays, interludes and common plays, condemned by ancient heathens, and much less to be tolerated amongst Professors of the Christian Religion, is the occasion of many and sundry great vices and disorders, tending to the high provocation of God's wrath and displeasure, which lies heavy upon this Kingdom, and to the disturbance of the peace thereof; in regard whereof the same hath been prohibited by Ordinance of this present Parliament, and yet is presumed to be practised by divers in contempt thereof.

Therefore, for the better suppression of the said stage plays, interludes, and common players, it is ordered and ordained by the Lords and Commons in this present Parliament assembled, and by authority of the same, that all stage players, and players of interludes, and common plays, are hereby declared to be, and are, and shall be taken to be Rogues, and punishable within the Statutes of the thirty-ninth year of the reign of Queen Elizabeth, and the seventh of the reign of King James, and liable unto the pains and penalties therein contained, and proceeded against according to the said Statutes, whether they be wanderers or no, and notwithstanding any licence whatsoever from the King or any person or persons to that purpose.

And it is further ordered and ordained by the Authority aforesaid, that the Lord Mayor, Justices of the Peace, and Sheriffs of the City of London and Westminster, and of the Counties of Middlesex and Surrey, or any two or more of them, shall, and may, and are hereby authorised and required to pull down and demolish, or cause or procure to be pulled down and demolished, all stage galleries, seats and boxes, erected or used, or which shall be erected and used, for the acting, or playing, or seeing acted or played such stage plays, interludes, and plays aforesaid, within the said City of London and Liberties thereof, and other places within their respective jurisdictions . . .

This Ordinance then proceeds to specify in great detail the several penalties for any proven infringements of its terms that will be meted out to four classes of person: first, actors; then, playhouse owners and owners of any other house used for a performance; thirdly, spectators caught attending performances; and lastly any 'Mayors, Bailiffs, Constables and other officials [and] Soldiers' who fail in future to enforce any of the provisions set out in this Ordinance.

(d) The title page of the published copy of 74c

AN

ORDINANCE

OF THE

LORDS and COMMONS

Aſſembled in

PARLIAMENT,

For,

The utter ſuppreſſion and aboliſhing

of all

Stage-Playes

AND

INTERLUDES.

With the Penalties to be inflicted upon

the Actors and Spectators, herein expreſt.

Die Veneris 11 *Februarii.* 1647.

ORdered by the Lords, *Aſſembled in Parliament, That this Ordinance for the ſuppreſſion of Stage-Playes, ſhall be forthwith printed and publiſhed.*

Joh. Brown Cler. Parliamentorum.

Imprinted at *London* for *John Wright* at the Kings Head in the old Bayley. 1647.

The wording of this Ordinance has a triumphalist finality built into it, leaving former players and play-goers alike in no doubt about the consequences of ignoring it or attempting to reverse it.

In short, from 1648 onwards, any dissidents brave or foolhardy enough to run the risks of incurring these penalties would have to do so clandestinely. In the event, while playhouses remained standing, many did.[1] Although it can be argued that this Ordinance applied only to Greater London, its classification of *all* actors as 'Rogues' as already defined by Statute, together with the abolition of any legitimacy attaching to the Royal Patents which had hitherto enabled them to tour the provinces, effectively destroyed their professional status and with it their former right to perform plays outside of London as well as in it.

[1] See Hotson, *CRS*, 16–69 and **457a–k**, **496a** and **516** below.

The provinces

The most remarkable feature of theatrical activity outside London revealed in the provincial records of the early Stuart era is the rapid erosion of both the number of companies touring the cities and towns and the number of civic corporations willing to allow actors to perform plays.

Since no systematic and comprehensive record of performances given by Jacobean and Carolean acting companies in provincial towns has yet been compiled, anything said here, or in subsequent pages of this book, about theatrical activity in the provinces during this period is likely to be subject to correction or adjustment after the editors of Records of Early English Drama have completed the transcription and publication of all such records for every county in England.

Meantime, it can be said with small fear of contradiction that James I's revision of the Statute governing Punishment of Rogues and Vagabonds, which passed through Parliament in 1604 (see **73a**) by withdrawing from noblemen the privilege of maintaining a private company of actors licensed to travel outside their own county boundaries, could only serve substantially to reduce the number of companies legally authorised to earn a living by touring long-established provincial circuits.[1] No less evident, even from such provincial records as have been made available for study to date, is the rapid decline from the 1620s onwards in the number of cities and towns still willing to welcome actors for extended and frequent visits.[2]

In some areas of the country, extreme Protestant opinion regarded any form of theatrical entertainment as little better than Black Mass: in others, attendance at plays was blamed for industrial absenteeism: and in others again it was the fear of outbreaks of plague (or spread of it) or the frequent damage caused to civic buildings hired out for performances which alienated the city fathers. Doubtless the arrogance of some actors in presuming upon their social status as members of Royal Households, together with the unpaid bills, and other indiscretions so often associated with travellers who are here today and gone tomorrow, also contributed to the mounting antipathy manifested in the surviving civic records towards plays and players in so many provincial cities.

The examples quoted below must thus all be regarded as illustrative rather than exhaustive, as much for limitations of space as for the reasons cited above.

[1] Correspondingly, several companies found it more profitable (and safer) to tour their plays in France, the Low Countries, Germany, Poland and Sweden, as they had already started to do in the 1580s and 1590s.
[2] In Canterbury, for example, the City Chamberlain's Accounts, now in the Cathedral Chapter Library, record visits by nine companies between 1621/2 and 1640/1, all of which received small gratuities 'not to play'; or, as in 1621/2, 'to rid them out of the City without acting'. See Giles E. Dawson, *Records of Plays and Players in Kent, 1450–1642*, MSC, VII, 20–1.

Enforcement of Sabbatarian legislation

Evidence that James I's Proclamation of May 1603, forbidding plays on Sundays (see **65**) was heeded outside London survives from the City of Leicester.

75 Entry in Leicester City Hall Book, 16 May 1603
Chamberlain's Accounts, BR/II/I/3, p. 277

Received of Henry Freeman, one of His Majesty's Messengers, four Proclamations by writ under His Highness's Seal, dated at Westminster, 9th day of May [1603] etc., prohibiting... And [one] also prohibiting all bear-baiting, bull-baiting, enterludes, common plays, or other like disordered or unlawful exercises or pastimes, to be kept or used upon any Sabbath day.

In this respect, the King's authority was reinforced as much by the ecclesiastical as by the civil courts. This was exercised through the annual visitations to parishes undertaken supposedly by the bishop of the diocese or, more often, by the archdeacon or his representative, when it became habitual to enquire into any breaches of the law alleged to have been committed by musicians, dancers, actors or other entertainers.

Instances of the disciplinary action that ensued from accusations, received from informers, are supplied here from two small towns in Worcestershire in 1611 – Alvechurch and Leigh.

76 (a) Alvechurch: the Lord (Judge) of the Diocesan Court sentences Edward Bartholomew, *alias* Heath, together with other actors for performing an Interlude on Sunday, 31 July 1611
St Helen's Record Office, Worcester. Visitation Act Book, SHRO: BA 2884, fo. 161.
Transcribed in REED, *Herefordshire and Worcestershire*, 355–6 and 555

Ralph Lyddiat, detected for playing a stage play upon the Sabbath days and upon St Peter's Day in time of divine service... The said Ralph Lyddiat appeared, and because he confessed his fault, the Lord (Judge) dismissed him with a warning.

The Certificate states that he was at first excommunicated but subsequently absolved. Similar proceedings were taken against John Lilley, Richard Davis and William More; but of these only More was actually excommunicated (22 November).[1]

---

[1] Similar proceedings were taken against players in Pershore a year later, and again in Leominster in Herefordshire in 1617, where Thomas Waucklen, a painter from neighbouring Kingsland by trade, was similarly excommunicated on conviction. See REED, *Herefordshire and Worcestershire*, 385–6, and 141 and 283.

(b) Leigh: proceedings against John Browning

St Helen's Record Office, Worcester. Visitation Act Book, SHRO: BA 2884, fo. 384b. 27 September 1611. Transcribed in REED, *Herefordshire and Worcestershire*, 381

... for being present at a play made in a house at service time on a Sabbath day.

The result of this examination is not recorded.

Royal Injunctions against performances in Lent were just as strictly enforced. Thus, when the Princess Elizabeth's players embarrassed the city fathers in Coventry by presenting themselves in that city during Lent in 1615, a ruling was sought from the Privy Council, whose secretary promptly supplied the reassurances required.

77 Letter from Sir Edward Coke to the mayor and justices of Coventry 'concerning the Lady Elizabeth's Players', 28 March 1615

Coventry Record Office, A79, p. 113. Transcribed in *Corporation Letter Book*, ed. Thomas Sharp and George Eld, 'Concerning Players in Lent', i.100, and in REED, *Coventry*, 394–5

Forasmuch as this time is by His Majesty's Laws and Injunctions consecrated to the service of Almighty God, and public notice was given on the last Sabbath for preparation to the receiving of the holy communion: These are to will and require you to suffer no common players whatsoever to play within your city for that it would lead to the hindrance of devotion, and drawing of the artificers and common people from their labours. And this being signified unto any such [*i.e.* the royal companies] they will rest therewith (as becometh them) satisfied: otherwise suffer you them not [*i.e.* to play], and this shall be your sufficient warrant.[1]

[1] This Order provides a very clear example of the manner in which Puritan zeal for piety became conjoined with the self-interest of employers of labour respecting absenteeism.

Twenty years later, however, a company of players possessed of a Royal Patent was either foolhardy or desperate enough to risk defying these 'Laws and Injunctions' when presenting themselves in Canterbury, where their conduct was provocative enough to oblige the mayor to inform the archbishop of the action taken against them: he in his turn informed the Privy Council in London.

78 The Privy Council thanks the Mayor of Canterbury for his firm but tactful action respecting players performing in Lent and at night in evident defiance of Injunctions to the contrary, 29 March 1636

See PC Register, Charles I, xii.59. Transcribed in MSC, 1.4 and 5.390–1

By your letter of the 25th of this month sent unto our very good Lord the Lord Archbishop of Canterbury his Grace, we understand with what respect you proceeded with the players that lately came to that city in regard of His Majesty's Commission which they carried, and we likewise take notice not only of the disorders occasioned by their playing at so unseasonable a time in the night, but also of their insolent behaviour to yourself, for which they deserve punishment, and shall smart when they shall be met withall; to which purpose we pray you to advertise the names of some of the chiefest of their company that further enquiry may be here made after them. And as we cannot but commend the great care you have expressed in the good and orderly government of that city, so we must let you know to your encouragement that His Majesty, being by his Grace made acquainted with your carriage in this particular, hath commanded us to give you notice of his gracious acceptance thereof; And for the future, if any stage-players shall come to play in your city in the time of Lent, you are not to give way unto it, without the special privity of his Grace of Canterbury.

A final illustration of the grip that Sabbatarian sects within the English church had acquired over all innocent entertainments undertaken on Sundays or in Lent during the last decade before the outbreak of the Civil War is supplied by the records from the quarter sessions held before the Justices of the Peace at Warrington in Lancashire in the summer of 1632. In this instance, the long arm of the law has reached beyond actual performances to ensnare a group of local amateurs caught either acting or rehearsing a play on a Sunday (see 79, note 1).

79 Depositions of Gregory Harrison, ale-house keeper, and others taken before Thomas Ireland, J P, 11 May, 1632

Lancashire Record Office, QSB 1/106/72. Reproduced in REED, *Lancashire*, 95

Gregory Harrison of Warrington within the County of Lancaster, Ale-house keeper, being ... examined the day and year above written before Thomas Ireland, Esquire, one of His Majesty's Justices of the Peace and Quorum within the County aforesaid, sayeth that upon Sunday last, being the 6th day of this instant May, about twelve or one of the clock, there came into his house in Warrington aforesaid some young men and desired him, this Examinate, that they might go into a loft which was in his house. The which this Examinate, not thinking that they would have stayed any longer than for the drinking of a can or two of ale, suffered them to go up ...

He goes on to claim that they had stayed there for an hour or more when they were arrested by the constables and churchwardens, and that he had heard subsequently that while in his loft 'they were acting a play'.

The magistrate then questioned the young men:

John Smith, Thomas Holebrook, John Wily of Overford, within the County of Lancaster; William Hardman, John Cadewell, William Wildigge, Robert Wick, John Choner and Randle Rylence of Warrington in the County aforesaid, being examined the day and year aforesaid, sayeth that they consented to go together, to meet at the house of one Gregory Harrison in Warrington aforesaid upon Sunday being the 6th day of May last past there to act a play called *Henry the Eighth*, which they accordingly did; and as they were in acting of it, were, in time of Divine Service, apprehended by the Churchwardens and Constable of Warrington, and so brought before a Justice of the Peace: and further say not.[1]

Bonds, varying in amount from £15 to £40, were taken as bail from each defendant, totalling £280, lest any of them abscond before appearing at the quarter sessions for trial. These were held at Ormskirk on 16 July, where they were all sentenced to 'condign punishment'; but special care was taken to ensure that they should then go free and not be liable to a second trial in the ecclesiastical courts.

As the latter part of this judgement reveals the sharp divergences of opinion surrounding all recreational sports and entertainments (and the degree of this offence in particular) upheld by the county squirearchy on the one hand and by strict Sabbatarians on the other, it merits quotation here (see 61 and 62). The vagueness of the phrase 'condign punishment' (i.e. adequate or suitable), suggests moreover that it was deliberately chosen to cover a minimal sentence rather than one of any great severity.

[1] Since these were the only people arrested and charged, and as no audience is said to have been present, their offence more nearly resembles a rehearsal than a performance.

80 Conclusion of the judgment awarded in the case of John Smith, Thomas Holebrook and others at the quarter sessions held at Ormskirk before Sir Charles Gerard and seven other magistrates, 16 July 1632

Lancashire Record Office, QSR 29 1632 mb 33. Transcribed in REED, *Lancashire*, 96–7 with comment in endnotes, 337–8

... for which misdemeanours the parties above named ... here received condign punishment. In respect whereof this Court doth order that they and every of them shall be freed and discharged of and from any further trouble in the Dean's or Ordinary's Court for the same offence; in respect by law they are not to be punished twice for one offence. And if the Dean do not, upon notice hereof, desist from any further proceeding against them, then upon complaint made to any Justice of Peace an attachment shall be awarded against him to answer his contempt at the next Sessions to be holden at Wigan.[1]

[1] It is further to be noted that no charge was brought against Gregory Harrison, the ale-house keeper, at the quarter sessions.

Local regulation of provincial acting companies

While it thus appears that Jacobean legislation forbidding performances of plays on Sundays and in Lent was enforced throughout the country and, in general, respected by most of the acting companies, it is harder to estimate the effects of the revised Statute of 1604 stripping noblemen of their former right to maintain a company of players. The fact is that several such companies continue to appear in provincial records as recipients of payments, if only sporadically, in most parts of the country throughout the period. Some indication, however, of the manner in which the government in London itself intended this Statute to be interpreted by city and town councils in the provinces survives in a memorandum preserved in the city chamberlain's account book at Leicester, where radical changes were made to the rules governing taxes to cover the costs of remunerating visiting players in 1607.

81   An Order governing payments for and attendance at performances of plays in the Town Hall before the Lord Mayor of Leicester, as they will affect all city councillors in future, 30 January 1607

Leicester, City Hall Book, p. 313. Transcribed in *Records of the Borough of Leicester, 1603–1608*, ed. Helen Stocks and W.H. Stevenson (Cambridge, 1923).

Plays. It is agreed that none of either of the Two Companies [*i.e.* City Livery Companies] shall be compelled at any time hereafter to pay towards any plays but such of them as shall be then present at the said plays: the King's Majesty's players, the Queen's Majesty's players, and the young Prince's players excepted: and also such players as do belong to any of the Lords of His Majesty's most honourable Privy Council also excepted: to these they are to pay according to the ancient custom, having warning by the Mace-bearer to be at every such play.

In other words, this Order releases all councillors in future from any obligation to respect any licences or commissions presented to them by visiting companies of professional actors other than those issued under the Privy Seal, or under the personal hand and seal of a Privy Councillor, ratified by the Master of the Revels. 'Obligation' was the key word; and, henceforth, advance warning of that would be issued to each councillor through the mace-bearer. Beyond that, the city could, if it saw fit to do so, license companies maintained by influential local noblemen to perform (but without any expectancy of a civic subsidy), or refuse to grant them even this modified permission.

Vague though this interpretation of the Statute may seem to us to be, it does conform with the situation that emerges nationwide from a study of recorded payments to players from 1604 onwards: it also accords with the abrupt reduction in the number of companies maintained by noblemen after 1614 from more than one hundred to approximately twelve. Of those that remained, moreover, some were certainly travelling on duplicate patents, or 'exemplifications' (see 86 and 87) and others as fragmented remnants of disbanded royal companies who had reorganised themselves under the patronage of an obliging nobleman with the tacit agreement of the Master of the Revels: and even these crop up in the documented records suddenly, and for only a few years, in strictly localised areas.

Major exceptions are companies under the patronage of such northern noblemen as the Earls of Leicester and Derby and the Lords Dudley and Stafford, and the Lord President of Wales (Lord Evers).

Further pressure was placed on all companies, no matter how valid and respectable their licences, to reconsider the desirability of undertaking extensive provincial tours after 1615, when many city and town councils by restricting the number of performances to be allowed to at most two or three in any one week in any one year followed the example set in Canterbury in 1595 (see 64). Worse still, companies were rewarded with gratuities for agreeing not to perform at all, most of which were worth half the fee previously paid for official performances, or less (see 64).

Three reasons for these increasingly restrictive local measures recur within the provincial records. The first was fear of plague, of the kind so familiar in the London records of the Elizabethan era, which was normally met by the payment to companies of fees for agreeing not to perform. The Chamberlain's accounts for the city of Canterbury offers a typical example under the year 1608/9, when two sums of 20 shillings each were paid to Lord Chandos and Lord Berkeley's players 'for that they should not play here by reason that the sickness was then in the city'[1]

The second was the damage done to civic buildings used for performances and the cost of repairing them after the actors had departed, an early example of which has already been cited from Liverpool in 1571/2 (see pp. 116–17 above; see also 82–85). The third was the growing awareness already commented upon that several seemingly respectable licensed companies were presenting themselves under duplicated Royal Patents which, by 1617, had become so frequent a cause of complaint that the Privy Council had to intervene to try to stop it (see 86).

[1] Murray, *English Dramatic Companies* II, 231.

Restricted use of civic buildings as playhouses

Both the nature of the damage done to civic buildings and the costs of repairing them are conveniently summarised in the Chamberlain's accounts for 1605 and 1608 now in the Leicestershire Record Office. Leicester; BR III/2/74, fo. 212 and BR III/2/75, fo. 102.

82 Repairs carried out to the Town Hall, Leicester, following performances given there by the Queen's company, January 1605 and in September 1608

Item: Given to the Queen's Majesty's players	40s
Item: Paid to Thomas Heyricke for lathes and for nails spent at the Hall at such time as the Queen's Players were there	9d
Item: Paid for mending the chair in the parlour at the Hall, more than was received of Ralph Edgerton, which was broken by the players	11d
Item: Paid to Richard Inge, glassier, for 70 quarrels of glass	3s 6d
Item: Paid him more for soldering of other panes of glass in the Hall	6d

The total bill for repairs on that occasion thus amounted to 5 shillings and 8 pence. In September 1608, the glass was again broken.

Item: Paid for mending of the shut windows in the
Town Hall   4d
Item: Paid for mending the glass windows at the Town
Hall more than was given by the players who
broke the same   2s
Item: Paid for mending the Latice Windows at the Town
Hall   13d

In July 1606 the town councillors at Cambridge reacted angrily to the damage done to their hall by this same company of actors.

83 Extract from the deposition of two members of the Queen's players on being arrested for performing without due authority in the Town Hall, July 1606

Commissiary's Court Book, CUA Ct. II 13, fo. 128b. Transcribed in REED, *Cambridge*, 1, 403

John Duke and Thomas Greene both say that Master Mayor did give them absolute authority to play in the Town Hall, and did give order to some to build their stage and take down the glass windows there; and did also [tak] give them the key to the Town Hall.

They were both bound over in the sum of £20, payable to the University, to agree not to play again in or near Cambridge (Court Book, fo. 107b).

Six years later the newly created Princess Elizabeth's company arrived in York and presented their Letters Patent to the city council. When these had been examined and found to authorise performances in 'moot halls, schoolhouses [and] town halls within any other cities or towns' (i.e. outside of London), the city council agreed that this company be permitted to perform in York. The city hall, however, if not specifically excluded, is not offered to them; and there is no record of any payment for a performance there before the mayor and council. Rather does the company appear to have been left to fend for itself elsewhere within the city.

84 York City Council licenses the Princess Elizabeth's players to perform in York, 13 August, 1612

York City Library, York House Books Y: B33, fo. 313v. Transcribed in REED, *York*, 1, 538.[1]

Whereupon it is thought good to permit them to play within this City in such places as they shall procure or get, so as they do not play on the Sabbath days or in the night time.

The onus of finding a building in which to perform their plays appears thus to have been shifted firmly on to the company.

---

[1] On an abortive attempt to build a playhouse in York in 1609, see REED, *York*, 1, 530–1. Payments were made to 'the late Queen's players' in 1620 and to 'the Prince's players' in 1623; but in 1626, when

'two several companies' sought permission to perform, both were refused and denied 'any benevolence'. See REED, *York*, I, 564 and 568–73.

A decade later, Worcester City Council was still willing to allow its town hall to be used for plays, but leave to perform in it was severely restricted: any civic official, moreover, found to have breached these new regulations, must expect to be fined for this offence.

85 Conditions governing use of the Town Hall in Worcester for the performance of plays, 1622

St Helen's Record Office, Worcester, Civic Miscellany, 2, SHRO: BA 9360/A.6, p. 24. Council Order. Transcribed in REED, *Herefordshire and Worcestershire*, 453–4.

Item: It is ordered that no plays be had or made in the upper end of the Town Hall of this City, nor Council Chamber used by any players whatsoever.[1] And that no plays to be had or made in Guild by night time. And if any players be admitted to play in the Guild Hall, to be admitted to play in the lower end only upon pain of 40s to be paid to Master Mayor to the use of the City if any shall be admitted or suffered to the contrary.

In 1626 this Order was extended to include Trinity Hall and all other civic buildings.[2] However, by that time even this sort of courteous compromise was already out of date in other provincial cities, where the only respect still accorded to the Royal Patents carried by the actors was a small gratuity paid to them in exchange for agreeing 'not to play' or, as frequently recorded in the annual accounts, 'to rid them out of this town'.[3]

[1] i.e. none of the adjacent rooms in the building.
[2] 9th October 1626 (Council Order) p. 39. Transcribed in REED, *Herefordshire and Worcestershire*, 455.
[3] See p. 119 n. 3 and p. 135 n. 2 above; also **175** below.

Duplication, exemplification and suspected forgery of actors' licences

A third reason contributing to the growing hostility displayed by town councils towards touring companies of professional actors was the discovery, made in 1616 if not before, that many of these companies were exploiting the goodwill of mayors and councillors by travelling under false pretences when presenting Patents that, on close inspection, proved to be duplicates of genuine originals.

86 The Lord Chamberlain writes to all mayors and county magistrates instructing them to arrest any actors suspected of travelling under dubious licences, and to send them to London for examination by the Privy Council, 4 June 1617

From the copy preserved in the Mayors' Court Books XV, NRO: 16a, fo. 133, Norfolk Record Office, Norwich. Transcribed in REED, *Norwich*, 151–2, and in *ES*, IV, 343–4.

Whereas Thomas Swynarton and Martin Slaughter, being two of the Queen's Majesty's company of players, having separated themselves from their said company, have each of them taken forth a several exemplification or duplicate of

His Majesty's Letters Patent granted to the whole company, and by virtue thereof they severally in two companies, with vagabonds and such like idle persons, have and do use and exercise the quality of playing in diverse places of this Realm to the great abuse and wrong of His Majesty's subjects in general and contrary to the true intent and meaning of His Majesty to the said company.

And whereas William Perry, having likewise gotten a warrant whereby he and a certain company of idle persons with him do travel and play under the name and title of the Children of Her Majesty's Revels to the great abuse of Her Majesty's service.

And whereas also Gilbert Reason, one of the Prince His Highness' players, having likewise separated himself from his company, hath also taken forth another exemplification or duplicate of the Patent granted to that company, and lives in the same kind & abuse.

And likewise one Charles Marshall, Humfrey Jeffes and William Parr: thereof [*sic?* three of] Prince Palatine's company of players, having also taken forth an exemplification or duplicate of the Patent granted to the said company and by virtue [of] thereof live after the like kind & abuse.

Wherefore, to the end such idle persons may not be suffered to continue in this course of life, these are [in his] therefore to pray, and nevertheless in His Majesty's name, to will and require you upon notice given of any of the said persons by the bearer hereof, Joseph More, whom I have specially directed for that purpose, that you call the said parties, offenders, before you, and thereupon take their said several exemplifications, or duplicates, or other their warrants by which they use their said quality, from them; and forthwith to send the same to me.

And also that you take good and sufficient bonds of every of them to appear before me at Whitehall at a prefixed day to answer their said contempts and abuses whereof I desire you not to fail. And these shall be your sufficient warrant in that behalf ... Dated 16th July ... 1616. Pembroke, Delivered to Mayor by Henry Sebeck, 4 June, 1617.

Despite this sabre-rattling in London, actors persisted in this practice. In 1624 the Corporation of Gloucester questioned a company of actors who had presented 'a commission under Sir Henry Herbert's hand and seal, Master of the Revels', possibly because its manager, Henry Sandes, had handed them a licence dated a mere month earlier. When examined, one of the actors confessed that his real name was Alexander Barker and not Baker as recorded in the Patent: it also became apparent that the company included 'one Jarvis Gennatt, a minstrel', who was not listed in this licence.[1] No record survives of what transpired in this case; but the mayor certainly possessed grounds enough, following this interrogation, to refer the authenticity of this licence back to the Privy Council for further assurance, just as the Mayor of Banbury did a decade later when confronted with a similar problem.

---

[1] City of Gloucester Record Office, Gloucester Corporation Memoranda Book. GRO: GBR 1435/1542, fo. 110v. Transcribed in REED, *Cumberland, Westmoreland and Gloucestershire*, 319–20.

87   The Privy Council acknowledges safe receipt of a Patent sent by the Mayor of Banbury that he suspected to be a forgery, and instructs him to send the actors concerned to London for examination, 22 May 1633

Transcribed in PC Register, Charles I, ix.51, 22 May 1633, and in MSC, 1.4 and 5.384–5

We have seen your Letters of the 6th of this instant month, as also a Patent of Licence pretended to be granted by His Majesty, a Commission from the Master of the Revels, and the examinations of those delinquents being (as you say) wandering rogues and dangerous persons: And as we concur with you in opinion that there may be forgery and erasure both in the said Patent and Commission, so we do approve and commend the discreet course you have taken in committing them to the common prison of your Borough. Now, to the end that this abuse may be farther searched into and examined, we do hereby require and authorise you to cause Jones and the rest of his [ac]complices (being five more) that are detained under restraint to be released, and forthwith delivered to this bearer, Robert Cross, one of the Messengers of His Majesty's Chamber, who hath warrant from this Board to receive them at your hands, and to bring them hither to answer before us for the crimes and misdemeanours wherewith they stand charged, and thereupon to be proceeded withall according to the quality of their offences and the Common Laws and Justice of this Kingdom.[1]

[1] Included in the PC Register are: (1) the Warrant issued to Robert Cross to take delivery of the players imprisoned at Banbury; (2) a list of the names of the offending actors on their arrival in London on 3 June; (3) a Warrant discharging the prisoners on bail pending their subsequent appearance before the council or the magistrates. All three documents are transcribed in MSC, 1.4 and 5.385. No record of the verdict on this case survives.

As official attitudes towards touring companies of actors hardened during James I's reign, it is understandable that actors' frustration should have increased proportionately. Tensions created by this situation reached crisis point in Norwich in 1624, where the Princess Elizabeth's players decided to challenge the mayor's authority to deny the validity of the Great Seal by ignoring or overruling the Letters Patent licensing them to perform 'within any Town Halls, Moot Halls, Guild Halls, School Houses or other convenient places within the liberty and freedom of any . . . City, University, Town or Borough whatsoever within our Realms and Dominions . . . without any your lets, hindrances, molestations or disturbances'.[1] All the documents relating to this notorious incident are quoted in full in 178a-f: but as this direct challenge to the local council represents a test case, the salient elements of it merit quotation here.

[1] See 178a-f. The full text is also given in *ES*, IV, 246–7.

88 Francis Wambus, leader of the Princess Elizabeth's men, challenges the Mayor of Norwich to test the strength of a Royal Patent against that of local powers of restraint backed only by an earlier letter from the Privy Council, 24 April 1624

Norfolk Record Office, Norwich, Mayors' Court Books, xv, NRO 16a, fo. 525. Transcribed in REED, *Norwich*, 180–1, and in *English Dramatic Companies*, II, 348–50. See also **178**.

Whereupon the said Wambus peremptorily affirmed that he would play in this City, and would lay [sic? lie] in prison here this twelve-month, but he would try whether the King's Command or the Council's be the greater. And this entry being read unto him [i.e. the respective dates of his own Patent (20 March 1621) and the Mayor's letter from the Privy Council (27 May 1623)] he said he denied nothing of that was here set down. And thereupon the said Wambus was, according to the Council's Order, commanded to forbear to play within the liberties of this City. And he nevertheless answered that he would make trial what he might do by the King's authority, for he said he would play.

Two days later (26 April 1624) the mayor was given a poster torn down off the gates of the White Horse inn which read:

Here within this place at one of the clock shall be acted an excellent new comedy called *The Spanish Contract* by the Princess's Servants. Vivat Rex.[1]

April 26. Whereupon Mr Mayor caused the several persons named in the Instrument shewed forth on Saturday last (April 24th) . . . to be warned forthwith to appear before him and the other Justices of Peace before mentioned. And the Officer, namely Henry Paman, returned that he could speak with no more of the said Company than only the said Francis Wambus who only appeared, and said confidently that he and his Company would play the comedy aforesaid. And being demanded whether the bill now showed unto him containing the words aforesaid was his handwriting or not, he said it was his handwriting and that he caused it to be set up this day. And the Council's Order being again read unto him, he said he would play whatsoever had been said to the contrary, and accused Mr Mayor to his face that he condemned the King's authority . . .[2]

After these heated and ill-tempered exchanges, Wambus was duly delivered to the city gaol, where he stayed for a month. At a hearing before the magistrates on 26 May it was explained on Wambus' behalf that his failure to produce bail was due to the fact that he was a visitor to the city and that he had sent his fellow-actor, John Townshend, to obtain it for him. Townshend returned that day with the money and Wambus was duly released that same afternoon. Wambus then returned to London, where he evidently discussed the whole situation with the Master of the Revels. He then came back to Norwich in time for the court hearing of his case on 18 September 1624 (Norfolk Record Office, Norwich, Mayors' Court Books XVI, NRO 16a, fo. 12b: transcribed in REED, *Norwich*, 182).

This day Mr Wambus showed forth a letter from Sir Henry Herbert dated June last purporting that it was my Lord Chamberlain's pleasure that he should be set at liberty ...

And there this dispute might have ended had either side been willing to let bygones be bygones and agree to compromise; but this was not to be. The court record thus proceeds:

And the said Wambus and Mr. Townshend being here in Court desired recompense for the imprisonment of Wambus, to whom it was answered that if they had occasion to depart this City before Wednesday next, Mr Mayor would call a meeting this afternoon, whereunto they replied they were willing to stay till Wednesday.

They got their answer, as promised, that same afternoon (25 September):

This day Mr Wambus and Mr Townshend, players, came into this Court and complained of wrongs done to the said Wambus and Bee by their imprisonment, and desired to have satisfaction for their charges. And because it was remembered and conceived that what was done concerning them was by consent of the whole Court, and that nothing was done any way injurious to them, but that their imprisonment was occasioned by their own miscarriage, therefore it was by general consent agreed that nothing should be given unto them in that respect.

Despite his courage and histrionic bravado, Francis Wambus, having put the King's authority as represented in his Patent to the test, thus found himself obliged to leave Norwich in the knowledge that it no longer carried any weight when provincial mayors and magistrates saw fit, for their own reasons, to require players to move on without playing. From then on the best that any company could hope for, when forced to leave London on a provincial tour, was to accept this situation as gracefully as it could, and compromise when necessary by accepting a token payment for its agreement 'not to play' in the form of a small gratuity to cover its travelling expenses. Sadly, the principal reason for the plight to which actors had thus been reduced in the English provinces must be attributed to those actors who by deceitfully duplicating, loaning or selling licences had devalued their currency to a point where the Privy Council lost patience with these escalating abuses, and decided to instruct all provincial mayors, sheriffs and magistrates to scrutinise all licences presented to them by players in future with greater care and rigour. Owners of licences thought to be suspicious, or of doubtful validity, were to be closely examined; meantime, permission to perform was then to be refused until proof was forthcoming from the Master of the Revels or his deputy that their licences were valid.

[1] In view of the widespread unpopularity of the proposed marriage between the Spanish Infanta and the Prince of Wales, this could only be regarded as a 'dangerous' play. See 70.
[2] See above note, and Norwich, Mayors' Court Books XV, NRO 16a, fos. 525b–6.

89 The Lord Chamberlain instructs provincial mayors and magistrates on how to handle companies of travelling actors presenting licences purporting to have been issued under the Privy Seal, 20 November 1622

Norfolk Record Office, Norwich. Copy preserved in the Mayors' Court Books XVI, NRO 16a, fos. 31–31b, dated 29 January 1625. Transcribed in REED, *Norwich*, 187–9, and in *English Dramatic Companies*, II, 351–2

Whereas I am credibly informed that there are many and very great disorders and abuses daily committed by diverse and sundry companies of stage players, tumblers, vaulters, dancers on the ropes, and also by such as go about with motions and shows and other the like kind of persons by reason of certain grants, commissions and licences which they have by secret means procured both from the King's Majesty and also from diverse noblemen, by virtue whereof they do abusively claim unto themselves a kind of licentious freedom to travel as well to show, play and exercise in eminent cities and corporations within this Kingdom, as also from place to place, without the knowledge and approbation of His Majesty's Office of the Revels, and by that means do take upon them at their own pleasure to act and set forth in many places of this Kingdom diverse and sundry plays and shows which for the most part are full of scandal and offence both against the Church and State, and do likewise greatly abuse their authority in lending, letting, and selling their said Commissions and Licences to others, by reason whereof diverse lawless and wandering persons are suffered to have free passage unto whom such grant and licences were never intended, contrary to His Majesty's pleasure and the laws of this land, His Majesty's grant and commission to the Master of the Revels and the first institution of the said office.[1] These are therefore in His Majesty's name straightly to charge and command you [and] every of you that whosoever shall repair to any of your Cities, Boroughs, Towns Corporate, villages, hamlets or parishes and shall show and present any play, show, motion, feats of activity and sights whatsoever, not having a licence now in force under the hand and seal of office of Sir John Astley, Knight, now Master of His Majesty's Office of the Revels, or under the hand of his Deputy, and sealed likewise with the seal of office, that you and every of you at all times forever hereafter do seize and take away every such grant, patent, commission or licence whatsoever from the bringer or bearer thereof, and that you forthwith cause the said grant or licence to be conveyed and sent to His Majesty's Office of the Revels there to remain at the disposition of the Master of the said Office. And that to the utmost of your power you do forbid and suppress all such plays, shows, motions, feats of activity, sights and every of them until they shall be approved, licensed and authorised by the said Sir John Astley, or his said Deputy, in manner aforesaid who are appointed by His Majesty under the great seal of England to that end and purpose. Herein fail not as you will answer the contrary at your perils. And for your more certainty, I advise you to take an exact copy of this my mandate. Given under my hand at Whitehall, the 25th day of November, 1622.

[1] The concluding clause of this sentence harks back especially to Edmund Tilney's revised Patent of 1581 (34) and helps to explain why its issue by Elizabeth I was received with such suspicion and hostility by the Common Council of the City of London (35 above).

This last instruction was certainly followed in Norwich. Receipt of it, and the recourse taken to the document in the case of Francis Wambus and the Princess Elizabeth's players between April and September 1624, marks the start of a swift decline in the number of professional acting companies receiving permission from city councils to perform their plays and being well paid for doing so. Many towns, like Canterbury for example (see **64a** and **78** above), consistently offered gratuities in return for an agreement 'not to play': others, like Coventry, continued to welcome them, if less often (see REED, *Coventry*, 421–48) until the outbreak of the Civil War. Either way, however, this means of redressing financial losses occasioned by enforced closures of their London playhouses became increasingly unreliable and uncertain until civil war and a parliamentary ban on acting finally divorced provincial audiences from all further contact with the licensed royal companies of players.

When professional acting was again legitimised in 1660, it was restricted to two companies based in London licensed to serve Charles II and his brother, James, Duke of York. On their return from exile, they and their entourage brought with them a demand for playhouses capable of accommodating Italianate changeable scenery and quasi-operatic tragicomedies of a kind that, before the Civil War, had been confined in England to Court Masques. These changes – architectural, scenic and stylistic – incurred costs which effectively prohibited any resumption of provincial touring by these London companies.

It was thus left to enterprising groups of strolling players to provide such recreational, theatrical entertainment outside London as local magistrates and town councils were prepared to sanction, where fit-up stages at fairgrounds, race meetings and in school halls and large farm barns would have to serve as playhouses for nearly a hundred years.

A detailed account of these changes and local regulation accompanying them has already been provided within this series by David Thomas and Arnold Hare in *Restoration and Georgian England, 1660–1788* (Cambridge, 1989).

Part two: players and playing

Edited by WILLIAM INGRAM

VI *Introduction*

In the strictest sense, 'professional' stage-playing seems to have been only a fitfully realised notion in the earliest years of the Tudor monarchy. There were, of course, people who performed in stage plays for money, and some who did so with regularity, even in the latter days of the Plantagenet kings. Yet until the reign of King Henry VIII such performers were in the minority. The surviving evidence suggests that the most active of them plied their trade by travelling in the countryside, but this may merely reflect the failure of similar activity in London to find its way into the records. In London in this period, stage-playing was for the most part engaged in by persons whose principal livelihood lay elsewhere, like the merchant tailor George Mayler or the stationer John Redman, mentioned below. 'Stage-playing' was not in this early period even a clearly defined activity; the normal repertory of a stage-player in the early sixteenth century might have included dancing, tumbling, clowning, juggling, fencing, mime and minstrelsy along with (or sometimes instead of) the declaiming of lines. 'Playing' is thus to be understood in its broadest sense in this early period as equivalent to 'performing' or 'entertaining' rather than as a synonym for 'acting' as we normally understand the term.

There were, of course – and had been for many years before the accession of the Tudors – guildsmen in various towns who celebrated the feast of Corpus Christi in the spring of each year by staging plays on biblical subjects for their fellow citizens. This tradition of religious pageantry lasted well into the reign of Queen Elizabeth, and thus is chronologically within the scope of the present volume; for a discussion of such plays and their performances see above, 30–33. But as the participants in such pageants were 'stage-players' in only a very specialised sense, in that they usually played only one role, and that only once a year, their enterprise is not dealt with here.

Apart from this group of guildsmen and their pageants, performers in the earlier 1500s may be conveniently if somewhat artificially divided into two categories determined by whether the players performed primarily in urban or rural settings. This distinction has to do with differences in the economics of performing and in the availability of audiences rather than with any differences in skills or techniques between urban and provincial players.[1] An urban setting, especially if it was London, might offer a degree of economic stability for a local troupe, enabling it to play more or less steadily in one place without exhausting its potential audience, and allowing its members to continue identifying themselves as ironmongers or haberdashers, pursuing those trades along with stage-playing. There would have been, in the early sixteenth century, little need for such urban stage-players to view their performing as anything other than an ancillary activity.

By contrast provincial performers, in their own quest for a continuing audience, were often forced to become itinerant, with the corollary that for such players a settled alternative employment would have been difficult and performing may have been at times their primary means of livelihood. Records of these early itinerant performers and their activities are increasingly coming to light, and while we know less about them than we do about the later and more famous London-based companies, we know enough to hazard some opinions. From the late fourteenth century onwards, most of them had identifiable patrons, and probably settled residences; the records of their appearances in various rural communities have some sort of regularity to them, but are not so numerous as to suggest that they were constantly on the road. Those who were truly the servants of some noble or gentle person would likely have had their domiciliar needs met by the person they served, and would have travelled with their occasional performances in a fairly small orbit and for reasons other than the necessity of making a living. For other troupes of players, not so happily situated, performing is likelier to have been an economic necessity, requiring more extensive travelling, and a greater dependence upon the income it produced.

These latter groups of provincial players were thus likely to have been 'professional' somewhat earlier than their counterparts in London. The professionalisation of the London-based stage-player's craft did not begin in earnest until after the death of King Henry VIII. But in the last decade or so of his reign both urban and rural groups of stage-players found themselves caught up in the doctrinal disputes attendant on the Reformation, and the involvement of some groups of players in the presentation of political subject matter led to a series of repressive measures across the land from the 1530s through the 1550s that silenced all but the most well connected or the most discreet of performers. London troupes wishing to carry on the business of playing through those troubled times found that protection from such statutory pressures soon became a necessity, and they sought the protection their provincial colleagues already had, the patronage of some noble or gentle person – not simply as a means of retiring into his household and becoming his domestic performers, but as a way to legitimate their continuing activity in the larger world.

The survival and financial success of those London companies of players that were able to find suitable patrons and to prosper under the new restrictions may have led in turn both to the growing profitability of stage-playing in London – a phenomenon that engendered its own resentments – and also to the erection, in the environs of the City, of purpose-built public playhouses some time after the accession of Queen Elizabeth. From this point onwards the part-time or amateur player increasingly disappeared from the urban setting, and the popularity of professional playing began to attract the notice of businessmen and investors as well as of writers, all of whom likely saw the activity as a potential source of income.

The consequent shift towards a greater commercialisation of stage-playing engendered an increasingly structured organisation for playing companies. The loose association of a few men and occasionally a boy that was characteristic of earlier troupes gave way to more formal relationships, with ownership of the company and its possessions vested in certain members called shareholders, who were bound to one another by indentures of association to meet the company's expenses and to share in its profits. For help with current production needs, shareholders could engage journeyman acting talent in the form of hired men to play adult roles in specific productions for a fixed wage; to fill the roles of women and children, as well as to prepare for the company's future, shareholders could take upon themselves the training of young boys in the craft of acting. Occasionally a group of shareholders might contemplate the outright purchase or erection of a playhouse, thereby becoming householders as well as shareholders; as their own landlords, they benefited from two kinds of income.

With the accession of King James I in 1603, the main companies of players were taken under royal patronage; from that point onwards they had the status of servants of the Crown. Some of them, like Edward Alleyn and the Burbages, grew rich during this period; others, like Andrew Cane, preserved the older tradition of maintaining a separate and second identity as freemen and tradesmen in the City of London while continuing to perform. The full commercialisation of London stage-playing was by this time virtually complete, and successful practitioners were able to earn a comfortable living and support their families on the proceeds of their craft. Throughout this period, English stage-playing remained an activity for males only, the cultural resistance to seeing women on the stage continuing strong until the Restoration.

One aspect of the developing professionalism of urban stage-players can be seen in their increasingly common practice of training up young boys in a kind of apprenticeship to the profession. As stage-players had no formal recognition as a guild, this sort of training conferred no rights of freedom upon its graduates, nor was it hedged round with the constraints of age and marital status imposed by the City on more formal kinds of apprenticeship.

In addition to the boy-players attached in this fashion to individual members of adult troupes, there were companies made up exclusively of boys. These companies of children performed before the public in London during the reigns of Queen Elizabeth and King James I, and their popularity was thought by some observers to threaten at times the hegemony of the adult players. The boys early attracted the notice of playwrights; a surprisingly large number of the surviving play-texts from this period were composed specifically for children to perform. Halfway through the reign of King James I, however, a combination of political misjudgements on the part of those who managed the children's companies and the waning of the public appetite for such performances resulted in the disappearance of companies of boy-players.

For the period covered by this volume, scholars have identified nearly five hundred people who were professional stage-players. Rudimentary biographical data is available for most of them, and quite full information for some forty or fifty. In addition, many documents speak of 'stage-players' or 'players of interludes' as a group. There is, in short, a fair amount of surviving evidence about these men and boys, though disparate rather than coherent in nature; accordingly, the documents in this section make no attempt at inclusiveness, but are rather chosen to be representative of the kind of data available for a study of stage-players.

Our modern notions about the increasing popularity of the theatre from the middle years of Queen Elizabeth's reign onwards are usually premised upon a belief in the increasing competence, even brilliance, of certain London-based playwrights; but it was due in perhaps equal measure to the performing skills of the best of the London players. This popularity was hard-won, achieved in the face of complex and shifting public attitudes about the appropriateness of stage-playing. At the beginning of our period, playing was inveighed against by cleric and layman alike. It was unnatural (some argued) that stage-players, idle drones whose stock-in-trade was mere public pretending, should be recompensed for contributing nothing to the common weal. It was immoral (others argued) that stage players should mouth salacious or seditious sentiments for the corruption of the masses while pretending to be other than what they were. But despite these attacks, noble and gentle persons quietly persisted in watching plays, and in rewarding players, against the tide of published opinion. In the latter half of the sixteenth century stage-playing found its public defenders, and was endorsed by some as being beneficial to the commonwealth. An active public

156   Players and playing

debate between these conflicting positions began, and was carried on at both the national and local level. Playing soon found itself authorised and prohibited in equal measure, but in the end it was finally accepted as part of the new social fabric. Some of the documents in the stage-player's quest for this acceptance follow.

[1] For an analogous set of classifications of players, see Samuel Cox's letter below (100).

VII The popular image of the stage-player

Co-existent with the statutory efforts to regulate stage-playing (as documented in the first section of this book) was a continuing articulation of strong emotional opposition to it. This hostility toward stage plays and stage-players arose for various reasons. The doctrinal opposition was based upon Scripture and the church fathers and stressed the immorality of playing, while the secular attacks centred upon its social and economic inutility. Proponents of the former view saw stage-players as lewd abominations, while to the latter group they were drones and parasites. The players and their defenders were more successful in answering attacks from the first group than from the second. The modern fashion of viewing these attacks as homogeneous, and of dismissing them all as the splenetic ranting of a joyless minority, is being dissipated in our own day, as social and cultural historians invite our attention to the legitimacy of many of the claims made by those who attacked stage plays. A reader of the texts generated by both sides in this debate about stage plays will inevitably find, embedded in the arguments of both factions, statements about the stage-players who brought those plays before the public. A sampling of such statements follows; interspersed among them are items of a more particular nature, attesting to specific instances in the lives of individual players and intended as a supplementary gloss on the more generalised remarks of the commentators.

90   Contention over the funeral obsequies for Henry VIII, 1547
PRO, SP10/1, fo. 8 (item 5), a letter from Stephen Gardyner, bishop of Winchester, to Sir William Paget, the Secretary of State

Using the recent death of Henry VIII as the grounds for his complaint, Gardyner here rehearses the common claim that stage-players have no sense of dignity or of the behaviour proper to certain occasions.

Master secretary, after my right hearty commendations; I sent unto you my servant yesterday, wherein by your advice I have had redress, and now I write unto you in another matter, somewhat greater, as it were, between game and earnest. Tomorrow the parishioners of this parish[1] and I have agreed to have solemn *dirige*[2] for our late sovereign lord and master, in earnest, as becometh us; and tomorrow certain players of my lord of Oxford's, as they say, intend on the other side within this borough of Southwark to have a solemn play, to try who shall have most resort, they in game or I in earnest; which me seemeth a marvellous contention, wherein some shall profess in the name of the commonwealth mirth and some sorrow at one time. Herein I follow the common determination to sorrow, till our late master be buried, and what the lewd fellows should mean in the contrary I cannot tell, nor cannot reform it, and therefore write unto you, who by means of my lord Protector may procure an uniformity in the commonwealth, all the body to do one thing, and in the interring of our old master to lament together and in the crowning of our now master to rejoice together; after which followeth incontinently a time of lamentation for sin [*i.e.* Lent], which is not to be neglected, and which I doubt not ye will, without me, consider your charge. I have herein spoken with master Acton, Justice of Peace, whom the players smally regard, and press him to a peremptory answer, whether he dare let them to play or not; whereunto he answereth neither yea nor nay, as to the playing; but as the assembly of people in this borough in this time, neither the burial finished nor the coronation done, he pleadeth to the players for the time Nay, till he have commandment to the contrary. But his Nay is not much regarded, and mine less, as party to players; and therefore I write unto you. Wherein if ye will not out of envy meddle, send me some word and I will myself sue to my lord Protector, for me thinketh it is most barbarous to play while in mourning, and too much money lost in blacks if we ought rather to play, as these playing beasts pretendeth, for Lucre, as in fortunate times it hath been accustomed, and in time of public rejoicing, so it is likewise honorable to proclaim mourning in misfortune, which shall set forth the coronation of our new master as black setteth forth white. But farewell to all these many players, and do as ye shall think good, and so fare you well. At my house in Southwark, the 5th of February.

    Your assured loving friend,
    Stephen Winton

[1] St Saviour's in Southwark, site of the bishop's London residence.
[2] A funeral mass.

91   Players and play-watchers equally corrupt, 1559

William Bavande, *A Work of Joannes Ferrarius Montanus Touching the Good Ordering of a Commonweal*, 1559 (STC 10831), fo. 100v

Ferrarius (actually Hans Eisermann) was a Marburg jurist whose 'work', entitled *De Republica bene instituenda Paraenesis*, was published in 1556, just two years before his death, and translated almost immediately into English by Bavande. Ferrarius dealt broadly with a number of topics, and attacks upon the theatre formed a very small part of his agenda.

For seeing we be naturally inclined to evil, and soon corrupt with naughty ensamples and talk, it is marvellous to consider, how that gesturing, which Tully elegantly termeth, the eloquence of the body, is able to move any man, and to prepare him to that which is evil, considering that such things be both disclosed to the eye and ear, as might a great deal more godlily be kept close, and to the greater benefit of the audience. Whereby a double offence is committed. First, by those dissolute players, which without any respect of innocency, without any regard of honesty, be nothing ashamed to exhibit the filthiest matters that they can devise. Secondly by the hearers, which vouchsafe to hear and behold such things, as only minister occasion of voluptuousness, to the great loss both of themselves and time.

92 Playing a dishonest and wicked occupation, 1569

Henry Cornelius Agrippa, *The Vanity and Uncertainty of Arts and Sciences*, 1569 (STC 204), sig. I4

Agrippa, a German physician, writer, and reputed magician, wrote his *De incertitudine et vanitate scientium et artium atque excellentia Verbi Dei declamatio* in 1526; it was Englished some forty years later by James Sandford, who had earlier translated Plutarch, Epictetus and many other authors into English. Like Ferrarius, Agrippa painted a large canvas, in which his few comments on stage plays seem perfunctory.

And therefore to exercise this art [of playing], is not only a dishonest and wicked occupation, but also to behold it, and therein to delight, is a shameful thing, because that the delight of a wanton mind is an offence. And to conclude, there was in times past no name more infamous than stage-players, and moreover, all they that had played an interlude in the theatre, were by the laws deprived from all honour.

93 Players offend the majesty of God, 1574

Geoffrey Fenton, *A Form of Christian Policy gathered out of French*, 1574 (STC 10793a), pp. 143–4

Fenton, like Edmund Spenser, spent much time as a civil servant in Ireland, and occupied himself in translating a number of works from other languages. The present text is a translation by him from the French of Jean Talpin.

All stage play[er]s, and interluders, puppet shows, and careless boys (as we call them) with all other sorts of people, whose principal end is in feeding the world with sights and fond pastimes, and juggling in good earnest the money out of other men's purses into their own hand, have been always noted of infamy, even in Rome, where yet was liberty enough to take pleasure in public sports ... Great then is the error of the magistrate to give sufferance to these players, whether they be minstrels or interluders, who, on a scaffold, babbling vain news to the slander of the world, put there in scoffing the virtues of honest men ... How often is the majesty of God offended in those two or three hours that those plays endure, both by wicked words, and blasphemy, impudent gestures, doubtful slanders, unchaste songs, and also by corruption of the wills of the players and the assistants. Let no man object here that by these public plays, many forbear to do evil, for fear to be publicly reprehended ... for it may be answered first, that in such disguised players given over to all sorts of dissolution, is not found a will to do good, seeing they care for nothing less than virtue.

94 A dialogue between Youth and Age, 1577

John Northbrooke, *A Treatise wherein Dicing, Dancing, vain Plays or Interludes, with other idle Pastimes, etc., commonly used on the Sabbath Day, are reproved by the Authority of the Word of God and Ancient Writers*, c. 1577 (STC 18670), pp. 58–9, 65, 69–71

Little is known about John Northbrooke. He was by his own account a Devonshire man, a sturdy Protestant, learned in the church fathers, and inspired every so often to set down a tract for the guidance of the less well informed. The present *Treatise* is cast, without any apparent sense of incongruity, in the form of a dramatic dialogue between Youth and Age, the former a naïve and eager enquirer, the latter a pious pedant of a familiar type. The narrowly specific focus of the *Treatise* is evident from its title; it is the earliest separate and systematic attack upon dramatic performances published in England, and contains the first known mention by name of the Theatre and Curtain playhouses.

YOUTH [Tell me about the men who play in] stage plays and interludes, which are now practised amongst us so universally in town and country.

AGE Those are called *Histriones*, or rather *Histrices*, which play upon scaffolds and stages interludes and comedies, or otherwise, with gestures, etc.

YOUTH What say you to those players and plays? Are they good and godly, meet to be used, haunted, and looked upon, which now are practised?

AGE To speak my mind and conscience plainly (and in the fear of God) they are not tolerable, nor sufferable in any commonweal, especially where the Gospel is preached; for it is right prodigality, which is opposite to liberality . . . prodigality is to bestow money and goods in such sort as it [is] spent either in banqueting, feasting, rewards to players of interludes, dicing, and dancing, etc., for the which no great fame or memory can remain to the spenders or receivers thereof . . . these are no examples for Christians to follow; . . . The like may I say of the gifts, buildings, and maintenance of such places for players, a spectacle and school for all wickedness and vice to be learned in. Saint Augustine saith, whosoever give their goods to interlude and stage-players is a great vice and sin, and not a virtue.

AGE [*After several classical examples of the profanity and immorality of stage plays*] Alas, my son, notwithstanding all this, are not almost all places in these our days replenished with jugglers, scoffers, jesters, and players, which may say and do what they list, be it never so filthily and fleshly, and yet are suffered, and heard with laughing and clapping of hands. Lactantius saith, 'those filthy and unhonest gestures and movings of interlude players, what other thing do they teach than wanton pleasure and stirring of fleshly lusters, unlawful appetites and desires, with their bawdy and filthy sayings and counterfeit doings?'

YOUTH Is there no laws, or decrees, that have been made against . . . players of interludes, sith they are so noisome a pestilence to infect a commonwealth?

AGE Very many laws, and decrees.

YOUTH I pray you, express some of them, for the better satisfying of my mind herein.

AGE [*After several classical examples*] Also there is a notable statute[1] made against vagabonds, rogues, etc., wherein is expressed what they are that shall be taken and accounted for rogues; amongst all the whole rabblement, common players in interludes are to be taken for rogues, and punishment is appointed for them to be burnt through the ear with an hot iron of an inch compass; and for the second fault, to be hanged as a felon, etc. The reason is, for that their trade is such an idle loitering life, a practice to all mischief, as you have heard before.

YOUTH If they leave this life, and become good true labourers of the commonwealth, to get their own livings with their own hands, in the sweat of their face, shall they not be admitted and taken again to the Lord's table, and afterward to be reputed and taken for honest men?

AGE Yes, truly.

[1] See 29.

95 Players a mixture of good and bad, 1579

Stephen Gosson, *The School of Abuse, containing a pleasant invective against poets, pipers, players, jesters and such like caterpillars of a commonwealth*, 1579 (STC 12097)

Like Christopher Marlowe (though ten years his senior), Stephen Gosson grew up in Canterbury, was educated at a Corpus Christi College (though at Oxford, not at Marlowe's Cambridge), and went on to write comedies and tragedies for the London stage; but there the resemblance ends. None of Gosson's plays have survived; probably none of them were printed. Gosson subsequently became a divine and a vocal moralist. Thomas Lodge, an opponent of Gosson's in the continuing controversy over the stage, suggests that in his earlier days Gosson had been a stage-player, but that later he turned 'from a player to become an envious preacher'(Thomas Lodge, 'A Defense of Poetry, Music, and Stage Plays'). In his later *Plays Confuted* (see below), Gosson warns his readers not to 'prefer the opinion of Lodge or any such like before the infallible testimony of your own senses' (sig G7v). Despite this coolness, some parts of Gosson's 'pleasant invective' are openly conciliatory to stage-players, and this strand of his thought is not normally given its due. Some representative passages follow.

[sigs. C3v–C4] I look still when players should cast me their gauntlets, and challenge a combat for entering so far into their possessions, as though I made them lords of this misrule, or the very schoolmasters of these abuses: though the best clerks be of that opinion, they hear not me say so. There are more houses than parish churches, more maids than Maulkin, more ways to the wood than one, and more causes in nature than efficients. The carpenter raiseth not his frame without tools, nor the devil his work without instruments; were not players the mean, to make these assemblies, such multitudes would hardly be drawn in so narrow room. They seek not to hurt, but desire to please; they have purged their comedies of wanton speeches, yet the corn which they sell is full of cockle; and the drink that they draw, overcharged with dregs.

[sig. C6r–v] Overlashing in apparel is so common a fault, that the very hirelings of some of our players, which stand at reversion of 6s by the week, jet under gentlemen's noses in suits of silk, exercising themselves to prating on the stage, and common scoffing when they come abroad, where they look askance over the shoulder at every man, of whom the Sunday before they begged an alms. I speak not this, as though every one that professeth the quality so abused himself, for it is well known, that some of them are sober, discreet, properly learned honest householders and citizens well thought on among their neighbours at home, though the pride of their shadows (I mean those hangbys whom they succour with stipend) cause them to be somewhat ill talked of abroad.

[sig. C8v] These [players] because they are allowed to play every Sunday, make four or five Sundays at least every week . . . to busy the wits of [the] people, for running a-woolgathering, and to empty their purses for thriving too fast.

[sig. D3] Were not we so foolish to taste every drug, and buy every trifle, players would shut in their shops, and carry their trash to some other country.

96 Players incline their audience to wickedness, 1580

?Anthony Munday, *A Second and Third Blast of Retrait from Plays and Theatres*, 1580 (STC 21677)

The author explains that 'the first blast' was Gosson's *School of Abuse* from the previous year. The present title continues with a description of the two sequent 'blasts': *the one whereof was sounded by a reverend bishop dead long since, the other by a worshipful and zealous gentleman now alive; one showing the filthiness of plays in times past, the other the abomination of theatres in the time present; both expressly proving that that commonweal is nigh unto the curse of God, wherein either players be made* [much] *of, or theatres maintained.* The 'reverend bishop' of the second blast was Salvianus, bishop of Massilia in the fifth century and a writer noted for his eloquence; the 'gentleman now alive' is conjectured to have been Anthony Munday, a prolific writer of ballads, romances and plays who was also employed as a heretic hunter by agents of the Crown, and was capable of turning his pen to either side of an issue. The selections which follow are all from the 'third' blast, many parts of which are indebted to Geoffrey Fenton and other writers in the anti-theatrical tradition. The writer's hope that stage-players will 'forsake their unlawful, ungodly and abominable exercise' (sig. A5) may be more formulaic and fashionable than fervently felt. The opening passage, on the inappropriateness of retaining stage-players as household servants, embodies a metaphor later used by Shakespeare.

[pp. 75–6] What credit can return to the noble[man], to countenance his men to exercise that quality which is not sufferable in any commonweal? Whereas it was an ancient custom that no man of honour should retain any man but such as was excellent in some one good quality or other, whereby if occasion so served, he might get his own living; then was every nobleman's house a commonweal in itself. But since the retaining of these caterpillars, the credit of noblemen hath decayed, and they are thought to be covetous by permitting their servants, which cannot live of themselves, and whom for nearness they will not maintain, to live at the devotion or alms of other men, passing from country to country, from one gentleman's house to another, offering their service, which is a kind of beggary.

[p. 95] It is marvellous to consider how the gesturing[1] of a player, which Tully termeth the eloquence of the body, is of force to move and prepare a man to that which is ill. For such things be disclosed to the eye, and to the ear, as might a great deal better be kept close. Whereby a double offence is committed: first by those dissolute players, which without regard of honesty, are not ashamed to exhibit the filthiest matters they can devise to the sight of men; secondly by the beholders, which vouchsafe to hear and behold such filthy things, to the great loss both of themselves and the time.

[pp. 110–17] When I see by them young boys, inclining of themselves unto wickedness, trained up in filthy speeches, unnatural and unseemly gestures, to be brought up by these schoolmasters in bawdry, and in idleness, I cannot choose but with tears and grief of heart lament ... And as for those stagers themselves, are they not commonly such kind of men in their conversation, as they are in profession? Are they not as variable in heart, as they are in their parts? Are they not as good practisers of bawdry, as enacters? Live they not in such sort themselves, as they give precepts unto others? Doth not their talk on the stage declare the nature of their disposition? Doth not everyone take that part which is proper to his kind? Doth not the ploughman's tongue [talk] of his plough; the seafaring man of his mast, cable, and sail; the soldier of his harness, spear, and shield; and bawdy mates of bawdy matters? Ask them, if in their laying out of their parts, they choose not those parts which is most agreeing to their inclination, and that they can best discharge? And look what every of them doth most delight in, that he can best handle to the contentment of others. If it be a roisting, bawdy, and lascivious part, wherein are unseemly speeches, and that they make choice of them as best answering, and proper to their manner of play; may we not say, by how much he exceed in his gesture, he delights himself in his part? And by so much it is pleasing to his disposition and nature? If (it be his nature) to be a bawdy player, and he delight in such filthy and cursed actions, shall we not think him in his life to be more disordered, and to abhor virtue?

But they perhaps will say, that such abuses as are handled on the stage, others by their examples, are warned to beware of such evils, to amendment ... I cannot by any means believe that the words proceeding from a profane player, and uttered in scorning sort, interlaced with filthy, lewd and ungodly speeches, have greater force to move men unto virtue, than the words of truth uttered by the godly preacher ... If the good life of a man be a better instruction to repentance than the tongue, or words, why do not players, I beseech you, leave examples of goodness to their posterity? ... Are they not notoriously known to be those men in their life abroad, as they are on the stage, roisters, brawlers, ill-dealers, boasters, lovers, loiterers, ruffians?... To conclude, the principal end of all their interludes is to feed the world with sights, and fond pastimes; to juggle in good earnest the money out of other men's purses into their own hands... Some have objected, that by these public plays many forbear to do evil for fear to be publicly reprehended.[2] And for that cause they will say it was tolerated in Rome, wherein emperors were touched, though they were present.

But to such it may be answered, first that in disguised players given over to all sorts of dissoluteness, is not found so much as a will to do good, seeing they care for nothing less than for virtue.

[p. 121] As for the players in these days which exhibit their games for lucre's sake ... they are, of the most part of men either of authority or learning, held for vagabonds and infamous persons; they may aptly be likened unto drones, which will not labour to bring in, but live of the labours of the painful gatherers.

[1] Note the indebtedness of this passage to the passage by William Bavande cited earlier (91).
[2] Geoffrey Fenton earlier offered the same argument (93).

97   Players are to be loathed, 1582

Stephen Gosson, *Plays Confuted in Five Actions*, 1582 (STC 12095)

Note the continued borrowing of language and phrase in the passages which follow. Gosson in this work becomes the most strident attacker of stage-players; their 'hearts are not right' (sig. B3), and they corrupt even potentially virtuous texts by performing them on the stage. In the dedicatory epistle to Sir Francis Walsingham, Gosson claims to have angered the players by his earlier attack, and professes to be concerned that 'the gentlemen players in the City of London are grown in such a heat that by their foaming, their fretting, their stamping, my friends to perceive how their hearts work [to my danger]' (sig. Av).

[sig. C7v] But whether plays, for the matter, or players, for their manners, be fit schoolmasters of honesty, I report me to them that by frequenting Theatres are very well acquainted with the argument of the one, the life of the other. If any goodness were to be learned at plays it is likely that the players themselves which commit every syllable to memory should profit most, because that as every man learneth so he liveth; and as his study is, such are his manners; but the daily experience of their behaviour showeth, that they reap no profit by the discipline themselves.

[sigs. D2v–3v] [Players, by their very nature, unfit to teach good morals:] For as they were forbidden in old time to expound any oracles which had any infection about their bodies; so have they no grace in rebuking others, that nourish a canker in their own souls. How are they able to pull us up that grovel as flat in the dust as we? What credit hath any good counsel in players' lips, when it works no amendment in themselves?... But neither the poets which pen the plays, nor the actors that present them upon the stage, do seek to do any good unto such as they rebuke, for the poet's intent is to wreak his own anger; . . . [and] the actors either hunt for their own profit, as the players in London; or follow the humour of their own fancies and youthful delights, as the students of the universities, and the inns of court.

[sig. E2] Sithence you see even by the examples of the Romans that plays are ratsbane to the government of commonweals, and that players by the judgement of them are infamous persons, unworthy of the credit of honest citizens, worthy to be removed from their tribe: if not for religion, yet for shame . . . withdraw your feet from Theatres, with noble Marius; set down some punishment for players, with the Roman censors; show yourselves to be Christians, and with wicked spectacles be not pulled from discipline to liberty, from virtue to pleasure, from God to Mammon.

[sigs. E3v–E4] The Law of God very straitly forbids men to put on women's garments, garments are set down for signs distinctive between sex and sex, to take unto us those garments that are manifest signs of another sex, is to falsify, forge, and adulterate, contrary to the express rule of the word of God, which forbiddeth it by threatening a curse unto the same.

All that do so are abomination un[to] the Lord, which way I beseech you shall they be excused, that put on, not the apparel only, but the gait, the gestures, the voice, the passions of a woman: all which like the writhings, and winding of a snake, are flexible to catch, before they speed; and bind up cords when they have possession. Some there are that think this commandment of God to be restrained to them, that go abroad in women's attire and use it for juggling, to shadow adultery.

[sig. E5] The proof is evident, the consequent is necessary, that in stage plays for a boy to put on the attire, the gesture, the passions of a woman; for a mean person to take upon him the title of a Prince with counterfeit port, and train, is by outward signs to show themselves otherwise than they are, and so within the compass of a lie, which by Aristotle's judgement is naught of itself and to be fled.

[sig. E6r–v] One [player] must learn to trip it like a lady in the finest fashion, another must have time to whet his mind unto tyranny that he may give life to the picture he presenteth, whereby they learn to counterfeit, and so to sin. Therefore whatsoever such plays as contain good matter are set out in print, may be read with profit, but cannot be played without a manifest breach of God's commandment.

[sig. G6v] Most of the players have been either men of occupations, which they have forsaken to live by playing, or common minstrels, or trained up from their childhood to this abominable exercise and have now no other way to get their living.

[sig. G7v] Let them that have no occupation at all ask God forgiveness for the time so evil spent, and apply themselves speedily to live within the compass of a commonweal. Let them not look to live by plays; the little thrift that followeth their great gain is a manifest token that God hath cursed it.

[sig. G8v] Plays are the inventions of the devil, the offerings of idolatry, the pomp of worldlings, the blossoms of vanity, the root of apostasy, the food of iniquity, riot, and adultery, detest them. Players are masters of vice, teachers of wantonness, spurs to impurity, the sons of idleness, so long as they live in this order, loathe them.

98 Players as painted sepulchres and double-dealing ambidexters, 1583

Philip Stubbes, *The Anatomy of Abuses*, 1583 (STC 23376)

Philip Stubbes attended both Cambridge and Oxford, but graduated from neither, preferring to continue his studies by travelling. He became a prolific writer, but not an opportunist like Munday; his point of view remained Christian and moral through all his works. His acknowledged aim in *The Anatomy* was not to abolish all amusements, but only the abuses of them. A temperate preface, attached to the first edition of the work, was struck from succeeding editions, lending them a sterner aspect. The present text is from the first edition.

[sig. ¶ 6r–v] Such is our gross and dull nature, that what thing we see opposite before our eyes, do pierce further and print deeper in our hearts and minds, than that thing which is heard only with the ears ... But being used (as now commonly they be) to the profanation of the Lord his sabbath, to the alluring and inveigling of the people from the blessed word of God preached, to theatres and unclean assemblies, to idleness, unthriftiness, whoredom, wantonness, drunkenness, and what not; and which is more, when they are used to this end, to maintain a great sort of idle persons, doing nothing but playing and loitering, having their livings of the sweat of other men's brows, much like unto dronets devouring the sweet honey of the poor labouring bees, then are they exercises (at no hand) sufferable.

[sigs. L5v–6] All the holy company of heaven ... do tremble and quake at the naming of God, and at the presence of His wrath, and do these mockers and flouters of his majesty, these dissembling hypocrites and flattering Gnatoes, think to escape unpunished? Beware therefore you masking players, you painted sepulchres, you double dealing ambidexters, be warned betimes, and like good computists cast your accounts before what will be the reward thereof in the end, lest God destroy you in his wrath; abuse God no more, corrupt his people no longer with your dregs, and intermingle not his blessed word with such profane vanities; for, at no hand, it is not lawful to mix scurrility with divinity, nor divinity with scurrility.

[sig. M1r–v] Therefore, I beseech all players and founders of plays and interludes, in the bowels of Jesus Christ, as they tender the salvation of their souls, and others, to leave off that cursed kind of life, and give themselves to such honest exercises, and godly mysteries, as God hath commanded them in his word to get their livings withal: for who will call him a wise man that playeth the part of a fool and a vice; who can call him a Christian, who playeth the part of a devil, the sworn enemy of Christ: who can call him a just man, that playeth the part of a dissembling hypocrite: and to be brief, who can call him a straight dealing man, who playeth a cozener's trick: and so of all the rest. Away therefore with this so infamous an art, for go they never so brave, yet are they counted and taken for beggars. And is it not true? Live they not upon begging of every one that comes? Are they not taken by the laws of the realm for rogues and vagabonds? I speak of such as travel the countries, with plays and interludes, making an occupation of it, and ought so to be punished, if they had their deserts. But hoping that they will be warned now at the last, I will say no more of them, beseeching them to consider what a fearful things it is to fall into the hands of God, and to provoke his wrath and heavy displeasure against themselves and others.

99 Players as unwholesome weeds, 1587

William Rankins, *A Mirror of Monsters, wherein is plainly described the manifold vices and spotted enormities that are caused by the infectious sight of plays*, 1587 (STC 20699)

Rankins, a professional writer, is here using his pen in the service of anti-theatrical interests, and in the process offering a thinly veiled challenge to royal morality. But his is no heartfelt outcry; a decade later Rankins was himself writing plays for Henslowe (all of them unfortunately lost), and was named in 1598 by Francis Meres as one of the three satirists of the age (the other two being Joseph Hall and John Marston). His case helps to remind us that anti-theatrical invective was a literary genre requiring only the adoption of a morally earnest persona by the writer. The popularity of the genre tells us more about the reading public than about its writers.

[fo. 2r–v] What men are these (nay, rather monsters) that thus corrupt so sweet a soil? Such are they, as in their outward show seem painted sepulchres, but dig up their deeds, and [you] find nothing but a mass of rotten bones.

Some term them Comedians, othersome Players, many Pleasers, but I Monsters, and why monsters? Because under colour of humanity they present nothing but prodigious vanity. These are wells without water, dead branches fit for fuel, cockle amongst corn, unwholesome weeds amongst sweet herbs, and finally, fiends that are crept into the world by stealth, and hold possession by subtle invasion.

But some of [them may] object that I chat beyond my charge . . . to speak against them that are privileged by a Prince, nay more, sworn servants to the anointed, allowed by magistrates, and commended by many. I easily answer: . . . the coat of a mighty and puissant Prince [cannot] privilege a subject to wander in error.

[fo. 9v] Of which sort of men (the more to be lamented) are these Players, who do not only exercise themselves in all kind of idleness, but minister occasion to many to incur the like? If then (as sure it is) idleness be the root of evil, and these men the root of idleness, it were pity but such a root should be fuel for the fire, to the intent the branches may flourish no longer.

100   Players as immoral profiteers, 1590
Samuel Cox, letter to an unknown recipient, dated 15 January 1590

Cox was personal secretary to Sir Christopher Hatton, and this letter is part of a collection of letters formerly belonging to the Hatton family; it is now in the British Library (Add. MS 15,891, fos. 184–5v). The letter is transcribed in full by Sir N. Harris Nicolas in his *Memoirs of the Life and Times of Sir Christopher Hatton, K.G.* (London, 1847), pp. xxix–xxxii, and excerpted by E. K. Chambers in *The Elizabethan Stage*, IV, 237. The occasion for the writing of the letter is unclear; though it purports to be the continuation of an earlier exchange, its arguments are the traditional ones rather than a subsequent set of more cogent ones. A principal issue is material gain; that players prosper seems to be Cox's chief source of resentment, and he makes several references to the immoral profits which accrue to playing.

Sir, your yesterday's letter reprehending me in some sort for my sharpness against the use of plays I received this day by your brother Mr Lewyn, for the which I heartily thank you, especially for your friendly care and regard which I find in them, to satisfy me in some points which I stood in doubt of; I must confess unto you I am somewhat scrupulous for the tolerating of these stage plays, which are nowadays without respect of persons, time, or place, so much used and allowed among us... What greater deformity can there be in any well-reformed state than to see the folly of a few fools bring divers wise men out of their wits? To see the gates of magistrates open for the one and shut up against the other? To see rich men give more to a player for a song, which he shall sing in one hour, than to their faithful servants for serving them a whole year? To see infinite numbers of poor people go a begging about the streets for penury, when players and parasites wax rich by juggling and jesting? It is said that the great and noble temple of Diana was built by the Amazons with the only money and riches taken from a player, and that the very pagans themselves did lament it, even in the time of blindness and ignorance: how much more may we Christians (enjoying the benefit of the Gospel) bewail the miseries of these times wherein we see more houses built for these lewd assemblies than for preaching or praying? This age requires other manners, another life. It was wondered at that two parasites gave more money to King Cadmus toward the building of the famous city of Thebes (which had a hundred gates unto it) than all his subjects did besides: and is it not as strange and much more lamentable in these days that (professing Christ as we do) we should suffer men to make professions and occupations of plays all the year long, whereby to enrich idle loiterers with plenty, while many of our poor brethren lie pitifully gasping in the streets, ready to starve and die of penury? In my poor opinion the building of Thebes with the parasites' ill-gotten goods cannot be more detestable: nor the pagans of that time more miserably wicked in this than ours: if we must needs tolerate these spectacles of folly for the vain recreation of the people. I could wish that players would use themselves nowadays, as in ancient former times they have done, which was only to exercise their interludes in the time of Christmas, beginning to play in the holidays and continuing until twelfth tide, or at the furthest until Ash Wednesday: of which players I find three sorts of people: the first, such as were in wages with the King, and played before him, some time at Hallowmass, and then in the latter Holy Days until twelfth-tide, and after that, only in Shrovetide; and these men had other trades to live of, and seldom or never played abroad, at any other times of the whole year. The second sort were such as pertained to noblemen, and were ordinary servants in their house, and only for Christmas times used such plays, without making profession to be players to go abroad for gain, for in such cases they were subject to the statute against retainers. The third sort were certain artisans in good towns and great parishes, as shoemakers, tailors, and such like, that used to play either in their town halls, or some time in churches, to make the people merry, where it was lawful for all persons to come, without exacting any money for their access, having only somewhat gathered of the richer sort by the churchwardens for their apparel and other necessaries, in which manner if our players nowadays used their sports and pastimes (not making their playing an occupation of idleness all the whole year, but an occupation only at certain festival times of rest when the people are free from labour), in my opinion they should less offend God in playing, and the magistrate for granting them the use of such a moderate kind of liberty. And so, praying pardon of you for my troubling of you so long with a matter of so idle and playing a subject, I commend you to God's merciful and richest blessings. From Westhall Hill the 15th of January 1590. Your very true friend, Samuel Cox

101 The adventures of Roberto, 1592

Robert Greene, *Greene's Groatsworth of Wit, bought with a Million of Repentance*, 1592 (STC 12245)

One of the best-known Elizabethan pamphleteers and playwrights, Greene was perhaps the first man to make his living by his pen. Though he professed to despise players, he supported himself largely by their readiness to buy his plays; the ambivalence of this situation seemed merely to be further grist for his prose writings. In the present tract, ostensibly 'written before his death and published at his dying request' (t.p.), Greene commences the story of one Roberto, a disinherited young man forced to make his way by his wits. [sigs. D4–E1v]

After suffering cruel rejection by his wealthy brother and a formerly kind courtesan, Roberto laid his head on his hand, and leaned his elbow on the earth, sighing out sadly, 'Alas, how I am wounded by my own weapons!!' On the other side of the hedge sat one that heard his sorrow; who, getting over, came towards him, and brake off his passion. When he approached, he saluted Roberto in this sort.

'Gentleman', quoth he, '(for so you seem), I have by chance heard you discourse some part of your grief; which appeareth to be more than you will discover, or I can conceipt. But if you will vouchsafe such simple comfort as my ability may yield, assure yourself that I will endeavour to do the best, that either may procure you profit or bring you pleasure; the rather for that I suppose you are a scholar, and pity it is men of learning should live in lack.'

Roberto, wondering to hear such good words, for that this iron age affords few that esteem of virtue, returned him thankful gratulations, and (urged by necessity) uttered his present grief, beseeching his advice how he might be employed. 'Why, easily', quoth he, 'and greatly to your benefit; for men of my profession get by scholars their whole living.' 'What is your profession?' said Roberto. 'Truly, sir,' said he, 'I am a player.' 'A player?' quoth Roberto. 'I took you rather for a gentleman of great living, for if by outward habit men should be censured, I tell you, you would be taken for a substantial man.' 'So I am where I dwell,' quoth the player, 'reputed able at my proper cost to build a windmill. What though the world once went hard with me, when I was fain to carry my playing fardel a footback; *tempora mutantur*; I know you know the meaning of it better than I, but I thus conster it: *it's otherwise now*; for my very share in playing apparel will not be sold for two hundred pounds.' 'Truly', said Roberto, ''tis strange that you should so prosper in that vain practice, for that it seems to me your voice is nothing gracious.' 'Nay then,' said the player, 'I mislike your judgement. Why, I am as famous for Delphrigus, and the King of Fairies, as ever was any of my time. The Twelve Labours of Hercules have I terribly thundered on the stage, and played three scenes of the Devil in the High Way to Heaven.' 'Have ye so?' said Roberto. 'Then I pray you pardon me . . . but how mean you to use me?' 'Why, sir, in making plays,' said the other, 'for which you shall be well paid, if you will take the pains.'

Roberto, perceiving no remedy, thought best in respect of his present necessity to try his wit, and went with him willingly; who lodged him at the town's end in a house of retail.

[Within a short time Roberto achieved fame as] an arch-play-making poet, his purse like the sea sometime swelled, anon like the same sea fell to a low ebb; yet seldom he wanted, his labours were so well esteemed.

[sigs. E3–F2; *Here Greene breaks off his narrative.*] Here (gentlemen) break I off Roberto's speech; whose life in most parts agreeing with mine, found one self-punishment as I have done. Hereafter suppose me the said Roberto, and I will go on with what he promised.

To those gentlemen his quondam acquaintance, that spend their wits in making plays, R. G. wisheth a better exercise, and wisdom to prevent his extremities . . . Base-minded men all three of you, if by my misery you be not warned; for unto none of you (like me) sought those burs to cleave; those puppets (I mean) that spake from our mouths, those antics garnished in our colours. Is it not strange that I, to whom they all have been beholding; is it not like that you, to whom they all have been beholding; shall (were ye in that case as I am now) be both at once of them forsaken? Yes, trust them not; for there is an upstart crow, beautified with our feathers, that with his *tiger's heart wrapped in a player's hide* supposes he is as well able to bombast out a blank verse as the best of you; and being an absolute *Johannes fac totum*,[1] is in his own conceit the only shake-scene in a country.[2] O, that I might intreat your rare wits to be employed in more profitable courses, and let those apes imitate your past excellence, and never more acquaint them with your admired inventions. I know the best husband of you all will never prove an usurer, and the kindest of them all will never prove a kind nurse; yet whilst you may, seek you better masters; for it is pity men of such rare wits should be subject to the pleasure of such rude grooms.

[1] Johnny Do-All.
[2] This passage is usually taken as a deprecating reference to Shakespeare.

102 The opinions of Pierce Penniless, 1592

Thomas Nashe, *Pierce Penniless his supplication to the Devil*, 1592 (STC 18373).

Nashe, like Greene, was a prolific writer of poems, pamphlets, and prose fiction as well as plays for the stage. In the following passage he aligns himself with the stage-player's defenders.

[sig. D4r–v] In Augustus' time (who was the patron of all witty sports) there happened a great affray in Rome about a player, insomuch as all the city was in an uproar; whereupon the Emperor (after the broil was somewhat overblown) called the player before him, and asked what was the reason that a man of his quality durst presume to make such a brawl about nothing. He smilingly replied, 'It is good for thee, O Caesar, that the people's heads are troubled with brawls and quarrels about us and our light matters; for otherwise they would look into thee and thy matters.' Read Lipsius or any profane or Christian politician, and you shall find him of this opinion. Our players are not as the players beyond sea, a sort of squirting bawdy comedians, that have whores and common courtesans to play women's parts, and forbear no immodest speech or unchaste action that may procure laughter; but our scene is more stately furnished than ever it was in the time of Roscius,[1] our representations honourable, and full of gallant resolution, not consisting, like theirs, of a Pantaloon, a Whore, and a Zany,[2] but of emperors, kings, and princes; whose true tragedies ... they do vaunt.

Not Roscius nor Aesop, those admired tragedians that have lived ever since before Christ was born, could ever perform more in action than famous Ned Alleyn.[3] I must accuse our poets of sloth and partiality, that they will not boast in large impressions what worthy men (above all nations) England affords. Other countries cannot have a fiddler break a string but they will put it in print; and the old Romans, in the writings they published, thought scorn to use any but domestical examples of their own home-bred actors, scholars, and champions, and them they would extol to the third and fourth generation: cobblers, tinkers, fencers, none escaped them, but they mingled them all in one gallimaufry of glory.

Here I have used a like method, not of tying myself to mine own country, but by insisting in the experience of our time: and, if I ever write any thing in Latin (as I hope one day I shall), not a man of any desert here amongst us, but I will have up. Tarlton, Ned Alleyn, Knell, Bentley,[4] shall be made known to France, Spain, and Italy: and not a part that they surmounted in, more than other, but I will there note and set down, with the manner of their habits and attire.

[1] A renowned Roman actor, later the archetype of the stage-player.
[2] Typical characters in the Italian *commedia dell'arte*.
[3] Edward Alleyn, perhaps the most famous actor of the 1590s, a member of the Lord Admiral's company of players.
[4] Richard Tarlton, William Knell and John Bentley were prominent members of the Queen's own company of stage-players, active in the 1580s and 1590s.

103 Accusations of sexual perversion and stage-playing, 1600

PRO, SP12/274, Item 126, 4 May 1600; the document is unpublished.

This affidavit, signed by eight Englishmen living in Sweden, lays charges of defamation against one Leonard Tucker, another Englishman. Tucker had apparently conceived a grudge against one James Hill, an agent of Sir Francis Walsingham's, and the writers of this document (presumably Hill's friends) wished to protest Tucker's conduct. They recount that Tucker's worst slanders against Hill involved charges that he was both a sexual pervert and a former stage-player. (For more on Hill, see Erik Wikland, *Elizabethan Players in Sweden 1591–92* (Stockholm: Almqvist and Wiksell, 1962).)

At Nyköping in Sweden this 4th of May in the year of Our Lord God 1600:

We whose names be hereunder written, remaining in Sweden, do certify unto those to whom these presents shall come that Leonard Tucker, our countryman, hath here in open court appeached the worshipful Mr James Hill for a 'shellom',[1] which is in these parts the greatest name of infamy that can be spoken to the meanest or vilest person;

And that Mr Hill hath also buggered a boy of his own, wherewith it appeared he charged him but in way of requital, for that Mr Hill, in the late Finland voyage, having him a shipboard with him [*i.e.* with Tucker], and seeing him to use more than ordinary familiarity towards his boy, did in friendly manner after give him warning thereof;

And that further, Mr Hill had been heretofore a player, and having stolen away their apparel, came into this country of Sweden, where he now remaineth in service by his excellency.

[1] Possibly *skálm*, a dwarf or fool; the word may have carried more opprobrium in 1600.

104 Cambridge students, aspiring to be stage-players, talk with Burbage and Kemp, c. 1601

The Return from Parnassus, London, 1606 (STC 19309). See J. B. Leishman, ed., *The Three Parnassus Plays* (London, 1949), 338–43.

The *Pilgrimage to Parnassus* and the two parts of the *Return from Parnassus* are the work of an unknown scholar of St John's College, Cambridge, at the turn of the century, and they dramatise the difficulties lying in the path of two students, Studioso and Philomusus, who wish to pursue the life of the mind and the muses. The following extract recounts their brief entrance into the world of the stage.

STUDIOSO, KEMP, BURBAGE, PHILOMUSUS

STUDIOSO Welcome, Mr Kemp, from dancing the Morris over the Alps.

KEMP Well, you merry knaves, you may come to the honour of it one day; is it not better to make a fool of the world as I have done, than to be fooled of the world, as you scholars are? But be merry my lads, you have happened upon the most excellent vocation in the world; for money, they come north and south to bring it to our playhouse, and for honour, who of more report than Dick Burbage and Will Kemp? He's not counted a gentleman that knows not Dick Burbage and Will Kemp, there's not a country wench that can dance Sellenger's Round but can talk of Dick Burbage and Will Kemp . . .

BURBAGE Mr Studioso, I pray you take some part in this book and act it, that I may see what will fit you best. I think your voice would serve for Hieronimo; observe how I act it and then imitate me:

  Who calls Hieronimo from his naked bed?

STUDIOSO Who calls Hieronimo from his naked bed?

BURBAGE You will do well after a while . . .

BURBAGE I like your face, and the proportion of your body for Richard the Third. I pray, Mr Philomusus, let me see you act a little of it.

PHILOMUSUS Now is the winter of our discontent
  Made glorious summer by the sun of York.

BURBAGE Very well I assure you. Well, Mr Philomusus and Mr Studioso, we see what ability you are of; I pray walk with us to our fellows, and we'll agree presently.

PHILOMUSUS We will follow you straight, Mr Burbage.

KEMP It's good manners to follow us, Master Philomusus and Master Otioso.

[*Exeunt* BURBAGE *and* KEMP]

PHILOMUSUS And must the basest trade bring us relief?
  Must we be practised to those leaden spouts
  That nought do vent but what they do receive?

(a) Woodcut of Will Kemp, 1600

From the title page of *Kemp's Nine Days' Wonder*, London, 1600 (STC 14923), a first-person narrative of Kemp's celebrated morris dance from London to Norwich (see Studioso's opening remark in the selection above (104)).

Kemps nine daies vvonder.

Performed in a daunce from London to Norwich.

Containing the pleasure, paines and kinde entertainment of William Kemp betweene London and that Citty in his late Morrice.

Wherein is somewhat set downe worth note; to reproove the slaunders spred of him: many things merry, nothing hurtfull.

Written by himselfe to satisfie his friends.

LONDON
Printed by E. A. for *Nicholas Ling*, and are to be solde at his shop at the west doore of Saint Paules Church. 1600.

105 Christopher Beeston accused of fornication, 1602

Bridewell Court Minute Books (King Edward School, Witley, Surrey), BK IV, folios as noted below. Beeston, a prominent stage-player, was not the only stage-player to have such accusations laid against him.

1602, October–November. Margery White, sent to Bridewell prison for having a child in whoredom by one Henry Noone of the Star and Cock in Fenchurch Street, deposes as follows . . .

[fo. 327v; court of 27 October 1602] And further she saith that one Christopher Beeston a player at one Winter's house in Star Alley without Bishopsgate had the use of her body, but as she saith he did it forcibly, for, said he, 'I have lain with a hundred wenches in my time.'

[fo. 330; court of 5 November 1602] Christopher Beeston, a player, accused by Margaret White, a prisoner of this house, to have had the use of her body at one Goodwife Winter's house without Bishopsgate on Midsummer Even last, being himself examined as touching the premises, utterly denieth it and saith it is done of malice. Ordered to put in sureties for his appearance within four days next after warning.

[fo. 332; court of 13 November 1602] [Mr Knevett, Sir Henry Billingsley's clerk,] utterly denieth that ever he used any such speeches that one Shepperd charged him to speak as concerning one Beeston, a player, which was to this effect, that Beeston himself said that he had lain with an hundred women in his time.

[fo. 332; court of 13 November 1602] And forasmuch as the said Christopher Beeston is by one Margaret White, a prisoner of this house, accused to have committed with her the abominable sin of adultery in most filthy and brutish manner in one Winter's house in an alley without Bishopsgate on Midsummer Eve last, for which he was convented before certain of the governors of this house, and he being examined utterly denieth the fact, notwithstanding she justifieth it to his face. At which time also the said Beeston and others his confederates players did very unreverently demean themselves to certain governors and much abused the place, and yet upon some reports made known to this court greatly suspected to have committed the fact. And because at this court also some in the said Beeston's behalf hath contrary to all good order taken exceptions against some of the governors of this house, it is ordered by a general consent that such a course shall be in law proceeded against him as is and shall be thought fit for so great a crime.

106 Players work in an ancient and honorable tradition, 1612

Thomas Heywood, *An Apology for Actors*, 1612 (STC 13309).

Heywood, a stage player as well as a playwright, addresses himself here not to a defence of plays but to an exoneration of 'my good friends and fellows, the City actors', hoping therein 'to touch some particulars concerning us, to approve our antiquity, ancient dignity, and the true use of our quality' (A3).

[sigs. B4, C3r–v] To turn to our domestic histories, what English blood seeing the person of any bold Englishman presented and doth not hug his fame, and honey at his valour, pursuing him in his enterprise with his best wishes, and as being rapt in contemplation, offers to him in his heart all prosperous performance, as if the personator were the man personated, so bewitching a thing is lively and well-spirited action, that it hath power to new mould the hearts of the spectators and fashion them to the shape of any noble and notable attempt ... [Ancient philosophers] that lived (as I may say) in the childhood and infancy of the world, before it knew how to speak perfectly, thought even in those days that action was the nearest way to plant understanding in the hearts of the ignorant.

Yea (but say some) you ought not to confound the habits of either sex, as to let your boys wear the attires of virgins, etc. To which I answer: the Scriptures are not always to be expounded merely according to the letter (for in such estate stands our main sacramental controversy), but they ought exactly to be conferred with the purpose they handle. To do as the Sodomites did, use preposterous lusts in preposterous habits, is in that text flatly and severely forbidden; nor can I imagine any man, that hath in him any taste or relish of Christianity, to be guilty of so abhorred a sin. Besides, it is not probable that plays were meant in that text, because we read not of any plays known in that time that Deuteronomy was writ, among the children of Israel, nor do I hold it lawful to beguile the eyes of the world in confounding the shapes of either sex, as to keep any youth in the habit of a virgin, or any virgin in the shape of a lad, to shroud them from the eyes of their fathers, tutors, or protectors, or to any other sinister intent whatsoever. But to see our youths attired in the habit of women, who knows not what their intents be? Who cannot distinguish them by their names, assuredly knowing they are but to represent such a lady, at such a time appointed?.

[sigs. E2–E3] Roscius, whom the eloquent orator and excellent statesman of Rome, Marcus Cicero, for his elegant pronunciation and formal gesture called his jewel, had from the common treasury of the Roman exchequer a daily portion allowed him of so many *sestertii* as in our coin amount to £16 and a mark, or thereabouts, which yearly did arise to any nobleman's revenues. So great was the fame of this Roscius, and so good his estimation, that learned Cato made a question whether Cicero could write better than Roscius could speak and act ... [*Heywood offers to omit discussion of French and Italian players in order*] to do some right to our English actors, as Knell, Bentley, Mills, Wilson, Cross, Laneham,[1] and others; these, since I never saw them, as being before my time, I cannot (as an eye-witness of their desert) give them that applause which no doubt they worthily merit, yet by the report of many judicial auditors their performance of many parts have been so absolute that it were a kind of sin to drown their worths in Lethe, and not commit their (almost forgotten) names to eternity. Here I must needs remember Tarlton,[2] in his time gracious with the Queen his sovereign, and in the people's general applause, whom succeeded Will Kemp,[3] as well in the favour of her Majesty as in the opinion and good thoughts of the general audience. Gabriel, Singer, Pope, Phillips, Sly,[4] all the right I can do them is but this, that though they be dead, their deserts yet live in the remembrance of many. Among so many dead let me not forget one yet alive in his time the most worthy famous, Master Edward Alleyn. To omit these, as also such as for divers imperfections, may be thought insufficient for the quality. Actors should be men picked out personable, according to the parts they present; they should be rather scholars, that though they cannot speak well, yet know how to speak, or else to have that volubility that they can speak well, though they understand not what, and so both imperfections may by instructions be helped and amended; but where a good tongue and a good conceit both fail, there can never be a good actor. I also could wish that such as are condemned for their licentiousness might by a general consent be quite excluded our society; for as we are men that stand in the broad eye of the world, so should our manners, gestures, and behaviours favour of such government and modesty, to deserve the good thoughts and reports of all men, and to abide the sharpest censures even of those that are the greatest opposites to the quality. Many amongst us I know to be of substance, of government, of sober lives, and temperate carriages, housekeepers, and contributary to all duties enjoined them, equally with them that are ranked with the most bountiful; and if so many of sort, there be any few degenerate from the rest in that good demeanour, which is both requisite and expected at their hands, let me entreat you not to censure hardly of all for the misdeeds of some, but rather to excuse us, as Ovid doth the generality of women.

[sigs. F2–F3] [Some who attack the profession or quality of stage-playing say that] the Romans in their time, and some in these days have abused it, and therefore we volley out our exclamations against the use. Oh shallow! Because such a man has his house burnt, we shall quite condemn the use of fire, because one man quaffed poison, we must forbear to drink, because some have been shipwrecked, no man shall hereafter traffic by sea. Then I may as well argue thus: he cut his finger, therefore must I wear no knife; yond man fell from his horse, therefore must I travel afoot; that man surfeited, therefore dare I not eat. What can appear more absurd than such a gross and senseless assertion? I could turn this unpointed weapon against his breast that aims it at mine, and reason thus: Roscius had a large pension allowed him by the Senate of Rome, why should not an actor of the like desert have the like allowance now? ... Playing is an ornament to the City, which strangers of all nations, repairing hither, report of in their countries, beholding them here with some admiration; for what variety of entertainment can there be in any city of Christendom more than in London? ... Our English tongue, which hath been the most harsh, uneven and broken language of the world, part Dutch, part Irish, Saxon, Scotch, Welsh, and indeed a gallimaufry of many, but perfect in none, is now, by this secondary means of playing, continually refined, every writer striving in himself to add a new flourish unto it; so that in process, from the most rude and unpolished tongue, it is grown to a most perfect and composed language.

[1] William Knell, John Bentley, Tobias Mills, Robert Wilson and John Laneham were all members of the Queen's company of players, active in the 1580s and 1590s; 'Cross' probably refers to Samuel Crosse, a stage-player in Shakespeare's company of whom virtually nothing else is known.
[2] Richard Tarlton was the most famous comedian of his day.
[3] Will Kemp was a noted comedian who played in many of Shakespeare's best-known plays.
[4] John Singer was another of the Queen's players; Thomas Pope, Augustine Phillips and Will Sly were

Lord Chamberlain's men. 'Gabriel' is probably Gabriel Spencer, a Lord Admiral's player, killed by Ben Jonson in a duel in 1598.

107 The proper name for a player is Hypocrite, 1615

I. G., *A Refutation of the Apology for Actors*, 1615 (STC 12214)

This work, by an unknown author supposed on insufficient evidence to be one John Greene, is a direct rebuttal to Thomas Heywood's *Apology for Actors* (for excerpts, see above). The chief characteristic of I.G.'s prose is its derivative nature; in it the reader may find recapitulated the arguments and the rhetoric of writers cited earlier in this section.

[pp. 55–7] All the whole company of heaven, angels, archangels, cherubim, seraphim, thrones, dominations, virtues, principalities, potestates, and all powers whatsoever, yea the devils themselves do tremble and quake at the naming of God, and at His presence. And do these mockers and flouters of His majesty, these dissembling hypocrites, think to escape unpunished? Beware, therefore, you players, hypocrites, and like good comptists cast up your accounts beforehand, what will be your reward in the end. Abuse God no more, corrupt his people no longer with your dregs, and intermingle not His blessed Word with your profane vanities.

[The efficient cause of plays is the devil; the material cause is their subject matter, inevitably blasphemous;] Hence ariseth the formal cause, or form of plays, which consisteth in the action, and in the actors. The action is twofold, in word and in deed. The action in words is lascivious speeches ... set forth ... with the grace, elegancy, and lustre of the tongue. The action in deed is the setting forth of all enormities and exorbitances, with the personating of the doers of them ... The form that consists in the actors is the parts they play ... And therefore these players, through the parts they act carrying the note and brand of all kind of cursed people on their backs, wheresoever they go, are to be hissed out of all Christian kingdoms, if they will have truth and not vanity, Christ and not the devil to dwell among them.

[p. 62] That man that giveth money for the maintenance of [stage-players] must needs incur the danger of *praemunire*, that is, severe judgement, except they repent. For the Apostle biddeth us beware lest we communicate with other men's sins, and this their doing is not only to communicate with other men's sins, and maintain evil to the destruction of themselves and many others, but also a maintaining of a great sort of idle and buzzing drones, to suck up and devour the good honey whereupon the poor bees should live. And therefore let all players and founders of plays, as they tender the salvation of their own souls and others, leave off that cursed kind of life, and betake themselves to such honest exercises and godly mysteries as God hath commanded in his word to get their living withal. For who will call him a wise man that playeth the fool and the vice? Who can call him a good Christian that playeth the part of a devil, the sworn enemy of Christ? Who can call him a just man that playeth the dissembling hypocrite? Who can call him a straight-dealing man, that playeth a cozener's trick? And so of all the rest. The wise man is ashamed to play the fool, but players will seem to be such in public view to all the world; a good

Christian hateth the devil, but players will become artificial devils excellently well; a just man cannot endure hypocrisy, but all the acts of players is dissimulation, and the proper name of Player (witness the *Apology* itself) is Hypocrite. A true-dealing man cannot endure deceit, but players get their living by craft and cozenage. For what greater cheating can there be than for money to render that which is not money's worth. Then seeing they are fools, artificial devils, hypocrites and cozeners, most evident it is that their art is not for Christians to exercise, as being diabolical, and themselves infamous; such indeed as the Lacedaemonians[1] had, and we also have great reason to extrude out of our commonwealth, for they are idle, vicious, dishonest, malicious, prejudicial and unprofitable to the same.

[1] The ancient Spartans.

108 Description of a common player, 1615

John Cocke, 'The Character of a Common Player', first published in 1615 in a collection of essays by John Stevens entitled *Satirical Essays Characters and Others* (STC 23250)

The book was reissued later the same year as *Essays and Characters, Ironical and Instructive*, in which many of the essays, including the one on the common player, were amplified. The text that follows is from this amplified edition (pp. 295–301), with one or two emendations carried over from the first edition.

A Common Player

Is a slow payer, seldom a purchaser, never a Puritan. The statute hath done wisely to acknowledge him a rogue errant, for his chief essence is a daily counterfeit. He hath been familiar so long with out-sides, that he professes himself (being unknown) to be an apparent gentleman. But his thin felt, and his silk stockings, or his foul linen, and fair doublet, do (in him) bodily reveal the broker: So being not suitable, he proves a motley: his mind observing the same fashion as his body: both consist of parcels and remnants: but his mind hath commonly the newer fashion, and the newer stuff: he would not else hearken so passionately after new tunes, new tricks, new devices: these together apparel his brain and understanding, whilst he takes the materials upon trust, and is himself the tailor to take measure of his soul's liking. He doth conjecture somewhat strongly, but dares not commend a play's goodness, till he hath either spoken, or heard the epilogue: neither dares he entitle good things *good*, unless he be heartened on by the multitude: till then he saith faintly what he thinks, with a willing purpose to recant or persist: so howsoever he pretends to have a royal master or mistress, his wages and dependence prove him to be the servant of the people. When he doth hold conference upon the stage, and should look directly in his fellow's face, he turns about his voice into the assembly for applause's sake, like a trumpeter in the fields, that shifts places to get an echo. The cautions of his judging humour (if he dares undertake it) be a certain number of saucy rude jests against the common lawyer; handsome conceits against the fine courtiers; delicate quirks against the rich cuckold a citizen; shadowed glances for good innocent ladies and gentlewomen; with a nipping scoff for some honest justice, who hath once imprisoned him; or some thrifty tradesman, who hath allowed him no credit: always remembered, his object is *a new play* or *a play newly revived*. Other poems he admits, as good fellows take tobacco, or ignorant burgesses give a voice, for company's sake; as things that neither maintain nor be against him. To be a player, is to have a *mithridate* against the pestilence; for players cannot tarry where the plague reigns; and therefore they be seldom infected. He can seem no less than one in honour, or at least one mounted; for unto miseries which persecute such, he is most incident. Hence it proceeds, that in the prosperous fortune of a play frequented, he proves immoderate, and falls into a drunkard's paradise, till it be *last* no longer. Otherwise when adversities come, they come together: for Lent and Shrove Tuesday be not far asunder, then he is dejected daily and weekly: his blessings be neither lame nor monstrous; they go upon four legs, but move slowly, and make as great a distance between their steps, as between the four terms. Reproof is ill bestowed upon him; it cannot alter his conditions: he hath been so accustomed to the scorn and laughter of his audience, that he cannot be ashamed of himself: for he dares laugh in the midst of a serious conference, without blushing. If he marries, he mistakes the woman for the boy in woman's attire, by not respecting a difference in the mischief: but so long as he lives unmarried, he mistakes the boy, or a whore for the woman; by courting the first on the stage, or visiting the second at her devotions. When he is most commendable, you must confess there is no truth in him: for his best action is but an imitation of truth, and an imitation is not the thing itself. It may be imagined I abuse his carriage, and he perhaps may suddenly be thought fair-conditioned: for he *plays above board*. Take him at the best, he is but a shifting companion; for he lives effectually by putting on, and putting off. If his profession were single, he would think himself a simple fellow, as he doth all professions besides his own: his own therefore is compounded of all natures, all humours, all professions. He is politic enough to perceive the commonwealth's doubts of his licence, and therefore in spite of Parliaments or statutes he incorporates himself by the title of a brotherhood. Painting and fine clothes may not by the same reason be called abusive, that players may not be called rogues: *For they be chief ornaments of his Majesty's Revels*. I need not multiply his character: for boys and every one, will no sooner see men of this faculty walk along but they will (unasked) inform you what he is by the vulgar title. Yet in the general number of them, many may deserve a wise man's commendation: and therefore did I prefix an epithet of *common*, to distinguish the base and artless appendants of our City companies, which often times start away into rustical wanderers and then (like Proteus) start back again into the City number.

109 The character of an excellent player, 1615

Sir Thomas Overbury, *New and Choice Characters of Several Authors, together with that exquisite and unmatched poem The Wife, written by Sir Thomas Overbury; . . . with other things added to this sixth impression*, 1615 (STC 18908).

The piece excerpted below appeared for the first time in the sixth edition of this work, and is thought to have been included as a response to J. Cocke's attack on players, above.

Overbury is generally presumed not to be its author; speculation has centred upon John Webster, though evidence is scant.

An Excellent Actor

[sigs. M5v–6v] Whatsoever is commendable in the grave orator is most exquisitely perfect in him; for by a full and significant action of body he charms our attention: sit in a full theatre and you will think you see so many lines drawn from the circumference of so many ears, whiles the *actor* is the *centre*. He doth not strive to make nature monstrous, she is often seen in the same scene with him, but neither on stilts nor crutches; and for his voice, 'tis not lower than the prompter, nor louder than the foil and target. By his action he fortifies moral precepts with example; for what we see him personate, we think truly done before us: a man of a deep thought might apprehend the ghosts of our ancient heroes walked again, and take him (at several times) for many of them . . . He adds grace to the poet's labours: for what in the poet is but ditty, in him is both ditty and music. He entertains us in the best leisure of our life, that is, between meals, the most unfit time either for study or bodily exercise . . . All men have been of his occupation: and indeed, what he doth feignedly, that do others essentially: this day one plays a monarch, the next a private person. Here one acts a tyrant, on the morrow an exile: a parasite this man tonight, tomorrow a precisian, and so of divers others. I observe, of all men living, a worthy actor in one kind is the strongest motive of affection that can be: for when he dies, we cannot be persuaded any man can do his parts like him. Therefore the imitating characterist was extreme idle in calling them rogues. His muse, it seems, with all his loud invocation, could not be worked to light him a snuff to read the Statute. For I would let his malicious ignorance understand that rogues are not to be employed as main ornaments to His Majesty's revels. But the itch of bestriding the press, or getting up on this wooden Pacolet,[1] hath defiled more innocent paper than ever did laxative physic. I value a worthy actor by the corruption of some few of the quality, as I would do gold in the ore; I should not mind the dross, but the purity of the metal.

[1] A fabulous horse capable of transporting its rider instantly to any place desired; from the old romance of *Valentine and Orson*.

110 Anonymous funeral elegy for Richard Burbage, 1619

Manuscript commonplace book, formerly in the Huth Library, now at the Huntington Library, shelfmark HM 198, 99–101; transcribed in Ingleby, *Shakespeare, the Man and the Book*, part II, 180–2, with an excellent preliminary discussion of the corrupted versions of the poem; and in Nungezer, *A Dictionary of Actors*, 74–6.

A Funeral Elegy on the Death of the famous Actor Richard Burbage who died on Saturday in Lent the 13th of March 1618 [/9]

>   Some skilful limner help me; if not so,
>   Some sad tragedian help t' express my woe.

But O he's gone, that could both best; both limn
And act my grief; and 'tis for only him
That I invoke this strange assistance to it,
And on the point invoke himself to do it;
For none but Tully, Tully's praise can tell,
And as he could, no man could act so well.
This part of sorrow for him no man draw,
So truly to the life, this map of woe,
That grief's true picture, which his loss hath bred.
He's gone, and with him what a world are dead,
Which he reviv'd, to be revived so
No more; young Hamlet, old Hieronimo,
Kind Lear, the grieved Moor, and more beside,
That liv'd in him, have now forever died.
Oft have I seen him leap into the grave,
Suiting the person, which he seem'd to have,
Of a sad lover, with so true an eye
That there I would have sworn he meant to die.
Oft have I seen him play this part in jest
So lively that spectators, and the rest
Of his sad crew, whilst he but seem'd to bleed,
Amazed, thought even then he died in deed.
O let not me be check'd, and I shall swear
E'en yet it is a false report I hear,
And think that he, that did so truly feign
Is still but dead in jest, to live again.
But now this part he acts, not plays; 'tis known
Other he play'd, but acted hath his own,
England's great Roscius, for what Roscius
Was unto Rome, that Burbage was to us.
How did his speech become him, and his pace
Suit with his speech, and every action grace
Them both alike, whilst not a word did fall
Without just weight to ballast it withal.
Hadst thou but spoke to death, and us'd thy power
Of thy enchanting tongue, at that first hour
Of his assault, he had let fall his dart
And been quite charm'd by thy all-charming art.
This he well knew, and to prevent this wrong
He therefore first made seizure on his tongue;
Then on the rest, 'twas easy by degrees;
The slender ivy tops the smallest trees.

Poets whose glory whilom 'twas to hear
Your lines so well express'd, henceforth forbear
And write no more; or if you do, let 't be
In comic scenes, since tragic parts you see
Die all with him. Nay, rather sluice your eyes
And henceforth wrote nought else but tragedies,
Or dirges, or sad elegies or those
Mournful laments that not accord with prose.
Blur all your leaves with blots, that all you writ
May be but one sad black, and open it.
Draw marble lines that may outlast the sun
And stand like trophies when the world is done,
Turn all your ink to blood, your pens to spears,
To pierce and wound the hearers' hearts and ears.
Enrag'd, write stabbing lines, that every word
May be as apt for murther as a sword,
That no man may survive after this fact
Of ruthless death, either to hear or act;
And you his sad companions, to whom Lent
Becomes more lenten by this accident,
Henceforth your waving flag no more hang out,
Play now no more at all, when round about
We look and miss the Atlas of your sphere.
What comfort have we (think you) to be there,
And how can you delight in playing, when
Such mourning so affecteth other men;
Or if you will still put 't out let it wear
No more light colours, but death livery there
Hang all your house with black, the hue it bears,
With icicles of ever-melting tears,
And if you ever chance to play again,
May nought but tragedies afflict your scene.
And thou dear Earth that must enshrine that dust
By Heaven now committed to thy trust,
Keep it as precious as the richest mine
That lies entomb'd in that rich womb of thine,
That after-times may know that much-lov'd mould
From other dust, and cherish it as gold.
On it be laid some soft but lasting stone
With this short epitaph endors'd thereon,
That every eye may read, and reading weep:
'Tis England's Roscius, Burbage, that I keep.

(a) Portrait of Richard Burbage

Dulwich College Picture Gallery, DPG 395. An early seventeenth-century portrait; the painter is unknown.

111   Players as exemplars of womanishness, 1621

Robert Burton, *Anatomy of Melancholy*, 1621 (STC 4159). This solitary and off-handedly unflattering reference to stage players occurs in a massive work whose theme is something altogether other.

[pp. 376–7] The riot in this kind [of artificial allurements] hath been excessive in times past; no man almost came abroad, but curled and anointed... and with perfumed hairs... Women are bad, and men are worse, no difference at all betwixt their and our times. Good manners (as Seneca complains) are extinct with wantonness, in tricking up themselves men go beyond women, they wear harlot's colours, and do not walk, but jet and dance, he-women, she-men, more like players, butterflies, baboons, apes, antics, than men.[1]

[1] The page reference is to the second edition, 1624 (STC 4160), from which this extract is taken.

112   Players as unfit subjects for legal redress, 1625

From a book of Decrees and Orders in the Court of Chancery (PRO, C33/149, fo. 844v, dated 23 June 1625)

The lawsuit in question is generally known as *Worth* v *Baskerville*, and involved several of the sharers of Queen Anne's company of players. Susan Baskerville had sued Ellis Worth and his companions at the common law for default on their performance bonds, and Worth and the others responded by appealing to the Lord Chancellor (through his Court of Chancery) to have the common law proceedings stayed. The decree of the judges in Chancery went against Worth and his fellows, for the reasons offered.

The matter in question between the said parties coming this day to be heard in the presence of the Council Learned on both parts – the Court being assisted by Mr Justice Dodderidge and Mr Justice Hatton – found that the substance of the plaintiffs' bill is to be relieved upon a parole [*i.e.* verbal] agreement against a deed in writing under hand and seal; and that the said agreement is made between players, which this Court conceived unfit to be relieved or countenanced in a court of equity; and also finding that the matter hath been several times heretofore dismissed, doth therefore order that the matter of the plaintiffs' bill be clearly and absolutely dismissed out [of] this Court but without any costs.

113   Players not to be confused with their roles, 1626

Philip Massinger, *The Roman Actor*, a play licensed on 11 October 1626 by Sir Henry Herbert, Master of the Revels, for performance by 'the King's Company', and printed in 1629 (STC 17642)

Joseph Taylor played the role of Paris, the tragedian who gives the play its title; Paris is pursued by Domitia, the Emperor's mistress (hence 'Augusta'), who wrongly praises his qualities; he corrects her misapprehension, rehearsing the standard arguments found earlier in Heywood (1612) and others. Massinger may have intended Paris's remarks

186   Players and playing

specifically as a reply to *A Short Treatise against Stage Players*, presented to Parliament in May 1625. The following excerpt is from IV.i.30–52.

DOMITIA   We could wish
  That we could credit thee, and cannot find
  In reason but that thou, whom oft I have seen
  To personate a gentleman, noble, wise,
  Faithful, and gamesome,[1] and what virtues else
  The poet pleases to adorn you with,
  But that, as vessels still partake the odour
  Of the sweet precious liquors they contained
  Thou must be really, in some degree,
  The thing thou dost present. Nay, do not tremble;
  We seriously believe it, and presume
  Our Paris is the volume in which all
  Those excellent gifts the stage hath seen him graced with
  Are curiously bound up.
PARIS   The argument
  Is the same, great Augusta, that I acting
  A fool, a coward, a traitor, or cold cynic,
  Or any other weak and vicious person,
  Of force[2] I must be such. O gracious madam,
  How glorious soever or deformed,
  I do appear in the scene, my part being ended
  And all my borrowed ornaments put off,
  I am no more nor less than what I was
  Before I entered.

[1] Spirited.
[2] Perforce.

114   Character of a virtuous player, 1628

John Earle, *Microcosmography, or a Piece of the World Discovered in Essays and Characters*, 1628 (*STC* 7439). Earle was, like Overbury, a writer of Characters. The following selection appears in its entirety.

22 A Player

[sigs. E3–E4v] He knows the right use of the world, wherein he comes to play a part and so away. His life is not idle for it is all action, and no man need be more wary in his doings, for the eyes of all men are upon him. His profession has in it a kind of contradiction, for none is more disliked, and yet none more applauded; and he has this misfortune of some scholar, too much wit makes him a fool. He is like our painting gentlewomen, seldom in his own face, seldomer in his clothes, and he pleases, the better he counterfeits, except only when he is disguised with straw for gold lace. He does not only personate on the stage, but sometime in the street, for he is masked still in the habit of a gentleman. His parts find him oaths and good words, which he keeps for his use and discourse, and makes show with them of a fashionable companion. He is tragical on the stage, but rampant in the tiring house, and swears oaths there which he never conned. The waiting-women spectators are over ears in love with him, and ladies send for him to act in their chambers. Your Inns of Court men were undone but for him, he is their chief guest and employment, and the sole business that makes them afternoon's men. The poet only is his tyrant, and he is bound to make his friend's friend drunk at his charges. Shrove Tuesday he fears as much as the bawds, and Lent is more damage to him than [to] the butcher. He was never so much discredited as in one act, and that was of Parliament, which gives hostlers privilege before him, for which he abhors it more than a corrupt judge. But to give him his due, one well-furnished actor has enough in him for five common gentlemen, and, if he have a good body, for six, and for resolution, he shall challenge any Cato, for it has been his practice to die bravely.

115   Players as the very dregs of men, 1632
William Prynne, Histriomastix, the Players' Scourge, 1632 (STC 20464).

More than a thousand pages in length, this numbing work is surely the longest anti-theatrical polemic in existence. The book caused an immediate furor because of a supposed aspersion upon Charles I and his queen; Prynne, a barrister of Lincoln's Inn, was sentenced by the court of Star Chamber to imprisonment in the Tower and a £5,000 fine, and his ears to be cropped as well.

[pp. 132–3] If we seriously survey the lives, the practices, the conditions of our common stage-players, we may truly write of them as William of Malmsbury doth of Edric: that they are the very dregs of men, the shame, the blemish of our English nation; ungracious helluoes,[1] crafty shifting companions, who purchase money not by their generosity but by their tongues and impudency; they being wise to dissemble, apt to counterfeit, prone to dive into the secrets both of King and state as faithful subjects, and more ready to divulge them on the stage as notorious traitors. [That they are slaves to every vice] may be truly verified of most common actors, who are usually the very filth and off-scouring, the very lewdest, basest, worst and most perniciously vicious of the sons of men; as all times, all authors have reputed them.

[pp. 904–10] I say it is altogether unlawful for any to act plays for gain or profit's sake, or to make a trade or living of it. First, because the profession of a player is no lawful warrantable trade of life, but a most infamous, lewd, ungodly profession . . . The acting therefore of plays for hire, gain or profit's sake (which ought not to be the end of any man's lawful calling, but only God's glory and the good of men, which plays and actors never aim at) must certainly be unlawful; which I would wish our players and play-haunters to consider.

[Another] ground of the unlawfulness of acting plays is the evil fruits that issue from it, both to the spectators . . . and likewise to the actors, which I shall here only name. As first, it makes the actors guilty of many sins, to wit, of vain, idle, ribaldrous, and blasphemous words, of light, lascivious, wanton gestures and actions, loss of time, hypocrisy, effeminacy, impudency, theft, lust, with sundry other sins, which they cannot avoid; secondly, it ingenerates in them a perpetual habit of vanity, effeminacy, idleness, whoredom, adultery, and those other vices which they daily act . . . When they shall have their minds, their memories and mouths full fraught with amorous, ribaldrous, panderly histories, pastorals, jests, discourses, and witty though filthy obscenities from day to day (the case of all our common actors, especially those who have been trained up to acting from their youth), no wonder if we discover a whole grove of all these notorious acted sins and villainies budding forth continually in their ungodly lives; in so much that those who in their younger days represented other men's vices only, fall shortly after to act their own, the better to enable them to personate other men's of the selfsame kind; he being best able to play the sins of others who hath ofttimes perpetrated the very selfsame crimes himself. Whence commonly it comes to pass that the eminentest actors are the most lewd companions.

The acting of stage plays, as it of right excludes all actors both from the privileges of the commonweal, from the church, the sacraments, and society of the faithful here, and draws a perpetual infamy upon their persons; so it certainly debars them from entering into heaven, and brings down an eternal condemnation on their souls and bodies hereafter, if they repent not in time; those being bound over to the judgement of the great general assizes and eternal torments even in heaven, who are thus bound and justly censured by the laws and edicts of the church or state on earth. Hence was it, that divers players and play-poets in the primitive church, and since, renounced their professions, as altogether incompatible either with Christianity or salvation. Yea, hence a late English player, some two years since, falling mortally sick at the city of Bath, whither he came to act;[2] being deeply wounded in conscience, and almost driven to despair with the sad and serious consideration of his lewd infernal profession, lying upon his death-bed ready to breathe out his soul, adjured his son, whom he had trained up to play-acting, with many bitter tears and imprecations, as he tendered the everlasting happiness of his soul, to abjure and forsake his ungodly profession, which would but enthrall him to the devil's vassalage for the present, and plunge him deeper into hell at last. Such are the dismal, execrable, soul-condemning fruits of play-acting; the profession therefore of a common player, and the personating of theatrical interludes, must needs be unlawful even in this respect.

[1] Gluttons.
[2] This player has not been plausibly identified.

116 Thomas Barnes, carpenter, pretends to be a player, 1632

PRO, LC5/132, p. 284. Transcribed in MSC, II(3).356–7.

William Prynne's shrillness in attacking stage-players was perhaps an index of their increasing social acceptance. Certainly Thomas Barnes, whose misfortune is recounted below, was eager to be mistaken for a stage-player, though for reasons that would seem to confirm Prynne's judgements.

Thomas Barnes discharged his service

Whereas, by virtue of a warrant under my hand, of the second of July, 1629, one Thomas Barnes was sworne his majesty's servant, in the place of a Groom of the Chamber in Ordinary, upon pretence that he was one of the company of players which, by his majesty's favour, had a licence to practice under the name of the Queen of Bohemia's servants; whereas, in truth, the said Barnes is by profession a carpenter, and never did nor doth profess the quality of a stage-player; but was dishonestly and sinisterly obtruded upon me, by the false and fraudulent suggestion of one Joseph Moore, that followed the business in the name of the company, out of a corrupt end to derive unto himself a benefit by entitling the said Barnes unto the privilege and protection of his majesty's service, as now appeareth unto me upon the several petitions of diverse persons of good credit; from some of whom the said Barnes doth most injuriously and scandalously detain their just and due debts, and others of them he hath drawn to be bound for him in great sums of money, which since, he hath suffered to be forfeited, and thereby hath exposed those which were engaged for him unto the danger of imprisonment and apparent ruin of their estates. For reformation hereof, and to the end that his majesty's service may be purged from the stain of so dishonest foul proceedings, these are to will and require you to call the said Barnes before you, and him to dismiss and discharge out of his majesty's service, and all relation thereunto, and to cause his name to be blotted and razed out of the list of his majesty's servants. Hereof you may not fail, and this shall be your warrant. Whitehall, the 23rd of January 1631[/2].

117 Players as speaking pictures, 1662

Richard Baker, *Theatrum Redivivum, or The Theatre Vindicated*, 1662

Baker's tract is a refutation of William Prynne's *Histriomastix* (1633), and was probably written a few years after Prynne's work appeared, though it was not published until after the restoration of the monarchy nearly three decades later. Baker himself died in 1645. For extracts from Prynne's work, see 115.

[pp. 42–5] When an actor presents himself upon the stage, until he speak he is but a picture, and when he speaks he is but a story (and therefore perhaps a player is called *histrio*, quasi *historio*); for, as one said well, that a judge is *lex loquens*, a speaking law; so we may say as truly that a player is a speaking picture, or a history in person; and seeing we know no hurt by a picture, and cannot but commend history, why should plays be condemned, which are but a composition made of these two. A history is not condemned if, recording the life of Julian, it set down his cruelty against Christians, and his blasphemies against Christ. And if an historian may lawfully write it, may not we as lawfully read it? And if we may lawfully read it, may not a player as lawfully pronounce it? And what doth a player else, but only say that without book, which we may read within book? A player acts the part of Solomon, but is never the wiser for acting his part; why should he be thought the wickeder for acting the part of Nero, or the more blasphemous for acting the part of Porphyry? . . . [*Gives examples of blasphemous and profane speeches;*] why then . . . shall players be thought either blasphemous or profane if sometimes they utter such speeches under the person of another? And indeed, to speak it plainly, they cannot avoid the using and uttering such speeches if they will be players. For as he who would lively portray a devil, or a deformed monster, must needs draw some ghastly lines, and use some sordid colours, so he who will delineate to the life the notorious lewdness of people in the world is necessarily enforced to such immodest phrases as may present it in its native ugliness; else he should but conceal or mask their horrid wickedness, that none may behold it; not rip it open that all may abhor it.

[pp. 48, 50] What hath Cicero recorded of Roscius, who was a famous player himself, and yet no less a famous honest man: 'So while he was most worthy of the stage because of his artifice, yet was he most worthy of the court because of his restraint'.[1] That his very adversary durst not speak of him at the bar without this addition, 'Whom I mention out of respect'. And lest he [*i.e.* Prynne] should say that the school of plays is degenerated and grown worse since that time, have we not seen in our own time a famous scholar come out of this school: Edward Alleyn, a player himself, famous as well for his honesty as for his acting, and who hath left behind him a worthy testimony of his Christian charity to all posterity?

[How is it] that players, in this man's [*i.e.* Prynne's] account, are most excessively vicious, unchaste, profane and dissolute men? Marry, because most of them (as he is credibly informed) are professed papists. A very necessary consequence; as though to be a professed papist were to be a professed atheist. For what but atheism could bring forth all such excessively vicious men as he would make them? Yet this makes well for plays, though it makes ill for players; for players, though the most excessively vicious men, yet are not so because players, but because papists. Let him take heed he pull not an old house upon his head.

[1] Cicero, *Oratio pro Quinto Roscio Amerino*, 2, 6.

VIII A representative life: Augustine Phillips

The life of a stage-player is usually more difficult to trace in the records than is the life of a playhouse. Sheer numbers are part of the problem; a handful of playhouses as against nearly 500 identifiable players, many of the latter virtually anonymous save for a single reference in a document. Even in the case of those players for whom a fair amount of biographical evidence is available, scholars often seem less certain about how to use it than they are in the correlative case of playhouses. But the value of such evidence is beyond question.

Augustine Phillips is a more useful figure to glance at than, for example, Edward Alleyn or Richard Burbage, for the careers of the latter two were so brilliant and unusual as to render them non-representative. Not that Phillips was a mere journeyman player; he was one of Shakespeare's fellows, and a well-known, though not one of the best-known, players of his day. The documents that follow provide a useful index to the kinds of evidence likely to survive for a stage-player in this period. The circumstances of Phillips's life, the circumstantial details in his will, and the legal entanglements attendant upon his death and his widow's remarriage, shed a useful light upon the personal relations among stage-players and their colleagues.

118 Augustine Phillips as Sardanapalus, 1590

Dulwich, MS xix; reproduced in Greg, *Henslowe Papers*, 130–2.

This is the earliest known reference to Phillips; it occurs in a theatrical 'plat' for a play conventionally referred to as 'the second part of the play of the seven deadly sins'. The play itself is lost, but its bare bones survive in this plat, in which players' entrances and exits are cued. Scholars date the play in or about 1590 and assign it to Lord Strange's players.

Enter Sardanapalus, Arbactus, Nicanor and Captains, marching; Mr Phillips, Mr Pope, Robert Pallant, Kit, John Sinckler, John Holland.

119 Phillips and his colleagues licensed to travel, 1593

PRO, PC2/20, p. 351. Reproduced in *ES*, II, 123. A licence issued by the Privy Council on 6 May 1593 to lord Strange's players, authorising them to travel in time of plague; Phillips is listed as one of the six members of the company.

Whereas it was thought meet that during the time of the infection and continuance of the sickness in the City of London there should no plays or interludes be used, for the avoiding of the assemblies and concourse of people in any usual place appointed near the said City; and though the bearers hereof, Edward Alleyn servant to the right honourable the lord high Admiral,[1] William Kemp, Thomas

Pope, John Heminges, Augustine Phillips and George Brian, being of one company, servants to our very good lord the Lord Strange, are restrained their exercise of playing within the said City and liberties thereof; yet it is not thereby meant but that they shall and may, in regard of the service by them done and to be done at the Court, exercise their quality of playing comedies, tragedies and such like in any other cities, towns and corporations where the infection is not; so it be not within seven miles of London or of the Court; that they may be in the better readiness hereafter for her majesty's service whensoever they shall be thereunto called. These therefore shall be to will and require you that they may without their let or contradiction use their said exercise at their most convenient times and places, the accustomed times of divine prayers excepted.

[1] The Lord Admiral was one of the five Privy Council members present at the meeting at which this licence was issued.

120   Phillips assessed by the subsidy commissioners, 1593

PRO, E179/186/349, lay subsidy roll, dated 21 August 1593; the document is unpublished. Phillips' worth was assessed at £3 by the subsidy commissioners, and a tax of 8s levied upon him in the Liberty of the Clink, where he was regarded by them as living.

Augustine Phillips £3 —————— 8s

121   Phillips resident in Horseshoe Court, 1593–1594

LMA, P92/SAV/244/6, the communion token book for 1593[/4]; the document is unpublished. Augustine Phillips was noted as living with his family at the end of Horseshoe Court, near Bullhead Alley, in the Liberty of the Clink, part of the parish of St Saviour's in Southwark, during the late winter of 1593/4. The number entered against his name indicates three adults in the household; presumably him, his wife, and a servant.

Horseshoe Court
   [*several names and numbers, including*]
   Augustine Phillips —————— 3

122   Phillips' first daughter baptised, 1594

LMA, P92/SAV/3001, the St Saviour's parish register; the register is unpublished

[*Under the date of 29 September 1594, the christening of*]
Magdalen Phillips, daughter of Austin, histrionis[1]

[1] *histrionis*: player.

123   Phillips' jig of the slippers, 1595

Registers of the Worshipful Company of Stationers, transcribed by Edward Arber (London, 1875–7), II, 298

Printers secured their rights to publish a text by registering its title with the Company of Stationers; copyright so established thus belonged to the printer (in this case, Ralph

Hancock) rather than to the author. The Phillips here referred to is generally assumed to have been the stage-player.

26 May 1595. Ralph Hancock. Entered for his copy under the hands of the wardens. Phillips' jig of the slippers . . . 6d

124 Phillips still resident in Horseshoe Court, 1595–1596

LMA, P92/SAV/245/10, the St Saviour's communion token book for 1595[/6]; the document is unpublished. The Phillips family was still living at the end of Horseshoe Court (now Alley) in St Saviour's during the late winter of 1595/6. The number again indicates three adults in the household.

Horseshoe Alley
  [*several names and numbers, including*]
  Augustine Phillips ——————— 3

125 Another daughter baptised, 1596

LMA, P92/SAV/3001, the St Saviour's parish register; the register is unpublished

[*Under the date of 11 July 1596, the christening of*]
Rebecca Phillips, daughter of Augustine, player of interludes

126 Phillips no longer resident in Horseshoe Alley, 1596–1597

LMA, P92/SAV/246/13, the St Saviour's communion token book for 1596/7; the document is unpublished. The Phillipses had vacated their premises in Horseshoe Alley by the late winter of 1596/7. The name was entered in the book, as before, but was then lined through.

Horseshoe Alley
  [*several names and numbers, including*]
  ~~Augustine Phillips~~ ——————— 3

127 A stillborn child buried, 1597

GL MS 9234/6, one of the day-books kept by the parish clerk of the church of St Botolphs without Aldgate, London; the document is unpublished. The Phillips family, now living in the parish of St Botolph without Aldgate at the eastern end of London, buried a stillborn daughter. The parish clerk noted that the body was coffined for burial.

A woman child, daughter to Augustine Phillips, a player of interludes, dwelling in Mr Hamond's Rents, being amongst the gardens near Houndsditch, was buried the 7th day of September anno 1597, being stillborn – 3s
  For the pit and knell,[1] coffined – 18d
  For the 2 searchers – 4d

[1] Digging the grave and ringing the bell.

128 Churching of Anne Phillips after the delivery of her stillborn child, 1597

GL, MS 9234/8, another of the day-books kept by the parish clerk of the church of St Botolph's without Aldgate, London; the document is unpublished

The wife of Augustine Phillips was churched the 5th day of October anno 1597.

129 Phillips a player in Jonson's Every Man in His Humour, 1598

The Works of Benjamin Jonson, London, 1616 (STC 14751)

Every Man in His Humour ... This comedy was first acted in the year 1598 by the then Lord Chamberlain's servants. The principal comedians were William Shakespeare, Richard Burbage, Augustine Phillips, John Heminges, Henry Condell, Thomas Pope, William Sly, Christopher Beeston, Will Kemp, John Duke. With the allowance of the Master of Revels.

130 Phillips living near the Swan playhouse in 1598/9?

A tradition begun by William Rendle ('The Bankside, Southwark, and the Globe Playhouse,' in F. J. Furnivall's 1878 edition of Harrison's *Description of England*, p. xxv) and subsequently repeated by others asserts that the token books of St Saviour's parish show Augustine Phillips living near the Swan playhouse in Paris Garden in the winter of 1598/9. The relevant token books do not support this claim.

131 Phillips a player in Jonson's Every Man Out of His Humour, 1599

The Works of Benjamin Jonson, London, 1616 (STC 14751)

This comical satire was first acted in the year 1599 by the then Lord Chamberlain's servants. The principal comedians were Richard Burbage, John Heminges, Augustine Phillips, Henry Condell, William Sly, Thomas Pope. With the allowance of the Master of Revels.

132 The Phillips family perhaps in a new dwelling, 1599

GL, MS 4449/1, the parish register of St Stephen's, Coleman Street; the register is unpublished. A third daughter was baptised, at St Stephen's Church, Coleman Street, near the Guildhall in London. The occurrence of a baptism in this church might, but need not, imply that the Phillips family had moved house.

[*Among the entries for 1599, the christening of*]
Anne Phillips, the daughter of Augustine Phillips, the 19th of August

133   Phillips examined about the Essex Rebellion, 1601

> PRO, SP12/278, fo. 153, item 85. Reprinted in *ES*, II, 205. As part of the enquiry into the Essex Rebellion, and the performance of Shakespeare's *Richard II* which was a preliminary to it, the queen's council arranged for Chief Justice Popham and Justice Fenner to examine Augustine Phillips on 18 February 1601 about the matter.

The Examination of Augustine Phillips, servant unto the Lord Chamberlain and one of his players, taken the 18th of February 1600[/1] upon his oath.

He saith that on Friday last was sennight[1] or Thursday Sir Charles Percy, Sir Jocelyn Percy, and the Lord Mounteagle, with some three more, spoke to some of the players in the presence of this Examinate, to have the play of the deposing and killing of King Richard the Second to be played the Saturday next, promising to get them 40s more than their ordinary to play it. Where this Examinate and his fellows were determined to have played some other play, holding that play of King Richard to be so old and so long out of use that they should have small or no company at it. But at their request, this Examinate and his fellows were content to play it the Saturday, and had their 40s more than their ordinary for it, and so played it accordingly.

Augustine Phillips

[1] That is, Friday of the week previous.

134   Phillips resettled in St Saviour's parish in Southwark, 1601

> LMA, P92/SAV/3001, the St Saviour's parish register; the register is unpublished.

The Phillips family resettled in St Saviour's parish in Southwark, where the parish register shows a son (their first) baptised. Nungezer (*Dictionary of Actors*) says that Phillips was living in Montague Close, at the eastern end of St Saviour's parish, in 1601/2. A 'Mr Phillips' is indeed recorded as living there, but his household contained only one adult; in all likelihood this was Edward Phillips, the minister, rather than Augustine the stage-player and his family. Subsequent records from this parish bear out the family's resettlement here, unlike the single occurrence (above) of a christening in St Stephen's, Coleman Street, which remains inconclusive.

[*Under date of 29 November 1601, the christening of*]
Austin Phillips, son of Austin, a player

135   Possible marriage of Elizabeth Phillips, 1603

> LMA, P92/SAV/3001, the St Saviour's parish register; the register is unpublished. Augustine Phillips's sister Elizabeth might have been married to the player Robert Gough. Phillips names a sister, Elizabeth Gough, in his will, and Robert Gough was one of the witnesses to the will.

[*Under date of 13 February 1603, the marriage of*]
Robert Gough and Elizabeth [*blank*]

136 Phillips resident again in Horseshoe Alley, 1602–1603

LMA, P92/SAV/252/14, the St Saviour's communion token book for 1602 [/3]; the document is unpublished. The return to St Saviour's was apparently to their former dwelling at the end of Horseshoe Alley, in a cluster of buildings occasionally labelled in the communion books as Bradshaw's Rents. They were there in the late winter of 1602/3. The number of adults in the household, first written as 4, was then altered to 6.

Horseshoe Alley
    [*several names and numbers, leading into*]
    Bradshaw's Rents
    [*a few names and numbers, including*]
    Augustine Phillips ——————— [4]6

137 Phillips still in Horseshoe Alley in 1603–1604

LMA, P92/SAV/253/9, the St Saviour's communion token book for 1603[/4]. The Phillips family was still in Horseshoe Alley in St Saviour's, Southwark, during the late winter of 1603/4, with the number of adults stabilised at six.

Horseshoe Alley
    [*several names and numbers, including*]
    Augustine Phillips ——————— 6

138 Phillips among those named to be the King's players, 1603

Augustine Phillips named, along with Lawrence Fletcher, William Shakespeare, Richard Burbage, John Heminges, Henry Condell, William Sly, Robert Armin, and Richard Cowley, as a member of the newly licensed royal players (see 66).

139 Phillips a player in Jonson's Sejanus, 1603

The Works of Benjamin Jonson, London, 1616 (STC 14751)

This tragedy was first acted in the year 1603 by the King's majesty's servants. The principal tragedians were Richard Burbage, William Shakespeare, Augustine Phillips, John Heminges, William Sly, Henry Condell, John Lowin, Alexander Cooke. With the allowance of the Master of Revels.

140 Phillips takes part in the royal coronation, 1604

PRO, LC2/4(5), Lord Chamberlain's records. Reproduced in *The New Shakspere Society's Transactions*, London, 1877–9, appendix ii, p. 16

Among those officers and servants of the royal chamber listed in the 'book of the account of the royal proceeding of our sovereign lord King James through his honourable City of London', dated 15 March 1604 and presented for audit by Sir George Home, knight of the wardrobe, the following names appear under the heading of 'Players' and are authorised to receive four and a half yards of red cloth each for their livery.

William Shakespeare, Augustine Phillips, Lawrence Fletcher, John Heminges, Richard Burbage, William Sly, Robert Armin, Henry Cundall, Richard Cowley.

141 Phillips' only son buried, 1604

LMA, P92/SAV/3001, the St Saviour's parish register; the register is unpublished. Augustine, the only son of Augustine and Anne Phillips, was buried at St Saviour's in Southwark.

[*Under date of 1 July 1604, the burial of:*]
Augustine Phillips a child

142 Augustine Phillips as a moneylender, 1604

PRO, C54/1797; the document is unpublished

On 2 November 1604 Phillips lent £100 to one John Baumfeld for six months, at the allowed interest rate of ten per cent per annum; hence a payment of £105 was due to Phillips in six months' time, on 4 May 1605. The recognizance or bond, in Latin, specifies that John Baumfeld, of Hardington in Somerset, owes £200 to Augustine Phillips of London, gentleman. On the back, in English, are the terms of the debt.

The condition of this recognisance is such that, if the above bound John Baumfeld, his heirs, executors and administrators, or any of them, do well and truly pay, or cause to be paid, to the above named Augustine Phillips, his executors, administrators or assigns, at the now dwelling house of the said Augustine Phillips, situate on the Bankside, in the county of Surrey, the sum of £105 of lawful money of England, on the fourth day of May next coming after the date above written, without fraud or coven, that then this recognisance to be void and of none effect; or else it to stand in full strength and virtue.[1]

[1] In the margin, in Latin, is written the notation that the debt, and its condition, are void. Phillips died within days of the bond's falling due, and John Heminges, his executor, affirmed before the probate court that the debt had been satisfied.

143 Vacating the premises in Horseshoe Alley, 1604–1605

LMA, P92/SAV/254/11, the St Saviour's communion token book for 1605; the document is unpublished. The Phillips family, presumably upon the death of Augustine, had vacated the premises in Horseshoe Alley by the late winter of 1604/5. The name is entered in the book, as before, but is lined through, and the name 'Bird' inserted above it.[1]

Horseshoe Alley
    Bird
    ~~Augustine Phillips~~

[1] In the token book for 1606 (LMA, P92/SAV/255/13) the new occupant is further identified as William Bird; this may be the stage-player William Bird *alias* Borne. Phillips names a sister, Margery Borne, in his will.

144 Augustine Phillips makes his will, 1605

PRO, Prob.11/105, fos. 241v–242. Reproduced in Collier, *History of English Dramatic Poetry*, III, 327–9

In the Name of God, Amen. The fourth day of May, anno domini 1605 . . . I, Augustine Phillips, of Mortlake in the county of Surrey, gentleman, being at this present sick and weak in body, but of good and perfect mind and remembrance, thanks be given unto almighty God, do make, ordain and dispose this my present testament and last will, in manner and form following; that is to say, first and principally I commend my soul into the hands of almighty God . . . and I commit my body to be buried in the chancel of the parish church of Mortlake aforesaid.

And after my body buried, and funeral charges paid, then I will that all such debts and duties as I owe to any person . . . shall be truly paid . . . [and that] my goods, chattels, plate, household stuff, jewels, ready money and debts [*i.e.* money owed to him] shall be divided by my executrix . . . into three equal and indifferent parts and portions, whereof one part I give and bequeath to Anne Phillips, my loving wife, to her own proper use and behoof. One other part thereof to and amongst my three eldest daughters, Magdalen Phillips, Rebecca Phillips, and Anne Phillips, equally amongst them, to be divided portion and portion like, and to be paid and delivered unto them as they and every of them shall accomplish and come to their lawful ages of twenty and one years, or at their days of marriage . . . And the other part thereof I reserve to myself and to my executrix to perform my legacies hereinafter following.

Item: I give and bequeath to the poor of the parish of Mortlake aforesaid, £5 . . . Item: I give and bequeath to Agnes Bennett, my loving mother, during her natural life every year yearly the sum of £5 . . . Item: I give to my brothers, William Webb and James Webb, if they shall be living at my decease, to either of them the sum of £10 . . . Item: I give and bequeath to my sister, Elizabeth Gough, the sum of £10 . . . Item: I will and bequeath unto Myles Borne and Phillips Borne, two sons of my sister Margery Borne, to either of them £10 . . .

Item: I give and bequeath unto and amongst the hired men of the company which I am of, which shall be at the time of my decease, the sum of £5 . . . to be equally distributed amongst them. Item: I give and bequeath unto my fellow William Shakespeare a 30s piece in gold; to my fellow Henry Condell one other 30s piece in gold; to my servant Christopher Beeston 30s in gold; to my fellow Lawrence Fletcher 20s in gold; to my fellow Robert Armin 20s in gold; to my fellow Richard Cowley 20s in gold; to my fellow Alexander Cooke 20s in gold; to my fellow Nicholas Tooley 20s in gold. Item: I give to the preacher which shall preach at my funeral the sum of 20s. Item: I give to Samuel Gilburne, my late apprentice, the sum of 40s, and my mouse-coloured velvet hose, and a white taffeta doublet, a black taffeta suit, my purple cloak, sword and dagger, and my bass viol. Item: I give to James Sands, my apprentice, the sum of 40s, and a cittern, and a bandore, and a lute, to be paid and delivered unto him at the expiration of his term of years in his indenture of apprenticehood.

Item: my will is that Elizabeth Phillips, my youngest daughter, shall have . . . my house and lands in Mortlake . . .

And I ordain and make the said Anne Phillips, my loving wife, sole executrix of this, my present testament and last will; provided always that, if the said Anne my wife do at any time marry after my decease, that then and from thenceforth she shall cease to be any more or longer executrix of this my last will, or anyways intermeddle with the same, and the said Anne to have no part or portion of my goods or chattels, to me or my executors reserved or appointed by this, my last will and testament. And that then and from thenceforth John Heminges, Richard Burbage, William Sly and Timothy Whithorne shall be fully and wholly my executors of this my last will and testament, as though the said Anne had never been named. And of the execution of this my present testament and last will, I ordain and make the said John Heminges, Richard Burbage, William Sly, and Timothy Whithorne overseers of this my present testament and last will, and I bequeath to the said John, Richard Burbage and William Sly, or either of them my said overseers, for their pains herein to be taken, a bowl of silver of the value of £5 apiece. In witness whereof to this my present testament and last will, I the said Augustine Phillips have put my hand and seal the day and year above written.

Sealed and delivered by the said Augustine Phillips as his last will and testament in the presence of us. Robert Gough. William Shepherd.

145 Death and burial of Augustine Phillips, 1605

The parish registers of Mortlake, in Surrey, have mostly survived for this period, but the record of marriages and burials between 1603 and 1613 have not; thus no record survives of the burial of Augustine Phillips.

146 Probate of the will; widow Anne Phillips named as executrix

PRO, Prob.8/12, unnumbered folio; the document is unpublished.

On 13 May 1605, administration of the goods and chattels of Augustine Phillips was awarded to his widow Anne, whom the probate court appointed as executrix.

147 Second probate of the will

PRO, Prob.8/13, p. 199; the document is unpublished.

On 16 May 1607 the will underwent a second probate, because of widow Anne's hasty marriage to John Witter, which invalidated her status as executrix in accordance with the terms of the will. John Heminges was sworn as executor in her place, with Richard Burbage, William Sly, and Timothy Whithorne named to serve with him.

148 Phillips' acting remembered and commended by Thomas Heywood, 1612

Thomas Heywood, *An Apology for Actors* (and see 106 for a fuller text)

Gabriel, Singer, Pope, Phillips, Sly, all the right I can do them is but this, that though they be dead, their deserts yet live in the remembrance of many.

149 Burial of Anne Phillips Witter, 1618

(i) GL, MS 9234/8, one of the day-books kept by the parish clerk of the church of St Botolph's without Aldgate, London; the document is unpublished. By 1618 the parish clerk had apparently forgotten Phillips' given name, initially writing it as 'Benjamin' then emending it.

Augustine
Anne Wittles, alias Phillips, sometime wife to ~~Benjamin~~ Phillips, one of the king's players . . . departed this life in the house of William Smith, surgeon, of Houndsditch, and was buried the 26th day of January, Anno Domini 1617[/8], coffined in the old churchyard.

(ii) GL, MS 9235/2, churchwardens' accounts of the church of St Botolph's without Aldgate, London; the accounts are unpublished

Received the 26th day for the burial of Anne Phillips of Houndsditch, who was coffined in the old churchyard and had the black cloth – 6s

150 John Witter's lawsuit, 1619

PRO, Req.4/1/1. Reprinted in Wallace, 'Shakespeare and his London Associates'. A player's affairs did not end with his death. Phillips' wife Anne remarried hastily, and John Witter, her second husband, sued John Heminges and Henry Condell in the Court of Requests on 20 April 1619 over Anne's inheritance, which included a share in the Globe playhouse.

(1) Witter's bill of complaint

To the King's most excellent Majesty:

Most humbly complaining sheweth unto your most excellent Majesty your most humble subject John Witter of Mortlake in the county of Surrey, gentleman, that whereas Augustine Phillips of London, gentleman, deceased, was in his lifetime lawfully possessed . . . of and in a sixth part of the moiety of the galleries of the playhouse called the Globe . . . and he the same Augustine Phillips . . . shortly after died so possessed . . . By virtue whereof . . . the said Anne Phillips, the executrix and relict of the said Augustine Phillips, into the said sixth part of the said galleries, ground and playhouse of the Globe and garden entered, and was thereof possessed accordingly . . . And she so being thereof . . . did during the time of her widowhood . . . grant and assign over unto your said subject all the same term therein then to come and unexpired, together with the original lease . . .

By force wherein[1] your said subject thereinto did enter and was thereof possessed accordingly and received the rents, issues and profits thereof . . . until now of late . . . your said subject, wanting money, was driven to mortgage the same lease and term unto John Heminges of London, gentleman, for the sum of £50 . . . upon a proviso or condition . . . for the repayment thereof with 50s more for the use or interest thereof at the end of six months then next ensuing. All which £52 10s the said Heminges then had and accepted of at the hands of your said subject at the said limited time . . .

But now . . . the said original lease, last will and testament, and the assignment and grant aforesaid, being . . . come to the hands and possession of the said John Heminges and one Henry Condell, gentleman, one of his fellows and familiar companions; being both servants to your Majesty, they, the said John Heminges and Henry Condell . . . not only . . . about five years last past entered into and upon the said sixth part of the said play house ground, galleries and gardens called the Globe, but also . . . detain and keep the same, and all the rents, issues and profits thereof, from your said subject . . . his wife[2] and children, unless your Majesty's accustomed aid to him be therein . . . extended. . . . as your said subject is not of ability and power to contend in law with the said John Heminges and Henry Condell, who are of great living, wealth and power, and have many more mighty and great friends than your said subject . . .

[1] Not 'forcibly', but by virtue of his supposed legal claim.
[2] As Anne Phillips Witter had died fifteen months before this suit was entered, the reference to a 'wife' is unclear.

(2) The answers of Heminges and Condell, 28 April 1619

The joint and several answers of John Heminges and Henry Condell, gentlemen, defendants to the bill of complaint of John Witter, gentleman, complainant.[1]

[The defendants] do say, and either of them for himself saith, that he thinketh it to be true that the said Augustine Phillips . . . was in his lifetime lawfully possessed of . . . a fifth part of the moiety of the said galleries of the said playhouse called the Globe in the said bill mentioned . . . [then] Augustine Phillips . . . made his last will and testament in writing and thereby made his then wife Anne his executrix of his said last will and testament . . .

[But this appointment] was not absolutely, but only with proviso or upon condition . . . that if the said Anne . . . should at any time marry after his decease, that . . . from thenceforth she should cease to be any more or longer executrix of his said last will, or any ways intermeddle with the same; and that . . . from thenceforth this defendant John Heminges, the said Richard Burbage, William Sly, and Timothy Whithorne should be fully and wholly his executors . . . And this defendant John Heminges further saith that the said complainant [Witter] . . . did come to this defendant and, making show and affirming that the said Anne and himself then stood in great need of money, did make offer to procure the said Anne to mortgage her said ... fifth part of the said playhouse, galleries, gardens and grounds ... unto this defendant for the sum of £50 or thereabouts, wherewith to relieve their wants, and would have had the said Anne by herself to have made the said mortgage ... But this defendant ... suspecting that [Witter] and Anne ... might then be secretly married, and so her assurance alone nothing worth; and [suspecting] that the said Anne had [already] assigned over the said ... fifth part of the said moiety to [Witter], this defendant required [Witter] to join in the said assurance of the ... said fifth part of the said moiety, in mortgage for his said money; which he ... yielded unto. And thereupon both [Witter] and the said Anne, then confessing themselves to be married, joined in the said mortgage to this defendant, and he paid unto them the said sum of £50 which, together with 50s for consideration for the forbearance thereof, this defendant confesseth was repaid unto him on the day limited in and by the said deed of assurance in mortgage for the repayment thereof ...

This defendant ... further saith that [because] the said complainant and the said Anne were intermarried ... the said condition in the said will of the said Augustine Phillips was broken ... [Heminges wished] especially to keep the complainant from receiving or recovering of the sum of £300 [part of Anne's legacy] ... lest he should spend the same, as he had before lavishly and riotously spent, wasted and consumed almost all the rest of the said goods and chattels which were of the said Augustine Phillips ... [So,] with the consent and entreaty of the said Anne, the administration of the goods and chattels of the said Augustine Phillips ... was committed to this defendant ... as executor of the said last will and testament of the said Augustine Phillips ...

[Heminges avers that] he hath also from time to time divers and many times in charity, and to relieve the said complainant his said wife and her children, delivered sometimes unto the said complainant himself, sometimes to his said wife, and sometimes to others for them, divers other sums of money, amounting to a further great sum of money, until about the said time of the burning of the said playhouse; and then the said complainant, divers years before the said Anne died, did suffer her to make shift for herself to live, and at her death this defendant, out of charity, was at the charges of the burying of her.

[1] Condell's share in the document seems to be minimal, Witter's quarrel being primarily with Heminges.

(3) Witter's replication, 10 May 1619

The replication of John Witter, gentleman, complainant, to the joint and several answers of John Heminges and Henry Condell, gentlemen, defendants.

[Witter claims] that the condition or proviso in the said will ... is not good nor available in our laws, nor yet in the ecclesiastical laws of this realm ... whereby no woman is to be bound or tied from lawful marriage, nor to lose or forfeit any executorship, legacy or other matter ... by reason of marriage. [But even if] the said proviso or condition [were] good and of force in the law, yet . . . it cannot bind or tie the said complainant [because] the said Anne the executrix, had first lawfully and duly proved the said will of her said former husband Phillips, and took upon her the execution thereof whilst she was his widow, and did also afterwards, and before her intermarriage with the complainant, assign and grant the same unto the said complainant (as she well and lawfully might do), before the said condition was broken, and before the said defendant Heminges any thing had or could have or claim therein . . .

(4) Final decree of the Court of Requests, 29 November 1620, settling the matter
PRO, Req.1/30

Whereas John Witter long sithence exhibited his bill of complaint unto the King's majesty and his highness' council in his honourable court of Whitehall at Westminster against John Heminges, gentleman, and Henry Condell, defendants; unto which bill the said defendants forthwith made their full and perfect answers; whereunto the complainant replied, and examined certain witnesses, above two terms now past, and hath ever sithence failed to proceed in his said cause as by the due and ordinary course of this court he ought to have done; it is therefore by his majesty's said council of this court ordered that the same matter be from henceforth out of this court clearly and absolutely dismissed forever, and the said defendants are licensed to depart at their liberties *sine die*; and it is further ordered that the complainant shall, upon sight or knowledge hereof, content and pay unto the said defendants the full sum of 20s for their costs herein most wrongfully sustained.

IX Patrons and playing companies

From the earliest years of the period most companies of players enjoyed the patronage of the wealthy or the well-connected. Such patronage became increasingly requisite as the sixteenth century wore on, and companies of players without recognised patrons or sponsors became increasingly rare. The number of identifiable persons of rank or standing who were patrons of playing companies in that century approached 100; most prominent among them were the various members of the royal family. We know so little about the details of theatrical patron–client relationships, however, that one cannot say with any confidence how a playing company whose patron was the monarch might have functioned differently in its day-to-day affairs than would a playing company whose patron was a member of the greater or lesser nobility. It is tempting to assume, as do some Shakespeareans, that the more prestigious the patron the more prominent the company; the truth is that for some companies this paradigm held true while for others it did not. For example, the company formed by Queen Elizabeth in 1583 was popular for a short while, then foundered in the late 1590s and did not outlast her reign, even as other companies were prospering. King James did not take over the Queen's players when he came to the throne in 1603 but instead took over the players belonging to the Lord Chamberlain.

The desire of a patron to be involved in the daily life of his company must have been minimal in most cases; the few instances cited below ought not be regarded as representing a norm.

THE EARL OF LEICESTER

The company of players taken under the patronage of the Earl of Leicester was in many ways not a typical playing company. Their patron seems to have been more interested in their welfare than were many other patrons, and his status as the Queen's favourite may have meant more opportunities for them than would have otherwise been the case. Further, the company consisted of some remarkably talented individuals. One of them, James Burbage, abandoned playing and built a playhouse; another, Robert Wilson, went on to be a playwright; still another, Will Kemp, achieved fame as a comedian. After the Earl's death in 1588, those members of the company who wished to continue performing had little trouble finding another patron.

151 Lord Robert Dudley intercedes for his company of stage-players, 1559

College of Heralds, Talbot MS E.f. 29, a letter from Lord Robert Dudley to the Earl of Shrewsbury, Lord President of the North. Reproduced in *ES*, IV, 264. Dudley did not become Earl of Leicester until 1564. Concern for the welfare of his players is made manifest in the letter that follows, and that concern may have been altruistic, but is as likely to have been occasioned by an awareness that his own dignity would be reflected in the reception accorded them.

My good lord,

Where my servants, bringers hereof unto you, be such as are players of interludes, and for the same have the licence of divers of my lords here under their seals and hands to play in divers shires within the realm under their authority, as may amply appear unto your lordship by the same licence, I have thought among the rest by my letters to beseech your good lordship's conformity to them likewise, that they may have your hand and seal to their licence for the like liberty in Yorkshire; being honest men, and such as shall play none other matters (I trust) but tolerable and convenient, whereof some of them have been heard here already before divers of my lords; for whom I shall have good cause to thank your lordship and to remain your lordship's to the best that shall lie in my little power. And thus I take my leave of your good lordship. From Westminster, the [*blank*] of June, 1559.

Your good lord's assured,
R. Dudley

152 Leicester's players petition to be his household servants, *c.* 1572

From MS F.10(213) in the Marquis of Bath's collection at Longleat. Transcribed in MSC, 1.348. For the Statute referred to, see 29

To the right honourable Earl of Leicester, their good lord and master:

May it please your honour to understand that forasmuch as there is a certain proclamation out for the reviving of a statute as touching retainers, as your lordship knoweth better than we can inform you thereof, we therefore, your humble servants and daily orators your players, for avoiding all inconvenience that may grow by reason of the said statute, are bold to trouble your lordship with this our suit, humbly desiring your honour that (as you have been always our good lord and master) you will now vouchsafe to retain us at this present as your household servants and daily waiters, not that we mean to crave any further stipend or benefit at your lordship's hands but our liveries as we have had, and also your honour's licence to certify that we are your household servants when we shall have occasion to travel amongst our friends as we do usually once a year, and as other noblemen's players do and have done in time past, whereby we may enjoy our faculty in your lordship's name as we have done heretofore. Thus being bound and ready to be always at your lordship's commandment we commit your honour to the tuition of the Almighty.

> Long may your lordship live in peace,
> > A peer of noblest peers;
> In health, wealth and prosperity
> > Redoubling Nestor's years.
>
> Your lordship's servants most bounden
> > James Burbage
> > John Perkin
> > John Laneham
> > William Johnson
> > Robert Wilson
> > Thomas Clarke

153 Royal Patent for the Earl of Leicester's players, 1574

PRO, C66/1116, memb. 36. Transcribed in MSC, 1.262.

Pro Iacobo Burbage et aliis de licencia speciali

Elizabeth by the grace of God, Queen of England, &c. To all justices, mayors, sheriffs, bailiffs, head constables, under constables, and all other our officers and ministers, greeting. Know ye that we of our especial grace, certain knowledge, and mere motion have licensed and authorised, and by these presents do license and authorise, our loving subjects James Burbage, John Perkin, John Laneham, William Johnson, and Robert Wilson, servants to our trusty and well beloved cousin and counsellor the Earl of Leicester, to use, exercise, and occupy the art and faculty of playing comedies, tragedies, interludes, stage plays, and such other like as they have already used and studied, or hereafter shall use and study, as well for the recreation of our loving subjects, as for our solace and pleasure when we shall think good to see them; as also to use and occupy all such instruments as they have already practised, or hereafter shall practise, for and during our pleasure. And the said comedies, tragedies, interludes, and stage plays, together with their music, to show, publish, exercise, and occupy to their best commodity during all the term aforesaid, as well within our City of London and liberties of the same, as also within the liberties and freedoms of any our cities, towns, boroughs, &c. whatsoever as without the same, throughout our realm of England. Willing and commanding you and every of you, as ye tender our pleasure, to permit and suffer them herein without any your lets, hindrance or molestation during the term aforesaid, any act, statute, proclamation, or commandment heretofore made, or hereafter to be made, to the contrary notwithstanding. Provided that the said comedies, tragedies, interludes, and stage plays be by the Master of our Revels for the time being before seen and allowed, and that the same be not published or shown in the time of common prayer, or in the time of great and common plague in our said City of London. In witness whereof &c. Witness our self at Westminster the xth day of May.

(a) Portrait of the Earl of Leicester, 1575

British Museum, Department of Prints and Drawings. Chalk sketch in red and black by Federigo Zuccaro, an Italian artist who spent the summer of 1575 in England. Written on the back (in Italian): 'Duke Robert of Leicester, my lord Leicester, favourite of the Queen of England, in 1575, London, Federigo Zuccaro.'

Players and playing

THE QUEEN

154 Formation of the Queen's players, 1583

PRO, AO3/907/9, 10 March 1583. Transcribed in *Office of the Revels, Eliz. I*, 359.

Royal companies could be constituted by fiat, that is, by royal warrant, a process not available to other patrons. Though the power was seldom used, Queen Elizabeth's company was formed in that manner in 1583, when the Master of the Revels was authorised to choose the twelve best players from among those companies already in existence.

Edmund Tilney, esquire, Master of the office,[1] being sent for to the court by letter from Mr Secretary[2] dated the 10th of March 1582[/3]. To choose out a company of players for her majesty; for money by him laid out for horse hire to the court and back again, 10s; for his own charges, his men's, and horsemeat there 2 days, 10s; viz. 20s.

[1] Of the Revels.
[2] Sir Francis Walsingham.

155 Comment on the Queen's players

Passage inserted by Edmund Howes into the 1615 and 1631 editions of John Stow's *Annals*. Howes' bias is evident in his disparaging comments about the competence of earlier players; he is also wrong about the Queen having had no players before 1583, as Elizabeth had inherited a company of royal players from her predecessor in 1558.

Comedians and stage-players of former times were very poor and ignorant in respect of these of this time; but being now grown very skilful and exquisite actors for all matters, they were entertained into the service of divers great lords, out of which companies there were twelve of the best chosen, and, at the request of Sir Francis Walsingham, they were sworn the Queen's servants and were allowed wages and liveries as grooms of the chamber. And until this year 1583, the Queen had no players. Among these twelve players were two rare men, viz. Thomas [*sic*; *i.e.* Robert] Wilson, for a quick, delicate, refined, extemporal wit, and Richard Tarlton, for a wondrous plentiful pleasant extemporal wit, he was the wonder of his time. He lieth buried in Shoreditch church. [*In a note*] He was so beloved that men use his picture for their signs.

(a) Drawing of Richard Tarlton

BL, MS Harl. 3885, fo. 19

Tarlton died in 1588. The drawing was probably made after that date, perhaps copied from an early broadside woodcut; see Astington, 'Rereading Illustrations of the English Stage', 161–4. The final sentence of the previous item affirms the ubiquity of images of Tarlton.

THE KING

156 Warrant to expand the King's company, 1633

PRO, LC5/132, p. 334. Transcribed in MSC, II(3).361. A memorandum from the Lord Chamberlain (Philip, Earl of Pembroke and Montgomery) to 'John Lowen and Joseph Taylor, two of the company of his Majesty's players'; another example of impressment, used this time not to create (as in 1583) but to sustain a royal troupe during an emergency.

Whereas the late decease, infirmity, and sickness of divers principal actors of his majesty's company of players hath much decayed and weakened them, so that they are disabled to do his majesty service in their quality, unless there be some speedy order taken to supply and furnish them with a convenient number of new actors; his majesty having taken notice thereof, and signified his royal pleasure unto me therein, these are to will and require you and in his majesty's name straitly to charge, command and authorise you, and either of you, to choose, receive and take into your company any such actor or actors belonging to any of the licensed companies within and about the City of London as you shall think fit and able to do his majesty service in that kind. Herein you may not fail, and this shall be your sufficient warrant and discharge in that behalf. Court at Whitehall the 6th of May 1633.

X   Players and their playing places

Stage-players were obliged to secure for their use not only costumes, properties and playbooks, but also access to playing places if they hoped to carry on their craft. Itinerant players, needing playing space only infrequently in any one location, faced different problems than did urban players, who would wish to play fairly persistently in the same localised vicinity. The tradition of inn-yard playing was a common factor for both urban and travelling companies, but beginning in the mid-1560s players in the vicinity of London began to find purpose-built structures available for their use, along with an owner or lessor willing to negotiate terms. These new playing spaces, and their landlords, soon became the emblematic norm, though playing in all the more traditional venues continued as well. Occasionally a consortium of stage-players might attempt to build or purchase their own playhouse, but for the most part the great majority of players throughout the period had to lease such premises from others. The documents that follow, most of them lawsuits, illustrate the kinds of difficulties stage-players encountered in attempting to keep themselves before the public.

157   The Swan playhouse and the Earl of Pembroke's players, 1597

PRO, Req.2/266/23, the suit, and Req.1/19, p. 405, the decree. Transcribed by Wallace, 'The Swan Theatre and the Earl of Pembroke's Servants', 345–55

On 28 July 1597 the Privy Council ordered all London's playhouses closed. At that time the Earl of Pembroke's company of stage-players was playing at Francis Langley's playhouse the Swan, on the Bankside, having contracted with Langley to do so. The players ceased playing in compliance with the order, but when the inhibition against playing was lifted, Pembroke's players did not return to the Swan, though their legal agreement still had some time to run; they chose to play instead at the Rose. Langley threatened to sue them at the common law to enforce his contract. The players responded with a countersuit in the Court of Requests, setting forth their reasons for avoiding Langley's playhouse.

(1) The players' bill of complaint, November 1597

To the Queen's most excellent majesty:

In most humble and dutiful manner showeth and beseecheth your highness your true, faithful and obedient subjects Robert Shaa, Richard Jones, Gabriel Spencer, William Bird alias Borne, and Thomas Downton, servants to the right honourable the earl of Pembroke . . . your highness's said subjects, together with others their accomplices and associates, have of long time used and professed the art of stage-playing, being lawfully allowed and authorised thereunto, during which time your highness's said subjects, being familiar and acquainted with one Francis Langley, citizen and goldsmith of London, about February [1597] . . . fell into conference and communication with the said Langley for and about the hiring and taking a playhouse of the said Langley, situate in the Old Paris Garden in the parish of St Saviour in the county of Surrey, commonly called . . . the Swan; which . . . they fully concluded and agreed therefore; and among the diverse other agreements between them in and about the same, the said Langley, craftily and cunningly intending . . . to circumvent and overreach your said subjects . . . required that your said subjects would become bound to him, the said Langley, in some great penalty with condition that they should not absent themselves nor play elsewhere but in the said playhouse called the Swan, as aforesaid, whereupon your highness's said subjects (nothing suspecting the said Langley's purpose and dishonest dealing and crafty complot . . . in or about the month of February [1597] . . . became bound severally, each by himself and for himself, in five several obligations in £100 apiece, with condition thereupon endorsed . . . to this or the like effect: that if your highness's said subject Robert Shaa, one of the said obligors, should until the twentieth day of February now next ensuing . . . continue and attend as one of the company of players which then were agreed to play in the said playhouse . . . called the Swan, without absenting himself at any time from the company when they should so play there, unless the said Robert Shaa . . . should in his place and stead bring in or procure a sufficient person (such as the same Langley or his assigns should like of) [to take his place] until the said twentieth day of February now next ensuing, as aforesaid; and further, it was contained in the said condition . . . that if your highness's said subject Robert Shaa, or [his replacement], should from time to time until the said twentieth day of February play in the said playhouse as one of the said company, and not in any other place . . . within five miles distant . . . from the City of London (except private places only), or that the company of players should not in the meantime play within the City of London, and so always should play in the said playhouse . . . that then the said obligation to be void; and so consequently each of your highness's said subjects became solely and severally bound by obligation in the sum of £100 . . . But now . . . sithence that time, as well your highness's said subjects as all other the companies of players in and about your highness's said City of London, have been prohibited and restrained from their liberty of playing[1] . . . [and] the said Francis Langley, of a greedy desire and dishonest disposition, endeavouring and seeking by all undue and indirect means to bring your said subjects into the danger and forfeiture of their said several obligations by severing of their company . . . procured from your said subjects two of their company so as they cannot continue their play and exercise as they should, nor as the condition of the said several obligations requireth; whereby the same are become forfeited, and now the said Langley, having thus lewdly and dishonestly procured your said subjects to incur the penalty of their said several obligations, and effected all things to his mischievous mind, hath of late published and given out (and still doth threaten) to commence suit at the common law against your said subjects upon their said several obligations, meaning by the rigour and strict course therof to recover the penalty of £500 . . . from your said subjects, against all right, equity, and good conscience, to their extreme impoverishing and utter undoing forever, unless your highness, of your wonted and accustomed clemency, mercy, and grace, relieve them herein . . . May it therefore please your highness . . . to grant to your said subjects your most gracious letters under your privy seal, to be directed to the said Francis Langley, commanding him . . . personally to be and appear before your highness's council in her honourable Court of Requests, then and there to answer to the premises, and to stand to and abide such order and direction therein as to your highness's council of the same court shall seem to stand with right and equity; and your said subjects, as they are already bound, shall daily pray for the preservation of your majesty in all prosperity and tranquillity long to reign and rule over us.

1 For the suspension of playing, see 54.

(2) Langley's answer, 24 November 1597

The answer of Francis Langley, defendant, unto the bill of complaint of Robert Shaa and others, complainants:

[Langley] for answer saith that the said Shaa and the rest . . . had been earnest suitors unto the defendant to have the defendant's house for to play in, [and] . . . it was concluded and fully agreed . . . that they should play in the defendant's said house for a year then next and immediately ensuing, and the defendant was to allow unto the complainants and the rest of their fellow players such benefit as was then likewise agreed between them, and the defendant, upon the said agreement giving credit unto their faithful promises, disbursed and laid out for making of the said house ready, and providing of apparel fit and necessary for their playing, the sum of £300 and upwards. And . . . they became bounden unto the defendant as in the bill is alleged; but the said Shaa and the rest of the complainants, not regarding their said promise and agreement, but contrariwise being resolute and, as it seemeth, meaning to defraud and to deceive the defendant, and to make him to lose most of the charges he had disbursed in and about the making ready of the said house and providing of the said apparel as aforesaid, they the said complainants have departed and so severed themselves from the rest of their company, without any just cause offered unto them by the defendant, and so have ever sithence absented themselves from the defendant's said house, and so now, sithence their liberty to play,[1] they have played in the house of one Philip Henslowe, commonly called . . . the Rose, on the Bankside; . . . true it is that there was a restraint, and that as well the complainants as all other the companies of players in and about the City of London were prohibited and restrained from playing for a time ... But ... the complainants were at liberty ever sithence the feast of All Saints last past [i.e. 1 November] (any restraint to the contrary to the defendant's knowledge notwithstanding), and might have played, if it had pleased them, in the defendant's house, as other of their fellows have done; but the complainants have, ever sithence, refused to play in the defendant's house, and thereby have wilfully forfeited their said bonds ... All which matters this defendant is ready to aver and prove, as this honourable court shall award, and prayeth to be dismissed with his reasonable costs and charges for his wrongful vexation herein sustained.

[1] That is, since the prohibition was lifted, on 1 November.

(3) The players' replication, 6 February 1598

The replication of Robert Shaa, Richard Jones, Gabriel Spencer, William Bird alias Borne, and Thomas Downton, complainants, to the answer of Francis Langley, defendant:

The said complainants, and every of them, do aver and maintain their said bill of complaint, and all and every the matters therein contained, to be true, certain, and sufficient in the law ... and say that the answer of the said defendant is very untrue, incertain, and insufficient in the law to be replied unto, for divers imperfections therein very manifestly appearing ... And as touching the departure and absence of these complainants from the house of the said defendant, the cause thereof was well known, as well to the said defendant as to others, for that by her majesty's authority and commandment a restraint was publicly made, as well of the said complainants as all other companies of players in and about her majesty's City of London, from playing in any of the said playhouses in or near the said City. And the owners of the same houses likewise prohibited to suffer any plays in the same several houses from about the feast-day of St James the Apostle [i.e. 25 July] until about the feast of All Saints [i.e. 1 November] last past; whereupon (after that these complainants had obtained licence to play again) they resorted to the said defendant, and offered themselves to play in the house of the said defendant, according to the condition of their obligation, as formerly they had done, if the said defendant would bear them out; who answered that he would not bear the complainants out, but said he had let to them his house, and bade them do what they would. The complainants then replied and said that they durst not play in his house without licence,[1] and that it was to their undoing to continue in idleness, and that Philip Henslowe ... had obtained licence for his house, and would bear the complainants out if they would go to him. Then the said defendant said that the complainants were best to go to him, which the complainants conceived and took for a licence of the said defendant, and that he meant well to the complainants that they should help themselves to get their living; since which time these complainants have exercised their playing at the house of the said Philip Henslowe, as lawfully they might, and these complainants are now persuaded that the said defendant used the said words, videlicet 'that then the said complainants might go and play in the house of the said Philip Henslowe', of policy to draw them into the penalty and danger of the forfeiture of their obligations, and not for any other purpose . . . [Further,] that the said defendant, giving credit unto the faithful promises of the complainants, disbursed and laid out for making of the said house ready, and providing for apparel fit and necessary for their playing, the sum of £300 and upwards, [is] very untruly . . . alleged; for the said complainants, for further replication, say that for the making of the said house ready and fit for the complainants to play in, the said defendant was at no cost at all, for the said house was then lately afore used to have plays in it; and if the said defendant were at charges for the providing of apparel, the said complainants say the same was upon his own offer and promise, that he by the same agreement was to provide the same, and afterwards to acquaint the complainants with the value thereof, and that the defendant should be allowed for the true value thereof out of the complainants' moiety of the gains for the several standings in the galleries of the said house, which belonged to them;[2] which the said complainants have faithfully performed from time to time . . . [We further deny] that the said defendant hath sustained any loss by reason of these complainants, for he the said defendant hath, ever since, had his said house continually . . . exercised with other players, to his great gains . . . therefore the said complainants humbly pray this honourable court to take some order whereby the defendant may be compelled to deliver such of the same apparel, so paid for by the complainants, to them the said complainants, or recover for the same, and to have their said obligation delivered unto them; with that, that the said complainants do and will aver and prove that the said defendant, of a greedy desire and dishonest disposition, did endeavour and sought by indirect and undue means to bring the complainants into the danger of forfeiture of their said several obligations, by severing of their companies, as before is truly declared; . . . all which matters the said complainants are ready to aver and prove, as this honourable court shall award, and pray, as before in the their said bill of complaint they have prayed.

[1] Playhouses as well as playing companies were supposed to be licensed; the players claim they cannot perform in an unlicensed playhouse, the Swan's licence not having been renewed after the inhibition.
[2] The income from admissions to the galleries was shared equally between Langley and the players; the players here offer money from their half, or moiety, to Langley as payment toward the apparel.

(4) Decree of the court, 29 May 1598

In the matter in variance depending before the Queen's majesty and her highness's council of her honourable court of Whitehall, at the suit of Robert Shaa, Richard Jones, Gabriel Spencer, William Bird alias Borne, and Thomas Downton, complainants, against Francis Langley, defendant, being for and concerning the stay of the defendant's proceedings at the common law against the said complainants upon five several obligations of £100 apiece, wherein the said complainants stand severally bounden to the said defendant, with condition for the performance of certain covenants and agreements ... it is this present day ... ordered that the said defendant, his councillors, attorneys, solicitors, and factors, and every of them, shall from henceforth surcease and stay, and no further prosecute or proceed at the common law upon the said obligations, or any of them, against the said complainants, until it shall please her majesty's said council to take further order for the final ending and determining of this cause; and it is further, by her majesty's said council, ordered that an injunction, under her majesty's privy seal, upon pain of £500, shall be awarded forth of this court and directed to the said defendant, his councillors, attorneys, solicitors, and factors, and every of them, for the due performance of this present order.

158 Lease of one thirty-second part of the income of the Fortune playhouse, 1608

Dulwich, Henslowe Papers, Mun. 33; followed by the counterpart, Mun. 34. Transcribed in Greg, *Henslowe Papers* 13–14

This lease, bearing neither seal nor signature, was in all likelihood never executed; but its terms are instructive. The intended lessors, Philip Henslowe and Edward Alleyn, spelled out with some care the duties and obligations Thomas Downton, a stage-player, would have to observe if he were to purchase the rights to one-eighth part of one-fourth of the profits.

[Lease, dated 1608, the day and month not being filled in, from] Philip Henslowe and Edward Alleyn of the parish of St Saviour's in Southwark, in the county of Surrey, esquires [to] Thomas Downton of the parish of St Giles without Cripplegate, London, gentleman ... in consideration of the sum of £27 10s ... in hand, [of] one-eighth part of a fourth of all such clear gains in money as shall hereafter, during the term hereunder demised, arise, grow, accrue or become due or properly belong unto the said Philip Henslowe and Edward Alleyn or either of them ... by reason of any stage playing or other exercise, commodity or use whatsoever used or to be used or exercised within the playhouse of the said Philip Henslowe and Edward Alleyn commonly called the Fortune ... [the said share to be paid] every day that any play or other exercise shall be acted or exercised in the playhouse aforesaid, upon the sharing of the monies gathered and gotten at every of the same, and exercises as heretofore hath been used and accustomed [from Michaelmas last past before the date of execution for the term of thirteen years, for the yearly rent of 10s payable quarterly; the said Thomas Downton covenanting to bear a proportionate part] of all such necessary and needful charges as shall be bestowed or laid forth in the new building or repairing of the said playhouse during the said term of thirteen years with[out] fraud or coven; [also that he will] not at any time hereafter during the said term give over the faculty or quality of playing, but shall in his own person exercise the same to the best and most benefit he can, within the playhouse aforesaid, during the time aforesaid, unless he shall become unable by reason of sickness or any other infirmity, or unless it be with the consent of the said Philip Henslowe and Edward Alleyn or either of them, their executors or assigns; [and further that he will] not at any time hereafter during the said term of thirteen years play or exercise the faculty of stage-playing in any common playhouse now erected or hereafter to be erected within the said City of London or two miles compass thereof other than in the said playhouse called the Fortune, without the special licence, will, consent and agreement of the said Philip Henslowe and Edward Alleyn or one of them . . . first therefore had and obtained, writing under their hands and seals; [and lastly that he will] not at any time hereafter during the said term give, grant, bargain, sell or otherwise do away or depart with the said eight part of a fourth part of the said clear gains before demised, nor any parcel thereof, to any person or persons whatsoever without the like consent, licence, will and agreement of them the said Philip Henslowe and Edward Alleyn or either of them . . . obtained in writing, under their hands and seals, for the same as aforesaid.

159 Agreement between a company of players and a playhouse owner, 1613

Dulwich, Henslowe Papers, Mun. 52. Transcribed in Greg, *Henslowe Papers* 23

In March 1613 a company of boy-players called the Children of the Queen's Revels (managed by Philip Rosseter, one of the King's lutanists) was absorbed into the Lady Elizabeth's company of players under Philip Henslowe, a playhouse owner. Nathan Field, the leader of the newly combined troupe, negotiated an agreement for the company's further activity with Henslowe and his business associate Jacob Meade. The document is undated, and may never have been executed, but its terms form the basis for the articles of grievance reproduced below (160).

?March 1613

Articles of agreement . . . on the part and behalf of Philip Henslowe, esquire, and Jacob Meade, waterman, to be performed, touching and concerning the company of players which they have lately raised, viz.:

Imprimis, the said Philip Henslowe and Jacob Meade . . . promise . . . by these presents to and with Nathan Field, gentleman, that they the said Philip Henslowe and Jacob Meade or one of them shall and will during the space of three years at all times (when no restraint of playing shall be) at . . . their own proper costs and charges find and provide a sufficient house or houses for the said company to play in, and also shall and will at all times during the said term . . . lay out all such . . . sums of money as four or five sharers of the said company, chosen by the said Philip and Jacob, shall think fitting, for the furnishing of the said company with playing apparel towards the setting out of their new plays; and further that the said Philip Henslowe and Jacob Meade shall and will at all times during the said term, when the said company shall play in or near the City of London, furnish the said company of players, as well with such stock of apparel and other properties as the said Philip Henslowe hath already bought, as also with such other stock of apparel as the said Philip Henslowe and Jacob Meade shall hereafter provide . . . and further shall and will at such . . . times during the said term as the said company of players shall, by means of any restraint or sickness, go into the country, deliver and furnish the said company with fitting apparel out of both the said stocks of apparel. And further the said Philip Henslowe and Jacob Meade do . . . covenant . . . with the said Nathan Field by these presents in manner and form following, that is to say, that they . . . or one of them shall and will . . . disburse and lay out such . . . sums of money as shall be thought fitting by four or five of the sharers of the said company, to be chosen by the said Philip and Jacob or one of them, to be paid for any play which they shall buy or condition or agree for; so always as the said company do and shall truly repay unto the said Philip and Jacob . . . all such . . . sums of money as they shall disburse for any play, upon the second or third day whereon the same play shall be played by the said company, without fraud or longer delay; and further that the said Philip Henslowe and Jacob Meade shall and will at all times, upon request made by the major part of the sharers of the said company . . . remove and put out of the said company any of the said company of players, if the said Philip Henslowe and Jacob Meade shall find the said request to be just and that there be no hope of conformity in the party complained of; and further that they the said Philip Henslowe and Jacob Meade shall and will at all times, upon request made by the said company or the major part thereof, pay unto them all such sums of money as shall come unto their hands [upon] . . . any forfeitures for rehearsals or such like payments; and also shall and will, upon the request of the said company or the major part of them, sue [any such] . . . persons by whom any forfeiture shall be made as aforesaid, and after or upon the recovery and receipt thereof (their charges disbursed about the recovery . . . [being] first deducted and allowed) shall and will make satisfaction of the remainder thereof unto the said company without fraud or guile.

[*The remainder of the document is badly damaged.*]

160 Players draft articles of grievance against Philip Henslowe, 1615

Dulwich, Henslowe Papers, MS 1, Art. 106. Transcribed in Greg, *Henslowe Papers* 86–90

Articles of [grie]vance against M[r Philip] Hinchlowe:

Imprimis, in March 1612, upon Mr Hinchlowe's joining companies with Mr Rosseter, the company borrowed £80 of one Mr Griffin and the same was put into Mr Hinchlowe's debt, which made it sixteen score pounds; who, after the receipt of the same or most part thereof, in March 1613 he broke the said company again and seized all the stock, under colour to satisfy what remained due to him; yet persuaded Mr Griffin afterwards to arrest the company for his £80, who are still in danger for the same. So now there was in equity due to the company: £80

Item: Mr Hinchlowe, having lent one Taylor £30 and £20 to one Baxter, fellows of the company, cunningly put their said private debts into the general account, by which means he is in conscience to allow them: £50

Item: Having the stock of apparel in his hands to secure his debt, he sold £10 worth of old apparel out of the same without accounting or abating for the same; here grows due to the company: £10

Also upon the departure of one Ecclestone, a fellow of the company, he recovered of him £14 towards his debt, which is in conscience likewise to be allowed to the Company: £14

In March 1613 he makes up a company and buys apparel of one Rosseter to the value of £63, and valued the old stock that remained in his hands at £63; likewise they upon his word accepting the same at that rate, which being prized by Mr Daborne justly, between his partner Meade and him, came but to £40; so here grows due to the company: £23

Item: he agrees with the company that they should enter bond to play with him for three years at such house and houses as he shall appoint, and to allow him half galleries for the said house and houses, and the other half galleries towards his debt of £126, and other such moneys as he should lay out for play apparel during the space of the said three years, agreeing with them in consideration thereof to seal each of them a bond of £200 to find them a convenient house and houses, and to lay out such moneys as four of the sharers should think fit for their use in apparel, which at the three years, being paid for, to be delivered to the sharers; who accordingly entered the said bonds; but Mr Hinchlowe and Mr Meade deferred the same, and in conclusion utterly denied to seal at all.

Item: Mr Hinchlowe, having promised in consideration of the company's lying still one day in fourteen for his baiting,[1] to give them 50s, he having denied to be bound as aforesaid gave them only 40s, and for that Mr Field would not consent thereunto he gave him so much as his share out of £50 would have come unto; by which means he is duly indebted to the company: £10

In June following the said agreement, he brought in Mr Pallant and shortly after Mr Dawes into the said company, promising one 12s a week out of his part of the galleries, and the other 6s a week out of his part of the galleries; and because Mr Field was thought not to be drawn thereunto, he promised him 6s weekly also; which in one month after, unwilling to bear so great a charge, he called the company together, and told them that this 24s was to be charged upon them, threatening those which would not consent thereunto to break the company and make up a new without them. Whereupon, knowing he was not bound, the three-quarters sharers advancing themselves to whole shares consented thereunto, by which means they are out of purse £30, and his part of the galleries bettered twice as much: £30

Item: having nine gatherers more than his due, it comes to this year from the company: £10

Item: the company paid for [Arra]s and other properties £40, which Mr Hinchlowe detaineth: £40

In February last 1614, perceiving the company drew out of his debt and called upon him for his accounts, he broke the company again, by withdrawing the hired men from them, and sells their stock (in his hands) for £400, giving under his own hand that he had received towards his debt: £300

Which, with the just and conscionable allowances before named made to the company, which comes to £267, makes £567

Articles of oppression against Mr Hinchlowe:

He chargeth the stock with £600 and odd, towards which he hath received as aforesaid £567 of us; yet sells the stock to strangers for £400, and makes us no satisfaction.

He hath taken all bonds of our hired men in his own name, whose wages though we have truly paid yet at his pleasure he hath taken them away and turned them over to others to the breaking of our company.

For lending of £6 to pay them their wages, he made us enter bond to give him the profit of a warrant of £10 due to us at Court.

Also he hath taken right gold and silver lace of divers garments to his own use without account to us or abatement.

Upon every breach of the company he takes new bonds for his stock and our security for playing with him; so that he hath in his hands bonds of ours to the value of £5,000 and his stock too; which he denies to deliver and threatens to oppress us with.

Also having appointed a man to the seeing of his accounts in buying of clothes (he being to have 6s a week) he takes the means away and turns the man out.

The reason of his often breaking with us he gave in these words: 'Should these fellows come out of my debt, I should have no rule with them.'

Also we have paid him for play books £200 or thereabouts and yet he denies to give us the copies of any one of them.

Also within three years he hath broken and dismembered five companies.

[1] The playhouse was also used for bear-baiting.

161 Edward Alleyn leases out the Fortune playhouse, 1618

Dulwich, Henslowe Papers, Mun. 56, followed (Mun. 57) by a bond in £60 of the same date from the lessees to observe covenants. Transcribed in Greg, *Henslowe Papers* 27–8. The lessees are stage-players of the company known as Palsgrave's Men because of their patronage by the Elector Palatine (*Pfalzgraf*) Friedrich V, who had married King James' daughter Elizabeth in 1613.

[Lease dated 31 October 1618, from] Edward Alleyn of Dulwich in the county of Surrey, esquire, [to] Edward Juby, William Bird *alias* Bourne, Frank Grace, Richard

Gunnell, Charles Massey, William Stratford, William Cartwright, Richard Price, William Parr and Richard Fowler, gentlemen, [of] All that his great building now used for a playhouse and commonly called . . . the Fortune, situate, lying and being between White Cross Street and Golding Lane, London . . . together with one messuage or tenement thereunto adjoining called the Taphouse . . . [from Michaelmas last past before the date above mentioned for the term of thirty-one years for the yearly rent of £200 payable quarterly.] And also two rundlets of wine, the one sack and the other claret, of 10s apiece price, to be delivered at the feast of Christmas yearly; [with provision that if the said Edward Alleyn die within the term of thirty-one years the rent be reduced to £120 for the residue; the lessees covenanting] that they nor any of them, their executors, administrators or assigns, shall not at any time hereafter alter, transpose, or otherwise convert the said playhouse to any other use or uses than as the same is now used . . . [Sealed and signed by Edward Juby, W. Bird, Frank Grace, R. Gunnell, Charles Massey, William Stratford, William Cartwright, Richard Price, William Parr, and Richard Fowler.]

162   The so-called 'Sharers' Papers', 1635

PRO, LC5/133, pp. 44–51. Transcribed in MSC, II(3), pp. 362–73

Even when playhouses were owned by stage players, so that performers were their own landlords, frictions might still develop. In 1635 certain of the King's players – Robert Benfield, Elliard Swanston, and Thomas Pollard – though already sharers in the profits of the company of players to which they belonged, wished also to become sharers in the profits of the playhouses that some of their colleagues owned among themselves. These three men petitioned the Lord Chamberlain in that year to authorise and permit them to purchase shares in the Globe and Blackfriars and thus become householders.

(1) Petition of Benfield, Swanston and Pollard

To the right honourable Philip, Earl of Pembroke and Montgomery, Lord Chamberlain of his majesty's household. Robert Benfield, Elliard Swanston and Thomas Pollard humbly represent these their grievances, imploring his lordship's noble favour towards them for their relief.

That the petitioners have a long time, with much patience, expected to be admitted sharers in the playhouses of the Globe and the Blackfriars, whereby they might reap some better fruit of their labours than hitherto they have done, and be encouraged to proceed therein with cheerfulness;

That [the present sharers] have . . . a full moiety of the whole gains arising thereby, excepting the outer doors, and such of the said housekeepers as be actors do likewise equally share with all the rest of the actors, both in the other moiety and in the said outer doors also;

That out of the actors' moiety there is notwithstanding defrayed all wages to hired men, apparel, poets, lights, and other charges of the houses whatsoever, so that, between the gains of the actors and of those few interested as housekeepers, there is an unreasonable inequality;

That the house of the Globe was formerly divided into sixteen parts, whereof Mr Cuthbert Burbage and his sisters had eight, Mrs Condell four, and Mr Heminges four;

That Mr Taylor and Mr Lowen were long since admitted to purchase four parts betwixt them from the rest, viz., one part from Mr Heminges, two parts from Mrs Condell, and half a part apiece from Mr Burbage and his sister;

That the three parts remaining to Mr Heminges were afterwards by Mr Shanks surreptitiously purchased from him,[1] contrary to the petitioners' expectation, who hoped that when any parts had been to be sold, they should have been admitted to have bought and divided the same amongst themselves for their better livelihood;

That the petitioners desire not to purchase or diminish any part of Mr Taylor's or Mr Lowen's shares ... [but] the petitioners' labours ... are equal to some of the rest, and for that others of the said housekeepers are neither actors nor his Majesty's servants, and yet the petitioners' profit and means of livelihood so much inferior and unequal to theirs, as appears before; they therefore desire that they may be admitted to purchase ... single parts ... from those that have the greatest shares and may best spare them; viz., that Mr Burbage and his sister, having three parts and a half apiece, may sell them two parts, and reserve two and a half apiece to themselves; and that Mr Shanks, having three, may sell them one and reserve two;

Wherein they hope your lordship will conceive their desires to be just and modest ...

That for the house in the Blackfriars, it being divided into eight parts amongst the aforenamed housekeepers, and Mr Shanks having two parts thereof, Mr Lowen, Mr Taylor and each of the rest having but one part apiece, which two parts were by the said Mr Shanks purchased of Mr Heminges together with those three of the Globe as before, the petitioners desire and hope that your Lordship will conceive it likewise reasonable that the said Mr Shanks may assign over one of the said parts amongst them three, they giving him such satisfaction for the same as that he be no loser thereby;

Lastly, that your lordship would to that purpose be nobly pleased, as their only gracious refuge and protector, to call all the said housekeepers before you, and to use your Lordship's power with them to conform themselves thereunto, the rather considering that some of the said housekeepers who have the greatest shares are neither actors nor his majesty's servants as aforesaid, and yet reap most or the chiefest benefit ... without taking any pains themselves; for which your petitioners shall have just cause to bless your lordship, as however they are daily bound to do with the devotions of most humble and obliged beadsmen.

Shares in the Globe			Shares in the Blackfriars	
Burbage	3½	of a lease of 9 years	Shanks	2
Robinson	3½	from our Lady Day last	Burbage	1
Condell	2	1635	Robinson	1
Shanks	3	not yet confirmed by	Taylor	1
Taylor	2	Sir Matthew Brend to	Lowen	1
Lowen	2	be taken to feoffees	Condell	1

[1] In his will, dated 30 December 1635, Shanks (who identified himself therein as both a freeman of the Weaver's Company and one of the King's players) stated that his estate consisted in part of 'a lease which I am to have of three-eighth parts in the moiety of the Globe Playhouse for the term of nine years from Christmas last, which I bought and paid dear for, and by means thereof have been put into debt' (PRO, Prob.11/170, fos. 53–4).

(2) Further petition of Benfield, Swanston and Pollard

Robert Benfield, Elliard Swanston, and Thomas Pollard do further humbly represent unto your lordship:

That the housekeepers, being but six in number, viz., Mr Cuthbert Burbage, Mrs Condell, Mr Shanks, Mr Taylor, Mr Lowen and Mr Robinson (in the right of his wife),[1] have amongst them the full moiety of all the galleries and boxes in both houses, and of the tiring-house door at the Globe;

That the actors have the other moiety, with the outer doors; but in regard the actors are half as many more, viz., nine in number, their shares fall short and are a great deal less than the housekeepers' and yet notwithstanding, out of those lesser shares the said actors defray all charges of the house whatsoever, viz., wages to hired men and boys, music, lights, &c., amounting to £900 or £1,000 per annum or thereabouts, being £3 a day one day with another, besides the extraordinary charge which the said actors are wholly at for apparel and poets, &c.;

Whereas the said housekeepers, out of all their gains, have not, till our Lady Day last, paid above £65 per annum rent for both houses, towards which they raise between £20 and £30 per annum from the tap-houses and a tenement and a garden belonging to the premises, &c., and are at no other charges whatsoever excepting the ordinary reparations of the houses;

So that upon a medium made of the gains of the housekeepers and those of the actors, one day with another throughout the year, the petitioners will make it apparent that when some of the housekeepers share 12s a day at the Globe, the actors share not above 3s; and then what those gain that are both actors and housekeepers, and have their shares in both, your lordship will easily judge, and thereby find the modesty of the petitioners' suit, who desire only to buy for their money one part apiece from such three of the said housekeepers as are fittest to spare them, both in respect of desert and otherwise; viz., Mr Shanks one part of his three; Mr Robinson and his wife, one part of their three and a half; and Mr Cuthbert Burbage the like.

And for the house of the Blackfriars, that Mr Shanks, who now enjoys two parts there, may sell them likewise one, to be divided amongst them three ...

[1] Richard Robinson, a stage-player, had married Richard Burbage's widow Winifred.

(3) John Shanks' answer

The answer of John Shanks to the petition of Robert Benfield, Elliard Swanston and Thomas Pollard, lately exhibited to the right honourable Philip, Earl of Pembroke and Montgomery, Lord Chamberlain of his majesty's household,

humbly showeth:

That about almost two years since, your suppliant, upon offer to him made by William Heminges, did buy of him one part he had in the Blackfriars, for about six years then to come, at the yearly rent of £6 5s, and another part he then had in the Globe for about two years to come, and paid him for the same two parts, in ready moneys, £156, which said parts were offered to your suppliant, and were as free then for any other to buy as for your suppliant;

That about eleven months since, the said William Heminges offering to sell unto your suppliant the remaining parts he then had, viz., one in the Blackfriars, wherein he had then about five years to come, and two in the Globe, wherein he had then but one year to come, your suppliant likewise bought the same, and paid for them in ready moneys more £350, all which moneys so disbursed by your suppliant amount to £506, the greatest part whereof your suppliant was constrained to take up at interest; and your suppliant hath besides disbursed to the said William Heminges divers other small sums of money since he was in prison.

That your suppliant did neither fraudulently nor surreptitiously defeat any of the petitioners in their hope of buying the said parts, neither would the said William Heminges have sold the same to any of the petitioners, for that they would not have given him any such price for the same, but would (as now they endeavour to do) have had the same against his will, and at what rates they pleased;

That your suppliant being an old man in this quality, who in his youth first served your noble father,[1] and after that the late Queen Elizabeth, then King James, and now his royal majesty, and having in this long time made no provision for himself in his age, nor for his wife, children, and grandchild, for his and their better livelihood, having this opportunity, did at dear rates purchase these parts, and hath for a very small time as yet received the profits thereof and hath but a short time in them, and is without any hope to renew the same when the terms be out, he therefore hopeth he shall not be hindered in the enjoying the profit thereof, especially when as the same are things very casual and subject to be discontinued and lost by sickness and diverse other ways and to yield no profit at all.

That whereas the petitioners in their complaint say that they have not means to subsist, it shall by oath (if need be) be made apparent that every one of the three petitioners for his own particular hath gotten and received, this year last past, of the sum of £180, which, as your suppliant conceiveth, is a very sufficient means to satisfy and answer their long and patient expectation, and is more, by above the one half, than any of them ever got or were capable of elsewhere; besides what Mr Swanston, one of them who is most violent in this business, who hath further had and received this last year above £34 for the profit of a third part of one part in the Blackfriars which he bought for £20, and yet hath enjoyed the same two or three years already, and hath still as long time in the same as your suppliant hath in his, who, for so much as Mr Swanston bought for £20, your suppliant paid £60.

That your suppliant, and other the lessees in the Globe and in the Blackfriars, are chargeable with the payment of £100 yearly rent, besides reparations, which is daily very chargeable unto them, all which they must pay and bear whether they make any profit or not; and so, reckoning their charge in building and fitting the said houses, yearly rent and reparations, no wise man will adventure his estate in such a course, considering their dealing, with whom they have to do, and the many casualties and daily troubles therewith.

That in all the affairs and dealings in this world between man and man, it was, and is ever, held an inviolable principle that in what thing soever any man hath a lawful interest and property, he is not to be compelled to depart with the same against his will, which the complainants endeavour.

And whereas John Heminges, the father of William Heminges, of whom your suppliant made purchase of the said parts, enjoyed the same thirty years without any molestation, being, the most of the said years, both player and housekeeper, and after he gave over playing, divers years; and his son, William Heminges, four years after, though he never had anything to do with the said stage, enjoyed the same without any trouble; notwithstanding, the complainants would violently take from your petitioner the said parts, who hath still, of his own purse, supplied the company for the service of his majesty with boys, as Thomas Pollard, John Thompson, deceased (for whom he paid £40), your suppliant having paid his part of £200 for other boys since his coming to the company – John Honyman, Thomas Holcombe and divers others – and at this time maintains three more for the said service. Neither lieth it in the power of your suppliant to satisfy the unreasonable demands of the complainants, he being forced to make over the said parts for security of moneys taken up as aforesaid of Robert Morecroft of Lincoln, his wife's uncle, for the purchase of the said parts, until he hath made payment of the said moneys, which he is not able to do unless he be suffered to enjoy the said parts during the small time of his lease, and is like to be undone if they are taken from him . . .

The humble suit of your suppliant is that your honour will be pleased that he may enjoy that which he hath dearly bought and truly paid for, and your suppliant (as in duty he is bound) shall ever pray for your lordship.

[1] The reference is to the company of players maintained in the 1590s by Henry Herbert, the Earl of Pembroke and father of the Lord Chamberlain to whom Shanks's appeal is addressed. This remark is our only evidence for Shanks having been a member of that company.

(4) Answer of Cuthbert and William Burbage and Winifred Robinson

To the Right Honourable Philip, Earl of Pembroke and Montgomery, Lord Chamberlain of his majesty's household:

Right Honourable, and our singular good lord: we, your humble suppliants, Cuthbert Burbage and Winifred his brother's [Richard's] wife and William his [Cuthbert's] son, do tender to your honourable consideration for what respects and good reasons we ought not, in all charity, to be disabled of our livelihoods by men so soon shot up, since it hath been the custom that they should come to it by far more antiquity and desert than those can justly attribute to themselves.

And first, humbly showing to your honour the infinite charges, the manifold lawsuits, the lease's expiration, by the restraints in sickness times and other accidents that did cut from them the best part of the gains that your honour is informed they have received:

The father of us, Cuthbert and Richard Burbage, was the first builder of playhouses, and was himself in his younger years a player. The Theatre he built with many hundred pounds taken up at interest. The players that lived in those first times had only the profits arising from the doors, but now the players receive all the comings in at the doors to themselves, and half the galleries, from the housekeepers. He built this house upon leased ground, by which means the landlord and he had a great suit in law, and by his death the like troubles fell on us, his sons. We then bethought us of altering from thence, and at like expense built the Globe, with more sums of money taken up at interest, which lay heavy on us many years; and to ourselves we joined those deserving men, Shakespeare, Heminges, Condell, Phillips, and others, partners in the profits of that they call the House; but making the leases for twenty-one years hath been the destruction of ourselves and others; for they dying at the expiration of three or four years of their lease, the subsequent years became dissolved to strangers, as by marrying with their widows, and the like by their children.

Thus, right honourable, as concerning the Globe, where we ourselves are but lessees. Now for the Blackfriars, that is our inheritance. Our father purchased it at extreme rates, and made it into a playhouse with great charge and trouble; which after was leased out to one Evans, that first set up the boys commonly called the Queen's Majesty's Children of the Chapel. In process of time the boys growing up to be men, which were Underwood, Field, Ostler, and were taken to strengthen the King's service; and the more to strengthen the service, the boys daily wearing out, it was considered that house would be as fit for ourselves, and so purchased the lease remaining from Evans with our money, and placed men players, which were Heminges, Condell, Shakespeare, &c.

And Richard Burbage, who for thirty-five years' pains, cost and labour, made means to leave his wife and children some estate (and out of whose estate so many of other players and their families have been maintained) these new men, that were never bred from children in the King's service, would take away with oaths and menaces that we shall be forced, and that they will not thank us for it; so that it seems they would not pay us for what they would have or we can spare, which, more to satisfy your honour than their threatening pride, we are for ourselves willing to part with a part between us, they paying according as ever hath been the custom and the number of years the lease is made for.

Then, to show your honour against these sayings that we eat the fruit of their labours, we refer it to your honour's judgement to consider their profits, which we may safely maintain; for it appeareth by their own accounts for one whole year last past, beginning from Whitsun Monday 1634, to Whitsun Monday 1635, each of these complainants gained severally, as he was a player and no housekeeper, £180. Besides, Mr Swanston hath received from the Blackfriars this year, as he is there a housekeeper, above £30, all which being accounted together may very well keep him from starving.

Wherefore your honour's most humble suppliants entreat they may not further be trampled upon than their estates can bear, seeing how dearly it hath been purchased by the infinite cost and pains of the family of the Burbages, and the great desert of Richard Burbage for his quality of playing, that his wife should not starve in her old age; submitting ourselves to part with one part to them for valuable consideration; and let them seek further satisfaction elsewhere, that is, of the heirs or assigns of Mr Heminges and Mr Condell, who had theirs of the Blackfriars of us for nothing. It is only we that suffer continually.

Therefore, humbly relying upon your honourable charity in discussing their clamour against us, we shall, as we are in duty bound, still pray for the daily increase of your honour's health and happiness.

(5) Order of the Lord Chamberlain, 12 July 1635

Court at Theobalds, 12 July, 1635

Having considered this petition and the several answers and replies of the parties, the merits of the petitioners and the disproportion of their shares, and the interest of his majesty's service, I have thought fit and do accordingly order that the petitioners, Robert Benfield, Elliard Swanston and Thomas Pollard, be each of them admitted to the purchase of the shares desired, of the several persons mentioned in the petition, for the four years remaining of the lease of the house in Blackfriars, and for five years in that of the Globe, at the usual and accustomed rates, and according to the proportion of the time and benefit they are to enjoy. And hereof I desire the housekeepers and all others whom it may concern to take notice, and to conform themselves therein accordingly; the which if they or any of them refuse or delay to perform, if they are actors and his majesty's servants, I do suspend them from the stage and all the benefits thereof; and if they are only interested in the houses, I desire my Lord Privy Seal to take order that they may be left out of the lease which is to be made upon the decree in the Court of Requests.

(6) Memorandum about John Shanks' petition

A petition of John Shanks to my Lord Chamberlain, showing that, according to his Lordship's order, he did make a proposition to his fellows for satisfaction, upon his assigning of his parts in the several houses unto them; but they not only refused to give satisfaction, but restrained him from the stage. That therefore his lordship would order them to give satisfaction, according to his propositions and computation.

(7) Memorandum about the Lord Chamberlain's response

Answered viz., I desire Sir H. Herbert, and Sir John Finett, and my solicitor Daniel Bedingfield, to take this petition, and the several papers hereunto annexed, into their serious considerations, and to speak with the several parties interested, and thereupon, and upon the whole matter, to set down a proportionable and equitable sum of money to be paid unto Shanks for the two parts which he is to pass unto Benfield, Swanston and Pollard; and to cause a final agreement and conveyances to be settled accordingly; and to give me an account of their whole proceedings in writing.[1] 1 August 1635.

---

[1] In the margin beside this entry is written 'Memorandum: all concerning this, and here entered, were delivered, annexed'; but no such 'account of their whole proceedings in writing' is annexed to these papers.

XI Costumes, properties and playbooks

Stage-players, whether early or late in our period and whatever the nature of the business arrangements between and among them, would have required for their continuance a dependable supply of playscripts on the one hand and reliable access to costumes and stage properties on the other. From the earliest days, the long-term needs of travelling players must have made group ownership of costumes and properties by the company itself seem prudent; in London, where several merchants stood ready to let such apparel on hire, group ownership may have seemed less urgent and may not have become standard practice until later; easy hiring of costumes and properties may, in its way, have contributed to the *ad hoc* nature of much early urban playing. But increasingly as the sixteenth century progressed, the growing stability and continuity of playing companies both urban and rural made group ownership of costumes and properties more the norm.

163 *Rastell* v *Walton*, a lawsuit about playing costumes, ?1530

PRO, Req.2/8/14; reproduced, with inaccuracies, in Pollard, *Fifteenth Century Verse and Prose*.

John Rastell, printer and playwright, had employed Henry Walton, a carpenter interested in theatrical business, to assist him in his preparations for the court performance of his interlude of *Love and Riches* at the royal banquet at Greenwich in 1527. He appears to have employed him also in erecting a stage for plays on the grounds of his house in Finsbury Fields. Further, he seems to have lent him some valuable theatrical costumes and other properties, including thirty yards of red buckram 'that went about my lord cardinal's great chamber'. He did this, he claimed, before he left England for a stay of 'half a year and more' in France. Walton seems to have interpreted the matter differently, taking the costumes as part payment for the cost of erecting Rastell's stage. When Rastell, upon his return from France in about 1530, protested this development, Walton sued in the Lord Mayor's court. Rastell, in turn, counter-sued in the Court of Requests. The text of this latter suit follows; it provides us with useful information about the range of people involved in the production of stage plays and interludes, the level of demand for costumes, and the kinds of costumes available, in the 1530s.

(1) Rastell's Bill of Complaint

To the King our Sovereign Lord:

Humbly complaineth unto your gracious Highness your poor orator and humble subject John Rastell, that where your said orator delivered to one Henry Walton certain parcels of stuff and goods to the value of 20 marks,[1] safely to keep to the use of your said orator, that is to say [*here follows a list of some twenty players' garments and pieces of fabric*]. Which said stuff and goods the said Walton promised to deliver again to your said orator, whensoever he should be . . . thereto required. Which said stuff and goods, after the said delivery to him made, the said Walton [had the use of for] half a year and more, during the time that your said orator was . . . in France. After whose coming home your said orator demanded of the said Walton delivery of the said stuff and goods, to whom the said Walton answered and said that he would bring him home the said goods and stuff [but Walton failed to do so for] two or three weeks, during which time the said Walton, unknown to your said orator . . . entered a false feigned plaint [in the Lord Mayor's court] against your said orator, supposing that your said orator should owe to the said Walton 40s sterling, wherein indeed your said orator owed him never a penny . . . [and Walton] made attachment of the said goods and stuff . . . and caused that one John Wilkinson, plasterer, and one Thomas Curtis, were assigned to be appraisers; which Wilkinson . . . appraised the said goods and stuff but to the value of 35s.9d., which goods and stuff at that time were well worth 20 marks and above. Upon which appraisement the said Henry had judgement to recover the said goods and stuff, for the which your said orator can never have remedy by course of the common law . . .

          Johannes Rastell

[1] A mark was worth 13s 4d.

(2) Walton's answer

The answer of Henry Walton to the bill of complaint of John Rastell gentleman

The said Henry Walton by protestation saith, that the said goods in the bill of complaint of the said John Rastell mentioned, be not of so great value as in his said bill of complaint is supposed . . . And where the said John Rastell . . . saith that the goods aforesaid were praised much under their value, the said Henry Walton saith that they were praised to as much as they at the time of the praisement were worth. And where the said complainant . . . saith that he oweth not the said defendant the said 40s and is without remedy, the said Henry Walton will aver that the said John Rastell oweth him the said 40s . . . And the said Henry Walton shall aver that the said goods were of no more value than they were appraised at, for they were rotten and torn players' garments . . .

(3) Rastell's replication

The replication of John Rastell to the Answer of Henry Walton

The said John Rastell saith that his said bill is true, and certain, and sufficient to be answered unto, and matter determinable in this honourable court, and will aver everything to be true contained in the said bill of complaint . . . [The goods were indeed] worth at that time 20 marks and above ... for the great part of the said goods were garments of silk and other stuff, fresh and newly made, with much workmanship done upon them, to the great cost and charge of your said orator ... [who denies] that they were then rotten and torn players' garments, for the said Rastell saith that the said Walton hath letten them out to hire to divers stage plays and interludes, and hath received and had for the hire of them since the said praisement of them the sum of 20 nobles[1] and above ...

[1] A noble was worth 10s.

(4) The list of costumes, with Rastell's valuations

The parcels confessed by Walton.[1]

In primis: A player's garment of green, lined with red tuke and with Roman letters stitched upon it, of blue and red sarcenet. 8 yds 22s

Item: One other garment, paned with blue and green sarcenet, lined with red buckram. 7 yds 20s

Item: Another garment, paned likewise, and lined as the other, with a cape furred with white cats. 7 yds 20s

Item: Another garment, paned with yellow, green, red, and blue sarcenet, and lined with old red buckram. 58 yds 22s

Item: Another garment, for a priest to play in, of red say. 12 yds 4s

Item: A garment of red and green say paned and guarded with gold skins lined with red buckram. 12 yards say and 7 yards buckram. 8s

Item: Two old short garments, paned of satin of Bruges, and of sarcenet of divers colours in the bodies. 20s

Item: A woman's garment, of green and blue sarcenet, checked and lined with red buckram. 24s

Item: An old remnant of red buckram, that was [in] a box [in] my Lord Cardinal's great chamber. 30 yds 6s 8d

[1] Only selected items are listed here.

(5) William Fishpole's deposition on behalf of Rastell

Deposition for the part of John Rastell against Henry Walton

William Fishpole of London, tailor, of the age of sixty years and above, sworn and examined upon his oath, saith that he made [many of the garments for Rastell including] two long gowns down to the ground, of sarcenet, one of them of blue and yellow sarcenet ... and another of green sarcenet ... which gowns coming to him in pieces contained in every piece 6 ells or thereabouts. And also he saith that if he should have bought out of the mercer's shop, every ell would have cost 5s;

and he saith that every gown was worth 20s and above . . . And also he saith he made a woman's gown of sarcenet, blue and yellow, as he remembereth, and it was made in quarrels or lozenges, he remembereth not whether, and was a busy work, and Mistress Rastell[1.] did help to sew that . . . [Some of the garments were] worth a noble the making. And how long he was in making of them he remembereth not, but he had 4d by the day, meat and drink . . .

[1] Rastell's wife Elizabeth was Sir Thomas More's sister.

(6) George Mayler's deposition on behalf of Rastell

George Mayler of London, merchant tailor, of the age of forty years, sworn and examined upon his oath, saith that he knew the said garments, but how many there be in number he remembereth not, for he hath occupied and played in them by the lending of Walton, and he saith they were worth 20s apiece and better. And he saith he knoweth well that [Walton] lent them out about twenty times to stage plays in the summer and interludes in the winter,[1] and used to take at a stage play for them and others, sometimes 40d, sometimes 2s, as they could agree, and at an interlude 8d for every time. But how many times he perfectly knoweth not, but by estimation twenty times a year in interludes . . . and further he saith that the summer when the King's banquet was at Greenwich, he saw the same garments occupied in divers stage plays, and occupied part of them himself by the lending of other players that Walton had lent them to hire, which then were fresh and little worse for the wearing; and more he knoweth not.

by me George Mayler

[1] This distinction is worth noting.

(7) George Birch's deposition on behalf of Rastell

George Birch of London, carrier, of the age of thirty-two years or thereabouts, sworn and examined saith, that he knew well a player's garment lined with red tuke and stitched with Roman letters upon it of blue and red sarcenet [and four other garments as well] . . . in which garments this deponent and his company played in while they remained in the hands of the said Rastell . . . [And he says] that Walton did let out the same garments to hire to stage plays and interludes sundry times . . . And further he saith that the common custom is at an interlude 8d for the garments, and at a stage play as the parties can agree. And he saith if they had been made of new stuff they had been much more worth . . . And further he saith that three or four years past, when the King's banquet was at Greenwich that summer, he saw the said garments played in three or four times, by the lending of the said Walton, and at that time they seemed fresh and good garments, and more he knoweth not.

by me George Birch

(8) John Redman's deposition on behalf of Rastell

John Redman of London, stationer, of the age of twenty-two years, sworn and examined upon his oath, saith that he knew the said garments... [because he had] played in the same divers times when Walton had them... And this deponent saith that he knoweth that the said Walton divers times lent them out...

      by me John Redman

(9) Roger Taylor's deposition on behalf of Walton

Roger Taylor of London, latten[1] founder, of the age of forty years, sworn and examined upon his oath, he saith he made part of the said players' garments, and some of them were made of say and some of sarcenet, which were not at that time of new stuff, for they had been occupied in other business, and they were occupied three or four years in playing and disguisings...

      by me Roger Taylor

[1] A brass-like metal.

(10) Thomas Curtis's deposition on behalf of Walton

Thomas Curtis of London, glazier, of the age of fifty-four years, sworn and examined upon his oath, saith that [he and] one John Wilkinson were commanded by the Mayor's clerk... to appraise the same garments indifferently... and the value or sum amounted unto... 35s 9d... And further he saith, that at the time of the said appraisement the said garments were old and torn, so that then they were not able to be worn nor occupied...

      [*the sign of* Thomas Curtis]

(11) John Wilkinson's deposition on behalf of Walton

John Wilkinson of London, plasterer, of the age of thirty-three years of thereabouts, sworn and examined, saith that he was commanded by... the Mayor's officer to appraise certain old playing garments which were broken and torn... and that he and Thomas Curtis appraised the said garments and stuff at 35s or 36s 9d, which in his conscience were no better worth, nor he would not have gladly given so much for them, and more he knoweth not.

      John Wilkinson

164 Getting costumes for a play before the King, 1552

Folger, Loseley MSS L.b.282, a letter from Thomas Darcy to the Master of the Revels. Transcribed in *Revels at Court, Ed. VI and Mary*, 86

For stage-players fortunate enough to be royal interluders, costumes and properties were matters of little concern, as whatever might be needed could simply be requisitioned from the Office of the Revels.

234   Players and playing

Twelfth Evening, 4 January 1552

After right hearty commendations, the King's Majesty's pleasure is that upon the sight hereof you deliver unto John Birche and John Browne, the King's interlude players, bringers hereof, such garments as you shall think meet and necessary for them and their three fellows to play an interlude in before His Highness tomorrow at night. And thus most heartily I bid you farewell. From Greenwich this twelfth even, 1551 [i.e. 1552].

165   A lawsuit about playscripts, 1572

PRO, C2/Eliz./D11/49. Transcribed by Benbow, 'Dutton and Goffe versus Broughton', 3–9

Many important documents of the period survive in damaged form. The record of legal proceedings in *Dutton and Goffe v Broughton*, commenced on 26 January 1573, is one such case. What follows is the text of the plea entered by the complainants – the Dutton brothers and Goffe – which is damaged along the right edge, resulting in some defective line endings. The answer of the defendant Broughton, which repeats much of the text of the complaint, makes possible the restoration of some of these missing phrases; restorations from this source are printed without comment and unmarked. Defects remedied by editorial conjecture, and transitional prose supplied to bridge omissions, are printed within brackets.

To the Right Honourable Sir Nicholas Bacon, Knight, Lord Keeper of the Great Seal:

Showing and in most humble wise complaining unto your honour, your poor and daily orators Lawrence Dutton and John Dutton of London, weavers, and Thomas Goffe, citizen and barber-surgeon of London, orators of the one part, and one Rowland Broughton of London, gentleman, of the other part . . . [that an indenture was drawn up for them by] one George Keavall of London, notary . . . [which read as follows:] . . .

This indenture made the second day of June anno domini 1572 . . . Between Lawrence Dutton and John Dutton of London, weavers, and Thomas Goffe, citizen and barber-surgeon of London on the one party and Rowland Broughton of London gentleman on the other party witnesseth that it is . . . agreed between the said parties . . . that they the said Lawrence, John and Thomas shall from the twelfth day of November next coming . . . for and during the space of two years and one half-year from thence next ensuing . . . play upon all Sundays and holidays in the year and otherwise as occasion shall serve, being not prohibited . . . some one history, comedy, or tragedy whatsoever of [the only device and making of the said] Rowland Broughton and none other as well within the City of London as elsewhere . . . [and to] pay or cause to be paid unto the said Rowland Broughton . . . [one] equal sixth part of all such sum or sums of money . . . [as] shall grow due or be payable by reason of any play aforesaid to be made, he the said Rowland Broughton bearing and paying one just sixth part of all charges . . . [growing out] of the wages or stipend of all such boys as shall be needful for players in and about the same play and plays . . . And the said Rowland Broughton . . . during the said term of two years and a half . . . [shall] truly deliver or cause to be delivered unto the said Lawrence Dutton, John Dutton, and Thomas Goffe . . . eighteen several plays of the only devise of the said Rowland Broughton and never before played in manner and form following: that is to say, [two plays by 12 November, another by 24 December, another by 16 February, another by Easter, another by Pentecost, and so on through the thirty months] in full delivery of all the said eighteen plays . . . in witness whereof the parties aforesaid . . . have put their seals. Given the day and years first above written.

[Performance bonds were sealed by all parties to this indenture and delivered] unto the said George Keavall . . . [but Broughton failed to uphold his end of the contract, and the others] divers and sundry times both before the said twelfth day of November and on the same day . . . [urged] the said George Keavall to procure the said Broughton to perform his promise and agreement . . . [but, that failing, they] requested divers and sundry times the said George Keavall . . . that he would redeliver unto your orators . . . as well the said writing indented as also the said obligation . . . which [Keavall, who holds the documents,] . . . still doth deny, contrary to the trust reposed in him and contrary to all equity and conscience . . . [so the complainants ask] the Queen's Majesty's most gracious writ of subpoena to be directed unto the same George Keavall commanding him by virtue thereof at a time certain to appear personally before your honourable Lordship in the Queen's majesty's highness's court of Chancery . . . to answer unto the premises . . .

166 Richard Jones and James Tunstall, players, buy gowns from Philip Henslowe, 1594

Account book of Philip Henslowe, fos. 15, 16. Transcribed in *Henslowe's Diary*, 35, 37

2 September 1594

Sold to Mr Richard Jones, player, a man's gown of peach colour in grain the 2nd of September 1594 to be paid by 5s a week immediately following and beginning as followeth:

Rd of Mr Jones the 7 of September	5s
Rd of Mr Jones the 13 of September	5s
Rd of Mr Jones the 20 of September	5s
Rd of Mr Jones the 4 of October	5s
Rd of Mr Jones the 11 of October	5s
Rd of Mr Jones the 18 of October	5s
Rd of Mr Jones the 24 of October	5s
Rd of Mr Jones the 2 of November	5s
Rd of Mr Jones the 9 of November	5s
Rd of Mr Jones the 16 of November	5s
Rd of Mr Jones the 23 of November	5s
Rd of Mr Jones in full payment the 30 of November 1594	5s

27 August 1595

Sold unto James Donstall, player, the 27th of August 1595, a man's gown of purple color cloth faced with coney and laid on the sleeves with buttons for 43s 4d to be paid 20s in hand and 23s 4d at Michaelmas next coming after the date above written, I say for: 43s 4d

Rd in part of payment the same day being the 27 of August 1595 of James Tunstall the sum of: 10s

Rd in part of payment the 28 of August 1595 in money of James Tunstall the sum of: 10s

Rest to pay: 23s 4d

167 Inventory lists belonging to Philip Henslowe, 1598

These inventory lists were found by Malone among the papers at Dulwich College and transcribed and printed by him in 1790. The originals have since disappeared. The lists are most recently reproduced in *Henslowe's Diary*, 316–25. Selected items from the lists are reproduced below.

The book of the inventory of the goods of my Lord Admiral's men, taken the 10th of March in the year 1598.

Item: 1 orange tawny satin doublet, laid thick with gold lace
Item: 1 blue taffeta suit
Item: 1 pair of carnation satin Venetians,[1] laid with gold lace
Item: 1 Longshanks' suit
Item: 1 Spaniard jerkin
Item: Harry the fifth's doublet
Item: Harry the fifth's velvet gown
Item: 1 friar's gown
Item: little doublet for boy

The inventory of the clowns' suits and hermits' suits, with divers other suits, as followeth, 1598, the 10th of March.

Item: 1 senator's gown, 1 hood, and 5 senators' caps. Item: 1 suit for Neptune; firedrake's suit for Dobe[2]
Item: 4 janissarys' gowns, and 4 torchbearers' suits
Item: 6 green coats for Robin Hood, and 4 knaves' suits
Item: 2 white shepherds' coats, and 2 Danes' suits, and 1 pair of Dane's hose
Item: the Moor's limbs, and Hercules' limbs, and Will Summers' suit[3]
Item: 4 friars' gowns and 3 hoods to them, and 1 fool's coat, cap, and bauble, and Branholt's[4] bodice, and Merlin gown and cap
Item: 2 black say gowns, and 2 cotton gowns, and 1 red say gown
Item: 1 red suit of cloth for Pig,[5] laid with white lace
Item: 5 pair of hose for the clown, and 5 jerkins for them

Costumes, properties and playbooks 237

Item: Eve's bodice, 1 pedant trouser, and 3 dons' hats
Item: 3 trumpets and a drum, and a treble viol, a bass viol, a bandore, a cittern, 1 ancient, 1 white hat
Item: 1 hat for Robin Hood, 1 hobby horse
Item: 5 shirts, and 1 furbelow, 4 farthingales
Item: 1 long sword

The inventory of all the apparel for my Lord Admiral's men, taken the 10th of March 1598, left above in the tire-house in the chest.

Item: 1 pair of hose for the Dauphin
Item: 1 murry leather jerkin, and 1 white leather jerkin
Item: 2 leather antics' coats with bosses, for Phaeton
Item: 1 pair of bodies[6] for Alice Pierce[7]

The inventory taken of all the properties for my Lord Admiral's men, the 10th of March 1598.

Item: 1 rock, 1 cage, 1 tomb, 1 Hell-mouth
Item: 1 tomb of Guido, 1 tomb of Dido, 1 bedstead
Item: 8 lances, 1 pair of stairs for Phaeton
Item: 2 steeples, and 1 chime of bells, and 1 beacon
Item: 1 globe, and 1 golden sceptre; 3 clubs
Item: 2 marchpanes, and the city of Rome
Item: 1 golden fleece; 2 rackets; 1 bay-tree
Item: 1 wooden canopy; old Mahomet's head
Item: 1 lion skin; 1 bear's skin; and Phaeton's limbs, and Phaeton chariot; and Argus' head
Item: Neptune fork and garland
Item: 8 vizards; Tamburlaine bridle; 1 wooden mattock
Item: Cupid's bow and quiver; the cloth of the sun and moon
Item: 1 boar's head and Cerberus' three heads
Item: 1 caduceus; 2 moss banks, and 1 snake
Item: 2 fans of feathers; Belin Dun's[8] stable; 1 tree of golden apples; Tantalus' tree; 9 iron targets
Item: 1 Mercury's wings; Tasso picture; 1 helmet with a dragon; 1 shield with 3 lions: 1 elm bowl
Item: 1 lion; 2 lion heads; 1 great horse with his legs; 1 sackbut
Item: 1 black dog
Item: 1 cauldron for the Jew[9]

The inventory of all the apparel of the Lord Admiral's men, taken the 13th of March 1598, as followeth:

Item: 1 moor's coat
Item: Tamburlaine's coat with copper lace
Item: Juno's coat

238   Players and playing

Item: Pierrot's suit, which William Sly[10] wore
Item: Tamburlaine's breeches of crimson velvet
Item: 1 flame coloured doublet, pinked
Item: 1 black satin doublet, laid thick with black and gold lace
Item: Dido's robe
Item: Harry the fifth velvet gown
Item: Harry the fifth satin doublet, laid with gold lace

A note of all such books as belong in the stock, and such as I have bought since the 3rd of March 1598.

Black Joan	Godwin
The Humours	Woman will Have her Will
Hardicanute	Welshman's Prize
Bourbon	Pythagoras
Cobbler of Queenhithe	Alexander and Lodowick
Friar Spendleton	Black Batman
Alice Pierce	Madman's Morris
Redcap	Pierce of Winchester
Phaeton	Vayvode
Triplicity of Cuckolds	

[1] Long breeches.
[2] Probably the name of a lost play.
[3] Will Summers was Henry VIII's fool.
[4] The company performed a play (now lost) called *Branholt*.
[5] John Pig, a boy-player with the company.
[6] A 'pair of bodies' is a bodice; see *OED* s.v. bodice.
[7] A play of that name was performed by the company.
[8] A play of that name was performed by the company.
[9] *Jew of Malta*, a play performed by the company.
[10] A stage-player.

168   Samuel Rowley asks Philip Henslowe to pay for playscripts, 1601

Dulwich, Henslowe Papers, MS i, Arts. 32–5. Transcribed in Greg, *Henslowe Papers* 56–7

4 April 1601

Mr Henslowe, I have heard five sheets of a play of the Conquest of the Indies, and I do not doubt but it will be a very good play; therefore I pray ye deliver them [*i.e.* to the playwrights] 40s in earnest of it [*i.e.* the play], and take the papers into your own hands, and on Easter eve they promise to make an end of all the rest.
        Samuel Rowley

?April 1601

Mr Henslowe, I pray you let Mr Hathaway have his papers again of the play of John of Gaunt, and for the repayment of the money back again he is content to give you a bill of his hand to be paid at some certain time as in your discretion you shall think good; which done, you may cross it out of your book and keep the bill; or else we'll stand so much indebted to you and keep the bill ourselves.

    Samuel Rowley

8 June 1601

Mr Henslowe, I pray you do so much for us, if John Day and Will Haughton have received but £3 10s, as to deliver them 30s more and take their papers.

    Yours to command
    Samuel Rowley

?June 1601

Mr Henslowe, I pray you deliver the rest of the money to John Day and Will Haughton due to them of the Six Yeomen of the West.

    Samuel Rowley

169 A dispute over ownership of costumes, properties, and playbooks, ?1619

PRO, C2.Jas.I/P16/14, a single-sheet plea torn at the upper left so that the first several letters of the opening lines are lost. Conjectural readings are supplied within brackets. The document is unpublished.

In this lawsuit Robert Lee, a former member of Queen Anne's company, is sued by his erstwhile fellows. The tale recounted by the complainants illustrates the hazards attendant upon any effort to reclaim from a departing colleague those playbooks, costumes, or other goods held to be the common property of a company of stage-players. The document is undated, but belongs probably to 1618 or 1619.

To the Right Honourable Sir Francis Bacon, Knight, Lord Chancellor of England

[In most humble wise] complaining show unto your lordship your lordship's daily orators Richard Perkins, John Cumber, William Robins, James Holt and Thomas Hayward,[1] of London, gentlemen, servants to the Queen's most excellent majesty in the quality of [stage-players; that] whereas your said orators, being lawfully authorised by his highness's letters patent ... for the showing and acting of plays and interludes, and having to that end furnished themselves in divers [clothes and play] books and other things fitting the state of such a business, one Robert Lee of London, gentleman, being about two years now last past, joined in fellowship with your orators, and, desiring to relinquish the same, did in [respect of certain money] paid him at certain days then following, promise and agree unto and with your said orators to dissolve and give over his fellowship with them, and to relinquish her majesty's service and all benefit in the patent aforesaid, and [to relinquish wholly] the practice of the said quality of playing, and to deliver up unto them all such clothes, books of plays, and other goods belonging thereunto, as he had then, or were trusted in his hands or custody; whereupon your orators, [taking the said Robert] Lee's promise and agreement in that behalf, did in respect and consideration thereof, by themselves and their friends, enter into three several bonds unto the said Robert of the penalties of £40 apiece, with conditions for payment of £20 apiece [to the aforesaid Robert] Lee, his executors and assigns, at certain days then following and now sithence past. Shortly after the making of which bonds, your said orators, sustaining great loss to the value of £500 in the riffling of their house called the [Cockpit, now by them] used for the showing of their interludes, and being thereby greatly weakened and disabled in their estates, and lost that in a moment which they had before with the labour of many years gleaned and gotten together, did yet in [   ]ly he the said Robert Lee, though in respect of that unexpected accident they might in conscience have been excused, they losing thereby the greater part of what he had bargained, satisfy and pay unto him nevertheless at several [different tim]es the satisfaction of the bonds aforesaid, divers several sums of money amounting in the whole to £50 or thereabouts, wherewith the said Robert Lee (seeming to compassionate your orators' loss aforesaid) rested then fully satisfied and [brought and deliver]ed up to be cancelled one of the bonds before mentioned, and promised to seek out and cancel the rest, and to deliver up unto your orators all such goods, apparel, books, and other things of theirs as he or any other to his use or by [his request or] appointment had in their custody, and to perform all other the points of his said promise and agreement, insomuch that your orators held themselves secure and free from any future trouble to ensue unto them in that behalf. [But so it is,] Right Honourable, that the said Robert Lee, having a purpose to overreach and defraud your orators, and having to that end drawn and wrapt them into the bonds aforesaid, and detained still in his hands, uncancelled, two of the said bonds, [now refuseth] to give them any security for performance of the said promise and agreement on his part; and presuming himself to be thereby free from any danger of suit at the common law in that behalf, hath thereupon of late denied his said promise [to them] and utterly refused to perform the same on his part, but in mere breach thereof hath betaken himself again to the practice and exercise of the said quality of playing, and erected and set up a new company, calling them by the name of the children [of her majesty]'s revels, and to furnish them hath not only enticed and drawn from your orators divers of their best respected young men to the number of seven or more, whom they had trained up and fitted for that quality, but also detaineth [some of your] orators' divers books, apparel and other goods of theirs to the value of £100 or thereabouts, and maketh use thereof to furnish his own new erected company; and having likewise in his custody your orators' letters patent aforesaid, refuseth to [restore] the same unto them, but hath of late offered to farm the same unto others, and so every way infringed and broken his promise and agreement aforesaid, and thereby benefited himself and endamaged your orators to above the value in the [whole of] £200; and yet not therewith content, but the more to prejudice your orators, and by their ruin to enrich himself, he the said Robert Lee hath of late also, for not payment of the remainder of the money undertaken by the bonds [aforesaid], commenced and presented suit against your orators at the common law upon the said two uncancelled bonds of £40 apiece, with purpose to recover from them the penalties thereof, and yet wholly detaineth from them the goods, and abridgeth [th]em of the bargain for which they were made, as aforesaid, and so every way seeketh to oppress your orators, and will neither restore unto them their said goods nor perform any part of his said bargain and promise, nor yet stay his suits [at law] and deliver up the said bonds though many entreaties have been made unto him by your orators in that behalf, but still detaineth the same, and proceedeth with his said suits against them at the common law upon the said bonds, with intent to recover from them the whole penalties thereof, contrary to all right and rules of equity, and to their (your said orators') apparent wrong, and the utter ruin of themselves and their fortunes, unless your lordship's accustomed favour be in equity extended unto them for their relief herein. In consideration . . . that your said orators are void of all remedy by the course of the common laws of this realm to relieve themselves in the said premises, and cannot thereby recover the goods detained from them, nor exact at the said Lee's hands the performance of his bargain and promise aforesaid, they having no writing under his hand proving the same, neither yet can your orators at the common law defend themselves against the suits there prosecuted against them upon the bonds aforesaid, or there plead the matters in equity before alleged or any other plea in bar or discharge of the said suits, but are for all those matters before your lordship in course of equity properly to be relieved. May it therefore please your good lordship, the premises considered, to grant unto your said orators the King's most gracious writ of subpoena to be directed to the said Robert Lee, commanding him thereby at a day and under a pain therein to be limited, personally to appear before your lordship in his majesty's high court of Chancery, then and there to answer directly all and singular the premises and to stand to and abide such further order and direction therein as unto your lordship in your grave wisdom shall seem consonant to equity and your orators shall perform the service of their hearts in praying for your Lordship's health and honourable estate.

[1] This is Thomas Heywood, the stage player and playwright.

170   Cast-off garments as costumes for players, 1629

Ben Jonson, *The New Inn*, II.i. The play was staged in 1629 and published in 1631 (*STC* 14780)

In the extract below, Lady Frampul examines some items in her wardrobe with an eye to giving them to her maid Prudence. When Prudence tires of them, Lady Frampul says offhandedly that they may be sold to players. Prudence remarks on the inappropriateness of such an action. Modern scholars have often assumed that some players' costumes were cast-off noblemen's clothing, but the extent of this practice is unknown; Prudence's observation about the unseemliness of such transactions is as likely to reflect the prevailing attitude as is Lady Frampul's readiness to countenance it.

PRUDENCE   This is well.
LADY FRAMPUL 'Tis rich enough! But 'tis not what I meant thee!
   I would ha' had thee braver than myself,
And brighter far. 'Twill fit the players yet,
   When thou has done with it, and yield thee somewhat.
PRUDENCE That were illiberal, madam, and mere sordid
   In me, to let a suit of yours come there.
LADY FRAMPUL Tut, all are players, and but serve the scene.

XII Players travelling in the provinces

When companies of players took to the road, whether by election or by constraint, and whether they were based in London or in the countryside, they incurred daily travelling expenses whether they performed or not; it was thus in their economic interest to maximise playing days while on the road, especially in those localities that had been hospitable and profitable to them in the past and where they hoped to find spectators still willing to pay. Most such visits were without incident. But often the very success of the players in drawing audiences at such locations aroused the opposition of local governing bodies, which might resent the arrival of a troupe of players, and the consequent disruption of civic life, for any of a variety of reasons. Now and again a struggle would develop between legitimate players, usually armed with proper authorisation for their travelling and playing, and magistrates, equally armed with the power to prohibit playing. Such confrontations were no less significant for being infrequent. While players were welcomed in provincial towns far more often than they were turned away, the periodic refusals perhaps illuminate more than the welcomings do. The extracts that follow illustrate selected moments in the history of that struggle.

171 What happened when players came to a town

Willis, *Mount Tabor* (1639) 110. Reprinted in *ES*, 1, 333. The happiest memories were of times when the players did play; the author of this passage recounts such a memory.

In the city of *Gloucester*, the manner is (as I think it is in other like corporations) that when players of interludes come to town, they first attend the mayor, to inform him what nobleman's servants they are, and so to get licence for their public playing; and if the mayor like the actors, or would show respect to their lord and master, he appoints them to play their first play before himself, and the aldermen and common council of the city; and that is called the mayor's play, where every one that will comes in without money, the mayor giving the players a reward as he thinks fit, to show respect unto them. At such a play my father took me with him, and made me stand between his legs, as he sat upon one of the benches, where we saw and heard very well.

172 A town's reasons for not wishing to welcome players, 1580

Gloucester Record Office, GRO: GBR B 3/1, Corporation Common Council Minute Book, fos. 71v–72. Transcribed in REED, *Cumberland, Westmoreland, Gloucester*, 306–7

At the council it was moved that some restraint might be had against common players of interludes. And for so much as daily experience teacheth and delivereth that the common players of interludes and plays draw away great sums of money from diverse persons, and allure servants, apprentices and journeymen and other of the worst disposed persons to lewdness and lightness of life, besides the maintenance of idleness and diverse other inconveniences which arise thereby, most necessary to be redressed, it is therefore at this council granted . . . that players of interludes and common players shall not be suffered within this city at any time hereafter, in any other sort of manner or otherwise than followeth . . . First, the Queen's majesty's players to be allowed to play three interludes or plays within three days or under, at every one time of their coming to, or being within, this city, and no more, nor oftener; and the players of any subject being a baron of the parliament, or of higher calling or degree, to be allowed to play two plays or interludes in two days or under at every one time of their coming to or within this city, and no more nor oftener; and any other subject's players, under the degree of a baron of the parliament, and being allowed by the statutes and laws of the realm to keep or have players, to be allowed to play but one play or interlude in one day at every one time of their coming to, or being within, this city, and no more nor oftener. And that none of the players above mentioned, be they her majesty's players or others, be suffered or allowed to play in the night season, nor at any unfit time, neither at any time without warrant or licence from Mr Mayor of this city. And it is like agreed and ordained that no burgess of this city shall at any time hereafter permit or suffer any plays to be played in his house without express licence of Mr. Mayor, nor . . . in other sort than is above declared, under pain of discommoning.[1]

[1] Losing the privileges of commonalty.

173 The Earl of Worcester's players told not to perform at Leicester, 1584

Leicestershire Record Office, Leicester Hall Papers, BR.II/18/1, fos. 38 and 42. Transcribed in *ES*, II,221–2. Chambers' text is based upon earlier printed sources and continues their errors. These entries recount a dispute at Leicester between Worcester's men and another company calling itself the Master of the Revels' men.

Tuesday the third day of March, 1583 [*i.e.* 1584]. Certain players, who said they were the servants of the Queen's Majesty's Master of the Revels, who required licence to play, and for their authority showed forth an indenture of licence from one Mr. Edmund Tilney esquire, Master of Her Majesty's Revels, of the one part, and George Hasell of Wisbech in the Isle of Ely in the county of Cambridge, esquire, on the other part.

The which indenture is dated the sixth day of February in the 25th year of Her Majesty's reign.

In which indenture there is one article that all justices, mayors, sheriffs, bailiffs, constables, and all other her officers, ministers and subjects whatsoever to be aiding and assisting unto the said Edmund Tilney, his deputies and assigns, attending and having due regard unto such persons as shall disorderly intrude themselves into any the doings and actions before mentioned, not being reformed, qualified and bound to the orders prescribed by the said Edmund Tilney. These shall be therefore not only to signify and give notice unto all and every her said justices, etc., that none of their own pretenced authority intrude themselves and presume to show forth any such plays, interludes, tragedies, comedies, or shows in any place within this realm, without the orderly allowance thereof under the hand of the said Edmund.

NOTA. No play is to be played, but such as is allowed by the said Edmund, and his hand at the latter end of the said book they do play.

The foresaid Hasell is now the chief player, etc.

Friday the 6th of March. Certain players came before Mr Mayor at the Hall ... who said they were the Earl of Worcester's men; who said the foresaid players were not lawfully authorised, and that they had taken from them their commission, but it is untrue, for they forgot their box at the inn in Leicester, and so these men got it; and they said the said Hasell was not here himself, and they sent the same to Grantham to the said Hasell who dwelleth there.

William, Earl of Worcester, etc., hath by his writing dated the 14th of January anno 25° Eliz. Reginae licensed his servants, viz. Robert Browne, James Tunstall, Edward Allen, William Harrison, Thomas Cooke, Richard Jones, Edward Browne, Richard Andrewes to play and go abroad, using themselves orderly etc. (in these words etc.) These are therefore to require all such Her Highness's officers to whom these presents shall come, quietly and friendly within your several precincts and corporations to permit and suffer them to pass with your furtherance using and demeaning themselves honestly and to give them (the rather for my sake) such entertainment as other noblemen's players have. [In witness etc.]

Mr Mayor	Mr Ja Clarke	Mr Robt Heyrycke
Mr Jo Heyrycke	Mr George Tatam	Mr Ellys
Mr Noryce	Mr Morton	Mr Newcome

Memorandum that Mr Mayor did give the aforesaid players an angel towards their dinner and willed them not to play at this present, being Friday the 6th of March, for that the time was not convenient.

The foresaid players met Mr Mayor in the street near Mr Newcome's house, after the angel was given about a 2 hours, who then craved licence again to play at their inn, and he told them they should not; then they went away and said they would play, whether he would or not, and in despite of him, with divers other evil and contemptuous words ...

More, these men, contrary to Mr Mayor's commandment, went with their drum and trumpets through the town, in contempt of Mr Mayor, neither would come at his commandment, by his officer ...

William Pateson my Lord Herbert's man
Thomas Powlton my Lord of Worcester's man

These two were they which did so much abuse Mr Mayor in the aforesaid words.

NOTA. These said players have submitted themselves, and are sorry for their words past, and craved pardon, desiring his worship not to write to their master against them, and so upon their submission, they are licensed to play this night at their inn, and also they have promised that upon the stage, in the beginning of their play, to show unto the hearers that they are licensed to play by Mr Mayor and with his good will and that they are sorry for the words past.

174 The Queen's players in an affray at Norwich, 1583
PRO, K.B.29/219 mm. 150–2. Transcribed in REED, *Norwich*, 70–6.

The Queen's players played at Norwich on the afternoon of Saturday 15 June 1583. The affray described in the following depositions took place shortly after they began playing. An inquisition was set up that very day, with some deponents questioned immediately and others questioned on the following Monday, 17 June.

The examination of Henry Brown ... [who] being at the play this afternoon, word was brought into the play that one of Her Majesty's servants was abused at the gate; whereupon this examinate, with others, went out; and one in a blue coat cast stones at Bentley and broke his head, being one of Her Majesty's servants; whereupon this examinate said 'villain, wilt thou murder the Queen's man?' and the fellow called this examinate 'villain' again, and thereupon this examinate struck him with his sword and hit him on the leg ...

Being examined how many of the players went from off the stage on Saturday to strike the man which was slain, he saith there were but two of the players which went, viz. Bentley and one other in a black doublet called Singer; and Tarlton also was going but he was stayed by the way. And being examined who did strike the man which was killed, besides this examinate, he saith the other man which went out with Bentley strake the man with an arming sword one blow upon the shoulder, and followed the fellow, which fled ...

[Brown also] saith that after that he this examinate had stricken the man, Singer did strike the man; and this examinate said to him, 'give him no more', for he doubted he had enough already; and when they came from the man again, Singer said to this examinate, 'be of good cheer, for if all this matter be laid on thee, thou shalt have what friendship we can procure thee'; and he further saith before he did strike the man he did see Bentley thrust at him twice with his naked rapier; the one thrust was about the knee, but he knoweth not where the other thrust was.

The examination of William Kilby of Pockthorpe, worsted weaver ... [who] saith that on Saturday last in the afternoon he was at a play in the yard at the Red Lion in St Stephen's, and he did see three of the players run off the stage with their swords in their hands, being in the scabbards, and heard a noise of scuffling at the Lion gate; whereupon this examinate went out of the gate to see what the matter was; and he did see a man at Mr Robert Davy's house, leaning against a stone, bleeding; which, as this examinate did then hear say, was hurt in the scuffling which was at the Lion gate; and one Edmund Kerrie told this examinate that two of the players did run after the man with their weapons drawn, and Kerrie took one of the players in his arms and would have stayed him, but one ran at him with his sword, and he, fearing some danger to himself, let the other go and fled himself. Being demanded whether they were in their play or no, he saith they had begun the play, and one of them ran out in his playing apparel, but he knoweth not the names of the players.

Thomas Holland of Norwich, carrier, examined the said day and year, saith that on Saturday last, in the afternoon, he being without the Red Lion gate, did see one of the Queen's players in his playing apparel, in the gatehouse, strike a man upon the head with the hilts of his sword, and brake his head; but what his name was whose head was broken he knoweth not; but as he heard, he was called Mr Wynsdon. And the said Wynsdon and a man in a blue coat went from the gate and stood over the way, and the people standing at the gate did stay the Queen's servant and desired him to be content; whereupon he, having his rapier drawn out of the scabbard, did put it up, and said he had done; and withdrawing himself a little from the people, ran over the way towards Wynsdon and him that had the blue coat; and they ran away, but the player overtook him that had the blue coat at the cockey[1] near Mr Davy's house, with his rapier drawn, and thrust at him that had the blue coat into the leg; whereat he that had the blue coat cried 'O, you have maimed me', and at the cockey took up a stone and threw at the Queen's servant; but whether he did hurt him or not he knoweth not. But then came one Brown, Sir William Paston's servant, and strake a blow at him that had the blue coat with his sword drawn; but whether he did hurt him or not he knoweth not. Then against Mr Davy's corner, one in a black doublet with an arming sword drawn strake at him in the blue coat, upon the shoulder, whereupon he that had the blue coat fell down, and then they all three which pursued him that had the blue coat came back again, and Brown said to the other two 'he is sped, I warrant him', and the other two men said 'whatsoever thou hast done, we will bear thee out'.

Edmund Brown of Norwich, draper, examined the said day and year, saith that on Saturday last he was at the play at the Red Lion, and while the players were playing, one Wynsdon would have entered in at the gate, but would not have paid until he had been within; and thereupon, the gate-keeper and he striking, Tarlton came out off the stage and would have thrust him out at the gate; but in the meantime one Bentley – he which played the Duke – came off the stage, and with his hilts of his sword he struck Wynsdon upon the head, and offered him another stripe, but Tarlton defended it; whereupon Wynsdon fled out of the gate, and Bentley pursued him; and then he in the black doublet, which kept the gate, ran up into the stage and brought an arming sword; and as he was going out at the gate, he drew the sword, and ran out at the gate; and this examinate went out to see the matter; and in the street, almost at Mr Robert Davy's house, he did see the man in the black doublet strike two blows upon the shoulder of the man in a blue coat; but this examinate, searching the man, did see his coat cut but not his flesh in that place; but he sayeth that he that had the blue coat had received his death's would before black doublet struck him; but who gave him his death's wound he knoweth not; and he sayeth the wound whereof he supposeth the man dyeth was a thrust above his knee.

Edmund Knee of Yelverton in the county of Norfolk, gentleman, examined the said day and year before the said mayor and justices, saith that on Saturday last he was at the play at the Red Lion in St Stephen's, and there was one Mr Wynsdon who would have come in at the gate, against the will of the gate-keeper, and in thrusting spilt the money out of the gate-keeper's hand, as this examinate did hear reported; but this examinate saith that he did see the money when it lay upon the ground, and was in gathering up; whereupon one Bentley, who played the Duke in the play, having a rapier in his hand, being upon the stage, and understanding of the strife at the gate, went off the stage; and one Tarlton, another of the players, went off the stage also; and one in a black doublet, and another in a tawny coat; but Wynsdon ran out of the gate into the street toward Mr Robert Davy's, and Bentley pursued him with his rapier drawn; but Tarlton would have stayed Bentley, and when he was without the gate Tarlton stayed, but the man in the black doublet and he in the tawny coat ran after Bentley; but between the Lion back gate and Mr Davy's back gate he did see a man in a blue coat cast stones; but he did not see the stones hit any man; but he did see Bentley's head bleed, and he did also see both the man in the black doublet and him in the tawny coat strike with their naked swords, and the man in the tawny coat did strike at his leg, but whether he did hurt the man in the blue coat or no, he knoweth not, because this examinate stood so far off as he could not well discern it. Being asked what men they were in the black doublet and tawny coat, he saith he knoweth not his name in the black doublet, but he in the tawny coat is Mr Paston's man, whose name is Henry Brown. Also this examinate did hear say that Brown, coming from the hurt man, should say that he had sped him; and he which told him this is Thomas Osborne of Kirby Bidon, gent.

Elizabeth, the wife of Robert Davy of Norwich, grocer, examined the said year and day, saith that on Saturday in the afternoon there was a man hurt and wounded at her gate, whom for pity sake she took in to comfort him; and there came in a woman who, as it was said, was farmer to the man's master, and she called him George; and the said George said he would fain speak with his master, and the woman desired this examinate to see well to him, and his charges should be answered; and one Mr Wynsdon, coming after, came in, and he denied him to be his master, but said he had been his servant about fifteen or sixteen years past, and the said George said it was not he, but it was his other master; and after a while one of the other Wynsdons came to him, and he also said he was not his servant, but he had been [with] him about three or four days. She saith he had two wounds or pricks, but she knoweth not who did hurt him.

Margery, the wife of Thomas Bloom, examined the said day and year, saith that on Saturday in the afternoon she found a man in a blue coat lie bleeding at Mr Atkin's back gate, and she went to him, and stopped his wound with her finger, and then sent for a surgeon; and after he spake, and called for his master, which was one Wynsdon; she saith that she asked him who did hurt him, and he said a fellow in a red coat, and she saith that he had two wounds or pricks, but she did see no man hurt him; but saith when he said it was a red coat that did hurt him, she thought it had been one of the Queen's servants, but none of them had on their coats at that time.

Nicholas Thurston, examined before the said mayor and justices &c. that being at the play on Saturday, and seeing one of the players which played the Duke go off the stage, he followed after, and in the street nigh the cockey, by Mr Robert Davy's house, this examinate standing by Mr Dawd's back gate, he did see the said player prick at the man which was slain, but whether he did hurt him or no he knoweth not.

Thomas Holland confesseth that one of the Queen's men, running out of their play, for that there was a quarrelling at the gate, the Queen's man drew his rapier at one that stood a little from the gate; which he, perceiving run away, and the Queen's man following him, thrust him into the leg; and the fellow said 'O, thou hast maimed me'; but recovering himself again threw a stone at the Queen's man, and hit him, and after that the Queen's man ran after him, and thrust at him, and Henry Brown, following, struck him on the leg, and turned back again and said to the Queen's man 'I have sped him', and the Queen's man said 'well done, boy, we will bear thee out in it'; and one other in a black doublet did strike at him before that, on the back, but he this examinate knoweth not him that struck him on the back.

Edmund Brown confesseth that he see one in a black doublet strike the man in the blue coat on the shoulder, but the fellow fell not down, and this examinate said to him 'you have done ill to cut the man,' and he said 'no, I have not cut him'.

George Jackson of Norwich, beer brewer . . . saith and deposeth that on Saturday last, being the xvth day of this instant June, he went toward the Red Lion in St Stephen's, and he did see a man running hastily out of the Lion gate, and another man in a black doublet did run out of the same gate after him, with a sword or rapier drawn in his hand, and running still after the party about the cockey by Mr Davy's house, because he could not overtake the party he pricked his weapon out of his hand at the party, but he did not hit him; he saith he knoweth neither of the said parties. After him came one of the players in his player's apparel, with a player's beard upon his face, with a sword or rapier in his hand, drawn, as far as the back gate of Thomas Bloom, and there a strange man in a blue coat, as he remembereth, fell at words, and the said man fled from the player, and he ran after him and struck him with his sword, but whether he did hurt him or no, he knoweth not; but thereupon he that had the blue coat, when he had got almost to the cockey, took up a stone and threw at the player, and the player did give two or three thrusts with his sword at the man, and hit him, but whether he drew blood or no, he knoweth not; but he that had the blue coat ran from him until he came almost at Mr Davy's corner, the player still pursuing him, and one Brown also, with his drawn sword, ran after the said man, and Brown struck a blow at the leg of him that had the said blue coat; and further he cannot say.

William Drake of Norwich, grocer, sworn and examined the said day and year, saith that his brother Stephen Drake, being at the play on Saturday last, did tell this examinate that there was a man slain, and this examinate asked him how it came to pass, and he said that a man in a white hat misused the players, and was thrust out at the doors, and did outrun the players, and the man which was slain did quarrel with the players, and threw stones at him, and, as he thought, the player was dazzled, for he could not strike him; whereupon one of Mr Paston's servants said 'wilt thou misuse the Queen's men?' and therewith ran after the man, and struck him as he ran from him, whereupon the people cried out to Brown, Mr Paston's man, saying 'huff him not'; then he turned his blow to a thrust, and gave him that thrust, and one other, with his naked sword, and this examinate saith that his brother said he never saw man bleed so much as he did after Mr Paston's man had pricked him; he saith his brother did not know Brown, nor whose servant he was, but three or four of Mr Paston's servants coming by this examinate's house, his brother said that he which killed the man had such a cognisance; and further he saith not.

[*Further corroborative depositions by Simon Sumpter, Thomas Crowe, and Stephen Drake.*]

[1] Meaning uncertain.

175 Various players discouraged from playing; twelve instances, 1580 to 1635

(i) 21 June 1580. PRO, S.P.12/139, fo. 76, letter from John Hatcher, Vice-Chancellor of Cambridge University, to William Cecil, Lord Burghley, the Lord Treasurer, 21 June 1580

My bounden duty remembered with most humble and hearty recommendations. Where it hath pleased your honour to commend unto me and the heads of the university my lord of Oxenford's players, that they might show their cunning in certain plays already practised by them before the Queen's Majesty, I did speedily counsel with the heads and others, viz. Dr Styll, Dr Howland, Dr Bing, Dr Legge, etc., and considering and pondering, that the seed, the cause and the fear of the pestilence is not yet vanished and gone, this hot time of the year; this midsummer fair-time having confluence out of all countries as well of infected as not; the commencement time at hand, which requireth rather diligence in study than dissoluteness in plays; and also that of late we denied the like to the right honourable the lord of Leicester's servants; and specially for that all assemblies in open places be expressly forbidden in this university and town, or within five miles compass, by her majesty's Council's letters to the Vice-Chancellor 30th October 1575; our trust is that your honour, our most dear loving Chancellor, will take our answer made unto them in good part; and being willing to impart something from the liberality of the university to them, I could not obtain sufficient assent thereto, and therefore I delivered them but 20s towards their charges. Also they brought letters from the right honourable the Lord Chancellor and the right honourable the lord of Sussex to the Vice-Chancellors of Cambridge and Oxford. I trust their honours will accept our answer. Thus leaving to trouble your honour any longer with my rude writing I take my leave, Cambridge the 21st of June 1580.

> Your Lordship's humble and unworthy
> deputy John Hatcher, Vice-Chancellor

> (ii) 7 June 1583. Norwich, Mayors' Court Books XI, NRO 16a, p. 157. Transcribed *English Dramatic Companies* II, 336, and in REED, *Norwich* 65–6

Whereas James Tunstall, Thomas Cook, Edward Brown, William Harrison and divers others, to the number of ten players of interludes, and servants as they say to the honourable the Earl of Worcester, made request to Mr Mayor and this house[1] to be licensed to play within this city, which Mr Mayor and this house refused to grant, as well to avoid the meetings of people this hot weather for fear of any infection, as also for that they came from an infected place, and for other causes moving this house. Nevertheless this house, for their lord and master's sake, did give them in reward 16s 8d, whereupon they promised to depart and not to play. Notwithstanding which promise, and contrary to the said prohibition, the said players did play in their host's house.[2] Wherefore it is ordered that their lord shall be certified of their contempt, and that henceforth the said players shall never receive any reward of the city whensoever they shall come again; and that they shall presently depart out of this city and not to play upon pain of imprisonment. But afterward, upon their submission and earnest entreaty, it is agreed that their lord shall not be certified thereof.

[1] That is, the Court of Aldermen.
[2] Probably the White Horse inn in Tombland.

> (iii) 10 June 1590. Norwich, Mayor's Court Books XII, NRO 16a, p. 441. Transcribed in *English Dramatic Companies* II, 337, and in REED, *Norwich* 96

This day John Mufford, one of the Lord Beauchamp's players, being forbidden by Mr Mayor to play within the liberties of this city, and in respect thereof gave them among them 20s, and yet notwithstanding they did set up bills to provoke men to come to their play, and did play in Christ Church; therefore the said John Mufford is committed to prison.

> (iv) March 1603. Chapter Library, Canterbury Cathedral, Chamberlains' Accounts of the City of Canterbury, accounts for 1602–3. Transcribed in MSC, VII.18

Item: paid to Thomas Downton, one of the Lord Admiral's players, for a gift bestowed upon him and his company; being so appointed by Mr Mayor and the Aldermen because it was thought fit they should not play at all, in regard that our late Queen was then either very sick or dead as they supposed.

(v) 25 July 1606. Cambridge University Archives, Comm. Ct. II.13, Commissary's Court Book, fo. 107v (*rev*). Transcribed in REED, *Cambridge*, I, 403–4

Thomas Greene and John Duke, stage-players (identified in the document as Thomas Greene of London, gentleman, and John Duke of London, gentleman), bind themselves to the Chancellor of the University of Cambridge in a performance bond of £50:

The condition of this obligation is such that, if at all times hereafter, the above bounden Thomas Greene and John Duke, and either of them, do wholly and altogether give over and leave off to act or play any manner of plays or interludes whatsoever, within the university and town of Cambridge, or within the compass of five miles of the said university and town of Cambridge, both by themselves and their whole company, then this present obligation to be void and of none effect, or else to be and abide in full force and virtue.

[*signed*] Thomas Greene
[*signed*] John Duke

(vi) 1608–9. Chapter Library, Canterbury Cathedral, Chamberlains' Accounts of the City of Canterbury, accounts for 1608–9. Transcribed in MSC, VII.18–19

Item: Given to the Lord Chandos' players for that they should not play here by reason that the sickness was then in this city; so appointed by Mr Mayor and the Aldermen 20s.

Item: Given to the Lord Berkeley's players for that they should not play here in this city by reason that the sickness being here; so appointed by Mr Mayor and the Aldermen 20s.

(vii) 21 March 1614. Norwich, Assembly Proceedings V, NRO 16d, fo. 19. Transcribed in REED, *Norwich* 140.

Whereas Joseph Moore and other stage-players, servants to the Lady Elizabeth, came lately to this city and here attempted to play without leave from Mr Mayor, at which their said plays were many outrages and disorders committed, as fightings, whereby some were wounded, and throwing about, and publishing of seditious libels, much tending to the disturbance and breach of his majesty's peace; for the preventing therefore of the like abuses and disorders hereafter, it is this day agreed that the law made in the time of Mr Bowde's mayoralty,[1] for restraining of citizens from going to stage plays and interludes, shall from henceforth be put in execution. And further it is agreed that such of the poorer sort which shall offend in that kind, not being of ability to contribute weekly towards the relief of the poor, shall be sent to Bridewell. And if any suit shall be brought against the mayor for the time being by any person or persons for the cause aforesaid, the said suit shall be defended at the charge of the city.

[1] Simon Bowde was mayor in 1579 and 1588.

(viii) 30 March 1616. Norwich, Mayor's Court Books xv, NRO 16a, fo. 62. Transcribed in *English Dramatic Companies*, II, 340–1, and in REED, *Norwich*, 145. See **88** above, and **178** for a subsequent set of documents

A patent was this day brought into the court [that is, the mayor's court] by Thomas Swinnerton, made to Thomas Green, Christopher Beeston, Thomas Heywood, Richard Perkins, Robert Pallant, Thomas Swinnerton, John Duke, Robert Lee, James Holt, and Robert Beeston, servants to Queen Anne, and the rest of their associates, bearing date 15th April [1609]. But the said Swinnerton confesseth that he himself and Robert Lee only are here to play; the rest are absent. He was desired to desist from playing and offered a benevolence in money, which he refused to accept. And Mr Reason,[1] one of the Prince's servants, came in at the same time affirming that they had a patent, and these two companies have leave to play four days this next week but not at Powle's,[2] but in the chapel near the new hall.[3]

[1] Gilbert Reason, one of Prince Charles' players.
[2] One Powle owned the White Horse, a playing inn.
[3] Part of the dissolved Blackfriars monastery.

(ix) 29 May 1616. Norwich, Mayor's Court Books xv, NRO 16a, fo. 70. Transcribed in *English Dramatic Companies*, II, 341, and in REED, *Norwich* 146

Thomas Swinnerton came this day into the court and affirmed himself to be one of the players to the Queen's majesty, and, bringing with him no patent, desired to have leave to play here. But because the same company had liberty to play here at Easter last, as by an order 30th March 1616 may appear, whereby they were restrained to the new hall (but that restraint was afterward mitigated and they had leave to play two of the four days then granted unto them at Powle's house and the other two at the new hall) yet they are again returned hither. Therefore there is no leave granted unto him. Whereupon it was said unto him 'if you will play, you must do it at your peril, without our leave'; his answer was 'we will adventure the peril, and we mean on Monday next to play in the city'. Yet afterward this house offered him a gratuity to desist. He was content to accept the same, and promised desistance accordingly.

(x) 20 July 1616. Norwich, Mayor's Court Books xv, NRO 16a, fo. 81. Transcribed in REED, *Norwich* 148

This day Martin Slater brought into this court a patent dated 17th January [1612] made to Thomas Green, Christopher Beeston, Thomas Heywood, Richard Perkins, Robert Pallant, Thomas Swinnerton, John Duke, Robert Lee, James Holt and Robert Beeston, to play &c. This patent hath been twice showed since Easter; this is the third time. The said Martin Slater is not named in the patent, therefore he hath no leave to play.

(xi) 13 November 1620. Devon Record Office, Exeter City Archives, G1/B1/7, City Council Chamber Act Book 7, fo. 207v. Transcribed in REED, *Devon*, 190

This day Mr Receiver is ordered to give unto certain players, which are licensed under the King's privy signet, the sum of 40s as a gratuity, and not to be suffered to play.

> (xii) 1634–5. County Achives Office, Maidstone, Kent, chamberlains' accounts of the town of Tenterden, accounts for 1634–5. Transcribed in MSC, VII.155

Item: to Mr Robert Woodball, being deputy, which he did give unto a company of players because they should not play in town. 10s

176 The Lord Chamberlain (the Earl of Pembroke) directs the Mayor of Norwich to confiscate exemplifications, June 1617

> Norwich, Mayor's Court Books xv, NRO 16a, fo. 133, 4 June 1617. Transcribed in *English Dramatic Companies*, II, 343–4, and in REED, *Norwich*, 151–2

Whereas Thomas Swinnerton and Martin Slater, being two of the Queen's majesty's company of players, having separated themselves from their said company, have each of them taken forth a several exemplification or duplicate of his majesty's letters patent granted to the whole company, and by virtue thereof they severally in two companies with vagabonds and suchlike idle persons have and do use and exercise the quality of playing in divers places of this realm to the great abuse and wrong of his majesty's subjects in general, and contrary to the true intent and meaning of his majesty to the said company; and whereas William Perry, having likewise gotten a warrant whereby he, and a certain company of idle persons with him, do travel and play under the name and title of the Children of Her Majesty's Revels, to the great abuse of her majesty's service; and whereas also Gilbert Reason, one of the Prince his highness' players, having likewise separated himself from his company, hath also taken forth another exemplification or duplicate of the patent granted to that company, and lives in the same kind and abuse; and likewise one Charles Marshall, Humfrey Jeffes and William Parr, thereof Prince Palatine's company of players, having also taken forth an exemplification or duplicate of the patent granted to the said company, and by virtue thereof live after the like kind and abuse; wherefore to the end such idle persons may not be suffered to continue in this course of life, these [instructions] are . . . in his majesty's name to will and require you . . . that you call the said parties offenders before you and thereupon take their said several exemplifications or duplicates, or other their warrants by which they use their said quality, from them; and forthwith to send the same to me. And also that you take good and sufficient bonds of every of them to appear before me at Whitehall at a prefixed day to answer their said contempts and abuses; whereof I desire you not to fail. And these [*i.e.* this letter] shall be your sufficient warrant in that behalf. Dated at the court at Theobalds this 16th day of July . . . 1616.

      Pembroke

To all justices of peace, mayors, sheriffs, bailiffs, constables, and other his majesty's officers to whom it may appertain

177 The Privy Council authorises the Mayor of Norwich to prohibit playing in his city, 1623

Norwich, City Revenues and Letters, NRO 17b, fo. 33, 27 May 1623. Transcribed in REED, *Norwich* 177–8

To our very loving friends the Mayor and Justices of the City of Norwich:

After our very hearty commendations: whereas we have received information from Master Glean, one of your aldermen, that you have been of late years, and are at this present, much pestered and disquieted in the orderly government of your city by the reason of several companies of players, tumblers, dancers upon the ropes, and the like, the suffering wherof is alleged to be more inconvenient and prejudicial to that city more than other places by reason it consists altogether of much and several manufactures, wherein multitudes of people and families are set on work, who, being apt to be drawn away from their business and labour by their occasions, the said manufactures are in the meantime in such sort neglected as causeth daily very great and apparent losses and damage to that city in particular, and by consequence no small hurt and prejudice to the commonwealth in general; we, taking the same into our considerations, and finding cause much to condemn the lawless liberty taken up and practised in all parts of the kingdom by that sort of vagrant and licentious rabble, by whose means and devices the purses of poor servants and apprentices and of the meaner sort of people are drained and emptied, and which pinches so much the more in these times of scarcity and death; and we, tendering the good and welfare of your city in particular, have thought good hereby to authorise and require you not to suffer any companies of players, tumblers, or the like sort of persons, to act any plays or to show or exercise any other feats and devices within that city or the liberty of the same until you shall receive further order from this board. And so we bid you very heartily farewell.

From Whitehall 27 May 1623

178 Francis Wambus, stage-player, contends with the Mayor of Norwich for the right to play, 1624

Norwich, Mayor's Court Books xv, NRO 16a, fos. 525, 525v, 526, 531, 531v, and xvi, fo. 12v. Transcribed in *English Dramatic Companies*, II, 348–50, and in REED, *Norwich* 180–83

The encounter of Francis Wambus with the town authorities at Norwich may serve as an exemplary instance. Most of what is known about Wambus, one of Lady Elizabeth's players, is contained in the following extracts. Wambus' known career spans little more than a decade; he is first heard of in 1611, when he and his fellows gave Philip Henslowe a bond of £500, and last heard of in 1624 in the final document cited below.

256   Players and playing

Wambus' experience at Norwich illustrates the way stage-players could become pawns or markers in the struggles for control among patrons, regulators and magistrates. As the extracts immediately above have shown the guarded and often firm attitude of town magistrates toward stage-playing in general, so the following items delineate a specific example of that firmness set within the general context. Wambus, who could have avoided the confrontation described below, chose to involve himself, to his own cost.

(i) Mayors' Court Books xv, fo. 525, 24 April 1624

This day Francis Wambus brought into this court a bill, signed with his majesty's hand and under his highness' privy signet, authorising John Townsend, Alexander Foster, Joseph Moore and the said Francis Wambus, servants to the Lady Elizabeth, to play interludes &c. dated the 20th day of March 1621 and in the 19th year of his highness' reign, whereupon there was showed forth unto him the letters directed from the lords of his majesty's most honourable privy council, dated the 27th of May 1623, whereby Mr Mayor and Justices of Peace are authorised and required not to suffer any players to show or exercise any plays within this city or liberties hereof. Whereupon the said Wambus peremptorily affirmed that he would play in this city, and would lay in prison here this twelve month but he would try whether the King's command or the council's be the greater. And this entry being read unto him, he said he denied nothing of that was here set down, and thereupon the said Wambus was, according to the council's order, commanded to forbear to play within the liberties of this city. And he nevertheless answered that he would make trial what he might do by the King's authority, for he said he would play.

(ii) Mayors' Court Books xv, fos. 525v-6, 26 April 1624

This day Wakefield, having brought to Mr Mayor a note which he found fastened upon the gate of the house of Thomas Marcon, being the sign of the White Horse near Tombland in Norwich, wherein was written these words, 'Here within this place at one of the clock shall be acted an excellent new comedy called *The Spanish Contract* by the Princess' servants; vivat rex.' Whereupon Mr Mayor caused the several persons named in the instrument showed forth on Saturday last, namely John Townsend, Alexander Foster, Joseph Moore, and Francis Wambus, to be warned forthwith to appear before him and the other Justices of Peace beforementioned; and the officer, namely Henry Paman, returned that he could speak with no more of the said company than only the said Francis Wambus, who only appeared, and said confidently that he and his company would play the comedy aforesaid; and being demanded whether the bill now showed unto him, containing the words aforesaid, was his handwriting or not, he said it was his handwriting, and that he caused it to be set up this day. And, the council's order being again read unto him, he said he would play, whatsoever had been said to the contrary, and accused Mr Mayor to his face that he contemned the King's authority. And when it was told him that the order of the council was the King's authority, he said notwithstanding that he would play, and taxed Mr Mayor very falsely and scandalously with untruths; and, being demanded to find sureties for his good behaviour, he said he would find none. Whereupon he was committed until he should find sureties for his appearance at the next sessions of the peace, to be holden for the county of this city, and in the meantime to be of good behaviour; or otherwise until further order shall be received from the lords of his majesty's most honourable privy council concerning him the said Wambus.

(iii) Mayors' Court Books xv, fo. 531, 24 May 1624

This day Mr Mayor and Justices of Peace of this city here assembled did offer to Francis Wambus, who was committed upon the 24th of April last until he should find sureties for his good behaviour, that inasmuch as he, being a stranger in this city, could not readily find bail, that therefore he might be discharged upon his own bond for his appearance at the next sessions of the peace to be holden after St Michael [29 September] next. And Mr Mayor, being further moved by Mr Ross in the behalf of the said Wambus, that because he, the said Wambus, seemed very desirous of enlargement, that therefore he might be enlarged without any bond for further appearance. The said Wambus, before any answer given thereunto by Mr Mayor, desired that he might have time of deliberation therein till the coming of his fellow Townsend, which should be this afternoon.

(iv) Mayors' Court Books xv, fo. 531v, 26 May 1624

This day a warrant was delivered to Richard Buller, directed to the keeper of the gaol, for the discharge of Francis Wambus and William Bee,[1] signed by Mr Mayor, Mr Blosse, Mr Mingay, Mr Ross, and Mr Birch.

[1] Bee, though not one of the four men named in Wambus' warrant, was probably a fellow-player. A William Bee was Will Kemp's 'servant' in 1599.

(v) Mayors' Court Books xvi, fo. 12v, 18 September 1624

This day Mr Wambus showed forth a letter from Sir Henry Herbert, dated in June last, purporting that it was my Lord Chamberlain's pleasure that he should be set at liberty, and should give his own security for payment of his charges in the beginning of August following. And the gaoler, being here in court, saith that upon his receipt of the warrant for discharging of the said Wambus and of Bee, he the said gaoler was contented to discharge them, for he said Mr Townsend had given his word to pay the charges. And the said Wambus and Mr Townsend, being here in court, desired recompence for the imprisonment of Wambus; to whom it was answered that, if they had occasion to depart this city before Wednesday next, Mr Mayor would call a meeting this afternoon. Whereunto they replied they were willing to stay till Wednesday.

258   Players and playing

(vi) Mayors' Court Books XVI, fo. 12v, 25 September 1624

This day Mr Wambus and Mr Townsend, players, came into this court and complained of wrongs done to the said Wambus and Bee by their imprisonment, and desired to have satisfaction for their charges. And because it was remembered and conceived that what was done concerning them was by consent of the whole court, and that nothing was done any way injurious to them, but that their imprisonment was occasioned by their own miscarriage, therefore it was by general consent agreed that nothing should be given unto them in that respect.

PERMISSIONS TO TRAVEL AND PROTECTIONS FROM ARREST

179   Request for a passport for players travelling through Holland, 1592

Letter of Sir Charles Howard, the Lord Admiral, to the States-General of the Netherlands, 10 February 1592. Printed in Van den Bergh, *'s Gravenhaagsche Bijzonderheden*, 41, from an unidentified manuscript in the Hague archives; reprinted with omissions and some errors in *ES*, II, 274, where the page is wrongly given as 51. The document is in French.

My Lords, forasmuch as the present bearers, Robert Browne, John Bradstreet, Thomas Saxfield, Richard Jones, with their companions, being my players and servants, have determined to make a voyage to Germany with intent to pass through the countries of Zeeland, Holland and Friesland, and intending while on their said voyage to exercise their qualities in music, tumbling, and playing of comedies, tragedies and histories, to maintain themselves and to offset their expenses during their said voyage; these are therefore to request you to show and lend every favour in your lands and jurisdictions, and to bestow upon them as a favour to me your full passport under the seal of the States, to the end that the magistrates of the towns under your jurisdiction do not impede them on their passage from exercising their said qualities everywhere. In so doing, I will remain obliged to you all, and you will find me fully disposed to return your courtesy in larger measure. From my chamber at the English Court, the 10th day of February 1591.

Your very devoted to do you pleasure and service,
C. Howard

180   Sir Henry Herbert's Protection from Arrest, 1624

Add. MS 19,256, fo. 44. Transcribed in Adams, ed., *Dramatic Records of Sir Henry Herbert*, 74–5

27 December 1624

These are to certify you that Edward Knight, William Patrick, William Chambers, Ambrose Byland, Henry Wilson, Jeffrey Collins, William Sanders, Nicholas Underhill, Henry Clay, George Vernon, Robert Pallant, Thomas Tuckfield, Robert Clark, John Rhodes, William Mago, Anthony Knight, and Edward Ashborne,

William Carver, Alexander Buklank, William Toyer, William Gascoyne are all employed by the King's majesty's servants in their quality of playing as musicians and other necessary attendants, and are at all times and hours to be ready with their best endeavours to do his majesty's service during the time of the revels, in which time they nor any of them are to be arrested, or detained under arrest, imprisoned, pressed for soldiers, or any other molestation whereby they may be hindered from doing his majesty's service, without leave first had and obtained of the Lord Chamberlain of his majesty's most honourable household, or of the master of his majesty's Revels; and if any shall presume to interrupt or detain them or any of them after notice hereof given by this my certificate, he is to answer it at his utmost peril. Given at his majesty's Office of the Revels under my hand and seal the 27th of December, 1624.

H. Herbert

181 Permission for players to travel and play, 1636

PRO, LC5/134, p. 124. Transcribed in MSC, II(3), 378–9. The Lord Chamberlain was Philip, Earl of Pembroke and Montgomery.

17 May 1636

Whereas William Penn, Thomas Hobbes, William Trig, William Patrick, Richard Baxter, Alexander Gough, William Hart and Richard Hanley, together with ten more or thereabouts of their fellows, His Majesty's comedians, and of the peculiar company of players in the Blackfriars, London, are commanded to attend His Majesty, and be nigh about the Court this summer progress, in readiness when they shall be called upon to act before His Majesty; for the better enabling and encouraging them whereunto, His Majesty is graciously pleased that they shall, as well before His Majesty's setting forth on his main progress as in all that time and after, till they shall have occasion to return homewards, have all freedom and liberty to repair unto all towns corporate, mercate towns and other, where they shall think fit; and there, in their common halls, moot-halls, schoolhouses, or other convenient rooms, act plays, comedies and interludes without any let, hindrance or molestation whatsoever (behaving themselves civilly). Wherein it is His Majesty's pleasure, and he doth expect that in all places where they come, they be treated and entertained with such due respect and courtesy as may become His Majesty's loyal and loving subjects towards his servants. In testimony whereof I have hereunto set my hand and seal at arms. Dated at Whitehall the 17th day of May 1636.

To all mayors, sheriffs, bailiffs, Justices of Peace, constables, headboroughs, and to all other His Majesty's officers and loving subjects whatsoever, whom this may concern.

XIII Companies of children

The history of public performances of plays by schoolboys during the later sixteenth and early seventeenth centuries is uneven. The performance of plays by children in grammar schools was of course an old tradition, and was sustained during this period not only in the schools themselves, as by Richard Mulcaster in the Merchant Taylors' School in London, but also by the schoolmasters appointed to supervise the children selected as royal choristers in the Chapel Royal and at Windsor, and by the Master of the Children at St Paul's Cathedral. Of these groups, the most influential were probably the Children of the Chapel Royal and the Children of Paul's. In 1576 Richard Farrant took over the management of the Chapel Children and they began offering public performances of plays, for an admission fee, in a house in Blackfriars. In the early 1580s the Children of Paul's began performing publicly as well. But the Chapel Children stopped these performances in 1584 with the loss of their lease, and Paul's Boys were stopped from playing in 1590, presumably for having meddled in the Marprelate Controversy. For the decade of the 1590s, plays by children were little more than a memory.

The practice was revived in 1599 when Paul's Boys began public performances again, though they stopped finally in about 1607. The children of the Chapel Royal began playing again in 1600 at Blackfriars, though their connection with the Chapel had become so tenuous that they were renamed the Children of the Queen's Revels in 1603. In 1609 this company moved to premises in Whitefriars, and in 1613 they were amalgamated with Lady Elizabeth's men.

Boys were recruited for the royal chapel in a variety of ways, not excluding forcible impressment by the choirmaster or his agents. Such impressment, not unlike the impressment of older males for military service, was employed ostensibly to serve the monarch's needs, in this case for a continuing choir.

182 William Hunnis seeks help in taking over the theatre at Blackfriars, 1580

SHC, Loseley MSS LM3/316. Reproduced in *ES*, II, 37–8

Under the direction of Richard Farrant, Master of the Children of Windsor Castle and later temporary or Acting-Master of the Children of the Chapel Royal, a company of Chapel children began staging plays for the general public in Blackfriars in 1576. When Farrant died in 1580 it fell to William Hunnis, Master of the Children of the Chapel Royal, to step in and try to carry on. He persuaded the Earl of Leicester to write on his behalf to Sir William More, who held the lease to the Blackfriars property.

Sir William More: Whereas my friend Mr Hunnis, this bearer, informeth me that he hath of late bought of Farrant's widow her lease of that house in Blackfriars which you made to her husband, deceased, and means there to practise the Queen's Children of the Chapel, being now in his charge, in like sort as his predecessor did for the better training them to do her majesty service; he is now a suitor to me to recommend him to your good favour, which I do very heartily as one that I wish right well unto, and will give you thanks for any countenance or friendship you shall show him for the furtherance of this his honest request. And thus with my hearty commendations, I wish you right heartily well to fare. From the court this 19th of September 1581.

        Your very loving friend,
        R. Leicester

183   William Hunnis appeals for more money, 1583
PRO, S.P.12/163 no. 88. Reproduced in *ES*, II, 37–8

To keep his project financially viable, Hunnis was forced to sell his lease of the Blackfriars premises to Henry Evans in 1582 or 1583, and thereafter was obliged to share his space with the Children of Paul's, in which Evans had a financial interest. The lease expired in any event in 1584, dispossessing both Hunnis and Evans, and the premises reverted to Sir William More. Anticipating these changes, Hunnis sought assurance from the Queen that support would continue. His petition, below, was apparently unpersuasive.

May it please your Honours, William Hunnis, Master of the Children of her Highness's Chapel, most humbly beseecheth to consider of these few lines.

First, her majesty alloweth for the diet of 12 children daily 6d apiece by the day, and £40 by the year for their apparel and all other furniture.[1]

Again, there is no fee allowed, neither for the Master of the said children nor for his usher, and yet nevertheless is he constrained over and besides the usher still to keep both a man-servant to attend upon them and likewise a woman-servant to wash and keep them clean.

Also there is no allowance for the lodging of the said children such time as they attend upon the Court, but the Master to his great charge is driven to hire chambers both for himself, his usher, children and servants.

Also there is no allowance for riding journeys when occasion serveth the Master to travel or send into sundry parts within this realm, to take up and bring such children as be thought meet to be trained for the service of her majesty.

Also there is no allowance nor other consideration for those children whose voices be changed, who only do depend upon the charge of the said master, until such time as he may prefer the same,[2] with clothing and other furniture, unto his no small charge.

And although it may be objected that her majesty's allowance is no whit less than her majesty's father of famous memory therefor allowed, yet considering the prices of things present to the time past, and what annuities the Master then had out of sundry abbeys within this realm, besides sundry gifts from the King and divers particular fees besides, for the better maintenance of the said children and office, and besides also there hath been withdrawn from the said children since her majesty's coming to the Crown 12d by the day which was allowed for their breakfasts, as may appear by the Treasurer of the Chamber his account for the time being, with other allowances incident to the office, as appeareth by the ancient accounts in the said office, which I here omit.

The burden hereof hath from time to time so hindered the Masters of the Children, viz., Mr Bower, Mr Edwards, myself and Mr Farrant, that notwithstanding some good helps otherwise, some of them died in so poor case and so deeply indebted that they have not left scarcely wherewith to bury them.

In tender consideration whereof, might it please your honours that the said allowance of 6d a day apiece for the children's diet might be reserved in her majesty's coffers during the time of their attendance. And, in lieu thereof, they to be allowed meat and drink within this honourable household, for that I am not able upon so small allowance any longer to bear so heavy a burden; or otherwise to be considered as shall seem best unto your honourable wisdoms.

[1] Furnishings.
[2] That is, secure another position for the same.

184   Thomas Giles' commission to impress children, 1585

BL, MS Sloane 2035b, fo. 73. Reproduced in *ES*, II, 17–18

Writs of impressment, such as the one reproduced below, were not uncommon; by their means, various royal choirmasters were enabled to sustain their choirs at an appropriate size and strength when voluntary recruitments were insufficient. That Giles was not a Master of a royal choir gives this document its principal interest.

By the Queen
Elizabeth

Whereas we have authorised our servant Thomas Giles, Master of the Children of the Cathedral Church of St Paul's within our City of London, to take up such apt and meet children as are most fit to be instructed and framed in the art and science of music and singing as may be had and found out within any place of this our realm of England or Wales, to be by his education and bringing-up made meet and able to serve us in that behalf when our pleasure is to call for them; we permit and suffer from henceforth our said servant Thomas Giles, and his deputy or deputies, and every of them, to take up in any cathedral or collegiate church or churches, and in every other place or places of this our realm of England and Wales, such child and children as he or they, or any of them, shall find and like of, and the same child and children by virtue hereof, for the use and service aforesaid, with them or any of them to bring away, without any your lets, contradictions, stay, or interruptions to the contrary; charging and commanding you and every of you to be aiding, helping, and assisting unto the above-named Thomas Giles and his deputy and deputies in and about the due execution of the premises, for the more speedy, effectual, and better accomplishing hereof from time to time, as you and every of you do tender our will and pleasure and will answer for doing the contrary at your perils. Given under our signet at our manor of Greenwich the 26th day of April in the 27th year of our reign.

To all and singular Deans, Provosts, Masters and Wardens of Colleges, and all ecclesiastical persons and ministers, and to all other our officers, ministers, and subjects to whom in this case it shall appertain; and to every of them greeting.

185 Nathaniel Giles' commission to impress children, 1597

PRO, C82/1608/[16], 3 July 1597. Reproduced in Wallace, 'Children of the Chapel at Blackfriars', 61

Nathaniel Giles, Master of the Children at Windsor, succeeded William Hunnis as Master of the Children of the Chapel Royal upon Hunnis' death in 1597. As part of his transition to these new duties, he was issued a writ of impressment, similar to those that had been issued to his predecessors.

Elizabeth, by the grace of God Queen of England, France and Ireland, defender of the faith, etc. To our right trusty and well-beloved Councillor Sir Thomas Egerton, Knight, Keeper of our Great Seal of England for the time being, greeting. We will and command you that under our said Great Seal ye cause our letters patents to be made forth in form following: Elizabeth by the grace of God &c. To all mayors, sheriffs, bailiffs, constables, and all other our officers, greeting. For that it is meet that our Chapel Royal should be furnished with well-singing children from time to time, we have and by these present do authorise our well-beloved servant Nathaniel Giles, Master of our Children of our said Chapel, or his deputy, being by his bill subscribed and sealed so authorised, and having this our present commission with him, to take such and so many children as he or his sufficient deputy shall think meet, in all cathedral, collegiate, parish churches, chapels, or any other place or places as well within liberty as without within this our realm of England whatsoever they be, and also at all times necessary horses, boats, barges, carts, cars, and wagons for the conveyance of the said children from any place, with all manner of necessaries appertaining to the said children by land or water at such reasonable prices as by the discretion of him or his said deputy shall be thought sufficient. And also to take up sufficient lodging for him and the said children, when they for our service shall remove to any place or places. Provided also that if our said servant or his deputy or deputies, bearers hereof in his name, cannot forthwith remove the child or children when he by virtue of this our commission hath taken him or them, that then the said child or children shall remain there until such time as our said servant Nathaniel Giles shall send for him or them.

Wherefore we will and command you and every of you to whom this our commission shall come, to be helping, aiding, and assisting to the uttermost of your powers, as you will answer at your uttermost perils. In witness whereof &c. Given under our privy seal at our manor of Greenwich the third day of July in the nine and thirtieth year of our reign.

186   Henry Clifton's son Thomas forced to be a stage-player, 1601

PRO, STAC.5/C46/39, the complaint of Henry Clifton, 15 December 1601. Reproduced in Fleay, *Chronicle History of the London Stage* 127–32

Only the initial bill of complaint survives from this lawsuit; there is no response from the named defendants, suggesting that the case proceeded no further than this, and that matters were settled out of court. The impressment of singing boys for the Chapel Royal was traditionally sanctioned by royal patent (as cited above) and justified by the monarch's presumed need for a continuing choir. The burden of Henry Clifton's complaint is that such impressment is authorised only for singing boys, and that the impressment of children solely to make stage-players of them falls outside the scope of the patent.

To the Queen's most excellent majesty. In all humbleness complaining, sheweth and informeth your most excellent majesty your highness's true, loyal and faithful subject, Henry Clifton, of Toftrees in your highness's county of Norfolk, esquire:

That whereas your excellent majesty, for the better furnishing of your Chapel Royal with well-singing children, by your majesty's letters patents ... authorised your highness's servant Nathaniel Giles, Master of the Children of your highness's said Chapel ... to take such children as he ... should think meet, in cathedral, collegiate, parish churches or chapels, for your majesty's said better service,

But so it is, most excellent sovereign, that the said Nathaniel Giles, confederating himself with one James Robinson, Henry Evans, and others ... conspiring and complotting how to oppress divers of your majesty's humble and faithful subjects and thereby to make unto themselves an unlawful gain and benefit, they the said confederates devised ... for their own corrupt gain and lucre, to ... furnish and maintain a playhouse or place in the Blackfriars ... and to the end they might the better furnish their said plays and interludes with children whom they thought most fittest to act and furnish the said plays, they the said confederates, abusing the authority and trust by your highness to him the said Nathaniel Giles ... by your highness's said letters patents given and reposed, hath sithence your majesty's last free and general pardon[1] most wrongfully, unduly and unjustly taken divers and several children from divers and sundry schools of learning and other places, and apprentices to men of trade from their masters, no way fitting for your majesty's service in or for your Chapel Royal; but the said children have so taken and employed in acting and furnishing of the said plays and interludes so by them complotted and agreed to be erected furnished and maintained against the wills of the said children, their parents, tutors, masters and governors, and to the no small grief and oppressions [of] your majesty's true and faithful subjects;

Amongst which numbers so by the persons aforesaid and their agents so unjustly taken, used and employed, they have unduly taken and so employed one John Chappell, a grammar school scholar of one Mr Spyke's school near Cripplegate, London; John Motteram, a grammar scholar in the free school at Westminster; Nathan Field, a scholar of a grammar school in London kept by one Mr Mulcaster;[2] Alvery Trussell, an apprentice to one Thomas Gyles;[3] one Philip Pykman, and Thomas Grymes, apprentices to Richard and George Chambers; Salomon Pavey, apprentice to one Peerce;[4] being children no way able or fit for singing, nor by any the said confederates endeavoured to be taught to sing, but by them, the said confederates, abusively employed, as aforesaid, only in plays and interludes.

... [And] your said subject, having Thomas Clifton his only son and heir, being about the age of thirteen years, and having for the better education of ... his said son, placed him in a grammar school in Christ Church, London, where for a good space he had ... been taught and instructed in the grounds of learning and the Latin tongue; and your said subject ... dwelling in a house ... near Great St Bartholomew's, London, where his said son also lay and had his diet, and had daily recourse from thence to the said grammar school; the same being well known to the confederates aforesaid, and they also well knowing that your subject's said son had no manner of sight in song nor skill in music, they the said confederates, about one year last past, and since your majesty's last free and general pardon, did under colour of their said authority and in abuse of your majesty's said commission ... surprise the said Thomas Clifton as he should pass between your said subject's house and the said grammar school and him with like violence and force to carry unto the said playhouse in the Blackfriars aforesaid, and there to sort him with mercenary players and such other children as by the abuse aforesaid they had there placed, and by like force and violence him there to detain and compel to exercise the base trade of a mercenary interlude player to his utter loss of time, ruin and disparagement;

And accordingly, about the thirteenth day of December [1600] ... the said confederates ... did waylay the said Thomas Clifton as he should pass from your said subject's house to the said school ... [as he was] walking quietly from your subject's said house towards the said school ... [and] with great force and violence did seize and surprise and him with like force and violence did, to the great terror and hurt of him the said Thomas Clifton, haul, pull, drag and carry away to the said playhouse in the Blackfriars aforesaid, threatening him that if he the said Thomas Clifton would not obey him the said Robinson, that he the said Robinson would charge the constable with him the said Thomas Clifton. By which violence, threats and terror the said James Robinson then brought the said Thomas Clifton into the said playhouse in the Blackfriars aforesaid, where the ... other confederates ...

committed [him] to the said playhouse amongst a company of lewd and dissolute mercenary players, purposing in that place (and for no service of your majesty) to use and exercise him the said Thomas Clifton in acting of parts in base plays and interludes, to the mercenary gain and private commodity of them the ... said confederates.

Of which abuse and oppression of your said subject and his said son, your said subject having notice, he your said subject forthwith repaired unto the said playhouse in the Blackfriars aforesaid, where he found the said Nathaniel Giles, James Robinson and Henry Evans, and in their violent custody your subject's said son, unto which said Nathaniel Giles, Henry Evans and James Robinson your said subject then and there divers times made request to have his said son released, which they the said Nathaniel Giles, Henry Evans and James Robinson utterly and scornfully refused to do; whereupon your said subject then and there affirmed unto them that if he should complain unto some of your majesty's most honourable privy council they, the said confederates, would hardly answer it;[5] whereupon the said Nathaniel Giles, James Robinson and Henry Evans in very scornful manner willed your said subject to complain to whom he would, and they would answer it; and in a most slight and scornful regard of your majesty's service and the duty they owe thereunto, they then and there said further that if the Queen (meaning your highness) would not bear them forth in that action, she (meaning likewise your highness) should get another to execute her commission for them, and then and there used divers other comtemptuous speeches, manifesting a very slight regard in them towards your majesty's service.

And your said subject ... [told them] that it was not fit that a gentleman of his sort should have his son and heir (and that his only son) to be so basely used, [but] they ... most arrogantly then and there answered that they had authority sufficient so to take any nobleman's son in this land, and did then and there use these speeches: that were it not for the benefit they made by the said playhouse, who would should[5] serve the Chapel with children for them; and the said Nathaniel Giles, Henry Evans and James Robinson then and there, to despite and grieve your said subject with an assurance that his said son should be employed in that vile and base manner of a mercenary player in that place, and in no other sort or manner, did then and there deliver unto his said son, in most scornful, disdainful, and despiteful manner, a scroll of paper containing part of one of their said plays or interludes, and ... commanded [him] to learn the same by heart; and in further grievance and despite of your said subject, the said Nathaniel Giles and James Robinson delivered and committed your subject's said son unto the custody of the said Henry Evans, with these threatening words unto the said Thomas Clifton: that if he did not obey the said Evans, he should be surely whipped. In which base restraint and misusage the said Thomas Clifton, by the practice, conspiracy and confederacy and violent dealing of the said Nathaniel Giles, James Robinson, Henry Evans and their said other confederates, continued by the space of about a day and a night, until such time as by the warrant of the right honourable Sir John Fortescue, knight, one of your majesty's most honourable privy council, he was set at liberty and freed from the same.

All which violent courses, despiteful usage of your subject and his said son, and the base restraint and employment of your subject's said son, and other the misdemeanours and offenses aforesaid, have been to the great grievance, wrong and vexation of your said subject and his said son, and have been so committed, perpetrated and done, both in abuse of the nobility of this your highness's realm, and in abuse of your majesty's said commission, and also to the great oppression and wrong of divers your majesty's loving and faithful subjects, and were so committed, perpetrated and done since your majesty's last free and general pardon, and contrary to divers your majesty's laws in this your highness's realm established. In tender consideration whereof, may it please your highness to grant unto your said subject your majesty's most gracious writ of *subpoena*, to be directed unto the said Nathaniel Giles, Henry Evans and James Robinson, commanding them and every of them, at a certain day and under a certain pain therein to be limited, personally to be and appear before your highness and the lords of your majesty's honourable council in your majesty's high court of Star Chamber, then and there to answer the premises, and further to stand to and abide such further order and punishment herein as your highness and the said your most honourable council shall seem most to agree with justice and the due reformation and punishment of such abuses; and your subject (as nevertheless) shall according to his bounden duty pray unto God for your highness in peace long to reign over us.

[1] The Queen had issued such a free and general pardon in August 1597; Clifton's son was taken up by Nathaniel Giles in December 1600; the Queen issued another such pardon in August 1601. Clifton's reference to the Queen's 'last free and general pardon' in his complaint of December 1601 is thus unclear; no doubt he meant to refer to the pardon of 1597.
[2] Richard Mulcaster was headmaster of Merchant Taylors' School. Field later became a famous adult stage-player.
[3] That is, one of the choristers at St Paul's while Thomas Giles was still master there.
[4] Perhaps Edward Pearce, Master of the Children of Paul's from 1600 to 1609. See below for Ben Jonson's elegy on Pavy.
[5] [would answer it rigorously]
[6] [whoever wished to should]

187 Ben Jonson's elegy for Salomon Pavy, a boy-player, ?1604

Ben Jonson, *Epigram cxx*, in *Works*, 1616 (STC 14751)

Salomon Pavy, named by Henry Clifton (above) as 'apprentice to one Peerce', may have begun his playing career with the Children of Paul's, where Edward Pearce was Master from 1600. If so, his abduction by Nathaniel Giles, as alleged by Clifton, must have remained permanent, for Jonson remembers Pavy as a child of the Queen's Chapel. The date of Pavy's death is unknown; but Jonson's comment that he had played for three years suggests that he died probably about 1603.

Epitaph on S. P. a child of Q. El. Chapel

> Weep with me, all you that read
> This little story:
> And know, for whom a tear you shed
> Death's self is sorry.
> 'Twas a child that so did thrive
> In grace and feature
> As heaven and nature seemed to strive
> Which owned the creature.
> Years he numbered scarce thirteen
> When fates turned cruel,
> Yet three filled zodiacs had he been
> The stage's jewel,
> And did act (what now we moan)
> Old men so duly,
> As, sooth, the Parcae thought him one,
> He played so truly.
> So, by error, to his fate
> They all consented;
> But, viewing him since (alas, too late),
> They have repented,
> And have sought (to give new birth),
> In baths to steep him;
> But being so much too good for earth,
> Heaven vows to keep him.

188 Abel Cooke's apprenticeship and reinstatement, 1607

PRO, K.B.27/1357, m. 582. Transcribed in Hillebrand, *The Child Actors* 197–8

In November 1606, Alice Cooke apprenticed her son Abel to Thomas Kendall at Blackfriars for three years so that he might be trained as a stage-player with the Queen's Revels company; but Abel left Kendall in May 1607, after only six months. Kendall claimed he was truant, and proceeded at law against Alice Cooke for the forfeiture of the indenture. Alice Cooke insisted that Abel had left with Kendall's written permission. Eventually an agreement was reached whereby Kendall took Abel Cooke again as an apprentice, with his mother agreeing to be bound for his continued good conduct. The condition of the bond is reproduced here.

The condition of this obligation is such that whereas our most gracious sovereign lord the King's majesty, by his letters patents under the great seal of England, bearing date at Westminster the fourth day of February [1604] ... hath appointed and authorised the within named Thomas Kendall, among others in the said letters patents nominated, from time to time to provide, keep, and bring up a convenient number of children, and them to practise and exercise in the quality of playing, by the name of the Children of the Revels to the Queen's Majesty, within the Blackfriars in his highness' City of London or in any other convenient place where they should think fit for that purpose, as by the same letters patents appeareth; and whereas the within bound Alice Cooke hath been an earnest suitor unto the said Thomas Kendall to receive, take, and entertain Abel Cooke her son to be one of the said children of her majesty's Revels, and to be practised and exercised in the said quality of playing, by the name of one of the children of her highness' Revels, for and during the term of three years now next ensuing; and thereupon the said Thomas Kendall hath received and entertained him the said Abel Cooke accordingly.

If therefore the said Abel Cooke shall from the day of the date within written, for and during the full term of three years from thence next and immediately ensuing, continue, abide with, and serve the said Thomas Kendall, and from time to time during the said term, when and so often as the said Thomas Kendall require or command, the said Abel shall practise and exercise himself in the quality of playing, as one of the Queen's majesty's children of her Revels aforesaid, and also shall, to the uttermost of his power and ability, at all times play at the direction and commandment of the said Thomas Kendall or his assigns, and shall not wittingly or willingly, during the said term, depart, absent, or prolong himself from the said service and practice and playing without the consent and licence of the said Thomas Kendall, his executors or assigns, first thereunto had, obtained in writing without fraud or coven; that then this present obligation to be void and of none effect; or else to stand or remain in full strength and virtue.

189   Articles of Agreement for a children's company, 1608

PRO, C2 Jas.I/A6/21, a lawsuit in Chancery brought by George Andrews against Martin Slater as a counter to a suit brought by Slater in the Court of King's Bench against Andrews and others.

In his bill of complaint, Andrews reproduces the text of an agreement between Slater and a syndicate of investors who planned to establish a company of boy-players to be called the Children of the King's Revels. These articles of agreement, though not the whole lawsuit, are reproduced in Hillebrand, *The Child Actors* 223–5. Martin Slater was a well-known stage-player, a servant of the Lord Admiral and later of Queen Anne. The syndicate included the poet Michael Drayton and two playwrights (Lording Barry and John Mason). The enterprise they launched by these articles of agreement was beset with troubles from the outset; their company was the last company of boy-players in London.

Articles of agreement indented, made the tenth day of March [1608] . . . between Martin Slater, citizen and ironmonger, of the one party, and Lording Barry, George Andrews, Michael Drayton, William Trevell, William Cooke, Edward Sibthorpe, and John Mason, of the city of London, gentlemen, on the other party, viz.:

Imprimis it is consented, concluded, and fully agreed by and between the said parties, that during all the term of years in the lease of the playhouse in the Whitefriars, which they hold of and from Robert, Lord Buckhurst, he the said Martin Slater shall have, receive, take and enjoy the sixth part, in six parts to be divided, and all such profit, benefit, gettings and commodity as shall at any time arise, come and grow by reason of any plays, shows, interludes, music, or such like exercises to be used and performed as well in the said playhouse as elsewhere, all manner of charges thereunto belonging being first defrayed and deducted.

Item: It is also covenanted, granted, concluded and fully agreed by and between all the said parties that he, the said Martin Slater, and all his family, shall have their dwelling and lodging in the said house, with free ingress, egress, and regress in, to, and from the same, or any part thereof, during the continuance of the said lease; the rooms of which house are thirteen in number, three below and ten above; that is to say, the great hall, the kitchen by the yard, and a cellar, with all the rooms from the east end of the house to the Master of the Revels' office, as the same are now severed and divided.

Item: It is further covenanted, granted, concluded and fully agreed between all the said parties that if any gain or profit can or may be made in the said house either by wine, beer, ale, tobacco, wood, coals, or any such commodity, that then he, the said Martin Slater, and his assigns, and none other, shall have the benefit thereof growing or arising during the continuance of the said lease.

Item: It is likewise covenanted, granted, concluded and agreed by and between the said parties that when their patent for playing shall be renewed, the said Martin Slater's name, with the said Michael Drayton's, shall be joined therein, in respect that if any restraint of their playing shall happen, by reason of the plague or otherwise, it shall be for more credit of the whole company that the said Martin shall travel with the children, and acquaint the magistrates with their business.

Item: It is also covenanted, granted, concluded and fully agreed between all the said parties that if at any time hereafter any apparel, books, or any other goods or commodities shall be conveyed or taken away by any of the said parties without the consent and allowance of the said residue of his fellow-sharers, and the same exceeding the value of 2s, that then he or they so offending shall forfeit and lose all such benefit, profit and commodity as otherwise should arise and grow unto him or them by their shares, besides the loss of their places and all other interest which they may claim amongst us.

Item: It is further covenanted, granted, concluded and fully agreed by and between all the said parties to these presents that during the said lease the whole charges of the house – the gatherers, the wages, the children's board, music, book-keeper, tireman, tirewoman, lights, the Master of the Revels' duties, and all other things needful and necessary – whatsoever one week's charge cometh unto, the sixth part of the same to be taken up every night; as, if one week's charge amounteth unto £10, then to take up every night 33s 4d, by which means they shall be still out of debt.

Item: It is likewise covenanted, granted, concluded and fully agreed by and between the said parties that whereas, by the general consent of all the whole company, all the children are bound to the said Martin Slater for the term of three years, he the said Martin Slater doth by these presents bind himself to the residue of the company in the sum of £40 sterling, that he shall not wrong or injure the residue of the said company in the parting with, or putting away, any one or more of the said young men or lads to any person or persons, or otherwise, without the special consent and full agreement of the residue of his fellow-sharers, except the term of his or their apprenticeship to be fully expired.

Item: It is also covenanted, granted, concluded and fully agreed between the said parties that all such apparel as is abroad shall be immediately brought in, and that no man of the said company shall at any time hereafter put into print, or cause to be put in print, any manner of playbook now in use, or that hereafter shall be sold unto them, upon the penalty and forfeiture of £40 sterling, or the loss of his place and share of all things amongst them, except the book of Torismond, and that play not to be printed by any before twelve months be fully expired.

Item: It is finally covenanted, granted, concluded and fully agreed by and between all the same parties that if at any time hereafter the same company shall be restrained from playing in the said house by reason of the plague, or otherwise, and that thereby they shall be enforced to travel into the country for the upholding of their company, that then the said Martin Slater, during the time of such his travel, shall have an allowance of one full share and a half.

Item: All the said parties before mentioned, in testimony hereof, have interchangeably set their hands and seals to these presents the day and year first above written.

190 The Queen sees to it that a company of children is allowed at Bristol, 1615–1618

(a) PRO, SP14/81/fo. 14, letter from Sir George Buck, the Master of the Revels, to John Packer, a secretary to the Lord Chamberlain, the Earl of Somerset. Transcribed in REED, *Bristol*, 202–3; (b) PRO, C66/2075, membs. 33–4. Transcribed in MSC, 1.279–80, and in REED, *Bristol*, 203–4; (c) PRO, SP14/97/fo. 307, letter from the Mayor of Exeter to Sir Thomas Lake, the King's Secretary of State, June 1618. Transcribed in REED, *Devon*, 188–9; (d) PRO, SP14/97/fo. 310. Transcribed in REED, *Bristol*, 209–10

(a) Letter from the Master of the Revels concerning a forthcoming patent for the Children of the Queen's Chamber of Bristol, 10 July 1615

Note the phrase 'children or youths', which recurs as a point of dispute in the following items in this series.

Good Mr Packer, Mr Samuel Daniel hath informed me that the King my master is pleased, at the mediation of the Queen in his behalf, that there shall be a company of children or youths prepared and licensed to play comedies and tragedies hence at Bristol and elsewhere and to go under the name and title of the Youths of Her Majesty's Royal Chamber of Bristol. And he hath desired my goodwill herein and he hath shewed to me a draft in parchment of the King's warrant in this behalf. Provided therefore that it be made in the same form (for I return the same draft to you here enclosed), I yield my consent, for I wish well to Mr Daniel and would be glad to do him any good, in any thing wherein I should not prejudice my own right, nor do wrong to my successors. And so I bid kindly farewell from the King's Office of the Revels. 10 July 1615.

>   Your very assured
>   friend George Buck

(b) Patent for the Children of the Queen's Chamber of Bristol, 17 July 1615

This is presumably the document mentioned in 190a. The John Daniel mentioned in the commission was the brother of the poet Samuel Daniel.

James by the grace of God etc. To all Justices of Peace, mayors, sheriffs, bailiffs, constables, headboroughs, and other our loving subjects and officers, greeting. Know ye that we, at the motion of our most dearly loved consort the Queen, have licensed and authorised, and by these presents do license and authorise, our well-beloved subjects John Daniel and his assigns to entertain and bring up a company of children and youths under the name and title of the Children of Her Majesty's Royal Chamber of Bristol; to use and exercise the art and quality of playing comedies, histories, interludes, morals, pastorals, stage plays, and such other like as they have already studied or hereafter shall study or use, as well for the solace and delight of our most dearly loved consort the Queen, whensoever they shall be called, as for the recreation of our loving subjects. And the said interludes or other to show and exercise publicly to their best commodity, as well in and about our said city of Bristol, in such usual houses as themselves shall provide, as in other convenient places within the liberties and freedoms of any other city, university town, or borough whatsoever within our realmes and dominions. Willing and commanding you and every of you, as you tender our pleasures, not only to permit and suffer them herein without any your lets, hindrances, molestations or disturbances during our said pleasure, but also to be aiding and assisting unto them if any wrong be done unto them or to them offered; and to allow them such further courtesies as have been given to other of the like quality. And also what further grace and favour you shall show unto them for our sakes, we shall take kindly at your hands. Provided always, and our will and pleasure is, all authority, power, privilege and profit whatsoever belonging and properly appertaining to the Master of the Revels in respect of his office shall remain and abide entire and in full force, effect, and virtue, and in as ample sort as if this our commission had never been made. In witness whereof etc. Witness ourself at Westminster the seventeenth day of July.

(c) The Mayor of Exeter's letter to Sir Thomas Lake, June 1618?

The patent in question is presumably the one cited in 190b.

Right honorable, my duty remembered, may it please you to be advertised that six days past there came to our city certain players, who came unto me desiring leave to play; whereupon I perused their patent, and finding that it is only for children and youths (for so are the words), I did with advice of some of the aldermen of this city, restrain them from playing here; for that there being fifteen of their company, there are but only five youths among them, and all the rest are men, some about 30 and 40 and 50 years as they have confessed unto me, as also of their age, upon which cause I prayed them to desist, and gave them four angels toward their expence, which seemed to me they were content. But since, I am informed that they purpose to inform the right honourable the lords of his majesty's privy council hereof, which if they do, I would humbly desire your Honour to make this known unto the right honourable the lords abovesaid, that they may not think I have done any thing of contempt, but to keep myself within the compass of the statutes. And if it be their Lordships' pleasure that they shall play, I shall be very well content therewith. I have, here enclosed, sent your honour the copy of their warrant,[1] that you may see the words of it. And, farther, we have in our city very many poor people, and they ordinarily are they that spend their money and time to those plays. Thus I have made bold to trouble your honour, praying you to excuse my boldness, and so most humbly do take my leave, and do commend you to the gracious protection of the Lord.

Your honour's to command
Ignatius Jurdain, Mayor
of the City of Exeter

[1] The 'enclosed . . . warrant' is presumably a copy of 190b.

(d) Letter confirming John Daniel's patent, undated

A more finished version of this letter may have been intended as an official response by the Privy Council to difficulties of the sort experienced at Exeter (190c above), as it specifically lists adult players as among those covered by John Daniel's patent. But this appears to be an unpolished draft; undated and possibly never sent. The original is archived with the original of the preceding item.

After our hearty commendations. Whereas it pleased his majesty by his letters patent under the great seal of England, bearing date the 17th day of July in the thirteenth year of his highness' reign, to grant unto John Daniel, gentleman, the prince his servant, authority to bring up a company of children and youths in the quality of playing interludes and stage plays; and we are informed that notwithstanding his majesty's pleasure therein, that there are some who oppugn and resist the said authority in contempt of his majesty's letters patent.

In consideration whereof, and for the further effecting and performance of his majesty's pleasure therein, we have thought good to grant unto the said John Daniel these our letters of assistance, thereby requiring you and in his majesty's name straitly charging and commanding you and every of you not only quietly to permit and suffer Martin Slatier, John Edmonds, and Nathaniel Clay, her majesty's servants, with their associates the bearers hereof, to play as aforesaid, as her majesty's Servants of her Royal Chamber of Bristol, in all playhouses, town halls, schoolhouses and other places convenient for that purpose in all cities, universities, towns and boroughs within his majesty's realms and dominions, freely and peaceably without any of your lets, troubles or molestations. But as occasion shall be offered (they or any of them having to show his letters patents and a letter of assignment[1] from the said John Daniel) to be likewise aiding and assisting unto them, they behaving themselves civilly and orderly like good and honest subjects and doing nothing therein contrary to the tenor of his majesty's said letters patents, nor staying to play in any one place above fourteen days together, and the times of divine service on the Sabbath days only excepted.

Whereof fail you not at your perils. Given at the court of Whitehall this [*blank*]

To all mayors, sheriffs, bailiffs,
constables and other his majesty's officers
and liege subjects to whom it may
belong or in any wise appertain.

---

[1] Presumably, a letter assigning Daniel's rights under the patent to Slatier, Edmonds and Clay.

XIV Some illustrative instances of professional theatrical life and practice

As one attempts to reconstruct a picture of theatrical activity in this period, every retrievable occurrence in the lives of stage-players and playing companies becomes potentially instructive. Unfortunately, the records of such occurrences often survive in isolation, and randomly rather than in a coherent order; as a result, the enclosing narrative of which the particular illuminating instance is a part is often lacking. Such is the case with the documents that follow; each records a moment in an on-going process whose outlines are sometimes clear, sometimes not. The intrinsic evidentiary value of the documents is beyond question, however, and in the selection that follows an appropriate series of problems can easily be discerned.

191 George Maller, glazier, and his apprentice Thomas Arthur, 1529

PRO, C1/546/77. Reproduced in *The New Shakspere Society's Transactions*, 425–8

The extracts below are from George Maller's bill of complaint, the only piece of pleading to have survived from this lawsuit. Maller's exact status is unclear; nominally a glazier, he seems to have been the manager of a company of players and may or may not have had connections with the Court. His apprentice Thomas Arthur seems to have had an agenda of his own. Maller's aim in this complaint is to seek relief from a series of lawsuits brought against him by Arthur in the Sheriffs' Court of the City of London. What follows provides an interesting glimpse of a strained relationship proceeding out of a promise of a career upon the stage.

To the most reverend father in God, Thomas, Lord Legate *a latere*, Cardinal Archbishop of York, Primate and Chancellor of England:

Most humbly showeth unto your good grace your daily orator George Maller, that where one Thomas Arthur, the 23rd day of November [1528] . . . made instant suit and labour to your said orator, him to teach in playing of interludes and plays, whereby he might attain and come to be one of the King's players, for which thing so to be done, the same Arthur faithfully promised well and truly to serve your said orator by the space of one whole year then next ensuing . . . [with your said orator] finding the said Arthur meat and drink and all other charges, giving him also 4d a day during the said year;[1] which Arthur, by the space of seven weeks in the beginning of the said year, served your said orator accordingly; and then he, intending untruly and craftily to hinder your said orator in his foresaid science of playing, procured three of the covenanted servants of your said orator, being expert in playing, to go away with him, without licence of your said orator; at whose request and procurement the said three servants went and departed with the said Arthur from your said orator without g[iving notice], going in sundry parts of England in playing of many interludes, getting and obtaining divers sums of money, amounting to the sum of £30, which they employed and converted to their own use, giving unto your said orator nothing thereof, contrary to their said covenants. And since the time of which departure of the said Arthur, and others before named, out of the service of your said orator, they have considered themselves together, going and perusing divers and many parts of the King's realm in uttering of plays and interludes, by means whereof your said orator hath not only lost their daily service, which they were bound to do unto him; but also the said Arthur and the others before named have continually gained, and yet daily do, great avail, profit and advantage, by reason of the aforesaid interludes and plays. All which profits and advantage thereof coming and growing, of very right ought to come and grow unto your said orator, by the reason of their said covenant, promise, and service, which they should have done and performed, as is before alleged, in consideration that your said orator taught the said Arthur and others, which said Arthur was right hard and dull to take any learning, whereby he was nothing meet or apt to be in service with the King's grace to make any plays or interludes before his highness. Nevertheless your said orator was agreeable to help and further the said Arthur into the King's service, to the intent to be one of his said players, so he would have tarried still with your said orator, and would have learned him the feat and cunning therof, which he refused to do, against his said promise. And so it is, gracious lord, the said Arthur, not regarding his said promise, covenants, or honesty, or yet good right and conscience, intending wrongfully to unquiet and trouble your said orator – because he should not take his remedy against the said Arthur for such wrongs and injuries that the said Arthur hath committed and done unto your orator – hath sued a feigned action of trespass upon his case, before the sheriffs of London, against your said orator . . .

Before which suit of the said feigned action, the said Arthur did commence and pursue another like action before the said sheriffs, and the process in the said former action continued unto such time that the said parties were at issue;[2] and so depending, it chanced your said orator to be in prison in Ludgate, within the City of London; and in the meantime the jury that was empanelled betwixt your said orator and the said Arthur were so wilfully set that they would not take any day or time to hear the witness of your said orator to speak in the premises;[3] but untruly found your said orator in the damage of[4] £4; howbeit, no judgement thereupon was given, because the pleading of the said surmised action was insufficient in the law. That notwithstanding, gracious lord, the inquest, that now is empanelled to pass betwixt your said orator and the said Arthur in the said second action, allege and say that they will lean unto the said verdict given by the other inquest, which they of right ought not to do, the same verdict being untrue, as your said orator shall by good and sufficient witness prove, if he may have granted unto him the King's writ of subpoena against the said witness, which in no wise will testify the truth in the premises, notwithstanding that your orator hath divers times required the said witness to depose the truth therein, which they always hath refused and yet do.

[1] A quite reasonable wage for the time.
[2] That is, the proceedings at law had reached the point where depositions from witnesses were to be taken.
[3] Presumably Maller means to claim that the jury would not hear his witness because Maller himself, being imprisoned, could not be present.
[4] At fault and liable for.

192 A woman and child reportedly killed at a play, 1587

BL, MS Egerton 2804, fo. 35; a letter of Philip Gawdy to his father, 16 November 1587. Transcribed in Jeayes, ed., *The Letters of Philip Gawdy*, 23. The event recounted in this letter is quite likely to be apocryphal, as no further record of such a mishap exists.

You shall understand of some accidental news here in this town, though myself no witness thereof, yet I may be bold to verify it for an assured truth. My Lord Admiral's men and players, having a device in their play to tie one of their fellows to a post and so to shoot him to death, having borrowed their calivers, one of the player's hands swerved; his piece, being charged with bullet, missed the fellow he aimed at and killed a child, and a woman great with child forthwith, and hurt another man in the head very sore. How they will answer it I do not study unless their profession were better, but in Christianity I am very sorry for the chance; but God's judgements are not to be searched nor enquired of at man's hands. And yet I find by this an old proverb verified, that never comes more hurt than comes of fooling.

193 Edward Alleyn, on tour, writes to his wife, 1593

Dulwich, Henslowe Papers, MS I, Art. 11; a letter from Edward Alleyn, a stage-player touring at Bristol, to his wife Joan on the Bankside in London, 1 August 1593 (?). Transcribed in *Henslowe's Diary*, 276–7

Philip Henslowe had acquired Joan Woodward as a step-daughter when he married Agnes, the widow of his former master Harry Woodward, dyer. Edward Alleyn and Joan Woodward were married on 22 October 1592. During the plague summer of 1593 Alleyn and many other stage players were obliged to travel in the provinces.

My good sweet mouse, I commend me heartily to you, and to my father, my mother, and my sister Bess,[1] hoping in God though the sickness be round about you, yet by his mercy it may escape your house, which by the grace of God it shall. Therefore use this course: keep your house fair and clean (which I know you will) and every evening throw water before your door and in your backside, and have in your windows good store of rue and herb of grace, and withal the grace of God, which must be obtained by prayers; and so doing, no doubt but the lord will mercifully defend you. Now good mouse, I have no news to send you but this, that we have all our health, for which the lord be praised. I received your letter at Bristol, by Richard Cowley,[2] for the which I thank you. I have sent you by this bearer, Thomas Pope's[3] kinsman, my white waistcoat, because it is a trouble to me to carry it; receive it with this letter, and lay it up for me till I come. If you send any more letters, send to me by the carriers of Shrewsbury, or to West Chester or to York, to be kept till my Lord Strange's players come. And thus, sweetheart, with my hearty commendation to all our friends, I cease. From Bristol this Wednesday after St James' day, being ready to begin the play of Harry of Cornwall.[4] Mouse, do my hearty commend to Mr Griggs,[5] his wife and all his household, and to my sister Phillips.[6] Your loving husband E. Alleyn.

Mouse, you send me no news of any things. You should send of your domestical matters, such things as happen at home, as how your distilled water proves, or this or that or any thing, what you will. And Jug I pray you, let my orange tawny stockings of woollen be dyed a very good black against I come home, to wear in the winter. You sent me not word of my garden, but next time you will; but remember this in any case, that all that bed which was parsley, in the month of September you sow it with spinach, for then is the time. I would do it myself but we shall not come home till All Hallowtide. And so sweet mouse, farewell, and brook our long journey with patience.

[1] These references would be to Alleyn's in-laws: Henslowe, his wife Agnes, and Joan's sister Elizabeth Woodward.
[2] A fellow stage-player.
[3] Thomas Pope was a fellow stage-player.
[4] A lost play.
[5] John Griggs, carpenter and playhouse builder.
[6] This person has not been identified with certainty.

(a) Portrait of Edward Alleyn, c. 1620

Dulwich College Picture Gallery, DPG 443. Alleyn was in his fifties at the time of this portrait. The painter is unknown.

(b) Portrait of Joan Woodward Alleyn, 1596

Dulwich College Picture Gallery, DPG 444. Joan and her husband had been married for four years at the time of this portrait. The painter is unknown.

194   Ben Jonson kills Gabriel Spencer in a duel, 1598

Dulwich, Henslowe Papers, MS I, Art. 24; a letter from Philip Henslowe to his son-in-law Edward Alleyn the stage-player, the latter being at Brill in Sussex. Transcribed in Greg, *Henslowe Papers* 47–8. Gabriel Spencer was a stage-player with the Lord Admiral's company at the time of his death; 'Benjamin Jonson bricklayer' is the actor and playwright Ben Jonson.

Son Edward Alleyn, I have received your letter, the which you sent unto me by the carrier, wherein I understand of both your good healths, which I pray to God to continue; and further I understand you have considered of the words which you and I had between us concerning the Beargarden, and according to your words you and I and all our friends shall have as much as we can do to bring it unto a good end . . . Now to let you understand news, I will tell you some, but it is for me hard and heavy; since you were with me I have lost one of my company, which hurteth me greatly, that is Gabriel, for he is slain in Hoxton Fields by the hands of Benjamin Jonson bricklayer; therefore I would fain have a little of your counsel if I could. Thus, with hearty commendations to you and my daughter, and likewise to all the rest of our friends, I end, from London the 26 of September 1598.

      Your assured friend
      to my power
      Philip Henslowe

To my well beloved son Mr Edward Alleyn at Mr Arthur Langworth's at the Brill in Sussex give this.

195   Indictment of Ben Jonson for the killing of Gabriel Spencer, 1598

LMA, MS MJ/SR/358/68. Transcribed in Jeaffreson, *Middlesex County Records*, I xxxix–xl. The presentment jury having found true grounds for bringing him to trial, Jonson was arraigned in the Justice Hall of the Old Bailey in October 1598 on the charge of killing his fellow-player Gabriel Spencer. The indictment is in Latin.

Middlesex: – The Jurors for the Lady the Queen present that Benjamin Jonson late of London, yeoman, on the twenty-second day of September in the fortieth year of the Lady Elizabeth, by God's grace Queen of England, France and Ireland, Defender of the Faith &c., made an assault with force and arms &c. against and upon a certain Gabriel Spencer, when he was in God's and the said Lady the Queen's peace, at Shoreditch in the aforesaid county of Middlesex, in the fields there, and with a certain sword of iron and steel called a Rapier, of the price of 3s, which he then and there had in his right hand and held drawn, feloniously and wilfully struck and beat the same Gabriel, then and there with the aforesaid sword giving to the same Gabriel Spencer, in and upon the same Gabriel's right side, a mortal wound, of the depth of six inches and of the breadth of one inch, of which mortal wound the same Gabriel Spencer then and there died instantly in the aforesaid fields at Shoreditch aforesaid in the aforesaid county of Middlesex. And thus the aforesaid Jurors say upon their oath that the aforesaid Benjamin Jonson feloniously and wilfully slew and killed the aforesaid Gabriel Spencer at Shoreditch aforesaid in the aforesaid county of Middlesex and in the aforesaid fields [in the year and day] aforesaid against the peace of the said Lady the Queen &c.

[*The heading of the document records the following disposition of the matter (also in Latin.*]

He confesses the indictment, asks for the book, reads like a Clerk, is marked with the letter T, and is delivered according to the form of the statute &c.

196 Edward Alleyn as moneylender, 1607

PRO, Req.2/397/132, an unexecuted and cancelled bond; the document is unpublished.

Moneylending, a widespread activity in this period, became even more ubiquitous after it was legalised with restrictions by the parliament of 1571; but it never quite lost the taint associated with its medieval proscriptions. Alleyn was not alone in being both a stage-player and moneylender; see above, 142, for another instance. Various kinds of evidence suggest that several stage-players engaged in moneylending. The recognisance or bond, in Latin, records the acknowledgement of John Churchill, Ellis Churchill, and John Tooke on 27 June 1607 that they owe £200 to Edward Alleyn of Dulwich, esquire. On the back, in English, are the terms or conditions of the debt.

21 June 1607

The condition of this obligation is such that if the within bound John Churchill, Ellis Churchill and John Tooke, or any of them, their executors, administrators or assigns, do well and truly pay or cause to be paid to the within named Edward Alleyn, his executors or assigns, the sum of £102 10s of lawful money of England, on the nine and twentieth day of September next coming after the date within written, at the now dwelling house of Philip Henslowe, esquire, in the parish of St Saviour's in Southwark, in the county of Surrey, without fraud or further delay, that then this obligation to be void and of none effect; or else it to be in full force strength and virtue.

197 Robert Dawes contracts to play for Philip Henslowe, 1614

Reproduced in Greg, *Henslowe Papers* 123. The original document was among the papers at Dulwich College, where it was seen by Malone and Boswell, who transcribed it; but it has been missing since the early nineteenth century.

7 April 1614

[Articles of agreement,] made, concluded, and agreed upon, and which are to be kept and performed by Robert Dawes of London, gentleman, unto and with Philip Henslowe, esquire, and Jacob [Meade, waterman,] in manner and form following, that is to say

Imprimis. The said Robert Dawes ... doth covenant, promise, and grant to and with the said Philip Henslowe and Jacob Meade ... in manner and form following, that is to say, that he the said Robert Dawes shall and will play with such company as the said Philip Henslowe and Jacob Meade shall appoint, for and during the time and space of three years from the date hereof for and at the rate of one whole share, according to the custom of players; and that he the said Robert Dawes shall and will at all times during the said term duly attend all such rehearsal, which shall the night before the rehearsal be given publicly out; and if that he the said Robert Dawes shall at any time fail to come at the hour appointed, then he shall and will pay to the said Philip Henslowe and Jacob Meade ... 12d; and if he come not before the said rehearsal is ended, then the said Robert Dawes is contented to pay 2s; and further that if the said Robert Dawes shall not every day, whereon any play is or ought to be played, be ready apparelled and ... to begin the play at the hour of three of the clock in the afternoon, unless by six of the same company he shall be licensed to the contrary, that then he, the said Robert Dawes, shall and will pay unto the said Philip and Jacob or their assigns 3s; and if that he, the said Robert Dawes, happen to be overcome with drink at the time when he [ought to] play, by the judgement of four of the said company, he shall and will pay 10s; and if he [the said Robert Dawes] shall [fail to come] during any play, having no licence or just excuse of sickness, he is contented to pay 20s; and further the said Robert Dawes ... doth covenant and grant to and with the said Philip Henslowe and Jacob Meade ... that it shall and may be lawful unto and for the said Philip Henslowe and Jacob Meade ... during the term aforesaid, to receive and take back to their own proper use the part of him, the said Robert Dawes, of and in one moiety or half part of all such moneys as shall be received at the galleries and tiring-house of such house or houses wherein he the said Robert Dawes shall play, for and in consideration of the use of the same house and houses; and likewise shall and may take and receive his other moiety [of] the moneys received at the galleries and tiring-house dues, towards the paying to them, the said Philip Henslowe and Jacob Meade, of the sum of £124, being the value of the stock of apparel furnished by the said company by the said Philip Henslowe and Jacob Meade [of] the one part of him the said Robert Dawes or any other sums [owed] to them for any apparel hereafter newly to be bought by the [said Philip Henslowe and Jacob Meade, until the said Philip Henslowe and Jacob Meade] shall thereby be fully satisfied, contented, and paid. And further the said Robert Dawes doth covenant [promise, and grant to and with the said Philip Henslowe and Jacob Meade, that if he, the said Robert Dawes] shall at any time after the play is ended depart or go out of the [house] with any [of their] apparel on his body, or if the said Robert Dawes [shall carry away any property] belonging to the said company, or shall be consenting [or privy to any other of the said company going out of the house with any of their apparel on his or their bodies, he, the said] Robert Dawes, shall and will forfeit and pay unto the said Philip and Jacob, or their administrators or assigns, the sum of £40 of lawful [money of England] ... and the said Robert Dawes, for him, his executors and administrators doth [covenant promise and grant to and with the said] Philip Henslowe and Jacob Meade, their executors, and administrators [and assigns] ... that it shall and may be lawful to and for the said Philip Henslowe and Jacob Meade ... to have and use the playhouse so appointed [for the said company ... one day of] every four days, the said day to be chosen by the said Philip and [Jacob] ... on which day it shall be lawful for the said Philip [and Jacob] ... to bait their bears and bulls there, and to use their accustomed sport and [games] ... and take to their own use all such sums of money as thereby shall arise and be received.

And the said Robert Dawes, his executors, administrators, and assigns [do hereby covenant, promise and grant to and with the said Philip and Jacob,] allowing to the said company day the sum of 40s money of England ... [in testimony] for every such, whereof I the said Robert Dawes have hereunto set my hand and seal this [sev]enth day of April 1614 ...

    Robert Dawes

Part Three: playhouses, 1560–1660
Edited by HERBERT BERRY

XV Introduction

Professional theatres in the English-speaking world were virtually invented in London during the first Elizabethan age. Permanent structures had been built for the professional acting of plays throughout the ancient world, and vestiges of a few are still to be seen in Britain. Such things had ceased to be built there, however, with the end of the Roman Empire, and more than a millennium was to pass before others were built.

Companies of players travelled from place to place acting plays for a living during the latter half of the fifteenth century, and the King himself was patron of one such company from at least the 1480s, perhaps the 1460s or earlier. People of means did not invest in theatres where these players could perform before the general public because plays were infrequent in any one place and the players did not stay long. In many places, groups of players had first to perform a sample of their wares, a 'mayor's play', before municipal officials and others, for which the municipality provided the place, often in the town hall and sometimes at night, and a fee. If the officials approved, the players then performed for a few days wherever they could hire space and collect money from spectators, in parish halls, for example, or the yards of inns, or even town halls. This way of working flourished in the provinces until the beginning of the seventeenth century and in some places until 1642. A small town like Bridgwater in Somerset usually paid for at least one or two mayor's plays a year from, it seems, 1461–2 to 1612 and sometimes for as many as five.

Investors had decided by the 1560s and 1570s that permanent theatres in and around London could yield great profits, though, presumably, players might come and go. The first such structure of which record has come to light was built there in 1567. Within twenty years, professional actors were regularly at work in no fewer than ten other structures there, and the erection of at least three of them had involved large amounts of capital.

These theatres (playhouses as they were usually called) belonged to either of two distinct types and so did their successors until the end of the so-called Shakespearean period, until, that is, 1642. They were public or private.

Public playhouses, except four built in inns, were outside the City of London to escape at least partly the jurisdiction of the mayor and aldermen, who were usually hostile to them. The essential features of these buildings were a yard open to the weather in which spectators stood, galleries around the yard in which spectators stood or sat, and a stage jutting out into the yard so that spectators in the yard stood around it on at least three sides. There were usually three tiers of galleries, one above the other, and the top one was roofed so that all were relatively protected from the weather. The floor of the bottom one was usually not much above the level of the yard. Behind the stage was a façade with a door or doors through which actors passed to get on and off the stage, and behind the façade was a tiring-house – one or more rooms that served for dressing and storage. Above the doors in the façade was a gallery for a few spectators who probably paid well to be seen as well as to see.

At first the stage seems not to have been roofed, but by the mid-1590s it was, and in the roof was usually machinery used to achieve spectacular effects by lowering actors and properties to the stage and taking them off again. Ordinary spectators first paid a small amount (a penny is mentioned several times) to get into the yard and then, if they wanted a better place, further small amounts to get into galleries.

The public playhouse was largely an English idea, and except for some playhouses in Spain, it was strikingly different from theatres elsewhere in Europe. Most of these public playhouses seem to have been sufficiently polygonal that people saw them as round, but some were square or rectangular, including, probably, those built in inns. Plays were acted in the afternoons by natural light, but, especially in the winter when darkness comes early in Britain, the last parts could be lighted by rope and pitch burning in cressets. Many public playhouses, and not just those in inns, had rooms or adjoining houses in which spectators could refresh and relieve themselves. These playhouses were open to the general public and, though their dimensions may seem modest nowadays, they accommodated huge audiences, several of them upwards of 3,000 people each.

The private playhouses were all built in large rooms in buildings already standing and originally meant for other things. Their audiences were, therefore, out of the weather and often saw the play by candlelight. In addition to stages and tiring-houses for actors, they had a place equivalent to the yard of the public playhouses (presumably lower than the stage) called the pit, galleries, and boxes for spectators. How these things related to one another architecturally is not clear, though modern writers usually prefer to see the private playhouse as the birthplace of the proscenium-arch theatre in Britain, hence akin to well-known theatres built after 1660. The private playhouses accommodated audiences comfortably in the pit as well as in the galleries and boxes. They also accommodated many fewer people than the public playhouses and charged much higher prices. Their customers, therefore, were usually people of pretension. All but one of these playhouses were in the City of London itself. Originally they were private because, in theory, they were not open to the general public. They housed companies of child musicians who were supposed to be kept ready to perform music and plays for the monarch, and their managers could allow people to attend rehearsals for a fee. Eventually the companies of children disappeared from these places as did the theory, to be replaced by the regular professional companies that performed also in the public playhouses.

Altogether, counting inns, seventeen public playhouses were built in London or its suburbs during the period, and at its close in 1642 at least three were still in business. For the ordinary play-goer, the plays of Elizabethan, Jacobean and Caroline times belonged almost wholly to these buildings. Six private playhouses were built during the period, and the first may antedate the first large-scale public playhouse by a year or two. Three of these private playhouses were also still in business in 1642.

Twenty-three professional theatres, then, were built in and around London during the seventy-five years from 1567 to 1642. Probably nothing of the kind had happened in any other city on earth.

Throughout the period, professional actors sometimes performed plays for private occasions in places in London other than these playhouses. Most such performances took place in large rooms in the royal palaces during the Christmas season, but others took place at various times in similar rooms in the inns of court and private houses. Professional actors continued to perform in makeshift places in the provinces, but towards the end of the sixteenth century, a scattering of permanent theatres began to appear in such places as

Liverpool, Bristol and Manchester. All seem also to have been in large rooms and therefore to relate to the private playhouses in London.

The people who invested in, and hence owned, playhouses were mostly small-scale capitalists – artisans, small traders, actors, musicians – but they included some large-scale financiers and a professional courtier. Most had the same goal, to make a lot of money quickly, and the same disability, not enough capital or patience to see their schemes through. A few made fortunes, Shakespeare, for example, the Burbages, Philip Henslowe and Edward Alleyn. But, when mutually antagonistic realities interfered with mutual aspirations, many of these people got into difficulties that led to losses and in some cases to ruin.

Luckily, the difficulties also led to lawsuits, and documents of most lawsuits of the time survive. Much of the primary evidence about the ownership of Shakespearean playhouses and about the buildings themselves comes from lawsuits among their investors and is couched, therefore, in fatiguing legal prose. Other, perhaps more direct, evidence comes from a few tourists who wrote about what they saw in and around London, from a few drawings showing the inside or outside of playhouses, and from three contracts drawn up by owner and builder before a playhouse was built. For some playhouses, especially those whose ownership was vexed, hence prone to litigation, there is a great deal more evidence than for others.

XVI The Red Lion

The Red Lion was, for practical purposes, the first structure now known to have been built as a regular professional theatre in the British Isles since Roman times. It has acquired its name because it was in a 'court or yard . . . belonging to' a farmhouse called the Red Lion. It was in Middlesex, in the parish of St Mary Matfellon, Whitechapel, evidently at the southeastern end of the parish,[1] perhaps 175 yards south of Whitechapel Road, on the north-west corner of Stepney Way and Halcrow Street, E.1. It was nearly a mile east of the City wall at Aldgate, near the grounds at Mile End where Londoners went to amuse themselves and where the musters of the City trained bands took place. Plays had been performed at Mile End before, and a record of one in 1501 survives. The Red Lion apparently had nothing to do with child-actors or private performances, hence must be thought of as a public playhouse.

John Brayne had the playhouse built in 1567. He was a grocer, who, nine years later, was to join his brother-in-law, James Burbage, in building the Theatre. Brayne hired one carpenter, William Sylvester, to build scaffolds for spectators and another, John Reynolds, to build a stage. The place was to be finished by 8 July 1567 and a play called *The Story of Samson* was then to be performed there. Brayne complained about the work of both carpenters, and the documents of his complaints provide everything known about the playhouse. On 15 July 1567, shortly after the playhouse was to be finished, Brayne complained about Sylvester's work to the Carpenters' Company, and in the autumn of 1568, more than a year later, he complained about Reynolds' work to the Court of King's Bench.

The amount of money Brayne was to pay Sylvester, £8 10s, and the amount involved in Reynolds' performance bond, £13 6s 8d (which should have been twice Brayne's risk), suggest that the place was not elaborate. Brayne evidently meant to use it for more than a performance or two, but he may have abandoned it by the time he sued Reynolds.[2]

Except for the amount of money involved, no hint survives of what the scaffolds were like. Reynolds, however, described the stage because he had his performance bond (dated 17 June 1567) copied into the court record, and the bond is, in effect, his and Brayne's contract for the work. The stage was a single scaffold, 5 feet high, 40 feet, 'in length' north to south, and 30 feet 'in breadth' east to west. It had 'a certain space . . . left unboarded' – for a trapdoor, one supposes; 'over' it was a 'turret' rising 30 feet from the ground with a floor 7 feet, 'under the top'. On top of the turret were four 'compass braces' whose purpose is unknown. Brayne may have had in mind the towers on some medieval stages. No one mentioned a roof, a tiring-house or walls.

[1] See Ingram, *Business of Playing* 105–10.
[2] See Berry, 'First Public Playhouses', 144–5.

198 Players perform at Mile End, 6 August 1501

PRO, E101/415/3/fo. 61v. Transcribed in Anglo, 'Court Festivals', 27–44

[An entry in the account book of John Heron, Treasurer of the King's Chamber:] Item: [Paid] to the players at Miles End, 3s 4d.

199 Brayne complains about the carpenter's work on the scaffolds, 15 July 1567

GL, MS 4329/1. Transcribed in *Records of the Worshipful Company of Carpenters*, III, 95–6. See Berry, 'First Public Playhouses', 142–3, 146

Court holden the 15th day of July 1567 ... by Master William Ruddoke, Master Richard More, Henry Whreste, and Richard Smarte, wardens, and Master Bradshaw. Be it remembered that ... where certain variance, discord, and debate was between William Sylvester, carpenter, on the one party and John Brayne, grocer, on the other party, it is agreed, concluded, and fully determined by the said parties, by the assent and consent of them both with the advice of the master and wardens above said, that William Buttermore, John Lyffe, William Snelling, and Richard Kyrby, carpenters, shall with expedition go and peruse such defaults as are and by them shall be found of, in, and about such scaffolds as he the said William hath made at the house called the Red Lion in the parish of Stepney, and the said William Sylvester shall repair and amend the same with their advice substantially as they shall think good. And that the said John Brayne on Saturday [19 July] next ensuing the date above written shall pay to the said William Sylvester the sum of £8 10s lawful money of England, and that after the play which is called *The Story of Samson* be once played at the place aforesaid the said John shall deliver to the said William such bonds as are now in his custody for the performance of the bargain. In witness whereof both parties hereunto hath [*sic*] set their hands.

200 Brayne complains about the carpenter's work on the stage, autumn 1568

PRO, KB 27/1229/m. 30. Transcribed in Loengard, 'An Elizabethan Lawsuit', 306–10, and in Berry, 'First Public Playhouses', 146–8

The document is a summary made towards the end of January 1569 of a lawsuit filed the previous autumn. Brayne sued John Reynolds, the carpenter, over a performance bond that Brayne had required Reynolds to draw up. The part of the bond on the front is alluded to in the second paragraph below, and the part on the back ('the condition') is quoted in the fourth.

In Michaelmas term last past [1568], John Brayne, citizen and grocer of London, came before the lady Queen at Westminster [*i.e.* the Court of King's Bench] by

Richard Heywood his attorney and brought . . . a certain bill against John Reynolds, citizen and carpenter of London, in the custody of the marshal, etc., of a plea of debt, . . . which bill follows in these words.

'. . . John Brayne, citizen and grocer of London, complains about John Reynolds, citizen and carpenter of London in the custody of the marshal of the Marshalsea of the lady Queen, before the Queen herself . . . concerning a plea that he pay him 20 marks [£13 6s 8d] of the legal money of England, which he owes him and unjustly detains from him. That is to say, whereas the said John Reynolds on the seventeenth day of June . . . [1567] at London in the parish of St Mary of the Arches in the Ward of Cheap, London,[1] by a certain obligatory writing [*i.e.* a bond] sealed with the seal of the John Reynolds himself, hereupon shown in the court of the now lady Queen, the date of which is the day and year aforesaid, acknowledged himself bound and firmly obligated to the aforesaid John Brayne in the said 20 marks, payable to the same John Brayne whenever the aforesaid should be demanded. Nevertheless John Reynolds, although very often demanded, etc., has not yet paid the said 20 marks to the same John Brayne, but has so far altogether refused to pay them to him and still refuses to the damage of the same John Brayne of £20, and the thereupon he brings the lawsuit, etc.

'And now, . . . namely the Monday next after the octave of St Hilary [24 January 1569] in that same term, from which day the said John Reynolds has had leave to imparl the same bill [*i.e.* to settle the matter amicably] and then to answer, etc., so the said John Brayne comes before the lady the Queen at Westminster by his said attorney as well as the said John Reynolds by his attorney, Hugh Russell, and the same John Reynolds denies force and damage at any time, etc. And he pleads the hearing of the said obligatory writing. And it is read to him, etc.; he also pleads the hearing of the endorsement of the same writing. And it is read to him in these words:

'"The condition of this obligation is such that if the within bounden John Reynolds, his executors, or assigns, or any of them, at his or their proper costs and charges do frame, make, or build and set up for the within named John Brayne within the court or yard lying on the south side of the garden belonging to the messuage or farmhouse called and known by the name of the sign of the Red Lion (about the which court there are galleries now building), situate and being at Mile End in the parish of St Mary Matfellon, otherwise called Whitechapel without Aldgate of London, sometime called Stark's House, one scaffold or stage for interludes or plays of good, new, and well-seasoned timber and boards, which shall contain in height from the ground five feet of assize and shall be in length north and south forty foot of assize and in breadth east and west thirty foot of assize, well and sufficiently stayed bounden and nailed, with a certain space or void part of the same stage left unboarded in such convenient place of the same stage as the said John Brayne shall think convenient; and if the said John Reynolds, his executors, or assigns do make, frame and set up upon the said scaffold one convenient turret of timber and boards which shall contain and be in height from the ground, set upon plates, thirty foot of assize, with a convenient floor of timber and boards within the same turret seven foot under the top of the same turret, and that the same turret be in all places sufficiently braced, pinned, and fastened for the binding together of the same turret, and do also make, frame, and set up upon the top of the same turret four sufficient compass braces of good and well-seasoned timber, and that the same turret so to be made, framed, and set up be fully finished, ended, and workmanly done in all things accordingly before . . . [24 June 1567], and also that the said scaffold or stage so to be made be fully finished, wrought and workmanly ended and done before the eighth day of July then next immediately ensuing without fraud or further delay: that then this obligation to be void and of none effect or else to stand and abide in full strength and virtue."

'To which reading and hearing the same John Reynolds says that the said John Brayne ought not to have or maintain his said action against him by virtue of the said obligatory writing, because he says that after the making of the said obligatory writing and before the said eighth day of July above specified in the said endorsement, that is on the first day of July . . . [1567], he did well and workmanly construct, make, and build of new, well-seasoned timber . . . of the same length, width, and height the structure called the scaffold specified in the said endorsement, and he was prepared to erect and put up the same structure at the said house called the Red Lion in the parish of Whitechapel to the size, form and effect of the said endorsement, but he says that finally the said John Brayne then and there impeded, disturbed and prohibited the same John Reynolds.

'And finally the same John Reynolds says that he made, joined, built the said tower specified in the said endorsement well and workmanly in the size, length and height with the same four braces[2] on the top of the same before . . . [24 June] specified in the said endorsement, namely on the twentieth day of June . . . [1567]. And he erected the same tower over the structure called the scaffold according to the form and effect of the said endorsement. And this he is ready to prove, whence he demands trial if the said John Brayne should thereupon have or maintain his said action against him.

'And the said John Brayne says that he ought not to be precluded from having his said action against the same John Reynolds by the things alleged by the said John Reynolds as pleading above, . . . protesting that the same John Reynolds has not performed some things specified above in the said endorsement on his part to be performed. For plea the said John Brayne says he did not impede, disturb and prohibit the said John Reynolds to erect and put up the said structure in the size and form specified in the said bar [*i.e.* the endorsement] as the said John Reynolds alleged in the pleading above. And he asks that it be inquired into by the country [*i.e.* come to trial]. And the said John Reynolds similarly, etc. Therefore let a jury thereupon come before the lady Queen at Westminster on the Wednesday next after the octave of St Hilary [26 January 1569]. And . . . the same day is given to the said parties at the same place.'

[1] The conventional place in London for sealing bonds.
[2] This phrase reads in the original, 'cum eisdem quatuor lez brases'. Because 'z' could represent 'us' in Latin ('partibz' in this document means 'partibus'), 'lez' is often read as 'leus' and translated as 'lewis'. But the word probably means only 'the'. People used undeclined English words, like 'brases', in Latin but in doing so observed certain conventions. One was to put the law French for 'the' before the word, 'le' for a singular (examples of which are legion), 'lez' for a plural (examples of which are not common). For example: 'apud le Sessions hall in le olde bailey' (twice) and 'versus Thomam Harrison de lez foure Milles in parochia de Bromeley' (LMA, MJ/SR 291/5, 6 and 301/51).

XVII–XX The Four Inns

Four London inns were made into playhouses but continued as inns. They were among the earliest playhouses, and one, at least, was a playhouse before the erection in 1576 of the Theatre in Shoreditch, which Cuthbert Burbage thought was the first playhouse. They have similar histories. All opened for theatrical business in the 1570s, and all had ceased being playhouses, but continued as inns, by about 1596. All were public playhouses: adult actors, not boy-choristers, played in them all. Their stages were, presumably, in their inn-yards, and their plays were performed in the open air. Well-known companies of actors played at one time or another in them all. Unlike other public playhouses, these were in the City; indeed three were within the walls. They were the Bel Savage (which was and still is spelled in various ways), the Bull, the Cross Keys and the Bell.

The Bel Savage was the earliest of them. It was on the north side of Ludgate Hill, about 100 yards outside (west of) Ludgate and about sixty west of Old Bailey. The site is now a garden-cum-parking lot behind no. 50 Ludgate Hill, a new building lying between Limeburner Lane and Old Bailey, E.C.4. People were going to plays there in 1575, if not several years earlier. The Bull was on the west side of Bishopsgate Street, E.C.2, where no. 51, Palmerston House, now is. It was used regularly for plays from at least 1577 and was, after its theatrical days, the inn from which Milton's carrier, Thomas Hobson, left weekly for Cambridge. The Cross Keys and the Bell adjoined one another on the west side of Gracechurch Street, north of Lombard Street. The site of the Cross Keys is occupied now by the northern part of the headquarters of Barclay's Bank, whose main entrance is in Lombard Street. The site of the Bell is marked now by an alley called Bell Inn Yard, E.C.3.[1] They were playhouses by 1577 or 1578.

Virtually nothing is known for certain about either the ownership of these places or what was done to make them playhouses. Nor is much known about how their owners contrived to carry on theatrical enterprises for twenty years and more on the home ground of mayors and aldermen who disapproved of such things.

One writer noted in 1576 that people paid to see plays at the Bel Savage by paying a penny to get in, another to go into 'the scaffold', and yet another for 'quiet standing'. People were doing as much to see plays in the purpose-built public playhouses twenty-five years later. The implication must be that so far as spectators were concerned, at least one of the inn/playhouses belonged to the same architectural and financial scheme of things as places like the Swan, Globe and Fortune. Another writer noted c. 1590 that the stage at the Bel Savage was high enough for a person 'to be in danger to break his neck' should he fall off it, and implied that the stage at the Bull was less dangerous. In 1579, incidentally, Stephen Gosson, who had written plays but now despised them, conceded that the Bel Savage and Bull could mount 'sweet plays'.

The Queen's men were at the Bull and the Bell during their first year, 1583, and they wanted to be at one of the inn/playhouses during their second. Lord Strange's men were at the Cross Keys in 1589, and the Lord Chamberlain's wanted to be there in 1594. The famous comedian, Richard Tarlton, sang his last 'theme' at the Bel Savage in, presumably, 1588.

From 1575 to 1590, the masters of defence (teachers of fencing) mounted at least nineteen of their 'prizes' at the Bull – public displays in which their students qualified as free scholars, provosts or masters of 'the noble science'. They mounted at least five at the Bel Savage and none at the other two inn/playhouses.

The Bel Savage, Cross Keys and Bell were all destroyed in the great fire of 1666. The Bull was not, and it survived until 1866, the last of the twenty-three Shakespearean playhouses.[2]

[1] On which is a memorial to the adjoining Cross Keys.
[2] On Ogilby and Morgan's map (1676), the yard of the Bull is perhaps 65 feet east to west by 25 feet north to south. The Bel Savage and Cross Keys had been rebuilt by then. The yard of the rebuilt Cross Keys is shown as 50 feet or so east by about 32 feet north to south. The rebuilt Bel Savage had two yards; the one closer to Ludgate Hill is shown as about 32 feet east to west by about 100 feet north to south; and the one farther north is about 82 feet north to south and some 63 feet dwindling to 38 feet east to west.

201   Fencers use the Bel Savage and Bull for their prizes, 1568, 1575

BL, Sloane MS 2530, fos. (a) 10, 33–4; (b) 11. Transcribed in Berry, *The Noble Science*; see also Brownstein, 'A Record of London Inn-Playhouses from *c.* 1565–1590', 17–24; Anglin, 'The Schools of Defense in Elizabethan London,' 393–410.

These entries are the first dated allusions to the Bel Savage and the Bull as places where the fencers mounted their prizes, but they could have used the Bel Savage for them as early as 1565 and the Bull as early as 1573. If prizes could be played in these places, perhaps plays could have been, too. All but two of the prizes mentioned in the manuscript as having been played in London from 1575 to 1590 were played at theatrical places: the Bull (19), the Bel Savage (5), and two purpose-built public playhouses – the Theatre and the Curtain (13).

(a) The Bel Savage, 13 June 1568

William Mucklowe played his provost's prize at the Bel Savage in Fleet Street with two provosts with three kind of weapons, the long sword, the sword and buckler, and the staff ... [and was admitted] as a provost ... the 13th day of June in the year of our Lord God 1568.

(b) The Bull, 7 June 1575

Isaac Kennard played his provost's prize at the Bull within Bishopsgate the 7th of June at three weapons, the long sword, the sword and buckler, and the staff ... in *anno domini* 1575.

202 The Bel Savage is in business as a playhouse, 1575

Gascoigne, *Glasse of Governement* (1575), the prologue

What man hath mind to hear a worthy jest,
Or seeks to feed his eye with vain delight,
That man is much unmeet to be a guest
At such a feast as I prepare this night.
Who list lay out some pence in such a mart,
Bel Savage fair were fittest for his purse.
I list not so to misbestow mine art,
I have best wares; what need I then show worse?
An interlude may make you laugh your fill,
Italian toys[1] are full of pleasant sport.

[1] *i.e.*, English plays in the manner of Terence and his Italian imitators, like Gascoigne's own *Supposes* (1573), a version of Ariosto's *I Suppositi*.

203 How spectators paid to see plays at the Bel Savage, 1576

Lambarde, *A Perambulation of Kent* (1576), sig. 4I–4Iv. 'The matter' mentioned below was the collecting of money from pilgrims at a shrine before the reformation.

The matter was so handled [by the monks at the shrine of St Rumwald in the abbey at Boxley in Kent] that without treble oblation (that is to say, first to the [pilgrim's] confessor, then to St Rumwald, and lastly to the gracious rood [of the abbey]) the poor pilgrims could not assure themselves of any good gained by all their labour. No more than such as go to Paris Garden [a bear-baiting ring], the Bel Savage, or some other such common place to behold bear-baiting, interludes, or fence play can account of any pleasant spectacle unless they first pay one penny at the gate, another at the entry of the scaffold, and the third for a quiet standing.

204 The Bell is in business as a playhouse, 12–21 February (Shrovetide) 1577

PRO, AO3/907/5, p. 272. Transcribed in *Office of the Revels, Eliz. I*, 277

[The Office of the Revels paid] for the carriage of the parts of the well counterfeit from the Bell in Gracious [*i.e.* Gracechurch] Street to St John's[1] to be performed for the play of Cutwell, 10d.

[1] The dissolved Priory of St John of Jerusalem in Clerkenwell, where the Office of the Revels was and 'our court plays have been . . . rehearsed, perfected, and corrected before they come to the public view of the prince and nobility' (Heywood, *Apology for Actors*, 1608, 40).

205 All four inns are probably in business as playhouses, 24 August 1578

Stockwood, *A Sermon Preached at Paules Crosse* . . . *24 of August 1578*, 24, 135–6

If you resort to the Theatre, the Curtain and other places of plays in the City, you shall on the Lord's day have these places, with many other that I cannot reckon, so full as possibly they can throng . . . If playing in the Theatre or any other place in London, as there are by six that I know too many, be any of the Lord's ways . . . then not only it may but ought to be used, but if it be any of the ways of man, it is no work for the Lord's Sabbath.

The six places should have been the Theatre, the Curtain and the four inns.

206 Italian tourists are to take note of playing at the Bull, 1578

Florio, *First Fruites* (1578), sig. A1

[In an English–Italian phrase book:] Where shall we go? To a play at the Bull, or else to some other place.

207 James Burbage attends a play at the Cross Keys, 23 June 1579

(a, b) PRO, C24/226/10/pt 1. Transcribed in Wallace, *First London Theatre*, esp. 82, 89–90; see also Berry, 'A Handlist of Documents About the Theatre in Shoreditch', 37 (*C–18*)

These statements are from depositions in Burbage's lawsuit against Margaret Brayne (the widow of his partner in the Theatre) and her supporter, Robert Miles. See **281**, **282**, **292–93**, etc.

(a) Burbage's question for a witness, John Hynd, 1592

Did you . . . about twelve years past, in *anno* 1579 the 23rd of June about two of the clock in the afternoon, send the sheriff, his officer, unto the Cross Keys in Gracious Street, being then the dwelling house of Richard Ibotson, citizen and brewer of London [the inn-holder], and there by virtue of precept to attach the body of this complainant [Burbage] for the sum of £5 1s 1d?

(b) Hynd's reply, 24 July 1592

True it is, he, this deponent, about twelve years past, which as he thinketh was in *anno domini* 1579 and, as he taketh it, about the 23rd day of June in the afternoon, did cause one Saunders, then one of the sergeants at mace to the sheriff of London or his yeoman, to arrest and attach the body of the now complainant [Burbage] as he came down Gracious Street towards the Cross Keys there to a play, for the sum of £5 1s 1d.

208 A despiser of plays approves of two at the Bel Savage and two at the Bull, 22 July 1579

Gosson, *Schoole of Abuse*, 1579 (STC 12097.5; SR, 22 July 1579), fos. 22v–23

Before he learned the error of his ways, Gosson wrote plays himself, which 'are daily to be seen upon stages as sufficient witnesses of mine own folly' ('To the Reader', sig.*6v).

And as some of the players are far from abuse, so some of their plays are without rebuke, which are as easily remembered as quickly reckoned: the two prose books played at the Bel Savage, where you shall find never a word without wit, never a line without pith, never a letter placed in vain; the *Jew* and *Ptolemy* shown at the Bull, the one representing the greediness of worldly choosers and bloody minds of usurers, the other very lively describing how seditious estates . . . are overthrown, neither with amorous gesture wounding the eye, nor with slovenly talk hurting the ears of the chaste hearers.

Gosson goes on to commend two more at the Theatre, one of which was his own (see **262**).

209 A fencer wants to play a prize at the Bull, 1–24 July 1582

CLRO, Remembrancia, I, (a) 359, 383; (b) 384. Transcribed in MSC, I.55-7

(a) The Earl of Warwick to the Lord Mayor of London, 1 July 1582

I am to request you and the rest whom it doth appertain that they would give licence to my servant, John David, this bearer, to play his provost prizes in his science and profession of defence [fencing] at the Bull in Bishopsgate Street or some other convenient place to be assigned within the liberties of London.

David took this letter to Guildhall, and, assuming that the Lord Mayor would agree, posted bills mentioning not only the Bull but the Earl. Because the Lord Mayor did not hasten to agree, the Earl wrote again, testily, on 23 July.

(b) The Lord Mayor replies to the Earl of Warwick, 24 July 1582

I did not expulse your servant from playing his prize, . . . only I did restrain him from playing in an inn, which was somewhat too close for infection, and appointed him to play in an open place of the Leadenhall, . . . which licence . . . he might well have used . . . before increase of peril by heat of the year. But about fourteen days afterward, when I thought he had taken the benefit and effect of my grant, the infection growing, . . . I was indeed enforced to restrain him from gathering public assembly of people to his play within the City, and never the less did allow him in the open fields . . . [Now,] I have herein yet further done for your servant what I may, that is that if he may obtain lawfully to play at the Theatre or other open place out of the City, he hath and shall have my permission with his company, drums, and show to pass openly through the City, being not upon the Sunday, which is as much as I may justify in this season, and for that cause I have with his own consent appointed him Monday next [July 30].[1]

[1] Although BL, MS Sloane 2530 records four prizes from 1 July to 10 August 1582 (fo. 12), it records neither a prize on 30 July nor a man named David in any connection.

210 The Queen's men are allowed to play at the Bull and Bell, 28 November 1583

(a) CLRO, Repertory 21, fo. 10; (b) BL, Lansdowne MS 20, fos. 36, 38v. (b) transcribed in MSC, I. 168; see ES IV, 298–302. Wallace mentioned (*First London Theatre*, 11) but did not publish the licence quoted in (a).

(a) The Queen's men may play at the Bull and the Bell, 28 November 1583

[In the margin:] Her Majesty's players licensed to play. [The text:] Item: This day, at the contemplation of the letters of the Right Honourable the Lords and others of her majesty's most honourable privy council written to this court [of aldermen] in the behalf of Robert Wilson, John Dutton, Richard Tarlton, John Laneham, John Bentley, Toby Mills, John Towne, John Synger, Lionel Cooke, John Garland, John Adams and William Johnson, her majesty's players, that, forasmuch as almighty God hath at this present stayed the infection of the plague within this city: that they may be suffered to play within the liberties thereof upon the work days only betwixt this and Shrovetide next [1–3 March 1584].

In consideration whereof, it is ordered by this court that the said Robert Wilson [etc.[1]] ... be permitted to use the exercise of playing at the signs of the Bull in Bishopsgate Street and the sign of the Bell in Gracious Street and nowhere else within this city betwixt this and Shrovetide next upon the holidays and upon the Wednesdays and Saturdays only, not in time of divine service, provided they play not upon the Sabbath days, nor upon any other days [of religious obligation], nor play any matter tending to the dishonour of almighty God, nor the disturbance of the quiet peace and government of this city. And that precepts be forthwith directed to every alderman within this city that they take present order that from henceforth no other players be suffered to play, or set up bills for players, within this city, nor the said players to play in any other place than [*i.e.* or] any other days than aforesaid.

[1] Here follows the same list of players as above.

(b) The City notes the result, *c.* November 1584

[When the Queen's men asked the privy council for a place to play a year later, the City wrote to the council:] It may please you to know that the last year when such toleration was of the Queen's players only, all the places of playing were filled with men calling themselves the Queen's players.

211   Richard Tarlton plays at the Bull and the Bell and jests at the Cross Keys, 1583–1588

Tarltons Jests (1613), sigs. (a) B2, C2v; (b) C2–C2v. Tarlton was the most famous comic of his time. He belonged to the Queen's men from their inception in 1583 until his death in 1588.

(a) At the Bull

At the Bull in Bishopsgate Street, where the Queen's men oftentimes played, Tarlton coming on the stage, one from the gallery threw a pippin at him . . . At the Bull at Bishopsgate was a play of Henry the Fifth wherein the judge was to take a box on the ear, and because he was absent that should take the blow, Tarlton himself (ever forward to please) took upon him to play the same judge, besides his own part of the clown.

(b) At the Bell and Cross Keys

There was one Banks in the time of Tarlton, who served the Earl of Essex and had a horse of strange qualities, and being at the Cross Keys in Gracious Street getting money with him, as he was mightily resorted to, Tarlton (with his fellows) playing at the Bell by, came into the Cross Keys (amongst many people) to see fashions, which Banks perceiving, to make people laugh, says, 'Signior', to his horse, 'go fetch me the veriest fool in the company.' The jade comes immediately and with his mouth draws Tarlton forth. Tarlton . . . said nothing but 'God a mercy, horse'. In the end, Tarlton, seeing the people laugh so, was angry inwardly and said, 'Sir, had I power of your horse as you have, I would do more than that.' 'What ere it be', said Banks to please him, 'I will charge him to do it.' 'Then', says Tarlton, 'charge him to bring me the veriest whoremaster in this company.' 'He shall,' says Banks. 'Signior,' says he, 'bring Master Tarlton here the veriest whoremaster in the company.' The horse leads his master to him. Then 'God a mercy, indeed,' says Tarlton. The people had much ado to keep the peace.

212 Tarlton sings his last 'theme' at the Bel Savage, c. 1588

The Company of Stationers of London, Register, fo. 246v. Transcribed in Arber, *Transcript of the Registers of the Company of Stationers of London* II, 526.

One of Tarlton's turns was to sing songs extempre on 'themes' that his audiences gave him. This is a licence of 2 August 1589 for a book of which no copy exists.

Licensed unto him [Henry Kirkham, a publisher] . . . a sorrowful new sonnet intituled Tarlton's recantation upon this theme given him by a gentleman at the Bel Savage without Ludgate, 'now or else never', being the last theme he sang.

213 The Lord Mayor stops playing in the City, but Strange's men defy him at the Cross Keys, 6 November 1589

BL, Lansdowne MS 60, fo. 47. Transcribed MSC, I. 180

[The Lord Mayor wrote to the privy council:] Where, by a letter of your lordship's [Lord Burghley, Secretary of State] directed to Mr [Richard] Young [a justice of Middlesex], it appeared unto me that it was your honour's pleasure I should give order for the stay of all plays within the City, in that Mr Tilney [Master of the Revels] did utterly mislike the same: according to which your lordship's good pleasure I presently sent for such players as I could hear of, so as there appeared yesterday before me the Lord Admiral's and the Lord Strange's players, to whom I specially gave in charge and required them in her majesty's name to forbear playing until further order might be given for their allowance in that respect. Whereupon the Lord Admiral's players very dutifully obeyed, but the others, in very contemptuous manner departing from me, went to the Cross Keys and played that afternoon, to the great offence of the better sort that knew they were prohibited by order from your lordship. Which as I might not suffer, so I sent for the said contemptuous persons who, having no reason to allege for their contempt, I could do no less but this evening commit some of them to one of the compters [prisons] and do mean according to your lordship's direction to prohibit all playing until your lordship's pleasure therein be further known.

214 The Bel Savage has a perilously high stage c. 1590

Silver, *Paradoxes of Defence* (1599), 66; see Berry, *The Noble Science*, 12 n. 5

[George Silver and his brother, Toby, challenged the two leading Italian teachers of fencing in London, Vincentio Saviolo and one Ieronimo,] to play with them at the single rapier, rapier and dagger, the single dagger, the single sword, the sword and target, the sword and buckler, and two-hand sword, the staff, battle axe, and morris pike to be played at the Bel Savage upon the scaffold, where he that went in his fight faster back than he ought, of Englishman or Italian, should be in danger to break his neck off the scaffold. We caused to that effect five- or six-score bills of challenge to be printed and set up.

The Silvers duly arrived at the Bel Savage 'with all these weapons . . . and a multitude of people there to behold the fight', but the Italians did not.

215 Diabolical events take place on the stage at the Bel Savage, c. 1590

Prynne, *Histrio-Mastix* (1633), fo. 556

[In a long and strenuous attack on drama for which Prynne famously lost his ears, he reported:] The visibile apparition of the devil on the stage at the Bel Savage playhouse in Queen Elizabeth's days (to the great amazement both of the actors and spectators), whiles they were there profanely playing the *History of Faustus*, the truth of which I have heard from many now alive who well remember it, there being some distracted with that fearful sight.

216 The Bull is noted as a place where actors speak fustian, 1592

Figueiro, *The Spaniards Monarchie*, translated from Spanish by H. O. (1592), sig. A2–A2v

H.O.'s remarks below about 'words running on the letter' and 'a fig for a Spaniard' allude to a work of 1591, reissued in 1592, G.B., *A Fig for the Spaniard*, 'or Spanish Spirits, wherein are lively portrayed the damnable deeds, miserable murders, and monstrous massacres of the cursed Spaniard'. H.O. thinks this title reminiscent of literary devices used in plays at the Bull and spuriously apt for his translation because of the surname of his author.

[The translated work] is no feather of fancy . . . If you expect extraordinary elegancy, I answer that a translator is bound rather to search fit words to express his author's meaning than invent words running on the letter to content over curious fancies, which I contemn as dictionary method. And thus much can I assure you, that albeit it [the work] hath no title fetched from the Bull within Bishopsgate, as a fig for a Spaniard, yet doth it discover so succinctly and briefly a Spanish imitation of Machiavellised axioms, that what other volumes at large, this in a less doth plainly demonstrate.

217 Francis and Anthony Bacon's mother warns Anthony of the dangers of living near the Bull, c. 1 May 1594

Lambeth Palace, MS 650, fo. 187. Transcribed in Berry, 'Chambers, the Bull, and the Bacons', 35–42. Lady Anne Bacon wrote from her house at Gorhambury in Hertfordshire to Anthony, who had just moved to Bishopsgate Street.

Having some speech with Mr Henshew [a clergyman] after you went hence touching your house taken in Bishopsgate Street, he very soberly said, 'God give him wit to be there, for this last plague that street was much visited and so was Coleman Street, large and wide streets both.' And asking him what ministry there, he answered it was very mean, the minister there but ignorant and, as commonly withal, careless, and he thought you should find the people thereafter given to voluptuousness and the more to make them so having but mean or no edifying instruction. The Bull inn there, with continual interludes, had even infected the inhabitants there with corrupt and lewd dispositions, and, so accounted of, he was even sorry on your behalf. I promise you, son, it hath been in my mind since with grief and fear for you and yours to dwell so dangerously every way. I marvel you did not first consider of the ministry as most of all needful, considering that street, and then to have so near a place haunted with such pernicious and obscene plays and [a] theatre able to poison the very Godly, and do what you can, your servants shall be enticed and spoiled.

218 The Lord Chamberlain's men want to continue playing at the Cross Keys, 8 October 1594

CLRO, Remembrancia, II, 33. Transcribed in MSC, 1.73. Lord Hunsdon, the Lord Chamberlain, wrote the letter below to the Lord Mayor.

Where my now company of players have been accustomed for the better exercise of their quality, and for the service of her majesty if need so require, to play this winter time within the City at the Cross Keys in Gracious Street: these are to require and pray your lordship (the time being such as, thanks be to God, there is now no danger of the sickness) to permit and suffer them so to do. The which I pray you the rather to do for that they have undertaken to me that, where heretofore they began not their plays till towards four o'clock, they will now begin at two and have done between four and five and will not use any drums or trumpets at all for the calling of people together and shall be contributories to the poor of the parish where they play, according to their abilities.

219 City authorities suppress the playhouses in the four inns, *c.* 1596

(a) Rawlidge, *A Monster Late Found Out and Discovered* (1628), sig. A3; (b) Lambarde, *A Perambulation of Kent* (1596), 233

It is usually said that the authorities of the City managed to suppress the four inns in 1596, though no document expressly says so. The evidence consists of the two remarks below and the remarks of a German tourist on 26 June 1596 and a Dutch one in about that year, who mentioned four public playhouses and no theatrical inns (see **352, 353**).

(a) The City did suppress the four inns

Whereupon some of the pious magistrates made humble suit to the late Queen Elizabeth . . . and her privy council and obtained leave from her majesty to thrust those players out of the City and to pull down the dicing houses, which accordingly was effected; and the playhouses in Gracious Street [the Bell and the Cross Keys], Bishopsgate Street [the Bull], nigh Paul's (that on Ludgate Hill) [the Bel Savage], the White Friars[1] were put down and other lewd houses quite suppressed within the liberties by the care of those religious senators.

[1] No playhouse, it seems, existed in Whitefriars in the time of the four inns. If the writer meant Blackfriars instead, the remark points to 1596. For in that year James Burbage bought a building there and erected the second Blackfriars playhouse in it (q.v.), but its neighbours and the authorities prevented him and his successors from allowing adult actors to use it until 1609.

(b) Three of them were out of business by 1596

[In the edition of his book dated 1576, Lambarde wrote of] such as go to Paris Garden [a bear-baiting ring], the Bel Savage, or some other such common place to behold bear-baiting, interludes, or fence play . . . [see 203]

[In the edition dated 1596, he wrote instead of] such as go to Paris Garden, the Bel Savage, or Theatre to behold bear-baiting, interludes or fence play.

220 The privy council administers a *coup de grâce* 22 June 1600

PRO, PC2/25, p. 223. Transcribed in *APC, 1599–1600*, 397

[In the Order decreeing that there should be one playhouse on the south bank of the Thames and one on the north (see 58), the privy council added:] And especially it is forbidden that any stage plays shall be played (as sometimes they have been) in any common inn for public assembly in or near about the City.

221 The playhouses in the four inns are remembered, and vestiges survive, 1664

Flecknoe, 'A short Discourse of the English Stage' (1664), sigs. G4v–5

From which [the Roman] time to the last age they acted nothing here but plays of the Holy Scripture, or saints' lives, and that without any certain theatres or set companies, till about the beginning of Queen Elizabeth's reign they began here to assemble into companies and set up theatres, first in the City (as in the inn-yards of the Cross Keys and Bull in Grace[church] and Bishopsgate Street[s] at this day is to be seen), till that fanatic spirit which then began with the stage and after ended with the throne banished them thence into the suburbs.

XXI St Paul's

St Paul's was a private playhouse having to do with old St Paul's Cathedral. Its actors were the ten boys who belonged to the choir school and were an important part of the musical establishment of the cathedral. Because, when they became skilful in music, they joined the lessons of the boys in the famous St Paul's grammar school, perhaps the grammar school boys could sometimes assist in the playhouse.

The playhouse was apparently in the almonry, where the master of the choristers (who was also the almoner) lived along with, presumably, his charges. The north wall of the almonry was at the south wall of the cathedral nave, between, on the west, the 'lesser' south door of the cathedral and, on the east, the west wall of the cloisters. The playhouse was probably at the north end of the almonry and in the middle storey, above rooms at street level and below others in the attic. (Both its great rivals, the first and second Blackfriars playhouses, were also in upper storeys.) People going to plays there would have proceeded along the east–west public street then and now called St Paul's Churchyard, turned north into the lane that led to the lesser south door, and at the top, near the cathedral wall, turned east into the almonry. The site of the playhouse is now mostly in the new cathedral: the middle of the north wall of the playhouse is probably on the north side of the south aisle of the nave, some 80 feet along from the top of the stairs at the west front.

Several contemporaries described the stage of the playhouse as small. The room where the playhouse probably was could have been about 29 feet west to east at the north end, but it could have been much bigger north to south. The boys could walk mostly unobserved between performances in the cathedral and the playhouse. For their master had the use of a hidden passage 4 feet wide that led from the 'backside' of the almonry, through a door in the cloister wall, and into the cloisters, from which a small door led into the nave at the crossing and a large door into the south transept.[1]

Boys from St Paul's performed at least one play in medieval times, and boys from the grammar school performed plays for dignitaries in the 1520s. The proper history of St Paul's as a theatrical entity in Shakespearean times, however, begins with the choristers' performances for dignitaries in the 1550s under their master, Sebastian Westcott, and the playwright, John Heywood. Neither Westcott nor Heywood accepted the Protestant dispensation in the country from 1558 onwards. Heywood left the country, but Westcott remained, and, despite some difficult periods, he flourished. From 1559 until his death in April 1582, he led his choristers in twenty-seven performances of plays at court, many more than any of the other companies of the time performed there.

The first notices that the boys were performing plays not only at court but publicly in London occur in December 1575 and December 1578, when, presumably, they were playing at their playhouse.[2] After Westcott's death in 1582, Thomas Bendbowe controlled the boys for the time being and in 1583 apparently had them playing jointly with boy choristers from two other choirs at the first Blackfriars playhouse (see the introduction to that playhouse). In 1584 the cathedral appointed Thomas Gyles as Westcott's successor.

The boys of St Paul's ceased to appear at court after three plays there during the Christmas season of 1589–90, and by 4 October 1591 they had ceased playing publicly. They are said to have been suppressed for performing plays having to do with Martin Marprelate, but the evidence for the idea is not overwhelming. Martin was the pseudonym of witty writers who mocked the ecclesiastical establishment in a series of tracts issued from 1588 to 1590. The bishops hired writers to reply in kind, who, in addition to tracts, wrote some anti-Martin plays. John Lyly probably wrote at least one anti-Martin tract, *Pappe with an Hatchet*, in which he proposed 'a fine tragedy' attacking Martin, and all but one of his surviving plays belonged to the boys of St Paul's. Thomas Nashe probably wrote anti-Martin tracts, too, in which he said that he was writing an anti-Martin play, *The May-game of Martinisme*, but he also said that he was still writing it in July 1590, long after a company could have got permission to play it. Although the anti-Martinists were defending the establishment, the privy council decided in November 1589 that any theatrical meddling in 'matters of divinity and of state' was 'unfit to be suffered'. The council, therefore, set up a scheme of censorship to prevent such meddling, but it did not order St Paul's or any other playhouse to close. Moreover, nobody said that any play of Lyly's, or any other play associated with St Paul's, attacked Martin, and none of Lyly's or Nashe's recognised plays has to do with Martin.

Gyles being terminally ill in the spring of 1599, St Paul's boys acquired a new master, Edward Peers,[3] and in the autumn they were acting publicly again. They were probably in their former playhouse and were financed by the Earl of Derby, an active patron of a company at the Boar's Head who had 'busied' himself in the summer of 1599 'only in penning comedies for the common players'.[4] From the Christmas season of 1600–1 onwards, the boys were also back at court, and when on 11 March 1601 the privy council suppressed playing for Lent, it had in mind 'especially' St Paul's and Blackfriars.[5]

Peers collected payments for these performances at court, but in 1603 he said that his role was teaching the boys, not producing plays. Plays were the province of a person whom Peers took as a partner. One such was Thomas Woodford, who would later have to do with the Whitefriars and Red Bull playhouses. Woodford was mounting plays at St Paul's from at least the end of 1602 to the middle of 1603, perhaps until December 1604, when he and Peers came to blows, or even the autumn of 1605, when he sued Peers for assaulting him. (In June 1606 he won £13 6s 8d from Peers in damages.) From at least the spring of 1606, Peers' theatrical partner was Edward Kirkham, who until recently had been one of the managers of the children's company at the second Blackfriars playhouse.[6]

The boys of St Paul's apparently ceased performing plays professionally once and for all in the summer of 1606. They performed their last recorded play at court then, and, so far as direct evidence goes, they did not play publicly after that, either.[7] Why they gave up playing is a mystery. Peers's rivals thought he could have resumed, for from 1608 to 1610 two of them bribed him to keep his playhouse closed.

St Paul's was notable for the quality of its playwrights. In addition to introducing all but one of Lyly's plays during its first period, up to *c.* 1590, it introduced plays by Marston and Middleton especially but also by Webster, Chapman, Dekker, Jonson and Beaumont among others during its second, from 1599 to 1606.

---

[1] Berry, 'Where was the Playhouse in which the Boy Choristers of St Paul's Performed Plays?'
[2] Moreover, in 1582, Gosson mentioned a play, *Cupid and Psyche*, as 'played at Paul's', probably the play

of the same title that the boys had played at Court during Christmas 1581–2 (*Plays Confuted in five Actions*, SR 6 April 1582, p. 188).
[3] Gair, 'The Conditions of Appointment for Masters of Choristers at Paul's (1553–1613)', 121–2. Marston's play, *Antonio and Mellida*, published in 1601 (SR 24 October 1601) as 'sundry times acted by the children of Paul's', contains topical allusions suggesting that it was written in the summer of 1599 (*ES*, III, 429–30).
[4] Berry, *Boar's Head Playhouse*, 34.
[5] PRO, PC2/26, p. 119, transcribed in *APC, 1600–1*, 218. Lent had begun on 25 February and Easter was on 12 April.
[6] Ingram believes that Woodford was not a manager of plays at St Paul's, merely the middle-man who bought one play for the place in 1603: 'The Playhouse as an Investment, 1607–1614', 227–8. Note, however, statements by Woodford and Peers (235) and Kirkham's becoming such a manager in 1606 (237).
[7] Because many plays produced at St Paul's were printed in 1607–8, one supposes that Peers had no further theatrical use for them, hence that the playhouse was closed. Gair, however, would have public performances continue until 'mid to late 1608'. In a sermon preached at Paul's Cross on 14 February 1608 (he argues), William Crashaw attacked one St Paul's play published in 1607 and so caused the authorities eventually to close the playhouse. The play was the anonymous *The Puritan* (SR 6 August 1607), in which two hypocrites bear the names of London churches. Crashaw described this aspect of the play as an example of abusing 'God himself . . . not on the stage only but even in print'. He did not, however, mention St Paul's or demand the closing of playhouses. After expressions of outrage, he demanded only that provincial magistrates end playing on Sundays, 'which generally in the country is their [actors'] play day'. See Crashaw, *Sermon Preached at the Crosse, Feb. xiiii, 1607[/8]*: 171–2; and Gair, *Children of Paul's*, 162–73.

222   Sebastian Westcott and John Heywood take boys to the court of Princess Elizabeth, 13 February 1552

Household Accounts of Princess Elizabeth. 37. The boys must have been from the choir school of St Paul's, since Westcott, the master of the choir school, was responsible for them.

Paid in reward to the King's majesty's [Edward VI's] drummer and fife, the 13th of February [1552], £1; Mr Heywood, £1 10s; and to Sebastian, towards the charge of the children, with the carriage of the players' garments, £4 19s. In the whole, as by warrant appeareth, £7 9s.

223   Westcott and Heywood lead the boys of St Paul's in a performance before Queen Elizabeth, 7 August 1559

BL, Cotton MS, Vitellius F.V, fo. 108v. Transcribed in Machyn, *Diary* 206. This was the first of twenty-seven plays the boys of St Paul's acted before the Queen from 1559 to 1582 under Westcott.

[The Earl of Arundel entertained the Queen at Nonsuch Palace with] At night . . . a play of the children of Paul's and their master, S[ebastian Wescott], Master Philips,[1] and Master Heywood, and after, a great banquet . . . with drums and flutes . . . till three in the m[orning].

[1] A Master Philip was an organist at St Paul's in 1557, and a John Philip wrote a play, *Patient Grissell* (c. 1566). See *ES*, II, 13 and note.

224 Westcott has the right to draft boys into his choir from anywhere, 30 June 1560

York, City Archives Dept., House Books XXIV, fo. 241. Transcribed in Raine, *York Civic Records*, 29.

The document is a letter from the Queen 'to all the deans, provosts, masters of colleges, and all ecclesiastical ministers, and to all other our officers, ministers, and subjects to whom in this it shall appertain'. It survives in York because, presumably, Westcott presented it there and an official copied it for the municipal records. It appears among documents dated in April and May 1571. Westcott's successor, Thomas Gyles, also had such a licence, dated 26 April 1585 (BL, Sloane MS 2035b, fo. 73; transcribed in Wallace, 'Children of the Chapel', 181).

Where this bearer, our servant Sebastian Westcott, master of the children of our church of Paul's, is by us appointed to repair unto sundry parts of this our realm for the taking up of certain apt children that may by his good education be framed in singing so as they may be meet to serve us in this behalf when we shall call for them: our pleasure and express commandment is that you, and every of you, to whom in this case it appertaineth be both aiding and assisting unto our said servant to the best of your powers in the doing hereof, and also suffer him quietly to have from you, without any your interruption, such children as he shall take up in any our cathedral or collegiate churches or other places within our realm. Whereof fail ye not as ye tender our favour and will answer for the contrary.

225 One of Westcott's boys is 'stolen', and the privy council tries seriously to find him, 3 December 1575

PRO, PC2/10, p. 408. Transcribed in *APC, 1575–7*, 56.

A letter to the Master of the Rolls and Master Dr Wilson [one of the masters of Requests: because] one of Sebastian's boys, being one of his principal players, is lately stolen and conveyed from him, they be required to examine such persons as Sebastian holdeth suspected and proceed with such as be found faulty according to law.

226 The London authorities find that the boys play for great gain at St Paul's, 8 December 1575

CLRO, Repertory 19, fo. 18. Transcribed in Hillebrand, 'Sebastian Westcote', 573. This is the earliest notice that the boys of St Paul's were playing professionally and in a playhouse having to do with the cathedral.

This court [of the common council of London] is informed that one Sebastian [Westcott], that will not communicate with the Church of England, keepeth plays and resort of the people to great gain and peril of the corrupting of the children with papistry. And, therefore, Master Norton[1] is appointed to go to the Dean of Paul's and to give him notice of that disorder and to pray him to give such remedy

310   Playhouses, 1560–1660

therein, within his jurisdiction, as he shall see meet for Christian religion and good order.

[1] An officer of the 'court', not one of the aldermen who attended its meetings regularly.

227 The privy council includes St Paul's boys among companies of professional players, 24 December 1578

PRO, PC 2/12, p. 349. Transcribed in *APC*, 1577–78, 436

[The privy council ordered that] A letter [be sent] to the Lord Mayor, etc., requiring him to suffer the children of her majesty's chapel, the servants of the Lord Chamberlain, the Earl of Warwick, the Earl of Leicester, the Earl of Essex, and the children of Paul's, and no companies else, to exercise playing within the City, whom their lordships [i.e. the privy council] have only allowed thereunto by reason that the companies aforenamed are appointed to play this time of Christmas before her majesty.

228 The playhouse at St Paul's and the Marprelate Controversy, October–November 1589

(a) Nashe?, *Returne of the renowned Caualiero Pasquill of England*, sig. D3v; (b) Lyly?, *Pappe with an Hatchet*, sigs. D2v, 3; (c) Harvey, 'An advertisement for Papp-Hatchett and Martin Mar-prelate', 75, 134; (d) BL, MS Lansdowne 60, fo. 47; (e) PRO, PC 2/16, pp. 388–9. Transcribed in (d) MSC, I. 180–1 (e) *APC*, 1589–90, 214–15

Following is much of the evidence used to argue that playwrights (mainly Nashe and Lyly) and players took the bishops' side in attacking Martin Marprelate and that the closing of the playhouse at St Paul's in 1590–1 resulted. See also **230**. The tracts quoted in (a) and (b) were printed anonymously.

(a) Nashe? 20 October 1589?[1]

[Pasquil (i.e. a lampoon) says that old comedy (knock-about stuff like the comedy in the plays of Aristophanes) has attacked Martin in London and adds:] I have a tale to tell her [i.e. old comedy] in her ear of the sly practice that was used in restraining of her.

[1] Pasquil lays down a mock challenge with a mock date, '20 Octobris, anno millimo, quillimo, trillimo' (sig. D3v), that may relate to the real one.

(b) Lyly? end of October 1589?[1]

Would those comedies might be allowed to be played that are penned, and then I am sure he [Martin] would be deciphered and so, perhaps, discouraged ... Would it not be a fine tragedy, when ... he that seeks to pull down those that are set in authority above him should be hoisted upon a tree above all other. [In the margin:]

If it be showed at Paul's, it will cost you 4d; at the Theatre 2d; at St Thomas à Waterings[2] nothing.

[1] *Pappe* must have appeared before the next item, in which Harvey (who assumed that Lyly had written *Pappe*) often mentioned and even quoted it.
[2] St Thomas à Waterings was a place of execution for Surrey, two miles south of London Bridge near the Old Kent Road. The chief writer of the Marprelate tracts, John Penry, was actually hanged there in 1593 (see Wheatley, *London Past and Present* III, 374–5).

(c) Harvey, 5 November 1589[1]

[Harvey did not defend Martin, but he did attack Lyly and Nashe. Had he been Martin, he would have been pleased that ecclesiastical officials should] entertain such an odd, light-headed fellow for their defence [as Lyly], a professed jester, a hickscorner,[2] a scoff-master, a playmonger, an interluder, once the foil of Oxford, now the stale of London . . . Martin [is] menaced with a comedy . . . All you that tender the preservation of your good names were best to please Pap-Hatchet and fee Euphues betimes for fear lest he be moved, or some one of his apes [*i.e.* perhaps Nashe] hired, to make a play of you. And then is your credit quite undone forever and ever. Such is the public reputation of their plays. He must needs be *discouraged* whom they *decipher*. Better anger an hundred other than two such, that have the stage at commandment and can furnish out vices and devils at their pleasure.

[1] Harvey dated this part of his book as 5 November 1589 (p. 140).
[2] One who scoffs, especially at religion.

(d) The Lord Mayor to Lord Burghley, 6 November 1589

[The Lord Mayor ordered playing in London to stop because] by a letter of your lordship's . . . it appeared unto me that it was your honour's pleasure I should give order for the stay of all plays within the City, in that Mr Tilney did utterly mislike the same. [See **48**. Tilney was the Master of the Revels.]

(e) The privy council Order, 12 November 1589

The privy council ordered that letters be written to the Archbishop of Canterbury, the Lord Mayor of London, and the Master of the Revels requiring them to appoint a committee to vet plays meant for performance in and about London. For the full text of the letters see **49**. The council gave its reasons as follows.

[The letter to the Archbishop was to explain that] there hath grown some inconvenience by common plays and interludes in and about the City of London in [that] the players take upon them to handle in their plays certain matters of divinity and of state unfit to be suffered.

[The letter to the Lord Mayor was to refer to] the plays daily exercised and presented publicly in and about the City of London, wherein the players take upon them, without judgement or decorum, to handle matters of divinity and state.

[And the letter to the Master of the Revels was to say that the committee should] strike out or reform such parts and matters as they shall find unfit and undecent to be handled in plays, both for divinity and state.

[If players did not conform,] they shall be not only severely punished but made [in]capable of the exercise of their profession forever hereafter.

229 Plays are no longer being performed publicly at St Paul's, 1591, 1596

(a) Lyly, *Endymion* (SR, 4 October 1591), the printer to the reader, sig. A2; (b) Nashe, *Have with you to Saffron Walden*, sig. G4v

In (b) Nashe supposes that his antagonist, Gabriel Harvey, might practice law in the Court of the Arches, the ecclesiastical court, which was part of the church of St Mary-le-Bow, in Cheapside a little east of St Paul's.

(a) Lyly, 4 October 1591

[The title page explains that the play was] played before the Queen's majesty at Greenwich on Candlemas Day [2 February in, perhaps, 1588] at night by the children of Paul's. [And the printer adds:] Since the plays in Paul's were dissolved, there are certain comedies come to my hands by chance which were presented before her majesty at several times by the children of Paul's.

(b) Nashe, 1596

Then we need never wish the plays at Paul's up again, but if we were weary with walking, and loath to go too far to seek sport, into the Arches we might step and hear him [Harvey] plead, which would be a merrier comedy than ever was old *Mother Bombie* [a play of Lyly's performed by the boys of St Paul's].

230 But the boys may perform for a private occasion in a private house, autumn 1592

Nashe, *Summer's Last Will and Testament* (SR, 28 October 1600), sig. Bv. See *ES*, III, 451–3

Allusions in the play suggest that boys performed it before Archbishop Whitgift at his palace in Croydon in the autumn of 1592. The boys may have been those of St Paul's, though their opening remark below suggests otherwise, since the boys of St Paul's were not novices. That and their following remarks may allude to the ending of public performance at St Paul's.

[In the prologue, spoken by 'the great fool, Toy', the boys say:] So fares it with us novices that here betray our imperfections: we, afraid to look on the imaginary serpent of envy, painted in men's affections, have ceased to tune any music of mirth to your ears this twelvemonth, thinking that, as it is the nature of the serpent to hiss, so childhood and ignorance would play the goslings, contemning and condemning what they understood not.

231 John Howe, a verger in the Cathedral, testifies about where the playhouse was, 1599

Malcolm, *Londinium Redivivum*, III, 73. See Berry, 'Where Was the Playhouse in which the Boy Choristers of St Paul's Performed Plays?'

In 1599, before the playhouse reopened, Howe made a remark that points to the location of the playhouse. The document in which the remark appeared is now lost, but Malcolm paraphrased and quoted it in a book of 1803. The playhouse is most likely to have been in the almonry, a 'mansion-house' that was, as many leases show (especially GL, MS 25, 630/4, fo. 100), against the south side of the nave and on the east side of the lane that led to the lesser south door of the cathedral. Both the original playhouse and the reopened one were there, for Thomas Woodford said in 1603 that the playhouse had 'of a long time' been in the same place (**235d**).

Howe testified that more than twenty buildings had been built against, and some actually into, the walls of the cathedral. The house of Thomas China stood against the church. Mr China had a closet in one of the rooms, four feet high, two feet deep, and two in width, which were [*sic*] literally dug in the wall. The house of John Gyles was partly formed by St Paul's and was 'lately used for a playhouse'. The house of John Wheeler was not only built upon the foundation of the church, but they had contrived a way through a window into a part of the steeple, where Mr Wheeler had a ware-room. John Francis, not less ingenious, baked his bread and pies in an oven excavated within a buttress. Those were on the south side. [The quotation marks are Malcolm's; and John Gyles is evidently a mistake for Thomas Gyles.]

232 The children of St Paul's have begun playing again, thanks to the Earl of Derby, 13 November 1599

Maidstone, Kent Archives Office, U1475/C 12/184. Transcribed in HMC, *De L'Isle and Dudley*, II, 415

This remark appears in a letter of court news from London written by Rowland Whyte to Sir Robert Sydney.

My Lord Derby hath put up the plays of the children in Paul's to his great pains and charge.

233 The children of St Paul's are playing old-fashioned plays, 8 September 1600

Marston? *Jack Drum's Entertainment* (SR, 8 September 1600), sig. H3v

The tenor of the passage suggests that the boys had only recently begun performing again. Brabant Senior is supposed to represent Ben Jonson.

SIR EDWARD FORTUNE: I saw the children of Paul's last night,
And, troth, they pleased me pretty, pretty well.
The apes [*i.e.* children] in time will do it handsomely.
PLANET: I'faith, I like the audience that frequenteth there
With much applause. A man shall not be choked
With the stench of garlic, nor be pasted
To the barmy jacket of a beer brewer.
BRABANT JUNIOR: 'Tis a good, gentle audience and I hope the boys
Will come one day into the Court of Requests.
BRABANT SENIOR: Aye, and [*i.e.* if] they had good plays. But they produce
Such musty fopperies of antiquity
And do not suit the humorous age's backs
With clothes in fashion.

234 People do not sit on the stage at St Paul's because it is very little, *c.* 1601

Marston, *What You Will*, the Induction (sig. A3)

[Before the play proper begins, Atticus says,] Let's place ourselves within the curtains, for, good faith, the stage is so very little, we shall wrong the general eye else very much.

235 The boys of St Paul's act a play about a vexed local matter, January and February 1603

PRO, STAC8/8/2. Discussed and partly transcribed in Sisson, *Lost Plays*, 12–79; see esp. 58–71

A series of lawsuits about who should marry Agnes Howe reveals some of the workings of the playhouse at St Paul's and concerns mainly people who lived nearby. The lawsuits were argued in the ecclesiastical courts and then, pursued by the Attorney General, in the Star Chamber. She was the daughter of a barber-surgeon. In 1600 she was a seventeen-year-old spinster who, thanks to the bequest of an aunt, would possess at her twentieth birthday a fortune that her father and many suitors coveted. The lawsuits arose because she agreed to marry three of her suitors and then went through a ceremony of marriage with a fourth. In January and February 1603, the boys of St Paul's often acted a play that George Chapman had written about the affair, *The Old Joiner of Aldgate* (now lost). By then the suitors were mainly John Flaskett, a stationer, and John Milward, doctor of civil law and preacher at Christchurch nearby, with whom she had gone through the ceremony. The courts successively arrived at three decisions: in the first two the lady was to be Flaskett's, in the third Milward's.[1] The second was arrived at while the play was running. Chapman received £13 6s 8d for the play, about twice the going rate, and after she and Milward were allowed to live together in November 1604, they soon had three sons.

[1] The decisions were in the ecclesiastical courts: 20 February 1602; 28 February 1603; 12 November 1604 (PRO, Del.5/3/ 13, 41, 67).

(a) The Attorney General's bill, 6 May 1603

[He charged:] That a stage play should be made, and was made, by one George Chapman, upon a plot given unto him concerning . . . Agnes Howe . . . And the same, under colourable and feigned names . . . so made and contrived, was sold to Thomas Woodford and Edward Peers [the master of the choir school] for twenty marks [£13 6s 8d] to be played upon the open stages in divers playhouses within the City of London to resemble and publish the dealing of her father towards her concerning his practice with several suitors to bestow her in marriage with one that might forgo her portion and that thereby she might shut up and conclude a match with . . . Flaskett rather than to suffer her name to be so traduced in every playhouse as it was like to be . . .

And the said confederates . . . caused the stage play . . . to be made and played . . . during all the last Hilary term until the very day wherein [the second] sentence should be given in that cause and upon the very same day also.[1]

[1] In 1603, Hilary term began on 24 January and ended on 12 February. Sentence was given on 28 February.

(b) Chapman's reply, 19 May 1603

Touching any combinations or confederacies upon a plot to him given . . . to make any such stage play to be played upon the open stages in divers playhouses within the City of London, . . . he . . . saith that he is not thereof, nor any part thereof, guilty.[1]

[1] In his testimony of 3 June 1603, Woodford was asked about the plot. He replied that 'he did once say there was a plot of the said play delivered unto Chapman, but [he] . . . doth not know who delivered that plot, nor whether there was any plot delivered to him or not. And [he] further saith that for anything this defendant knoweth, the said play was conceived and contrived by the said Chapman only' (Interrogatories and depositions, fo. 163v).

(c) Chapman's testimony, 30 May 1603

[He] did hear it reported by a general report that there was a suit in the ecclesiastical court between a doctor [Milward] and one Flaskett and a barber's daughter for her marriage . . . [And] he did make a stage play called *The Old Joiner of Aldgate*, and . . . he finished the same presently after Christmas last, [but nobody instructed him] . . . by writing nor otherwise, but [he] . . . made the same of his own invention . . . [and he] never saw the same acted and played publicly upon a stage . . .

He hath heard it reported that a doctor of Paul's [Milward] did entreat or speak to have the play forborne to be played for four or five days, but otherwise [he] . . . doth not know that the same was forbidden to be played.[1]

Before Christmas last past . . . Woodford coming to this defendant and, being then acquainted that this defendant was about a play called *The Old Joiner of Aldgate*, this defendant then told the said Woodford that he should have the same play of this defendant when it was finished, and so this defendant then sold the same to the said Woodford but did not finish it until after Christmas last, and then this defendant delivered the same out of his hands. [Interrogatories and depositions, fos. 171–2.]

[1] By 'special procurement', Milward got Peers to deliver the playbook to him 'to peruse over, who had and detained the same for the space of two weeks', at the end of which he declared 'that there was not anything in the said playbook that touched him at all' (Woodford's reply).

(d) Woodford's reply, 23 May 1603

True it is that he bought one playbook of . . . George Chapman, being licensed by the master of our late sovereign lady, the Queen's majesty's revels, he not knowing that it touched any person living. And further [he] . . . saith that the said playbook was played by the children of Paul's in a private house of a long time kept, used, and accustomed for that purpose.

(e) Woodford's testimony, 3 June 1603

He did buy a stage play of George Chapman . . . and paid for the same twenty marks, which play was called *The Old Joiner of Aldgate* and was played at some several times the last Hilary term by the children of Paul's by this defendant's means and appointment. But before the playing thereof, the same was licensed to be played by the Master of the Revels. And, further, this defendant saith that he hath the book itself without altering of it, to this defendant's knowledge, since the last of February last. [Interrogatories and depositions, fo. 163.]

(f) Peers' reply, 7 June 1603

Whereas . . . [the Attorney General's bill charges] that a certain playbook . . . was sold unto one Thomas Woodford and this defendant for twenty marks, this defendant . . . saith that he neither bought the . . . playbook, neither doth he at any time disburse any money for buying the plays which usually are acted by the children of Paul's, but his care is otherwise employed for the education of the said children and to instruct them as appertaineth to his place and charge. And, therefore, if it shall be thought an offence by this honourable court to buy a playbook in this manner, the defendant . . . is not guilty.

236 William Percy may offer five of his plays to the children of St Paul's, 1603–ff.

Huntington Library, MS HM 4, fo. 190. Transcribed in Collier, *History*, III, 377, n.

Percy wrote six plays, dating two 1601, two 1602, one 1603 and one 1632. He thought that the first five could be performed at St Paul's, for he implied in 1647 that he had sent a copy of them to the master of the children with a note about how the master could shorten them.[1] The note survives only as Percy wrote it in 1647. It seems doubtful that any of Percy's plays was performed anywhere, or, since he spent his life at Oxford, even that he knew much about St Paul's.

[1] The 'note' is at the end of a copy of all six plays, which Percy wrote out and dated 1647. Remarks in three of the first five plays allow the players to do one thing 'if for Paul's' and another if 'for [adult] actors'. See Berry, 'Sebastian Westcott', 80–2.

A note to the Master of the Children of Paul's

Be it remembered that if any of the five and foremost of these pastorals and comedies contained in this volume shall but overreach in length (the children not to begin before four, after prayers, and the gates of Paul's shutting at six) the time of supper, that then, in time and place convenient, you do let pass some of the songs and make the consort the shorter. For I suppose these plays be somewhat too long for that place. Howsoever, on your own experience, and at your best direction, be it. Farewell to you all.

237 Peers and Woodford quarrel, and Edward Kirkham becomes a master of the boys of St Paul's, 1604–1606

PRO, (a) KB27/1396/m. 536; (b) E351/543/m. 163. Transcribed in (a) Hillebrand, *Child Actors*, 213–14 n.; (b) Cunningham, *Extracts*, xxxviii

(a) Peers assaults Woodford, 2 December 1604

[A year later, Woodford sued Peers for damages in the King's Bench. Woodford claimed that:] On ... 2 December in the second year of James, now King of England [1604], ... he [Peers] assaulted with force and arms, etc., the same Thomas Woodford at London ... [who was] then and there going about in God's and the said King's peace. And he [Peers] then and there struck, wounded, and badly treated the same Thomas so that he despaired of his life. And he [Peers] inflicted other enormities on him against the said present King's peace to Thomas's cost of £100 ...

[And on 20 June 1606, the court awarded Woodford] Damages: £13 6s 8d [20 marks].

(b) Kirkham is a master, spring 1606

[The Treasurer of the chamber paid] To Edward Kirkham, one of the masters of the children of Paul's, upon the council's warrant dated ... the last day of March 1606, for bringing the said children and presenting by them two plays or interludes before the Prince his grace [*i.e.* Prince Henry] and the Duke of York [*i.e.* Prince Charles] upon nights mentioned in a schedule annexed unto the said warrant . . . in all, the sum of £16 13s 4d.

238 The boys of St Paul's perform before two kings at Greenwich, 30 July 1606

The King of Denmark's Welcome, 16

The kings were James I of England and Christian IV of Denmark. This is the boys's last performance for which contemporary notice has been found. The play is otherwise unknown.

On Wednesday at night the youths of Paul's, commonly called the children of Paul's, played before the two Kings a play called *Abuses* containing both a comedy and a tragedy, at which the Kings seemed to take delight and be much pleased.

239 Rival companies of players bribe the people at St Paul's to keep the playhouse closed, 1608–1610

PRO, Req.4/1, replication and rejoinder. Transcribed in Wallace, 'Shakespeare and his London Associates', 350, 355–6

On 8 February 1610 Robert Keysar (who, with Philip Rosseter, managed the children of the Queen's revels) sued the King's men (who owned the Blackfriars playhouse) about matters that at first had nothing to do with St Paul's (**409e**). But he made an assertion later in the lawsuit that caused the King's men to explain an arrangement by which Peers, the master of the choir school, received £20 a year to keep his playhouse closed.

(a) Keysar's assertion, 2 May 1610

Then also did they [the King's men], in further testimony of their malice, privately contract with the owners of all the private playhouses within the City of London for one whole year, and for the same did satisfy and pay a dead rent to the owners thereof to their own great loss and hindrance, intending nothing thereby but the advancement of their exceeding malice to this complainant [Keysar], . . . who all that time had a company of the most expert and skilful actors within the realm of England to the number of eighteen or twenty persons, all or most of them trained up in that service in the reign of the late Queen Elizabeth for ten years together, . . . until now . . . they are enforced to be dispersed and turned away to the abundant hurt of the said young men, the disappointing of her majesty's service, and . . . the loss and hindrance of this complainant at least of £1,000.

(b) The King's men's answer, 19 June 1610

These defendants [the King's men] have credibly heard and do verily believe . . . that there being . . . but only three private playhouses in the City of

London, the one of which being in the Blackfriars and in the hands of these defendants, or of their assigns, one other being in the Whitefriars in the hands or occupation of the said complainant [Keysar] himself, his partners, or assigns,[1] and the third near St Paul's church then being in the hands of one Mr Peers but then unused for a playhouse: one Mr Rosseter, a partner of the said complainant, dealt . . . and compounded with the said Mr Peers to the only benefit of him, the said Rosseter, the now complainant, the rest of their partners and company (and without the privity, knowledge, or consent of these defendants, or any of them) . . . that thereby they . . . might advance their gains and profit . . . in their said house in the Whitefriars, that there might be a cessation of playing and plays to be acted in the said house near St Paul's church aforesaid, for which the said Rosseter compounded with the said Peers to give him, the said Peers, £20 per annum. But these defendants afterwards coming to play at their said house in the Blackfriars and the said Rosseter perceiving that the benefit of the said cessation of plays at Paul's did, or was likely to, turn as well to the benefit of these defendants and their company as to the benefit of the said complainant, the said Rosseter, and the rest of their company, . . . he, the said Rosseter, came unto these defendants, or some of them, and intreated them [that they would] . . . be content to bear and pay one half of the charge of the said rent of £20 per annum. Whereunto these defendants, in all love and as well for the benefit of the said complainant . . . as of any other person or persons, willingly did yield and accordingly have paid their part of the said rent. Wherein also the malice and ingratitude of the said complainant is most perspicuous and plain, who can be contented to receive daily benefit, not only by the cessation of the plays in the said house near Paul's but also out of these defendants' purses in ready money, and yet cannot bridle his envy toward these defendants.

[1] See 432.

XXII Newington Butts

Newington Butts was a public playhouse whose proper name, if it had one, is now unknown. Newington Butts refers simply to the street in which it stood, the high street of Newington. The street was, and part of it still is, called the Butts, a name, it seems, that has nothing to do with butts used in archery. The playhouse was on the east side of the street, a few yards from the famous inn, the Elephant and Castle. It was a mile south of London Bridge, in Surrey, at the southern end of Southwark, and well out of the City of London. The site is on the east side of Walworth Road near its junction with the New Kent Road, S.E.17.

In 1566, Richard Hicks, a grocer who had become 'one of the yeomen of her majesty's guard', leased thirty-five acres in Newington from the owners, the Dean and Chapter of Canterbury Cathedral, for sixty years. Part of the property was a field, somewhat bigger than ten acres, called Lurklane, which was bounded on the west by Newington Butts.[1] A common sewer (part of the drainage system of the low-lying lands south of the Thames, not a sewer in the modern sense) ran under Newington Butts and through Lurklane. Hicks enclosed part of this field and built a 'messuage or tenement' there.

Hicks subleased his enclosed part of Lurklane to Richard Thompson for nineteen years, and when fourteen of the nineteen remained, Thompson further subleased the place to Jerome Savage, a leading player in a new company bearing the name of the Earl of Warwick, first recorded on 14 February 1575 for a performance at court. Savage presently paid Hicks £10 for a new sublease dated 25 March 1576, which was in Savage's name rather than Thompson's and for thirty years rather than fourteen.

Savage apparently made Hicks' messuage into a playhouse, probably after getting his new sublease, but conceivably earlier, even in 1575. The playhouse, therefore, could well have existed before the Theatre in Shoreditch, which Cuthbert Burbage and many since have thought of as the first playhouse. The enclosed property in which messuage and playhouse stood was 33 yards 'in breadth' on the west side along Newington Butts, 42 yards in breadth on the east side, and 48 yards deep on both the north and south sides. It also contained a garden and orchard.

Savage and his men were using the playhouse in May 1577 when Hicks and his son-in-law, Peter Honingborne, tried to drive him out of it, alleging among other things that Savage was 'a very lewd fellow and liveth by no other trade than playing of stage plays and interludes'. Hicks and Honingborne may not have succeeded, but Honingborne had acquired Hicks' main lease and so had become Savage's landlord. By 1590, he held the playhouse, when, despite his opinion of Savage's trade thirteen years before, he was allowing the place to be used for plays.

Savage may have used the playhouse until his company dissolved in 1580. The company was reborn, without Savage, as the Earl of Oxford's men, who may have carried on at Newington Butts led by John and Lawrence Dutton. The rebirth occurred, it seems, with indecent haste, for when Oxford's men 'wrote themselves his comedians . . . certain gentlemen altered and made [the word] chamelions'.[2]

Great companies eventually played at Newington Butts but were anxious to leave because the way to it from the City was tedious and it had for a long time not been used on working days. Before 25 September 1593, Lord Strange's men played there for three days, and in June 1594 the two companies into which they had by then divided, the Lord Chamberlain's and Lord Admiral's men, played unprofitably there for ten days.

A month later, the Dean and Chapter of Canterbury Cathedral had had enough. They agreed that Paul Buck, who may have been a player, should have the lease on the playhouse on condition that he 'not suffer any plays there after Michaelmas next' – 29 September 1594. They granted a formal renewal in Buck's name on 5 April 1595 without mentioning either the playhouse or condition, suggesting that Buck had brought playing to an end as he was bound to do. The playhouse certainly was no more in 1599.

Nothing is known of the size or shape of the building, but since it was used by adult players rather than children, it must have been a public playhouse rather than a private one.

Ingram treats the playhouse at length in *The Business of Playing*, 150–81, where he revises an earlier article, 'The Playhouse at Newington Butts: A New Proposal', *SQ*, 21 (1971), 385–98.

[1] Canterbury Cathedral, Chapter Library, Register V3, fos. 172v–73v.
[2] *ES*, II, 98–9.

240 The officers of Canterbury Cathedral describe the playhouse plot, 30 November 1590; 5 and 6 April 1595

Canterbury Cathedral, Chapter Library, Register W23, fos (a) 36v–37, 292v, (b, c) 266.
Transcribed in Ingram, *Business of Playing*, (a) 157, (b) 157–8, (c) 158

The lease of 26 November 1566 by which Richard Hicks acquired a lease for sixty years on thirty-five acres in Newington went through many transactions, including several in which the owners, the Dean and Chapter of Canterbury Cathedral, renewed it. For (b) and (c) see also **249**.

(a) The playhouse

[The Dean and Chapter took notice of the playhouse in a renewal they granted on 30 November 1590, and then in another of 1 November 1596, where they quoted the lease as Hicks had acquired it but with one addition:] Except and always to the said Dean and Chapter and their successors reserved, one messuage or tenement heretofore by one Richard Hicks, deceased, erected and built upon parcel of the said lands, now called the playhouse,[1] with all houses, gardens or orchards thereto adjoining, as they be now enclosed and in the occupation now or late of one Peter Honingborne or his assigns.

[1] Hence, evidently, Hicks built a 'house or tenement' that somebody else (Jerome Savage, presumably – see **241**) made into a playhouse.

(b) The plot

[And in yet another renewal, on 5 April 1595, the Dean and Chapter described this plot as:] That house and tenement lately built by the aforesaid Richard Hicks upon a parcel of land lying, situate, and being in Newington near Southwark in the county of Surrey called Lurklane, which parcel was letten as aforesaid to the said Richard Hicks among other lands, together with one garden or garden plot, as it is now enclosed out of the said land called Lurklane. All which said house and garden containeth in length along by the lands of the said Dean and Chapter now in the tenure of the said Richard Hicks or his assigns towards the north 46 yards and like length along by the common sewer[1] there towards the south 44 yards, and in breadth along by the Queen's highway there towards the west 36 yards, and in breadth along by the lands of the said Dean and Chapter towards the east twenty [*illegible words*] . . .

[1] That is, one of the drains by which the low-lying lands south of the Thames were kept dry.

(c) The plot revised

[On the next day, 6 April 1595, the Dean and Chapter corrected the dimensions of the plot. They declared the day-old lease faulty:] The full content of the lands enclosed in [the] said garden and garden plot [are] not fully set down in the said former lease as it was enclosed and taken in by the said Richard Hicks in his lifetime, bearing the content of 48 yards towards the north and south, and in breadth towards the east 42 yards, and in like breadth to the west 33 yards, be it more or less.

241 An actor, Jerome Savage, has the part of Hicks' land including the playhouse, 1576–1578

LMA, SKCS18, fo. 87v. Transcribed in Ingram, *Business of Playing*, 162

[On 13 July 1576, the Surrey and Kent Commissioners for Sewers ordered] Jerome Savage and John Hills to scower and cast deeper ten rods of their common sewer leading from the grate at Newington Butts to the end of Jerome Savage's orchard corner . . . The inhabitants of the parish of Newington to cleanse and cast deeper one rod [of the sewer] before the grate at Jerome Savage's door.

Savage and Hills were similarly charged with ten rods on 5 July 1577 and 3 November 1578 (fos. 95v, 105v).

242 Hicks and his son-in-law try to remove Savage from the playhouse property, and Savage sues them, May 1577

PRO, Req.2/266/8. See Ingram, *Business of Playing*, 164–5

What the court did about this lawsuit does not appear, but Savage probably survived it, since he was still responsible for the playhouse in November 1578 and playing continued there.

(a) Savage's bill of complaint, undated

Your majesty's humble and obedient subject, Jerome Savage, [showeth] that one Richard Thompson had by good conveyance fourteen of nineteen years [*i.e.* a lease of nineteen years of which fourteen were yet to come] in and to one messuage with the appurtenances in Newington in the county of Surrey, wherein your said subject [Savage] now inhabiteth. And he, the said Thompson, being thereof so possessed, conveyed his interest aforesaid therein to your said subject, by force whereof your said subject entered and was possessed accordingly. And your said subject, having had the premises by such title, was desirous to procure further years, as also to have estate in his own right, from him that claimed the inheritance of the premises, that is to say of one Richard Hicks. And thereupon your said subject moved the said Richard Hicks, who then affirmed to have the very fee simple of the premises and ... full power to grant the same to your said orator [Savage], for ... term of thirty years. And thereupon, for the sum of £10 paid by your said orator, the said Richard Hicks at or about [25 March 1576] ... did by his sufficient deed let the said messuage and one orchard and garden with the appurtenances for term of thirty years then next following, reserving yearly during the said term four marks [£2 13s 4d] of good and lawful money of England, payable quarterly at four terms in the year, that is to say at the feasts of the nativity of St John Baptist [24 June] and St Michael the archangel [29 September] and the nativity of our lord God, and the annunciation of our Lady [25 March], by even portions.

And in the said lease there was one condition or proviso by the which it was provided that if the said rent or any part thereof were behind in part or in all at any feast or day aforesaid wherein the said rent ought to be paid and by fourteen days after, being lawfully demanded, that then it should be lawful for the said Richard, his heirs, and assigns to enter and it to have repossessed as in his first and former estate. And by force of such lease your said subject entered and was possessed.

Now ... the said Richard Hicks, seeking to defeat your said subject of the premises, contrary to his own grant, and to prefer one Peter Honingborne, his son-in-law, to the same, pretendeth that the said Peter had and hath of the said Richard a former grant before the said second lease. And [he] publisheth the said lease, where either there is no such lease or, if there were any, the same was antedated or made only upon trust between the said parties and not to the use of the said Peter but by fraud and coven to deceive such to whom the said Richard should let the premises. And the said Richard and Peter, fearing and suspecting that such former lease as they published, if any there be, will not be sufficient to defeat such the estate of your highness's subject so made *bona fide* for good considerations, the said Richard by secret practice with the said Peter, as the said Peter affirmeth, hath made secret estate to the said Peter of the reversion of the premises to the end that he, the said Peter, by some art and practice might the sooner come to his determined purpose to procure the possession of the premises to himself and to defeat by craft your said subject's lease, by reason that your said subject knew not of any such assurance as the said Peter now pretendeth.

And ... after the feast of the annunciation of our Lady last past [1577] and before the fourteenth day after, your said subject left the said rent due at the said feast with one Thomas Whaston, whom your ... [subject], having occasion to go about his affairs, left in the said house, commanding him to pay the said rent to the said Richard Hicks before or at the said fourteenth day. Which the said Richard and Peter, understanding, came not to demand the same rent, so that thirteen days passing, ... the said Thomas Whaston, suspecting no fraud, upon the fourteenth day went to London about his affairs as also hoping to meet there with the said Richard Hicks to pay the said sum, not knowing that the same was to be tendered on the land, nor suspecting such the practice of the said Richard and Peter. And your said subject hopeth to prove that by secret means used by the said Peter ... the said Thomas was procured to go to the said city that day, he the said Thomas nothing suspecting such practice. And ... after ... the said Thomas was departed to London, the aforesaid Honingborne, having knowledge thereof, came to the aforesaid messuage and there demanded the said rent, sometimes, as it is said, in his own and sometimes in the name of the said Richard, and for default of payment, as he, the said Peter, reporteth, made his entry into the said messuage.

And ... the said Thomas, coming to the said messuage within half an hour after and hearing of the same demand, returned to the house of the said Peter in London immediate[ly], the same day, and there offered to pay the same rent, and declared that he had the same long before ready to have paid it by the delivery and commandment of your majesty's said subject [Savage]. But at the first the said Peter refused to receive the same, and, ... the same day, your highness' said subject likewise after came to the house of the said Peter and made tender of the said rent, which the said Peter awhile refused. Nevertheless, the same Peter afterwards, the same day, by his wife received the same rent and she delivered it to the said Peter, who yet hath the same and the premises.

Notwithstanding, the said Peter and Richard by such continual practice seek still to frustrate and make void the interest of your said subject by such their indirect and extreme dealing, notwithstanding the receipt of the said rent. And for that in extremity of law some peril in the premises may ensue to your said subject unless the truth in the premises may appear by the corporal oath of the said ... Richard and Peter, may it ... please your most excellent majesty to grant your majesty's writ of privy seal to be directed to the said Richard and Peter, commanding them, and either of them, thereby, at a certain day [and] under a certain pain therein to be limited, personally to appear before your majesty's honourable Court of Requests then and there to answer the premises.

(b) The reply of Honingborne, 10 May 1577

[Savage has set forth his bill] of craft, envy and malice to entrap, charge and vex [Hicks, who leased one messuage, or house, in Newington Butts to Richard Thompson, a silk weaver, and when Thompson left it, Jerome Savage occupied it, Savage then sought] by all means that he could [to get a lease of thirty years from

Hicks, the chief landlord for many years yet to come, which Hicks granted. The fine for the lease, the rent, and provisions against default are all as Savage has stated.]

[Savage, however, tried to entrap Hicks,] a simple and plain-dealing man whom the said complainant [Savage], as well therein as other ways, hath greatly abused. [Savage] did cause to be inserted in the said indenture of lease a covenant whereby ... [Hicks] did stand bound that he had full power, right and authority to demise and grant the said messuage ... in such sort as in the said deed is expressed. [Hicks,] being simple and giving overmuch credit to the fair words of the said complainant, [sealed a bond of £100 to perform the covenant,] and Jerome Savage meant to make him forfeit the bond immediately after the sealing.

Hicks, being by obligation under his hand and seal lawfully and justly indebted to this defendant [Honingborne] in the sum of £50, for the payment whereof he stood bound to the said defendant in one obligation of 100 marks [£66 13s 4d], and for non-payment thereof being sued at the common law by this defendant, and the matter ready to come to trial, ... fell to composition with this defendant. And for satisfaction thereof, amongst other things, the said Richard Hicks did grant a reversion of the said premises to the said defendant for divers years yet to come, whereunto the said complainant [Savage] consented and did accordingly [recognise] the said defendant as his landlord.

And afterwards, this defendant coming to the foresaid messuage, or tenement, as aforesaid demised, gently demanded his rent on the fourteenth day after [Lady Day, 1577], ... and there tarried for the same one whole hour in the latter part of the day, even until the sun was set and the day finished, and yet could get no rent or other money due. Whereupon this defendant immediately re-entered ...

And further, this defendant saith that he with workmen, according to a covenant and condition contained in the said lease, came to view the reparations and could not be suffered to enter and view according to the said covenant and condition. But those that kept the house utterly denied him so to do and shut the door against him, by reason whereof also the lease was void ... And when this defendant cometh thither, meaning to talk friendly and deal courteously with the said complainant [Savage], although he in truth be otherwise, the same complainant giveth unto the defendant threatening words and fetcheth his sword to the intent, as this defendant is induced to believe, to strike this defendant. And the same complainant braggeth and boasteth that he hath such friends as shall compel this defendant to deal in such sort as pleaseth him.

And in truth, the complainant himself is a very lewd fellow and liveth by no other trade than playing of stage plays and interludes, to the knowledge of this defendant. And for his lewd and loose life [Savage] hath commandment from the ordinary [i.e. the parish priest – Stephen Bateman, a well-known puritan[1]], as is credibly reported, to avoid out of that parish, which his lewd behaviour would soon make an honest man weary of so wicked and idle a living tenant, and so much the more because the honest neighbours in that place do so mislike his behaviour as they will not suffer him to dwell there any longer ...

[Besides, Honingborne cannot conveniently allow Savage's tenancy to continue] because, in truth, this defendant is in great need of a house and therefore meaneth to dwell there himself . . . And because he [Savage] could not hold the same by himself, he did set a bill on the door to sell or do away the same . . . [Honingborne] did not procure Thomas Whaston to go to London that day whereon the said demand was made . . . for in very truth this defendant tarried a great while for his rent, could get none or heard of any such fellow . . . [nor was the rent paid to Honingborne as Savage says].

[1] See Ingram, *Business of Playing*, 169.

(c) Hicks' reply, 14 May 1577

It is nearly a verbatim copy of Honingborne's reply. Hicks adds that he granted Honingborne the reversion of two houses in St Olave's, Southwark, leased to Thomas Cranage, as well as that of the messuage in Newington Butts.

[He insists that he did not try] to defeat the complainant of his interest in the premises but did grant the reversion of the premises *bona fide* to the said Peter Honingborne.

243 The playhouse is to stop alluring people to plays, 10 November 1578

PRO, PC2/12, p. 300. Transcribed in *APC*, 1577–8, 381

[Since the playhouse was the only theatrical establishment then in Southwark and Surrey, the privy council must have had it in mind when it ordered that a letter be written] to restrain certain players within the Borough of Southwark and other places near adjoining within that part of Surrey, who by means of the alluring of the people to their plays do augment the infection of the plagues in London.

244 The playhouse has been defying an order to stop playing, 13 May 1580

PRO, PC2/13, p. 10. Transcribed in *APC*, 1580–1, 15

[The privy council ordered that a letter be written to the justices of Surrey:] that whereas their lordships do understand that notwithstanding their late order given to the Lord Mayor [of London] to forbid all plays within and about the City until Michaelmas next for avoiding of infection, nevertheless certain players do play sundry days every week at Newington Butts on that part of Surrey without [i.e. outside] the jurisdiction of the said Lord Mayor, contrary to their lordships' order: their lordships require the justices not only to enquire who they be that disobey their commandment in that behalf, and not only to forbid them expressly for playing in any of these remote places near unto the City until Michaelmas, but to have regard that within the precinct of Surrey none be permitted to play.[1]

[1] See 37.

245 The playhouse is closed, like its competitors nearer to the City of London, 11 May 1586

PRO, PC2/14, p. 84. Transcribed in *APC*, 1586–7, 99

[The privy council had already ordered that playing stop 'in and about the City of London ... for the avoiding of the infection' and now turned to Newington. The Surrey justices were] required in like sort to take order that the plays and assemblies of the people at the theatre or any other places about Newington be forthwith restrained and forborne as aforesaid.

246 Peter Honingborne has the playhouse and Richard Cuckow the rest of Hicks' property, 1590, 1591

(a) Canterbury Cathedral, Chapter Library, Register W23, fos. 36v–37, 292v; (b) LMA, SKCS18, fo. 172. Transcribed in Ingram, *Business of Playing*, (a) 157, (b) 176

(a) 30 November 1590

By this time, Honingborne had acquired the playhouse property and got the Dean and Chapter to separate it from Hicks' other property in Newington. See **240a**.

(b) 26 February 1591

[The commissioners for sewers ordered that Peter Honingborne is] to open the sluice by the playhouse that the water may have a free passage, [and] Richard Cuckow [is] to make a sluice or thorough at his gate leading into his field next adjoining to the playhouse.

247 The playhouse is disused, but Lord Strange's men play there briefly, before 25 September 1593

Dulwich, MS I, fo. 27. Transcribed in *Henslowe's Diary*, 285

Evidently Lord Strange's men went to Newington because the privy council closed the Rose. The document below is an undated privy council order among the papers at Dulwich College. Accompanying it are two other documents, also undated, that may or may not relate to it: (1) a petition by Lord Strange's men to the privy council 'now in this long vacation [*i.e.* summer]' to be allowed to return to a playhouse on the Bankside because 'travelling the country' is unprofitable and the watermen depend for a living on people crossing the Thames to see plays there; (2) a petition by the watermen for the reopening of the Rose

(Dulwich, MS I, fos. 23, 25, transcribed in *Henslowe's Diary* 283–5; see also *ES*, IV, 311–13). The date of these documents has long been a problem. The first two should belong to a time before 25 September 1593, because Lord Strange became Earl of Derby on that day.

Whereas not long since upon some considerations we did restrain the Lord Strange his servants from playing at the Rose on the Bankside and enjoined them to play three days at Newington Butts, now for as much as we are satisfied that by reason of the tediousness of the way and that of long time plays have not there been used on working days, and for that a number of poor watermen are thereby relieved, you [*i.e.* authorities in Southwark] shall permit and suffer them or any other there to exercise themselves in such sort as they have done heretofore, and that the Rose may be at liberty without any restraint, so long as it shall be free from infection of sickness, any commandment from us heretofore to the contrary notwithstanding.

248 The Lord Admiral's and Lord Chamberlain's men play jointly at Newington Butts, 3–13 June 1594

Dulwich, MS VII, fo. 9. Transcribed in *Henslowe's Diary*, 21–2

Evidently, Philip Henslowe hired the playhouse from 3 to 13 June 1594 for the players who had used his Rose, which for some reason the privy council kept closed from 16 May to 15 June. They were the former Lord Strange's men, who during the long closings from 22 June 1592 to 14 May 1594 had broken into two separate companies: the Lord Admiral's with Edward Alleyn and the Lord Chamberlain's with Richard Burbage. The two companies did not now reunite but took turns playing their own plays. The figures below are Henslowe's profits recorded in his 'diary'. They are a small fraction of the sums he usually got at his own playhouse and may partly result from his deducting what he had to pay to sublet Newington Butts. See 344.

In the name of God, amen, beginning at Newington, my Lord Admiral's Men and my Lord Chamberlain's Men as followeth, 1594:

3 of June 1594	Received at *Hester and Ahasuerus*		8s
4 of June 1594	Received at *The Jew of Malta*		10s
5 of June 1594	Received at *Andronicus*		12s
6 of June 1594	Received at *Cutlack*		11s
8 of June 1594	ne – Received at *Bellendon*	x	17s[1]
9 of June 1594	Received at *Hamlet*		8s
10 of June 1594	Received at *Hester*		5s
11 of June 1594	Received at *The Taming of a Shrew*		9s
12 of June 1594	Received at *Andronicus*		7s
13 of June 1594	Received at *The Jew*		4s

[1] Henslowe's 'ne' followed by 'x' is often taken to mean that the play was new and he had paid a fee to the Master of the Revels for it.

249 Paul Buck, perhaps a player, acquires the playhouse on condition that he ends playing there, 6 July 1594

Canterbury Cathedral, Chapter Library, Chapter Act and Minute Book, 1581–1607, fo. 153. Transcribed in Ingram, *Business of Playing*, 176

The document is merely an agreement entered in the act and minute book of the Dean and Chapter. For the formal renewal of the lease nine months later, see above, **240b, c**. A Paul Bucke, player, had children buried in Blackfriars in 1580 and 1599, and the name occurs, for no apparent reason, at the end of Wilson's *Three Ladies of London* (1584) (see *ES*, II, 304).

[The Dean and Chapter] Agreed that Mr Paul Buck shall have the leases of the tenement and playhouse thereto adjoining in Newington renewed up to twenty-one years, with covenants as before and with a clause that he shall convert the playhouse to some other use upon the said ground and not suffer any plays there after Michaelmas next.

250 The playhouse has been replaced by houses, 5 October 1599

LMA, SKCS18, fo. 294av. Transcribed in Ingram, *Business of Playing*, 176–7

[The commissioners for sewers noted:] We find that the sewer leading from the houses where the old playhouse did stand at Newington all along unto the bridge going from Bermondsey across the highway unto St Thomas Waterings[1] is needful to be cast, cleansed and scoured.

[1] St Thomas à waterings was the place of execution for Surrey, two miles south of London Bridge, near the Old Kent Road.

251 The playhouse is remembered, 1631

Stow, *Annales*, 'continued and augmented . . . by Edmund Howes' (1631), 373

One [playhouse built] in former time at Newington Butts.

XXIII The Theatre

The Theatre was a public playhouse in Shoreditch, a little west of Shoreditch High Street and some 500 yards beyond the north-eastern boundary of the City of London. Its site is now occupied by buildings on the east side of Curtain Road, E.C.2, extending north from the corner of that road and New Inn Yard, from no. 86 (on which are two memorials) to no. 100 (the London College of Fashion).

A joiner turned actor, James Burbage, set out in 1576 to build a large, costly building that he meant from the start to be a public playhouse. The place opened before it was fully complete, probably in the latter half of the year, and Burbage dominated its affairs until he died in 1597. Thinking of this building in 1635, his son, Cuthbert, described his father as 'the first builder of playhouses', in effect the originator of the Shakespearean theatre, a remark much echoed since. Several other playhouses, however, preceded it. The Red Lion had been built as a public playhouse in 1567, and at least one of the four theatrical inns had become a playhouse before 1576. A place associated with St Paul's had probably been converted into a private playhouse in 1575, and another private playhouse, the first Blackfriars, opened, like the Theatre, towards the end of 1576. A public playhouse in Newington Butts could have opened earlier in 1576 or even in 1575. But if cost, size, permanence and influence are important, one can probably still think of Burbage's building as the first playhouse. Appropriately, he called it the Theatre.

Giles Allen granted him a lease dated 13 April 1576 on part of the dissolved priory of Holywell in Shoreditch. The leased property included several old buildings and an open space where the playhouse would go. Burbage paid Allen £20 for the lease and was to pay him £14 a year in rent. The lease was for twenty-one years from 25 March (Lady Day) 1576 until 25 March 1597, but Burbage probably thought of it as for thirty-one, because a clause provided that if he spent £200 on the old buildings within ten years, he could renew the lease for twenty-one years from the date of the renewal. Another clause provided that he could dismantle and remove the theatre while the lease was in force.

The playhouse was beset by quarrels throughout its history. The most serious arose because Burbage had nothing like enough money to finance his project. He took in his brother-in-law, John Brayne, the grocer who had built the Red Lion. They agreed that Brayne would supply most of the money needed to erect the building, and Burbage would have the lease put into both their names. Once the playhouse was open, the takings would pay the running costs and yield profits, most of which would go to Brayne until his investment and Burbage's were the same. Then the two men would share costs and profits. Brayne, who was childless, spoke of leaving his share of the enterprise to Burbage's children (the Braynes had had four children between 1565 and 1573, but all had died soon after birth). The scheme presumed an ample flow of takings and goodwill between the Burbage family and the Brayne family, especially because at the outset the parties committed nothing to written contracts.

The scheme went awry from the beginning. Burbage and Brayne had planned to spend about £200, which would probably have made their playhouse much more costly than any of the earlier places, but they actually spent about £700. Even between them, they did not have that much money. They had to borrow money and then mortgage the lease. Brayne, even Brayne's wife, had to join in putting up the building, and Brayne had to sell his house and business. They soon fell into bitter and even violent quarrels about who had spent how much and taken how much in profits. Because the lease was mortgaged, Burbage could not add Brayne's name to it. Instead, he gave Brayne bonds guaranteeing that he would do so. The name was never added, however, and the bonds proved uncollectable.

Brayne died a bankrupt in 1586, partly because he had also invested in the George Inn in Whitechapel and his dealings with his partner there, Robert Miles, were equally feckless. Brayne's widow, Margaret Brayne, convinced herself that her husband had died because Miles had struck him. She began an attempt to collect on Burbage's bonds in the courts in 1587, first at common law then in Chancery, and presently Miles became not only her supporter and mentor in her lawsuits but eventually her heir. She apparently had a child, Katherine, some months after her husband's death, and the Burbages seem to have decided that the child was Miles' and that the two had conspired in her husband's death.

The Burbages squeezed Margaret Brayne out of the ownership of the Theatre in 1589. The mortgage was by then well and truly forfeit, and the mortgagee, John Hyde, legally owned the lease. He, however, was ready to return it to Burbage and Brayne's widow in return for his money, of which only about £30 was still owning. Burbage's son, Cuthbert, got his patron, Walter Cope, an official in the entourage of the Lord Treasurer, to ask Hyde to turn the lease over to Cuthbert if Cuthbert paid the money. Cuthbert did so, and Hyde gave him the lease. The Burbages now argued that both James Burbage and Brayne had lost the lease when it became forfeit and that Cuthbert owned lease and playhouse outright.

Margaret Brayne died of plague in 1593, leaving to Miles her goods and Katherine Brayne, who soon also died of plague. Her lawsuit in Chancery continued voluminously until her death and was carried on by Miles until 1595, when the Burbages effectually won. Miles began another lawsuit against them on her behalf in 1597, but soon dropped it.

The landlord, Allen, caused another quarrel at the Theatre that continued from 1585 to 1602. He refused to renew the lease in 1585, arguing that James Burbage had not spent £200 on the old buildings and had been a bad tenant. In 1596, as the lease was running out, the Burbages began seriously negotiating with Allen for a new lease. These negotiations took place on or about the quarter days when Allen, who lived at Hazeleigh in Essex, was in Shoreditch to collect his rents. James Burbage died in February 1597, and Cuthbert Burbage continued negotiating. When the lease ran out, Allen allowed the Burbages to hold the place year by year.

The parties discussed a ten-year renewal, in keeping with the original lease, but they eventually thought of twenty-one years. As in 1585, Allen complained that James Burbage had not spent £200 on the old building. He wanted compensation, £24 a year in rent, and a guarantee that he would get his rent without trouble. He wanted £30 that he said James Burbage had not paid in rent.[1] He also wanted an end to theatricals on the property and the conversion of the playhouse to some other use. The Burbages agreed to pay the new rent and £30 in cash. They at first rejected the idea that the Theatre should cease to be a playhouse but may have acquiesced when Allen conceded that they could use it as such for five more years. Allen had a draft lease drawn up, but he then demanded that the Burbages provide £100 for the buildings other than the playhouse. They refused to sign, Allen dropped his demand for £100 in favour of a promise that they would improve the buildings, and another draft lease was drawn up. The Burbages offered James' other son, the actor Richard Burbage, as their guarantor for the rent, but Allen would have none of that. They also may have decided to insist that the Theatre should be a playhouse for all twenty-one years, which Allen 'misliked'. At Michaelmas 1598 the Burbages decided that further negotiations were useless, though Allen seems to have thought they would go on.

Cuthbert Burbage hired a carpenter, Peter Street, and twelve of his workmen to dismantle the Theatre. The work went on, it seems, during two to four days, beginning on 28 December, a Saturday, in the presence of members of the Burbage family and friends. The useful parts of the building – mainly its timbers (girders) and wood (wainscoting, doors, facings, etc.) – were taken to a site in Southwark where Street would use them to build a new playhouse, the Globe.

As soon as he could, probably on 20 January 1599, Giles Allen sued Street in King's Bench for trespass. Cuthbert Burbage had probably paid the rent for the property until Lady Day 1599 and so, even though the lease had expired, he could use the Theatre and other buildings there until then. According to the terms of the lease of 1576, however, the Theatre actually belonged to Allen, because the Burbages could remove it only while the lease was still in force.

Cuthbert Burbage countersued Allen in an equity court, Requests, in 1600 to stop Allen's lawsuit in King's Bench and have the dismantling of the Theatre judged as a matter of equity rather than common law. He argued that he could remove the Theatre because James Burbage had spent £200 on the old buildings in the first ten years of the lease and Allen should have renewed it. Burbage won his case in the autumn of 1600. Allen sued him twice more, but these cases disappeared in 1602, and Allen's role in theatrical history ended.

The documents about the Theatre do not provide much information about the building itself. It was a large timber building with tile roofs. Into it also went wainscoting, brick, sand, lime, lead and iron. It was built mainly by carpenters and plasterers, and a painter came to be a regular employee in it. It had a yard, tiring-house, galleries in which spectators sat and stood, and a door leading up to the galleries at which a gatherer stood to take money from people going to the galleries. One surprised foreign tourist, de Witt, described it as an amphitheatre, and another, Kiechel, said it had three galleries, one above the other.[2] It was, that is, a typical, probably the archetypical, Shakespearean public playhouse. It yielded something like 29 per cent of capital a year and, in a sense, survived even demolition. For its timbers were used in the Globe, which must, therefore, have been much the same size and shape.

Leicester's men (the company to which James Burbage belonged) evidently played in the Theatre for a time, as did Warwick's, Oxford's, the Queen's, the Lord Admiral's, and the company that included Shakespeare, belonging successively to Lord Strange, the Earl of Derby, and the Lord Chamberlain.

The bitter quarrels over the Theatre created more documentation than exists for any other playhouse, and nearly all has been in print since 1913 in Wallace's *First London Theatre*. Given for the documents mentioned below are the relevant pages in that book and, in italics, the numbers assigned the documents in a descriptive catalogue of them in Berry, *Shakespeare's Playhouses*.

---

[1] Burbage withheld the money in 1582 because he paid men that much to keep off people who disputed Allen's title.
[2] See *353* and *325a*. For a drawing of a playhouse that may be the Theatre but is probably the Curtain, see the introduction to chapter 25.

252 James Burbage leases property in Holywell from Giles Allen in which to build a playhouse, 13 April 1576

PRO, Req. 2/87/74, the answer. Transcribed in Wallace, *First London Theatre*, 187–91. D–2

The lease does not survive, but five long statements about it do: (1) a summary in Latin, used by Allen in 1599; (2) a lengthy description, used by the Burbages in 1599, of a draft lease of 1585, which was supposed to be a verbatim copy of most of the original lease; (3) a summary of the original lease, used by the Burbages in 1600; (4) a summary of the original lease, used by Allen in 1600; (5) a translation into Latin of the first part of the original lease, used by Allen in 1601. These statements do not much disagree except where they omit sections. All are at the PRO, the first two in KB27/1362/m. 587 (transcribed in Wallace, *First London Theatre*, 165–8, 169–78; D–1), the third in Req. 2/87/74, the bill (transcribed in Wallace, *First London Theatre*, 181–3; D–2), and the fifth in KB27/1373/m. 257 (transcribed in Wallace, *First London Theatre*, 267–72; D–16). Below is the fourth, which seems to report all the sections. The 'defendant' was Allen.

He, the said defendant, together with Sarah, his wife, did by their indenture of lease bearing date ... [13] April [1576] for and in consideration of the sum of £20 of lawful money of England ... in hand at the ensealing thereof by the said James Burbage ... truly paid, ... amongst other things did demise unto the said James Burbage: all those two houses or tenements with the appurtenances then being in the several tenures or occupations of Joan Harrison, widow, and John Dragon; and also all that house or tenement with the appurtenances, together with the garden ground lying behind part of the same, then being in the occupation of William Garnett, gardener; and also all that house or tenement with the appurtenances called ... the mill house, together with the garden ground lying behind part of the same, then being in the tenure or occupation of Ewan Colfoxe, weaver, or of his assigns; and also all those three upper rooms with the appurtenances next adjoining to the foresaid mill house, then being in the occupation of Thomas Dancaster, shoemaker, or of his assigns; and also all the nether rooms with their appurtenances lying under the same three upper rooms and next adjoining also to the foresaid ... mill house, then being in the several tenures or occupations of Alice Dotridge, widow, and Richard Brackenburye, or of their assigns, together also with the garden ground lying behind the same; and also one great barn with the appurtenances, then being in the occupations of Hugh Richardes, inn-holder, and Robert Stoughton, butcher. Except and reserved to the said defendant and Sarah, his wife, and to their heirs and assigns, and to such other person or persons as then did or should inhabit or make abode in the capital messuage or tenement there, or any part thereof, then or late in the occupation of the said defendant, and to and for the said defendant which did and should dwell in Holywell aforesaid, free liberty to fetch and draw water at the well there from time to time during the said term.

To have and to hold all the said houses or tenements, barn, gardens, grounds and all other things by the said indentures demised (except before excepted) unto the said James Burbage, his executors, and assigns from the feast of the annunciation of our Lady [25 March 1576] . . . unto the full end and term of twenty and one years from thence next immediately following and fully to be complete and ended, yielding and paying therefor yearly during the said term unto the said defendant and Sarah, his wife, or to one of them, and to the heirs and assigns of the said defendant and Sarah, £14 of lawful money of England at four feasts or terms of the year, that is to say at the feasts of the nativity of St John Baptist [24 June], St Michael the archangel [29 September], the birth of our Lord God, and the annunciation of our Lady, or within the space of eight and twenty days next after every of the same feast days, by even portions.

And the said James Burbage, for him, his executors, administrators and assigns, did by the said indentures covenant with the said defendant and Sarah, his wife, their heirs and assigns, that he, the said James Burbage, his executors, administrators or assigns, at his or their own proper costs and charges, the said houses or tenements, barn, gardens and all other things by the said indenture demised, in all manner of needful reparations well and sufficiently should repair, uphold, sustain, maintain and amend from time to time when and so often as need should require, and the same so well and sufficiently repaired and amended in the end of the said term of one and twenty years should leave and yield up.

And the said defendant and Sarah, his wife, did covenant by the said indentures that it should be lawful for the said James Burbage, his executors, administrators and assigns, or any of them, at any time during the first ten years of the said term of one and twenty years, to alter, change, remove or take down any of the houses, walls, barn or buildings then standing and being in and upon the premises, or any part thereof, and the same to make, frame and set up into what form or fashion for dwelling house or houses it should seem good to the said James Burbage, his executors or assigns for the bettering thereof, so that the premises demised and the new buildings afterwards to be made should or might be reasonably, from time to time, set at a more value and greater rent than by the said indentures they were let for.

Towards the doing and finishing whereof in form aforesaid, the said defendant and Sarah, his wife, did covenant with the said James Burbage, his executors, administrators, and assigns . . . that it should be lawful for the said James Burbage, his executors and assigns to have and to take to his and their own proper use and behoof forever all the timber, tile, brick, iron, lead and all other stuff whatsoever of the said old houses or buildings which should come by reason thereof.

And further, the said James Burbage, for him, his executors, administrators and assigns, did by the said indentures covenant with the said defendant and Sarah that he, the said James Burbage, his executors, or assigns, as well in consideration of the said lease and term of years before . . . granted, as also for and in consideration of all the timber, brick, tile, lead and all other stuff coming of the said tenements, barn and all other the premises to be had and enjoyed in form aforesaid, should and would, at his and their own costs and charges, within ten years next ensuing the date of the said indentures employ and bestow in and upon the building, altering and mending of the said houses and buildings for the bettering thereof, as is aforesaid, . . . the sum of £200 . . . at the least, the value of so much of the said old timber and stuff as should be employed and bestowed thereabouts to be accounted parcel of the said sum of £200. And the same buildings so to be made, should, at all times after the making thereof, at the costs and charges of the said James, his executors and assigns, ... [be repaired, kept, made and maintained] from time to time as oft as need should be during the said term. And all the said messuages, buildings, gardens, tenements and other the premises, and every part thereof, sufficiently repaired, made and amended, [he and they] in the end the said term should leave and yield up.

And it was further conditioned ... that if it should happen the said yearly rent of £14 to be behind unpaid in part or in all after or over any feast day of payment thereof at which the same rent ought to be paid by the space eight and twenty days, being lawfully asked, and no sufficient distress or distresses in or upon the said premises, or any part thereof, for the said rent and the arrearages thereof could or might be found,[1] or if the foresaid sum of £200 should not be employed or bestowed within the time and space aforesaid, ... that then it should be lawful for the defendant and Sarah, his wife, and to the heirs and assigns of the defendant, into the said houses or tenements, barn and all other things by the said indentures granted to re-enter.

And furthermore, the defendant and Sarah, his wife, did covenant with the said James Burbage, his executors and assigns, ... that they, the said defendant and Sarah, his wife, or one of them, should and would at any time within ten years next ensuing the date of the said indentures, at and upon the lawful request or demand of the said James Burbage, his executors, administrators or assigns, at his and their costs and charges in the law, make or cause to be made to the said James Burbage, his executors or assigns a new lease or grant like to the former of all the foresaid houses or tenements, barn, gardens, grounds or soil, and of all other things by the said indentures granted, for the term of one and twenty years to begin and take commencement from the day of the making of the same lease so to be made, yielding therefore yearly the foresaid yearly rent of £14 at the feasts before mentioned and under such like covenants, grants, conditions, articles and agreements as were in the said indentures mentioned and expressed and none other (except the covenant for making a new lease within ten years and the covenant for employing the foresaid sum of £200).

And further, the defendant and Sarah, his wife, did covenant with the said James Burbage, his executors and assigns, by the said indentures, that it should be lawful to the said James Burbage, his executors or assigns in consideration of the employing and bestowing of the foresaid sum of £200 in form aforesaid, at any time before the end of the said term of one and twenty years, ... or before the end of the foresaid one and twenty years thereafter by virtue of the said indentures to be granted, to take down and carry away to his and their own proper use all such buildings and other things as should be builded, erected or set up in or upon the gardens and void ground by the said indentures granted, or any part thereof, by the said James, his executors, or assigns, either for a theatre or playing place, or for any other lawful use, for his or their commodities (except such buildings as should be after made ... by reason of the employing and bestowing of the said sum of £200), as the complainant [Cuthbert Burbage] in his bill of complaint in part hath alleged, and as in and by the said indentures (whereunto the defendant referreth himself) more fully may and doth appear.

[1] That is, if Allen could not have a bailiff seize and sell enough of Burbage's goods to pay the amount owing.

253 The playhouse has been in business for some time, 1 August 1577

PRO, PC2/11, p. 223. Transcribed in *APC*, 1575–7, 388

Apart from an assertion by one of Margaret Brayne's witnesses in 1592 that the building was open before it was finished (PRO, C24/226/11 [pt. 1], transcribed in Wallace, *First London Theatre*, 135, C–23), the first surviving notice that the playhouse was open occurs in a privy council minute.

[The privy council ordered that:] A letter [be sent] to the Lord Wentworth, Master of the Rolls, and Mr Lieutenant of the Tower, signifying unto them that for the avoiding of the sickness likely to happen through the heat of the weather and assemblies of the people of London to plays, her highness's pleasure is that as the Lord Mayor hath taken order within the City, so they immediately ... shall take order with such as are and do use to play ... within that county [Middlesex], ... as the Theatre and such like, shall forbear any more to play until Michaelmas be past at the least ...

254 Burbage is to share the lease with John Brayne but cannot because it has been pawned, 9 August 1577

PRO, C24/226/11 [pt 1]. Transcribed in Wallace, *First London Theatre*, 150–1. C–23. This remark is from a deposition of 31 July 1592, on Margaret Brayne's behalf in her lawsuit against James Burbage.

James Burbage and one John Brayne ... came to this deponent [William Nicoll, a notary public] to his then shop ... in the Old Jewry in London and required to have a lease and covenants drawn between them of the moiety of certain houses, ... barn, stable, Theatre, gardens and other premises ... held by lease of one Giles Allen ... at Holywell near unto Finsbury Fields ... At which time the said James Burbage and John Brayne did declare to this deponent that though the lease was taken in the name only of the said James Burbage, yet it was meant to be for both their uses, and, therefore, he, the said James Burbage was willing to assure the one moiety of the premises to the said John Brayne. Whereupon this deponent did draw and engross an indenture of lease between them dated the 9th day of August [1577] ... to the effect of their then agreements. Which lease so engrossed this deponent thinketh ... was not sealed by the same James Burbage, for that the original lease ... was then at pawn for money which was borrowed for the building of the said Theatre.

255 A 'brabble' over a matter at the Theatre, 5 October 1577
BL, Lansdowne MS 24, fo. 196. Transcribed in MSC, I. 152

[William Fleetwood, Recorder of London, writing to the Lord Treasurer, Burghley:] Yesterday ... I was at London with the Master of the Rolls at my Lord Mayor's at dinner ... After dinner we heard a brabble between John Wotton and the lieutenant's son of the one part and certain freeholders of Shoreditch for a matter at the Theatre. I mistrust [*i.e.* suspect] that Wotton will be found in the fault, although he complained.

256 Clergymen find the Theatre a sumptuous school for wickedness and vice, 3 November and 2 December 1577
(a) T. W., *A Sermon Preached at Pawles Crosse on Sunday the Thirde of November 1577*, 46; (b) Northbrooke, *A Treatise wherein Dicing, Daunsing, Vaine playes ... are reproued by the Authoritie of the word of God* (SR, 2 December 1577), 59

(a) T. W., 3 November 1577
Behold the sumptuous Theatre houses ...

(b) Northbrooke, 2 December 1577
A spectacle and school for all wickedness and vice to be learned in ... [are] those places ... which are made up and builded for such plays and interludes, as the Theatre and Curtain is [*sic*] and other such like places.

257 Burbage bonds himself to give Brayne half the Theatre, but they argue and violence ensues, 22 May 1578
PRO, C24/226/11 [pt 1]. Transcribed in Wallace, *First London Theatre*, 151–2, C–23. Another part of Nicoll's testimony. See 254.

John Brayne ... about the 22nd of May [1578] ... did require this deponent [William Nicoll, the notary public] to draw an obligation wherein the said James Burbage should be bound to the said John Brayne in £400 for the making unto the said John Brayne ... a good and lawful lease, grant and other assurance of the moiety ... of all and singular the said Theatre and other the premises granted to the said James Burbage by the said original lease, and of all the benefit of the covenants, grants and agreements comprised in the said lease. Which bond or obligation this deponent made and engrossed according to the agreement between the said parties. And afterwards the said James Burbage did seal and deliver as his deed the said obligation to the said John Brayne in the presence of this deponent and one John Gardiner, as by the said obligation and teste[1] thereof (whereunto he, this deponent, referreth himself, being showed unto him at this his examination) doth appear.

And further this deponent saith that shortly after the sealing of the said bond there grew some contention between the said James Burbage and John Brayne touching the indifferent dealing and collecting of the money for the galleries in the said Theatre, for that he well remembreth the said John Brayne did think himself much aggrieved by the indirect dealing of the said James Burbage therein. And coming then both together in the shop of this deponent . . . they, the same James Burbage and John Brayne, fell a-reasoning together of the ill-dealing of the said James Burbage. At which time this deponent was present and doth well remember that the said John Brayne did declare these words or the like, in effect, how he had left his trade and sold his house by the means of the said James Burbage to join with him in the building of the said Theatre, and that he had disbursed a great deal more money about the same than the said James Burbage had and there repeated what he had laid out and what the said Burbage had laid out (the certain sums the deponent doth not now certainly remember, but he thinketh that the sum then disbursed by the said John Brayne was three times, at the least, as much more as the sum then disbursed by the said James Burbage), and in the end declared so many words of the ill-dealing of the said Burbage towards him in that dealing of the Theatre that Burbage did there strike him with his fist. And so they went together by the ears in so much that this deponent could hardly part them.

[1] The part of the bond stating that Nicoll and Gardiner had witnessed Burbage's signing it.

258 Burbage and Brayne seek arbitration of their disagreements, 12 July 1578

PRO, (a, c) C24/226/11 [pt 1]; (b) C24/228/10. Transcribed in Wallace, *First London Theatre*, (a) 143–4, (b) 119–20, (c) 151–2, (a, c) C–23, (b) C–22

All these remarks are from Margaret Brayne's lawsuit against James Burbage. She called upon Robert Miles, her supporter and heir, and Nicoll (whose remark is from the deposition also quoted in 254 and 257) to testify, and James Burbage called upon Ralph Miles, Robert's son.

(a) Robert Miles, 30 July 1592

He hath been privy and present at . . . divers variances and contentions between the said John Brayne and James Burbage for and concerning the matters and profits of the said Theatre. And that they did submit themselves therein to the award and arbitrament of one Richard Turner and John Hill, men of great honesty and credit, to make a final end of all matters in question between them, who upon great discretion and indifferency between them both, having thoroughly heard their griefs and demands, did arbitrate and award in writing indented between them, ready to be seen, that from thenceforth the said John Brayne, his executors and assigns should have, receive and enjoy to them and their own uses during the said lease the one-half, or moiety, of the profits that should grow and rise by the plays to be used there, and also of the rents, fines and other yearly profits of such other tenements and places there as should yearly grow due for the same, and the said James Burbage, his executors and assigns to have also the other moiety of the premises during the said lease in like manner . . .

The said arbitrators did also award between them that if occasion should move them, the said James Burbage and John Brayne, to mortgage the said lease upon the borrowing of any sum of money to pay debts concerning the said Theatre, that then they both should join in the same mortgage, and that money coming of the profits of the said plays and the other said rents and fines to go to the redemption of the said lease, as by the said award may appear . . .

(b) Ralph Miles, 26 April 1592

And . . . before those debts were satisfied and discharged, neither the said Brayne nor the said Burbage, nor their executors should have nor enjoy any part or parcel thereof to his own or their own use, but only that the said Brayne should have 10s by the week for and towards his housekeeping [*i.e.* ownership of the playhouse] and the said Burbage to have 8s, as he remembreth, weekly out of the same for and towards his housekeeping, of the profits of such plays as should be played there upon Sundays, and that when the said debts were discharged, that then the said Brayne should take and receive all the rents and profits of the said Theatre to his own use till he should be answered such sums of money which he had laid out for and upon the same Theatre more than the said Burbage had done.[1]

[1] The Burbages said that the arbitrament was not carried out by either party and never could be – probably because it fudged the real quarrel, which was over how much each man had spent (PRO, C24/226/10, transcribed in Wallace, *First London Theatre*, 73; C–18).

(c) Nicoll, 31 July 1592

This deponent saith that . . . the 12th day of July [1578] . . . the said Richard Turner and John Hill did make, enseal and give up their award between the said James Burbage and John Brayne in the presence of this deponent and George Gosse, then his apprentice, as by the said award indented and teste thereof (which was showed to this deponent at this his examination) doth appear . . .

259 The gorgeous Theatre, 24 August 1578

Stockwood, *A Sermon at Paul's Cross on 24 August 1578*, 23, 133

The Theatre, the Curtain and other places of plays in the City . . . The gorgeous playing place erected in the [Finsbury] Fields, . . . as they please to have called it, a Theatre.

260 Swordsmen in the Theatre, 25 August 1578

BL, Sloane MS 2530, fo. 11. Transcribed in Berry, *The Noble Science*. This is the first dated allusion to the Theatre as a place where fencers played their prizes. Others were played there in 1582 (2 or 3), 1583 and 1585 (2). See fos. 12 (2), 46, 6 (2).

Edward Harvie played his provost's prize the 25th . . . of August at the Theatre at three weapons, the two-hand sword, the back sword, and the sword and buckler. There played with him one provost, whose name is John Blinkinsop, and one free scholar, called by name Francis Calvert, who had a provost's licence for that time. And so the said Edward Harvie was made a provost under Richard Smyth, master, 1578.

261 Burbage and Brayne mortgage the lease on the property for £125, 26 September 1579

PRO, C24/218/93 [pt 2]. Transcribed in Wallace, *First London Theatre*, 53–4, C–10. The quotation below is from the deposition of John Hyde, grocer, who testified on 8 December 1590 for Burbage in Margaret Brayne's lawsuit against Burbage.

John Brayne . . . and one John Prynn, a broker, did take up, borrow, and owe unto him, this deponent, about the 26 day of September 1579 the sum of £125 8s 11d or thereabouts, as this deponent remembreth, and he doth also well know and remember that the said James Burbage, the now defendant, did about the same time mortgage and convey unto him, this deponent, the lease and all his title therein of and in the Theatre and other buildings in Holywell in . . . Middlesex, the which he had of one Giles Allen and Sarah his wife, upon condition to this effect, that if the said sum of £125 were repaid to him, this deponent, or to his assigns within twelve months and one day next ensuing after the said September 1579 by the said James Burbage, that then he, this deponent, should reconvey to him, the said James, the lease and Theatre and other the premises again. And, as he remembreth, the lease and other bonds made by Giles Allen for the enjoying thereof were delivered into his hands and possession at the time of the said conveyance sealed by the defendant, which was done with the consent and appointment of the said John Brayne . . . [James Burbage], for this deponent's better security, stood bound to him, this deponent, jointly with the said Brayne and Prynn in a bond of £200 (as this deponent remembreth) with condition endorsed as well for the repayment of the said money at the time appointed as for the performance of the covenants and performing the said mortgage.

262 Wholesome plays at the Theatre, 1579

Gosson, *The School of Abuse* (STC 12097, 5; SR, 22 July 1579), fo. 23v

Gosson despised plays and everything to do with them, but he had written them himself and now found six worthy of praise. Two of them (one his own) were usually played at the Theatre. For the other four, see **208**.

And as some of the players are far from abuse, so some of their plays are without rebuke, which are easily remembered and as quickly reckoned: ... *The Blacksmith's Daughter* and *Catiline's Conspiracies*, usually brought into the Theatre, the first containing the treachery of Turks, the honourable bounty of a noble mind, and the shining of virtue in distress. The last, because it is known to be a pig of mine own sow, I will speak the less of it, only giving you to understand that the whole mark which I shot at in that work was to show the reward of traitors in Catiline and the necessary government of learned men in the person of Cicero, which foresees every danger that is likely to happen, forestalls it continually ere it take effect ... These plays are good plays and sweet plays.

263   Unwholesome Plays at the Theatre, 1579

Harvey, *Letter Book* (1579), 67 (cf. 4)

Leicester's, Warwick's, Vaux's or Rich's men or some other fresh start up comedians [may ask Harvey] for some malt-conceived comedy fit for the Theatre or some other painted stage.[1]

[1] Similar remarks at the time appear in T.F., *News from the North* (1579), sig. F4; Twyne, *Physic for Fortune* (1579), I, 130; Stubbes, *The Anatomy of Abuses* (1583), I, 144; Field, *A Godly Exhortation* (1583), sig. B4; and Rankins, *A Mirror of Monsters* (1587), fo. 4v.

264   Burbage and Brayne are indicted for malefactions at plays at the Theatre, 21 February 1580

LMA, MJ/SR 225/4. Transcribed in Jeaffreson, *Middlesex County Records*, II, xlvii–xlviii

The juries on behalf of our lady the Queen present [*i.e.* charge] that John Brayne ... and James Burbage ... on 21 February [1580], ... and divers other days and times before and after, congregated and maintained illicit assemblies of people to hear and see certain ... plays or interludes put into effect and practised by the same John Brayne and James Burbage and divers other persons unknown at a certain place called the Theatre in Holywell ... On account of which illicit assembly of people, great affrays, reviling, tumult and near insurrections, and divers other malefactions and enormities were then and there made and perpetrated by a great many ill-disposed people in a great disturbance of the peace of our lady the Queen, and also subversion of good order and government, and also to the peril of the lives of divers good subjects of the said lady Queen being in the same place, and also contrary to the peace of the same lady Queen and likewise the form of the statute for that purpose decreed and provided, etc.

265   An earthquake shakes the Theatre, 6 April 1580

Gardiner, *Doomes-Day book* (1606), xx. The earthquake, which is reported in many places, does not seem to have damaged any playhouses.

The earthquake ... shaked not only the scenical Theatre but the great stage and theatre of the whole land.

266 Another riot at the Theatre, 10 April 1580

CLRO, Remembrania 1, 9. Transcribed in MSC, 1. 46

Where it happened on Sunday last that some great disorder was committed at the Theatre, I [the Lord Mayor of London writing to the Lord Chancellor] sent for the under sheriff of Middlesex to understand the circumstances, to the intent that by myself or by him I might have caused such redress to be had as in duty and discretion I might, and, therefore, did also send for the players to have appeared afore me, and the rather because those plays do make assemblies of citizens and their families of whom I have charge . . .

267 The mortgage on the Theatre property is forfeit, 27 September 1581

PRO, (a) C24/218/93 [pt 2]; (b) C24/221/12; (c) C24/228/10; (d) C24/228/11. Transcribed in Wallace, *First London Theatre*, (a) 53–4, (b) 62, (c) 107, (d) 111. (a) C–10, (b) C–12, (c) C–21, (d) C–22

The mortgage was dated 26 September 1579 (see 261). The evidence here is from four depositions in Margaret Brayne's lawsuit against James Burbage, three by John Hyde (the man who lent the money) and the other by Burbage.

(a) Hyde deposes, 8 December 1590

After the said lease became forfeited to him, this deponent, it was agreed on both sides that if the said Burbage and Brayne, or either of them, did pay this deponent £5 a week till all the foresaid mortgage money were paid with some reasonable consideration for the forbearing of it, that then they should have their lease again, which they performed by the space of 4 or 5 weeks after. But they performed no more, and so suffered their lease to be once again forfeited to this deponent.

(b) Burbage deposes, 16 February 1591

The said [John] Brayne . . . did procure this deponent to mortgage the lease of the said Theatre . . . for one year, and after that for another year with a proviso that for the non-payment of the said sum . . . the said lease to be forfeited, which was forfeited accordingly by the non-payment of the money.

(c) Hyde deposes, 12 February 1592

Not only the said lease but the said James Burbage['s], the defendant's, title therein was absolutely forfeited and lost to him, this deponent, for the non-payment of the said sum of £125 8s 11d or thereabouts according to the time limited for the payment thereof and to the effect of the said deed of mortgage. And he, this deponent, did account and repute himself to be thereby rightful owner of the said lease and title therein of the said James Burbage.

(d) Hyde deposes, 21 February 1592

[He] did many and sundry times tell both the said John Brayne, the said James Burbage, [Margaret Brayne], . . . and others her friends that if he . . . were paid his money that was behind due [and reasonable consideration] for the forbearing thereof, that he would never take any advantage of the said forfeiture.

268   A scurvy play at the Theatre set out by a virgin, 22 February 1582

BL, Cotton MS 47, fo. 6v. Transcribed in *ES*, I, 371 n. 4. The remark is one of the very rare indications that a woman might appear on a regular, professional stage in London.

[Richard Madox] went to the Theatre to see a scurvy play set out all by one virgin, which there proved a freemartin ['fyemarten' – *i.e.* an imperfect female] without voice, so that we stayed not the matter.

269   James Burbage hires men to prevent Edmund Peckham from seizing the Theatre, spring 1582

PRO, (a) Req.2/87/74; (b, c) Req.2/184/45. Transcribed in Wallace, *First London Theatre*, (a) 201, (b) 240, (c) 242. (a) *D–2*, (b, c) *D–7*

One of Giles Allen's complaints against James Burbage was that he had not paid all his rent. In a lawsuit against Allen in Requests, Cuthbert Burbage and two of his witnesses eventually explained why James Burbage might not have done so. Allen said that the sum involved was £30 (302b). See *A–10, 11*.

(a) Cuthbert Burbage's bill, 26 January 1600

There was much variance and controversy between [Giles Allen] . . . and one Edmund Peckham touching the title of the premises, . . . by reason whereof the said James Burbage, this complainant's [Cuthbert Burbage's] father, was very much troubled and often charged to find men to keep the possession of the said premises from the said Edmund Peckham. Neither could this complainant's said father enjoy the said premises according to the lease to him made by the said defendant. For which causes (if any part of the rent were unpaid) it may be this complainant's said father detained some part of the rent in his own hands.

(b) Deposition of Randolph May, a painter, 15 May 1600

This deponent saith he well remembreth that about eighteen years now last past there were suits between the defendant, Allen, and one Edmund Peckham touching the title of the Theatre and lands in the deceased James Burbage his possession. And by reason thereof the said James Burbage was much hindered and troubled, and was often charged to find men to keep the possession of the premises in controversy between Allen and Peckham, and was once in danger of his own life by keeping possession thereof from Peckham and his servants. And [James Burbage] could not enjoy the premises peaceably and quietly according to his lease. And ... he [May] knoweth the same to be true for that he was then there, a servant in the house called the Theatre. And [he] knoweth that the said James Burbage lost much money by that controversy and trouble, for it drove many of the players thence because of the disturbance of the possession.

(c) Deposition of Oliver Tilte, a yeoman, 15 May 1600

This deponent saith that ... James Burbage ... did pay him, this deponent, and others wages for keeping the possession of the Theatre from the said Mr Peckham and his servants. Whereby he saith he verily thinketh that the said James Burbage was at great charge, for he paid men wages for keeping possession so long as the controversy was between Mr Allen and Mr Peckham.

270 Hyde attempts to collect money owing for the mortgage on the Theatre, June 1582

PRO, C24/218/93 [pt 2]. Transcribed in Wallace, *First London Theatre*, 54–5. C–10. The remark is from the deposition of John Hyde, the mortgagee, 8 December 1590.

He [Hyde] was offended that the said [James] Burbage and Brayne did not repay him the said sum of £125 8s 11d, and did thereupon threaten to put the said Burbage out of possession of the said Theatre and buildings ... and thereupon did cause the said James Burbage to be arrested by process out of ... [King's] Bench about June, as he remembreth, 1582. And the said Burbage did thereupon come to this deponent's [Hyde's] house with the officer or bailiff that had him arrested, and this deponent's wife in his absence did accept of £20 paid unto her to this deponent's use by the defendent [Burbage]. And the same defendant was thereupon either by him, this deponent, or his wife (but precisely by whether of them he doth not now remember) discharged from the bailiff upon condition that he, the same defendant, should come unto him, this deponent, whensoever he, the same deponent, did send for him to take order in the premises. And the said defendant did accordingly repair unto him and did give unto him, this deponent, new bonds with a surety for his forthcoming to this deponent's house at an hour's warning to be subject to his, this deponent's, actions ...

Burbage did complain unto him that the said Brayne had received and gotten into his hands a great portion of money levied in the said Theatre at the play times and that he would catch what he could and that he [Burbage] ... could not enforce him to deliver any part thereof neither to him [Burbage] ... nor unto him, this deponent, towards an agreement with him, this deponent, in the premises ...

He thereupon did send his servants to charge the said Brayne not to deal any further with anything concerning the said Theatre except he would deliver unto him, this deponent, the money he received. And this deponent remembreth that he did appoint one of his servants with the said James Burbage, as in his, this deponent's, right, title and interest, to discharge, dismiss, and put out the said Brayne from the said Theatre...

By reason the said Brayne would not depart [*i.e.* part] with the money he had received, he, this deponent, was constrained to appoint one of his servants and the said James Burbage ... to gather up £5 weekly during the time of plays, thinking by that means to have paid himself with the profits of the Theatre, for that he saw the said Brayne to be so bad a fellow.[1] And this deponent by that rate did receive in money to the sum of £20 or £30 as he remembreth.

[1] Hyde was testifying here for the Burbages and defending himself for having given the lease to Cuthbert Burbage. He was kinder to Brayne when he testified for Margaret Brayne a little more than a year later, saying, for example, that before getting involved with the Theatre, Brayne was 'a man well thought of in London' (PRO, C24/228/11, transcribed in Wallace, *First London Theatre*, 109; C–21).

271 Richard Tarlton and the Queen's men are at the Theatre, 1583–ff.

Harington, *Metamorphosis of Ajax* (1596), 10. Tarlton, the best-known comic of his time, played with the Queen's men, who were at the Theatre from time to time from 1583 (see 273).

[Harington mentions a vulgar word,] 'prepuce', which word was after admitted into the Theatre with great applause by the mouth of Master Tarlton, the excellent comedian.

272 One Browne causes a brawl at the door of the Theatre, 10 June 1584

BL, Lansdowne MS 41, fos. 32–3. Transcribed in MSC, 1. 163

[William Fleetwood, recorder of London, writes to Lord Burghley, the Queen's principal minister:] Upon Wednesday, one Browne, a serving man in a blue coat, a shifting fellow having a perilous wit of his own, intending a spoil if he could have brought it to pass, did at [the] Theatre door quarrel with certain poor boys, handicraft apprentices, and struck some of them, and lastly he with his sword wounded and maimed one of the boys upon the left hand. Whereupon there assembled near . . . 1,050 people. This Browne did very cunningly convey himself away, but . . . he was taken after.

273 James Burbage resists an attempt by the City of London to suppress the Theatre, 14 June 1584

BL, Lansdowne MS 41, fo. 31. Transcribed in MSC, 1. 163

Quoted below is another part of Fleetwood's letter to Lord Burghley. The players mentioned, the Queen's and Lord Arundel's men, were presumably at the Theatre and Curtain respectively. See 271 and 324.

Upon Sunday my Lord [Mayor] sent two aldermen to the court [*i.e.* Whitehall] for the suppressing and pulling down of the Theatre and Curtain. All the lords [of the privy council] agreed thereunto, saving my Lord Chamberlain and Mr Vice-Chamberlain,[1] but we obtained a letter to suppress them all. Upon the same night I sent for the Queen's players and my Lord of Arundel his players, and they all willingly obeyed the lords' letters. The chiefest of her highness's players advised me to send for the owner of the Theatre [James Burbage], who was a stubborn fellow, and to bind him [*i.e.* make him sign a bond guaranteeing, presumably, that he would close the Theatre]. I did so. He sent me word that he was my Lord Hunsdon's man and that he would not come at me, but he would in the morning ride to my Lord [Mayor]. Then I sent the under-sheriff for him and he brought him to me. And at his coming he stouted [*i.e.* braved] me out very hasty. And in the end I showed him my Lord [Hunsdon's], his master's hand, and then he was more quiet. But to die for it, he would not be bound. And then I minding to send him to prison, he made suit that he might be bound to appear at the [sessions of] oyer and terminer [at Newgate], the which is tomorrow, where he said that he was sure the court would not bind him, being a [privy] councillor's man. And so I have granted his request, where he shall be sure to be bound or else is like to do worse.

[1] The Lord Chamberlain was Lord Howard of Effingham, the future Lord Admiral, who was the patron of a notable company of players. The Vice-Chamberlain was Sir Christopher Hatton.

274 Allen denies that Burbage has observed the terms of the lease and refuses to extend it, 1 November 1585

PRO, (a, b) Req.2/87/74; (c–e) Req.2/184/45. Transcribed in Wallace, *First London Theatre*, (a) 183, (b) 191–5, (c) 210, (d) 218–19, (e) 237–8. (a, b) *D–2*, (c–e) *D–7*

The documents are from Cuthbert Burbage's lawsuit in Requests against Giles Allen. The original lease provided that if James Burbage spent £200 on the buildings other than the Theatre within the first ten years, Allen would grant a new lease that in effect extended the old one for another twenty-one years beginning on the date of the new lease. Burbage had a new lease drawn up, dated 1 November 1585, which is quoted, supposedly verbatim, in KB27/1362/m. 587, transcribed in Wallace, *First London Theatre*, 169–78; *D–1*. Baker and Johnson were witnesses for Allen.

(a) Cuthbert Burbage's bill, 26 January 1600

The said first term of ten years drawing to an end, the said James Burbage did oftentimes in gentle manner solicit and require the said Giles Allen for making a new lease of the said premises according the purport and effect of the said covenant [in the old lease] and tendered unto the said Allen a new lease devised by his [Burbage's] counsel, ready written and engrossed with labels and wax thereunto affixed, agreeable to the covenant before recited, which he, the said Allen, made show that he would [sign and] deliver yet by subtle devices and practices did from time to time shift of the finishing thereof. [For other parts of Burbage's bill, see **302a**.]

(b) Allen's answer, 4 February 1600

Allen said that he made no 'showe' that he would accept the new lease and utterly refused to sign it, because it differed materially from the old one. Moreover, Burbage was a 'troublesome' tenant and had not spent £200 on the buildings other than the Theatre. The reply is quoted in **302b**.

(c) Deposition of Philip Baker, 26 April 1600

Saith he hath heard the defendant [Allen] and others say that the complainant's father [James Burbage] did . . . tender and deliver unto the defendant a draft of a new lease of certain houses and grounds which the said defendant had before that time formerly demised unto him, the complainant's father. And that the complainant's father did upon the delivery thereof require the defendant to seal and deliver the same according to form of law in those cases provided. And the defendant said in his, this deponent's, presence that he refused the same for that the lease which the complainant's father so tendered unto him was not verbatim agreeable with the old lease before demised, as their agreement was together. And for that there was some rent behind and unpaid for the premises upon the old lease.

(d) Deposition of Henry Johnson, 26 April 1600

Saith that . . . the defendant refused to seal the lease tendered for that he said it was not according to the same covenants contained in the old lease, and for that the said complainant's father (as the defendant then affirmed) was behind with the payment of part of his rent reserved upon the old lease. And . . . he knoweth the same to be true for that he was present when the same lease was tendered by James Burbage to the defendant to seal, at which time the said James Burbage answered the defendant that whatsoever was amiss in the new lease was not long of him but the scrivener who drew the same.

(e) Deposition of William Smyth, 15 May 1600

Saith he hath heard the defendant . . . confess that James Burbage aforesaid did tender unto him, the defendant, a new lease ready written and engrossed, ready to seal according [to] the covenants and provisos contained in the first lease. And he, the defendant, upon the same tender, asked the said James Burbage and the scrivener (who brought the same lease with them, ready to be sealed) if they would give him leave to advise of it. Whereupon they answered 'no', 'Then,' said the defendant, 'if you will not give me leave I will take leave', and [he] took the said lease and since then kept it in his own possession and never sealed the same.

275 James Burbage shows that he has indeed spent £200 on buildings other than the Theatre, 20 November 1585

PRO, Req.2/184/45. Transcribed in Wallace, *First London Theatre*, 234. D–7

When Allen refused to sign the new lease of 1 November 1585, claiming, among other things, that Burbage had not spent £200 on buildings other than the Theatre (see **274**), James Burbage had a group of builders take a formal view of the work.

[Thomas Osborne, a carpenter who testified for Cuthbert Burbage on 15 May 1600,] saith that ... he did hear the said Bryan Ellam, William Bothan and William Clerke affirm and say that they had taken a ... view of Mr James Burbage his buildings, and costs bestowed upon the premises, which view, they said they made about the twentieth day of November ... 1585, and that they had confirmed the same under their hands in a book of account of the said Mr James Burbage, and that then the same came ... to £220, and that he thinketh it could be no less, for that it seemed there had been great cost bestowed upon and about the same by the said Mr James Burbage, and for that they who were viewers thereof were workmen of good judgement in building and had wrought upon the same for the said James Burbage at his charge. [See also **288** and **306**.]

276 The Theatre is tied commercially to its neighbour, the Curtain, for seven years from Michaelmas 1585

PRO, (a) C24/221/12; (b) C24/228/10; (c) C24/226/11 [pt 1]. Transcribed in Wallace, *First London Theatre*, (a) 62, (b) 125–6, (c) 149. C–12, C–22, C–23

Why Burbage and Brayne made this curious arrangement is a puzzle.[1] Three people described it, all in Margaret Brayne's lawsuit against James Burbage.

[1] See Ingram, *The Business of Playing*, 227–36.

(a) James Burbage, 16 February 1591

[He and Brayne] join[ed] in a grant to one Henry Lanman, gentleman, of the one moiety of the said Theatre and of the profits and commodities growing thereby for certain years yet enduring, as by the deed thereof may appear, and bound themselves in great bonds for the performance thereof.

(b) John Allein, an actor, 6 May 1592

[He knew that] one Henry Lanman had ... part of the profits of the ... [Theatre] and so must till Michaelmas now next coming. [Moreover, he had seen Burbage pay some of the profits of the Theatre to Lanman,] which profits, as this deponent hath heard the said James Burbage say, were due unto the said Lanman and that he and the said Brayne were both bound by writing to pay the same unto him in consideration that the said Lanman did grant unto them the one-half of the profits of the other playhouse thereby, called the Curtain.

(c) Henry Lanman, owner of the Curtain, 30 July 1592

About seven years now shall be this next winter, they, the said Burbage and Brayne, having the profits of plays made at the Theatre and this deponent having the profits of the plays done at the house called the Curtain near to the same, the said Burbage and Brayne, taking the Curtain as an easer[2] to their playhouse, did of their own motion move this deponent that he would agree that the profits of the said two playhouses might for seven years' space be in divident between them. Whereunto this deponent, upon reasonable conditions and bonds, agreed and consented and so continueth to this day. And [Lanman] saith that at the first motion of this agreement the said Brayne had his portion duly answered him of the said profits and until he died.

[2] The word is spelled 'Esore' in the document. Lanman meant, presumably, easement, which is 'a Service or Convenience which one Neighbour has of another by Charter [*i.e.*, a written contract] or Prescription [*i.e.* use], without profit' (Cowel, *A Law Dictionary*, 1727).

277 John Brayne dies, apparently childless; his widow accuses Robert Miles of murder, July–August 1586

PRO, (a) C3/222/83; (b) C24/226/10 [pt 1]. Transcribed in Wallace, *First London Theatre*, (a) 42; (b) 86. (a) *C–3*, (b) *C–18*

Brayne may have thought himself childless when he died, but his wife was, it seems, pregnant at the time (see **281** and **290**). Despite Burbage's remarks here, Brayne did not leave his interest in the Theatre to Burbage's children. Margaret Brayne probated her husband's will (dated 1 July 1578) on 10 August 1586 (GL, MSS 9171/17/fos. 29v–30, 9168/14/fo. 101). Henry Bett was a lawyer who testified for James Burbage in the lawsuit against Margaret Brayne quoted in (a).

(a) James Burbage's bill, 1588

In the time of his sickness and not long before his death [Brayne] promised, confessed and agreed with ... James Burbage and his said wife ... that as well the moiety of the premises and all matters whatsoever concerning the said Theatre and buildings and his moiety therein to be assured ... were and should be and remain if he died (for that he had no children) ... to your orator's [*i.e.* James Burbage's] the children aforesaid, whose advancement he then seemed greatly to tender.

(b) Deposition of Henry Bett, 30 September 1591

At his [Brayne's] death ... he [Brayne] charged Miles with his death by certain stripes [*i.e.* blows] given him by Miles, who was afterwards called by the suit of the said Margaret [Brayne] before an inquest held by the coroner for the county of Middlesex for the inquiry thereof.

278 Margaret Brayne collects her husband's share of profits at the Theatre and Curtain, autumn 1586–87?

PRO, (a) C24/226/10 [pt 1]; (b) C24/228/11; (c) C24/226/11 [pt 1]. Transcribed in Wallace, *First London Theatre*, (a) 87–8, (b) 104, (c) 146. C–18, C–21, C–23. For Bett, see **277** above. Robert and Ralph Miles (father and son) testified for Margaret Brayne in her lawsuit against James Burbage.

(a) Deposition of Henry Bett, 30 September 1591

[He] saith that . . . after . . . [John Brayne's] death the said Margaret did take up some money at the playhouse called the Curtain, but by what right or by whose sufferance she so received the same, this deponent knoweth not.

(b) Deposition of Ralph Miles, 10 February 1592

He did hear say since the decease of the said Brayne that the said James Burbage did earnestly persuade the said complainant [Margaret Brayne] to bestow all the money that she was able to make in repairing and building about the said Theatre. And in that respect he suffered her a certain time to take and receive the one-half of the profits of the galleries of the said Theatre until she had spent and bestowed upon the same all that she had received and a great deal more. And then, on a sudden, he would not suffer her to receive any more of the profits there, saying that he must take and receive all, till he had paid the debts. And then she was constrained as his servant to gather the money and to deliver it unto him, and shortly after he would not suffer her any way to meddle in the premises but thrust her out of all and so useth her to this day.

(c) Deposition of Robert Miles, 30 July 1592

He doth well remember that the said James Burbage, after the death of the said Brayne and before the redemption of the said lease, did for a time suffer the complainant to take some of the profits of the said plays, so long as she was able to lay out money to the necessary use of the said playhouse to the sum of £30 or thereabouts, as she reported, and no longer. Whereupon this deponent on the complainant's behalf, both before and since the redemption of the same, charged them [the Burbages] with the same, and the said James made answer that she should have her moiety according to the said award when all their debts were paid.[1]

[1] These remarks are supported by remarks of John Allein and Henry Lanman; PRO, C24/228/11 and C24/226/11 [pt 1], transcribed in Wallace, *First London Theatre*, 100, 149; C–21, C–23.

279 Margaret Brayne and Robert Miles sue one another, then combine against the Burbages, 1586–1588

PRO, C24/226/10. Transcribed in Wallace, *First London Theatre*, 88. C–18

Miles must have sued Margaret Brayne at common law for her husband's debts and expelled her from the George Inn in Whitechapel, where he and Brayne had been partners and lived. For she tried to have him prosecuted for common barratry and sued him in Chancery in April 1597 for readmission to the George (PRO, C2/Eliz. /B13/5, C–1). When Miles did not reply to her lawsuit, the court ordered him to do so by 14 May 1597 (PRO, C33/74/fo. 372, C–2), but since nothing more is heard of the lawsuit, she must have dropped it. Presumably he dropped his lawsuit against her and readmitted her to the George.[1] She then sued James Burbage at common law over the bonds he had given her husband; Burbage sued her in Chancery to stop her lawsuit at common law (see **281** below); and she countersued him in Chancery (bill and answer[s] missing, but many ancillary documents exist). Miles had become her protector and the force behind these and her later legal actions against the Burbages. Note some of Burbage's remarks in his bill (**281**) and a remark of Henry Bett on 30 September 1591:

He [Bett] hath heard it reported that the said Miles hath made great boast that it is he that will maintain and defend her herein [*i.e.* Margaret Brayne in her lawsuits], albeit she did procure his trouble before the coroner's inquest and did impute to him the death of her husband and procured him to be indicted as a common barrator. But of his own knowledge herein he knoweth nothing.

[1] She was probably living in the George when she died in 1593 (see **290**).

280 John Hyde, the mortgagee, tries to collect the money owing on the mortgage, 1587–1588

PRO, C24/218/93 [pt 2]. Transcribed in Wallace, *First London Theatre*, 55–7. C–10. The quotations are from the depositions of two witnesses for Burbage in Margaret Brayne's lawsuit against him.

(a) Hyde, 8 December 1590

After the death of the said Brayne and after the receipts as aforesaid, he [Hyde] did say and gave it out in speech that he had set over and assigned the said lease and bonds to one George Clough, his , this deponent's, father-in-law, but in truth he did not so . . . But this deponent [Hyde] thinketh that the said Clough, his father-in-law, did go about to put the said defendant [James Burbage] out of the Theatre, or, at least, did threaten him to put him out. And, as this deponent remembreth, the said Burbage did tell him that he could not accomplish such order as he, this deponent, and his said father-in-law, Clough, had set down and prescribed to him for the redemption of his said lease.

(b) George Clough, 8 December 1590

On a time, but certainly how long sithence he [Clough] remembreth not, one John Hyde of London, grocer, who had married this deponent's wife's daughter, told him, this deponent, that he had certain money owing unto him by one Burbage and one Brayne, as this deponent remembreth, and that for his security of the payment thereof he had assigned unto him a lease of the Theatre, and told this deponent that he could not have his money paid and therefore requested him, this deponent, being his father-in-law, to go unto the said Burbage to demand of him the money he owed him and to say that he had assigned over the said lease to him, this deponent. And this deponent thereupon went divers and sundry times to the said Burbage and received money of him due to the said John Hyde, whereof he made unto the same John Hyde an account from time to time as he received the same, but how much the same moneys did amount unto this deponent remembreth not. Neither did he at any time to his remembrance . . . [go] about to put the now defendant out of the Theatre.

281   James Burbage countersues Margaret Brayne in Chancery, autumn 1588

PRO, C3/222/83. Transcribed in Wallace, *First London Theatre*, 39–44. C–3

The quotations below are from Burbage's bill, the date of which is illegible except for the last digit, which is 8 and suggests 1588. A large piece of the left side has been torn off and lost, so that each line is missing six or more inches, indicated below by square brackets enclosing three dots.

One John Brayne, late of Whitechapel, [. . .] he practised to obtain some interest therein [*i.e.* the Theatre property and the buildings on it], presuming that he might easily compass the same by reason that he was natural brother [of your said orator's wife . . .] divers sums of money) he made means to your said orator, James Burbage, that he might have the moiety of the above-named Theatre and [. . .] that in consideration thereof he would not only bear and pay half the charges of the said buildings then bestowed and thereafter to be bestowed [. . .] your orator's aforesaid, her children should have the same moiety so to him to be conveyed and assured, making semblance that his industry was [. . .] children of his sister as is aforesaid. Whereupon your said orator, James Burbage, did become bound to the said Brayne in £400 [. . .] effect that your said orator should at the request of the said John Brayne his executors or assigns convey to him the said John Brayne, his [executors and assigns . . .] to be erected upon the premises demised by the said Giles Allen to your said orator with such covenants and warranties as your orator might [. . .] lease made by the said Giles Allen was then, or thereafter should be, charged with by any act then done, or thereafter to be done, by your [said orator . . .] money borrowed by your said orator, as by the same obligation and condition more at large it doth and may appear.

And after the [. . .] amounting unto exceeding charges about the said buildings than of ability to support the same and having gotten your said orator to be bound [. . .] to redeem the said lease, nor had wherewith to proceed in those manner of buildings wherein he had procured your orator to enter into [. . .] charge any sums of money grown due for the said buildings, nor pay the moiety of the rent aforesaid, but with your orator's money the profits [. . .] wealth of the said Brayne before, being conferred and weighed with the costs upon the said inn [*i.e.* the George in Whitechapel] by him bestowed after it manifestly appeared and [. . .] and finishing of the said buildings to his great hindrance, as is well to be proved.

And after, for that your said orator, James Burbage, had no bond [. . .] so by him to be received out of the premises from thenceforth upon the said buildings and maintenance thereof, he, the said Brayne, and the said James Burbage, your [said orator . . .] arbitrament of certain arbitrators, who thereupon, according to the said submission, did deliver up an award or arbitrament in writing dated about the year [1578 . . .] John Brayne should not be comprised within the compass of the said arbitrament, but that as well by force thereof as by virtue of the said arbitrament your said orator [. . .] Theatre and buildings and of the moiety of the profits thereof whensoever the said Brayne would demand the same, with such exception of acts as is aforesaid [. . . with] which arbitrament your said orator did content himself and did permit and suffer the said John Brayne to receive the moiety of the profits of the said Theatre and [. . .] on his part.

But the said John Brayne, being a very subtle person and confederating himself with one Robert Miles of London, goldsmith, [blank: *i.e.* William] Tomson of [. . .] they might impoverish your said orator and to deprive him of his interest and term for years in the said Theatre and buildings and to bring him into the danger [. . .] same, he, the said Brayne, not meaning to give the said moiety nor his interest therein to your said orator's the children aforesaid nor the lease of the said George [. . .] the moiety of the profits of the premises as is aforesaid, the which promise was made as well before as after the said arbitrament made as is aforesaid. But practising to deprive [. . .] again made a deed of gift to the said Tomson and thereby did give and grant to him all his goods and chattels whereof he was then, or thereafter should be, possessed. Whereby [. . .] for the recovery of the bond of £200 to him forfeited by the said Brayne for the not performing of the said arbitrament, nor to levy the same out of his goods and chattels [. . .] against the body of the said Brayne for the same, the which during his life he was loath to do for that he was his brother-in-law, as is aforesaid. The benefit [. . .] the said Tomson, the said Brayne, for the maintenance of his said fraud and devices, procured the executors or administrators of the said Tomson to convey to the said Robert [Miles . . .] so granted to the said Tomson by the said Brayne with the lease of the said inn called the George also at his own death or not long before, he fearing [. . .] ample conveyance of all his goods and chattels which he then had to the said John Gardiner and to others, to the intent that he or they by force thereof should or might enter into [. . .] or other the premises, or that the said Miles by virtue of the same deed of gift made to the same Tomson should challenge or demand the same or to incur the danger [. . .] in the time of his sickness and not long before his death promised, confessed, and agreed with your said orator, James Burbage, and his said wife in the presence [. . .] of the said Miles that as well the moiety of the premises and all matters whatsoever concerning the said Theatre and buildings and his moiety therein to be assured and [. . .] had received of and by the premises, as namely the lease of the George in Whitechapel, were and should be and remain if he died (for that he had no children and for [. . .] premises) to your orator's the children aforesaid, whose advancement he then seemed greatly to tender, and further promised to your said orator that his said bonds should be [. . .] of your said orator, James Burbage.

And after the said John Brayne died in anno 1586. By means whereof, now so it is, if it may please your honour, the [. . .] administration of the goods of her said late husband, the which she practised then to have) by the said John Gardiner and Robert Miles by reason that they claimed the same goods and chattels [. . .] conveyances) under the colour of a will supposed to be made by the said Brayne long before the said conveyances so made to the said Gardiner and Tomson, the which is supposed to be rased [. . .] that any such will should be maintained or produced. Yet by virtue thereof and being therein nominated to be executor to her said husband, she now as executor goeth about to arrest your said [orator . . .] pretending that he did not perform the said arbitrament (as in truth he did) and for the said bond of £400, pretending that your orator hath also forfeited the same, as in truth he hath not. And [. . .] said husband denying that her said husband made any such promises as is aforesaid, either for the cancelling or conveying of the premises to your orators aforesaid. And the said Robert Miles by [. . .] then to sue your said orator, James Burbage, for the said bonds but hath entered into and upon the said Theatre and buildings and troubleth your orator and his tenants in their peaceable possession [. . .] both the issues and profits thereof by virtue of the conveyances made to him thereof. And the administrators of the said John Gardiner, who deceased in anno 1587, to whom the said bond [. . .] made to the said Gardiner demand and go about to sue your said orator, James Burbage, for the two several bonds. And amongst them by reason of multiplicity of [. . .] their conveyances and sometime denying the same to be good) they do all join together to imprison your said orator, James Burbage, thereby to enforce him to yield to their requests. And [. . .] impertinent actions only to procure him to great charges and to his impoverishment forever, the rather because by these devices he cannot have the said £200 due to him by the said [. . .] Brayne.

In tender consideration of the premises, and for that the said Margaret Brayne, Robert Miles, and [blank] Gardiner, the administrator of the said John Gardiner [. . .] said lease so being mortgaged and forfeited as is aforesaid and have the said lease to them reconveyed, do now demand the same moiety and will not permit the children aforesaid [. . .] all the said promises, the which now your said orators are unable to do by reason that the same promises were done in secret and in the presence only of the said Robert [. . .] or gone beyond the seas so that your orators cannot have their testimony in the premises, by which means your said orator, James Burbage, is without [. . .] the said bonds or to enforce them to cancel the same, nor the children aforesaid, by the ordinary course of the common law aforesaid cannot procure the [. . .] the premises so promised to them by the said John Brayne, the which to do the said Brayne was bound in conscience to so perform, and that the said bonds should [. . .] done by the said John Brayne and by your said orator James Burbage jointly in contradiction of the matters contained in the said bond and arbitrament so [. . .] not be performed if they, or any of them, had lawful interest therein, as they have not.

282 Margaret Brayne and Robert Miles respond in Chancery, autumn 1588

PRO, C3/222/83. Transcribed in Wallace, *First London Theatre*, 44–5. C–3

Margaret Brayne and Robert Miles demurred. They said, that is, that James Burbage's complaint was irrelevant as well as 'very untrue and insufficient in the [law]', the untruths 'over tedious to be recited'.

283 Cuthbert Burbage pays off the mortgage and takes possession of the lease, 7 June 1589

PRO, (a, b) C24/228/11; (c) KB27/1373/m.257. Transcribed in Wallace, *First London Theatre*, (a) 99, (b) 108–9, (c) 272. (a, b) C–21, (c) D–16

The first two quotations below are from depositions taken on behalf of Margaret Brayne in her lawsuit against James Burbage; the third is from the summary of Giles Allen's lawsuit in King's Bench against Cuthbert Burbage. From now on, Cuthbert Burbage at least nominally owned the property and buildings, and the lawsuits were in his name as well as his father's.

(a) Ralph Miles, 10 February 1592

He was present with others when the said complainant, the widow Brayne, offered to the said John Hyde that if he would deliver up the lease unto her she would make shift for the money that was behind[1] and would be bound to assure to the said James Burbage the one-half thereof, although he went about to do her wrong in it. Whereunto the said John Hyde made answer that he would not do so, 'but when', quoth he, 'I have my money I will deliver it up to you both, as I had it of your husband and him'. And then she told him, saying, 'Mr Hyde, if you do otherwise, you undo me.' 'Fear not, Mrs Brayne,' quoth he, 'I will be as good as my word when I am paid my money, for had it not been for your husband, whom I knew to be of credit, I would not have dealt with the other', or words to this effect.

[1] Margaret Brayne thought this amount was about £30, but Hyde, though asked directly, avoided giving any figure. She argued that James Burbage did not complete paying off the mortgage on the lease because if he did Hyde would return it to her as well as to Burbage. PRO, C24/228/11, transcribed in Wallace, *First London Theatre*, 94, 99, 108. C–21.

(b) John Hyde, 12 February 1592

It may be the said complainant [Margaret Brayne] did offer this deponent [Hyde] the money behind unpaid unto him of the said mortgage, for she came many and oftentimes unto him concerning the same, but, in truth, he doth not remember she made him any such offer. But he saith that if she had, and had performed the same, he would rather have put it over unto her than to the same Burbages, for that she did greatly complain unto him that James Burbage did her wrong and sought to put her from it. And saith that to his remembrance he did not hear her say that if this deponent did put it over to her she would be bound to convey the one moiety of it to the said James Burbage. And otherwise to this interrogatory he saith he cannot depose . . .

The said James Burbage was sundry times in hand with this deponent that upon the payment of the money behind and some consideration for the forbearing thereof he, this deponent, should convey over the premises to his son, Cuthbert Burbage, and this deponent was very loath so to do without the consent of the complainant. And at the last, he and his son brought to this deponent a letter from one Mr Cope, one of the Lord Treasurer's gentlemen, the said Cuthbert's master, [saying] that he, this deponent, . . . (at his request and as he might be able to do this deponent any friendship or pleasure in any [of] his occasions to his lord and master) should convey over his interest of and in the premises to his servant, Cuthbert Burbage, the son of the said James, upon the payment of such money as was due unto him and unpaid and upon some consideration for the forbearing of it. And this deponent (partly at the said gentleman's request and partly at instant [*i.e.* pressing] entreaty of the said James Burbage and his said son) did indeed upon the considerations aforesaid convey over the premises to the said Cuthbert . . . But he well remembreth that he wished the said Burbages to do the complainant no wrong [since] her husband was dead and had left her in great lack, and that he did undo himself by entering in the doings of the Theatre. And they said, and many times have said, that they would do her no wrong . . .[1]

The said Burbages did promise this deponent that . . . what was the complainant's [*i.e.* Margaret Brayne's] right and due to have, that she should have it at their hands.

[1] On another occasion, Hyde explained the transaction this way: 'Mr Walter Cope, being attendant upon the Lord Treasurer, did write his letters to him, this deponent, thereby entreating him that he would sell to his, the same Mr Cope's servant, Cuthbert Burbage, his title and interest of the said lease, the rather for that he might help discharge his father (meaning the defendant [James Burbage]) out of many troubles which Brayne and his said father might have sustained about conveyances and bonds made by them concerning the Theatre'. PRO, C24/218/93 [pt. 2], transcribed in Wallace, *First London Theatre*, 55–6; C–10.

(c) Giles Allen, January 1601

John Hyde afterwards, namely on 7 June . . . [1589] at the aforesaid Holywell, assigned all his interest and term of years that he had yet to come of and in the said tenements by the aforesaid James [Burbage] before acquired and demised, with the appurtenances, to the said Cuthbert Burbage by virtue of which the aforesaid Cuthbert entered those said tenements with the appurtenances and was thereupon possessed.

284 A play against Martin Marprelate is played at the Theatre, 1589

Nashe, *Martins Months Minde* (1589), To the Reader

Martin... being... sundry ways very cursedly handled, as... wormed and lanced, that he took very grievously to be made a May game upon the stage. [In the margin:] The Theatre.

285 Chancery orders that the arbitrament of 1578 be observed, 13 November 1590

PRO, C33/81/fo. 145. Transcribed in Wallace, *First London Theatre*, 48. C–8

See 258. The 'sequestration' refers to Margaret Brayne's demand on 4 November 1590 that the court collect half the profits of the Theatre and other places on the property (PRO, C33/81/fo. 109, transcribed in Wallace, *First London Theatre*, 47–8; C–7).

Forasmuch as upon the opening of the matter this present day by Mr Sergeant Harris, being of the defendant's [*i.e.* Burbage's] counsel, and seeking for stay of a sequestration prayed by a former order on the plaintiff's [*i.e.* Margaret Brayne's] behalf, and also upon the hearing of Mr Scott, being of the plaintiff's counsel, what he could say touching the cause: it seemed unto this court that there was an arbitrament heretofore made between the plaintiff's late husband and the said James Burbage the 12th day of July in ... [1578] by one Richard Turner and John Hill touching the same matter which is now again brought in question, and that neither of the parties did now show any sufficient cause wherefore the same arbitrament or award should not be performed. It is therefore ordered that the said award or arbitrament shall be well and truly observed and performed according to the tenor and true meaning thereof, as well by the plaintiff and all claiming from, by, or under her, as also by the defendants and every of them and all claiming from, by, or under them or any of them, and the said order for sequestration shall be stayed.

286 The Burbages suspect Miles and Margaret Brayne of murdering John Brayne and of adultery, November 1590

PRO, C24/226/10 [pt 1]. Transcribed in Wallace, *First London Theatre*, 81 (see also 88, 89, 92). C–18

According to Margaret Brayne's allies, James Burbage several times called her a 'whore' and a 'murdering whore', and his wife, Ellen, and son, Richard (the actor), called Miles a 'murdering knave' and 'other vile and unhonest words' (see **287c–e**). For his part, James Burbage asked Henry Bett and two others:

> How often, to your knowledge, is the said Robert Miles indicted . . . for . . . adultery, or as you have heard? And . . . was he called before the Coroner's Inquest for the death of Brayne, yea or no? [But all three avoided saying anything about adultery.[1]]

[1] See also Berry, 'Shylock, Robert Miles, and Events at the Theatre,' pp. 193–5.

287 Margaret Brayne tries to claim half the Theatre, and the Burbages defy her, 14 November 1590–spring 1591

PRO, (a, b) C24/221/12; (c–e) C24/228/11, C24/228/10. Transcribed in Wallace, *First London Theatre*, (a) 59–60, (b) 61–3, (c) 97–8, 114–15, (d) 100–2, 126–7, (e) 105, 121–2. (a, b) C–12, (c–e) C–21, C–22

Margaret Brayne thought the order of 13 November 1590 (**285**) justified her claim to half the Theatre property. In the days following, therefore, she and friends visited the Theatre several times to claim the fruits of ownership. The Burbage family reacted sharply, as five people explained. First, the court summoned James and Cuthbert Burbage to answer questions that she proposed about the affair – see (a, b). Then on 13 November 1591 the court allowed her and the Burbages to propose questions for three other people, each of whom responded to her questions and then to the Burbages' – see (c–e).[1]

[1] The court also allowed her and the Burbages to question John Hyde, the mortgagee, who explained how and why he returned the lease to Cuthbert Burbage (see **283b**).

(a) Cuthbert Burbage, 16 February 1591

It is true indeed that Robert Miles . . . and others with him came to this deponent's [Cuthbert Burbage's] father's dwelling house in Holywell by Shoreditch upon or about the 16th day of November . . . for and in the name of the now complainant [Margaret Brayne], as he said, and demanded rent and the performance of the said award [*i.e.* the arbitrament of 1578] according to the said order [of 13 November 1590]. And what answer this deponent's said father made unto him he saith he remembreth not, but this deponent made him answer that he should have no rent there, [and] he would sufficiently answer the court the cause why when he were called, and withal told him that Brayne nor his wife had no right there, for it was his, this deponent's, and he had bought it with his own proper money, as they well knew . . .

When the said Miles came to this defendant's father's house as aforesaid . . . he came in such rude and exclamable sort as indeed his said father threatened to set him away off his ground if he would not go his way quietly . . .

He cannot certainly depose what answer or speech . . . [his] father made or uttered to the complainant at any time she came to him or to the Theatre for any rent or other demand concerning the moiety of the same, for he did not hear the same. Or, at the least, he did [not] heed the same . . .

(b) James Burbage, 16 February 1591

Robert Miles . . . with two other persons with him, whose names he [James Burbage] knoweth not, in November last past (the certain day he now remembreth not) did in the behalf of the now complainant [Margaret Brayne] come to this deponent's [James Burbage's] dwelling house near the Theatre in Shoreditch and there did demand first of this deponent's son [Cuthbert Burbage] the moiety of the said Theatre and the rents of the same to her use and of the performance of the said award [i.e. the arbitrament of 1578]. And what answer this deponent's said son made him thereunto he cannot certainly tell. But he saith that this deponent, being within the house [and] hearing a noise at the door, went to the door and there found his son, the said Cuthbert, and the said Miles speaking loud together; and asking what the matter was, the said Miles did as a afore[said], demand the moiety of the said Theatre and the rent thereof and the performance of the said award on the complainant's behalf. And then this deponent told him that the order [of 13 November 1590] did not warrant any such demand of rent nor of any moiety of the said Theatre; and for the performance of the said award, he told him that he, this deponent, for his part, could not perform it better than he had done.

And then the said Miles said that by the said award the moiety of the Theatre and the rent thereof are to be had and received by and to the use of the said complainant. So it was indeed, quoth this deponent, before John Brayne himself and he, this deponent, did, after the making of the said award, join in a grant to one Henry Lanman, gentleman, of the one moiety of the said Theatre and of the profits and commodities growing thereby for certain years yet enduring, as by the deed thereof may appear, and bound themselves in great bonds for the performance thereof. And [he] further saith that long after the said arbitrament and award and before the grant made to the said Lanman, the said Brayne, the complainant's said husband, did procure this deponent to mortgage the lease of the said Theatre for the sum of £125 and odd money to one John Hyde of London, grocer, for one year, and after that for another year, with a proviso that for the non-payment of the said sum at a day the said lease to be forfeited, which was forfeited accordingly by the non-payment of the money. So as then the said Hyde was fully and absolutely possessed thereof to dispose of the same at his will and pleasure, by which means he, this deponent, doth verily take it that the said arbitrament and award was determined and dissolved . . .

But he, this deponent, being nearly urged and dared by the said Miles with great threats and words that he would do this and could do that to the undoing and great disgrace of this deponent and his son, he, this deponent, told him that it was too much to face him so on his own ground and that he [Miles] knew he could not answer it. And that if he would not leave his railing and quietly depart, he, this deponent, would send him away . . .

The said complainant with the said Miles and others came to the said Theatre, to the tenants thereof, and there very imperiously, since the said order, did challenge and demand rents of the same as due unto her for the moiety of the same according to the said arbitrament. And answer was made unto her and them that came with her, both by the said tenants and Cuthbert, this deponent's son, that she had nothing to do there and that they never knew her to have any interest in the same.

(c) Nicholas Byshop, 29 January and 6 April 1592

[In answer to Margaret Brayne:] he doth ... know that the said Margaret Brayne with one Robert Miles came at several times to the said Theatre, and namely upon one of the play days, and entreated James Burbage, one of the now defendants, that she might enjoy her moiety of the premises according to the award and order of the Chancery [i.e. the arbitrament of 1578 and order of 13 November 1590]. And the answer which James Burbage made thereunto was that before she should have anything to do there she should show good order for it. And then the said Miles said that he had a sufficient order of the Chancery for the same and showed him some papers. And then the said Burbage called him rascal and knave and said before he would lose his possession he would make twenty contempts [of court]. And then the wife of the said James and their youngest son, called Richard Burbage, fell upon the said Miles and beat him and drove both him and the complainant [Margaret Brayne] away, saying that if they did tarry to hear the play as others did they should, but to gather any of the money that was given to go upon [the galleries?], they should not, and saith that Cuthbert Burbage, the other of the defendants, was not there to his remembrance.

[In answer to the Burbages:] he was requested by the said Margaret Brayne and Robert Miles, the father of the said Ralph Miles, to go with them to the Theatre upon a play day to stand at the door that goeth up to the galleries of the said Theatre to take and receive for the use of the said Margaret half the money that should be given to come up into the said galleries at that door, according to the foresaid award and an order made thereupon by the Court of Chancery, requesting this deponent [Byshop], in very earnest manner, to resist no violence or other withstanding of him so to do that should be made to or against him in so doing by the said Burbages. At which time, for the better authority of the said Margaret so to do, there was showed forth in the hand of the said Miles to the said Burbages both the said arbitrament and order of the Chancery, and required the said Burbages to suffer the performance thereof. But ... the said James Burbage and his wife and his son, Richard Burbage, did with violence thrust this deponent and the said Margaret and Robert Miles away from the said door going up to the said galleries with vehement threats and menacing that if they departed not from the place they would beat them away.

And so, indeed, upon some words uttered by the said Robert Miles to the said Burbage wishing them to obey the said order, the said Richard Burbage and his mother fell upon the said Robert Miles and beat him with a broom staff, calling him 'murdering knave' with other vile and unhonest words. At which time the said

James Burbage told the said Robert Miles that he had but a paper which he might wipe his tail with, and rather than he would lose his possession he would commit twenty contempts. And by cause this deponent spoke then somewhat in the favour of the poor woman that she did nothing then but by authority of the said order, the said Richard Burbage, scornfully and disdainfully playing with this deponent's nose, said that if he [Byshop] dealt in the matter he would beat him also and did challenge the field of him at that time. And the cause why the said Robert Miles kept fast in his hand the said order was for that the said Burbages would have torn the same in pieces if they had had the same in their hands . . .

(d) John Allein, an actor, 6 February and 6 May 1592

[In answer to Margaret Brayne:] he hath seen the . . . complainant with one Miles come divers times to the said Theatre and hath desired the said defendants [James and Cuthbert Burbage] that, according to the said arbitrament and order of the Chancery [i.e. the arbitrament of 1578 and order of 13 November 1590], she might take, receive and enjoy her moiety of the said profits. And the said defendants and one other of the said James Burbage's sons, called Richard, did rail upon the complainant and the said Miles and with violence drove them out, saying that she should have no moiety there. And then this deponent, being there, did, as a servant, wish the said Burbage to have a conscience in the matter, saying unto him that he himself knew that the woman had a right in the same by her husband, and it was her husband's wealth that built the Theatre, as everybody knoweth. And he then did answer: 'Hang her, whore', quoth he, 'she getteth nothing here. Let her win it at the common law and bring the sheriff with her to put her in possession,' and then he would tell her more of his mind.

Then this deponent [Allein] told him that though he overreached her husband, being but a plain and simple man, 'yet she, being enforced to seek remedy against you, hath the Chancery, being the highest court and a court of conscience, on her side and hath an order out of the same to have her moiety thereof'. 'Conscience', quoth he, 'God's blood, what do you tell me of conscience or orders.' 'No,' quoth this deponent, 'remember yourself well, for if my Lord Chancellor make an order against you, you were best to obey it, otherwise it will prove a contempt and then you shall purchase my Lord Chancellor's displeasure.' And he made answer that he cared not for any contempt, saying that if there were twenty contempts and as many injunctions he would withstand them all before he would lose his possession.

And [he] further saith that when this deponent, about eight days after, came to him for certain money which he detained from this deponent and his fellows of some of the divident money between him and them growing also by the use of the said Theatre, he denied to pay the same, he, this deponent, told him that belike he meant to deal with them as he did with the poor widow, meaning the now complainant, wishing him he would not do so, for if he did they would complain to their lord and master, the Lord Admiral. And then he in a rage, little reverencing his honour and estate, said by a great oath that he cared not for three of the best lords of them all.

And [he] further saith that at the time when the complainant and the said Miles required (as is beforesaid) her moiety of the said Theatre and premises, this deponent found the foresaid Richard Burbage, the youngest son of the said James Burbage, there with a broom staff in his hand, of whom when this deponent asked what stir was there, he answered in laughing phrase how they come for a moiety, 'but', quoth he (holding up the said broom's staff), 'I have, I think, delivered him a moiety with this and sent them packing'. And then this deponent said unto him and his father that the said Miles might have an action against the said Richard. 'Tush,' quoth the father, 'no, I warrant you, but where my son hath now beat him hence, my sons, if they will be ruled by me, shall at their next coming provide charged pistols with powder and hemp seed to shoot them in the legs.' But to his remembrance he saw not Cuthbert, the other defendant, there.

[In answer to the Burbages:] And [he] saith that the words mentioned in his former examination . . . spoken by the said James Burbage, viz. 'Conscience? God's blood, what tell you me of conscience or orders', that he cared not for any contempt, and if there were twenty contempts and as many injunctions he would withstand and break them all before he would lose his possession, were uttered within the Theatre yard when the complainant and the said Miles came to desire him to perform the said arbitrament and order, which he thinketh to be about a year past, in the hearing of one Nicholas Byshop, this deponent [Allein], and others. And the other words spoken by him . . . viz., 'I care not for three of the best lords of them all,' were uttered by him in the attiring-house, or place where the players make them ready, about seven days next after, in the hearing of one James Tunstall, this deponent, and others.

(e) Ralph Miles, 10 February and 26 April 1592

[In answer to Margaret Brayne:] he doth know there was such an order [of 13 November] . . . the which Order the said complainant [Margaret Brayne], being very willing to perform the same, went divers times with sundry her friends and neighbours to the now defendants [James and Cuthbert Burbage] and demanded of them her moiety of the rents and profits of the said Theatre and premises according [to] the said order. And they did utterly deny so to do in the hearing of this deponent and others of credit and reputation, the said James Burbage saying he would obey no such order, nor cared not for them, reviling the complainant with terms of 'murdering whore' and otherwise and charged her and her company to get them off his ground or else he would set them off with no ease. At which time, Cuthbert Burbage, the other defendant, came to them and then the said complainant demanded of him the performance of the said order, and he made answer he would not stand to any such order and willed her and her company to get them thence, saying 'thou hast nothing to do here', and so with much threatening and menacing, she and her company went away.

[In answer to the Burbages:] at such time this deponent and others went at the complainant's request with her to the now defendants to require them to perform the said award as by an order made in the Chancery they were ordered to do, the said James Burbage's wife charged them to go out of her ground or else she would make her son break their knaves' heads and so hotly railed at them. And then the said James Burbage, her husband, looking out at a window upon them, called the complainant 'murdering whore', and this deponent and the others 'villains, rascals, and knaves'. And then the complainant said unto him that she was come to require of him the performance of the award [*i.e.* the arbitrament of 1578], as the Court of Chancery had ordered to do. And then he cried unto her, 'go, go, a cart, a cart for you. I will obey no such order, nor care I not for any such orders, and, therefore, it were best for you and your companions to be packing betimes, for if my son come he will thump you hence.' With that, in manner, his son [Cuthbert] came home, of whom the complainant did also require the performance of the said award, according to the said order of the Chancery, and then he in very hot sort bid them get them hence or else he would set them forwards, saying 'I care for no such order. The Chancery shall not give away what I have paid for. Neither shalt thou have anything to do here while I live, get what orders thou canst.' And so with great and horrible oaths uttered by both him and his father that they would do this and that, the complainant and her company went their ways.

288 The Burbages have the work done on buildings other than the Theatre valued again, July 1591

PRO, C24/226/9 [pt 2]. Transcribed in Wallace, *First London Theatre*, 77. C–17

The Burbages were trying to show here that James Burbage rather than Brayne had spent a lot of money on work done on buildings other than the Theatre. Three builders, Bryan Ellam, Richard Hudson[1] and William Clerke valued the work. Ellam and Clerke had gone through a similar exercise in 1585, when James Burbage was trying to show that he had spent £200 on those buildings and so, according to the terms of his lease, should have an extension (see **274, 275, 306**).

[1] Hudson had to do with the Burbage theatrical enterprises for most of their history, from 1580 or so until at least 1634 (Berry, *Shakespeare's Playhouses*, 166–7, 232–3).

[Hudson, given here as bricklayer but elsewhere as carpenter, said on 29 February 1592:] That he was one amongst others that in July last past [1591] did survey and view the new buildings and the reparations done by the now defendants [the Burbages], or one of them, in and upon certain decayed houses and places in Holywell, near Shoreditch without Bishopsgate, London. And [he] saith that in their judgement they could reckon it to no less than £240 [Ellam said '£240 or £230'] or thereabouts, as by a memorandum under their hands and marks written in the defendants' book of the same may more plainly appear.

289 The Burbages spend £30 to £40 on 'further building and repairing' the Theatre, winter 1591–2

PRO, C24/226/9 [pt 2]. Transcribed in Wallace, *First London Theatre*, 76, 77. C–17. These are further quotations from the depositions quoted in 288.

(a) Bryan Ellam, carpenter, 25 February 1592

Saith that the said defendants [James and Cuthbert Burbage], or one of them, have bestowed in further building and reparations of the Theatre there within this six or seven weeks past to the value of £30 or £40, as this deponent doth estimate the same.

(b) Richard Hudson, 25 February 1592

Saith that the said defendants, or one of them, hath since that view [in July 1591] bestowed in further building and repairing of the Theatre or playhouse there, wherein he, this deponent, was one of the workmen, to the value of £30 or thereabouts.

290 Margaret Brayne dies leaving her child and lawsuits to Robert Miles, 8–13 April 1593

GL, MSS 9172/16, fo. 26v and 9171/18, fo. 26. Transcribed in Wallace, *First London Theatre*, 153–4. C–24

Margaret Brayne wrote her will (quoted below) on 8 April 1593, and Miles proved it on 3 May 1593. She was buried at St Mary Matfellon (Whitechapel) on 13 April 1593, and Katherine Brayne was buried there on 23 July 1593, both probably having died of the plague (the parish register, LMA, P93/MRY/1).

I, Margaret Brayne of the parish of St Mary Matfellon alias Whitechapel, . . . being whole in mind, sick of body, but of a perfect memory, . . . do make and ordain this . . . my last will and testament in manner and form following . . . Item: I give and bequeath unto Robert Miles, citizen and goldsmith of London, in consideration that I am greatly indebted unto him in such great sum and sums of money that all the goods I have in the whole world will nothing countervail the same, all such interest, right, property, claim and demand whatsoever which I, the said Margaret Brayne have, should, or ought to have of, in, or to the one moiety, or half part, of the playhouse commonly called the Theatre, near Holywell in the county of Middlesex. And also my mind and will is that the said Robert Miles shall have all the benefit, profit and commodity thereof . . . coming or growing or which by any means may descend or come by virtue of the said moiety, or half part, of the Theatre to me in right belonging as aforesaid. Item: I give and bequeath unto the said Robert Miles all . . . manner of bonds, specialties, debts, sum and sums of money whatsoever as I now have or which by virtue of any such bonds or specialties may be gotten, won or obtained, or which now and hereafter shall grow due and payable. And lastly, I give and bequeath unto the said Robert Miles all and singular my goods, chattels, household stuff and other of my goods whatsoever. Item: my will is, in consideration partly of the premises [*i.e.* the foregoing], that the said Robert Miles shall keep, educate and bring up Katharine Brayne, my husband's daughter,[1] of whom I hope he will be good and have an honest care for her preferment. And I make and ordain the said Robert Miles sole executor of this my said testament and last will . . .[2]

[1] Professor Ingram has taken these words to mean that Katharine Brayne was John Brayne's child by a woman other than his wife (*Business of Playing*, 216), but the remarks in **286** and **287** suggest otherwise. If she was legitimate, she would have been born by March 1587, hence seven years old when Margaret Brayne wrote her will.
[2] She probably died at the George Inn, since she gave herself as of, and was buried in, Whitechapel, and four of the five people who signed her will were probably associated with the George. They were George Harrison, the notary public who wrote it, and Nicholas and Barbara Byshop (PRO, C3/245/85; C33/87/fo. 704v (A book) and /88/fo. 711 (B book); C24/244/pt 1/89), and John Patteson, who would marry Miles' widowed daughter on 1 November 1593 (the parish register, LMA, P93/MRY/1, and Miles' will, PRO, PROB.11/123, fo. 255).

291 Robert Miles takes up Margaret Brayne's lawsuit against James Burbage in Chancery, 11 February 1594

PRO, C33/85/fo. 758 (A book) and C33/86/fo. 785 (B book). Transcribed in Wallace, *First London Theatre*, 155. C–25

Forasmuch as this court was the present day informed by Mr Scott, being of the plaintiff's [*i.e.* Robert Miles'] counsel, that the matter wherein Margaret Brayne was lately plaintiff against the above-named defendants [the Burbages], standing heretofore referred unto Mr Dr Stanhope and Mr Dr Legg, two of the masters of the court, and they being ready to make their report, the said Margaret, then plaintiff, died. Since which time the said Robert Miles hath exhibited a bill and served process upon the defendants to answer the same to revive the said former suit and the orders of referment made thereupon in the same state it stood at the time of the former plaintiff's death. It is, therefore, ordered that the said masters of this court shall, at the now plaintiff's suit, take the like consideration as they were to do of the matters to them before referred at the former plaintiff's suit and make such report thereof as, by the former orders made in that behalf, they were appointed to do . . .

292 Chancery combines the two lawsuits about the Theatre, 14 March 1595

PRO, C33/87/fo. 857v (A book) and C33/88/fo. 862 (B book). Transcribed in Wallace, *First London Theatre*, 155–6. C–26

Forasmuch as the right honourable Sir John Pickering, knight, lord keeper of the great seal of England, was this present day informed on the plaintiff's [James

Burbage's] behalf by Mr Borne, being of his counsel, that the said parties [Burbage and Robert Miles] have cross bills, the one against the other, and that witnesses in the said several causes are examined and publication at one time by consent of the said parties was long since had, and that the cause wherein the said Burbage is plaintiff for the most part concerneth the other, and that the cause wherein the said Miles is plaintiff is appointed to be heard at the Rolls chapel on Monday, the 28th day of May next [1595], it was therefore most humbly desired by the said Mr Borne, for that the matter wherein the said Burbage is plaintiff against the said Miles was first commenced and is also ready for the hearing as aforesaid, might be also heard together with the other cause wherein the said Miles is plaintiff on the 28th day of May next at the said chapel of the Rolls. It is ordered by his lordship that if the said Miles shall not by the second return [day – *i.e.* 5 May] of the next term show unto this court good cause to the contrary, then the said cause wherein the said James Burbage is plaintiff is set down to be heard on the said 28th day of May without further motion to be made on that behalf, and the said Miles or his attorney is to be warned hereof.

293 Robert Miles effectually loses his case against James Burbage, 28 May 1595

PRO, C33/89/fo. 130 [A book] and C33/90/fo. 140–41v (B book). Transcribed in Wallace, *First London Theatre*, 156–7. C–27

By deciding that it would not consider the lawsuits about the Theatre further until Robert Miles had sought redress in the courts of common law, the Court of Chancery returned him to the state of affairs in 1587–8. It therefore delayed him, increased his costs, and, for the time being, at least, denied him his best arguments, which could not be used at common law because they had to do with imprecise agreements between Brayne and Burbage. Miles now abandoned this lawsuit.

The matter in question between the said parties [Robert Miles and the Burbages], touching the moiety of the lease of the Theatre in the bill mentioned and the profits thereof, coming this present day to be heard in the presence of counsel learned on both parts, it was alleged by the defendants' [the Burbages'] counsel that the said plaintiff [Miles] had not only a bond of £400 made unto him by the defendants for the assigning over of the same moiety unto him, whereupon a demurrer is now joined at the common law, but also another bond of £200 made for the performance of an arbitrament made between the said parties, which the said plaintiff pretendeth to be also forfeited by the defendant. And, therefore, as the said counsel alleged, the plaintiff hath no need of the aid of this court for the said lease and profits. It is thereupon thought fit and so ordered by this court that the said plaintiff shall proceed at the common law against the said defendant upon the said bonds to the end it may be seen whether the plaintiff can relieve himself upon the said bonds or not. But if it fall out that the plaintiff cannot be relieved upon the said bonds, then the matter shall receive a speedy hearing in this court, and such order shall be given thereupon as the equity of the cause shall require. And in the meantime the matter is retained in this court.

294   *Hamlet* is being acted at the Theatre, 1595–1596
Lodge, *Wits Miserie* (1596), xx. This play is probably the so-called *Ur-Hamlet* by, perhaps, Thomas Kyd.

Pale as the vizard of the ghost which cried so miserably at the Theatre, like an oyster wife, 'Hamlet, revenge.'

295   The Burbages negotiate with Giles Allen to renew the lease on the Theatre property, 1596–1598
PRO, (a–d) Req.2/87/74; (e–g) Req.2/184/45. Transcribed in Wallace, *First London Theatre*, (a) 184, (b) 295–6, (c) 254, (d) 256–7, (e) 258, (f) 220–1, 246, (g) 250. (a–d) D–2, (e–g) D–7

Evidence about the manoeuvring from 1596 until the autumn of 1598 over a new lease on the Theatre property appears mostly in Allen's response to Cuthbert Burbage's lawsuit against him in Requests in 1600. The matter was not useful to Burbage's case. In his replication (302c), therefore, he denied the assertions in Allen's answer, and he asked only one relevant but not very revealing question of his witnesses, to which only one of them replied.[1]

[1] Burbage argued only that Allen should have made the lease in 1598 that he had not made in 1585 (**274** and **275**). His question was, in effect: did Burbage ask Allen for such a lease in 1598 and divers times since, did not Allen deny to make it, and why. William Smyth, gentleman, agreed that Burbage had asked and Allen denied and gave Allen's reasons as 'arrearages of rent'. Smyth added: Allen 'did tender . . . a new lease, . . . with improvement of rent and very strict and unreasonable covenants, . . . for which causes the plaintiff refused the same' (PRO, Req.2/184/45; transcribed in Wallace, *First London Theatre*, 224, 238; D–7. Burbage's replication is Req.2/87/74, transcribed 200–5; D–2).

(a)   Cuthbert Burbage's bill, 26 January 1600
[Cuthbert Burbage said that he:] did often require the said Allen and Sarah, his wife, to make unto him the said new lease of the premises, according to the agreement in the said indenture, which the said Giles Allen would not deny but for some causes which he feigned did defer the same from time to time but yet gave hope to your subject and affirmed that he would make him such a lease . . .

But after the said first term of one and twenty years ended [on 25 March 1597], the said Allen hath suffered your subject to continue in possession of the premises for divers years and hath accepted the rent reserved by the said indenture from your subject.

(b)   Allen's answer, 4 February 1600
A little before the death of the said James Burbage [in February 1597], through great labour and entreaty of the said James Burbage and the complainant

[Cuthbert Burbage] and other their friends, who often moved the defendant [Allen] in their behalf, and the said James Burbage pretending and making show unto the defendant with many fair speeches and protestations that he would thereafter duly pay his rent and repair the houses and buildings and perform all his covenants, as a good and an honest tenant ought to do, and that he would likewise pay the said arrearages of £30: the defendant and the said James Burbage grew to a new agreement that the said James Burbage should have a new lease of the premises contained in the former lease for the term of one and twenty years, to begin after the end and expiration of the former lease, for the yearly rent of £24 ...

And it was likewise further agreed between them ... that the said Theatre should continue for a playing place for the space of five years only after the expiration of the first term [*i.e.* until 1602], and not longer, by reason that the defendant saw that many inconveniences and abuses did grow thereby, and that after the said five years ended it should be converted by the said James Burbage and the complainant, or one of them, to some other use, and be employed ... whereby the benefit and profit thereof, after the term of the said James Burbage ended, should remain and be unto the defendant.

But before that agreement was perfected (by reason that the said James Burbage had not procured such security for the performance of his covenants as the defendant did require), the said James Burbage died. After whose death the complainant did again often move and entreat the defendant that he might have a new lease of the premises according to the former agreement made between the said James Burbage, the father of the complainant, and the defendant, the said complainant promising the defendant the payment of the said £30 rent which was behind in the time of the complainant's father, and that he would put in good security to the defendant for the payment of the rent during the term and the repairing of the houses and the performance of all other covenants on his part to be performed, touching which matter there was oftentimes communication had between the complainant and the defendant, who, for his part, was contented to have made the said lease unto the complainant, who likewise seemed very willing to have it in such manner and under such covenants as were formerly agreed upon between the defendant and the said James Burbage. And so the matter was at the last concluded between the complainant and the defendant, and (as the defendant remembreth) a lease was drawn accordingly by the complainant, which the defendant thinketh he can show forth unto this honourable court. And yet, notwithstanding, the complainant found means by colourable shifts and delays to defer the accomplishing and execution thereof from time to time.

Howbeit, the defendant, hoping that the complainant had meant honestly and faithfully, and to have taken the lease according to their agreement, ... was contented to suffer the complainant to enjoy the premises after the first lease expired for the space of a year or two, paying only the old rent of £14.

(c) Two of Allen's interrogatories, 5 June 1600

[Allen asked if there were not two different proposals.] Was there not an agreement . . . to this effect: that the defendant [Allen] should make a new lease to the complainant [Cuthbert Burbage] of the houses and grounds which were formerly demised unto James Burbage . . . for one and twenty years from and after the expiration of that former lease, and that the complainant should pay yearly for the same the sum of £24? And . . . was it not likewise agreed . . . that the Theatre there erected should continue for a playing place by the space of five years only? . . . And did not the complainant, upon that agreement, promise the defendant to pay him . . . £30 which was due to the defendant for rent, and to put the houses and buildings in good reparations? And how long is it sithence such agreement was made?

[And] was it agreed between the defendent and the complainant that the complainant should take a new lease of the said houses and grounds for the term of ten years and that the complainant should give . . . £100 for the said lease, and £24 rent yearly? . . . And at what time [was] any such agreement made?

(d) Robert Vigerous, lawyer, replies, 14 August 1600

[He assisted both sides in the negotiations.] The said complainant [Cuthbert Burbage] together with James Burbage, his father, and the said defendant [Allen] were in communication about the making and taking of a new lease of the houses and grounds and Theatre mentioned in this interrogatory. And at the last it was concluded and agreed between all the said parties that the defendant should make a new lease of the same to the said complainant for the term of ten years for and under the yearly rent of £24, which (as this deponent remembreth) was an increase of £10 more than was reserved in a former lease heretofore made to the said James and then expired or near to be then expired. And that at the ensealing of the said new lease so to be had the said James and Cuthbert, the complainant, or one of them, should pay unto the defendant certain arrearages of rent reserved upon the said former lease amounting to the sum (as this deponent verily thinketh) of £30.

All which this deponent knoweth to be true for that he was of counsel with the said parties in the said agreement, and by all their mutual consents was appointed and especially named to draw, pen and write the said new lease according to their said agreement. And this examinant saith that he did write a draft . . . lease to be made of the premises accordingly, which, being done, he delivered the same into the hands of the said complainant when he came to this deponent's chamber to demand and see the same, and paid him his fees with promises of further reward for his pains about the effecting of the same new lease to be made, which should be a satin doublet. Howbeit, he never had it. But whether the complainant should give . . . £100 for the same lease or whether the said lease took effect, or what other agreement passed between the said complainant and defendant, this deponent, by reason of his discontinuance from the Temple, knoweth not. But he saith that he hath seen a draft ... lease to be made of the same premises wherein it is inserted that ... £100 should be paid by the complainant to the defendant, which draft (as the defendant informeth this deponent) was made or caused to be made by the complainant and by him brought and delivered to the defendant at his house in the country.

And this deponent, being asked by the said commissioners [*i.e.* examiners] if he knew upon what consideration the said £100 was inserted, said that he remembreth not the consideration mentioned in the said draft. But he saith upon the first communication had between the said complainant and defendant and the said James before this deponent, as is aforesaid, the defendant did demand recompense at the hands of the said James, for that the defendant said the said James had not bestowed £200 in the building or repairing of the said houses according to a covenant mentioned in the said former lease, nor half so much, or words to the like effect. But whether the said £100 was inserted upon that consideration or no, this deponent knoweth not.

(e) Thomas Nevill, gentleman, replies 10 October 1600

There was an agreement had between them, the said complainant [Cuthbert Burbage] and the said defendant [Allen], for the houses and grounds with the Theatre, which were formerly demised unto James Burbage, the father of the said complainant, with an increasing of the rent from £14 by the year unto £24 by the year. Which lease should begin at the expiration of the old lease made unto the said complainant's father and should continue for the space of one and twenty years.

And this deponent further saith that the said defendant was at the first very unwilling that the said Theatre should continue one day longer for a playing place, yet, nevertheless, at the last he yielded that it should continue for a playing place for certain years, and that the said defendant did agree that the said complainant should after those years expired convert the said Theatre to his best benefit for the residue of the said term then to come, and that afterward it should remain to the only use of the defendant. And further this deponent saith that the said James Burbage, the father, did acknowledge the sum of £30 mentioned in this interrogatory to be due unto the said defendant for rent then behind and unpaid, and that the complainant, Cuthbert Burbage, did oftentimes sithence promise payment of the said sum of £30 at the ensealing of the new lease. And he further saith that the said agreement was made between the said complainant and the defendant now two years sithence or thereabouts, at Michaelmas term now next coming [*i.e.* in 1598].

(f) Henry Johnson answers other questions, 26 April 1600

[He was another of Allen's witnesses, one of his tenants, and a silk weaver.] About Michaelmas term last past was twelvemonth [1598], the complainant [Cuthbert Burbage] ... and he, this deponent, met at the defendant's [Allen's] lodging, with the defendant, at the sign of the George in Shoreditch, ... at which time there passed between the complainant and the defendant divers speeches touching a new lease of the premises to be made by the defendant to the complainant for one and twenty years. Which speech and communication was to this or like effect: viz., the complainant demanded of the defendant a lease of the houses and grounds for one and twenty years to commence after the expiration of the lease which had been before made unto his father, James Burbage; and that the Theatre, which then was upon part of the said grounds, might for this term of one and twenty years remain for place to play in, as it was wont; and in consideration thereof, he, the complainant, then promised to give the defendant £24 per annum for a yearly rent for the premises and would take upon him[self] to pay the defendant the sum of £30 which the defendant claimed for arrearages of rent due in James Burbage his lifetime, and would undertake to put the mansion-houses [i.e. the major buildings other than the Theatre] upon the premises in reparation.

And the defendant was contented and did accept of the complainant's proffer in all, except his demand for the Theatre to stand as a playhouse, which he misliked ... Whereupon the complainant requested the defendant that he would suffer it to stand for a playhouse but the five first years of the one and twenty years, and afterwards he would convert the same to some other, better use, viz., into tenements or repairing the other premises demised unto him, and afterwards leave the same upon the premises for the defendant's benefit, which the defendant then agreed unto, and then demanded of the complainant sufficient security for the payment of his, the complainant's, rent during his term of one and twenty years. Whereupon he [the complainant] made proffer unto the defendant of his brother, Richard Burbage, with whom the defendant misliked, and so thereupon they left off and parted.

[Johnson added on 23 May 1600:] He knoweth that the complainant [Cuthbert Burbage] hath many times laboured and entreated the defendant [Allen] to make him a new lease of the premises in question. For this deponent saith that many times when the defendant hath come up to London to receive his rents, he, this deponent, hath been with him paying him certain rent and then he hath seen the plaintiff with his landlord [i.e. Allen] paying his rent likewise. And then finding opportunity, the plaintiff would be entreating the defendant to make him a new lease of the premises in question. And [he] saith it is at least three years since he, this deponent, first heard the plaintiff labour and entreat the defendant for a new lease, and that it was at the sign of the George in Shoreditch that the defendant lay when he came to London to receive his rents, and there the plaintiff solicited him for a new lease.

(g) John Goburne answers, 23 May 1600

[He was another of Allen's witnesses, one of his tenants, and a merchant tailor.] He never heard that the said James Burbage and the defendant [Allen] had at any time any speeches together touching the continuance of the Theatre for a playing house for the space of but five years only after the expiration of his old lease. But the defendant would fain have had the said James Burbage to have converted the said Theatre to some other use upon the premises demised unto him, which the said James Burbage would not agree unto but told the defendant that he would increase his rent £10 per annum if he might have his lease renewed for one and twenty years more after the expiration of the old lease, and the Theatre to continue during that time for a playing-house... And... after the new lease which he then entreated for were expired he or the now complainant [Cuthbert Burgage] would convert the said Theatre upon the premises to some other use for the benefit as well of the defendant as for the lessee then in possession. But upon all that conference nothing was absolutely agreed upon because the defendant would not consent to suffer the same Theatre to continue so long for a playhouse.

296 Robert Miles sues Cuthbert Burbage and Giles Allen, April–May 1597

PRO, Req.2/241/14. Transcribed in Wallace, *First London Theatre*, 158–62, C–28

After James Burbage died in February 1597 Robert Miles took his lawsuit against the Burbages to another court of equity, the Court of Requests. Because the court would not consider a lawsuit already decided, Miles made it seem new by including Giles Allen in his complaint. Only the bill of complaint survives, filed between 13 April (when Easter term began) and 9 May (see **297**) 1597.

Robert Miles... executor of the last will and testament of Margaret Brayne, deceased, executrix of the last will and testament of John Brayne, her husband, also deceased, [complains] that whereas one Giles Allen, gentleman, and Sarah, his wife, ... for a fine of £20 (whereof one-half was paid by the said John Brayne and the other by one James Burbage, deceased) by their deed indented demised and leased to... James Burbage in... [1576] divers messuages and tenements and vacant pieces of ground in Holywell... for the term of twenty and one years, rendering the yearly rent of £14, in which demise or lease the said James did covenant to bestow £200 in buildings in and upon the demised premises...

The said Giles and Sarah did covenant to and with the said James and his assigns that he, the said Giles and Sarah and their heirs and assigns, within ten years following the beginning of the said demise, would make a new demise or lease of the premises to the said James or his assigns for one and twenty years to begin at the making of the said demise, rendering the like rent as aforesaid and upon like covenants as the former demise was made, except as in the said covenants is excepted, for the making of which said lease the said Giles also became bound to the said James in a sum of money unknown to the said Robert.

And also the said Giles and Sarah did further covenant to and with the said James and his assigns that, at any time before the end of the first lease aforesaid, the said James and his assigns might have taken down and carried away all such buildings as should be builded by the said James and his assigns in a garden and void ground demised by the said former lease, except such buildings as should be built by the expense of the said £200.

And whereas also the said James, being not able to build according to the agreement made and to his desire upon the demised premises, did, both before and after the said first demise and lease so taken, agree and promise to and with the said John Brayne that the said John and his executors should have the benefit and profits both of the first demise and likewise of the second demise which was to be made, and also of the covenant and covenants aforesaid and of all other covenants and bonds by the said Giles and Sarah or any of them, for or concerning the premises to the intent and in consideration that the said John should disburse a moiety both of the said £200 and of all other charges which should arise and grow in buildings or otherwise concerning the premises.

Now, . . . since the first demise and agreement as aforesaid, the said John Brayne did join with the said James in the building aforesaid and did expend thereupon greater sums than the said James, that is to say at least £500 or £600, after which time the said John did for a time perceive [*i.e.* receive] and take the profits of the moiety of the said demised premises by the assent of the said James, as also by an arbitrament between them made by Richard Turner and John Hill, until the said James did mortgage the said lease unto one John Hyde for £125 or thereabouts and did forfeit the said lease unto the said John Hyde for non-payment of £30 only, all the which money, £30 excepted, was paid by the said John Brayne unto the said John Hyde, who always made faithful promise that upon the payment of the said £30, and some consideration beside for the forbearing of the money, he would assure the lease back again unto the said John Brayne and the said James Burbage and their assigns, all the which he was moved unto by the reason that he, the said John Hyde, did know of the said agreement and joint expenses and perception of the profits by the said John and James before the said mortgage. After the which time, the said Hyde, by covin of the said James and one Cuthbert Burbage, his son, contrary to his faithful promise that he would assure the said lease unto the said John Brayne and to the said James Burbage, not any way taking advantage of the said mortgage, did convey the said lease, upon payment of the said £30, to the said Cuthbert only to defeat the said agreement, which said conveyance was some seven years ago or thereabout.

Since which time the said Cuthbert hath taken all the profits of the said lease. The which said lease is now expired, and the said James Burbage is deceased. And the said Brayne, being indebted in the sum of £500 to this complainant, made his wife, Margaret, his executrix and died, which Margaret, also remaining in the debt as aforesaid to your said subject [*i.e.* Miles], made him to that end her executor and died. Sithence which time the said Robert as executor to the said Margaret, the executrix of the said John Brayne, hath often required the said Cuthbert and Giles and Sarah to permit and suffer him to take down such buildings as by the covenant aforesaid were to be taken down and to allow this complainant the moiety of the timber and other things, or the value of the moiety thereof. And also this complainant hath often required the said Giles and Sarah, according to their covenant aforesaid, to make to him, as executor of Margaret Brayne aforesaid, executrix of the said John, a lease of the moiety of the premises before demised, according to the covenant and agreements aforesaid. And also, although the said Robert hath required the said Cuthbert to allow him the arrearages of the moiety of the profits of the demised premises aforesaid received by the said Cuthbert sithence the conveyance thereof to him made by John Hyde aforesaid, yet that to do they utterly deny, contrary to all equity and good conscience.

And whereas also the said James had taken all the profits of the said demised premises, contrary to the trust aforesaid, until the assignment made by Hyde as aforesaid to the said Cuthbert; and because he was otherwise indebted to the said Brayne in obligations in £600, and sithence died intestate, and one Ellen Burbage hath taken administration of the goods of the said James and hath gotten goods and chattels of his into her hands amounting to £1,000 [and] refuseth to pay and allow to this complainant the arrearages of the moiety of the profits taken by the said James before the said assignment and also to pay the said other debts, alleging she hath no goods in her hands unadministrated: whereby your majesty's poor subject [*i.e.* Miles] is likely every way to be defeated except he may have some relief . . . in this honourable court.

And forasmuch also as your majesty's poor subject is altogether without his remedy at the common law for the recovery of the moiety of the profits of the Theatre and other the lands and tenements so wrongfully taken by the said James and Cuthbert Burbage, by reason that the said John Brayne had no assignment made unto him of the said lease so taken by the said James Burbage of the said Giles Allen, although it were taken as well to the use of the said John Brayne as unto the use of the said James, and so likewise of the said benefit of all the covenants contained in the said lease. And forasmuch also as your majesty's poor subject hath no remedy by the common law to compel the said Giles Allen and the said Sarah to make a new lease according to his covenants contained in the said lease for a longer time, although he is interested in all equity in the same as executor unto the said Margaret Brayne, the executrix of the said John Brayne, who bestowed all the cost, in effect, upon the buildings and stood upon the faithful promise of the said James and Cuthbert to have a moiety of the said lease to be assigned.

And forasmuch also as your majesty's poor subject is altogether without his remedy upon the said bonds of £600 as aforesaid, they being made void by the cunning practices of the said James Burbage, Cuthbert Burbage, and the said Ellen by attachments and other device. And forasmuch also as the said Giles Allen and Sarah have been required to make a lease of the moiety of the premises as aforesaid, who hath refused so to do.

In tender consideration whereof, may it please your majesty, the premises considered, to grant unto your poor subject your most gracious writ of privy seal to be directed unto the said Ellen Burbage, Giles Allen and Sarah, his wife, and Cuthbert Burbage, commanding them personally to appear before your majesty's council of your highness' Court of Requests... there to answer the premises and also to abide such order and direction as shall seem to stand with good conscience.

297   Requests hesitates to accept Miles' lawsuit, 9 May 1597

PRO, Req.1/48/9 May 39 Eliz. Transcribed in Wallace, *First London Theatre*, 162. C–29

[A court order:] Robert Miles, complainant; Cuthbert Burbage and others, defendants. Upon the motion of Mr Walter, being of counsel with the said defendants, it is ordered that the attorneys on both sides confer [*i.e.* compare] the bill preferred by the plaintiff into her majesty's high Court of Chancery against the said defendants together with his bill here depending in this court. And if upon report thereof to be made it shall appear that they both contain one matter in substance and effect, then the same matter shall be from hence dismissed.

298   Requests accepts Miles' lawsuit, 27 May 1597, but Miles evidently drops it

PRO, Req.1/48/27 May 39 Eliz. Transcribed in Wallace, *First London Theatre*, 163. C–30

[A court order:] In the cause at the suit of Robert Miles, complainant, against Giles Allen and others, defendants, Mr Scott, being of counsel with the said complainant, hath this day informed... this court that the persons named in the bill which formerly depended in Chancery concerning this cause and in the bill now depending in this court concerning the same cause are not all one but several and distinct. Therefore upon motion of Mr Scott aforesaid it is ordered (notwithstanding any former order) that this cause shall be retained in this court to be heard in the same, and that the said defendants shall make their full and perfect answers upon their oaths unto the said complainant's bill in this court without delay, at their perils. [But nothing more is heard of the lawsuit.]

299   The Theatre is abandoned, before 8 September 1598

Guilpin, *Skialetheia* (1598), SR, 15 September 1598, satire V, sig. D6

When the Privy Council ordered the destruction of all the London playhouses (but specifically only the Theatre and Curtain) on 28 July 1597 (see **54**), the company at the Theatre was the Lord Chamberlain's men. They were probably there, too, in the autumn of 1597, when all the playhouses reopened, but they moved to the Curtain for the autumn season of 1598 and left the Theatre 'unfrequented'. The first sign that they were at the Curtain occurs in Marston's satire, *Scourge of Villainy* (1598), SR, 8 September 1598, where their play, *Romeo and Juliet*, is said to have received 'Curtain plaudities'. The next is Guilpin's remark:

> but see yonder,
> One, like the unfrequented Theatre,
> Walks in dark silence and vast solitude.[1]

[1] See 328, 346.

300 Cuthbert Burbage has the Theatre dismantled so that parts can be used in a new playhouse, Christmas 1598

PRO, (a) KB27/1362/m. 587; (b, d) Req.2/87/74; (c) STAC5/A12/35; (e-g) Req.2/184/45;. Transcribed in Wallace, *First London Theatre*, (a) 164, (b) 197, (c) 278–9, (d) 184, (e) 222, (f) 217–18, (g) 238. (a) *D–1*, (b, d) *D–2*, (c) *D–17*, (e–g) *D–7*

The evidence for this famous event comes from the lawsuits about it: Allen's in King's Bench against Peter Street (the chief carpenter), Cuthbert Burbage's in Requests against Allen, and Allen's in the Star Chamber against the Burbages and some of their supporters.

(a) Allen in King's Bench, January 1599?[1]

On the twentieth day of January ... [1599], with force and weapons, he [Peter Street] broke and entered Giles' yard called the inner courtyard, parcel of the former priory of Holywell now dissolved ... And going and coming he trampled underfoot and consumed the same Giles' grass then growing in the said yard, to the value of 40s. And then and there he pulled apart, tore asunder, seized and took away a certain structure of the same Giles, framed and erected in the same place, called the Theatre, to the value of £700. And he caused other enormities against the peace of the said lady, the Queen, to the same Giles' damage of £800.

[1] The date of this lawsuit and the date it gives for the pulling down of the Theatre (20 January 1599) defy other evidence. The lawsuit says that Allen filed it in Easter term 1599, and the surviving summary belongs to Trinity term after that. Allen, however, said that he filed it in Hilary term 1599, and the Burbages agreed with him (in the Star Chamber). Moreover, Allen said in one place that the Theatre was pulled down 'about' Christmas 1598, meaning the season; he said in another that it was pulled down on about 28 December 1598; and two of his witnesses who saw the work being done said it was done at Christmas 1598. Because 20 January was one of the return days for Hilary term before the term proper began, hence one of the earliest moments after the pulling down when Allen could file the lawsuit, the date given in the summary for the pulling down may be a mistake for the date of filing. In addition to (b, c) below, see in Wallace, *First London Theatre*, 279, 284; 216, 221.

(b) Allen's reply in Requests, 4 February 1600

But now by the dealing of the complainant [Cuthbert Burbage] it appeareth that he never in truth meant to take the lease as he pretended but only sought to take occasion when he might privily, and for best advantage, pull down the said Theatre, which about the feast of the nativity of our Lord God in the [one and] fortieth year of her majesty's reign [1598–9] he hath caused to be done without the privity or consent of the defendant, he being then in the country. [Allen lived at Hazeleigh in Essex.]

(c) Allen in the Star Chamber, 23 November 1601

The said Cuthbert Burbage ... unlawfully combining and confederating himself with the said Richard Burbage and one Peter Street, William Smyth [a friend of the Burbages] and divers other persons to the number of twelve to your subject [Allen] unknown, did about the eight and twentieth day of December ... [1598] riotously assemble themselves together and then and there armed themselves with divers and many unlawful and offensive weapons, as namely swords, daggers, bills, axes and such like. And so armed, [they] did then repair unto the said Theatre and then and there, armed as aforesaid, in very riotous, outrageous and forcible manner, and contrary to the laws of your highness's realm, attempted to pull down the said Theatre.

Whereupon divers of your subject's servants and farmers [tenants] then going about in peaceable manner to procure them to desist from that their unlawful enterprise, they, the said riotous persons aforesaid, notwithstanding, ... with great violence, not only then and there forcibly and riotously resisting your subject's servants and farmers but also then and there pulling, breaking and throwing down the said Theatre in very outrageous, violent and riotous sort to the great disturbance and terrifying not only of your subject's said servants and farmers but of divers others ... there near inhabiting. And having so done [they] did then, also in most forcible and riotous manner, take and carry away from thence all the wood and timber thereof unto the Bankside ... and there erected a new playhouse with the said timber and wood.

(d) Cuthbert Burbage in Requests, 26 January 1600

Whereupon of late your said subject having occasion to use certain timber and other stuff which were employed in making and erecting the said Theatre upon the premises (being the chiefest profit that your subject hoped for in the bargain thereof [*i.e.* a new lease]) did to that purpose, by the consent and appointment of Ellen Burbage, administratrix of the goods and chattels of the said James Burbage, take down and carry away part of the said new building ... and the same did employ to other uses.

(e) Allen's tenant, Henry Johnson, in Requests, 26 April 1600

This deponent [Johnson] saith he went to the Theatre when it was in pulling down to charge the workmen and the complainant [Cuthbert Burbage] not to pull the same down for that it was not according to any agreement or communication of agreement in his presence. And being there, he, this deponent, did perceive that the same Theatre was appointed to be so pulled down by the complainant, by his brother (Richard Burbage), and one Thomas [*i.e.* William] Smyth, and one [Peter] Street, who was head carpenter that gave assistance therein. And when he had so charged them not to pull the same Theatre down, they, the said complainant and Thomas Smyth and Street, the carpenter, told him, this deponent, that they took it down but to set it up upon the premises in another form, and that they had covenanted with the carpenter to that effect, and showed this deponent the decays about the same as it stood there, thereby colouring their deceit. And more he cannot depose, save only that, notwithstanding all their speeches, they pulled it down and carried it away.

(f) Allen's tenant, John Goburne, in Requests, 26 April 1600

This deponent [Goburne] saith that he heard that the Theatre was in pulling down, and, having a letter of attorney from the defendant [Allen] to forbid them, did repair thither and did find there, at the pulling down of the same, and that commanded and countenanced the same, one Thomas [i.e. William] Smyth, the complainant [Cuthbert Burbage] and Peter Street, the chief carpenter. And the other that were there were labourers and such as wrought for wages, whose names he perfectly remembreth not.

(g) The Burbages' friend, William Smyth, in Requests, 15 May 1600

This deponent [Smyth] saith that he knoweth the said complainant's mother [Ellen Burbage] did give her consent that the plaintiff should take down and carry away the timber and stuff employed for the Theatre or playhouse in the bill mentioned, for she was there and did see the doing thereof and liked well of it and did allow thereof. [She was the ostensible owner of the Theatre.]

301 Giles Allen sues Burbages for trespass, 20 January 1599?

PRO, KB27/1362/m. 587. Transcribed in Wallace, *First London Theatre*, 163–80. *D–1*

The dismantling of the Theatre led inevitably to lawsuits. Allen promptly sued Peter Street, who led the workmen, in King's Bench for trespass. After explaining what happened (see 300a), Allen went on at length to explain why, according to the lease, Street had no right to pull the place down and take it away.

302 Cuthbert Burbage countersues Giles Allen in Requests, 26 January 1600

PRO, Req.2/87/74. Transcribed in Wallace, *First London Theatre*, (a) 184–6, (b) 191–5, 197–8, (c) 201–5. *D–2*

Cuthbert Burbage countersued Giles Allen in an equity court in order to stop Allen's lawsuit in King's Bench and have the dismantling of the Theatre judged as a matter of equity rather than common law.

(a) Cuthbert Burbage's bill of complaint, 26 January 1600

He recited the lease James Burbage had taken from Allen in 1576 (**252**), said that James Burbage had tried to get Allen to renew it in 1585 (**274a**) and that he himself had tried recently (**295a** and **300d**).

[He went on:] Giles Allen, minding to take advantage of his own wrongful and unconscionable dealing in not making the said new lease, [and] finding the words of the said covenant to be that the said James Burbage, his executors, administrators or assigns might, before the end of the said term of one and twenty years granted by the said indenture (or before the end of the said one and twenty years after by virtue of the said agreement to be granted), take down and carry away the said timber and stuff used for making of the said Theatre, [saith] that, therefore, (in regard your subject [Cuthbert Burbage], trusting to his promises to have a new lease, did not take the same away at the end of the said term of one and twenty years granted by the said indenture and that no new term being granted by the said Allen to the said James Burbage or his assigns by the words of the said covenant) he [Cuthbert Burbage] hath not liberty to take the same away afterwards in strictness of law.

Thereupon, he, the said Giles Allen, hath brought an action of trespass in your majesty's court ... called the ... [King's] Bench against Peter Street, your subject's servant, who by your subject's direction and commandment did enter upon the premises and take down the said building, [Allen] minding most unconscionably to recover the value of the said building in damages, which must ... light upon your said subject if he [Allen] should therein prevail. And there [Allen] doth prosecute the same with all rigour and extremity, which will tend to your subject's great loss and hindrance, except your majesty's favour and aid in such cases used be to him herein extended.

In tender regard whereof, forasmuch as it is against all equity and conscience that the said Giles Allen should, contrary to his covenant and agreement aforesaid, through his own wrong and breach of covenant, hinder your subject to take the benefit of the said agreement in the foresaid indenture expressed to take away the said timber and buildings before the end of the said one and thirty years; and for that your said subject or his servant can minister no perfect plea at the common law in bar of the said action, and yet in all equity and conscience ought to be relieved according to the true meaning [of the agreement]; and the said Giles Allen ought to be stayed of his said suit: may it therefore please your most excellent majesty, the premises considered, to grant unto your said subject your highness's writ of privy seal to be directed to the said Giles Allen, commanding him thereby, at a certain day and under a certain pain therein to be limited, to be and personally to appear before your majesty in your highness's court of Whitehall at Westminster [*i.e.* Requests], then and there to answer to the premises and to abide such further order and direction therein as to the masters of the said court shall be thought meet and convenient, and also to grant your majesty's most gracious writ of injunction to be directed to all the counsellors, attorneys, solicitors and factors of the said Allen commanding them to cease all proceedings in the said action until the matter in equity (wherein your poor subject humbly prayeth to be relieved) be first heard before the masters of your highness's said court ...

(b) Giles Allen's answer, 4 February 1600

[He, too, recited the original lease, then:] And further, the defendant [Allen] saith that true it is that the said James Burbage ... did require the said defendant to make him a new lease and did [in 1585] tender unto the defendant a draft of a new lease written and engrossed, as the complainant hath alleged, which lease so tendered the defendant did not make show that he would deliver [*i.e.* sign] it . . . [nor] by subtle devices shift of the finishing thereof, as the complainant most untruly hath alleged. But contrarily the defendant did upon many and very just and reasonable causes and considerations (as he hopeth it shall appear unto this honourable court) utterly refuse to seal and deliver the same. For the plain and true declaration whereof, first the defendant saith that (as he taketh it and as he is by his counsel informed) the draft of the said lease so tendered unto the defendant was in many material points varying and differing from the lease which the defendant and his wife had formerly made to the said James Burbage and, therefore, in respect that the second lease should be made like unto the former and under the like covenants, articles and agreements, and no other, as before is shown, the defendant was in no wise (as he taketh it) either in law or conscience bound to seal the same . . .

And further, the defendant saith that such was the bad dealing of the said James Burbage towards the defendant from time to time before the time of the said new lease tendered, and the said James Burbage had been such a troublesome tenant unto the defendant, that there was no cause in conscience to make the defendant to yield to anything in favour of the said James Burbage, further than by the law he might be compelled to do. For first, whereas the said James Burbage was bound to pay unto the defendant the sum of £20 for a fine for the lease formerly made unto him, the said James Burbage neglected the payment thereof at the time appointed and long time after, and hardly could the defendant, after much delay and trouble by suit in law, obtain the same. And further, the said James Burbage continually failed in the payment of this rent and never duly paid the same, whereby the defendant was often driven, to his great trouble, to go about to distrain for the same, and yet could not the defendant that way help himself, for either the door and gates were kept shut that he could not enter to take any distress, or [James Burbage] otherwise the matter so handled that the defendant could not find any sufficient distress to satisfy him for the arrearages thereof. And at the time of the said new lease tendered by the said James Burbage, he, the said James, did then owe unto the defendant £30 for the rent of the said houses and grounds demised unto him, which as yet remaineth unpaid . . .

And further, touching the repairing of the houses and buildings which the said James Burbage ought to have repaired and maintained, that was likewise by the said James Burbage much neglected. For whereas amongst the houses and buildings demised to the said James Burbage there was one great tiled timber barn of 80 feet of assize in length and 24 feet of assize in breadth, or very near thereabouts, very substantially built, for the which the defendant had formerly received a rent of good value, the said James Burbage did divide the same into eleven several tenements (as the defendant now remembreth) and did let out the same severally to poor persons for the several rents of 20s by the year to be paid by every tenant, who were and are unable to do any reparations upon them. For such was, and now is, their poverty that, as the defendant is informed, they usually beg in the fields and streets to get money for the payment of their rents, by reason whereof the defendant hath been much blamed, and by the parishioners there very hardly censured that he should be an occasion to bring so many beggars amongst them, to their great trouble and annoyance, which proceeded not from any fault of the defendant, but from the covetous humour of the said James Burbage, who respected more his own commodity than the good report and credit either of the defendant or himself.

And the like evil disposition appeareth to be in the complainant, who since the death of his father hath continued these poor people there, and still doth, and yet doth in no wise repair the said tenements, whereby they are grown in great decay, and are almost utterly ruinated, and are now by the complainant under-propped with shores to keep them from falling down, instead of repairing and amending the same, as by the covenant of the said James Burbage ought to be done, insomuch that the said poor people have complained unto the defendant that they were so decayed both without and within that they were in fear that they would fall upon their heads, whereby it appeareth that the complainant hath small regard either of the credit or the commodity of the defendant but seeketh only to enrich himself by the rents and other profits which he unconscionably receiveth for the same...

And the said James Burbage and the complainant, or one of them, have likewise heretofore placed other poor people in other tenements there, which still continue in the same. Which tenements are by reason thereof so decayed that the defendant seeth not how he shall well be answered the old rent of £14 of such tenants as be of ability to pay the same. So that howsoever the complainant hath furnaced [*i.e.* urged] that by the said £200 supposed to be bestowed by the said James Burbage, his father, that the houses and buildings were greatly amended and bettered (as in truth they ought to have been), yet the defendant taketh it that he shall be able to make it appear unto this honourable court that they are rather impaired and in worse plight for the benefit and profit of the defendant, all things considered, than they were at the time when the said James Burbage first took them. Neither yet in truth had the said James Burbage, at the time of the said second lease tendered, or at any time after (as the defendant hopeth he shall be able to prove to this honourable court), bestowed the said sum of £200, or near thereabouts, for the bettering of the houses and buildings demised. Neither was there any likelihood that the said James Burbage should perform the same within the time limited by the said indentures, the said second lease being tendered but a very short time before the expiration of the said term of ten years within which time the said sum of £200 should have been bestowed, as before is shown. For all which causes the defendant did refuse to seal the said lease, as he thinketh he had just cause, both in law and conscience, so to do[1]...

But now by the dealing of the complainant it appeareth that he... only sought to take occasion when he might privily, and for best advantage, pull down the said

Theatre, which ... he hath caused to be done without the privity or consent of the defendant, he being then in the country. For the which the said defendant hath brought an action of trespass in her majesty's bench against him [Peter Street] who, by the commandment of the complainant, was the doer thereof, which action the defendant thinketh he had very good and just cause, both in law and conscience, to prosecute. For, first, it appeareth that the liberty which the said James Burbage had by the said first lease to pull down the said Theatre at any time during the term was granted unto him in consideration only of the said sum of £200 to be employed and bestowed by the said James Burbage upon the houses and buildings that were demised unto him, which sum not being by him bestowed accordingly, and other covenants broken, there was no colour (as the defendant taketh it) either in law or conscience for the complainant to take away the same ...

And further, whereas the complainant supposeth that the said James Burbage, his father, did to his great charges erect the said Theatre and thereby pretendeth that there should be the greater cause in equity to relieve him, the complainant, for the same: hereunto the defendant saith that considering the great profit and benefit which the said James Burbage and the complainant in their several times have made thereof, which (as the defendant hath credibly heard) doth amount to the sum of £2,000 at the least, the defendant taketh it they have been very sufficiently recompensed for their charges which they have bestowed upon the said Theatre or upon any other buildings there, had they been much greater than they were.

[1] See 295b.

(c) Cuthbert Burbage's replication, 27 April 1600

[He denied many of Allen's other assertions, then:] And whereas the said defendant [Allen] allegeth in his said answer that the said James Burbage neglected to do reparations upon the said houses and buildings, and that the said James did divide the said barn in the answer specified into eleven several tenements and did let the same severally to poor persons (for the several rents of 20s, by year) who were unable to do reparations upon the same: this complainant thereunto replieth and saith that true it is that the said James Burbage, being possessed, amongst other things, of the said barn by virtue of the lease to him made as aforesaid, which barn stood and lay empty a long time in the hands of ... the said James without yielding any profit or commodity, and the said James, being desirous to convert the same for his benefit, did therefore to his great charges divide the same into several tenements, as, in the bill [*i.e.* lease] is expressed, was lawful ... for him, the said James, to do (as he, this complainant taketh it), and so much the rather for that he, the said James, was not restrained by his said lease to build or convert any part of the premises to him demised thereby. And this complainant further saith that he ... very well knoweth and can well and sufficiently prove and make manifest to this honourable court that the said James Burbage hath for divers years during the said term bestowed and disbursed in and about the reparations of the same tenements a great sum of money. Without that [*i.e.* he denies] that the said tenants are so poor that they usually beg in the fields and streets to get money for the payment of their rents, or that that there were any causes the said defendant should be much blamed or hardly censured by the parishioners, or that the said James respected more his own commodity than the good report and credit of the defendant or himself, as in the said answer most slanderously is alleged.

Without that also that he, this complainant, hath not since the death of his said father repaired the said tenements, or that the said tenements are grown in great decay or almost utterly ruinated, or that there is any cause that the said poor people should complain to the said defendant that the said tenements would fall upon their heads as in the said answer is untruly surmised . . .

Without that that the said James Burbage had not at the time of the said second lease tendered, or any time after, bestowed the sum of £200 or near thereabouts for the bettering of the houses and buildings demised, or that there was not any likelihood that the said James Burbage should perform the same within the time limited by the said indentures, as in the said answer is also surmised. For this complainant saith and can well and sufficiently prove and make manifest, as well by divers good workmen [as] . . . other persons, that the said James Burbage before the tendering of the said second lease to the said defendant did bestow and disburse for the bettering of the said houses and buildings above the sum of £200. And, therefore, he, the said defendant, had no just cause to refuse to seal the said lease, as by his said answer he pretendeth . . .

And this complainant doth not deny but that he hath pulled down the said Theatre, which this complainant taketh it was lawful for him so to do, being a thing covenanted and permitted in the said former lease to this complainant's said father made as aforesaid.

Without that that . . . the said James Burbage or this complainant hath made £2,000 profit and benefit by the said Theatre, as in the said answer is also alleged.

303 Requests stops Allen's lawsuit in King's Bench, 10–22 April, 1600

PRO, Req.1/49, (a) 10 April, (b) 22 April 1600. Transcribed in Wallace, *First London Theatre*, (a) 205, (b) 205–6. D–4, D–6

(a) A court order, 10 April 1600

Cuthbert Burbage, gentleman, complainant, against Giles Allen, gentleman, defendant. It is ordered upon the motion of Mr Walter, of counsel with the said complainant, that an injunction (without further motion in that behalf to be made) shall be awarded forth of this court against the said defendant for the stay of his proceedings at the common law in the action of trespass there depending until this court shall take further order to the contrary, if he, the said defendant (having notice of this order in convenient time) shall not upon Thursday next coming [17 April] show good matter in this court in stay thereof.

(b) A court order, 22 April 1600

It is ordered that the said complainant (according to the offer of his counsel this day made) shall by or before Monday next coming [28 April] put in a perfect and issuable plea to the defendant's action depending at the common law, or else, in default thereof, shall take no benefit by his suit in this court ... If it shall be put in accordingly, then the defendant's counsel doth consent, and it is so ordered, that he, the said defendant, shall stay his further proceedings at the common law until the matter be heard [in this court].

304 Cuthbert Burbage accuses Allen of pressing the lawsuit in King's Bench despite a court order, 11 June 1600

PRO, Req.1/211, 11 June 1600. Transcribed in Wallace, *First London Theatre*, 252. *D–11*

The order below suggests that Cuthbert Burbage (because of 303b) demurred in reply to Allen's case in King's Bench, that on 31 May Requests noted as much and ordered again that Allen stop his proceedings in King's Bench, and that Allen pressed on regardless.

[An affidavit of Cuthbert Burbage.] Whereas in the cause at the suit of Cuthbert Burbage, gentleman, plaintiff, against Giles Allen, gentleman, defendant, it was ordered the last day of May last past that the said defendant, his counsellor, attorney and solicitor should surcease and stay and no further proceed in an action of trespass at and by the order of her majesty's common laws and not cause the demurrer there tendered upon the defendant's plea in that suit to be joined up or entered until the hearing of the said cause and other order taken and made to the contrary: the said Cuthbert Burbage maketh oath that he, the said defendant [Allen], hath since the said order, contrary to the effect thereof, caused the said demurrer to be joined up and entered a rule thereupon for this deponent to stand to his plea at and by the order of the common law.

305 Requests orders Giles Allen arrested for contempt as a result of Cuthbert Burbage's accusation, 11 June 1600

PRO, (a) Req.2/372/pt 1 [bottom]; (b) STAC5/A12/35. Transcribed in Wallace, *First London Theatre*, 252–3, 280–1. *D–12, D–17*

(a) A court order, 11 June 1600

Because Giles Allen has defied an order made by the council [*i.e.* the privy council, which in theory was the Court of Requests] in the cause between Cuthbert Burbage, gentleman, plaintiff, and the aforesaid Giles Allen, defendant, dated 31

May last past: therefore it is now ordered that a writ of attachment be directed to the lieutenant of the county of Essex and also Hugh Barbon, gentleman, to attach the body of the said Giles, returnable immediately, etc.

(b) Allen's recollection of being arrested

... Whereupon your subject [Allen] for that supposed contempt was in the vacation time then next following [*i.e.* summer 1600], by the procurement of the said Cuthbert Burbage and by the confederacy aforesaid, fetched up to London by a pursuivant to his great vexation and trouble (being a man very aged and unfit to travel) and to his excessive charges in his journey and otherwise to his great discredit and disgrace in the country. And your said subject, then by the said pursuivant brought before one of the masters of your highness's said court [of Requests], did (by the said master's order then made) become bound unto the said Cuthbert Burbage in a bond of £200 to appear in the said Court of Requests in the beginning of the term of St Michael [*i.e.* in October 1600] then next following to answer the said supposed contempt and to stand to the order of the said court upon the hearing of the cause. And ... your said subject ... appeared in the said court accordingly, and the matter aforesaid being opened ... your subject was thereupon by order of that court discharged of the supposed contempt ...

306 Requests decides for Cuthbert Burbage in his lawsuit against Giles Allen, 18 October 1600

PRO, STAC5/A12/35. Transcribed in Wallace, *First London Theatre*, 281–2. D–14, D–15, D–17. The order of the court recording the trial and decision is lost, but Giles Allen described both in a lawsuit he filed in the Star Chamber on 23 November 1601.

And ... in the term of St Michael, at the day appointed for the hearing of the said cause [18 October 1600], your subject [Allen] appearing in your highness's said court [of Requests] and having divers witnesses there present to testify *viva voce* on the behalf of your subject: the said Cuthbert Burbage and the said Richard Burbage, still persisting in their unlawful and malicious courses against your subject, did by the confederacy aforesaid then and there very shamefully and unlawfully revile with many reproachful terms your subject's said witnesses and affirmed that they had formerly testified in the said cause divers untruths and threatened to stab some of your subject's said witnesses because they had testified of the fraudulent deed of gift made by James Burbage to the said Cuthbert Burbage and Richard Burbage as aforesaid.[1] By which their furious and unlawful threats, your subject's witnesses were then so terrified that they durst not testify the truth on the behalf of your subject in the said cause.

And further ... the said Cuthbert Burbage did very maliciously and corruptly, and contrary to the laws and statutes of your highness's realm, suborn and procure one Richard Hudson of the parish of St Alban in London, carpenter, and

Thomas Osborne of the parish of Fenchurch in London, carpenter, to commit very grievous and wilful perjury in the said suit in your highness's Court of Requests in divers material points concerning the said suit: the said Richard Hudson testifiying and deposing in the said suit on the behalf of the said Cuthbert Burbage that he was present at a view and estimate made of the costs bestowed by the aforementioned James Burbage ... upon the houses and tenements demised unto him by your subject, which view was taken the eighteenth day of July ... 1586 by himself and others, and that then it did appear unto them that before that time the said James Burbage had bestowed upon the said houses and tenements the sum of £240; and the said Thomas Osborne in like manner testifying and deposing in the said suit on the behalf of the said Cuthbert Burbage, that he likewise was present at the same view and that it did then appear that within four or five years before that view taken there had been bestowed upon the said houses and tenements by the said James Burbage the sum of £240.

Whereas in truth the said Richard Hudson was not present at any view taken in the year aforesaid, but only at [a] view taken in the three and thirtieth year of your highness's reign [1590–1] as by the deposition of the said Richard Hudson himself heretofore made in your highness's Court of Chancery and there remaining of record it doth evidently appear.[2] Neither had the said James Burbage at the time of the said view supposed to be made the eighteenth day of July ... 1586 bestowed anything near the sum of £240, whereof your subject hopeth he shall be able to make very sufficient proof. By which unlawful practices of the said Cuthbert Burbage your subject did then lose his said cause.

[1] Allen had claimed that at James Burbage's death his sons frustrated his creditors, including Allen, by making his wife executrix but conveying his goods to them, so that she had little substance of her own and so could not be profitably sued (PRO, Req. 2/87/74, the answer, transcribed in Wallace, *First London Theatre*, 197–8; D–2).

[2] Allen is right, but if Cuthbert Burbage's witnesses perjured themselves they probably did so inadvertently, as the Star Chamber may have agreed (see 307). The Burbages had two 'views' taken, the first in November 1585, the second in July 1591. Witnesses, whose remarks comprise the evidence, confused the two. They described that of 1585 mainly in 1600, when Cuthbert Burbage wanted to show that Allen should have extended the lease, and that of 1591 in 1592, when the Burbages wanted to show that they, not Brayne, had spent money for repairs. See **274, 275, 288** and the depositions of Bett, Ellam, Hudson, and Clerke in the fall and winter of 1591–2, and of Hudson and Osborne in May 1600: PRO, C24/226/9 [pt 2] and Req.2/184/45, transcribed in Wallace, *First London Theatre*, 69–70, 72, 76, 77, 78, 228–9, 233–4; C–17, D–7.

307 Giles Allen files two more lawsuits against Cuthbert Burbage, 1601–1602

PRO, (a) KB27/1373/m. 257; (b) STAC5/A12/35, STAC5/A. 33/32. Transcribed in Wallace, *First London Theatre*, (a) 267–75. (b) 275–97, (a) D–16, (b) D–17, D–18

Having lost in Requests (and, therefore, in King's Bench) over Cuthbert Burbage's removing the Theatre, Giles Allen could not sue him again about that matter. He could, however, sue him about allied matters.

(a) Early 1601

Allen sued Cuthbert Burbage in King's Bench again, accusing him of having failed to keep the terms of the lease of 1576. Nothing is heard of the lawsuit after Easter term 1602.

(b) 23 November 1601

Allen sued Cuthbert Burbage and some of his supporters in the Star Chamber, accusing them of having won the case in Requests by extra legal means. Allen's bill is quoted in 306. In reply, Burbage and his supporters filed demurrers that, on behalf of the court, a noted lawyer, Francis Bacon, found sufficient, noting 'that the said [*i.e.* Allen's] bill is very uncertain and insufficient, and that no further answer needeth to be made thereto'.

In this lawsuit, Allen also accused the deputy registrar of the Court of Requests, Richard Lane, of allowing Burbage to determine how the order of 31 May 1600 was recorded (see 304). That was the order that led to Allen's arrest for contempt. Lane denied the accusation, Allen prepared questions for Lane on 1 May 1602 and Lane answered them on 11 May 1602, after which this lawsuit disappears.

XXIV The first Blackfriars

The first Blackfriars playhouse was a private playhouse in the nine-acre compound that had been the convent of the Dominican, or black, friars in London. That compound lay, roughly, between Ludgate Hill, E.C.4, and the Thames, just within the south-west end of the old wall of the City. The area is still called Blackfriars. In Elizabethan, even Jacobean times it retained some of the freedom from control by the City that the friars had exercised until their convent was dissolved in 1538.

The playhouse was in 'the house . . . late in the Lord Cobham's hands', which consisted, it seems, mainly of six rooms in two convent buildings on the western side of the compound.[1] The buildings were rectangular, their long dimensions lying north to south, and the south end of one adjoined the north end of the other, so that people could pass between them without going outside. The northern one was the old buttery, and the southern one was the old refectory, containing a great medieval hall called the parliament chamber. Two of the rooms were in the south end of the upper storey of the old buttery, and four were in the north end of the upper storey of the old refectory. The rooms were adjacent to one another in a line north to south. Those in the old buttery measured 46½ feet north to south and about 26 feet east to west. The other four measured 110 feet north to south and 22 feet east to west, and they probably occupied part of the space where the second Blackfriars playhouse would eventually be. All these rooms were served by an external 'great' staircase that had recently been built on the western side. The playhouse was probably in the two rooms of the old buttery. The Society of Apothecaries acquired that building in 1632, long after the time of the playhouse, and, the building having been destroyed in the great fire of 1666, built the present Apothecaries Hall, Black Friars Lane, E.C.4, on the site.

On 27 August 1576 Richard Farrant asked the owner, Sir William More, for a lease on the 'house', and on 20 December More officially granted it. It required Farrant to pay £14 a year in rent and was to run for twenty-one years beginning the previous Michaelmas day, when Farrant may well have moved in. He was a musician, master of the children (that is, boy choristers) of the chapel at Windsor Castle and deputy to William Hunnis, master of the children of the Chapel Royal. In asking for the lease, Farrant told More that he wanted the rooms for teaching the children of the Chapel Royal and would pull down only one partition so as to make two rooms into one – presumably the partition between the two rooms in the old buttery. He said nothing of plays or a playhouse, nor does the lease, and he promised in the lease that he would not sublet any of the property. Yet he opened a playhouse there in the winter of 1576/7, if not a little earlier, where he led a company of boys, perhaps from both his choirs. He also pulled down other partitions, and eventually let out two parts of the place. He should have had 46½ feet by about 26 feet for his playhouse, but how he might have arranged that space is unknown. This private playhouse probably opened in the same year as two of the earliest public playhouses, that in Newington Butts and the Theatre.

More tried to evict Farrant from the property in 1580, saying that Farrant had greatly damaged it, lied about how he meant to use it, and sublet part of it. Farrant evidently tried to mollify More but died soon after 30 November 1580, leaving the problem to his widow, Anne, together with ten small children and little, if any, income. The playhouse may have closed for a time. Then she sublet most of the property to Hunnis and John Newman for the years left in the main lease, and Hunnis got the Earl of Leicester to write to More suggesting that More wink at the illegality of the sublease. The Earl mentioned Hunnis' 'honest request' to train children as Farrant had done, 'to do her majesty service'.

The sublease included the upper rooms in which the playhouse probably was, but not 'divers other little parcels'.[2] Hunnis would present plays in the playhouse acted by the boys of the Chapel Royal, of whom there were twelve. Newman would provide finance. They would pay Anne Farrant £6 13s 4d more in rent than she had to pay More, and they would keep the place in repair. Newman paid her £30 for the lease, according to More, and Hunnis and Newman gave her a bond in which they agreed to pay her £100 if they did not keep the terms of the sublease. Hunnis had control of the property by mid-September 1581, though the documents were not signed until 20 December, the fifth anniversary of Richard Farrant's lease.

Early in 1583, Hunnis and Newman conveyed the sublease to Henry Evans, who had a connection with the children of St Paul's Cathedral. Evans sold it to the Earl of Oxford, who gave it to John Lyly. These transactions must have been collusive, because a company of boys from the Chapel Royal and St Paul's then appeared in the playhouse under Oxford's patronage playing plays by Lyly.[3]

The scheme, however, ended the playhouse. For if More had allowed Anne Farrant to sublet most of the playhouse property to Hunnis and Newman contrary to the terms of the main lease, he would not allow a further alienation. In May or June 1583, therefore, More granted a new lease of the property to a creature of his, Thomas Smalepeece, who sued Evans for possession in the Court of Husting at Guildhall.[4] Meanwhile, nobody paid Anne Farrant her rent, so that in the autumn she sued Hunnis and Newman for their bond, and in the winter they countersued her, having first paid their rent. More won his case in Easter term 1584, evicting not only Evans, and therefore Hunnis, Newman, the Earl of Oxford, Lyly[5] and the players, but also Anne Farrant. She had lost her lease in a lawsuit having nothing to do with her and of which she did not know until it was nearly over, and, it seems, she got nothing for Hunnis and Newman's bond. She complained formally at least twice and in 1587 may have received some compensation.

[1] Which building or buildings and which rooms in it or them housed the playhouse is a complex and uncertain matter. The remarks here follow Smith, *Blackfriars Playhouse*, esp. 83–129, but see also, for example, *ES*, II, 480–96.
[2] More evidently assumed that the sublease included the whole of the playhouse property (318), but Anne Farrant described the main lease as 'her said lease whereby she holdeth the premises [in the sublease] and divers other little parcels'. Otherwise, she described the sublet property as 'the said roomeths' or 'rooms', and Hunnis and Newman described it as 'certain rooms'.
[3] See *ES*, II, 39–40.
[4] No one mentioned the name of the court, but More's remark that 'the recorder argued against me' there indicates that it was the court of Husting, in which the recorder of the City of London was the 'assessor'; the court concerned itself largely with 'pleas of land' in the City (see Hall, 'Court of Husting', 156–61).
[5] Lyly had subleased parts of the place to at lest two neighbours, Lord Hunsdon (who was mainly interested in the water supply mentioned in Farrant's lease) and Rocco Bonetti (who got a 'house' on which he foolishly spent a lot of money). More refused to renew Hunsdon's sublease in 1586, despite

Hundson's annoyance, and tried to expel Bonetti, 1584–6, despite the pleas of several well-placed mutual friends. SHC, LM VIII, 58, transcribed in MSC, 11.i.123; see also Smith, *Blackfriars Playhouse*, 155–6; and SHC, MS LM, Cor 3/372, 383, 386–8.

308 Richard Farrant asks Sir William More for a lease on a 'house' in Blackfriars, 27 August 1576

Folger, MS L.b.446. Transcribed in Wallace, *Evolution of the English Drama*, 131 n. 2, and Smith, *Blackfriars Playhouse*, 135. On the same day, a former tenant of More's, Sir Henry Neville, wrote to More introducing Farrant.[1]

[Farrant asked for the lease in a letter to more:] My duty done, these are to signify unto you that where your worship doth mind to let your house in the Blackfriars, late in the Lord Cobham's hands, I am earnestly to request your worship if I may be your tenant there – if the Italian may be removed, as it appeareth somewhat to me it were easily done.[2] If it be your pleasure so to accept of me, though unacquainted unto you, I hope in God you will not mislike with me in any dealings concerning the rent or any other things to be performed. If it be my chance to have that favour at your hands, this yet farther am I to request, that I may pull down one partition and so make of two rooms one, and will make it up again at my departure or when my lease shall end. Thus craving your worship's answer by this bringer, either to me or your man, the keeper of your said house, with my humble and hearty commendations I commit you to the Almighty.

[1] SHC, LM II, 71, transcribed by Wallace, *Evolution of the English Drama*, 131 n. 1, and Smith, *Blackfriars Playhouse*, 135.
[2] Presumably the Italian had been a subtenant of the previous holder of the lease, Lord Cobham, and was easily removed. He was probably Rocco Bonetti, a teacher of fencing. If so, he was back in part of the property by 1584 and from at least 1585 leased other places from More in Blackfriars (see note 5 in the chapter introduction above and Folger, MS L.b.352).

309 More leases the playhouse property to Farrant for twenty-one years, 29 September and 20 December 1576

Folger, MS L.b.350.[1] Transcribed in Wallace, *Evolution of the English Drama*, 132–6, and MSC, 11.i. 28–35

This indenture made ... [20] December ... [1576] ... between Sir William More of Loseley in the county of Surrey, knight, ... and Richard Farrant of New Windsor in the county of Berkshire, gentleman, ... witnesseth that the said Sir William More hath demised, granted and to farm letten ... unto the said Richard Farrant all those his six upper chambers, lofts, lodgings or rooms lying together within the precinct of the late dissolved house or priory of the Blackfriars, ... which ... were lately, amongst others, in the tenure and occupation of the right honourable Sir William Brooke, knight, Lord Cobham, and do contain in length from the north end thereof to the south end of the same 156½ feet, ... whereof two of the said six upper chambers, lofts, lodgings or rooms in the north end of the premises, together with the breadth of the little room under granted, do contain in length 56½ feet, and from the east to the west part thereof in breadth 25 feet ... ;[2] and the four other chambers or rooms, residue of the said six upper chambers, do contain in length 110 feet and in breadth from the east to the west part thereof 22 feet... Of which four chambers last recited, one of them is ceiled with wainscot on the east part, south part and a part of the west, with a great round portal contained within the same chamber and ceiling, which ceiling over and besides the said portal doth contain fourscore and fourteen yards.[3] And the north end of the premises... doth abut upon the south part of the now dwelling house of the said William Lord Cobham. And also the said Sir William More... doth demise, grant and to farm let unto the said Richard Farrant all the said wainscot and round portal contained within the said chamber above demised.

And [he doth demise] also all that his new kitchen lately built by Sir Henry Neville, knight, with the stair leading out of the same kitchen up into the premises before letten, with the little void room wherein the foot of the said stairs standeth, and the wood yard to the same kitchen adjoining, situate... together,... between the entry being under part of the premises above demised on the east part, and a certain way called Water Lane leading to the Blackfriars bridge [i.e. stairs] at the Thames-side on the west part, and the said dwelling house of the said William Lord Cobham on the north part, and a certain void ground and a way of the said Sir William More leading from the said Water Lane towards and unto the dwelling house or tenement and garden of the said Sir William More... on the south part.

And [he doth demise] also... the great stairs lately erected and made by the said Sir Henry Neville upon part of the said void ground and way last above expressed, with the little void room under the same great stairs, which said great stairs do serve and lead into the premises before demised; and also the use and commodity of one quill of conduit water issuing and running from the conduit and water of the said Sir William More, together with the cocks thereof, set and being in the little void room at the said stair foot,... for the only use of the said Richard Farrant and his family;... also free ingress, egress and regress to and from the said great new stairs lately erected and made by the said Sir Henry Neville in and upon the said void ground and way leading from the said way called Water Lane unto the said great new stairs...

And [he doth demise] also... all those two rooms with the two cellars directly under part of the upper chambers, lodgings or rooms above demised, which said two rooms and two cellars... do lie between the said void ground on the west part, and an entry leading from the said void ground into the garden of the said Sir William More on the north part, and an entry leading from the said void ground into the said dwelling house or tenement of the said Sir William More on the south part, and the garden of the said Sir William More on the east part, with free and quiet ingress, egress and regress into and from the said two rooms and two cellars...

And [he doth demise] also... one little room, sometime two little rooms, lying within the limits and bounds first above expressed, whereof one part was sometime used for a withdraught or privy and the other part thereof was lately used for a coal-house.

Except and always reserved unto the said William More . . . all that great room now used for a washing-house, being directly under parcel of the premises first above demised and adjoining unto the said two rooms last above [demised], bounden on the east part of the same two rooms. And also except . . . all the leads covering the premises before demised, and the use of them, saving that it shall and may be good and lawful for the said Richard Farrant . . . to have free ingress, egress and regress to and from the said leads to repair, maintain and amend the same . . .

To have and to hold all and singular the premises before demised . . . with their appurtenances (except before excepted) unto the said Richard Farrant . . . from the feast of St Michael [29 September] . . . last past . . . unto the end and term of twenty-one years, . . . yielding and paying therefore yearly . . . unto the said Sir William More . . . £14 of lawful money of England at four usual terms of the year [i.e. Lady Day, St John Baptist, Michaelmas and Christmas], . . . or within fifteen days next after every of the same feasts, by even portions yearly to be paid.

And the said Richard Farrant doth covenant, promise and grant . . . that . . . he . . . shall well and sufficiently repair . . . all manner of reparations whatsoever to the premises above demised, . . . and also shall repair . . . all such defaults and reparations as shall at any time hereafter be in the leads above excepted and in the timberwork and roof that beareth the same leads, . . . together with the said wainscot and great round portal . . .

And also the said Richard Farrant doth covenant and grant . . . that he . . . shall at all times hereafter . . . bear and pay all manner of charges and payments from henceforth due to be paid unto the church and scavenger, . . . and also shall scour, cleanse and make clean the privy or withdraught being in the wood yard aforesaid,[4] . . . and . . . shall well and sufficiently house, cover and keep dry the said privy . . . and, as much as conveniently may be, [keep it] from annoying of the inhabitants there next adjoining . . .

And if it shall happen the said yearly rent of £14 to be behind unpaid in part or in all . . . by the space of fifteen days, that then it shall be lawful unto the said Sir William More . . . into all the said . . . premises above demised . . . to enter and distrain [Farrant's goods], and, the distress thereof taken, lawfully to lead, drive, bear and carry away . . . and keep until the said yearly rent . . . shall be . . . paid. And if it shall happen the said yearly rent . . . to be behind unpaid . . . by the space of twenty days, . . . it shall be lawful unto the said Sir William More . . . into all and singular the premises . . . to re-enter, and all the same . . . to have again, repossess, and enjoy . . . and the said Richard Farrant, his executors and assigns from thence utterly to expel . . .

Provided always . . . that it shall and may be lawful unto the said Sir William More . . . to shut, lock, bar or open the gate joining upon the said way called Water Lane from time to time at such . . . hours of the night and of the mornings as to the said Sir William More . . . shall seem meet and convenient . . . Provided also that the said Richard Farrant . . . shall not alter nor cut the pipe of the said conduit or water, nor . . . employ any the water aforesaid but only to the use of the said Richard Farrant and his family, . . . nor shall suffer the same water to run to waste . . .

Provided also that the said Richard Farrant, his executors or assigns, ... shall not in anywise demise, let, grant, assign, set over or by any ways or means put away his or their interest or term of years, or any part of the same years of or in the said premises, ... or any part, parcel or member thereof, to any person or persons ... without the especial licence, consent and agreement of the said Sir William More ... first had and obtained in writing, ... but only by the last will and testament of the said Richard Farrant in writing to the wife of the said Richard or to his children ... And that the said wife or child ... shall or may ... have the use and commodity of the said quill of water ... And further it is agreed ... that the said Richard Farrant, his executors and assigns shall and may ... for his and their only use ... open and unlock the said gate joining upon the said way called Water Lane so often as occasion shall serve ...

[1] This is More's copy of the original indenture, formerly in SHC, LM 348. He also kept a copy of the lease in a book of such things, SHC, 1438, fos. 120v–23 (transcribed in MSC, II. i. 28–35, and Smith, *Blackfriars Playhouse*, 163–6).
[2] In an earlier lease of the first two rooms, they are 46½ feet long. The 'little room under [*i.e.* later in this document] granted', part of which had been and perhaps was still a privy, must have added 10 feet to the length, but if so, the total length given for all the rooms, 156½ feet, is 10 feet short. In earlier leases, the first two rooms are 26 feet 7½ inches and 27 feet wide, 'averaging', as Smith says, 'about 26 feet' (*Blackfriars Playhouse*, 461, 89–90).
[3] The words 'ceiled' and 'ceiling', refer to the walls. 'To ceil' (*OED*, 2) was, among other things, 'to cover with a lining of woodwork', hence 'to wainscot'. The 94 yards of wainscot must be square, not linear, measure, and if the wainscoting was 3 feet high and the round portal 4 feet across, the room (given as 22 feet east to west) was exactly 27 feet north to south. The sentence says that the portal was 'contained within' the wainscot, which was on the east, south and part of the west sides of one of the four southern rooms. Smith, however, puts the portal on the north side of the northernmost of these rooms (*Blackfriars Playhouse*, 92).
[4] Despite the word 'aforesaid', this is the first, and last, allusion to a wood yard.

310 Farrant makes his will, leaving the playhouse property to his wife, 30 November 1580

PRO, PROB.11/63/fo. 67v. Transcribed in Wallace, *Evolution of the English Drama*, 152 n. 3

[Farrant made his will when 'sick in body'. He named his wife as his executrix then wrote:] Item: I give and bequeath to my wife, Anne Farrant, the lease of my house in the Blackfriars in London, which lease is in a chest at my house in Greenwich, to have and enjoy the same for and during her natural life, if she live so long as the years yet unexpired do continue. And if not then I give and bequeath the residue of the said years unto which of my children she shall think meet. [He also left her his house and other property in Greenwich. She proved the will on 1 March 1581.]

311 Farrant's widow pleads with More for permission to sublet the playhouse property, 25 December 1580

Folger, MS L.b.448. Transcribed in Wallace, *Evolution of the English Drama*, 153 n. 2

After my humble commendations and my duty also remembered: where it hath pleased your worship to grant unto my husband ... one lease of your house within the Blackfriars for the term of twenty-one years with a proviso . . . that he cannot neither let nor set [over] the same without your worship's consent under your hand . . . And now for that it hath pleased God to call my said husband unto his mercy, having left behind him the charge of ten small children . . . and my husband besides greatly indebted, [I] not having the revenue of one groat any way coming in but by making the best I may of such things as he hath left behind him to relieve my little ones: may it therefore please your worship of your abundant clemency and accustomed goodness to consider a poor widow's distressed estate and for God's cause to comfort her with your worship's warrant under your hand [to allow me] to let and set [over] the same to my best commodity during the term of years in the said lease contained . . . In all which doing I shall evermore . . . pray unto God for the preservation of your worship's long continuance.

312 Anne Farrant sublets the playhouse to William Hunnis and John Newman, just before 19 September 1581

SHC, MS LM Cor 3/316. Transcribed in Wallace, *Evolution of the English Drama*, 154 n. 2

In a letter to Sir William More of 19 September 1581, the Earl of Leicester hinted at what Anne Farrant did with the playhouse after her own letter to More of 25 December 1580 (311). Evidently More did not agree that she could sublet the playhouse, and she sublet it anyway to Hunnis and Newman, who knew that More's approval was necessary. For the Earl wrote his letter at the behest of Hunnis, who delivered it himself, and its purpose must have been to suggest that More wink at the sublease, as, it seems, he did. The sublease does not survive, but it is alluded to in a lawsuit (316), and the accompanying bond is quoted in another lawsuit (315).

[The Earl wrote:] Whereas my friend, Mr Hunnis, this bearer, informeth me that he hath of late bought of Farrant's widow her lease[1] of that house in Blackfriars which you made to her husband, deceased, and means there to practise the Queen's children of the Chapel, being now in his charge, in like sort as his predecessor did for the better training them to do her majesty service: he is now a suitor to me to recommend him to your good favour, which I do very heartily as one that I wish right well unto and will give you thanks for any countenance or friendship you shall show him for the furtherance of this his honest request.

[1] Leicester is wrong here. She continued to hold the lease and pay the rent for it.

313 A great many comedies have been played in the first Blackfriars playhouse, 6 April 1582

Gosson, *Playes Confuted in fiue Actions* (SR, 6 April 1582)

This remark of 1582 is the first direct notice that plays were performed at the first Blackfriars playhouse, though one of six companies allowed 'to exercise playing within the City' during the Christmas season of 1578–9 was the children of the Chapel Royal playing, presumably, at Blackfriars.[1] Moreover, no title page of a printed play says that the play was performed at Blackfriars, and for only two surviving plays is there evidence otherwise that they were performed there, Lyly's *Campaspe* and *Sapho and Phao* (both 1584).

[1] PRO, PC2/12, p. 349 transcribed in *ES*, IV, 278.

In plays, . . . those things are feigned that never were, as *Cupid and Psyche* played at Paul's and a great many comedies more at the Blackfriars and in every playhouse in London, which for brevity's sake I overskip . . .

314 Hunnis pleads impoverishment because of the expenses of the children of the Chapel Royal, November 1583

PRO, SP12/163/fo. 209. Transcribed in Wallace, *Evolution of the English Drama*, 156 n. 3

Hunnis' enterprise at the Blackfriars playhouse was evidently not a financial success. He and Newman, according to Anne Farrant (316b), paid their bills slowly from the beginning, sometimes not for six months. Moreover, while More's lawsuit in the court of Husting (318) was in progress and nobody was paying rent to her, Hunnis declared his financial troubles to officials of the royal household, which the Chapel Royal served.

[The money he received, 6d a day for the 'diet' of each of the twelve children and £40 a year for their 'apparel and all other furniture', had long been inadequate:] the burden hereof hath from time to time so hindered the masters of the children, viz., Master Bower, Master Edwardes, myself and Master Farrant, that, notwithstanding some good helps otherwise, some of them died in so poor case and so deeply indebted that they have not left scarcely wherewith to bury them.

In tender consideration whereof, might it please your honours that [the royal household keep] the said allowance of 6d a day apiece for the children's diet . . . and in lieu thereof they to be allowed meat and drink within this honourable household. For that I am not able upon so small allowance any longer to bear so heavy a burden.

315 Anne Farrant sues William Hunnis and John Newman in Common Pleas for not paying their rent, autumn 1583

PRO, CP40/1418/m. 301. Transcribed in Wallace, *Evolution of the English Drama*, 159 nn. 1–2

Anne Farrant knew nothing about More's case against Evans in the court of Husting until January 1584 (317). She did know, however, that neither Hunnis and Newman nor anybody else had paid the rent due on 25 March, 24 June, and 29 September 1583 (316b). So she sued Hunnis and Newman in the autumn of 1583, separately but at the same time and in the same words, claiming that the bond of £100 that they had given her when they acquired the lease was forfeit for non-payment of rent.

[She added to the case against Newman a quotation of the condition of the bond:] The condition of this obligation is such that if the within bound William Hunnis and John Newman ... do well and truly observe, perform, fulfil and keep all and every the covenants, grants, articles, payments and agreements which on the part and behalf of the said William, John, their executors, administrators and assigns, or any of them, are or ought to be observed ... and mentioned in one pair of indentures bearing date with these presents, made between the within-named Anne Farrant on the one party and the said William and John of the other party according to the tenor, purport, effect and true meaning of the said indentures, that then this present obligation to be void or else to stand and abide in full force and effect.

Arguing, probably, that they were countersuing (316), Hunnis and Newman got these cases postponed until January 1584 and then until Easter term following, when the cases disappear.

316 Hunnis and Newman countersue Anne Farrant in Requests, 20 January 1584

PRO, (a–c) Req.2/246/25; (d) Req.1/13/fos. 41v, 43v, 120. Transcribed (a–d) in Wallace, *Evolution of the English Drama*, 160–8. Hunnis and Newman had paid the outstanding rent on about 1 November 1583 – see (b) below.

(a) Newman and Hunnis' bill of complaint, 20 January 1584

John Newman and William Hunnis of the City of London, gentlemen, [complained] that whereas one Anne Farrant, late of Greenwich, widow, by indenture bearing date the twentieth day of December ... [1581] did demise and let certain rooms, parcel of the dissolved house of Blackfriars, ... unto your said subjects for divers years yet enduring, yielding and paying for the same such yearly rent and at such days and times as in the said indenture is expressed with other covenants by your said subjects to be performed ... And for the performance of the said covenants your said subjects became bound by obligation, jointly and severally, in the sum of £100: ... so it is ... that although your said subjects and their assigns have from time to time paid the said yearly rents ... and, as they verily think, have observed the covenants, ... yet, notwithstanding, the said Anne Farrant, of a covetous and greedy mind, ... hath of late ... commenced her several suits at the common law upon the said bond of £100 against your said subjects in your majesty's Court of Common Pleas, surmising and making speech that the said rent hath not been duly paid, ... which your said subjects do think to have been paid at the said days or at least very shortly after ...[1]

May it therefore please your most excellent majesty ... to grant your highness's most gracious writ of privy seal to be directed to the said Anne Farrant, commanding her ... personally to appear before your majesty in your highness's Court of

Requests, then and there to answer to the premises, and farther to grant your most gracious writ of injunction, ... enjoining her thereby not to proceed any farther to sue and vex your subjects, or either of them, ... touching the premises ...

[1] Here follows the reason Hunnis and Newman offered for moving their case from Common Pleas to Requests. It was the one commonly offered and was, as commonly, no doubt fictitious: they did not have the indenture and so could not defend themselves in a court that, like Common Pleas, required precise details.

(b) Anne Farrant's answer, 27 January 1584

By this time, she had learned of More's lawsuit in the court of Husting, but only at the end of her answer did she realise the threat it posed to her. Yet her lawsuit and their countersuit required her to argue here mainly that they had forfeited their bond for non-payment of rent, not for imperilling her main lease by passing the sublease to Evans.

The defendant ... for answer in and to the said bill of complaint ... saith that long time before that the said defendant did demise and grant by her indenture the said roomeths, parcel of the said dissolved house of the Blackfriars ... to the said complainant[s], ... one Sir William More of Loseley in the county of Surrey, knight, was thereof seized ... And so being seized, by his indenture of lease bearing date the twentieth day of December ... [1576, he] did amongst other things demise grant and to farm let unto one Richard Farrant, ... then husband to this defendant, the said roomeths ... for the term of one and twenty years ... yielding and paying therefor yearly to the said Sir William More ... £14 of lawful money of England at the [four usual feasts] ... by even portions ... in and by which indenture the said Richard Farrant did covenant ... to repair, sustain and amend the said rooms, and the buildings, tilings, leads and other things in or about the same ... and that neither he nor any of his assigns should asign, demise or let the premises or any part thereof ...

And the said Richard ... about three years now last past died intestate,[1] after whose decease the administration of all the goods and chattels of the said Richard were committed to this defendant ... By virtue of which letters of administration, the said defendant did enter and was possessed of the things in and by the said indenture demised, and by virtue thereof was chargeable with the same rent, condition, covenants, articles. And being a sole woman, unable of herself to use the said roomeths to such purposes as her said husband late used them, ... nor being able to sustain, repair and amend the said rooms according to the ... articles in the said indenture, ... at the earnest request and desire of the said complainants, she, this defendant, was content to let the rooms ... to the said complainants, yielding and paying therefor to her yearly the sum of twenty nobles [£6 13s 4d] more than the said £14 due to the said Sir William More. Which lease the scrivener which by their appointment made the indenture of the same lease did make yielding only the yearly rent of £20 6s 8d ... at the said four feasts ... or within eight days then next following. Whereby this defendant is driven by oversight to lack one noble [6s 8d] yearly of the rent she meant to have, for which the complainants promised her a satisfaction which she never yet could get of them.

By which indenture also the said complainants did covenant, grant and agree with the said defendant to repair, sustain and amend . . . the said rooms and the buildings, tilings, leads and other the premises which her said husband by his said covenant was charged to do. And further the said complainants became bound by obligation in £100 to this defendant, with condition well and truly to observe . . . all the covenants . . . which in the said indenture of lease by her to them made are mentioned. In and by which indenture also the said now defendant hath covenanted not only to save these complainants harmless of the said rent reserved to the said Sir William More, but also to pay or tender the same . . .

Since which demise and grant made to the said complainants, . . . [they], as this defendant hath credibly been advertised, have granted all their estate and term in and to the premises unto one Henry Evans, citizen and scrivener of London, and they have . . . by virtue thereof had and reaped far greater profit than the said yearly rent amounteth unto. And, as this defendant by divers good presumptions hath good cause to suspect, they, or some of them, have sought . . . to avoid and defraud this defendant of and from the rent . . . [They] have not at any time since, to this defendant's now remembrance, paid their quarter rent due at any of the quarter days . . . and many times have withholden the said rent for and by the space of half a year and more. And this defendant, being left very bare and poor and with great charge of children and debts of her said late husband, . . . having great lack of money and not having money in hand to satisfy the rent due to the said Sir William More, she hath been driven . . . by humble and pitiful suit to the right honourable Lord Cobham to obtain such favour and help of his good lordship that one of his men would and might offer and tender to pay the rent then due . . . And at another time this defendant hath been urged to crave and obtain of Master Henry Sackford, esquire, of her majesty's privy chamber,[2] to lend to this defendant so much money as would and did pay the said quarter's rent . . . And other times this defendant hath been . . . driven for the payment of the said rent . . . to sell divers of her goods and chattels at far lesser price than they were worth, as at one time a dozen of gold buttons and at another time a set of viols. And at some time when this defendant for extreme need hath borrowed of some of them some money and laid some of her plate and jewels to them or some of them in pawns, they have at the payment of the said rent to her defalked from the rent the money to her lent and yet detained the said pawns. And this last year . . . three-quarters' rents due . . . [at 25 March, 24 June and 29 September] last past were not paid until near about All Saints Day last past [1 November 1583].

And further, the said complainants being earnestly required by this defendant to do needful reparations upon the house, being greatly decayed by their not repairing thereof, they did drive the time so long until Sir William More was determined to come to London. Whereby the said defendant . . . was constrained to amend and repair the leads of the said house, being before blown up with wind, the charges whereof did come to 15s 6d, and the said complainants never would pay the same. Whereupon the workman did retain one of the Knight Marshal's men for arrest [of] this defendant for the same, for the avoiding whereof this defendant paid the same 15s 6d. And further, this defendant hath divers other manifest matters ... which do persuade her that the said complainants intend to cause this defendant to forfeit or lose her said lease whereby she holdeth the premises and divers other little parcels ...

Besides that the said Sir William More hath since made some entry and a new lease of the premises to one[3] who by colour thereof hath sued the said Evans, who hath, without the privity of this defendant, so faintly and falsely pleaded and defended the cause that judgement is like to be given against the said Evans, to the great prejudice of this defendant.[4] And they, or some of them, have at some times falsely protested that they ... had satisfied the rent due to Sir William More, when in truth the rent ... hath not been paid. The which cause, besides divers other unfriendly and hard dealings by them, or some of them, used to this defendant, this defendant thinketh to be such ... as this court will vouchsafe ... that she shall not be stayed or hindered to persecute her just and lawful actions and suits at the common law against the said complainants ...

[1] The document is mistaken, as Hunnis and Newman pointed out in their replication. Richard Farrant did leave a will (310). The mistake, however, is not important because the effect of the will was the same as that stated in the following remarks.
[2] Sackford was master of the tents and keeper of the privy purse.
[3] Thomas Smalepeece (317).
[4] Evans merely demurred and judgement did go against him (318).

(c) Newman and Hunnis' replication, 27 May 1584

[Newman and Hunnis say that everything in their bill of complaint is true and deny that they or Evans have tried to defraud the defendant of her rent. On the contrary, they have paid] the whole sum of £20 13s 4d according to the true intent and meaning of the said parties touching their said bargain. And ... they have done from time to time, and were ready to have done, sufficient reparations in and upon the said premises as need required, but in one time when the said defendant wilfully obtruded herself into some botching and unfit dealing in the same reparations and did let [i.e. hinder] the sufficient and due performing thereof by the said complainants ... to their great loss and hindrance ... [They also deny that] by their negligence in not payment of rent ... [she was] driven to sell divers of her goods and chattels at a far lesser price than they were worth.

(d) Court orders, January–June 1584

The court made three orders about the case, on 27 and 30 January and 23 June 1584. According to the first, the lawyers for both sides were to argue on 29 January 'concerning the maintenance of the bill of complaint'; and according to the second, the parties and lawyers on both sides were to argue one point only on 1 February, whether the court should grant the injunction Hunnis and Newman were seeking. What if anything happened on these occasions does not appear.

[According to the third order, made on the motion of the lawyer representing Hunnis and Newman:] both parties shall attend with their counsel learned upon Saturday next [27 June], then to be heard upon the points of the breach of the obligation mentioned in the answer of the said defendant [Anne Farrant], which is in the same answer assigned to be for non-payment of the rent . . . payable by force of the indenture of lease made to the complainants, and whether that thereupon an injunction shall be awarded out of this court for the stay of the defendant's proceedings in [Common Pleas].

What happened on this third occasion does not appear, either, but the order suggests what might have happened. Hunnis and Newman protested that the only real issue before this court and Common Pleas was whether they had paid their rent, and they had indeed paid it, though usually, no doubt, very late. The court might have decided that they should pay Anne Farrant some interest on overdue rent, which could not have amounted to more than a pound or two, and that she should stop her lawsuit in Common Pleas on the bond. Such a sum was by this time, however, derisory. More had won his case against Evans in the court of Husting a month or so before, in Easter term, and the court had ordered a sheriff to seize the playhouse property for him. More had evicted everybody. They had caused her to lose the main lease, worth £6 13s 4d a year to her.

317 Anne Farrant appeals to Sir Francis Walsingham about More's seizure of the playhouse property, autumn? 1584

SHC, LM 412. Transcribed in Wallace, *Evolution of the English Drama*, 158 n. 1

Anne Farrant had lost her lease on the playhouse property without being able to argue her claim to it, but she probably saw little point in suing More for possession or Hunnis and Newman again on their bond. More would have argued that everybody concerned with the lease had violated its terms, hence nullified it. Hunnis and Newman would have argued either that she had failed once already to collect on the bond or that her husband's violations of the lease and her own had rendered it at least dubious before they bought it. So instead she used her influence as the worthy widow of a conspicuous man at court. She asked Walsingham to intervene with More, phrasing her request as though it were a bill of complaint in a lawsuit. Walsingham was the more prominent of the two secretaries of state and the most ardent Protestant in the upper reaches of the government.

In most humble wise showeth . . . your poor oratrix, Anne Farrant, widow, that whereas Sir William More, knight, the twentieth day of December . . . [1576] did demise unto Richard Farrant, your said oratrix's late husband, and to his executors and assigns, one house with other appurtenances . . . in the Blackfriars for the term of twenty-one years then next ensuing,[1] as by the indentures appeareth, so it is . . . that now of late this last Hilary term [January 1584][2] Sir William More, upon a supposal of a lease to be made by your oratrix unto one Henry Evans, hath entered upon the demised premises and made over a lease thereof unto his own man, Thomas Smalepeece, to try the said Evans his right therein, who hath recovered it against Evans and seeketh by the supposed lease made to Evans to take forfeiture also against your said oratrix, which might be her utter undoing.

Whereas your said oratrix never made any lease to Evans nor admitted any forfeiture, but truly paid her rent from time to time unto Sir William More and repaired the house. Which house did greatly indebt your said oratrix's late husband to make it commodious for his purpose. Which debt, had not her majesty been gracious and bountiful unto your said oratrix,[3] [she] had never [been] able to discharge, ... who hath paid all her majesty's bounty ... for his debts and for the relief of your said oratrix and her poor ten children since it pleased God to call ... [her] late husband, so that your said oratrix hath nothing left to relieve her and her poor children.

May it therefore please your honour of your abundant compassion, the rather for that your said oratrix is a poor widow and hath a great charge of children and is not able without great charges and hindrance to defend the truth of her cause, to grant your honour's letter unto Sir William More that he would stay his proceeding and suffer the cause to be heard by indifferent persons, lest, through mistaking your said oratrix her cause and intent, both she and hers be causeless put from their only stay and relief.

[1] Anne Farrant is inexact here. The twenty-one years began on the previous 29 September (309).
[2] Anne Farrant is wrong here. More said that he began the attempt to evict the people at the playhouse in Trinity term (May–June) 1583 (318). Her mistake suggests that she did not know of More's case at Guildhall until January 1584. So do her statement about it in Hunnis and Newman's case in Requests (27 January 1584 – 316b) and More's remark that he 'never heard of' her throughout the case at Guildhall.
[3] In 1582 the Queen had granted Anne Farrant gratis a lease in reversion on lands, etc., worth £20 a year clear (Hatfield House, Cecil MS 162/96, calendared in HMC, *Salisbury*, II, 539).

Walsingham sent this letter to More, who wrote on it 'Anne Farrant supplication'. More did not mention it in his explanation of how and why he seized the playhouse property (318), but he could have confused this moment with that after Richard Farrant's death. If so, he suggested now that she and he submit the argument to two indifferent lawyers or judges and she refused.

318 More explains how and why he seized the playhouse property, *c.* summer–autumn 1584

SHC, LM 425/11. Transcribed in Wallace, *Evolution of the English Drama*, 174 n. 2, 175–6

Perhaps in response to Anne Farrant's appeal to Walsingham (317), More jotted down a statement of his views (SHC, LM Cor 3/649, now mostly illegible), which a secretary made into a formal document (quoted here). Some of the secretary's work is also now illegible, but Wallace could supply a few missing words from More's jottings.

First I let the said house to Sir Henry Neville for a term of one and twenty years and took of him no fine for the same. Sir Henry added a new kitchen and set up [blank] partitions in the house. Afterward, Sir Henry sold me his lease thereof for an hundred pounds, which I paid him at one payment, besides forbearing of two or three years' rent, so far as I remember.[1]

Afterward, Sir Henry Neville desired me by his letter to let the said house to Farrant, which I did upon condition that he should not let nor set [over] the same, nor any part thereof, to any person without my consent had and obtained in writing under my hand and seal.

Farrant pretended unto me to use the house only for the teaching of the children of the Chapel but made it a continual house for plays, to the offense of the precinct, and pulled down partitions to make that place apt for that purpose, which Sir Henry Neville had set up. And, contrary to the condition, [he] let out part of the said house, for the which I charged him with the forfeiture of his lease, whereunto he yielded and offered composition. But before I could take remedy against him he died.

After whose death I entered upon the said house and refused to receive any rent but conditionally, nevertheless offering Farrant's widow that if she would commit the cause to two lawyers indifferently chosen, or to any two judges, I would yield to whatsoever they should determine therein, which she utterly refused.

Immediately after, she let the house to one Hunnis and afterward to one Newman or Sutton, as far as I remember, and then to Evans,[2] who sold his interest to the Earl of Oxford, who gave his interest to Lyly. And the title thus was posted over from one to another from me, contrary to the said condition.

... [When] Evans was so possessed of it, I brought my action against him for the same [in the court of Husting], and when it came to be tried he demurred in law upon it, which was done in Trinity term [*i.e.* May or June 1583]. The demurrer being drawn, the said Evans kept the same [*i.e.* the house] in his hands all Michaelmas term [*i.e.* the autumn] next following, using many delays.

After the demurrer had, I caused my learned counsel in Hilary term [23 January to 12 February 1584] to demand judgement, arguing the case at the usual place, but the recorder argued against me.

The judges would not then give judgement but required to have books of the whole proceeding delivered them, whereof I delivered one to every of them.[3]

At the end of Easter term following I had judgement against Evans and process awarded to the sheriff to give me possession. In all which time of my suit I never heard of Farrant's widow, but only by her said means I was put to this great charges of suit, very injuriously.

My charges in following the said suit and lying in London for that business stand me in not less than £40.

The house is much impaired by the pulling down the partitions thereof.

She had of the said Newman or Sutton £30 in money at his entry into [*i.e.* taking possession of] the said house, as he told me.

---

[1] More bore these costs presumably because of Neville's improvements to the place, which included also two stairways from the yard up to the main rooms, one the 'great' stairway and the other a lesser one from the kitchen.

[2] In saying that Anne Farrant had sublet the 'house' to Evans, More gave himself a reason for evicting her. She insisted that Hunnis and Newman had passed their sublease to Evans without her involvement (317).

[3] The court of Husting met and meets on the dais at the east end of Guildhall, and its officials were and are the Lord Mayor and the sheriffs as judges, the recorder as 'assessor', and the aldermen as the jury, if needed.

319 Anne Farrant appeals to the privy council about More's seizure of the playhouse property, 13 January 1587

SHC, LM Cor 3/395. Transcribed in Wallace, *Evolution of the English Drama*, 177 n. 1. This is part of a letter More received from his son-in-law, Sir John Wolley, who wrote mainly of the progress of a petition to the Queen in which people protested that Blackfriars should be free from control by the City.

Likewise Mr [William] Wade, clerk of the [privy] council, telleth me of Farrant's widow's renewing of her complaint, which he prayeth me at your coming to London may be ended between you and me and her, which at your coming I have promised him for my part to do.

The Privy Council did not mention Anne Farrant or her case in the minutes of its meetings, though on 24 June 1587 it did mention the petition (PRO, PC2/14, p. 378, transcribed in *APC, 1587–8*, 137–8). Perhaps Wolley and More offered and she accepted some money, so that the history of the first Blackfriars playhouse finally ended early in 1587.

XXV The Curtain

The Curtain was a public playhouse in Shoreditch in Middlesex, perhaps 300 yards beyond the north-eastern boundary of the City of London and 200 south or south-east of another public playhouse, the Theatre. It was somewhere in a large former pasture on the south side of Holywell Lane, E.C.2, that, like the land on which the Theatre stood, had belonged to Holywell Priory. The playhouse probably opened in the autumn of 1577, a year after the Theatre. It remained in theatrical use longer than any other Shakespearean playhouse, from 1577 to 1625, and evidently was still standing in 1698.

The name of the playhouse had nothing to do with theatrical curtains. The pasture had been called the Curtain, meaning that it was enclosed by a wall, long before the playhouse existed. The playhouse is often supposed to have been on the eastern side of the present Curtain Road, E.C.2, about where Hewett Street is, because in his map of the area of 1745 Peter Chassereau, the local curate, shows a large, more or less square, building there called 'Curtain Court'.[1] The playhouse, however, could have been elsewhere in the pasture, closer, for example, to Holywell Lane and, or, Shoreditch High Street. A difficulty in locating the playhouse is that the word, 'Curtain', referred not only to the playhouse but to the pasture

Fig. 1. The Curtain playhouse (?), from *The View of the Cittye of London from the North towards the Sowth*, c. 1600–10 or later.

and the many structures eventually built in it. One such structure was described as 'the house, tenement, or lodge commonly called the Curtain' in 1567 and 1572, before the playhouse was built, and in 1581 some four years after. This building may well have been 'the Curtain house' in 1640,[2] and the origin of Chassereau's 'Curtain Court'.

When the Priory was dissolved in 1539, the Crown assumed ownership of the pasture and sold it as a single freehold 'in capite', that is subject to an annual 'free-farm rent' and other charges paid to the Crown. The people who came to own the freehold then leased out parts of the pasture so that it became the Curtain estate, often called Curtain close. By 1 July 1611 sixteen people held thirteen 'messuages' (including the playhouse), one 'house', a 'parcel of pasture ground', and properties held by three people and lumped together as 'all other the messuages, lands, tenements and hereditaments'. If 'the house, tenement or lodge' of 1567–81 was 'the Curtain house' in 1640, it should have been the 'house' of 1611, held then by Richard Pooley.

Maurice Longe, cloth-worker, and one of his sons, William, also a cloth-worker, bought the freehold of the Curtain estate for £60 on 20 February 1567, and Maurice and his wife mortgaged it for £200 on 23 August 1572. Maurice having died in 1577, William sold it 'for a certain sum' on 18 March 1581 to Thomas Harberte of Cheapside, girdler. Then Peter and Richard Payne, the one of Shrewsbury, butcher, the other of London, girdler, and William Harries of London, porter, owned it. On 31 January 1609 they passed it to Thomas Catchmay of Barnard's Castle, London, esq., and Thomas Wood of Saint Swithin's Lane, London, gentleman, who sold it on 1 July 1611 to Edward Morris of London, embroiderer, for £450 'and other good causes'. These people probably saw the estate as merely an investment in a group of leases, and the men who sold it in 1611 thought the playhouse defunct, though clearly it was not.

Who built the playhouse and how he, she or they financed it are unknown, as is its ownership for most of its history. Henry Lanman, a yeoman of the Queen's guard, is usually said to have built it. He owned it, hence probably a lease of the land on which it stood, from at least 1585 to at least 1592, and he could well have owned it in 1581, when he was mentioned as one of the tenants in the Curtain estate.[3] On 22 July 1603, Thomas Pope, an actor among the Lord Chamberlain's men, owned a share of the playhouse. In 1611, it was Thomas Greene, the leading actor among Queen Anne's men, who held, or had lately held, the whole playhouse, and he was also one of the three men who held 'all other the messuages, lands, tenements and hereditaments' in the Curtain estate. In October 1624, John Underwood, an actor among the King's men, owned a share of the playhouse. Two other people involved in the playhouses of the time are also said to have had a hand in it, but one of them, and perhaps both, merely had leases on other properties in the estate. In 1581, Richard Hicks, who had to do with the playhouse at Newington Butts, was a tenant in the estate. In 1611, Christopher Beeston, who was to create the Phoenix playhouse, held the 'parcel of pasture ground' near the Curtain estate and was also one of the three men who held 'all other the messuages, lands, tenements and hereditaments' there.[4]

At Michaelmas 1585, Lanman and the two owners of the Theatre, John Brayne and James Burbage, agreed to pool and share equally the profits of the two playhouses for seven years. Why they should do so is a puzzle. When Burbage and Lanman alluded to the arrangement in 1591 and 1592, neither said he was dissatisfied with it, and they and an actor all implied that it was being carried out. Lanman suggested that it was a mutual convenience rather than an ordinary commercial transaction.

For many years contemporaries mentioned the two playhouses together as representing all the purpose-built playhouses in and around London. The arrangement for pooling their profits implies that they accommodated about the same number of people, hence were of similar size. The few surviving contemporary remarks about the shape of the Curtain suggest that the place, like the Theatre, conformed to the general idea of public playhouses. It was a timber-frame building, but, unlike the Theatre, it was covered with thatch. It was polygonal so that it seemed round, an 'amphitheatre'. It had three galleries, one over the other, around an open yard. The playhouse shown near the left edge of *The View of the Cittye of London from the North towards the Sowth* (fig. 1) is probably the Curtain, though it is often said to be the Theatre.[5] This building is an octagon three storeys high. On top is a large rectangular hut with a pitched roof, behind the ridge of which rises a short round, apparently battlemented tower with a flagpole from which a large flag flies. The hut, whose long dimension lies east and west, is probably over the south side of the unseen yard. The building has two large external staircases serving all three storeys, one on the east side, the other on the west. The only doorway visible is on the ground floor of the middle side of the three sides facing north.

The Curtain was never one of the great playhouses. Its use is as imperfectly known as its ownership. No company is definitely known to have played there during the first twenty years, though Lord Arundel's men were probably there in 1584. Three companies are known to have used it for only about five of the next twenty-eight years. After the Lord Chamberlain's men abandoned the Theatre in the autumn of 1598, they played at the Curtain until they moved into the Globe in May 1599. When playing resumed after the great plague of 1603–4, Queen Anne's men used the Curtain and probably meant to stay there for more than a season or two, since Greene acquired the lease on it. But at the same time they also meant to use the Boar's Head, the lease on which Greene's wife had just inherited (389), and probably after the summer of 1607, they abandoned both places for the new Red Bull. Prince Charles's (I) men played at the Curtain from 1620 to 1623. Yet the place was clearly in theatrical use in at least most of the intervening plague-free years and until 1625.

The Curtain was then used for a time for fencing displays. Thereafter the building seems to have been converted to domestic use. One of the reasons for its survival may be the same as that for the lack of evidence about it. Its owners and landlords may have given lawyers little occasion (so far as is presently known) to create documents about it.

[1] Tomlins ('Origin of the Curtain Theatre', 34) suggested the idea in 1844, and Halliwell-Phillipps promoted it in 1882 (*Outlines*, 361), but Chambers (*ES*, II, 401–2) dismissed it as have others.

[2] The registers of the parish church, St Leonard, Shoreditch, record that Margery Banister was buried on 31 January and John Hyemarsh baptised and buried on 15 March 1640, both as 'from the Curtain house'. The registers identify many others as belonging to the Curtain without the addition of the word 'house'. On 7 June 1619 'John Edwards, being excommunicated, was buried ... in the King's highway in Holywell Lane near the Curtain'. See GL, MSS 7499 (burials), 7493 (baptisms); also Tomlins, 'Origin of the Curtain Theatre', 33, and Halliwell-Phillipps, *Outlines* (1881), 365.

[3] See Ingram, *The Business of Playing*, 219–38.

[4] Beeston's pasture ground adjoined the estate on two sides and contained three rods and ten perches. Because in his will in 1638 he mentioned property in Shoreditch (see 492) and Hotson found that it was near the Curtain estate, writers sometimes say that Beeston had a stake in the Curtain playhouse (*J and CS*, VI, 138; *CRS*, 92), but this document suggests that he did not (PRO, C54/2075/17).

[5] See H. Berry, 'The View of London from the North and the Playhouses in Holywell'.

The Curtain 407

320 The Curtain estate is described in 1567, 1572 and 1581

PRO, (a) C54/742/34, 35; (b) C54/884/m. 17–19 from the bottom; (c) C54/1098/m. 8 from the bottom. Transcribed (a–c) in Tomlins, 'Origin of the Curtain Theatre', 29–31

Quoted below are the descriptions of the Curtain estate in the contracts by which it was sold, mortgaged and sold again in 1567, 1572 and 1581. The names at the ends are of people who held leases in the estate.

(a) 20 February 1567

Maurice Longe and one of his sons, William, bought the Curtain estate from James Blount, Lord Mountjoy, and his wife, Katherine (who had inherited it from her father, Sir Thomas Leigh).

[The contract describes the estate as:] All that the house, tenement or lodge commonly called the Curtain, and all that parcel of ground and close, walled and enclosed with a brick wall on the west and north parties called also the Curtain close, sometime appertaining to the Priory of Holywell, now dissolved, set lying, and being in the parish of St Leonard in Shoreditch in the county of Middlesex, together with all the gardens, fishponds, wells, hereditaments and brick wall, and all other profits, appurtenances and commodities to the premises or any part or parcel thereof in any way appertaining or belonging, now in the tenures or occupations of [blank] Wilkinson and Robert Manne.

(b) 23 August 1572

Maurice Longe and Jane, his wife, mortgaged the Curtain estate and a warehouse in Milk Street to Sir William Allyn, the Lord Mayor, for £200 (£100 to be repaid on 23 August 1573 and £100 a year later). The mortgage describes the estate word for word as the contract of 1567 does, except that the mortgage gives Wilkinson's Christian name as Richard.

(c) 18 March 1581

[William Longe, son of Maurice Longe, sold the Curtain estate to Thomas Harberte, the estate described in the contract as:] All that the house, tenement, or lodge commonly called the Curtain, and also all that parcel of ground and close, walled and enclosed with a brick wall on the west and north parts, and in part with a mud wall at the west side or end towards the south, called also the Curtain close, sometime appertaining to the late Priory of Holywell, now dissolved, set lying, and being in the parish of St Leonard in Shoreditch . . . in the county of Middlesex, together with all the gardens, fishpond, well and brick wall to the premises, or any of them, belonging or appertaining, and also all and singular other messuages, tenements, edifices and buildings, with all and singular their appurtenances, erected and builded upon the said close called the Curtain, or upon any part or parcel thereof, or to the same near adjoining, now or late in the several tenures or occupations of Thomas Wilkinson, Thomas Wilkins, Robert Medley, Richard Hicks, Henry Lanman and Robert Manne, or any of them . . . and also all other messuages, lands, tenements and hereditaments, with their appurtenances, set, lying and being in Holywell Lane.

321 The Curtain playhouse and its neighbour, the Theatre, are in business, 2 December 1577

The Curtain playhouse is first heard of in John Northbrooke's treatise on 'vain plays' and 'other idle pastimes', SR, 2 December 1577, in which it and its neighbour, the Theatre, are schools for 'wickedness and vice to be learned in'. The Curtain is supposed to have been built after the Theatre mainly because, unlike the Theatre, it is not mentioned in a privy council order of 1 August 1577 forbidding 'assemblies of the people of London to plays' in order to prevent 'sickness.'[1]

[1] See 253, 256b.

322 The Curtain and the Theatre represent London playhouses in general, 1577–1592

(a) T. F., *Newes from the North* (1579), sig. F4, and Twyne, *Physic against Fortune* (1579), 1, 30; (b) Stubbes, *Anatomie of Abuses* (1583), 143–4; (c) CLRO, Remembrancia, 1, 538; (d) Rankins, *A Mirrour of Monsters* (London, 1587), fo. 4v; (e) Nashe, *Martins Months Minde* (1589), sigs. F–F2; (f) PRO, PC2/19, p. 415. Transcribed in (c) MSC, 1, 63; (f) APC, 1591–2, 550

The Theatre and Curtain evidently caught the public imagination as other playhouses did not. For though six other public playhouses and two private playhouses operated in London during at least part of the time, the Theatre and Curtain were often mentioned together as representing them all from 1577 until 1592 and beyond. For further instances, see 256b and 259.

(a) 1579

I call to witness the Theatres, Curtains, . . . bowling alleys, and such places where time is so shamefully misspent, namely the Sabbath days, unto the great dishonour of God and the corruption and utter destruction of youth. [And:] JOY   I am delighted with sundry shows. REASON   Perhaps with the Curtain or Theatre, which two places are well known to be enemies to good manners . . .

(b) 1 March 1583

For so often as they go to those houses where players frequent, they go to Venus' palace and Satan's synagogue. [And in the margin:] Theatres and Curtains Venus' palaces . . . [And:] mark the flocking and running to Theatres and Curtains daily and hourly, night and day, time and tide, to see plays and interludes.

(c) 3 May 1583

Among other[s], we find one very great and dangerous inconvenience, the assembly of people to plays . . . [and other] profane spectacles at the Theatre and Curtain and other like places.

(d) 1587

The Theatre and Curtain may aptly be termed for their abomination the chapel of adultery.

(e) August 1589

[The supposedly dying Martin Marprelate speaks to his sons:] I perceive that every stage-player, if he play the fool but two hours together, hath somewhat for his labour, and I . . . nothing . . . [People are] now weary of our stale mirth, that for a penny may have far better by odds [of finding mirth] at the Theatre and Curtain and any blind [i.e., private?] playing house every day [than by buying a pamphlet of Martin's consisting of] twittle-tattles that indeed I had learned in ale-houses and at the Theatre of [John] Laneham [a player among the Queen's men] and his fellows.

(f) 23 June 1592

[The Privy Council ordered:] that there be no plays used in any place near thereabouts, as the Theatre, Curtain, or other usual places . . . where the same are commonly used.

323 Fencers play their 'prizes' at the Curtain, 1579–1583

BL, Sloane MS 2530, fos. (a) 43, (b) 4 (also 44, 12 (2), 13, 46). Transcribed in Berry, *The Noble Science*, (a) 127, (b) 49 (also 129, 65, 67, 133)

Between 1575 and 1590 the London schools of fencing mounted at least seven of their 'prizes' at the Curtain (see **201**). Prizes were public displays-cum-examinations that students had to perform successfully in order to proceed from one rank to another. Quoted are the first and last references to the Curtain in a manuscript devoted mainly to prizes from the 1540s to 1590.

(a) 25 August 1579

Richard Fletcher played his scholar's prize at the Curtain in Holywell . . . at two weapons, the long sword and the sword and buckler. There played with him at long sword six, and one free scholar, *videlicet* Thomas Noble, at both weapons. And there played at the sword and buckler eighteen. And so he was allowed under Isaac Kennard, master, the 25 of August 1579.

(b) 30 April 1583

Alexander Reyson played his master's prize the last day of April 1583 at the Curtain in Holywell at four kind[s] of weapons, that is to say, the long sword, the back sword, the sword and buckler, and the staff. There played with him four masters, *videlicet* William Mathewes, Francis Calvert, John Goodwen and Isaac Kennard. And so the said Alexander Reyson was admitted master under William Joyner, master.

324 The City of London tries to suppress the Curtain, 14 June 1584

Though both the Theatre and Curtain were outside the City, the City could exercise control over them if the privy council allowed. On Sunday 14 June the City authorities persuaded most of the council then in Whitehall to agree that the City could pull down the two playhouses. In the end, however, the City could do little more than harrass two companies of players and James Burbage, who was one of the owners of the Theatre. The players were the Queen's and Lord Arundel's men. They were, presumably, using the two playhouses, and if so, it was probably Lord Arundel's who were at the Curtain. See 273.

325 Contemporaries describe the Curtain, 1585–1611

(a) Hassler, *Die Reisen des Samuel Kiechel*, 29; (b) University of Utrecht Library, MS Var. 355, fos. 131v–32; (c) William Rowley, Day, Wilkins, *Travels of the The Three English Brothers* (1607), sig. H4v; (d) PRO, C54/2075/17. Transcribed in (b) Gaedertz, *Zur Kenntniss der altenenglischen Bühne*, 6. See also the second paragraph of 329 below. For (b) below, see also 353.

(a) Samuel Kiechel, 1585

Kiechel was a German who visited London in the autumn of 1585 and noted the 'daily comedies' to be seen.

[He added:] There are some peculiar houses that are so made as to have about three galleries one over another so that a great number of people always come in to see such entertainment. [In 1585 two (perhaps three) purpose-built playhouses could be so described, and one of them was the Curtain.]

(b) Johannes de Witt, 1596

De Witt was a Dutchman who visited London in, probably, 1596. He mentioned four 'amphitheatres', two of which:

are outside the City towards the north [*i.e.* the Theatre and Curtain], on the street going through the episcopal gate ['episcopalem portam'], vulgarly called Bishopsgate.[1]

[1] The street going through Bishopsgate is itself called Bishopsgate; it becomes Norton Folgate and then, near the playhouses, Shoreditch.

(c) John Day, William Rowley, George Wilkins, 1607

The epilogue of a play acted at the Curtain addresses the audience (see 333 and 437):

> Some that fill up this round circumference...
> Might justly call the authors travellers.

(d) The owners, 1611

See below, 335.

326 The owners of the Curtain and Theatre agree to share the profits of the two playhouses, 1585–1592

At Michaelmas 1585, Henry Lanman, who owned the Curtain at the time, agreed with the two owners of the Theatre that he and they would pool and share the profits of their two playhouses for seven years, and the arrangement (called an 'easer') was evidently carried out. See 276.

327 The privy council orders the Theatre and Curtain to be speedily pulled down, 28 July 1597

See 54. This most drastic of inhibitions was aimed at all playing places within three miles of the City of London but specifically mentioned only the Theatre and Curtain. Neither, however, was pulled down, nor was any of the others, and by the autumn the Curtain and the others were back in business, though the Swan (see introduction and 355) was troubled.

328 The Lord Chamberlain's men move from the Theatre to the Curtain, autumn 1598

(a) Marston, *Scourge of Villainy* (1598), sig. H4 (SR, 8 September 1598); (b) Guilpin, *Skialetheia* (1598), sig. B8v (SR, 15 September 1598); (c) Armin, *Foole vpon Foole* (1600, 1605), title pages

It is often argued that the Lord Chamberlain's men moved into the Curtain in the autumn of 1597. The Burbages' lease on the Theatre ran out on 25 March 1597, and (so the argument goes) they would not have reopened the playhouse when other owners reopened playhouses after the inhibition of 28 July 1597 (327). The landlord at the Theatre, however, allowed the Burbages to remain there paying their usual rent for 'a year or two' according to him, 'for divers years' according to Richard Burbage. Moreover, allusions to the Lord Chamberlain's men at the Curtain begin in September 1598, when the Burbages gave up their attempts to renew their lease (see 295 and 299).

(a) Marston, 8 September 1598

Luscus says to a companion, hinting that *Romeo and Juliet*, a play of the Lord Chamberlain's men, had been played at the Curtain:

> I set thy lips abroach, from whence doth flow
> Naught but pure Juliet and Romeo.
> Say who acts best, Drusus or Roscio?
> Now I have him that ne'er of ought did speak
> But when of plays or players he did treat,
> Hath made a commonplace book out of plays,
> And speaks in print: at least whate'er he says
> Is a warranted by Curtain plaudities.

(b) Guilpin, 15 September 1598

In his collection of epigrams and satires, Guilpin says that Thalia, the muse of comic poetry,

> Edgeth some blunted teeth and fires the breast
> Of many an old, cold, grey-beard citizen,
> Medea-like making him young again,
> Who, coming from the Curtain, sneaketh in
> To some odd garden noted house of sin.

And he says later in the same book that the Curtain is busy but the Theatre 'unfrequented' (see **299** and **346**).

(c) Armin, 1600, 1605

[He was an actor who joined the Lord Chamberlain's men c. 1599. In the first edition of his book, he called himself] Clonnico de Curtanio Snuff, [and in the second, referring to the Globe,] Clonnico del mondo Snuff. [In the third, the book now enlarged and titled A Nest of Ninnies (1608), he used his own name].[1]

---

[1] See *ES*, II, 403. Moreover, Thomas Pope, another member of the company, mentioned owning a share of the Curtain in his will, dated 22 July 1603 (PRO, PROB.11/103/fos. 95–6).

329 A Swiss sees a play at the Curtain, September or October 1599

Basle University Library, Platter's Journey 1595–1600, fo. 683. Transcribed in Binz, 'Londoner Theater und Schauspiele im Jahre 1599', 458–9

The Lord Chamberlain's men moved from the Curtain to the Globe when the Globe opened in May 1599, but the Curtain soon received other players. The Swiss, Thomas Platter of Basle, was in England from 18 September to 20 October 1599. He wrote of going to the Globe on 21 September to see *Julius Caesar* (no. **396**) and to the Curtain 'at another time':

I also saw after dinner a comedy not far from our inn in the suburb, if I remember right, in Bishopsgate. [The only playhouse near Bishopsgate at the time was the Curtain.] Here they represented various nations with whom on each occasion an Englishman fought for his daughter and overcame them all except the German, who won the daughter in fight. He then sat down with him and gave him and his servant strong drink so that they both got drunk, and the servant threw his shoe at his master's head and they both fell asleep. Meanwhile, the Englishman went into the tent, robbed the German of his gains, and thus he outwitted the German also. At the end, they danced very elegantly both in English and in Irish fashion.

And thus every day at two o'clock in the afternoon in ... London two and sometimes three comedies are performed at separate places wherewith folk make merry together, and whichever does best gets the greatest audience. The places are so built that they play on a raised platform, and everyone can well see it all. There are, however, separate galleries and there one stands more comfortably and, moreover, can sit, but one pays more for it. Thus anyone who remains on the level standing pays only one English penny, but if he wants to sit, he is let in at a further door and there he gives another penny. If he desires to sit on a cushion in the most comfortable place of all, where he not only sees everything well but can also be seen, then he gives yet another English penny at another door. And in the pauses of the comedy, food and drink are carried round amongst the people, and one can thus refresh himself at his own cost.

330 A barber is charged with stealing a purse at a play at the Curtain, March 1600

LMA, MJ/SR 378/7. Transcribed in Jeaffreson, *Middlesex County Records*, I, 259

A Middlesex justice, Nicholas Collyns, took a bond of £10 from Richard Fletcher, a pewterer of Norwich, to guarantee Fletcher's appearance at the next general sessions of the peace to give evidence against William Haukins, a barber of St Giles without Cripplegate. At the bottom of the court copy of the bond, the clerk noted the case against Haukins:

Charged with a purse taken at a play at the Curtain with 26s 6d in it.

331 The privy council allows the Fortune to open provided that the Curtain is closed, 22 June 1600

PRO, PC2/25, p. 223. Transcribed in *APC, 1599–1600*, 397

Because of objections to the building of the Fortune (418), the privy council decided briefly to limit the number of playhouses to two, one on each side of the Thames – the Fortune and the Globe (418,58). So among the reasons the council offered for allowing the Fortune was:

It is likewise ordered that the said [play]house of [Edward] Alleyn shall be allowed ... so as the house called the Curtain be (as it is pretended) either ruinated or applied to some other good use.

Alleyn seems to have had no stake in the Curtain, hence could not close it, but because it was much the oldest playhouse in London, he and the privy council might have expected it to close soon in any event. If they did, however, they were wrong.

332 But playing continues at the Curtain: the privy council suppresses a play there, 10 May 1601

PRO, PC2/26, p. 193. Transcribed in *APC, 1600–01*, 346. The privy council was concerned only about the play, apparently unaware that the playhouse was supposed to be no more.

[It addressed 'certain justices of the peace in . . . Middlesex':] We do understand that certain players that use to recite their plays at the Curtain . . . do represent upon the stage . . . the persons of some gentlemen of good desert and quality that are yet alive, under obscure manner but yet in such sort as all the hearers may take notice both of the matter and the persons that are meant thereby.

This being a thing very unfit, offensive and contrary to such direction[s] as have been heretofore taken that no plays should be openly showed but such as were first perused and allowed and that might minister no occasion of offence or scandal, we do hereby require you that you do forthwith forbid those players . . . that do play at the Curtain . . . to represent any such play, and that you will examine them who made that play and to show the same unto you, and as you in your discretions shall think the same unfit to be publicly showed, to forbid them from henceforth to play the same either privately or publicly. And if upon view of the said play you shall find the subject so odious and inconvenient as is informed, we require you to take bond of the chiefest of them to answer their rash and indiscreet dealing before us.

333 The privy council allows Queen Anne's men to play at the Curtain after the plague of 1603–4, 9 April 1604

Dulwich, MS I, fo. 54. Transcribed in Collier, *Memoirs of Edward Alleyn*, 66

[The Privy Council ordered the Lord Mayor and justices of Middlesex and Surrey to:] permit and suffer the three companies of players to the King, Queen and Prince publicly to exercise their plays in their several and usual houses for that purpose and no other, viz., the Globe situate in Maiden Lane on the Bankside, . . . the Fortune in Golden Lane, and the Curtain in Holywell.

The Queen's men also used the Boar's Head at the time, and by the autumn of 1607 had moved into the Red Bull, where they stayed for many years. See **389, 390, 437**.

334 Entertainments continue at the Curtain after the departure of the Queen's men, 1605–1615

(a) G.S. Gargano, *Scapigliatura Italiana a Londra sotto Elisabetta e Giacomo I*, 125–6 (see also *CSP, Ven.*, 1615–17, 593–ff.); (b) Smith, *The Hector of Germany* (1615), SR, 24 April 1615; (c) I.H., *This World's Folly* (1615), sig. B2v

Although the Curtain was now the oldest playhouse in London by many years, and the owners of the freehold thought it decayed and disused in 1611 (see **335**), it remained a working playhouse. John Heath mentioned it as a regular playhouse along with the Globe and Fortune in 1610, and George Wither disparaged the plays produced in it in two of his satires in 1613.[1] What players used it from 1605 to 1615, indeed to 1619, is unknown, except for those who performed one play (b below). Other signs that the old place was still a working playhouse during these years follow.

[1] *Epigrams* (1610), century 2, no. 39 (sig. E3v); *Abuses Stript and Whipt* (1613), sigs. C4v, P8v.

(a) The Venetian ambassador in London, 1611–1615

From 1611 to 1615, he was Antonio Foscarini, who was accused of many things on his return home, among them trying to seduce a penitent lady attached to an English nun belonging to the embassy, 'sometimes attending the public comedies and standing among the people on the chance of seeing her'. Writing an undated letter to Andrea Cioli, Secretary of State at Florence, Antimo Galli described an exploit of Foscarini's at the Curtain:

Finally, I want to tell you how our Pantalone has been up to a most Pantalonean adventure.[1] He is now in the habit of often going out alone, that is with a trusted servant who walks a little ahead of him and shows him which way to go, and he says he is going incognito. Where he is going, who would know? In this fashion he often goes to a playhouse, and, not counting others, he went the other day to a playhouse that is called the Curtain, which is the other way from his house, a place as dubious as they come, and where you would never see the face of a gentleman, let alone a nobleman. And what made it worse, so as not to have to pay sixpence ['un reale'] or a [MS mutilated] [he chose not] to go to one of the boxes and not even to be seated in one of the degrees [*i.e.* galleries] they have there but preferred to stand below in the middle, among the rabble of porters and carters, pretending that he needed to stay close by because he was hard of hearing, as if he really understood what was being recited.

But that is not all, for in the end, when one of the actors took leave of the audience and invited it to come back the next day and to pick a play, he actually named one. But the crowd wanted another and began to shout '*Friars, Friars*' because they wanted one that usually took its name from the friars, meaning [in Italian] 'frati'. Whereupon our blockhead[2] turned to his interpreter [who] explained that this was the name of a comedy about friars. So loosening his cloak, he began to clap his hands just as the mob did and to shout, 'frati, frati'. As he was shouting this, the people turned to him and, assuming he was a Spaniard, began to whistle in such a way that I cannot imagine that he would ever want to return to that place. But he has not given up visiting the other theatres and almost always with a single servant.[3]

[1] In *commedia dell'arte*, Pantalone is a lean, elderly, and foolish Venetian who wears slippers, pantaloons and glasses.
[2] 'Tamballone', i.e. Tambellone?
[3] The translation is by Professor Peter Bietenholz, University of Saskatchewan.

(b) Wentworth Smith, 1615

[The title page of a play describes it as:] A new play, an honourable history, as it hath been publicly acted at the Red Bull and at the Curtain by a company of young men of this city.

(c) 1615

[Among much else, actors:] were wont to Curtain over their defects with knavish conveyances and scum off the froth of all wanton vanity to qualify the eager appetite of their slapping favourites. [And in the margin just above is 'Greene's baboon' – an allusion to a part played by Thomas Greene, who had held the lease on the Curtain playhouse (335) and had died in 1612.]

335 The Curtain is decayed and, as the freeholders think, is no longer a playhouse, 1 July 1611

PRO, C54/2075/17. The contract by which the freehold of the Curtain estate changed hands in 1611 explains not only the recent history of the freehold but something of the playhouse itself.

[The playhouse is:] All that large messuage or tenement [*i.e.* holding] built of timber and thatch, now in decay, called the Curtain, with a parcel of ground adjoining thereto, wherein they use[d] to keep stage plays, now or late in the tenure and occupation of Thomas Greene, his assignee or assigns.

The contract adds that Greene (the leading figure among the Queen's men) was also one of three men who held properties lumped together as 'all other the messuages, lands, tenements and hereditaments' in the Curtain estate.

336 Prince Charles' (I) men are at the Curtain, early 1620–1623

(a) Bodleian Library, MS Eng. Misc. c. 4, fos. 5, 6; (b) Sir Henry Herbert, Office Book (now lost), reported by Malone in *Plays and Poems of William Shakespeare* (1821), III, 57–9; (c) *Vox Graculi* (1623), sigs. Iv–I2. Transcribed in (a) MSC, VI. 148. There are several indications in addition to those below that the Prince's men were at the Curtain for several years in the early 1620s.[1]

[1] See *J and CS*, VI, 134–8.

(a) February 1620

John Drew, one of the ordinary grooms[1] of the Prince his chamber, being sent in his highness's service . . . from the court at St James into London so far as Shoreditch with a message to [William] Rowley, one of his highness's players . . . [and] he returned with answer . . . Therefore he prayeth to have allowance for the charges . . . to and fro.

[And] William Price, one of the grooms of the Prince his chamber, being sent . . . [with] one message from the court at Whitehall to the Prince his players in Shoreditch to warn them to attend his highness, . . . he prayeth to have allowance for himself, his pains and charges. [The only playhouse in Shoreditch after 1598 was the Curtain.]

[1] A groom in ordinary was paid for being a groom, unlike an extraordinary one.

(b) 1622

[Herbert, the Master of the Revels, alluded several times to the Prince's men at the Curtain at least in 1622. Malone, who had the Office Book before him, noted:] It appears from the office book of Sir Henry Herbert . . . in the year 1622 there were but five principal companies of comedians in London, . . . [among them] the Prince's Servants, who performed then at the Curtain.

(c) 1623

[A mock almanac for 1623:] About this time new plays will be more in request than old, and, if company come current to the [Red] Bull and Curtain, there will be more money gathered in one afternoon than will be given to the Kingsland Spittle[1] in a whole month. Also if at this time, about the hours of four and five, it wax cloudy and then rain downright, they shall sit drier in the galleries than those who are the understanding men in the yard.

[1] There was a leper house in Kingsland, which is north of Shoreditch.

337 Prince Charles' (I) men leave the Curtain to lesser companies, 1623–1625

Sir Henry Herbert, Office Book (now lost), quoted in Halliwell-Phillipps' scrapbook at the Folger, 'Fortune', 85. Transcribed in *J and CS*, VI, 137–8.

On 19 August 1623 the Master of the Revels licensed Prince Charles' (I) men to perform a play at the Red Bull, and in the same month he licensed an unknown company to perform a play at the Curtain, 'the profaneness left out'. This second company was probably not an experienced London company because the Master also 'commanded a reformation in all their other plays'. Then in March 1624, William Perry, of the Children of the Revels to the late Queen Anne, a provincial company,[1] got a licence for his company to continue for a year, and to use the Curtain for some days.

[1] *J and CS*, II, 529.

It determines [*i.e.* ends] 9 March 1625, a licence to Perry and others in confirmation of a patent from the Revels for a year after date hereof: this 9th April 1624, £3.

He [Perry] hath given his bond for £6 more to be paid in six months in respect of the weakness of his commission for the Revels, their having a latter grant of more force; at the same time [blank] days liberty to act with his company in this town of London at the Curtain, 10s; of this hath been paid for the composition by Mrs Fleming this 17 April 1624, £2.

338 The Curtain ceases to be a playhouse but continues to house other entertainments and then people, 1625–1698

(a) Sir Henry Herbert, Office Book (now lost), reported by Malone in *Plays and Poems of William Shakespeare* (1821), III, 54 n. 2; (b) Garfield, *The Wandring Whore Continued* (1660), 13; (c) PRO, T54/16, p. 32. Transcribed in (c) *Calendar of Treasury Books*, XIII, 311

Nobody, it seems, mentioned plays at the Curtain after 1625, and Malone is supposed to have written the first item below with Herbert's Office Book before him. Although Malone often cited that book, however, he did not do so here.

(a) Fencers at the Curtain, 1625–ff.

[Malone wrote:] Soon after that period [the accession of King Charles on 27 March 1625], it [the Curtain] seems to have been used only by prize fighters [i.e. probably fencers].

(b) The Curtain is still standing, 1660

[One of a list of 'common whores, night-walkers, pickpockets, wanderers and shoplifters and whippers' in London in 1660 is:] Mrs Mails by the Curtain playhouse.

(c) The playhouse is a garden and houses, 1698

[In 1698, Samuel Newton bought the Crown's right to collect fee-farm rents on many properties, one of them described as:] Garden and houses called the Curtain playhouse in Holywell Lane in Shoreditch [on which the rent was 1s 7½d a year].

XXVI The Rose

The Rose was the first of the five public playhouses built on Bankside in Southwark, near the south bank of the Thames. It was on the east corner of Maiden Lane (now Park Street) and Rose Alley, S.E.1. Most of its foundations were unearthed in 1989, and more of them probably lie under a part of the site not yet excavated. Eventually, when some way has been found to preserve them, they will be on public display in a large hall comprising the ground floor and basement of an office building, Rose Court, now built over them. The name of the playhouse derives from the property on which it stood, which was called the Little Rose, perhaps because it had once been a rose garden.

The freehold of that property had belonged since 1552 to the parish of St Mildred Bread Street in the City of London. On 20 November 1574 the parish leased it to William Gryffyn, vintner, for thirty-one years. Gryffyn's successor, Robert Withens, vintner, assigned the lease to Philip Henslowe on 24 March 1585 and Henslowe had John Griggs, carpenter, build the playhouse in 1587, when eighteen years remained in the lease. The playhouse opened in the autumn of 1587.

Henslowe was ostensibly a dyer but actually a successful financier who invested in many things, including animal-baiting and companies of players. He eventually involved himself in three other playhouses, the first Fortune, Whitefriars, and Hope. From 19 February 1592 he kept a 'diary' in which he recorded not the social comings and goings that one might expect, but financial transactions having to do with the Rose and its players. On 22 October 1592 his step-daughter, Joan Woodward, married the most noted actor of the time, Edward Alleyn, who eventually became Henslowe's collaborator in financial ventures and heir. Alleyn was to found the College of God's Gift, now called Dulwich College, to which he left Henslowe's papers, including the diary, and they are still there.

When the erection of the Rose was about to begin, Henslowe made a curious agreement with John Cholmley, grocer. Cholmley evidently wanted to sell food and drink in a building on the south-west corner of the Rose property. Henslowe was willing. Cholmley would have a lease on the building for eight years and three months beginning on 10 January 1587 (the date of the agreement), during which Henslowe would not allow anybody else to sell food and drink at the Rose. But Henslowe, it seems, pressed on Cholmley something more.

Cholmley would pay the enormous rent of £25 10s a quarter for eight years, the first payment on 24 June 1587, or £816 during the term of the lease. Henslowe paid only £7 a year for the whole property.[1] In return, Cholmley would get not only his food and drink business, but a half-interest in the playhouse itself until 10 April 1595. Henslowe would continue to erect the playhouse at his own expense, and from 29 September 1587 when, presumably, it would be open, Cholmley would be Henslowe's partner in it, the two of them sharing both its profits and expenses equally. Both would be able to appoint gatherers and go to plays with friends *gratis*. Together they would appoint players to use the playhouse.

420   Playhouses, 1560–1660

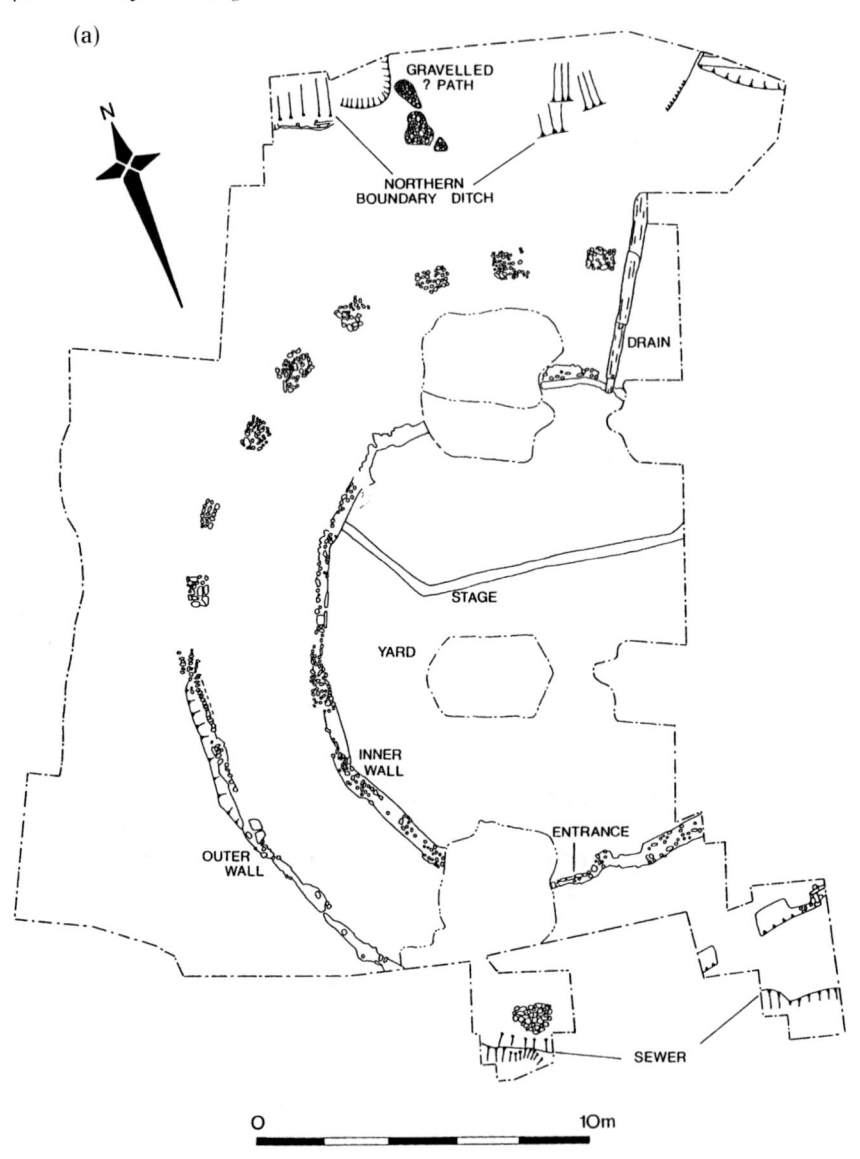

(a)

Fig. 2. The remains of the Rose playhouse, (a) as built in 1587, (b) as rebuilt in 1592, from the provisional plans of the excavation in 1989. The five large blank spaces, three down the middle and two on the right, have to do with a building erected on the site in the 1950s and since removed.

The Rose 421

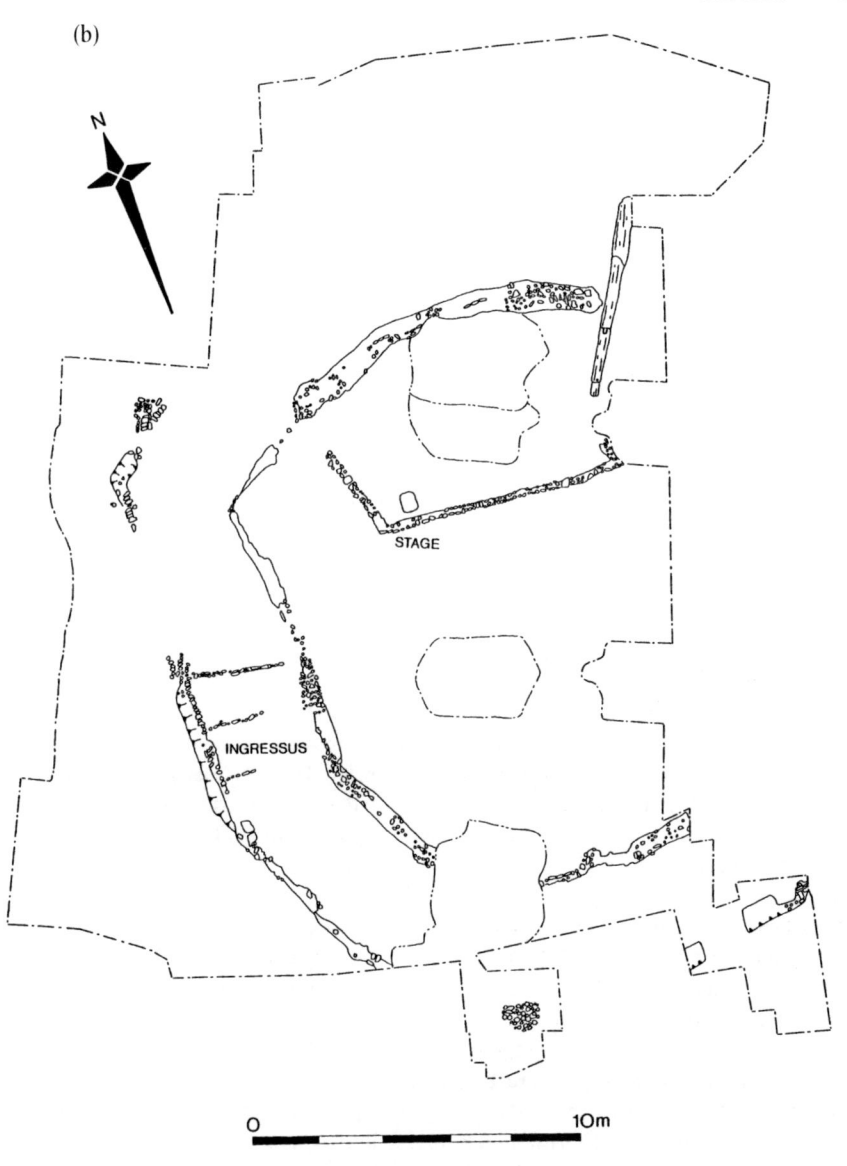

(b)

Cholmley, however, could get out of the agreement at any time by simply not paying the rent. Henslowe was committed to it as long as Cholmley liked. At first, the agreement would also end if either of them should die during the eight years and three months, but a later clause provides that either could leave his interest to a survivor.

The two men had 'great zeal and good will' towards one another and entered into the agreement 'better [to] increase their substance'. Cholmley, that is, expected the profits of his business and half the owner's profits to exceed £102 a year and half the expenses of a working playhouse; and if some disaster happened, he could withdraw. Henslowe must have seen the agreement as a way of protecting the money he was spending to erect the playhouse. If he could ordinarily expect, say, £20 a year for the food and drink business and costs of £50, he would have to make more than £214 in profits before he could do better without Cholmley than with him. Moreover, the greater the costs the greater the profits would have to be to render Cholmley a liability. The agreement, however, was probably not being observed from at least 1592 onwards, for Henslowe did not mention Cholmley in the diary, apart from scribbling his name on the front page.

The Rose was built on a piece of ground about 94 feet square. As the excavated parts of its foundations suggest, the Rose was a timber-frame building originally of thirteen or fourteen somewhat irregular sides and could be seen as round. It may have been some 73 feet across and so probably smaller than its competitors. It consisted of three tiers of galleries one above the other (as representations of the place in map views suggest), the lowest about 14 feet deep, around an open yard perhaps 45 feet across. The stage was on the northern side of the yard and was evidently unroofed.[2] It was nearly 37 feet wide at the widest, tapered to about 27 feet at the front, and extended about 16 feet 6 inches into the yard. The northern half of the yard sloped downward towards the stage, probably to give spectators at the back a better view and to drain water to a wooden drain that began under the stage and led away north towards a ditch. The building had a brick foundation, much of which under the outer wall sat on piles made of bricks and rubble sunk into the ground, and the rest of which sat on chalk and flint footings. The tiring-house was apparently in the lower gallery behind the stage.

From February to April 1592 Henslowe spent well over £100 enlarging the Rose so that it could hold many more people. He rebuilt the northern half of the galleries to extend the yard some 10 feet northward and some 10 feet on each side at the northern end. As a result, the playhouse and its yard became rather egg shaped, the widest part east and west no longer across the middle but beside the stage. He rebuilt the stage so that it was much the same size as before but more like a rectangle. In 1592 if not in 1587 the place was at least partly thatched (Henslowe's accounts in 1592 mention a thatcher but neither a tiler nor tiles). It had a 'room over the tiring-house' and a 'lord's room' for pretentious spectators, since both had been ceiled – the walls or ceilings or both covered, as the accounts suggest, with plaster. There was also a lean-to behind the tiring-house. If Henslowe did not provide a roof over the stage in 1592, he did in 1595, when he further improved his playhouse by installing in the roof a throne that could be lowered onto the stage. In 1596 there were in London 'four amphitheatres of obvious beauty', and 'The two more remarkable of these are situated to the south, on the far side of the Thames, named the Rose and Swan' (see 353).

It is not known what players used the Rose before Henslowe began his diary. The company there while he was paying for rebuilding it, and still there on 22 June 1592, when plague closed all the playhouses, was Lord Strange's men, a combination of two former companies whose leading figure was Alleyn. Except for several brief reopenings, plague kept the playhouses closed for two years. Lord Strange's were at the Rose for the first reopening, from 29 December 1592 to 1 February 1593, but by the next they and other London companies had dissolved. Temporary amalgamations of players used the Rose from 26 December 1593 to 6 February 1594 and for a week in April. Lord Strange's men then resolved themselves into their two constituent parts, one now called the Lord Admiral's men, led by Alleyn, and the other the Lord Chamberlain's men, led by the Burbages. The Admiral's men moved into the Rose in May 1594, but the playhouse soon closed again for a month. When it reopened, they returned, and they stayed there until 13 July 1600, after which they moved to Alleyn and Henslowe's new playhouse, the Fortune.

Henslowe mentioned two companies at the Rose after the Admiral's men, Pembroke's men briefly in October 1600, and Worcester's from August 1602 until 12 March 1603, when they went into the provinces presumably because of Lent, which had just begun. A few days later, the sickness and death of the Queen closed the playhouses, and the horrendous plague that soon followed kept them closed for over a year. When they reopened in 1604, the Rose was evidently finished as a playhouse. Henslowe seems not to have renewed his lease in 1605, and a successor may have pulled it down in 1606. If not, the successor or others used it until the 1620s for entertainments other than plays.

[1] In 1603, when Henslowe sought to renew his lease, the landlord proposed a new lease requiring Henslowe to pay £20 a year for the whole property with the playhouse on it, and spend £66 13s 4d on the place during the term of the lease. Henslowe thought such sums so outrageous that he said he would pull the Rose down rather than pay them, and in the end he did not renew the lease.
[2] See Wickham, '"Heavens", Machinery, and Pillars in Early Playhouses', 1–15.

339 Philip Henslowe acquires the lease on the property where he will build the Rose, 24 March 1585

Dulwich, Mun. 15. Transcribed in *Henslowe Papers*, ed. Greg, 1–2. In the assignment by which Henslowe acquired the lease, the property is described as follows ('her' refers to Thomasin Symonds, who gave the property to the parish of St Mildred Bread Street on 3 December 1552):

All that her messuage or tenement then called the little Rose with two gardens to the same adjoining . . . in the parish of St Saviour in Southwark . . . and all her houses, shops, cellars, solers, chambers, entries, gardens, ponds, easements, lands, soil and hereditaments whatsoever with their appurtenances in the parish of St Saviour in Southwark aforesaid to the messuage or tenement belonging or in any wise appertaining.[1]

[1] This description of the property was copied from that in the assignment by which Gryffyn had acquired the property in 1574 (Dulwich, Muniment 8).

340 Henslowe provides for food and drink at the Rose and takes a partner, 10 January 1587

Dulwich, Mun. 16. Transcribed in *Henslowe Papers*, ed. Greg, 2–4, and *Henslowe's Diary*, 304–6.

[A contract between Henslowe and John Cholmley, grocer, who:] for the great zeal and goodwill that is between them, and to the intent that they may the better increase their substance, are entered into partnership and are become co-partners together ... in the ... possessing ... of all that parcel of ground or garden plot containing in length and breadth square every way 94 feet of assize, little more or less, as also ... of all the benefit, sums of money, profit and advantage of a playhouse now in framing and shortly to be erected and set up upon the same ground or garden plot from the day of the date of these presents [10 January 1587] for ... and until the end and term of eight years and three months from thence next ensuing ... if the said parties do so long live.

Whereupon it is ... agreed between the said parties ... that it shall and may be lawful to and for the said John Cholmley ... to have ... the moiety or one half of all such ... sums of money, gains, profit and commodity which shall arise, grow, be collected, gathered or become due for the said parcel of ground and playhouse when and after it shall be erected and set up, by reason of any play or plays that shall be shown or played there or otherwise howsoever, and ... the said Philip Henslowe ... to have ... the other moiety ...

And further, the said Philip Henslowe ... doth ... grant that he, the said John Cholmley, ... shall ... possess and enjoy all that small tenement or dwelling house situate and standing at the south end or side of the said parcel of ground or garden plot to keep victualling in or to put to any other use or uses whatsoever, with the whole benefit ... which he ... shall or may receive or make ... by the same house near adjoining unto a lane there commonly called Maiden Lane, now in the tenure of the said John Cholmley or his assigns, with free ... passage ... as well in, by, and through the alley there called Rose Alley, leading from the river of Thames into the said parcel of ground, as also in, by, and through the way leading into the said Maiden Lane ...

And likewise that he, the said Philip, ... shall ... at his ... own proper cost and charges, with as much expedition as may be, erect, finish and set up, or cause to be erected, finished and set up by John Griggs, carpenter, his servants or assigns the said playhouse, with all furniture thereunto belonging ... all which premises ... are situate ... on the Bankside in the parish of St Saviour's in Southwark in the county of Surrey.

In consideration whereof the said John Cholmley ... doth covenant ... with the said Philip Henslowe ... to pay or cause to be paid unto the said Philip Henslowe ... for a yearly annuity the sum of £816 ... in manner and form following: that is to say, on the feast day of the nativity of St John Baptist [24 June] next coming ... £25 10s ... and so further after that from feast day to feast day, quarter to quarter, and year unto year, ... until all the said sum of £816 be ... truly contented and paid ...

And if it shall happen the said ... quarterly payments ... to be behind and unpaid in part or in all by the space of twenty and one days ... after any feast day, ... being lawfully demanded at the said playhouse after the same shall be erected, ... that then and from thenceforth the said co-partnership ... shall be void, ... and

... it shall and may be lawful to and for the said Philip Henslowe ... to re-enter and the said John Cholmley ... utterly to expel ...

And further, ... if it happen either of the said parties ... die ... before the end of the said term, ... it shall ... be lawful ... for the executors or administrators of the party so deceasing to have ... the part ... of him so deceasing as co-partner with the survivor ...

And further, the said parties ... do ... grant either with other by these presents that it shall and may be lawful to and for the said Philip Henslowe and John Cholmley ... jointly to appoint and permit ... players to use, exercise and play in the said playhouse ... at their wills and pleasures, being for the profit and commodity of them both.

And likeway, that the said Philip Henslowe and John Cholmley, when any play or plays shall be played or shown in the said playhouse, ... shall and will be there present themselves, or appoint their sufficient deputies or assigns, with themselves or otherwise at their choice to collect, gather and receive all such ... sums of money of every person ... resorting and coming to the said playhouse to view, see and hear any play or interlude at any time or times to be showed and played during the said term of eight years and three months, except it please any of the said parties to suffer their friends to go in for nothing.

And that all such ... sums ... so collected ... shall immediately that night, after account made by themselves, their deputies or assigns, be equally divided, ... whereof the said Philip Henslowe ... to have the one-half ... and ... John Cholmley ... to have the other ...

And further, the said Philip Henslowe ... shall ... pay or cause to be paid ... all manner of quit rents and other rent charges due and payable to the lord or lords of the premises, ... and likeways [he] shall ... repair and amend all the bridges and wharfs belonging to the said parcel of ground ... at or before the 29th day of September next coming [1587] ...

And likeways, the said John Cholmley and Philip Henslowe ... do ... grant either with other ... that they ... shall ... after the said 29th day of September next coming at their equal costs ... repair, amend, sustain, maintain and uphold the said playhouse, bridges, wharfs and all other the ways and bridges now leading ... into, out and from the said parcel of ground ... when and as often as need shall require ...

And further, the said Philip Henslowe ... doth ... grant to and with the said John Cholmley ... that he ... will not permit or suffer any person or persons other than the said John Cholmley ... to utter, sell or put to sale in or about the said parcel of ground, playhouse or garden plot ... any bread or drink other than such as shall be sold to and for the use and behoof of the said John Cholmley.

341 The Rose is open, and the government takes an interest, 29 October 1587 and 12 April 1588

(a) PRO, PC2/14, p. 477; (b) LMA, SKCS18/fo. 148v. Transcribed in (a) *APC, 1587–8*, 271–2; (b) Gomme, 'Story of London Maps', 628

In (a) below, the privy council's allusion to a letter it had written about playing on Sundays is puzzling. The only recent letter about playing mentioned in the records of the council went to the Surrey justices, the Lord Mayor and the Master of the Rolls on 7 May 1587, but it restrained all playing because of disorders and infection and said nothing of playing on Sundays (PRO, PC2/14, p. 339, transcribed in *APC, 1587–8*, 70). In (b) below, the sewer commission for Surrey and Kent was interested in the Rose because drainage ditches ran by the playhouse along Maiden Lane and Rose Alley (hence the bridges mentioned in the Henslowe–Cholmley contract [340]).

(a) The privy council writes to the Surrey justices, 29 October 1587

[The plays performed, as the council says, in Southwark must have been performed at the Rose because it was the only playhouse there at the time.] Whereas the inhabitants of Southwark had complained to their lordships declaring that the order by their lordships set down for the restraining of plays and interludes within that county on the Sabbath days is not observed, and especially within the liberty of the Clink and in the parish of St Saviour's in Southwark, which disorder is to be ascribed to the negligence of some of the justices of peace in that county:

They are required to take such strict order for the staying of said disorder as is already taken by the Lord Mayor within the liberties of the City, so as the same be not hereafter suffered at the times forbidden in any place of that county.

(b) The sewer commission alludes to the Rose, 12 April 1588

Philip Henslowe, Morgan Pope, and John Napton[1] . . . [are] to cleanse and scour, and to lop the willows that hang over, the common sewer . . . ten pole[s], more or less [*i.e.* 165 feet], lying against their ground at the new playhouse, to be done by the last day of July next coming upon pain of [paying] 20s for every pole then undone. [In the margin:] not done.

[1] Pope and Napton had to do with the Beargarden nearby.

342 Henslowe rebuilds the Rose, February – April 1592 and Lent 1595

Dulwich, MS VII, fos. (a) 4–5v. (b) 2v. Transcribed in *Henslowe's Diary*, (a) 9–13, (b) 6–7

Henslowe's accounting of the money he spent to rebuild the Rose is incomplete because the cost of many items is blank, a few sums are illegible and part of a leaf is torn away. Omitted below is the word 'Item', with which each entry begins. Sums in square brackets are an attempt to fill in some of Henslowe's blanks: where, for example, he bought 400 threepenny nails (by definition, 3d a hundred) and left the amount blank, one may write 1s, though he sometimes paid less than the notional amount, as 4s 6d for 1,000 sixpenny nails instead of 5s.

(a) 1592

A note of such charges as I have laid out about my playhouse in the year of our Lord 1592 as followeth:

Paid for a barge	£3	10s	
Paid for breaking up and paling	£1		
Paid for wharfing		8s	
Paid for timber and bringing by water	£7	9s	
Paid for lime		9s	2d
Paid for wages		19s	
Paid for bringing of deal boards		2s	6d
Paid for 200 [weight] of lime		11s	
Paid for 75 of deal boards	£3		
Paid for a mast		12s	
Paid for a sum [i.e. a horse-load] of lath nails and half	[blank]		
Paid for wages	£4	10s	
Paid for 400 of threepenny nails		1s	
Paid for 1 load of rafters	[blank]		
Paid for 1 load of quarters[1]	[blank]		
Paid for 1,000 of lath nails	[blank]		
Paid unto the thatcher		7s	
Paid for bringing stuff			6d
Paid for 100 [weight] of lime		5s	6d
Paid for 3 days for a workman		3s	6d
Paid for a nailer [i.e. maker of nails] for four days		3s	4d
Paid unto the thatcher	£1		
Paid for sand		4s	6d
Paid for 1,000 of lath nails	[blank]		
Paid for 26 fir poles [scaffolding?]		10s	6d
Paid unto my workmen for a week's wages	£6		
Paid for a hundred of single tens [i.e. tenpenny nails]		10d	
Paid for 4 load[s] of sand		4s	
Paid unto the thatcher's man		3s	
Paid for 200 of sixpenny nails		1s	
Paid for half a load of laths	[blank]		
Paid for half a sum [i.e. a load] of lath nails	[blank]		
Paid for 250 of double tens [i.e. twenty-penny nails]		[4s	2d]

Paid for 500 of sixpenny nails	[2s	6d]
Bought half a load of laths of J. Griggs[2]	[blank]	
Paid for 300 of sixpenny nails to Brader	18s	
Paid for chalk[3] and bricks	3s	4d
Paid for 100 of double tens [nails]		10d
Paid for 200 [weight] of lime	11s	
Paid unto the thatcher	[illegible]	
Paid for sand	1s	
Paid for wages	6s	1d
Paid for turned ballusters 2d apiece, 2 dozen [*i.e.* 26?]	4s	6d
Paid for wages	3s	4d
Bought 20 fir poles [scaffolding?] at 6d apiece	10s	
Paid unto the thatcher	10s	
Paid for nails to Brader	2s	4d
Paid the 6th of February for wages £4	3s	4d
Paid for 500 of sixpenny nails	[2s	6d]
Paid Stephen Coke 3s for his man's wages	[3s]	
Bought of J. Griggs 285 foot boards [*i.e.* 1 foot wide]	19s	
Bought of J. Griggs 2 bundle[s] of laths	2s	
Paid the thatcher	5s	
Bought of the ironmonger in Southwark one half [illegible: a sum (load)?] of lath nails	[blank]	
Bought at the Frying Pan 500 of tens [nails]	2s	6d
Bought at the Frying Pan 200 double tens [nails]	3s	4d
Bought at the Frying Pan 1,000 of sixpenny nails	4s	6d
Paid for 1,000 of sixpenny nails	[5s]	
Paid for one-half sum of twopenny nails	[blank]	
Bought 1 load of rafters and 1 load of quarters	[blank]	
Paid for 2 load[s] of lime and 1 load of sand	3s	
Paid for bricklaying	2s	2d
Bought at the Frying Pan one-half sum of twopenny nails	[blank]	
Paid the labourers' wages	8s	9d
Bought at the Frying Pan 500 sixpenny nails	[2s	6d]
Bought at the Frying Pan 250 single tens [nails]	[2s	1d]
Paid for 100 [weight] of lime	5s	6d
Bought 400 of quarter boards [*i.e.* 9 inches – a quarter of a yard – wide]	£1	
Bought 500 of inch boards [*i.e.* an inch thick]	£1 5s	
Bought half a load of rafters	[blank]	
Paid the thatcher	10s	
Paid for nails		8d
Bought of J. Griggs half a load of laths	15s	

Bought at the Frying Pan 250 double tens [nails]	[4s	2d]
Paid unto the carpenters for wages	£4 5s	
Paid for the carriage of timber		7d
Paid for 3 fir bords sawed	4s	6d
Paid for painting my stage	11s	
Paid for 500 of sixpenny nails at [the] Frying Pan	[2s	6d]
Paid for 250 of double tens at [the] Frying Pan [nails]	[4s	2d]
Paid for 250 of single tens [at the] Frying Pan [nails]	[2s	1d]
Bought of Brader 200 of fourpenny nails		8d
Paid for two dozen of turned ballusters	4s	
Bought at Brader's 350 fourpenny nails	[1s	2d]
Bought at the Frying Pan 500 sixpenny nails	[2s	6d]
Bought at the Frying Pan 250 double tens [nails]	[4s	2d]
Bought at the Frying Pan 250 single tens [nails]	[2s	6d]
Bought at the Frying Pan 250 single tens [nails]	[2s	6d]
Bought at the Frying Pan a 1,000 of sixpenny nails	[5s]	
Bought at the Frying Pan a quarter of [a] sum of lath nails	[blank]	
Bought 1 load of single quarters	[blank]	
Paid for bringing stuff by water	[blank]	
Bought of Brader 500 of fourpenny nails	[1s	8d]
Bought 69 coarse deal [boards] at 3½d	20s	
Paid for bringing them by water		8d
Paid the thatcher	5s	
Bought at the Frying Pan 125 of single tens [nails]	[1s	½d]
Bought at the Frying Pan 125 double tens [nails]	[2s	1d]
Bought at the Frying Pan 250 sixpenny nails	[2s	3d]
Bought at the Frying Pan 50 of single tens [nails]	[5d]	
Bought at the Frying Pan 250 single tens [nails]	1s	5d
Bought of Brader 200 of fourpenny nails	[8d]	
Bought of J. Griggs 300 of quarter boards [9 inches wide]	16s	
Bought at the Frying Pan 250 single tens [nails]	1s	5½d
Bought at the Frying Pan 250 double tens [nails]	[4s	6d]
Bought at the Frying Pan 250 sixpenny nails	[1s	3d]
Bought of Brader 200 fourpenny nails	[8d]	
Bought at the Frying Pan 250 single tens [nails]	1s	5d
Bought at the Frying Pan 250 sixpenny nails	[1s	3d]
Paid unto the thatcher [for] a bundle of laths	1s	
Of Brader 50 of sixpenny nails	[3d]	
[Illegible] Locks [here the bottom third of the leaf is torn away]		
...		
Paid in full payment the 7 of March 1592, unto the ironmonger in Southwark at the Frying Pan	£3	12s

430   Playhouses, 1560–1660

Paid in full payment the 28 of March 1592 unto Mr Lee, timberman, for rafters and quarters and laths and boards	£5	14s
...		
Paid unto the painters the 28 of March 1592	£1	6s
...		
Paid for ceiling[4] the room over the tire-house		10s
Paid for wages to the plasterer		4s
Paid for ceilings [of] my lord's room		14s

Paid for making the penthouse shed at the tiring-house door as followeth:

Paid for old timber	10s	
Paid for boards and quarters	18s	6d
Paid for boards	13s	6d
Paid for nails and hinges and bolts	19s	
Paid the carpenters' wages	9s	

[1] Quarters were pieces of timber either 2 × 4 inches (single quarters) or 4 × 4 inches (double quarters).
[2] John Griggs was the carpenter who built the Rose in 1587.
[3] Chalk and bricks were used in the foundations.
[4] i.e. covering or lining the walls or roof or both.

(b) 1595

A note [of] what I have laid out about my playhouse for painting and doing it about with elm boards and other reparations as followeth, 1595 in Lent:

Bought 325 of elm boards	£1	4s	
Paid the carpenters their wages		8s	
Given the painter in earnest	£1		
Given the painter more		10s	
Given more unto the painter	£1		
Paid unto the painter		10s	
Paid the carpenters their wages		16s	
Paid for 3 hinges		2s	
Paid for a board		2s	2d
Paid for 5 lb[s] of spikes		1s	3d
Paid the carpenters		5s	4d
Paid the painter		5s	
Paid for 2 bundle[s] of laths		2s	2d
Paid for 1 load of sand		1s	2d
Paid for half a thousand of lath nails			8d
Paid the painter		6s	
Paid the painter		4s	

Paid for 1 load of lime	1s	2d
Paid for wages	4s	6d
Paid the painter	5s	
Paid the painter in full	16s	
Paid for nails	2s	4d
Paid the smith for nails in full	12s	3d
...		
Paid for carpenters' work & making the throne in the heavens the 4 of June 1595	£7	2s

343 Henslowe takes Lord Strange's men into the Rose and begins his 'Diary', 19 February 1592

Dulwich, MS VII, fo. 7. Transcribed in *Henslowe's Diary*, 16

This accounting of plays is the earliest in the diary. It shows day by day for a week how much money Henslowe received for performances of plays by Lord Strange's men at the Rose.

In the name of God, amen, 1592, beginning the 19 of February, my Lord Strange's men, a[s] followeth, 1592:

Received at *Friar Bacon* the 19 of February, Saturday	17	3d
Received at *Muly Mollocco* the 20 of February	£1	9s
Received at *Orlando* [*Furioso*] the 21 of February	16s	6d
Received at *Spanish Comedy Don Horatio* the 23 of February	13s	6d
Received at *Sir John Mandeville* the 24 of February	12s	6d
Received at *Harry of Cornwall* the 25 February 1592	£1	12s
Received at *The Jew of Malta* the 26 of February 1592	£2	10s

This listing continues until 22 June 1592, when a riot and then the plague caused the privy council to restrain playing for six months. It resumes from 29 December 1592, when the plague abated, until 1 February 1593, when the plague increased.

344 After the plague of 1592–1594, Henslowe takes the Lord Admiral's men into the Rose, 14 May, 15 June 1594

Dulwich, MS VII, fo. 9. Transcribed in *Henslowe's Diary*, 21–2

The Admiral's men first appeared at the Rose on 14 May 1594, but after three performances the playhouse closed for an unknown reason until 15 June, when the Admiral's men returned and stayed there until 1600. While the playhouse was closed, Henslowe sponsored ten performances at Newington Butts by, more or less, resurrecting Lord Strange's men – a combination of the Admiral's and Chamberlain's men (see **248**). Below is Henslowe's accounting of the Admiral's brief stay at the Rose and of the first week of their long one.

In the name of God, amen, beginning the 14 of May 1594, by my Lord Admiral's men:

Received at the *Jew of Malta* 14 of May 1594	£2	8s
Received at *The Ranger's Comedy* the 15 of May 1594	£1	13s
Received at *Cutlack* the 16 of May 1594	£2	2s
...		
15 of June 1594, received at *Bellendon*	£3	4s
17 of June 1594, received at *Cutlack*	£1	15s
18 of June 1594, received at *The Ranger's Comedy*	£1	2s
19 of June 1594, received at *The Guise* [i.e. *Massacre at Paris*]	£2	14s
20 of June 1594, received at *Bellendon*	£1	10s
22 of June 1594, received at *The Ranger's Comedy*	£2	18

[And so on to 13 July 1600.]

345 The parish tries, and apparently fails, to raise money from its playhouses, 1 May, 19 July 1598

LMA, P92/SAV/450/pp. 323, 324, 325. Transcribed by (1 May) Rendle, 'The Bankside, Southwark, and the Globe Playhouse', vi; (19 July) Malone in *Plays and Poems of William Shakespeare*, ed. Boswell (1821), III, 452

The vestry of St Saviour's resolved:

(a) On 20 April 1598, and again on 1 May

that . . . the churchwardens . . . shall speak to Mr Langley and Mr Henslowe and Jacob Meade[1] for money for the poor in regard of their plays.

[1] Francis Langley owned the Swan. Henslowe not only owned the Rose, but with Meade had to do with the Beargarden, near the Rose.

(b) On 19 July 1598

that a petition shall be made to the body of the [privy] council concerning the playhouses in this parish [i.e. the Rose and Swan], wherein the enormities shall be showed that come thereby to the parish, and that in respect thereof they may be dismissed and put down from playing, and that four or two of the [four current] churchwardens [and four or two named other vestrymen and two or one named others] . . shall prosecute the cause . . .

The parish raised the matter again on 28 March 1600, by which time the Globe was also in the parish: LMA, P92/SAV/450, p. 339, transcribed by Malone in *Plays and Poems of William Shakespeare*, ed. Boswell (1821), III, 452.

346 The Rose is busy, August – September 1598

Guilpin, *Skialetheia* (1598), SR, 15 September 1598, sigs. D4v–5

Skialetheia is a collection of epigrams and satires. When it was licensed, the Lord Chamberlain's men were playing at the Curtain and would soon be the Rose's neighbours at the Globe.

> If my dispose
> Persuade me to a play, I'll to the Rose,
> Or Curtain ...

347 The first Globe is built across the street from the Rose, May 1599, and Henslowe's receipts diminish

Dulwich, MS VII, fos. 48v, 62v. Transcribed in *Henslowe's Diary*, 95, 120

See 395c. Henslowe's receipts in March and April 1599, before the Globe opened, averaged £7 19s 4d a week (and for January and February, £9 4s 6d). His receipts for 20 October to 25 November 1599, when the Globe was fully open, averaged £5 10s 6d a week.

Received the 26 of March 1599	£3	18s
Received the 1 of April 1599	£2	2s
Received the 8 of April 1599	£3	8s
Received the 15 of April 1599	£13	7s
Received the 22 of April 1599	£13	16s
Received the 29 of April 1599	£11	5s
...		
Received the 20 of October 1599	£4	3s
Received the 27 of October 1599	£3	14s
Received the 3 of November 1599	£8	16s
Received the 10 of November 1599	£6	9s
Received the 18 of November 1599	£2	17s
Received the 25 of November 1599	£7	4s

348 Henslowe builds the Fortune, moves the Admiral's men into it, and finds new players for the Rose, 1600–1603

Dulwich, MS VII, fos. (a) 82, (b) 115, 113v, 114. Transcribed in *Henslowe's Diary*, (a) 164, (b) 212–13

See 419, 383. Henslowe recorded his last receipts from the Admiral's men at the Rose on 13 July 1600 (*Henslowe's Diary*, 121), and mentioned two companies of players who succeeded them there.

(a) 28–29 October 1600

My Lord's of Pembroke's men began to play at the Rose the 28 of October 1600 as followeth:

October 28, received at *The* ['*Devil*' crossed out] *Like unto Like* [*i.e. The Devil's Dam?*]	11s 6d
October 29, received at *Roderick*	5s

(b) August 1602 to 12 March 1603

[Henslowe did not note his receipts from performances of the next company he mentioned at the Rose, which was the last, but he did note money he lent them, the list beginning:]

Lent unto my Lord of Worcester's players as followeth, beginning the 17 day of August 1602

Lent unto the company the 17 of August 1602 to pay unto Thomas Dekker for new additions in *Oldcastle*, the sum of	£2

[on 12 March 1603 he noted three similar loans, one of which reads:]

Lent unto Richard Perkins the 12 of March 1603 when he rode with the company to play in the country, in ready money the sum of	10s

349 Henslowe inquires about renewing his lease of the property where the Rose stood, 25 June 1603

Dulwich, MS VII, fo. 114v. Transcribed in *Henslowe's Diary*, 213. The landlord was the parish of St Mildred Bread Street in London, and Henslowe's lease was to run out in 1605.

[Henslowe noted:] Memorandum: that the 25 of June 1603 I talked with Mr Pope at the scrivener's shop where he lies concerning the taking of the lease anew of the Little Rose, and he showed me a writing betwixt the parish and himself which was to pay £20 a year rent and to bestow 100 marks [£66 13s 4d] upon building, which I said I would rather pull down the playhouse than I would do so, and he bade me do and said he gave me leave and would bear me out, for it was in him to do it.

350 Henslowe does not renew his lease, and the Rose comes to an end, 1604–1622

(a) LMA, SKCS18/fos. 388, 426v, 436, 441; (b) Malone in *Plays and Poems of William Shakespeare*, ed. Boswell (1821), XIII, 56n.; (c) Dulwich, MS IX, fo. 59v. Transcribed in (c) Young, *History of Dulwich College*, II, 241. For (a) see Wallace, 'Shakespeare and the Globe', 9–10

No players seem to have used the Rose after the departure of Worcester's men, who, when the great plague of 1603–4 ended, went to the old Curtain rather then back to the Rose (see

333). The most reliable documents about the end of the Rose are those of the sewer commissioners in (a) below. The context of their allusion to 'the late playhouse' in 1606 suggests that the place still stood but was no longer used as a playhouse, rather than that it had been pulled down.

(a) 25 January 1604 – 25 April 1606

[The commissioners for sewers in Surrey and Kent decided:]

[On 25 January 1604 that] Francis Henslowe, gentleman [Philip's nephew], before the 20th day of March next shall board up two poles [*i.e.* 33 feet], more or less, of his wharf lying against the playhouse in Maiden Lane upon pain to forfeit for either pole then undone: [in the margin] 6s 8d, not done [and a note that the fine had been pursued].

[On 4 October 1605, that] Philip Henslowe shall before St Andrew's Day next [30 November] [1] well and sufficiently pile and board three poles [*i.e.* 49 feet 6 inches], more or less, of the bank against his playhouse in Maiden Lane upon pain to forfeit for every pole then undone: [in the margin] 40s, not done, out of his hands; [2] pull up and take clean away his two posts which stand in the sewer under his bridge against his said playhouse upon pain to forfeit: [in the margin] £4, not done, out of his hands. [The commissioners had made the same demands the previous 20 August, the work to be done by Michaelmas and the penalties 20s and 40s. They had noted that Henslowe had not done the work but not that he no longer owned the playhouse (fo. 442v).]

[On 30 January 1606 that Edward] Box[1] of Bread Street in London shall before the 20th day of April next pile, board and fill up five poles, more or less [*i.e.* 82 feet 6 inches], of the bank against the sewer by the playhouse in Maiden Lane called the Rose, upon pain to forfeit for every pole then undone: [in the margin] 5s, not done, a court decree on 17 October 1606.

[On 25 April 1606 that] Edward Box of Bread Street in London shall before the first day of June next pile, board, and fill up five poles, more or less, of the bank against the sewer by the late playhouse in Maiden Lane called the Rose upon pain to forfeit for every pole then undone: [in the margin] 15s, not done, [and the decree] at court increased on 27 October 1606.

[1] Presumably someone to whom the parish had recently leased the property, which the parish continued to own well into the 1850s (GL, MS 11,011A).

(b) After 1620

[Edmond Malone noted that:] The Swan and the Rose are mentioned by [John] Taylor, the water poet, but in 1613[/4] they were shut up[1] ... After the year 1620, as appears from Sir Henry Herbert's office book, they were used occasionally for the exhibition of prize-fighters.

Herbert was Master of the Revels and would have noted in his office book that he had granted permission for the use of the Rose. Malone had the office book before him, but it is now lost.

[1] Malone is alluding to Taylor's *The True Cause of the Watermen's Suit concerning the Players* (1614), reprinted in *All the Workes of John Taylor* (1630), sigs. Pp4–6v, in which Taylor complains about the lack of work for watermen now that plays take place on the south bank only at the Globe.

(c) June 1622

[Edward Alleyn, Henslowe's heir, noted in his diary that he paid:]
The tithe due for the Rose　　　　　　　　　　　　　　　　　　　1s

The diary does not suggest why Alleyn should pay anything for the Rose seventeen years after Henslowe's lease had run out. Perhaps the parish of St Saviour demanded money that Henslowe had not paid when he held the lease.

XXVII The Swan

The Swan was the second of the five public playhouses built on Bankside – in Southwark, that is, near the south bank of the Thames. The Rose was already there, and the two Globes and Hope would be. But these other places were all relatively near the southern end of London Bridge; the Swan was more than 500 yards west of them, hence that much farther from the City proper on the north bank and the large number of people who lived and did business near the southern end of the bridge. The Swan was in the manor of Paris Garden, some 120 yards directly south of a landing place on the Thames called Paris Garden stairs. It was evidently built over a ruined chapel, and its site may be under the present Hopton Street, opposite the northern half of Sampson House, S.E.1.[1]

Fig. 3. The interior of the Swan playhouse, from Arend van Buchell's copy in the Library of the University of Utrecht of a lost letter of Johannes de Witt, c. 1596.

Its builder was Francis Langley, a nephew of a lord mayor, who spent his adult life as a money broker and speculator in dubious ventures, two of which had to do with other playhouses, the Boar's Head and the Theatre.[2] Officially, he was a draper, but like others of his kind he was often called a goldsmith. Having bought Paris Garden in November 1589 for £850, he probably began building the Swan towards the end of 1594 and finished it in 1595.[3]

On 26 June 1596 a German tourist implied that the Swan was one of the four public playhouses then doing business in London, and at perhaps much the same time a Dutch tourist found it 'the largest and most distinguished' of the London playhouses. The Dutchman, Johannes de Witt, described it as a large timber-frame building whose interstices were filled not with the usual wattle and daub but with flints and cement. He said that it held 3,000 spectators and that its posts were skilfully painted to look like marble.

He also drew a picture of it from the inside, the famous surviving copy of which shows the familiar scheme of public playhouses at the time, and is one of the chief pieces of evidence for that scheme. In the picture the Swan is round[4] and consists mainly of three tiers of galleries, one over the other, surrounding an open yard. Interrupting the galleries and rising above them is a tiring-house, 'mimorum ædes' – house of the players. A rectangular stage extends from the tiring-house perhaps half way across the yard, so that spectators could stand on three sides of it. The tiring-house probably consists of three storeys, one at stage level with two doors leading onto the stage, another just above with a window right across at which sit, it seems, spectators, and the third at the top with two windows facing the yard and a door on the right side out of which steps a man probably blowing a trumpet. A flag flies on top with a swan on it. The galleries, tiring-house and part of the stage all have thatched roofs, and that over the stage is held up by two pillars on the stage. The lowest gallery is labelled 'orchestra' – a place for dignitaries – the middle gallery 'sedilia' – benches – and the top one 'porticus' – gallery. All the galleries seem to have benches in the drawing, though in 1598 players described the galleries as 'the several standings'.[5]

The players also said that they had half the takings in the galleries and Langley the other half, the usual arrangement at the time, according to which the players also had all the takings in the yard. A famous non-event at the Swan in 1602 suggests that the place was capable of staging a fight of twelve gentlemen at barriers, an ascent 'up into heaven', a descent of 'a throne of blessed souls', 'strange fireworks', and the rising from beneath the stage of 'divers black and damned souls . . . in their several torments'.

Players were evidently using the Swan in 1595 and 1596, but which players does not appear. Some writers argue that the Lord Chamberlain's men, Shakespeare's company, used it for a time in 1596.

Pembroke's men then agreed to use the playhouse for a year beginning on 20 February 1597, and five of them said that it was 'lately afore used to have plays in it'. Langley agreed to put the place in order and provide apparel 'fit and necessary for their playing', for which they would reimburse him out of their takings in the galleries. (He said he spent £300 doing these things; they said he 'was at no cost at all' in getting the place ready and defalked £100 from their takings for apparel.) Evidently, Langely had had trouble keeping players in the Swan, for he required at least eight of these players to sign bonds of £100 apiece guaranteeing that each would play nowhere else within five miles of London without supplying a 'sufficient' substitute of whom Langley or his assigns approved.

This arrangement foundered on 28 July, when the privy council issued a drastic order against playhouses in and around London. Their owners had not only to close them but to destroy them so 'as they may not be employed again' for plays. The council offered one reason, 'very great disorders committed in the . . . playhouses', and defined 'disorders' as 'lewd matters' played there and the 'confluence' there of 'bad people'. By 10 August Philip Henslowe thought that the real reason was a play, now lost, *The Isle of Dogs*, written by Thomas Nashe, Ben Jonson and others and performed by Pembroke's men at the Swan. Nashe came to think so (he fled the City), as, by 15 August, did the privy council itself, which had Jonson and two players at the Swan arrested. No playhouse was pulled down, however, and by 11 October the Rose was back in business. So, by 1 November, was the Swan.[6] Although the council may well not have had the play or the Swan in mind on 28 July, the affair had serious consequences at the Swan.

For some reason, Langley cancelled the bonds of three of Pembroke's men, who soon joined Henslowe's enterprise at the Rose. Then five more also joined Henslowe, arguing that Langley had given them permission and that they 'durst not' play at the Swan because its licence had not been renewed. Langley set about suing these five on their bonds early in November, and they promptly countersued. Licence or no licence, the remaining Pembroke's men resumed at the Swan, with, no doubt, some additions, though not under a name that survives. They or equally unnamed successors were still there in the summer of 1598, and by September Henslowe was helping his new players buy off Langley's claims against them.

After the summer of 1598, it seems, regular playing ceased at the Swan for twelve years, but why it ceased is not known. Playing went on again there from 1610 to 1614, and from 1620 to 1621, when it ended altogether. The Swan had been a regular playhouse for only nine years, and except for Pembroke's men, who were there for five months, one must guess at who its players were. It was farther from the centres of population than other playhouses of its time, and in order to get to it, its spectators who went by road had to pass the offerings of the strong company at the Rose and eventually of the stronger one at the Globe.

Langley died a bankrupt and was buried on 9 July 1602. In January he had sold the manor of Paris Garden, including the Swan, for £2,500 to Hugh Browker (pronounced 'Brooker'), a prothonotary in the Court of Common Pleas.[7] Browker and his heirs continued to own much of Paris Garden until 1655. By 1606 or so, however, he had disposed of the Swan, the manor-house and some other things, for they were then in the hands of Alexander Walshe, fruiterer. The Swan is last heard of in use in 1634, when officials from the Court of Requests examined witnesses there for a lawsuit about the second Globe (475, 477, 479), and it was still standing in 1637.[8]

Writers sometimes say that the Swan was also called the Prince's Arms,[9] but no contemporary said so, at least unequivocally. The idea rests on some facts and some presumptions. The facts are: (1) two licences of 1623 allowed performances 'at the Prince's Arms or the Swan', one 'a prize' (presumably a display of fencing), the other 'Italian motions' (presumably a puppet show); (2) an entry in SR, 4 July 1620, says that a masque was performed 'At the Prince's Arms by the Prince His Highness's servants'; and (3) the masque, according to its address to the reader, was 'born on the Bankside of Helicon'. The presumptions are: (1) the licences mean that the performances could take place at the Swan *alias* the Prince's Arms, not at either the Swan or the Prince's Arms; (2) the Prince's men would have performed the masque at a playhouse rather than some other kind of house. The masque was Middleton and William Rowley's *The World Tossed at Tennis* (1620). They had written it for the Prince's men to perform at a royal occasion in Denmark House, but the occasion did not take place and they then rewrote it for public performance.

440 Playhouses, 1560–1660

[1] Cf. a map of Paris Garden, 1627 (noting its scale bar) and: Morgan, *London &c, Actually Survey'd* (1682); Rocque, *A Plan of the Cities of London and Westminster, and the Borough of Southwark* (1746); Greenwood, *Map of London* (1827); and modern maps. The map of 1627 has been reproduced several times, first by Rendle in 1878 and more accurately, it seems, by Norman, 'The Accounts of the Overseers of the Poor of Paris Garden', facing 55, and others.
[2] Berry, *Shakespeare's Playhouses*, 30–1, 32–3.
[3] Ingram, *A London Life in the Brazen Age*, 66–72, 106–11.
[4] On the map of Paris Garden of 1627 the Swan consists of a circular outer band divided into nine unequal sections and an inner band and centre, both blank. It has a small rectangular attachment on the north-east – an entrance and stairway, perhaps. The playhouse is also round on views of London. But like other public playhouses it is usually thought of as sufficiently multi-sided to seem round.
[5] Because the Hope was modelled on the Swan, the contract for building the Hope (**459**) can yield suggestions about the Swan, except that the stage was to be removable at the Hope but not the Swan.
[6] See Ingram's persuasive study of the affair, *A London Life in the Brazen Age*, 167–91, 205–10.
[7] Browker died early in 1608. See *ibid.*, 280, 251–63, 267, 287.
[8] Among Inigo Jones' designs for Davenant's *Britannia Triumphans* (performed 7 January 1638) are two views of London both of which seem to show the Swan. The designs are at Chatsworth and are reproduced in Shapiro, 'The Bankside Theatres: Early Engravings', plate XIV A and B. Plate IX B reproduces part of the map of Paris Garden of 1627.
[9] Greg, *A Bibliography of the English Printed Drama to the Restoration*, II, 365; *J and CS*, IV, 907–11.

351 The playhouse is being built, and the City objects, 3 November 1594

CLRO, Remembrancia, II, 73; Transcribed in MSC, I. 74. The Lord Mayor took an interest in Southwark because it had been part of the City since 1556, though still outside his jurisdiction for some things.

[The Lord Mayor wrote to the Lord Treasurer, Lord Burghley, who was a leading member of the privy council:] I understand that one Francis Langley . . . intendeth to erect a new stage or theatre (as they call it) for the exercising of plays upon the Bankside. And, forasmuch as we find by daily experience the great inconvenience that groweth to this city and the government thereof by the said plays, I have emboldened myself to be an humble suiter to your good l[ordship] to be a means for us rather to suppress all such places built for that kind of exercise than to erect any more of the same sort . . . I thought it my duty, being now called to this public place, to inform your good l[ordship] . . . humbly beseeching you to vouchsafe me your help for the stay and suppressing, not only of this which is now intended, by directing your letters to the justices of peace of Middlesex and Surrey, but of all other places, if possibly it may be, where the said plays are showed and frequented.

352 A German prince includes the Swan among the active playhouses in London, 26 June 1596

Becmann, *Accessiones Historiae Anhaltinae* (1716), 172

Prince Ludwig of Anhalt-Cöthen wrote an account in verse of his journey through Germany, the Netherlands, England and France, 1596–7. In a passage dated 26 June 1596 he wrote of London:

Here one may see four playhouses,
In which people counterfeit princes, kings, emperors;
In fitting greatness of life, in splendour of beautiful garments,
Also of deeds, as they take place, they are remembered.

In 1596 the four playhouses should be the Swan, Rose, Curtain and Theatre.

353   A Dutchman describes the playhouses in London, especially the Swan, *c.* 1596

Library of the University of Utrecht, Ms Var. 355, fos. 131v–32. Transcribed in Gaedertz, *Zur Kenntniss der altenglischen Bühne*, frontispiece and 3–18

Johannes de Witt described the playhouses in a letter to his friend, Arend van Buchell, in Utrecht. De Witt meant his famous drawing of the Swan to explain the letter (note the passage at the end of the quotation below). Both letter and drawing survive only in van Buchell's copy of them.

In London are four amphitheatres of obvious beauty, which from their diverse signs receive their diverse names. In them a different play is daily presented to the people. The two more remarkable of these are situated to the south, on the far side of the Thames, named the Rose and Swan, from the suspended signs. Two others are outside the City towards the north, on the street going through . . . Bishopsgate[1] . . . Of all the theatres, however, the largest and most distinguished is the one whose sign is a swan (commonly, the Swan theatre), which, to be sure, accommodates three thousand people in seats. [It is] built of an accumulation of flint stones (of which in Britain there is a vast abundance), supported by wooden columns which, on account of the colour of marble painted on them, can deceive even the most acute, whose form, at least, since it [the playhouse] seems to represent the general notion of Roman work, I have drawn above.

[1] *i.e.*, the Theatre and Curtain.

354   A play at the Swan, *The Isle of Dogs*, has disastrous results there, 28 July 1597

See 54

The play or the Swan may or may not have been the true cause of a stern order of the privy council against playhouses, but the order led to the break up of Pembroke's men and a lawsuit. See the introduction and the next item.

355   Francis Langley sues players who have abandoned the Swan for the Rose, November 1597–1598

PRO, (a–c) Req.2/266/23; (d) Req.1/19, p. 405. Transcribed (uncited) by Wallace, 'The Swan Theatre and the Earl of Pembroke's Servants', 340–95. Early in November 1597 Langley threatened to sue, or actually sued, five players in one of the common law courts, and they promptly countersued in Requests to stop him, as follows.

(a) The bill, 1–16 November 1597[1]

[Five of Pembroke's men, Robert Shaa, Richard Jones, Gabriel Spencer, William Bird (alias Borne) and Thomas Downton, complained:] That whereas ... [they], together with others their accomplices and associates, have of long time used and professed the art of stage-playing, being lawfully allowed and authorised thereunto, during which time, ... being familiar and acquainted with one Francis Langley, citizen and goldsmith of London, about February last [1597] ... fell into conference and communication with the said Langley for and about the hiring and taking a playhouse of the said Langley, situate in the Old Paris Garden, ... commonly called and known by the name of the sign of the Swan. Which said speech and communication took such effect ... as they fully concluded and agreed therefor. And among the divers other agreements between them in and about the same, the said Langley craftily and cunningly intending and going about to circumvent and overreach your said subjects [i.e. the five players], ... required that your said subjects would become bound to him, the said Langley, in some great penalty with condition that they would not absent themselves nor play elsewhere but in the said playhouse ...

Whereupon your highness's said subjects (nothing suspecting the said Langley his purpose and dishonest dealing and crafty complot, which now appeareth very palpable) ... in or about the month of February last ... became bound severally, each by himself and for himself, in five several obligations in £100 apiece, with condition ... to this or the like effect: that if ... Robert Shaa, one of the obligors, should until ... [20 February 1598] in good sort and manner and from time to time continue and attend as one of the company of players which then were agreed to play in the said playhouse, ... without absenting himself at any time from the company when they should so play there, unless the said Robert Shaa ... should in his place and stead bring in or procure a sufficient person (such as the said Langley or his assign should like of), which as one of the said company should play there until the said [20 February] ... as aforesaid, and further ... that if ... Robert Shaa, or any other sufficient person so by him to be appointed and procured, should from time to time until the said [20 February] ... play in the said playhouse as one of the said company and not in any other place or places within five miles distant of and from the City of London (except private places only), or that the company of players should not in the meantime play within the City of London and so always should play in the said playhouse ... without fraud or coven: that then the said obligation to be void.

And so consequently each of your highness's said subjects became solely and severally bound by obligation in the sum of £100 with condition to the effect before mentioned.

But now ... sithence that time, as well your highness's said subjects as all other the companies of players in and about ... the City of London have been prohibited and restrained from their liberty of playing for some time together. And also the said Francis Langley, of a greedy desire and dishonest disposition, endeavouring and seeking by all undue and indirect means to bring your said subjects into the danger and forfeiture of their said several obligations by severing of their company, he, the said Langley, . . . hath procured from your said subjects two of their company so as they [*i.e.* the five players] cannot continue their play and exercise as they should, nor as the condition of the several obligations requireth, whereby the same are become forfeited. And now the said Langley, having thus lewdly and dishonestly procured your said subjects to incurr the penalty of their said several obligations and effected all things to his mischievous mind, hath of late published and given out, and still doth threaten, to commence suit at the common law against your said subjects upon their said several obligations, meaning by the rigour and strict course thereof to recover the penalty of £500 of and from your said subjects, against all right, equity and good conscience to their extreme impoverishing and utter undoing forever, unless your highness, of your wonted and accustomed clemency, mercy and grace, relieve them herein.

The players repeated their remarks about 'the restraint lately published' and Langley's causing 'some' of the company 'to be sequestered from the rest whereby they could not continue . . . playing', so that their bonds are forfeited and they have no recourse at common law. They wanted the court to make Langley appear 'to answer to the premises'.

[1] The date on the bill is illegible. The bill, however, mentions 'this nine and thirty year' of Elizabeth, which ended on 16 November 1597, and was the result of Langley's forfeiting the bonds of five players because they were not playing at the Swan from 1 November 1597, onwards.

(b) Langley's answer, 24 November 1597

[Langley said that Shaa and the rest of Pembroke's men were 'about the time in the bill mentioned . . . earnest suitors . . . to have the' Swan to play in, and Langley and they agreed] that they should play in the . . . said house for a year then next and immediately ensuing . . . And the defendant [*i.e.* Langley] upon the said agreement, giving credit unto their faithful promises, disbursed and laid out for making of the said house ready and providing of apparel fit and necessary for their playing the sum of £300 and upwards. And thereupon true it is that they became bounden unto the defendant as in the bill is alleged.

But the said Shaa and the rest of the complainants [*i.e.* the five players], not regarding their said promise and agreement, but, contrariwise, being resolute and, as it seemeth, meaning to defraud and to deceive the defendant and to make him to lose most of the charges he had disbursed in and about the making ready of the said house and providing of the said apparel as aforesaid, they . . . have departed and so severed themselves from the rest of their company without any just cause offered unto them by the defendant. And so [they] have ever sithence absented themselves from the defendant's said house. And so now, sithence their liberty to play, they have played in the house of one Philip Henslowe, commonly called . . . the Rose on the Bankside.

[Langley agreed that all the companies were restrained from playing in and about London 'for a time', but] the complainants were at liberty ever sithence the feast of All Saints [1 November] last past (any restraint to the contrary, to the defendant's knowledge, notwithstanding), and might have played, if it had pleased them, in the defendant's house as other of their fellows have done, but the complainants have ever sithence refused to play in the defendant's house and thereby have wilfully forfeited their said bonds.

And, therefore, the defendant hopeth that in law, equity, and conscience he may lawfully sue . . . them, the said complainants, upon their said bonds, for and in respect of the great costs and charges he hath disbursed and laid out at and by their appointment and direction for the making ready of the playhouse and furnishing himself with sundry sort of rich attire and apparel for them to play withal, whereof the defendant hath ever sithence had little use.

[Langley denied that he meant to defraud Pembroke's men, or that he had severed the company so that he could forfeit the bonds, or that he] hath procured from the complainants two of their companions so as they could not continue their play and exercise as they should, or as they were bound in and by their said several obligations.

(c) The replication of the five players, 6 February 1598

[They declared that their bill is 'true . . . and sufficient' and that Langley's answer is 'untrue . . . and insufficient'. They added:] that the said defendant, upon agreement between him and three of the company of the said complainants, did deliver unto them their said obligations [whereb]y they were emboldened to depart from the society of these complainants, so that these complainants could not, according to the condition of the said obligation, continue in the same society . . . in the said [play]house of the said defendant.

And as touching the departure and absence of these complainants from the house . . . the cause thereof was well known as well to the said defendant [as] to others, for that by her majesty's authority and commandments a restraint was publicly made as well of the said complainants as all other companies of players in and about . . . London from playing in any of the said playhouses in or near the said city. And the owners of the same houses [were] likewise prohibited to suffer any plays in the same several houses, from about the feast of St James the Apostle [25 July 1597] until about the feast of All Saints [1 November 1597] . . .

Whereupon (after . . . these complainants had obtained licence to play again) they resorted to the said defendant and offered themselves to play in the house of the said defendant, according to the condition of their obligation, as formerly they had done, if the said defendant would bear them out . . . [Langley] answered that he would not bear the complainants out but said he had let to them his house and bade them do what they would. The complainants then replied and said that they durst not play in his house without licence, and that it was to their undoing to continue in idleness, and that Philip Henslowe . . . had obtained licence for his house [the Rose] and would bear the complainants out if they would go to him. Then the said defendant said that the complainants were best to go to him. Which the complainants conceived and took for a licence [*i.e.* permission] of the said defendant, and that he meant well to the complainants that they should help themselves to get their living. Since which time, these complainants have exercised their playing at the house of the said Philip Henslowe, as lawfully they might.

And these complainants are now persuaded that the said defendant used the said words, *videlicet* 'that then the said complainants might go play in the house of the said Philip Henslowe', of policy to draw them into the penalty and danger of the forfeiture of their obligations and not for any other purpose.

[The five players denied that they 'were earnest suitors' to Langley for his playhouse but that he 'desired' them to play in the playhouse. They also denied that Langley spent £300 and upwards making the playhouse ready] and providing for apparel fit and necessary for their playing, . . . for the said complainants . . . say that for the making of the said house ready and fit for the complainants to play in the said defendant was at no cost at all, for the said house was then lately afore used to have plays in it. And if the said defendant were at charges for the providing of apparel, . . . the same was upon his own offer and promise that he by the same agreement was to provide the same, and afterwards to acquaint the complainants with the value thereof, and that the defendant should be allowed for the true value thereof out of the complainants' moiety of the gains for the several standings in the galleries of the said house, which belonged to them. Which the said complainants have faithfully performed from time to time.

And the complainants further say that the said house of the defendant might have long continued without gains if they, the said complainants, had not, upon request of the defendant, exercised their playing therein, whereby the defendant hath gained at least £100 and more by these complainants and hath also received for apparel . . . £100 and above out of the said moiety which was due to the complainants as aforesaid. And [he] hath all the said apparel to himself, part whereof the complainants have truly paid for and, therefore, ought to have the same again of the said defendant or consideration for the same . . .

These complainants desired to see the bill of account of the defendant and he should have such money [as] he had disbursed according to the agreement between these complainants and him, which he refused and took the said apparel and converted the same to his best profit by lending the same for hire, whereby he hath received great gains.

[The five players denied] that the said defendant hath sustained any loss by reason of these complainants, for he . . . hath ever since had his said house continually from time to time exercised with other players to his great gains.

[The five players then summarised their case and denied Langley's. They concluded with two demands:] for that they truly paid for part of the same apparel which the defendant maketh no little gains of, [the court should] . . . take some order whereby the defendant may be compelled to deliver such of the same apparel

(d) An Order of the court, 29 May 1598

It is this present day, . . . in presence of counsel on both sides, ordered that the said defendant . . . shall from henceforth surcease and stay and no further prosecute or proceed at the common law upon the said obligations, or any of them, against the said complainants until it shall please [the court] . . . to take further order for the final ending . . . of this cause. And it is further . . . ordered that an injunction under her majesty's privy seal upon pain of £500 shall be awarded forth of this court and directed to the said defendant . . . for the due performance of this present order.

356 The churchwardens of St Saviour's assume that the Swan is still in business, 20 April – 19 July 1598

See 347

The Swan was as obliged to provide money for the poor (hence was as much in business) as were the other places of entertainment in the parish, the Rose and the Beargarden.[1]

[1] Moreover, a German who was in London from 31 August to 8 September 1598 assumed that the Swan was one of the regular playhouses. He concluded a remark about the playhouses outside the City of London by noting that 'Not far from one of these theatres, which are all made of wood, is the royal barge', which was moored in the Thames near the Swan. See Hentzner, *Itinerarium Germaniae, Galliae, Angliae, Italiae* (1612), 132, and *ES*, II, 362–3.

357 A challenge in extemporaneous versifying takes place at the Swan, before 7 September 1598

Meres, *Palladis Tamia*, SR, 7 September 1598. This is one of Meres' many items in which he compares classical and English literary figures.

As Antipater Sidonius was famous for extemporal verse in Greek, and Ovid [in Latin], . . . so is now our witty [Robert] Wilson, who for learning and extemporal wit in this faculty is without compare or compeer, as, to his great and eternal commendations, he manifested in his challenge at the Swan on the Bankside.

358 Peter Bromvill, a French acrobat, performs at the Swan, 15 May 1600

PRO, PC2/25, p. 179. Transcribed in *APC, 1599–1600*, 327. Bromvill had 'danced on the rope' before the Queen three days earlier (see *ES*, IV, 112 and n.).

[The privy council sent an open letter to the justices of the peace in Surrey and others:] Whereas the bearer, Peter Bromvill, hath been recommended unto her majesty from her good brother, the French king, and hath showed some feats of great activity before her highness, her majesty is pleased to afford him her gracious favour and leave to exercise and show the same in such public place as may be convenient for such exercises and shows, and because for the present he hath made choice of a place called the Swan in Old Paris Garden, being the house of Francis Langley, these shall be to let you understand her majesty's good pleasure in his behalf and to require you not only to permit him there to show his feats of activity . . . without let or interruption but to assist him (as there shall be occasion) that no abuse be offered him.

359 Richard Vennar uses the Swan for a celebrated fraud, 6 November 1602

PRO, SP12/285, fo. 149v. Calendared in *CSP, Dom.*, 1601–3, 264, transcribed in *Letters of John Chamberlain*, I, 172. See also *ES*, III, 500–3, and Berry, 'Richard Vennar, England's Joy'.

Vennar was an educated bankrupt who proposed to mount a spectacular play called *England's Joy* at the Swan on 6 November 1602. He issued a prospectus explaining that the play was to deal with famous events from the reign of Edward III to that of Elizabeth (who was England's Joy).[1] One scene was to be 'a great triumph . . . with fighting of twelve gentlemen at barriers', and another was to show the Queen 'taken up into heaven, when presently appears a throne of blessed souls and beneath under the stage, set forth with strange fireworks, divers black and damned souls wonderfully described in their several torments'. What followed became a joke remembered for many years by, among many others, Ben Jonson, Sir John Suckling and William Davenant.

[Chamberlain wrote to Dudley Carleton on November 19:] I must . . . tell you of a cozening prank of one Vennar, of Lincoln's Inn, that gave out bills of a famous play on Saturday was seven-night on the Bankside to be acted only by certain gentlemen and gentlewomen of account. The price at coming in was 2s or 18d at least. And when he had gotten most part of the money into his hands, he would have showed them a fair pair of heels, but he was not so nimble to get up on horseback but that he was fain to forsake that course and betake himself to the water, where he was pursued and taken and brought before the Lord Chief Justice, who would make nothing of it but a jest and merriment and bound him over in £5 to appear at the sessions. In the meantime, the common people, when they saw themselves deluded, revenged themselves upon the hangings, curtains, chairs, stools, walls and whatsoever came in their way, very outrageously, and made great spoil. There was great store of good company, and many noblemen.[2]

[1] *The Plot of the Play Called England's Joy*, 'to be played at the Swan this 6th of November 1602 (1602), a broadside.
[2] In *An Apology* of 1614, Vennar explained that he had meant to have a play performed but that bailiffs seized him for debt 'before the first entrance, [and] spoke an epilogue instead of a prologue'. To show that a play did exist, he had it performed at an unknown place in the spring of 1615, a performance judged worse than the fiasco 'at the Swan'.

448 Playhouses, 1560–1660

360 A display of fencing at the Swan has a tragic result, 7 February 1603

PRO, SP12/287/fo. 44v. Calendared in *CSP, Dom.*, 1601–3, 290; transcribed in *Letters of John Chamberlain*, I, 184. Below is Chamberlain's account in his letter to Dudley Carleton, 11 February 1603, but the affair was much reported.[1]

On Monday last, here was a great prize and challenge performed at the Swan between two fencers, [John] Dun and [John] Turner, wherein Dun had so ill luck that the other ran him into the eye with a foil and so far into the head that he fell down stark dead and never spake word nor once moved.

[1] See, for example, Manningham's diary, BL, Harl. MS 5353, fo. 98, transcribed in *The Diary of John Manningham*, 187.

361 Alexander Walshe, a fruiterer, occupies the Swan, *c*. March 1606

PRO, SP14/19, fos. 184–5. Calendared in *CSP, Dom.*, 1603–10, 307 (no. 100).

The quotation below is from a study of 'concealed' lands in the manor of Paris Garden that the writer thought the King might claim because anciently they had belonged to the Knights Templar, whose lands the Crown had seized. The document is undated but calendared as 'March? 1606'.

[People who dwelt in the vicinity of] the old Paris Garden stairs . . . [were] parishioners to the Temple and had their temple of ease to the Temple,[1] whereupon is now built the sign of the Swan and is in the occupation of one Alexander Walshe, a fruiterer. [The document adds that Walshe dwells in the manor house and some tenants of the manor pay their rents to him.]

[1] That is, a local chapel belonging to the Knights Templar that people might attend in order not to have to cross the Thames to go to their parish church, which was the Temple church.

362 Players use the Swan from perhaps May 1610 to the summer of 1614

(a) BL, Add. MS 34,110, fos. 8, 9, 10, 11, 12; (b) Middleton and Dekker, *The Roaring Girl* (1611), sig. L2; (c) Middleton, *A Chaste Maid in Cheapside* (1630). Transcribed in (a) Norman, *Accounts of the Overseers of the Poor of Paris Garden*, 27, 29, 30, 31, 33

Players paid fees to the overseers of the poor of Paris Garden for the use of the Swan in every year from that ending in April 1611 to that ending in April 1615. One can, however, only guess at which players they were. Lady Elizabeth's men may have been there for a time soon after they were formed in the spring of 1611, but they also used the Hope and perhaps Whitefriars during the period.

(a) Accounts of the overseers of the poor, April 1610 – April 1615

The small amount the overseers received for the year ending on 20 April 1615 suggests that little playing went on in that year.

[Up to 5 April 1611] from the playhouse	£4	6s	8d ...
[Up to 16 April 1612] received from the players of the Swan	£5	3s	4d ...
[Up to 16 April 1613] from the Swan playhouse	£5	5s	...
[Up to 25 April 1614] item, from the players of the Swan playhouse	£3	0s	10d ...
[Up to 20 April 1615] received from the Swan playhouse		19s	2d

(b) An allusion to a new play at the Swan, 1610

[*The Roaring Girl* was acted at the Fortune in, probably, 1610. In it, the Roaring Girl says:] There's a knight, to whom I'm bound for many favours, lost his purse at the last new play i' the Swan, seven angels in't ...

(c) A play perhaps acted at the Swan by Lady Elizabeth's men, c. 1611

[The title page, printed long after the event, describes the play as:] A pleasant conceited comedy never before printed, as it hath been often acted at the Swan on the bankside by the Lady Elizabeth her servants.

363 The players have forsaken the Swan to play in Middlesex, spring – summer 1614

Taylor, *True Cause of the Watermen's Suit concerning Players* (first printed in *Workes* [1630], 172, second pagination)

Taylor (the water poet) presented a petition on behalf of his fellow watermen c. May 1614. Their trade of ferrying people across the Thames to playhouses on the south bank had collapsed because little playing was going on in them. He mentioned the Globe, which had burned in 1613 but was being rebuilt, and the Rose and Swan, where, he implied, there was no playing. He did not mention the Hope, which was probably not yet fully in business. The petition led nowhere because one member of the commission appointed to look into it died in the summer of 1614 and another was appointed to do other work.[1]

[The petition read in part:] I have known three companies [of players], besides the bear-baiting, at once there: to wit, [at] the Globe, the Rose and the Swan, [but] ... the players have all (except the King's men) left their usual residency on the Bankside and do play in Middlesex, far remote from the Thames, so that every day in the week they do draw unto them three or four thousand people that were used to spend their monies by water.

---

[1] See *ES*, II, 371–2.

364 A Swan song at the Swan: players perform there again, 1620 – spring 1621

BL, Add. MS 34, 110, fo. 19. Transcribed in Norman, *Accounts of the Overseers of the Poor of Paris Garden*,. 41. The overseers of the poor reported that they had for the year ending:]

[9 April 1621] received of the players[1]   £5   3s   6d[2]

[1] Bentley (*J and CS*, VI, 251) suggested that they were the men of Lady Elizabeth or Prince Charles (I).
[2] Norman mistakenly gives £3 19s 4d because he confused the amount for this item with that for another.

365 The Swan is used occasionally after 1620, but for fencing, not playing

Sir Henry Herbert, Office Book (now lost). Reported by Malone in *Plays and Poems of William Shakespeare* (1821), III, 56 n. 5

[According to Malone, the entries in the Office Book showed that:] After the year 1620, . . . they [the Swan and Rose] were used occasionally for the exhibition of prize fighters [*i.e.* probably fencers[1]].

[1] After an entry in the Office Book dated 23 August 1623, an undated one evidently read, 'For a prize played at the Prince's Arms or the Swan by Thomas Musgrave and Renton – 10s' (according to a copy of some of the book at least parts of which Halliwell-Phillipps cut up and pasted into his scrapbook at the Folger, 'Theatres in Shakespeare's Time', 127).

366 The Swan is decayed in 1632, but used by the Court of Requests, 1 October 1634

(a) Nicholas Goodman, *Holland's Leaguer* (1632), fo. 2v; (b) PRO, Req. 2/706/[bottom], introductory remarks to depositions for the King's men and for Brend. Transcribed in (b) Berry, *Shakespeare's Playhouses*, 229, 235. These are the latest remarks in which contemporaries said that the Swan was in existence.

(a) 1632

The writer wrote that 'three famous amphitheatres . . . stood so near situated' to Holland's Leaguer, a brothel, that one 'might take view of them from the lowest turret'.

[One was the Globe, one the Hope, and one –] which stood, and, as it were, shaked hands with this fortress, being in times past as famous as any of the other – was now fallen to decay and, like a dying Swan hanging down her head, seemed to sing her own dirge.

(b) 1 October 1634

The Court of Requests appointed a commission to take evidence in a case between the King's men and Sir Matthew Brend (see **475, 477**). Two sets of the resulting depositions are headed:

Depositions of witnesses taken before us, George Bingley, Thomas Mainwaringe . . . and Henry Withers, . . . this present first day of October 1634 . . . at the house commonly called or known by the name or sign of the Swan on the bankside in the county of Surrey.

Presumably an official body of the court would not take evidence in a hovel.

XXVIII The Boar's Head

The Boar's Head playhouse was a public playhouse in the Boar's Head Inn, which was in the parish of St Mary Matfellon (Whitechapel) in Middlesex. The inn consisted of numerous buildings around a scheme of open yards. The main entrance and some of the buildings were along the north side of Whitechapel High Street, near the western end at the corner of Hog Lane – later Petticoat Lane, and now Middlesex Street, E.1. Its other buildings and its yards were behind the buildings in the high street and also behind those on the eastern side of Hog Lane and the western side of the present Goulston Street. The high street was and is part of the main road leading east from the City of London towards Essex, and both Middlesex and Goulston Streets lead north from it. The inn was only a few yards beyond the City of London, the eastern boundary of which ran along the middle of Hog Lane. On sunny afternoons the City literally cast its shadow over the Boar's Head. The sidewalk now on the eastern side of Middlesex Street at its southern end lies on the sites of buildings that stood along Hog Lane and the inn-yard, and it extends eastwards to, roughly, where the middle of the stage was.

The inn had existed in the 1530s, perhaps long before, and people had thought of producing plays in it in 1557, but no evidence shows that a play was actually produced there until it became a playhouse in 1598. The Boar's Head does not belong in the group of four theatrical inns described above, because it did not share important aspects common to them. They were among the earliest playhouses, ceased to be playhouses by 1596, were in the City, and remained inns despite their plays. When the Boar's Head became a playhouse, it ceased to be an inn.

For four years beginning in the autumn of 1599, the owners of the Boar's Head fought a legal war with one another from which many documents survive. More is known about the place, therefore, than about other playhouses.

The playhouse was originally the project of Oliver Woodliffe, officially a haberdasher, actually a financier. In November 1594 he took a lease on much of the inn for twenty-one years from Lady Day (25 March) 1595. His rent was £40 a year, and he bonded himself to build a playhouse in the main ('great') inn-yard. He did nothing about the project until Christmas 1597, when he took a partner, Richard Samwell the elder, a yeoman of means. On 13 April 1598 Woodliffe subleased most of his part of the inn to Samwell for £40 a year for eighteen years from the previous Christmas, but not specifically the yard where spectators would stand nor the buildings along the west side of the yard.

In the yard, Woodliffe would build a stage and in his buildings a tiring-house and a gallery for spectators above it. Samwell would build a similar gallery on the north side of the yard and another on the south side, both of which would join the existing gallery that served for access to the rooms in the upper storey of his building on the east side. Samwell's galleries would be above the yard on posts so that people could come and go under them. Woodliffe and Samwell would have half the takings in their galleries; the players would have the other half and the takings in the yard. Samwell would see to the building of Woodliffe's structures as well as his own and manage the playhouse. Woodliffe would be a silent partner and soon went abroad.

The playhouse probably opened in the summer of 1598. It was primitive and tentative. Samwell had spent only about £40. His galleries were narrow, and people stood in them. The stage was in the middle of the yard, like a boxing ring.

The place must have prospered, for when Woodliffe returned the next summer he proposed and Samwell agreed to an expensive enlargement of the scheme. The new work was done in July and perhaps the first part of August 1599, and Samwell spent a further £260. The galleries became wider and people were to sit in them. A new gallery was added above the existing one on the eastern side. The stage was moved westwards so that it adjoined the tiring-house and gallery above. The drainage in the yard was improved.

The playhouse was now recognisably a public playhouse, but it was smaller than others. The yard was roughly 55 feet square. On the north and south sides, single galleries stood over it on posts so that people could stand under them. On the east side were two galleries, one above the other, the lower also over the yard on posts. The north and south galleries were some 6 feet deep and ran along the whole of the north and south sides of the yard, from the lower east gallery, into which they led, to the west gallery, which they abutted but did not lead into. The two eastern ones were about 8 feet deep and the western one about 7 feet deep. All the galleries had roofs as did the stage. The stage was about 39 feet 7 inches wide (north to south) by perhaps 25 feet deep (east to west). Behind and above it was the western gallery, and beside it were strips of the yard about 8 feet wide, in which spectators could stand, mostly under the north and south galleries. No spectator was more than about 40 feet from the stage. See the appendix below.

Samwell soon had to borrow money from Robert Browne, who led a company of players, Derby's men; then, probably in mid-October 1599, Samwell turned his share of the project over to Browne for £360 in all. On 7 November Woodliffe sold his part of the venture to Francis Langley for £400, much more than it was worth. Langley paid £100 in cash and the rest in three bonds of £100 (worth £200 if forfeit) each, all guaranteed by his nephew, Richard Langley. The first was due on 2 November 1600.

Langley was a rash financier who had built and burned his fingers in the Swan. He paid so much because he and Woodliffe thought that he could seize Samwell's galleries and so own the whole playhouse. They would argue that the Woodliffe–Samwell lease gave Samwell only the right to come and go in the yard, not ownership of it. The posts holding up Samwell's galleries, hence the galleries themselves, therefore, rested on Woodliffe's and then Langley's ground and so belonged to Woodliffe or Langley. Woodliffe made the point evidently while in Samwell's galleries in about October 1599. Then after buying Woodliffe's property, Langley set out to harass Samwell and later Browne into submission.

Langley proceeded mainly in a court suited to the purpose, the Marshalsea. It was meant for disputes among servants in the royal household (who included neither Langley nor Samwell), but it was eager to expand its repertoire, and it demanded huge fees of the people its tipstaffs arrested. To multiply legal complications, Langley leased part of the yard to a Thomas Wolleston, who on 15 December leased part of that part to a Richard Bishop. Between mid-November 1599 and mid-April 1600, Langley launched six lawsuits against Samwell in the Marshalsea and one in King's Bench. Members of Samwell's household were arrested seven times, including Winifred, wife of Samwell's son, another Richard, with her six-week old child, Rebecca, 'sucking at her breast'. Langley bound the younger Samwell to the peace in King's Bench and then his father in Chancery. Samwell paid £40 in fees to release people from arrests and to satisfy other legal charges. Worse, Langley and a team of followers, including tipstaffs from the Marshalsea and usually Woodliffe's wife, invaded the playhouse four times between 13 and 26 December 1599, once to serve papers, once to arrest Samwell (he was rescued by his son), once to arrest his son and take money from people who went up into Samwell's galleries at a play, and once to cut a door from Langley's part of the playhouse into Samwell's. 'Nor', as Samwell complained, was 'any suit prosecuted' to a decision, 'nor any costs upon the non-suit of any action could be recovered'.

In reply, Samwell sued Woodliffe in King's Bench for trespass and Woodliffe and Langley in Chancery for title to the yard. Finally, on 11 April 1600, he sued all his antagonists in the Star Chamber. What that court did with the lawsuit does not appear, but neither Langley nor the people from the Marshalsea bothered Samwell or his family again. Samwell may have had to pay Langley something, for in October 1600, he began a lawsuit in Chancery against Browne and Browne's financier, Israel Jordan, attempting, perhaps, to get out of them whatever Langley had got out of him. He soon abandoned the lawsuit but continued with his lawsuit in Chancery against Woodliffe. He died during the winter or spring following. Langley now turned his attention to Browne, taking his legal business to King's Bench where his creature, Bishop, filed a lawsuit against Browne and his carpenter, John Mago, in May 1600.

Langley did not pay Woodliffe the £100 due on 2 November 1600. The first of Langley's bonds, therefore, was forfeit. Woodliffe lost little time suing Richard Langley in Common Pleas for £200 plus £40 in damages. Trial was set for the end of April 1601, but on the appointed day Richard Langley did not appear. The court decided that Woodliffe should have only his debt and £7 in damages and awarded him a judgement against Richard Langley for £107.

At the end of April 1601 the two Langleys sued Woodliffe in Chancery to stop him from executing his judgement in Common Pleas and to get the court to sanction a device by which they could get out of the Boar's Head cheaply. Woodliffe, however, shrank from cancelling bonds, giving up a judgement of £107, and giving back £100 in cash in exchange for the future half profits of the western gallery and whatever he could get out of Browne because the posts holding up Browne's galleries rested in Woodliffe's yard.

While the Langleys and Woodliffe were at one another's throats in Common Pleas and Chancery in the spring of 1601, Browne sued them all and Bishop in Chancery. He argued that he, not they, owned the yard. He conceded that according to the Woodliffe–Samwell lease of 1598 Woodliffe owned the yard. But the discussions between Woodliffe and Samwell in July 1599 amounted to a verbal lease according to which the yard passed to Samwell, who had included it among the parts of the playhouse he had sold to Browne. Samwell had acquired the yard in return for spending a good deal of money to rebuild his galleries. This argument proved durable, for Browne was still using it two years later.

Professing that he did not know whether Langley or Woodliffe owned the stage, tiringhouse and western gallery, Browne ceased on 22 August 1601 to pay the half-profits from the gallery to either of them. He then leased the Boar's Head to Worcester's men, and, it seems, his own men went into the provinces. The rent Browne demanded for his playhouse was 'shares due in their plays', and to guarantee payment of them Browne took bonds from six members of the company.

Soon after Worcester's men settled into the Boar's Head, Francis Langley again appeared there with 'rude fellows' to demand that the players pay him £3 a week for using his and Woodliffe's stage, tiring-house and western gallery. Worcester's men agreed and ceased to pay Browne, who promptly sued them, it seems, at common law on their bonds. They countersued in Chancery, then negotiated a compromise with him and gave up their lawsuit. But on 13 May 1602 he pointed out in Chancery that they had not formally closed their lawsuit against him and so owed him costs. He got costs, and they went to the Rose.

After Francis Langley's death early in July 1602, Richard Langley agreed to a scheme by which he would escape the Boar's Head. Woodliffe would cancel the two remaining bonds but keep the £100 Langley had paid him at the outset and be free to do what he could to execute his judgement for £107. Langley would return Woodliffe's part of the Boar's Head but first get Browne out of it – a project with which Woodliffe was willing to help. He got an elegit against Langley, a writ directing a bailiff to seize Langley's goods to satisfy the judgement for £107, and at Christmas 1602 a bailiff appeared at the Boar's Head to seize the goods in Langley's part of the place and collect money people paid to go into his gallery. Browne thought that Langley and a Henry Sibdall had paid the costs of the elegit. He closed the playhouse and kept it closed for some time. Woodliffe had regained his part of the Boar's Head by the end of the January 1603, but Browne was soon mounting plays there again.

Except for a week or two in May 1603, all the playhouses were closed from 19 March 1603 until 9 April 1604 because of the Queen's illness and death and then the great plague of 1603–4. Browne's company went to the provinces along with other companies, but Browne remained at the Boar's Head pursuing lawsuits. In April he sued Woodliffe in Common Pleas; in May, Woodliffe countersued in Requests; and in June, Browne sued Woodliffe and Richard Langley in Chancery. They sued in vain, however, for Woodliffe soon died of the plague and then Browne. Woodliffe was buried in Whitechapel churchyard on 30 July, Browne on 16 October, and nobody revived their lawsuits.

Tranquillity thus achieved, the playhouse continued until the leases expired in 1616, after which it was converted into a collection of small-holdings. The companies who had used it included Derby's men, the company known as Worcester's and later the Queen's men, evidently the Duke of Lennox's men, and Prince Charles's (I) men.

367 The privy council prevents a lewd play from being performed at the Boar's Head, 5 and 6 September 1557

PRO, PC2/7, pp. (a) 695, (b) 696. Transcribed in *APC, 1556–8* 168, 169

(a) 5 September 1557

[The privy council ordered the Lord Mayor of London] to give order forthwith that some of his officers do forthwith repair to the Boar's Head without Aldgate where the lords [of the privy council] are informed a lewd play called *A Sack Full of News* shall be played this day, the players whereof he is willed to apprehend and to commit to safe ward until he shall hear further from hence, and to take their playbook from them and to send the same hither.

(b) 6 September 1557

The Mayor arrested the players that day, sent them to prison, and presumably sent their playbook to Westminster. The playbook must have been innocuous, for on the next day, the privy council ordered the Mayor to set the players free. They and others, however, were not to be allowed to play until 1 November and then only if their plays were officially allowed.

368 Oliver Woodliffe leases most of the Boar's Head so that he can build a playhouse in it, 28 November 1594

PRO, Req.2/466/pt 11 [/1], the bill. See Berry, *Boar's Head Playhouse*, 24

[The lease does not survive, but in May 1603, Woodliffe explained] That . . . Jane Poley, widow, and Henry Poley, son of the said Jane, did, by their indenture of lease bearing date [28 November 1594] . . . demise and unto farm let unto . . . [Woodliffe] all that tenement, messuage, or inn commonly called the Boar's Head in Whitechapel in Middlesex, together with all the edifices, barns, buildings, stables, yards, ways and passages with their appurtenances . . . then used and occupied to and with the said messuage by the said Jane or her assigns. And the said Jane and Henry did further demise unto . . . [Woodliffe] and Susan, his wife, the garden and back yard then used and occupied by the said Jane and Henry with the said tenement or inn, together with all the ways and passages then used and occupied with the said garden and back yard. To have and to hold . . . during the term of twenty-one years,[1] yielding and paying therefore yearly unto the said Jane and Henry or their assigns the sum of £40 of lawful English money at four terms in the year. In which indenture of lease aforesaid is contained a special proviso that . . . [Woodliffe] should bestow £100 in building of the larder, the larder parlour, the well parlour, the coal-house, the oat loft, the tiring-house, and stage within seven years or the said lease to be forfeited, with divers other covenants specified in the said lease. And . . . [Woodliffe] did enter into a bond of £300 to perform the covenants in the said indenture contained.

[1] In April and May 1600 both Richard Samwell and the Woodliffes explained that the twenty-one years were to begin at Lady Day 'next ensuing after the date' of the lease – on, that is, 25 March 1595: PRO, STAC5/S74/3, the bill and the Woodliffes' reply.

369 Woodliffe subleases most of the Boar's Head to Richard Samwell for eighteen years, 13 April 1598

PRO, (a) Req.2/466/pt 2[/1], the bill; (b) Req.2/466/pt 2[/1], Browne's answer; (c) STAC5/S74/3, the bill; (d) C24/278/71/Moxlay, 3. See Berry, *Boar's Head Playhouse*, 30–2, 95–6

The sublease does not exist, but people who disputed its implications did not seriously dispute its terms. Lengthy descriptions of it, by Woodliffe, his opponent Robert Browne and Browne's ally the younger Richard Samwell are similar, and shorter descriptions by these and other people add a few details that no one disputed either. Below are Woodliffe's lengthy description (compared in footnotes with Browne's and the younger Samwell's[1]), and three shorter descriptions.

[1] Both are at the PRO, C24/290/3, interrogatory 2 and Samwell 2.

(a) Woodliffe, 20 May 1603

[Woodliffe said that he,] by indenture bearing date the 13th day of April in . . . [1598, did] demise and let unto Richard Samwell the elder certain particular parcels of the said inn, viz.: [1] a hall, a parlour, a kitchen (being of one floor), with a cellar underneath part of the hall, and over the hall and kitchen three several chambers,[1] situate on the west side of the entry of the said inn; and [2] over the entry of the said inn one chamber; and [3] on the east side of the great yard[2] of the said inn one room to drink in, three parlours, a cellar and three stables, and over the[3] parlour[s], cellar and stables one gallery with seven chambers, with the said east end of the great barn there; and [4] on the west side of the great yard one[4] hostry with a loft over it to lay hay in, and a back room behind the hostry, and a stable under two houses reserved by the said Jane and Henry Poley;[5] and [5] certain name[d] stuff belonging to divers rooms contained in a schedule indented to the said indenture annexed, with a garden, all which were then in the occupation of the said Richard Samwell the elder.

Whereupon was reserved unto . . . [Woodliffe] a yearly rent of £40 payable at four terms in the year, with a clause of re-entry for non-payment of the said rent, and a covenant for the said Samwell to uphold and maintain the said demised premises, with a special covenant to suffer the said Jane and Henry Poley or their assigns twice every year unto the demised premises to enter to view and see the reparations. And further the said Samwell did especially covenant to and with . . . [Woodliffe] and Susan, his wife, to suffer them or their assigns to enter into the said inn at all times convenient with cart and carriage for the building of the west part of the great yard of the said in, which . . . [Woodliffe] was tied to build in seven [years] or else the original lease to be forfeited, with divers other covenants in the said indenture contained.

[1] Browne said instead, 'two chambers over the said hall and a chamber over the kitchen', and the younger Samwell agreed.
[2] The younger Samwell said 'thereof' instead of 'of the great yard'.
[3] Browne added 'said drinking rooms' and the younger Samwell 'said drinking room'.
[4] Browne and the younger Samwell said 'the' instead of 'one' before 'hostry' and Browne also before 'back room'.
[5] Browne and the younger Samwell mentioned the garden and the rent but none of the other matters from here on. Instead, both mentioned the term of the lease and a clause allowing the elder Samwell 'free ingress, egress and regress into and from all and every the said premises in, by and through the ways and passages thereunto then used'. The younger Samwell added that the lease included 'one back yard to lay dung in'. Though Woodliffe mentioned neither the clause nor the back yard here, he mentioned both in May 1600 (PRO, STAC5/S74/3, the Woodliffes' reply).

(b) Browne, 30 May 1603

[Browne soon agreed:] True it is that . . . [Woodliffe] did demise . . . by indenture unto the said Richard Samwell the elder, deceased, all the said premises as in the said bill is mentioned, for such term and rent as in the said bill is recited. [But the term is not recited, though it is elsewhere, for example just below.]

(c) The elder Samwell, 11 April 1600

[He said that he was uncertain about the lease because he no longer had it, but he noted several things about it that others did not:] Oliver and Susan [Woodliffe] . . . did demise and let unto . . . [Samwell] divers parcels of the said messuage or inn, as divers chambers, a hall, an hostry, a barn and divers stables, a privy, and the said garden and back yard . . . To have and to hold . . . from the feast of Christmas last past before the date of the said indenture [*i.e.* 1597] unto the end and term of eighteen years next ensuing . . . In and by which indenture so made to . . . [Samwell] there was a covenant therein contained whereby . . . [Samwell] did covenant, promise and grant to and with the said Oliver and Susan to let the said Oliver build on the west part of the said great yard near adjoining to certain rooms excepted in the said indenture to the said Oliver and his wife a full yard further in length into the great yard aforesaid.

(d) Moxlay, 22 October 1600

[Nicholas Moxlay was an apprentice notary public. He said:] that he remembreth that when the said lease was to be sealed, this deponent [Moxlay] carried it to a lower room next adjoining unto the hall of the said house [*i.e.* inn], as he remembreth, where the said lease was read openly [by Moxlay] and sealed.

370 Samwell and Woodliffe build a primitive playhouse in the Boar's Head, summer 1598

(a, b) PRO, C24/290/3/Samwell 3, 5. See Berry, *Boar's Head Playhouse*, 32–3, 108–10, 159–62. Other witnesses confused the playhouse of 1598 with that of 1599 or spoke only of that of 1599, but not the younger Richard Samwell.

(a) The date of building

[In June 1601, the younger Samwell said:] that he well knoweth that his father, the said Richard Samwell [the elder], after the said lease to him made by Woodliffe and his wife [on 13 April 1598], did (when the said Woodliffe was at sea or abroad) erect and set up in the great yard of the said inn certain galleries or rooms for people to stand in to see the plays. And . . . afterwards, when Woodliffe came home again, Woodliffe found fault because the said galleries or rooms were made so little.

(b) The cost of building

The elder Samwell's part of the first playhouse apparently cost about £40, a figure arrived at by subtracting a reliable figure for his part of the second playhouse from a reliable figure for his part of both. John Mago, the chief builder of the second playhouse, said in February 1600 that Samwell's part of that playhouse cost about £260 (see below). In June 1601 the younger Samwell said that his father's part of both playhouses cost about £300:

the timber, nails, stuff and workmanship which was employed and spent in setting up the said little galleries, and afterwards in taking the same down again and setting up the larger as aforesaid, cost his father, the said Richard Samwell, and the complainant [Browne] £300 or thereabouts. The which he knoweth to be true because he, this deponent [the younger Samwell], by the appointment of his father, and for him, did keep the book of the expenses about the same, viz., of the timber, nails, boards, tiles, laths and other stuff which was employed about the said galleries, together with the workmanship, and [he] hath the same book still in his keeping.[1]

[1] At the same time, William Hoppdale, a carpenter, agreed with this figure as, then and later, did Browne, who contributed much of the money. See PRO, C24/290/3, interrogatory 5, Hoppdale 5; Req.2/466/pt. 2[/1], the reply.

371 Woodliffe and Samwell build a new and much more expensive playhouse, July 1599

PRO, (a) STAC5/S74/3, the bill; STAC5/S18/8; C24/290/3, Hoppdale, Samwell 4; (b, c) C24/278/71, Rodes 2, 3, and Mago 1, 4, 5; C24/290/3, Bagnall 7. See Berry, *Boar's Head Playhouse*, 33–5, 159–62, 163–70, 175–6

(a) The date of building

[On 11 April 1600, the elder Samwell said that] abouts July in . . . [1599] it was agreed between [Samwell] . . . and the said Oliver and Susan [Woodliffe] that . . . [Samwell should rebuild his parts of the playhouse, and he] did in July last past or thereabouts build in the said great yard for the necessary use of [himself] . . . divers rooms, galleries, chambers and other necessary buildings.

[Samwell spoke eleven days later of his] charges and expenses . . . bestowed upon new buildings in the said messuage or inn sithence midsummer last past [24 June 1599] for and towards the erecting and setting up of the galleries.

[On 11 June 1601, Hoppdale said] the said Oliver [Woodliffe] and Richard Samwell made an agreement about St James tide [25 July 1599] . . . that he, the said Richard Samwell, should pull down certain new galleries and rooms which he had formerly set up in the great yard of the said inn and should sett up again the same galleries and roomths larger out, into and upon the said yard, viz., so far as the said Oliver Woodliffe did then measure and sett out in the presence of this deponent [Hoppdale] and Mr Cuckow and others.

[At the same time, the younger Samwell said that the arrangement between his father and Woodliffe to rebuild the playhouse] was made ... betwixt midsummer [24 June] and Bartholomew-tide [24 August] last was twelvemonth [*i.e. c.* 24 July 1599].

(b) Sequence of events

When Woodliffe returned to the Boar's Head after having been abroad, Walter Rodes, a carpenter, was taking measure for an upper eastern gallery that had evidently been part of the scheme of 1598 but, probably because it would have been expensive, had been put off. Woodliffe proposed, and Samwell agreed, that they pull down the work of 1598 and build, in effect, a proper public playhouse, which in Samwell's case meant pulling down the galleries of 1598 and building newer and bigger ones. The builders probably took on the south gallery first, because their wagons had to pass under it to get to the rest of the work. Then they took on the north gallery, and as they were at work on that, they moved the stage to make more room for their next project, the two east galleries, which were massive. They turned last to Woodliffe's structures on the west side of the yard.

[On 2 February 1600, Rodes said that Woodliffe,] coming to the deponent [Rodes] as he was taking measure for a story to be made over the long old [*i.e.* the eastern] gallery, said these words or the like in effect to him, 'If the case were mine, as it is Samwell's, I would pull down this older gallery to the ground and build it four feet forwarded toward the stage into the yard,' and with a lath or some other thing which he then had in his hand did point how far he would wish the said old long gallery to be built.

[Rodes added] that while the said John Mago and this deponent [Rodes] and the rest of the workmen were in hand with a gallery which standeth on the north side of the said yard, the said defendant [Woodliffe] caused the stage which stood in the yard to be removed and pulled inwards to make more room for the long [eastern] gallery and the yard;[1] [and] that the said stage was removed inwards about five or six feet, as he taketh it for the enlargement of the said yard and to give the complainant [Samwell] the more scope for the better enlarging of his galleries.

[John Mago, the chief builder, said at the same time:] that about the time of the removing of the said stage, there lay a great deal of dung and rubbish in the said yard, most part whereof was thrown from under the stage.

[On 10 June 1601, the man who carried away the rubbish, Richard Bagnall, said:] that ... he, this deponent [Bagnall], was procured by the said Oliver Woodliffe to carry away out of the yard of the said house certain rubbish which was cast under the stage, and after such time as he had carried away the same rubbish and had made clean the yard, he repaired to the said Woodliffe for his money for his work, ... but ... Woodliffe made answer that he had nothing to do with it, nor would pay him anything, willing this deponent to go to Mr Browne [i.e. it seems, Samwell] for it.

[On 2 February 1600, Mago said that Woodliffe did not] deny the plaintiff's [Samwell's] right [to build in the yard] ... until such time as the said galleries were all finished saving one storey of the gallery on the west side of the said yard, which when this deponent [Mago] began to fall in hand withal and to take off the roof, he willed this deponent to forbear and go no forwarder till Samwell and he had talked together ... for that storey which then was to be done.

[1] In June 1601, however, the younger Samwell said that they moved the stage 'after or at such time as the said east galleries were finishing or finished': PRO, C24/290/3, no. 7.

(c) The cost of building

[On 2 February 1600 Mago said] that he knoweth that Richard Samwell [the elder] ... did [in 1599] build certain rooms or galleries in the yard of the messuage or inn called the Boar's Head, ... for this deponent [Mago] was his chief workman in the making of the same galleries. And [he] saith that ... the timber which was employed and used about those galleries came to about £140, the which was provided by this deponent and upon his credit ... And [he] further saith that the nails which the plaintiff [Samwell the elder] bought to be employed and were employed about the said galleries came to about £20, and the workmanship he verily thinketh could not come to less than £100, but the certainty thereof he cannot justly sett down because he never kept any account of it, but only of the stuff.[1]

[1] Mago's figure must be reliable because he gave it only a few months after doing most of the work, and was (as he also said) still owed some of the money. There were, however, other figures. In February 1600 Samwell's servant, Edward Willys, quoted his master as saying that the work on Samwell's part of the second playhouse had cost £280 'or thereabouts', and the carpenter, Rodes, who said he did not know, thought the materials and labour had 'stood' Samwell 'in little less' than £300. In July 1603 Mago put the cost of both years at 'almost £200 or £300', and John Marsh, a carpenter, said 'at least' instead of 'almost'. Samwell himself said in April 1600 that the work on the second playhouse had cost him £300 'and more' (PRO, C24/278/71, Rodes, Willys 1; C24/304/27, Mago, Marsh 6; STAC5/S74/3, the bill).

372 Samwell sells his part of the Boar's Head to Robert Browne, mid-October 1599

PRO, (a, b) C24/290/3/interrogatory 6, Samwell 6, 8; (b) C24/278/71/Moxlay 3. See Berry, *Boar's Head Playhouse*, 35–6, 40–1, 177–8

When Browne acquired Samwell's part of the Boar's Head is a puzzle. Samwell and Browne probably found it legally convenient to obscure the details of the transaction, and Samwell may have lost control of the place gradually because he mortgaged his sublease to Browne, or Browne's moneylender, Israel Jordan, or others before he formally assigned it to Browne. Various people said various things about the matter, but the younger Samwell, who should have known, hinted that his father controlled the place until mid-October 1599.

(a) The transaction

[Early in June 1601 Browne asked the younger Samwell to confirm that because] the said complainant [Browne] ... disbursed for the said Samwell [the elder] ... the sum of £100 and upwards, he, the said Richard Samwell, in consideration thereof, and for the sum of £260 more by the said complainant to him, the said Richard Samwell, then paid, being in the whole sum of £360, did by good conveyance in the law assign and set over unto the said complainant all and every the said rooms and premises so to him demised by the said Oliver Woodliffe as aforesaid, and also the said galleries and rooms so built as aforesaid.

[On 11 June the younger Samwell confirmed the thrust of the question but reversed the numbers:] the said Richard Samwell, growing indebted unto the complainant [Browne] for moneys which the complainant had disbursed for him in setting up the said galleries or rooms, and for moneys which the complainant had lent to and disbursed for the said Richard Samwell to the value of £200 or thereabouts in the whole, and being not able to make the complainant satisfaction thereof, he, the said Richard Samwell, in consideration thereof and of £160 more or thereabouts paid by the complainant to him, did by a conveyance in writing under his hand and seal assign and set over unto the complainant all and every the said rooms and premises so to him demised aforesaid [*i.e.* by Woodliffe on 13 April 1598] ... and all the right, title, interest, estate and term of years which he, the said Richard Samwell, then had to come of and in the same, which this deponent [the younger Samwell] knoweth to be true because he was present both at the bargain making betwixt his father and the complainant and at the ensealing of the writings which passed betwixt them about the same.

(b) The date

[On 22 October 1600, the apprentice notary public, Nicholas Moxlay, said:] when in the reading [aloud] of the said lease [of 13 April 1598] and in rehearsing the several roomths specified ... they came to name the parlour or roomth ... wherein the defendant [Woodliffe] and his wife then lodged, the said defendant willed this deponent [Moxlay], who was reading the said indenture, to stop there, and directing his speech to the complainant [Samwell the elder], used these or the like words in effect, viz., 'Mr Samwell, you know that it was our bargain that I should have this parlour to myself till I have built on the other side of the yard.' 'You shall have it,' quoth the complainant, 'with all my heart.'

[On 11 June 1601, the younger Samwell said] that the said Woodliffe did withhold from this deponent's said father one parlour called the upper parlour, parcel of the premises which were demised to his father by the said Indenture [of 13 April 1598] and withheld the same from him by the space of a year and [a] half or thereabouts, and the same as yet standeth locked up, and his father never, to his knowledge, could get the key thereof from Woodliffe, though he oftentimes demanded it within the said year and [a] half.

If Samwell acquired the parlour on 13 April 1598, and Woodliffe kept it from him for a year and a half until Samwell no longer controlled his part of the inn, Samwell had controlled his part until mid-October 1599.[1]

[1] In April 1600 Samwell said that he no longer had his lease but still had possession of his parts of the Boar's Head at 'abouts' Christmas 1599. In April 1601 Francis Langley thought Browne had possession by 15 December 1599. In May 1603 Woodliffe said that Brown acquired possession 'by indirect means'. In July 1603 Browne, Mago and Marsh all said that Samwell had possession at the time of the Woodliffe–Langley lease (7 November 1599), and Browne added that at Christmas 1602 he had had possession 'for two years before' (PRO, STAC5/S74/3, the bill; KB27/1367/m. 199d; Req. 2/466/pt 2[/1], the bill; C24/304/27/interrogatories 7, 8, Mago, Marsh 7; see Berry, *Boar's Head Playhouse*, 177–8).

373 Woodliffe sells his part of the Boar's Head to Francis Langley for £400, 7 November 1599

PRO, (a) STAC5/S74/3, reply of Langley and Roberts; (b) CP40/1655/m. 724d; (c) C33/99/464v (A book) and C33/100/452v (B book); (d) Req.2/466/pt 2[/1], the bill. See Berry, *Boar's Head Playhouse*, 37–40. Without disagreement, the two Langleys, Woodliffe and the Court of Chancery all explained how and when Francis Langley bought Woodliffe's part of the Boar's Head.

(a) Francis Langley, 17 April 1600

Francis Langley further saith that he did buy (as was lawful for him, as he thinketh and hopeth to make manifest to this honourable court, without any offense to any law or statute) the whole interest of the said Woodliffe and his said wife of and to the said inn called the Boar's Head by an indenture bearing date the 7th day of November last [1599] ... in which indenture to avoid all ambiguities and doubts is rehearsed what was formerly granted or demised by the said Woodliffe and his wife to the complainant [Samwell] and all therein not granted; and the rent thereby reserved is granted to this defendant [Langley] as by the same indenture ... may appear.

(b) Richard Langley, January 1601

Each of the three bonds that Langley and his nephew, Richard Langley, gave Woodliffe towards the purchase price would have had two parts, the first saying that the Langleys owed Woodliffe £200 payable whenever Woodliffe demanded and the second that the bond would be void if the Langleys paid Woodliffe £100 on a specified day. Richard Langley said that the second part of the first bond read:

The condition of this obligation is such that if the within bounden Francis Langley and Richard Langley, or either of them, or the heirs, executors, administrators or assigns of them, or either of them, do well and truly pay or cause to be paid unto the within named Oliver Woodliffe, his executors or assigns, the sum of £100 of good and lawful money of England on the second day of November [1600][1] ... at the now dwelling house of the said Oliver situate and being within the messuage or inn called the Boar's Head ... without further delay; and also if it shall happen the said Francis and Richard, or either of them, to die or decease before the said sum of £100 shall be fully paid, then if the survivor of them, his executors, administrators

464   Playhouses, 1560–1660

or assigns shall find and put in one other good and sufficient surety or person of ability to become bounded to the said Oliver, his executors or assigns with him, the same survivor, for the payment of the said £100 on the said second day of November without further delay: that then this present obligation to be void and of none effect, or else it to stand and remain in full strength.

[1] In the earlier part of the document (a lawsuit in Common Pleas), Woodliffe said that Langley entered into the bond on 12 November 1599. The second and third bonds were presumably due on 2 November in 1601 and 1602, in any event well before 20 May 1603, when Woodliffe said they were due 'at several days long since past' (PRO, Req.2/466/pt 2[/1], the bill).

(c) An order of Chancery, 6 May 1601

The said Francis Langley ... bought a lease of an inn ... of the defendant [Woodliffe] for £400, whereof he paid £100 in hand and ... entered into three ... bonds of £200 apiece for payment of the other £300 at several days specified in the conditions of the same bonds, and the plaintiff [Langley took] ... a bond of 1,000 marks [£666 13s 4d] of the defendant for his security of the same lease.

(d) Woodliffe, 20 May 1603

[He and his wife on 7 November 1599:] did for and in consideration of the sum of £400 ... set over unto one Francis Langley ... all his right, title and interest of the said inn ... [and Richard Langley] ... stood bound with the said Francis unto ... [Woodliffe] in three several bonds of £200 apiece for payment of £300.

374   Langley tries to seize Samwell's galleries, autumn 1599 – April 1600

(a–g) PRO, STAC5/S74/3, the bill and replies; STAC5/S13/8. See Berry, *Boar's Head Playhouse*, 41–5

Langley aimed first at Samwell, not knowing, perhaps, the extent of Browne's involvement in Samwell's galleries nor wanting to interrupt Browne's performances. Below are quotations from Samwell's lawsuit in the Star Chamber. The lawsuit explains much of what happened, and it effectually ended Langley's attacks on the Samwells. Its documents are in two groups:

(1) Samwell's bill, 11 April 1600, and three replies: of the two Woodliffes, 10 May 1600; of Langley and Owen Roberts (Langley's carpenter), 17 April 1600; and of Alexander Foxley and John Johnson (officers of the Marshalsea court), 24 April 1600;

(2) Samwell's interrogatories, 22 April 1600, and the depositions of Langley, 30 April 1600, and Roberts, 1 May 1600.

(a) The argument

[Samwell declared in his bill:] The said Oliver [Woodliffe] and Susan [his wife] ... did demise and let unto [Samwell] ... divers parcels of the said messuage or inn

... together with a great yard in the said house, excepting ingress, egress and regress to the said Oliver and Susan and their assigns into the great yard to such rooms as the said Oliver and Susan excepted to themselves [as] mentioned in the said indenture of demise unto [Samwell] ... the certainty whereof [Samwell] ... knoweth not for want of having the said indenture[1] ...

[The Woodliffes replied:] Neither the great yard nor the backyard mentioned in the bill was or is conveyed or demised or intended to be demised unto him, the said complainant [Samwell], but only ingress, egress and regress into and from the same great yard and all and singular the demised premises in, by, and through the ways and passages thereunto there used and accustomed ... As by the indenture between the said defendants [the Woodliffes] and the complainant made may at large appear, whereunto these defendants to refer themself [sic] ...

[Samwell asked Langley in the interrogatories:] Did you buy the right of the said Oliver Woodliffe and his wife of the said galleries newly erected and who was in possession of these galleries at the time that you bought the same and how long had they been in possession thereof, and who built the said galleries and who kept the possession thereof until you bought the same of the said Woodliffe?

[And Langley deposed:] Galleries were built in the yard of the said inn, which yard was not demised by the said Woodliffe unto the said complainant [Samwell] and therefore, as this defendant [Langley] taketh it, the said galleries were in the possession of the said Woodliffe at such time as he did sell his interest in the said inn to this defendant, as by the said indenture [of 7 November 1599] may appear.

[1] By this time, Browne or Browne's moneylender, Israel Jordan, would have had Samwell's copy of the Woodliffe–Samwell lease. If Samwell really believed that it gave him the yard and Woodliffe only the right to come and go in it, he had forgotten an essential aspect of it. Not only did Woodliffe and Langley quickly point out that the reverse was the case, but Browne and the younger Samwell conceded it in June 1601, as did Browne again in 1603 (PRO, C24/290/3, interrogatory 2, Samwell 2; Req.2/466/pt 2[/1], the reply) Moreover, later in the document here Samwell allowed that he might hold the yard 'by disseisin' – illegally – but if so, he argued, he had had actual possession of it long enough that Woodliffe could not simply sell it, the law being that Woodliffe had to have such possession when he sold it and for one whole year before.

(b) Events, September – November 1599

[Samwell declared in his bill:] The said Oliver Woodliffe and Susan, his wife, being confederated with one Francis Langley to cozen and defraud [Samwell] ... of the said galleries, rooms and new building, did abouts Michaelmas [29 September] last past deny [Samwell] ... to enjoy the same galleries and did seem to interrupt [his] ... possession of the said galleries. Whereupon [Samwell] ... did in Michaelmas term last past commence his action of trespass against the said Oliver for entering into the said galleries so built and other the premises ... in [the King's Bench]. And [Samwell] ... did then also exhibit his bill of complaint into [the] ... Court of Chancery against the said Oliver and his wife and the said Francis Langley and others. Depending [i.e. pending] which suits, the said Francis Langley nothing regarding the penalties and forfeitures provided and set forth against unlawful maintenance, champerty and buying of pretended rights and titles, nor the unlawful maintenance of any suits in any ... courts of records, the said Oliver and Susan did in Michaelmas term last past [1599] or shortly after ... pretend title to the said galleries and new buildings then being in the possession of [Samwell] ... And thereupon [the Woodliffes] did abouts Christmas last past[1] bargain and sell to the said Francis Langley all the right, estate and title ... in the said galleries or new buildings erected by [Samwell] ...

[1] Samwell seems not to have known yet that the Woodliffe–Langley lease was sealed on 7 November 1599.

(c) Langley invades the playhouse, 13 December 1599

[Samwell declared in his interrogatories:] After such unlawful conveyance so made and contrived of the said galleries and buildings to the said Francis Langley, he, the said Francis Langley, being a man heretofore questioned and convicted in your majesty's high court of Star Chamber for many offences and being a man also well known to be a common disturber of your majesty's subjects by prosecuting suits of sinister vexation of your subjects and upon buying of many other pretended rights and titles to lands and tenements and of divers debts and rights in actions of divers of your Majesty's subjects, did abouts the 13th day of December last past, being accompanied with the said Susan [Woodliffe] and one Owen Roberts, Alexander Foxley, John Johnson, Peter Boulton and Anthony Strayles,[1] most forcibly with bills, staves, swords and daggers enter into the possession of the said premises ...

[1] Boulton and Strayles were 'servants' to Foxley and Johnson (see below).

(d) Langley invades the playhouse, 16 December 1599

[Samwell declared in the interrogatories:] And not so satisfied, the said Francis Langley intending by vexation to oppress [Samwell], ... the said Francis Langley, Owen Roberts, Anthony Strayles, being accompanied with the said Alexander Foxley, John Johnson and Peter Boulton, all armed with weapons as swords, daggers, rapiers, pistols and other weapons, did abouts the 16th day of December last past in the night-time of the said day, abouts seven of the clock in the afternoon, most riotously and forcibly enter into the said dwelling house of [Samwell] ... called the Boar's Head and then and there, with their weapons drawn, did assault [Samwell] ... and Richard Samwell, your subject's only son and child, and did then and there very sore beat and hurt [Samwell] ... and his son in their arms and legs and divers parts of their bodies. And intending to murder and kill [Samwell], ... they, the said riotous persons, did in the dark throw divers daggers and other weapons at [Samwell] ... and his son, which weapons, hardly missing, ... did stick in the walls of the said house so as [Samwell] ... and his son hardly escaped [with] their lives by shifting and flying away from their assaults.

[Samwell asked Langley in the interrogatories:] Did you procure Anthony Strayles, Alexander Foxley, John Johnson and Peter Boulton, all armed, in or abouts the 16th day of December last past in the night-time of the said day riotously to enter into the said messuage or inn? And did you or any of the said persons then and there assault and hurt the complainant and Richard Samwell, his son, and what weapons had they then and there, and who was it that did hurt the said complainant and his son, or either of them? And did you or any of the said riotous persons in the night-time of the said day throw a dagger at the complainant or his son to the intent to have hurt them, or one of them, and who was it that did throw the said dagger? And for what intent and upon what occasion, as you know or have heard, was their assembly then and there against the complainant and his servants?

[And Langley deposed:] He ... did not to his remembrance procure Anthony Strayles, Alexander Foxley, John Johnson or Peter Boulton, or any of them, to enter into the said messuage or inn upon or about the 16th day of December last past, or in the night-time of the said day. Neither did this defendant, nor any of the said persons to his knowledge, ... assault or hurt the complainant or Richard Samwell, his son. But this defendant saith that upon or about the said 16th day of December the said Foxley and Johnson, being the marshal's men, ... accompanied with the said Strayles and Boulton, their servants, as they said, came to the said inn upon the possession of this defendant, where the said Samwell, the complainant, was and there did arrest ... Samwell at the suit of the said Woodliffe, who at the first did yield unto the said arrest and promised them to put in bail and afterwards, being gone out of this defendant's presence towards his own house, was rescued by his son, Richard Samwell, and others his servants, who, as this defendant hath heard, did shrewdly beat the said marshal's men and their servants. And further than that neither he, this defendant, nor any other to his knowledge, did about the same time throw a dagger at the complainant or any other as in the interrogatory is supposed. And [he] saith that he, this deponent, for his own part, had not any weapon at that time nor doth usually carry any weapons at all. And what weapons any of the other persons had at that time he saith he doth not remember.

(e) Langley invades the playhouse, 24 December 1599

[Samwell declared in his bill:] Abouts Christmas last past, the said Francis Langley, for further vexation to [Samwell] ... and his people, did conspire with the said Foxley and Johnson, Owen Roberts, Anthony Strayles and Peter Boulton to arrest [Samwell] ... and all his servants, without cause of suit into your majesty's Court of Marshalsea, to the end, only by colour of those troubles and arrests and the charges thereof, to compel [Samwell] ... to agree with the said Langley and to yield to his desires. According to which confederacy ... the said Foxley, Johnson, Boulton and Strayles the 24th day of December last past forcibly entered into the said inn called the Boar's Head and then and there, being a stage play, the said riotous persons, together with Owen Roberts, Francis Langley, Susan Woodliffe and others, most forcibly gathered and took away the money of those persons that were to go up into the said galleries to the said stage play, amounting to the value of £4 or thereabouts, and the said Foxley and Johnson, Bolton and Strayles then and there alleged that they had a warrant from the lords of your majesty's most honourable privy council, or some of them, authorising them thereby to take and arrest [Samwell] . . . and his son and one Winifred, the wife of [Samwell's] . . . son, having a young infant then of the age of three weeks or thereabouts[1] sucking at her breast, and Edward Willys, [Samwell's] . . . servant, at which time they did arrest . . . the said Winifred and did . . . show some paper as a warrant to carry her away, by colour whereof they did then and there carry away the said Winifred into the county of Surrey and her detained in the house of the said Foxley in Southwark with her said young infant until [Samwell] . . . did put in bail to answer to such suits as should be objected, [on] which warrant the said Foxley and Johnson, or one of them, if they had any, forged or caused to be forged the name or names of some of the lords of your majesty's privy council. And thereupon [Samwell] . . . paid unto the said Johnson and Foxley for the said arrest of [Samwell] . . . and his son and the said Winifred, his wife, the sum of £4 or thereabouts. And afterwards the said Foxley, Johnson and Boulton arrested the said Edward Willys, servant to [Samwell], . . . and him detained long in the prison of the Marshalsea, which money they took by extortion directly against your majesty's laws to the sum of £8 or thereabouts, or else [Samwell] . . . and his son should not have been enlarged out of the said prison called the Marshalsea, which the said Johnson and Foxley claimed as due to them for their fees for the said arrests of your said subject and his servants and family as aforesaid, being indeed taken by extortion and unlawful corruption by colour of their offices and not for any due fees to them due to be paid. Which suits were only practised by the said Francis Langley and others by his procurement . . . (the defendants . . . not being any of your majesty's household [the ordinary clientele of the Marshalsea Court]) . . . for vexation to put [Samwell] . . . to charges.

[Samwell asked Langley in the interrogatories:] Did you in or abouts the 23rd or 24th day of December last past, being accompanied with the said Susan Woodliffe, Owen Roberts and Anthony Strayles and others, forcibly with weapons enter into the possession of the said premises? . . . And did those persons then enter by your means, and to what end as you remember, and what money was then gathered by you and carried away and by what title?

[And Langley deposed:] Neither he, this defendant, nor any other in his company did in or about the 23rd or 24th day of December last forcibly with weapons enter into the possession of the premises. But this defendant confesseth that upon or about the 24th day of December last he did set Anthony Strayles to gather money there of such as came then hither to hear the play and saith that they did gather so much money as their part came to, 5s or thereabouts, as this defendant now remembreth, and that they did so gather the same money for that the said galleries sat upon this defendant's ground, as he hopeth to prove.

[Roberts deposed:] This deponent saith that upon or about the time . . . mentioned [23 or 24 December] this deponent, being in Francis Langley's work in part of the said inn, he was sent for by the said Langley to come to open a door at the stair's foot leading up to the said galleries. And thereupon this deponent came thither, and . . . [there were no more] but the said Langley, and they, being without weapons, did set their hands to the said door and did thrust it open. And so this deponent departed, and otherwise neither he, this deponent, nor any other in his . . . [company], did about the 23rd or 24th day of December last forcibly with any weapons enter into the possession of the premises, neither did this deponent gather any . . . [money] there at that time.

[1] The child was Rebecca, baptised 11 November 1599, hence about six weeks old at the time: LMA, P93/MRY/1 (the parish register).

(f) Langley invades the playhouse, 26 December 1599

[Samwell declared in his bill:] The said Francis Langley, . . . after the last day of Christmas last past, being accompanied with the said Owen Roberts, Alexander Foxley and Peter Boulton, Anthony Johnson [*i.e.* Strayles], John Johnson and Susan Woodliffe most forcibly and riotously entered into the said galleries and rooms and cut part of the said galleries down with axes and saws. And [they] did break the doors of the said galleries and . . . buildings [and] would have most forcibly and unlawfully cut and pulled down the same if they had been suffered to do, directly against your majesty's laws and statutes.

[Langley said in his reply to the bill:] He did command . . . Owen Roberts, being a carpenter and working in other work of this defendant's in some parcel of the said inn, . . . to leave that work and to go to cut down quarters [*i.e.* studs] and boards in the wall of the new gallery built in the said great court for to make a doorway from this defendant's house into the said gallery, which the said Owen quietly did without wrong to the plaintiff [Samwell] and, in his understanding, without offence to the law.

[And Roberts said in his reply to the bill:] He did neither use force nor unlawfully do any act to his knowledge. And if in the cutting down of the said quarters and boards mentioned in the answer of the said Francis Langley, by the commandment of the said Langley, he, . . . Owen Roberts, did commit an offence, it is more than this defendant conceiveth.

[Samwell asked Langley and Roberts in the interrogatories:] Did you take or procure any money to be taken on St Stephen's Day last past [26 December 1599] of those that came to the said galleries to see the said plays then and there . . . ? And what title had you to do the same, and why did you and Strayles and the said Owen Roberts and Susan Woodliffe stand there at the gallery doors to take the money of those that came in to see the said plays . . . ? And did the said defendant, Owen Roberts, break open a door in the said galleries with an axe abouts Christmas last past, and did the said Owen Roberts with axes, chisels, saws and other tools cut down the walls of the said galleries and make a new door, saying, 'Who dare deny the same', and was the said Langley, Strayles, Susan Woodliffe and the said Owen Roberts then present at the doing thereof?

[Langley deposed:] He did not gather or procure any money to be gathered or taken of any person or persons that came to the said galleries to see the play upon St Stephen's Day last past, but saith that he and the said Strayles did offer to gather money the same day of such as came hither to see the said play but were refused by the said Richard Samwell the younger, son to the complainant. And . . . the reason why they did so offer to gather money of such as came to the said galleries that day was for that the said galleries do stand upon this defendant's ground, as he, this defendant hopeth to prove. And this defendant further saith that the said Owen Roberts did by the commandment of this defendant cut down certain quarters in the end of the said galleries with such tools as carpenters do use in such case and made a doorway into the said galleries. And [he] saith that he, this defendant, or the said Owen Roberts by his appointment, did pull open one of the said gallery doors about Christmas last without resistance, and saith that it may be he did use such speeches as in the interrogatory are mentioned but saith there was none present at the cutting down of the said quarters and making of the said door but this defendant and the said Owen Roberts, being a carpenter.

[And Roberts deposed:] He . . . did neither take nor procure any money to be taken upon St Stephen's Day last past of any that came to the said gallery or to see the play. Neither did this deponent stand at any door to the intent to gather any money. But this deponent saith that about Christmas last he was commanded by the said Langley to cut down a wall and to make a doorway into the said galleries, which this deponent did accordingly with such tools as are necessarily used in such like works and no other. And . . . there was nobody present to the cutting down of the said wall but this deponent and the said Langley, . . . being without weapons. And [he] saith that as this deponent was cutting down the said wall the complainant's son came unto them and did forbid this deponent to work there, and thereupon the said Langley willed this deponent to go forward in his said work and he would bear him out in it, but neither he, this deponent, nor any other in his hearing did utter any such words as in the interrogatory is mentioned nor any words to such effect.

(g) Arrests

[Samwell declared in his bill:] The said Alexander Foxley and John Johnson, servants unto Sir Thomas Gerrard, knight, marshal of your majesty's household, . . . [affirmed on 16 December] that they had process out of the Marshal's Court for your majesty's household to arrest [Samwell] . . . and his son at the suit of the said Langley and Woodliffe; whereas in truth they only before conspired upon their pretensed malice to kill and murder [Samwell] . . . and his son, or one of them, to satisfy and revenge the malice of the said Langley . . . conceived against [Samwell]

... for denying to enjoy the said new buildings. Whereupon [Samwell], ... understanding that the said Foxley and Johnson pretended arrests, did put in sureties to answer to any actions brought against [Samwell] ... in the said court ...

One Richard Bishop, a child of the age of eight years, declared [*i.e.* sued] upon an action of *ejectione firme* against [Samwell's] ... servant, Edward Willys, in your majesty's Court [of] Marshalsea for ejecting the said Bishop out of the said house called the Boar's Head.[1] And no other declaration was had against [Samwell] ... and the other persons arrested ([Samwell's] ... servants), whose charges [Samwell] ... paid. Which actions was [*sic*] ... not tryable in your majesty's Court of Marshalsea but tryable at your majesty's common laws. For which suits [Samwell] ... hath little remedy elsewhere than before your majesty's ... most gracious high court [of Star Chamber for the] ... wrongful arrests ... at the suit of the said Langley and Woodliffe and for other arrests had and made against [Samwell] ... and his servants at the suit of the said Bishop and at the suit of the [said] Strayles to the number of ... seven[2] arrests in the said Court of the ... Marshalsea ... [And Strayles] and Johnson arrested ... [Samwell] and his son and servants to make their [Strayles and Johnson's] gain and [Samwell's] ... spoil to his utter undoing, and no suit there prosecuted or perused to be good. And ... [Samwell's] ... son ... in Michaelmas term last past ... [was] bound to the peace in your majesty's Court of [King's] ... Bench at Westminster and had put in sufficient sureties there, whereat the said Francis Langley, knowing the same, for vexation sake procured a *supplicavit*[3] against ... [Samwell] in your majesty's high Court of Chancery to be further there bound to the peace at his suit in abuse of your majesty's laws, for very vexation. And after, [he] procured the riots ... of purpose to cause [Samwell] ... and his son to break the said several recognisances [*i.e.* bonds] for the peace ...

And the said Anthony Strayles and Langley, ... Foxley, Johnson and Boulton gave out words that when they wanted money they would arrest [Samwell] ... or his servants to supply their wants to pay their rents and charges if [Samwell] ... or his servants went out of the doors into the yard or elsewhere. And also they affirmed ... that they had arrested many persons within short time before to answer in your majesty's Marshal's Court, who had been undone by the charges of the fee of every arrest which they took, amounting to the sum of 9s 8d for every arrest and other charges. And neither ... those persons arrested or the plaintiffs therein [were] servants to your majesty. Nor [was] any suit prosecuted, nor any costs upon the non-suit of any action could be recovered ... By colour of which several suits [Samwell] ... hath ... been put [to] the expenses of £40 sithence Michaelmas last past, and the said Langley refuseth to bring any action at the common law but useth other men's names ... for the said arrests in the said Marshal's Court without their privity or knowledge and without cause of action.

And the said Foxley, Johnson and Peter Boulton, not so satisfied, but upon the 4th day of this instant month of April [1600] ... did by the practice and procurement of the said Langley again arrest the said Richard Samwell, [Samwell's] ... son, upon ... [a] supposed warrant in the names of the lords of your majesty's most honourable privy council, or some of them, having in truth no such warrant to do the same, and then and there brought [Samwell's] . . . son to the prison of the Marshalsea, but they refused to show the said warrant nor any warrant for the said arrest or otherwise to accept any bail for the arrest of [Samwell's] . . . son to answer to any action, and by colour of that arrest they do detain [Samwell's] . . . son in the said prison of the Marshalsea. And . . . Johnson and Boulton being commanded by one Rowland Rosse, [Samwell's] . . . servant, to see the warrant of the lords of your majesty's council to arrest the said Richard Samwell the younger, the said Johnson and his fellow presently, near unto [Samwell's] . . . house [called the Boar's] Head without Aldgate, did most riotously assault the said Rowland Rosse and with their weapons and fists did then and there sore beat, wound and evil intreat the said Rowland Rosse, . . . and then and there likewise they did assault and sore beat the said Winifred, threatening to arrest her also with the said forged warrant, which they afterwards would have done if she had not flown and shifted away. [Samwell and] his family are enforced to keep their houses to avoid the continual arrests and excessive charges of those suits and arrests, being too great a spoil to be suffered.

[The Woodliffes replied:] These defendants say to the multiplicity of suits objected in the bill, that that is not in their judgement any offence, for that multiplicity of wrongs cannot otherwise, to their understanding, be righted. And if any of these have just cause hereof to complain, it is these defendants, for they say that the complainant, without any good cause hath caused the said defendant Oliver Woodliffe to be arrested by a bailiff of Middlesex upon an action of trespass [in the King's Bench] as he was coming to his learned counsel for the penning and engrossing of this his answer, to his great charge, discredit, vexation and hinderance and to the manifest contempt of this most honourable court. [And they plead innocent to] all . . . the offences and misdemeanours laid by the said bill to these defendants or to either of their charge . . .

[In his reply to the bill, Langley said:] And further this defendant saith to the multiplicity of suits objected in the bill, it is not, in his judgement, any offence, for that multiplicity of wrongs cannot otherwise be (to his understanding) righted.

[In their reply to the bill, Foxley and Johnson said:] They [are] . . . but poor men and inferior officers of the Marshalsea of our sovereign lady the Queen . . . And first, the said Alexander Foxley . . . saith that he hath often arrested the plaintiff [Samwell] at many men's suits by writs out of the Court of the Marshalsea and hath taken the ordinary fees every time for the knight marshal, which is due and accustomed and hath been ever taken time out of memory of man . . . And other . . . than due fees he hath not . . . taken. And these defendants, Alexander Foxley and John Johnson, say that at or about the time that the riots complained of against them in the bill are laid to their charge to be committed, they did lawfully and peaceably execute the writs of the said Court of Marshalsea and thereby arrested the parties therein commanded to be arrested, without doing any riot or offence against the peace, as they doubt not will manifestly appear to this honourable court . . .

[Samwell asked Langley in the interrogatories:] Did any by your procurement arrest the said Richard Samwell [the younger] . . . and Winifred, his wife, and Edward Willys, the complainant's [Samwell's] servants? And if you so did arrest them, upon what action were they arrested and when and how often and at whose suits, as you remember? And what money was taken of them or either of them, or of the complainant for those arrests, and what fees they claim and take of the plaintiff for those arrests, as you remember, or any other by your privity or consent? And did you or any other with your knowledge forge or cause to be forged any warrant soever in the name of the lords of her majesty's honourable council . . . sithence Christmas last past, whereby the said complainant, his son or any other of his servants or household were arrested? And how many arrests have you made and caused to be made before and sithence Christmas last past? And what warrants have you, or any other by your privity, whereby the said complainant, his son and Winifred, the plaintiff's son's wife, and others of the plaintiff's household have been arrested? And how many arrests have been made by you, or any other by your privity, upon the plaintiff and his household before and sithence Christmas last past? And what fees have been paid by the plaintiff for the said several arrests by your means or privity and upon what actions? . . . And whether have you said you would undo the plaintiff by arrests?

[Langley deposed:] About Christmas last past or somewhat before, the said Richard Samwell the younger was arrested two several times, whereof one was at the suits of Richard Bishop and the other at the suit of Thomas Wolleston upon action of trespass . . . upon such grounds as this defendant had let unto the said Bishop and Wolleston, and saith that about the same time Richard [i.e. Edward] Willys was also arrested upon an action of trespass at the suit of the said Bishop and be in suit at this instant. And [he] saith that this defendant was acquainted with the said arrests but neither this defendant nor any by his procurement did arrest the said Winifred as in the interrogatory is supposed. Neither doth this defendant know what money was taken or demanded for fees for any of the said arrests. And this defendant further saith that neither he, this defendant, nor any other to his knowledge, did forge or cause any warrant or warrants to be forged in the name of the lords of her majesty's privy council . . . whereby the said plaintiff [Samwell] or his son or any other of his servants or household were arrested. Neither doth this defendant know or remember of any more arrests made upon the complainant or any of his servants or household than such as before he hath set down, though one action which this defendant caused to be brought against the complainant for certain goods which he wrongfully holden from this defendant, but what money the said complainant hath paid for the said several arrests he saith he knoweth not. And [he] saith that he did never say that he would undo the complainant by arrests nor did use any words to such effect.

[Samwell also asked Langley in the interrogatories:] Did you enter any actions in the Court of the Marshalsea against the complainant and Richard Samwell, the plaintiff's son, and Winifred, his wife, and Edward Willys? And at whose suits were those actions brought against them and for what causes? And who procured these actions to be entered? And ... was there any action tried against the said Willys at the suit of Richard Bishop and upon what actions? And who made your declarations thereupon in the Marshal's Court upon an *ejectione firme* against the said Edward Willys at the suit of Richard Bishop, and who gave you directions therein? And ... was Richard Bishop privy to the entering of these actions and suits in his name and prosecuting the same suits? And what age is the said Bishop and what estate had he in the said messuage or house?

[To which Langley deposed:] This defendant saith ... that the said actions of trespass are now depending in the said Marshal's Court at the suit of the said Richard Bishop against the complainant's son and the said Willys, and saith that the said declarations were drawn by an attorney of that court and by ... [another] there whose names this defendant more remembreth not. And [he] saith that the said Richard Bishop was privy to the entering and prosecuting of so many actions as were entered in his name, and further saith that the said Bishop is about twenty years of age or upwards and had a lease of parcel of the said inn from the said Wolleston bearing date the 15th day of December last [1599] as by the same lease doth and may appear.

[Samwell further asked Langley:] Hath there been six actions of late entered in the marshal's court at your suit and at the suit of the said Bishop and at the suit of the said Woodliffe and at the suit of one John Johnson against the complainant, his son and wife, and the said Edward Willys and Rowland Rosse, the complainant's servants ... ? And did you procure actions and suits to be entered and prosecuted against them at your charges ... ? And did you bring those actions of purpose to vex the complainant and his family and to charge them with the fees of arrests ... ? And did you cause Richard Samwell the younger to be arrested at the suit of one Wolleston into her majesty's Court of [King's] ... Bench ... ? And what was the cause of the suit of the said Wolleston as you know, and did you procure the same and for what cause?

[And Langley deposed:] He ... did not enter, or cause any actions to be entered, against the complainant or any other in the interrogatory named other than such as before he hath declared. Neither did this defendant bear the charges of the said actions other than of such as concerned the title of the said inn or trespasses there ... upon such grounds as this defendant had interest in. And [he] denieth that he did bring the said actions of purpose to vex the complainant or his family, or to charge them with the fears of arrests. But [he] confesseth he was acquainted with the arresting of the said Richard Samwell the younger at the suit of the said Wolleston into her majesty's Court of [King's] ... Bench upon an action of trespass ... upon the premises as before is declared.

[Samwell further asked Langley:] Did you know that the defendants Alexander Foxley, John Johnson and Peter Boulton did arrest the said Winifred upon any warrant from any of the lords of the council or from the Lord Chief Justice of England, and had they any such warrant to arrest her, and did you procure the same arrests, and did you affirm that you had such a warrant to arrest the complainant or his servants?

[And Langley deposed:] He hath heard that Alexander Foxley, John Johnson and Peter Boulton did arrest the said Winifred by a warrant out of the Marshal's Court for rescuing of the complainant when he was arrested, but this defendant did not procure the said Winifred to be arrested, neither did this defendant affirm that he had any such warrant or other warrant to arrest the complainant or his servants.

[1] That is, Willys had ejected Bishop from a part of the Boar's Head on which Bishop claimed to have a valid lease. So Bishop obtained a writ (*ejectione firme*) to eject Willys and prosecuted it in the Marshalsea Court.
[2] Only 'ven' survives of the word, which, therefore, could also be 'eleven'.
[3] A writ asking a court to order Samwell (in this case) to make a bond guaranteeing that he would keep the peace against Langley.

375 Bishop accuses Browne and Mago of damaging posts and fixed seats at the Boar's Head, 20 May 1600

PRO, (a) KB27/1364/m. 259; (b) KB27/1367/m. 199d. See Berry, *Boar's Head Playhouse*, 45–6, 48–9

Langley's creature, Richard Bishop, filed a lawsuit against Browne and his carpenter, John Mago, in King's Bench in the autumn of 1600. Bishop, who had leased part of the Boar's Head yard from Langley's other creature, Thomas Wolleston, pursued his case to a trial, but he did not appear on 21 November 1600, when the trial was to take place. He filed the lawsuit again in the spring of 1601 and this time abandoned it at an earlier stage. His case was as follows:

(a) Autumn 1600

Robert Browne and John Mago [who were probably making repairs to Browne's galleries] ... came on 20 May 1600 ... with force and arms to the house of the said Richard [Bishop] in ... Whitechapel [*i.e.* the Boar's Head] ... and broke and entered. And then and there they threw and cast down certain posts and fixed seats in the said house and made mayhem in the same house to the value of 100s. They then and there seized and conveyed ['apportauer*unt*'; *i.e.* stole the seats and posts?] and committed other enormities against the peace of the now Queen to the damage of the same Richard of £20.

(b) Spring 1601

On 15 December 1599, ... Robert Browne ... with a certain Thomas Wolleston,[1] demised and granted to Richard Bishop a messuage called the Boar's Head with a garden in Whitechapel, to hold from that date for ... three years, and Richard entered and took possession of the same. And afterwards, on 20 May 1600, Robert Browne came with force and arms and entered the same and ejected and expelled Richard from possession and committed upon him other enormities against the Queen's peace to his damage of £20.

[1] Bishop must have been wrong to associate Browne with this transaction. Langley himself said only that his other creature, Wolleston, had leased it to Bishop (see 374g).

376 Francis Langley forfeits his first bond, and Woodliffe sues Richard Langley, 19 January – 12 February 1601

PRO, CP40/1655/m. 724d. See Berry, *Boar's Head Playhouse*, 46, 47–8. Richard Langley had guaranteed the bond, which was for £100 or if forfeit (as it was after 2 November 1600) £200.

[Woodliffe declared to the court:] that on 12 November [1599] . . . he [Richard Langley] was obliged, and he conceded by a certain writing held by Oliver [Woodliffe], that he would pay the said £200 when required, but when it was required Richard did not pay it, to Oliver's damage of £40 . . . [Then follows the 'condition' of the first bond, see 373b.]

Richard says that he does not owe Oliver because he did pay him £100 on 2 November at the said mansion-house, the Boar's Head . . . The said Oliver says that on that day Richard did not pay him £100 but owed it according to the terms of the writing.

Trial was set for the end of April 1601, but on the appointed day Richard Langley did not appear. The jury decided that Woodliffe should have only his debt of £100 and £7 in costs and damages and awarded him a judgement for £107.

377 Francis and Richard Langley seek a way to escape Woodliffe and the Boar's Head, late April – May 1601

PRO, C33/99/fos. (a) 464v, (b) 526, (c) 577v in the A book, and C33/100/fos. 452v, 518, 564v in the B book. See Berry, *Boar's Head Playhouse*, 48–50.

The two Langleys sued Woodliffe in Chancery at the end of April 1601 to stop Woodliffe from proceeding with his judgement in Common Pleas, and, in general, to escape from the Boar's Head. The bill and answers seem not to survive, but numerous court orders do.

(a) 6 May 1601

This court was this present day informed by . . . the plaintiffs' [the Langleys'] counsel [that] . . . he [Francis Langley] . . . cannot quietly enjoy the said lease [of Woodliffe's part of the Boar's Head] by reason of an encumbrance done by the defendant [Woodliffe].[1] And yet the defendant now prosecuteth suit at the common law against Richard Langley upon the first of the . . . bonds, notwithstanding the defendant doth offer by his answer [to this lawsuit] to deliver up the said three bonds and to repay to the plaintiff the said £100 [that Langley paid in cash] so as he [Woodliffe] may have his said lease, . . . which the plaintiff is likewise content to do, and also to deliver up his said bond of 1,000 marks, so as he [Woodliffe] may pay up[2] his said bonds and the said money which he hath received, together also with such costs and charges as he [Langley] hath been at in and about the building and repairing of the said house. Wherefore, it was most humbly desired that some of the masters of this court might hear and end the cause to that effect, which this court thought reasonable. It is, therefore, ordered that this day sevennight be given to the defendant to show cause wherefore the matter should not be referred to Master Hunt, one of the masters of this court, for the purpose aforesaid, and wherefore all suits at the common law should not be stayed. And in the meantime . . . the same suits are stayed.

[1] The encumbrance was, no doubt, his being unable to get rid of Samwell and then Browne.
[2] *i.e.*, cancel the bonds and pay back the money. For 'pay up', the B book has 'have up'.

(b) 20 May 1601

[In response, Woodliffe's counsel tried:] to show cause wherefore the matter should not be referred to Master Hunt . . . and wherefore the defendant's suits at the common law upon the bonds in question should not be stayed . . . But [he] showed no such cause as this court allowed of. It is, therefore, ordered that the matter be referred to Master Hunt to the end he may consider of the cause and make report to this court . . . And in the meantime, . . . the defendant's said proceedings at the common law upon the said bonds are stayed.

(c) 22 May 1601

[Woodliffe's counsel returned to the court,] alledging divers causes wherefore the said defendant [Woodliffe] should be at liberty to proceed at the common law upon the bond in question, . . . and . . . the plaintiff's [the Langleys'] counsel speaking for maintaining of the former order . . . and alledging that the said defendant hath refused to attend Master Hunt: . . . it is ordered that Master Dr Carew and Master George Carew, two of the masters of this court,[1] shall consider the whole state of the cause . . . and thereupon make report to this court what they think meet to be done . . . And in the meantime the defendant's said proceedings at the common law is stayed . . . And if the said masters of this court shall think it . . . meet, the plaintiffs shall bring the £100 into this court . . . which should have been paid unto this defendant in November last.

[1] Dr Matthew Carew (father of Thomas Carew, the poet) was one of the oldest and most experienced masters and his nephew, George Carew, one of the youngest and least experienced. Francis Langley and Woodliffe now set about negotiating before them how Langley might return his part of the Boar's Head to Woodliffe.

378 Browne argues in Chancery that the galleries belong to him by a verbal lease, late April – June 1601

PRO, (a) C33/99/fo. 473v in the A book, C33/100/fo. 461 in the B book; (b, c) C24/290/3, interrogatory 4, Samwell 4. See Berry, *Boar's Head Playhouse*, 48, 50

In this lawsuit, Browne sued Woodliffe, the Langleys and Bishop, probably as a response to Bishop's two futile lawsuits in the King's Bench (375). Browne's bill and the answers seem

478   Playhouses, 1560–1660

not to survive, but a court order, Browne's interrogatories, and the depositions of five of his witness do. Browne's arguments appear especially in his interrogatories and in the deposition of his ally, the younger Samwell.

(a) The court order, 9 May 1601

Robert Browne plaintiff, Richard . . . and Francis Langley, defendants. Saturday next [16 May] is given to the defendant to make answer or else an attachment is awarded against him.

(b) One of Browne's questions

Do you know or have you heard that in consideration of the pulling down and the new building and setting up again of the said galleries and rooms as aforesaid, he, the said Oliver Woodliffe, then agreed with the said Richard Samwell [the elder] and by word did demise and let unto him, the said Samwell, the said great yard, galleries and rooms so by him to be built in the said great yard as aforesaid from that time forward for and during the whole residue of the said term of years granted in and by the said indenture of lease made by the said Oliver Woodliffe and Susan, his wife, unto the said Richard Samwell . . . without any rent to be paid for the same save only the said £40 by the year to him reserved in and by the said former indenture of lease? . . . And about what time was the same lease parole so made?

(c) The younger Samwell's answer, 11 June 1601

At the time of the said agreement betwixt the said Richard Samwell [the elder] and the said defendant, Woodliffe, for the pulling down of the said little galleries, the said Woodliffe did agree and promise to and with the said Richard Samwell that in consideration that he the said Richard Samwell should pull down the same and set up larger galleries . . . that he, the said Richard Samwell, should enjoy the said yard and galleries so to be built and set up peaceably, together with the rest of the premises demised as aforesaid, for and during the residue of the said term of years that then were to come without paying any rent for the same save only the said yearly rent of £40 reserved upon the lease before mentioned . . . And this he knoweth to be true because he was also present at the said agreement betwixt his father and the said Woodliffe.

379   **Browne ceases to pay the half-profits of the western gallery to Woodliffe or Langley, 22 August 1601**

PRO, (a) C33/101/fo. 207v and (b) C33/103/fo. 43–43v in the A book (C33/102/fo. 249v and C33/104/fo. 44v in the B book); (c) Req.2/466/pt 2[/1], the bill and reply. See Berry, *Boar's Head Playhouse*, 51, 65–7. This matter is reported in two court orders in Langley's case against Woodliffe in Chancery (377) and in Woodliffe's lawsuit of May 1603 against Browne in Requests.

(a) A court order, 15 January 1602

Mr Ayloff [Woodliffe's counsel said] that ... one Browne, who is tenant of part of the house or inn in question [the Boar's Head], taketh the profits of the whole house and payeth nothing either to the plaintiffs [the Langleys] or defendant [Woodliffe] for the same.

(b) A court order, 15 October 1602

Mr Ayloff [said that] ... one Robert Browne, tenant of part of the said inn, perceiving controversy between the plaintiff [Francis Langley] and defendant [Woodliffe], hath by force entered into [*i.e.* has ceased paying for] the said stage, tiring-house and galleries for the which the said Browne paid before better than £4 a week ... and ... hath ... made oath and thereby confessed that he is to render an account to the plaintiff or defendant of the profits made therein to him that shall prevail in suit.

(c) Woodliffe's bill, 20 May 1603

The said Browne paid unto your subject [Woodliffe] £6 8s 8d ... [but] doth detain from ... [Woodliffe] great sums of money, which amount to better than £200, due for the stage, tiring-house and galleries, to his great loss and hindrance and utter undoing forever unless your majesty of your gracious pity and clemency extend your relief unto your highness's subject [Woodliffe] in this behalf ... And ... the said Browne hath and doth detain in his hands the sum of £5 the week for the stage, tiring-house and galleries which hath been due unto your subject ever since 22 August [1601][1] ...

[1] Hence, Woodliffe supposed here and in (b) that the Boar's Head was used for about 41 – or, using his figure in (a), 51 – of the 82 weeks from 22 August 1601 to 19 March 1603 (when all the playhouses closed for a protracted time).

(d) Browne's reply, 30 May 1603

That ... [he] hath detained from the complainant [Woodliffe] great sums of money which doth amount to £200 due for the stage, tiring-house and galleries, as the complainant in his bill hath most impudently surmised, and that ... this defendant doth detain in his hands the sum of £5 a week for the stage, tiring-house and galleries, which hath been due to the complainant ever sithence 22 August [1601] ... in manner and form as by the complainant [is alleged] in his bill is most untruly surmised.

380 Browne leases the Boar's Head to Worcester's men for shares in their plays, late summer 1601

See 383

To guarantee payment of the shares, Browne took bonds from six members of the company, including John Duke and the playwright, Thomas Heywood. These bonds led to two lawsuits, one in which he seems to have sued them at common law in the autumn of 1601 and the other in which they sued him in Chancery soon after. The two lawsuits apparently survive only in a series of court orders in Chancery.

381 Langley raids the playhouse and Worcester's men agree to pay him £3 a week for twenty weeks, autumn 1601

PRO, (a) Req.2/466/pt 2[/1], the reply; (b–d) C24/304/27, interrogatory 14, Mago 8, 14, Marsh 14. See Berry, *Boar's Head Playhouse*, 51–2. Browne and his allies explained this adventure of Francis Langley's in two lawsuits of 1603: Woodliffe's against Browne in Requests in May, and Browne's against Woodliffe and Richard Langley in Chancery in June and July.

(a) Browne replies to Woodliffe's lawsuit, 30 April 1603

The said Richard Langley[1] ... abouts two years past ... unlawfully entered into the said stage, tiring-house and galleries and offered to disturb the said plays and comedies to be acted on the said stage ... And for fear thereof [he] extorted from the players there divers sums of money to permit the said comedies there quietly to be acted and done by the said players without disturbance of the said Richard Langley, against all right, equity and conscience.

[1] The eye-witnesses, Marsh and Mago, said it was Francis Langley who led the rude fellows. Browne probably mentioned Richard Langley because by 1603, when Browne made the remarks, Francis was dead and Richard was Browne's antagonist.

(b) Browne questions Mago and Marsh, carpenters, July 1603

Did the defendant [Richard Langley] cause rude fellows to break into the tiring-house and on the stage, swearing and threatening to kill any that should come there, and ... were the players enforced by that means to enter into bonds to pay £3 a week from Michaelmas [29 September 1601] or thereabouts until Shrovetide then next following [14–16 February], and what were the words you heard them threaten?

(c) Marsh replies, 25 July 1603

At one time the said Francis Langley (by what means he knoweth not) got the possession of the said stage and tiring-houses from the complainant [Browne] and with a company of rude fellows kept the same, some of them swearing and vowing that they would kill or murder any that should resist them. And this he hath cause to remember for that one of the said company with halberd or suchlike weapon had almost maimed this deponent [Marsh] in the thigh, being then there at work for the complainant [Browne].

(d) Mago replies on the same day

At one time . . . the said Francis Langley or his assigns did . . . get . . . by force [the stage, tiring-house and gallery,] which some rude company . . . [kept], swearing and protesting to kill or slay any that that should resist them . . . And further, . . . some of the company of the players . . . were forced to enter into a bond to pay £3 a week for a certain time, which they were constrained to do because . . . the players for that winter had no other winter house licensed for them to play in. And, as he hath heard, the said weekly payments began at Michaelmas time or thereabouts and were to continue until Shrovetide then next following. And . . . this deponent [Mago] with his man [Marsh] was working in the said great yard for the complainant [Browne] at the time of the said possession taking and before. And one of the said Langley's company with a halberd or suchlike weapon struck at this deponent's servant then working and almost wounded him, but, as God would, he hurt him not.

382 Worcester's men legalise themselves and make the Boar's Head their permanent home, 31 March 1602

CLRO, Remembrancia, II, 189. See Berry, *Boar's Head Playhouse*, 56–7

When Francis Langley ceased to collect his £3 a week in mid-February 1602, Worcester's men evidently decided that they were secure in the Boar's Head. Prompted by one of their patrons, the Earl of Oxford, and perhaps by the other, the Earl of Worcester, the privy council told the Lord Mayor that it had granted 'toleration' to the company, 'and because we are informed the house called the Boar's Head is the place they have especially used and do like best of, we do pray and require you that the said house, namely the Boar's Head, may be assigned unto them'. Three months before, the privy council had decreed that only two companies should play in London in only two playhouses, the Lord Admiral's at the Fortune and the Lord Chamberlain's at the Globe. For the full text of the document, see **59**.

383 Worcester's men quarrel with Browne, he sues them, and they move to the Rose, autumn 1601 – 17 August 1602

PRO, C33/101/fos. (a) 573, (b) 611, (c) 643–43v, (d) 735 in the A book and C33/102/fos. 577v, 616, 648v, 798v in the B book. See Berry, *Boar's Head Playhouse*, 51–2, 58–60

The only documents that survive to explain this confrontation are four orders belonging to Worcester's men's case against Browne in Chancery. In these orders, Worcester's men go by the names of two of their members, John Duke and Thomas Heywood. For their appearance at the Rose, see **348b**.

(a) 13 May 1602

Forasmuch as the defendant [Browne] put in his answer to the plaintiff's [Duke's] bill in Michaelmas term last and yet he, the plaintiff, . . . hath not replied thereunto: therefore the plaintiff is adjudged to pay to the [defendant] . . . 40s costs.

(b) 29 May 1602

William Stavely [Browne's counsel] made oath for the serving of a subpoena on the ... [plaintiff, Duke] for costs, who hath not paid the same. Therefore attachment is awarded against [Duke] by the sheriff of London.

(c) 8 June 1602

Forasmuch as this court was this present day informed by Mr Stavorton, being of the plaintiffs' [Duke's and Heywood's] counsel, which information was also verified by the oath of the said John Duke, that he and the other plaintiffs having exhibited a bill into this court against the defendant [Browne] for the bringing in of six several bonds into this court made by the said plaintiff to the said defendant, he, the said defendant, after his answer made to the said bill, sent unto the plaintiff, and after some conference between him and the plaintiff, he, the said defendant, did promise to deliver up the said bonds unto them. Whereupon the said plaintiff left the further prosecution of their suit ... and therefore did forbear to reply, by means whereof the said defendant hath now ... got costs against the plaintiff ... It is thereupon ordered that the matter shall be retained in this court, ... and Master Dr [Matthew] Carew, one of the masters of this court, shall consider of the said bill and answer and thereupon report to this court whether the said answer be sufficient.

(d) 28 June 1602

Forasmuch as the Lord Keeper [*i.e.* the judge, Sir Thomas Egerton] was this present day informed ... that the suit between the parties ... is for certain bonds which were made between them, being players, for shares due in their plays, which his lordship thinks no meet matter for this court: ... [he] doth order that the matter touching the same bonds be clearly dismissed out of this court and the plaintiffs [Duke, Heywood and others] left to take their remedies for the same elsewhere. And because the defendant [Browne] was put to charge in maintaining his answer, wherewith the plaintiffs found fault and yet the same is found sufficient by Master Dr Carew, ... therefore the plaintiffs shall pay to the defendant 26s 8d [*i.e.* two marks] costs.

384 The Langleys escape from the Boar's Head, July – 15 October 1602

PRO, C33/103/fo. 43–43v in the A book; C33/104/fo. 44v in the B book. See Berry, *Boar's Head Playhouse*, 52–3, 55–6, 58–9, 60–2.

In the autumn of 1601 the Langleys and Woodliffe agreed to a complex scheme by which the Langleys could escape from the Boar's Head, but they did not complete it. Francis Langley escaped by dying early in July 1602. Richard Langley began his escape three months later by agreeing to a compromise that would lead to the end of his lawsuit against Woodliffe in Chancery. See **385–386**.

[A Court Order in Chancery, 15 October 1602:] This court was this present day informed by Mr Ayloff, being of the defendant's [Woodliffe's] counsel, that the matter in question concerning an inn called the Boar's Head is now agreed between the said parties and that the plaintiff [Richard Langley] . . . is to reassign to the defendant the lease of the said inn [free] of all incumbrances and also to deliver each to other all bonds, bills and specialties concerning the same, according to a report of Master Dr Carew and Master George Carew, . . . who heard the said cause. And upon the said agreement, the plaintiff is to deliver to the defendant the possession of the stage, tiring-house and galleries situate on the west side of the great yard of the said inn lately built by the defendant . . . It was therefore desired that an injunction might be awarded against . . . [Robert] Browne and all others in possession of the rooms aforesaid for the said defendant. It is . . . ordered that Master Dr Carew . . . shall . . . consider . . . whether he think fit an injunction shall go against the said Browne for the said defendant['s] possession, and if he think fit then a subpoena shall be awarded [returnable] immediate against the said Browne to show cause why an injunction should not be granted for the defendant['s] possession as aforesaid.

385 A bailiff effectually closes down the Boar's Head, Christmas 1602

PRO, C24/304/27, interrogatories 8, 9, 12, 15. See Berry, *Boar's Head Playhouse*, 61–2

In June 1602 Woodliffe got an elegit by which he could have a bailiff seize Richard Langley's goods to satisfy Woodliffe's judgement for £107. Woodliffe did nothing about his elegit until the Christmas following, when Langley still owned the stage, tiring-house and western gallery. Information about the effect of the elegit comes mainly from four questions Browne asked on 25 July 1603 of his carpenters, Mago and Marsh, who agreed with the point of the questions but could not add anything to them.[1] The questions follow.

[1] Elegits were issued for limited periods. Woodliffe's elegit, which was directed to the sheriff of London, expired first in October, then in November, January and April 1602–3, after which the record trails off. Woodliffe's counsel appeared each time to renew it, and the sheriff, who was also sheriff of Middlesex, reported each time that he had done nothing about it (PRO, CP40/1655/m. 724d).

8. Do you know of the any extent [i.e. seizure of goods] had upon an elegit abouts Christmas last past by the said defendant Oliver Woodliffe against the defendant Richard Langley, . . . and . . . was the said stage, tiring-houses and galleries over the stage extended by that elegit as the possession and estate for years [*i.e.* by lease] of the defendant Richard Langley? . . . And . . . was that extent of covin and confederacy had by sinister counsel to take away by extent the possession of the said stage, tiring-houses and galleries over the stage? . . . And was the suit upon the said obligation brought by the defendant Woodliffe against the defendant Langley by agreement to extend the said stage, tiring-houses and galleries?

9. Did the said defendants [Woodliffe and Langley] practice the said elegit to extend the said premises, or any part thereof, for that they could not recover the

same by any actions [at law], and were all the defendants of conspiracy with that elegit? And . . . did the defendant[s] Sibdall and Langley bear the charge of that elegit and also maintain that suit to dispossess [Browne] . . . of the premises, or any part thereof, by the said covin?

12. Was there any persons in possession of the said tiring-houses and new galleries when the bailiff of the liberty of Stebonheath [*i.e.* Stepney] abouts Christmas last past delivered the possession of the said premises by force of the said elegit, . . . and were those persons removed out of possession at the delivery of such possession by the said bailiff?

15. Did they . . . practice this confederacy about the elegit because they could not recover the premises by due course of law?

386 Woodliffe regains the stage, tiring-house and western gallery from Richard Langley, before 28 January 1603

PRO, C33/103/fo. 346 in the A book, C33/104/fo. 359 in the B book. See Berry, *Boar's Head Playhouse*, 63–4

The evidence is an order in Chancery. Since 'the sum', was the only matter remaining unresolved in the deal by which Richard Langley would escape from the Boar's Head (see **384**), Woodliffe must have got back his parts of the place and cancelled the two remaining bonds. The sum was probably the amount Woodliffe would take to give up his elegit, for the 'umpire', Thomas Walmesley, was a judge of Common Pleas, where the elegit had originated.[1]

[1] Langley evidently did not pay the sum immediately, for Woodliffe was still aiming the elegit at him in April 1603 (see **385**).

Upon the opening of the matter this present day [28 January 1603] by Mr Stavorton, being of the plaintiff's [Richard Langley's] counsel, and by Mr Ayloff, being of the defendant's [Woodliffe's] counsel, it is ordered by assent of the said counsel on both parts that the matter be referred unto Mr Towse and to the said Mr Ayloff to hear, end, and finally determine the sum if they can. If not, that then they certify their differences . . . unto Mr Justice Walmesley, who is required by this court as umpire to end the same, and what order shall be taken by him therein shall be performed by the said parties accordingly.

387 Browne has regained the use of the stage, tiring-house and western gallery, 20 May 1603

PRO, Req.2/466/pt 2[1], (a) the bill; (b) the reply. See Berry, *Boar's Head Playhouse*, 64

(a) Woodliffe's bill, 20 May 1603

The said Robert Browne, a common stage-player . . . hath by force entered in and upon the stage, tiring-house and galleries on the west side of the great yard of the said inn, lately belonging to the said Richard Langley and now belonging to your subject [Woodliffe], . . . and hath and doth detain and keep by force the said stage, tiring-house and galleries on the west side of the said inn without any right, title or interest.

(b) Browne's reply, 30 May 1603

[Browne denied that he] hath by force entered unto the said stage, tiring-houses and galleries and detained and kept the same by force without any right, title or interest . . . [And he remembered how Francis Langley had extorted money from Worcester's men] against all right, equity and conscience, which the complainant [Woodliffe] would by like wrong now exact and get from this defendant and his fellows if he by any undue course might procure the same.

388   The Boar's Head takes leave of the law courts, July, October 1603

Dulwich, MS I, fo. 52. Transcribed in *Henslowe's Diary*, 297; see Berry, *Boar's Head Playhouse*, 64–71

The great plague of 1603–4 drove the Boar's Head out of the law courts. For while Browne and Woodliffe were launching a final flurry of lawsuits against one another from 24 April to July 1603,[1] the plague was on the march in London scattering the theatrical industry, but not Browne, into the countryside. Woodliffe was buried in Whitechapel churchyard on 30 July, only five days after Browne examined witnesses in his final lawsuit, and Browne was buried there on 16 October.[2]

[1] PRO, CP40/1701/m. 1109 (*Browne v. Woodliffe*, 24 April); Req.2/466/pt 2[/1] (*Woodliffe v Browne*, 20 May); C24/304/27 (*Browne v Woodliffe, Henry Sibdall, Richard Langley*; only Browne's interrogatories and two depositions survive, all dated 25 July).
[2] LMA, P93/MRY 1 (registers of St Mary Matfellon).

[Joan Alleyn in London wrote to her absent husband, the actor Edward Alleyn, on 21 October 1603:] About us the sickness doth cease and likely more and more by God's help to cease. All the companies be come home and well for aught we know, but that Browne of the Boar's Head is dead and died very poor; he went not into the country at all.

389   Worcester's men plan to return to the Boar's Head, winter – spring 1603–4

PRO, SP14/2/fo. 247. Transcribed in MSC, 1. 265. See Berry, *Boar's Head Playhouse*, 73

Browne's and Woodliffe's parts of the Boar's Head now belonged to their widows, two Susans, who probably came to some agreement about the use of the place since they seem not to have sued one another. Both soon remarried, Susan Browne an actor, Thomas Greene, and Susan Woodliffe a financier, James Vaughan. Greene, who was a clown, was in the process of joining and becoming the leader of Worcester's men, who were renaming themselves the Queen's men. They drafted a patent – never made official – that confirms them as the Queen's men and proclaims that after the plague they would play 'as well within their now usual houses called the Curtain and the Boar's Head . . . as in any other playhouse not used by others, by the said Thomas Greene elected or by him hereafter to be built'.

390 The Queen's men are at the Boar's Head, 1604–1607, and Prince Charles' (I) men are there, 1609

(a) CLRO, Remembrancia, II, 283; (b) LMA, DL/C/217, pp. 214–17; (c) Leicester Record Office, BR III/2/75/fos. 98–100. Transcribed in (a) MSC, I. 87 (b) Eccles, 'Elizabethan Actors II', 456; (c) Berry, *Boar's Head Playhouse*, 74–5

When the government allowed playing to resume on 9 April 1604 the Queen's men duly reappeared at the Boar's Head, and also at the Curtain. They probably used both places until the autumn of 1607, when they settled into the Red Bull. They were using the Boar's Head (if not also the Curtain) in the winter of 1606–7 and perhaps until the summer following (see 438). The Boar's Head may then have housed the Duke of Lennox's men, and after them Prince Charles' (I) men.[1]

[1] The Duke of Lennox's men seem in 1608 to have become Prince Charles' (I) men (see c): Lennox's men disappeared about when Charles' (I) men appeared, and a member of the former, John Garland, was a leader of the latter.

(a) 12 April 1607

[The Lord Mayor wrote to the Lord Chamberlain, who was the Earl of Suffolk, and in effect, to the privy council, of which the Earl was a member:] Whereas it pleaseth God that the infection of sickness is for these two or three weeks of late somewhat increased in the skirts and confines of this city and by the untimely heat of this season may spread further than can hereafter be easily prevented, my humble desire is that your lordship . . . will vouchsafe your honourable favour in two special points concerning this matter: first, in restraining such common stage plays as are daily shown and exercised and do occasion the great assemblies of all sorts of people in the suburbs and parts adjoining to this city; . . . secondly, whereas it appeareth . . . that the said skirts and out-places of the city are more subject to the infection than any other places, that your honours [*i.e.* the privy council will please to give order to the justices of Middlesex to put in due execution such ordinances as are formerly by your lordships recommend unto them in this behalf, especially that there may be a better care had of Whitechapel, Shoreditch, Clerkenwell [*i.e.* the Boar's Head, Curtain and Red Bull], and such other remote parts than formerly hath been accustomed.

(b) 16 June 1607

[Thomas Greene testified on this day, while he was still living in Whitechapel, presumably at the Boar's Head, that the Queen's men had hired someone to keep the gallery doors] in the winter time last at such time as plays were used to be played and acted at the Boar's Head.

(c) 1609

[A reward given to players who visited Leicester in the summer of 1609:] Item: given to the Prince's players of the Whitechapel, London, 20s.

The Prince must have been Charles, because the players of the other Prince, Henry, had long been established at the Fortune in Golden Lane, St Giles without Cripplegate.

391 The leases fall in, Christmas 1615 and Lady Day 1616, and the playhouse ends, before 23 June 1618

(a) Folger, MS Z.c. 22(23), attachment; (b) PRO, C54/2471/17. See Berry, *Boar's Head Playhouse*, 76–9, 189–90

Samwell and Browne's lease expired at Christmas 1615, and Woodliffe's grand lease at Lady Day 1616. Coincidentally or not, Prince Charles' (I) men joined a consortium in June 1615 to build a new playhouse in Blackfriars, and when that venture proved abortive, they contracted themselves to play at the Hope – on 20 March 1616, when the grand lease on the Boar's Head had only five days to run. From 25 March the Boar's Head belonged to Sir John Poley, the son of the woman who had leased it to Woodliffe, and he set about making it into a housing estate.

(a) 23 June 1618

[In the contract by which Poley enfranchised the Boar's Head from the manor of Stepney, the place is:] All that messuage or tenement called or known by the name of the Boar's Head, now divided into several tenements or cottages, and one barn thereunto adjoining or belonging.

(b) 27 December 1621

[In a contract by which Poley sold the part of the Boar's Head where the playhouse had been to William Browne, citizen and cooper of London, a complex list of holdings includes:] so much of the said Boar's Head ground as lately was builded and known for a tiring-house or stage and two tenements late in the several occupations of Humphrey Plevy and John Walford and have been lately pulled down to be re-edified and builded in a better form.

392 The Boar's Head is remembered, *c.* 1660

Strong, *A Catalogue of Letters ... in the Library at Welbeck*, 226. See Berry, *Boar's Head Playhouse*, 75

[In a letter of advice to Prince Charles (soon to be Charles II), the Marquess of Newcastle remembered the playhouses 'in my time'. He mentioned eight of them and then:] Some [players] played at the Boar's Head and at the Curtain in the fields and some at the Hope ... and some at Whitefriars.

Appendix: The buildings and the theatrical enterprise in them

The evidence comes entirely from legal documents at the PRO, dating from 1600 to 1603. The people who created the documents were usually intent upon something other than the structures or the enterprise, so that the evidence often appears as asides or hints, but there is a great deal of it and almost none is contradictory. Quoted and discussed below are important parts of it.

(a) Woodliffe's (later Langley's) part of the playhouse: the stage, tiring-house and gallery on the west side of the yard

In May 1603, Woodliffe said that his lease of 28 November 1594 required him to spend £100 'in building of the larder, the larder parlour, the well parlour, the coal-house, the oat loft, the tiring-house, and stage'; and when he described the sublease of 13 April 1598 by which he conveyed most of the inn to Richard Samwell, he mentioned 'the building of the west part of the great yard of the said inn, which [he] . . . was tied to build' (Req.2/466/pt2[/1], the bill; see **368, 369a**). Samwell recalled in April 1600 that the sublease allowed Woodliffe to 'build on the west part of the said great yard near adjoining to certain rooms . . . a full yard further in length into the great yard' (STAC5/S74/3, the bill; see **369c**). A court order in October 1602 mentions 'the stage, tiring-house and galleries[1] situate on the west side of the great yard of the said inn lately built by [Woodliffe]' (C33/103/fo. 43–43v; see **384**).

Referring to the rebuilding of the playhouse in 1599, John Mago, the chief carpenter, spoke in February 1600 of 'one storey of that gallery on the west side of the said yard, which . . . [Mago] began to fall in hand withal and to take off the roof' (C24/278/71, no. 4; see **371b**). In July 1603, Mago described Woodliffe's structures as 'the stage, tiring-houses and the galleries over and about the stage with the coverings over them which the said Woodliffe builded' (C24/304/27, no. 3). And in answer to a lawsuit mainly about the profits derived from spectators in Woodliffe's gallery, Browne described it four times in May 1603 as 'the said west galleries over the said stage' (Req.2/466/pt2[1]).

The larder and other non-theatrical places mentioned in the lease of 1594, therefore, were the 'certain rooms' on the west side of the yard in the sublease of 1598, and they amounted to a two-storey building (since it had a loft) that became the tiring-house. The 3 feet of the yard into which Woodliffe could build in 1598 must have been the width of his gallery in the first playhouse; and because he urged that all the galleries, including his own, be made 4 feet wider in the rebuilding of 1599, his rebuilt gallery was probably 7 feet wide (see (b) below). His gallery had a roof in its first form and its second.

Berry, *Boar's Head Playhouse*, 108–10, 163–5

[1] The copy of the order in the B book (C33/104/fo. 44v) has 'gallery'; at the time, the plural and singular were often used interchangeably.

(b) Samwell's two galleries on the eastern side of the yard

The sublease of 1598 specified that on the east side of the yard, before the playhouse was built, were 'a room to drink in, three parlours, a cellar and three stables, [and] one gallery with seven several chambers or rooms over the said drinking room, parlours, cellars, and stables' (C24/290/3, interrogatory 2; see **369a**). These things, therefore, consisted of one two-storey building with a gallery along the upper storey serving for access to seven upper rooms. Relative to the rest of the playhouse, the gallery was both long and old.

A second eastern gallery was to be built above the long old one in the first playhouse, but the work was put off and was just getting underway when Woodliffe returned to the Boar's Head in the summer of 1599. In February 1600, Mago's foreman, Walter Rodes, explained what happened then: Woodliffe 'coming to the deponent [Rodes] as he was taking measure for a storey to be made over the long old gallery said these words or the like in effect to him: "If the case were mine, as it is Samwell's, I would pull down this older gallery to the ground and build it four feet forwarder toward the stage into the yard," and with a lath or some other thing which he then had in his hand did point how far he would wish the said long gallery to be built, and quoth he, "if it were built so far forwarder then would there be room for three or four seats more in a gallery and for many more people and yet never the less room in the yard" ... And upon his speeches the complainant [Samwell] caused the said old long gallery to be pulled down and to be built and placed according to [Woodliffe's] ... direction, saving that it was not set out so far into the said yard as [Woodliffe] ... did appoint it by a foot at least' (C24/278/71, no. 2; see **371b**).

In July 1603, Mago described the eastern galleries as 'the great new galleries ... in the yard next the parlours' (C24/304/27, no. 3). The lower eastern gallery may have been about 5 feet wide in 1598 and before and, as Ogilby and Morgan's map suggests, 8 feet in 1599 and after.

See Berry, *Boar's Head Playhouse*, 113–14, 165–8

(c) Samwell's single galleries on the north and south sides of the yard

In February 1600, Mago said that Samwell had built 'certain rooms or galleries in the yard of the messuage or inn called the Boar's Head ... [and] there were three galleries so made there, one on the east side of the said yard, another on the north side, and the third on the south' (C24/278/71, no. 1).

The northern and southern galleries, like the lower eastern one, were evidently above the yard on posts so that people could come and go under them.

As Rodes quoted it (see (b) above), Woodliffe's remark of the summer of 1599 referred only to the eastern gallery, but others associated the remark with all Samwell's galleries. Mago alluded to the remark twice in February 1600: (1) Woodliffe 'appointed' him 'how far forth the [*i.e.* Samwell's] galleries should [stand[1]] ... when he took measure for the framing of the timber according to the proportion of the ground which he, the said Oliver [Woodliffe], appointed for the situation of the galleries, and did help this deponent to measure out the said ground, one Walter Rodes, then this deponent's chief workman, being present at the same time'; and (2) 'Woodliffe found fault with the [*i.e.* Samwell's] galleries because they were made no bigger, using these words to this deponent, or words to the like effect, "if they were mine, as they been Samwell's, I would pull down that long gallery and bring it forwarder into the yard" and . . . pointed with a rod which he then had in his hand how far forth he would set that gallery'. Edward Willys, Samwell's servant, said at the same time that Woodliffe 'gave them [the carpenters] direction how wide to make the same [i.e. Samwell's] galleries, and how far forth to set the posts . . . viz., "if the case were mine, as it is Mr Samwell's, I would set the posts and other things in this and this manner"' (C24/278/71, no. 2, 3). In June 1601 the younger Samwell also alluded to the remark: 'Woodliffe found fault because the said [i.e. his father's] galleries or rooms were made so little. Whereupon it was afterwards agreed by and between this deponent's father and Woodliffe that this deponent's father should pull the said new galleries down again and should build or set up larger galleries and further into the yard, viz., so far forth into the yard as the said Woodliffe did measure or set out with a rule or lath which he had in his hand, which, so far as he remembreth, was some 3 feet or 4 feet or more further into the said yard than the said little galleries did stand' (C24/290/3, no. 3).

The elder Samwell also suggested that all the galleries were above the yard by asserting in April 1600 that Francis Langley and others 'most forcibly gathered and took away the money of those persons that were to go up into the said [Samwell's] galleries to the said stage play' (STAC5/S74/3, the bill; see 374e), as did Owen Roberts, Langley's carpenter, who 'was sent for by the said Langley to come to open a door at the stair's foot leading up to the said galleries' (STAC5/S13/8, no. 3). See also (d) below.

In June 1601 the younger Samwell described all three of his father's galleries in the first playhouse as 'certain galleries or rooms for people to stand in to see the plays. And . . . afterwards . . . Woodliffe found fault because the said galleries or rooms were made so little' (C24/290/3, no. 3; see 370a). If Woodliffe's gallery was 3 feet deep to start with, so perhaps were Samwell's two galleries that abutted it on its north and south ends (see (d) below). And if Samwell added 3 feet to these two in 1599 in order to add rows of seats as Rodes said (see (b) above), the galleries became 6 feet wide and were meant for persons sitting, not standing. Moreover, Francis Langley's creature, Richard Bishop, said that on 20 May 1600 Robert Browne and Mago pulled down 'certain posts and fixed seats' in the Boar's Head, while, presumably, repairing Samwell's galleries (KB27/1364/m. 259; see 375a).

Berry, *Boar's Head Playhouse*, 109, 168–9

[1] Several words are illegible here.

(d) The layout of Samwell's and Woodliffe's (later Langley's) galleries

In April 1600, Langley said he had Roberts 'cut down certain quarters [2 (or 4) × 4 inch studs] and boards in the wall of the new gallery built in the said great court for to make a doorway from this defendant's [Langley's] house into the said [Samwell's] gallery' (STAC5/S74/3, Langley and Roberts' answer). And, Langley added, Roberts 'cut down certain quarters in the end of the said galleries with such tools as carpenters do use in such case and made a doorway into the said galleries' (STAC 5/S13/8, no. 10; see 374f).

These remarks, together with those of the elder Samwell and Roberts (in (c) above) implying that one stairway led up to all Samwell's galleries, define the layout not only of Samwell's but probably also of Woodliffe's galleries. Since Langley's 'house' must have belonged to Woodliffe's premises on the west side of the yard, Roberts probably cut a doorway from Woodliffe's western gallery into Samwell's northern or southern one. So the northern and southern galleries were connected with the lower eastern gallery and extended along the yard to Woodliffe's premises, which they abutted but did not originally lead into. And all these galleries were more or less on a level with one another.

Berry, *Boar's Head Playhouse*, 113, 169

(e) The location of the stage in 1598 and 1599 and its size

In February 1600, Samwell asked Mago, Rodes and Willys, 'Did the said Oliver Woodliffe remove [in the summer of 1599] a certain stage in the yard of the said inn to the end to give more room to the plaintiff [Samwell] thereby to erect and build the said galleries . . . and how much was the same stage removed?'

Mago replied that Woodliffe 'caused to be removed a stage which stood in the yard of the said inn to give the plaintiff [Samwell] more scope or room for the erecting or building of the said galleries, and . . . the same stage was removed about 6 feet from the gallery further than it stood before'. Rodes said that Woodliffe 'caused the stage which stood in the yard to be removed and pulled inwards to make more room for the long [hence eastern] gallery and the yard . . . The said stage was removed inwards about 5 feet or 6 feet, as he taketh it, for the enlargement of the said yard and to give the complainant [Samwell] the more scope for the better enlarging of his galleries.' Willys said that Woodliffe 'caused to be removed a stage which stood in the said yard to give more scope and room . . . to the plaintiff [Samwell] for the erecting and building of the said galleries . . . The said stage was removed some three-quarters of a yard or more inwards towards the house' (C24/278/71, no. 3, and, for Rodes, also 2). The 'house' seems to have been the tiring-house.

If the stage was moved 6 feet westward and Woodliffe's western premises were enlarged 4 feet eastwards in 1599, the stage stood more or less in the middle of the yard in 1598. Some nineteen remarks put the stage under Woodliffe's western gallery from 1599 on, hence adjacent to the tiring-house in the usual way (see, for example, (a) above).

The dimensions of the plot on which the stage and tiring-house stood are derived from a deed of 27 December 1621 by which William Browne bought part of the Boar's head. Among other things, he bought 'so much of the said Boar's Head ground as lately was builded and known for tiring-house or [*i.e.* and] stage and [*i.e.* or] two tenements late in the several occupations of Humphrey Plevy and John Walford and have been lately pulled down to be re-edified and builded in a better form, as the same by measure do contain at the north and next the tenement wherein Thomas Milles, butcher, now dwelleth in breadth from the pale belonging to the copyhold tenements of Samuel Rowley west to the corner of the said tenements wherein the said Thomas Milles now dwelleth 36 feet 6 inches of assize, and in breadth at the south end next the garden of the said William Browne the like assize of 36 feet 6 inches and do contain on the east and west side thereof 39 feet 7 inches, (C54/2515/71).

This 39 feet 7 inches was the width of the stage itself. To the 36 feet 6 inches for the other dimension of the plot one must add the 8 feet taken from the plot for an alley that Browne was to make running along the western side of the plot,[1] of which 44 feet 6 inches the stage could have occupied some 25 feet. If the stage did not have a roof in 1598, it acquired one in the rebuilding of 1599 (C24/304/27, interrogatories, Mago, and Marsh nos. 3).

See Berry, *Boar's Head Playhouse*, pp. 98–103, 108, 110–12, 167, 170, 189–90

---

[1] The alley is described in the deed as 'one passageway of the breadth of 8 feet . . . to be made, laid out, and maintained passageable by the said William Browne . . . in and through the said parcel of ground

where the stage was built right descending [*i.e.* southwards] from the way along out of Hog Lane'. Browne's 'passageway' was made and is shown on maps until the eighteenth century. The 'way out of Hog Lane' was also made – along the north side of the stage and tiring-house plot – and remained in public use until 1882.

(f) Arrangements among the owners and players for managing the playhouse

In June 1601 the younger Samwell said that his father had the right 'to shut the gates of the said inn or messuage at 11 of the clock, or at such other times as the players or the said Richard Samwell should think convenient' (C24/290/3, no. 4).

In May 1603, Browne said that he and his predecessor, Samwell, had the right to use 'the said stage, tiring-houses and galleries over the stage during all such time and term of years as the said Richard Samwell had the other part of the premises', *i.e.* until Christmas 1615. In return, Samwell should pay Woodliffe 'the one-half of the profits coming, arising and to be taken out of the said west galleries over the said stage at such time and times as there should be any plays or comedies acted and played upon the stage aforesaid' (Req.2/466/pt 2[1], the answer). In July 1603, Browne added 'clearly discharged, the gatherers being first paid', and his witnesses, Mago and another carpenter, John Marsh, added 'and the players the other half'.

On the same occasion, Browne and his witnesses explained some of the incidental costs he, and Samwell before him, paid as manager of the playhouse. Browne said that they paid 'the charges for all the licences for warrants from the Master of the Revels, . . . [which] cost £10 a warrant'; and 'all weekly payments to the said Master of the Revels', which, as Mago added, 'was affirmed to be 15s a week when they played'; and 'for the weekly payment to the poor' of the parish, which, according to Mago, 'was said to be 5s a week'; and 'the wages of the stage-keepers', which, Mago said, 'was said to be 6s a week'; and for 'all rushes and cresset lights', or, as Mago put it, 'rushes and cresset lights in winter, which some weeks came to 10s or 12s a week, as they said' – a remark that indicates how the playhouse was lighted on dark winter afternoons.

Browne said that he and his predecessor also paid 'all charges of suits concerning the upholding and maintaining of the playing there'. These suits were not lawsuits, for Mago and Marsh described them as 'all suits at court to uphold playing in the said house, which', Mago said, 'came to much money'. Browne added that the suits were 'to have toleration from time to time to uphold the house to play in'. (C24/304/27, interrogatories 3, 16, Mago and Marsh 3).

Berry, *Boar's Head Playhouse*, 171–4

XXIX The First Globe

The first Globe was the third of the five public playhouses built on Bankside – in Southwark, near the south bank of the Thames. It was on the south side of Maiden Lane (now Park Street), more or less across the street from the Rose. Its site is mostly under a listed building called Anchor Terrace on the east side of Southwark Bridge Road, S.E.1, partly under the parking lot behind and partly, perhaps, under the east side of Southwark Bridge Road itself. (See the second Globe.)

The first Globe was built by a consortium into which the Burbage family and the leading men in the Lord Chamberlain's company of actors had formed themselves for the purpose. The members (sharers) were James Burbage's two sons, Cuthbert and Richard, who had half the venture (25 per cent each), and William Shakespeare, Augustine Phillips, Thomas Pope, John Hemmings and William Kempe, who had the other half (10 per cent each). Except for Cuthbert Burbage, all were actors and members of the company.

Before Christmas 1598 the sharers negotiated a lease on two adjoining plots of ground in Southwark. The lease began at Christmas, but it was not signed until 21 February 1599. The plots belonged to a large estate there that Nicholas Brend had inherited three months before from his father, Thomas. Nicholas' wife was a cousin of Sir John Stanhope, the Treasurer of the Chamber, hence paymaster of actors who played before the Queen.[1]

A few days after Christmas, the Burbages had the Theatre pulled down and the parts they could use again carried to the new site (see **300**, **302a**), a manoeuvre Brend must have approved in advance, since he had not yet signed the lease. There, using those parts and beginning, probably, after the signing of the lease, the consortium erected the first Globe, which was probably complete or nearly so by 16 May 1599. The builder who led the workmen in pulling down the Theatre, Peter Street, probably led those who built the Globe (he was soon also to lead those who built the first Fortune).

The sharers apparently thought of the Globe as a kind of renewal of James Burbage's scheme for the Theatre in 1576. As they eventually said, they spent £700 on the building, about what James Burbage and John Brayne had spent on the Theatre. Because the parts of the Theatre used in the first Globe included the timber, presumably the girders that made up the skeleton of the Theatre, the first Globe must have been much the same size and shape as the Theatre. James Burbage meant that his lease (**252**) should be for thirty-one years, and he paid £14 a year in rent. The new lease was indeed for thirty-one years – expiring at Christmas 1629 – and the annual rent was £14 10s 0d. Brend, however, did not require the consortium to pay a fee for the lease, nor did he allow that the consortium could remove the playhouse while the lease was in force.

The financial arrangements between players and consortium were probably those explained in documents for the second Globe. The sharers owned the lease on the property, hence the buildings on it, including the playhouse, which they had erected. They paid the rent for the property and the costs of keeping up the buildings and grounds. They collected rents from buildings other than the playhouse. The players, many of whom were not sharers, paid all the costs of producing plays, including their own wages. In return for using the playhouse, they gave the sharers half the money people paid at the doors leading to the galleries and boxes and (in the second Globe, at least) at the tiring-house door – leading, presumably, to the gallery above and behind the stage and to the stage, where people could sit. The players kept the other half and all the money people paid at 'the outer doors', which led to the yard and the other doors.

Cuthbert and Richard Burbage continued to own 25 per cent of the enterprise each throughout the life of the first Globe. The five players who originally owned the other half, however, proved less constant. Four of them absorbed Kempe's share when he left the company in 1599, so that for a time each owned 12.5 per cent. They then added two more players, Henry Condell and William Sly (so that each owned 8.33 per cent) and finally in 1612 another, William Ostler (so that each owned 7.14 per cent). The first Globe was then effectually owned in fourteen shares, of which the two Burbages held seven, and players and others held seven more in various combinations. Hemmings had eventually acquired Phillips' share after Phillips' death in 1605 and leased it out to a non-player, and Hemmings and Condell had eventually bought Sly's share and divided it between them after Sly's death in 1608. Hemmings, therefore came to own 17.9 per cent (of which 7.14 per cent was out of his control), Condell 10.7 per cent and Shakespeare, Pope's heirs, and Ostler 7.14 per cent each.[2]

The first Globe was a stable and successful enterprise. From beginning to end, its players were the Lord Chamberlain's men, who in 1603 became and then remained the King's men. Unlike its contemporary, the Boar's Head, it did not become the subject of lawsuits. Brend died in great financial difficulty in 1601, leaving an heir less than two years old, but the sharers had no trouble about their lease as long as the first Globe stood. Nor did legal disputes arise among sharers until long after the playhouse had ceased to exist.

As a result, few documents of the time point to details of the building. Its relationships with the Theatre and the second Globe, together with drawings on maps, suggest that it was a large, polygonal timber-frame building that seemed round. It was laid out as other public playhouses were: three galleries, one above the other, surrounded an open yard; a roofed stage stood in part of the yard against the gallery structure; and a tiring-house occupied that structure behind the stage. Fatally, the gallery structure had a thatched roof. Little else is certainly known about the building and nothing about its details.[3]

Other playhouses of the time are as slightly known, but because the first Globe had to do with many of Shakespeare's plays, writers have been eager to supply the lacunae of information about it. Moreover, in recently building 'Shakespeare's Globe', a supposedly authentic version of the first Globe, some 225 yards west of the site of the original one, the late Mr Sam Wanamaker and associates have had to supply all the lacunae. Information about the first Globe may lie in the contract for the first Fortune (417), because the same carpenter probably built both places, and the contract instructed him to use the Globe as a model for things that the contract did not spell out. Information probably also lies in evidence having to do with the second Globe. But major and lesser matters must inevitably continue to rely on conjecture, among them the number of sides in the polygon and the size even of those aspects for which there is some evidence.

The first Globe ended abruptly in the afternoon of 29 June 1613 when during a performance of Shakespeare's *Henry VIII* it burned spectacularly to the ground. The burning wad from a small cannon fired as a salute in the play flew into the thatched roof and was ignored until a great deal of thatch was alight.

[1] Berry, *Shakespeare's Playhouses*, 84–8.
[2] See *ES*, II, 417–19. Three people came to have an interest in Pope's share, one of them a player among the Queen's men.
[3] Edmond Malone thought the Globe was named 'only from its sign, which was a figure of Hercules supporting the globe, under which was written, *Totus mundus agit histrionem* [the whole world plays the actor]' (*Plays and Poems of William Shakespeare*, 1821, III, 66–7). He did not say where he had found this information, but in the Folio version of *Hamlet* (p. 263), Hamlet says, 'Do the boys carry it away' (*i.e.*, are companies of boy-actors driving companies of adult actors out of business), and Rosencrantz replies, 'Aye, that they do, my lord, Hercules and his load, too.'

393 A consortium leases two plots of ground in Southwark for the site of the Globe, Christmas, 1598

PRO, (a) KB27/1454/m. 692; (b) Req.2/789/[top]. Transcribed in (a) Wallace, *Advance Sheets*, 5–16; (b) Berry, *Shakespeare's Playhouses*, 221

The lease does not survive, but important parts of it are paraphrased and, probably, quoted in lawsuits of 1616, 1619 and 1632–7. Below are quotations from the first lawsuit, which describes the property in the lease more fully than the other two, and the third, which mentions things in the lease omitted from the first and second.[1]

[1] Wallace translated the first lawsuit (the original of which is in Latin) in 'Shakespeare in London', 9. He announced the second in 'Shakespeare's Money Interest', 508, and transcribed it in 'Shakespeare and his London Associates', 307–36; it is at the PRO, Req.4/1/2.

(a) The lawsuit of 1616

[The lease was for two pieces of property:] [1] All that parcel of ground lately ... enclosed and formed into four several gardens formerly in the tenure and occupation of Thomas Burt and Isbrand Morris, dyers, and Lactantius Roper, salter [and] citizen of London, containing in length from east to west 220 feet ... or thereabouts, lying and adjoining on a way or lane there on one side and abutting on a piece of land called the Park on the north, and on a garden then or formerly in the tenure or occupation of a certain John Cornishe towards the west, and on another garden then or formerly in the tenure or occupation of a certain John Knowles towards the east, with all the houses, buildings, structures, ways, easements, commodities and appurtenances thereto belonging ... Which said premises are ... in the parish of St Saviour in Southwark in the county of Surrey.

[2] And also all that parcel of land lately ... enclosed and formed into three separate gardens, of which two ... [were] formerly in the tenure or occupation of a certain John Robertes, carpenter, and the other formerly in the occupation of a certain Thomas Ditcher, citizen and merchant tailor of London, situated ... in the said parish ... containing in length from east to west, by estimation, 156 feet ... or thereabouts and in breadth from north to south 100 feet ..., by estimation, or thereabouts, lying and adjoining on the other side of the way or lane aforesaid and abutting on a garden there then or lately ... in the occupation of William Sellers

towards the east and on one other garden there then or lately in the tenure of John Burgram [*i.e.* Bingham?], sadler, towards the east, and on the lane there called Maiden Lane towards the south [*i.e.* north], with all the houses, structures, ways, easements, commodities and appurtenances . . . together with liberty of ingress, egress and regress . . . by and through the said way or lane lying and being between the said premises.[1]

[1] A description of the property also appears in the bill of the third lawsuit (where the parties to the lease are said to have been 'Nicholas Brend on the first part, . . . Cuthbert Burbage and Richard Burbage of the second part, and William Shakespeare, Augustine Phillips, Thomas Pope, John Hemmings, and William Kempe, gentlemen, on the third part'), which is accepted as true in the answer: Req.2/706/[bottom], transcribed in Berry, *Shakespeare's Playhouses*, 197–8, 203–4 (see also 86–7, 178–80).

(b) The lawsuit of 1632–1637

[And, the lease went on,] the said Nicholas Brend doth covenant that it shall be lawful for the lessees, their executors and assigns to take and pull down, alter, or change any houses, sheds, pales, fences or other buildings which then were or after should be in or upon the premises, so as there be as good or better re-edified and built on the premises within a year then next ensuing. And the lessees covenant for them, their executors, and assigns at their costs and charges to maintain and support as good and better buildings and fences as then were upon the premises in and with all necessary reparations during the said term, and [to leave] the same so repaired, made, maintained and amended, together with all such edifices and buildings whatsoever as should be built and set up in or upon the premises, or others as good and convenient for the place, . . . at the end of the said lease . . . unto the said Nicholas, his heirs and assigns. [Evidently the lease also said that the consortium meant to build a playhouse on the site.[1]]

[1] PRO, Req.2/706/[bottom], interrogatories for Burbage *et al.* (1634) 3, and depositions for Burbage *et al.* (1634), John Atkins, 3; transcribed in Berry, *Shakespeare's Playhouses*, 227, 230 (see also 179–80).

394 The Theatre is pulled down so that much of it can be used in building the Globe, 28–ff. December 1598–9

See the Theatre, 300–ff.

The materials were taken to the just-leased property in Southwark.

395 The consortium builds the Globe for £700 and opens it, spring 1599

(a) PRO, LC5/133, p. 50; (b) Req.2/789/[top]; (c) C142/257/68. Transcribed in (a) MSC, 11.iii. 362–73; (b) Berry, *Shakespeare's Playhouses*, 221; (c) Wallace, 'New Light on Shakespeare', 4. For the full text of the document quoted in (a), see **162**.

(a) The consortium raises money

[In 1635, Cuthbert Burbage together with Richard Burbage's widow, Winifred, and son said that in the winter of 1598–9 'we' – meaning Cuthbert and Richard –] then bethought ourselves of altering from thence [i.e. the site of the Theatre in Shoreditch] and at like expense [like, that is, the sum spent on the Theatre] built the Globe with more sums of money taken up at interest, which lay heavy on us many years, and to ourselves we joined those deserving men, Shakespeare, Hemmings, Condell,[1] Phillips and others, partners in the profits of that they call the house [i.e. the playhouse].

[1] Condell was not one of the original shareholders. He first acquired an interest in the Globe between 1605 and 1608.

(b) The consortium spends about £700

[In a statement of fact dated 5 February 1634, the consortium stated that] the lessees thereupon [i.e. after leasing the property] spent about £700 in building a playhouse called the Globe upon the premises.

(c) The playhouse is newly built, 16 May 1599

[Nicholas Brend's father, Thomas, had died on 21 September 1598, and the inquisition post-mortem taken on him, dated 16 May 1599, describes a building, presumably the playhouse, on the Brend estate in Southwark as] one house newly built with a garden pertaining to the same in the parish of the said St Saviour in the said county of Surrey in the occupation of William Shakespeare and others.

396 A Swiss sees Julius Caesar at the Globe, 21 September 1599

Basle University Library, Platter's Journey, 1595–1600, fos. 682v–83. Transcribed in Binz, 'Londoner Theater und Schauspiele im Jahre 1599', 458

This is the first notice of a specific play performed at the Globe. While the passage does not mention the Globe, *Caesar* belonged to the company at the Globe, which was 'over the water' and had a thatched roof.

After dinner on 21 September, at about two o'clock I [Thomas Platter of Basle, who had recently arrived in England] went with my companions over the water [i.e. the Thames] and in the thatched-roof house ['in dem streuwinen Dachhaus'] saw the tragedy of the first Emperor Julius with at least fifteen characters very pleasingly acted. At the end of the comedy, they danced, according to their custom, exceedingly gracefully: two attired in men's clothes and two in women's performed wonderfully with one another.

397 The privy council licenses the Lord Chamberlain's men to play at the Globe, 22 June 1600

PRO, PC2/25/p. 223. Transcribed in *APC, 1599–1600*, 397

The arrangement explained here was brought on by the building of the Fortune (418) and involved also the Curtain (331) and eventually the Boar's Head (382). See also 58.

There shall be about the City two [play]houses, . . . of the which houses one shall be in Surrey . . . and the other in Middlesex [*i.e.* the Fortune] . . . And for the . . . [playhouse] allowed to be on the Surrey side, whereas their lordships [of the privy council] are pleased to permit . . . the company of players that shall play there to make their own choice which they will have of divers houses that are there, choosing one of them and no more, and the said company of players, being the servants of the Lord Chamberlain, . . . have made choice of the house called the Globe, it is ordered that the said house and none other shall be there allowed.

The council repeated the order a year and a half later and, as regards the Lord Chamberlain's men and the Globe, in March 1602. The government further allowed the company to use only the Globe in London when it made them the King's men in 1603. See 66.

398 The Globe has its share of critical spectators, 1610

Heath, *Two Centuries of Epigrammes* (1610), 39. Momus was the god of sarcasm and mockery.

Momus would act the fool's part in the play,
And cause he would be exquisite that way,
Hies me to London, where no day can pass
But that some playhouse still his presence has:
Now at the Globe with a judicious eye
Into the vice's action doth he prie,
Next to the Fortune . . .

399 Foreign tourists visit the Globe, 30 April 1610; 1611

(a) Rye, *England as Seen by Foreigners in the Days of Elizabeth and James*, 61; (b) Feyerabend, 'Zu K.H. Schaible's Geschichte der Deutschen in England', 440

(a) Prince Lewis Frederick of Württemberg[1]

Monday, 30 [April 1610]. His excellency went to the Globe, the ordinary place where they play comedies, and there the story of the Moor of Venice was presented.

---

[1] This passage is from a manuscript journal kept in French by the Prince's secretary, Hans Jacob Wurmsser, of a journey from the Rhineland to England and Scotland, but Rye did not say where the manuscript is (Rye, pp. cxv–xxi, 57).

(b) Prince Otto of Hesse-Cassel, 1611

In London are seven theatres where daily, except for Sundays, comedies are performed, among which the most important is the Globe, which lies over the water.

400 The Globe burns to the ground during a performance of *Henry VIII*, 29 June 1613

(a) Birch, *Court and Times of James the First*, I, 253; (b) *Letters of Sir Henry Wotton to Sir Edmund Bacon* (1661), 30–1; (c) Somerset Record Office, Taunton, DD/SF 3066; (d) Jonson, *Works* (1640), Underwoods 42. Transcribed in (c) Cole, 'A New Account of the Burning of the Globe', 352; for (b) see also Smith, *Life and Letters of Sir Henry Wotton*, II, 32

Shakespeare's *Henry VIII* was also known as *All is True*. A chamber is 'A small piece [of ordnance] without a carriage, standing on its breech, used to fire salutes' (*OED*). The fire became famous, at least partly because it lent itself to witty irony. Some of the many surviving remarks about it follow.

(a) Letter, Thomas Lorkin to Sir Thomas Puckering, 30 June 1613

No longer since than yesterday, while [Richard] Burbage's company were acting at the Globe the play of *Henry VIII* and there shooting off certain chambers in way of triumph, the fire catched and fastened upon the thatch of the house, and there burned so furiously as it consumed the whole house, all in less than two hours, the people having enough to do to save themselves.

(b) Letter, Sir Henry Wotton to Sir Edmund Bacon, 2 July 1613

I will entertain you . . . with what happened this week at the Bank's side. The King's players had a new play, called *All is True*, representing some principal pieces of the reign of Henry VIII, which was set forth with many extraordinary circumstances of pomp and majesty, even to the matting of the stage: the knights of the order with their Georges and garters, the guards with their embroidered coats, and the like – sufficient in truth within a while to make greatness very familiar, if not ridiculous. Now King Henry making a masque at the Cardinal Wolsey's house, and certain chambers being shot off at his entry, some of the paper or other stuff wherewith one of them was stopped did light on the thatch, where being thought at first but an idle smoke, and their eyes more attentive to the show, it kindled inwardly and ran round like a train [*i.e.* of powder], consuming within less than an hour the whole house to the very grounds. This was the fatal period of that virtuous fabric wherein yet nothing did perish but wood and straw and a few forsaken cloaks. Only one man had his breeches set on fire that would perhaps have broiled him if he had not by the benefit of a provident wit put it out with bottle ale.

(c) Letter, Henry Bluett to Richard Weeks, 4 July 1613

On Tuesday last [June 29] there was acted at the Globe a new play called *All is True*, which had been acted not passing two or three times before. There came many people to see it, insomuch that the house was very full, and as the play was almost ended the house was fired with shooting off a chamber which was stopped with tow [*i.e.* fibres of flax or hemp] which was blown up into the thatch of the house and so burned down to the ground. But the people escaped all without hurt except one man who was scalded with the fire by adventuring to save a child which otherwise had been burned.

(d) Ben Jonson, 'Execration upon Vulcan', after 1621

But O those reeds. Thy [Vulcan's] mere disdain of them
Made thee beget that cruel stratagem,
Which some are pleased to style but thy mad prank,
Against the Globe, the glory of the bank,
Which though it were the fort of the whole parish,
Flanked with a ditch and forced out of a marish,
I saw with two poor chambers taken in
And razed, ere thought could urge this might have been.
See the world's ruins, nothing but the piles
Left, and wit since to cover it with tiles.

Vulcan was the god of fire.

XXX The second Blackfriars

The second Blackfriars playhouse, like the first, was a private playhouse in an ancient building belonging to the former convent of the Dominican, or black, friars in London, south of Ludgate Hill. The building of the second playhouse adjoined that of the first. Indeed, the space occupied by the auditorium of the second probably adjoined the space occupied by the auditorium of the first, and some of the space of the second had been rooms belonging to the first. Both playhouses were in the upper storey of rectangular buildings whose longer dimensions lay north to south, and people in the upper storey of one could pass into the upper storey of the other. The second playhouse was in the northern end of the southern building, the first in the southern end of the northern one. In London as it is now, the second playhouse extended southwards from the southern end of Apothecaries Hall (which replaces the building in which the first playhouse was), across a street called Playhouse Yard, and along the eastern side of Black Friars Lane, E.C.4.

The second was in a large medieval hall known as the parliament chamber because at least three parliaments had met there.[1] It was, therefore, a much grander place than the first. It was probably a great deal higher – the height of at least two rooms built one over the other at the northern end – and its ceiling could have been a hammer beam roof in the manner of other medieval halls, like Westminster Hall. At floor level it measured 66 feet north to south and 46 feet east to west. It comprised, therefore, 3,036 square feet, more than two and a half times the size of the first one. The main entrance was at its northern end, served, apparently, by the 'great' stone staircase that had served the first playhouse. Because this staircase and the two rooms one over the other were at the northern end of the room, the stage must have been at its southern end.

If more information is available about the interior of the second playhouse than about that of the first, not enough is available to sustain the usual assertion that the proscenium-arch stage in professional English playhouses had its origin in the second. Below the level of the stage was a pit where people sat on benches. Somewhere there was a tiring-house.[2] There were galleries, perhaps a single level of them, running around three sides of the room above the pit. There were boxes adjacent to and on a level with the stage, perhaps at the back. The stage was famous for the spectators on it, standing, sitting (on three-legged stools) and even reclining. But its size and shape are unknown.

On 4 February 1596, James Burbage bought the parliament chamber and allied places outright from Sir William More for £600. The Burbages would have no difficulties with leases and landlords at this venture. He and his brother-in-law, John Brayne, had effectually begun the history of public playhouses, the brother-in-law by building the first one (the Red Lion) in 1567, both by building the first large, permanent one (the Theatre) in 1576. Now, in his declining years Burbage would make the private playhouse a worthy competitor. The two earlier private playhouses had been small and meant for performances by boy-choristers. They had, moreover, been closed for years. Burbage meant to build a new and much finer one meant for a regular professional company of men.[3]

He promptly made a playhouse out of the seven rooms into which the parliament chamber had been divided. Unlike his earlier scheme, however, this one was ahead of its time. His influential and wealthy neighbours in Blackfriars objected to a playhouse for adult players in their midst, not for familiar religious or moral reasons but for the inconvenience that large numbers of play-goers could cause. As a result, Burbage could not open his new playhouse. When he died in 1597, the family decided that his younger son, Richard, the chief actor among the Lord Chamberlain's men, should control the playhouse rather than the heir, Cuthbert, who took over other parts of the property. Richard leased the playhouse in 1600 for twenty-one years at £40 a year to Henry Evans, who with two partners meant to present plays acted by the boys of the Chapel Royal. If adult players could not act in Blackfriars, boys apparently could, as they had done from 1576 to 1584. Besides, the boys of St Paul's had recently begun public playing again there.

Evans was the main entrepreneur. He was the man whose subleasing of the first Blackfriars in 1583 had ultimately caused its closing. His partners now were Nathaniel Giles, who in 1597 had succeeded William Hunnis as master of the children of the Chapel Royal and would provide the boys, and James Robinson, who held several rooms adjoining the playhouse.

Rosencrantz' 'little eyases' who 'are most tyrannically clapped' and 'are now the fashion' probably allude to these revived companies of boys. The enterprise at the second Blackfriars playhouse, however, was no luckier than that at the first had been. It, too, was fraught with legal problems, which came to involve virtually everybody concerned with it, including Richard Burbage. The problems began almost at once, when Evans again attempted more than the rules allowed and again lost control of his playhouse though not of his lease. The children may not have earned enough money to pay their expenses and gratify the financial aspirations of their investors, because they may have played only once a week, on Saturdays. The child-actors in the second Blackfriars, like those in the first, went on for eight years. They ended in March 1608 not, however, because of lawsuits or poverty but because of plays that caused offence.

The Burbage family now concluded that they could move the King's men (as the Lord Chamberlain's men had become) into the playhouse and so accomplish James Burbage's purpose in building it. The playhouse would become the first private playhouse in which adult players regularly performed. The Burbages organised a new consortium whose documents Richard Burbage sealed on 9 August 1608, and the next day he formally regained the lease from Evans in return for giving up Evans' bond of £400 and a 'consideration'. This consortium was different from that at the Globe because the Burbages owned this playhouse outright. In effect, Richard Burbage divided Evans' lease into seven parts and reissued it. He kept a seventh of the playhouse for himself and granted each of six people an identical lease on a seventh of the playhouse for twenty-one years from 24 June 1608 at £5 14s 4d a year in rent ($\times 7 = £40$ 0s 4d). Six of the seven had shares in the Globe and five were members of the King's men: Richard and Cuthbert Burbage (who was not a member of the King's men), John Hemmings, Shakespeare, William Sly and Henry Condell. The seventh was Thomas Evans. He may have been Henry Evans or an agent for him, and his share may have been his 'consideration'. Unlike the scheme at the Globe, each of the sharers (lessees) at the Blackfriars began with an equal stake, and the Burbage family had two sevenths of the venture, not half.

The consortium kept the playhouse in repair, paid Richard Burbage his rent, and allowed the players to use the playhouse in return for half the takings in the galleries and boxes. The players kept the other half and all the takings in the pit,[4] out of which they paid their own wages, those of hired men, and all other costs of playing – for boys, plays, music, lights, costumes, properties and the like. Since Richard Burbage was landlord, sharer and player, he paid his part of the consortium's and the company's costs, and he received not only his annual rent from the other sharers (34 6s 0d), but a seventh of the consortium's part of the takings, and his part of the players' takings.

The King's men apparently did not begin at the second Blackfriars until late in 1609 because of plague. They continued until the closing of all the playhouses in 1642. Their neighbours objected repeatedly, and not without cause, but did not prevail again. The King's men came to use the playhouse mainly in the winter months and the Globe in the summer ones. When the original leases ran out on 24 June 1629, they were renewed by Richard Burbage's widow, Winifred, who had inherited the playhouse in 1620.[5] The rent was now £50 rather than £40 a year, the term ten years rather than twenty-one, and the number of leases seven rather than six, each for an eighth part of the playhouse rather than a seventh. By 1635, they were held by Winifred (who in 1632 was the wife of an actor among the King's men, Richard Robinson), Cuthbert Burbage and five actors or former actors among the King's men, John Shanks (who had two leases), Joseph Taylor, John Lowin, Henry Condell and John Underwood. The leases were probably renewed again in 1639, but no notice of such a renewal survives.

Neither the consortium nor the company was troubled by disabling lawsuits or serious financial problems. The playhouse became the most important playhouse of its time and one of the most important in the whole history of English drama. Regular playing ceased there on 2 September 1642, when Parliament ordered all public acting to cease, but unlike other playhouses, Blackfriars seems not to have housed surreptitious performances after that.[6] Richard Burbage's son, William, sold it as a playhouse in 1651 for £700. The building in which it was should have been destroyed in the great fire of 1666, like the rest of Blackfriars.

[1] Evidence in a lawsuit of 1611–12 (403a, 409f) shows that Smith and Bentley were right to put the playhouse in the parliament chamber rather than, as others have done, in the rooms under it. See Smith, *Blackfriars Playhouse*, 165–6, and *J and CS*, VI, 5–6.

[2] Many contemporary writers alluded to the pit, or cockpit, at Blackfriars, among them Leonard Digges in a commendatory poem for Shakespeare's *Poems* (1640):

> let but Beatrice
> And Benedick be seen, lo in a trice
> The cockpit, galleries, boxes all are full
> To hear Malvoglio, that coarse gartered gull.

Thomas Carew alluded to the benches in his poem on Davenant's 'misunderstood' play, *The Just Italian*, produced at Blackfriars in 1629 (the poem published with the play, London, 1630). People throng to other stages:

> Whilst the true brood of actors, that alone
> Keep natural unstrained action in her throne
> Behold their benches bare ...

Fitz-Geoffrey alluded to the tiring-house in his *Satyres and Satyricall Epigrams*, the section called 'Notes from Black-Fryers':
> I know him well. Did he not drop
> Out of the Tyring-house?

See *J and CS*, VI, 44.

[3] He must also have thought of the Blackfriars property as a hedge against the possibility of his losing the Theatre, because his lease on the ground under the Theatre had only a year to run and his landlord was refusing to renew.
[4] *J and CS*, VI, 36–7.
[5] PRO, E112/221/1215; see Berry, 'Miltons and the Blackfriars Playhouse', 510–14.
[6] *J and CS*, VI, 41–2.

401 James Burbage buys the parliament chamber and allied properties from Sir William More, 4 February 1596

Folger, MS L.b.348.[1] Transcribed in MSC, II.i. 60–9, and in Smith, *Blackfriars Playhouse*, 471–5

Though the contract was signed on 4 February 1596, its terms were probably settled during the previous Christmas season, for on 9 January 1596 Lord Hunsdon wanted to buy part of More's property in Blackfriars, 'understanding that you [More] have already parted with part of your house to some that means to make a playhouse in it' (Folger, MS L.b.38, transcribed in Wallace, *Evolution of the English Drama*, 195 n. 7, and MSC, II.i. 123).

This indenture made the fourth day of February . . . [1596] between Sir William More of Loseley in the county of Surrey, knight, of the one party and James Burbage of Holywell in the county of Middlesex, gentleman, of the other party, witnesseth that the said Sir William More, for and in consideration of . . . £600 of lawful money of England to him by the said James Burbage . . . truly paid, . . . hath bargained, sold, aliened, enfeoffed and confirmed . . . to the said James Burbage, his heirs and assigns forever:

All those seven great upper rooms as they are now divided, being all upon one floor and sometime being one great and entire room, with the roof over the same covered with lead, together also with all the lead that doth cover the same seven great upper rooms; and also all the stone stairs leading up unto the leads or roof over the said seven great upper rooms out of the said seven great upper rooms; and also the great stone walls and other walls which do enclose, divide and belong to the same seven great upper rooms; and also all that great pair of winding stairs, with the staircase thereunto belonging, which leadeth up unto the same seven great upper rooms out of the great yard there which doth lie next unto the Pipe office.[2] Which said seven great upper rooms were late in the tenure or occupation of William de Laune, doctor of physic, or of his assigns, and are situate, lying and being within the precinct of the late Blackfriars Preachers near Ludgate in London. Together also with all the wainscot, glass, doors, locks, keys and bolts to the same seven great upper rooms and other the premises by these presents bargained and sold . . .

Together also with the easement and commodity of a vault, being under some part of the said seven great upper rooms or under the entry or void room lying between those seven great upper rooms and the said Pipe office, by a stole [*i.e.* a small room such as could contain a privy] and tunnel to be made into the same vault in and out of the great stone wall in the inner side thereof, next and adjoining to the said entry or void room, being towards the south.

And also all those rooms and lodgings, with the kitchen thereto adjoining, called the middle rooms or middle storeys, late being in the tenure or occupation of Rocco Bonetti and now ... of Thomas Bruskett, gentleman, or of his assigns, containing in length 52 feet of assize more or less and in breadth 37 feet of assize more or less, lying and being directly under part of those of the said seven great upper rooms which lie westwards. Which said middle rooms or middle storeys do extend in length southwards to a part of the house of Sir George Carey, knight. And also all the stone walls and other walls which do enclose, divide and belong to the same middle rooms or middle storeys. Together also with the door and entry which do lie next unto the gate entering into the house of the said Sir George Carey and used to and from the said middle rooms or middle storeys out of a lane or way leading unto the house of the said Sir George Carey, with free way, ingress, egress and regress ... through the ways now used to the said house of the said Sir George Carey.

And also all those two vaults or cellars late being in the occupation of the said Rocco Bonetti, lying under part of the said middle rooms or middle storeys at the north end thereof, as they are now divided and are now in the tenure or occupation of the said Thomas Bruskett and of John Favor, and are adjoining to the two little yards now in the occupations of Peter Johnson and of the said John Favor, together also with the stairs leading into the same vaults or cellars out of the foresaid kitchen in the occupation of the said Thomas Bruskett.

And also all those two upper rooms or chambers with a little buttery, at the north end of the said seven great upper rooms and on the west side thereof, now being in the occupation of Charles Bradshaw, together with the void room, way and passage now thereunto used from the said seven great upper rooms.

And also all those two rooms or lofts now in the occupation of Edward Merry, the one of them lying and being above or over the said two upper rooms or chambers in the occupation of the said Charles Bradshaw and on the east and north part thereof and having a chimney in it, and the other of them lying over part of the foresaid entry or void room next the foresaid Pipe office; together with the stairs leading from the foresaid rooms in the occupation of the foresaid Charles Bradshaw up unto the foresaid two rooms in the occupation of the said Edward Merry.

And also all that little room now used to lay wood and coals in, being about the middle of the said stairs westwards, which said little room last mentioned is over the foresaid buttery now in the occupation of the said Charles Bradshaw, and is now in the occupation of the said Charles Bradshaw.

And also all that room or garret lying and being over the said two rooms or lofts last before mentioned in the occupation of the said Edward Merry, together with the door, entry, void ground, way and passage and stairs leading or used to, with, or from the said rooms in the occupation of the said Edward Merry up unto the said room or garret over the said two rooms in the occupation of the said Edward Merry.

And also all those two lower rooms now in the occupation of the said Peter Johnson, lying directly under part of the said seven great upper rooms; and also all those two other lower rooms or chambers now being also in the tenure or occupation of the said Peter Johnson, being under the foresaid rooms or chambers in the occupation of the said Charles Bradshaw; and also the door, entry way, void ground, and passage leading and used to and from the said great yard next the said Pipe office into and from the said four lower rooms or chambers.

And also all that little yard adjoining to the said lower rooms as the same is now enclosed with a brick wall and . . . in the occupation of the said Peter Johnson. Which said four lower rooms or chambers and little yard do lie between the said great yard next the said Pipe office on the north part, and an entry leading into the messuage which Margaret Pooly, widow, holdeth for term of her life, now in the occupation of the said John Favor, on the west part, and a wall dividing the said yard now in the occupation of the said Peter Johnson, and the yard now in the occupation of the said John Favor on the south part.

And also the stairs and staircase leading from the said little yard now in the occupation of the said Peter Johnson up unto the foresaid chambers or rooms now in the occupation of the said Charles Bradshaw.

And also all that little yard or piece of void ground with the brick wall thereunto belonging, lying and being next the Queen's highway leading unto the river of Thames wherein an old privy now standeth, as the same is now enclosed with the same brick wall and with a pale, next adjoining to the house of the said Sir William More now in the occupation of the right honourable the Lord Cobham on the east part, and the street leading to the Thames there on the west part, and the said yard next the said Pipe office on the south part, and the house of the said Lord Cobham on the north part.

All which premises before in these presents mentioned to be hereby bargained and sold are situate, lying and being within the said precinct of the said late Blackfriars Preachers, together also with all liberties, privileges, lights, water courses, easements, commodities and appurtenances to the foresaid rooms, lodgings and other the premises . . . belonging or in any wise appertaining.

And also the said Sir William More . . . by these presents doth . . . confirm unto the said James Burbage . . . free and quiet ingress, egress and regress to and from the street or way leading from Ludgate unto the Thames, over, upon and through the said great yard next the said Pipe office, by the ways now thereunto used into and from the said seven great upper rooms and all other the premises, . . . together also with free liberty for the said James Burbage . . . to lay and discharge . . . his wood, coal and all other carriages, necessaries and provisions in the same great yard . . . for convenient time until the same may be taken and carried away from thence, . . . leaving convenient ways and passages to go and come . . . through the said great yard . . . to and from the said Pipe office and to and from the garden and other houses and rooms of the said Sir William More not hereby bargained and sold, . . . so that the said wood, coal, carriages and provisions so laid and discharged . . . be removed and avoided out of and from the said yard within three days next after it shall be brought thither, without fraud or further delay.

The second Blackfriars 507

And further, the said Sir William More . . . doth . . . sell unto the said James Burbage . . . the reversion and reversions, remainder and remainders, of all . . . the premises . . . mentioned to be . . . sold, . . . except and reserved unto the said Sir William More, his heirs and assigns one room, or stole, as the same is now made in and out of the foresaid wall next the said entry adjoining to the said Pipe office into the foresaid vault . . . [3]

In witness whereof, the parties first above named to these indentures sunderly [*i.e.* separately] have set their seals the day and year first above written . . .

[1] This is Sir William More's part of the original indenture and still bears James Burbage's signature and seal. A copy is at the PRO, on the close roll, C54/1540/m. 28–30 (transcribed by Halliwell-Phillipps, *Outlines*, I, 299-304), which must derive from Burbage's part of the original indenture, since, according to the indenture, Burbage was to have a copy put there at his expense; the roll says that More approved the copy in person before a Chancery official.
[2] The Pipe office was a branch of the Exchequer having to do with the collection of taxes. It occupied the space where the first Blackfriars playhouse had been.
[3] Here follow statements by More explaining, among other things, that he owned the property outright, that he was selling it to Burbage so, and that two agents of his, George Austen, gentleman, and Henry Smith, merchant tailor, would deliver possession.

402 Neighbours petition the privy council to prevent the playhouse from opening, November 1596

PRO, SP12/260/fo. 176. Transcribed in Halliwell-Phillipps, *Outlines*, I, 304; *ES*, IV, 319–20; and in Smith, *Blackfriars Playhouse*, 481

This undated copy of a petition has been thought a forgery because J.P. Collier, the forger, announced it and added a reply by the Lord Chamberlain's men that is certainly a forgery (see Collier, *History* [1837], I, 219, 287, and *CSP, Dom.*, 1595–7, 310). The petition is not mentioned in the records of the privy council, but it is both mentioned and dated in a similar petition of 1618–19 (**410a**).

To the right honourable the lords and others of her majesty's most honourable privy council:

Humbly showing and beseeching your honours, [we] the inhabitants of the precinct of the Blackfriars, London, [show] that whereas one Burbage hath lately bought certain rooms in the same precinct near adjoining unto the dwelling houses of the right honourable the Lord Chamberlain and the Lord of Hunsdon, which rooms the said Burbage is now altering and meaneth very shortly to convert and turn the same into a common playhouse, which will grow to be a very great annoyance and trouble, not only to all the noblemen and gentlemen thereabout inhabiting, but also a general inconvenience to all the inhabitants of the same precinct, both by reason of the great resort and gathering together of all manner of vagrant and lewd persons that, under colour of resorting to the plays, will come thither and work all manner of mischief, and also to the great pestering and filling up of the same precinct if it should please God to send any visitation of sickness as heretofore hath been. For that the same precinct is already grown very populous, and besides that the same playhouse is so near the church that the noise of the drums and trumpets will greatly disturb and hinder both the ministers and parishioners in time of divine service and sermons.

In tender consideration whereof, as also for that there hath not at any time heretofore been used any common playhouse within the same precinct,[1] but that now all players being banished by the Lord Mayor from playing within the City by reason of the great inconveniences and ill rule that followeth them, they now think to plant themselves in liberties: that therefore it would please your honours to take order that the same rooms may be converted to some other use, and that no playhouse may be used or kept there. And your suppliants, as most bounden, shall and will daily pray for your lordships in all honour and happiness long to live.

The second of the thirty-one people who signed the petition was, curiously, Lord Hunsdon, who had just become patron of the players, including Richard Burbage and Shakespeare, for whom James Burbage probably meant the playhouse. Hunsdon was evidently more intent on his own convenience than that of his players, for he lived next to the playhouse in the same building. The privy council responded to the petition (according to that of 1619) by noting on the back that it 'forbade the use of the said house for plays'.

[1] The first Blackfriars playhouse was not a 'common playhouse' because it was meant for private performances by children.

403 Richard Burbage leases the playhouse to Henry Evans for twenty-one years, 2 September 1600

PRO, (a) KB27/1432/m. 359; (b) C2/Jas. I/K5/25, Evans' reply. Transcribed in (a) Berry, *Shakespeare's Playhouses*, 59–60, 68–9; (b) Fleay, *Chronicle History*, 223–51, and in Smith, *Blackfriars Playhouse*, 176. The lease does not survive, but it was quoted and paraphrased in several lawsuits, especially one in which Evans dealt mainly with the playhouse and another in which he dealt mainly with the term and rent.

(a) May 1612

[The lease included:] all that great hall or room with the rooms above the same as then were erected, furnished and built with a stage, galleries[1] and seats of a quantity specified in a schedule annexed thereto, situate and being at the northern end of certain rooms then in the tenure and occupation of one John Robinson or his assigns within the precinct of Blackfriars, London, and being part and parcel of those houses and edifices in the same place that were then lately acquired and bought ... by James Burbage ... containing by estimation in length from the south to the northern part of the same 66 feet of assize, be it more or less, and in width from the west to the eastern part of the same 46 feet of assize, be it more or less, together with all lights, easements and commodities whatsoever pertaining to the same hall or rooms ...

[The lease did not include:] all the vaults and rooms under the said great hall ... then in the tenure or occupation of Thomas Bruskett or his assigns[2] and those rooms situated and being on the western side of the door of the stairs leading up into the said great hall ... then in the occupation of Henry Duncalf or his assigns.

[1] Not only these lawsuits but also the sharers' papers (411 and 162) and several contemporary poems mention galleries. No contemporary writer, however, noted how many or where they were. Wallace and others have supposed that there were three galleries, one over the other, as in public playhouses like the Swan and Fortune, because all the contemporary writers used the word in the plural and two alluded to 'the middle region' (Marston in *The Dutch Courtesan*, 1605, v. iii. 162, and Fitz-Geoffery in his 'Notes from Blackfriars', 1617, sig. E7v). At the time, however, the word usually appears in the plural when modern writers would use the singular, and neither writer connected the middle region to galleries. There could well have been a single level of galleries on three sides of the room, built over the pit so that people could sit under them. See Smith, *Blackfriars Playhouse*, 290–4; ES, II, 514; and Berry, *Shakespeare's Playhouses*, 62–3.
[2] This exclusion signifies that the playhouse must have been in the parliament chamber and had nothing to do with the storey under it.

(b) 5 November 1612

Richard Burbage of the parish of St Leonard's in Shoreditch in the county of Middlesex, gentleman, by his indenture and lease bearing date the second day of September ... [1600] hath leased and to farm letten unto ... Henry Evans all that great hall or room, with the rooms over the same in the said indenture mentioned, situate in the precinct of the Blackfriars, London, ... to hold unto the said Henry Evans, his executors and assigns from ... [Michaelmas] next ensuing after the date of the said indenture unto the end and term of one and twenty years from thence next ensuing and fully to be complete and ended, yielding and paying therefor yearly during the said term unto the said Richard Burbage, his executors and assigns ... [£40] at four feasts or terms in the year, that is to say at ... [Christmas, Lady Day, St John Baptist, and Michaelmas] by even and equal portions to be paid.

The lease also had a clause preventing Evans from subletting the place or any part of it and another requiring him to keep it in repair (PRO, Req.4/1, the defendants' reply and rejoinder; transcribed in Wallace, 'Shakespeare and his London Associates', 340–60). Moreover, accompanying the lease was a bond in which Evans and his son-in-law, Alexander Hawkins, promised to pay Richard Burbage £400 if they did not pay the rent and keep their other promises (C2/Jas. I/K5/25, John Hemmings and Richard Burbage's reply, transcribed in Fleay, as above).

404 Evans stumbles a second time at a Blackfriars playhouse, December 1600 – January 1602

PRO, (a) STAC5/C46/39; (b) C2/Jas. I/K5/25, Kirkham's replication; (c) C66/1708/m. 6d–7d). Transcribed in (a–b) Fleay, *Chronicle History*, 127–32, 223–51; (a–c) Smith, *Blackfriars Playhouse*, 484–6, 545, 185

The earliest notices that the children of the Chapel Royal were playing at the second Blackfriars playhouse belong to the winter of 1600–1,[1] and one of the first concerns an event that ended the venture of Evans and his partners, Nathaniel Giles and James Robinson. As master of the choristers, Giles, like his predecessors, had been granted a patent enabling him to impress children into his choir.[2] He unluckily seized a boy for acting whose father was not only no lover of plays but was articulate and determined. Worse, he found a good lawyer who a year later, on 15 December 1601, took the partners to the Star Chamber. That court soon arrived at a judgement. Although the judgement itself does not survive, notices of it do.

[1] See for example, Smith, *Blackfriars Playhouse*, 177–80, 183
[2] PRO, C66/1476/m. 7d; transcribed in Smith, *Blackfriars Playhouses*, 482–3.

(a) Giles seizes a child to make an actor of him, 13 December 1600

[The father, Henry Clifton, explained what happened in his lawsuit in the Star Chamber.] Whereas your said subject [Henry Clifton] having Thomas Clifton [as] his only son and heir, being about the age of thirteen years, and having for the better education of him . . . placed him in a grammar school in Christ Church, London, where for a good space he had continued and been taught and instructed in the grounds of learning and the Latin tongue; and your said subject being resident and dwelling in a house which he had taken in or near Great St Bartholomew's, London, where his son also lay and had his diet and had daily recourse from thence to the said grammar school; the same being well known to the confederates aforesaid [Evans, Giles and Robinson], and they also well knowing that your subject's said son had no manner of sight in song nor skill in music: they . . . about the 13th day of December . . . [1600] did . . . waylay the said Thomas Clifton as he should pass from your subject's house to the said school . . . and him . . . did . . . haul, pull, drag and carry away to the said playhouse in the Blackfriars, . . . where the said Nathaniel Giles, Henry Evans and the said other confederates . . . him, the said Thomas Clifton, as a prisoner committed to the said playhouse amongst a company of lewd and dissolute mercenary players, purposing in that place (and for no service of your majesty) to use and exercise him . . . in acting of parts in base plays and interludes to the mercenary gain and private commodity of them, the said . . . confederates.

Of which abuse and oppression . . . your said subject having notice, he . . . forthwith repaired unto the said playhouse . . . where he . . . then and there divers times made request to have his son released, which they, the said Nathaniel Giles, Henry Evans and James Robinson, utterly and scornfully refused to do . . . And your said subject . . . using many persuasions unto them . . . to have his said son released, alleging therein that it was not fit that a gentleman of his sort should have his son and heir (and that his only son) to be so basely used, they . . . most arrogantly then and there answered that they had authority sufficient to take any nobleman's son in this land. And . . . [they] did then and there deliver unto his said son in most scornful, disdainful and despiteful manner a scroll of paper containing part of one of their said plays or interludes, and him, the said Thomas Clifton, commanded to learn the same by heart. And in further grievance and despite of your said subject, [they] delivered and committed your subject's said son unto the custody of the said

Henry Evans with these threatening words... that if he did not obey the said Evans he should be surely whipped. In which base restraint and misusage the said Thomas Clifton ... continued by the space of about a day and a night, until such time as, by the warrant of the right honourable Sir John Fortescue, knight, one of your majesty's most honourable privy council, he was set at liberty ...

(b) The decision about Evans, 23–30 January 1602

[Evans was fined £100,[1] and as Edward Kirkham, a litigant against Evans, explained in 1612:] That the said Evans in or about the three and fortieth year of the reign of the late Queen Elizabeth[2] was censured by the right honourable Court of Star Chamber for his unorderly carriage and behaviour in taking up gentlemen's children against their wills and to employ them for players and for other misdemeanours in the said decree contained, and further that all assurances made to the said Evans concerning the said house or plays or interludes should be utterly void and to be delivered up to be cancelled, as by the said decree more at large it doth and may appear.

The court may have pronounced similarly about Robinson, since he disappeared from the venture with Evans.

[1] PRO, E159/423/Trin. 44 Eliz. /84.
[2] Kirkham is slightly wrong here. The Queen's forty-third year ended on 16 November 1601, but the bill is dated 15 December 1601, and a note on it gives the hearing as in the octave of Hilary term (23–30 January) 1602.

(c) The decision about Giles and the children, 23–30 January 1602

[In 1606, Giles' right to impress children was confirmed in a patent, but with this proviso:] We [*i.e.* the King] do straightly charge and command that none of the said choristers or children of the Chapel so to be taken by force of this commission shall be used or employed as comedians or stage-players or to exercise or act any ... stage plays, interludes, comedies or tragedies, for that it is not fit or decent that such as should sing the praises of God almighty should be trained up or employed in such lascivious and profane exercises.

405   **Evans distances himself from the playhouse and his other possessions, 21 October 1601, 20 April 1602**

PRO, (a) KB27/1432/m. 359 (also /1414/m. 456 and C2/Jas. I/K5/25, Evans' reply); (b) KB27/1408/m. 303; (c) C66/1614/m. 31. Transcribed in (a) Wallace, 'Children of the Chapel', 206 n. 2, Hillebrand, *Child Actors*, 180–1, and Fleay, *Chronicle History*, 240–1; (b) Wallace, 'Children of the Chapel', 216 n. 3, and Hillebrand, *Child Actors*, 187–8, 332–3; (c) *ES*, II, 49, and MSC, I. 267–8 (a–c) Smith, *Blackfriars Playhouse*, 508–10, 511, 488

On 21 October 1601, it seems (**409h**), Evans assigned all his possessions except the lease on the playhouse to his son-in-law, Alexander Hawkins. He was probably protecting himself should his investment in the playhouse become a liability. He said that he kept the lease to protect Hawkins, should the bond for £400 become forfeit. When the Star Chamber fined him and required him to give up his interest in the playhouse (404), he set about giving it up in public but hanging on to half of it in private. He signed a contract on 20 April 1602, in which Giles and Robinson disappeared from the playhouse and a new partnership of three men took over: Edward Kirkham (the main one, who may have been a yeoman of the Revels), William Rastall (a merchant), and Thomas Kendall (a haberdasher). Evans would continue to own the lease, pay half the rent and other charges, and receive half the profits – but all in Hawkins' name. The three partners would pay and receive the other half. They would invest money in the venture, which in one place Kirkham said was £300 and in another £400. They would also manage it, and, it seems (409c, h), for that privilege they would pay Evans 8s a week on the Saturdays of weeks in which the children played. Should Kirkham, Rastall or Kendall die, his interest would pass to the survivors among them, not, except for the final survivor, to heirs. Evans and Hawkins bonded themselves for £200 to keep their side of the contract, and the other three bonded themselves for £50 to pay Evans his 8s a week. This contract does not survive, but the bonds, which explain most of it, are quoted and other aspects are mentioned in surviving lawsuits (409a, c, f).

Kirkham and associates raised money to equip the children's company with apparel, properties and playbooks by selling shares in the company to, among others, the playwright John Marston and a musician, Martin Peerson.[1] Evans decided that disappearing from public view at Blackfriars was not enough. A month after signing the contract, he went into the country for fear, as he said (409g), of the Lord Chamberlain's displeasure, also for fear, perhaps, of the fine in the Star Chamber. If Giles disappeared from Blackfriars, so, in a sense, did the children of the Chapel Royal. The children at the playhouse were increasingly separate from those at the Chapel and on 4 February 1604 were renamed the Children of the Queen's Revels and were to have their plays approved by Samuel Daniel, the poet. Eventually, because their plays offended the authorities, they lost their royal connection altogether and became simply Children of the Revels, or of Blackfriars.

[1] See Hillebrand, *Child Actors, passim*, and Eccles, 'Martin Peerson and the Blackfriars', 100–6.

(a) Evans and Hawkins' bond for £200, 20 April 1602

[The first part of the bond would have read that Evans and Hawkins owed Kirkham, Rastall and Kendall £200. As quoted by both Hawkins (in 1609) and Evans (in 1612, also in 1609), the second part reads:] The condition of this obligation is such that . . . if . . . William Rastall, Edward Kirkham and Thomas Kendall and every of them, their and every of their executors, administrators and assigns shall or may from henceforth during the continuance of the said lease have the joint use, occupation and profit, together with the within bounden Henry Evans and Alexander Hawkins . . . of and in the said great hall or room and other the premises, without the let or trouble of the said Henry and Alexander . . . or of any other person or persons by their or any of their means or procurement, they, the said William, Edward and Thomas . . . paying unto the said Henry and Alexander . . . from henceforth yearly during the continuance of the said lease the moiety or one-half of the said yearly rent [*i.e.* £20] at the four usual feasts in the year or within one and twenty days next after every of the same feasts by even portions, and also bearing and paying the moiety of such charges as from time to time shall be laid out or disbursed for, in, or about the reparations of the premises by and according to the purport, true meaning, and limitation of the said lease, and also permitting and suffering the said Henry and Alexander . . . to have joint use, occupation and profit together with them, the said William, Edward and Thomas . . . of and in the said great hall and premises without their or any of their lets, troubles and interruptions: that then this present obligation to be void and of none effect, or else it to stand in full force and virtue.

(b) Kirkham, Rastall and Kendall's bond for £50, 20 April 1602

[The first part of the bond would have read that Kirkham, Rastall and Kendall owed Evans and Hawkins £50. As quoted by Evans (in 1608), the second part reads:] The condition of this obligation is such that if the within bounden William Rastall, Edward Kirkham and Thomas Kendall, or any of them, their or any of their executors, administrators or assigns, every week, or weekly, on Saturday during the space of fifteen years next ensuing the date within written, when and so often as any interludes, plays or shows shall be played, used, shown or published in the great hall and other the rooms situate in the Blackfriars, London, or any part thereof mentioned to be demised by one Richard Burbage, gentleman, to the within named Henry Evans in and by one indenture of lease bearing date the second day of September . . . [1600], or elsewhere, by the children or any called by the name of the children of the Queen's Majesty's Chapel, or by any other children which, by the consent of the said William, Edward, Thomas, Henry, and one Alexander Hawkins, gentleman, their executors or administrators or any three of them, whereof the said Henry or Alexander, their executors, or administrators to be one, shall be dieted, kept or retained for the exercise of the said interludes or plays, do and shall well and truly pay, or cause to be paid, unto the said Henry Evans, his executors or assigns at or in the said great hall the sum of eight shillings of lawful money of England, the first payment thereof to begin and to be made on Saturday, being the four and twentieth day next coming of this present instant month of April within written: that then this present obligation to be void and of none effect, or else it to stand in full force and virtue.

(c) The Children of the Queen's Revels, 4 February 1604

[The document is a patent.] Whereas the Queen, our [*i.e.* the King's] dearest wife, hath . . . appointed her servants, Edward Kirkham, Alexander Hawkins, Thomas Kendall and Robert Payne to provide and bring up a convenient number of children who shall be called the Children of her Revels, know ye that we have appointed and authorised ... the said Edward Kirkham, Alexander Hawkins, Thomas Kendall and Robert Payne from time to time to provide, keep and bring up a convenient number of children and them to practice and exercise in the quality of playing ... within the Blackfriars in our City of London or in any other convenient place where they shall think fit for that purpose ... Provided always that no such plays or shows shall be presented before the said Queen, our wife, by the said children, or by them anywhere publicly acted, but by the approbation and allowance of Samuel Daniel, whom her pleasure is to appoint for that purpose.

406 Spectators who sit on the stage are a source of revenue at the playhouse, 1603–1604

PRO, C24/351/pt 1/48, Outlawe 11. Transcribed by Eccles, 'Martin Peerson', 104–5

[On 22 June 1609 Henry Outlawe deposed on Kirkham's behalf that:] By the space of about fifteen weeks together in the first year of the King's majesty's reign in England [24 March 1603 to 23 March 1604], the said Evans, or others by his appointment, did receive and take to the value of 30s a week or thereabouts to his own use for the use of the stools standing upon the stage at Blackfriars ... And ... he [Outlawe] verily thinketh that he [Evans] did never give accompt thereof to the sharers of that house.

Because, on other evidence, people paid 6d per stool, Outlawe was suggesting that sixty people hired stools per week, unknown to Kirkham *et al.* Moreover, because Kirkham *et al.* could hardly have failed to know that people hired stools, Outlawe was also suggesting that people other than Evans' sixty must have hired stools of whom Kirkham and associates did know. Do such throngs of people on stage per week suggest that the children performed once a week, or twice, or three times, or more – or that the witness was exaggerating? From the mid-1590s spectators were common on the stages of London playhouses, especially the private ones and more especially Blackfriars, until King Charles eventually ordered them off in 1639. Spectators not only sat on stools on stage but reclined and stood there (see **413a**) as well.[1]

[1] Eccles used the remark to argue that the children performed three times a week, despite evidence that they performed less often. See also *ES*, II, 535; *J and CS*, VI, 7–8; and Smith, *Blackfriars Playhouse*, 220–3. In his *Gull's Hornbook* (1609), Dekker tells his gallant to sit on the stage where 'you may ... have a good stool for sixpence', and may 'salute all your gentle acquaintance that are spread either on the rushes or on stools about you' (ch. vi). Stages were commonly covered with rushes.

407 The King ends the career of the child-actors in the Blackfriars playhouse, shortly after 11 March 1608

PRO, SP14/31/fo. 166v. Transcribed in *ES*, II, 53–4; Hillebrand, *Child Actors*, 200; and in Smith, *Blackfriars Playhouse*, 193

The children often acted plays that could offend influential people and counted on such plays to attract audiences. Several times the children's playwrights had to appear before the authorities, who sent some playwrights to prison. In 1606, Day's *Isle of Gulls* caused the playhouse to close for a time, and, like Evans before them, Kirkham and his associates had to give up their public connection with the place. They, too, became silent partners – Kirkham also became manager at the St Paul's playhouse (237b) – and Robert Keysar, a goldsmith, took charge at Blackfriars. Then early in March 1608 the children acted two plays within a few days that finished them at Blackfriars. One, now lost, mocked the King's Scottish friends and a Scottish mine operated in his name; the other, one of the parts of Chapman's *The Conspiracy and the Tragedy of Charles, Duke of Byron*, mocked the Queen of France. When the French ambassador complained about the latter play, the English King readily agreed with him.

[The Earl of Montgomery conveyed the King's wishes to the Earl of Salisbury, who directed the work of the privy council, and on 11 March 1608 Sir Thomas Lake wrote to the Earl to repeat them:] His majesty was well pleased with that which your lordship advertiseth concerning the committing of the players that have offended in the matters of France and commanded me to signify to your lordship that for the others who have offended in the matter of the mines and other lewd words, which is the Children of the Blackfriars,[1] that though he had signified his mind to your lordship by my Lord of Montgomery, yet I should repeat it again: that his grace had vowed they should never play more, but should first beg their bread, and he would have his vow performed. And therefore my Lord Chamberlain by himself, or your lordships at the table [*i.e.* in the privy council], should take order to dissolve them and to punish the maker [*i.e.* the playwright] besides.

Several of the children went to prison for a time, and Kirkham (Rastall and Kendall being dead) decided to abandon the venture. He gave up his commission authorising the children to play, discharged poets, and on 26 July 1608 divided the children's goods with Evans (409g). Keysar, however, kept the company together, so that, despite the King's annoyance in March, they played at court during the Christmas season following (1608-9), and with a new partner, Philip Rosseter, he had them playing at the Whitefriars playhouse in 1609.

[1] Lake is probably wrong to imply that the children at Blackfriars acted the play alluding to Scottish mines and another company acted the one alluding to the Queen of France. The ambassador, Antoine de la Boderie, said the same players acted both plays and the play to which he objected concerned the Duke of Byron (his letter of 8 April at the Bibliothèque Nationale, Fr. 15,984; transcribed by Jusserand, 'Ambassador La Boderie and the "Compositeur" of the Byron Plays', 204, and *ES*, III, 257–8). According to the title page (1608) both parts of Chapman's play were acted at Blackfriars. The other play may have been by Marston, whom the privy council sent to prison on 8 June (BL, Add. MS 11,402, fo. 141; transcribed by Wilson, 'Marston, Lodge, and Constable', 99).

408 Richard Burbage regains the playhouse and moves the King's men into it, 9–10 August 1608

PRO, (a) KB27/1454/m. 692; (b) Req.4/1. Transcribed in (a) Wallace, *Advance Sheets*, 5–16, and Chambers, *William Shakespeare*, 62–4; (b) Wallace, 'Shakespeare and his London Associates', 346–7, and Smith, *Blackfriars Playhouse*, 522–3

Five months after the King ended the performances of the choristers at Blackfriars, Richard Burbage, Evans' wife (on his behalf and with the involvement of Hawkins) and the King's men arrived at two transactions that moved the King's men into the playhouse (see also 409g, h).

(a) Richard Burbage leases the playhouse to a consortium, 9 August 1608

This arrangement is mentioned in a lawsuit of 1629 between people into whose hands the lease of William Sly fell or should have fallen.

By a certain ... indenture of lease bearing date 9 August [1608], ... Richard Burbage leased and to farm let to a certain William Sly ... one full seventh part of all that playhouse and of divers other things of the said Richard Burbage particularly specified in the said indenture of lease as well as in five other indentures of lease of the same date separately granting parcels of the said playhouse and premises situated in the precinct of Blackfriars, London (excepting as is excepted by the said separate indentures), for and to the said Richard Burbage, the said John Hemmings, a certain William Shakespeare, Cuthbert Burbage, Henry Condell, Thomas [i.e. Henry?] Evans of London aforesaid, gentlemen, for the term of twenty-one years and for and under an annual rent of £5 14s 4d [each].

Later in the lawsuit, in another connection, the twenty-one years are said to end on 24 June 1629 – hence they began on 24 June 1608.

(b) Evans surrenders the old lease, 10 August 1608

[Because] the said premises lay then [in August 1608] and had long lain void and without use for plays, whereby the same became not only burdensome and unprofitable unto the said Evans but also ran far into decay for want of reparations done in and upon the premises, they ... [Richard Burbage and the King's men] entered into communication with the said Henry Evans, as well for satisfaction of the said bond [for £400] and covenants then forfeited [because Evans had not kept up repairs] unto the said Richard Burbage, as for the repairing of the premises and so maintaining the same, ... which he, the said Henry Evans, finding himself ... unable to perform and being unwilling any longer to charge himself with so great and unnecessary a burden, he, the said Evans, began to treat with the said Richard Burbage about a surrender of the said Evans his said lease, which finally, for and in regard of some competent consideration given him in recompense of his, the said Evans his charge formerly bestowed in buildings in and about the premises, was accomplished, and the said Evans his whole estate of, in , and to the premises was surrendered by the said Evans, unto the said Burbage, who accepted the same surrender accordingly ... as he hopeth it lawful was for him to do, especially the premises being in such decay for want of reparations as then they were ... The said surrender ... was about the tenth of August [1608].[1]

[1] See Smith, *Blackfriars Playhouse*, 208 n. 33. As for the bond of £400, Evans said on 5 November 1612 that when Richard Burbage received the lease back 'he, the said Richard Burbage, delivered up the said obligation of £400 to be cancelled, which this defendant's [Evans'] wife . . . delivered unto the said Hawkins': PRO, C2/Jas. I/K5/25, Evans' reply (**409h**).

409 People concerned with the playhouse in the time of the child-actors sue one another, spring 1608–1612

PRO, (a) KB27/1408/m. 303; (b) KB27/1414/m. 456; (c) C24/351/pt 1/48; (d) C2/Jas. I/K4/33; (e) Req.4/1; (f) KB27/1432/m. 359; (g) C2/Jas. I/E4/9; (h) C2/Jas. I/K5/25, C33/123/fo. 165, C33/124/fo. 171. Transcribed in (a, b, d) Hillebrand, *Child Actors*, 332–4, 180–5, 334–8, and Smith, *Blackfriars Playhouse*, 512–13, 516–19, 514–15; (e) Wallace, 'Shakespeare and his London Associates', 340–60, and Smith, *Blackfriars Playhouse*, 520–6; (f) see Berry, *Shakespeare's Playhouses*, 58–60, 68–9; (g, h) Fleay, *Chronicle History*, 210–22, 223–51, and Smith, *Blackfriars Playhouse*, 527–33, 534–46

People began suing one another over interests in the playhouse a few weeks after the King ended the children's performances there in March 1608, though people had been in court over interests in the children's company since 1605. The surviving legal documents are voluminous. Below are summaries of lawsuits about the playhouse and one other allied lawsuit, and quotations of passages in them that reveal information about the building.

(a) Evans sues Kirkham, Rastall and Kendall in King's Bench, spring 1608

Evans said that because the children had acted a play at Blackfriars on Saturday 16 June 1604 the three new partners should have paid him 8s for the week ending on that day but had not. Their bond of £50 was, therefore, forfeit (**405b**). Kendall said that he had paid the money when appropriate from the beginning, and that no play was played on the day in question. This lawsuit goes no further, but the matter is explained more fully in another (**h** below). The week in question was only one of many for which Kirkham and his associates did not pay Evans. He said they owed him £54, hence had not paid him for 135 weeks. They may have stopped paying him when they resumed playing after the plague of 1603–4 and not paid him again. If so, the week of resumption would have been that ending on 16 June 1604, and from then until early March 1608 the children would have played in 135 weeks. When the lawsuit in King's Bench was ready for trial, Evans settled out of court (**c, h** below): they gave him a new bond for £80 on 4 June 1608 in which they promised to pay him later, and he cancelled the old one and eventually received £48 10s (= 121.35 weeks).

(b) Kirkham and Rastall sue Hawkins in King's Bench, autumn 1608

Kirkham and Rastall (Kendall being dead) sued Hawkins on the bond of £200 given them by Evans and Hawkins (**405a**). Kirkham and Rastall declared that the bond was forfeit, hence that Hawkins owed them £200, but they did not at first say why it was forfeit. Both sides then made some confusing and probably inaccurate statements. Hawkins thought the bond was forfeit because: on 1 July 1604 the playhouse needed repairs for which Evans paid £10 on 18 December 1604; the next day he asked Kirkham for half, £5, and, the money not forthcoming, on 20 December he prevented the three new partners from using the playhouse. Kirkham and Rastall denied that the place had needed repairs, that Evans had spent £10, and that he had asked them for £5. The bond was forfeit, they said, because on 29 February 1604 Evans locked and for some months refused to let them use a room above the room called the schoolhouse. Hawkins replied that Evans did not lock the room or shut the three out of it. Here, Kirkham and Rastall apparently let the lawsuit lapse, probably because Rastall died. Kirkham renewed it against Evans in 1611, and in reply Evans refined or corrected these statements (f below).

Hawkins described the playhouse here as Evans had acquired it in 1600 and the repairs necessary in 1604, but in the lawsuit of 1611 Evans refined these remarks, too (see f below).

In another confusing remark here, Rastall and Kirkham said that

there was a certain chamber called the schoolhouse above part of the said great hall, and certain other chambers above the chamber called the schoolhouse ... The said chamber [was] above the chamber called the schoolhouse.

Evans refined this remark in a lawsuit of 1612 (g below).

(c) Kirkham sues Evans in Chancery, spring 1609

The parts of this lawsuit that seem to survive are interrogatories and depositions for two witnesses on Kirkham's behalf, which show that Kirkham had taken the arguments of the two King's Bench lawsuits above (a, b) to Chancery. One witness, Henry Outlawe, gentleman, said that Evans had detained two rooms from Kirkham *et al.*, 'the one called the schoolhouse and the other room being over the schoolhouse'. He also, unbidden, accused Evans of cheating his colleagues in 1603–4 (see 406). The other witness, Percival Golding, also gentleman, offered on 22 May 1609 a reason why Kirkham *et al.* promised to pay Evans 8s a week: because 'they were desirous that the said Henry Evans should no further intermeddle with the affairs of the playhouse of Blackfriars but should leave them to be managed by the said Alexander Hawkins'. He also offered a reason why Kirkham *et al.* entered into the bond of £50 for the payment of the 8s a week (405b): because the parties agreed to submit their differences to an arbitrator, who, as Kirkham *et al.* hoped, would award them more money from Evans and Hawkins than the £50 they would have to pay if they forfeited the bond.

(d) Kirkham and Kendall's widow sue Samuel Daniel in Chancery, 9 May 1609

For Daniel's acting as censor of plays performed by the Children of the Queen's Revels, Kirkham and Kendall agreed to pay him £10 a year if the children played regularly for six months and other sums if they played less or more. Kirkham and Kendall gave Daniel a bond of £100 guaranteeing that they would pay him. Eventually, the three of them agreed to change the sum to 5s for every week in which the children played (suggesting that they played in about forty weeks a year). Kirkham and Kendall were to give Daniel a new bond, and Daniel was then to return the old bond to them, but Kirkham and Kendall did not carry out their promise. Daniel, moreover, assigned the old bond to John Gerrard on 28 April

1605, whereupon Kirkham and Kendall stopped making regular payments. Declaring the old bond forfeit, therefore, Gerrard sued Kirkham and Kendall in Daniel's name for £100, and they countersued Daniel in this lawsuit.

(e) Keysar sues the Blackfriars consortium in Requests, 8 February 1610

Keysar claimed that Richard Burbage and the rest of the Blackfriars consortium had: (1) deprived him of a share in the playhouse amounting to a sixth of its value, and (2) kept his child-actors out of all the private playhouses so that they had to disperse. For the first claim: Keysar argued that Evans had sold a sixth of his interest in his lease and in the goods of the child-actors to John Marston, the playwright, and in the late spring or early summer of 1608 Keysar had bought that interest from Marston for £100. Moreover, Keysar had first asked the consortium for, and got, a promise that it would not regain the lease from Evans unless all interested parties were treated fairly, but it had regained the lease without reference to Keysar. For the second claim: Keysar argued that the consortium had paid the owners of all private playhouses in London to close their places for one whole year so that Keysar's children had no place to play.

The consortium flatly denied the first claim. Evans did not and, according to his lease, could not sell an interest in the playhouse to Marston; Keysar did not make any arrangements with the consortium; and Marston did not sell an interest to Keysar.[1] Evans did have goods belonging to the children and was willing to give Keysar a proper share of them. As to the second claim: Keysar and his partner, Rosseter, now had child-actors at another private playhouse, Whitefriars. Moreover, Rosseter gave the appropriate official at another, St Paul's, £20 a year to keep the place closed, and when the King's men began to play at Blackfriars, Rosseter asked them to pay half the £20, to which they agreed. See **239** and **432**.

[1] Marston and others owned shares not in the lease but in the children's company and their effects. See Eccles, 'Martin Peerson', 100–6.

(f) Kirkham sues Evans in King's Bench twice, summer 1611

Rastall and Hawkins having died, Kirkham sued Evans twice in King's Bench in the summer of 1611 on the bond of £200 (**405a**). In one lawsuit, a continuation of his and Rastall's lawsuit of 1608 (**b** above), Kirkham said the bond was forfeit because Evans and Hawkins had locked doors in the playhouse. In the other, he said it was forfeit because Evans did not allow Kirkham to resume at the playhouse in 1608 after, presumably, the King's annoyance had abated. Either way, Kirkham was also owed £1,000 in damages. Evans soon responded to the second lawsuit, but it did not go to trial because of delays that the parties blamed on each other. This lawsuit seems not to survive, but comments about it survive in another (**g** below). Evans replied to the lawsuit about locked doors early in May 1612, and corrected or refined statements of 1608. The repairs were necessary on 1 July 1603, not a year later. They cost £11 0s 2d, not £10. Evans paid the money on 18 December 1603, not on that day in 1604. He demanded half (£5 10s 1d) from Kirkham and associates on 19 January 1604, and when they did not pay, he closed both the schoolhouse and the room above it on the next day. When this lawsuit was tried *c*. 25 May 1612, the Lord Chief Justice decided that Kirkham had no case (**g** below).

Evans also refined descriptions of the playhouse (see **403a**) and repairs to it. On 1 July 1603 the playhouse needed repairs (was 'in decay and least in repair') as follows:

> in the outside door leading to the said leased premises and in the walls on the right side of the same door; in the pavement along the eastern part of the said hall and in the pavement under the eastern end of a certain stage in the said hall; and in the walls in the same place above the stairs: and in the glass and in the wooden windows above as well as below on both sides of the said hall; and in the walls on both sides and ends of the said hall; and in the lead gutters and in the roofing of the said premises; ... and in the large purlin[s] on the southern side of the said hall; and in the ceiling in the schoolhouse at the northern end of the said hall.

(g) Evans sues Kirkham in Chancery, 5 May 1612

Evans probably lacked confidence when he replied early in May 1612 to Kirkham's lawsuit in King's Bench (**f** above), since he countersued at the same time in Chancery saying nothing about repairs. He had locked the schoolhouse and room above it from 20 January to 1 May 1604 because they contained goods of his, and he unlocked them whenever Kirkham and his associates asked. Those men, therefore, could not have lost much and need not have lost anything. Moreover, they had promised never to take advantage of the bond for £200 for small breaches of it.

Then, on about 25 May 1612, Evans won the case in King's Bench: Kirkham had not succeeded in showing that the bond was forfeit because Evans had locked rooms.

When Kirkham replied in Chancery on 19 July 1612, therefore, he said little about locked rooms and turned to his other lawsuit of 1611 (**f** above) instead. The bond was forfeit, and his damages were £1,000, because Evans turned him out of the playhouse in the autumn of 1608 and had kept him out ever since. Evans, that is, would not let the children resume at Blackfriars when the authorities might have. In his answer to this answer, Evans pointed to the decision in King's Bench: since his locking of rooms had not caused the bond of £200 to be forfeit, that locking could have cost Kirkham very little. More important, Kirkham himself (presumably through his agent, Keysar) had voided the contract with Evans, hence the bond, by causing the King to prohibit the children's plays and imprison some of the children. As a result, there was no profit at the playhouse, and without plays the place was worth almost nothing, yet Evans had to pay the rent and other expenses. Besides, Kirkham then abandoned the venture by giving up his commission authorising the children to play and discharging poets and divers partners. Evans had the children's goods appraised on 26 July 1608, and Kirkham accepted half of them and seemed satisfied. So assuming that Kirkham had voided the contract, Evans dealt with Richard Burbage and the King's men and was right in law and equity to do so.[1]

Remarks here and in **f** above (see also **403a**) about the 'schoolhouse' and room over suggest that the playhouse was at least two storeys high. Evans said, and Kirkham agreed, that:

> there was a certain room called the schoolhouse and a certain chamber over the same demised and letten ... in and by the said indenture of lease [*i.e.* the

Burbage–Evans lease] . . . which said schoolhouse and chamber over were severed from the said great hall and made fit by . . . [Evans] to dine and sup in.

[1] Evans also argued that Kirkham, Rastall and Kendall had caused him to lose 'at least' £300 when he went 'into the country' a month after he had signed his contract with them (on 20 April 1602) and left them to manage the playhouse 'for a long space of time'. Kirkham replied that Evans lost nothing when he went 'into the country' because he left Hawkins behind to deal for him and take his profits. Evans then enlarged his story: Kirkham, Rastall and Kendall gave the Lord Chamberlain false information against him, so that the Lord Chamberlain commanded him to leave the playhouse, and for fear of his displeasure Evans also left 'the country' and so, because Hawkins was negligent, lost 'near' £300.

(h) Kirkham sues Edward Painton in Chancery, 1 July 1612

Before he replied to Evans in Chancery (g above), Kirkham turned to Hawkins' part in the enterprise, now represented by Edward Painton, gentleman, who had married Hawkins' widow, Margaret. Kirkham advanced a new reading of his contract with Evans: the contract required that Kirkham and associates spend £400 'about the premises', and, in return, that Hawkins (to whom Kirkham thought Evans had assigned the lease) assign them a half-interest in the lease on request.[1] They had spent the money, and Kirkham, as their survivor, should now own half the lease and receive half the profits.[2] Moreover, Hawkins had died without a will so that his widow had effectually owned the lease before Evans surrendered it to Burbage; Evans, therefore, could not surrender it to Burbage, and Painton was now the rightful owner who should convey half to Kirkham. In reply, Painton agreed that he should own the whole lease but denied that he should assign half to Kirkham, though Kirkham and associates had spent money on 'such trash' as plays and players.

Evans, Burbage and the consortium (represented by John Hemmings, the King's men's treasurer) made common cause. They argued that the court should dismiss Kirkham's case because it concerned playhouses and plays, which, as courts had occasionally decided, were unworthy of legal attention. The court, however, did not accept the argument. They then denied all Kirkham's and Painton's statements in detail, especially that Hawkins was to assign half the lease to Kirkham and his associates and that Hawkins still had anything to do with the lease when he died. Evans denied that he had assigned the lease to Hawkins along with his other goods. He argued, as he had done six months earlier (g above), that his contract with Kirkham and associates ended when their actions caused the King to banish the children from the playhouse, and he said that Kirkham himself had once thought so.

The court dismissed Kirkham's case on 14 November 1612. If Hawkins was to assign half the lease to Kirkham and the others, such an assignment was never sealed, and neither Evans nor Kirkham had paid Burbage the rent for the playhouse since 1608. Moreover, the court now decided that the case did concern those unworthy matters, playhouses and plays.

Kirkham declared in this lawsuit that he and his associates made £100 a year above expenses when they ran the playhouse and more than £150 when their agent, Keysar, did. He also declared that Burbage and the consortium made £160 a year clear from 1608 onwards (which Burbage, Hemmings and Evans all denied) and, wildly defying arithmetic, £1,000 more 'in one winter . . . than they were used to get' from the Globe. In the previous lawsuit (g above) Kirkham had implied that he and his associates had made £60 a year.

[1] In the previous lawsuit (g above) Kirkham said that he and associates had to spend £300 'for divers employments' in the playhouse, but not that in return Hawkins was to give them a half-interest in

the lease. Kirkham's new case was that he and associates had spent money on the building, hence should have a share of it. Evans, in the previous lawsuit, and Burbage and Hemmings now, said that Kirkham and associates had spent money only on 'playing apparel and other implements and properties touching and concerning the furnishing and setting forth of players and plays', as Kirkham eventually admitted. He and associates had spent their £400 and £200 besides 'towards the apparel of the players and other necessaries for their provision'.

[2] Kirkham declared that he and his associates also paid Evans 8s a playing week in return for Hawkins' assigning half the lease to them. Evans replied that Kirkham and associates paid the money 'because . . . [they] would at their directions have the dieting and ordering of the boys used about the plays there, which before . . . [Evans] had and for the which he had weekly . . . disbursed and allowed great sums of money'. Writers (for example, Smith, *Blackfriars Playhouse*, 187) have taken the remark to mean that Kirkham and associates were to reimburse Evans for money he had paid before they had anything to do with the playhouse. The remark makes more sense if it means, as one of Kirkham's witnesses said (c above), that they paid the money to have control of the boys and their work without interference from Evans, even though Evans owned half the venture. Evans added that arrearages built up until £54 was owing, for which he sued Kirkham and the others, who settled out of court and eventually paid him £48 10s (see **a** above).

410 Neighbours repeatedly try to have the playhouse closed, 1618–1641

(a) CLRO, Remembrancia, v, 28, 29 and Repertory 34, fo. 38v; PRO, C66/1608/m. 4 and PSO2/40/24–30 March 17 Jas. I/2. (b) PRO, PC2/43/fos. 137, 175, 213, and SP16/250/fo. 195; *Strafforde's Letters and Dispatches*, I, 175. Transcribed in (a) MSC, I. 91–4, 264, 281, and *J and CS*, VI, 18–20; Halliwell-Phillipps, *Outlines* (1887), I, 311; (b) MSC, I.386–9, and *J and CS*, VI, 27, 29–30.

The argument for all these attempts to close the playhouse was the one used for the first attempt in 1596 (402): that the playhouse caused inconveniences in the neighbourhood, as it really did[1] and would still if the playhouse were there now. No one mentioned moral or religious arguments, even though a prime mover was the puritan writer, William Gouge, who became rector of the parish in 1621. These attempts occurred in 1618–19, 1625–6, 1631, 1633 and 1641, and none succeeded. Below are quotations from the first and fourth of them.

[1] On 19 January 1638 'a beggar child', William Jordan, was buried in Blackfriars, having been 'killed with a coach coming from the play' (GL, MS 4510/1; see *J and CS*, VI, 18n.).

(a) December 1618 – March 1619

[The officers of the parish, led by Gouge, petitioned the Lord Mayor and Corporation of London, probably in December 1618 or just after:] May it please your lordship and your brethren . . . that contrary to the said orders [forbidding the opening of the playhouse in 1596 (402)], the owner of the said playhouse doth, under the name of a private house, . . . convert the said house to a public playhouse, unto which there is daily such resort of people and such multitudes of coaches (whereof many are hackney [*i.e.* hired] coaches bringing people of all sorts), that sometimes all our streets cannot contain them . . . They clog up Ludgate also in such sort that both they endanger the one the other, break down stalls, [and] throw down men's goods from their shops. And the inhabitants there cannot come to their houses nor bring in their necessary provisions of beer, wood, coal or hay, nor the tradesmen or shopkeepers utter their wares, nor the passenger [*i.e.* pedestrian] go to the common water stairs without danger of their lives and limbs. Whereby also many times quarrels and effusion of blood hath followed. And what further danger may be occasioned by broils, plots or practices of such an unruly multitude of people if they should get head, your wisdoms can conceive. These inconveniences falling out almost every day in the winter time (not forbearing the time of Lent) from one or two of the clock till six at night, . . . being the time also most usual for Christenings and burials and afternoons service, we cannot have passage to the church for performance of those necessary duties, the ordinary passage for a great part of the precinct aforesaid being close by the playhouse door.

[Then twenty-four other citizens of the parish also petitioned the Lord Mayor, desiring:] your lordship and your brethren to help us to some remedy therein [*i.e.* about the playhouse 'in that unfit place'], that we may go to our houses in safety and enjoy the benefit of the streets without apparent danger, which now, we assure your lordship, neither we that are inhabitants nor any other of his majesty's subjects having occasion that way, either by land or water, can do. For such is the unruliness of some of the resorters to that house and of coaches, horses and people of all sorts gathered together by that occasion in those narrow and crooked streets that many hurts have heretofore been thereby done. And [we] fear it will at some time or other hereafter procure much more if it be not by your wisdoms prevented.

[On 21 January 1619 the City considered these petitions and] doth think fit and so order[s] that the said playhouse be suppressed and that the players shall from henceforth forbear and desist from playing in that house in respect of the manifold abuses and disorders complained of as aforesaid.

[The playhouse remained open, however, and on 27 March 1619 the King's men had their Patent of 1603 renewed so that it effectually allowed them to play at Blackfriars in the King's name. In 1603, one section of the patent had allowed them to play:] within their now usual house called the Globe within our county of Surrey.

[In 1619, the same section allowed them to play:] within their two . . . now usual houses called the Globe within our county of Surrey and their private [play]house situate in the precincts of the Blackfriars within our City of London.

(b) October–December 1633

[At a meeting on 9 October 1633, the privy council debated] the great inconvenience and annoyance occasioned by the resort and confluence of coaches to the playhouse in Blackfriars [at play times], whereby the streets, being narrow thereabouts, are at those times become impassable to the great prejudice of his majesty's subjects passing that way upon their several occasions and in particular to divers noblemen and councillors of state whose houses are that way, whereby they are many times hindered from their necessary attendance upon his majesty's person and service. Their lordships [*i.e.* members of the council], calling to mind that formerly upon complaint hereof made . . . [they were] of opinion that the said playhouse was fit to be removed from thence, and that an indifferent recompence and allowance should be given them [*i.e.* the consortium and players] for their interests in the said house and buildings thereunto belonging, did therefore think fit and order that Sir Henry Spiller and Sir William Becher, knights, the aldermen of the ward; Lawrence Whitaker, esq.; and [blank] Child, citizen of London, or any three of them, be hereby required to call such of the parties interested before them as they shall think fit, and, upon hearing their demands and view of the place, . . . make an indifferent estimate and value of the said house and buildings and of their interests therein, and . . . agree upon and set down such recompence to be given for the same as shall be reasonable, and thereupon . . . make report to the . . . [council] of their doings and proceedings therein by the 26th of this present [month].

[The unstated idea was that the residents of Blackfriars would provide the money necessary to buy the playhouse. The committee made their report, and on 20 November the council considered it, noting that] The players demand £21,000. The commissioners (Sir Henry Spiller, Sir William Becher and Lawrence Whitaker) valued it at near £3,000. The parishioners offer towards the removing of them £100.[1] [The council, therefore, gave up the idea of buying out the enterprise and turned to a cheaper way of dealing with:] the great inconveniences that grow by reason of the resort to the playhouse of the Blackfriars in coaches, whereby the streets near thereunto are at playtime so stopped that his majesty's subjects going about their necessary affairs can hardly find passage and are oftentimes endangered. Their lordships [*i.e.* councillors], remembering that there is an easy passage by water unto that playhouse without troubling the streets and that it is much more fit and reasonable that those which go thither should go thither by water or else on foot rather than the necessary businesses of all others and the public commerce should be disturbed by their pleasure, do therefore order that if any person . . . of what condition whatsoever repair to the aforesaid playhouse in coach, so soon as they are gone out of their coaches the coachmen shall depart thence and not return till the end of the play, nor shall stay or return to fetch those whom they carried any nearer with their coaches than the farther part of St Paul's Churchyard on the one side and Fleet conduit on the other side, and in the time between their departure and return shall either return home or else abide in some other streets less frequented with passengers, . . . which order if any coachman disobey, the next constable or officer is hereby charged to commit him presently to Ludgate or Newgate. And the Lord Mayor of the City of London is required to see this carefully performed . . . And, to the end that none may pretend ignorance hereof, it is lastly ordered that copies of this order shall be set up at Paul's chain, by direction of the Lord Mayor, also at the west end of St Paul's church, at Ludgate, and the Blackfriars gate, and Fleet conduit.

[The cheaper way, however, did not please everyone, as the council noted at a meeting on 29 December, attended by the King himself:] Upon information this day given to the board [*i.e.* council] of the discommodity that divers persons of great quality, especially ladies and gentlewomen, did receive in going to the playhouse of Blackfriars by reason that no coaches may stand within the Blackfriars gate or return thither during the play, and of the prejudice the players, his majesty's servants, do receive thereby, but especially that the streets are so much the more encumbered with the said coaches: the board, taking into consideration the former order of the 20th of November last concerning this business, did think fit to explain the said order in such manner that as many coaches as may stand within the Blackfriars gate may . . . enter and stay there or return thither at the end of the play.

[And so things were back to normal when George Garrard wrote to Lord Wentworth in Ireland on 9 January 1634:] Here hath been an order of the lords of the council hung up . . . near Paul's and the Blackfriars to command all that resort to the playhouse there to send away their coaches and to disperse abroad in Paul's Churchyard, Carter Lane, the conduit in Fleet Street, and other places and not to return to fetch their company, but they must trot afoot to find their coaches. 'Twas kept very strictly for two or three weeks, but now I think it is disordered again.

[1] Collier printed (*New Facts*, 27–8), Bentley reprinted (*J and CS*, VI, 28), and Chambers summarised (*ES*, II, 512 n., see also MSC, I. 386) a document that purports to be the actual report of the committee. One might doubt its authenticity, however, because Collier said he owned it and nobody else has seen it. Moreover, it says that the people mainly concerned with the playhouse, including, presumably, Richard Burbage, other members of the consortium and actors, had equal interests in it, as they clearly did not (see **408**). The document also says wrongly that the playhouse was 'the inheritance' of Cuthbert and William Burbage; on 20 November 1633 it was the inheritance of Richard Burbage's widow, Winifred Robinson, and would eventually be that of their then seventeen-year-old son, William (see **411**, **415a**). Cuthbert owned property in Blackfriars, but not having to do with the playhouse. The document gives the sum demanded by 'the company' as £21,990 (including £2,400 for the interests of sixteen people at £150 each) and that proposed by the committee as £2,900 13s 4d (£700 for the playhouse, £1,134 for allied properties, £1,066 13s 4d for the interests of the sixteen people at £66 13s 4d each). The document does not mention the sum raised by parishioners.

411 The consortium renews the leases, 24 June 1629

PRO, LC5/133, pp. 44–51. Transcribed in Halliwell-Phillipps, *Outlines* (1882), 476–86, and MSC, II.i.362–73

The terms of the new leases at Blackfriars and other aspects of the ownership and management of the Blackfriars and Globe playhouses appear in the so-called Sharers' Papers of 1635. Three players (Robert Benfield, Thomas Pollard and Eyllaerdt Swanston) protested to the Lord Chamberlain that though they were leading actors among the King's men they could not own shares in either of the company's playhouses. Below are quoted the parts of the papers relating to the Blackfriars playhouse. See also **478** and, for the full document, **162**.

526   Playhouses, 1560–1660

[The players said:] That for the house in the Blackfriars, it being divided into eight parts amongst the ... housekeepers [*i.e.* the consortium] and Mr Shanks having two parts thereof, Mr Lowin, Mr Taylor and each of the rest having but one part apiece, which two parts were by the said Mr Shanks purchased of Mr Hemings, ... the petitioners desire and hope that your lordship [the Lord Chamberlain] will conceive it ... reasonable that the said Mr Shanks may assign over one of the said parts amongst them three, they giving him such satisfaction for the same as that he be no loser thereby.

[In his reply, Shanks alluded to the term of the new leases and the annual rent when he explained that he had bought both his leases from William Hemings, the heir of the actor, John Hemmings.]

That about two years since [in 1633] ... [he] upon offer to him made by William Hemings did buy of him one part he had in Blackfriars for about six years then to come at the yearly rent of £6 5s ... That about eleven months since [in 1634] the said William Hemings offering to sell ... the remaining ... [part] he then had ... in the Blackfriars, wherein he had then about five years to come ... [he, Shanks] likewise bought the same. [If the rent paid for one lease was £6 5s, that for all eight was £50.]

[Winifred Robinson (Richard Burbage's widow) and Cuthbert Burbage replied:] Now for the Blackfriars, that is our inheritance. Our father purchased it at extreme rates and made it into a playhouse with great charge and trouble, which after was leased out to one Evans that first set up the boys commonly called the Queen's majesty's Children of the Chapel ... In process of time ... the boys daily wearing out, it was considered that house would be fit for ourselves and so [we] purchased the lease remaining from Evans with our money and placed men players, which were Hemmings, Condell, Shakespeare, etc. [there].

The Lord Chamberlain decided on 12 July and 1 August 1635 that the three actors should buy one of Shanks' shares in Blackfriars, which now had four years to run, at the 'usual and accustomed' rate to be decided by a committee of three.

412   Actresses appear at Blackfriars with a French troupe, autumn 1629

Sir Henry Herbert, Office Book (now lost). Transcribed by Malone in *Plays and Poems of William Shakespeare* (1821), III, 120; Prynne, *Histrio-Mastix*, sigs. Ee3–4, Ggg3v. See J and CS, VI, 23, 225–7

[On 4 November 1629 the Master of the Revels noted receiving a fee] For the allowing of a French company to play a farce at Blackfriars ... £2 0s 0d.

[And four years later Prynne noted:] They have now their female players in Italy and other foreign parts ... [And] in imitation of these, some French women, or monsters rather, on Michaelmas term 1629 attempted to act a French play at the playhouse in Blackfriars – an impudent, shameful, unwomanish, graceless, if not more than whorish attempt.

413 Fashionable people quarrel at plays at Blackfriars, 1632–1636

(a) PRO, C115/M35/8391; (b) HMC, *Various*, VII, 408; (c, d) *Strafforde's Letters and Dispatches*, I, 426, 511. Transcribed in (a) Berry, *Shakespeare's Playhouses*, 48–9. See *J and CS*, VI, 33–4

At least four quarrels took place at the playhouse from 1632 to 1636. They show the kind of people who made up what Bentley called 'the coterie character of the audience' there (*J and CS*, VI, 33). More important, two of the quarrels yield information about the places from which these people watched plays.

(a) Lord Thurles and Captain Essex, late January 1632

[Describing recent cases in the Star Chamber, a writer of newsletters, John Pory, noted on 4 February 1632:] Their lordships [*i.e.* judges of the court] made my Lord of Thurles . . . to do the like satisfaction[1] to Captain Essex. The occasion was this. This captain attending and accompanying my Lady of Essex in a box in the playhouse at the Blackfriars, the said lord, coming upon the stage, stood before them and hindered their sight. Captain Essex told his lordship they had paid for their places as well as he and therefore entreated him not to deprive them of the benefit of it. Whereupon the lord stood up yet higher and hindered more their sight. Then Captain Essex with his hand put him a little by. The lord then drew his sword and ran full butt at him, though he missed him, and might have slain the Countess as well as him.[2] [Hence the boxes were contiguous to the stage and on a level with it, and people stood on stage as well as sat there on joint stools.]

[1] Pory alluded here to his remark just above this one, that the judges had recently compelled Walter Steward to give Sir Miles Fleetwood 'such satisfaction' in their presence as 'they thought reasonable'. Steward had called Fleetwood, treasurer of the Court of Wards, 'a briber . . . yea more, that he was a base knave' who went to two sermons on Sunday and would sell his friend on Monday for 2s.
[2] The Countess was the new wife of the Earl of Essex and the Captain was Charles Essex, a professional soldier and follower of the Earl. Lord Thurles was the future Duke of Ormond.

(b) Sir John Suckling and John Digby, 18 November 1634

[In a letter dated 25 November 1634, Robert Leake told Sir Gervase Clifton:] I make no doubt but you have heard that *actus secondus* played on Tuesday last [18 November] at Blackfriars between Sir John Suckling and Mr Digby: both of them with their companies was committed to the King's Bench [prison], but surely Sir John was bailed, for a I saw him this day in a coach.

(c) Lord Digby and Will Crofts, spring 1635

[In a letter dated 19 May 1635, George Garrard told Lord Wentworth, the Lord Deputy in Ireland:] The quarrel that lately broke out betwixt my Lord Digby and Will Crofts in the Blackfriars at a play stands as it did when your brother went hence. Crofts stands confined to his father's house because by striking he broke his bonds of £5,000, but there was a great difference in the parties that stood bound. My Lord of Bedford and Sir John Strangwick stipulated for my Lord Digby, [and] Tom Eliot and Jack Crofts, men of small fortunes, for the other, that they should keep the peace during the suit depending in the Star Chamber. The lords [*i.e.* judges] have heard it and reported their opinions to the King and there it rests.

(d) The Duke of Lennox and the Lord Chamberlain, January 1636

[In a letter dated 25 January 1636, Garrard also told Lord Wentworth:] A little pique happened betwixt the Duke of Lennox and the Lord Chamberlain about a box at a new play in the Blackfriars of which the Duke had got the key, which if it had come to be debated betwixt them, as it was once intended, some heat or perhaps other inconvenience might have happened. His majesty hearing of it, sent to the Earl of Holland to command them both not to dispute it but before him, so he heard it and made them friends.

414 The Queen joins the audience at Blackfriars, 1634–1638

Alnwick Castle, MS 506/132. Transcribed in HMC, *Third Report*, 118. See *J and CS*, VI, 34–5

Queen Henrietta attended at least four performances in the playhouse, the first early in May 1634 and the last on 23 April (St George's Day) 1638.

[The King's nephew, Charles, wrote of an occasion that took place in the winter of 1635 or spring following. In a letter to his mother, the former Princess Elizabeth, who lived in the Netherlands and had been patron to a company of actors, Charles reported that the King sat 'yesterday' for a portrait by Anthony Van Dyke, commissioned by the Prince of Orange, and added that Van Dyke's] house is close by Blackfriars, where the Queen saw Lodowick Carlell's second part of *Arviragus and Felicia* acted, which is hugely liked of everyone.

415 The Blackfriars playhouse comes to an end, 1642–1655?

(a) PRO, C54/3579/m. 39–40; (b) Flecknoe, *Miscellania*, sig. 16–6v; (c) Folger, MS V.b.275, p. 16. Transcribed in (a) Berry, *Shakespeare's Playhouses*, 69; (c) Collier, *Works of William Shakespeare*, I, ccxli–ii, n.

The document quoted in (c) below is probably a forgery and is in any case unreliable, though Chambers (*ES*, II, 374–5), Bentley (*J and CS*, VI, 41–2) and others have accepted it at face value. If the playhouse was not pulled down in 1655, it could have been made into something else about then. See Berry, 'Folger Ms V.b.275'.

(a) The Burbages sell the playhouse, 1651

[William Burbage sold the playhouse building on 13 August 1651 to George Best, merchant, for £700, as follows:] All that great hall or room heretofore divided into seven rooms and since converted into a playhouse and lately furnished with a stage, galleries and seats, and for many years together of late heretofore used for showing and acting of plays therein . . . together with the stairs and staircase thereunto belonging and leading up into the late playhouse out of the great yard or street there now commonly called . . . the playhouse yard. And also all the rooms under the said late playhouse and all other rooms, chambers, galleries, cellars, solers, vaults, curtilages, yards and hereditaments whatsoever, situate and being within the said stone wall. And also all that other large messuage or tenement with the appurtenances near adjoining to the said late playhouse on the south side thereof, late in the tenure or occupation of John Bill or his assigns[1] and enclosed likewise with a stone wall and abutting upon the lane leading into the yard called the printing house yard towards the south. And all shops, rooms, cellars, solers, vaults, withdraughts [*i.e.* privies], courtyards, curtilages, backsides, lights, easements, ways, passages, liberties, privileges, annuities, profits, commodities, advantages, emoluments, hereditaments and appurtenances whatsoever to the said great hall, messuages and premises . . . belonging . . .

[1] Bill was the King's printer. His printing house was in Hunsdon House, which was the southern part of the building in which the playhouse was. Lord Hunsdon had lived there in the early days of the playhouse.

(b) The playhouse in 1652

[In 'A whimsey written . . . about the end of the year 52' (i.e. 1652), Richard Flecknoe described a walk from Smithfield to St Paul's and then:] passing on to Blackfriars and seeing never a play bill on the gate, no coaches on the place, nor doorkeeper at the playhouse door with a box like a churchwarden desiring you to remember the poor players, I cannot but say for epilogue to all the plays were ever acted there:

> Poor house that in days of our grandsires
> Belongst unto the mendiant friars
> And where so oft in our fathers' days
> We have seen so many of Shakespeare's plays,
> So many of Jonson's, Beaumont's, and Fletcher's,
> Until I know not what puritan teachers . . .

Have made with their railings the players as poor
As were the friars and poets before.

(c) The playhouse pulled down, 1655?

The Blackfriars players' playhouse in Blackfriars, London, which had stood many years, was pulled down to the ground on Monday the 6th of August, 1655, and tenements built in the room.

XXXI The first Fortune

The first Fortune playhouse was a public playhouse in Middlesex, about quarter of a mile north of the north-west corner of the London wall and a hundred yards or so beyond the north-west parts of the City boundary. It lay between two streets that ran (and run) south from Old Street towards St Giles Cripplegate, in the parish of which it was. The streets are Golden (or Golding) Lane and Whitecross Street, and the playhouse was where the present Fortune Street, E.C.1, runs east and west between them. The main entrance to the playhouse was probably via Golden Lane.

The playhouse was the project of Philip Henslowe and his stepdaughter's husband, the actor Edward Alleyn, mainly the latter. They were moving their theatrical enterprises from the Rose in Southwark, which was relatively small and a short distance from a new playhouse built in the spring of 1599, the Globe. On 22 December 1599, Alleyn paid £240 for a lease until 25 March 1625 on the property where the Fortune was to be built, and on 8 January 1600 he and Henslowe engaged Peter Street to build it. Street was the carpenter who with his men had pulled down the Theatre a year earlier and then had probably built the Globe. Alleyn set about overcoming the objections of neighbours, and Henslowe dealt with Street and paid sums as required. The work of building began during the spring of 1600 and was to be finished by 25 July, but it took several months longer, one of them the result of objections by neighbours. Alleyn later noted that he had spent £520 on the building. That sum must have comprised the £440 for which Street had agreed to build the building, plus £80 for painting and other finishing work excluded from the arrangements with Street and, perhaps, for cost overruns.[1] Alleyn also paid £680 for leases and, in 1610, the freehold on the property, but these transactions included neighbouring properties that had nothing to do with the Fortune and in which he carried on ventures of his own.

Henslowe and Alleyn's copy of their contract with Street survives, because Alleyn left it to the school he eventually founded, the College of God's Gift in Dulwich, where it still is. More, therefore, is reliably known about the structure of the playhouse than about that of any other, and aspects of the place often figure in theorising about its less well-documented competitors and the Renaissance playhouse in general.

Like the Globe and most other public playhouses of the time, the first Fortune was a timber-frame building, but unlike them it was square. It consisted of a roofed 'frame' standing around an open yard in which was a roofed stage. This 'frame' sat on foundations rising at least a foot above ground and was 80 feet square on the outside, 55 feet square on the inside. It was three storeys high, the lower one 12 feet high, the middle one 11 feet high, and the top one 9 feet high. The lower storey was 12 feet 6 inches deep, and because each of the other two had a 'jutty' of 10 inches (that is, extended that much more over the yard than the storey below), the middle storey was 13 feet 4 inches deep and the upper one 14 feet 2 inches. The 'frame' was mainly to provide galleries for spectators. Four 'convenient divisions' of the galleries were 'gentlemen's rooms' and other divisions were 'twopenny rooms'. All the galleries contained 'seats'. The bottom gallery was paled inside with oak boards and 'laid over and fenced with iron pikes', perhaps to keep spectators from climbing into that gallery from the yard. The floors of the galleries were new deal boards, and the gentlemen's and twopenny rooms were 'ceiled with' – that is, their walls and ceilings were of – lath and plaster.

At least part of one side of the 'frame' was a tiring-house, which had glazed windows and 'lights'. The stage extended from the tiring-house to the middle of the yard, 27½ feet. It was 43 feet wide, so that 6 feet of the yard lay between each side and the 'frame'. It was paled in below with oak boards, and its floor consisted of new deal boards. It, too, was 'ceiled with' – presumably had a ceiling of – lath and plaster.

The roofs were covered with tiles. A lead gutter carried water backwards off the stage roof to a good drain, and other gutters, probably, carried water away from the frame and staircases to the same drain.

Helpful though it is, however, the contract leaves much to be desired because for many things it directs Street merely to do as he had done at the Globe, about which little is reliably known, or to follow a separate 'plot' that is missing. The stage was to be 'placed' and 'set' according to the plot, but 'in all other proportions' it was to be like the one at the Globe. Similarly, the staircases were explained in the plot but also to be like those at the Globe; the contract suggests in passing that they were outside the 'frame', enclosed, and roofed with tiles. In the galleries, the aisles ('conveyances') and partitions ('divisions without and within') were to be like those at the Globe. And for details throughout the playhouse about which the contract is silent, the model was to be the Globe.

The contract specifies two improvements on the Globe. The main posts of the galleries and stage facing the yard were to be 'square and wrought plasterwise with carved . . . satyrs . . . placed and set on the top' of each. And all the lesser beams of the frame were to be bigger than those in the Globe.

Henslowe and Alleyn's company left the Rose and opened the new playhouse in the autumn of 1600. The company stayed there throughout the history of the playhouse, as the Lord Admiral's men, then Prince Henry's men, and finally the Palsgrave's men.

In 1601, some six months after the opening, Henslowe and Alleyn drew up a document in which they formalised their partnership in the playhouse. The document was a lease in which Alleyn granted half the playhouse to Henslowe until 25 March 1625, when Alleyn's current lease on the land under the playhouse ran out. Henslowe paid £8 a year in rent, which should represent the amount by which Alleyn's investment was greater than Henslowe's; at 8 per cent interest, hence twelve and a half years purchase, that amount would be £100.

Henslowe left his lease to his widow when he died early in 1616, and, after thinking of selling it to three others, she left it to Alleyn when she died the next year. In 1618 he leased the whole playhouse to the Palsgrave's men for £200 a year.

Like the first Globe before it, the first Fortune was destroyed by fire. It was 'quite burnt down in two hours' late on the night of 9 December 1621.

---

[1] Dulwich, MS VIII, fo. 6v, transcribed in *Henslowe Papers*, ed. Greg, 108. See also Orrell, 'Building the Fortune', 129–44.

416 Edward Alleyn acquires the property on which he builds the playhouse, 22 December 1599

Dulwich, Muniments (a) 20, (b) 38. Transcribed in (b) *Henslowe Papers*, ed. Greg, 17–18 (see also 15–16)

In 1584 a goldsmith, Patrick Brewe, bought a lease for forty-one years on the property where the playhouse would stand from the people who owned the freehold, a family named Gill. Brewe paid £13 6s 8d for the lease, and his rent was £12 a year (Muniment 12). Alleyn bought Brewe's lease in 1599. In 1601 the Gills leased the property to John Garrett, cloth worker, for twenty-one years beginning when Brewe's forty-one years were up in 1625 (Muniment 23). Alleyn bought this lease, too, on 1 May 1610, for £100 (Muniment 36), and soon after, with the help of Brewe, he bought the freehold of the property from the Gills. Below are quotations from two of these transactions.

(a) Alleyn buys Brewe's lease, 22 December 1599

[For 'a certain sum of . . . money' and a bond in which Brewe undertook to pay Alleyn £250 if he, Brewe, did not perform his part of the bargain, Alleyn acquired a lease comprising:] All those his [Brewe's] six messuages or tenements with all and singular shops, cellars, chambers, halls, parlours, roomeths, gardens, void grounds, lights, easements, water courses, wells, paths, ways, entries, outgates [*i.e.* exits], profits, commodities and appurtenances whatsoever to the same six messuages or tenements, or any of them, belonging or in any wise appertaining, . . . five of which said premises are situate and being on the east side of Golden Lane and the other messuage or tenement on the west side of the Whitecross Street in the said parish of St Giles Cripplegate.

In the section beginning 'To have and to hold', the contract repeats some of these aspects of the property and adds kitchens, sollars (*i.e.* upper rooms), orchards, and backsides.

(b) Alleyn buys the freehold, 30 May 1610

[Daniel Gill the elder and his two sons, four daughters, and their husbands sold to Edward Alleyn for £340:] all those their twelve tenements, be they more or less, and all that their playhouse commonly called or known by the name of the Fortune, or by what other name it be known or called, with their and every of their several appurtenances, situate and being in the parish of St Giles without Cripplegate, London, and in the county of Middlesex . . . Six of which said twelve tenements are situate and being on the east side of Golden Lane in the parish and county aforesaid and the other six . . . are situate and being on the west side of Whitecross Street in the parish and county aforesaid. All which said tenements, playhouse, and other the premises abut upon Whitecross Street aforesaid on the east part and upon Golden Lane aforesaid and the lands and tenements now or late of Thomas Langham, fishmonger, . . . on the west and north, that is to say part on the west and part on the north, and upon the lands and grounds now or late called the Rose and Crown . . . towards the north, and the lands and tenements now or late of Richard Roper, baker, and Godfrey Isburd, haberdasher, and a piece of ground appertaining to the Chamber of London towards the south.

[Alleyn wrote a summary on the back of the document:] An Indenture of bargain and sale from all the Gills, and the four daughters co-heirs, and their husbands to Edward Alleyn, date the 30th of May [1610].

417 Henslowe and Alleyn contract with a carpenter, Peter Street, to build the first Fortune, 8 January 1600

Dulwich, Mun. 22. Transcribed in *Henslowe Papers*, ed. Greg, 4–7; *ES*, II, 436–9; *J and CS*, VI, 141–3; *Henslowe's Diary*, 307–10, and in many other places. The original is reproduced as an attachment in *Henslowe Papers*, ed. Foakes, I. Malone knew of the contract in the eighteenth century and printed it, with the contract for the Hope, in *Plays and Poems of William Shakespeare* (1821), III, 338.

This indenture made the eighth day of January [1600] . . . between Philip Henslowe and Edward Alleyn of the parish of St Saviour's in Southwark, in the county of Surrey, gentlemen, on the one part and Peter Street, citizen and carpenter of London, on the other part.

Witnesseth, that whereas the said Philip Henslowe and Edward Alleyn . . . have bargained, compounded and agreed with the said Peter Street for the erecting, building and setting up of a new house and stage for a playhouse in and upon a certain plot or parcel of ground appointed out for that purpose, situate and being near Golden Lane in the parish of St Giles without Cripplegate of London, to be by him, the said Peter Street, or some other sufficient workmen of his providing and appointment, and at his proper costs and charges (for the consideration hereafter in these presents expressed), made, erected, builded and set up in manner and form following:

That is to say, the frame of the said house to be set square and to contain 80 feet of lawful assize every way square without and 55 feet of like assize square every way within, with a good sewer and strong foundation of piles, brick, lime and sand, both without and within to be wrought 1 foot of assize at the least above the ground. And the said frame to contain three storeys in height: the first or lower storey to contain 12 feet of lawful assize in height, the second storey 11 feet of lawful assize in height, and the third or upper storey to contain 9 feet of lawful assize in height. All which storeys shall contain 12½ feet of lawful assize in breadth throughout, besides a jutty forwards in either of the said two upper storeys of 10 inches of lawful assize, with four convenient divisions for gentlemen's rooms and other sufficient and convenient divisions for twopenny rooms, with necessary seats to be placed and set as well in those rooms as throughout all the rest of the galleries of the said house, and with suchlike stairs, conveyances, and divisions without and within as are made and contrived in and to the late erected playhouse on the Bank in the said parish of St Saviour's called the Globe.

With a stage and tiring-house to be made, erected and set up with the said frame, with a shadow or cover over the said stage. Which stage shall be placed and set, as also the staircases of the said frame, in such sort as is prefigured in a plot thereof drawn. And which stage shall contain in length 43 feet of lawful assize and in breadth to extend to the middle of the yard of the said house. The same stage to be paled in below with good strong and sufficient new oaken boards, and likewise the lower storey of the said frame withinside, and the same lower storey to be also laid over and fenced with strong iron pikes. And the said stage to be in all other proportions contrived and fashioned like unto the stage of the said playhouse called the Globe.

With convenient windows and lights glazed to the said tiring-house. And the said frame, stage and staircases to be covered with tile and to have a sufficient gutter of lead to carry and convey the water from the covering of the said stage to fall backwards. And also all the said frame and the staircases thereof to be sufficiently enclosed without with lath, lime and hair, and the gentlemen's rooms and twopenny rooms to be ceiled[1] with lath, lime and hair, and all the floors of the said galleries, storeys and stage to be boarded with good and sufficient new deal boards of the whole thickness where need shall be.

And the said house and other things before mentioned to be made and done to be in all other contrivitions [*i.e.* contrivances], conveyances, fashions, thing, and things effected, finished and done according to the manner and fashion of the said house called the Globe, saving only that all the principal and main posts of the said frame and stage forward shall be square and wrought plasterwise with carved proportions [*i.e.* figures] called satyrs to be placed and set on the top of every of the same posts. And saving also that the said Peter Street shall not be charged with any manner of painting in or about the said frame, house or stage or any part thereof, nor rendering the walls within, nor ceiling any more or other rooms than the gentlemen's rooms, twopenny rooms, and stage before remembered.

Now thereupon the said Peter Street doth covenant, promise and grant for himself, his executors and administrators to and with the said Philip Henslowe and Edward Alleyn and either of them and the executors and administrators of them and either of them by these presents in manner and form following: that is to say that he, the said Peter Street, his executors, or assigns shall and will at his or their own proper costs and charges well, workmanlike, and substantially make, erect, set up and fully finish, in and by all things according to the true meaning of these presents, with good, strong and substantial new timber and other necessary stuff, all the said frame and other works whatsoever in and upon the said plot or parcel of ground (being not by any authority restrained and having ingress, egress and regress to do the same) before the five and twentieth day of July next coming after the date hereof. And [he] shall also at his or their like costs and charges provide and find all manner of workmen, timber, joists, rafters, boards, doors, bolts, hinges, brick, tile, lath, lime, hair, sand, nails, lead, iron, glass, workmanship and other things whatsoever which shall be needful, convenient and necessary for the said frame and works and every part thereof.

And [he] shall also make all the said frame in every point for scantlings[2] larger and bigger in assize than the scantlings of the timber of the said new erected house called the Globe.

And also . . . he, the said Peter Street, shall forthwith, as well by himself as by such other and so many workmen as shall be convenient and necessary, enter into and upon the said buildings and works, and shall in reasonable manner proceed therein without any wilful detraction until the same shall be fully effected and finished.

In consideration of all which buildings and of all stuff and workmanship thereto belonging, the said Philip Henslowe and Edward Alleyn and either of them, for themselves [and] their and either of their executors and administrators, do jointly and severally covenant and grant to and with the said Peter Street, his executors and administrators by these presents that they, the said Philip Henslowe and Edward Alleyn, or one of them, or the executors, administrators or assigns of them, or one of them, shall and will well and truly pay or cause to be paid unto the said Peter Street, his executors or assigns at the place aforesaid appointed for the erecting of the said frame the full sum of £440 of lawful money of England in manner and form following: that is to say at such time and whenas the timber work of the said frame shall be raised and set up by the said Peter Street, his executors or assigns, or within seven days then next following, £220, and at such time and whenas the said frame and works shall be fully effected and finished as is aforesaid, or within seven days then next following, the other £220, without fraud or coven.

Provided always, and it is agreed between the said parties, that whatsoever sum or sums of money the said Philip Henslowe and Edward Alleyn, or either of them, or the executors or assigns of them or either of them, shall lend or deliver unto the said Peter Street, his executors, or assigns, or any other by his appointment or consent, for or concerning the said works or any part thereof, or any stuff thereto belonging, before the raising and setting up of the said frame, shall be reputed, accepted, taken and accounted in part of the first payment aforesaid of the said sum of £440. And all such sum and sums of money as they, or any of them, shall, as aforesaid, lend or deliver between the raising of the said frame and finishing thereof, and of all the rest of the said works, shall be reputed, accepted, taken and accounted in part of the last payment aforesaid of the same sum of £440, any thing abovesaid to the contrary notwithstanding.

As its first ten and last seven words suggest, this last section of the contract is an addendum deliberately at odds with the rest, especially with the section just above. The three men had agreed that Street would pay for wages and materials and that Henslowe and Alleyn would pay him in two instalments, but as the final draft of the contract was being written, Street must have said that he could not finance his part of the scheme. Henslowe and Alleyn must then have agreed to a new scheme without rewriting the contract. They would provide money for materials and labour as the work went on, and they added the last section to protect themselves. On the back of the contract, Henslowe and others noted seventy-one payments made from the day the contract was signed (when Street received £10 for 'stuff') to 11 June. Payments ranged from 4s to £40, often to Street or his agents, sometimes directly to suppliers of materials, occasionally to workmen for their wages. By 20 March the sums came to £180 18s 0d, as Henslowe noted and Street subscribed. By 11 June the payments came to £170 3s 8d more, or £351 1s 8d altogether. The payment on 10 June was 4s 'to Street to pacify him'. Henslowe noted other payments in his diary for, among other things, dining with Street virtually daily from 2 June to 8 August, presumably to discuss the progress of the work. (See *Henslowe's Diary*, 310–15, 191–3, 188–90, 236.)

[1] The word has as much to do with walls as ceilings.
[2] Scantlings are studs, small timbers used to frame partitions and the like.

418 Neighbours object to the building of the playhouse, 12 January – 8 April 1600

(a, c, d) Dulwich, MS I, fos. 40, 41v, 43; (b) PRO, PC2/25, p. 78. Transcribed in (a, c, d) *Henslowe Papers*, ed. Greg, 49–52, and *Henslowe's Diary*, 288–91; (b) APC, 1599–1600, 146

The objections must have begun almost as soon as Alleyn acquired the property on which the playhouse would be built, for on 8 January the builder, Street, promised to finish the work by 25 July provided he was 'not by any authority restrained' (see **417** above). Presumably it was Alleyn who dealt with the objections because the relevant correspondence mentions him and not Henslowe. The Lord Admiral was the Earl of Nottingham, a privy councillor and patron of Henslowe's and Alleyn's company at the Rose that was to use the new playhouse. He signed the letter of the privy council allowing the work on the playhouse to proceed, along with Lord Hunsdon (the patron of the company at the Globe) and Robert Cecil. That letter did not end the affair, for the privy council continued to reflect about the objections until 22 June, when it gave them as the reason for a new regime of playhouses in London. There were to be two officially sanctioned, the Fortune (still being built) on the north bank and the Globe on the south, an order that the patrons of the two companies involved and Cecil also signed (see **58**).

(a) The Lord Admiral writes to the Middlesex justices, 12 January 1600

Whereas my servant, Edward Alleyn (in respect of the dangerous decay of that house [*i.e.* the Rose] which he and his company have now on the Bank, and for that the same standeth very noisome for resort of people in the winter time), hath therefore now of late taken a plot of ground near Redcross Street [the southern continuation of Golden Lane], London, very fit and convenient, for the building of a new house there and hath provided timber and other necessaries for the effecting thereof, to his great charge:

Forasmuch as the place standeth very convenient for the ease of people, and that her majesty (in respect of the acceptable service which my said servant and his company have done and presented before her highness to her great liking and contentment as well this last Christmas as at sundry other times) is graciously moved towards them, with a special regard of favour in their proceedings:

These shall be, therefore, to pray and require you, and every of you, to permit and suffer my said servant to proceed in the effecting and finishing of the said new house without any your let or molestation towards him or any of his workmen. And so not doubting of your observation in this behalf, I bid you right heartily farewell.

(b) The privy council writes to the Middlesex justices, 9 March 1600

We are given to understand by our very good lord, the Lord Willoughby, and other gentlemen and inhabitants in the parish of St Giles without Cripplegate that there is a purpose and intent in some persons to erect a theatre in Whitecross Street, near unto the bars [marking the City boundary], in that part that is in the county of Middlesex,[1] whereof there are too many already not far from that place; and, as you know, not long sithence [in 1597 – see 54] you received special direction to pluck down those and to see them defaced. Therefore, if this new erection should be suffered it would not only be an offence and scandal to divers but a thing that would greatly displease her majesty.

These are, therefore, to will and require you in any case to take order that no such theatre or playhouse be built there, or any other house to serve for such use, both to avoid the many inconveniences that thereby are likely to ensue to all the inhabitants and the offence that would be to her majesty, having heretofore given sufficient notice unto you of the great mislike her highness hath of those public and vain building[s] for such occasions that breed increase of base and lewd people and divers other disorders. Therefore, we require you not to fail [and] forthwith to take order that the foresaid intended building may be stayed, and if any be begun to see the same quite defaced.

[1] The parish of St Giles Cripplegate was partly outside ('without') the City of London in the county of Middlesex and partly inside ('within') the City.

(c) Parishioners petition the privy council, c. 1 April 1600[1]

In all humbleness, we the inhabitants of the lordship of Finsbury within the parish of St Giles without Cripplegate, London, do certify unto your honours that where the servants of the right honourable Earl of Nottingham [i.e. the lord Admiral] have lately gone about to erect and set up a new playhouse within the said lordship, we could be contented that the same might proceed and be tolerated (so it stand with your honours' pleasures) for the reasons and causes following:

First, because the place appointed out for that purpose standeth very tolerable near unto the [Finsbury] Fields and so far distant and remote from any person or place of account as that none can be annoyed thereby.

Secondly, because the erectors of the said house are contented to give a very liberal portion of money weekly towards the relief of our poor, the number and necessity whereof is so great that the same will redound to the continual comfort of the said poor.

Thirdly and lastly, we are the rather contented to accept this means of relief of our poor because our parish is not able to relieve them, neither hath the justices of the shire taken any order for any supply out of the country as is enjoined by the late act of Parliament. [Twenty-seven people signed the petition.]

[1] Foakes and Rickert date this document 'about January 1600', but one might better date it as between 9 March (when the privy council apparently did not know of it) and 8 April (when that body did know of it). See (b) and (d) here, and *Henslowe's Diary*, 289.

(d) The privy council writes the Middlesex justices, 8 April 1600

Whereas her majesty (having been well pleased heretofore at times of recreation with the services of Edward Alleyn and his company, servants to me, the Earl of Nottingham, whereof of late he hath made discontinuance[1]) hath sundry times signified her pleasure that he should revive the same again, forasmuch as he hath bestowed a great sum of money not only for the title of a plot of ground situate in a very remote and exempt place near Golden Lane, there to erect a new house, but also is in good forwardness about the frame and workmanship thereof, the conveniency of which place for that purpose is testified unto us under the hands of many of the inhabitants of the liberty of Finsbury, where it is, and recommended by some of the justices themselves:

We, therefore, having informed her majesty likewise of the decay of the house wherein this company lately played, situate upon the Bank, very noisome for the resort of people in the winter time, have received order to require you to tolerate the proceeding of the said new house near Golden Lane and do hereby require you, and every of you, to permit and suffer the said Edward Alleyn to proceed in the effecting and finishing of the same new house without any your let or interruption towards him or any of his workmen, the rather because another house is pulled down instead of it.[2] And so not doubting of your conformity herein, we commit you to God.

[1] Alleyn had retired from the stage in 1597 but returned to it when the Fortune opened. This passage suggests that he offered to return as an inducement for the authorities to allow the erection of the Fortune to proceed.
[2] The Curtain was to be 'ruinated or applied to some other good use', as the privy council wrote on 22 June 1600 (see 331, 58), but it remained a playhouse for many years.

419   Alleyn and the Lord Admiral's men are performing in the first Fortune playhouse, autumn 1600

Henslowe's Diary, 137

The evidence for the opening of the first Fortune consists of three of Philip Henslowe's remarks in his diary. His last payment from the Lord Admiral's men at the Rose was for

13 July 1600 (121). His next payment at the Rose was from Pembroke's men for 28 October (164, and see 348a). Between entries dated 11 November and 14 December he noted without a date:

Paid unto my son, Alleyn, for the first week's play . . . 32s.

420 Henslowe and Alleyn formalise their partnership in the playhouse, 4 April 1601

Dulwich, Mun. 53. Transcribed in *Henslowe Papers*, ed. Greg, 25–6

The lease in which Henslowe and Alleyn formalised their partnership does not exist, but an extensive quotation of it does. The quotation is in an unexecuted document of 15 February 1616, by which Henslowe's widow contemplated conveying three of her husband's leases to three London men.

[On 4 April 1601, Alleyn leased to Henslowe:] the moiety or one-half of a playhouse and of a certain plot of ground whereupon the said playhouse was built and of all the necessaries and appurtenances thereof within the compass of the said plot;

And the moiety or one-half of all such other grounds adjoining to the said house as then were enclosed to be belonging to the said house on the north and west side thereof;

And the moiety or one-half of [a] parcel of the plot of ground on the south side of the said house, extending from the outmost bounds thereof at the west eastward 30 feet of assize, and from the uttermost bounds thereof on the south towards the north 14 feet of assize, with a competent way the breadth of a cart-way at the least on the south side aforesaid of the said house from one door of the said house to another, to be used in common by and between the said parties, their executors and assigns, with free ingress, egress and regress into and from the said house by the way and ways thereunto now used and accustomed, in so large and ample manner and form as the said Edward Alleyn then had or enjoyed the same way and ways;

And also the moiety or one-half of all the gains, commodity, sum and sums of money and profits whatsoever which from time to time should clearly come, arise and be gotten in or by the use and occupation of the said playhouse with the appurtenances, either by reason of playing there or otherwise howsoever by the grant, demise, using or letting of the said Edward Alleyn and Philip Henslowe, their executors, or assigns, or any of them . . .

[Excepted from the arrangement was:] the allowance and part of the company which for the time being shall play there, which shall be allowed to them by the joint consent and agreement of both the said parties, their executors and assigns. [Also excepted were other grounds and properties adjoining, particularly a house Alleyn had newly erected] adjoining and fixed to the south side of the said playhouse.

421 Alleyn lays out about £120 a year on the first Fortune, 1602–1608

Dulwich, MS XVIII, fo. 76. Transcribed in *Henslowe Papers*, ed. Greg, 110, and *Henslowe's Diary*, 303–4

Alleyn drew up a summary of the money spent on the Fortune from 1602 to 1608. It shows that in seven years almost twice as much had been spent as Street had received to build the playhouse, and in one year, 1604, more than half as much had been spent.

[Year]	£	s	[d]
1602	089	05	0
1603	004	02	0
1604	232	01	8
1605	108	14	3...
1606	127	00	00
1607	163	00	00
1608	121	06	00...
Total	845	08	11

422 Alleyn and Henslowe contemplate sharing profits with leading members of the company at the Fortune, 1608

Dulwich, Mun. 33. Transcribed in *Henslowe Papers*, ed. Greg, 13–14

In 1608, Henslowe and Alleyn contemplated leasing some of the profits of the playhouse to perhaps eight players for thirteen years as a way of both capitalising the place and tying players to play only there except when touring away from London. Henslowe and Alleyn drew up a lease to an actor, Thomas Downton, but they did not fill in the day and month or sign it. If they had executed eight such leases, they would have given up a quarter of the profits in return for £220 at once and then £4 a year.

[In return for £27 10s 0d in cash and 10s a year payable quarterly, Henslowe and Alleyn would grant to Downton for thirteen years from 29 September last past:] one-eight part of a fourth of all such clear gains in money as shall hereafter, during the term hereunder demised, arise, grow, accrue or become due or properly belong unto the said Philip Henslowe and Edward Alleyn, or either of them, their or either of their executors or assigns for or by reason of any stage-playing or other exercise, commodity or use whatsoever used or to be used or exercised within the playhouse of the said Philip Henslowe and Edward Alleyn, commonly called the Fortune, situate and being between Whitecross Street and Golden Lane in the parish of St Giles without Cripplegate, London in the county of Middlesex ... [the share to be paid] every day that any play or other exercise shall be acted or exercised in the playhouse aforesaid upon the sharing of the moneys gathered and gotten at every of the same and exercises as heretofore hath been used and accustomed ...

[Downton was to pay a proportionate share of:] all such necessary and needful charges as shall be bestowed or laid forth in the new building or repairing of the said playhouse during the said term of thirteen years with[out] fraud or covin . . .

[Downton was] not at any time hereafter during the said term [to] give over the faculty or quality of playing but shall in his own person exercise the same to the best and most benefit he can within the playhouse aforesaid during the time aforesaid, unless he shall become unable by reason of sickness or any other infirmity, or unless it be with the consent of the said Philip Henslowe and Edward Alleyn, or either of them, their executors or assigns . . . [Nor will he] exercise the faculty of stage-playing in any common playhouse now erected or hereafter to be erected within the said City of London or two miles compass thereof other than in the said playhouse called the Fortune without the special licence, will, consent and agreement of the said Philip Henslowe and Edward Alleyn, or one of them, their or one of their heirs, executors or assigns first therefor had and obtained in writing . . .

[Downton was not] at any time hereafter during the said term [to] give, grant, bargain, sell or otherwise do away or depart with the said eight part of a fourth part of the said clear gains before demised, nor any parcel thereof, to any person or persons whatsoever without the like consent, licence, will and agreement of them, the said Philip Henslowe and Edward Alleyn, or either of them, or their or either of their heirs, executors, administrators or assigns first therefor had and obtained in writing.

If not this scheme, Henslowe and Alleyn may have carried out another like it. For when asking Alleyn for money in *c.* 1612,[1] an actor, Charles Massey, mentioned 'that litt[le] mote I have in the playhouses, which I would willing[ly] pass over unto you by deed of gift or any course you [w]ould set down for your security' (Dulwich, MS I, fo. 94, transcribed in *Henslowe Papers*, ed. Greg, 64–5).

[1] Massey mentioned the actor Thomas Towne, as dead, who was buried on 9 August 1612. See *ES*, II, 347.

423 A character in a play describes the first Fortune and its audience, *c.* 1610

Dekker and Middleton, *The Roaring Girl*, sig. B3. See Sampson, 'Interior of the Fortune', 195

Early in the play, Sir Alexander Wengrave shows friends around his house. In describing it to them, he evidently alludes to the first Fortune and its audience, where and before whom, according to the title page of 1611, the play was 'lately' acted. Adam's remark alludes ironically to the breath of the audience.

ALEX: How do you like
 This parlour, gentleman?
OMNES: Oh, passing well . . .
ADAM: What a sweet breath the air casts here, so cool.
LAXTON: See how 'tis furnished . . .
ALEX: The furniture that doth adorn this room

Cost many a fair gray groat ere it came here,
But good things are most cheap when they're most dear.
Nay, when you look into my galleries –
How bravely they are trimmed up – you all shall swear
You're highly pleased to see what's set down there:
Storeys of men and women mixed together,
Fair ones with foul, like sunshine in wet weather.
Within a square a thousand heads are laid
So close that all of heads the room seems made.
As many faces there (filled with blithe looks)
Show like the promising titles of new books
(Writ merrily), the readers being their own eyes,
Which seem to move and to give plaudities,
And here and there (whilst with obsequious ears
Thronged heaps do listen) a cutpurse thrusts and leers
With hawks' eyes for his prey. I need not show him
By a hanging villainous look: yourselves may know him,
The face is drawn so rarely. Then, sir, below,
The very flower (as 'twere) waves to and fro
And like a floating island seems to move
Upon a sea bound in with shores above.

424 Criminal acts are perpetrated at the Fortune, 1611–1613

LMA, (a) MJ/SR 499/86, 87; (b) MJ/SBR 1, pp. 559, 543; (c) MJ/SR 522/211. Transcribed in (a–c) Jeaffreson, *Middlesex County Records*, II, 71, 83, 88–9. The Middlesex justices had to consider events at the Fortune several times.

(a) Two butchers abuse gentlemen, c. 26 February 1611

A justice took two recognisances (*i.e.* bonds) on 26 February from four butchers to guarantee the appearance in court of two of them. The first recognisance was:

of John Shawe of Grub Street, butcher, and Gilbert Borne of Whitecross Street, butcher, in the sum of £20 each and of Ralph Brewyn of St Clement Eastcheap, butcher, in the sum of £40 for the appearance of the said Ralph Brewyn at the next sessions of the peace for Middlesex to answer . . . for abusing certain gentlemen at the playhouse called the Fortune. [The second recognisance is nearly identical, except that for Brewyn it substitutes John Lynsey of St Andrew Undershaft, butcher.]

(b) Jigs attract ill-disposed persons, 1 October 1612

[The bench of nineteen justices, among them Nicholas Bestney, issued a declaration reading:] Whereas complaint[s] have been made at this last general sessions that by reason of certain lewd jigs, songs and dances used and accustomed at the playhouse called the Fortune in Golden Lane, divers cutpurses and other lewd and ill-disposed persons in great multitudes do resort thither at the end of every play, many times causing tumults and outrages whereby his majesty's peace is often broke and much mischief like to ensue thereby: it was hereupon expressly commanded and ordered by the justices of the said bench that all actors of every playhouse ... [in London and Middlesex] utterly abolish all jigs, rhymes and dances after their plays ... upon pain of imprisonment and putting down and suppressing of their plays, and such further punishment to be inflicted upon them as their offences shall deserve.

And ... if any outrage, tumult or like disorder as aforesaid should be committed or done, ... then the parties so offending should forthwith be apprehended and punished according to their demerit for the better suppressing of which abuses and outrages ...

(c) A justice's son is stabbed, 5 June 1613

[A jury found the following indictment a true bill:] On the said day at the Fortune near ... Golden Lane ... Richard Bradley, late [since he was now in gaol] of St James Clerkenwell, yeoman, assaulted Nicholas Bestney the younger, gentleman [evidently son of the justice in (b) above], and with a knife gave him two grievous wounds by stabbing him with the said weapon, in the first place on the right breast and then in the left part of his belly, of which two wounds the said Nicholas languished and still remains in danger of death.

Notes add that Bradley confessed and was remanded while the court awaited the outcome of Bestney's wounds.

425 Alleyn inherits Henslowe's part of the Fortune then leases the playhouse to the players, 1616–1618

Dulwich, Mun. 56. Transcribed in *Henslowe Papers*, ed. Greg, 27–8. See *J and CS*, VI, 149–50

After Henslowe's death, on 9 January 1616, and that of his widow, Agnes, in April 1617, his property, including his lease on the Fortune (420) and his papers, passed to Alleyn, who then owned the whole place outright. Having apparently wearied of being directly responsible for the Fortune, however, he soon leased it (but not most of his other holdings on the site) to his old company, now called the Palsgrave's men, who were still in the playhouse. Coincidentally, the lease provides a kind of bequest to his old colleagues, for their rent was to be much diminished after his death.

The lease is dated 31 October 1618. In it, Alleyn grants to ten actors among the Palsgrave's men (Edward Juby, William Bird alias Borne, Frank Grace, Richard Gunnell, Charles Massey, William Stratford, William Cartwright, Richard Price, William Parr and Richard Fowler):

All that his great building now used for a playhouse and commonly called by the name of the Fortune, situate, lying and being between Whitecross Street and Golden Lane in the county of Middlesex in the parish of St Giles without Cripplegate, London, together with all lights, ways, passages, easements, commodities and appurtenances to the same belonging, or appertaining, or therewith now used, occupied or enjoyed, together with one messuage or tenement thereunto adjoining, called the taphouse, now in the occupation of one Mark Brigham or his assigns:

And also one piece of ground as it is now impaled, containing in length east and west 123 feet of assize more or less and in breadth north and south 17 feet of assize more or less, and rangeth with the passage on the south side of the said playhouse . . .

[The lease was to run for thirty-one years from 29 September 1618. The rent was £200 a year, payable quarterly,] and also two roundlets [*i.e.* small casks] of wine, the one sack and the other claret, of 10s apiece price, to be delivered at the feast of Christmas yearly . . . [If Alleyn should die within the thirty-one years, the rent would be reduced to £120 a year for the remaining years.]

[The lessees agreed] that they nor any of them, their executors, administrators or assigns shall not at any time hereafter alter, transpose or otherwise convert the said playhouse to any other use or uses than as the same is now used.

The lessees were to receive rent of 24s a year, to be reduced to 4s at Alleyn's death, from John Russell, who held a lease for ninety-nine years from 20 June 1617 on a tenement of two rooms adjoining the playhouse.[1]

[1] Alleyn had appointed a John Russell as a gatherer for the players at the Fortune. They rejected him because he was 'often false', but to please Alleyn they would allow him to be an 'attendant on the stage' and mender of their garments (Dulwich, MS I, fo. 149, transcribed in *Henslowe Papers*, ed. Greg, 85–6).

426 The players feast the Spanish ambassador at the Fortune, 16 July 1621

PRO, SP14/122/fos. 43v–44. Transcribed in *Letters of John Chamberlain*, II, 391

Chamberlain reported the feast to his regular correspondent, Sir Dudley Carleton, in a letter dated 21 July 1621. The feast may have taken place in the paled ground, 123' × 17', mentioned in Alleyn's lease to the players in 1618 (**425**).

On Monday [16 July, the Spanish ambassador, Gondomar], with his whole train, . . . went to a common play at the Fortune in Golden Lane, and the players (not to be overcome with courtesy) made him a banquet when the play was done in the garden adjoining.

427 The first Fortune is destroyed by fire, 9 December 1621

PRO, SP14/124/fo. 92v. Transcribed in *Letters of John Chamberlain*, II, 415. Chamberlain reported the fire in a letter to Sir Dudley Carleton of 15 December 1621.

On Sunday night [9 December 1621], here was a great fire at the Fortune in Golden Lane, the fairest playhouse in this town. It was quite burned down in two hours, and all their apparel and playbooks lost, whereby those poor companions are quite undone. There were two other houses on fire, but with great labour and danger [they] were saved.[1]

[1] In his diary, Alleyn noted for 9 December that 'this night at 12 of the clock the Fortune was burnt': Dulwich, MS IX, fo. 56, transcribed in Young, *History of Dulwich College*, II, 225.

XXXII Whitefriars

The Whitefriars playhouse was a private playhouse in the City of London but outside the walls. It was in 'the great hall' of the dissolved priory of the Carmelite, or white, friars. The priory lay between Fleet Street on the north and the Thames on the south, and between Water Lane (the present Whitefriars Street and its southern extension, Carmelite Street) on the east and the Temple on the west. The area was a so-called liberty whose residents, like those of Blackfriars, claimed freedom from the jurisdiction of the City. The great hall was apparently the rectangular building called 'The Hale' on an early seventeenth-century survey of Whitefriars. Its longer dimension extended east from the Temple wall, and its northern side was 330 feet south of Fleet Street.[1] Much of the site is now no. 11 Bouverie Street, E.C.4, which lies between that street and the part of Temple Lane running north and south along the Temple wall, and on the south side of the part of Temple Lane running east and west to Bouverie Street.

The early history of the playhouse is also that of a company of child-actors (who were not choristers), the children of the King's Revels, and the origin of both probably had to do with events at other playhouses in 1606.[2] In that year one of the two companies of children, that at St Paul's, ceased playing, and the other, at Blackfriars, was threatened with closure because one of its plays, Day's *The Isle of Gulls*, had caused great offence.

Company and playhouse may have begun during the Christmas season of 1606–7, when, it seems, Thomas Woodford took a sublease on the great hall from Sir Anthony Ashley for eight years beginning on 1 December 1606 at £50 a year. Ashley's lease may have ended shortly after the sublease did. Woodford had had to do with the boy-players of St Paul's at least in the winter of 1602–3 (**235**, **237**) and was to buy a stake in the Red Bull in 1612 (**440**). Ashley was the brother-in-law of the man who had built the Swan, Francis Langley.

Woodford engaged the poet and playwright, Michael Drayton, to lead the children. Then, with the help of Ashley, he set about capitalising his sublease during the summer of 1607. The sublease, hence the whole venture, would be divided into six sub-subleases, or shares, of which Drayton came to hold three and Lording Barry three. Barry wrote one of the company's plays, *Ram Alley*, named for a notorious street in Whitefriars a little north and west of the playhouse. Drayton assigned two of his shares to businessmen, William Trevell, a chandler, and Edward Sibthorpe, and he, they and Barry all borrowed money from Woodford to finance the venture, giving Woodford several bonds dated 12 August 1607 as guarantees of repayment.[3] Barry sold a half-share to John Mason, who also wrote one of the company's plays, *The Turk*, and another, for £45, to William Cooke, a haberdasher.

The first notices that the playhouse existed and was in business belong to the summer and autumn of 1607. People were buried 'out of the playhouse' on 29 and 30 September; Sharpham's *Cupid's Whirligig* (SR, 29 June 1607) was published later that year as 'sundry times acted by the children of the King's majesty's Revels'; and Middleton's *The Family of*

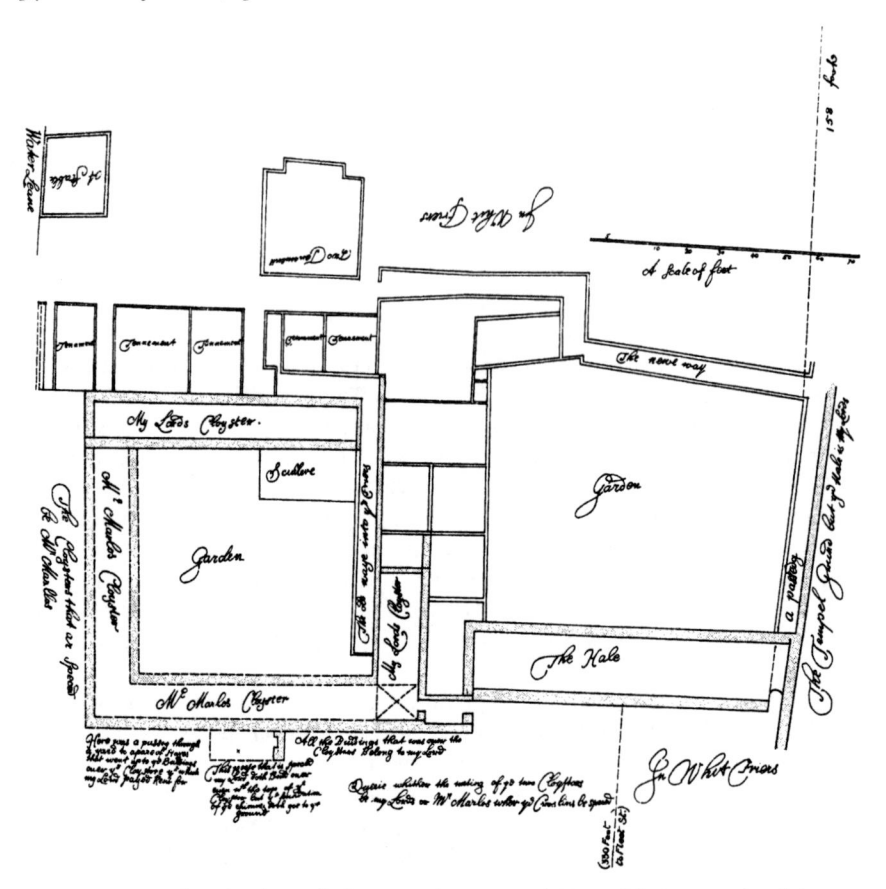

Fig. 4. The Whitefriars playhouse (?), from A. W. Clapham, 'The Topography of the Carmelite Priory of London', p. 26, a reproduction of a plan at the British Museum now lost. The playhouse must have been in the 'Hale', i.e., hall. The Thames is beyond the top of the drawing and Fleet Street beyond the bottom.

Love (SR, 12 September 1607) was published the next year as 'lately acted by the children of his majesty's Revels'.

The sharers could not, however, pay their expenses. Cooke lent them £6 13s 4d in return for a bond, and on 16 October 1607 he lent them £20 more for four months without interest so that they could feed and board the boys. He said that others would not lend money because of the plague, implying that the plague prevented the boys from earning money by performing, as between 24 September and 19 November it probably did. In return he got not only a bond, but 'an assurance of two' half-shares – a document, presumably, that assigned the half-shares to somebody else and that Cooke was to keep as security until his £20 was repaid.

Early in 1608 the sharers embarked on a reorganisation of the venture, again, it seems, assisted by Ashley, since Woodford did not pay the rent at Christmas and Ashley did not seize the building. They brought in a new man of substance, George Androwes, a silk weaver, who bought one of Barry's shares for £70 in February 1608. They then gave a share, evidently half of Drayton's remaining share and half of one of Barry's shares, to the veteran actor, Martin Slatier, who would take over the company. (He had thought to lead a company at the Red Bull in the spring of 1605 – **436**.) The full sharers were now Trevell, Sibthorpe, Androwes and Slatier, and the half-sharers were Drayton, Barry, Mason and Cooke. These people spent a lot of money on the venture: Androwes said he spent £300 altogether, and Slatier said all the sharers contributed 'ratably'.

The sharers made their reorganisation formal on 10 March 1608, when they signed three documents. One was a new sublease specifying that they had six years, eight months and twenty days remaining in their building (until 30 November 1614) and, no doubt, spelling out the arrangement of shares. Another was a contract between Slatier and the other sharers making him leader of the company. It survives word for word. Its first clause awarded him his share, and its second allowed him and his family of ten to live above the playhouse. Other clauses provided that his name would be joined to Drayton's in the company's patent, that the boy-actors would be Slatier's apprentices, and that Slatier and his fellow-sharers would be businesslike in the conduct of the company and its property. The third document was a bond of £200 in which the other sharers 'jointly and severally' guaranteed to Slatier that they would abide by the contract.

This commendable scheme endured less than a month. A few days before its signing, the rival company at Blackfriars had performed two scandalous plays, and, as a result, shortly after 11 March the King closed all the playhouses and threatened to keep them closed (**407**). When Woodford did not pay the rent due at Lady Day (25 March), so that it was now half a year behind, Ashley gave up on the venture. He declared the first sublease void and expelled the players from the building, leaving them without a playhouse and their sharers much out of pocket and, inevitably, in the law courts. Slatier was 'riotously, wilfully, violently and unlawfully . . . put and kept out of his said rooms'. He sued Androwes on the bond of £200 – not the others, because, presumably, Androwes was the only one of them worth that much money. Trevell had financed his share by borrowing not only from Woodford but from fourteen others, all of whom sought money he could not pay. His widow finally silenced Woodford in the courts in 1642.

Sometime in 1609 the company that had helped to cause the collapse of the King's Revels moved into Whitefriars. They were the children who had been at Blackfriars and had regrouped under Robert Keysar, goldsmith, and Philip Rosseter, a musician. They probably caused the constables of St Dunstan in the West to 'present' the playhouse in December 1609 as not 'now tolerable', but they played in it apparently peaceably and successfully until 1614. They began there as the children of Whitefriars, regained their connection with the Queen in 1610 (having lost it in 1606), and, it seems, effectually combined with Lady Elizabeth's men in March 1613, one of Philip Henslowe's enterprises.[4] If so, the playhouse became, like the second Blackfriars, a private playhouse where adults acted.

The playhouse must have been long and narrow and much less grand than the one in Blackfriars. Slatier's contract describes the building as having thirteen rooms, 'three below and ten above, that is to say [below,] the great hall, the kitchen by the yard, and a cellar, with [above,] all the rooms from the east and of the house to the Master of the Revels' office'. The playhouse could only have been in the great hall, which obviously took up much of the ground floor and was one storey high. The cellar would have been a storeroom above ground, associated, perhaps, with the kitchen. The building called the hall in the early seventeenth-century survey, and no other building in it is so-called, had stone walls. Its ground floor was according to the scale bar, about 90 feet by 17 feet inside and the upper one about 94 feet by 17 feet. A passage about 4 feet wide, running north and south along the Temple wall, went through the ground floor at the far western end. The upper floor extended over the passage, and it was there and in rooms adjoining that the office of the Master of the Revels apparently was. The 'yard' would have been the garden on the south side of the building.

The Whitefriars playhouse apparently ended in 1614 because Ashley's lease ran out. No contemporary mentioned drama there after that. An assertion that Ashley expelled players from it in 1621 is the result of Cunningham's mistakenly combining two remarks that Trevell made in 1640.[5]

[1] The play-goer walking along Fleet Street would turn south through the little gate of the priory, now Pleydell Court, and proceed south along and to the bottom of the present Lombard Lane. The survey, which was huge, 60" × 18½", is said to be in the Print Room of the British Museum, but it cannot now be found there or in the Map Room. The relevant part of it, however, has been reproduced at least twice: by Clapham, 'The Topography of the Carmelite Priory of London', facing p. 26; and, less satisfactorily, by Adams, *Shakespearean Playhouses*, facing p. 312. Moreover, a careful nineteenth-century copy of it is in the Crace Collection in the Map Room, Crace Port. 8, no. 104. The survey shows walls as grey or red, probably meaning stone or brick.

[2] Rawlidge wrote that in Elizabethan times the City 'quite suppressed' playhouses 'within the liberties', including one in Whitefriars (*A Monster Late Found Out and Discovered*, 1628, sig. A3). But since there is no other evidence of an earlier playhouse and Rawlidge did not mention Blackfriars, Chambers credibly suggested that Rawlidge wrote 'White' when he meant 'Black' (*ES*, II, 359–60, 515).

[3] For a fuller account of these and later transactions, see Ingram, 'The Playhouse as an Investment, 1607–14', 210–13. See also Hillebrand, *Child Actors*, 220–36.

[4] For an indication that Henslowe had an interest in a private playhouse at this time, see *ES*, II, 257–8.

[5] 'The Whitefriars Theatre, the Salisbury Court Theatre, and the Duke's Theatre in Dorset Gardens', 89–90, and *ES*, II, 517. Trevell said, without mentioning a date, that Ashley expelled the players; a little later he said that Woodford formally released him from debt on 21 May 1621 (see **431**: Trevell's first remark is quoted at the end; his second follows in the original but is omitted here).

428 The playhouse exists, 29 September 1607

GL, MS 10,343. Transcribed in Jonas, *Shakespeare and the Stage*, 132, and in Ingram, 'The Playhouse as an Investment, 1607–1614', 211

Whitefriars was extra-parochial, but the names of residents often appear in the registers of two parish churches, St Dunstan in the West (on the north side of Fleet Street and a little west of Whitefriars), and St Bride (east of Whitefriars). The one nearer the playhouse was St Dunstan. What Gerry had to do with the playhouse does not appear, but since plague was prevalent from 24 September onwards, he, his son and wife may well have been among its victims.

[Four entries in the burial register of St Dunstan in the West, September 1607:]

8 Jeffrey Daviges, servant to Mr Woodford, out of the Friars, buried . . .
29 [Blank] Gerry, out of the playhouse in the Friars, buried.
29 Francis, the son of the said Gerry, likewise buried . . .
30 [Blank] the wife of [blank] Gerry, out of the playhouse, buried.

Whitefriars

429 The investors in the playhouse experience difficulties, autumn 1607

PRO, (a) Req.2/405/136; (b) Req.2/414/139, Cooke 6. See also Ingram, 'The Playhouse as an Investment, 1607–1614', 211–12, 223

These two documents and the two in the next item resulted from the collapse of the first venture at the Whitefriars playhouse in the spring of 1608. All four deal with some of the same matters, but those here focus on the events of the summer and autumn of 1607. They belong to a lawsuit in which William Trevell sued William Cooke and others in the Court of Requests on 16 May 1610 over money borrowed and not repaid. When the people of whom Trevell complained did not reply, he got the usual injunction against them but did nothing about it until the winter of 1614–15. Cooke then replied in January 1615, and on 5 February 1616 he answered questions (in a deposition) about his failure to reply sooner and also augmented his account of the events of 1607. Richard Jobber, mentioned in both documents, was the agent through whom Cooke preferred to do business.

(a) Cooke's reply, January 1615[1]

[Cooke said] that he ... by insinuation, allurement and often and urgent importunity of the said Trevell and others, was drawn to disburse ... certain moneys upon the only persuasion that the said playhouse would yield a great benefit to him ... and did upon the said Trevell and others their persuasions disburse at times to the sum of £45 or thereabouts. But so far was this defendant [Cooke] from receiving of any benefit, profit or commodity by his said money for and in respect of the said playhouse that this defendant was by the said Trevell and others, his associates sharers in the said playhouse, directly defrauded of his said money and never received to this day either principal or benefit by the principal.

Notwithstanding which, the said Trevell, persisting still to draw from this defendant more moneys, treated with this defendant for the loan of more moneys, ... and, ... seeing that no denial would serve the said Trevell, this defendant did cause to be delivered unto the said Trevell the sum of twenty nobles [£6 13s 4d], and the said Trevell did become bound to one Jobber by obligation for payment thereof.

And not yet satisfied, [Trevell] importuned this defendant to procure the sum of £20 more, which this defendant did accordingly, for which said sum of £20 the said Trevells [*sic*] with others did likewise enter into bond to the said Jobber for payment of the said £20 at the end of four months or thereabouts without any interest or consideration at all. But ... short time after, the said Trevell, having, as this defendant verily believeth, ... gotten divers men's money and goods into his hands, became insolvent, as he made show to the world ...

This defendant did about the year ... 1607 once cause the said Trevell in the name of the said Jobber to be arrested upon the said bond for the payment of the said twenty nobles, and judgement was obtained in the Guildhall, London, upon the same ... [Jobber agreed to take the money in quarterly instalments of 20s], but such was the carelessness and dishonesty of the said Trevell [that he] hath not as yet performed the said order nor paid his said money but there is still remaining 17s 8d or thereabouts unpaid of the said judgement. [Cooke, in the name of Jobber, has delayed suing Trevell for the £20] till of late, . . . for that the said Trevell is now grown into good estate and worth . . . £400 or near thereabouts.

[1] The place on the document where the date is has partly perished: the day has gone, but 'Januarij' survives as does part of the year, 'xi[j]' James. Cooke noted in the document that Trevell had 'exhibited' the bill on 16 May 1610, and that the matter had lain 'dormant ever since, being almost five years'.

(b) Cooke's deposition, 5 February 1616

This deponent [Cooke] saith that the complainant [Trevell] and divers others were suitors to this deponent for the sum of £20, which this deponent was very unwilling to have done, but being very much laboured and importuned by the plaintiff [Trevell] and divers others of them [named] in the bond for the same, [he] granted that he would move a friend [presumably Jobber] to furnish them with £20. And thereupon, on or about the 16th day of October 1607, at Mr [Randall] Hanmer his shop in Friday Street, London, he, this deponent, carried £20 in money for the plaintiff and his partners named in the bond and found there for his security a bond sealed and delivered by the complainant and one Lording Barry, one Edward Sibthorpe, one [John] Mason and one John Cooke to the use of Richard Jobber. Which bond this deponent received for his security for his said £20, as also an assurance of two twelve parts of the lease of the Whitefriars playhouse and of a part of the shares, as may appear by the writings thereof made by Barry and Sibthorpe remaining with this deponent for his better security if then this deponent would have paid and delivered them, the plaintiff and Barry and Sibthorpe or any of them, the said £20.

But they would not receive the same but requested this deponent to pay . . . to Mason, then in the scrivener's shop, £2 3s and to the said Sibthorpe the sum of £3 for the boys of the playhouse their board and diet, the £3 then paid being for their week's diet aforehand, as they affirmed. And [they] wished this deponent to keep the rest until they or any of them did call for it from time to time to pay for the boys' diets, being in the sickness time when no person would trust them, as he thinketh. So that after that, viz. on the 22nd of October following, this deponent paid the said Sibthorpe for a week's diet and board more aforehand for the said play boys' diet (as he said) the sum of £3 more, and after to the said Mason 20s more in the scrivener's shop. Then after, on the 27th day of October aforesaid, he paid unto the foresaid Mason in the said scrivener's shop the sum of £10 17s, which made the just sum of £20. And [he, Cooke,] saith the money was his own and not Mr Jobber's.

And [Cooke] further saith that he had half a share of the Whitefriars playhouse, which cost him about £45, which he hath lost amongst them.

430 The investors in the playhouse try to run it in a businesslike way, spring 1608

PRO, C2/Jas, I/A6/21. Transcribed in Greenstreet, *The Whitefriars Theatre in the Time of Shakespeare*, 272–84. See Ingram, 'The Playhouse as an Investment, 1607–1614', 210–13

George Androwes' lawsuit against Martin Slatier concerns mainly the events of February and March 1608. The numbered items in the bill are the clauses in the contract between Slatier and the other sharers.

(a) Androwes' bill of complaint, 9 February 1609

[George Androwes, of London, silk weaver, complained:] That whereas one Lording Barry about February . . . [1608], pretending . . . to be lawfully possessed of one moiety of a messuage or mansion-house parcel of the late dissolved monastery called the Whitefriars in Fleet Street in the suburbs of London by and under a lease [to be] made thereof about March then next following from the right honourable Robert, Lord Buckhurst [the landlord],[1] unto one Michael Drayton and Thomas Woodford for the term of six years, eight months and twenty days then following for and under the yearly rent of £50, . . . the moiety of which said lease and premises by mesne assignment[2] from the said Thomas Woodford was lawfully settled in the said Lording Barry, as he did pretend, together with the moiety of divers playbooks, apparel and other furnitures and necessaries used and employed in and about the said messuage . . . [by] the Children of the Revels there being, in making and setting forth plays, shows and interludes and suchlike.

And the said Lording Barry, so pretending . . . to be of the moiety of the said messuage and premises possessed and being desirous to join others with him . . . who might be contributory to such future charges as should arise in setting forth of plays and shows there, and sharers in the gain and benefit to be made thereof, did thereupon, by himself and by the means of one Martin Slatier, citizen and ironmonger of London, and other his confederates, solicit and persuade your orator [*i.e.* Androwes] to take from the said Barry an assignment of a sixth part of the messuage, premises and profits aforesaid, alledging the great benefit that would redound unto your orator by means thereof, and that the very apparel which lay then in the said house he pretended cost £400, whereof this complainant should have one-sixth part, falling into terms of bargaining with your orator demanding of him . . . [£90] for a sixth part therein, adding . . . that if it had not been in love to the complainant that they would not have parted so easily with it, considering the benefit which they affirmed would be to your orator, the clear sum of £100 yearly above charges.

With which fair and false flattering speeches of the said Lording Barry, Martin Slatier and others, your orator was most notably abused and drawn unto a good opinion thereof and did accept of the said bargain and went through with Barry for the purchase of a sixth part thereof and accepted an assignment from the said Barry of a sixth part of the said lease and of all the gain and profit of the premises to be had or gotten upon or by reason of the said messuage and premises, or any new building thereupon to be made, and of all the plays, shows, interludes or other exercises therein to be acted or done for and during the residue of the said term of six years, eight months and twenty days then to come. And your orator did, therefore, justly and truly satisfy unto the said Lording Barry and others by his appointment the full sum of £70 current money of England, presuming and hoping to have the benefit of the said bargain . . .

But after your orator had better considered of his bargain, he found himself to be very much abused and overreached therein, for that the apparel, which was affirmed by the said Barry, Slatier and others to be worth £400 and was the chief cause of your orator's bargaining, was not worth above £5 in true value, and the charges of building and other charges in maintaining the children and other incidents to the said business, whereof the most part or almost all did fall upon your orator, considering the small gain which came thereby and your orator being cut short of his share, were an exceeding great loss, in all amounting to £300 or thereabouts. And besides, the said original lease made by the said Robert, Lord Buckhurst, for non-payment of the rent due, before any assignment of the said sixth part of the same made to your orator, was forfeited and, in extremity of law, lost, and your orator was threatened to lose his said sixth part and premises.

And . . . the said Lording Barry, Michael Drayton, William Trevell, William Cooke, Edward Sibthorpe and John Mason, of London, gentlemen, being likewise interest[ed] of and in all the rest and residue of the parts of the messuage and of all other the gains, profits and commodities that should at any time arise, come or grow by reason of any shows, plays, interludes, music or suchlike exercises as should be used or performed in the said playhouse: on the tenth day of March . . . [1608], there were certain articles of agreement . . . made between the said Martin Slatier of the one party and your orator, Lording Barry, Michael Drayton, William Trevell, William Cooke, Edward Sibthorpe and John Mason of the other party, the tenor whereof, word for word, doth hereafter ensue . . . :

[1] . . . During all the term of years in the lease of the playhouse in the Whitefriars, . . . he, the said Martin Slatier, shall have, receive, take and enjoy the sixth part, [the whole lease] in six parts to be divided, of all such profit, benefit, gettings and commodity as at any time shall arise, come and grow by reason of any plays, shows, interludes, music or suchlike exercises to be used and performed as well in the said playhouse as elsewhere, all manner of charges thereunto belonging being first defrayed and deducted.

[2] . . . He, the said Martin Slatier, and all his family shall have their dwelling and lodging in the said house with free ingress, egress and regress to and from the same, or any part thereof, during the continuance of the said lease. The rooms of which house are thirteen in number, three below and ten above, that is to say, [below] the great hall, the kitchen by the yard, and a cellar, with [above,] all the rooms from the east end of the house to the Master of the Revels' office, as the same are now severed and divided.

[3] ... If any gain or profit can or may be made in the said house either by wine, beer, ale, tobacco, wood, coals or any such commodity, that then he, the said Martin Slatier, and his assigns and none other shall have the benefit thereof ... during the continuance of the said lease.

[4] ... When their patent for playing shall be renewed, the said Martin Slatier ... with the said Michael Drayton shall be joined therein, in respect that if any restraint of their playing shall happen by reason of the plague or otherwise, it shall be for more credit of the whole company that the said Martin shall travel with the children and acquaint the magistrates with their business.

[5] ... If at any time hereafter any apparel, books or any other goods or commodities shall be conveyed or taken away by any of the said parties without the consent and allowance of the residue of his fellow-sharers, and the same exceeding the value of 2s, that then he or they so offending shall forfeit and lose all such benefit, profit and commodity as otherwise should arise and grow unto him or them by their shares, besides the loss of their places and all other interest which they may claim amongst us.

[6] ... During the said lease the whole charges of the house (the gatherers, the wages, the children's board, music, book-keeper, tireman, tirewoman, lights, the Master of the Revels' duties, and all other things needful and necessary), whatsoever one week's charge cometh unto, the sixth part of the same to be taken up every night: as if one week's charge amounteth unto £10, then to take up every night 33s 4d, by which means they shall be still out of debt.

[7] ... Whereas by the general consent of all the whole company all the children are bound to the said Martin Slatier for the term of three years, he the said Martin Slatier doth by these presents bind himself to the residue of the company in the sum of £40 sterling that he shall not wrong or injure the residue of the said company in the parting with or putting away any one or more of the said young men or lads to any person or persons, or otherwise, without the special consent and full agreement of the residue of his fellow-sharers, except the term of his or their apprenticeship be fully expired.

[8] ... All such apparel as is abroad shall be immediately brought in, and ... no man of the said company shall at any time hereafter put into print, or cause to be put into print, any manner of playbook now in use or ... hereafter shall be sold unto them, upon the penalty and forfeiture of £40 sterling, or the loss of his place and share of all things amongst them, except the book of *Torrismount*,[3] and that play not to be printed by any before twelve months be fully expired.

[9] ... If at any time hereafter the same company shall be restrained from playing in the said house by reason of the plague or otherwise, and ... thereby they shall be enforced to travel into the country for the upholding of their company, ... then the said Martin Slatier during the time of such travel shall have an allowance of one full share and a half.

[10] ... All the said parties ... in testimony hereof have interchangeably set their hands and seals to these presents the day and year first above written.

And your orator, together with the said Lording Barry, Michael Drayton, William Trevell, William Cooke, Edward Sibthorpe and John Mason, by their obligation made the tenth day of March . . . [1608] became jointly and severally bound unto the said Martin Slatier in the sum of £200, endorsed with condition that if the said obligors and every of them, their executors, administrators and assigns should well and truly observe, perform, fulfill and keep all and singular the covenants, grants, articles and agreements whatsoever contained and specified in the . . . articles and covenants before expressed on the obligors' parts, their executors', and administrators', to be performed and kept, that then the said obligation of £200 should be void.

But so it is . . . that your orator at the time when he did seal and deliver the said . . . bond for performance of covenants, himself being ignorant in the law but yet being purposed to covenant and be bound for himself only and for his own acts and not for any other the parties obliged or bound . . . he did demand of a scrivener which did make the same and of the said Martin Slatier whether the same did extend to charge your orator any farther than for his own acts. And thereupon the said Slatier did affirm to your orator that he had no meaning at all to charge your orator but only for his own acts and breach of covenant for . . . your orator's own particular act and part and not for the breach of covenant which should be committed or done by the other obligors, or any of them, well knowing that the true and plain meaning of the said agreement was such and no otherwise, howsoever the said covenants and bond are made and in law do extend to charge your orator otherwise. And, for further manifestation of the truth herein, the said Martin Slatier did then bind himself by his promise not to take any advantage of the said bond and covenants, or either of them, against your orator . . . unless your orator should by his own act, or in his own default, break any the agreements aforesaid.

Upon which agreements and true declaration of the true meaning of the said covenants and bond, and faithful promise of the said Slatier, your orator, . . . little suspecting any such matter as hath since fallen out, . . . did unadvisedly seal and deliver the said articles of agreement and bond. And your orator doth verily believe that the rest of the obligors have broken some small covenant by some act of theirs, altogether against your orator's liking and without his consent, act or privity, and yet there is no good cause in conscience wherefore your orator should be endamaged by the covenants or bond aforesaid, having himself done nothing contrary to the true meaning of the agreement aforesaid, whereby the said obligation of £200 is become forfeit in extremity of the common law.

And the said Slatier hath caused your orator to be arrested into the King's Bench at Westminster and declared against your suppliant [Androwes] upon the said bond of £200, intending to take the penalty thereof against your orator to his utter undoing, unless your lordship, according to your accustomed goodness extended to others in the like case, do relieve him herein, . . . [because he] is void and destitute of all remedy at the common law . . . [Besides, Slatier absents himself so that

Androwes cannot have him arrested. Slatier does not have enough money to pay any damages, and if he should get the £200, Androwes could never get it back again by any subsequent action.] And forasmuch also as there is no breach at all of any covenant made by your orator's own act, and all that which is made by the other obligors, or some of them, is but of small importance, nothing answerable to the said penalty of the said bond, . . . [Androwes especially asks the court to stop Slatier's proceedings in King's Bench.]

[1] After Thomas Sackville, the first Lord Buckhurst, was created Earl of Dorset in 1604, the heirs of the Earls of Dorset were called Lord Buckhurst by courtesy. The man called so in February 1608 was Thomas Sackville's son and heir, Robert Sackville, who became second Earl of Dorset on 19 April 1608, when his father died.
[2] An assignment meant to be passed on to somebody else.
[3] The play is otherwise unknown.

(b) Slatier answers, 17 February 1609

This defendant, for answer unto the said bill and the surmised matters therein contained, saith that he thinketh it to be true that the said Lording Barry . . . about the time . . . in the bill mentioned . . . [was] possessed of a moiety of the said messuage or mansion-house in the bill also mentioned, for such term and under such yearly rent as by the bill is a[lledged, for] anything this defendant now conceiveth to the contrary. And this defendant also thinketh it to be true that the moiety of the said lease, playbooks, apparel and other furnitures and necessaries in the bill men[tioned] was by mesne assignment from the said Thomas Woodford settled in the said Lording Barry.

But this defendant denieth that ever he did solicit or persuade the said complainant [Androwes] to take from the said Barry an assignment of the sixth part of the said messuage, premises and profits, for that the same was fully effected before this defendant did know the said complainant and the said Barry, or either of them . . . The said complainant, as this defendant verily thinketh and hath credibly heard, did accept of the said bargain in the bill mentioned, and went through with Barry for the purchase of a sixth part thereof, and accepted an assignment from the said Barry of a sixth part of the said lease and of all the gain and profit to be had or gotten upon or by reason of the said messuage and premises . . . and of all plays, shows, interludes or exercises therein to be acted or done for and during the residue of the said term of six years, eight months and twenty days then to come, before this defendant did know the said complainant, or Barry, or any of them . . .

[Slatier, therefore, did not know what Barry or anybody else said to entice Androwes, nor did he know the value of apparel, or Barry's asking price for a share.] Yet he thinketh it to be true that the said complainant did satisfy unto the same Lording Barry the sum of £70 and no more . . .

And as touching that senseless part of the complainant's bill touching the complainant's charge and £300 loss, to which this defendant is as ready to give full answer as his understanding, by reason of the confused and dark setting forth of the same [in the bill], will serve and permit him. That is, that the charge in building by the complainant alledged was no way thought upon, that ever this defendant heard of, until long after the bargain finished with the said Barry. And, therefore, if any charge were sustained by the complainant, as this defendant doth think there was, the same was done by his own direction or with his own consent. And, therefore, [it is] absurd, in this defendant's understanding, that the complainant should seek relief at the hands of this defendant for his, the complainant's, own voluntary act[s] in case they prove not profitable, especially the charge thereof being as great unto this defendant as unto the said complainant, each of them being interested in a several sixth part of the said house and so chargeable with an equal, ratable and several sixth part of the charge thereof.

And this defendant denieth that all or the most part of the charges in maintaining the children and other incidents to the said business . . . did fall upon the complainant, or any charge to the value of £300, to the knowledge or thinking of this defendant. [Even if] . . . the plaintiff's allegations were true touching the profits and gains of his said sixth part, and his greedy and covetous desires (except they exceed all reasonable expectation) were allowed him thereunto, [nevertheless] . . . there is no cause in course of equity or otherwise to allow any man for default of his hoped-for gains, how necessary or likely soever, especially out of or against . . . an equal or greater loser by many degrees than the complainant, and yet [who] . . . no way persuaded the complainant to deal in the said sixth part, the pretended cause of the complainant's loss, nor yet [was] any causer of . . . his losses sustained thereby, for that this defendant was no worker nor causer of neither.

Neither doth it concern this defendant if the said original lease were forfeited before the assignment of the said sixth part so made unto the said complainant, for that this defendant was no causer of the complainant's dealing therein nor acquainted with the said forfeiture, if any were, which whether any such forfeiture were or no, this defendant knoweth not.

Yet [he] confesseth that the said complainant, the said Lording Barry, Michael Drayton, William Trevell, William Cooke, Edward Sibthorpe, John Mason and this defendant were likewise interested of and in all the parts of the said messuage and of all other the gains, profits and commodities that should at any time arise, come or grow by reason of any shows, plays, interludes, music or suchlike exercises as should be used or performed in the said playhouse. And [he] confesseth it to be true that the tenth day of March . . . [1608] there were certain articles of agreement indented and made between this defendant on the one party and the complainant, Lording Barry, Michael Drayton, William Trevell, William Cooke, Edward Sibthorpe and John Mason of the other party, the tenor whereof is in substance as by the bill is pretended, for anything this defendant now conceiveth to the contrary, but for certainty [he] referreth himself to the deed thereof. And [he] confesseth that the said complainant and the other parties in the bill mentioned did become bound unto this defendant in the penal sum of £200, conditioned as by the bill is pretended, for anything this defendant now perceiveth, yet for certainty [he] likewise referreth himself to the said obligation and the condition thereof, dated as by the bill pretended.

And this defendant marvelleth that the said plaintiff will offer so frivolous, false and weak a plea for his relief as ignorance of the law, the plaintiff well knowing that the agreement of all the parties to the same obligation was that the said obligation should be *verbatim*, as it is. But . . . this defendant . . . confidently affirmeth that his verbal agreement in that behalf [was] as is aforesaid. And this defendant denieth that either the scrivener, . . . to this defendant's knowledge, or this defendant ever affirmed that the said plaintiff was bound but only for his own acts. [But i]f this defendant did affirm to the plaintiff that he had no meaning at all to charge the plaintiff but only for his own acts and breach of covenants, for . . . the complainant's own particular act and part, [the same] is not material as the case now is, for that this defendant did . . . covenant with the complainant to the same effect, which in case the complainant hath by his own act no way broken the condition or forfeited [the said] bond, then is this defendant's . . . covenant a sufficient shield or defence for the complainant against this defendant and the said obligation of £200.

And if, on the contrary part, he the said complainant, by his own act hath forfeited the said bond, then, under favour of this honourable court, as this case is, is there no cause in conscience or equity to relieve the complainant, by whose means, amongst others', this defendant is riotously, wilfully, violently and unlawfully, contrary to the said articles and pretended agreement, put and kept out of his said rooms of habitation for him, this defendant, and his family, and all other his means of livelihood, thereby leaving this defendant and his whole family, being ten in number, to the world to seek for bread and other means to live by, tending to a far greater loss than the penalty of the said £200 bond, or any advantage to be had thereupon, can extend unto.

[Slatier denied that the other obligors had broken covenants against Androwes' liking and without his consent, and that Androwes had done nothing contrary to the agreement so that the bond of £200 was not forfeit. Slatier admitted that he had caused Androwes to be arrested and had begun a lawsuit in King's Bench on the bond,] as he hopeth, under favour of this honourable court, is lawful for him to do. And [Slatier] further saith that . . . [he] hath or should have a sufficient estate to satisfy anything the complainant could justly demand of him, . . . in case the said complainant and others did not fully, unlawfully and unconscionably withhold the same from this defendant. And . . . this defendant often and commonly goeth where he is subject to any arrest the said complainant can lay upon him.

431 The children of the King's Revels lose their lease on the playhouse, *c.* late March – early April 1608

PRO, Req.1/37/fo. 247. Transcribed in Hillebrand, *Child Actors*, 227

Thomas Woodford got a good deal of money out of William Trevell in 1611 for the bonds Trevell had given him in August 1607 towards a share of the playhouse. He then got more in 1621. When he tried to get yet more in 1640, Trevell sued him in the Court of Requests.

Trevell died soon after filing his bill in the autumn of that year, but his widow, Susan, carried on the case and won a complete victory on 11 June 1642. In its final decree, the court summarised Trevell's case, describing the events at the Whitefriars playhouse much as, no doubt, Trevell had done in his bill, which evidently does not survive:

The scope of the said William Trevell his bill . . . [is] to be relieved against two several judgements by the defendant [Woodford] obtained against the said William Trevell in the sixth year of . . . King James [*i.e.* 24 March 1608 to 23 March 1609], the one being for £40 debt and £1 costs and the other for £20 debt and £1 costs. And both of them grounded upon two several obligations wherein the said William Trevell became bound to the defendant.

The consideration which induced the said William Trevell to become bound in the said bonds . . . [was] only for a sixth part of the lease of a playhouse in the Whitefriars, whereunto the said William Trevell was drawn by the persuasion of Sir Anthony Ashley, knight, and one Mr Smith, and the defendant, who likewise prevailed with the said Trevell (being ignorant in the course of sharers in a playhouse) to become engaged in several other bonds and bills to divers persons for payment of divers sums only to make a stock for supply of the playhouse.

And although that the said Sir Anthony Ashley . . . [was] the landlord on [*sic*] the playhouse,[1] by combination with the defendant upon pretence that half a year's rent for the playhouse was unpaid, [he] entered into [*i.e.* seized] the playhouse and turned the players out of doors and took the forfeiture of the lease, whereby the said William Trevell was frustrated of all benefit which he was to have by the said lease.

[1] The freehold apparently belonged to the Sackville family, specifically in February 1608 to Robert Sackville (who was called Lord Buckhurst from 1604 to 19 April 1608, when he became second Earl of Dorset), from whom Ashley held a lease. See **430**.

432 The children of Blackfriars succeed those of the King's Revels at Whitefriars, 1609

See **239, 409e**

Although the King had driven the children of Blackfriars out of that playhouse in March 1608 vowing that 'they should never play more' (**407**), they performed at court three times during the Christmas season following, at least once before the King himself.[1] They were still described as of Blackfriars, and Robert Keysar was still responsible for them. Soon after, it seems, they moved into Whitefriars, where they were led by Keysar and Philip Rosseter, a noted musician. At first, they were probably merely living there, because of the plague of 1609.

[1] *ES*, IV, 175.

433 The constables of St Dunstan in the West file a complaint about the playhouse, 21 December 1609

GL, MS 3018/1, fo. 86. Transcribed in Jonas, *Shakespeare and the Stage*, 132

The constables presented their complaint before the wardmote inquest for the parish. What, if anything, happened as a result of the complaint does not appear.

We [the constables] present one playhouse in the same precinct [Whitefriars] not fitting there to be now tolerable.

434 The Blackfriars children become the Children of the Queen's Revels at Whitefriars, 4 January 1610

PRO, C66/1801/15. Transcribed in MSC, I. 271. See *ES*, II, 56 n. 2

The former Blackfriars children presumably began playing regularly at Whitefriars when the plague abated late in 1609 and were quite successful. For they were paid for playing no fewer than five times at court during the Christmas season of 1609–10,[1] calling themselves the children of Whitefriars. Just before the season was over they acquired a patent that made them the Children of the Queen's Revels (the title they had lost in 1606) who played at Whitefriars.

[The patent, 4 January 1610:] Whereas the Queen, our [*i.e.* the King's] dearest wife hath, for her pleasure and recreation when she shall think it fit to have any plays or shows, appointed her servants Robert Daborne, Philip Rosseter, John Tarbuck, Richard Jones and Robert Browne to provide and bring up a convenient number of children who shall be called Children of her Revels:[2] know ye that we have appointed and authorised ... [these men] from time to time to provide, keep and bring up a convenient number of children and them to practice and exercise in the quality of playing ... within the Whitefriars in the suburbs of our City of London or in any other convenient place where they shall think fitt for that purpose.

Since Ashley had cancelled Woodford's sublease shortly after 25 March 1608, Ashley must eventually have granted Keysar and Rosseter a new one about which nothing is known. However the Blackfriars children acquired the right to use the Whitefriars playhouse, they seem to have had no trouble there until the playhouse came to an end when Ashley's lease evidently ran out in 1614.

[1] *ES*, IV, 175.
[2] Daborne was or became a playwright; Jones and Browne were veteran actors. Who Tarbuck was is unknown, as is what had happened to Keysar.

435 Sheriffs stop a play being performed by apprentices at the Whitefriars playhouse, 21 February 1613

Wotton, *Letters of Sir Henry Wotton to Sir Edmund Bacon*, 155–6. See *ES*, III, 496

Sir Henry Wotton told his friend, Sir Edmund Bacon, of this débâcle in a letter written on 23 February 1613. The play was by Robert Tailor and printed in 1614 as 'Divers times publicly acted by certain London prentices'.

On Sunday last [21 February 1613] at night, . . . some sixteen apprentices (of what sort you shall guess by the rest of the story), having secretly learned a new play without book, intituled *The Hog Hath Lost His Pearl*, took up the Whitefriars for their theatre, and having invited thither (as it should seem) rather their mistresses than their masters, who were all to enter *per bullettini* [i.e. by tickets] for a note of distinction from ordinary comedians: towards the end of the play the sheriffs (who by chance had heard of it) came in (as they say) and carried some six or seven of them to perform the last act at Bridewell [a prison nearby]. The rest are fled. Now, it is strange to hear how sharp-witted the City is, for they will needs have Sir John Swinnerton, the Lord Mayor, be meant by the hog and the late Lord Treasurer [the Earl of Salisbury, d. 1612] by the pearl.

436 The lease runs out at Whitefriars, the players leave, the playhouse dies, 1613–1615

PRO, C66/2075/18. Transcribed in MSC, I. 277–9

In 1610 and 1611 the people at Whitefriars toyed with a dubious scheme to renew their lease with the help of Woodford, who invested some money in vain.[1] In the summer of 1613, however, they must have supposed that the playhouse would end with the lease, for on 13 June Rosseter, Philip Kingman 'and others' paid the Master of the Revels for permission to build a new playhouse in a garden in Whitefriars. Residents objected, however, and the privy council quashed the scheme.[2] On 3 June 1615 the lease having run out, Rosseter, Kingman, Jones and Ralph Reeve[3] got a patent allowing them to build another new playhouse. This one was to be in Blackfriars in a place called Porter's Hall. The work went ahead there until it was nearly finished, but residents complained again and had their way again. See *ES*, II, 472–4.

[The patent of 1615 begins by reciting the terms of the one of 4 January 1610 (434), then adds] and . . . the said Philip Rosseter and the rest of his said partners have ever since trained up and practiced a convenient number of children of the Revels for the purpose aforesaid [i.e. to play before the Queen] in a messuage or mansion-house being parcel of the late dissolved monastery called the Whitefriars near Fleet Street in London, which the said Philip Rosseter did lately hold for a term of a certain years expired.

---

[1] PRO, C2/Jas. I/W11/21. See Ingram, 'The Playhouse as an Investment, 1607–1614', 213–17.
[2] The Master of the Revels noted on 13 June that he had received £20 from an unnamed person for per-

mission to build a new playhouse in Whitefriars. The privy council noted on 29 July that it sided with residents and rejected a plan by Rosseter and Philip Kingman (apparently a former player) to build a playhouse in a garden they had sublet from one Sturgis, who had leased it from Sir Edward Gorge. See Herbert's office book (now lost), as reported by Malone in *Plays and Poems of William Shakespeare* (1821), III, 52; and PRO, PC2/27/fo. 55v, transcribed in *APC, 1613–14*, 166.

[3] Reeve was a former player who had managed the Whitefriars company on a tour in the provinces in 1611.

XXXIII The Red Bull

The Red Bull was a public playhouse in Clerkenwell in Middlesex, some 575 yards north of the City boundary at Smithfield. It was built in and around the yard of a former inn that lay behind buildings along the west side of St John Street, and its main entrance was a passageway through those buildings. Its name was probably that of the inn. The site is closely marked now by the eastern half of Hayward's Place, E.C.1, which also begins with a passageway through the buildings along the west side of St John Street.[1] The model for the Red Bull must have been the Boar's Head, which had been built six years before in, and named for, an inn.

The builder of the Red Bull was an illiterate, Aaron Holland, who leased the inn for perhaps thirty years from Christmas 1604.[2] He acquired the help of Martin Slatier, an actor among the Queen's men, who proposed to found a company of players belonging to the Duke of Holstein and to lead them at the Red Bull. The Duke was the Queen's brother. He was visiting England from Denmark and wanted to remain in England. According to the Venetian ambassador, however, he annoyed his sister by treating her chambers as his own, was asked to leave, and did so on 31 May 1605, when Slatier's enterprise must have collapsed.[3] The work of converting the inn to a playhouse was nearly finished – 'all framed and almost set up' – while, it seems, the Duke was still in England, but the privy council then ordered the work to stop. Slatier petitioned the council to let the work proceed, and eventually it did proceed.

The playhouse may have opened in 1605 or 1606, but it was not demonstrably in use until about the autumn of 1607, when the Queen's men had settled in for a long stay. They had used the Boar's Head in the winter of 1606–7, perhaps until the summer of 1607, having used it in 1601–2 and, with the Curtain, from 1604 until their arrival at the Red Bull. Slatier joined the same company as an actor for a time, but early in 1608 he sought again to lead a company, the one then in the Whitefriars playhouse, and he failed again.

Although the Red Bull was a playhouse for nearly sixty years, very little is known about its ownership or buildings. Holland seems to have avoided trouble with his landlords and associates, hence stayed out of revealing lawsuits. Eventually, however, he did get into trouble with Thomas Woodford, who invested in the Red Bull in June 1612.[4] Woodford had been managing St Paul's at least in 1602–3 and had been one of the main financiers at the Whitefriars. At the Red Bull, he paid £50 for a lease on, in effect, an 'eighteenth part' of the money collected from spectators in the galleries and on the stage (after the players had had their share). The lease was to run until 1634, and he was to pay £2 10s a year as rent. Holland had originally sold the lease in 1605 for £25. Woodford thought that he had also leased a gatherer's place worth 3d a day, or 18d a week, out of which he would pay a gatherer.

Woodford sued Holland repeatedly about these things in three courts from April 1613

Fig. 5. The Red Bull playhouse during a performance of drolls in the 1650s (?), from Francis Kirkman, *The Wits, or Sport upon Sport*, frontispiece

until 3 May 1624 (see the appendix and 441). In the lawsuits, Woodford referred to Holland 'and the rest of his partners, players of the said playhouse', and Holland referred to 'the partners and sharers of the said playhouse'. If Holland could sell leases on each of eighteen parts for £25, he had £450 with which to build his playhouse, and if each yielded £2 10s a year in rent, he had an income of £45 a year. But he must not have sold leases on all the parts, for he repeatedly claimed, and the courts did not deny, that, in effect, the 3d a day belonged to the enterprise as represented by him, not to associates. The lawsuits also suggest that the usual arrangement at the time between players and owners applied at the Red Bull. The players, that is, took the money collected in the yard and some (customarily half) of that in the galleries and on the stage. The owners took the rest of the money for the galleries and stage, and they hired at least one gatherer for the purpose.

How much did an eighteenth part amount to and how much the 3d a day? While sums mentioned by Woodford and Holland are too imprecise to provide an exact accounting, they do not differ wildly and they do suggest the scale of things. In 1619, Woodford said that the two together were yielding about £30 a year when he bought his lease, that is from the end of February 1609 to Michaelmas 1612, and he should have meant that amount clear of the rent, or £32 10s altogether. In 1623 he said that the eighteenth part had yielded, on average, £1 a week for three years (evidently 1609–12). On 22 June 1613 one arbitrator fixed the 3d a day from the end of February 1609 to Christmas 1612 as the same as the eighteenth part for the first two-quarters of 1613,[5] and on 9 October 1613 another (according to Holland in 1623) agreed. The first also fixed Holland's legal expenses at £5 8s 4d, and in 1623 Holland said that these two sums came to twenty marks (£13 6s 8d), meaning that the eighteenth part for two-quarters came to £7 18s 4d, as did the 3d a day for nearly sixteen-quarters. In 1623, Woodford put the amount of the eighteenth part for the two-quarters at £7 18s.

Though neither Woodford nor Holland said so, these figures must have applied only while players were using the playhouse. The figures suggest, therefore, that from 1609 to 1612 the players were averaging only some thirty weeks a year at the playhouse, thanks, presumably, to closings because of plague in 1609–10. The galleries and stage yielded about £3 a day to the owners, and probably a like amount to the players. Thomas Heywood said that the whole playhouse, the yard as well as the galleries and stage, 'received' £8 or £9 a day at about this time. During an ordinary year of forty odd weeks, the eighteenth part must have yielded about £40 clear, and the 3d a day might have amounted to something like £3.[6]

After a victory – which came to nothing – in the first lawsuit, Woodford lost every time. The lawsuits, however, finished Holland at the Red Bull, or so he said. In order to pay his legal bills, he had by 6 November 1623 sold his lease on the place and some adjoining houses, together with his interest in the profits of the playhouse, for £100 and an annuity on his and his wife's lives. That sum, as he also said, was a good deal less than he could have got if he had been able to sell at leisure. But though he no longer owned the playhouse, a year later he was still going to plays there. It is not known who succeeded him.

Not much is known about the playhouse proper. According to Slatier in 1605, Holland 'altered some stables and other rooms, being before a square court[yard] in an inn, to turn them into galleries', and according to Holland in 1623, he 'set up . . . divers buildings and galleries for a playhouse'. Slatier also remarked that the playhouse cost £500, including, presumably, any fees involved in acquiring the lease. Both Woodford and Holland referred to the 'great gate' leading to the playhouse from, presumably, St John Street, and to spectators who stood and sat in the galleries and on the stage.

The Queen's men were at the Red Bull until 1617, and were there again from 1619 until 1623, when, as the Revels company (the Queen having died in 1619), they broke up. Prince Charles' (I) men, who had replaced the Queen's men in 1617, replaced them again in 1623. That company broke up in 1625 and were succeeded by an obscure group called the King's players on the road and the Red Bull company in London. A notable company, Prince Charles' (II) men arrived in 1634 and stayed until 1640, when the Red Bull company returned and stayed until the closing of the playhouse in 1642.

The playhouse was 're-edified' sometime in the 1620s. It was, however, never a playhouse of great plays, and, with other public playhouses, it was increasingly seen as in an unfashionable part of the City and lacking in the refinement of the private playhouses.

After 1642 it was used for entertainments even more than other playhouses, especially after the drastic order of 9 February 1648. Towards the end of the interregnum, it was the only playhouse associated with the performance of 'drolls', groups of excerpts from famous plays of former times. In his second collection of them, Francis Kirkman wrote that he had 'seen the Red Bull playhouse, which was a large one, so full [at such performances] that as many went back for want of room as had entered'. Langbaine wrote that Robert Cox, the only actor associated with drolls, 'betook himself to making drolls or farces ... which under the colour of rope-dancing were allowed to be acted at the Red Bull playhouse by stealth and the connivance of those straight-laced governors'.[7]

For a frontispiece, Kirkman's book has a famous drawing of a candle-lit performance of drolls in what should be the Red Bull in the 1650s. A stage adjoins a tiring-house façade in which, above the back of the stage, is a gallery. Actors enter the stage through, apparently, a single door covered with two arrases. In front of the gallery are drawings of a cavalry battle on the left side and soldiers with lances and a flag on the right side. The middle of the gallery is bowed out over the stage door, has balusters instead of a drawing, and is covered top to bottom with four pieces of striped cloth. Four spectators sit, it seems, on the left side of the gallery and four more on the right, and many stand in the yard around three sides of the stage.

Two candelabra with sixteen lighted candles hang above the stage, and twelve lighted candles lie across the front of the stage. Because of this artificial light, writers have supposed that the yard was roofed. But Hotson has argued convincingly that the yard of the Red Bull was never roofed, and *Historia Histrionica* reports that the Globe, Fortune and Red Bull 'were large houses and lay partly open to the weather, and there they always acted by daylight'.[8] The contradiction may be more apparent than real. The candles should signify a surreptitious performance at night and the candelabra could well hang from the stage roof that the Red Bull, like its coevals, must have had

When playing resumed legally in 1660, the Red Bull was available. It became an important playhouse in August, because Thomas Killigrew installed his company there, but this importance did not last long, for the company left early in November. Other actors played there for two more years but with little success. The place was empty in 1663 and used for fencing in 1664. It escaped the great fire of 1666, and the main part of 'Red Bull Yard' is shown as about 38′ × 70′ on Ogilby and Morgan's map (1676). The yard is also shown on Morgan's map (1682, c. 1720) and Rocque's map (1746).

[1] So Ogilby and Morgan's *Large and Accurate Map of London* (1676) shows 'Red Bull Yard', its surrounding buildings, and its entrance into St John Street. Another entrance led south from the south-west corner of the property into Clerkenwell Green (now Aylesbury St). In both Morgan's (1682, c. 1720) and Rocque's (1746) maps, the entrance into St John Street is directly opposite Compton Street, as is the present entrance to Hayward's Place.
[2] In the lawsuit of 1623 (see 441 and the appendix), both Woodford and Holland said that the lease for a share of the profits ended at Michaelmas 1634, and in 1619 Woodford said that it began in the third year of James I. One can guess, therefore, that it began at Michaelmas 1605 and was for twenty-nine years. Since Holland granted the lease, his own grand lease on the property should have begun sooner (it was evidently in being in May 1605) and ended later.
[3] *CSP, Ven, 1603–7*, 248.
[4] For Woodford, see Ingram, 'The Playhouse as an Investment, 1607–1614', 225–8.
[5] Wallace, 'Three London Theatres', 299–300.
[6] Yet Holland said in 1623 that the 3d a day 'was far more worth than the said eighteenth part'.
[7] Kirkman, *The Wits, or Sport upon Sport*, sig. A2v; Langbaine, *An Account*, 89.
[8] CRS, 86–7; Wright (?), *Historia Histrionica*, 7.

437 Martin Slatier asks the privy council to let the work on the playhouse continue, before 31 May 1605

Hatfield House, Cecil Papers, MS 197, fo. 91 (2). Calendared in HMC, *Salisbury*, XVII, 234. Slatier's petition is undated, but since it implies that the Duke of Holstein was still in England, it should have been written before 31 May 1605, when the Duke left.

The humble petition of Martin Slatier, one of her majesty's servants

... Whereas it pleased the right gracious, the Duke of Holstein, to make choice of your supplicant, as by his grace's warrant appeareth, to select and gather a company of comedians to attend his grace here or elsewhere at his commandment, and, having made choice of them, [they] being unprovided of a house to play in, as others of their profession have:

Your supplicant [is] very willing to show himself in the best manner he could for his grace's service, together with one Aaron Holland, servant to the ... Earl of Devonshire, having jointly the lease of the house betwixt them for thirty years; [Holland] hath altered some stables and other rooms, being before a square court[yard] in an inn, to turn them into galleries, first having in general the parish's consent, who have subscribed their names to a petition already exhibited to your honours at the [privy] council table, with due consideration for divers causes, and especially towards the poor of the parish, who [*i.e.* Holland] hath allowed them 20s a month towards their maintenance and, likewise, for the amending and maintaining of the pavements and highways thereabouts. And your supplicants have bestowed upon the same the sum of £500.

Since which time there is a letter come from your honourable lordships to stay the finishing of the same, being all framed and almost set up, to your supplicants's utter undoing forever, without it shall please God to move your honours' hearts to pity us.

May it, therefore, please your honours, the premises considered, to grant unto your poor supplicants your lawful favours and allowances to finish the same and to have such privilege as others of their quality have, and the rather that many poor men are left destitute of living and are utterly overthrown forever ...

438 The Red Bull is first mentioned as open when the Queen's men are there, autumn 1607

Beaumont and Fletcher, *The Knight of the Burning Pestle* (1613), IV, i

The evidence is a remark in *The Knight of the Burning Pestle* (published in 1613 but first performed probably late in 1607), which refers to a play the Queen's men played at the Red Bull probably in the autumn of 1607. Thomas Dekker alluded to the Red Bull as a working playhouse twice in 1609: *Raven's Almanack* (London, 1609), sig. D3; and *Work for Armourers* (1609), sig. Bv. In *The Knight of the Burning Pestle*:

CITIZEN: Why so, sir, go and fetch me him [Ralph, the Citizen's apprentice] then, and let the Sophy of Persia come and Christen him a child.
BOY: Believe me, sir, that will not do so well: 'tis stale, it has been had before at the Red Bull.

The Sophy of Persia Christens a child in the last scene of the Queen's men's play, Day, William Rowley and Wilkins, *The Travels of Three English Brothers*, published in 1607 (SR, 29 June 1607) and apparently based on a book of 1607: Nixon, T*he Three English Brothers* (SR, June 8, 1607).[1]

[1] The entry for the play in Stationer's Register says that the Queen's men performed it at the Curtain, and a remark in the epilogue about the 'round circumference' of the playhouse suggests the Curtain, too. The title page, however, mentions no playhouse. As Bentley (*J and CS*, VI, 216–17n.) guessed, the play could have been written for the Curtain and later played at the Red Bull. The company used both the Curtain and the Boar's Head from 1604 until their arrival at the Red Bull. They were demonstrably at the Boar's Head in the winter of 1606–7 and possibly until the summer of 1607. See 325c, 333, 389, 390b.

439 Notable outrages are committed at the Red Bull, May 1610 – c. 1623

(a) LMA, MJ/SR 489/9, 11,101, 103, 105; (b) LMA, MJ/SR 519/53; (c) *Dice, Wine, and Women, or the Unfortunate Gallant Gulled at London* (c. 1623). Transcribed in (a, b) Jeaffreson, *Middlesex County Records*, II, 64–5, 86

(a) 29 May 1610

[One man was bonded on 29 May for £60 and four on 3 July for £40 to guarantee their appearance at the next sessions of the peace in Middlesex: William Tedcastle, yeoman; and John Fryne (29 May), Edward Brian, Edward Purfett and Thomas Williams, felt makers. Each bond explained in much the same language:] For that he and others made a notable outrage at the playhouse called the Red Bull.

(b) 3 March 1613

[Alexander Fulsis was bonded to guarantee his appearance at the next gaol delivery of the Middlesex sessions of the peace because he was] suspected to have picked a purse and £3 in money in the same, being out of the pocket of one Robert Sweete at the Red Bull in St John Street.

(c) c. 1623

[In a ballad, a young man newly arrived in London from Cornwall says that 'a pander' took him to a brothel, where he lost £10, then:]

Most of my money being spent,
  To St John's Street to the [Red] Bull I went,
Where I *The Roaring Rimer*[1] saw,
  And to my face was made a daw [*i.e.* fool];
And pressing forth among the folk,
  I lost my purse, my hat, and cloak.

[1] The writer could have meant a playwright rather than a play.

440 Fools learn a fool's eloquence at the Red Bull, 1613, 1615

(a) Wither, *Abuses Stript and Whipt* (1613), Satire 1; (b) Tomkis, *Albumazar* (1615), sigs. C4v–D

(a) 1613

Of a foolish, courting lover:

His poetry is such as he can cull
From plays he heard at Curtain or at [Red] Bull,
And yet is fine, coy Mistress Marry-muff
The soonest taken with such broken stuff.

(b) 1615

[A clown describes how he means to woo a lady:] I [will] confound her with compliments drawn from the plays I see at the Fortune and Red Bull, where I learn all the words I speak and understand not.[1]

[1] Bentley (*J and CS*, VI, 241–3) mentions other instances in which sophisticates mock what was said on the stage at the Red Bull: the man who gathers 'musty phrases from the [Red] Bull'; a silly romantic device drawn 'from a play at the [Red] Bull t'other day'; a 'solecism' like 'the Red Bull phrase, . . . "enter seven devils *solus*"'.

441 Thomas Woodford sues Aaron Holland over the profits of the galleries and stage at the Red Bull, 1613–1624

PRO, (a, b) C3/390/47; (c) C33/146/fo. 948a. Transcribed in *CRS*, 327–47

Woodford sued Holland repeatedly in three courts between 1613 and 1624 (see the appendix). Below is a summary of the bill and quotations from the rest of the final lawsuit, where the issues of the dispute are more clearly stated than elsewhere.

(a) Woodford's bill of complaint, 25 October 1623

Woodford began his bill with an explanation of events up to 1612, with much of which Holland agreed. Woodford admitted that Swinnerton and Stone after him had received 3d a day for a gatherer's place not by contractual means but 'by the usual custom' and 'certain orders' between players and owners. Woodford's non-payment of the rent at Christmas 1612, he then argued, was Holland's fault. Woodford's agent had asked Holland to let him know when the rent should come due, and Holland had replied that the agent 'need not trouble' himself because Holland's love for Woodford was such that 'he would do anything for' Woodford's 'content and good'. When the agent finally tendered the money, Holland told him to keep it until Woodford returned. Holland's avoiding the order of 23 June 1613 (see appendix, (a) and (b)), Woodford protested, was an underhanded conspiracy between Holland and his lawyer. The 'release' (appendix (d)) allowing Holland to avoid a lawsuit in which Woodford sued in Stone's name was the result of a 'fraudulent combination' between Holland and Stone. It was also a matter that especially annoyed Woodford.

(b) Holland's answer, 6 November 1623

He, the defendant, saith that . . . he . . . was lawfully possessed for the term of years yet to come of and in the said messuage or tenement now commonly called or known by the name or sign of the Red Bull at the upper end of St John's Street,[1] with the courts, gardens, cellars, ways and liberties thereunto belonging or appertaining, situate, lying and being in the parish of St James at Clerkenwell in the county of Middlesex. And [he saith] that this defendant, to his great charge and expenses, did erect and set up in and upon part of the said premises divers buildings and galleries for a playhouse[2] to present and play comedies, tragedies and other matters of that quality, . . . as in the said bill of complaint is set forth . . .

And . . . [he saith] that he, being of the said premises so possessed, and having erected and made such buildings and galleries as aforesaid, did by deed indented, as in the bill is alledged, grant unto Thomas Swinnerton, . . . being then one of the players and servant to the late Queen Anne, for divers years then unexpired the eighteenth penny, or just eighteenth part of all such sum and sums of money and commodities that should be collected of every person that should come and take place, stand or sit in any the said galleries or rooms belonging to the said playhouse (excepting and deducting as in the said indenture is excepted and deducted), as in the said bill of complaint is also set forth. To which deed for more certainty hereof this defendant referreth himself. But this defendant utterly denieth that there is, or ever was, . . . belonging to the said eighteenth part, by any usual custom, a gatherer's place in respect of any orders made between the said company of players and the partners and sharers of the said playhouse in such sort as in the said bill of complaint is untruly surmised. Neither doth this defendant know of any such 3d a day profit arising to the said Thomas Swinnerton, or to such gatherers as he did appoint during the time of playing by reason of any such gatherer's place . . . belonging to the said eighteenth part, as in the said bill is alledged.

But . . . if the said Swinnerton did receive any such 3d a day, he did not receive the same as incident to the eighteenth part but rather in respect of some special words contained in his said grant which are not mentioned or contained in the grant afterwards made to the said Philip Stone, as will hereafter appear. Or, if there were no such special words in the said grant, as this defendant remembreth not certainly after so long time and the deed being now cancelled, then he saith he permitted him, the said Swinnerton, to take the same out of his love and favour towards him, in respect of the hard pennyworth the said Swinnerton then affirmed he had thereof.

And this defendant further saith that . . . the said Swinnerton, . . . being possessed of the said eighteenth part as aforesaid, some agreement was between the said Thomas Swinnerton and the said Philip Stone . . . for the buying of the said eighteenth part of him, the said Thomas Swinnerton. But this defendant denieth, to his knowledge, that the said Philip Stone did pay £50 beforehand to the said Thomas Swinnerton for the said eighteenth part . . . in such sort as in the said bill of complaint is surmised. Neither doth this defendant think it to be true that the said Philip Stone did pay any such sum for the same, in respect this defendant upon the making of the first grant thereof to him, the said Thomas Swinnerton, had and received only . . . £25 or thereabouts, and that by divers and several small payments, . . . some thereof by £5 quarterly and . . . some thereof by £2 10s and £2 and suchlike small sums severally at many payments, and the said Swinnerton then saying that it was not worth so much.

And this defendant further saith . . . that he, this defendant, upon the request . . . of the said Thomas Swinnerton and Philip Stone, and upon the surrendering up of the said former deed, did by a new indenture bearing date the said 30 February [*sic*], . . . 1608[/9] . . . covenant and grant to pay and deliver to the said Philip Stone, his executors and assigns the said eighteenth penny or just eighteenth part of all such sum or sums, commodities and benefits during the said term of twenty-five years and three-quarters of a year (except as before is excepted) that should be collected or received of any person that should come to take place, sit or stand in the said rooms or galleries, or upon the stage, in the said playhouse weekly or at the end of every week in such sort as in the said bill of complaint is set forth . . . And this defendant saith that . . . in the same indenture made to the said Philip Stone as aforesaid there is a covenant or reservation whereby the said Philip Stone, his executors, or assigns should yearly well and truly pay, or cause to be paid, to this defendant, his executors, administrators or assigns at the great gate of the said playhouse the sum of £2 10s of lawful money of England at such feasts and day, and in such sort, manner and form as in the said bill of complaint is set forth.[3] And [he saith] that in the same indenture there is likewise a proviso contained that if default of payment thereof were made . . . the said benefit to the said Philip Stone by the said indenture granted, together with the same indenture, should cease, determine and be utterly void, . . . as in and by the same indenture, whereunto this defendant for more certainty referreth himself, more at large appeareth.

In which said indenture so made to the said Philip Stone there is no mention made of a gatherer's place . . . belonging to the said eighteenth penny or eighteenth part granted to the said Philip Stone as aforesaid. Neither was there any such thing by the same indenture granted, nor was it the intent or meaning of this defendant to grant any such gatherers's place to him, the said Philip Stone. And this defendant saith that if such a gatherer's place . . . were incident or belonging to the said eighteenth penny or eighteenth part, as, indeed, there is none but by the said complainant's presumption, it is very likely . . . that the said Philip Stone, at the time of the making of the said indenture to him by this defendant, would have specially mentioned the same in the said indenture.

All which notwithstanding, he, the said Philip Stone, and the said complainant have and did for a long time, upon pretence of such a gatherer's place to be incident or belonging to the said eighteenth part or eighteenth penny as aforesaid, receive and take divers sums of money for and in respect of 3d a day by them pretended to be due and appertaining to the said gatherer's place daily to be paid out of the profits arising of the said playhouse over and besides the said eighteenth part or eighteenth penny covenanted by this defendant to be paid to the said Philip Stone as aforesaid. To which said gatherer's place and the said 3d a day thereto belonging, as by the said complainant is pretended, he, the said Philip Stone, nor the said complainant, nor either of them, hath or ever had any just or lawful right, title or interest. But [they] have and did intrude themselves thereinto and wrongfully receive the same to the great loss and prejudice of him, this defendant, to whom the same of the right did and doth truly belong . . .

And he, this defendant, thereupon demanded restitution of the said Philip Stone of the said sums so by him wrongfully received, which the said Philip Stone refusing, this defendant then said he would bring his action at the common law against him, the said Stone, for the same, as under favour of this honourable court this defendant thinketh it was lawful for him to do. Upon which occasion, he, the said Stone, imagining this defendant would have molested him for the said sums so by him wrongfully received, and perceiving that he should not, nor could not, any longer quietly receive the said profits in respect he had no just nor lawful title, right, or claim thereunto, did thereupon, as this defendant thinketh, conceiveth [*sic*] to be rid of further trouble for some good consideration [and did] bargain, sell or assign over the eighteenth part or eighteenth penny to the said complainant to be by him received and taken during the residue of the said years to come. But by what conveyance or what manner of assurance this defendant saith he knoweth not, nor was made privy thereunto.

And this defendant further saith and denieth that . . . the said Anthony Payne, in the bill of complaint named to be substitute to the complainant for the receiving of the said eighteenth part or eighteenth penny and to pay the said £2 10s yearly to this defendant, . . . did, before the day limited for the payment of the said £2 10s yearly, resort to this defendant in the absence of the said complainant concerning the same payment, or that this defendant did thereupon say that he should not need to trouble himself touching the payment thereof, for that he, this defendant, would do nothing to hinder the complainant by taking advantage against the said complainant's payments, as in the said bill of complaint is untruly surmised. For this defendant saith that he never had any meddling or dealing with the said complainant concerning the said eighteenth part or eighteenth penny or other the premises, nor ever accounted him as his tenant thereunto but only the said Philip Stone . . .

According to which clause [that the deed would be void if the rent were not paid within fourteen days of being due], this defendant at . . . [Christmas] 1612 and within fourteen days after, expecting payment of the quarter's rent . . . then due from the said Philip Stone, and no payment thereof being then, or within the said fourteen days after, made or tendered by the said Philip Stone or by any in his behalf: according to the said clause, . . . the said deed . . . concerning the payment of the said eighteenth part or eighteenth penny to the said Philip stone did cease and become absolutely void, frustrate, and of none effect to all intents and purposes. And although the said complainant supposeth in his said bill of complaint that the said Anthony Payne, his substitute, did shortly after the said fourteen days next after . . . [Christmas] 1612 in the said complainant's absence tender the said quarter's rent to this defendant, this defendant saith that the same was tendered to be paid to this defendant in the name of Philip Stone, which this defendant then refused to accept of. And this defendant saith . . . that he then had, and yet hath, good reason to take and hold the forfeiture of the said eighteenth part or eighteenth penny so forfeited as aforesaid, for that the said sums of money intruded upon and wrongfully received by the said Philip Stone in respect of the benefit and profit of the said gatherer's place (which of right did belong to this defendant) was far more worth than the said eighteenth part or eighteenth penny of the profits and sums aforesaid. And this defendant could not but with much suit, trouble and expenses remedy or help himself therein. And, therefore, this defendant . . . hopeth this honourable court will think it reasonable that he, this defendant, for his relief and satisfaction therein did take the said forfeiture in manner and form aforesaid.

And although this defendant did upon the reasons aforesaid take the said forfeiture, yet at the time of the foresaid tender, this defendant did offer that if the said Philip Stone or the said complainant would have . . . paid the said defendant all and every such sums as were by him, the said Philip Stone, and the said complainant wrongfully received as aforesaid and which truly belonged to him, this defendant, that then he, this defendant, would have made good the said grant of the said eighteenth part or eighteenth penny to him, the said complainant, for and during the said residue of the said term then to come, which the said complainant refused to accept of.

But thereupon . . . the said now complainant exhibited his bill of complaint into the . . . Court of Requests [in the spring of 1613]. To which bill this defendant . . . in his answer thereunto . . . did not deny the said assignment of the . . . eighteenth part or eighteenth penny from the said Philip Stone to him the said complainant. And . . . he, this defendant, for avoiding of tedious suits and costs and expenses thereupon, did in his answer . . . offer that if the said Philip Stone, or such as claimed under him, would satisfy this defendant all such sums of money as were then justly due to this defendant by the said Stone or by any claiming under him for the sums so wrongfully received, that then this defendant would make a new covenant of the said eighteenth part or eighteenth penny to the said complainant in his own name with the like covenants and agreements as were in the said indenture made to the said Philip Stone, to which answer this defendant for more certainty referreth himself. But this defendant denieth that any mention was therein . . . assented unto for the granting of any such gatherer's place or of any such 3d a day, or that the said gatherer's place was incident and belonging to the said eighteenth part or eighteenth penny, as by the same answer more at large appeareth.

And this defendant further saith that, during the dependency of the said suit in the said Court of Requests, the said now complainant and defendant, upon some conference had between them concerning the premises, did refer themselves to stand to the arbitrament of Clement Goldsmith of Gray's Inn . . . and Anthony Dyott of the Middle Temple, . . . arbitrators equally and indifferently chosen by the said parties for the final determining and ending of the said controversies . . . between them. And [they] did then assure and promise each to other to stand to the same award and arbitrament . . . The said arbitrators . . . did amongst other things award (as this defendant hopeth to prove to this honourable court) that the sum of twenty marks [£13 6s 8d] should be paid to this defendant for the said sums so wrongfully received by the said Stone and the said complainant for the said 3d a day or gatherer's place . . . and for this defendant's great charges expended in suits concerning the same.

But the said complainant, well perceiving there was no bond nor other consideration given each to the other . . . whereby the said complainant was bound or compellable in law to stand and obey the same award and therefore might easily avoid the same, . . . did accordingly utterly refuse to stand to or perform the same award. And thereupon [he] did, whilst this defendant was busied and employed about the said awards or arbitrament, not thinking of any further suit or proceedings in the said Court of Requests, and before this defendant could be sufficiently provided to withstand the same or to give his counsel directions or informations concerning the said business, . . . obtain an order in the same Court of Requests against this defendant, by force whereof the said complainant again entered into and had and enjoyed the said eighteenth part or eighteenth penny of the profits aforesaid, and by colour thereof intruded and took likewise the profits of the said gatherer's place, or 3d a day, as incident to the said eighteenth part for some time, until this defendant, upon good reasons therefor showed by his counsel, obtained a writ of prohibition out of the Court of King's Bench, . . . as hereafter is more at large showed.

And this defendant confesseth that the said complainant did tender an indenture to him, this defendant, to be sealed, which he, the said complainant, told this defendant was drawn up according to the said former deed . . . made to the said Stone of the said eighteenth part or eighteenth penny, which this defendant did not deny to seal but desired respite of time to be advised thereupon by his counsel whether the same were drawn up according to the said former deed and the true meaning of the said order. At or about which time, or shortly after, there being some treatise or conference between the said complainant and this defendant of a new reference to be had of all the said differences to Ralph Wormleighton of Gray's Inn, . . . the said indenture so tendered was not afterwards much uged upon this defendant to be sealed. And, therefore, this defendant, hoping all the said differences would have been ended upon the said arbitrament, did thereupon forbear to seal the same indenture so tendered.

And this defendant further saith that he, being still desirous of an arbitrament and peaceable end concerning the premises for the avoiding of multiplicity of suits and the great charges and expenses in law upon a second treaty of agreement had between the said complainant and this defendant, they both referred themselves to the arbitrament of the said Ralph Wormleighton, . . . chosen between them to end and determine all matters and differences between them. And [they] became bound by several obligations each to other in the penal sum of £20 . . . to stand by the arbitrament . . . of the said Ralph Wormleighton, to be given . . . at or before 9 October then next following [1613], as by the said obligation bearing date 15 September [1613] . . . more at large appeareth. And thereupon the said Ralph Wormleighton, taking upon him the making of the said award and hearing the allegations and proofs of both parties, and being willing to set them at unity, did arbitrate [firstly] that this defendant, upon the said complainant's request, should make a new grant to the said complainant of the said eighteenth part of the sums and profits to be gathered in the said playhouse (the players' parts and other duties being first deducted); secondly that this defendant should enjoy the gatherer's place; thirdly that this defendant should be absolutely discharged against the complainant for the mean profits of the said eighteenth part by him received since the said forfeiture; and fourthly that the said complainant should pay to this defendant £2 in discharge of arrearage of rent due to this defendant; and [fifthly] that the said suit in the said Court of Requests and all other suits between them should cease and determine – as by the said award under the hand and seal of the said Ralph Wormleighton, bearing date . . . 9 October . . . [1613], ready to be showed to his honourable court, more at large appeareth.

After which said award and arbitrament so made, this defendant, thinking that the said complainant would not refuse but stand to and obey the same as he, this defendant, was then willing to obey and perform the same of his part, did accordingly divers times require him, the said complainant, to perform the said award of his part. But he, the said complainant, being a contentious person and being more desirous of suits and controversies than of peace and unity, did refuse to obey or perform the contents of the said award.

And notwithstanding the said complainant had enjoyed and received the said eighteenth part or eighteenth penny of the profits aforesaid by force of the said order made in the said Court of Requests and thereupon wrongfully intruded upon the said gatherer's place and received the profits thereof which of right belonged to this defendant, yet the said complainant detained and refused to make payment of the quarter's rent of the said yearly rent of £2 10s payable to this defendant for the rent of the premises at [Michaelmas 1613] . . . after the said order made. Whereupon this defendant, having no other present remedy for his said wrongs, was enforced to make means for the said prohibition, and by his counsel moved in the said Court of King's Bench, where, the full and whole matter being plainly and truly set forth and opened to the said court, it pleased the said court, upon the just reasons there showed, to grant the said writ of prohibition to this defendant for the avoiding of the said order and proceedings in the Court of Requests concerning the premises, as by the said writ of prohibition, ready to be showed to this honourable court, more at large appeareth.

After which time, the said defendant, although the said prohibition was had and obtained upon good matters and reasons grounded as well upon law as equity, he, the said complainant, having a desire and delight to variety of suits and controversies, did afterwards . . . make divers motions in the said Court of King's Bench for the making void . . . of the said prohibition, and thereby put this defendant to great and unnecessary expenses in answer of the said several motions.

And at last, perceiving he could not prevail therein, he, the said complainant, thinking himself (as this defendant conceiveth) to be an excellent tragedian and purposing to vex and undo this defendant (being an aged man) with suits and controversies, exhibited another bill of complaint in the . . . Court of Requests in the name of the said Philip Stone against this defendant, containing in effect . . . the self-same matters before in his said former bill complained of in the said Court of Requests. And thereupon this defendant, being served with his majesty's writ of privy seal out of the said Court of Requests to appear and answer the said bill exhibited in the name of the said Philip Stone, he, this defendant, meeting with the said Philip Stone and upon conference had between him and this defendant, he, the said Philip Stone, well perceiving how he had formerly wronged this defendant in intruding upon and taking the profits of the said gatherer's place, . . . and likewise perceiving how this defendant was molested and wronged without any just cause, he, the said Stone, then said this defendant should be no further troubled therein, neither should his [Stone's] name be used as an instrument to vex and trouble this defendant. And thereupon he, the said Philip Stone, upon the request of him, this defendant, did seal and deliver unto him, this defendant, a general release of all actions, claims and demands whatsoever from the beginning of the world until the time of the date of the same release, as by the said general release bearing date 16 May . . . [1614], ready to be showed to this honourable court, appeareth.

And this defendant confesseth [that] he pleaded the said release to the complainant's said second bill in the Court of Requests, which this defendant hopeth

... this honourable court will think it was lawful for him to do. Which release this defendant ... did not obtain in respect he, this defendant, knew not how otherwise to answer the said complainant's second bill in the said Court of Requests, ... as in the said bill of complaint in this court is untruly surmised, but because this defendant, being wearied out with costs and expenses in suits, was grown unable to maintain defence against such tedious suits with such a perverse and contentious adversary ... And this defendant denieth that he gave or promised to give to the said Philip Stone any gratuity for ... the making of the said release, ... nor that the same was made for and upon any other causes and reasons than are before alledged. And this defendant likewise saith that if he, the said complainant, received any prejudice ... by reason of the said release, then [he] ... might have had or may have his remedy by action at the common law or otherwise against the said Philip Stone upon his, the said Stone's, covenants between him and the said complainant upon the assigning of the said eighteenth part, as aforesaid.

But the said complainant, not resting but still persevering in the vexing and molesting of this defendant, caused an action ... to be brought in the Court of King's Bench in the name of the said Stone against this defendant upon a supposed assumpsit,[4] ... made by this defendant to the said Stone at the time of the making of the said release, to discharge him, the said Stone, of a bond of £100 wherein the said Stone stood bound to the said complainant. Which action coming to trial by *nisi prius*[5] before the Lord Chief Justice of the King's Bench, the said complainant was therein overthrown and this defendant found to have made no such promise for and in consideration of the said release, but that the same release was freely made from the said Stone to this defendant upon causes and reasons before herein set forth ...

By reason of all which said tedious suits and vexations prosecuted by the said complainant against this defendant, he, this defendant, for the defence and maintaining of his right, hath been put to great charges and expenses and, therefore, compelled to borrow many sums of money. And for satisfaction thereof, [he] hath been enforced not only to sell his whole benefit and profit in the said playhouse, but also all his interest and term of years in the said messuage called the Red Bull and in divers tenements thereunto near adjoining for the sum of £100, reserving a small annuity for the maintenance of him and his wife for the term of their several lives. Whereby it may plainly appear that, the whole benefit of the said playhouse, together with the messuage and divers other tenements, being sold by this defendant for such small consideration, ... the said eighteenth penny or eighteenth part of the benefit and profit aforesaid, for which the said complainant hath so wrongfully molested and sued this defendant and put him to such unjust costs and expenses as aforesaid, can be by all probability but of small worth or consequence.

And this defendant likewise hopeth that it will ... appear to this honourable court, the passages and circumstances aforesaid being duly weighed and considered, that the said complainant (after this defendant hath now been for the space of these eight years in quiet[6]) hath no just cause to complain in this honourable court, but that the said bill of complaint now exhibited into this court is merely framed of purpose to scandalise and vex this defendant upon some hope to wrest or gain a sum of money upon some composition from this defendant and not upon any just or lawful ground . . .

[1] In reciting the same information in 1619, Woodford added here 'by force of a lease thereof for many years yet enduring to him . . . made by Anne Bedingfield, late wife . . . of Christopher [?] Bedingfield, deceased'. In 1623 he added instead, 'sometimes in the tenure of one John Waintworth or his assigns'.
[2] In reciting the same information in 1619, Woodford added here that Holland then 'leased [the place] for a playhouse'.
[3] *i.e.*, on the usual quarter days, Lady Day (25 March), St John Baptist (24 June), Michaelmas (29 September) and Christmas.
[4] *i.e.* an unkept promise to seal a contract. Woodford argued that Stone had given Holland a bond for £100 on, presumably, another occasion and that Holland had promised to cancel the bond in return for the release.
[5] *i.e.* the hearing of a civil matter by a judge in a court of common law, like King's Bench.
[6] Holland, or his lawyer, forgot the lawsuit in Requests in 1619.

(c) the court's decision, 3 May 1624

The plaintiff [*i.e.* Woodford] is adjudged to pay to the defendant [*i.e.* Holland] £2 6s 8d costs for want of a replication,[1] and the matter of the plaintiff's bill is from henceforth clearly and absolutely dismissed out of the court.

[1] *i.e.* a reply to Holland's answer.

442 The Queen's men get into difficulties at the Red Bull because of negligent management, 1615

PRO, C24/500/9, no. 33. Transcribed in Sisson, 'The Red Bull Company and the Importunate Widow', 64.

[In a lawsuit of 1623, the Queen's men's playwright, Thomas Heywood, said that:] The now complainants [the leaders of the Queen's men] and the rest of their then company, both before and since the decease of . . . Thomas Greene [who led them until he died in 1612], did repose their main trust and confidence in . . . [Christopher] Beeston, for and concerning the managing of their affairs, he having a kind of powerful command over the now complainants and their said then fellow-actors in that behalf, [Heywood then said, but deleted when he saw the written version:] insomuch as at one time they trusted him three years together or thereabouts with their moneys gotten by their labours and pains in acting or playing, without any accompt thereof by him made unto the . . . complainants or company to this deponent's knowledge, when there hath been £8 or £9 in a day received at the doors and galleries [of the Red Bull].

443 The Queen's men leave the Red Bull, and Prince Charles' (I) men arrive, spring 1617

PRO, E407/62. Transcribed in MSC, VI. 146–7

The Queen's men were playing at the Phoenix when apprentices wrecked it on Shrove Tuesday, 4 March. They then returned to the Red Bull while the Phoenix was being repaired and were back at the Phoenix on about 3 June (see chapter 36, introduction and 483–485).[1] Prince Charles' (I) men seem to have been at the Red Bull as early as April 1617 (sharing the place, presumably, with the Queen's men), since the Prince's establishment at St James' Palace recorded the following payment. See also chapter 34, introduction and 463b.

[In April 1617, for the delivery of:] one other message from St James' to the Red Bull with a message to the players.

[1] Apprentices threatened to pull down the Red Bull, Phoenix and Fortune the following Shrove Tuesday but were prevented. See 484 n. 1.

444 Prince Charles' (I) men and the Queen's men, now the company of the Revels, swap playhouses, 1619

I.C., *A Pleasant Comedy Called the Two Merry Milkmaids, or the best Words Wear the Garlands* (1620)

When the Queen died on 2 March 1619, the owner of the Phoenix joined prince Charles' (I) men and took them into his playhouse. The remnant of the Queen's men reorganised themselves as the Revels company and moved to the Red Bull (see chapter 36, introduction and 487).

In the prologue to one of their first plays back at the Red Bull, the men of the Revels announced that they meant to raise the standard of plays, acting and the taste of audiences there, and they admitted that what they were doing was risky ('We stand a hazard now ...').

> This day we entreat all that are hither come
> To expect no noise of guns, trumpets, nor drum,
> Nor sword and target, but to hear sense and words
> Fitting the matter that the scene affords,
> So that, the stage being reformed and free
> From the loud clamours it was wont to be
> Turmoiled with battles, you, I hope, will cease
> Your daily tumults and with us wish peace.
> We stand a hazard now. Yet, being prepared,
> We hope, for your own good, you in the yard
> Will lend you ears attentively to hear
> Things that shall flow so smoothly to your ear,
> That you, returning home, t'your friends shall say,
> Howe'er you understand't, 'Tis a fine play.'

445 A felt maker's apprentice sitting on the stage is injured by an actor's sword, 10 March 1623

LMA, MJ/SR 617/30. Transcribed in Jeaffreson, *Middlesex County Records*, II, 175–6

The apprentice was John (or Richard) Gill, and the actor was Richard Baxter, who belonged to the Revels company (the former Queen's men). The matter is on record because Gill wrote 'a turbulent and rebellious' letter to Baxter on 16 March (a Sunday) and Baxter gave it to the Middlesex authorities, whose offices were nearby in St John Street. The letter is quoted in a true bill, where it is partly illegible:

Mr Baxter: So it is that upon Monday last . . . [I happened] to be upon your stage intending no hurt to anyone, where I was grievously wounded in the head as may appear, and in the surgeon's hands, who is to have 10s for the cure, and in the meantime my master refuses to give me maintenance . . . [I suffered] great loss and hindrance, and, therefore, in kindness I desire you to give me satisfaction, seeing I was wounded by your own hand [and] weapon. If you refuse, then look to yourself and avoid the danger which shall this day ensue upon your company and [play]house . . . as you can, for I am a felt maker's prentice and have made it known to at least one hundred and forty of our . . . [fellow apprentices], who are all here present, ready to take revenge upon you, unless willingly you will give present satisfaction . . . And as you have a care of our own safeties, so let me have answer forthwith.

The authorities went to the Red Bull and found Gill, another felt maker named Roger Edgill, and a hundred persons 'assembled riotously . . . to the terror and disquiet' of the neighbours. They arrested Gill and Edgill, whereupon the others, it seems, went home. Gill was bailed on 19 April, and at a trial on 19 July Edgill was found not guilty. What happened to Gill does not appear. Since one of the two witnesses at the trial was Richard Gill, apparently the scrivener's servant who had bonded himself to bail the culprit Gill, the latter was not friendless at the trial (Baxter was the other witness).[1]

[1] The court accepted bonds from Richard Gill, 'servant of Thomas Helme, . . . scrivener' of £20 and from two coopers of £10 each to guarantee that the culprit Gill appear at the trial. On the same day the court took a bond of £20 from Baxter to guarantee that he appear to give evidence against the culprit Gill 'for threatening Mr Baxter and the other Red Bull players to ruin their [play]house and persons' (LMA, MJ/SR 616/89). In the true bill, the culprit Gill is called John several times, but in the bonds he and the scrivener's servant are both Richard. Jeaffreson, strangely, mistook the dates of both the bonds (II, 165–6) and true bill.

446 The Red Bull is used for a fencing prize, 21 March 1623

Sir Henry Herbert, Office Book, now lost. Transcribed in Adams, *The Dramatic Records of Sir Henry Herbert*, 48

[A note of payment for a licence to use the playhouse:] 1623, 21 March. For a prize at the Red Bull, for the house (the fencers would give nothing): 10s[1]

[1] For a similar, but undated, licence for the Red Bull, see Sir Henry Herbert's Office Book, reported by Halliwell-Phillipps in his scrapbook at the Folger, 'Theatres of Shakespeare's Time', 53.

447 The Revels Company disappears, and Prince Charles' (I) men return to the Red Bull, before 30 July 1623

Sir Henry Herbert, Office Book, now lost. Reported in Adams, *The Dramatic Records of Sir Henry Herbert*, 24. Prince Charles' (I) men had been at the Curtain, 1620–3 (see 336–337).

[They were at the Red Bull on 30 July 1623, when the Master of the Revels licensed a play, now lost, for them:] For the Prince's players, a French tragedy of *The Bellman of Paris*, written by Thomas Dekker and John Day, for the company of the Red Bull.[1]

[1] Halliwell-Phillipps reported the same entry from Herbert's Office Book, adding that the manuscript of the play contained forty sheets and the licence cost £1: his scrapbook at the Folger, 'Theatres of Shakespeare's Time', 51.

448 A play at the Red Bull combines two current sensational events, 3–15 September 1624

(a–c) PRO, STAC8/31/16. Transcribed in (a–c) Sisson, 'Keep the Widow Waking', 240, 257, 258; see also his *Lost Plays of Shakespeare's Age*, 80–124

The company at the Red Bull paid Thomas Dekker, John Webster, John Ford and William Rowley to write a play, now lost, called *The Late Murder of the Son upon the Mother, or Keep the Widow Waking*. Its main plot dealt with a matricide in Whitechapel on 9 April 1624. Its subplot dealt with the abuse of a widow of sixty-two years whom scoundrels kept drunk for five days in late July and early August during which they forced her to marry one of them and stole her goods said to have been worth some £3,000. Both the murderer and the abusers were tried at the Middlesex sessions on 3 September: the murderer, Nathaniel Tindall, confessed and was hanged near the scene of his crime; the chief abuser, Tobias Audley, was remanded and was still in gaol when he died in 1625, but some of his colleagues were found not guilty. Because the case against the abusers had proved inconclusive at the sessions, the government, in the person of the Attorney General, laid charges against them in the Star Chamber in November, and Dekker was among those charged. This case, too, proved inconclusive, probably because three principals – Audley, the clergyman who had performed the marriage, and the widow – were all dead by the spring of 1626.

The play was, according to the licence granted by the Master of the Revels, 'a new tragedy',[1] but the subplot was comic. In order to promote the play, Aaron Holland (according to the charge) had a ballad about it sung under the widow's window. On 10 May 1626, however, he denied having anything to do with the ballad, though a singer of ballads had tried to sell him a copy on the street; nor did he have anything to do with the play, though he had seen it once or twice. The ballad, written by Richard Hodskyns, explains the subplot and survives in the Attorney General's bill.

[1] Sir Henry Herbert, Office Book, as reported in Adams, *The Dramatic Records of Sir Henry Herbert*, 29. The licence is undated, but it is between entries dated 3 and 15 September.

(a) The ballad concludes

Thus in four hours the youth was sped,
   In such a mood her taking.
They wooed, were married, went to bed

> To keep the widow waking.
>
> ...
>
> And you who fain would hear the full
>   Discourse of this matchmaking,
> The play will teach you at the [Red] Bull
>   To keep the widow waking.

(b) Dekker answers, 3 February 1625

Whereas in the said information [*i.e.* the Attorney General's bill], mention is made of a play called . . . *Keep the Widow Waking*, this defendant saith that true it is [that] he wrote two sheets of paper containing the first act of a play called *The Late Murder in Whitechapel, or Keep the Widow Waking* and a speech in the last scene of the last act of the boy who had killed his mother, which play (as all others are) was licensed by Sir Henry Herbert, knight, Master of his majesty's Revels, authorising thereby both the writing and acting of the said play . . . [And] he is no ways guilty of any the crimes specified other than the making part of the said play, which he hopeth is no crime.

(c) Dekker deposes, 24 March 1626

John Webster, William Rowley, John Ford and this defendant were privy, consenting and acquainted with the making and contriving of the said play called *Keep the Widow Waking* and did make and contrive the same upon instructions given them by one Ralph Savage.[1] And this defendant saith that he . . . did often see the said play or part thereof acted but how often he cannot depose.

[1] Savage must have had to do with the management of the company at the Red Bull, but nothing more is known of him.

449   The Red Bull is re-edified and perhaps enlarged, 1622–1630

Prynne, *Histriomastix*, first Epistle Dedicatory, sig. *3v

In 1633, Prynne's 'lately' could mean more than a decade. The book was entered in the Stationer's Register on 16 October 1630, and the re-edifying of the Fortune, also embraced in the remark, must be the rebuilding of 1622. A book of 1625 may hint that the re-edifying had already taken place (see *J and CS*, VI, 222–3). Salisbury Court was built in 1629. The asterisks below are Prynne's.

*two old playhouses being also lately re-edified, enlarged and one *[*] new theatre erected, the multitude of our London play-haunters being so augmented now that all the ancient devil's chapels (for so the fathers style all playhouses), being five in number, are not sufficient to contain their troops, whence we see a sixth now added to them.
*The Fortune and Red Bull.
*[*] Whitefriars Playhouse [*i.e.* Salisbury Court].

584   Playhouses, 1560–1660

450   Prince Charles' (I) men disband and the Red Bull company moves into the Red Bull, 1625

Sir Henry Herbert, Office Book, now lost. Transcribed by Malone in *Plays and Poems of William Shakespeare* (1821), III, 229

The Prince's men broke up in 1625 because the prince became Charles I and adopted his father's company, the King's men, whom several of the Prince's men joined. The men who succeeded them at the Red Bull were called the King's players on tour and the Red Bull company in London, where, apparently, they played from November 1625, when the great plague of that year ended, until 1634. But though many records attest to their playing in the provinces, very few do to their work at the Red Bull. The first is a curious note in the office book of the Master of the Revels saying that the King's men were willing to pay the Master a great deal of money to have him prevent the people at the Red Bull from playing Shakespeare's plays, which the King's men owned. Evidently the Red Bull people were playing those plays because they had to pay nothing to do so.

[A payment] From Mr [John] Hemmings [the King's men's treasurer] in their company's name to forbid the playing of Shakespeare's plays, to the Red Bull Company, this 11th of April 1627: £5.

451   A French company with women plays at the Red Bull, 22 November 1629

Sir Henry Herbert, Office Book, now lost. Transcribed by Malone in *Plays and Poems of William Shakespeare* (1821), III, 120

So far as his fragmentary surviving records show, the Master of the Revels took £2 to allow a French company with 'female players' to perform for one day each at three playhouses, the second of them the Red Bull. When he allowed them to play at the third, the Fortune, on 14 December he took only £1, noting that 'in respect of their ill fortune, I was content to bestow a piece back'. Did the audience at the Red Bull contribute to their ill fortune? See 412.

452   A notable company, Prince Charles' (II) men, have taken up residence at the Red Bull, 18 July 1634

Crosfield, *Diary*, 72

When the men of the King's Revels were playing at Oxford on 18 July 1634, their wardrobe keeper told Thomas Crosfield, a fellow of Queen's College, about five London companies, and Crosfield noted in his diary what he had heard. The third of the five was Prince Charles' (II) men, who had been at Salisbury Court and were now at the Red Bull. For the quality of the new company at the Red Bull, see 502.

3. The Prince's servants at the Red Bull in St John's Street, the chief Mr [Andrew] Cane, a goldsmith; Mr [Ellis] Worth, Mr [Matthew] Smith.

453 Great disorders occur at the Red Bull, January – August 1638

LMA, MJ/SR (a) 839/73; (b) 842/133. Transcribed in Jeaffreson, *Middlesex County Records*, III, 168.

(a) 16 January 1638

[The authorities in Middlesex took bonds worth £40 for the appearance at the next sessions of Thomas Pinnocke] for menacing and threatening to pull down the Red Bull playhouse and striking divers people with a great cudgel as he went along the streets.

(b) 23 August 1638

[The same authorities took bonds worth £40 for the appearance at the next sessions of Thomas Jacob] for committing a great disorder in the Red Bull playhouse and for assaulting and beating divers persons there.

454 Players at the Red Bull get into trouble for acting a play that mocks officials, 29 September 1639

PRO, (a) PC2/50, fo. 322; (b–c) SP16/429/fos. 92, 91. Transcribed in (a) MSC, I. 394–5; (b–c) *CSP, Dom.*, 1639, 529–30

The play was called *The Whore New Vamped*; its author is unknown and it is now lost. Versions of the documents quoted below survive on both the privy council register and among the State Papers.

(a) The complaint

Complaint was this day made ... that the stage-players of the Red Bull have lately for many days together acted a scandalous and libellous play wherein they have audaciously reproached and in a libellous manner traduced and personated some[1] persons of quality and scandalised and defamed the whole profession of proctors belonging to the court of the civil [*i.e.* ecclesiastical] law and reflected upon the present government.

[1] The version among the State Papers inserts here 'of the aldermen [of the City of London] and some other'.

(b) The specific charges

In the play called *The Whore New Vamped*, where there was mention of the new duty upon wines, one that personates a justice of peace says to [Andrew] Cane [the actor], 'Sirrah, I'll have you before the alderman'. Whereto Cane replied, ... 'The alderman, the alderman is a base, drunken, sottish knave. I care not for the alderman. I say the alderman is a base, drunken sottish knave'. Another said, 'How now, sirrah, what alderman do you speak of?' Then Cane said, 'I mean alderman the blacksmith in Holborn [*i.e.* William Abell].' Said the other, 'Was he not a vintner?' Cane answered, 'I know no other.' In another part of the same play, one speaking of projects and patents that he had gotten amongst the rest, said that he had a patent for 12d apiece upon every proctor and proctor's man that was not a knave. Said another, 'Was there ever known any proctor but he was an arrant knave?'

(c) The action taken

[The Privy Council ordered that:] Master Attorney General should be hereby prayed and req[uired] forthwith to call before him not only the poet that made the play and the actors that played the same, but also the person [that] licensed it, and, having diligently examined the truth of the said complaint, to proceed roundly against such of them as he shall find to have been faulty, and to use such effectual exp[edition to] bring them to sentence, as that their exemplary punishment may [check] such insolencies betimes.[1]

[1] Yet within six weeks the same players gave a play at the court at Richmond, and it was Cane who eventually received payment (MSC, II. 394).

455 Sophisticates mock the plays and playing at the Red Bull, 1638–1641

(a) Jasper Mayne in *Jonsonus Virbius* (1638), sig. E4; (b) Ralph Bride-Oak in Randolph, *Poems, with the Muses Looking-Glass* (1638), sig. **; (c) *The Late Will and Testament of the Doctors Commons* (1641). Although memorable actors were at the Red Bull from 1634 to 1640 (see **502**), sophisticates mocked the goings-on at the place more than those at any other playhouse except, perhaps, the second Fortune.[1]

[1] After the closing of the playhouses in 1642, one writer remembered the Red Bull for plays that depended on 'Drums, trumpets, battles and heroes', and another remembered it and the second Fortune for actors who 'were terrible tear-throats' (see *J and CS*, VI, 245–7).

(a) 1638

Ben Jonson wrote no

> Pitched [battle]fields, as Red Bull wars.

(b) 1638

Thomas Randolph was not one of

> The sneaking tribe that drink and write by fits
> As they can steal or borrow coin or wits,
> That Pandars fee for plots and then belie

The paper with – 'An Excellent Comedy,
Acted' (more was the pity) 'by th' Red Bull
With Great Applause', by some vain City gull;
That damn philosophy and prove the curse
Of emptiness, both in the brain and purse.

(c) 1641

[A testator makes a mock will, leaving:] All my great books of acts to be divided between the Fortune and the [Red] Bull, for they spoil many a good play for want of action.

456 The players at the Red Bull and the second Fortune swap playhouses, Easter 1640

(a) Sir Henry Herbert, Office Book, now lost; (b) Tatham, *Fancies Theater* (1640) (SR 15 October 1640), sigs. H2v–3. Transcribed (a) by Malone in *Plays and Poems of William Shakespeare* (1821), III, 241. The new company at the Red Bull were the King's players/Red Bull company, for which see 450.

(a) The swap

At Easter 1640, the Prince's company went to the Fortune and the Fortune company to the Red Bull.

(b) The new company asks the Red Bull audience to be civil

The new company at the Red Bull addresses audiences there in 'A Prologue Spoken upon the Removing of the Late Fortune Players to the [Red] Bull' (the play for which the prologue was written is unknown):

Only we would request you to forbear
Your wonted custom, banding [*i.e.* throwing] tile or pear
Against our curtains, to allure us forth.

457 After the closing of the playhouses in 1642, the Red Bull is often used for illegal performances

(a) *Perfect Occurrences*, 28 January to 4 February 1648; (b) *A Perfect Diurnal*, 7–14 February 1648; (c) *The Kingdom's Weekly Intelligencer*, 2–9 January 1649; (d) *A Perfect Diurnal*, 17–24 December 1649; (e) *The Man in the Moon*, 23–31 January 1650; (f) *The Laughing Mercury*, 15–22 September 1652; (g) *Mercurius Democritus*, 1–8 June 1653; (h) *Mercurius Fumigosus*, 15–22 November 1654; (i) *The Weekly Intelligencer*, 26 December – 2 January 1654–5; (j) *Mercurius Fumigosus*, 9–16 May 1655; (k) *The Weekly Intelligencer*, 11–18 September 1655

Like the other playhouses, the Red Bull officially ceased to be a place where plays could be performed on 2 September 1642 by order of Parliament. Most of the playhouses housed illegal performances from time to time thereafter, but the Red Bull seems to have housed them more persistently than the others.

(a) 3 February 1648

Tickets [*i.e.* leaflets] were thrown into gentleman's coaches thus, 'At the [Red] Bull this day you may have wit without money', meaning a play.[1]

[1] The play was, presumably, John Fletcher's *Wit Without Money*.

(b) 9 February 1648

[In response, it seems, the House of Commons passed and sent to the House of Lords this ordinance for approval:] for the better suppression of . . . stage-players, interludes and common players, it is ordained . . . that all stage plays and the players of interludes and common players shall be taken to be rogues . . . and liable to the pains and penalties . . . [in the statutes against rogues and vagabonds enacted in the thirty-ninth year of Elizabeth and the seventh of James I (see 74c)].

And it is further ordained that the Lord Mayor [of London], justices of the peace and sheriffs of the City of London and Westminster and the counties of Middlesex and Surrey, or any two or more of them . . . are authorised to pull down and demolish, [or] to cause or procure to be pulled down and demolished, all stages, galleries, seats and boxes . . . within their respective jurisdiction . . .

And that every person which shall be present and a spectator at any such stage play or interlude . . . [shall be fined] for every time he shall be so present . . . 5s.

(c) 2 January 1649

See 516b.

(d) 20 December 1649

There being some actors privately playing near St John's Street, whereof one giving information to some soldiers, some troopers went from the Mews,[1] seized upon the players, and took away their sword and clothes.

[1] The King's Mews, where Trafalgar Square now is, was ordinarily the royal stables but during the interregnum barracks for the parliamentary army.

(e) 22 January 1650

['The tragedians at Westminster Hall' (*i.e.* members of Parliament) sent 'to those other comedians in St John's Street'] two or three companies of the rebels [*i.e.* parliamentary soldiers, who] seized on the poor players, uncased them of their clothes, disarmed the lords and gentleman [*i.e.* the audience] of their swords and cloaks . . . They hung the poor players' clothes upon their pikes and very manfully marched them away with them as trophies of so wonderful a victory. There was taken at this fight about seven or eight of the chief actors, some wounded, all their clothes and properties, without the loss of one man on our side.[1]

[1] Another account of the affair appeared for 22 January 1650 in *Mercurius Pragmaticus*, 22–29 January 1650, mentioning Andrew Cane, formerly the leading figure among Prince Charles' (II) men.

(f) 22 September 1652

A report of a preposterous race that will take place this week between two pairs of oars in silver boats from one northern suburb of London, Islington, to another, Barnet. Each boat will be steered by a monkey attended by two jackanapeses.

[On the way back to London from the race,] The jackanapeses . . . [are to meet] the players . . . as they come from Stourbridge Fair in a galley-foist [*i.e.* a state barge] and to sail with them to the Red Bull, where they are to act a bloody sea fight before them in a land water work written by the ghost of Friar Bacon at the very instant that the brazen head spake to him and said, 'Times past.'[1]

[1] An allusion to Greene's play, *Friar Bacon and Friar Bungay*, produced *c.* 1589, IV, i.

(g) 9 June 1653

[Perhaps a coded advertisement for a performance of drolls – see the introduction above:] At the Red Bull in St John's Street on Thursday next, being the ninth of June, . . . there is a pretty conceited fellow that hath challenged the dromedary[1] lately come out of Barbary to dance with him cap-à-pie on the low rope, . . . as also running up a board with rapiers, and a new country dance called the horn-dance, never before presented, performed by the ablest persons of that civil quality in England. There will also appear a merry conceited fellow which hath formerly given content.[2]

And you may come and return with safety.

[1] 'A stupid, bungling fellow' (*OED*), but which such fellow does not appear.
[2] Perhaps Robert Cox, who wrote and acted in drolls. In the issue for 22–29 June the same journal reported (without mentioning the Red Bull) that 'The rope-dancers, having employed one Mr Cox, an actor (a very honest though impoverished man who is not only, as well as others, put by the practice of his calling but charged with a poor wife and five helpless infants) to present a modest, harmless jig called 'Swobber', yet two of his own quality, envying their poor brother should get a little bread for his children, basely and unworthily betrayed him to the soldiers and so abused many of the gentry that formerly had been their benefactors, who were forced to pay to the soldiers 5s apiece for their coming out, as well as for their going in.' For other notices of a rope-dancer at the Red Bull, see CRS, 86.

(h) 15–22 November 1654

[A remark suggesting that actors regularly used the Red Bull:] Two cross-legged creatures called sutorians [*i.e.* shoemakers], having a great mind to learn the right art of preaching, would the other day needs go to the Red Bull to learn speech and action of the players before they come to exercise or hold forth.

(i) 29 December 1654

The players at the Red Bull were on the last Saturday despoiled of their acting clothes by some of the soldiery, they having not so full a liberty as they pretended.[1]

[1] Another journal gives the name of the play as Fletcher's *Wit without Money*, and yet another says that the actors were in their costumes at the time of the raid and that the soldiers, for once, 'carried themselves very civilly towards the audience' (*A Perfect Account of the Daily Intelligence*, 27 December – 3 January 1654–5, and *Mercurius Fumigosus* for the same week).

(j) 16–23 May 1655

A dumb comedy is next week to be acted at the Red Bull, if the players can but agree and be honest among themselves, which will be the best, though hardest, scene they can act.

(k) 14 September 1655

This day proved tragical to the players at the Red Bull . . . The soldiers secured the persons of some of them who were upon the stage and in the tiring-house; they seized also upon their clothes in which they acted, a great part whereof was very rich. It never fared worse with the spectators than at this present, for those who had monies paid their [fines of] 5s apiece, those who had none to satisfy their forfeits did leave their cloaks behind them. The tragedy of the actors and the spectators was the comedy of the soldiers. There was abundance of the female sex, who, not able to pay 5s, did leave some gage or other behind them, . . . all which [the next day], their poverty being made known, and after some check for their trespass, were civilly restored to the owners.[1]

[1] Jerome Bankes wrote of this raid that 'many were put to rout by the soldiers and had broken crowns (PRO, SP18/100, fo. 287, transcribed in *CSP, Dom.*, 1655, 336), and another journal reported that 'some prisoners [were] taken' (*Mercurius Fumigosus*, 12–19 September 1655). A ballad published the next year added that tiremen and musicians were involved as well as players, and that the musicians saved their instruments ([Phillips], *Sportive Wit* [1656], sigs. Ff4v–5).

458 The regular playing of plays is legal again, and the Red Bull resumes, then ends as a playhouse, 1660–1664

(a–b, d) Pepys, *Diary*, II, 58; III, 93; V, 132–3; (c) Davenant, *The Playhouse to be Let*, performed summer 1663, printed in *The Works of Sr William D'avenant K^t*, p. 71 (2nd pagination).

(a) Pepys, 23 March 1661

[Pepys went to a play at the Red Bull for the first time 'since plays came up again', and found:] the clothes . . . very poor and the actors but common fellows. At last into the pit, where I think there was not above ten more than myself, and not 100 in the whole house. And the play, . . . [William Rowley's] *All's Lost by Lust* [first performed in 1619 or 1620], poorly done and with . . . much disorder.

(b) Pepys, 26 May 1662

[I took] my wife to the Red Bull, where we saw [Marlowe's] *Dr Faustus*, but so wretchedly and poorly done that we were sick of it.

(c) Davenant, summer 1663

Tell 'em the Red Bull stands empty for fencers.
There are no tenants in it but old spiders.
Go, bid the men of wrath allay their heat
With prizes there.

(d) Pepys, 25 April 1664

[On his last visit to the Red Bull, Pepys saw] a rude prize fight – but with good pleasure enough.

Appendix: Woodford's lawsuits against Holland

Holland's troubles with Woodford originated in a lease by which Holland sold a stake in the playhouse to Thomas Swinnerton, one of the Queen's men, for £25 paid in dribs and drabs. The lease may have begun at Michaelmas 1605, and it was to end at Michaelmas 1634.[1] It yielded Swinnerton an eighteenth of the money that spectators paid to stand or sit in the galleries and on stage (after the players had had their share), and he paid £2 10s a year as rent. Finding the lease a 'hard pennyworth', according to Holland, Swinnerton sold it to Philip Stone at the end of February 1609 for more than £50 according to Woodford, or much less than £50 according to Holland. Swinnerton surrendered the lease to Holland, and Holland drew up a new one for Stone. Then in 1612, Holland noticed that some of the money he had paid regularly to Swinnerton and Stone was not actually mentioned in the lease. By some extra contractual arrangement eventually forgotten, Swinnerton had collected 3d a day for a gatherer's place, and Stone was doing so, too. Holland threatened to sue Stone to get the money back. So on 17 June 1612 Stone assigned the lease to Woodford, who paid £50 for it.

Woodford's ownership evidently began at Michaelmas, for he collected the eighteenth part and the 3d a day from Michaelmas to the next quarter-day, Christmas 1612. Then, Woodford being abroad, his agent, Anthony Payne, was two days late paying the quarterly rent of 12s 6d. Holland forfeited the lease, as a clause in it entitled him to do, and declared that he would renew the lease only if somebody paid him the money that Stone and Woodford had collected for the gatherer's place since 1609. When Woodford returned, he refused to pay and began a series of lawsuits against Holland that would continue for more than a decade. Woodford demanded that Holland renew the lease with the gatherer's place in it and pay all the money the lease should have yielded since the forfeiture. Holland was willing to renew the lease, but not with a gatherer's place in it and not with the 3d a day that Stone and Woodford had collected.

Below is a list of these lawsuits (see also 441 and the introduction above). Letters in parentheses refer to lawsuits in this list.

(a) April–November 1613

Woodford sued Holland first in the Court of Requests. He must have filed his bill of complaint in April because he said (e) that Holland filed his answer on 1 May. Neither the bill nor answer has been found, but ancillary papers have, which, among other things, summarise the bill and answer, as do statements in later lawsuits. Towards the end of May, Woodford and Holland agreed that their lawyers should act as arbitrators, but when Woodford knew what was in the arbitration, he refused to abide by it, because it provided that Holland should have the 3d a day and that Woodford should repay Holland the 3d a day that Stone and Woodford had collected since 1609. Holland's lawyer presented the arbitration on 22 June, saying that Woodford's lawyer had agreed to it but then had withdrawn from it 'to the grave and judicious censure' of the court. On the next day Woodford's lawyer successfully pressed the court to grant Woodford an order compelling Holland to give Woodford a new lease yielding everything that Philip Stone had received. The reason offered was that Holland 'hath not made apparent to this court' how much Woodford owed him; Holland said that he had not done so because he was satisfied with the arbitration and thought the case at an end (f). The court issued an injunction against Holland on 3 July and soon ordered the sheriff of London to arrest him. These orders were Woodford's only successes.

See PRO, Req.1/26/fos. 729v, 779v*, 835, 889v–91*; Req.1/128/6 July 1613*; Req. 1/183/fos. 377, 378v. Greenstreet had transcribed the starred items in 'The Red Bull Playhouse in the Reign of James I', 709–10, and Wallace transcribed all these documents in 'Three London Theatres', 293–303. He also transcribed one (the arbitration of 22 June) that nobody else has seen; he had found it among the uncalendared proceedings of the court in the reign of James I (Req.2) but did not give a further number, either in 'Three London Theatres' or in his notes now at the Huntington (Wallace Collection, Box 5, no. 15).

Woodford and Holland then agreed to another arbitration, and on 15 September each bonded himself for £20 to abide by it. On 9 October this arbitrator reported much as his predecessor had done, but Woodford again refused to accept the arbitration.

These documents have not been found, but Holland (not Woodford) mentioned them and laid them before a court in 1623 (f).

(b) 9 November 1613 and Winter 1613–14

Holland went to the Court of King's Bench on 9 November 1613, perhaps about Woodford's bond, certainly about the order of 23 June. He got a writ of prohibition that prevented Requests from carrying out the order. Holland did not say why the court granted the writ, but Woodford said twice (e, f) that it did so because what the order termed a lease, was, legally, something else. The order (Req.1/26/fos. 889–91), however, refers only to an 'indenture or deed indented' and does not contain the word 'lease' (a).

During the winter of 1613–14 Woodford tried to get the King's Bench to withdraw the writ but failed, so that the writ ended Woodford's lawsuit of 1613 (a).

The documents of Holland's manoeuvre have not been found, but both Holland and Woodford mentioned it (e, f). Those of Woodford's response have not been found, either, but Holland (not Woodford) mentioned it (f).

(c) Spring 1614

Woodford, in the name of Philip Stone, sued Holland again in Requests. Holland did not answer the bill. Instead, he got Stone to sign a 'release' on 16 May 1614, which caused the case to collapse. The document released Holland from legal actions in Stone's name up to the date of the document. Woodford said that he had secured Stone's permission in writing but had lost the document, also that Holland had got the release 'by covin and deceit' (e, f); Holland said that Stone had given him the release freely, and that Woodford had used Stone's name without Stone's 'privity' (f).

The documents of this manoeuvre have not been found, but both Woodford and Holland mentioned it twice (e, f).

(d) 1614–1615?

Woodford, in the name of Stone again, sued Holland in King's Bench on an 'assumpsit'. Woodford, that is, argued that Holland had paid Stone for the release by promising to cancel a bond for £100 that Stone had given him on, presumably, some other occasion. The case came to trial and Woodford was 'overthrown', found nonsuit, because the court accepted that there had been no promise or payment.

The documents of the case have not been found, but Holland (not Woodford) mentioned it twice (e, f).

(e) 31 March – 7 June 1619

Woodford sued Holland yet again in Requests. His case was much the same as it would be in 1623 (f), but he repeatedly described his share of the profits as a seventh rather than an eighteenth. Holland did not correct the statements because his answer was a demurrer: he argued, that is, that Woodford's case was irrelevant and that he, Holland, had no need to make a proper answer. The court sent for Holland, who appeared with his lawyer on 1 June. His lawyer appeared again on 7 June, when, it seems, the court allowed the demurrer and the case collapsed.[2]

Curiously, in 1623 (f) neither Woodford nor Holland mentioned this lawsuit among their lists of legal actions, and Holland even said that Woodford had not troubled him for eight years.

PRO, Req.2/411/149 (the bill), 148 (the answer),[3] and Req.1/110/fo. 132v (the ancillary document noting the appearances of Holland and his lawyer), all of which Wallace transcribed in 'Three London Theatres', 303–15.

(f) 25 October 1623 – 3 May 1624

Woodford sued Holland again, now in the Court of Chancery, and repeated his old case, parts of which, especially about the non-payment of the rent in 1612, must have seemed silly. Holland had neatly avoided Woodford's previous lawsuits, but he confronted this one head-on, laid all the documents before the court, and won decisively. See **441**.

---

[1] In 1619, Woodford said that the lease began in the third year of James I but left the day and month blank (e). Holland did not give a date.

[2] After noting that Holland personally appeared in court with his counsel on 1 June 1619, the ancillary document adds: 'afterwards, that is on the seventh day of the present month, it [the demurrer?] is allowed, by means of counsel' ('postea viz Septimo Die mensis instantis Admissus est per Co[nsilium]'), and counsel is named as Ralph Wormleighton, who had signed Holland's demurrer.

[3] On the back of the bill Wallace read 'xxxj die' of an illegible month, 'Anno . . . Regis Jacobi . . . xvij'. Because the events mentioned in the ancillary document are dated 1 and 7 June 1619 and the 17th year of James began on 24 March 1619, he concluded that the illegible month must be March. Wallace's date no longer exists, having, perhaps, been lost when the document was repaired after he had seen it. No date appears on the answer, either.

XXXIV The Hope

The Hope was a public playhouse and animal baiting house, designed and built to serve as either as its owners chose. It was the fourth of the five playhouses built on Bankside, that is in Southwark near the south bank of the Thames. It was on the north side of Maid Lane (now Park Street), in effect across the road from the Globe, which was some 150 yards south and east. It was only a few yards west along Maid Lane from where the Rose had been or, perhaps, at least part of it still was. The site is now a short street called Bear Gardens, S.E.1.

It was the project of Philip Henslowe – his fourth (if one includes Whitefriars) and last playhouse – and Jacob Meade, waterman. Both, together with Edward Alleyn, the actor who had married Henslowe's stepdaughter, had been involved in the animal baiting business at the Beargarden from 1594. Henslowe and Alleyn came to own the Beargarden and to own or control much of the property nearby. They used the royal animals by licence of their master. To save themselves fees, presumably, Henslowe and Alleyn tried repeatedly from 1597 to acquire the mastership themselves, first in reversion and then, on the deaths of two masters in quick succession, outright. Finally in 1604 they paid yet another master £450 to become joint masters and keepers, offices they kept for the rest of their lives. Meade was a keeper of the royal bears in 1599. He apparently held an interest in the Beargarden by lease from Henslowe and Alleyn.

Alleyn sold his part of the Beargarden to 'my father, Henslowe', for £580 in February 1611. On 29 August 1613, two months after the destruction of the first Globe, Henslowe and Meade drew up a contract with a carpenter, Gilbert Katherens, according to which Katherens would pull down the Beargarden and build the Hope 'near or upon the said place where the said game place' stood. The contract survives, like the one for the first Fortune, among Alleyn's papers at Dulwich College. The work, which also included taking down a building for bulls and horses and putting up another, was to cost £360 and be finished in three months, by 30 November.

Less is known about the Hope, however, than one might expect. The contract often specifies merely that the builder do what had been done at the Swan nearly twenty years before, and only a rough sketch survives to show what the Swan was like. The Hope was to be 'fit and convenient . . . both for players to play in and for the game of bears and bulls to be baited in'. Its stage was not to be permanently fixed but to stand on trestles so that it could be carried away, and the roof over the stage ('the heavens') was to be held up so that no posts stood on the stage. There were, however, to be 'turned columns upon and over the stage', perhaps a banistered railing around it. The place was to have three galleries, one above the other, and the bottom one was (like that at the Fortune) to be 12 feet high. If the size of the timbers holding up the other two galleries are a guide, the middle one was to be less high and the top one less high yet, also as at the Fortune. There were to be a tiring-house and, somewhere in the bottom gallery, 'two boxes . . . fit and decent for gentlemen to sit in'. The galleries were to rest on a brick foundation rising at least 13 inches above ground level, and people were to get into them via two staircases adjoining outside. The building was to have lead gutters, and its roof was to be tiled. The materials used in it included plaster. Much of the place was made of second-hand materials – the useful parts of the Beargarden and 'old timber' supplied by Henslowe from an 'old house in Thames Street'.

Wenceslas Hollar persuasively represented both the Hope and second Globe in his famous engraving often called the Long Bird's-Eye View of London (1647) (see figs 6a and b in chapter 35), and in a preliminary drawing for part of the engraving. In each, the two buildings are similar in layout, though the Hope may be smaller. The galleries of the Hope are round inside and out and lie around an open yard.[1] The roof over the stage and tiring-house, however, is only a cowl-like continuation of the roof over the galleries.

Like the Fortune, the Hope was apparently not finished when the contract provided that it should be. The playhouse was open in the spring of 1614, when Henslowe and Meade engineered the reorganisation of Lady Elizabeth's men and set them to work there, some three months before the rebuilt Globe was open. One of the first events associated with the Hope was an abortive 'trial of wit' that was to have taken place there on 7 October 1614. To appease angry spectators, the resident actors, presumably Lady Elizabeth's men, mounted an act of a play extempore, as John Taylor wrote,

> And such a company (I'll boldly say)
> That better (nor the like) e'er played a play.

Another early event was the premiere of Ben Jonson's *Bartholomew Fair*, performed there by Lady Elizabeth's men on 31 October, the Hope's one brush with literary fame. The new playhouse did not impress Jonson. In his induction to the play, he told the spectators that he had 'observed a special decorum', because the playhouse was 'as dirty as Smithfield [the setting of the play] and as stinking every whit'.

Lady Elizabeth's men soon fell out with Henslowe, and he 'broke' them in February 1615, after, according to them, they had played there forty weeks. Henslowe then put Prince Charles' (I) men into the Hope, having reorganised them so that they included four of Lady Elizabeth's men, but they, too, fell out with him and, after he died on 6 January 1616, with Meade. They left the Hope of their own accord early in 1617. Both companies objected to the financial conditions Henslowe and Meade imposed on them, one of which required them to lose money because animals periodically displaced plays.

Henslowe was evidently wrong to think that plays and animals would mix well. After the departure of Prince Charles' men only three years after the Hope had opened, no important company played regularly there again. Alleyn inherited Henslowe's part of it, but Meade managed it, his interest in 1619 being a lease on it for which he paid Alleyn £100 a year. Its contemporaries came increasingly to think of the place as a beargarden, not a playhouse. Whatever claim it still had to be a playhouse ceased on 2 September 1642, when Parliament ordered all playing to cease. Then on 12 December 1642 Parliament ordered an end to baiting there 'in these times of great distractions' – in vain apparently, for on 30 November 1643 Parliament issued a sterner order to the same effect.[2]

Animal baiting attracted audiences of all classes and was probably more profitable than playing.[3] In 1623 the Spanish ambassador was delighted by the baiting at, and in the river outside, the Hope, and in 1661 a north countryman complained in retrospect about the use of the Hope for plays rather than baiting:

> When Ise come there, I was in a rage.
> I railed on him that kept the bears:
> Instead of a stake was suffered a stage,
> And in Hunks[4] his house a crew of players.

The Beargarden stood, and the Hope was meant to stand, on land belonging to the Crown, not on adjacent land belonging to the Bishop of Winchester. While Henslowe and Alleyn had interests in leases on both pieces of land, trouble could ensue if the new buildings stood on land held by different leases. Yet in 1620 it was argued that the Hope had been partly built and then enlarged on the bishop's land. Alleyn seems to have survived this argument, for in 1664 it was assumed that the Hope was wholly on Crown land. Alleyn's interest in the place must have expired long before then. James I renewed the lease on the Crown land until Michaelmas 1675, and in about 1634 Charles I granted the freehold to Sir Edward Sydenham when the lease should expire.[5]

A dubious document proclaims that the Hope was pulled down 'to make tenements' in 1656. The Hope does seem to have been pulled down sometime during the period, but it was replaced in 1663 by a beargarden that had nothing to do with plays, though it was still sometimes called the Hope. This place was built by Thomas Davies, who then held the lease on the Crown land and whose son, James, had succeeded Thomas Godfrey as master of the royal animals in 1662. Baiting resumed there until enthusiasm for the 'game' waned in the 1680s, after which the new building disappeared and the site became Beargarden Square.[6]

---

[1] In his pamphlet, *Bull, Beare, and Horse, Cut, Curtaile, and Longtaile* (1638), John Taylor, the water poet, describes the Hope (which he calls the Beargarden) as 'a sweet rotundious college' and adds that it is 'circular or round, / Where Jackanapes his horse doth swiftly run / Her circuit like the horses of the sun' (sigs. D5, E3v). The preliminary drawing is in the Mellon Collection at Yale University.

[2] *Journals of the House of Commons*, II, 885; III, 325.

[3] In his diary, Henslowe mentioned his receipts from both the Beargarden and Fortune for the three days after Christmas 1608: those at the Beargarden averaged £4 11s 4d, those at the Fortune £1 18s 3d (p. 127).

[4] The writer probably means the name to refer generally to bears. In the 1590s famous bears were called Tom and Harry Hunks, and other bears were probably called Hunks later. The verses are from *Wit and Drollery* (1661), sig. F6v. See *J and CS*, VI, 210–13.

[5] PRO, E112/126/185; E134/18 Jas. I/M. 10; PC2/56, pp. 348–9; C10/79/28. See Kingsford, 'Paris Garden and the Bear-baiting', 155–78; *ES*, II, 463–65; and *J and CS*, VI, 202–5.

[6] PRO, PC2/55/fo. 319, and SP44/13, pp. 331–2. See also Adams, *Shakespearean Playhouses*, 339, and *CRS*, 69–70.

459 Henslowe and Jacob Meade engage a carpenter to build the Hope, 29 August 1613, and work gets under way

(a) Dulwich, Mun. 49; (b) PRO, E134/18 Jas. I/M10, Baxter 10. Transcribed in (a) Malone in *Plays and Poems of William Shakespeare* (1821), III, 343, also in *Henslowe Papers*, ed. Greg, 19–22, and many other places; (b) *J and CS*, VI, 202. The original of (a) is reproduced as an attachment to *Henslowe Papers*, ed. Foakes, 1. By agreeing to pay the carpenter at specific points in the fulfilling of the contract, Henslowe and Meade avoided the detailed accounting that Henslowe had got into during the building of the Fortune.

(a) The contract

Articles . . . agreed upon [29 August 1613] . . . between Philip Henslowe of the parish of St Saviour in Southwark within the county of Surrey, esquire, and Jacob Meade of the parish of St Olave's in Southwark aforesaid, waterman, on the one party, and Gilbert Katherens of the said parish of St Saviour in Southwark, carpenter, on the other party, as followeth, that is to say:

Imprimis, the said Gilbert Katherens for him, his executors, administrators and assigns doth covenant, promise and grant to and with the said Philip Henslowe and Jacob Meade, and either of them, the executors, administrators and assigns of them and either of them, by these presents in manner and form following. That he, the said Gilbert Katherens, his executors, administrators or assigns shall and will, at his or their own proper costs and charges, upon or before the last day of November next ensuing [1613], . . . not only take down or pull down all that game place or house where bears and bulls have been heretofore usually baited, and also one other house or stable wherein bulls and horses did usually stand, [which are] sett, lying and being upon or near the bankside in the said parish of St Saviour in Southwark, commonly called or known by the name of the Beargarden; but shall also, at his or their own proper costs and charges, upon or before the said last day of November, newly erect, build, and set up one other game place or playhouse fit and convenient in all things, both for players to play in and for the game of bears and bulls to be baited in the same: and also a fit and convenient tire [*i.e.* tiring-] house and a stage to be carried or taken away, and to stand upon trestles, good, substantial and sufficient for the carrying and bearing of such a stage; and shall new build, erect and set up again the said playhouse or game place near or upon the said place where the said game place did heretofore stand.

And . . . [he shall] build the same of such large compass, form, wideness and height as the playhouse called the Swan in the liberty of Paris Garden . . . now is. And shall also build two staircases without and adjoining to the said playhouse in such convenient places as shall be most fit and convenient for the same to stand upon, and of such largeness and height as the staircases of the said playhouse called the Swan now are or be. And shall also build the heavens all over the said stage, to be borne or carried without any posts or supporters to be fixed or set upon the said stage. And all gutters of lead needful for the carriage of all such rainwater as shall fall upon the same. And shall also make two boxes in the lowermost story fit and decent for gentlemen to sit in. And shall make the partitions between the rooms as they are at the said playhouse called the Swan. And . . . [shall] make turned columns upon and over the stage.

And [he] shall make the principals and forefront of the said playhouse of good and sufficient oaken timber, and no fir timber to be put or used in the lowermost or middle storeys, except the upright posts on the back part of the said storeys; all the binding joists to be of oaken timber. The inner principal posts of the first storey to be 12 feet in height and 10 inches square, the inner principal posts in the middle storey to be 8 inches square, the innermost posts in the upper storey to be 7 inches square. The prick posts [*i.e.* braces between the principal posts and horizontal beams] in the first storey to be 8 inches square, in the second storey 7 inches square, and in the uppermost storey 6 inches square. Also the breastsummers [*i.e.* the main horizontal beams] in the lowermost storey to be 9 inches deep and 7 inches in thickness, and in the middle storey to be 8 inches deep and 6 inches in thickness. The binding joists of the first storey to be 9 inches and 8 inches in depth and thickness, and in the middle storey to be 8 inches and 7 inches in depth and thickness.

Item, . . . [he shall] make a good, sure, and sufficient foundation of bricks for the said playhouse or game place, and . . . make it 13 inches at the least above the ground.

Item: . . . [he shall] new build, erect and set up the said bull house and stable with good and sufficient scantling timber [*i.e.* studs], planks and boards, and partitions of that largeness and fitness as shall be sufficient to keep and hold six bulls and three horses and geldings, with racks and mangers to the same, and also a loft or storey over the said house as now it is. And [he] shall also at his . . . own proper costs and charges new tile with English tiles all the upper roof of the said playhouse, game place and bull house or stable. And shall find and pay for, at his like proper costs and charges, . . . all the lime, hair, sand, bricks, tiles, laths, nails, workmanship and all other things needful and necessary for the full finishing of the said playhouse, bull house and stable. And the said playhouse or game place to be made in all things and in such form and fashion as the said playhouse called the Swan (the scantling [*i.e.* measuring] of the timbers tiles, and foundation as is aforesaid without fraud or covin).

And the said Philip Henslowe and Jacob Meade, and . . . the executors, administrators and assigns of them, or either of them, do covenant and grant to and with the said Gilbert Katherens, his executors, administrators and assigns in manner and form following: . . . That he the said Gilbert or his assigns shall or may have and take to his or their use . . . all the timber, benches, seats, slates, tiles, bricks and all other things belonging to the said game place and bull house or stable, and also all such old timber which the said Philip Henslowe hath lately bought, being of an old house in Thames Street, London, whereof most part is now lying in the yard or backside of the said Beargarden.

And . . . [Henslowe and Meade shall] satisfy and pay unto the said Gilbert Katherens, his executors, administrators or assigns for the doing and finishings of the works and buildings aforesaid the sum of £360 of good and lawful money of England, in manner and form following. That is to say: in hand at the ensealing and delivery hereof, £60, which the said Gilbert acknowledgeth himself by these presents to have received; and moreover to pay . . . weekly, during the first six weeks unto the said Gilbert or his assigns, when he shall set workmen to work upon or about the building of the premises, the sum of £10 of lawful money of England to pay them their wages (if their wages doth [*sic*] amount unto so much money); and when the said playhouse, bull house and stable are reared, then to make up the said wages [to] £100 of lawful money of England, and to be paid to the said Gilbert Katherens or his assigns; and when the said playhouse, bull house and stable are reared, tiled, walled, then to pay unto the said Gilbert Katherens or his assigns one other £100 of lawful money of England; and when the said playhouse, bull house and stable are fully finished, builded and done in manner aforesaid, then to pay unto the said Gilbert Katherens or his assigns one other £100 of lawful money of England in full satisfaction and payment of the said sum of £360 . . .

(b) The work gets under way

[In 1620, John Baxter, a witness in a lawsuit, deposed:] He verily believeth that those buildings aforesaid were set upon the King's land for that at the first driving of the piles for the foundation of the Hope playhouse the workmen had encroached upon the Bishop of Winchester's land, whereof Mr Alleyn being advertised that it would breed discord thereafter, coming thither advised Mr Henslowe to alter his circle of the playhouse and set it altogether upon [the] King's lands, which was accordingly done.

460 Henslowe and Meade raise a company of actors for the Hope and arrange for animal baiting, March – April 1614

Dulwich, missing. Transcribed by Malone in *Plays and Poems of William Shakespeare* (1821), XXI, 413; and by Greg in *Henslowe Papers*, 123–5

In about March 1614, Henslowe and Meade drew up a contract making Nathan Field a sharer for three years in 'the company of players which they [*i.e.* Henslowe and Meade] have lately raised', and which must be Lady Elizabeth's men. A similar document, dated 7 April 1614, makes Robert Dawes a sharer in Lady Elizabeth's men for three years, but unlike Field's contract, this one provides for the use of the Hope for animal baiting. Both contracts were among Alleyn's papers at Dulwich, and the first still is (Muniment 52, transcribed in *Henslowe Papers*, ed. Greg. 23–4). The second has disappeared, but Malone printed a transcription of it quoted below, with many gaps (indicated by '[. . .]' below) and bracketed words. The gaps must represent words that could not be read, but the bracketed words, it seems, represent interlineations as well as guesses about illegible words.

[The part about the use of the playhouse:] And the said Robert Dawes, for him, his executors, and administrators, doth [covenant, promise, and grant to and with the said] Philip Henslowe and Jacob Meade, their executors, and administrators, [and assigns] [. . .] that it shall and may be lawful to and for the said Philip Henslowe and Jacob Meade, their executors, and assigns to have and use the playhouse so appointed [for the said company [. . .] one day of] every four days, the said day to be chosen by the said Philip and [Jacob] [. . .] Monday in any week, on which day it shall be lawful for the said Philip [and Jacob, their administrators,] and assigns to bait their bears and bulls there and to use their accustomed sport and [games]

[...] and take to their own use all such sums of money as thereby shall arise and be received.

461 A projected 'trial of wit' at the Hope becomes a fiasco, 7 October 1614

Taylor, *Taylor's Revenge* (1615), sig. A3–3v, A5, A7v, A8v, B, Bv

In this tract and *A Cast Over the Water* (1615), Taylor treated in prose and then twice in verse satire one of the first events known to have taken place at the Hope, though Lady Elizabeth's men seem to have been acting there since the spring of 1614 (**463a**). Taylor, the so-called water poet, was a prolific versifier and self-publicist.

Be it therefore known unto all men that I, John Taylor, waterman, did agree with William Fennor (who arrogantly and falsely entitles himself the King's majesty's rhyming poet) to answer me at a trial of wit on the seventh of October last, 1614, on the Hope stage, ... and the said Fennor received of me 10s in earnest of his coming to meet me. Whereupon I caused 1,000 bills to be printed and divulged my name 1,000 ways and more, giving my friends and divers of my acquaintance notice of this Beargarden banquet of dainty conceits. And when the day came that the play should have been performed, the house being filled with a great audience who had all spent their moneys extraordinarily, then this companion for an ass ran away and left me for a fool amongst thousands of critical censurers, where I was ill thought of by my friends, scorned by my foes, and, in conclusion, in a greater puzzle than the blind bear in the midst of all her whip-broth ...

> What damned villain would forswear and swear,
> As thou [Fennor] didst, 'gainst my challenge to appear
> To answer me at Hope upon the stage?
> And thereupon my word I did engage
> And to the world did publish printed bills
> With promise that we both would show our skills,
> And then your rogueship durst not show your face
> But ran away and left me in disgrace.
> To thee ten shillings I for earnest gave
> To bind thee that thou shouldst not play the knave ...
> Hadst thou the conquest got, I had not cared,
> So thou unto thy word hadst had regard.
> Then, sure, the players had not played a play,
> But thou or I had borne away the day ...
> But when I saw the day away did fade
> And thy looked-for appearance was not made,
> I then stepped out their angers to appease,
> But they, all raging like tempestuous seas,

Cried out their expectations were defeated . . .
One swears and storms, another laughs and smiles,
Another madly would pluck off the tiles, . . .
One valiantly stepped out upon the stage
And would tear down the hangings in his rage . . .
And first I played A *maundering roguish creature*, . . .
Which act did pass and please and filled their jaws
With wrinkled laughter and with good applause.
Then came the players, and they played an act
Which greatly from my action did detract,
For 'tis not possible for anyone
To play against a company alone,
And such a company (I'll boldly say)
That better (nor the like) e'er played a play.
In brief, the play my action did eclipse
And, in a manner, sealed up my lips.

462 Ben Jonson comments on the Hope in the induction to *Bartholomew Fair*, 31 October 1614

The play was printed in 1631 but not published until that edition was included in *The Workes of Benjamin Jonson* (1640), II.

The play was first 'Acted in the year 1614 by the Lady Elizabeth's servants', according to the title page in 1631, and at the Hope, according to the induction. A stage-keeper first comes out, then the book-holder and a scrivener. The book-holder chases off the stage-keeper as fit only for 'sweeping the stage, or gathering up the broken apples for the bears within'. He then asks the scrivener to read:

certain articles drawn out in haste between our author and you [the audience], which if you please to hear, and, as they appear reasonable, to approve of, the play will follow presently. [The scrivener reads] Articles of agreement, indented between the spectators or hearers at the Hope on the Bankside in the county of Surrey on the one party, and the author of *Bartholomew Fair* in the said place and county on the other party, the one and thirtieth day of October 1614. [The articles are a witty and ironical recital of Jonson's usual opinions about audiences in general, but the penultimate remark concerns the Hope:] The play shall presently begin. And though the fair be not kept in the same region that some here, perhaps, would have it, yet think that therein the author hath observed a special decorum, the place being as dirty as Smithfield and as stinking every whit.[1]

[1] Bartholomew Fair was held at Smithfield, which is just within the north-west corner of the City and on the north side of the river. Jonson allows that some spectators might prefer that the fair of the play take place at Smithfield, like the real fair, rather than at the Hope.

463 Players quarrel with the management partly about baiting and then leave, 1615–1617

Dulwich, MS I, (a) fo. 151, and (b) fo. 157. Transcribed in (a) by Malone in *Plays and Poems of William Shakespeare* (1821), XXI, 416, and *Henslowe Papers*, ed. Greg, 88; (b) *Henslowe Papers*, ed. Greg, 93.

Evidence about how often baiting took place is confusing. Henslowe seems at first to have wanted one day in four (**460**), then one day in fourteen, for which he was willing to compensate the players; and his successors seem to have settled on two or three days a week (see *J and CS*, VI, 207–8).

(a) Lady Elizabeth's men quarrel with Henslowe, 1615

When 'in February' 1615 the company 'called upon' Henslowe 'for his accounts, he broke' them. They then drew up an arduous document claiming that Henslowe had cheated them of some £1,134. They quoted him as saying, 'Should these fellows come out of my debt, I should have no rule with them', and added that 'within three years he hath broken and dismembered five companies'. Their complaint about baiting reads:

Item: Mr Henslowe having promised, in consideration of the company's lying still one day in fourteen for his baiting, to give them 50s, [but] he having denied to be bound as aforesaid, gave them only 40s. And for that Mr Field would not consent thereunto, he [Henslowe] gave him so much as his [presumably Field's] share out of £50 would have come unto. By which means he is duly indebted to the company £10.[1]

[1] So the document reads, but £50 may be a mistake for 50s. The company is accusing Henslowe of having bribed Nathan Field, the first and leading sharer in the company, to accept 40s rather than 50s on behalf of the company. If Henslowe cheated the company of 10s every fourteen days and owed them £10 altogether, the company played at the Hope forty weeks until Henslowe 'broke' them in February 1615. Hence they began at the Hope in the spring of 1614.

(b) Prince Charles' men leave, winter of 1616–17

The company moved into the Hope in 1615 and drew up a formal contract with Alleyn and Meade on 20 March 1616. But probably in the winter following, one of them (on behalf of seven) wrote to Edward Alleyn,

Sir, I hope you mistake not our removal from the Bankside. We stood the intemperate weather till more intemperate Mr Meade thrust us over, taking the day from us which by course was ours [presumably for animal baiting. They then asked Alleyn to find them another playhouse and in the meantime to lend them £40. They went to the Red Bull (**443**).]

464 The Hope is a place mainly for baiting bears and bulls, 1621–1622

(a) Farley, *St Pavles-Church her Bill for the Parliament* (1621), SR, 20 May 1621, sig. E4–E4v; (b) PRO, E112/126/185, Alleyn's answer. See *J and CS*, vi, 209–10

(a) Henry Farley, before 20 May 1621

In admonishing Londoners for letting St Paul's Cathedral decay, Farley's character, Zeale, runs through a list of popular entertainments on which 'the bounty of our age' is spent rather than on 'any pious motion'. People spend money:

> To see a strange outlandish fowl,
> A quaint baboon, an ape, an owl,
> A dancing bear, a giant's bone,
> A foolish engine move alone,
> A morris dance, a puppet play,
> Mad Tom to sing a roundelay,
> A woman dancing on a rope
> Bull-baiting also at the Hope,
> A rhymer's jests, a juggler's cheats,
> A tumbler showing cunning feats,
> Or players acting on the stage.

(b) Edward Alleyn, 5 February 1622

[In his answer to a lawsuit, Alleyn said that:] The said Philip Henslowe... did erect and build the house called the Hope now employed and used for a game place for baiting his majesty's bears and bulls and for a playhouse, to which use it is employed and used at this day.

465 The Spanish ambassador takes delight in animal baiting at the Hope, *c.* 5 July 1623

PRO, SP14/148,fo. 99v. Transcribed in *Letters of John Chamberlain*, ii, 507. Chamberlain reported the event in a letter to Sir Dudley Carleton, 12 July 1623.

The Spanish ambassador is much delighted in bear-baiting. He was the last week at Paris Garden [*i.e.* the Hope], where they showed him all the pleasure they could, both with bull, bear and horse, besides jackanapes [*i.e.* a monkey or monkeys] and then turned a white bear into the Thames, where the dogs baited him swimming, which was the best sport of all.

466 The Hope is used for entertainments other than plays and baiting, 1631–1632

(a) Stow, *Annales* (1631), sig. Iiiiv; (b) Goodman, *Holland's Leaguer* (1632), sig. F2v; (c) Sir Henry Herbert, Office Book, now lost. Transcribed in (c) Halliwell-Phillipps, in his scrapbook at the Folger, labelled 'Hope', 46. See *ES*, II, 376

(a) Edmund Howes, 1631

[Howes brought Stow's book up to date for the editions of 1615 and 1631. He names six London playhouses and adds:] besides the new-built bear garden [*i.e.* the Hope], which was built as well for plays and fencers' prizes as bull-baiting.

(b) Nicholas Goodman, 1632

[From 'the lowest turret' of a famous brothel in Southwark, Holland's Leaguer, one could see 'three famous amphitheatres' in Southwark, one of which was:] a building of excellent Hope, and though wild beasts and gladiators [*i.e.* fencers and/or wrestlers] did most possess it, yet the gallants that came to behold those combats, though they were of a mixed society, yet were many noble worthies amongst them. [The other amphitheatres were the Globe and Swan.]

(c) Sir Henry Herbert, June 1632

Herbert was Master of the Revels and William Blagrave was his deputy. Herbert kept track of the fees he received, two of which concerned the Hope in 1632.

For a [fencing] prize, from Blagrave, played at the Hope the 13 June 1632 ... [And] 1632, for a warrant to Grimes for showing the camel for a year from 20 June.

467 The Hope is said to have been pulled down, 25 March 1656

Folger, MS V.b.275, p. 16. Transcribed in Collier, *Works of William Shakespeare*, I, ccxli–ii, n. See Berry, 'Folger Ms. V.b.275'

The manuscript from which these remarks come is probably a forgery, though Chambers (*ES*, II, 470), Bentley (*J and CS*, VI, 214) and others have accepted it as genuine. Nonetheless, the passage in it about the end of the Hope could well be mostly right.

The Hope on the Bankside in Southwark, commonly called the Beargarden, a playhouse for stage plays on Mondays, Wednesdays, Fridays and Saturdays and for the baiting of the bears on Tuesdays and Thursdays, the stage being made to take up and down when they please. It was built in the year 1610 [*i.e.* 1613–14] and now pulled down to make tenements by Thomas Walker, a petticoat maker in Cannon Street, on Tuesday the 25 day of March 1656. Seven of Mr Godfrey's bears, by the command of Thomas Pride, then high sheriff of Surrey, were then shot to death on Saturday the 9 day of February 1656 by a company of soldiers.[1]

[1] This episode became famous. Thomas Godfrey was a keeper of the King's game. In February 1656 Pride had 'the poor' bears and sixty cocks killed, not on moral grounds, it was said, but 'for preventing any great meeting of the people' who might rise against the government. See *CRS*, 69–70; Carte, *Collection of Original Letters and Papers*, II, 83 (where 'beavers' must be a misreading for bears); and Alexander Brome's mock-heroic poem 'On Col. Pride' in *Rump: or an Exact Collection of the Choycest Poems and Songs* (1662), 199–302, sts. 14–18.

XXXV The second Globe

The second Globe was the fifth and last public playhouse built on Bankside – in Southwark, west of the south end of London Bridge and near the south bank of the Thames. It occupied the same lines on the ground as the first Globe had done.[1] It was, therefore, on the south side of Maid Lane, now Park Street, some 150 yards across the street and south-east from the Hope, which was opened while the Second Globe was being built. In 1989 archaeologists found fragments of its foundations under the carpark behind Anchor Terrace, a listed building on the east side of the Southwark Bridge Road, S.E.1. The rest must lie under the building and perhaps the road.

After the famous destruction of the first Globe (q. v.) by fire on 29 June 1613, the consortium that had built it was required by its lease to replace it within a year with a building as good or better. Cuthbert and Richard Burbage comprised half the consortium and players and others, including Shakespeare, the other half. They reckoned apparently that if they were to spend large sums they should have a lease like the one they had when they spent £700 building the first Globe: for thirty-one years at £14 10s 0d a year rent. Only sixteen years of that lease remained, and they had no right to demand an extension. Still, they asked John Bodley, who controlled the property in trust for Nicholas Brend's son and heir, Matthew, to extend the lease for fifteen years, until Christmas 1644. He did extend the lease on 26 October 1613, but for only six years, until Christmas 1635. So on 15 February 1614 the principal sharers – the two Burbages, John Hemmings and Henry Condell – together with Hemmings's son-in-law, John Atkins, a scrivener, went to the heir, who lived in the family mansion at West Molesey in Surrey, across the Thames from Hampton Court. He had just celebrated his fourteenth birthday and could not therefore, legally bind himself. Nonetheless, they got him to sign a document saying that when he was twenty-one he would, in effect, confirm Bodley's extension and grant them one of his own for the other nine years. In return, they would pay him £10 and in the meantime spend £1,000 rebuilding the Globe. The heir's mother and uncle countersigned the document.

Relying on this dubious device, the consortium set out to rebuild the playhouse. Its sharers, who owned fourteen shares, meant to tax themselves £50 or £60 a share, hence to spend £700 to £840. But in the end they taxed themselves £120 a share and spent £1,400 on the playhouse, twice as much as their lease required them to spend and much more even than they had promised the heir. They spent another £200 building an adjoining house in which to refresh their customers. Hemmings, who acted as their treasurer, took charge of the project, assisted by Atkins, who looked after contracts with builders. The work must have begun after the visit to Matthew Brend on 15 February 1614 and was finished by the end of June following, when the new playhouse was open.

Matthew Brend got control of his property in Southwark on 21 February 1622[2] and did

Figs 6a and b. (a) The Hope playhouse and baiting house, (b) the second Globe playhouse, from Wenceslas Hollar, Long Bird's-Eye View (1647). Hollar reversed the labels for the buildings.

nothing to alter Bodley's six-year extension of the Globe lease. The sharers promptly offered him £10 for a further nine years, but he (shortly Sir Matthew) refused, pointing out that the document he had signed in 1614 was invalid because of his then age. He decided that the rent of £14 10s 0d was too little and that the property would be worth much more if it had 'fit dwelling houses' rather than a playhouse on it. Eventually, he said that he would sell the Globe to others when Bodley's extension ran out at Christmas 1635.

The sharers sued him in January 1632, trying not to make him honour the document of

1614 but to manoeuvre him into a court-supervised agreement by which they would get a new lease for nine years at an increased rent they could afford. On 18 November 1634 Brend and the sharers agreed in court that he would grant the lease for the nine years, from Christmas 1635 to Christmas 1644, at £40 a year. He then, however, held out for better terms, and after Christmas 1635 the sharers offered to pay him either the new rent in return for the new court-approved lease or the old rent. Brend refused both. Eventually he returned to the court, which, on 28 November 1637, again ordered that he draw up the new lease. It also ordered that the sharers pay the old rent for the first of the years after Christmas 1635 (so that Brend had lost £25 10s) and £40 thereafter.

The sharers managed the second Globe as they had the first Globe. They continued to own the lease on the property and to pay the rent and the costs of keeping the place in repair. They continued to collect rents from buildings other than the playhouse, and, for letting the players use the playhouse, they continued to collect half the money people paid at the doors leading to the galleries and boxes. At the second Globe, if not at the first Globe, they also collected half the money people paid at the tiring-house door, which led, presumably, to a gallery above and behind the stage and to the stage, where people could sit. As before, the players kept the other half and all the money paid at 'the outer doors', through which people passed to get to the yard and to the doors leading to the galleries and boxes. The players continued to pay the costs of producing plays.

At least two disputes about the ownership of shares reached the courts, and one reached the Lord Chamberlain. Shares increasingly fell into the hands of people who were not actors. By the early 1630s, indeed, the consortium seems to have had almost no direct connection with the players at the Globe. The non-Burbage half then comprised eight shares, four owned by Condell's widow and four by Hemmings' son, William, who was not an actor. The Burbage half was owned by Cuthbert Burbage and Richard Burbage's widow and young son. The only actor among the King's men who had any legal interest in the consortium was Richard Robinson, who had married the widow. Actors complained, and rearrangements of shares then occurred, so that by 1635 five actors held seven shares, though shortly, it seems, persons who were not actors again held more shares than persons who were.

For the whole of its history, the second Globe was the home of the King's men and the property of the consortium associated with that company. By 1616, if not virtually from the beginning, the King's men regarded it as secondary to their private playhouse, the second Blackfriars. The Globe was used only in the summer, roughly from mid-May to early September, and its audiences were seen as crude in comparison with those in Blackfriars. Both sharers and players, however, continued to think it a valuable piece of theatrical real estate. The King's men had been using Blackfriars for more than five years when they spent vastly more to build the second Globe than their lease required. At least two plays were huge successes at the Globe in August, *A Game at Chess* in 1624 and *The Late Lancashire Witches* in 1634, and both attracted large numbers of nobility and 'fine folk' when such people were supposed to be out of town.

Wenceslas Hollar included a persuasive engraving of the exterior of the second Globe in his so-called Long Bird's-Eye View, a panorama of London from the south published in Amsterdam in 1647 (see figs. 6a and 6b). He based the part of the View showing Bankside on a drawing of his that survives in two states, the pencil original drawn when the playhouse was nearing the end of its life, and a working over in ink. Recently these images have been minutely studied as part of the attempt to rebuild the first Globe, on the assumption that what is true of the second Globe is also true of the first Globe. Even though Hollar clearly did not mean to draw with mathematical precision (he showed the playhouse as round, not polygonal, for example), his images have been made to yield information as though he achieved such precision. Actually, one can only describe the impression the exterior of the building made on a great graphic artist and say almost nothing for certain about the building as a spectator at a play would have seen it. Still, it is clear that the second Globe was a large, polygonal timber building that appeared round and, according to the Spanish ambassador, could accommodate 3,000 people. It was laid out much as the first Globe and other public playhouses were, and its galleries were covered with tiles. Over its stage and tiring-house was a large roof of two gables, and over that was a small polygonal tower covered by an onion dome. It had at least one external staircase leading up into its galleries.

Digging under Anchor Terrace could supply crucial information about the second Globe: exact measurements, for example, the number of sides, the shape of the stage. Because Anchor Terrace, now made into expensive flats, is also of historical interest, however, archaeologists cannot attempt such digging until they find, and can fund, a way to keep it from falling down as they dig.

The second Globe ceased to be used as a playhouse on 2 September 1642, along with all the other playhouses, because Parliament ordered an end to professional, public acting. It may have been pulled down c. 1644–5, and other buildings were certainly standing on its site in 1655.

If the Theatre and first Globe were much the same size and shape, as they probably were, the first Globe and second Globe must also have been much the same size and shape because the two occupied the same lines on the ground. The scheme James Burbage and John Brayne had followed in 1576, therefore, was still in use when the playhouses closed in 1642, having endured throughout the whole of the golden age of English Renaissance drama. Moreover, since the second Globe cost twice as much to build as the first Globe, it must have been a more refined place. And since two contemporary carpenters thought its timbers and lead inferior,[3] its refinement may have lain in cosmetic manipulations of carpentry and plaster. One of its contemporaries called it 'the fairest playhouse that ever was in England'.

[1] In January 1635 the government asked officials of St Saviour's parish, where the Globe was, to say whether buildings put up since 1605 were on new or old foundations. On 27 February 1635 the officials reported that 'The Globe playhouse near Maid Lane [was] built by the company of players with timber about twenty years past upon an old foundation' and 'one house thereto adjoining built about the same time with timber' (LMA, P92/SAV/1325–7; see Berry, *Shakespeare's Playhouses*, 185–7, and *J and CS*, VI, 185). Neither the government nor the officials meant that foundations were literally old, but that they followed the lines of former foundations. In their lawsuit against Sir Matthew Brend, the sharers said that the second Globe was 'erected, built, and set up ... in the same place where the former house stood'.
[2] Berry, *Shakespeare's Playhouses*, 95.
[3] Ibid., 235, 189–92.

468 The sharers add six years to their lease, 26 October 1613, and are promised nine more, 15 February 1614

PRO, Req.2/789/[top]. Transcribed in Berry, *Shakespeare's Playhouses*, 220–2. Bodley's extension and Brend's promise apparently do not survive, but they are described (in reverse order) in a statement of fact to which the sharers and Brend agreed on 5 February 1634.

(a) Bodley adds six years to the lease, 26 October 1613

Sir John [as he was in 1634] Bodley, taking notice of the said loss by fire and charge of new building, . . . by his indenture dated 26th of October 1613 for good considerations him moving, made thereupon unto the said lessees [the sharers] a lease of the premises for six years to begin from the end of the said lease of thirty-one years under the like rent and covenants as are in the said lease for one and thirty years. Whereupon they new built the said playhouse and expended about £1,400 thereupon and have ever sithence quietly enjoyed the same.[1]

[1] George Archer, Brend's rent gatherer, added, 'and . . . the indenture in parchment now showed to this deponent . . . is the counter-part of the same lease' (PRO, Req.2/706/[bottom], transcribed in Berry, *Shakespeare's Playhouses*, 219).

(b) Brend promises to add nine years, 15 February 1614

A playhouse called the Globe upon the premises . . . being burnt down by casualty of fire that happened therein, . . . Sir Matthew [as he was in 1634] Brend . . . by his deed poll[1] dated 15th February 1614, reciting the said lease made by his father and the burning down of the said playhouse by casualty of fire and the lessees' intention to lay out £1,000 . . . upon the re-edifying of the said playhouse, in consideration of their said loss and expense and for their encouragement to re-edify the same and for £10 to be paid him at his full age of twenty-one years (if he shall then make them the lease hereinafter mentioned) covenants that when he shall attain his said full age . . . [he shall] make them a further lease of fifteen years to begin after the expiration of the said lease of one and thirty years under the like rent and covenants as were in the said lease of one and thirty years.[2] At the ensealing of which deed, the mother and uncle of the said Sir Matthew were present, and were privy and acquainted with the said Sir Matthew his covenant and agreement in and by the same deed poll made, and did subscribe their names as witnesses to express their consents thereunto. And at the time of the ensealing of the said deed poll, the said Sir Matthew was within one month of the age of fourteen years.[3]

[1] A deed poll is a contract made by one party only.
[2] That is, he would confirm the six years his trustee had already given and add nine more.
[3] Atkins described this event at greater length: PRO, Req.2/706/[bottom], transcribed in Berry, *Shakespeare's Playhouses*, 213–15.

469 To raise money for rebuilding the Globe, the sharers tax themselves £120 for each share, 1613–1614

PRO, Req.4/1/2, the answer. Transcribed in Wallace, 'Shakespeare and his London Associates', 320–1

The documents involved in raising the money do not survive, but in a lawsuit of 1619, the treasurer of the consortium, John Hemmings, implied how much each sharer, including Shakespeare, paid for each full share. Hemmings was describing his dealings with John Witter, who had held one share when the first Globe burned. For the full text of the document, see **150**.

Shortly after [the fire] . . . this defendant [Hemmings] and his partners [the other sharers] in the said playhouse resolved to re-edify the same, . . . the rather because they were, by covenant on their part in the said original lease contained, to maintain and repair all such buildings as should be built or erected upon the said gardens or ground . . . as by the said original lease may appear. And thereupon this defendant did write . . . to the said complainant [Witter] signifying the same unto him and therein required him to come and bring or send £50 or £60 by a day therein mentioned for and towards the re-edifying . . . in regard of his . . . part of the said ground . . . But the said complainant neither brought nor sent any money towards the re-edifying of the said playhouse, nor did this defendant ever receive any answer by or from him . . . And thereupon this defendant did enter into the said part [*i.e.* seized the share], . . . and because he found that the re-edifying of the said playhouse would be a very great charge and doubted what benefit would arise thereby and for that the said original lease had then but a few years to come, he, this defendant, did give away . . . one moiety of the said part of the said moiety . . . to . . . Henry Condell gratis. [And] the re-edifying . . . hath sithence cost the said defendants [Hemmings and Condell] about the sum of £120.

By this last remark Hemmings must have meant that he and Condell, having divided Witter's share between them, were taxed £60 each for it, £120 altogether. The owners of other shares, therefore, should also have paid £120 for each share, so that all the shares together yielded £1,680. Since Hemmings and Condell each had a share before they divided Witter's (Wallace, 'Shakespeare and his London Associates', 313, 317), each should have paid £180 in all.[1]

[1] Other interpretations of the remark make less sense. If Hemmings meant that his and Condell's three shares were taxed £120 in all, and if at the time there were seven such shares in half the enterprise (as he also said, Wallace, 'Shakespeare and his London Associates', 321), the tax would have raised only £560. If he meant that he and Condell had been taxed £120 each for a share and a half, the tax would have raised only £1,120. Witter thought there were six shares and each was taxed £50 (Wallace, 'Shakespeare and his London Associates', 309, 331), yielding only £600. See ES. II, 423, and Baldwin, *Organization and Personnel of the Shakespearean Company*, 100–2.

470 Hemmings directs the building of the second Globe; it costs £1,400 and a house adjoining £200: spring 1614

PRO, (a) Req.2/706/[bottom]; (b) Req.2/789/[top]. Transcribed in Berry, *Shakespeare's Playhouses*, (a) 230, (b) 222. How the sharers proceeded in rebuilding the Globe and how much they spent are shown in remarks they and their scrivener, John Atkins (Hemmings' son-in-law), made twenty years later in their lawsuit against their landlord, Sir Matthew Brend.

(a) Atkins, 1 October 1634

This deponent [Atkins] hath heard and doth believe that the playhouse at the last building thereof did cost . . . the sum of £1,300 or £1,400 and that the other tenement adjoining thereunto... did cost in building the sum of £200.[1] And this deponent is the rather induced so to believe for that this deponent married the daughter of the said John Hemmings, who was a principal agent employed in and about the oversight of the building of the said playhouse and bore part of the charge, and this deponent was by him used in and about the making of certain covenants between the carpenters and the plaintiffs [the sharers].

[1] In the trial of their lawsuit, the sharers said they spent £1,400 on the playhouse and £200 on the house (see 477).

(b) A statement of fact for both sides, 5 February 1634

They [the sharers] new built the said playhouse and and expended about £1,400 thereupon and have ever sithence quietly enjoyed the same.

471 Plays are being performed at the second Globe, the fairest playhouse that ever was in England, 30 June 1614

(a) PRO, SP14/77/fo. 107v; (b) Taylor, *Taylors Water-work or The Sculler Travels from Tiber to Thames* (1614), sig. G4 (epigram 22). Transcribed in (a) *Letters of John Chamberlain*, I, 544

(a) John Chamberlain writes to Alice Carleton, 30 June 1614

I have not seen your sister Williams since I came to town, though I have been there twice. The first time she was at a neighbour's house at cards and the next she was gone to the new Globe to a play. Indeed, I hear much speech of this new playhouse, which is said to be the fairest that ever was in England, so that if I live but seven years longer, I may chance take a journey to see it.

(b) The water poet's tribute, 1614

As gold is better that's in fire tried,
So is the Bankside Globe that late was burned,
For where before it had a thatched hide,
Now to a stately theatre is turned,
Which is an emblem that great things are won
By those that dare through greatest dangers run.

472 The King's men use the second Globe only during the summer, and its audiences prefer crude plays, *c.* 1616–ff.

(a) Goodman, *Holland's Leaguer* (1632), sig. F2v; (b) Queen's College, Oxford, MS 390, fo. 68v; (c) Davenant, *Works of Sir William Davenant, Kt.* (1673), sig. Aaaa; (d) Shirley, *Poems &c.* (1648), sigs. D4v–D5. Transcribed in (b) *The Diary of Thomas Crosfield*, 72. See also *J and CS*, VI, 12–17, 179, 192–4, 196. Below are a few of the many evidences.

(a) Goodman, 1632

[The Globe] was the continent of the world, because half the year a world of beauties and brave spirits resorted unto it.

(b) Crosfield, 18 July 1634

[In July 1634, Thomas Crosfield described the King's men as] The King's company at the private house of Blackfriars.

(c) Davenant, August 1635

In the prologue for his play, *News from Plymouth*, licensed 1 August 1635 and meant for the Globe, Davenant had the actor who spoke the prologue say:

> Each spectator knows
> This house and season does more promise shows,
> Dancing, and Buckler fights than art or wit.
> Yet so much taxed of both as will befit
> Our humble theme, you shall receive, and such
> As may please those who do not expect too much.

(d) Shirley, 1640

In his play, *The Doubtful Heir*, produced in 1640 at the Globe over his objections, Shirley had the actor who spoke the prologue say:

> Gentlemen, I am only sent to say
> Our author did not calculate this play
> For this meridian. The Bankside, he knows,
> Is far more skilful at the ebbs and flows
> Of water than of wit. He did not mean
> For the elevation of your poles[1] this scene.
> No shows, no frisk, and what you most delight in
> (Grave understanders), here's no target fighting
> Upon the stage, all work for cutlers barred,
> No bawdry, nor no ballads; this goes hard.
> The wit is clean and what affects you not,
> Without impossibilities the plot:
> No clown, no squibs, no devil's in't . . .
> But you that can contract yourselves and sit
> As you were now in the Blackfriars pit,
> And will not deaf us with lewd noise or tongues,
> Because we have no heart to break our lungs,

Will pardon our vast scene and not disgrace
This play, meant for your persons, not the place.

[1] *i.e.* latitudes. Being round (or seeming so), the Globe suggested a level dial and its poles a gnomon, whose elevation was the angle it made with a celestial body.

473 An ambassador objects to a play at the second Globe and says the place could hold 3,000 people, 6–17 August 1624

(a) PRO, SP14/171/fo. 103; (b) Biblioteca Nacional, Madrid, MS 18,203; (c) Spanish State Archives, Simancas, Registro de Cartas, Libro 375. Transcribed in (a) *Letters of John Chamberlain*, II, 577–8; (b, c) Wilson and Turner, 'The Spanish Protest Against *A Game at Chesse*', 477, 478, 480, 482. See also *J and CS*, IV, 870–9; VI, 183–4

Middleton's play, *A Game at Chess*, opened at the Globe on 6 August 1624 and ran nine straight days to full houses. It was one of the greatest theatrical successes of the age, in general because it is sharply anti-Spanish and in particular because its actors mocked a former Spanish ambassador in London, Gondomar. The current ambassador informed his government in Madrid and protested to the English one. The privy council summoned Middleton and the actors on 18 August and ordered the actors not to perform the play again.[1] The number of people that the ambassador said could attend a play at the second Globe is the number de Witt had said could attend a play at the Swan. Many notices of the affair survive (see *J and CS*, IV, 871–6), including two of the ambassador's allusions to the capacity of the Globe.

[1] PRO, PC2/32, pp. 421, 424, transcribed in *APC, 1623–5*, 303, 305.

(a) John Chamberlain to Sir Dudley Carleton, 21 August 1624

I doubt not but you have heard of our famous play of Gondomar, which hath been followed with extraordinary concourse and frequented by all sorts of people, old and young, rich and poor, masters and servants, Papists and puritans, wisemen etc., churchman and statesmen, . . . and a world besides. The Lady Smith would have gone if she could have persuaded me to go with her. I am not so sour nor so severe but that I would willingly have attended her, but I could not sit so long, for we must have been there before one o'clock at the farthest to find any room.

(b) A Spanish account of the ambassador's protest, 10 August 1624

The actors whom they call here the King's men have recently acted and are still acting in London a play that so many people come to see that there were more than 3,000 persons there on the day that the audience was smallest. There was such merriment, hubbub and applause that even if I had been many leagues away it would not have been possible for me not to have taken notice of it.

(c) Another Spanish account of the ambassador's protest, 10 August 1624

It cannot be pleaded that those who repeat and hear these insults [in the play] are merely four rogues, because during these last four days more than 12,000 persons have all heard the play of *A Game at Chess*, for so they call it, including all the nobility still in London.

474 The second Globe is used for things other than plays, February 1631 and March 1635

(a, b) Sir Henry Herbert, Office Book (now lost). Reported by Halliwell-Phillipps in his scrapbooks at the Folger, 'Lowin', 19, and 'Globe', 133; transcribed in *J and CS*, VI, 194

These are payments to the Master of the Revels for permission to perform during Lent. The 'their house' of the first could, of course, refer to Blackfriars, except that a 'vaulter' seems more suitable for the Globe. John Lowin was one of the treasurers of the King's men, and William Blagrave was an assistant of the Master of the Revels.

(a) February 1631

Received [a fee] of Mr Lowin for allowing of a Dutch vaulter at their house, 18 February 1631

(b) March 1635

From the Dutchman – at the Globe, [a fee received] by Blagrave, 16 March 1635.

475 The sharers sue Sir Matthew Brend for an extension of their lease, 28 January – 10 May 1632

PRO, Req.2/706/[bottom]. Transcribed in Berry, *Shakespeare's Playhouses*, 197–208; see also 156–67

Brend refused to grant the nine-year extension of the lease on the Globe property that, as a minor in 1614, he had promised to grant in return for £10 when he should be of age and have control of the property (468b). So the sharers sued him in the Court of Requests well before their current lease ran out at Christmas 1635. Their bill of complaint, his reply, and their replication were the opening gambits of a game that continued until 1637.

(a) The sharers' bill of complaint, 28 January 1632

[The sharers rehearsed the terms of the original lease (393) and Brend's promise, then recited their own doings. They] have sithence [*i.e.* since Brend's promise], at their own proper costs and charges, erected, built and set up thereupon the demised premises, in the same place where the former house stood, a very proper, new and fair house or playhouse called the Globe to their further charge of £1,500 [later reduced to £1,400] of lawful English money at the least, being the greatest part of your said subjects' and servants' [*i.e.* the sharers'] substance and estates. And sithence the said Sir Matthew Brend hath accomplished his age of one and twenty years, your said subjects and servants, . . . in all gentle and courteous manner, have tendered the same £10 unto the said Sir Matthew Brend and have requested him to accept thereof and according to his said promise, grant and covenant in writing to make, grant and confirm unto them a new lease or estate of the said house and ground for the said term of fifteen years [*i.e.* to confirm the six years the trustee, Bodley, had given and grant nine more] to commence after the expiration of their said old lease under the like yearly rent of £14 10s 0d and other the covenants and agreements contained in the same old lease.

But . . . he, the said Sir Matthew Brend, taking advantage of his said then minority when he did make, seal and deliver the said writing, hath and doth refuse to accept of the said . . . £10 and to grant and confirm unto your said subjects and servants such further term of years as he promised . . .

[The sharers next rehearsed the Bodley extension, according to which they now occupied the property, then turned to their current problem.] The said lease made by the said Sir John Bodley drawing on and coming near to an end, being to end about four years hence, the said Sir Matthew Brend doth not only refuse to make the said new lease for the remainder of the said term of fifteen years . . . but doth threaten when the said lease made by the said Sir John Bodley is ended to dispossess your said subjects and servants of the said house and grounds . . . and to sell it to others, . . . which is contrary to all equity and will be to your said subjects' and servants' utter undoing, having disbursed and laid out their whole stocks and estates in and upon the re-edifying and new building thereof.

[Finally, they asked the court to provide them a remedy at equity, since they could have none at common law.] And your said subject and servants are become remediless at law therein, for that [*i.e.* because] the said promise . . . of the said Sir Matthew Brend was by him . . . made in his minority, and the same neither doth nor can bind . . . him at common law . . . But nevertheless in equity the said Sir Matthew Brend ought to be bound thereunto, for that the inheritance of the said Sir Matthew Brend is advanced and bettered thereby to the sum of £1,500 which hath been . . . laid out by your said subjects and servants . . . in the new building and re-edifying thereof, and your said subjects and servants were thereunto drawn to expend and disburse the said moneys (which otherwise they would not have done) but by and upon the promise . . . of the said Sir Matthew Brend as aforesaid; and for that . . . the said house is for their exercise and practice of their quality very fit and commodious, the better to enable your majesty's servants to do their service to your highness; and [for] that your most excellent majesty by . . . letters patents under the great seal of England for the purposes aforesaid hath also licensed and authorised your said servants to exercise their said quality of acting and playing of interludes, comedies and tragedies in the same house called the Globe.

(b) Brend's reply, 6 February 1632

[Brend also rehearsed the old lease and Bodley's extension, then explained why the court should not require him to extend it further.] This defendant [doth not] know that the same [*i.e.* the Globe] was by fire burned down, as in the bill is pretended, neither is the same material unto this defendant . . . for that the said original lessees, their executors and assigns were by covenant as aforesaid bound to erect buildings upon the said parcels of ground and premises and for that consideration the same were let unto them at such small yearly rents by this defendant's said late father as aforesaid. And in case any casualty happened thereunto, they were to maintain, repair, rebuild and amend the same buildings and in the end of their said old lease to leave and yield up the same in good repair to this defendant. And therefore their negligence or ill-keeping . . . ought not, as this defendant conceiveth, in law or equity to move this defendant to make them any longer lease of it or grant them any longer term in the said playhouse called the Globe than they had by virtue of the said first lease.

And as the covenant in the bill suggested to be entered into by this defendant in . . . [1614], this defendant saith that in case any such covenant was entered into by this defendant, the same was . . . when this defendant was either within the age of fourteen years or when this defendant had but newly attained thereunto. And this defendant was greatly abused therein, as he also conceiveth. And therefore as he is not by law bound to perform the same, so he conceiveth, under the favour of this most honourable court, he is not compellable in equity to make the same good or perform the same covenant in any part, especially seeing by the complainants' own showing it appears that without any consideration at all they have obtained a further term of six years from the said Sir John Bodley, . . . which this defendant agreeth to confirm. And in regard that thereby the complainants are to enjoy the same playhouse and premises for so many years more at so small yearly rents without any valuable benefit or advantage at all to this defendant, whereby this defendant hath sustained so much loss in the improvement he might raise the yearly value and rents of the said playhouse and premises unto, this defendant is not willing to agree to make any further estate therein unto the said complainants than they have by the said lease of the said Sir John Bodley . . . [by which] they have had and received much more profit and advantage than this defendant was bound either by law or equity to give unto them . . .

And [he] therefore hopeth, under the favour of this honourable court, it shall and may be lawful for him, after the end of the said new lease of six years, to dispose of the same playhouse and premises as pleaseth him and to whom he will and at such better yearly rents as he can get for the same, notwithstanding the said covenant abusively and surreptitiously obtained from him when he had not discretion to know what he did or wherefore he did it . . .

And this defendant doth not believe that his inheritance is advanced or bettered by any buildings now upon the premises, but verily thinketh that if fit dwelling houses had been erected upon it in value answerable to the long term of years the complainants and their predecessors have enjoyed it, and are to enjoy it, at such mean yearly rents as aforesaid, it had been far better for this defendant's inheritance than now it is or can be.

(c) The sharers' replication, 10 May 1632

[The sharers decline to reply to anything in Brend's answer and 'aver' that] every the matters and things... contained... [in their bill are] just, certain and sufficient in the law to be answered unto, and that defendant's answer... is very uncertain, untrue and insufficient in the law to be replied unto.

476 A play about witchcraft is a great success at the Globe, 11–15 August 1634

Somerset Record Office, Taunton, DD/PH 212/no. 12. Transcribed in Berry, *Shakespeare's Playhouses*, 123–4; see also 121–43

In the summer of 1634 the King's men were evidently urged by a faction of the privy council to mount a play about people recently accused and convicted of witchcraft in Lancashire. The company was provided with material from official depositions and was promised that no other play about witchcraft would be licensed until their play had finished its run. The company engaged Thomas Heywood and Richard Brome to write it, opened it at the Globe some six weeks later, on 11 or 12 August, ran it for three days, and allowed it to be licensed for printing on 28 October. It was a huge success, and a letter written on 16 August by a spectator contains what amounts to a review of it, one of the earliest things of the kind.

Here hath been lately a new comedy at the Globe called *The Witches of Lancashire*[1] acted, by reason of the great concourse of people, three days together. The third day I went with a friend to see it and found greater appearance of fine folk, gentlemen and gentlewomen, than I thought had been in town in vacation. The subject was of the slights and passages done or supposed to be done by these witches sent form thence hither[2] and other witches and their familiars; of their nightly meetings in several places; their banqueting with all sorts of meat and drink conveyed unto them by their familiars upon the pulling of a cord; the walking of pails of milk by themselves...; the transforming of men and women into the shapes of several creatures, and especially of horses by putting an inchanted bridle into their mouths; their posting to and from places far distant in an incredible short time; the cutting off of a witch-gentlewoman's hand in the form of a cat by a soldier turned miller, known to her husband by a ring thereon (the only tragical part of the story); the representing of wrong and putative fathers, in the shape of mean persons, to gentlemen by way of derision; the tying of a knot at a marriage (after the French fashion) to cassate [*i.e.* annul] masculine ability; and the conveying away of the good cheer and bringing in a mock feast of bones and stones instead thereof; and the filling of pies with living birds and young cats; etc.

And though there be not in it (to my understanding) any poetical genius or art or language or judgement to state our tenet of witches (which I expected), or application to virtue, but full of ribaldry and of things improbable and impossible; yet in respect of the newness of the subject (the witches being still visible and in prison here) and in regard it consisteth from the beginning to the end of odd passages and fopperies to provoke laughter, and is mixed with divers songs and dances, it passeth for a merry and excellent new play.

[1] It was printed and is now known as *The Late Lancashire Witches*.
[2] The jury at the Lancashire assizes found the witches guilty, but the circuit judges who presided over the trial refused to sentence them and laid the matter before the King. He and the privy council then had four of the witches brought to London.

477 The sharers and Brend reach a compromise in their lawsuit, 18 November 1634

PRO, Req.1/157/fo. 65v. Transcribed in Berry, *Shakespeare's Playhouses*, 237; see also 169–76

By 22 November 1632 the sharers and Sir Matthew Brend had examined their witnesses and were ready to proceed to a formal hearing of their lawsuit in the Court of Requests. Both parties, however, then lost interest in the case until February 1634, when the sharers (with less than two years left of their lease) began to drive an unwilling Brend to a conclusion. Lawyers for both sides signed a statement of the facts, and an official commission tried in vain to resolve the case. On 18 November 1634 the court formally heard it. The resulting Order issued by the court does not survive, but an account of the hearing does survive in the court notebook.

The first six years allowed them [*i.e.* the sharers] by Sir Matthew urged as a sufficient recompence for their charge in building and re-edifying the playhouse. £1,400 bestowed in re-edifying the playhouse and £200 upon the house. The charge of the plaintiffs induced by the hopes given them for enjoying the further term by the defendant's covenant in his infancy. The defendant's mother and his uncle witnesses to the covenant. The straight of the case: how the covenant of the infant shall bind him. Where the person is disabled, there no court can make him able. For an end to the cause, it is ordered by consent of the defendant that the plaintiffs shall enjoy their term of nine years after the expiration of the six years in ... their lease upon the increase of their rent to £40 per annum during the continuance of the said nine years. Upon full hearing in presence of counsel and parties. And they to put in sufficient [security] for keeping of the house[s] in the repair and leaving them sufficiently in repair at the end of the term. And the ... [defendant] to make a lease accordingly to the said complainants.

Brend, however, soon thought better of this arrangement and refused to make the new lease. After the existing lease ran out at Christmas 1635, the King's men remained at the Globe protected by the court order. The sharers offered Brend the new rent in return for a new lease, but he refused to accept the one or make the other; they then offered him the old rent, but he refused to accept it. He, therefore, received no money from his tenants and could not remove them.

478 Financial arrangements between sharers and players are explained, summer 1635

PRO, LC5/133, pp. 44–51. Transcribed in MSC, II. 362–73; see also *J and CS*, I, 43–7

In the summer of 1635 three players among the King's men complained to the Lord Chamberlain that they could not own shares in the Globe or the Blackfriars playhouses because non-playing sharers would not sell shares to them. This and subsequent statements by the players, sharers and the Lord Chamberlain comprise the so-called Sharers' Papers, for the full text of which see **162**. Two remarks by the players and one by the Burbages explain financial arrangements between owners and players at both Globes, the second Blackfriars, the Theatre, and probably other places. The players asked that the sharers be compelled to sell shares to them or to change the way players paid for the use of the playhouse: instead of paying a share of gate receipts, players might pay simple rent. The Lord Chamberlain ordered that sharers sell shares to the three players at the going rates.

[The three players complained:] That those few interested [*i.e.* having a share] in the [Globe and Blackfriars] houses have (without any defalcation or abatement at all) a full moiety of the whole gains arising thereby, excepting the outer doors. And such of the said housekeepers [*i.e.* the sharers] as be actors do likewise equally share with all the rest of the actors both in the other moiety and in the said outer doors also.

[The players later explained:] That the housekeepers ... have amongst them the full moiety of all the galleries and boxes in both houses and of the tiring-house door at the Globe,[1] [and] that the actors have the other moiety with [all the money collected at] the outer doors.

[In reply the Burbages said that:] The players that lived in those first times [*i.e.* when the Theatre in Shoreditch was in business] had only the profits arising from the doors, but now the players receive all the comings in at the doors to themselves and half the galleries from the housekeepers.

[1] Despite the words used here and in the two other remarks, it is said (see, for example, *J and CS*, VI, 180) that the sharers had all the takings at the tiring-house door.

479 Brend returns to court, and the sharers' lawsuit against him ends, 28 November 1637

PRO, Req.1/160/fo. 181. Transcribed in Berry, *Shakespeare's Playhouses*, 239–40; see also 176–8

On 9 November 1637, Sir Matthew Brend told the Court of Requests that he was ready to make a new lease in return for the new rent from Christmas 1635, but the sharers were refusing to pay the new rent. The court ordered them to pay the money and accept the lease. On 28 November, however, they explained what Brend had omitted to say, and the court issued another and final order. This order does not survive, but the account of the hearing in the court notebook does.

The improved rent tendered and refused by the defendant [Brend], who would rather that the plaintiffs [the sharers] should continue it at the old rent than to be pressed to make a new lease. The plaintiff's prayer: that they may be discharged of the increase of rent for those two years ... The defendant prays performance of the decree for the increase of rent. The plaintiffs to pay it for one of the two years and to be discharged thereof for the other year. And for the remnant of the term the plaintiffs to accept a new lease at the improved rent and Mr Lane[1] to consider whether it be fit that there be one or two [*i.e.* probably, bonds to guarantee that the sharers leave the property in good repair at the end of the term].

[1] Three people named Lane were involved with the case: Richard, the sharers' counsel; Richard, the sharers' attorney (the best guess); and William, the deputy registrar of the court (see Berry, *Shakespeare's Playhouses*, 178).

480 The second Globe is closed, 2 September 1642, and comes to an end, 1644–1655

(a) Folger, MS V.b.275, p. 16; (b) PRO, C5/448/137, the bill. Transcribed in (a) Collier, *Works of William Shakespeare*, I, ccxli–ii, n.; see Berry, 'Folger Ms. V.b.275'

Like all the other playhouses, the second Globe fell silent on 2 September 1642, when Parliament ordered all professional, public acting to cease. It was pulled down and replaced by other buildings, perhaps in April 1644, more likely *c.* 1645, certainly by 1655. The document quoted in (a) below is probably a forgery and is in any case unreliable. The Globe appears in the first edition of Dankerts' map of London (*c.* 1633) but has been removed from the second (*c.* 1645).

(a) 15 April 1644

The Globe playhouse on the bankside in Southwark was burnt down to the ground in the year 1612 [*i.e.* 1613], and new built up again in the year 1613 [*i.e.* 1614] at the great charge of King James and many noblemen and others. And now [it has been] pulled down to the ground by Sir Matthew Brend on Monday the 15 of April 1644 to make tenements in the room of it.[1]

[1] Not only are the two dates wrong, but so is the remark about the King and noblemen. Only the sharers should have, and seem in fact to have, provided the money to rebuild the Globe (see **469**). Moreover, though the sharers' papers say that the lease was to finish on March 25, 1644, it was actually to finish at Christmas, 1644, and Sir Matthew Brend should not have had control of the property until then. Chambers (*ES*, II, 427) and Bentley (*J and CS*, VI, 200), however, accepted this document as reliable.

(b) 17 October 1655

[Sir Matthew Brend included the site of the Globe in the contract for the marriage of his son, Thomas, and Judith Smith, as:] all those messuages or tenements ... in or near Maiden Lane in the parish of St Saviour ... most of which ... messuages or tenements were erected and built where the playhouse called the Globe stood and upon the ground thereunto belonging.

XXXVI The Phoenix

The Phoenix Playhouse (often called the Cockpit) was a private playhouse in the City of Westminster and the parish of St Giles in the Fields. It was about three-eighths of a mile west of the western boundary of the City of London at Temple Bar. It was and is usually said to be in Drury Lane, but it was actually about midway between Drury lane and Wild Street, both of which ran and run north and south. It was served by a now-defunct Cockpit Alley, which ran east and west from Drury Lane to Wild Street about midway between Great Queen and Princes (now Kemble) Streets, also running east and west. The entrance to Cockpit Alley was about opposite the present entrance to Martlett Court on the west side of Drury Lane. The site of the playhouse is in the northern part of the Peabody housing estate that now lies between Drury Lane and Wild Street, W.C.2.[1]

The Phoenix was the first professional playhouse in the so-called west end, now the main theatrical district of London. It was also the first of many theatres in or a few yards from Drury Lane itself. Five are there now and two others are not far away.

A veteran actor among the Queen's men, Christopher Beeston, had the playhouse built in the autumn and winter of 1616–17, and he owned and managed it until he died in 1638. In his hands, it attracted much the same sophisticated clientele as the private playhouse in Blackfriars and achieved an artistic standard second only to the one that playhouse achieved.

On 9 August 1616, Beeston took a sublease on a piece of property where a cock-fighting enterprise stood, and in 1633 he paid £5 to extend the sublease. It was to begin at Michaelmas 1616 and to continue at first for thirty-one years, then for nine more, at £45 a year. It would finally expire, that is, on 28 September 1656. The buildings on the property were a cockpit (built in 1609 or thereabouts), cock-houses and sheds. The property also included a house and garden and a piece of ground behind the cockpit. Beeston was already at work 'converting' the Cockpit into a playhouse on 15 October 1616, when the benchers of Lincoln's Inn complained (vainly, it seems) about having a playhouse little more than a quarter-mile west of their Inn.

The Queen's men, who were to open the playhouse, were still at the Red Bull on 23 February 1617, but they were performing a play at the Phoenix on 4 March when rioting apprentices broke into and wrecked the place. That was Shrove Tuesday, the apprentices' annual holiday on which such riots often occurred. The Queen's men then returned to the Red Bull for three months while Beeston repaired the Phoenix.

The building apparently had brick walls. Little else is known for certain about it, but writers have recently advanced two quite different ideas. According to one, Inigo Jones designed the playhouse, and two unlabelled and undated architectural drawings from his workshop (which are now at Worcester College, Oxford) represent his plan.[2] These show a two-storey building whose ground plan consists of a rectangle joined to an apse. The rec-

Fig. 7. The Phoenix playhouse (?), from Wenceslas Hollar, the Great Map, as reproduced in *A Collection of Early Maps of London 1553–1667*, sheet 19. The playhouse is probably the larger of the two buildings in the middle that have three pitched roofs. The street in the lower left corner is Drury Lane, and that across the top is Wild Street.

tangle contains the tiring-house, stage and space for spectators on the left and right sides of the stage; the apse contains a pit and gallery for spectators. An external rectangular staircase adjoins the main rectangle and another the apse.

The other idea is more persuasive. Here, the playhouse is a building shown on a map-view drawn by Wenceslas Hollar *c.* 1658.[3] The building is in the right place, and the buildings and grounds around it match those mentioned in a series of deeds and in a lawsuit of 1647 partly about the playhouse. The map is the only sheet printed of a proposed 'Great Map' of London that Hollar said was to be 10 feet by 5 feet and in 1660 sought funds to finish. The map, he wrote, was to show not only streets, lanes and alleys 'proportionably measured, but also the buildings (especially of the principal houses, churches, courts, halls, etc.) as much resembling the likeness of them as convenience of the room [on the map] will permit'. Hollar was a considerable graphic artist, and this sheet of his map 'represents the zenith of the art of the map-view'.[4] The building that should be the playhouse is square, about 40 feet by 40 feet. It has at least two main storeys and three pitched roofs whose ridges are side by side and parallel to Drury Lane. On its north side is an alley that should be Cockpit Alley, and on its south side is an open space. On perhaps two-thirds of its west side is a building facing but set back from Drury Lane. At its south-east corner is a two-gabled structure from which a garden extends east to Wild Street. The map does not show a building resembling Inigo Jones' design.

The Queen's men remained at the Phoenix, not very profitably, it seems, until the death of their patroness on 2 March 1619, when the company dissolved. Beeston then abandoned his fellows, seizing (so they said) 'all the furniture and apparel', presumably to equip his playhouse, and refusing to help pay their debts. He took Prince Charles' (I) men into his playhouse, and by 7 May 1622 replaced them with Lady Elizabeth's men, a company he had reconstituted for the purpose. Then he apparently used the cessation of playing caused by the plague of 1625 to create a new company partly out of the membership of Lady Elizabeth's – Queen Henrietta Maria's men, whom he seems to have taken into his playhouse when playing resumed. From Lady Elizabeth's he also acquired the playwright James Shirley, who had already written one play for the playhouse and went on to write twenty more.

Beeston removed Queen Henrietta Maria's men during the plague of 1636–7 and formed yet another new company for the place, the King and Queen's Young Company. They performed at Court on 7 and 14 February 1637, and Beeston was sworn 'Governor of the new company of the King's and Queen's boys' a week later. He got into trouble for presenting the company to an invited audience at the Phoenix in May 1637, before the plague was over. This company was not like the boys' companies in the private playhouses at the turn of the century and before. It was a regular adult company with a large number of boys, and part of its purpose was to train the boys as players. It remained at the Phoenix until the closing of the playhouses in 1642.

From 1622 onwards, if not from 1617, Beeston saw himself not as one of a group of players but as owner and manager of a playhouse who could take on and dispose of players as he liked. It was a new dispensation that would also apply at Salisbury Court before the closing of the playhouses and everywhere during the Restoration and later. One aspect of the scheme was that the plays performed in his playhouse belonged not to the players but to him. Another was that it was his responsibility to keep the Master of the Revels and the parish content with what went on at the playhouse. Towards that end, Beeston offered gift after gift to both from 1623; while Henrietta Maria's men were still at the Phoenix, he and they gave Sir Henry Herbert, the Master, a share in the company, which Herbert sold to his assistant, William Blagrave, for £100.

Beeston died late in 1638, leaving the Phoenix to his widow, who installed their son, William Beeston, in the playhouse as 'Governor and instructor of the King's and Queen's young company of actors'. After Easter 1639, William Beeston enticed the playwright, Richard Brome, to abandon a contract to write plays for Salisbury Court (512) and to write them for the Phoenix instead. He undid himself early in May 1640, however, by allowing his company to perform an unlicensed and now unknown play mocking some of the King's doings that led to the second bishops' war. The Phoenix was closed for only three days, but Beeston and two players went to prison, and a poet and playwright, William Davenant, was put in charge of the company and perforce of the playhouse. A year later Davenant also got into political trouble over the Army Plot and fled London. Whereupon Beeston returned to the Phoenix and remained in charge until 2 September 1642, when Parliament closed all the playhouses.

The Phoenix was, like other playhouses, occasionally used illegally after that, the last recorded occasion being in 1649. For a few months beginning in October 1650, Beeston tried vainly but expensively to buy the freehold of the Phoenix. His mother's interest there ended with her sublease on 28 September 1656. Davenant used the Phoenix more or less legally in 1658 and 1659 for his famous plays-cum-operas, and John Rhodes was in charge in 1660 when it was the first playhouse after 1642 to offer regular plays legally. It fell out of use after a few years, partly because of competition from the Drury Lane Theatre, which opened in 1663 and was (as its successor is) about a hundred yards south along the street. The Phoenix may have ended its days converted to domestic uses.[5]

[1] For the Phoenix in general, see *J and CS*, VI, 47–77, and *CRS*, 88–100. For its location, see Rocque's *Map of London* (reproduced in Adams, *Shakespearean Playhouses*, facing 350).
[2] Orrell, *Theatres of Inigo Jones and John Webb*, 39–77. The idea depends on the inevitably tenuous dating of the architectural drawings to 1616.
[3] Barlow, 'Wenceslas Hollar', 30–44.
[4] The sheet of the map and the 'Propositions' (in which Hollar described the map and asked for funds) survive in a single copy each, the first at the British Library, the other at the Folger. Both are reproduced in *A Collection of Early Maps of London 1553–1667*, the sheet on plate 19, the 'Propositions' in the introduction, where John Fisher describes the 'Great Map'. See also Ralph Hyde's introduction (1976) to Ogilby and Morgan's *Large and Accurate Map*. Hotson (*CRS*, 91) wrote that the building shown on Hollar's map could be the playhouse, but did not pursue the idea.
[5] Barlow, 'Wenceslas Hollar', 37–8.

481 Christopher Beeston subleases property for the playhouse, 9 August 1616 and 4 May 1633

PRO, (a) C2/Chas. I/H44/66, the bill; (b) /H28/26, answer of the Kirkes. See *CRS*, 88, 89. The original subleases do not survive, but quotations or paraphrases of the main parts of them do survive in lawsuits of 1647.

(a) Buildings erected 1609–ff.

[John Best, grocer, acquired the property on 9 October 1609 and:] did shortly after erect or cause to be erected upon the said parcels of ground about seven or eight several messuages or dwelling houses with necessary outhouses and other appurtenances, as namely one messuage, house or tenement called a cockpit and afterwards used for a playhouse and now called the Phoenix with divers buildings thereto belonging, and one other messuage, house or tenement with the appurtenances adjoining to the said messuage called the Phoenix, wherein one William Sherlock sometimes dwelt and now one John Rhodes dwelleth.[1]

[1] Sherlock was an actor at the Phoenix in Lady Elizabeth's and then Henrietta Maria's men. Rhodes was a draper turned bookseller who involved himself with the Fortune in the 1630s; he formed a company at the Phoenix in 1659 and led it there when legal playing resumed in 1660 (see *J and CS*, II, 544–6).

(b) The property in 1616

[When Beeston subleased it from Best on 9 August 1616 the property consisted of:] all that edifices [*sic*] or building called the cockpits and the cockhouses and sheds thereunto adjoining, late before that time in the . . . occupation of John Atkins, gentleman, or his assigns, together also with one tenement or house and a little garden thereunto belonging next adjoining to the said cockpits, then in the occupation of Jonas Westwood or his assigns, and one part or parcel of ground behind the said cockpits, cockhouses, three tenements and garden divided as in the said indenture [*i.e.* the original sublease] is expressed: to have and to hold . . . from the feast day of St Michael the Archangel next coming after the date of the said recited indenture unto the end and term of one and thirty years . . . next ensuing . . . [Beeston] paying therefor yearly . . . £45 . . . at four of the most usual feasts in the year by equal portions . . .

[After Best's death, his widow, Katherine, on 4 May 1633] did . . . demise, grant and to farm let the same premises . . . unto the said Christopher Hutchinson, alias Beeston, . . . from the end and expiration of the said one and thirty years . . . for and during the full end and term of nine years from thence next coming, . . . [Beeston] paying therefor . . . £45 per annum.[1]

[1] In 1650 Thomas Hussey, who had acquired Katherine Best's interest in the Cockpit, said that Beeston had paid her £5 for extending the lease: PRO, C2/Chas. I/H108/34.

482 Beeston is converting the cockpit into a playhouse, 15 October 1616

Lincoln's Inn, Black Books, VI, fo. 628. Transcribed in *The Records of the Honourable Society of Lincoln's Inn, Black Books*, II, 186

[At a meeting on 15 October 1616 the benchers of Lincoln's Inn decided to send a committee to] the Queen's council, with others of the Inns of Court, touching the converting of the cockpit in the fields into a playhouse.[1]

In approaching the Queen's council rather than the privy council, the benchers evidently assumed that Beeston meant the playhouse for his own company, the Queen's men.

[1] Howes also noted that the cockpit was made into a playhouse, rather than pulled down so that a new playhouse could be built on the site: in his additions to Stow's *Annales* (1631), 1004.

483 The Queen's men are still at the Red Bull, 23 February 1617

PRO, Req.2/459/pt 1 [7th in the box], the bill. Transcribed in Wallace, 'Three London Theatres', 319

This information comes from a lawsuit in which John Smith sued the Queen's men on 10 November 1619 over material that he had supplied for costumes and for which they had not paid. For some answers to the lawsuit, see 487 below.[1]

John Smith, citizen and fishmonger of London, . . . did heretofore, between the 27th day of June in . . . 1612 and the 23rd day of February *anno domini* 1617, at the earnest request and entreaty of one Christopher Beeston, deliver or cause to be delivered ... unto and for the use of the company of players at the Red Bull, ... viz. unto Ellis Worth, Richard Perkins and John Cumber and others, divers tinsel stuffs and other stuffs for their use in playing, amounting in the whole to £46 5s 8d or thereabouts.

[1] The players and Beeston all said that they knew nothing of the transaction. Smith, however, said that the lawsuit was collusive, its purpose to have the court decide how much Beeston should pay and how much the others (PRO, Req.1/130/13 Nov. 1620; Wallace, 'Three London Theatres', 336–7). Four witnesses confirmed that the material was delivered to the Queen's men at Beeston's behest, and two of them mentioned the Red Bull.

484 Apprentices wreck the Phoenix on Shrove Tuesday during a performance by the Queen's men, 4 March 1617

PRO, (a) PC2/28, pp. 574–5; (b) SP14/90, fo. 192; (c) SP14/90, fo. 193v. Transcribed in (a) MSC, I. 374–75; (b) *Letters of John Chamberlain*, II, 59–60; (c) *J and CS*, VI, 54

The wrecking of the Phoenix during the apprentices' Shrove Tuesday riots in 1617 was much noted.[1] Below are three reports.

[1] In addition to Chamberlain and Sherburne, Howes and Camden also described the playhouse as new in their reports of the event: Howes – 'And that afternoon they spoiled a new playhouse' (his edition of Stow's *Annales* (1631), 1026); and Camden – 'A playhouse lately erected in Drury Lane was destroyed by the fury of the multitude and equipment torn in pieces' (*Annales Ab Anno 1603 ad Annum 1623*, 24). The privy council feared that the next year the apprentices would destroy the Phoenix, Fortune and Red Bull, but they did not (PRO, PC2/29, p. 268, transcribed in MSC, I, 377).

(a) By the privy council, 5 March 1617

[Writing to the Lord Mayor:] It is not unknown unto you what tumultuous outrages were yesterday committed near unto the City of London in divers places by a rout of lewd and loose persons, apprentices and others, especially in Lincoln's Inn Fields and Drury Lane, where, in attempting to pull down a playhouse belonging to the Queen's majesty's servants, there were divers persons slain and others hurt and wounded, the multitude there assembled being to the number of many thousands, as we are credibly informed.

(b) By John Chamberlain, 8 March 1617

[Writing to his regular correspondent, Sir Dudley Carleton:] Being assembled in great numbers, they [the apprentices] fell to great disorders in pulling down of houses and beating the guards that were set to keep rule, specially at a new playhouse (sometime a cockpit) in Drury Lane, where the Queen's players used to play. Though the fellows defended themselves as well as they could and slew three with shot and hurt divers, yet they [the apprentices] entered the house and defaced it, cutting the players' apparel all in pieces and all other their furniture, and burned their playbooks, and did what other mischief they could.

(c) By Edward Sherburne, 8 March 1617

[Writing also to Sir Dudley Carleton:] On Shrove Tuesday last, . . . three or four thousand [apprentices] committed extreme insolencies. Part of this number, taking their course for Wapping, did there pull down to the ground four houses . . . and a justice of peace coming to appease them, while he was reading a proclamation had his head broken with a brickbat. Th'other part, making for Drury Lane (where lately a new playhouse is erected), they beset the house round, broke in, wounded divers of the players, broke open their trunks, and what apparel, books, or other things they found they burned and cut in pieces. And not content herewith, [they] got on the top of the house and untiled it, and had not the justices of peace and sheriff levied an aid and hindered their purpose, they would have laid that house likewise even with the ground. In this skirmish one prentice was slain, being shot through the head with a pistol, and many others of their fellows were sore hurt . . .

485 The Queen's men return to the Red Bull, then reopen the Phoenix on or about 3 June 1617

PRO, C2/Jas. I/W2/67, the reply. Transcribed in Greenstreet, 'Documents Relating to the Players', 504.

The evidence that the Queen's men returned to the Red Bull after the wrecking of the Phoenix on 4 March and then reopened the Phoenix on or about 3 June appears in a lawsuit of 1623. It concerned money that the Queen's men owed to Susan Baskervile, the widow of one of their members. She said that the company agreed to repay her by means of a 'pension' paid to her and her son, William Browne, for the life 'of the longest liver of them'. When any four or more of the company should play at a playhouse within two miles of London they would pay 3s 8d a day for six days a week to an agent of the lady and her son.

[Twelve named and probably one or two other] fellows and sharers of the said company and now come or shortly to come from the said playhouse called the Red Bull to the playhouse in Drury Lane called the Cockpit, by their deed indented bearing date on or about the third day of June . . . [1617, agreed to make the payments,] . . . at the playhouse called the Cockpit in Drury Lane or at such other place or playhouse within two miles of London where the said players or any four of them should play together.

486 Contemporary playwrights allude to the nature of the building, 1619–1640

(a) Middleton, *Inner Temple Masque*, sig. B3v; (b) Heywood, *Loves Maistresse*, sig. B2, and Shirley (or Fletcher), *The Coronation*, the prologue; (c) Nabbes, *Covent Garden*

Information about the playhouse building is scanty and vague. For a dubious remark of 1699 that the Phoenix was the same shape and size as Blackfriars (which was a rectangle, 66' × 46') and Salisbury Court, see **509** n. 1.

(a) The Phoenix is made of bricks, and the Queen's men do not prosper there

In Middleton's masque, Dr Almanack says to Shrovetuesday, alluding to 1619,

> 'Tis in your charge to pull down bawdyhouses,
> To set your tribe awork, cause spoil in Shoreditch,
> And make a dangerous leak there, deface Turnbull,
> And tickle Codpiece Row, ruin the Cockpit, the
> Poor players ne'er thrived in't; a my conscience, some
> Quean pissed upon the first brick.[1]

[1] The Masque alludes to February 1619, because Candlemas complains that he 'dwells so near' to Shrovetuesday: the two days were only a week apart in 1619, 2, 9 February, and had not been so close since 1611. Turnbull, (*i.e.* Turnmill) Street and its northern extension, Codpiece Row, were notorious for the brothels in them.

(b) The auditorium is compared to a sphere

[In the frame of Heywood's play, performed at the Phoenix, Apuleius introduces Midas to the playhouse, where Apuleius will present a play about Cupid and Psyche:] Seest thou this sphere spangled with all these stars? [and in another play at the Phoenix, the female prologue tells the ladies in the audience that they:] . . . make a harmony this sphere of love.

(c) The stage may have had three doors and a balcony

[In Nabbes' play, played in 1633, many of the exits and entrances are described as] by the right scene, [or] by the middle scene, [or] by the left scene [or] in the balcony.

This play also suggests, as do two other plays by Nabbes, that scenes were changed between the acts. See *J and CS*, IV, 934; VI, 53.

487 When the Queen dies, Beeston removes the Queen's men to put Prince Charles' (I) men into the Phoenix, 1619

PRO, Req.2/459/pt I [7th in the box]. Transcribed in Wallace, 'Three London Theatres', 324, 326. These remarks are from the answers to John Smith's bill of complaint against the Queen's men, for which see 483. The Queen died on 2 March 1619.

(a) The answer of three Queen's men, 18 November 1619

[Ellis Worth, Richard Perkins and John Cumber remarked in reply] that the said Beeston, having from the beginning a greater care for his own private gain and not respecting the good of these defendants and the rest of his fellows and companions, hath in the place and trust aforesaid much enriched himself and hath of late given over his coat and condition and separated and divided himself from these defendants, carrying away not only all the furniture and apparel . . . but also suffering the complainant [Smith] to sue, molest and trouble these defendants.

(b) Beeston's answer, 23 November 1619

[Beeston said:] The company of comedians . . . supposed in the plaintiff's bill to have contracted with him, the said defendant, for the said stuffs [is] . . . since altered and the parties separated and dispersed amongst other companies . . . True it is that, about the time mentioned in the said bill, the said defendant was one of the said company of comedians attending upon the late Queen's majesty, until, after her majesty's decease, he entered into the service of the most noble Prince Charles.

488 Beeston removes Prince Charles' (I) men and installs Lady Elizabeth's, 1622

Bodleian Library, Oxford, Malone's MS note on the flyleaf of his copy of Middleton and Rowley, *The Changeling*. Transcribed by Lawrence, 'New Facts', 820. The first indication that a new company was at the Phoenix is in a note written by Malone, who was apparently transcribing an entry in the office book, now lost, of Sir Henry Herbert, the Master of the Revels:

[Herbert] Licensed [*The Changeling*] to be acted by the Lady Elizabeth's Servants at the Phoenix, 7 May 1622.

In another note, Herbert mentioned the seven principal actors at the Phoenix in 1622. They included only one who had been a member of Lady Elizabeth's before, five who had not been known as actors before, and Beeston. See *J and CS*, VI, 59.

489 Beeston removes Lady Elizabeth's men and installs Henrietta Maria's during the plague of 1625

(a) Sir Henry Herbert, Office Book (now lost); (b) Shirley, *The Wedding*, title page. Transcribed in (a) by Malone in *Plays and Poems of William Shakespeare* (1821), III, 230

This familiar assertion is largely guesswork. Lady Elizabeth's men do not appear in London after the closing for the plague of 1625; Henrietta Maria's men may have been at the Phoenix in 1626 but were not certainly there until 1629.

(a) Henrietta Maria's men are first recorded, 5 July 1627

[Malone apparently transcribed an entry under that date in Herbert's Office Book, now lost:] *The Great Duke* [by Massinger] was licensed for the Queen's [*i.e.* Henrietta Maria's] servants.

(b) They are at the Phoenix, 1629

[Though Shirley's play was published in 1629, it was first played in 1626. The title page describes it as:] lately acted by her majesty's servants at the Phoenix in Drury Lane.

490 A French company, including actresses, plays at the Phoenix without apparent objections, Lent 1635

Sir Henry Herbert, Office Book (now lost). Transcribed by Malone in *Plays and Poems of William Shakespeare* (1821), III, 121, 122

The company was Floridor's, which had just performed at Somerset House and Whitehall and, like other French companies, numbered women among its members. If women played with the company at the Phoenix, however, they created no stir that survives, unlike the French women who played at Blackfriars in 1629 (**412**). Bentley reckoned that the company played at the Phoenix about fourteen times on days when the resident company would ordinarily not have been allowed to play (*J and CS*, VI, 65–6).

[On 20 February 1635 as Herbert noted:] The King told me his pleasure and commanded me to give order that this French company should play ... in Lent and in the house of Drury Lane, where the Queen's players usually play.

The King's pleasure I signified to Mr Beeston the same day, who obeyed readily ...

They ... got £200 at least, besides many rich clothes were given them.

They had freely to themselves the whole week before the week before Easter, which I obtained of the King for them.

491 Beeston removes Henrietta Maria's men and installs the King's and Queen's boys, 1636–1637

(a) House of Lords, MS 3488; (b) Sir Henry Herbert, Office Book (now lost); (c) PRO, LC5/134, p. 151; (d) PRO, SP16/339/fo. 21. Transcribed in (a) HMC, *House of Lords*, XI, 243; (b) Malone in *Plays and Poems of William Shakespeare* (1821), III, 239; (c) MSC, II. 382; (d) *CSP, Dom.*, 1636–7, p. 254

The first remark below describes events that must have occurred after the privy council closed the playhouses on 10 May 1636 because of plague (PRO, PC2/46, p. 144, transcribed in MSC, II. 391–2). They remained closed almost continuously until 2 October 1637.

(a) Beeston expels Henrietta Maria's men, after 10 May 1636

[In an undated petition to the House of Lords of, probably, 1640, the widow of Sir Henry Herbert's assistant, William Blagrave, recalled that:] Mr Beeston, being master of the said playhouse [the Phoenix], . . . takes occasion to quarrel with the company to the end he might have a company that would take what he would be willing to give them. And upon this falling out, some of them go to Blackfriars and some to Salisbury Court playhouses, and those of Salisbury Court are made the Queen's [i.e. Henrietta Maria's] company. [See 513.]

(b) Beeston leads a new company at court, 7, 14 February 1637

[Sir Henry Herbert noted two performances at Court: Fletcher's] *Cupid's Revenge*, at St James, by Beeston's boys, the 7 February [1637 and Beaumont and Fletcher's] *Wit Without Money*, by the B boys at St James, the 14 February [1637].

(c) Beeston is made governor of the boys, 21 February 1637

[The Lord Chamberlain's office noted that it had issued:] A warrant to swear Mr Christopher Beeston his majesty's servant in the place of governor of the new company of the King's and Queen's boys.

(d) Beeston tries the boys out in public, c. 12 May 1637

He, his son, William, and three others at the Phoenix were arrested on 12 May 1637 for performing a play before the plague was over (PRO, PC2/47, p. 403, transcribed in MSC, I, 392). So he wrote to the privy council:

Your petitioner, being commanded to erect and prepare a company of young actors for their majesties' service and desirous to know how they had profected [i.e. advanced] by his instructions, he invited some noble gentlemen to see them act at his house, the Cockpit. For which (since he perceives it is imputed a fault) he is very sorry, humbly craving . . . pardon and promiseth not to offend in the like nature [again].

492 Beeston dies, leaving the Phoenix to his widow and son, William, late 1638

PRO, PROB. 11/178/fos. 450v–51v. Transcribed in *CRS*, 398–400

At his death, Beeston owned not only the sublease on the site of the playhouse, hence the playhouse itself, but also two-thirds of the shares in the company that played there (the company owned the other third). Beeston drew up his will disposing of these possessions on 4 and 7 October 1638 and died before 3 December, when his widow proved the will.

[Beeston did not mention the Phoenix in his will but did] give unto my said executrix [his wife], after my debts paid, legacies performed and funeral charges defrayed, the residue of all and singular my goods and chattels whatsoever [including his sublease on the Phoenix] . . .

[As to his shares in the company, he wrote on 4 October:] Whereas I stand possessed of four of the six shares in the company for the King's and Queen's service at the Cockpit in Drury Lane, I declare that two of my said four shares shall be delivered up for the advancement of the said company and the other two to remain unto my said executrix as fully and amply as if I lived amongst them. And I will that my said executrix shall for the two said shares provide and find for the said company a sufficient and good stock of apparel fitting for their use, she allowing and paying to my son, William Hutchinson [alias Beeston], for his care and industry in the said company, £20 . . . per annum.

[And on 7 October he added:] Now my will and mind is, and I do hereby order and devise, that my said executrix, in lieu of the said £20 per annum, shall allow unto him, my said son, . . . one-half share of the two shares in the said company within mentioned for his care in the business, she finding and providing a stock of apparel for the said company as is within declared.

493 William Beeston is confirmed as director of the company at the Phoenix, 5 April 1639

PRO, LC5/134, p. 326. Transcribed in MSC, II, 389

[The Lord Chamberlain recorded] A warrant to swear Mr William Beeston . . . in the quality and under the title of governor and instructor of the King and Queen's young company of actors.

494 William Beeston gets into trouble and is replaced at the Phoenix by William Davenant, early May – June 1640

(a) Brome, *The Court Beggar*, sig. S8–8v; (b) PRO, LC5/134, p. 392; (c) Sir Henry Herbert, Office Book (now lost); (d) PRO, LC5/134, p. 405. Transcribed in (b, d) MSC, II, 393–4, 395; (c) Malone in *Plays and Poems of William Shakespeare* (1821), III, 241

William Beeston's management was threatened, it seems, even before his actors performed a play that caused the Lord Chamberlain to remove him and put Davenant in charge of the company at the Phoenix. Despite this event, Beeston and his mother continued to own their two shares in the company and she to own the playhouse itself.

(a) Beeston is threatened but is a success, spring 1640

[Brome addressed the epilogue of his play (probably played in the spring of 1640) to William Beeston:] And to be serious with you [the audience], if, after all this, by the venomous practice of some who study nothing more than his [Beeston's] destruction, he should fail us, both poets and players would be at a loss in reputation . . . But this small poet [Brome] vents but his own [wit], and his [Beeston's], by whose care and directions this stage is governed, who has for many years, both in his father's days and since, directed poets to write and players to speak till he trained up these youths here to what they are now, ay, some of 'em from before they were able to say a grace of two lines long to have more parts in their pates than would fill so many dryfats [large containers used to hold dry goods].

(b) Beeston mounts a play criticising the King, 1–2 May 1640

[On 3 May 1640 the Lord Chamberlain ordered:] Whereas William Beeston and the company of the players of the Cockpit in Drury Lane have lately acted a new play without any licence from the Master of his majesty's Revels, and, being commanded likewise to forbear all manner of playing, have, notwithstanding, in contempt of the authority of the said Master of the Revels and the power granted unto him under the great seal of England, acted the said play and others to the prejudice of his majesty's service and in contempt of the Office of the Revels [by which] he and they and all other companies have been and ought to be governed and regulated: These are, therefore, in his majesty's name and signification of his royal pleasure, to command the said William Beeston and the rest of that company of the Cockpit players from henceforth and upon sight hereof to forbear to act any plays whatsoever until they shall be restored by the said Master of the Revels unto their former liberty, and conform accordingly, as they and every one of them will answer it at their peril.

(c) Beeston is imprisoned and the playhouse closed, 4–6 May 1640

[On or after 7 May 1640 the Master of the Revels noted:] On Monday the 4 May 1640 William Beeston was taken by a messenger and committed to the Marshalsea [prison] by my Lord Chamberlain's warrant for playing a play without licence. The same day the company at the Cockpit was commanded by my Lord Chamberlain's warrant to forbear playing, for playing when they were forbidden by me, and for other disobedience, and [they] lay still Monday, Tuesday and Wednesday. On Thursday at my Lord Chamberlain's entreaty . . .and upon their petition of submission subscribed by the players, I restored them to their liberty . . . The play I called for and, forbidding the playing of it, keep the book, because it had relation to the passages of the King's journey into the north and was complained of by his majesty to me with command to punish the offenders.

(d) Davenant is director at the Phoenix, 27 June 1640

[The Lord Chamberlain formally appointed Davenant:] to take into his government and care the said company of players, to govern, order and dispose of them . . . and all their affairs in the said house as in his discretion shall seem best to conduce to his majesty's service in that quality. And I do hereby enjoin and command them all . . . that they obey the said Mr Davenant and follow his orders and directions as they will answer the contrary, which power of privilege he is to continue and enjoy during that lease which Mrs Elizabeth Beeston . . . hath . . . in the said playhouse, provided he be still accountable to me for his care and well ordering the said company.

495 Davenant flees London because of the Army Plot, and William Beeston resumes at the Phoenix, May 1641

PRO, LC3/1. Transcribed in MSC, II. 326

Nothing is known of Davenant's regime at the Phoenix, but on 7 July, shortly after he took over, Beeston's mother mortgaged the playhouse for £150 to an actor, William Wilbraham (PRO, C2/Chas. I/H108/34). Then a year after Beeston's debacle, Davenant suffered one, too. He was caught up with the poet, Sir John Suckling, and other royalists in the Army Plot, an attempt to use the army to suppress Parliament, and with them he fled London (see Gardiner, *History of England from the Accession of James I to the Outbreak of the Civil War*, IX, 312–60). The only evidence of what happened at the Phoenix after Davenant's flight is the following.

Establishment list of servants of the chamber in 1641
Governor of the Cockpit players, William Beeston.

496 The Phoenix is closed with all the other playhouses, 2 September 1642, then is sometimes used illegally

(a) PRO, C2/Chas. I/H108/34, and *Mercurius Elencticus*, 19–26 January 1648; (b) Folger Library, MS V.b.275, p 16; (c) PRO, C2/Chas. I/B160/113 (the bill), C10/35/29, and C10/128/27 (the bill). Transcribed in (b) Collier, *Works of William Shakespeare*, I, ccxli–ii

Parliament closed all the playhouses on 2 September 1642, but the Phoenix, like others, occasionally housed illegal performances thereafter. Quarrels arose over the payment of the rent for the sublease and who should collect it (see CRS, 94–100), and a dubious manuscript reported that the playhouse was pulled down in 1649. It was not pulled down, however, nor, probably, even damaged. It was worth a good deal of money in 1650–1, was available for performances in 1658 and 1659, and became a proper playhouse again in 1660, not under William Beeston, who had acquired Salisbury Court in 1652, but John Rhodes (see 481 n. 1).

(a) Illegal performances, 1647–1648

[Thomas Hussey, the man to whom William Beeston's mother and her then husband, Sir Lewis Kirke, were to pay the rent for the sublease, said on 10 May 1650 that they had not paid a good deal of it:] Although they do make a very great constant yearly profit [by renting out parts of the premises] . . . and sometimes a very extraordinary profit, for in several nights since the . . . feast of St Michael [29 September] 1647 they have gained by acting of plays there about £30 or £40 a night.

[And in the week of 19–26 January 1648 a newspaper remarked:] Where a dozen coaches tumble after Obadiah Sedgewick [a preacher], three-score are observed to wheel to the Cockpit. [See **516b** and **503c**.]

(b) The Phoenix is said to have been pulled down, 1649

[This passage follows and alludes to one about Salisbury Court (**517b**).] The Phoenix in Drury Lane was pulled down also this day, being Saturday the 24 day of March 1649 by the same soldiers.

(c) Beeston tries to buy the Phoenix, October – March 1650–1651[1]

William Beeston set out in October 1650 to buy the freehold of the Phoenix and as a result eventually made a remark that Hotson took as confirming the remark in (b) above (*CRS*, 95, 99). The seller and Beeston agreed that Beeston would take possession of the Phoenix in 1653 or 1657 or at some time in between, depending partly whether the seller could remove the sitting tenant, Beeston's mother.[2] Beeston paid £151 (or £150) on 2 January 1651, but could not pay the remaining £201 on 24 March as agreed. He filed a lawsuit on 2 June to get his down payment back and returned to a scheme to buy Salisbury Court. In the lawsuit he said nothing of damage, soldiers, having possession of the Phoenix or spending money on it; and in a reply his mother said that she still possessed it and knew nothing of his scheme to buy it. The lawsuit failed because he was an 'outlaw' – had not paid sums awarded against him in previous lawsuits. He filed much the same lawsuit in 1672, therefore, but added a claim for damages: he said that he 'entered upon' the Phoenix after 2 January 1651 and spent nearly £200 'repairing and fitting the same for . . . [his] occasions, and [he] took apprentices' and hired men 'to instruct them in the quality of acting and fitting them for the stage, for which the said premises were so repaired and amended'. Even in 1672 he did not mention damage caused by soldiers or anybody else. These remarks of 1672, therefore, probably had to do with Salisbury Court (on which he did spend a good deal of money) rather than the Phoenix. See **517**.

[1] See Berry, 'Folger Ms. V.b.275'.
[2] If Beeston could not have possession at Christmas 1653, he was to receive £45 a year until the seller could give him possession, the latest date for which was 18 December (Beeston thought Christmas) 1657, when the main lease expired (PRO, C5/21/89, Hussey's answer). Beeston's mother's sublease expired at Michaelmas 1656 (**481b**).

XXXVII The second Fortune

The second Fortune playhouse was a new building that replaced the first, which had been destroyed by fire on the night of 9 December 1621. The second was built on much the same site as the first, between Whitecross Street and Golden Lane where Fortune Street, E.C.1, joins them. It was, therefore, in Middlesex about a hundred yards north of the City boundary, and in the parish of St Giles Cripplegate. The main entry, like that of the first, seems to have been via Golden Lane. In July 1656, after its theatrical life was over, the second enterprise consisted of a playhouse and tap-house on a piece of ground 127 feet east to west and 129 feet north to south.[1]

At the time of the fire, Edward Alleyn owned the playhouse and buildings around it, having acquired much of the place on his own and inherited Philip Henslowe's part in 1616 and 1617. He was organising the building of a new playhouse some four months after the fire: he paid for dinner 'with the builders of the Fortune' on 16 April 1622, and ten days later he paid for wine with them.[2] The chief builders were Thomas Wigpitt, a bricklayer, and Anthony Jarman, a carpenter.

Alleyn meant that the company burned out of the first Fortune, his old company now called the Palsgrave's men, should return to the second, and he continued to own the land on which the second stood. He simply abandoned, however, the scheme of finance and management that he had devised for the first in 1618 (425), with, presumably, the approval of the others involved.

He organised instead a consortium whose members held twelve shares, one of which he initially kept for himself. All the shares were in the form of leases on the ground where the new playhouse would stand, which were for fifty-one years beginning on 24 June 1622. The holder or holders of each share paid Alleyn £10 13s 10d a year in rent and the builders £83 6s 8d towards the cost of building the playhouse. He, she or they received a twelfth of the profits of the playhouse, paid a twelfth of the expenses, and agreed not to convert the place into something other than a playhouse. The playhouse, therefore, was to continue until 1673. The sharers were to provide £1,000 to build the playhouse, and Alleyn was to receive £128 6s a year in rent, both sums including money for Alleyn's own share. According to the arrangement of 1618 for the first Fortune, he had received £200 a year in rent, and his heirs were to receive £120 a year after his death.

The initial leases were dated 20 May 1622, by which time Alleyn had settled the design of the playhouse but the builders had not begun work. Alleyn granted six leases for a twenty-fourth each, six for a twelfth each, and one for two-twelfths (reissued in June 1623 as two for a twelfth each), plus the twelfth he kept for himself. Half the shares belonged to Alleyn and others who had to do with the playhouse in other ways. Players among the Palsgrave's men held three shares – Charles Massey a share and a half, Richard Gunnell one share, and Richard Price a half-share. Frances Juby, the widow of a Palsgrave's man, held a half-share.

Jarman, the carpenter, held one share and Wigpitt, the bricklayer, half a share. The six other sharers were, apparently, merely investors.

By March 1623 plays were being performed in the new playhouse. Between then and the spring of 1624 sharers surrendered four shares of a twelfth each, presumably because they preferred not to make the payments the leases required, especially to the builders. Alleyn recruited new sharers, mostly from 29 January to 21 April 1624, to take up new leases with the same conditions as the old. Three of these new leases were for a twelfth each and three for a twenty-fourth each, so that Alleyn's own stake became a half-share. The sharers must now have finished paying for the erection of the playhouse, making all the leases partly obsolete and the granting of further leases unnecessary, for Alleyn seems to have granted no others.[3]

As at the first Fortune and other playhouses, the sharers at the second must have collected rents on buildings other than the playhouse and kept the place in repair. The players must have paid the costs of productions and used the playhouse in return for giving the sharers half the takings in the galleries and other privileged places.

Little is known about the physical aspects of the second Fortune because the contract with its builders (a 'plotform') does not survive and contemporary descriptions of it are few and far between. It was not, it seems, a copy of the first. Unlike the first Fortune, which was a square timber-frame building, the second was apparently a round brick building. It had, like other playhouses, two gates, and, inevitably, its sign was a picture of Dame Fortune.

The Palsgrave's men used their new playhouse for only two years. The closing of all playhouses for the death of King James in the spring of 1625 and then for the horrific plague that immediately followed finished them and every other company except the King's men. For fifteen years thereafter, the Fortune housed a series of 'shadowy' and undistinguished companies: the King and Queen of Bohemia's men (partly made up of remnants of the Palsgrave's men, including the three sharers), then the men of the King's Revels, then the 'Red Bull–King's players'. When this last company and the company at the Red Bull exchanged playhouses in April 1640, the Fortune at last acquired notable actors in the men of Prince Charles (II), who remained until the closing of the playhouses on 2 September 1642.[4]

Alleyn died on 25 November 1626, leaving his interest in the Fortune to the college he had founded at Dulwich. That body, therefore, became the landlord of the property and a sharer holding a twenty-fourth of the playhouse and other buildings until 1673. By 1656, however, the College had become not only landlord but holder of all the shares, because, no doubt, the other sharers had long since stopped paying their rent.

As at other playhouses, illegal performances took place at the Fortune after 1642, the last recorded one in 1649. The building was ruinous in 1656 for lack of repair, and the College decided in 1660 to redevelop the site as a housing estate, even though playing was legal again. Beginning in 1661, a builder 'totally demolished' the playhouse and by the spring of 1662 had built twenty 'messuages' where it had stood and on 'other ground thereunto belonging'. The playhouse, however, refused to die in the mind's eye. People thought in 1653 and 1658 that it would be refurbished. A historian of London assured his readers in 1739 that its ruins were 'still to be seen'. And George Shepherd issued an engraving in 1811 and 1819 of a building in Golden Lane – almost certainly on the wrong site – whose façade and other walls and at least part of an upper floor were supposed to have belonged to the playhouse.

---

[1] Dulwich, MS I, fo. 225, transcribed in *Henslowe Papers*, ed. Greg, 95–6.
[2] Dulwich, MS IX, fo. 58v, transcribed in Young, *History of Dulwich College*, II, 234, 235.

[3] For a list of the leases, see *Henslowe Papers*, ed. Greg, 28–30, 112.
[4] *J and CS*, VI, 159–60, 162–9.

497 Alleyn forms a consortium to own the second Fortune playhouse for fifty-one years, 20 May 1622

Dulwich, Mun. 58. Transcribed in *Henslowe Papers*, ed. Greg, 28–30. The quotations below are from one of the thirteen similar leases by which Alleyn organised the ownership of the playhouse into twelve parts. Alleyn leased to Charles Massey, an actor, a twelfth and a twenty-fourth part (share) of the playhouse.

[His twenty-fourth share was of:] all that part or parcel of ground upon part whereof lately stood a playhouse . . . called the Fortune, with a taphouse belonging to the same, a tenement in the occupation of Mark Brigham, one other tenement heretofore demised to one John Russell, one other tenement in the occupation of William Bird, alias Bourne, and one other tenement in the occupation of John Parson: containing in breadth from east to west 130 feet and in length 131 feet 8 inches or thereabout . . . [also] one other messuage or tenement containing a shop or chamber and a garret towards the street and two rooms and a garret behind the same, and one yard thereto belonging, late in the tenure of William Garrell and now in the occupation of Henry Smith, situate on the north side of a way leading to the said playhouse. All situate . . . between Whitecross Street and Golden Lane, . . . upon part of which said ground there is intended to be erected and set up a new playhouse.

[The term was fifty-one years from 24 June 1622 and the rent was £5 6s 11d a year. Moreover,] the said Charles Massey is to pay, or cause to be paid, unto Anthony Jarman and Thomas Wigpitt [the builders of the new playhouse] for the new building and erecting of a playhouse in Golden Lane aforesaid, according to a plotform by them already drawn, the sum of £41 13s 4d, proportionably according to the four and twentieth part thereof and according to such days and times as [are explained] in one pair of indentures . . . bearing date with these presents [*i.e.* 20 May 1622], made between Thomas Wigpitt [½], citizen and bricklayer of London, and Anthony Jarman [1], citizen and carpenter of London, of the one part; and Thomas Sparkes [1], citizen and merchant tailor of London, William Gwalter [2], citizen and innholder of London, Richard Gunnell [1] of London, gentleman, Charles Massey [1½] of London, gentleman, Richard Price [½] of London, gentleman, Adam Islipp [1] of London, stationer, John Fisher [½] of London, barber surgeon, Edward Jackson [1] of London, gentleman, and Frances Juby [½] of Southwark, . . . widow, of the other part.[1]

[Massey was also to pay a proportionate part of all repairs, and] not at any time hereafter [to] divide, part, alter, transport, or otherwise convert the . . . edifices and buildings that now are or shall be hereafter erected and set up as is aforesaid to any other use or uses than as a playhouse for recreation of his majesty's subjects, his heirs', and successors'.

[1] These people, including Wigpitt and Jarman, were the original sharers (their shares shown in brackets), plus Alleyn himself, who had a full share. The list omits George Massey, citizen and merchant tailor, who had half a share.

498 The playhouse may open in March, and the Palsgrave's men are there *c.* 23 May 1623

(a) *Vox Graculi, or Iacke Dawes Prognostication . . . For this yeere 1623* (1623), sig. D2; (b) PRO, Req.1/132/29 Jan., 21 Jac. I. See *J and CS*, VI, 157

No evidence specifically describes the opening of the second Fortune playhouse, but a witty almanac for 1623 and an affidavit suggest that it was to open in March and that the Palsgrave's men were there on 23 May 1623. The Palsgrave's men had been at the first Fortune from its beginning.

(a) The almanac

The dugs of this delicate young bedfellow to the sun [*i.e.* the spring] will so flow with the milk of profit and plenty that (of all other) some players (if fortune turned phoenix fail not of her promise) will lie sucking at them with their fulsome forecastings for pence and twopences like young pigs at a sow newly farrowed . . .

[And for March the jackdaw says, among other things,] As for thunder and lightning, you shall be sure to have . . . store this month at the Fortune in Golding Lane . . .

(b) The affidavit

[Paul Tey, an official of the Court of Requests, swore on 29 January 1624] that on or about 23 May last, he warned Richard Clayton, Richard Grace, William Stratford and Abraham Pedel, all actors at the Fortune near Golden Lane [and all Palsgrave's men] . . . in their several persons . . . that [together with three other men who were not actors] all and every of them should upon the 25th day of the same month make their personal appearances in this court.

499 Contemporaries describe the second Fortune playhouse, 1627–1699

(a) Heywood, *The English Traveller* (1633), sigs. I3v–I4; (b) Stow, *Annales* (1631), sig. Iiiiv; (c) *The Weekly Account* (4 October 1643), 1; (d) Dulwich, MS I, fo. 225; (e) Wright? *Historia Histrionica* (London, 1699), 6. Transcribed in (d) *Henslowe Papers*, ed. Greg, 96. See *J and CS*, VI, 154–6, 174, 177, and *ES*, IV, 371–2

Nobody described the playhouse at large during the seventeenth century and few people alluded even to parts of it. The information that it was round, the most interesting way in which it may have differed from its predecessor, depends entirely on a remark made fifty years after the last recorded performance in the place.

(a) The playhouse sign, c. 1627
In a play produced c. 1627, Thomas Heywood alluded to:

the picture of Dame Fortune
Before the Fortune playhouse.

(b) The second Fortune is far fairer than the first, 1631
[In his continuation of Stow's *Annales*, Edmund Howes wrote of both Fortunes:] a fair, strong, new-built playhouse near Golding Lane called the Fortune by negligence of a candle was clean burned to the ground but shortly after rebuilt far fairer.

(c) The playhouse has two gates, 1643
[A report of a raid on an illegal performance at the Fortune on 2 October 1643:] The players at the Fortune in Golding Lane . . . persevering in their forbidden art, this day there was set a strong guard of pikes and muskets on both gates of the playhouse, and in the middle of their [the players'] play they [the guard] unexpectedly did press into the stage upon them . . .

(d) The playhouse has, among other things, brick walls, 1656
[Dulwich College hired two surveyors to report on the state of the building in 1656, and they reported on 18 July 1656 that:] by reason the lead hath been taken from the said building, the tiling not secured, and the foundation of the said playhouse not kept in good repair, . . . the timber thereof much decayed and rotten, and the brick walls so rent and torn, . . . and . . . much shaken, [the structure could not be repaired; it would be dangerous to demolish and its materials worth only £80].

(e) The playhouse was round, 1699
[A character in a dialogue says that Edward Alleyn] built the Fortune playhouse from the ground, a large, round, brick building.

500 Naval seamen riot at the Fortune, mid-May 1626; and apprentices catch Dr Lambe there, 13 June 1628

(a) LMA, MJ/SR 649/53–8; (b) *A Briefe Description of the notorious Life of . . . Doctor Lambe. Together with his Ignominious Death* (1628), sigs. C3v–C4. See (a) Jeaffreson, *Middlesex County Records*, III, 161–3; (b) *J and CS*, VI, 161–2

The Middlesex authorities gaoled six sailors from the Royal Navy (one not directly involved in the riot) and released them when each gave bonds of £66 13s 4d to guarantee that he would appear in court and, in the meantime, keep the King's peace. The affair of Dr Lambe is reported in many places, including several letters, a pamphlet (quoted below), a popular ballad, and probably a play.[1] Lambe was an astrologer patronised by the Duke of Buckingham, and both were unpopular. Some apprentices saw Lambe at a play at the Fortune. After the play, they and others pursued him into the City and, though he hired sailors to protect him, beat him to death.

[1] The play is lost. In 1634 it was described as an old play called *Dr Lambe and the Witches* (see *J and CS*, v, 1455).

(a) Men of the Royal Navy

The bonds relate to the same event and are dated 16 or 18 May 1626. Each sailor bonded himself for 100 marks (£66 13s 4d) and got two others to bond themselves for £50 each. The bonds describe the sailors as taking part in

a dangerous and great riot committed in Whitecross Street at the Fortune playhouse, [and each then adds a particular charge against the particular man: 1. James Carver, 16 May,] especially for striking, beating and assaulting Francis Foster, the constable, and Thomas Faulkner, an inhabitant at the Fortune playhouse. [2. Thomas Alderson, 16 May,] for joining with the rest of the rioters in beating and assaulting of Thomas Faulkner . . . and, being charged in the King's name to yield and keep the peace, he said he cared not for the King, for the King paid them no wages and therefore he cared not; and further saying he would bring the whole navy thither to pull down the playhouse. [3. Patrick Gray, 18 May, for] calling to his fellow-sailors to knock them all down that were present. [4. Robert Franke, 18 May,] for giving out that if they, the sailors, were not put in a stronger house than the New Prison they would all be fetched out before the next morrow. [5. William Collinson, 18 May,] for assaulting and striking of Edward Heather, the headborough [*i.e.* a policeman].

[6. Richard Margrave, 16 May, was gaoled] for publishing certain discoveries of an intended assembly at the Beargarden [*i.e.* the Hope] for revenge of an injury done to a sailor and that there would be a captain, a drum and colours to go with them, and afterwards for denying it upon examination . . .

(b) Apprentices and Dr Lambe

Upon Friday, being the 13 of June . . . 1628, he [Dr Lambe] went to see a play at the Fortune, where the boys of the town and other unruly people,[1] having observed him present, after the play was ended flocked about him and (after the manner of the common people, who follow a hubbub when once it is afoot) began in a confused manner to assault him and offer violence. He, in affright, made for the City as fast as he could out of the fields.

[1] Identified in other accounts as apprentices.

501 The Fortune is compared unfavourably with the Blackfriars, 1632

Bodleian, Ashmole MS 38, p. 15. Transcribed in *J and CS*, vi, 163

When Ben Jonson's *Magnetic Lady* failed at Blackfriars in October 1632, Alexander Gill thought the play might have succeeded among the less discriminating audience at the Fortune. The 'loadstone' was both the magnetic lady who drew all to her and the play itself.

> Is this your loadstone, Ben, that must attract
> Applause and laughter at each scene and act?
> Is this the child of your bed-ridden wit,[1]
> And none but the Blackfriars to foster it?
> If to the Fortune you had sent your lady,
> Mongst prentices and apple-wives, it may be
> Your rosy fool might have some sport begot . . .

[1] Jonson was paralysed in 1628 and spent much of his life thereafter in his chamber.

502 Memorable players perform at the Fortune during the last two years of legal playing there, 1640–1642

(a) *Mercurius Pragmaticus (for King Charls II)*, 22–9 January, 1650; (b) Gayton, *Pleasant Notes upon Don Quixot* (1654), 271; (c) Tatham? *Knavery in all Trades: or the Coffee-House* (1664), sigs. D4v–E; (d) Chapman, *Thermae redivivae: the City of Bath Described* (1673), 16. See *J and CS*, vi, 170–3. Prince Charles' (II) men, who played at the Fortune from 1640 until Parliament closed the playhouses in 1642, would be long remembered, especially Andrew Cane (the clown), Richard Fowler, Matthew Smith and Ellis Worth.

(a) Cane, 1650

[A pamphleteer complained in 1650 that the only players and stages now allowed were Members of Parliament and the places where they gathered:] those are the men now in request. Andrew Cane is out of date and all other his complices.

(b) Fowler and Cane, 1654

A writer remembered what used to happen (at, perhaps, the Fortune) during certain festivals like Shrovetide if players did not perform as audiences wished.

The benches, the tiles, the laths, the stones, oranges, apples, nuts flew about most liberally, and as there were mechanics of all professions who fell every one to his own trade and dissolved a house in an instant and made a ruin of a stately fabric. It was not then the most mimical nor fighting man, Fowler nor Andrew Cane, could pacify. Prologues nor epilogues would prevail. The devil and the fool were quite out of favour. Nothing but noise and tumult fills the house . . .

(c) Smith, Worth and Fowler, 1664

In a play, unnamed gentlemen trade anecdotes about former players.

[THE FOURTH GENTLEMAN, REFERRING TO A PRODUCTION OF JANUARY 1664:] 'tis impossible they [*i.e.* modern players] should do anything so well as I have seen things done:
FIFTH: When Taylor, Lowin, and Pollard [all King's men at Blackfriars and the Globe] were alive.
FOURTH: Did you not know Benfield and Swanston [also King's men]?
FIFTH: Did I not know 'em? Yes and hummed them off a hundred times.
FOURTH: But did you know Mat Smith, Ellis Worth, and Fowler at the Fortune?
FIFTH: Yes... [and he tells an anecdote about Fowler, who 'was appointed for the conquering parts'.]

(d) Cane, 1673

[A writer mocked the fashion of equipping pamphlets with appendices:] THE APPENDIX, Without which a pamphlet nowadays finds as... small acceptance as a comedy did formerly at the Fortune playhouse without a jig of Andrew Cane's into the bargain.

503 The playhouse is closed with all the others in 1642 but is used for illegal performances, 1643–1649

(a) *Mercurius Veridicus*, 19–26 April 1645; (b) *The Ladies, A Second Time Assembled in Parliament* (1647), 279; (c) *Kingdom's Weekly Intelligencer*, 18–25 January 1648; (d) *Kingdom's Weekly Intelligencer*, 12–19 September 1648 (see *J and CS*, VI, 176–8)

Although Parliament ordered the playhouses closed on 2 September 1642, players and others continued to use the Fortune occasionally until at least January 1649. Knowledge of these performances derives from the authorities' many attempts to stop them, for one of which see 499c.

(a) Fencing, 19–26 April 1645

A waterman and a shoemaker met at the Fortune playhouse to play at several weapons, at which (though they had but private summons) many were present. And in the midst of their pastime, divers of the trained bands [*i.e.* London militia] beset the house and, some constables being present, had choice of fit men to serve the King and Parliament [as soldiers].

(b) Plays, 2 August 1647

[A witty account of a session of a fictitious parliament of ladies: when the house assembled,] the first thing they fell upon was a complaint... against players, who, contrary to an ordinance, had set up shop again and acted divers plays at the two houses, the Fortune and Salisbury Court. Whereupon it was demanded what plays they were, and the answer being given that one of them was *The Scornful Lady*, the house took it in high disdain . . . [1]

[1] The fictitious goings-on in the ladies' parliament were probably based on fact, for a newspaper, *Perfect Occurrences*, 6–13 August 1647, reported that a complaint arrived at the real Parliament on 11 August, about 'players acting plays publicly at the Fortune and Salisbury Court. The House wondered at the neglect of the justices of the peace therein to permit them . . . [and] passed a vote that order be given to the justices to take care speedily to suppress them.' And for the week of 30 August – 4 September 1647 *Mercurius Melancholicus* reported 'the unfortunate accident which happened at the Fortune playhouse, the actors . . . being taken away by some industrious officers to prevent such dangerous assemblies, and so the play was spoiled'.

(c) A play, 20 January 1648

It is very observable that on Sunday 23 January there were ten coaches to hear Dr Ussher [Archbishop of Armagh] at Lincoln's Inn, but there were about six-score coaches on the last Thursday in Golden Lane to hear the players at the Fortune. [See also 496a.]

(d) Plays, 12–19 September 1648

Despite an ordinance of 9 February 1648 (see 457b), in which Parliament ordered the destruction of all buildings used for playing or watching playing, the arresting and whipping of actors, the fining of spectators, and the confiscation of money taken at plays, playing at the Fortune continued:

Stage plays were daily acted either at the [Red] Bull or Fortune or the private house at Salisbury Court.

(e) Rope-dancing, 2–9 January 1649

The last notice of a performance at the Fortune refers to rope-dancing. See Salisbury Court, 516b.

504 The second Fortune playhouse comes to an end, 1649–1739

(a) Folger, Ms. V.b.275, p. 16; (b) Sir Aston Cokayne, verses for Brome's *Five New Plays* (1653), 16; (c) Dulwich, MS I, fo. 225; (d) HMC, *Le Fleming*, 23; (e) *Mercurius Publicus*, 14–21 February 1661; (f) Dulwich, Ms. I, fos. 234, 256, 257; (g) Maitland, *History of London* (1739), II, 1370. Transcribed in (a) Collier, *The Works of William Shakespeare*, I, ccxli–ii, n.; (c) *Henslowe Papers*, ed. Greg, 96. Reproduced in (f) *Henslowe Papers*, ed. Foakes, II

The document quoted in (a) was accepted as genuine by, for example, Chambers (*ES*, II, 443) and Bentley (*J and CS*, VI, 177), but it is probably a forgery and is in any event unreliable. Information about the end of the Fortune is better sought in such documents as those quoted in (b) and following. See Berry, 'Folger Ms. V.b.275'.

(a) The Fortune is said to have been pulled down on the inside, 1649

The Fortune playhouse between Whitecross Street and Golding Lane was burned down to the ground in the year 1618 [*i.e.* 1621], and built again with brickwork on the outside in the year 1622. And now pulled down on the inside by these soldiers this 1649.[1]

[1] No other remark about the end of the Fortune says that the building was pulled down on the inside. This one may do so because in 1811 and 1819 the walls of a building in Golden Lane, especially the façade, were supposed to be those of the playhouse, as was at least part of an upper floor. That building, however, was almost certainly on the wrong site. See the sheet containing a picture drawn by George Shepherd and a map, published by Robert Wilkinson in 1811 and, with an explanatory essay, as part of his *Londina Illustrata* (London, 1819), I. 2, fos. 188–9 in the pencilled foliation of the copy at the BL, MAPS 24.b.4, 5.

(b) A prediction that the place would reopen, 1653

In a poem for an edition of Brome's plays (for Jack Pudding, see 516 n. 2):

> Our Theatres of lower note in those
> More happy days shall scorn the rustic prose
> Of a Jack Pudding and will please the rout
> With wit enough to bear their credit out.
> The Fortune will be lucky, see no more
> Her benches bare, as they have stood before.

(c) The building is ruinous, 18 July 1656

In 1656, Dulwich College, now the sole owner of the Fortune, hired two men to investigate the state of the building. The men reported in July that:

great part of the said playhouse is fallen to the ground.

More of their remarks are quoted in 499d.

(d) But a man says it is being refurbished, 15 October 1658

A letter from Dr Thomas Smith at Cockermouth in Cumberland to Sir Daniel Fleming at Rydal Hall in Westmorland, reporting news received from Humphrey Robinson in London:

Sir William Davenant, the poet laureate, has obtained permission for stage plays, and the Fortune playhouse is being trimmed up.

Davenant was organising theatricals at the time, but if he meant to use the Fortune, he changed his mind.

(e) The site is to be redeveloped, 1660–1661

[Having decided on 5 March 1660 to redevelop the site, Dulwich College placed this advertisement in a journal of 14–21 February:] The Fortune playhouse . . . with the ground thereto belonging is to be let to build upon, where twenty-three tenements may be erected, with gardens, and a street may be cut through [presumably from Whitecross Street to Golden Lane] for the better accommodation of the building.

No one hastened to take up the lease, and on 16 March the College sold the useful material of the playhouse for £75 (Dulwich, MS I, fo. 231, transcribed in *Henslowe Papers*, ed. Greg, 95 n.).

(f) The Fortune is no more, 1661–1662

[On 24 July 1661 officials of Dulwich College noted that the playhouse had been demolished and new buildings erected on part of the site, and on 4 March 1662 that:] The said playhouse was very ruinous, decayed and fallen down and is since totally demolished . . . [And] William Beaven . . . hath . . . new built and erected on the ground whereon the said late playhouse stood and on certain other ground thereunto belonging twenty messuages or tenements with backsides, gardens and other conveniences . . . [And, on 28 July 1662 one official noted that Beaven] hath lately erected [several tenements] upon the ground [on] which the late demolished Fortune playhouse stood and the ground thereunto belonging.

(g) But the ruins of the playhouse are said still to exist, 1739

[A playhouse] was situate between Whitecross Street and Golden Lane in a place still denominated Playhouse Yard, where on the north side are still to be seen the ruins of that theatre.

XXXVIII Salisbury Court

Salisbury Court was a private playhouse in the City of London but outside the walls, in the ward of Farringdon Without, and in the parish of St Bride's. It was on the east side of Water Lane, which ran and runs from Fleet Street to the Thames and is now called Whitefriars Street (its northern half) and Carmelite Street (its southern half). The playhouse may have been near the present junction of the street with Tudor Street, E.C.4,[1] perhaps 150 yards south-east of the site of the Whitefriars playhouse, which, in a sense, it replaced.

It was the last regular playhouse opened in or near London during the so-called Shakespearean period and the only one in which politicians took part. The deputy to the Master of the Revels, William Blagrave, and a veteran actor, Richard Gunnell, built and owned it, and behind Blagrave, it seems, was the Master of the Revels himself, Sir Henry Herbert.[2] Moreover, the landlord was the Earl of Dorset, the Queen's Chamberlain, who took an interest in it at critical moments.

The site of the playhouse was evidently the result of the Earl's need for a great deal of cash in the summer of 1629. He leased his London house, Dorset House in Salisbury Court, to the Queen and, on 6 July, a piece of its grounds to Gunnell and Blagrave on condition that they build a playhouse there. The piece stretched 42 feet north and south along the east side of Water Lane and 140 feet east from that street to the wall of the garden of Dorset House. On its northern side was a barn, in which Gunnell and Blagrave were to build the playhouse. The lease was for forty-one and a half years (until 1670), the rent £25 for the first half-year and £100 a year thereafter. Nine days later, on 15 July, the Earl further leased the playhouse property to John Herne of Lincoln's Inn as part of a mortgage. This lease provided that Herne was to have the property for sixty-one years from 8 July (until 1690) at a peppercorn a year, but that the Earl could have it back if he paid Herne £950 plus interest on 16 July 1634. Herne, therefore, was to receive Gunnell and Blagrave's rent, and though the Earl did not pay the £950 in 1634, he remained the ultimate landlord.

Gunnell and Blagrave spent something like £1,000 making the barn into a playhouse and also building a dwelling on the property. They organised a new company for the playhouse, the King's Revels, ostensibly made up of children like the long-defunct company of the name that had been at the Whitefriars playhouse, but actually made up mainly of men. This enterprise seems to have opened with Thomas Randolph's *The Muses' Looking Glass* in November 1630, when playing in London resumed after having been closed since April because of plague.

The playhouse was small and earned small profits.[3] It was in many ways the third private playhouse of Caroline times, behind the second Blackfriars and the Phoenix. Since it eventually had a room 40 feet square built above it, it must have been rectangular and both its linear dimensions were at least that long. It had seats, boxes and 'viewing rooms', as other

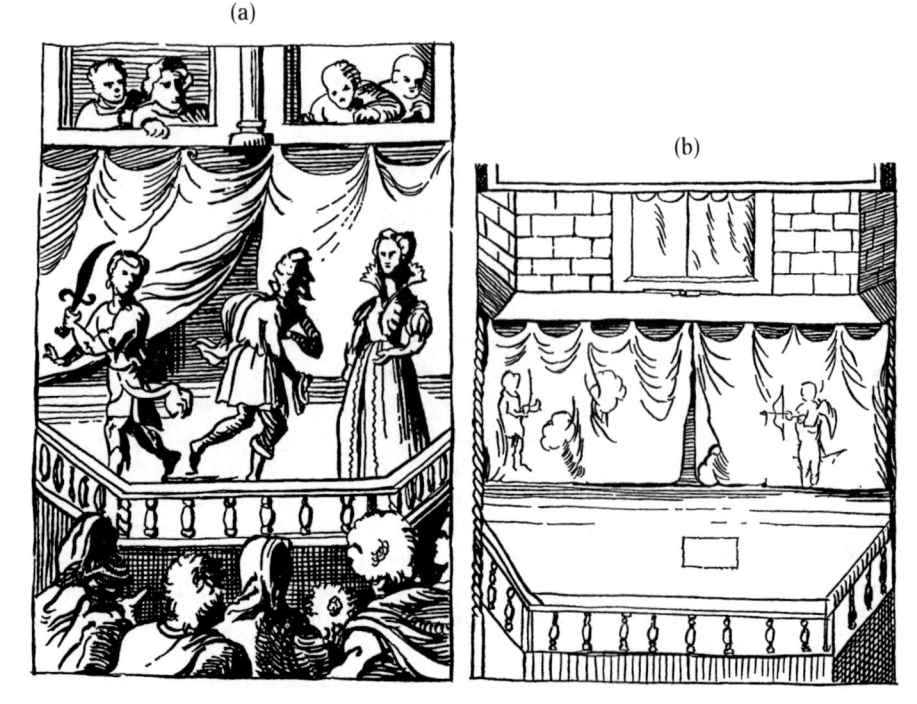

Figs 8a and b. Unidentified playhouses of Caroline times, (a) from the title page of William Alabaster, *Roxana*, a Latin play, (b) from the title page of Nathaniel Richards, *Messallina*. The second drawing is probably derived from the first.

private playhouses did, and in 1637 it was capable of staging a masque requiring (in the printed text, at least) machines and perspective scenery.

The King's Revels stayed at Salisbury Court for about a year. They were succeeded by another new company, evidently introduced to the playhouse by the Earl of Dorset, the men of the new Prince Charles, whose best-known player was Andrew Cane, their clown.[4] They stayed there for about two and a half years. The King's Revels had returned by July 1634 and remained until the plague of 1636–7 caused them and other companies to break up. Gunnell and Blagrave remained in control of the playhouse during the tenure of both companies, until Gunnell died early in October 1634 and Blagrave towards the end of 1636, during the plague.[5]

Gunnell had tried to hire a rising playwright, Richard Brome, to write exclusively for the playhouse. It was a successor, however, who signed a contract with Brome on 20 July 1635, providing that Brome would write three plays a year for the playhouse and not write for any other. The contract was to continue for three years, and Brome was to receive 15s a week as 'salary', plus the profit of one performance of each play, which Brome said was £5. The earliest fruit of this scheme was *Sparagus Garden*, which Brome said made the reputation of the company in the playhouse and £1,000 in profit.

The owners and actors fell out with Brome during the plague of 1636–7, when the playhouse was yielding no money and they stopped paying Brome's salary. In August 1638, though four plays were then 'in arrears', they offered Brome a new contract for three plays a year for seven years at a weekly salary of 20s and with a requirement that Brome write three of the four plays. Brome started to carry out this contract but did not sign it and after Easter 1639 joined William Beeston at the Phoenix. Some people at the playhouse, it seems, thought highly of Brome's plays, but others did not.

Richard Heton took over management of the playhouse before the plague of 1636–7 was over and continued until playing became illegal in 1642. With the help of the Earl of Dorset again, Heton assembled another new company to use the playhouse after the plague. This one was made up of men from the King's Revels and the company that had been at the Phoenix, Queen Henrietta Maria's men, whose name the new company resumed. It occupied the playhouse from October 1637 until Parliament closed all the playhouses on 2 September 1642. If Gunnell and Blagrave had not already, Heton certainly tried to impose on the playhouse the new form of management that Christopher Beeston had already essayed at the Phoenix. Heton would be in complete charge not only of the playhouse itself but of the company using it. The players would satisfy him or not play there.

After the closing in 1642, Gunnell and Blagrave's successors eventually stopped paying their rent, and Herne ejected them. Plays took place illegally in the playhouse from the latter half of 1647 to the first days of 1649. Herne then decided to make it into a brewery. The Earl of Dorset objected because of the nearness of his house and persuaded William Beeston, Christopher's son, to buy Herne's lease on the property, of which forty years remained. The Earl offered Beeston forty more years at a peppercorn rent if he would allow no brewery.

Beeston and Herne agreed on a price, £700, of which Beeston paid £100, the rest payable in six months. Soldiers, however, 'utterly defaced' the interior of the playhouse before the six months were up, the damage worth, Beeston said, £200. So he did not pay the £600. Herne died before 17 October 1649 leaving the affair to his son, another John, who thought of returning Beeston's down payment and getting on with the brewery. For a few months beginning in October 1650, Beeston tried instead to acquire the Phoenix (see **496c**). The Earl now offered Beeston new inducements to acquire the Hernes' lease on the Salisbury Court playhouse, not only forty more years but additional pieces of land, a right of way and some money. So in April 1651, Beeston and the younger Herne made a new agreement. Herne, it seems, reduced the price £200 because of the soldiers' damage, and Beeston paid all the remaining money but £80.

Later, not having received his £80, Herne allowed the brewer to take down the roof of the playhouse towards achieving a brewery. After further urging by the Earl, Beeston finally completed purchase of the lease on 25 March 1652. He had paid £400, plus, presumably, his original £100, plus £8 (interest, it seems, on the £80) for the by now 'ruined buildings of the playhouse'.

At the demand of a new Earl of Dorset (the old one having died on 17 July 1652), Beeston had some repairs done to make the building fit 'to entertain persons of honour in'. This Earl, however, not only refused to carry out his family's promises to Beeston, but in 1658 tried to evict him, since Beeston paid only the peppercorn rent for the property that the Hernes had paid. Beeston sued the new Earl, and the Court of Chancery allowed Beeston to remain for the rest of the Herne lease – until 7 July 1690. At the end of 1659, sensing that the interregnum was about to be over, Beeston set about restoring and enlarging the building in earnest. It became a regular playhouse again in 1660 but was destroyed in the great fire of London in 1666 and not rebuilt.

[1] The site of the playhouse is under either Fleetbank House, which occupies the land from Whitefriars Street east to Salisbury Square and south almost to Tudor Street, or the buildings and public places just south of that. See Bordinat, 'A New Site for the Salisbury Court Theatre', who has argued for the southernmost site.
[2] Herbert may have had a ninth share in the playhouse. See *J and CS*, vi, 90 and n.2, and 507 and 508b.
[3] See *J and CS*, vi, 93.
[4] A draft patent for the company is at the BL, Add. Charter 9291. It names ten members of the company and allows them to play in London only at 'their new playhouse in Salisbury Court'. The day and month of the date are left blank, and the year is given as the seventh of Charles I (27 March 1631 to 26 March 1632). See Bawcutt, 'Documents', 181–4.
[5] See *J and CS*, vi, 94, 103 (where, coincidentally, he wrongly gives a different date for Gunnell's death).

505 Richard Gunnell and William Blagrave lease land and buildings for the playhouse, 6 July 1629

BL, Add. MS 5064, fo. 222. Transcribed by Cunningham, 'The Whitefriars Theatre', 102

The original lease of the playhouse property is lost, but at least two summaries exist, one of 25 June 1658, partly damaged (PRO, C10/53/7, the bill), and another of 2 July 1667. Quoted below is the latter.

The Right Honourable Edward, late Earl of Dorset, and his trustees, by indenture dated the sixth day of July . . . [1629], in consideration that Richard Gunnell and William Blagrave should at their own costs and charges erect a playhouse and other buildings at the lower end of Salisbury Court in the parish of St Bridget in the ward of Farringdon Without, did demise to the said Gunnell and Blagrave a piece of ground at the same lower end of Salisbury Court containing 140 feet in length and 42 feet in breadth, to hold to the said Gunnell and Blagrave, their executors and assigns from thenceforth for forty-one years and a half, paying therefore to the said trustees, or the survivors of them, £25 for the first half-year and £100 per annum for the remainder of the term by quarterly payments.

506 The Earl of Dorset leases the playhouse property to John Herne, 15 July 1629

BL, Add. Charter 9290. Transcribed by Cunningham, 'The Whitefriars Theatre', 91–5. See Bawcutt, 'Documents', 181. This lease describes the property in greater detail than other documents do.

[The property concerned is:] all that soil and ground whereupon the barn at the lower end of the great back court, or yard, of Salisbury Court now stands; and so much of the soil whereupon the whole south end of the great stable in the said court or yard stands, . . . [containing,] from that end of that stable towards the north end thereof, 16 feet of assize; and the whole breadth of the said stable and all the ground and soil on the east and west side of that stable lying directly against the said 16 feet of ground at the south end thereof, between the wall of the great garden belonging to the mansion-house called Dorset House and the wall that severs the said court from the lane called Water Lane; and all the ground and soil . . . between the said walls on the east and west parts thereof and the said barn, stable and ground on both sides the same on the south and north parts thereof.

Which said several parcels of soil and ground . . . demised [to Gunnell and Blagrave] contain in the whole in length, from the brick wall of the said garden at the east end thereof to the said wall dividing the said court or yard from the said . . . Water Lane at the west, 140 feet of assize, and in breadth, from the outside of the said barn towards the south into [*i.e.* unto] the said stable and ground on both sides thereof towards the north, 42 feet of assize and lies [*sic*] together at the lower end of the said court . . .

Together with . . . free ingress, egress and regress for the said John Herne . . . and every other person and persons in, by, through and on . . . Salisbury Court, and also any the utter courts belonging to the said mansion-house . . . there now commonly used or which at any time hereafter shall be made or commonly used during the term . . . granted . . . unto Richard Gunnell and William Blagrave.

507 The playhouse is to be built, 24 October 1629

Williams, ed., *Court and Times of Charles I*, II, 35

The document is a letter from Sir George Gresley at Essex House in London to Sir Thomas Puckering about the Earl of Dorset's attempts to raise money. Williams printed it without saying where he had found it and so did Rimbault ('Salisbury Court Theatre', 145). The £1,000 that Gresley says Gunnell and Blagrave paid as a 'fine' (*i.e.* fee) for their lease is a mistake, probably for the amount the Earl received for his lease (effectually a mortgage) of 15 July 1629 (506). Gunnell and Blagrave apparently paid no fine for their lease.

My Lord of Dorset is become a great husband. For he hath let his house in Salisbury Court unto the Queen for the ambassador lieger [*i.e.* resident] of France, which is daily expected to come over, to lie in, and [she] giveth for it £350 by the year; and . . . the rest of his stables and outhouses towards the water side he hath let for £1,000 fine and £100 by the year rent unto the Master of the Revels to make a playhouse for the Children of the Revels.

508 Gunnell and Blagrave spend about £1,000 converting the barn into a playhouse, 1629–1630

(a) PRO, C10/53/7, the bill; (b) Kent Archives Office, Maidstone, U2269 E 136/1. Transcribed in (b) Rosenfeld, 'Unpublished Stage Documents', 92. For (a) see *CRS*, 100–6

In a lawsuit of 1658 and an undated petition of *c.* 1657–8, William Beeston and Gunnell's and Blagrave's heirs and successors explained how much money the lease required Gunnell and Blagrave to spend in building the playhouse (an aspect of the lease not reported elsewhere) and how much they actually spent.

(a) Beeston, 25 June 1658

[The Earl of Dorset granted the lease of 1629 (505) on Salisbury Court:] in consideration that ... Richard Gunnell and William Blagrave should at their own proper costs and charges erect a playhouse and other buildings upon some part of the said ground ... [And] they, the said Gunnell and Blagrave, by the consent of the said Edward, Earl of Dorset, did erect and build upon the said premises one dwelling house and playhouse wherein plays and interludes were usually acted, the building whereof cost the said Gunnell and Blagrave the sum of £1,000.

For more of this document, see 517d.

(b) The successors (in a petition to the Earl of Dorset), c. 1658

[Speaking for themselves and their predecessors, Elizabeth Heton, William Wintersall and Mary Young (now the wife of William Jones) explained:] that ... about thirty years past [they] did, by Sir Henry Herbert's interest in your ... [the Earl of Dorset's] late father, take a lease from him of an old barn standing in Salisbury Court. [On] which barn they were tied by covenants to lay out ... £800 for converting the same into a playhouse and to pay for the same playhouse the rent of £100 per annum for the full term of forty-one years, which was duly paid to your late father until the profits and privileges of the said house were absolutely taken from your petitioners and they made incapable of continuing the said payment.

[And they added] that ... [they spent] near the sum of £1,200 in building and finishing the said playhouse and have paid near £300 since their house was taken from them.

That is, after September 1642 they may have paid the rent for a time and made some repairs.

509 Contemporaries describe the playhouse

(a) Nabbes, *Tottenham Court* (London, 1638), the epilogue, and Sharpe, *The Noble Stranger* (London, 1640), the prologue; (b) PRO, C10/80/15. See *J and CS*, VI, 91–3 and, for (b), *CRS*, 107–13

What the original playhouse was like is hinted at in two plays of the 1630s and, less reliably, in a lawsuit of 1666. The latter describes repairs and additions made to the building in 1660, after soldiers had defaced it in 1649, a brewer had altered it in 1651, and William Beeston had repaired it before June 1658. The remark in the lawsuit that a room 40 feet square was to be built above the theatre suggests that the original theatre was rectangular and at least that big.

(a) The playhouse was small[1]

[In a play acted at Salisbury Court in 1633, the hostess says to neglected playwrights:] When others' [*i.e.* playhouses'] filled rooms with neglect disdain ye, My little house (with thanks) shall entertain ye.

And in another, acted there c. 1638, the prologue says:

Blest fate protect me! What a luster's here?
How many stars deck this our little sphere!

[1] But in *Historia Histrionica*, usually attributed to James Wright, p. 7, the second Blackfriars, the Phoenix and Salisbury Court are dubiously said to have been 'all three built almost exactly alike for form and bigness'.

(b) Size, shape, seats, boxes and viewing rooms[1]

[In the lawsuit Beeston alleged that:] about the latter end of 1659, when it was known that His Majesty was like to return, . . . your orator [Beeston] was minded to repair and amend the said house and make it fit for the use aforementioned [*i.e.* 'stage-playing'. He, therefore, engaged Thomas Silver and Edward Fisher, carpenters, who] should . . . build and erect on the said theatre or stage[2] a large room or chamber for a dancing school 40 feet square, which was to be done with good, sufficient and substantial timber; and should also well and substantially and firmly repair and amend the said theatre and all the seats and boxes and viewing rooms thereto belonging.

[1] The lawsuit also mentions external walls that 'were then [before the reparations of 1660] already built or almost built with brick', and, twice, 'the timber belonging to the private house ['dwelling house' on the second occasion] and over the stage'. These things, however, could have more to do with alterations and repairs in the 1650s than with the original playhouse. A house over the stage would, presumably, be the domain of the manager.

[2] The two words were sometimes used together because 'theatre' could refer to a stage as well as a building. Beeston meant the building here, in view of his carpenter's remark below about having to roof 'the full extent of the same building'. See *OED*: 'Stage', 1, 5, and 'Theatre', 3a, 4. In Latin, 'theatrum' could also refer to a stage as well as a building: Lewis and Short, *A Latin Dictionary*, 'Theatrum', II.

510 The playhouse opens, *c.* 25 November 1630

(a) Prynne, *Histrio-Mastix*, sigs. *3v, Iiiii; (b) Randolph, *The Muses' Looking Glass, or The Entertainment*, 1–2, 93; (c) Bodleian Library, Malone's MS note in his copy of Langbaine, *An Account*, II, 415. Transcribed in (c) Lawrence, 'New Facts', 820. See *J and CS*, VI, 94–8

The playhouse could have opened sometime between 24 October 1629 (see 507) and 17 April 1630, when all the London playhouses closed because of plague. Some remarks by William Prynne, however, suggest that Randolph's *The Muses' Looking Glass* was the first play, and that play was evidently performed in a new playhouse some two weeks after the London playhouses reopened on 12 November 1630.

(a) Prynne's book

In the first Epistle Dedicatory of his *Histrio-Mastix*, Prynne said that 'one new Theatre' had 'lately' been erected in Whitefriars – the area immediately west of Salisbury Court with which Salisbury Court was often confused.

[Then in the work proper he said with heavy irony] that none but a company of puritans and precisians speak against . . . [plays]; all else applaud and eke frequent them. Therefore certainly they are very good recreations, since none but puritans disaffect them. [And he explained his irony in a note:] This objection, as I have heard, was much urged in a most scurrilous and profane manner in the first play that was acted in the new-erected playhouse, a fit consecration sermon for that devil's chapel.

(b) Randolph's play

Bird and Mrs Flowerdew, 'two of the sanctified fraternity of Blackfriars' – that is, puritans – sit on stage throughout the play commenting sourly (at first) on things around them. They begin with the audience, who are 'the lewd reprobate', then turn to the playhouse, evidently newly built,

BIRD: Sister, were there not before inns –
   Yes, I will say inns, for my zeal bids me
   Say filthy inns – enough to harbour such
   As travelled to destruction the broad way?
   But they build more and more, more shops of Satan.
FLOWERDEW: . . . Had we seen a church,
   A new-built church, erected north and south,
   It had been something worth the wondering at.

By the end of the play, however, they have been converted to the love of plays:

FLOWERDEW: Most blessed looking glass
   That didst instruct my blinded eyes today;
   I might have gone to hell the narrow way.
BIRD: Hereafter I will visit comedies
   And see them oft: they are good exercises.

(c) Edmond Malone quoting the Master of the Revels

[Alluding to Sir Henry Herbert's Office Book (now lost), Malone wrote in his copy of Langbaine's *An Account* that] *The Muses' Looking Glass* was not printed till 1638 (at Oxford by Leonard Lichfield and Francis Bowman), and the title page has only 'by T. R.', without any preface or mention of the theatre where it was acted. But it was acted by the Children of the Revels [who were then at Salisbury Court] under the title of *The Entertainment* in the summer of 1630 [evidently in the provinces] and licensed by Sir Henry Herbert, 25 November 1630.

511 Awkward events at the playhouse, 1634–1635

(a) GL, MS 6538; (b) Sir Henry Herbert, Office Book (now lost). Transcribed in (a) *J and CS*, VI, 99; (b) Malone in *Plays and Poems of William Shakespeare* (1821), III, 237. The Salisbury Court playhouse did not usually figure in violent or scandalous events, but it was not completely immune from them.

(a) Violence, 27 March 1634

[The burial register of St Bride's, the parish church of Salisbury Court:] George Wilson killed at the playhouse in Salisbury Court.

(b) Blasphemy on stage, 16 February 1635

[The Maser of the Revels noted:] I committed Cromes, a broker in Long Lane, the 16th of February . . . 1635 to the Marshalsea [prison] for lending a church robe with the name of JESUS upon it to the players in Salisbury Court to present a flamen, a priest of the heathens. Upon his petition of submission and acknowledgement of his fault, I released him the 17th of February . . . 1635.

512 Richard Brome is contracted to write plays for Salisbury Court, 20 July 1635 – Spring 1639

PRO, Req. 2/662/pt 1 [near the bottom of the box] (the bill) and Req.2/723 [top of the box] (the answer). Transcribed by Haaker in 'The Plague, the Theatre, and the Poet', 296–306. Brome's arrangements with the owners and players of Salisbury Court were ill-starred and are explained in a lawsuit in which the owners and players sued him for not writing as many plays for them as he had contracted to write.

(a) The owners and players' bill, 12 February 1640

The owners at the time were Richard Heton, John Robinson and Nathaniel Speed. The players were the Queen Henrietta Maria's men, named as Richard Perkins, Anthony Turnor, William Sherlocke, John Younge, John Sumpner, Edward May, Curtis Grevill, William Wilbraham, Timothy Reade and William Cartwright the younger. These owners and players argued as follows.

Richard Brome, . . . well knowing that it would be very beneficial for him . . . to write and compose plays for the actors and owners of the said house, did by himself and others whom he employed therein make means unto . . . the then owners and actors in the said house to entertain him in that business. And after many parleys and treaties therein, it was at the last by articles of agreement indented bearing date on or about the twentieth day of July . . . 1635 agreed . . . that he, the said Brome, should for the term of three years the next ensuing with his best art and industry write every year three plays and deliver them to the company of players there acting for the time being. And that the said Richard Brome should not nor would write any play or any part of a play to any other players or playhouse but apply all his study and endeavours therein for the benefit of the said company of the said playhouse. And that the said covenantees [*i.e.* the owners and players] should pay unto the said Richard Brome the sum of 15s per week during the said term of three years and permit the said Brome to have the benefit one day's profit of playing such new play as he should make, ... the ordinary charges of the house only deducted.

In pursuance of which articles, he, the said Richard Brome, did put himself into the said business and received all his said pay of 15s per week thenceforth until it pleased God that, by reason of the ... plague in the year following, public acting of plays on the stage in or about London were [*sic*] prohibited. By reason whereof the said covenantees did forbear (as in such cases is usual) to pay the said 15s ... for a while. Whereupon the said Brome did come to an agreement ... to accept of £10 for the satisfaction of all demands for salary from the time of the said prohibition until allowance should be obtained for acting of plays again. The which agreement was ... set down in a note ... bearing date on or about the six and twentieth day of October ... 1636, as in and by the said writing ... appeareth. The which £10 was ... well and truly paid unto or for the said Richard Brome. And, nevertheless, at the end of the said term of three years your subjects [the owners and actors], or some of them, made full payment unto the said Brome of all the said salary after the rate of 15s per week for all the time of cessation, which continued a full year and a half, save only £5 ...

But ... the said Brome, having gotten so much money of your subjects as aforesaid, did fail to deliver unto your subjects the number of plays which ... he was ... to have delivered them, being then in arrear with them four plays. And, moreover, your subjects discovered that the said Richard Brome did, in the three years beforementioned, sell and deliver one of the plays which he made for your subjects in the said time unto Christopher Beeston ... and William Beeston [at the Phoenix], or one of them, which was to your subjects great prejudice.

Howbeit, upon the said Brome's promise to deliver the other plays behind as aforesaid and apply himself wholly unto your subjects, it was in ... August in ... 1638 concluded and agreed by and between your subjects and the said Richard Brome ... that he ... should for the space of seven years thence next ensuing write and present unto your subjects and the company of players acting at the said house for the time being three plays yearly ... and that he should not write, invent or compose any play, tragedy or comedy, or any part thereof, for any other playhouse. And that he should not suffer any play made or to be made or composed by him for your subjects or their successors in the said company in Salisbury Court to be printed by his consent ... without the licence from the said company or the major part of them. And that if he, the said Brome, should not bring in three new plays of his own composing ... within every year of the said seven years, that then half his pay or salary hereafter mentioned should be detained ... until he had brought in such plays ... And that the said Richard Brome should bring in two of the said new plays wherewith he was so in arrear so conveniently as that they might be studied to be presented unto public view upon the stage at the said house in the term of . . . [Michaelmas] next ensuing the time of the said articles, for each of which the said Brome was to have of your subjects or their successors in the said company £2 10s apiece in full satisfaction and discharge of the £5 so [in] arrear and due unto him as aforesaid for the said plays in arrear during the said first mentioned three years. And that he should bring [in] the third play of the said four plays behind . . . at any time within three years next ensuing the said agreement. And that in case the said Brome performed the said last mentioned agreement in every respect, that then the fourth play of the said plays behind with your subjects as aforesaid should be remitted to him freely. And . . . upon performance of the said agreement on . . . Brome's part to be performed, and in case your subjects and their successors there continued playing at the said playhouse without restraint, that then they should pay unto or for the said Richard Brome the sum of 20s per week and permit and suffer him to have one day's profit of the said several new plays (except as before excepted) . . . as in the said first recited articles of agreement is mentioned . . .

Unto which agreement, he, the said Richard Brome condescended, vowed and promised the performance thereof and willed that the same might be reduced into writing to that end and purpose. Whereupon your subjects did cause the said . . . agreement to be put into writing by way of articles indented. Whereunto the said Richard Brome seemed very desirous to seal and execute the same in due form of law, but from time to time delayed the same with asseveration of his willingness to perform the said agreement and to seal the said articles, . . . and in expectation of the performance thereof your subjects did continue payment of the said 20s per week, according to the said later agreement, from the time of the said later agreement-making until a fortnight after Easter last past. And your subjects expected that the said Brome would have sealed the said articles . . . or at the leastwise to have stood unto and performed the same in every respect accordingly.

But now . . . the said Richard Brome, by and through the persuasions and enticement of the said William Beeston, or some other by him in that behalf employed to defeat your subjects of such benefit and profit as shall or may accrue and come unto them by the said Brome's study and performance in the said business, and upon the said Beeston's promise to be his good friend and to give him more salary than your subjects by the agreement aforesaid, he, the said Richard Brome, did voluntarily fail to present unto your subjects any more of the said plays for which he was in arrear with your subjects as aforesaid than only one play instead of two which he was to bring in in the term of [Michaelmas] . . . 1638 . . . Howbeit, your subjects paid or caused to be paid unto the said Richard Brome, according to the said last mentioned articles, the sum of £2 10s and permitted him to have one day's profits of the said new play so by him newly made . . . And the said Brome promised to compose, make and present unto your subjects the residue of the said plays in arrear . . .

But the said Brome, being tampered withal by the said Beeston as aforesaid, hath and doth refuse and deny to compose, make or present unto your subjects the said three plays which by the first articles he is in arrear in . . . with your subjects as aforesaid, but wholly applies himself unto the said Beeston and the company of players acting at the playhouse of the Phoenix in Drury Lane. And, notwithstanding he hath received of your subjects . . . his salary and wages of 20s per week from or about the twentieth day of July 1638 until the thirty [*i.e.* twenty] -sixth day of April following or thereabouts, being nine months and upwards, which amounts to £40 and better, . . . yet he refuseth and denieth to present unto your subjects the residue of the said plays in arrear . . . with your subjects . . . or any satisfaction for the aforesaid salary of 20s per week received as aforesaid, which tendeth unto your subjects' loss, prejudice and damage of £500 at the least, as is well known unto the said Brome.

[As the convention was, the owners and players went on to explain why they had to sue at equity rather than common law.]

(b) Brome's answer, 6 March 1640

Eighteen months or thereabouts before the date of the said articles in July 1635 in the bill mentioned, one Richard Gunnell and others, . . . being of the company known by the name of Salisbury Court actors, . . . did make means unto this defendant and, upon their specious pretences and promises of reward and bountiful retribution and love, did entice and inveigle this defendant to depart and leave the company of the Red Bull players, being the Prince's Highness's servants, and where this defendant was then very well entertained and truly paid without murmuring or wrangling and to come and write and compose and make plays for the said complainants [the owners and players at Salisbury Court] . . . Upon which enticements and inveiglements this defendant, upon hope and confidence of the complainants' performance of their said undertakings and promises, . . . did compose and make for the said complainants divers plays which the said complainants and their company did act, which plays proved very fortunate and successful to the said complainants and their said company, and, being in the infancy of their setting up and first playing at Salisbury Court, . . . did bring them into esteem and fame. And one of the said plays, styled and called *The Sparagus Garden*, was worth to them by general conjecture and estimation, and as by their own books and writings being produced this defendant verily believeth may appear, the sum of £1,000 and upwards.

And this defendant further saith . . . that . . . finding how useful and profitable this defendant's labours in that kind might and was apparently like to prove unto them, the complainants, out of a large pretence of love and courtesy as aforesaid, did first entreat and persuade this defendant to agree to write three plays for . . . [them] yearly for the space of three years together, which this defendant at the first proposition thereof was unwilling to undertake as being more than he could well perform. But some of the complainants on the behalf of the residue of them did undertake and assuredly affirm unto this defendant that howsoever they had desired to have three plays yearly for three years . . . to be undertaken and promised by this defendant, yet upon trust and confidence and by the true and fair intent and plain meaning of all parties, the plaintiffs neither should nor would exact nor expect from this defendant the performance or composition of any more plays than . . . this defendant could or should be able well and conveniently to do or perform, and that their main purpose in expressing such a number of plays was but only to oblige this defendant to dedicate all his labour and plays totally unto their sole profits. Upon which trust, . . . this defendant, by articles in writing indented made between the said complainants or some of their company on the one part and this defendant on the other part, and bearing date in or about the said month of July 1635, . . . did agree to compose and write three plays yearly by the space of three years together then next following for the said complainants or the said company, and that he would write for no other company, but apply his labours totally unto them . . .

In consideration whereof, the said complainants, or some [of] them, . . . did agree to pay 15s weekly upon every Saturday unto this defendant and to permit this defendant to have the clear benefit of any one day's playing unto himself within the space of ten days after the first playing of any such play at this defendant's election (the common charge deducted) . . .

And this defendant further saith that his purposes and intents were always . . . to perform the said articles, . . . albeit the same were left, in effect, unto himself upon trust as aforesaid. And the said complainants, or some of the chief of the said company, did oftentimes confidently affirm . . . that this defendant's best endeavours in writing plays for them should be always accepted; and that they would expect no more from him than he could well and conveniently do therein as aforesaid; and also that they would be more grateful and beneficial unto this defendant for his endeavours than by their said written articles and agreement they had engaged themselves to be.

Whereupon this defendant also showeth that he, in pursuance and part of performance of the said articles on his part, did compose and deliver unto the said complainants or their company two plays within the first three-quarters of the year after the date of the said articles, and . . . that this defendant for the first of the said two plays had one day's clear profit, as they affirmed by their account, deducting as aforesaid according to the said articles. But this defendant also saith that albeit this defendant's said labours brought the said company into their first and chiefest estimation, accompanied with very great profits and gains as aforesaid, yet the plague shortly afterwards increasing . . . in and about London, this defendant's said second play was first played by the said company near or about the time of their restraint from playing by reason of the said sickness. And this defendant's said clear day's profit of the said second new play was never allowed unto him to the damage of £5 and upwards.

And this defendant also saith that the complainants and their said company, being shortly afterwards wholly restrained from playing, and this defendant intending in the time of vacancy of the said playing to compose and prepare more new plays for them according to the said articles and agreement for their future use and commodity when they should play again, and in recompense and requital thereof, this defendant expected the due and true performance and payment of the said 15s weekly from the said complainants' company according to their agreement aforesaid in the vacancy, in which time he was to write for them as well as when they had permission to play, there being no exception at all either in the said treaty, agreement or articles of any time or such casualty whatsoever nor intention, to this defendant's knowledge. Neither is there any such mention made in the said bill of complaint that this defendant should not be paid in case of such restraint. But the complainants or their said company, intending covenously or fraudulently to deceive and defraud this defendant of the said weekly payment, did first begin to quarrel and take occasions of distaste against this defendant and did deny to pay the same 15s weekly to this defendant against all equity and good conscience and expressly against their agreement and articles aforesaid.

And the said company, or some part of the chiefest of them on behalf of the residue, in the said time of vacancy willed this defendant to take what course he could or would for himself, for they neither could nor would continue the weekly payment of 15s unto him . . . And about the month of May 1636 . . . this defendant was offered by the said complainants or company or some of them that the said articles bearing date in July as aforesaid should be delivered up unto this defendant to be cancelled, so as this defendant was . . . put to his shifts in that hard, sad and dangerous time of the sickness, both for himself and his family.

Whereupon, . . . about the month of August then next following, this defendant, by necessity constrained and being left in such distress and want as aforesaid by their sole defaults, did repair unto the said William Beeston . . . and acquainted him with his then present case and condition, who then lent this defendant £6 . . . upon this defendant's agreement to compose and write a play for the Cockpit company. Whereof when some of the complainants and their company understood, being in hope that the sickness would in a short time . . . cease, . . . some of them offered this defendant money and did earnestly solicit this defendant to desert the said William Beeston and [his] company and to return to the complainants again, which this defendant at the present refused in regard of his said former bad and uncharitable usage. Yet upon their earnest persuasion and promises of better usage afterwards, and partly upon threats of [law]suits and troubles, this defendant did resolve to make further trial of them. And thereupon the complainant Richard Heton on the company's behalf did undertake, agree and promise to take this defendant off from the said William Beeston and to give him, the said Mr Beeston, satisfaction whereby this defendant might be freely released from him. And likewise they then agreed and promised to pay this defendant £10 . . . towards the satisfaction of the then arrearages of the said weekly payment of 15s due and behind unpaid unto this defendant upon the said former agreement and articles. But the same was not all paid unto this defendant until he brought them a new play, and then it was made up with several small sums and petty dribbling payments which did small pleasure unto this defendant.

And this defendant also saith that afterwards, the sickness still continuing, the said 15s per week was still stopped from this defendant, whereby this defendant was in a kind enforced to treat again and to make some agreement with the said William Beeston touching the premises. Whereupon the complainants or some of their company became suitors to Sir Henry Herbert, knight, Master of the Revels, to hear and examine the cause between them. And the said Master of the Revels, taking the trouble upon him, did afterwards award that the defendant should be paid 6s weekly and £5 for every new play which he should bring until such time as the sickness should cease and the plaintiffs should have leave to play again. Which award the plaintiffs and company did but in part perform, for when they began to play again, which was in the month of October 1637, they were then indebted upon that award and account to this defendant the sum of £11 11s 6d or thereabouts.

And this defendant also saith that he brought the said company ... six new plays within the space of three years next after the first agreement and articles, and more he was not able possibly to perform, as well through sickness as by other hindrance which he then had. And this defendant, upon the last agreement in the bill mentioned for 20s a week, namely in Hilary term 1639, composed another new play for the said complainants, and before Easter term 1639 this defendant brought them another new play, written all but part of the last scene.

But this defendant found that divers of the company did so slight the last mentioned plays and used such scornful and reproachful speeches concerning this defendant, and divers of them did advise the rest of them to stop all weekly payments towards this defendant, so as this defendant understood that they took occasions daily to weary the defendant from and out of their employment, which this defendant well perceiving did again leave them to their own dispose through their own only default as aforesaid. And ... this defendant sithence that time hath contracted and made other agreements with the said William Beeston, with whom he hopeth to enjoy the fruits of his labours more beneficially and peaceably.

And this defendant also saith that ... of late time when he was in the complainants' employment, being very sick, [he] did send unto the said complainants ... for some weekly means at that time to supply his necessity, but they uncharitably refused to send him any. And for their further trial, this defendant did two or three times, week after week, importune and solicit them with letters imagining that [he] might and would work remorse and pity from them. Whereupon some of the company, by the assent of the residue as he conceiveth, sent him word that they had given him ... wholly over and meant to employ him no further and wished him to shift for himself again as aforesaid and refused utterly to yield any payment or relief unto this defendant in his said great sickness, want and misery, saying they would have no more to do with him. Whereby this defendant was again enforced through their mere default as aforesaid to provide for himself as aforesaid. Which when the complainants observed this defendant to have done, they do now, out of malice and evil will, only molest and vex this defendant with suits of law, intending thereby to crush and ruin him.

[Brome then formally denied many of the assertions in the bill, and he] saith that he is only behind with them two plays, in lieu of which he hath made divers scenes in old, revived plays for them and many prologues and epilogues to such plays of theirs, songs and one introduction at their first playing after the ceasing of the plague – all which he verily believeth amounted to as much time and study as two ordinary plays might take up in writing – which happened by the accidents and through their own defaults as aforesaid. And as to the new play which the complainants suppose this defendant to have sold unto the said Christopher or William Beeston: this defendant confesseth it to be true that the stoppage of his weekly means and unkind carriages aforesaid forced this defendant to contract and bargain for the said new play with the said William Beeston, but yet the said complainants and their company had it and acted it and by common estimation got £1,000 and upwards by it.

[He admitted that he and the complainants had agreed to a new arrangement by which he would receive 20s a week, but he said he had not signed it because during the plague he was badly used] and his labours and plays cavilled at and rejected and himself discharged and left at liberty as aforesaid. [He denied that he had received 20s a week] from July 1638 until April 1639 or that [he] ... is, in effect, any plays behind upon agreement with the complainants.

513 Richard Heton becomes manager at Salisbury Court, 1636–1637, and establishes a new regime there, 1639

BL, Add. Charter 9292 A–C. Transcribed in Cunningham, 'The Whitefriars Theatre', 95–100. Reprinted in *J and CS*, II, 684–7 (see also VI, 103–4, 104 n.). See Bawcutt, 'Documents', 184–6

In October 1637, when the playhouses reopened after having been closed almost continuously for seventeen months because of plague, Heton had already been manager of the Salisbury Court playhouse for at least eight months, perhaps for well over a year. In 1639 he meant to secure a patent that would create a more dictatorial regime at Salisbury Court, and drew up five statements as a guide to what the patent should contain. The company he had in mind was the one then in the playhouse, the reformed Queen Henrietta Maria's men (see 491a).

(a) 'Instructions' for the patent, early 1639

That the patent for electing her majesty's company of comedians be granted only to myself, [so] that I may always have a company in readiness at Salisbury Court for her majesty's service, and that if all or any of the company go away from Salisbury Court to play at any other playhouse . . . they from thenceforth to cease to be her majesty's servants, and only the company remaining there to have that honour and title. Myself to be sole governor of the company.

The company to enter into articles with me to continue there for seven years upon the same conditions they have had for a year and half last past, and such as refuse, to be removed and others placed in their rooms. For if they should continue at liberty as they now are and have power to take her majesty's service along with them, they would make use of our house but until they could provide another upon better terms and then leave us as in one year and half of their being here they have many times threatened, when they might not exact any new impositions upon the housekeepers at their pleasure. And some of them have treated upon conditions for the Cockpit [i.e. Phoenix] playhouse, some gone about to beg our house from the King, and one now of the chief fellows, an agent for one that hath got a grant from the King for the building of a new playhouse which was intended to be in Fleet Street . . .

When her majesty's servants were at the Cockpit, being all at liberty, they dispersed themselves to several companies, so that had not my Lord of Dorset taken care to make up a new company for the Queen, she had not any at all . . .

And whereas my Lord of Dorset had gotten for a former company at Salisbury Court the Prince's service, they, being left at liberty, took their opportunity of another house and left the house in Salisbury Court destitute both of a service and company.

This settling of the service and company upon conditions certain, and . . . a known governor, would be the occasion to avoid many differences and disturbances that happen both between the company and housekeepers, amongst the company themselves, and many general discontents – to the great credit of the house and profit of the company.

(b) Draft of the first part of the patent, 1639

[After the usual opening:] Whereas our [i.e. the King's] servant, Richard Heton, one of the sewers [i.e. waiters at table] of the chamber to our dear consort, the Queen, hath disbursed great sums of money in providing a convenient playhouse in Dorset House yard for her majesty's comedians to practice and act plays in [so] that they may be there resident and in readiness for the said service when they shall be commanded, and hath likewise disbursed good sums of money for the maintaining and supporting the said actors in the sickness time, and other ways to keep the said company together, without which a great part of them had not been able to subsist but the company had been utterly ruined and dispersed:

And whereas upon every small occasion for their own benefit, companies of actors have removed from their residence and dispersed themselves into several places, so that no certain place of abode is known where they may be found when we are pleased to command their attendance for our own or our dear consort's solace, pleasure, and disport:

Now know ye that we . . . have licensed and authorised . . . our said servant, Richard Heton, or his assigns . . . at all times hereafter to select, order, direct, set up and govern a company of comedians in the said private house in Dorset House yard for the service of our dear consort, the Queen, and there to exercise their quality of playing . . . stage plays and suchlike, . . . as well for the solace and pleasure of our dear consort, the Queen, and ourself, when we shall think fit to see them, as the recreation of our loving subjects; and the said . . . stage plays and suchlike to show, act and exercise to their best profit and commodity, as well within their foresaid playhouse in Dorset House yard as in any city, university, town or borough of our said realms and dominions, there to sojourn and abide, if at any time they with their company and associates (whom our said servant Richard Heton, shall think fit to select) shall have occasion by reason of sickness in London or otherwise, to travel; to exercise publicly to their best profit . . . their aforesaid comedies, tragedies, etc., at all time or times (the time of divine service only excepted), before or after supper, within any town halls, guild halls, moot halls, schoolhouses or any other convenient places whatsoever. And the same comedies, tragedies, etc., with the times they are to be acted, to proclaim in such places as aforesaid with drums, trumpets and by public bills . . .

(c) 'My intention for the rest' of the patent, 1639

That such of the company as will not be ordered and governed by me, or shall not by the Master of his majesty's Revels and myself be thought fit comedians for her majesty's service, . . . I may have power to discharge from the company and, with the advice of the Master of the Revels, to put new ones in their places. And those who shall be so discharged [are] not to have the honour to be her majesty's servants but only those who shall continue at the foresaid playhouse. And the said company not to play at any time in any other place but the foresaid playhouse without my consent under my hand in writing (lest his majesty's service might be neglected), except by special command from one of the lord chamberlains or the Master of the Revels, etc.

(d) 'Instructions', dated 14 September 1639

[Summarising differences between the old regime and the new one:] The housekeepers enjoy not any one benefit in the last [*i.e.* new articles] which they had not in the first; and they paid only by the first:

1. All repairs of the house
2. Half the gathering places, half to the sweepers of the house, the stagekeepers, to the poor, and for carrying away the soil.

By the last articles, we first allow them:

[1.] a room [*i.e.* box?] or two more than they formerly had
[2.] all that was allowed by the former articles
[3.] and half the poets' wages which is 10s a week
[4.] half the licensing of every new play, which half is also 20s
[5.] and one day's profit wholly to themselves every year in consideration of their want of stools on the stage, which were taken away by His Majesty's command.

We allow them also that was in no articles:

[1.] half for lights, both wax and tallow, which half all winter is near 5s a day
[2.] half for coals to all the rooms
[3.] half for rushes, flowers and strowings on the stage
[4.] half for all the boys' new gloves at every new play and every revived play not lately played.

(e) A note

All the rest of the articles are some indifferent rules fit to be observed for the general credit of the house and benefit of both housekeepers and players.

514 An elaborate production mounted on the stage at Salisbury Court, 1637

Nabbes's masque, *Microcosmus*, sigs. B2, Cv. See *J and CS*, VI, 107–9

Nabbes wrote the masque while the playhouses were closed for the plague of 1636–7, since in commendatory verses Richard Brome mentions the plague as current. The masque was, as the title page says, mounted at Salisbury Court 'with general liking', presumably soon after the reopening of the playhouses in October 1637. If the stage directions were even partly carried out, the stage at Salisbury Court was capable of elaborate effects having more to do with stages of Restoration times than those of Shakespeare's.

[The text requires a special proscenium, or 'Front', and five elaborate 'scenes'. The proscenium was to be:] Of a workmanship proper to the fancy of the rest, adorned with brass figures of angels and devils with several inscriptions: the title in an escutcheon supported by an angel and a devil. Within the arch a continuing perspective of ruins, which is drawn still before the other scenes whilst they are varied ...

[Five pages into the play the first scene appears:] Whilst the following song is singing, the first scene appears, being a sphere in which the four elements are figured, and about it they sit embracing one another. [Then, presently,] they return to the scene and it closeth.

515 The stage at Salisbury Court is itself on stage there, *c.* 1638

Goffe, *The Careless Shepherdess*, sigs. B–B4v. The setting for the 'Praeludium' at the beginning of Goffe's play is the playhouse stage itself.

(The Scene: Salisbury Court. BOLT, a door-keeper, sitting with a box on the side of the stage. To him THRIFT, a citizen.)

THRIFT: Now for a good bargain. What will you take to let me in to the play?

BOLT: A shilling, sir.

THRIFT: Come, here's a groat [4d]. I'll not make many words . . .

(Enter SPRUCE, a courtier.)

SPRUCE: How oft has't sounded?[1]

BOLT: Thrice, an't please you, sir . . .

(Enter LANDLORD, a country, gentleman.)

LANDLORD: God save you, gentlemen. 'Tis my ambition
   To occupy a place near you. There are
   None that be worthy of my company
   In any room beneath the twelve penny . . .
   Why I would have the fool in every act.
   Be it comedy or tragedy, I 'ave laughed
   Until I cried again to see what faces
   The rogue will make . . .

THRIFT: I never saw [Timothy] Reade peeping through the curtain
   But ravishing joy entered into my heart . . .

[Landlord decides to leave and have his money back because the play has no fool.]

BOLT: But hist, the prologue enters, Landlord. Now it chimes,
   All in, to the play, the peals were rung before . . .

[They sit on the stage. Two prologues forget their lines and leave in confusion.]

SPRUCE: Perhaps our presence daunteth them. Let us
   Retire into some private room for fear
   The third man should be out . . .

LANDLORD: I'll follow them, though it be into a box.
   Though they did sit thus open on the stage
   To show their cloak and suit, yet I did think
   At last they would take sanctuary 'mongst
   The ladies, lest some creditor should spy them.
   'Tis better looking o'er a lady's head
   Or through a lattice window than a grate [*i.e.* in prison].

THRIFT: And I will hasten to the money box
   And take my shilling out again, for now
   I have considered that it is too much.
   I'll go [to] th' [Red] Bull or Fortune and there see
   A play for tuppence, with a jig to boot.

---

[1] Bells rang three separate times to warn spectators that the beginning of the play was increasingly imminent.

516 The playhouse is closed with all the others in 1642 but is used for illegal performances, 1647–1649

(a) *Perfect Occurrences*, 1–8 October 1647; (b) *The Kingdom's Weekly Intelligencer*, 2–9 January 1648/9

After Parliament closed all the playhouses on 2 September 1642 most were used occasionally for illegal performances, especially in 1647, 1648 and early 1649, when Salisbury Court was so used, twice with notable results. See also **503b, d**.

(a) 5 or 6 October 1647[1]

A stage play was to have been acted in Salisbury Court this day (and bills stuck up about it) called *A King and No King*, formerly acted at the Blackfriars by His Majesty's servants about eight years since, written by Francis Beaumont and John Fletcher.

The sheriffs of the City of London with their officers went thither and found a great number of people, some young lords and other eminent persons, and the men and women with the [money] boxes . . . fled. The sheriffs brought away Tim Reade, the fool, and the people cried out for their moneys but slunk away like a company of drowned mice without it [*sic*].

[1] The incident was reported in three journals. In the one used here it took place on 'this day', 6 October, in another on 5–12 October, and in the third 'on Tuesday last', 5 October. See *Mercurius Pragmaticus*, 5–12 October 1647 and *Mercurius Melancholicus*, 2–9 October 1647.

(b) 2 January 1649

The soldiers seized on the players on their stages at Drury Lane [the Phoenix] and at Salisbury Court. They went also to the Fortune in Golden Lane, but they found none there but John Pudding[1] dancing on the ropes, whom they took along with them. In the meantime, the players at the Red Bull, who had notice of it, made haste away and were all gone before they came and took away all their acting clothes with them.

But at Salisbury Court they were taken on the stage, the play being almost ended, and with many . . . lighted torches they were carried to Whitehall with their players' clothes upon their backs. In the way, they oftentimes took the crown from his head who acted the king and in sport would oftentimes put it on again. Abraham [evidently a boy playing a woman] had a black satin gown on, and before he came into the dirt he was very neat in his white-laced pumps. The people not expecting such a pageant looked and laughed at all the rest, and not knowing who he was, they asked what had that lady done.

They made some resistance at the Cockpit in Drury Lane, which was the occasion that they were bereaved of their apparel and were not so well used as those in Salisbury Court, who were more patient, and, therefore, at their releasement they had their clothes returned to them without the least diminution. After two days'

670   Playhouses, 1560–1660

confinement, they were ordered to put in bail and appear before the Lord Mayor to answer for what they have done according unto law.

[1] Apparently a name for any undistinguished performer. See *J and CS*, vi, 171–2n.

517   William Beeston buys the playhouse to save it from becoming a brewery, 1649–1652

(a) BL, Add. Charter 9393; (b) Folger, Ms. V.b.275, p. 16; BL, Add. Charter 9294; (d) PRO, C10/53/7. Transcribed in (b) Collier, *Works of William Shakespeare*, i, ccxli–ii; (c) Cunningham, 'The Whitefriars Theatre', 101. For (d) see *CRS*, 100–6. See also **496c**; Berry, 'Folger Ms. V.b.275'; and Bawcutt, 'Documents', 189–91

Much of what is known about the history of the playhouse from the winter of 1648–9 to its demise in 1666 derives from two indentures and two lawsuits in the Court of Chancery. The indentures and the first of the lawsuits are noticed below. The second lawsuit, in which Beeston sued two builders on 8 May 1666 is quoted in **509b**. The document quoted in (b) below was accepted as genuine by Bentley (*JCS*, vi, 114) among others, but it is probably a forgery and is unreliable; the passage quoted here reports inaccurately an event mentioned in the authentic document quoted in (d).

(a)   Beeston agrees to buy the lease on the playhouse, winter 1648–1649

The document is an uncompleted indenture saying that Beeston has bought the lease for £600. It is unsigned, and the day and month of its date are left blank; its year is given twice: as the twenty-fourth of Charles I (which began on 27 March 1648 and ended with his execution on 30 January 1649), and as 1648, which would include January 1648/9.[1] The document does not mention Beeston's down payment of £100, which could have been a separate transaction recorded in another document.

[1] The six months in which Beeston was to complete payment had begun and probably not ended by 12 April 1649 when the elder Herne wrote his will, for he noted in it that his lease in Salisbury Court was 'subject to my contract to be performed with Mr Beeston' (PRO, PROB.11/209/fos.215v–17). The younger Herne proved the will on 17 October 1649.

(b)   Soldiers are said to have pulled down the playhouse, 24 March 1649

The playhouse in Salisbury Court in Fleet Street was pulled down by a company of soldiers set on by the sectuaries of these sad times. On Saturday the 24 day day [*sic*] of March 1649.

(c)   Beeston completes purchase, 25 March 1652

The document is a completed indenture saying that Theophilus Bird has bought the lease on the playhouse property from the younger Herne for 'four [two spacing devices] hundred pounds'. After 'hundred' someone wrote, in different ink, a caret in the line and '& eight' above the line. Bird was an actor and Beeston's brother-in-law. His name was used, presumably, to prevent Beeston's creditors from getting their hands on the place.

(d) Beeston explains his purchase, 25 June 1658

This is the bill by which Beeston sued the new Earl of Dorset. Much of it is illegible, especially along the right side and at the bottom, where the parchment has perished (illegible places are shown here by three periods within square brackets). The document is so prolix, however, that the legible parts leave little doubt about the meaning of the whole. After a recital of the leases of 1629 and other preliminary matters (quoted in 508a), Beeston alleged that

The said Gunnell and Blagrave [*i.e.* their heirs and successors, being] disabled to pay the said rent of £100 a year, [John Herne] did intend and was resolved to make the same [playhouse] into a brewhouse, which the said Earl perceiving . . . the same would be a great annoyance to him being so near his dwelling [. . .] did earnestly importune him, your orator [*i.e.* Beeston], to agree with the said Mr Herne about the premises and [to] buy the said latter lease¹ of the said Mr Herne, promising your orator that for so doing your orator should have a new lease of the said playhouse and premises for eighty years at the rent of a peppercorn.

Whereupon [. . .] [your orator, not] doubting of the performance, agreed with the said Mr Herne for the same for £700 and paid him . . . £100 in part payment of the said £700, and your orator was to pay the remainder of the said sum about six months after. But before the remainder was to be paid [. . .] house by reason of which divers soldiers by force and arms entered the said playhouse, cut down the seats, broke down the stage, and utterly defaced the whole buildings [*sic*]. In regard whereof your orator did not pay the residue of the said money to the said Mr Herne, the said house being become [. . .] . . . And your orator further showeth . . . that within a short time after, he, the said John Herne died and left the premises to his son, John Herne, who sealed a lease of ejectment upon the premises.²

Whereupon the assigns of the said Gunnell and Blagrave, finding plays [. . .] unto the said John Herne [Jr] . . . who entered thereupon and shortly after contracted with one Lightmaker, a brewer, for the converting of the said playhouse into a brewhouse, and thereupon the said John Herne designed to return to your orator his £100 disbursed as aforesaid [. . .]. Whereupon the said Earl of Dorset, knowing what an annoyance a brewhouse would be so near his own house, tried many ways to prevent it, and, finding he could not prevail therein, sent for your orator and told him . . . that if your orator would go on with your orator's former bargain and [. . .] him, the said Earl, the said house should not be made a brewhouse, your said orator should find him, the said Earl, his great friend.

But your orator, excusing himself, did allege to the said Earl . . . that the aforesaid bargain was worse by £200 than at the time your orator did give the said [. . .] Whereupon the said Earl promised . . . that in case your orator would conclude his said bargain with the said John Herne that your orator should have the . . . time which was then unexpired, forty years or thereabout, made up [to] eighty years and that the said [. . .] his son, Richard then Lord Buckhurst, now Earl of Dorset, unto your orator, and that your orator should likewise by the said lease have a passage to the water stairs through Dorset Garden, then the said late Earl's, and also have the place where the dunghill now is in Salisbury Court with a coach house adjoining to [. . .]. [The Earl] also promised that so soon as he could receive the money which was due to him from the Earl of Middlesex, he would pay your orator £700 which he, the said Earl, did owe to Thomas Bowen, mercer of London, for wares, whose relict and executrix your orator married, all which aforesaid [. . .] . . .

Your orator acquainted Richard, then Lord Buckhurst, now Earl of Dorset, the then Earl's eldest son, with, and did demand of the said Lord Buckhurst if he would promise your orator to make good, the said Earl Edward's his promise in joining with his father in making your orator a lease of the [. . .] named place where the dung-hill is and the coach house next it, and also the passage to the water, all which the said Richard Lord Buckhurst promised to perform with his said father in consideration your orator should take the said playhouse and premises of the said Mr Herne and [. . .] [if] the making the said playhouse a brewhouse would be offensive to his father, whom [sic], he did believe, would very seldom stir out of his chamber, it would be much more inconvenient to him, the said Lord Buckhurst and to his posterity.

And the said Lord Buckhurst then promised to your orator to use his [. . .] said Lord Buckhurst went to the said Mr Herne, the son, and treated with him concerning the premises in the behalf of your orator. And [he] so far prevailed with him, the said Mr Herne, that the said Herne was willing to treat with your orator for the same. And thereupon, and upon the aforesaid premises, he, the said Earl, and Lord Buckhurst his son [. . .] after many meetings between the said Herne and your orator, the said Herne promised your orator if your orator would pay him, the said Herne, the money that his father and your orator agreed upon for the same, your orator should have the said house and premises. And thereupon your orator condescended to accept [. . .] Buckhurst would perform their promise made to your orator as aforesaid. And two months after, in the presence of the said Edward Earl of Dorset, your orator having sold and pawned his most necessary goods and having took up money upon ill conditions, he paid Mr Herne for the premises all the money agreed upon except £80 [. . .] by promise to your orator that his son, Richard Lord Buckhurst, should make your orator a lease of the premises for eighty years.

And your orator further showeth . . . that about two months after, which was in June 1651, the said Earl of Dorset being then very sick, your orator came to the said Lord Buckhurst [. . .] informing your orator that his father could not live two days. Wherefor your orator did desire him, the said Lord Buckhurst, in case the said Earl died to make your orator a lease of the premises for eighty years as he had formerly promised your orator. Whereupon [he] . . . repeated again his former promise and that he would make the same good unto [. . .] and formerly the playhouse in Salisbury Court and the ground belonging to the said playhouse for eighty years, and your orator should have the ground where now lieth a dung-hill in Salisbury Court and the coach house adjoining to the said dung-hill and a freedom to go to Dorset Garden to his Lordship's water stairs upon condition your orator would [. . .] playhouse or any part of the ground belonging to it. And the said Lord Buckhurst then further told your orator that his father, the Earl of Dorset, that day had desired him, the said Lord Buckhurst, particularly to perform his, the said Earl's, aforesaid promise to your orator, the said Earl being then upon his death-bed. And your orator [. . .] Dorset . . . and your orator . . . repaired to the said Richard now Earl of Dorset and desired that he would make good by lease the former promise of his father and himself, and he replied unto your orator that what his father promised in his lifetime and what he, the said now Earl, then promised . . . was to please [. . .] hearing what words the new Earl of Dorset had given your orator.

And your orator not having paid the said Mr Herne the said £80, the remainder of the said purchase money, the said Lightmaker treated with the said Mr Herne for the said house and premises, the said Lightmaker being at that time to lease his brewhouse [. . .] Lightmaker concluded for the same. And the said Lightmaker entered upon the said house and premises and took down the roof of the said house and was disposing of it to a brewhouse. Whereupon the said Richard Earl of Dorset caused one Mr Mastock, a gentleman belonging to him, to write a letter to your orator [. . .] the said house at the desire and promise of the late Earl of Dorset . . . Which letter the said Earl did see and did read and approve thereof and did cause the same to be read to him before the same was so sent to your orator. The substance of which letter was that if your orator would use [. . .] by lease confirm his former promise concerning the playhouse and premises upon condition your orator would be tied by covenant in the said lease not to make the same a brew-house. Upon which letter, your orator, by the assistance of his friends and selling and pawning all that he could [. . .] the brewer to assign the premises to your orator and also paid the present John Herne his £80.

Whereupon the said John Herne, by the direction of your orator, did the five and twentieth day of March 1652 assign the said playhouse and premises to Theophilus Bird [in trust for your orator] [. . .] said playhouse in the presence of the said Richard, now Earl of Dorset, who persuaded your orator to repair the ruined buildings of the playhouse and to make a convenient house to entertain persons of honour in, and promised your orator that your orator should have, after it was done, his lease confirmed [. . .] And the said Earl promised if your orator would build the house as aforesaid the said Earl would make it worth at least £300 a year to your orator. Upon which encouragement your orator upon several engagements procured £300 and laid [it out in repairs] [. . .] . . .

Beeston continued his recital of futile negotiations with the Earl and then with his Countess and his agent, Sir Kenelm Digby (both of whom Beeston thought sympathetic to him). He declared finally that the Earl had recently sued him in Common Pleas to eject him in favour of one Henry Wheeler, to whom the Earl had given a new lease. He asked Chancery to stop that case, and Chancery did so.

In reply, the Earl argued mainly (and, it seems, correctly) that the property belonged to his father only for life, hence that the leases ended at his father's death on 17 July 1652 (see also BL, Add. MS 5064, fo. 225). Chancery decided on 6 November 1658, however, that Beeston should continue to hold the property for the years remaining in the Dorset–Herne lease (until 7 July 1690) because the Earl had not objected to Beeston for five years after his father's death (PRO, C33/211/fo. 49v).

[1] i.e., the Dorset–Herne lease of 15 July 1629 (506).
[2] After his father's death, evidently, the younger Herne formally ejected Gunnell's and Blagrave's heirs and successors from Salisbury Court. They may have paid the rent for a year or two and made some repairs after Parliament closed the playhouses in 1642. Then they supposed that even though they were no longer paying the rent they still had an interest in the place, for eventually they petitioned the Earl of Dorset to reinstate their lease, perhaps when he was trying to remove Beeston in 1658. The Earl probably could do little about the petition because Chancery ordered that Beeston continue to possess the playhouse. The petition is quoted in 508b.

Bibliography

Acts of the Privy Council of England, ed. J. R. Dasent. London: HMSO. Volumes for 1542–7 (1890); 1547–50 (1890); 1550–2 (1891); 1552–4 (1892); 1554–6 (1892); 1556–8 (1893); 1558–70 (1893); 1571–5 (1894); 1575–7 (1894); 1578–80 (1895); 1580–1 (1896); 1581–2 (1896); 1586–7 (1897); 1587–8 (1897); 1589–90 (1899); 1590 (1899); 1591 (1900); 1591–2 (1901); 1592–3 (1901); 1597 (1903); 1597–8 (1903); 1599–1600 (1905); 1600–1 (1906); 1601–4 (1907).

Adams, Joseph Q. *Shakespearean Playhouses*. Boston, 1917.

Adams, Joseph Q., ed. *The Dramatic Records of Sir Henry Herbert, Master of the Revels, 1623–1673*. New Haven, 1917.

Agrippa, Henry Cornelius. *The Vanity and Uncertainty of Arts and Sciences*. London, 1569.

Andrews, C.E. *Richard Brome*. New York, 1913.

Anglin, Jay P. 'The Schools of Defense in Elizabethan London.'. *Renaissance Quarterly*, 37.3 (autumn 1984).

Anglo, Sydney. 'The Court Festivals of Henry VII: A Study Based Upon the Account Books of John Heron, Treasurer of the Chamber'. *Bulletin of the John Rylands Library*, 43.1 (1960).

'An Early Tudor Programme for Plays and Other Demonstrations Against the Pope'. *Journal of the Warburg and Courtauld Institutes*, 20 (1957).

Spectacle, Pageantry and Early Tudor Policy. Oxford, 1969.

Armin, Robert. *Foole vpon Foole*. London, 1600, 1605. And with another title, *A Nest of Ninnies*. London, 1608.

Astington, John. 'Rereading Illustrations of the English Stage'. *Shakespeare Survey*, 50 (1997).

B., G. *A Fig for the Spaniard*. London, 1591, 1592.

Baker, Richard. *Theatrum Redivivum, or The Theatre Vindicated*. London, 1662.

Baldwin, Thomas W. *The Organization and Personnel of the Shakespearean Company*. Princeton, 1927.

Bale, John. *King Johan, I and II*. Ed. Barry B. Adams. San Marino, CA: Huntington Library Publications, 1969.

The Chief Promises of God unto Man. Ed. J. S. Farmer. In *Tudor Facsimile Texts*, vol. XXI. London, 1908.

The Temptation of our Lord. Ed. J. S. Farmer. In *Tudor Facsimile Texts*, vol. XXII. London, 1909.

Three Lawes of Nature, Moses and Christ. In *The Dramatic Writings of John Bale*, ed. J. S. Farmer. London, 1907.

Barlow, Graham F. 'Wenceslas Hollar and Christopher Beeston's Phoenix Theatre in Drury Lane'. *Theatre Research International*, 13.1 (spring 1988).

Bavande, William. *A Work of Joannes Ferrarius Montanus Touching the Good Ordering of a Commonweal*. London, 1559.

Bawcutt, N.W. 'Documents of the Salisbury Court Theater in the British Library'. *Medieval and Renaissance Drama in England*, 9 (1997).

Beaumont, Francis and John Fletcher. *Cupid's Revenge*. London, 1615.

A King and No King. London, 1619.

The Knight of the Burning Pestle. London, 1613.

Becmann, Johann Christoff. *Accessiones Historiae Anhaltinae*. Zerbst, 1716.

Benbow, R. Mark. 'Dutton and Goffe Versus Broughton: A Disputed Contract for Plays in the 1570s'. *REED Newsletter*, 2 (1981).

Bentley, Gerald Eades. *The Jacobean and Caroline Stage*. 7 vols. Oxford, 1941–68.

Berry, Herbert. *The Boar's Head Playhouse*. Washington, DC, 1986.
   The Noble Science. Newark, DE, 1991.
   Shakespeare's Playhouses. New York, 1987.
   'Chambers, the Bull, and the Bacons'. *Essays in Theatre* (November 1988).
   'The First Public Playhouses, Especially the Red Lion'. *Shakespeare Quarterly*, 40.2 (summer 1989).
   'Folger Ms. V.b.275 and the Deaths of Shakespearean Playhouses'. *Medieval and Renaissance Drama in England*, 10 (1998).
   'A Handlist of Documents About the Theatre in Shoreditch'. In *Shakespeare's Playhouses*. New York, 1987.
   'The Miltons and the Blackfriars Playhouse'. *Modern Philology*, 89.4 (May 1992).
   'Richard Vennar, England's Joy', *English Literary Renaissance*, forthcoming.
   'Sebastian Westcott, the Children of St Paul's, and Professor Lennam'. *Renaissance and Reformation*, 14.1 (1978).
   'Shylock, Robert Miles, and Events at the Theatre'. *Shakespeare Quarterly*, 44.2 (summer 1993).
   'The View of London from the North and the Playhouses in Holywell'. *Shakespeare Survey*, 53 (2000).
   'Where was the Playhouse in which the Boy Choristers of St Paul's Performed Plays?' *Medieval and Renaissance Drama in English*, 13 (2000).
Binz, Gustav. 'Londoner Theater und Schauspiele im Jahre 1599'. *Anglia*, 22 (1899).
Birch, Thomas. *Court and Times of James the First*. London, 1848.
Blackfriars Records. *See* Feuillerat, Albert.
Bordinat, Philip. 'A New Site for the Salisbury Court Theatre'. *Notes and Queries*, n.s. 3.201 (1956).
Bride-Oak, Ralph. A commendatory poem. In Thomas Randolph, *Poems, with the Muses Looking-Glass*. London, 1638.
Briefe Description of the notorious Life of . . . Doctor Lambe, A. Together with his Ignominious Death. Amsterdam, 1628.
Brome, Richard. *The Court Beggar*. London, 1653.
   Five New Plays. London, 1653.
Brownstein, Oscar L. 'A Record of London Inn-Playhouses from *c*. 1565–1590'. *Shakespeare Quarterly*, 22.1 (1971).
Bucer, Martin. 'De honestis ludis'. Part of *De Regno Christi Jesu*. Printed in *Scripta Anglicana*, 1557.
Burton, Robert. *Anatomy of Melancholy*. London, 1621.
C., I. *A Pleasant Comedy Called the Two Merry Milkmaids, or the best Words Wear the Garlands*. London, 1620.
Calendar of Letters and Papers, Foreign and Domestic, Henry VIII. London: HMSO.
   January–May 1537, ed. J. Gairdner, 1890.
   January–July 1539, ed. J. Gairdner and R. H. Brodie, 1894.
   August–December 1539, ed. J. Gairdner and R. H. Brodie, 1896.
   1542, ed. J. Gairdner and R. H. Brodie, 1900.
Calendar of State Papers, Domestic. London: HMSO.
   1547–80, ed. R. Lemon, 1858.
   1595–7, ed. Mrs Everett Green, 1869.
   1601–3, ed. Mrs Everett Green, 1870.
   1603–10, ed. Mrs Everett Green, 1857.
   1636–7, ed. John Bruce, 1867.
   1639, ed. W. D. Hamilton, 1873.
   1655, ed. Mrs Everett Green, 1882.
Calendar of State Papers, Venetian. London: HMSO.
   1603–7, ed. H. F. Brown, 1900.
   1615–17, ed. A. B. Hinds, 1908.
Calendar of Treasury Books. 32 vols. Compiled by William A. Shaw. London: HMSO.
   Vol. XIII, 1933.
The Cambridge Modern History, Ed. A. W. Ward, G. W. Prothero and Stanley Leathes. Cambridge, 1934.
   Vol. III.
Camden, William. *Annales Ab Anno 1603 ad Annum 1623*. London, 1691. Published with the *Epistolae*.
Cardwell, Eward. *Documentary Annals of the Reformed Church of England . . . from the year 1546 to the year 1716*. 2 vols. Oxford, 1844.

Carew, Thomas. A commendatory poem. In William Davenant, *The Just Italian*. London, 1630.
Carlell, Lodowick. *Arviragus and Felicia*. London, 1639.
Carte, Thomas. *A Collection of Original Letters and Papers*. London, 1739.
Chamberlain, John. *The Letters of John Chamberlain*. Ed. Norman E. McClure. Philadelphia, 1939.
Chambers, E.K. *The Elizabethan Stage*. 4 vols. Oxford, 1923.
  Notes on the History of the Revels Office Under the Tudors. London, 1906.
  William Shakespeare. 2 vols. Oxford, 1930.
Chapman, George. *The Conspiracy and the Tragedy of Charles, Duke of Byron*. London, 1608.
Chapman, George, Ben Jonson and John Marston. *Eastward Ho!* London, 1605.
Chapman, Henry. *Thermae redivivae: the City of Bath Described*. London, 1673.
Clapham, A. W. 'The Topography of the Carmelite Priory of London'. *The Journal of the British Archaeological Association*, 2nd series, 16 (1910).
Clode, C.M. *The Early History of the Guild of Merchant Taylors of the Fraternity of St John the Baptist*. London, 1888.
Cocke, John. 'The Character of a Common Player'. *See* Stevens, John.
Cole, M. J. 'A New Account of the Burning of the Globe'. *Shakespeare Quarterly*, 32.3 (autumn 1981).
A Collection of Early Maps of London, 1553–1667, Ed. John Fisher. Lympne Castle, Kent, 1981.
Collier, John Payne. *History of English Dramatic Poetry*. London, 1831, 1837.
  Memoirs of Edward Alleyn. London, 1841.
  New Facts Regarding the Life of Shakespeare. London, 1835.
  The Works of William Shakespeare. London, 1844.
Cooper, Charles Henry. *Annals of Cambridge*. 5 vols. (vol. v ed. John Williams Cooper). Cambridge, 1842–1908.
Cowel, John. *A Law Dictionary*. London, 1727.
Crashaw, William. *The Sermon Preached at the Crosse, Feb. xiiij. 1607[/8]*. London, 1608.
Crosfield, Thomas. *The Diary of Thomas Crosfield*, Ed. F. S. Boas. London, 1935.
Cunningham, Peter. *Extracts from the Accounts of the Revels at Court*. London, 1842.
  'The Whitefriars Theatre, the Salisbury Court Theatre, and the Duke's Theatre in Dorset Gardens'. *Shakespeare Society's Papers*, 4 (1849).
Daniel, Samuel. *Tethys' Festival*. London, 1604.
  The Vision of the Twelve Goddesses. London, 1623.
Dankerts, Cornelius. *London*. Amsterdam, *c.* 1633, *c.* 1645. (*a map*)
Davenant, Sir William. *Britannia Triumphans*. London, 1638.
  News from Plymouth. In *The Works*. London, 1673.
  The Play-house to be Let. In *The Works*. London, 1673.
  The Witts. London, 1636.
  The Works of Sir William Davenant, Kt. London, 1673.
Day, John, William Rowley and George Wilkins. *The Travels of Three English Brothers*. London, 1607.
Day, John. *Isle of Gulls*. London, 1606.
Dekker, Thomas. *The Guls Hornebooke*. London, 1609.
  Ravens Almanacke. London, 1609.
  Worke for Armorours. London, 1609.
Dekker, Thomas, John Ford and William Rowley. *The Witch of Edmonton*. London, 1658.
Dekker, Thomas, and Thomas Middleton. *The Roaring Girl*. London, 1611.
Dice, Wine, and Women. Or, the Unfortunate Gallant Gulled at London. London, *c.* 1623.
Digges, Leonard. A commendatory poem. *See* Shakespeare, William.
Earle, John. *Microcosmography, or a Piece of the World Discovered in Essays and Characters*. London, 1628.
Eccles, Mark. 'Elizabethan Actors II: E–J'. *Notes and Queries*, 38.4 (1991).
  'Martin Peerson and the Blackfriars'. *Shakespeare Survey*, 11 (1958).
English Dramatic Companies. *See* Murray, John Tucker.
'English Literature and History, London, 16 and 17 December 1996'. Sale catalogue. London: Sotheby's.
F., T. [Francis Thynne?] *News from the North*. London, 1579.
Farley, Henry. *St Pavles-Church her Bill for the Parliament*. London, 1621.

Fenton, Geoffrey. *A Form of Christian Policy gathered out of French*. London, 1574.
Feuillerat, Albert. *Documents Relating to the Office of the Revels in the Time of Queen Elizabeth*. Louvain, 1908.
    Documents Relating to the Revels at Court in the Time of King Edward VI and Queen Mary. Louvain, 1914.
Feyerabend, Karl. 'Zu K. H. Schaible's Geschichte der Deutschen in England'. *Englische Studien*, 14 (1890).
Field, John. *A Godly Exhortation*. London, 1583.
Figueiro, Vasco. *The Spaniards Monarchie*. London, 1592.
Fitch, Robert. 'Norwich Pageants'. *Norfolk Archaeology*, 5 (1856).
Fitz-Geoffrey, Henry. 'Notes from Black-Fryers'. In his *Satyres and Satyricall Epigrams*. London, 1617.
Fleay, F.G. *A Chronicle History of the London Stage, 1559–1642*. London, 1890.
Flecknoe, Richard. *Miscellania*. London, 1653.
    'A Short Discourse of the English Stage'. Attached to his *Love's Kingdom*. London, 1664.
Fletcher, John. *Wit Without Money*. London, 1639.
    See James Shirley.
Florio, John. *First Fruites*. London, 1578.
Foakes, R.A. *Illustrations of the English Stage, 1580–1642*. London, 1985.
Foxe, John. *Actes and Monuments of these latter and perillous dayes touching matters of the Church*. 2 vols. London, 1570.
G., I. *A Refutation of the Apology for Actors*. London, 1615.
Gaedertz, K.T. *Zur Kenntnis der altenglischen Bühne*. Bremen, 1888.
Gair, Reavley. *The Children of Paul's: The Story of a Theatre Company, 1553–1608*. Cambridge, 1982.
    'The Conditions of Appointment for Masters of Choristers at Paul's (1553–1613)'. *Notes and Queries*, 225 (1980).
Gardiner, Samuel. *Doomes-Day Book*. London, 1606.
Gardiner, Samuel R. *History of England from the Accession of James I to the Outbreak of the Civil War*. London, 1883–4.
Gardner, Harold C., SJ. *Mysteries' End: An Investigation of the Last Days of the Medieval Religious Stage*. Yale Studies in English, 103. New Haven, 1967.
Garfield, John. *The Wandring Whore Continued*. London, 1660.
Gargano, G. S. *Scapigliatura Italiana a Londra sotto Elisabetta e Giacomo I*. Florence, 1923.
Gascoigne, George. *The Glasse of Governement*. London, 1575.
    Supposes. London, 1573.
Gayton, Edmund. *Pleasant Notes upon Don Quixot*. London, 1654.
Gildersleeve, Virginia C. *Government Regulation of the Elizabethan Drama*. New York, 1908.
Goffe, Thomas. *The Careless Shepherdess*. London, 1656.
Goldyng, Arthur. *A brief treatise of the burning of Bucer and Phagius at Cambridge in the tyme of Queen Mary, with their restitution in the time of our moste gracious souerayne Lady that now is . . . translated into Englyshe*. London, 1562.
Gomme, Laurence. 'The Story of London Maps'. *The Geographical Journal*, 31 (January–June 1908).
Goodman, Nicholas. *Holland's Leaguer*. London, 1632.
Gosson, Stephen. *Plays Confuted in fiue Actions*. London, 1582.
    The School of Abuse, containing a pleasant invective against poets, pipers, players, jesters and suchlike caterpillars of a commonwealth. London, 1579.
Greene, Robert. *Greene's Groatsworth of Wit, bought with a Million of Repentance*. London, 1592.
    The Honorable Historie of Friar Bacon and Friar Bungay. London, 1627.
Greenstreet, James. *The Whitefriars Theatre in the Time of Shakespere*. London, 1888.
    'Documents Relating to the Players at the Red Bull . . . and the Cockpit in Drury Lane in the time of James I'. *The New Shakspere Society's Transactions* (1880–6).
    'The Red Bull Playhouse in the Reign of James I'. *The Athenaeum*, 28 November 1885.
Greenwood, C. and J. *Map of London*. London, 1827.
Greg, W. W. *A Bibliography of the English Printed Drama to the Restoration*. London, 1951.
Guilpin, Everard. *Skialetheia*. London, 1598.
H., I. *This World's Folly*. London, 1615.

Haaker, Ann. 'The Plague, the Theatre, and the Poet'. *Renaissance Drama*, n.s. 1 (1968).
Hall, Norman L. 'The Court of Husting'. *Transactions of the GHA*, 5 (1981).
Halliwell-Phillipps, James Orchard. *Outlines of the Life of Shakespeare*. London, 1881, 1882, 1887. The one cited is 1887 unless otherwise noted.
Halliwell (later Halliwell-Phillipps), James O, ed. *Letters of the Kings of England*. 2 vols. London, 1848.
Harington, Sir John. *Metamorphosis of Ajax*. London, 1596.
Harvey, Gabriel. *Letter Book*. London, 1579.
'An Advertisement for Papp-Hatchett and Martin Mar-prelate'. In his *Pierces Supererogation*. London, 1593.
Hassler, Conrad. *Die Reisen des Samuel Kiechel*. Bibliothek des literarischen Vereins in Stuttgart, 86. Stuttgart, 1866.
Hazlitt, William Craven. *The English Drama and Stage under the Tudor and Stuart Princes, 1543–1664*. The Roxburghe Library, 1869: reprint Burt Franklin, NY (Research Source Works Series, 49), n.d.
Heath, John. *Two Centuries of Epigrammes*. London, 1610.
Henslowe, Philip. *Henslowe's Diary*. Ed. R.A. Foakes and R.T. Rickert. Cambridge, 1961. This is the edition cited, unless otherwise noted.
Henslowe's Diary. Ed. W.W. Greg. 2 vols. London, 1904, 1908.
The Henslowe Papers. Ed. R.A. Foakes. London, 1977. (*facsimile*)
Henslowe Papers, being documents supplementary to Henslowe's Diary. Ed. W.W. Greg. London, 1904–8.
Hentzner, Paul. *Itinerarium Germaniæ, Galliæ, Angliæ, Italiæ*. Nuremberg, 1612.
Heywood, Thomas. *An Apology for Actors*. London, 1612.
The English Traveller. London, 1633.
Loves Maistresse. London, 1635.
Heywood, Thomas, and Richard Brome. *The Late Lancashire Witches*. London, 1634.
Hillebrand, Harold N. *The Child Actors*. Urbana, IL 1926.
'Sebastian Westcote, Dramatist and Master of the Children of Paul's'. *Journal of English and Germanic Philology*, 14 (1915).
Historical Manuscripts Commission. London: HMSO.
Calendar of the Shrewsbury and Talbot Papers. Ed. G.R. Batho (1971).
De L'Isle and Dudley. Vol. II, 1934.
Eighth Report (vol. 2, 1908).
House of Lords. Vol. XI, 1962.
Le Fleming. 1890.
Salisbury. Vol. II, 1888; vol XVII, 1938.
Third Report. 1872.
Various. Vol. VII, 1914.
Holinshed, Raphael. *Chronicle*. 3 vols. London, 1577. Ed. Allardyce and Josephine Nicoll, New York, 1995.
Hollar, Wenceslaus. The Long Bird's-Eye View of London. Antwerp, 1647. (*a map view*)
Hotson, Leslie. *The Commonwealth and Restoration Stage*. Cambridge, MA, 1928.
Household Accounts of Princess Elizabeth. Ed. Viscount Strangford. Camden Society 55 [2]. London, 1853.
Ingleby, C. M. *Shakespeare, the Man and the Book*. London, 1877.
Ingram, William. *The Business of Playing*. Ithaca, NY, 1992.
A London Life in the Brazen Age: Francis Langley, 1548–1602. Cambridge, MA, 1978.
'The Playhouse as an Investment, 1607–1614: Thomas Woodford and Whitefriars'. *Medieval and Renaissance Drama in England*, 2 (1985).
'The Playhouse at Newington Butts: A New Proposal'. *Shakespeare Quarterly*, 21 (1971).
Jeaffreson, John Cordy. *See Middlesex County Records*.
Jeayes, I. H., ed. *The Letters of Philip Gawdy*. London, 1906.
Jonas, Maurice. *Shakespeare and the Stage*. London, 1918.
Jonson, Ben. *The Workes of Benjamin Jonson*. London: 1616, 1640.
Bartholomew Fair. In *The Workes* (1640).

Catiline his Conspiracy. London, 1611.
Epicoene. London, 1609.
The Magnetic Lady. In *The Workes* (1640).
The Masque of Blackness. London, 1608.
The Masque of Queens. London, 1609.
The New Inn. London, 1631.
Oberon, the Fairy Prince. London, 1616.
Sejanus. London, 1604.
'Underwoods'. In *The Workes* (1640).
The Journals of the House of Commons. London, 1742.
Jusserand, J.J. 'Ambassador La Boderie and the "Compositeur" of the Byron Plays'. *Modern Language Review*, 6 (1911).
Kemp, Will. *Kemps Nine Daies Wonder*. London, 1600.
The King of Denmark's Welcome. London, 1606.
The Kingdom's Weekly Intelligencer. 18–25 January, 12–19 September, 1648; 2–9 January, 1649.
Kingsford, C.L. 'Paris Garden and the Bear-baiting'. *Archaeologia*, 2nd series, 20 (1920).
Kirchmayer, Thomas. *Pammachius*. 1538.
  Tragoedia nova Pammachius. Basel, 1541.
Kirkman, Francis. *The Wits, or Sport upon Sport*. London, 1662, 1673.
The Ladies, A Second Time Assembled in Parliament. London, 1647.
Lamb, John. *A Collection of Letters, Statutes and other Documents* etc.. London, 1838.
Lambarde, William. *A Perambulation of Kent*. London, 1576, 1596.
Langbaine, Gerard. *An Account of the English Dramatick Poets*. London, 1691.
Larkin, J.F. and Paul Hughes. *Stuart Royal Proclamations*. 2 vols. Oxford, 1973–83.
The Late Will and Testament of the Doctors Commons. London, 1641.
The Laughing Mercury. 15–22 September, 1652.
Lawrence, W.J. 'New Facts From Sir Henry Herbert's Office Book'. *Times Literary Supplement*, 29 November 1923.
Leishman, J.B., ed. *The Three Parnassus Plays*. London, 1949.
Lewis, C.T. and C.S. Short. *A Latin Dictionary*. Oxford, 1896.
Lodge, Sir Edmund. *Illustrations of British History, Biography and Manners in the Reigns of Henry VIII, Edward VI, Mary, Elizabeth and James I*. 3 vols. London, 1791.
Lodge, Thomas. *Wits Miserie*. London, 1596.
Loengard, Janet. 'An Elizabethan Lawsuit: John Brayne, his Carpenter, and the Building of the Red Lion Theatre'. *Shakespeare Quarterly*, 34.3 (autumn 1983).
Lyly, John. *Endymion*. London, 1591.
?Lyly, John. *Pappe with an Hatchet*. London, 1589.
Machyn, Henry. *The Diary of Henry Machyn, Citizen and Merchant-Taylor of London, AD 1550–1563*. Ed. John Gough Nichols. Camden Society, 1st series, 42. London, 1848.
Maitland, William. *History of London*. London, 1739.
Malcolm, J. P. *Londinium Redivivum*. London, 1803.
Malone Society *Collections*. Oxford University Press.
  I.1 (1908). *Dramatic Records: The Remembrancia*. Ed. E.K. Chambers and W.W. Greg.
  I.2 (1909). *Dramatic Records from the Landsdowne Manuscript*. Ed. E.K. Chambers and W.W. Greg.
  I.3 (1910). *Dramatic Records from the Patent Rolls. Company Licences*. Ed. E.K. Chambers and W.W. Greg.
  I.4–5 (1911). *Dramatic Records from the Privy Council Register, 1603–1642*. Ed. E.K. Chambers and W.W. Greg.
  II.1 (1913). *Blackfriars Records*. Ed. Albert Feuillerat.
  II.3 (1931). *Players at Ipswich*. Ed. V.B. Redstone and E.K. Chambers.
  III (1954). *A Calendar of Dramatic Records in the Books of the Livery Companies of London, 1485–1640*. Ed. Jean Robertson and Donald J. Gordon.
  VI (1961). *Dramatic Records in the Declared Accounts of the Treasurer of the Chamber, 1558–1642*. Ed. David Cook.

VII (1965). *Records of Plays and Players in Kent, 1430–1642*, Ed. Giles Dawson.
VIII (1969). *Records of Plays and Players in Lincolnshire, 1300–1585*, Ed. Stanley Kahrl.
Malone, Edmond. 'Enlarged History of the Stage'. In *The Plays and Poems of William Shakespeare*, ed. James Boswell the Younger. London, 1821. ('The third variorum.')
The Man in the Moon. 23–31 January 1650.
Manningham, John. *The Diary of John Manningham*, Ed. R.P. Sorlien. Hanover, NH, 1976.
Marlowe, Christopher. *Dr Faustus*. London, 1604, 1616.
Marston, John. *Antonio and Mellida*. London, 1601.
  The Dutch Courtesan. London, 1605.
  The Scourge of Villainy. London, 1598.
  What You Will. London, 1607.
?Marston, John. *Jack Drum's Entertainment*. London, 1601.
Massinger, Philip. *The Great Duke of Florence*. London, 1636.
  The Roman Actor. London, 1629.
Mayne, Jasper. A commendatory poem. In *Jonsonus Virbius*. London, 1638.
Mercurius Democritus. 1–8 June 1653.
Mercurius Elencticus. 19–26 January 1648.
Mercurius Fumigosus. 15–22 November 1654; 27 December – 3 January 1654/5; 9–16 May, 12–19 September 1655.
Mercurius Melancholicus. 4 September, 2 – 9 October 1647.
Mercurius Pragmaticus. 5–12 October 1647; 22–9 January 1650.
Mercurius Publicus. 14–21 February 1661.
Mercurius Veridicus. 19–26 April 1645.
Meres, Francis. *Palladis Tamia*. London, 1598.
Middlesex County Records, Ed. John Cordy Jeaffreson. 4 vols. London, 1886–92.
Middleton, Thomas. *A Chaste Maid in Cheapside*. London, 1630.
  The Family of Love. London, 1608.
  A Game at Chesse. London, n.d. [1624 or 1625].
  Inner Temple Masque. London, 1619.
Middleton, Thomas, and Thomas Dekker. *The Roaring Girl*. London, 1611.
Middleton, Thomas, and William Rowley. *The Changeling*. London, 1653.
Morgan, William. *London &c. Actually Survey'd*. London, 1682, c. 1720.
?Munday, Anthony. *A Second and Third Blast of Retrait from Plays and Theatres*. London, 1580.
Murray, John Tucker. *English Dramatic Companies, 1558–1642*. 2 vols. London, 1910.
Nabbes, Thomas. *Covent Garden*. London, 1638.
  Microcosmus. London, 1637.
  Tottenham Court. London 1638.
Nashe, Thomas. *Have with you to Saffron Walden*. London, 1596.
  Martins Months Minde. London, 1589.
  Pierce Penniless his supplication to the Devil. London, 1592.
  Summer's Last Will and Testament. London, 1600.
?Nashe, Thomas. *The Returne of the renowned Caualiero Pasquill of England*. London, ?1589
The New Shakspere Society's Transactions. London, 1877–9.
Nicholl, J. *Some Account of the Worshipful Company of Ironmongers compiled from their own Records and other authentic sources of information by John Nicholl*. London, 1851.
Nicolas, Sir N. Harris. *Memoirs of the Life & Times of Sir Christopher Hatton, K.G.* London, 1847.
Nixon, Anthony. *The Three English Brothers*. London, 1607.
Norman, Philip. *The Accounts of the Overseers of the Poor of Paris Garden*. London, 1901.
  'The Accounts of the Overseers of the Poor of Paris Garden'. *Surrey Archaeological Collections*, 16 (1901).
Northbrooke, John. *A Treatise wherein Dicing, Dancing, vain Plays or Interludes, with other idle Pastimes, etc., commonly used on the Sabbath Day, are reproved by the Authority of the Word of God and Ancient Writers*. London, c. 1577.

Nungezer, Edwin. *Dictionary of Actors and Other Persons Associated with the Public Representations of Plays in England Before 1642*. New Haven, 1929.
Ogilby, John and William Morgan. *A Large and Accurate Map of the City of London*. London, 1676.
A Large and Accurate Map of the City of London, Ed. Ralph Hyde. Lympne Castle, Kent, 1976.
Orrell, John. *The Theatres of Inigo Jones and John Webb*. Cambridge, 1985.
  'Building the Fortune'. *Shakespeare Quarterly*, 44.2 (summer 1993).
Overbury, Sir Thomas. *New and Choice Characters of Several Authors, together with that exquisite and unmatched poem The Wife, written by Sir Thomas Overbury; . . . with other things added to this sixth impression*. London, 1615.
Oxford English Dictionary, Ed. J.A.H. Murray, et al.; J.A. Simpson, E.S.C. Weiner. Oxford, 1928, 1989.
Parker, Matthew. *Correspondence of Matthew Parker, DD, Archbishop of Canterbury, comprising Letters written by and to him from AD 1535 to his Death, AD 1575*, Ed. John Bruce and Thomas Thomason Perowne. Publications of the Parker Society, 49. Cambridge, 1853.
Pepys, Samuel. *Diary*, Ed. Robert Latham and William Matthews. London, 1971.
A Perfect Account of the Daily Intelligence. 27 December – 3 January 1654–5.
A Perfect Diurnal. 7–14 February 1648; 17–24 December 1649.
Perfect Occurrences. 6–13 August, 1–8 October 1647; 28 January – 4 February 1648.
Philip, John. *Patient Grissell*. London, c. 1566.
?Phillips, John. *Sportive Wit*. London, 1656.
Pollard, A.W. *Fifteenth-Century Verse and Prose*. London, 1903.
Prynne, William. *Histrio-mastix*. London, 1633.
The Puritan. London, 1607.
Raine, Angelo. *York Civic Records*, 115 (1950).
Randolph, Thomas. *The Muses' Looking Glass, or The Entertainment*. Oxford, 1638.
Rankins, William. *A Mirror of Monsters, wherein is plainly described the manifold vices and spotted enormities that are caused by the infectious sight of plays*. London, 1587.
Rawlidge, Richard. *A Monster Late Found Out and Discovered*. London, 1628.
Records of Early English Drama. University of Toronto Press.
  Bristol, Ed. Mark C. Pilkinton, 1997.
  Cambridge, Ed. Alan H. Nelson, 2 vols., 1989.
  Chester, Ed. Lawrence M. Clopper, 1979.
  Coventry, Ed. R.W. Ingram, 1981.
  Cumberland, Westmoreland, Gloucester, Ed. Audrey Douglas and Peter Greenfield, 1986.
  Devon, Ed. John Wasson, 1986.
  Herefordshire, Worcestershire, Ed. David N. Klausner, 1990.
  Lancashire, Ed. David George, 1991.
  Norwich 1540–1642, Ed. David Galloway, 1984.
  York, Ed. Alexandra F. Johnston and Margaret Rogerson, 2 vols., 1979.
The Records of the Honourable Society of Lincoln's Inn, Black Books. London, 1898.
Records of the Worshipful Company of Carpenters, Ed. Bower Marsh. Oxford, 1915.
Rendle, William. 'The Bankside, Southwark, and the Globe Playhouse'. In F. J. Furnivall's 1878 edition of William Harrison's *Description of England*.
The Return from Parnassus. London, 1606.
Rimbault, Edward F. 'Salisbury Court Theatre'. *Notes and Queries*, 2nd series, 2 (1856).
Rocque, John. *A Plan of the Cities of London and Westminster, and the Borough of Southwark*. London, 1746.
Rosenfeld, Sybil. 'Unpublished Stage Documents'. *Theatre Notebook*, 11 (1956–7).
Rowley, William. *All's Lost by Lust*. London, 1633.
Rowley, William, John Day and George Wilkins. *The Travels of The Three English Brothers*. London, 1607.
Rump: Or an Exact Collection of the Choycest Poems and Songs. London, 1662.
Rye, W.B. *England as Seen by Foreigners in the Days of Elizabeth and James*. London, 1865.
Rymer, Thomas. *Foedera, conventiones, literae, et cujuscunque generis Acta publica inter Reges Angliae*. London, 1704–32. (Better known as Rymer's *Foedera*.)
Sackville, Thomas and Thomas Norton. *Gorboduc*. London, 1566.

Sampson, Martin W. 'The Interior of the Fortune'. *Modern Language Notes* (June 1915).
Shakespeare, William. *The Plays and Poems of William Shakespeare*. Ed. James Boswell the Younger. London, 1821. (The 'third variorum'.)
   Shakespeare's Poems. London, 1640. Contains a commendatory poem by Leonard Digges.
Shapiro, I. A. 'The Bankside Theatres: Early Engravings'. *Shakespeare Survey*, 1 (1948).
Sharpe, Lewis. *The Noble Stranger*. London, 1640.
Sharpham, Edward. *Cupid's Whirligig*. London, 1607.
Shirley, James. *The Doubtful Heir*. London, 1652.
   Poems &c. London, 1648.
   The Wedding. London, 1629.
Shirley, James (or John Fletcher). *The Coronation*. London, 1640.
A Short-Title Catalogue of English Books, 1475–1640. Compiled by A.W. Pollard and G.R. Redgrave; Oxford, 1926. Revised edn, 3 vols., ed. Katharine Pantzer, 1991.
Sidney, Sir Philip. *The Defense of Poesy*. London, 1595.
Silver, George. *Paradoxes of Defence*. London, 1599.
Sisson, C.J. *Lost Plays of Shakespeare's Age*. Cambridge, 1936.
   'Keep the Widow Waking'. *The Library*, 4th series, 8 (1927).
   'The Red Bull Company and the Importunate Widow'. *Shakespeare Survey*, 7 (1954).
Smith, Irwin. *Shakespeare's Blackfriars Playhouse*. New York, 1964.
Smith, Logan Pearsall. *Life and Letters of Sir Henry Wotton*. London, 1907.
Smith, Wentworth. *The Hector of Germany*. London, 1615.
Stationers' Register. *See Transcript of the Registers of the Company of Stationers of London.*
Statutes of the Realm, 9 vols. in 10 with alphabetical index, 1810–22 and 1824 (index).
Stevens, John. *Satirical Essays Characters and Others*. London, 1615. Contains the essay by John Cocke.
Stocks, Helen and W.H. Stevenson. *Records of the Borough of Leicester, 1603–1608*. Cambridge, 1923.
Stockwood, John. *A Sermon Preached at Paules Crosse . . . 24 August 1578*. London, 1578.
Stow, John. *Annales or Generall Chronicle of England*, 'continued and augmented . . . by Edmund Howes'. London, 1631.
Strafford, the Earl of (Thomas Wentworth). *The Earl of Strafforde's Letters and Dispatches*. Ed. William Knowler. London, 1739.
Strong, S.A. *A Catalogue of Letters . . . in the Library at Welbeck*. London, 1903.
Strype, John. *Ecclesiastical Memorials relating chiefly to Religion and the Reformation of it, and the emergencies of the Church of England under King Henry VIII, King Edward VI and Queen Mary I*. 3 vols. London, 1721.
Stubbes, Philip. *The Anatomy of Abuses*. London, 1583.
Tarltons Jests. London, 1613.
Tatham, John. *Fancies Theater*. London, 1640.
?Tatham, John. *Knavery in all Trades: Or the Coffee-House*. London, 1664.
Taylor, John (the water poet). *All the Workes of Iohn Taylor*. London, 1630.
   Bull, Beare, and Horse, Cut, Curtaile, and Longtaile. London, 1638.
   A Cast Over the Water. London, 1615.
   Taylors Revenge. Rotterdam (i.e., London), 1615.
   Taylors Water-work or The Sculler Travels from Tiber to Thames. London, 1614.
   The True Cause of the Watermens' Suit concerning Players. In *All the Workes*. London, 1630.
Thomas, David and Arnold Hare. *Restoration and Georgian England, 1660–1788*. Cambridge, 1989. (Theatre in Europe: A Documentary History series.)
Tomkis, Thomas. *Albumazar*. London, 1615.
Tomlins, Thomas Edlyne. 'Origin of the Curtain Theatre, and Mistakes Regarding it'. *Shakespeare Society's Papers*, 1 (1844).
Transcript of the Registers of the Company of Stationers of London, Ed. Edward Arber. London, 1875.
Twyne, Thomas. *Physic against Fortune*. London, 1579.
   Physic for Fortune. London, 1579.
?Udall, Nicholas. *Respublica*, Ed. W. W. Greg. London, 1952
Van den Bergh, L. Ph. C. *'s Gravenhaagsche Bijzonderheden*. 1857.

Vennar, Richard. *An Apology* (for *England's Joy*). London, 1614.
The Plot of the Play Called England's Joy. London, 1602.
The View of the Cittye of London from the North towards the Sowth. c. 1600–1610 or later
Vox Graculi, or Iacke Dawes Prognostication . . . For this yeere 1623. London, 1623.
W., T. *A Sermon Preached at Pawles Crosse on Sunday the Thirde of November 1577*. London, 1577.
Wallace, Charles William. Advance Sheets from *Shakespeare, the Globe, and Blackfriars*. Stratford-upon-Avon, 1909.
  The Evolution of the English Drama up to Shakespeare. Berlin, 1912.
  The First London Theatre. Lincoln, NE, 1913.
  'The Children of the Chapel at Blackfriars, 1597–1603'. *University Studies of the University of Nebraska*, 8.2–3 (April–July 1908).
  'New Light on Shakespeare'. *The Times*, 1 May 1914.
  'Shakespeare and his London Associates as Revealed in Recently Discovered Documents'. *University Studies of the University of Nebraska*, 10.4 (October 1910).
  'Shakespeare and the Blackfriars'. *Century Magazine*, 80.5 (September 1910).
  'Shakespeare and the Globe'. *Times*, 30 April 1914.
  'Shakespeare in London'. *Times*, 4 October 1909.
  'Shakespere's Money Interest in the Globe Theater'. *Century Magazine*, 80.4 (August 1910).
  'The Swan Theatre and the Earl of Pembroke's Servants'. *Englische Studien*, 43 (1911).
  'Three London Theatres of Shakespeare's Time'. *University Studies of the University of Nebraska*, 9.4 (October 1909).
The Weekly Account. 4 October 1643.
The Weekly Intelligencer. 26 December – 2 January 1654/55; 11–18 September 1655.
Wentworth, Thomas. *See* Strafford, the Earl of
Westfall, Suzanne R. *Patrons and Performance: Early Tudor Household Revels*. Oxford, 1990.
  'The Chapel: Theatrical Performance in Early Tudor Great Households.' *English Literary Renaissance*, 19 (1989).
Wheatley, H. B. *London Past and Present*. London, 1891.
White, Paul Whitfield. *Theatre and Reformation: Protestantism, Patronage and Playing in Tudor England*. Cambridge, 1993.
Wickham, Glynne. *Early English Stages*. 4 vols. London, 1959–81.
Wickham, Glynne. '"Heavens", Machinery, and Pillars in the Theatre and Other Early Playhouses'. In *The First Public Playhouse*, ed. H. Berry. Montreal, 1979.
Wikland, Erik. *Elizabethan Players in Sweden, 1591–1592*. Stockholm, 1962.
Wilkinson, Robert. *Londina Illustrata*. London, 1819.
Williams, R.F., ed. *The Court and Times of Charles I*. London, 1848.
Willis, R. *Mount Tabor* (1639).
Wilson, Edward M. and Olga Turner. 'The Spanish Protest Against A Game at Chesse'. *Modern Language Review*, 44 (1949).
Wilson, F. P. 'Marston, Lodge, and Constable'. *Modern Language Review*, 9 (1914).
Wilson, Robert. *Three Ladies of London*. London, 1584.
Wit and Drollery. London, 1661.
Wither, George. *Abuses Stript and Whipt*. London, 1613.
  Epigrams. London, 1610.
Wotton, Sir Henry. *Letters of Sir Henry Wotton to Sir Edmund Bacon*. London, 1661.
?Wright, James. *Historia Histrionica*. London, 1699.
York Archaeological Society. *Index of Wills in the York Registry*. Vol. VI, 1594–1602. In *Record Series*, vol. xxiv (1898).
Young, William. *The History of Dulwich College*. London, 1889.
Youngs, Frederic A. Jr. *The Proclamations of the Tudor Queens*. Cambridge, 1976.

Index

Note: search under 'London and Environs'; 'Playing Companies'; 'Playhouses'; and 'Stage Characters' for individual entries appropriate to those categories.

Abell, William (alderman), 586
Abuses, 318
Acton, Mr (justice of the peace), 158
Actors. *See* Players
Adams, John (player), 300
Adams, Joseph Quincy. *Shakespearean Playhouse*, 550n, 597n, 626n; *Dramatic Records of Sir Henry Herbert*, 581, 582, 582n
Admiral, Lord. *See* Lord Admiral
Admiral's players. *See* Playing Companies
Aesop, 171
Agrippa, Henry Cornelius (writer), 159
Alabaster, William (playwright), 650
Aldermen of London. *See* London
Alderson, Thomas (sailor), 643
All Hallowtide, 100
All Saints Day, 35
Allen, Giles, 330–2&n, 333–6&n, 340, 343–4, 346–7, 348, 352, 355, 356–7, 367–72, 372–5, 376–8&n, 378–83, 383–4, 384–5, 385–6&nn, 386–7, 411
Allen, Sarah, 333–6, 340, 367, 372–5
Alleyn, Edward (player), 13, 65, 80, 106, 107, 124, 155, 171, 172, 177, 190, 191, 216–17, 220–21, 245, 277–8, 281, 282, 289, 328, 413–14, 419, 422–3, 436 485, 531–2, 533–4, 534–7, 537–9&n, 539–40, 541, 541–2, 544–5&n, 595–7, 600, 603, 604, 638–9, 640, 641n, 642; his Diary, 436, 546n; his portrait, 279
Alleyn, Joan (wife of Edward), 13, 277–8, 419, 485, 531, 595; her portrait, 280
Alleyn, John (player), 348–9, 350n, 361–2
Alvechurch (Worcestershire), 136
Amsterdam, 609
Anatomy of Abuses (Stubbes), 166
Anatomy of Melancholy (Burton), 185
Andrews (Androwes), George (silk weaver, playhouse investor), 269–71, 548–9, 353–9

Andrews, Richard (player), 245
Anglin, Jay P., 'The Schools of Defense', 296
Anglo, Sydney, 20; 'Court Festivals', 291
Annals of England. *See* Stow, John
Anne, Queen, 119, 122, 125, 513–14, 561, 562, 564, 580, 625, 630–1; her company of players, *see* Playing Companies
Apothecaries, 388, 501
Arber, Edward, 192
Archer, George (rent gatherer), 611n
Arches, Court of the, 292, 294n, 312
Ariosto, Ludovico, *I Suppositi*, 297n
Armin, Robert (player and writer), 123, 196, 197, 198; *Foole vpon Foole*, 411–12
Army Plot, The, 625, 636
Arthur, Thomas (apprentice player), 275–7
Arundel, Earl of (Henry Fitzalan, twelfth Earl), 73, 308; his company of players, *see* Playing Companies
Ash Wednesday, 169
Ashborne, Edward (musician or stage attendant), 258–9
Ashley, Sir Anthony, 547–50&n, 560&n, 561
Astington, John, 209
Astley, Sir John, 128, 148
Atkin, Mr (of Norwich), 248
Atkins, John (occupier of the cockpit in Drury Lane before 1616), 627
Atkins, John (scrivener), 607, 611n, 612
Atlas, 183
Attorney General, 314–5, 316, 582–3, 586
Audiences and auditoria, 3, 4, 5, 6, 10, 11, 12, 22, 46, 60, 76, 84, 85, 92, 116, 122, 135, 137, 139, 149
Audley, Tobias, 582
Augustus (Roman emperor), 171
Austen, George, 507n
Ayloff, Mr (lawyer), 479, 483, 484

685

B., G. (writer), *A Fig for the Spaniard*, 303
Backwell, 54–60
Bacon, Anthony, 303–4
Bacon, Francis (lawyer), 239, 303, 387
Bacon, Lady Anne, 303–4
Bacon, Sir Edmund, 499, 562
Bagnall, Richard, 460
Baker, Philip, 346–7
Baker, Richard (writer), 189
Baldwin, T.W., *Organization and Personnel of the Shakespearean Company*, 612n
Bale, John (playwright), 21, 24, 33
Ballads, songs and rhymes, 24, 34, 50, 52
Banbury (Oxfordshire), 145
Banister, Margery, 406n
Bankes, Jerome, 590n
Banks, one (horseman), 301
Barbon, Hugh (pursuivant), 385
Barclays Bank. *See* London
Barker, Alexander (player), 144
Barker, Richard, 119
Barlow, Graham F., 'Wenceslas Hollar', 626nn
Barne, John, 100
Barnes, Lord, 73
Barnes, Thomas (pretended player), 189
Barnet (Hertfordshire), 589
Barry, Lording (playwright, playhouse investor), 269–71, 547–9, 552, 553–9; *Ram Alley*, 547
Bartholomew (alias Heath), Edward, 136
Bartholomewtide, 80
Baskervile, Susan. *See* Greene, Susan
Basle (Switzerland), 412, 497
Bateman, Stephen (clergyman and writer), 325
Bath, 188
Baumfeld, John (of Somerset), 197
Bavande, William (writer), 158, 164n
Bawcutt, N. W., 'Documents', 652&n, 664, 670
Baxter, John, 600
Baxter, Richard (player), 259, 581&n
Baxter, Robert (player), 219
Bear-baiting, 84, 86–7, 88, 112, 124, 136, 220n, 305 449. *See also* Beargarden, Paris Garden, Hunks, and (under Playhouses) Hope
Beargarden, The, 426n, 432n, 446, 595, 597, 598–9, 601. *See also* (under Playhouses) Hope
Bears and Beasts, Master of the King's, 13
Bearwards, 62
Beauchamp, Lord; his company of players, *see* Playing Companies
Beaumont, Francis (playwright), 529; (and with John Fletcher:) *A King and No King*, 669; *Knight of the Burning Pestle*, 568–9; *The Scornful Lady*, 646; *Wit Without Money*, 588, 590n, 633

Beaven, William (builder), 648
Becher, Sir William, 524
Becmann, J. C., *Accessiones Historiae Anhaltinae*, 440
Bedford, Earl of (Francis Russell, fourth earl), 528
Bedingfield, Anne, 569n
Bedingfield, ?Christopher, 569n
Bedingfield, Daniel, 228
Bee, William (player), 257–8
Beeston, Robert (player), 253
Beeston alias Hutchinson: Alice, 672
Beeston, Christopher (player), 125, 128, 129, 175, 194, 198, 253, 405, 406n, 579, 623, 625, 626–7&n, 628n, 630–1, 632–3, 633, 635, 651, 658, 664
Beeston, Elizabeth, 625–6, 633–4, 636, 636–7&n
Beeston, William, 625–6, 633, 633–4, 634–5, 636, 636–7&n, 651, 653, 654–5&n, 658–60, 662–4, 670–4&n
Bel Savage Inn. *See* Playhouses
Bell Inn. *See* Playhouses
Bendbowe, Thomas (clergyman), 306
Benfield, Robert (player), 221–8, 525–6, 621, 645
Benger, Sir Thomas, 69, 70
Bentley, G.E., *The Jacobean and Caroline Stage*, 406n, 416n, 418n, 440n, 450n, 503n, 504nn, 514&n, 522&n, 525n, 527, 528, 534, 544, 569n, 570n, 583, 586n, 597nn, 597, 603, 604, 605, 610n, 613, 615, 616, 621&n, 622n, 626nn, 628, 630, 631, 640n, 641, 642, 643n, 644, 645, 646, 652nn, 654, 655, 657, 664, 667, 670
Bentley, John (player), 172, 176, 246–50, 300
Bergomasks, 93
Berkeley, Lord, 73, 92, 141; his company of players, *see* Playing Companies
Berkshire, 390
Berry, Herbert, *The Boar's Head Playhouse*, 308n, 456, 458, 459, 461, 463n, 463, 464, 475, 476, 477, 478, 480, 481, 482, 483, 484, 485, 486, 487, 488, 489, 490, 491, 492; 'Chambers, the Bull, and the Bacons', 303; 'First Public Playhouses', 290n, 291; 'Folger Ms. V.b.275', 529, 605, 622, 637n, 646, 670; 'A Handlist of Documents About the Theatre in Shoreditch', 298; 'Miltons and the Blackfriars Playhouse', 504n; *The Noble Science*, 296, 340, 409; 'Richard Vennar, England's Joy', 447; 'Sebastian Westcott', 317n; *Shakespeare's Playhouses*, 332, 363n, 440n, 450, 495n, 496&nn, 508, 509n, 517, 527, 528, 610&nn, 611nn, 612, 616, 619, 620, 621, 622n;

'Shylock, Robert Miles, and Events at the Theatre', 358n; 'The View of London from the North', 406n; 'Where was the Playhouse in which the Boy Choristers of St Paul's Performed Plays?' 307n, 313
Best, George (merchant), 529
Best, John (grocer), 626–7
Best, Katherine, 627&n
Bestney, Nicholas the elder (judge), 543, 544
Bestney, Nicholas the younger, 544
Bett, Henry (lawyer), 349–50, 351, 358, 386n
Bibliothèque Nationale (Paris), 515n
Bietenholz, Peter, 416n
Bill posters and posting, *see* Playing Companies; Playbills
Bill, John (the King's printer), 529&n
Billingsley, Sir Henry, 175
Binden, Viscount, 73
Bing, Dr. (of Cambridge), 250
Bingham, John (sadler), 496
Bingley, George, 451
Binz, Gustav, 'Londoner Theater und Schauspiele', 412, 497
Birch, George (carrier), 232
Birch, Thomas, *Court and Times of James the First*, 499
Birche, John (player), 234
Bird, William, *alias* Borne (player), 197, 211–16, 220–1, 438, 442–6, 544, 640
Bird, Theophilus (player), 670–1, 673
Biron, Charles, Duke of, 126
Bishop. *See* Byshop
Bishop of London, 46, 54
Bishop, Richard, 453–4, 471, 473–4, 475n, 475, 476n, 477, 490
Blackfriars. *See* Playhouses; *See* London
Blagrave, Dorothy, 632–3
Blagrave, Sir Thomas, 70
Blagrave, William (deputy Master of the Revels), 605, 616, 625, 632, 649–51, 652, 653, 653–4, 671, 674n
Blakewell, William (Lord Mayor of London), 42, 44–5, 54–60, 63–4, 73–7, 80–4, 93–9
Blinkinsop, John (fencer), 340
Bloom, Margery (of Norwich), 248
Bloom, Thomas (of Norwich), 248–9
Bluett, Henry, 500
Boar's Head Inn. *See* Playhouses; *see* London
Boderie, Antoine de la (French ambassador), 515n
Bodley, John (later Sir John), 607–8, 610–11, 617–18
Bohemia, King and Queen of. Their company of players, *see* Playing Companies

Boleyn, Ann, 17, 48
Bonds and fines, 50, 57–8, 74, 75, 76, 90, 118–19, 128, 131, 133–5, 139, 142–3, 144
Bonetti, Rocco (fencer), 389–90n, 390&n, 505
Book of Common Prayer, 34, 50
Books and Booksellers, 17, 23, 24, 36, 40, 50–3, 87
Bordinat, Philip, 'A New Site for the Salisbury Court Theatre', 652n
Borne, Mr (lawyer), 366
Borne, Gilbert (butcher), 543
Borne, William, 101
Boston (Lincolnshire), 73
Bothan, William (carpenter), 348
Boulton, Peter (servant), 466–9&n, 471–2, 471–2, 474–5
Bowde, Simon (Mayor of Norwich), 252
Bowen, Alice. *See* Beeston, Alice
Bowen, Thomas (mercer), 672
Bower, Richard (musician, Master of the Chapel), 262, 395
Bowler, Mr, 100
Bowling alleys, 408
Bowman, Francis (printer), 656
Box, Edward, 435&n
Boxley Abbey (Kent), 297
Boy players. Companies of, 155; as apprentices to adult players, 155; wearing women's garments, 165, 176. *see also* John Chappell; Thomas Clifton; Abel Cooke; Thomas Grymes; Thomas Holcombe; John Honyman; John Motteram; Salomon Pavy; Philip Pykman; John Thompson; Alvery Trussell
Brackenburye, Richard, 333
Brader, one (ironmonger), 428–9
Bradley, Richard, 544
Bradshaw, one (carpenter), 291
Bradshaw, Mr, his Rents on the Bankside, 196
Bradshaw, Charles, 505–6
Bradstreet, John (player), 258
Brayne, John (grocer, playhouse investor), 290, 294, 298, 330–1, 336, 337–9, 340, 341, 342–3, 344–5&n, 348–9, 349–50, 351–2, 352–5, 355–6&n, 357, 358–9, 361, 363, 365&n, 366, 372–5, 386n, 405, 411, 493, 501, 610
Brayne, Katherine, 331, 364–5&n
Brayne, Margaret, 298, 330–1, 336, 338, 340, 342–3, 345n, 348, 349–50, 351–2, 352–5, 355–6, 357, 357–8, 358–63&n, 364–5&n, 372–5
Brend, Matthew (later Sir Matthew), 223, 450, 494, 607–9, 610n, 610–1, 612, 616–19, 620–1, 621–2, 622&n

Brend, Nicholas, 493–4, 496n, 497, 607, 611, 618
Brend, Thomas (Nicholas Brend's father), 493, 497
Brend, Thomas (Sir Matthew Brend's son), 622
Brewe, Patrick (goldsmith), 533
Brewyn, Ralph (butcher) 543
Brian, Edward (feltmaker), 569
Bride-Oak, Ralph (writer), 586
Bridewell prison, 562
Bridgwater, Somerset, 287
Brief Description of the notorious Life of . . . Doctor Lambe, 642
Brigham, Mark, 545, 640
Bristol (City of), 118–19, 289; Guildhall, 118–19
British Library, 626n; Map Room, 550n
British Museum, 548, 550n; Print Room, 550n
Brome, Alexander (writer), 606n
Brome, Richard (playwright), 625, 650–1, 657–64, 667. *The Court Beggar* 634–5; *Five New Plays*, 646–7; *Sparagus Garden*, 650, 660
Bromvill, Peter (acrobat), 446–7
Brooke, Robert, 65
Broughton, Rowland, 234–5
Browker, Hugh (prothonotary), 439&n
Brown, Edmund (of Norwich), 247, 249–50
Brown, Henry (of Norwich), 246–50
Browne, one (servant), 345
Browne, Edward (player), 245, 251
Browne, John (player), 234
Browne, Robert (player, Worcester's, Admiral's), 245, 258
Browne, Robert (player, of the Boar's Head, d. 1603), 105–6, 109, 453–5, 456–8&nn, 459&n, 460, 461–2, 463n, 464, 465n, 475, 476n, 477n, 477–8, 478–9, 470–80, 480–1&n, 481–2, 483, 483–4, 484–5, 487, 488, 490, 492
Browne, Robert (player, of Whitefriars *et al.*, alive in 1610), 105–6, 245, 258, 561&n
Browne, Susan. *See* Greene, Susan
Browne, William (cooper), 487, 491&n
Browme, William (player), 629
Browning, John, 137
Brownstein, Oscar, 'A Record of London Inn-Playhouses', 296
Bruskett, Thomas, 505, 508
Bryan, George (player), 192
Bucer, Martin, 37, 38
Buchell, Arend van, 437, 441
Buck, Paul (player?), 321, 329
Buck, Sir George (Master of the Revels), 271–2
Buckhurst, Lord (Thomas Sackville, first lord), 557n

Buckhurst, Lord (Robert Sackville, second lord), 270, 553–4, 557n, 560n
Buckingham, Duke of (George Villiers, first Duke), 643
Buklank, Alexander (musician or stage attendant), 258–9
Bull Inn. *See* Playhouses
Bull-baiting, 84, 122, 136
Buller, Richard (of Norwich), 257
Burbage, family of, 155
Burbage, Cuthbert (businessman), 221–8, 289, 295, 320, 330, 331–2, 333, 343, 345n, 346–7, 352–5, 355–7&n, 358–63&n, 364, 365, 366–7, 367–72, 372–5, 376–8&n, 378–83, 383–4, 384–5, 385–6&nn, 386–7, 405, 411, 493–4, 496n, 497, 502–3, 516, 522, 525n, 526, 607, 609, 621; his sisters, 222; his son William, 226
Burbage, Ellen (wife of James), 357–8, 360–3, 374, 377–8, 386n
Burbage, James (joiner, player), 63, 92, 127, 204, 206, 226, 289, 290, 298, 305, 330–1, 332&n, 333–7&n, 337–9, 340, 341, 342–3, 343–4, 344–5&n, 346, 346–7, 348, 348–9, 350, 351, 351–2, 352–5, 355–7&nn, 358, 358–63&n, 364, 365, 365–6, 366–7, 367–72, 372–5, 377, 378–83, 385–6&nn, 410, 411, 493, 501–2, 504n, 504, 506–7&nn, 507–8, 526, 610
Burbage, Richard (player), 173, 191, 194, 196, 197, 199, 201, 227, 289, 328, 332, 352–5, 357–8, 360–2, 371, 376–7, 385, 386n, 411, 423, 493–4, 496n, 497, 499, 502–3, 508, 508–9, 513, 515–16, 517n, 519, 520–1, 522n, 526, 607, 609; his portrait, 184; funeral elegy, 181
Burbage, William, 503, 525n, 529, 609
Burbage, Winifred (wife of Richard), 226, 497, 503, 525n, 526, 609, 621
Burghley, Lord (William Cecil, first Lord, Lord Treasurer), 70, 87, 92–3, 105, 108–9, 111–13, 250, 302, 311, 331, 337, 345–6, 356&n, 440
Burgram, John. *See* Bingham, John
Burt, Thomas (dyer), 495
Burton, Robert (writer), 185
Buttermore, William (carpenter), 291
Byland, Ambrose (musician or stage attendant), 258–9
Byron, Duke de, 515n
Byshop, Barbara, 365n
Byshop, Nicholas, 360–2, 365n

C., I., *A Pleasant Comedy Called the Two Merry Milkmaids*, 580

Cadewell, John, 138–9
Cadmus, king of Thebes, 168
Cadwood, John, 51–2
Calfhill, Mr, 55
Calvert, Francis (fencer), 340, 410
Calvin, John, 33, 37, 85
Cambridge (City of), 11, 12, 17, 21, 24–9, 37, 112–16, 142, 295; Guildhall, 142
Cambridge (University), 161; St John's College, 173
Camden, William, *Annales Ab Anno 1603 ad Annum 1623*, 628n
Campion, Thomas, 8
Cane, Andrew (player and goldsmith), 155, 584, 585–6&n, 589n, 644–5, 650
Canterbury (City of), 21, 23, 44, 45, 117, 135, 137–8, 141, 149, 161; Guildhall, 117–18; Fuller, John (Mayor), 44–5
Canterbury Cathedral, Dean and Chapter of, 320, 321, 322, 327, 329
Canterbury, Archbishop of, 3, 52, 53, 94–8, 104, 137–8, 311, 312. *See also* Thomas Cranmer, John Whitgift
Cardwell, E., 52–3
Carew, Dr Matthew (master in Chancery), 477&n, 482, 483
Carew, George (master in Chancery), 477&n, 483
Carew, Thomas (the poet), 477n, 503n
Carey, Henry, Lord Hunsdon. *See* Hunsdon
Carey, Sir George, 505
Carlell, Lodowick (playwright), *Arviragus and Felicia* (part 2), 528
Carleton, Alice, 613
Carleton, Dudley (later Sir Dudley), 447, 448, 545, 546, 604, 615, 628–8
Carlisle, 61
Carpenters, 22, 290, 291; *Records of the Worshipful Company of Carpenters*, 291
Carte, Thomas, *Collection of Original Letters and Papers*, 606n
Cartwright, William, the elder (player), 221, 544
Cartwright, William, the younger (player), 657–64
Carver, James (sailor), 643
Carver, William (musician or stage attendant), 258–9
Catchmay, Thomas, 405
Catholic League, 78
Cato, Marcus Porcius, 176, 187
Cawarden, Sir Thomas, 32, 69
Cecil, Robert. *See* Salisbury, Earl of
Cecil, William. *See* Burghley, Lord
Censorship, 4, 17, 35, 40, 44, 48–9, 51, 126–7

Chamber, Treasurer of the, 262, 317
Chamberlain, John, 610; *Letters*, 447, 448, 545, 546, 604, 613, 615, 628
Chamberlain, Lord. *See* Lord Chamberlain
Chambers, E.K., *The Elizabethan Stage*, 42–3, 308n, 312, 328, 389nn, 395n, 406n, 412n, 449n, 511, 514n, 514, 515n, 525n, 528, 542n, 550nn, 560n, 561n, 562 605, 605, 612n, 622n, 646; *William Shakespeare*, 515
Chambers, George, 265
Chambers, Richard, 265
Chambers, William (musician or stage attendant), 258–9
Chancery, Court of, 331, 351, 352, 357, 358–63&n, 365, 365–6, 366–7, 375, 386, 389nn, 454–5, 463–4, 465, 471, 476–7, 477–8, 480, 481–2, 482–3, 484, 507n, 518, 520, 521, 559, 573–5, 578–9, 594, 651, 670, 674&n
Chandos, Lord, 117, 141; his company of players, *see* Playing Companies
Chapel Royal, 388, 502; Master of the, *see* Richard Bower; Richard Edwards; Richard Farrant; Nathaniel Giles
Chapels, 49
Chapman, George (playwright), 126, 307, 314–16&n; *The Old Joiner of Aldgate*, 314–16&nn; *The Conspiracy and Tragedy of Chrles Duke of Byron*, 515&n
Chapman, Henry (writer), *Thermae redivivae*, 644
Chapmen, 62
Chappell, John (imprest boy player), 265
Charles Lewis, Prince (son of Princess Elizabeth), 528
Charles, Prince, later King Charles I, 5, 120, 121–2, 125, 127, 128–32, 187, 318, 418, 514, 524–5, 528, 597, 617, 620n, 635–6, 643, 645, 665–7, 670; his company of players, *see* Playing Companies
Charles, Prince, later King Charles II, 6, 149, 487, 655; his company of players, *see* Playing Companies
Chassereau, Peter (clergyman), 404–5
Chatsworth House (Derbyshire), 440n
Cheshire, 111, 117
Chester, Bishop of, 111
Chester (City of), 17–20, 41, 64–8; Hankey, John (Mayor), 65, 67–8; Hardware, Henry (Mayor), 67–8; Savage, Sir John (Mayor), 66, 68
Chesterton (Cambridgeshire), 112–13, 116
Child, Mr, 524
Children of Paul's, 306–7, 308&n, 309–10, 312, 313, 314, 316, 317, 389, 502, 547

690 Index

Children of the Chapel Royal, 310, 388–9, 394, 394–5, 402, 502, 509–11, 512, 514&n, 517, 518, 526; *see also* Children of the Queen's Revels
Children of the King's Revels, 547–9, 553–5, 558, 559–60
Children of the Queen's Revels (also called Children of the Revels, of Blackfriars, and of Whitefriars), 307, 318, 512, 512–13, 514–5&n, 515, 517, 519&n, 520, 547, 549, 560, 561, 562, 563n
Children of the Revels to Queen Anne, 417–18
China, Thomas, 313
Cholmley, John (grocer), 419, 422, 423–5, 426
Choner, John, 138
Christchurch (Hampshire), 127
Christian IV, King of Denmark, 318
Christmas, 1, 82, 83, 103, 105, 109
Church of England, 309
Churchill, Ellis, 282
Churchill, John, 282
Cicero, Marcus Tullius, 158, 163, 176, 182, 190, 341
Cioli, Andrea (secretary of state at Florence), 415
Civil War, 1, 6, 130, 132, 133, 138, 149
Clapham, A. W., 'The Topography of the Carmelite Priory of London', 548, 550n
Clark, Robert (musician or stage attendant), 258–9
Clarke, Thomas (player), 206
Clay, Henry (musician or stage attendant), 258–9
Clay, Nathaniel (player), 274
Clayton, Richard (player), 641
Clerke, William (carpenter), 348, 363, 386n
Clifton, Henry (of Norfolk), 264–7, 510–11
Clifton, Sir Gervaise, 527
Clifton, Thomas (imprest boy player), 264–7, 510–11
Clough, George, 351–2
Cobb, Richard, 113
Cobham, Lord (William Brooke, seventh lord), 388, 390&n, 390–1, 398, 506
Cocke, John (writer), 179, 180
Cockpit. *See* Playhouses
Cokayne, Sir Aston (writer), verses for Brome's *Five New Plays*, 646–7
Coke, Sir Edward, 137
Coke, Stephen, 428
Cole, M. J., 'A New Account of the Burning of the Globe', 499
Colfoxe, Ewan (weaver), 333

College of Arms, 42–3
College of God's Gift. *See* Dulwich College
Collier, John Payne, 34, 198, 507; *History*, 317, 507; *New Facts*, 525n; *Works of William Shakespeare*, 528, 605, 622&n, 636, 646, 670
Collins, Jeffrey (musician or stage attendant), 258–9
Collinson, William (sailor), 643
Collyns, Nicholas (judge), 413
Comedies, 23, 37, 71, 74, 75, 76, 95, 118, 123, 127–8, 146
Commedia dell'arte, 63, 172n, 416n
Common Council, Court of. *See* London
Common Pleas, Court of, 395, 396–400&n, 439, 454–5, 464n, 476, 484, 674
Compass braces (in a playhouse), 293
Condell, Elizabeth (wife of Henry), 222–3, 609
Condell, Henry (player), 123, 194, 196, 197, 198, 200–3, 226–7, 494, 497&n, 502–3, 516, 526, 607, 612&n
Constables, 35, 36, 40, 56–7, 113–14, 138–9
Cooke, Abel (boy player), 268–9
Cooke, Alexander (player), 196, 198
Cooke, Alice, 268–9
Cooke, Lionel (player), 300
Cooke, Thomas (player), 245, 251
Cooke, William (haberdasher, playhouse investor), 269–71, 547–9, 551–2&n, 554–9
Cope, Walter, 331, 356&n
Cornishe, John, 495
Cornwall, 569
Cornwall, Duke of, 123
Corpus Christi, feast of, 1, 33, 41, 48–9, 61, 64–5, 110, 153
Costumes, 443–6, 515, 519&n, 520, 522n, 546, 553–5, 588–9, 590&n, 628–9, 631, 634, 669
Court, The Royal (at Whitehall), 306–7, 320, 346, 400, 417, 492, 515, 560
Court of Aldermen. *See* London
Court of the Arches, 292, 294n, 312
Court of Common Council. *See* London
Courts of Law. *See* Common Pleas, King's Bench, Marshalsea, Requests, Star Chamber
Coventry (City of), 41, 69, 117, 137, 149
Cowel, John, *A Law Dictionary*, 349n
Cowley, Richard (player), 123, 196, 197, 198, 278
Cox, Robert (player), 567, 589n
Cox, Samuel, 168
Cranage, Thomas, 326
Crane, John, 27
Cranmer, Thomas (Archbishop of Canterbury), 2–3, 18, 20–1, 33, 37

Crashaw, William, *Sermon Preached at the Crosse*, 308n
Crime, immorality and corruption of youth, 30, 53, 73–4, 87, 95–6, 99–100, 111
Crofts, Jack, 528
Crofts, Will, 528
Cromes, one (broker), 657
Cromwell, Thomas, Lord Chancellor, 2, 21–2
Crosfield, Thomas (academic), 584; Diary, 584, 613–14
Cross Keys Inn. *See* Playhouses
Cross, Robert, 145
Crosse, Samuel (player), 176
Crowe, Thomas (of Norwich), 250
Crown, The (i.e. the government), 405, 448, 597
Croydon Palace, 312
Cuckow, Mr (carpenter?), 459
Cuckow, Richard, 327
Cumber, John (player), 239–41, 628, 630–1
Cunningham, Peter. *Extracts*, 317; 'The Whitefriars Theatre, the Salisbury Court Theatre, and the Duke's Theatre', 550&n, 652, 664, 670
Cupid and Psyche (the story), 630
Curtis, Thomas (glazier), 230, 233

Daborne, Robert (playwright), 219, 561&n
Dancaster, Thomas (shoemaker), 333
Daniel, John, 119, 272–4
Daniel, Samuel (writer), 8, 119, 125, 271, 512, 514, 518–19
Dankerts, Cornelius (map-maker), *London*, 622
Davenant, William (playwright), 121, 128–30, 447, 625–6, 634–6, 647; *Britannia Triumphans*, 440n; *The Just Italian*, 503n; *News from Plymouth*, 614; *The Playhouse to be Let*, 590–1; *Works*, 590, 613
David, John (fencer), 299–300
Davies, James (master of the royal animals), 597
Davies, Thomas, 597
Daviges, Jeffrey (servant), 550
Davis, Richard, 136
Davy, Elizabeth (of Norwich), 248
Davy, Robert (of Norwich), 246–9
Dawd, Mr (of Norwich), 249
Dawes, Robert (player), 219, 282–4, 600
Day, John (playwright), 126, 239; *Isle of Gulls*, 514, 547
Dekker, Thomas (playwright), 307, 434, 514n, 582–3; (with John Day) *The Bellman of Paris*, 582&n; (with John Webster, William Rowley, John Ford) *The Late Murder ... or Keep the Widow Waking*, 583–3; *Raven's Almanack*, 568; *Work for Armourers*, 568
DeLaune, William (physician), 504
Denmark, 125, 564
Derby, Earls of, 73
Derby, Earl of (Ferdinando Stanley, fifth Earl). His company of players. *see* Playing Companies
Derby, Earl of (William Stanley, sixth Earl). His company of players. *see* Playing Companies
Derby, Elizabeth, Countess of, 105
Description of England (Harrison), 194
Deuteronomy, 176
Devon, 40–1
Devonshire, Earl of (Charles Blount, first earl), 568
DeWitt, Joannes. *See* Witt, Joannes de
Dice, Wine, and Women, 569
Dicing houses, 304
Digby, John, 527
Digby, Lord (Robert Digby, first baron), 528
Digby, Sir Kenelm, 673
Digges, Leonard (writer), commendatory poem for Shakespeare's *Poems*, 503n
Ditcher, Thomas (merchant tailor), 495
Divine Services. *See* Feast Days; Sabbatarians; Sundays
Dodderidge, Mr (justice in Chancery), 185
Dorset, Countess of (Frances Sackville, wife of the fifth earl), 673
Dorset, Earl of (Thomas Sackville, first earl), 557n
Dorset, Earl of (Robert Sackville, second earl), 270, 553–4, 557n, 560n
Dorset, Earl of (Edward Sackville, fourth earl), 649–51, 652, 653, 654, 665, 671–4
Dorset, Earl of (Richard Sackville, fifth earl), 651, 654, 671–4&n
Dorset, Marquis of, 37
Dotridge, Alice, 333
Downton, Thomas (player), 211–17, 251, 438, 442–6, 541–2
Dragon, John, 333
Drake, Stephen and William (of Norwich), 250
Drayton, Michael (playwright, playhouse investor), 269–71, 547–9, 553–9; (with Richard Hathaway, Anthony Munday, Robert Wilson) *Sir John Oldcastle*, 434
Drew, John (groom to Prince Charles), 417
Drolls, 567, 589&n
Dudley, Robert. *See* Leicester, Earl of
Duke of Holstein. *See* Holstein, Duke of
Duke of Lennox. *See* Lennox, Duke of

692   Index

Duke, John (player), 142, 194, 252, 253, 479–80, 481–2
Dulwich College, 13, 327, 419, 531, 595, 600, 639, 647–8
Dun, John (fencer), 448
Duncalf, Henry, 509
Dutton, John (weaver, player), 234–5, 300, 320
Dutton, Lawrence (weaver, player), 113, 234–5, 320
Dyott, Anthony (lawyer), 575, 593

Earle, John (writer), 186
Earthquake (1580), 341
Easement? ('Esore') at the Theatre and Curtain, 348–9, 359, 411
Easter, 1
Eccles, Mark, 'Elizabethan Actors', 486; 'Martin Peerson and the Blackfriars', 512n, 514&n, 519n
Ecclesiastical Commissions, 4, 44, 52, 53, 64, 68–9, 78, 94
Ecclesiastical Courts, 46, 136, 139
Ecclestone, William (player), 219
Edgerton, Ralph, 141
Edgill, Roger (feltmaker), 581
Edmonds, John (player), 274
Edric, 187
Edward III, King, 447
Edward VI, King, 3, 10–11, 33–7, 39–40, 48, 50
Edwardes, John, 406n
Edwardes, Richard (musician, Master of the Chapel), 262, 395
Egerton, Sir Thomas (lord keeper), 263, 482
Eisermann, Hans (writer), 158
Eliot, Tom, 528
Elizabeth (Tudor), Princess, later Queen of England, 3, 4, 5, 8, 11, 13, 48–119, 120, 122, 124, 133, 137, 142, 145–6, 149, 304, 308, 309, 310, 312, 318, 341, 376, 379, 394 401&n, 403, 423, 444, 446–7, 455, 466–8, 470–2, 474, 475, 493, 511&n, 537–9. *Household Accounts of Princess Elizabeth*, 308. Her company of players, *see* Playing Companies
Elizabeth (Stuart), Princess, later Queen of Bohemia, 528; her company of players, *see* Playing Companies
Elizabeth, Countess of Derby, 105
Ellam, Bryan (carpenter), 348, 363, 364, 386n
English, John, 1
Epictetus, 159
Epiphany, 1
Essex (County of), 41, 44, 61, 385, 452; Lord Lieutenant of, 44

Essex, Earls of, 73
Essex, Earl of (Robert Devereux, second Earl), 301
Essex, Earl of (Robert Devereux, third Earl), 527n; his rebellion, 195
Essex, Countess (Elizabeth, wife of the third earl), 527&n
Essex, Captain Charles, 527&n
Evans, Mrs. (wife of Henry), 515
Evans, Henry, 226, 261, 264–7, 389, 395, 397–400&n, 400–1, 402&n, 502, 508–9, 509–11, 511–13, 514, 515, 515–16, 517n, 517–21&n, 522nn, 526
Evans, Thomas, 502, 516
Evers, Lord (President of Wales), 140
Excommunication, 49, 61, 136
Exeter (City of); Jurdain, Ignatius (Mayor), 273

F., T., *News from the North*, 341n, 408
Fairs and fairgrounds, 1, 7, 149
Farley, Henry (writer), *St Pavles-Church her Bill for the Parliament*, 604
Farrant, Anne (wife of Richard), 261, 389&n, 391–3, 393–4, 395, 395–6, 396–400, 400–1&nn, 401–2&n, 403
Farrant, Richard (musician, Master of the Chapel), 260–62, 388–9, 390, 390–3, 393–4, 395, 397–400&n, 400–1, 402, 403
Faulkner, Thomas, 643
Favor, John, 505–6
Feast Days. *See* Holy Days; Sunday; All Hallowtide; All Saints; Bartholomewtide; Christmas; Corpus Christi; Easter; Epiphany; Lammas; Lent; May Day; Michaelmas; Pentecost; Shrovetide; Whitsun
Feats of activity. *See* Games
Feltmakers (apprentice), 581
Fencers and fencing prizes. *See* Games
Fenner, Mr (justice in King's Bench), 195
Fennor, William, 601–2
Fenton, Geoffrey (writer), 159, 162, 164n
Ferrarius, Joannes (writer), 158
Feyerabend, Karl, 'Zu K.H. Schaible's Geschichte', 498
Field, John (writer), *A Godly Exhortation*, 341n
Field, Nathan (player), 217–19, 226, 265, 600, 603&n
Figueiro, Vasco (writer), *The Spaniards Monarchie*, 303
Fines. *See* Bonds
Finett, Sir John, 228
Fire, the great fire of London (1666), 296
Fisher, Edward (carpenter), 655

Fisher, John (barber surgeon), 640
Fisher, John, intro. to *A Collection of Early Maps of London*, 624, 626n
Fishpole, William (tailor), 231
Fitz-Geoffrey, Henry, 'Notes from Black-Fryers', 503n, 509n
Flaskett, John (stationer), 314–15
Fleay, F.G., *Chronicle History*, 508, 509, 511, 517
Flecknoe, Richard (writer), *Miscellania*, 528–30; 'A Short Discourse of the English Stage', 305
Fleetwood, Edward, 111
Fleetwood, Sir Miles, 527n
Fleetwood, William (recorder of London), 100, 337, 345–6
Fleming, Mrs., 418
Fleming, Sir Daniel, 647
Fletcher, John (playwright), 529; *Cupid's Revenge*, 633; (and with Francis Beaumont:) *A King and No King*, 669; *Knight of the Burning Pestle*, 568–9; *The Scornful Lady*, 646; *Wit Without Money*, 588, 590n, 633
Fletcher, Lawrence (player), 123, 196, 197, 198
Fletcher, Richard (fencer), 409
Fletcher, Richard (pewterer), 413
Florio, John (writer), *First Fruites*, 298
Foakes, R.A., 13, 91
Folger Shakespeare Library (Washington, D.C.), 417, 450n, 581, 582, 626n
Football. *See* Games
Ford, John (playwright), 582–3
Form of Christian Policy, A (Fenton), 159
Fortescue, Sir John, 267, 511
Foscarini, Antonio (Venetian ambassador), 415–16
Foster, Alexander (player), 256
Foster, Francis (constable), 643
Four Inns, The, 295–6, 298, 304–5, 340, 452. *See also* (under Playhouses) the Bell, Bel Savage, the Bull, the Cross Keys
Four Mills (in Bromley, ?Kent), 294n
Fowler, Richard (player), 221, 544, 644–5
Fowler, Thomas, 100
Foxe, John, 22
Foxley, Alexander (tipstaff), 464, 466–72, 474–5
France, 126, 135, 440, 515; King of, 447; Queen of, 515&n; Ambassador of, 653. *See also* Boderie, Antoine de la
Francis, John, 313
Franke, Robert (sailor), 643
Freeman, Henry, 136
Fryer, Robert (goldsmith), 57
Fryne, John (feltmaker), 569
Fuller, John (Mayor of Canterbury), 44–5

Fulsis, Alexander, 569
Furnivall, F.J., 194

Gaedertz, K. T., *Zur Kenntniss der altenenglischen Bühne*, 410, 441
Gair, Reavley, 'The Conditions of Appointment for Masters of Choristers at Paul's', 308n; *Children of Paul's*, 308n
Galli, Antimo (an Italian), 415–16
Games, 43, 89, 112, 116, 139; Archery, 30, 87; Bowling, 84; Feats of activity (acrobatics, juggling, rope-dancing, tumbling, vaulting), 62, 148; Fencing and fencing prizes, 62, 82, 86, 92, 148, 296, 297, 305, 340, 406, 409, 418, 435–6, 439, 450&n, 581, 591, 605, 614, 645; Football, 81
Gardens, 49, 54, 58
Gardiner, John, 338&n, 353–4
Gardiner, Samuel (writer), *Doomes-Day book*, 341
Gardiner, S.R., *History of England*, 636
Gardiner, Stephen (Bishop of Winchester), 25–6, 27–9, 34, 57, 69, 157–8
Gardiner, William, 100–1
Gardner, H.C., 69
Garfield, John, *The Wandring Whore Continued*, 418
Gargano, G.S., *Scapigliatura Italiana a Londra*, 415
Garland, John (player), 300, 486n
Garnett, William (gardener), 333
Garrard, George (clergyman), 525, 528
Garrell, William, 640
Garrett, John (cloth-worker), 533
Gascoigne, George, *The Glasse of Government*, 297; *The Supposes*, 297n
Gascoyne, William (musician or stage attendant), 258–9
Gawdy, Philip, 277
Gayton, Edmund (writer), *Pleasant Notes upon Don Quixot*, 644
Gennatt, Jarvis (minstrel), 144
Gerard, Sir Charles, 139
Germany, 17, 105, 126, 135, 440
Gerrard, John, 518–19
Gerry, one (of Whitefriars playhouse), 550
Gilburne, Samuel (player), 198
Giles, Nathaniel (Master of the Chapel), 264–7, 502, 509–11, 512
Giles, Thomas (Master of the Children of Paul's), 262–3, 265
Gill, family of, 533–4
Gill, Alexander (writer), 644
Gill, Daniel the elder, 533
Gill, John (or Richard) (feltmaker), 581&n

Gill, Richard (apprentice scrivener), 581&n
Glean, Mr (alderman of Norwich), 255
Gloucester, 144
Gnatho, 166
Goburne, John (merchant tailor), 371–2, 378
Godfrey, Thomas (master of the royal animals), 597, 605, 606n
Goffe, Thomas (barber-surgeon, player, playwright), 234–5; *The Careless Shepherdess*, 668
Golding, Percival, 518
Goldsmith, Clement (lawyer), 575, 593
Gomme, Laurence, 'The Story of London Maps', 426
Gondomar, Sarmiento de Acuña, Count (Spanish ambassador), 127, 545, 610, 615
Goodman, Nicholas, *Holland's Leaguer*, 450, 605, 613–14
Goodwen, John (fencer), 410
Gorge, Sir Edward, 563n
Gorhambury (Hertfordshire), 303
Gosse, George (apprentice notary public), 339
Gosson, Stephen (writer), 161, 162, 164, 295, 340; *Catiline's Conspiracies*, 341; *Plays Confuted in five Actions*, 308n, 394; *Schoole of Abuse*, 299, 340–1
Gouge, William (clergyman), 522
Gough, Alexander (player), 259
Gough, Robert (player), 195, 199
Grace, Frank (player), 220–1, 544
Grace, Richard (player), 641
Grafton, Richard, 35–6
Gray, Patrick (sailor), 643
Greene's Groatsworth of Wit, 169
Greene, John (writer), 178
Greene, Robert (writer), 11, 169, 171; *Friar Bacon and Friar Bungay*, 431, 589; *Orlando Furioso*, 431
Greene, Susan (formerly Browne and later Baskervile), 185, 406, 485, 629
Greene, Thomas (player), 142, 252–3, 405–6, 416, 485–6, 579
Greenstreet, James, 'Documents Relating to the Players', 629; 'The Red Bull Playhouse', 593; *The Whitefriars Theatre in the Time of Shakespeare*, 553
Greenwell, Nicholas, 27
Greenwood, C. and J., *Map of London*, 440n
Greg, W.W., *A Bibliography of the English Printed Drama*, 440n
Gresley, Sir George, 653
Greville, Curtis (player), 657–64
Grey, Lady Jane, 39

Griffin, Mr, 218–19
Griggs, John (carpenter), 278, 419, 424, 428–30
Grimes, one (showman), 605
Grindal, Edmund (Bishop of London, later Archbishop of York), 53, 55, 64–6
Grocers, 97
Gryffyn, William (vintner), 419, 423n
Grymes, Thomas (imprest boy player), 265
Guildhall, London. *See* London
Guildhalls, Provincial, 7, 110, 121, 123, 141–3, 145–7. *See also* Bristol; Cambridge; Canterbury; Leicester; Liverpool; Worcester
Guilds. *See* Apothecaries; Carpenters; Feltmakers; Grocers; Ironmongers; Mercers; Merchant Taylors; Stationers
Guilpin, Everard (writer), *Skialetheia*, 375, 411–12, 433
Gunnell, Richard (player), 220–1, 544, 638, 640, 649–51, 652&n, 653, 653–4, 660, 671, 674n
Gwalter, William (innholder), 640
Gyles, John, 313
Gyles, Thomas, 307, 309, 313

H., L., *This World's Folly*, 415–16
Haaker, Ann, 'The Plague, the Theatre, and the Poet', 657
Haddington, Lord, 126
Hadley (Suffolk), 110
Hall, Joseph (writer), 167
Hall, Norman L., 'The Court of Husting', 389n
Halliwell (later Halliwell-Phillipps), James O., 21–22; *Outlines*, 406nn, 507n, 507, 522, 525; Scrapbooks (at the Folger), 417–18, 450n, 581, 582, 605, 616
Hammond, Mr, his Rents near Houndsditch, 193
Hancock, Ralph (printer), 192–3
Hankey, John (Mayor of Chester), 65, 67–8
Hanley, Richard (player), 259
Hanmer, Randall (scrivener), 552
Harberte, Thomas (girdler), 405, 407
Hardman, William, 138–9
Hardware, Henry (Mayor of Chester), 67–8
Harington, Sir John, *Metamorphosis of Ajax*, 345
Harries, William (porter), 405
Harris, Mr (Serjeant, a lawyer), 357
Harrison, George (notary public), 365n
Harrison, Gregory, 138
Harrison, Joan, 333
Harrison, Thomas, 294n
Harrison, William (writer), 194, 245, 251
Hart, William (player), 259
Harvey, Gabriel, 312; 'An advertisement for

Papp-Hatchett and Martin Mar-prelate', 310–11&nn; *Letter Book*, 341
Harvie, Edward (fencer), 340
Hasell, George (player), 244–5
Hassler, Conrad, *Die Reisen des Samuel Kiechel*, 410
Hatcher, John (Vice-Chancellor of Cambridge University), 250–1
Hatfeld-Bradock (Essex), 41
Hathaway, Richard (playwright), 238
Hatton, Mr (justice in Chancery), 185
Hatton, Sir Christopher, 168, 346&n
Haughton, William (playwright), 239
Haukins, William (barber), 413
Hawkins, Alexander, 509, 511–14, 515&n, 517–18, 521&nn, 522nn
Hawkins, Margaret, 521
Hayrick, Thomas, 141–2
Hazeleigh (Essex), 331, 376
Heath, John (writer), 415, 498
Heather, Edward (headborough), 643
Helme, Thomas (scrivener), 581n
Heminges, John (player), 192, 194, 196, 197, 199, 200–3, 222, 226–7, 493–4, 496n, 497, 502, 516, 521, 522n, 526, 584, 607, 609, 611–12&n, 612–13
Heminges, William, 224–5, 526, 609
Henrietta Maria, Queen, 528, 649, 653, 665–6; her company of players, *see* Playing Companies
Henry the Fifth. *See* (under Plays) The Famous Victories of Henry V
Henry VI, King of England, 33–7 passim, 48, 50
Henry VII, King of England, 1, 48; his company of players, *see* Playing Companies
Henry VIII, King of England, 1–2, 5, 17–62 passim, 31, 33–4, 39, 48, 62, 69–70, 73, 499; his funeral, 157; his company of players, *see* Playing Companies
Henry, Prince (son of King James), 5, 120, 125, 318, 487; his company of players, *see* Playing Companies
Henshew, Mr (clergyman), 303–4
Henslowe Papers (ed. Foakes), 534, 597, 646
Henslowe Papers (ed. Greg), 423, 532n, 533, 534, 537, 540, 541, 542, 544, 545n, 597, 600, 639n, 640&n, 641, 646, 648
Henslowe, Agnes, 277–8, 532, 540, 544
Henslowe, Francis, 435
Henslowe, Philip (dyer, financier), 13, 80, 84, 91, 100–1, 105–6, 108–9, 124, 167, 213, 215, 216–17, 218–20, 235–9, 255, 277–8, 281, 282–4, 289, 328&n, 419, 422–3&n, 423–5, 426–31, 431–2, 433, 433–4, 435–6, 439, 443–5, 531–2, 534–7, 539–40, 541–2, 544, 549, 550n, 595–7&n, 597–601, 603&n, 604, 638; *Diary*, 327–8, 419, 423, 426, 431, 433, 434, 534, 537, 539n, 539–40, 597n
Hentzner, Paul (German tourist), *Itinerarium Germaniae, Galliae, Angliae, Italiae*, 446n
Herbert, Sir Henry (Master of the Revels), 127–8, 144, 185, 228, 257–9, 417–18, 436, 583, 625, 649, 652n, 654, 656, 663; his Office Book, 416–17, 417–18, 435–6, 450&n, 526, 563n, 581&n, 582&nn, 584, 587, 605, 616, 631, 632–3, 634, 656, 657. *See also* Revels, Master of the
Hercules, 495n
Hercules, twelve labours of, 170
Hereford, 33, 136
Heresy, 17, 35, 37, 41, 42, 46–7, 48, 49, 50, 62
Herne, John the elder, 649, 651, 652–3, 670n, 671–2, 674n
Herne, John the younger, 651, 670n, 671–3, 674n
Heron, John (treasurer of the King's chamber), 291
Heton, Elizabeth, 654
Heton, Richard (playhouse manager), 651, 657–64, 664–7
Hewet, one (martyr), 22–3
Heywood, John (writer), 306, 308
Heywood, Richard (lawyer), 292
Heywood, Thomas (playwright, player), 175, 178, 200, 239–41, 253, 479–80, 481–2, 566, 579; *An Apology for Actors*, 200, 297n; *The English Traveller*, 641–2; (with Richard Brome) *The Late Lancashire Witches*, 609, 619–20&n; *Loves Maistresse*, 620–30
Hicks, Richard (grocer, yeoman of the Queen's guard), 320, 321&n, 322, 323–6, 327, 405, 408
Hill, James, 172
Hill, John (arbitrator), 338–9, 357, 373
Hillebrand, Harold N., 'Sebastian Westcote', 309; *Child Actors*, 317, 511, 512n, 514, 517, 550n, 559
Hills, John (property holder in Newington), 322
Historical Manuscripts Commission *Reports*, 313, 401n, 568, 632, 646
Histrio, histriones, 160, 189, 192
Histriomastix, the Players' Scourge (Prynne), 187
Hobbes, Thomas (player), 259
Hobson, Thomas (carrier), 295
Hodskyns, Richard (writer), *Keep the Widow Waking* (ballad), 582

Holcombe, Thomas (boy player), 225
Holebrook, Thomas, 138–9
Holinshed, Raphael, 50
Holland's Leaguer (a brothel), 450, 605
Holland, Earl of (Henry Rich, first earl), 528
Holland, Aaron, 564–6, 567nn, 568, 570–9&nn, 582, 592–4&nn
Holland, John (player), 191
Holland, Thomas (of Norwich), 247, 249
Hollar, Wenceslas (graphic artist), 'The Great Map', 624–5, 626n; 'Long Bird's-Eye View', 596, 608–10
Holstein, Duke of (Ulric Oldenburg), 564, 568; his company of players, see Playing Companies
Holt, James (player), 239–41, 253
Holy Days, 1, 20, 30, 42, 55, 57, 73, 75, 80, 83, 112, 136
Home, Sir George (Knight of the Wardrobe), 196
Honingborne, Margaret (wife of Peter), 324
Honingborne, Peter, 320, 321, 323–6, 327
Honyman, John (boy player), 225
Hoppdale, William (carpenter), 459n, 459
Horne, William (Master of the Grocer's Company), 97
Hotson, Leslie, *The Commonwealth and Restoration Stage*, 406n, 567&n, 570, 589n, 597n, 606n, 626&nn, 633, 636–7, 654
Household Order Books, 17
Howard, Lord (Charles Howard, first Lord Howard of Effingham). *See* Admiral, Lord
Howe, Agnes, 314–15
Howe, John (verger in St Paul's cathedral), 313
Howes, Edmund (writer), 208, 329, 605, 627n, 628n, 642
Howland, Dr (of Cambridge), 250
Hudson, Richard (carpenter), 363&n, 364, 385–6&n
Hunks, Harry (a bear), 597n
Hunks, Tom (a bear), 597n
Hunnis, William (musician), 260–1, 388–9&n, 394, 395, 395–6, 396–400&nn, 400&n, 402&n, 502
Hunsdon, Lord (Henry Carey, first Lord), 73, 80–1, 304, 346, 389–90n, 504, 507–8, 529n, 537; his company of players, *See* Playing Companies
Hunt, John (master in Chancery), 477&n
Huntingdon, Earl of, 66
Huntington Library (San Marino, California), 593
Hussey, Thomas, 627n, 636

Husting, Court of. *See* London
Hutton, Dr. (Dean of York), 64, 69
Huxton (Suffolk), 22
Hyde, John (grocer), 331, 340, 342, 344–5&n, 351–2, 358n, 359, 373–4
Hyde, Mrs. (wife of John), 344, 352, 355–7&nn
Hyde, Ralph, intro. to a reprinting of Ogilby and Morgan's *Large and Accurate Map*, 626n
Hyemarsh, John, 406n
Hygiene and infections diseases, 49, 54, 60, 86–7, 100, 107, 114; *see also* Plague
Hynd, John, 298

Ibotson, Richard (inn-holder), 298
Ieronimo (fencer), 302–3
Immorality. *See* Crime; Lewd Persons
Inge, Richard, 141
Ingleby, C.M., 181
Ingram, William, 290, 308n, 321; *The Business of Playing*, 321, 322, 326n, 327, 329, 348n, 365n, 406n; *A London Life in the Brazen Age*, 440nn; 'The Playhouse as an Investment', 550&n, 551, 553, 562n, 567n; 'The Playhouse at Newington Butts', 321
Inns, taverns and their keepers, 11, 54, 56, 57, 59, 73, 74, 75, 76, 86, 90, 107, 108, 118, 121, 138–9; The Four Inns, 295–6, 298, 304–5, 340, 452. *See also* (under Playhouses) Bell, Bel Savage, Bull, Cross Keys
Inns of Court. *See* London
Interludes, 9, 10, 17, 21, 30–2, 34–6, 40–1, 42, 43, 49, 50, 51, 54, 55, 58–60, 71, 74, 76, 78, 82, 88, 90, 94, 116, 118, 122, 127, 131, 132–5, 136
Ipswich (Suffolk), 18
Ireland, 525, 528
Ireland, Thomas, 138
Ironmongers, 85
Isburd, Godfrey (haberdasher), 534
Islipp, Adam (stationer), 640
Italian stage players, 63
Italy, 526; Italian Renaissance, 10

Jackson, Edward, 640
Jackson, George (of Norwich), 249
Jacob, Thomas, 585
James I, King, 11, 13, 49, 72–3, 85, 120–31 *passim*, 133, 135, 318, 448, 479, 511, 513, 514, 514–15, 517, 519, 520, 521, 523, 549, 560, 561, 567n, 597, 600, 601, 622&n, 639; his company of players, *see* Playing Companies
James VI, King of Scotland, 5, 85
James, Duke of York, 6, 149

Jarman, Anthony (carpenter), 638–9, 640, 641n
Jeaffreson, J.C., *Middlesex County Records*, 341, 413, 543, 569, 581&n, 585, 642
Jeffes, Humfrey (player), 144–5, 254
Jobber, Richard, 551–2
Johnson, Henry (silk weaver), 347, 370–1, 377
Johnson, John (tipstaff), 464, 466–72, 474–5
Johnson, Peter, 505–6
Johnson, William (player), 206, 300
Jonas, Maurice, *Shakespeare and the Stage*, 550, 561
Jones, Inigo (architect), 8–9, 11, 125, 440n, 623–4
Jones, Mary. See Young, Mary
Jones, Richard (player), 101, 211–16, 235, 245, 258, 438, 442–6, 561&n, 562
Jones, William, 654
Jonson, Ben (playwright, player), 8–10, 11, 80, 92, 95, 101–2, 104, 121, 125–6, 178, 194, 241, 267–8, 307, 314, 447, 586, 596, 602, 644n; kills Gabriel Spencer, 281–2. *Bartholomew Fair*, 596, 602&n; *Catiline*, 11; 'Execration upon Vulcan', 500; *Magnetic Lady*, 644; *The Works of Benjamin Jonson*, 194, 499, 602
Jordan, Israel (moneylender), 454, 461, 465n
Jordan, William, (a beggar child), 522n
Journals of the House of Commons, 597n
Joyner, William (fencer), 410
Juby Frances, 638, 640
Juby, Edward (player), 220–1, 544, 638
Jugg, Richard, 51–2
Jugglers. See Games
Jurdain, Ignatius (Mayor of Exeter), 273
Jusserand, J.J., 'Ambassador La Boderie', 515n
Justices of the Peace. See Magistrates

Kahrl, Stanley, 41
Katherens, Gilbert (carpenter), 595, 598–600
Katherine of Aragon, Queen, 17, 39
Keavall, George (notary), 234–5
Kemp, William (player), 173, 176, 191, 194, 204, 493–4, 496n; his picture, 174. *Kemp's Nine Days' Wonder*, 174
Kendall, Mrs (wife of Thomas), 518
Kendall, Thomas (haberdasher), 268, 512–14, 515, 517–19, 521n
Kennard, Isaac (fencer), 296, 409–10
Kent, 41, 44, 61
Kerrie, Edmund (of Norwich), 246–7
Keysar, Robert (goldsmith), 318–19, 515, 519, 520, 521, 549, 560, 561&n
Kiechel, Samuel (German tourist), 332, 410
Kilby, William (of Pockthorpe), 246

Killigrew, Thomas, 567
King and Queen of Bohemia, their company of players. See Playing Companies
King and Queen's Young Company of players. See Playing Companies
King of Denmark's Welcome, The, 318
King's Bench Prison, 527
King's Bench, Court of, 290, 291, 317, 332, 344, 355, 376, 378, 379, 382, 383–4, 386–7, 453–4, 465, 471–2, 474, 475, 477, 518, 519, 520, 556–7, 559, 575, 577–8, 579n, 593–4
King's Revels, men and boys of the. See Playing Companies
Kingdom's Weekly Intelligencer, The, 587, 645, 669
Kingman, Philip (player), 562, 563n
Kingsford, C.L., 'Paris Garden and the Bear-baiting', 597n
Kirchmayer, Thomas (playwright), 24–5
Kirke, Elizabeth, Lady. See Beeston, Elizabeth
Kirke, Sir Lewis, 636–6
Kirkham, Edward, 120–1, 307, 317, 511&n, 512–14, 515, 517–21&nn, 522nn
Kirkham, Henry (publisher), 302, 308n
Kirkman, Francis, The Wits, 565, 567&n
Knee, Edmund (of Yelverton), 248
Knell, William (player), 172, 176
Knevett, Mr, 175
Knight Marshal, 399
Knight, Anthony (musician or stage attendant), 258–9
Knight, Edward (musician or stage attendant), 258–9
Knights Templar, 448&n
Knollys, Baron, 73
Knowles, John, 495
Kyrby, Richard (carpenter), 291

Lactantius, 160
Lake, Sir Thomas, 126, 273, 515&n
Lamb, John, 29
Lambarde, William (writer), *A Perambulation of Kent*, 297, 304–5
Lambe, Dr John (astrologer), 642–3
Lammas, 22
Lancashire, 111, 115, 117, 138, 141, 619, 620n
Lancaster, Duchy of, 111, 112
Lane, Richard (lawyer), 387, 622&n
Lane, William (lawyer), 622n
Laneham, John (player), 176, 206, 300, 409
Langbaine, Gerard, *Account of the English Dramatick Poets*, 567&n, 655–6
Langham, Thomas (fishmonger), 533

Langley, Francis (draper, playhouse owner), 102–3, 104, 211–16, 432&n, 438–9, 440, 441–6&n, 447, 453–5, 463n, 463–4&n, 464–75&nn, 476n, 476, 476–7&n, 477–8, 478–9, 480–1&n, 482, 485, 488, 490, 547
Langley, Richard, 453–5, 463–4, 476, 476–7, 477–8, 479, 480&n, 482–3, 483–4, 484&n, 485
Langworth, Arthur, 281
Lanman, Henry, 348–9, 350n, 359, 405, 408, 411
Late Will and Testament of the Doctors Commons, 586–7
Laughing Mercury, The, 587
Laune, William de (physician), 504
Law Courts. *See* Common Pleas, King's Bench, Marshalsea, Requests, Star Chamber
Law Schools, London. *See* Inns of Court
Lawrence, W.J., 'New Facts', 631, 655–6
Leake, Robert, 527
Lee, Mr (timberman), 430
Lee, Robert (player), 239–41, 253
Leeke (or Leke), Sir Francis, 42–3
Legg, Dr Thomas (master in Chancery), 365
Legge, Dr. (of Cambridge), 250
Leicester (City of), 136, 140–2, 487; Guildhall, 136, 140–2
Leicester, Earl of (Robert Dudley, first earl), 61, 63, 70, 71, 76–7, 80–1, 90–1, 140–1, 204–7, 260–1, 389, 394&n; his portrait, 207; his company of players, *see* Playing Companies
Leigh (Worcestershire), 137
Leigh, Sir Thomas, 407
Lennox, Duke of (James Stuart, fourth duke), 5, 120–1, 123–4, 528; his company of players, *see* Playing Companies
Lent, 26, 77, 79, 80, 85–91, 104, 107, 111, 121, 137–8, 139, 180, 181, 183, 187, 188
Leominster (Herefordshire), 136
Lewd persons, plays and treatises, 43, 44, 45, 57, 78, 99, 100, 102, 112
Lewis Frederick, Prince (of Württemberg), 498
Lewis, C.T. and C.S. Short, *A Latin Dictionary*, 655n
Lewyn, Mr, 168
Licensing Commission, 49–50, 80, 92, 93–8
Lichfield, Leonard (printer), 656
Lieutenant of the Tower of London, 336
Lightmaker, Mr (brewer), 671, 673
Lilley, John (of Worcestershire), 136–7
Lincoln's Inn. *See* London. *Records of the Honourable Society of Lincoln's Inn*, 627
Lincoln, 41

Ling, Nicholas, printer, 174
Lipsius, Justus (Flemish writer), 171
Liverpool (Lancashire), 117, 141, 289; Guildhall, 117
Livery, 1, 5, 43, 48, 61
Livery Companies. *See* Apothecaries; Carpenters; Feltmakers; Grocers; Ironmongers; Mercers; Merchant Taylors; Stationers
Livery Halls, 1, 49, 97–8, 121, 140
Lockwood, Doctor, 27
Lodge, Sir Edmund, 42–3
Lodge, Thomas (writer), 11, 161
Loengard, Janet, 'An Elizabethan Lawsuit', 291
London, Bishop of, 46, 54
London: Aldermen, Court of, 31, 32, 42, 50–51, 53, 54, 56, 58, 60, 74, 75, 77, 79, 81, 83, 300; Abell, William (alderman), 586; Chamber of, 30–1, 534; Common Council, Court of, 4, 35–6, 40, 55–6, 71, 74, 76, 78, 85, 97, 99, 309; Corporation of, 522–3; Husting, Court of, 389&n, 395, 397, 400, 401n, 402&n, 551; Lord Mayor, 299, 302, 304, 310, 311–12, 326, 336, 337, 342, 346, 402n, 407, 414, 426, 440, 455, 481, 486, 508, 522–5, 588, 628, 670. *See also* William Blakewell; John Swinnerton; Lord Mayor's court, 230; Recorder of London, 402&n; Sheriff's Court, 275. *see also* Sheriffs
London and environs: City of, 4, 6, 7, 11, 30–1, 32, 44, 48, 53–61, 63, 67, 71–8, 79, 81–103, 104–10, 112, 120–4, 126–8, 130, 132, 134, 142, 143, 145, 146, 287, 298, 299–301, 302, 304, 305, 310, 311, 315, 318, 320, 321, 324, 326–7, 330, 336, 339, 345n, 371, 385, 388, 389n, 394, 395, 396–7, 403, 404–6, 408, 410, 411, 413, 419, 437, 440, 442, 444, 446n, 452, 485, 486, 498, 501, 504, 508, 510, 514, 523, 531, 533, 534, 538&n, 542, 544, 545, 547, 550n, 553, 561, 562, 564, 569, 585, 589, 599, 602n, 620n, 623, 625, 628, 631, 636, 638, 643, 649, 658, 661; Aldgate, 290, 455, 472; Anchor Terrace, 493, 607, 610; Arches, Court of the, 292, 294n, 312; Aylesbury Street, 567n; Bankside, 99, 102, 107, 327–8, 377, 414, 419, 424, 437, 439, 440, 443, 446, 447, 449, 451, 493, 499–500, 534, 537, 539, 595, 602, 603, 605, 607, 609, 613, 614; Barclays Bank in Lombard Street, 295; Barnard's Castle, 405; Bear Gardens, 595; Beargarden Square, 597; Bel Savage Inn, 295–7, 299, 302–3, 304, 305, 330; Bell Inn, 295–6, 297, 300, 301, 304; Bermondsey, 329; Bishopsgate, 296, 303, 363, 411n, 413, 441; Bishopsgate Street, 295, 300, 303–4, 305, 411n;

Index

Blackfriars, 92, 121, 123, 124, 126–7, 221–8, 259–61, 264–7, 268–9, 305, 329, 388, 390&n, 393, 394, 403, 487, 502, 507, 508–9, 513, 514, 516, 524, 525n, 529, 530, 547, 550n, 562, 656; Blackfriars (the convent), 388, 390, 396, 501, 504, 506; Blackfriars Gate, 525; Blackfriars Lane, 501; Blackfriars Stairs, 391; Boar's Head Inn, 452, 494 (*see also* Playhouses); Bouverie Street, 547; Bread Street, 435; Bridewell, 175, 252, 562; Bull Inn, 295–6, 298, 300, 301, 304, 305; Bullhead Alley (Bankside), 192; Cannon Street, 605; Carmelite Priory, *See* Whitefriars Priory; Carmelite Street, 547, 649; Carter Lane, 525; Charing Cross Road, 73; Cheap (Ward of), 292; Cheapside, 56, 312, 405; Christ Church, 510; Christ Church grammar school, 265; Clerkenwell, 124, 486, 564; Clerkenwell Green, 567n; Clink Liberty (Bankside), 91, 192, 426; Cockpit Alley, 623–4; Codpiece Row (i.e., Town's End Lane), 630&n; Coleman Street, 303; Compton Street, 567n; Curtain Close (the estate), 405, 407–8, 416; Curtain House (or Lodge? or Court?), 404–5, 406n, 407; Curtain Road, 330, 404; Denmark House, 439; Dorset Garden, 672–3; Dorset House, 649, 651, 652–3, 665–6, 671; Drury Lane, 623–6, 628–9, 631, 634, 635, 637, 660, 669; Drury Lane Theatre, 626; Elephant and Castle (tavern), 320; Essex House, 653; Farringdon Without (Ward of), 649, 652; Finsbury, 91, 106; Finsbury Fields, 229, 336, 339, 538; Finsbury, Lordship of, 538–9; Fleet Conduit, 524–5; Fleet Street, 125, 130, 547–9, 550n, 562, 649, 665; Fleetbank House, 652n; Fortune Street, 531, 638, 648; Friday Street, 552; Frying Pan (Southwark), 428–9; George Inn (Whitechapel), 331, 351&n, 353–4, 365n; George, sign of the (Shoreditch), 371; Golden (or Golding) Lane, 221, 414, 487, 531, 533, 534, 537, 539, 541, 544, 545, 546, 638–9, 640, 641, 642, 646, 647–8&n, 669; Goulston Street, 452; Gracechurch Street, 295, 297, 298, 300, 301, 304; Great Queen Street, 623; Greenwich, 129, 391, 396; Greenwich Palace, 312, 318; Grub Street, 543; Guildhall, 4, 7, 55, 56, 59, 73, 76, 78–9, 81, 85, 92, 97, 98, 109, 124, 145, 299, 389, 401n; Halcrow Street, 290; Hampton Court (Middlesex), 607; Hayward's Place, 564, 567n; Hewett Street, 404; Hog Lane, 452, 492n; Holland's Leaguer (Bankside brothel), 450, 605; Holywell, 333, 336, 340, 341, 356, 358, 363, 364, 372, 409–10, 414, 504; Holywell Lane, 404, 406n, 408, 418; Holywell Priory, 330, 376, 404–5, 407; Hopton Street, 437; Horseshoe Alley or Court (Bankside), 192, 196; Houndsditch, 193; Hoxton Fields, 281; Hunsdon House, 529n; Inns of Court, 3, 11, 187, 627; Islington, 46, 589; Kemble Street, 623; King's Bench Prison, 527; King's Mews, 588&n; Kingsland leper house, 417&n; Lambeth Palace, 43; Leadenhall, 299; Liberties, 54, 79, 91, 118, 133, 145; Limeburner Lane, 295; Lincoln's Inn, 187, 447, 623, 627, 646, 649; Lincoln's Inn Fields, 628; Lombard Lane, 550n; Lombard Street, 295; London Bridge, 311n, 320, 329, 437, 607; London College of Fashion, 330; London Wall, 295, 388, 531, 547; Long Lane, 657; Ludgate, 295, 302, 504, 506, 522, 524–5; Ludgate Hill, 295, 296n, 304, 388, 501; Ludgate Prison, 276; Lurklane (Newington, Surrey), 320, 322; Marshalsea Prison, 292, 468, 472, 635, 657; Maiden (or Maid) Lane, 414, 419, 424, 426, 435, 493, 496, 595, 607, 610n, 622; Martlett Court, 623; Merchant Taylors' School, 260; Middlesex Street, 452; Mile End, 290, 291, 292; Milk Street, 407; Moorfields, 79, 108; New Inn Yard, 330; New Kent Road, 320; Newgate, 346; Newgate Prison, 62, 162, 524; Newington (Surrey), 320, 321, 322, 325, 326, 329; Newington Butts (Surrey), 81, 83, 320, 323; Nightingale Lane, 106; Norton Folgate, 411n; Old Bailey, 294n, 295; Old Jewry, 336; Old Kent Road, 311n, 329; Old Street, 531; Palmerston House in Bishopsgate Street, 295; Park Street, *See* Maiden Lane; Paris Garden Stairs, 437, 448; Paul's Churchyard and Cross, 68, 87; Peabody Housing Estate, 623; Petticoat Lane, 452; Playhouse Yard (Blackfriars), 501; Playhouse Yard (St Giles Cripplegate), 531, 638, 648; Pleydell Court, 550n; Porter's Hall (Blackfriars), 562; Prince's Arms, 439, 450n; Princes Street, 623; Ram Alley, 547; Red Lion Farmhouse (Middlesex), 290, 291, 292, 293, 501; Redcross Street, 537; Rose Alley, 419, 424, 426; 'The Little Rose' (plot of land), 419, 423, 424, 434; Rose and Crown, 534; Rose Court (a building), 419; Salisbury Court, 649, 652n, 652–3, 654, 655, 657, 670n, 672–3; Sampson House, 437; Shoreditch, 31, 92, 110, 281–82, 295, 320, 330, 331, 337, 358–9, 363, 371, 406n, 418, 486, 497, 509, 630&n; Shoreditch High Street, 330, 404, 411n, 417&n; Smithfield, 47,

700   Index

London and environs (*cont.*)
529, 564, 596, 602&n; Southwark, 46, 110, 123, 126, 157, 320, 322, 326, 328, 332, 419, 423, 424, 426, 428–9, 437, 440, 493, 495, 497, 531, 534, 595, 598, 605, 607, 622; Southwark Bridge Road, 493, 607; St James's Palace, 580, 633; St John of Jerusalem (Priory of), 297&n; St John Street, 564, 566, 567n, 569–70, 571, 581, 584, 588, 589; St Paul's Chain, 524; St Paul's Churchyard (a street), 306, 524, 525; St Paul's Cross, 308n; St Swithin's Lane, 405; Stark's House, *See* Red Lion Farmhouse; Stepney, 487; bailiff of, 484; Stepney Way, 290; Temple, The, 369, 448, 547, 575; Temple Bar, 623; Temple Church, 448n; Temple Lane, 547; Thames Street, 596, 599; Thames (river), 305, 320, 322n, 388, 391, 419, 422, 424, 437, 446n, 448n, 449, 493, 497, 499, 506, 524, 547–8, 595, 596, 602n, 604, 607, 649; Tower of London, Lieutenant of the, 336; Tudor Street, 649, 652n; Turnbull or Turnmill Street, 630&n; Walworth Road, 320; Wapping, 629; Water Lane (Blackfriars), 391–3; Water Lane (Whitefriars), 547, 649, 653; West End, 623; Westminster, 471, 557, 623; Westminster Hall, 501, 588; Whitechapel, 290, 292, 293, 351, 352, 353–4, 364, 365n, 452, 455, 456, 475, 476n, 485, 486, 582; Whitechapel High Street, 452; Whitechapel Road, 290; Whitecross Street, 221, 531, 533, 538, 541, 543, 545, 638, 640, 643, 647–8; Whitefriars, 305&n, 547–8, 550&n, 554, 560, 561, 562, 563n, 655; Whitefriars Priory, 547, 553, 562; Whitefriars Street, 547, 649, 652n; Whitehall, 410, 669; Wild Street, 623–5
Longe, Jane, 407
Longe, Maurice (cloth-worker), 405, 407
Longe, William (cloth-worker), 405, 407
Lord Admiral (Charles Howard, Lord Howard of Effingham and Earl of Nottingham), 73, 80, 84, 90, 91, 92, 93, 102–5, 106, 107, 109, 120, 123, 258, 346&n, 537–8; his company of players, *see* Playing Companies
Lord Arundel, his company of players. *See* Playing Companies
Lord Chamberlain, 5, 48, 70, 75–6, 83–104, 107, 109–10, 117, 120–3, 126, 143–4, 147–8, 210, 221, 224, 226n, 227, 254, 257, 259, 486, 507, 512, 515, 521n, 525–6, 528, 609, 621, 633, 634, 635; his company of players, *see* Playing Companies
Lord Chancellor, 251, 342, 361
Lord Chief Justice, 447, 474, 520, 578

Lord Derby, his company of players. *See* Playing Companies
Lord Rich, his company of players. *See* Playing Companies
Lord Strange, his company of players. *See* Playing Companies
Lord Vaux, his company of players. *See* Playing Companies
Lorkin, Thomas, 499
Loseley (Surrey), 390, 397, 504
Low Countries, 41
Lowin, John (player), 196, 210, 222–3, 503, 526, 616, 645
Ludwig, Prince (of Anhalt-Cöthen), 304, 438, 440–1
Luther, Martin, 17
Lyddiat, Ralph, 136–7
Lyffe, John (carpenter), 291
Lyly, John (writer), 93, 307, 310, 389&n, 402; *Campaspe*, 395; *Endymion*, 312; *Mother Bombie*, 312; *Pappe with an hatchet*, 307, 310–11&n; *Sapho and Phao*, 395
Lynsey, John (butcher), 543

Machiavelli, Niccolò, 303
Machyn, Henry, 46; his *Diary*, 308
Madox, Richard, 343
Madrid, 615
Magistrates, 4, 35, 43–4, 48, 51, 62–3, 68, 70, 77–8, 81, 84–5, 87, 88–90, 99, 103, 104, 108, 110–11, 112, 115, 121, 124, 132, 133, 138–9
Mago, John (carpenter), 454, 459, 460–1&n, 463n, 475, 476n, 480–1&n, 483, 488–9, 491, 492
Mago, William (musician or stage attendant), 258–9
Mails, Mrs. (prostitute?), 418
Mainwaringe, Thomas, 451
Maitland, William, *History of London*, 646
Malcolm, J.P., *Londinium Redivivum*, 313
Maller, George (glazier), 275–7
Malone Society *Collections*, 310, 390, 393n, 408–9, 416, 440, 504, 511, 522, 525n, 525, 562, 580, 585, 586n, 621, 628&n, 632–3, 634, 636
Malone, Edmond, 236, 417, 418, 435–6, 534, 631, 655–6; *Plays and Poems of William Shakespeare*, 416–17, 418, 432, 434, 450, 495n, 526, 534, 563n, 584, 587, 597, 600, 603, 631, 632, 634, 657
Man in the Moon, The, 587
Manchester, 289
Manne, Robert, 407–8
Manningham, John, The *Diary*, 448n

Index 701

Marcon, Thomas (of Norwich), 256
Margrave, Richard (sailor), 643
Marlowe, Christopher (playwright), 11, 13, 161; *Doctor Faustus*, 303, 591; *The Jew of Malta*, 328, 431, 432; *Massacre at Paris (The Guise)*, 432
Marmion, Shakerley, *Holland's Leaguer*, 450
Marprelate, Martin (pseudonym), 92–3, 260, 307, 310–11&n, 357, 409
Marsh, John (carpenter), 461n, 463n, 480–1&n, 483, 492
Marshall, Charles (player), 144, 254
Marshalsea, Court of the, 453–4, 464, 467–8, 470–5&n
Marshalsea, Marshal of the (i.e., marshal of the royal household), 292, 467, 470, 472
Marston, John (playwright), 11, 126, 127, 128, 167, 307, 512, 515n, 519&n; *Antonio and Mellida*, 308n; *The Dutch Courtesan*, 509n; *Jack Drum's Entertainment*, 313; *What You Will*, 314; *Scourge of Villainy*, 375, 411–12
Martyrs, 2, 3, 22, 37, 46–7
Mary Stuart, Queen of Scots, 49, 61–3, 78
Mary Tudor, Queen, 1, 3, 10–11, 37, 39–47 *passim*, 48, 78; as Princess 39
Maskewe, Mr, 65
Mason, John (playwright, playhouse investor), 269–71, 547–9, 552, 554–9; *The Turk*, 547
Massey, Charles (player), 221, 542&n, 544, 638, 640
Massey, George (merchant tailor), 641n
Massinger, Philip (playwright), 129, 185; *The Great Duke*, 631
Mastock, ?Mr (a gentleman of the Earl of Dorset), 673
Mathewes, William (fencer), 410
Maulkin, 161
May Day games and plays, 22, 93, 112, 131
May, Edward (player), 657–64
May, Randolph (painter), 343–4
Mayler, George (merchant tailor, player), 153, 232
Mayne, Jasper (writer), 586
Mayor's plays, 287
Meade, Jacob (waterman), 217–18, 282–4, 432&n, 595–6, 597–600, 600–1, 603
Medea, 412
Medley, Robert, 408
Medwall, Henry (playwright), 2
Mellon Collection (Yale University), 597n
Mercers, 97–8
Merchant Taylors, 97–8
Mercurius Democritus, 587
Mercurius Elencticus, 636–7

Mercurius Fumigosus, 587, 590nn
Mercurius Melancholicus, 646n, 669n
Mercurius Pragmaticus, 589n, 644, 669n
Mercurius Publicus, 646
Mercurius Veridicus, 645
Meres, Francis (writer), 167; *Palladis Tamia*, 446
Merry, Edward, 505
Michaelmas, 79, 81, 82, 113
Microcosmography (Earle), 186
Middlesex, 63, 76–86, 88–9, 99–101, 103, 104, 106, 110–11, 121, 132, 133, 336, 340, 364, 404, 407, 449, 452, 456, 472, 498, 504, 509, 531, 533, 538&n, 541, 544, 545, 564, 571, 581, 585, 638; Justices of, 414, 440, 486, 537–9, 543, 642, 645, 646n
Middlesex, Earl of (Lionel Cranfield, third earl), 672
Middleton, Thomas (playwright), 127, 128, 307; (with William Rowley) *The Changeling*, 631; *A Chaste Maid in Cheapside*, 448–9; *The Family of Love*, 547–8; *A Game at Chess*, 609, 615–16; *Inner Temple Masque*, 629–30; (with Thomas Dekker) *The Roaring Girl*, 448–9, 542–3; (with William Rowley) *The World Tossed at Tennis*, 439
Miles, Ralph, 338–9, 350, 355, 362–3
Miles, Robert (goldsmith), 298, 331, 338–9, 349–50, 351, 353–4, 355, 357–8, 358–63, 364–5&n, 365–6, 366–7, 372–5
Milles, Thomas (butcher), 491
Mills, Tobias (player), 176, 300
Milton, John (poet), 295
Milward, Agnes. *See* Howe, Agnes
Milward, John (Dr. of Civil Law), 314–16&nn
Minstrels, 20, 62, 144
Mirror of Monsters, A (Rankins), 167
Mithridate, 180
Momus, 498
Montgomery, Earl of (Philip Herbert, first earl), 515
Moore, Joseph (player), 189, 252, 256
Moot-halls. *See* Guildhalls, provincial
More, Joseph, 144
More, Richard (carpenter), 291
More, Sir Thomas, 232n
More, Sir William, 260–1, 388–9&nn, 390&n, 390–3&n, 393–4, 395, 397–400, 400–1&nn, 401–2&n, 403, 501, 504, 506–7&nn
More, William (of Worcestershire), 136–7
Morecroft, Robert (of Lincoln), 225
Morely, Baron, 144
Morgan, William, *London &c, Actually Survey'd*, 440n, 567&n; *see also* John Ogilby
Morris dances, 112

Morris, Edward (embroiderer), 405
Morris, Isbrand (dyer), 494
Morrison, Sir Richard, 20–1
Mortlake (Surrey), 198, 200
Motteram, John (imprest boy player), 265
Mount Tabor (Willis), 243
Mounteagle, Lord, 195
Mountjoy, Lady (Katherine Blount), 407
Mountjoy, Lord (James Blount, sixth lord), 407
Moxlay, Nicholas (apprentice notary public), 458, 462
Mucklowe, William (fencer), 296
Mufford, John (player), 251
Mulcaster, Richard (Headmaster of Merchant Taylors' School), 260, 265
Munday, Anthony (writer), 162
Murray, Mr W., 129
Musgrave, Thomas (fencer), 450n

Nabbes, Thomas (writer), *Covent Garden*, 620–30; *Microcosmus*, 667; *Tottenham Court*, 654
Napton, John, 426
Nashe, Thomas (writer), 9–10, 80, 92–3, 95, 101, 102, 104, 171, 307, 310–311&n, 439; *Have with you to Saffron Walden*, 312; (with Ben Jonson and others) *Isle of Dogs*, 439, 441; *The May-game of Martinisme*, 307; *Martins Months Minde*, 357, 408–9; *Returne of the renowned Caualiero Pasquill of England*, 310; *Summer's Last Will and Testament*, 312
Nelson, Alan, 29
Nero, 190
Nestor, 206
Netherlands, The, 41, 440, 528
Nevill, Thomas, 370
Neville, Sir Henry, 390, 391, 401–2&n
New and Choice Characters of Several Writers (Overbury), 180
New Windsor (Berkshire), 390
Newcastle, Marquess of (William Cavendish, first marquess), 487
Newhall, William (Town Clerk of Chester), 18–19
Newman, John, 389&n, 394, 395, 395–6, 396–400&nn, 400&n, 402&n
Newmarket (Cambridgeshire), 129
Newton, Samuel, 418
Nichols, John Gough, 46
Nicoll, William (notary public), 336, 337–9&n
Nixon, Anthony, *Three English Brothers*, 569
Noble, Thomas (fencer), 409
Nonsuch Palace (Surrey), 308

Noone, Henry, 175
Norfolk, 61, 82, 100
Norfolk, Duke of, 22, 61–2, 73
Norman, Philip, 'Accounts of the Overseers of the Poor', 440n; *Accounts of the Overseers of the Poor*, 448–9, 450&n
Normanton, Earl of, 73
North, Lord, 113, 116
Northbrooke, John (clergyman), *A Treatise wherein Dicing, Dauncing, Vaine playes, etc.*, 160, 337, 408
Northern Rebellion, 48, 61, 69
Northumberland, Duke of, 39
Norton, Thomas (playwright), 52
Norwich (City of), 61, 82, 145–7, 149, 413; Bowde, Simon (Mayor), 252; White Horse Inn, 251n, 253n, 256
Nottingham (City of), 6, 9, 20
Nottingham, Earl of (Charles Howard, first earl). *See* Lord Admiral
Nottingham, Sheriff of, 20
Nyköping, Sweden, 172

Oaths, 128–129, 131
Ogilby, John and William Morgan, *A Large and Accurate Map of the City of London*, 296n, 489, 567&n, 626n
Old Comedy, 310
Orange, Prince of (Frederick Henry of Nassau), 528
Ordinances, Bristol, 118–119; London, 132–5
Ormond, Duke of, 527
Ormskirk (Lancashire), 139
Orrell, John, 'Building the Fortune', 532n; *Theatres of Inigo Jones and John Webb*, 626n
Osborne, Thomas (carpenter), 348, 386&n
Osborne, Thomas (of Kirby Bidon), 248
Ostler, William (player), 226, 494
Otto, Prince (of Hesse-Cassel), 499
Outlawe, Henry, 514, 518
Overbury, Sir Thomas, 180, 186
Ovid, 177, 446
Oxford (City of), 11, 12, 17, 20, 27, 30, 36, 40, 51, 69–70, 311, 317, 584
Oxford, Earl of (Edward de Vere, seventeenth earl), 90, 92, 105, 109–10, 389, 402, 481; his company of players, *see* Playing Companies
Oxford, University of, 161
Oxford English Dictionary, 393n, 499, 589n, 655n

Packer, John, 271–2
Pacolet (fabulous horse), 181
Pageants, 1, 131

Paget, Sir William, 34, 157
Painton, Edward, 521
Painton, Margaret. *See* Hawkins, Margaret
Pallant, Robert (player), 191, 219, 253, 258–9
Palsgrave (Count Palatine), his company of players. *See* Playing Companies
Paman, Henry (of Norwich), 146, 256
Papal Bulls, 48, 49, 61; Papal Legate, 41; Papal Supremacy, 1, 3
Paris Garden, Manor of, 212, 437–9&nn, 442, 447, 448, 448–9, 598; bear baiting there, 87, 297, 305, 604
Parishes: St Alban, Wood Street, 385; St Andrew Undershaft, 543; St Anne Blackfriars, 508, 522n, 522–3; St Bartholomew the Great, 510; St Botolph without Aldgate, 193, 194; St Bride Fleet Street, 550, 649, 652, 657; St Clement Eastcheap, 543; St Dunstan in the West, 549, 550, 561; St Giles in the Fields, 623; St Giles without Cripplegate, 216, 413, 487, 531, 533, 534, 538, 541, 545, 638; St James, Clerkenwell, 544, 568, 571; St Leonard Shoreditch, 208, 406n, 407, 509; St Mary Matfellon, *see* (under London) Whitechapel; St Mary le Bow, 312; St Mildred, Bread Street, 419, 423n, 423, 434; St Olave Southwark, 326, 598; St Saviour Southwark, 88, 195, 197, 212, 216, 282, 423, 424, 426, 432, 436, 446, 495, 497, 534, 598, 610n, 622; St Stephen Coleman Street, 195
Park, The (Bishop of Winchester's estate, Southwark), 495
Parker, Matthew, 25–9
Parliament, 503, 587, 588, 596, 610, 622, 625, 636, 644, 645–6&n, 651, 669, 674n; House of Commons, 588; House of Lords, 588, 632; members of, 644
Parliament, Acts of: Advancement of True Religion (1543), 23–5, 26, 33; Chantries (1549), 33; Punishment of Beggars, Rogues and Vagabonds (1531), 48, 62–3, 79, 81, 103, 120, 131, 133, 139–40; Royal Supremacy (1531–36), 40, 48, 53; Suppression of Plays and Playhouses (1647–8), 132–5; Uniformity of Service and Administration of the Sacraments (1549), 34, 40, 50. *See also* Statutes of the Realm
Parr, William (player), 144, 221, 254, 544
Parson, John, 640
Paston, Sir William, 247–50
Pateson, William (player), 245
Patrick, William (musician or stage attendant), 258–9
Patteson, John, 365n

Paul's, Master of the Children of: *See* Thomas Giles; Edward Pearce
Pavy, Salomon (imprest boy player), 265, 267–8
Payne, Anthony, 573–4, 592
Payne, Peter (butcher), 405
Payne, Richard (girdler), 405
Payne, Robert, 513–14
Peace, disturbances of, 18, 35–6, 41, 43, 44, 53, 73, 76, 77, 79, 80, 87, 88, 89, 92–93, 116, 138, 148–9
Pearce (Peers), Edward (musician, Master of the Children of Paul's), 265, 307, 308n, 315, 316&n, 317, 318–19
Peckham, Edmund, 343–4
Pedel, Abraham (player), 641
Pedlars. *See* Vagrants
Peele, George (playwright), 11, 431
Peers, Edward. *See* Pearce
Peerson, Martin (musician), 512
Pembroke, Earl of, 9, 101–2, 104, 108, 144, 226, 254; his company of players, *see* Playing Companies
Pembroke and Montgomery, Earl of, 210, 221, 224, 259
Penn, William (player), 259
Penry, John (Martin Marprelate?), 311n
Pentecost, 34
Pepys, Elizabeth, 591
Pepys, Samuel, 590–1; Diary, 590
Percy, Sir Jocelyn, 195
Percy, William (writer), 317
Perfect Account of the Daily Intelligence, A, 590n
Perfect Diurnal, A, 587
Perfect Occurrences, 587, 646n, 669
Perkin, John (player), 206
Perkins, Richard (player), 239–41, 253, 434, 628, 630–1, 657–64
Perry, William (player), 144, 254, 417–18
Pershore (Worcestershire), 136
Philip II, King of Spain, 3, 39, 40
Philips, Mr (Master, musician?), 308&n
Phillips, Augustine (player), 123, 176, 191–203, 226, 493–4, 496n, 497; his brothers James Webb and William Webb, 198; his daughter Anne, 194, 198; his daughter Elizabeth, 199; his daughter Magdalen, 192, 198; his daughter Rebecca, 193, 198; his Jig of the Slippers, 193; his mother Agnes Bennett, 198; his nephews Miles Borne and Phillips Borne, 198; his sister Elizabeth Gough, 195, 198; his sister Margery Borne, 197n, 198; his son Augustine, 197; his wife Anne, 194, 198, 199, 200–03

Phillips, Edward (of St Saviour's parish), 195
Phillips, John (writer), *Sportive Wit*, 590n
Pickering, Sir John (Lord Keeper), 365–6
Pierce Pennilesse his Supplication to the Devil (Nashe), 171
Pig, John (player), 236
Pilgrimage of Grace, 22
Pinnocke, Thomas, 585
Pipe Office, 504–7&n
Plague, 49, 54, 55, 59, 60, 74, 75, 76, 79, 80–5, 86, 87, 89, 107, 111, 112, 116, 123, 135, 141, 299, 326–8, 336, 406, 408, 414, 431, 434, 455, 486, 503, 507, 548, 552, 555, 560, 632–3, 649, 658, 661–4, 664–6, 667
Platter, Thomas (Swiss tourist), 412–13, 497
Players (in general), 207–8, 287, 299, 305, 306–7, 308n, 311–12, 317, 326–7, 341, 395, 409, 449, 531; as caterpillars, 162; as drones, 178; as hypocrites, 179; Italian, 63; to be burnt through the ear with a hot iron, 161; wearing women's garments, 165
Players. *See* John Adams; Edward Alleyn; John Alleyn; Richard Andrews; Robert Armin; Thomas Arthur; Alexander Barker; Thomas Barnes; Richard Baxter; Robert Baxter; William Bee; Christopher Beeston; Robert Beeston; Robert Benfield; John Bentley; John Birche; Theophilus Bird; William Bird; John Bradstreet; Edward Browne; John Browne; Robert Browne; William Browme; George Bryan; Paul Buck; James Burbage; Richard Burbage; Andrew Cane; William Cartwright; John Chappell; Thomas Clarke; Nathaniel Clay; Richard Clayton; Thomas Clifton; Henry Condell; Abel Cooke; Alexander Cooke; Lionel Cooke; Thomas Cooke; Richard Cowley; Robert Cox; Samuel Crosse; John Cumber; Robert Dawes; Thomas Downton; John Duke; John Dutton; Lawrence Dutton; William Ecclestone; John Edmonds; Nathan Field; Lawrence Fletcher; Alexander Foster; Richard Fowler; John Garland; Samuel Gilburne; Thomas Goffe; Alexander Gough; Robert Gough; Frank Grace; Richard Grace; Thomas Greene; Curtis Greville; Thomas Grymes; Richard Gunnell; Richard Hanley; William Hart; George Hasell; John Heminges; Thomas Heywood; Thomas Hobbes; John Holland; James Holt; Humfrey Jeffes; William Johnson; Richard Jones; Ben Jonson; Edward Juby; William Kemp; Philip Kingman; William Knell; John Laneham; Robert Lee; John Lowin; Charles Marshall; Charles Massey; Edward May; George Mayler; Tobias Mills; Joseph Moore; John Motteram; John Mufford; William Ostler; Robert Pallant; William Parr; William Pateson; Salomon Pavy; Abraham Pedel; William Penn; John Perkin; Richard Perkins; William Perry; Augustine Phillips; John Pig; Thomas Pollard; Thomas Pope; Thomas Powlton; Richard Price; Philip Pykman; Timothy Reade; Gilbert Reason; John Redman; Ralph Reeve; William Robins; Richard Robinson; William Rowley; Thomas Sackville; James Sands; Jerome Savage; Robert Shaa; William Shakespeare; John Shanks; William Sherlock; John Sinckler; John Singer; Martin Slater; William Sly; Matthew Smith; Gabriel Spencer; William Stratford; John Sumpner; Elliard Swanston; Thomas Swinnerton; Richard Tarlton; Joseph Taylor; Nicholas Tooley; John Towne; Thomas Towne; John Townsend; William Trig; Alvery Trussell; James Tunstall; Anthony Turnor; John Underwood; Francis Wambus; William Wilbraham; Robert Wilson; Ellis Worth; John Younge

Playhouses
Admissions and local taxes, 3–4, 6, 90–1
Demolition, threats of, 9, 92, 99, 100–3, 104, 111, 133–5
Private (in general), 287–8, 318, 409, 519; stage, 288, 544; tiring-house, 288; pit, 288; galleries, 288; boxes, 288; sitting on stage, 514&n
Public (in general), 287–8, 315, 332, 339, 341, 405–6, 408–9, 542, 544, 566; yard, 287–8, 413; galleries, 287, 410, 413; stage, 288, 413; tiring-house, 287; stage machinery, 288; lighting, 288, 492; sitting on stage, 514&n

Playhouses (London and environs):
Bear Garden, 87, 92, 124, 281 (see also Hope)
Bel Savage Inn, 295–7, 299, 302–3, 304, 305, 330
Bell Inn, 295–6, 297, 300, 301, 304
Blackfriars (the first playhouse), 288, 306, 307, 330, 388–403, 501, 507n, 508n
Blackfriars (the second playhouse), 288, 305, 306, 307, 318, 319, 501–30, 549, 560, 609, 614, 616, 621, 623, 629, 633, 644, 645, 649, 655n; sharers in, 502–3, 519, 521, 525n, 525–6
Boar's Head, 45, 92, 105, 107, 108, 109, 110, 124, 307, 406, 414, 438, 452–92, 494, 498, 564, 569n
Bull Inn, 295–6, 298, 300, 301, 304, 305

Index 705

Cockpit, 125, 240, 288, 405, 580&n, 623–37, 649, 651, 655n, 658, 660, 662, 665, 669
Cross Keys Inn, 93, 295–6, 298, 301, 302, 304
Curtain, 81, 92, 99, 100, 105, 107, 108, 109, 124, 160, 296, 298, 332n, 337, 339, 345–6, 348–9, 350, 375, 404–18, 433, 434, 441, 441n, 486, 487, 498, 539&n, 564, 569n, 570, 582
Drury Lane, 626
Fortune (the first playhouse), 13, 80, 90, 91, 106, 107, 216–17, 220–1, 295, 413–14, 415, 419, 423, 449, 481, 487, 493–4, 498, 509n, 531–46, 570, 580n, 595, 597n, 597, 628n, 638–9, 642
Fortune (the second playhouse), 288, 567, 583, 584, 586–7&n, 626n, 638–48, 668, 669
Globe (the first playhouse), 90, 106, 107, 123, 295, 332, 376, 406, 412, 414, 415, 432, 433, 436n, 437, 439&n, 449, 481, 493–500, 521, 523, 525, 531–2, 534–6, 595, 607, 609–10, 611–12; sharers in, 493–4, 495, 497, 502–3, 607–9, 610n, 613, 621
Globe (the second playhouse), 200–3, 221–28, 288, 439, 450, 493–4, 567, 596, 605, 607–22, 645; sharers in, 607–9, 610–11, 611–12, 612–13&n, 616–19, 620–1, 621–2&n
Hope, 124, 419, 437&n, 448, 449, 450, 487, 534, 595–606, 607, 643
Newington Butts, 81, 83, 320–9, 330, 388, 405, 431
Phoenix. *See* Cockpit
Red Bull, 124, 125, 288, 299, 303, 307, 406, 414, 416, 417, 486, 547, 549, 564–94, 603, 623, 627–8&nn, 629, 646, 660, 668, 669
Red Lion, 287, 290–4, 330
Rose, 13, 80, 84, 92, 101, 103, 106, 107, 109, 211, 213, 327–8, 419–36, 437, 439, 441, 441n, 441, 443–5, 446, 449, 450, 455, 481, 493, 531–2, 537, 539, 539–40, 595
Salisbury Court, 125, 288, 583, 584, 625, 629, 633, 637, 646&n, 649–74
Swan, 11, 92, 102–3, 104, 105, 108, 124, 211–26, 295, 411, 422, 432n, 437–51, 453, 509n, 595, 598–9, 605
St Paul's, 120–1, 306–19, 330, 395, 515, 519, 547, 564
Theatre, 81, 92, 99, 100, 103, 105, 160, 226, 290, 295, 296, 298, 299, 300, 305, 311, 320, 330–87, 388, 404–6, 408–9, 410, 411, 411–12, 438, 441, 441n, 493, 497, 501, 504n, 532, 610, 621
Whitefriars, 121, 122, 125, 260, 307, 319, 419, 448, 487, 515, 519, 547–63, 564, 595, 649
Playhouses (Provincial)
Bristol: Redcliffe Hill (1631–2 to 1640), 119; Wine Street (1604–5 to 1628–9), 119
Norwich: White Horse Inn, 146
Playing Companies, general
Amateur, 4, 8, 48–9, 61, 69, 125–6
Boys: General, 110, 123; Chapel Royal, 260–1, 264–7; King's Revels, 121, 124, 269–71; Paul's, 260, 261; Queen's Chamber at Bristol, 119, 271–4; Queen's Chapel, 226; Queen's Revels, 121, 124, 125, 126–7, 144, 217–18, 240, 254, 260, 268–9
Men: Managers, 78, 88, 89–90, 98, 109; Patents, 96, 119, 120, 124, 125, 126, 130–1, 135, 140; Performances at night, 57–8, 86, 117–19, 137, 142–3; Playbills and bill posting, 6, 31, 77, 81–2, 90, 114, 146; Players paid 'not to play', 119, 121, 135, 140–1, 143, 147, 149; Players' economy, 82–3, 84, 114; Playmakers, 3, 5, 8, 10, 11, 17, 41, 45, 71, 98, 104, 109, 121
Playing Companies
Admiral, Lord, 84, 90, 91, 92, 93, 102, 103, 104, 105, 120, 123, 178n, 191, 236–8, 251, 258, 277, 302, 321, 328, 332, 361–2, 410, 423, 431–2, 433, 481, 532, 537–9, 539–40
Anne, Queen, 122, 123, 140–3, 185, 239–41, 253–4, 406, 414, 415, 416, 455, 486, 486–7, 495n, 564, 566, 568–9, 579, 580, 581, 623, 625, 627, 627–8&n, 629, 630, 630–1. *See also* Revels; Palsgrave
Arundel, Earl of, 345–6, 406
Beauchamp, Lord, 251
Berkeley, Lord, 92, 141, 252
Bohemia, King and Queen of, 639
Bohemia, Queen of, 189. *See also* Elizabeth, Princess
Chamberlain, Lord, 80, 103, 104, 106, 107, 109, 120, 178n, 195, 204, 296, 304, 310, 321, 332, 375, 406, 411–12, 412, 423, 431, 433, 438, 481, 493–4, 497, 498, 502, 507
Chandos, Lord, 117, 252
Charles, Prince, later King Charles I, 124, 128, 140, 141–3, 253–4, 259, 406, 416–17, 439, 450&n, 455, 486–7&n, 503, 566, 580, 582, 583n, 584, 596, 603, 609, 614, 616, 619, 620–1, 625, 630–1, 639, 645, 669
Charles, Prince, later King Charles II, 566, 584, 585–6, 587, 589n, 639, 644–5, 650, 652n, 660, 665
Derby, Earl of (fifth earl), 328, 332

Index

Playing Companies (cont.)
   Derby, Earl of (sixth earl), 105, 108–9, 111–12, 140, 307, 313, 453–5
   Elizabeth, Princess (Lady Elizabeth's players), 124, 137, 142, 145–7, 149, 189, 217–18, 252, 255–8, 260, 448–9, 450n, 549, 596, 600, 601–2, 603&n, 625, 626, 631
   Elizabeth, Queen, 92, 96, 177nn, 204, 208, 244, 246–50, 295–6, 300, 301, 332, 345–6, 409, 410
   Essex, Earl of, 310
   Henrietta Maria, Queen, 625, 626, 631, 632–3, 651, 657–64, 664–7
   Henry VII, King, 1
   Henry VIII, King, 2, 48, 275
   Henry, Prince, 123, 414, 487, 532
   Holstein, Duke of, 568
   Hunsdon, Lord, *See* Lord Chamberlain
   James, King, 122, 123, 127, 140, 196, 204, 210, 221–8, 307, 318–19, 414, 449, 494, 498, 499, 502–3, 515–16, 519, 520, 523, 525&n, 584, 609, 610n, 613–14, 615
   King's Players. *See* Red Bull company
   King's Revels, men and boys of the, 639, 649–51, 653, 656, 657–8, 660
   King and Queen's Young Company, 625, 632–3, 633–4, 635, 660, 662
   Leicester, Earl of, 78, 90, 205–6, 250, 310, 332, 341
   Lennox, Duke of, 123–4, 455, 486&n
   Nottingham, Earl of. *See* Admiral, Lord
   Oxford, Earl of, 90, 92, 109, 157, 250–1, 320–1, 332
   Palsgrave (Count Palatine), 144, 220, 254, 532, 544, 545, 546, 638–9, 641
   Pembroke, Earl of (Henry Herbert, second earl), 101, 102, 105, 108, 211–16, 423, 434, 438–9, 441, 442–6, 540
   Red Bull company, 566, 584, 587, 639
   Revels, 580, 581&n, 582
   Rich, Lord, 341
   Strange, Lord, 191–2, 278, 296, 302, 321, 327–8, 332, 422–3, 431
   Vaux, Lord, 341
   Warwick, Earl of, 310, 320, 332, 341
   Worcester, Earl of, 244–5, 251, 423, 434, 454–5, 479–80, 480–1, 481–2, 484, 485–6
Playing: arguments against, 155; as ornament to the City, 177; on Sundays, 162; restraint of (1597), 211–16
Plays, 327, 328n, 408–9, 410, 413; *Alexander and Lodowick* (Anon), 238; *Alice Pierce* (Anon), 237–8; *All is True*, see *Henry VIII*; *Albumazar* (Tomkis), 570; *Antonio and Mellida* (Marston), 308n; *Arviragus and Felicia* (Carlell), 528; *Bartholomew Fair* (Jonson), 602; *The Battle of Alcazar* (Peele), 431; *Bellendon* (or *Belin Dun*) (Anon), 328, 432; *The Bellman of Paris* (Dekker & Day), 582&n; *Black Batman* (Chettle et al.), 238; *Black Joan* (Anon), 238; *The Blacksmith's Daughter* (Anon), 341; *Bourbon* (Anon), 238; *Britannia Triumphans* (Davenant), 440n; *Campaspe* (Lyly), 395; *The Careless Shepherdess* (Goffe), 668; *Catiline* (Jonson), 11; *Catiline's Conspiracies* (Gosson), 341; *The Changeling* (Middleton & Rowley), 631; *A Chaste Maid in Cheapside* (Middleton), 448–9; *The Cobbler of Queenhithe* (Anon), 238; *The Conquest of the Indies* (Day et al.), 238; *The Conspiracy and Tragedy of Charles, Duke of Biron* (Chapman), 126; *The Coronation* (Shirley? Fletcher?), 629–39; *The Court Beggar* (Brome), 634–5; *The Creed Play* (York), 33, 64; *Cupid and Psyche* (Anon), 307, 395; *Cupid's Whirligig* (Sharpham), 547; *Cutlack* (Anon), 328, 432; *Cutwell* (Anon), 297; *The Devil's Dam* (Haughton), 434; *Doctor Faustus* (Marlowe), 13, 303, 591; *Doctor Lambe and the Witches* (Anon), 643&n; *The Doubtful Heir* (Shirley), 614; *The Dutch Courtesan* (Marston), 509n; *Eastward Ho!* (Chapman, Jonson, Marston), 126; *Endymion* (Lyly), 312; *The English Traveller* (Heywood), 641–2; *Epicoene, or The Silent Woman* (Jonson), 11; *Every Man in His Humour* (Jonson), 194; *Every Man Out of His Humour* (Jonson), 194; *Play of the Fall* (Norwich Grocers), 61; *The Family of Love* (Middleton), 547–8; *The Famous Victories of Henry V* (Anon), 301; *Five New Plays* (Brome), 646–7; *Friar Bacon and Friar Bungay* (Greene), 431, 589; *Friar Spendleton* (Anon), 238; 'Friars' (Anon), 415; *A Game at Chess* (Middleton), 127, 609, 615–16; *God's Promises* (Bale), 21; *Godwin* (Chettle et al.), 238; *Gorboduc* (Sackville & Norton), 52; *The Great Duke* (Massinger), 631; *The Guise* (Marlowe), 432; *Hamlet* (the ur-*Hamlet*), 328; *Hamlet* (Shakespeare), 495n, 502; *Hardicanute* (Anon), 238; *Harry of Cornwall* (Anon), 278, 431; *Henry VIII* (Shakespeare), 139, 494, 499–500; *Hester and Ahasuerus* (Anon), 328; *Hieronimo* (Kyd), 13; *The Hog Hath Lost His Pearl* (Tailor), 562; *The Humours* (Anon), 238; *Inner Temple Masque* (Middleton), 629–30; *The Isle of Dogs* (Nashe, Jonson et al.), 9–10, 80, 92, 95, 101, 102, 104, 439, 441; *The Isle of*

Gulls (Day), 126; *Jack Drum's Entertainment* (Marston), 313; *The Jew* (Anon), 299; *The Jew of Malta* (Marlowe), 237, 328, 431, 432; *John of Gaunt* (Anon), 238; *Julius Caesar* (Shakespeare), 412, 497; *The Just Italian* (Davenant), 503n; *Keep the Widow Waking, see* Late Murder; *A King and No King* (Beaumont & Fletcher), 669; *The King and the Subject* (Massinger), 129; *Knavery in all Trades* (?Tatham), 644; *The Knight of the Burning Pestle* (Beaumont & Fletcher), 568–9; *Kyng Johan* (Bale), 21; *Ladies A Second Time Assembled in Parliament* (Anon), 645–6&n; *The Late Lancashire Witches* (Heywood & Brome), 609, 619–20&n; *The Late Murder . . . or Keep the Widow Waking* (Dekker, Ford, Rowley, Webster), 583–3; *Like unto Like* (Anon), 434; *Love and Riches* (Rastell), 229; *Loves Maistresse* (Heywood), 620–30; *The Madman's Morris* (Anon), 238; *A Masque of Blackness* (Jonson), 125; *The Massacre at Paris* (Marlowe), 432; *Messallina* (Richards), 650; *Mother Bombie* (Lyly), 312; *Much Ado About Nothing* (Shakespeare), 503n; 'Muly Mollocco' (Peele)), 431; *The Muses' Looking Glass* (Randolph), 656; *The New Inn* (Jonson), 241; *News from Plymouth* (Davenant), 614; *Oberon* (Jonson), 125; *Orlando Furioso* (Greene), 431; *Othello* (Shakespeare), 498; *Pammachius* (Kirchmayer), 24–5; *Pater Noster Play* (York), 64–5; *Patient Grissell* (Philip), 308n; *Phaeton* (Anon), 238; *Pierce of Winchester* (Anon), 238; *The Pilgrimage to Parnassus* (Anon), 173; *Playhouse to be Let* (Davenant), 590–1; *Ptolemy* (Anon), 299; *The Puritan* (Anon), 308n; *Pythagoras* (Anon), 238; *The Ranger's Comedy* (Anon), 432; *Redcap* (Anon), 238; *Respublica* (Udall), 41; *The Return from Parnassus* (Anon), 173; *Richard II* (Shakespeare), 195; *The Roaring Girl* (Middleton & Dekker), 448–9, 542–3; 'Roaring Rimer' (Anon), 570; *The Roman Actor* (Massinger), 185; *Romeo and Juliet* (Shakespeare), 375, 412; *Roxana* (Alabaster), 650; *Sacrament, Croxton Play of the*, 33; *Samson* (Anon), 290, 291; *Sapho and Phao* (Lyly), 395; *The Scornful Lady* (Beaumont & Fletcher), 646; *The Scourge of Villainy* (Marston), 375, 411–12; *Sejanus* (Jonson), 11, 196; *The Seven Deadly Sins* (Anon), 191; *The Six Yeomen of the West* (Day & Haughton), 239; *The Spanish Contract* (Anon), 146–7, 256; *The Spanish Tragedy* (Kyd), 431; *The Sparagus Garden* (Brome), 650, 660; *Summer's Last Will and Testament* (Nashe), 312; *Tamburlaine* (Marlowe), 13; *The Taming of a Shrew* (Anon), 328; *The Temptation of our Lord* (Bale), 21; *Tethys' Festival* (Daniel), 125; *Three Ladies of London* (Wilson), 329; *The Three Lawes* (Bale), 21; *Titus Andronicus* (Shakespeare), 328; *Torismond* (Anon), 271; *The Travels of The Three English Brothers* (Day, Rowley, Wilkins), 569; *A Triplicity of Cuckolds* (Anon), 238; *Two Merry Milkmaids* (?Cumber), 580; *Twelfth Night* (Shakespeare), 503n; *Vayvode* (Anon), 238; *A Vision of the Tudor Goddesses* (Daniel), 125; *The Wedding* (Shirley), 631–2; *The Welshman's Prize* (Anon), 238; *What You Will* (Marston), 314; *The White Devil* (Webster), 125; *The Whore New Vamped* (Anon), 585–6; *Wit Without Money* (Beaumont & Fletcher), 588, 590n, 633; *The Witch of Islington* (Anon), 101; *The Witts* (Davenant), 128, 129; *A Woman will Have her Will* (Anon), 238; *The World Tossed at Tennis* (Middleton & Rowley), 439

Plays Confuted in Five Actions (Gosson), 164
Plevy, Humphrey, 487, 491
Plutarch, 159
Pole, Cardinal Reginald, 3, 41
Poley, Henry, 456, 457
Poley, Jane, 456, 457, 487
Poley, Sir John, 487
Polish Ambassador, 104
Pollard, Thomas (player), 221–8, 525–6, 621, 645
Pooley, Richard, 405
Pooly, Margaret, 506
Pope, the, 1, 2, 18–19, 20–1, 27–8, 61, 62
Pope, Mr, 434
Pope, Morgan, 426
Pope, Thomas (player), 176, 191–2, 194, 200, 278, 405, 412n, 493–4, 496n
Popham, Sir John (Lord Chief Justice), 195
Porphyry, 190
Porter, Endymion, 128–9
Pory, John (writer of newsletters), 527&n
Powle, Mr (of Norwich), 253
Powlton, Thomas (player), 245
Praemunire, 178
Price, Richard (player), 221, 544, 638, 640
Price, William (groom to Prince Charles), 417
Pride, Col. Thomas (sheriff of Surrey), 605, 606n
Prince Charles, his company of players. *See* Playing Companies
Prince Henry, his company of players. *See* Playing Companies
Printers. *See* Stationers

Prisons: *See* (under London) Bridewell; King's Bench; Ludgate; Marshalsea; Newgate
Privy Council, 9, 17, 28, 34, 36, 37, 39, 45–6, 49, 57, 61, 63, 67–8, 70, 71, 76, 78–9, 80–4, 86–90, 92, 99–103, 105–10, 111–13, 120–1, 127, 137, 140, 141, 144–7, 211, 266, 273, 301, 302, 304, 307, 309, 310, 311, 326–8, 336, 346, 375, 403, 408, 409, 410, 411, 413–14, 414, 426, 431, 432, 438–9, 440, 441, 446–7, 455–6, 468, 472–4, 481, 486, 498, 507–8, 511, 515&n, 523–5, 537–9&nn, 562, 563n, 564, 568, 585–6, 615, 619, 610n, 627, 628n, 632–3; Queen Henrietta Maria's, 627
Privy Seal, writs of, 324, 374, 379, 396, 446, 577
Proclamations, Royal, 3, 34–7, 39–41, 50–2, 55, 110, 120, 122–3, 130, 136; Civic (London), 30, 59; Civic (Provincial), 18–19
Proscenium-arch theatres, 288, 501
Proteus, 180
Prynn, John (broker), 340
Prynne, William (writer), 187, 190, 303; *Histriomastix*, 303, 526–7, 583, 655–6
Puckering, Sir Thomas, 499, 653
Pudding, John (or Jack) (a name for an undistinguished performer?), 647, 669, 670n
Puppets, 60
Purfett, Edward (feltmaker), 569
Puritans, 5, 6, 53, 60, 85, 111, 112, 121, 133, 135, 137
Pykman, Philip (imprest boy player), 265

Queen Anne, her company of players. *See* Playing Companies
Queen Elizabeth, her company of players. *See* Playing Companies
Queen Henrietta Maria, her company of players. *See* Playing Companies
Queen's College, Oxford, 584

Raine, Angelo, *York Civic Records*, 309
Ramsay, martyr, 22–3
Randolph, Thomas (writer), *The Muses' Looking Glass*, 649, 655–6; *Poems, with the Muses' Looking Glass*, 586–7
Rankins, William (writer), 167; *A Mirror of Monsters*, 341n, 408–9
Rastall, William, 512–14, 515, 517–9, 521n
Rastell, John (printer, playwright), 229–33; his wife, 232
Rawlidge, Richard, *A Monster Late Found Out and Discovered*, 304–5, 550n
Reade, Timothy (player), 657–64, 668, 669
Reason, Gilbert (player), 144, 253–4

Rebellion, 17, 41, 44; *see also* Northern Rebellion
Red Lion Inn, Norwich, 246–50
Redman, John (stationer, player), 153, 233
Reed, Oliver, 113
Reeve, Oliver, 113–14
Reeve, Ralph (player), 562, 563n
Refutation of the Apology for Actors, 178
Rendle, William, 194; 'The Bankside, Southwark, and the Globe Playhouse', 432, 440n
Renton, Mr (fencer), 450n
Requests, Court of, 313, 324, 332, 346, 367, 372–5, 376, 378, 379–81, 383–4, 384–5, 395–6, 386–7, 396–400, 401n, 439, 441, 443, 445–6, 450–1, 455, 478, 480, 519, 551, 560, 574–8, 592–4, 616–18, 620, 621, 622n, 628n, 641
Return from Parnassus, The, 173
Revels, Office of the, 5, 32, 48–50, 69–71, 297&n, 635; Master of the, 5, 32, 63, 69–70, 74, 83, 93–8, 103, 104, 106, 109, 110, 120–121, 124, 127–128, 129, 140, 145, 146–147, 148, 194, 196, 206, 270, 302, 311–12, 316, 328n, 426, 492, 526, 549–50, 554, 555, 562&n, 582, 582–3, 584, 616, 625, 635–6, 649, 653, 656, 657, 666. *See also* William Blagrave; Sir George Buck; Sir Henry Herbert; Edmund Tilney
Revels, Royal, 180, 181
Reynolds, John (carpenter), 290, 291–4
Reyson, Alexander (fencer), 410
Rhineland, The, 498n
Rhodes, John (musician or stage attendant), 258–9, 626&n, 636
Rich, Richard, Lord, 41–2, 44–5; his company of players, *see* Playing Companies
Richards, Hugh (inn-holder), 333
Richards, Nathaniel (playwright), *Messallina*, 650
Richmond Palace (Surrey), 586n
Ridolfi, Roberto, 62
Rimbault, Edward F., 'Salisbury Court Theatre', 653
Riots and other malefactions at playhouses, 341, 342, 345, 413, 431, 466–72, 522–3, 527–8, 543–4, 569–70, 581, 585, 628–9&n, 642–3, 644, 657
Robertes, John (carpenter), 495
Roberts, Owen (carpenter), 464, 466–70, 490
Robins, William (player), 239–41
Robinson, Humphrey, 647
Robinson, James, 264–7, 502, 509–11, 512

Robinson, John, occupied in 1600 part of the building in which the second Blackfriars playhouse was, 508; in 1640 an owner of the Salisbury Court playhouse, 657–64
Robinson, Richard (player), 223, 503, 609
Robinson, Winifred. *See* Burbage, Winifred
Rocque, John, *A Plan of the Cities of London and Westminster*, 440n, 567&n, 626n
Roderick, 434
Rodes, Walter (carpenter), 460, 461n, 489–90, 491
Rolls Chapel (Chancery Lane, London), 366
Rolls, Master of the, 336, 337
Rope dancing, 446–7, 567, 589&n, 604, 614, 646, 669
Roper, Lactantius (salter), 495
Roper, Richard (baker), 534
Roscius (Roman actor), 171, 176, 177, 182, 183, 190
Rose, John, 60
Rosenfeld, Sybil, 'Unpublished Stage Documents', 653
Ross, Mr (of Norwich), 257
Rosse, Rowland (servant), 472, 474
Rosseter, Philip (musician), 124, 217, 218–19, 515, 519, 549, 560, 561, 562, 563n
Rowley, Samuel (playwright), 238–39, 491
Rowley, William (player and writer), 417, 582–3; *All's Lost by Lust*, 591; (with John Day and George Wilkins) *Travels of The Three English Brothers*, 410–11, 569
Royal Household, 395
Royal Navy, 642–3
Ruddoke, William (carpenter), 291
Ruff (or Rough), Sir John, 46–7
Rump: or an Exact Collection of the Choycest Poems and Songs, 606n
Russell, Hugh (lawyer), 292
Russell, John, 545&n, 640
Russian Ambassador, 104
Rye, W.B., *England as Seen by Foreigners*, 498&n
Rylence, Randle, 138–9

Sabbatarians, 111, 118, 122, 138
Sabbath, profanation of, 166
Sack Full of News, A, 455–6
Sackford, Henry (master of the tents and keeper of the privy purse), 398&n
Sackville family. *See* Buckhurst, Lords
Sackville, Thomas (playwright), 52
Sackville (Saxfield), Thomas (player), 258
Sacraments, 26, 33, 69; *see also* Act of Uniformity

Saint. *See* Parishes
Salisbury (City of), 22, 24, 30–1
Salisbury, Earl of (Robert Cecil, first earl), 26, 515, 537, 562
Salvianus (bishop of Massilia), 162
Sampson, Martin W., 'Interior of the Fortune', 542
Samwell, Rebecca, 453–4, 468, 469n
Samwell, Richard the elder, 104–5, 106, 452–4, 456n, 456–8, 458–9, 459–61&n, 461–3&n, 463, 464–75&nn, 477n, 478, 487, 488, 489, 490, 491, 492
Samwell, Richard the younger, 453–4, 456–8&nn, 458–9, 460–1&n, 461–2, 465n, 466–8, 470–4, 478, 490, 492
Samwell, Winifred, 453–4, 468, 472–5
Sanders, William (musician or stage attendant), 258–9
Sandes, Henry (manager), 144
Sandford, James (writer), 159
Sands, James (player), 198
Satirical Essays Characters and Others (Stevens), 179
Saunders Mr (sergeant at mace), 298
Savage, Jerome (player), 320, 321, 322–6
Savage, Sir John (Mayor of Chester), 66, 68
Savage, Ralph, 583&n
Saviolo, Vincentio (fencer), 302–3
Saxfield, Thomas (player), 258
Scenery, stage, 8, 12, 125, 130, 149
School of Abuse, The (Gosson), 161
Scotland, 120, 123, 126, 498n, 515&n
Scott, Mr (lawyer), 357, 365, 375
Scott, Bartholomew, 100–1
Scott, Master Cuthbert, 25, 27–9
Scroop, Baron, 73
Sebeck, Henry, 144
Sebright, William, 77–8
Second and Third Blast of Retrait from Plays and Theatre, 162
Sedgewick, Obadiah (preacher), 637
Sedition, rumours and slanders, 3, 26, 35, 39, 40, 42, 43, 49, 53, 62, 73, 74, 76
Sellenger's Round, 173
Sellers, William, 495
Seneca, Lucius Annaeus, 185
Sessions of oyer and terminer (for Midlesex and London), 346, 447, 543, 569, 582, 643
Sewers (for water runoff), 320, 322&n; Surrey and Kent Commissioners for, 322, 327, 329, 426, 435
Seymour, Edward, duke of Somerset, the Lord Protector, 3, 33, 36, 158

Shaa (or Shaw), Robert (player), 77–8, 211–16, 438, 442–6
Shake-scene, 171
Shakespeare, the Man and the Book, 181
Shakespeare, William (playwright, player), 123, 191, 194, 196, 197, 198, 226, 289, 438, 493–4, 496n, 497, 502, 508, 516, 526, 529, 584, 607, 611, 667. *Hamlet*, 495n; *Henry VIII*, 494, 499–500; *Julius Caesar*, 412, 497; *Othello*, 498; *Romeo and Juliet*, 375, 412; *Poems*, 503n; *Titus Andronicus*, 328
'Shakespeare's Globe' (London), 494
Shanks, John (player), 222–4, 228, 503, 526
Shapiro, I.A., 'The Bankside Theatres: Early Engravings', 440n
Sharers' Papers, 221–8
Sharpe, Lewis, *The Noble Stranger*, 654
Sharpham, Edward, *Cupid's Whirligig*, 547
Shaw, John (butcher), 543
Sheffield, Baron, 73
Shepherd, George, 639, 647n
Shepherd, William, 199
Sherburne, Edward, 628n, 629
Sheriffs of London and Middlesex, 342, 346, 361, 402&n, 482, 483n, 562, 588, 593, 669; of Surrey, 588, 605. *See also* Magistrates
Sherlock, William (player), 626&n, 657–64
Shermons (of Carpenter's Hall), 22–3
Shirley, James (playwright), 625; *The Coronation* (or by John Fletcher?), 629–39; *The Doubtful Heir*, 614; *The Wedding*, 631–2
Shrewsbury, 405
Shrewsbury, Earl of, 42–3, 205
Shrove Tuesday, 180, 187
Shrovetide, 25, 41, 57, 79, 83, 103, 105, 109, 169
Sibdall, Henry, 455, 484
Sibthorpe, Edward (playhouse investor), 269–71, 547, 552, 554–9
Sidney, Sir Philip, 11
Sidonius, Antipater, 446
Silver, George (fencer), 302–3; *Paradoxes of Defence*, 302–3
Silver, Thomas (carpenter), 655
Silver, Toby (fencer), 302–3
Sinckler, John (player), 191
Singer, John (player), 176, 200, 246, 300
Sir John Mandeville, 431
Sisson, C.J., *Lost Plays*, 314, 582; 'Keep the Widow Waking', 582; 'The Red Bull Company', 579
Skelton, John, 2
Skevington, Richard, 100–1

Slater (Slatier), Martin (ironmonger, player), 120–1, 143–4, 253–4, 269–71, 274, 549, 553–9, 564, 566, 567n, 568
Sly, William (player), 122–3, 176, 194, 196, 197, 199, 200–1, 238, 494, 502, 516
Smalepeece, Thomas, 389, 399&n, 401
Smarte, Richard (carpenter), 291
Smith, Mr, 560
Smith, Henry (merchant tailor), 507n
Smith, Henry (occupier of a shop near the second Fortune), 640
Smith, Irwin, *Blackfriars Playhouse*, 389–90nn, 390&n, 393nn, 503n, 504, 507, 508&n, 509, 510nn, 511, 514&n, 515, 517n, 517, 522n
Smith, John (fishmonger), 627–8&n, 630–1
Smith, John (of Lancaster), 138–9
Smith, Judith (fiancée of Thomas Brend), 622
Smith, Judith Lady (née Lytton), 615
Smith, Logan Pearsall, *Life and Letters of Sir Henry Wotton*, 499
Smith, Matthew (player), 584, 644–5
Smith, Thomas (of Cambridge), 25–6
Smith, Dr Thomas (of Cumberland), 647
Smith, Wentworth, *The Hector of Germany*, 415–16
Smyth, Richard (fencer), 340, 367n
Smyth, William, 347, 376–8
Snelling, William (carpenter), 291
Sneyd, William, 18–19
Sodomites, 176
Solomon, 190
Some, Robert, 112–13
Somerset, Duke of (Edward Seymour), the Lord Protector, 3, 33, 36, 158
Sophocles, 29
Spain (the Spanish ambassador), 61, 127, 604. *See also* Gondomar, Count
Spanish Armada, 78
Sparkes, Thomas (merchant tailor), 640
Spartans, 179n
Speed, Nathaniel, 657–64
Spencer, Gabriel (player), 102, 176, 200, 211–16, 438, 442–6; his death, 281–2
Spencer, Richard, 22–3
Spiller, Sir Henry, 524
Spyke, Mr (schoolmaster), 265
St. *See* Parishes
St Mary of the Arches. *See* Court of the Arches
St Paul's Cathedral, 304, 306, 312, 313, 525, 529, 604; almonry, 306, 313; choir school, 306, 308; cloisters, 306, 389; grammar school, 306
St Paul's, Dean of, 309–10

St Rumwald. *See* Boxley Abbey (Kent)
St Thomas à Waterings (London), 93, 311&n, 329&n
Stafford, Lord, 73, 140
Stage characters: Adam, 542–3; Alice Pierce, 237; Apuleius, 630; Argus, 237; Bacon, Friar, 589; Beatrice, 503n; Belin Dun, 237; Benedick, 503n; Bird, 656; Bolt, 668; Boy, 569; Branholt, 236; Candlemas, 630; Cerberus, 237; Citizen, 569; Cupid, 237; Dauphin, 237; Delphrigus, 170; Dido, 237, 238; Doctor Almanack, 630; Domitia, 185; Eve, 237; Flowerdew, 656; Friar Tuck, 20; Gentlemen, 644; Guido, 237; Hamlet, 182, 495n; Hercules, 236; Hieronimo, 173, 182; Juno, 237; King Henry V, 236, 238; Lady Frampul, 241; Landlord, 668; Lear, 182; Longshanks, 236; Mahomet, 237; Maid Marian, 20, 93; Malvolio, 503n; Mercury, 237; Merlin, 236; Midas, 630; Moor, 237; Neptune, 236, 237; Othello, 182; Pantaloon, 171; Paris, 185; Don Pedro (King of Spain), 129; Phaeton, 237; Philomusus, 173; Pierrot, 238; Prudence, 241; Ralph, 569; Robin Hood, 20, 236, 237; Rosencrantz, 495n, 502; Sardanapalus, 191; Scrivener, 602; Shrovetuesday, 630; Sophy of Persia, 569; Spruce, 668; Studioso, 173; Tamburlaine, 237, 238; Tantalus, 237; Tasso, 237; Thrift, 668; Sir Alexander Wengrave, 542–3; Whore, 171; Will Summers, 236; Zany, 171
Stage players. *See* Players; *see* individual names
Stanhope, Dr Edward (master in Chancery), 365
Stanhope, Sir John (treasurer of the chamber), 493
Star Chamber, Court of, 44–5, 187, 267, 314, 376&n, 386n, 387, 454, 464, 466, 471–2, 510–11, 512, 527&n, 528, 582–3
Stationers, 35–36, 40, 52, 129, 192
Statute for the punishment of vagabonds (1572), 161
Statutes of the Realm, 9, 30, 41, 43, 50, 52, 53, 63, 103, 110, 131, 135, 139, 140. *See also* Acts of Parliament; Ordinances
Stavely, William (lawyer), 482
Stavorton, Mr (lawyer), 482, 484
Stevens, John (writer), 179
Steward, Walter, 527n
Stockwood, John (clergyman), *A Sermon Preached at Paules Crosse*, 298, 339
Stone, Philip, 570–5, 577–8, 579n, 592–4
Stoughton, Robert (butcher), 333
Stourbridge Fair, 589

Stow, John (writer), 208; *Annales*, 329, 605, 627n, 628n, 641–2
Strafford, Earl of (Thomas Wentworth, first earl), 525, 528; *Strafforde's Letters and Dispatches*, 522, 527
Strange, Lord (Ferdinando Stanley), 84, 92–94, 328; his company of players, *see* Playing Companies. *See also* Derby, fifth Earl of
Strangwick, Sir John, 528
Strasbourg, 50
Stratford, William (player), 221, 544, 641
Strayles, Anthony (servant), 466–71&n
Streatham, 13, 72–3
Street, Peter (carpenter), 332, 376–8, 379, 382, 493–4, 531–2, 534–7, 537, 541
Strong, S.A., *A Catalogue of Letters*, 487
Strype, John, 42–43
Stuart, Henry, Prince of Scotland, 123
Stuart, Ludovic. *See* Lennox, Earl of
Stubbes, Philip (writer), *The Anatomy of Abuses*, 166, 341n, 408
Sturgis, Mr, 563n
Styll, Dr (of Cambridge), 250
Suckling, Sir John (poet), 447, 527, 636
Suffolk (county), 24, 28, 30, 61, 82
Suffolk, Duke of, 22, 73
Suffolk, Earl of (Thomas Howard, first earl), 486
Suffolk, High Sheriff of, 110
Sumpner, John (player), 657–64
Sumpter, Simon (of Norwich), 250
Sundays, 30–32, 42, 46, 49, 54, 57–9, 60, 73, 75, 76, 79, 83, 84, 85–91, 107, 111, 112–13, 117–18, 120, 122, 131, 136, 142
Suppression of plays and playhouses, 132–5
Surrey, 76, 78, 79, 81, 83–4, 88–9, 106, 111, 121, 123, 132, 133, 311n, 320, 322, 323, 326–7, 329, 390, 397, 424, 451, 495, 497, 498, 504, 523, 534, 598, 602; Justices of, 326–7, 414, 426, 440, 446–7; Sheriffs of, 588, 605
Sussex, Earl of, 251
Sutton, one, 402
Swanston, Elliard or Eyllaerdt (player), 6, 221–8, 525–6, 621, 645
Sweden, 135
Sweete, Robert, 569
Swinnerton, Sir John (lord mayor), 562
Swinnerton, Thomas (player), 143–4, 253–4, 570–2, 592
'Swobber' (a jig), 589n
Sydenham, Sir Edward, 597
Sydney, Sir Robert, 313
Sylvester, William (carpenter), 290–1

Symonds, Thomasin, 423
Synger, John (player), 176, 200, 246, 300

Talpin, Jean (writer), 159
Tarbuck, John, 561&n
Tarlton, Richard (player), 172, 176, 200, 246–50, 296, 300, 301–2, 345; his picture, 209
Tatham, John (writer), *Fancies Theater*, 587; (?) *Knavery in all Trades*, 644
Taylor, John (the water poet), 435&n, 449, 596, 601; *All the Workes*, 436, 449; *Bull, Beare, and Horse*, 597n; *A Cast Over the Water*, 601; *Taylor's Revenge*, 601–2; *Taylors Water-work*, 613; *The True Cause of the Watermen's Suit*, 436, 449
Taylor, Joseph (player), 185, 210, 219, 222–3, 503, 526, 645
Taylor, Roger (latten founder), 233
Tedcastle, William, 569
Terence, 297n
Tey, Paul (legal official), 641
Thalia (muse of comic poetry), 412
Theatrum Redivivum (Baker), 189
Thebes in Greece, 168
Thomas, David, 7, 149
Thompson, John (boy player), 225
Thompson, Richard (silk weaver), 320, 322
Thomson, William, 353–4
Thorndon (Suffolk), 28
Thorpe, Sir Simond, 73
Thurles, Lord (James Butler), 527
Thurston, Nicholas (of Norwich), 249
Tilney, Agnes, 73
Tilney, Edmund (Master of the Revels), 5, 13, 70–3, 78–9, 82–3, 75, 98, 103, 108, 110–11, 148–9, 208, 244–5
Tilney, Frederick, 73
Tilney, Hugh, 73
Tilney, Sir Philip, 73
Tilte, Oliver, 344
Tindall, Nathaniel (matricide), 582
Tobacco, 180
Tomkis, Thomas (writer), 570
Tomlins, Thomas E., 'Origin of the Curtain Theatre', 406nn, 407
Tooke, John, 282
Tooley, Nicholas (player), 198
Topcliffe, Richard, 101–2
Torrismount, 555
Touching the Good Ordering of a Commonweal (Ferrarius), 158
Towne, John (player), 300

Towne, Thomas (player), 542n
Townsend, John (player), 147, 256–8
Towse, William (lawyer), 484
Toyer, William (musician or stage attendant), 258–9
Tragedies, 25–9, 37, 71, 74, 75, 76, 95, 114, 118, 123
Trained bands (of London), 290, 645
Transcript of the Registers of the Company of Stationers, 302
Treasurer of the Chamber, 262, 317
Treatise Wherein Dicing, Dancing, Vain Plays [etc] are Reproved (Northbrooke), 160
Trevell, Susan, 549, 560
Trevell, William (chandler, playhouse investor), 269–71, 547–50&n, 551–2&n, 554–9, 559–60
Trewe, Andrew, 65
Trig, William (player), 259
Trinity Hall, Worcester, 143
Trussell, Alvery (imprest boy player), 265
Tucker, Leonard, 172
Tuckfield, Thomas (musician or stage attendant), 258–9
Tunstall, James (player), 235–6, 245, 251, 362
Turner, John (fencer), 448
Turner, Olga. *See* Edward M. Wilson
Turner, Richard (arbitrator), 338–9, 357, 373
Turnor, Anthony (player), 657–64
Twyne, Thomas (writer), *Physic for Fortune*, 341n; *Physic against Fortune*, 408
Tyndale, William, 24

Udall, Nicholas (playwright), 41
Underhill, Nicholas (musician or stage attendant), 258–9
Underwood, John (player), 226, 405, 503
Upstart crow, 171
Ussher, James (archbishop of Armagh), 646
Utrecht, University of, 437, 441

Vagrants (Pedlars, tinkers and wanderers), 48, 53, 62, 81, 115, 133, 144
Van Buchell, Arend, 437, 441
Van Dyke, Sir Anthony, 528
Vanity and Uncertainty of Arts and Sciences, The (Agrippa), 159
Vaughan, James (financier), 485
Vaughan, Susan. *See* Woodliffe, Susan
Vaulters in playhouses, 616
Vaux, Lord, his company of players. *See* Playing Companies
Venice, 564; Teatro San Cassiano, 130

Vennar, Richard (writer), 438, 447&n; *An Apology*, 447n; *England's Joy*, 447; *The Plot of the Play Called England's Joy*, 447n
Vernon, George (musician or stage attendant), 258–9
View of the Cittye of London from the North towards the Sowth, The, 406
Vigerous, Robert, 369–70
Vox Graculi, 416–17, 641
Vulcan, 500

W., T. (clergyman), *A Sermon Preached at Pawles Crosse*, 337
Wade, William (clerk of the privy council), 403
Waintworth, John, 569n
Wakefield (Yorkshire), 41, 64, 69
Wales, President of, 140
Wales, Prince of, 33, 127, 147
Walford, John, 487, 491
Walker, Thomas (petticoat maker), 605
Wallace, Charles W., 401, 495n, 509n; Advance Sheets, 495, 515; 'Children of the Chapel', 309, 511; Evolution of the English Drama, 390&n, 393, 394, 395, 396, 400, 401, 403 504; First London Theatre, 298, 300, 300, 301, 302, 332, 333, 336, 337, 338, 339n, 340, 342, 343, 344, 345n, 346, 348, 349, 350&n, 351, 352, 355&n, 356n, 357, 358, 363, 364, 365, 366, 367&n, 372, 375, 376&n, 378, 383, 384, 385, 386&nn; 'New Light on Shakespeare', 496; 'Shakespeare and his London Associates', 318, 495n, 509, 515, 517, 612&n; 'Shakespeare and the Globe', 434; 'Shakespeare in London', 495n; 'Shakespeare's Money Interest', 495n; 'The Swan Theatre and the Earl of Pembroke's Servants', 441; 'Three London Theatres', 567n, 593, 594&n, 627, 628n, 630
Walmesley, Thomas (judge), 484
Walshe, Alexander (fruiterer), 439, 448
Walsingham, Sir Francis (secretary of state), 86–7, 90, 164, 172, 208, 229–33, 400–1
Walter, Mr (lawyer), 375, 383–4
Wambus, Francis (player), 146–9, 255–8
Wanamaker, Sam, 494
Warrington (Lancashire), 138–9
Warwick, Earl of (Ambrose Dudley, first Earl), 92, 299–300; his company of players, *see* Playing Companies
Watermen (of London), 327–8, 449
Waucklen, John, 36
Webster, John (playwright), 125, 181, 307, 582–3

Weekly Account, The, 641
Weekly Intelligencer, The, 587
Weeks, Richard, 500
Wendey, Doctor, 27
Wentworth, Lord (Thomas Wentworth, second lord), 336; *see also* Strafford, Earl of
West Molesey (Surrey), 607
Westcott, Sebastian (musician), 306, 308–9
Weston, Doctor, 31
Westwood, Jonas, 627
Wharton, Mr (Duke of Norfolk's Comptroller), 22
Whaston, Thomas, 324, 326
Wheatley, H.B., *London Past and Present*, 311n
Wheeler, Henry, 674
Wheeler, John, 313
Whitaker, Lawrence, 524
White, Margaret, 175
White, Rowland, 313
Whitgift, John (Archbishop of Canterbury), 95–96; *see also* Canterbury, Archbishop of
Whithorne, Timothy, 199, 201
Whitsun, 1, 18, 65–8, 69, 110
Whreste, Henry (carpenter), 291
Wickham, Glynne, '"Heavens", Machinery, and Pillars in Early Playhouses', 423n
Wigan (Lancashire), 111, 139
Wigan, Master Doctor, 27
Wigpitt, Thomas (bricklayer), 638–9, 640, 641n
Wikland, Erik, 172
Wilbraham, William (player), 636, 657–64
Wildigge, William, 138–9
Wile, John, 138–9
Wilkins, George. *See* Rowley, William
Wilkins, Thomas, 408
Wilkinson, John (plasterer), 230, 233
Wilkinson, Richard, 407
Wilkinson, Robert, *Londina Illustrata*, 647n
Wilkinson, Thomas, 408
William of Malmsbury, 187
Williams, Elizabeth (née Carleton), 613
Williams, R.F., *Court and Times of Charles I*, 653
Williams, Thomas (feltmaker), 569
Willis, R (writer), 243
Willoughby, Lord (Peregrine Bertie, ninth lord), 538
Willys, Edward (servant), 461n, 468, 471, 473–4, 475n, 490, 491
Wilson, Dr, 31
Wilson, Dr Thomas (a master of Requests), 309
Wilson, Edward M., (with Olga Turner) 'The Spanish Protest Against A Game at Chesse', 615–16

Wilson, F.P., 'Marston, Lodge, and Constable', 515n
Wilson, George, 657
Wilson, Henry (musician or stage attendant), 258–9
Wilson, Robert (playwright, player), 176, 204, 206, 208, 300, 446; *Three Ladies of London*, 329
Winchester, Bishop of, 600; Stephen Gardiner, 25–26, 27–29, 34, 57, 69, 157–8
Winchester, Marquis of, 73
Windsor Castle, choristers in the chapel of, 388
Wintersall, Williams, 654
Wit and Drollery, 597n
Witchcraft, 619–20&n
Withens, Robert (vintner), 419
Wither, George (writer), *Abuses Stript and Whipt*, 415&n, 570; *Epigrams*, 415&n
Withers, Henry, 451
Witt, Johannes de (Dutch tourist), 11, 304, 332, 410, 437–8, 441, 615
Witter, John, 199, 200–3, 611–12
Wolf, John, 106
Wolleston, Thomas, 453, 473–4, 475, 476n
Wolley, Sir John, 403
Wolsey, Cardinal Thomas, 18, 499
Women on stage in playhouses, 343, 584, 632
Wood, Thomas, 405
Woodball, Robert (of Maidstone), 254
Woodford, Thomas (financier), 307, 308n, 313, 315&n, 316, 317, 547–9, 550, 553, 557, 559–60, 561, 562, 564–6, 567nn, 570–9&nn, 592–4&n
Woodliffe, Oliver (haberdasher, playhouse speculator), 105, 106, 452–5, 456&n, 456–8, 459–61, 461–3&n, 463–4&n, 464–7&nn, 470–2, 474, 476, 476–7&n, 477–8, 478–9&n, 480, 482–3, 483–4&n, 484&n, 484–5, 487, 488, 489, 490, 491, 492
Woodliffe, Susan, 454, 456&n, 457–8, 459, 462, 463, 464–6, 468–70, 472, 478, 485
Woodward, Elizabeth, 277
Woodward, Joan. *See* Alleyn, Joan
Woolfe, Nicholas, 119
Worcester (City of), 143; Guildhall, 143
Worcester College, Oxford, 623
Worcester, Earl of (Edward Somerset, fourth earl), 109, 120, 123, 481; his company of players, *see* Playing Companies
Worcestershire, 136–7
Wormleighton, Ralph (lawyer), 576, 593, 594n
Worth, Ellis (player), 185, 584, 628, 630–1, 644–5
Wotton, John, 337
Wotton, Sir Henry, 499; Letters, 499, 562
?Wright, James, *Historia Histrionica*, 567&n, 641, 655n
Wrothe, Robert, 100
Wurmsser, Hans Jacob, 498n
Wynsdon, Mr (of Norwich), 247–50

York, Archbishop of. *See* Grindal, Edmund
York, City of, 21, 44, 61, 64, 142, 309
York, James, Duke of, 6
Young, Mary, 654
Young, Mr, 93–4
Young, Richard (justice of Middlesex), 302
Young, William, *History of Dulwich College*, 434, 546, 639n
Younge, John (player), 657–64

Zeale (character). *See* Farley, Henry
Zuccaro, Federigo (Italian artist), 207

Lightning Source UK Ltd.
Milton Keynes UK
28 November 2010

163545UK00002B/72/P